Neither Angels Nor Thieves: Studies in Deinstitutionalization of Status Offenders

Joel F. Handler and Julie Zatz, *editors*

Panel on the Deinstitutionalization of
Children and Youth
Committee on Child Development Research and
Public Policy
Assembly of Behavioral and Social Sciences
National Research Council

NATIONAL ACADEMY PRESS
Washington, D.C.   1982

NOTICE: The project that is the subject of the report was approved by the Governing Board of the National Research Council, whose members are drawn from the Councils of the National Academy of Sciences, the National Academy of Engineering, and the Institute of Medicine. The members of the Committee responsible for the report were chosen for their special competences and with regard for appropriate balance.

This report has been reviewed by a group other than the authors according to procedures approved by a Report Review Committee consisting of members of the National Academy of Sciences, the National Academy of Engineering, and the Institute of Medicine.

The National Research Council was established by the National Academy of Sciences in 1916 to associate the broad community of science and technology with the Academy's purposes of furthering knowledge and of advising the federal government. The Council operates in accordance with general policies determined by the Academy under the authority of its congressional charter of 1863, which establishes the Academy as a private, nonprofit, self-governing membership corporation. The Council has become the principal operating agency of both the National Academy of Sciences and the National Academy of Engineering in the conduct of their services to the government, the public, and the scientific and engineering communities. It is administered jointly by both Academies and the Institute of Medicine. The National Academy of Engineering and the Institute of Medicine were established in 1964 and 1970, respectively, under the charter of the National Academy of Sciences.

This project was supported by Grant Nos. 78-JC-AX-001 and 79-JC-AX-002, awarded by the Office of Juvenile Justice and Delinquency Prevention. The contents do not necessarily reflect the views and policies of the grantor.

Library of Congress Cataloging in Publication Data
Main entry under title:

Neither angles nor thieves.

Bibliography: p. 240
Includes index.
1. Status offenders—United States—Case studies.
2. Status offenders—Government policy—United States.   I. Handler, Joel F.   II. Zatz, Julie.
HV9104.N34   364.6'8   82-2171
ISBN 0-309-03192-3   AACR2

Available from

NATIONAL ACADEMY PRESS
2101 Constitution Avenue, N.W.
Washington, D.C. 20418

Printed in the United States of America

PANEL ON THE DEINSTITUTIONALIZATION OF CHILDREN AND YOUTH

JOEL F. HANDLER, *Chair*, School of Law, University of Wisconsin

AUGUSTINE C. BACA, New Mexico Youth Development, Inc.

BARBARA BLUM, New York State Department of Social Services

ROBERT H. BREMNER, Department of History, Ohio State University

ROBERT B. HILL, National Urban League, Inc., Washington, D.C.

PAUL LERMAN, Graduate School of Social Work, Rutgers University

ROBERT C. MAYNARD, Oakland Tribune

JOANNE MITCHELL, Illinois Commission on Delinquency Prevention

WILLIAM POLLAK, School of Social Service Administration, University of Chicago

JULIAN RAPPAPORT, Department of Psychology, University of Illinois

MARGARET K. ROSENHEIM, School of Social Services Administration, University of Chicago

GERALD J. STRICK, Maricopa County, Arizona, Superior Court

DEBORAH KLEIN WALKER, Graduate School of Education and School of Public Health, Harvard University

CAROL K. WHALEN, Department of Social Ecology, University of California, Irvine

JULIAN WOLPERT, School of Architecture and Urban Planning, Princeton University

MAYER N. ZALD, Center for Research on Social Organization, University of Michigan

Staff

JULIE ZATZ, Study Director
SALLY A. KORNEGAY, Research Associate
TIMOTHY C. MACK, Research Associate
SUZANNE S. MAGNETTI, Research Associate
VIRGINIA PETERSON, Administrative Secretary

Field Staff

WAYNE M. ALVES	RICHARD E. JOHNSON	JOSEPH F. SHELEY
JOANNE A. ARNAUD	JEAN ANN LINNEY	MICHAEL SOSIN
STANLEY FELDMAN	STEVEN L. NOCK	JOHN A. STOOKEY

iii

iv

CONTRIBUTORS

WAYNE M. ALVES *is a statistician in the Department of Neurosurgery at the University of Virginia.*

JOANNE A. ARNAUD *is a political scientist.*

MICHAEL J. CHURGIN *is a professor of law at the University of Texas.*

STANLEY FELDMAN *is an assistant professor of political science at the University of Kentucky.*

JOEL F. HANDLER, *Vilas research professor of law at the University of Wisconsin, served as Chair of the Panel on the Deinstitutionalization of Children and Youth.*

RICHARD E. JOHNSON *is an associate professor of sociology at Brigham Young University.*

SALLY A. KORNEGAY, *an economist, served as research associate to the project.*

JEAN ANN LINNEY *is an assistant professor of psychology at the University of Virginia.*

TIMOTHY C. MACK, *a lawyer, served as research associate to the project.*

SUZANNE S. MAGNETTI, *a lawyer, served as research associate to the project.*

STEVEN L. NOCK *is an assistant professor of sociology at the University of Virginia.*

WILLIAM POLLAK, *an economist, is an associate professor in the School of Social Service Administration at the University of Chicago.*

JOSEPH F. SHELEY *is an assistant professor of sociology at Tulane University.*

MICHAEL SOSIN *is an assistant professor of social work at the University of Wisconsin.*

DAVID STEINHART *is an attorney and codirector of Social Advocates for Youth in San Francisco, California.*

JOHN A. STOOKEY *is an associate professor of political science at Arizona State University.*

MARK TESTA *is a research associate at the National Opinion Research Center and the School of Social Service Administration at the University of Chicago.*

JOAN L. WOLFLE *is a criminal justice specialist.*

JULIE ZATZ, *a political scientist, served as study director to the project.*

Contents

Preface   xi

PART I

1   Introduction   3

2   Problems and Issues in Deinstitutionalization: Historical
Overview and Current Attitudes
Julie Zatz   14

3   Problems and Issues in Deinstitutionalization: Laws,
Concepts, and Goals
Julie Zatz   41

4   The Implementation System: Characteristics and Change
Joel F. Handler and *Julie Zatz*   66

5   Deinstitutionalization in Seven States: Principal Findings
Joel F. Handler, Michael Sosin, John A. Stookey, and
Julie Zatz   88

6   Alternative Facilities for Youth in Trouble: Descriptive
Analysis of a Strategically Selected Sample
Jean Ann Linney   127

7   The Role of Federal Programs in Efforts to
    Deinstitutionalize Status Offenders
    Sally A. Kornegay and *Suzanne S. Magnetti*   176

8   Conclusions   200

9   Recommendations   230

    References   240

PART II

    Overview   251

    STATE PROGRAM ANALYSES

10 Deinstitutionalization of Status Offenders in Arizona:
    State and Local Initiators of Policy Change
    Timothy C. Mack and *John A. Stookey*   255

11 Deinstitutionalization Efforts in Louisiana
    Joseph F. Sheley and *Steven L. Nock*   296

12 The Deinstitutionalization of Status Offenders in
    Massachusetts: The Role of the Private Sector
    Joanne A. Arnaud and *Timothy C. Mack*   335

13 The Deinstitutionalization of Status Offenders in
    Pennsylvania
    Stanley Feldman   372

14 Deinstitutionalization in Utah: A Study of Contrasts
    and Contradictions
    Richard E. Johnson and *Timothy C. Mack*   419

15 Competing Definitions of Troublesome Children
    and Youth in Virginia
    Steven L. Nock and *Wayne M. Alves*   464

16 Deinstitutionalization of Status Offenders and Dependent
    and Neglected Youth in Wisconsin
    Michael Sosin   513

FEDERAL PROGRAM ANALYSES

17 Services for Status Offenders Under the LEAA, OJJDP,
    and Runaway Youth Programs
    Sally A. Kornegay and *Joan L. Wolfle*   561

18 Title XX and Social Services for Status Offenders
    Sally A. Kornegay   598

19 Federal Child Welfare Funds and Services for Status
    Offenders
    Sally A. Kornegay   621

20 State Use of the AFDC-Foster Care Program for Status
    Offenders
    Sally A. Kornegay   641

21 Impact of the Medicaid Program on the Treatment of
    Status Offenders
    Suzanne S. Magnetti   663

22 Title I of the Elementary and Secondary Education Act:
    Implications for the Deinstitutionalization of Status
    Offenders
    Suzanne S. Magnetti   681

23 Effects of the Education for All Handicapped Children Act
    on the Deinstitutionalization of Status Offenders
    Suzanne S. Magnetti   699

APPENDIXES

A Research Design   723

B Data Analysis: Methods and Problems in the State Case
   Studies   732

C Multicomponent Assessment of Residential Services for
   Youth (MARSY)
   Jean Ann Linney   740

D Data Issues and Problems in the Federal Program Analyses   780

E   The Politics of Status Offender Deinstitutionalization in California
    David Steinhart   784

F   Child Placement and Deinstitutionalization: A Case Study of Social Reform in Illinois
    Mark Testa   825

G   Mandated Change in Texas: The Federal District Court and the Legislature
    Michael J. Churgin   872

H   Services for Status Offenders: Issues Raised by Private Provision of Publicly Financed Services
    William Pollak   899

    Index   939

Preface

This report is the product of a three-year study sponsored by the Office of Juvenile Justice and Delinquency Prevention of the U.S. Department of Justice. It was undertaken to assess what has been happening to youth who commit status offenses (e.g., truants, runaways, incorrigibles) in the aftermath of the 1974 Juvenile Justice and Delinquency Prevention Act. That legislation generally mandates, in part, the removal of these youth from secure confinement, prohibits their subsequent incarceration, and calls for the development of alternative types of community-based programs and services.

This research project was comparatively large and far-flung for an undertaking of the Assembly of Behavioral and Social Sciences. It involved a good deal of on-site work in the 7 states and 14 localities that were selected for study, as well as research on the activities of several federal agencies. As is true of many studies of this size and complexity, a great many debts were incurred.

Most of the members of our panel were strangers to one another, known perhaps only by reputation. They came from different disciplines and had varying research interests. Shortly, however, they became a close-knit, enthusiastic working group. Many members participated willingly and actively in every phase of the study. Individually and collectively the panel was continually involved in the design, execution, review, and critique of the study. When asked, members took on extra assignments despite their own busy schedules. There was a good climate with this panel. Views were expressed forcefully but respectfully, and we all learned in the process. The atmosphere of this study was both stimulating and pleasurable. I very much enjoyed working with the panel, and I welcome the opportunity to express my thanks to them.

As shown in the table of contents, most of the chapters of this study were individually authored. The panel has signed three chapters. The panel, however, is fully apprised of the entire contents of the study and stands behind the report as a whole.

The research involved a sizable number of people. Most of the field staff were young scholars with university appointments in sociology, political science, social work, and psychology. They not only authored several of the chapters, but they also participated effectively in panel deliberations and from time to time helped out on various special assignments. As with the panel members, the staff also quickly developed a cooperative spirit that contributed to the good atmosphere of this project. All of the field staff deserve our thanks. I would especially like to commend four who took on special assignments that were crucial to the study: Steven Nock worked on difficult problems of design; Michael Sosin and John Stookey helped make sense out of the state findings; and Jean Ann Linney was in charge of the very complex facility analysis.

We also had an in-house staff. As with the field staff, these people had major substantive responsibilities and their names also appear as authors. In addition, they performed many other services, both large and small, that were essential to the project and made life a lot easier for all of us. They spent a great deal of time working with the field staff and troubleshooting the myriad issues and problems that always appear. They were loyal, intelligent, and productive good friends: Sally Kornegay, Timothy Mack, and Suzanne Magnetti. I thank them.

Besides the panel and the staff, a wide network of people helped this project in various ways. A great many federal, state, and local officials and other interested persons generously gave of their time. The list is too long to be mentioned here, but many of their names appear after each of the state case-study chapters. On behalf of the panel, I express my appreciation to them. They supplied the necessary data and a good many ideas as well.

Closer to home, we are particularly appreciative of the support of the Office of Juvenile Justice and Delinquency Prevention. John Rector was the administrator of that office at the start of this study. His enthusiastic interest and encouragement were essential in getting the project under way. Despite subsequent staff changes within that office, our dealings have been more than cordial and we never lacked for assistance.

Within the National Research Council, the members of the Committee on Child Development Research and Public Policy were supportive and constructive throughout. We would particularly like to thank Laurence E. Lynn, Jr., who was chair of the committee for most of the period of this project. We also thank Cheryl D. Hayes, executive officer of the committee. She was always available to explain procedures, and in countless ways eased the project along. In a similar vein, we appreciate the support and efforts of David A. Goslin, executive director of the Assembly of Behavioral and Social Sciences.

This project generated a lot of paper and involved a lot of people coming and going. Anyone in the least familiar with a project of this size knows the value of a good administrative secretary and we had the best. Ginny Peterson not only turned the work out, but she willingly and cheerfully put in numerous after hours and weekends so that we could meet our deadlines. She was a very important part of the task, and we are all most grateful for her help. We also appreciate the care and attention of Sherry Snyder in editing the final draft of the report.

Julie Zatz was the study director. It would be hard to exaggerate the scope and quality of her contributions to the entire study. Everything, both major and minor, passed through her hands. Throughout the project, she displayed great scholarly and administrative skill. She made important intellectual contributions to the original conceptualization of the study, its design, and execution, and she authored several of the chapters. She kept the project going—stimulating, encouraging, cajoling, and sometimes taking stronger measures. She did everything. Many people contributed to this project. Julie Zatz was indispensable.

Joel F. Handler, *Chair*
Panel on the
Deinstitutionalization of
Children and Youth

PART I

1 Introduction

Adolescence is a time of stress, and the range of reactions to that stress is vast. For some youth, coping is a private affair, barely noticeable even to family and friends. It may be a time of preoccupation, moodiness, and introspection (Blum 1969; Daedalus 1971; Erikson 1965, 1968; President's Science Advisory Committee 1973; Weiner 1970). Others show more visible signs of emotional distress, including engaging in socially unacceptable behavior. Such youth fight with their parents, stay out all night, do poorly or are disruptive in school, hang out on street corners, become sexually promiscuous, engage in drug use, and run away or commit criminal acts. The actual proportion of youth in distress is controversial (Rutter et al. 1976, Weiner 1970). More to the point, the differential impact of this stage of development on youth and their families is little understood. What today is generally regarded as nuisance behavior, in another day might have been viewed as a first step toward a life of crime. Although disobedience and other forms of acting out are, at present, less likely to be viewed as protocriminal, there is a good deal of disagreement as to the appropriate response (Rubin 1976, Sosin 1981). Some people, feeling that a certain amount of adolescent turmoil is a necessary and desirable part of the maturation process, are inclined to endure youthful disobedience (Erikson 1959, 1968; Freud 1962; Group for the Advancement of Psychiatry 1968; Schur 1973). Others see these same youth as needing professional services (Juvenile Justice Standards Project 1980, National Advisory Committee for Juvenile Justice and Delinquency Prevention 1980) or as needing corrective

3

measures (Arthur 1975). How best to define the limits of acceptable behavior on the part of young people and what, if anything, to do about youth who exceed those limits has been a topic of enduring public concern.

This study is concerned with a certain portion of these youth—those known as status offenders. This group is hard to define, at least with any precision. They are youth who have been charged with or found to have committed offenses that would not be regarded as wrongdoing if committed by an adult. Characteristically, they are labeled ungovernables, truants, and runaways. Their offenses are not so much ones at law as affronts to their parents, schools, and communities that may or may not prove harmful to themselves as well. They engage in activities that probably are engaged in by large numbers of youth in our society, but for a variety of reasons this particular class comes to the attention of the authorities. Many status offenders are "push-outs"—their families can no longer tolerate their behavior and seek the help of the juvenile justice system. For others, the demands may be the opposite—for example, they run away and their parents seek to have them returned home. In any case, the dilemma for the state is what to do to or for these youth, or whether to become involved with them or their families at all. Because of shifts in attitudes as to the tolerable limits of behavior, and because of changing ideas as to the appropriateness of a given response, the resulting process is highly uneven: Youth who engage in identical behavior may receive different dispositions while youth engaging in different activities may be dealt with in the same way.

Ambiguities, vagaries, and changes in public attitudes are reflected in statutory definitions, administrative procedures, and the allocation of resources. For this reason alone, it is virtually impossible to fix with any precision the number and characteristics of status offenders. For example, it is claimed that truancy is epidemic in larger urban areas; yet it has disappeared as a status offense statistic in those jurisdictions that have decided to consider this form of behavior a problem for the schools rather than the juvenile court. In any event, it is probably safe to assume that youth who commit status offenses are ubiquitous (President's Commission on Law Enforcement 1967c). It is probable that those who are identified and labeled as status offenders constitute a substantial percentage of all youth dealt with by juvenile courts (National Advisory Commission 1973). However, this number is quite small when compared with the total youth population (President's Commission on Law Enforcement 1967c). To parents, neighbors, police, courts, and practitioners, status offenders are hardly strangers; and whether they are youth who represent a tide of troublemaking or a normal, albeit irritating, response to parental and societal authority depends on one's point of view.

The most recent public response has been to deinstitutionalize status offenders. Shortly, we will have much to say about the meaning and ramifications of deinstitutionalization, but for present purposes it means removing status offenders from secure detention or correctional facilities or preventing their placement in such settings. Wherever possible or appropriate, these youth are to be diverted from the juvenile justice system and provided alternative services.

In 1974 the federal government enacted the Juvenile Justice and Delinquency Prevention Act (P.L. 93-415), which was intended, in part, to bring about the deinstitutionalization of status offenders. The act was amended in 1977 (P.L. 95-115) to apply to dependent and neglected children as well as status offenders.[1] The Office of Juvenile Justice and Delinquency Prevention (OJJDP) was established to explore ways to coordinate federal programs and policies in the states. This study originates out of that mandate, for its initial aim was to assist OJJDP with its task by examining a range of public policies and programs contributing to the institutionalization and deinstitutionalization of status offenders and, to a lesser extent, dependent and neglected youth.[2]

The initial research question was cast in this form: What has been the impact of federal programs on the deinstitutionalization of status offenders? This form of the question is characteristic of conventional impact or implementation analysis and implicitly assumes that federal rules, programs, and policies play a leading role in bringing about change at state and local levels. (See chapter 4 for an extended discussion of the styles of implementation analysis. See also Elmore 1980, Hargrove 1975, Sabatier and Mazmanian 1980, and Zald 1980). Deinstitutionalization policies are part of a larger concern for the welfare of children and other disenfranchised groups. The origins of these policies extend back over time and reflect the broader influences of related social movements.

---

[1] The act was again amended in 1980 (P.L. 96-509) following completion of our research. Some of the provisions of the act, particularly those pertaining to the use of secure detention or correctional facilities, were modified. See chapter 17 for a discussion of these changes.

[2] Major reductions of dependent and neglected children housed in large state facilities were essentially accomplished in the majority of states well before the passage of the federal act. Although constituting only a small part of our story, the dependent and neglected child population was still of some concern to us because the federal programs providing foster care and protective, homemaker, and similar services to status offenders were originally designed to help these younger, less troublesome children.

Like many other major social welfare programs, these policies were shaped and developed primarily at the state and local levels; federal influence came late and, although important, did not alter the fundamental allocation of responsibility and power. The federal government provides standards and a variety of incentives; these may or may not be important in stimulating change, but essentially the federal government is reactive to state and local initiatives.

For this reason, we recast the question: What has been happening with deinstitutionalization at state and local levels, and what, if anything, has been the impact of federal policies and programs on these developments? This reformulation is based on a theory of social processes and change that applies more generally to social welfare and education programs that have the federal-state, grant-in-aid structure. That theory is set forth in detail in chapter 4.

Our field research began in the spring of 1979 and was essentially completed by the fall of 1980. Three questions were asked: What has happened to status offenders in terms of detention and placement in state correctional institutions? To what extent are status offenders handled by diversion programs? Where are status offenders going and what services, if any, are they receiving? The definition of deinstitutionalization is operational. It takes meaning from what the state and local governments and communities are doing. In chapter 5 we discuss the extent to which these questions were answered.

WHAT THE STUDY DOES AND DOES NOT DO

The research began by trying to understand what was happening at the state and local levels, what directions were being taken and why, and what influence federal programs and policies had on this direction. The working hypothesis is that change comes quite incrementally, at uneven rates, in different localities, and that many factors usually have to work in combination to produce that change. We looked at how the various public policies and programs helped or hindered that process of change, recognizing that different combinations of forces are operating in any particular locality. A detailed description of the study's research design is contained in appendix A.

Because the states and even localities within states move at uneven rates, it was necessary to select a sample of states that represented different deinstitutionalization postures. Resource limitations required selecting only a small number of states for intensive analysis. Basically, we tried to select those which, on the basis of available data, seemed to represent differences in change in populations in juvenile institutions, and then, from among those that shared the same patterns of change, to weigh other factors such as geographical distribution, urban-rural dimensions, minority populations, and so forth. Seven states were finally selected: Arizona, Louisiana, Massachusetts, Pennsylvania, Utah, Virginia, and Wisconsin. In each of the seven states, two local jurisdictions were selected. Criteria here also varied, but generally jurisdictions were selected in terms of a contrast between a major urban setting and a more rural setting, or in terms of some contrast in progress toward the deinstitutionalization of status offenders. Modified research on California, Illinois, and Texas was also commissioned.

In addition, we wanted to learn something about the situation of status offenders who were placed out of their homes. A small, purposive sample of facilities was selected and divided into four predominant program types that provide the bulk of residential services to status offenders: detention, the alternative to detention (typically, an emergency shelter care facility or nonsecure detention facility), a group home, and a residential treatment facility. Generally, we tried to discover what these facilities are like. To what extent are they "community-based" and "nonsecure"? What are their goals, philosophy, sources of financial support, and policies of admission, programming, and discharge? What kinds of youth are served by these programs and in what ways? Although resources did not permit a larger random survey, and the findings must be treated cautiously, the research does shed light on some of the important policy implementation issues of this study.

While the weight of the research effort focused on understanding what was happening and why in these seven states and in the local areas within those states, research simultaneously was conducted on nine federal programs that seemed to have the most relevance for this population, including Title XX social services, Title IV-B child welfare services, Title IV-A foster care grants under AFDC, Title I of the Elementary and Secondary Education Act (ESEA), Medicaid, and the Education for All Handicapped Children Program (referred to as P.L. 94-142). The study also reviewed the Runaway Youth Act and the Juvenile Justice and Delinquency Prevention Act and other programs operating out of the Law Enforcement Assistance Administration (LEAA) that dealt with juveniles.[3] Ultimately, the two foci of research were brought together in order to assess the impact of the federal efforts.

---

[3] Title XX Grants to States for Services, P.L. 93-647 S2, 88 Stat. 2337 (1976), codified at 42 USC 1397-1397S. Title IV-B Child Welfare Services, P.L. 90-248, Title II, S240(c), 81 Stat. 911 (1968), codified at 42 USC SS620-626. Medicaid Social Security Amendments

The study looks at social and political institutions—courts, police, legislatures, administrators, interest groups—to see how policy is shaped and implemented. Because of resource limitations, this focus precluded taking a more specific individualized approach. Theoretically, a study of public policies that affect deinstitutionalization of these juveniles could be conducted by drawing a large enough sample of families and youth and by then tracing out the actual effects and impacts of deinstitutionalization programs on them. This is needed research. In truth, very little is known in a systematic way about what is happening to youth who come into the system, to youth who are in fact diverted away from the system, or to youth who go through various parts of the system and then return home. A large sample could begin to answer some of these questions, but it would not answer others. For example, little would be learned about how institutions and agencies operate on levels higher than the street-level or first-line decisionmakers. Furthermore, no information would be generated on the role of interest groups in the formation of public policy or the role of other key forces, such as court decisions, laws and regulations, and legislative politics. One of the major findings of this study is the importance of local variation and how federal influence, in its variety of forms, operates in different ways depending on local conditions. It would be unlikely that such a finding would arise out of a study of youth and their families even if large enough samples were drawn from all the relevant local areas. The availability of appropriate alternative out-of-home placements would be an important research finding, but a study of these youth and their families would shed no light on why these placements are available in some communities and not others, and what role, if any, federal or state policy had in the creation of these facilities.

As in all social science research, choices had to be made as to which questions should be addressed, leaving others to subsequent efforts. In this study we have explained some of the important determinants of

---

of 1965, P.L. 89-97, 79 Stat. 286, codified at 42 USC 1396 (1976) "Grants to States for Medical Assistance Programs." Title IV-A Aid to Families with Dependent Children codified at 42 USC SS601-610. The Education for All Handicapped Children Act of November 25, 1975, P.L. 94-142, 89 Stat. 774, 20 USC 1401 *et seq.* Title I Elementary and Secondary Education Act Title 1, codified at 20 USC 241a *et seq.* Runaway Youth Program Juvenile Justice & Delinquency Prevention Act of 1974, Title III, 91 Stat. 1058, 42 USC 5711 "Runaway Youth Act." OJJDP Juvenile Justice & Delinquency Prevention Act of 1974, P.L. 93-415 (amended by P.L. 95-115, The Juvenile Justice Amendments of 1977; by P.L. 96-157, the Justice System Improvement Act of 1980, and by P.L. 56-509, the Juvenile Justice Amendments of 1980) 42 USC 5601 *et seq.*

deinstitutionalization policy, provided insights on some questions involved in deinstitutionalization research, and supplied a framework for further analysis of these additional questions. Given the institutional and organizational characteristics and constraints that we have identified, we can make more intelligent estimates as to the kinds of policy goals that might be pursued and the kinds of research that should be undertaken. Present research indicates that foster care is looming large as an alternative out-of-home placement for status offenders; thus, if research is to be done on actual impacts on youth and families, samples should be drawn to capture the variation in foster care placements and its closely related alternatives. Similarly, we have also found that there is resurgent interest in the use of secure detention for short periods of time; samples should be drawn to capture the impact of detention as well.

While we believe that institutional research is necessary and important, it also has its limitations. It tends to be qualitative, which inevitably raises questions of validity and generalization. In this study, for instance, states were not randomly selected. Rather, they were picked as representatives of trends based on estimates of changes in juvenile populations in institutions, plus other socioeconomic characteristics. We think the states that were selected do in fact represent important variations, but caution must be exercised in drawing inferences about deinstitutionalization nationwide. The same caveat holds true for the local areas and out-of-home placement facilities that were studied.

There is another limitation specific to this particular study, and that has to do with the nature of the statistical data. States differ in their definitions and classifications of youth and their actions, and this fact increases the difficulty of drawing comparisons both across and within states. In addition, agencies and organizations gather and publish information about their work for their own purposes and not necessarily for the purposes of the researcher or, for that matter, any other organization that might be looking over their shoulders (see Kaufman 1973). In this study, we wanted to know which youth are entering the system, which are not, what happens to the ones who do enter the system, and what have been the changes over time. Relying on the data supplied by the key agencies in the field has been troublesome, to say the least, and later we discuss in detail the difficulties of data gathering and analysis (see appendixes B and D).

Given the resources of this study, only a limited amount of original data gathering could be undertaken; we could not analyze individual case records of youth who came into contact with the system. This was a basic research decision, and it should be understood that this decision limits the ability of the study to answer certain important questions. One important question is whether there has been relabeling; that is, have law enforcement personnel and the courts, in efforts to avoid deinstitutionalization mandates, upgraded status offenses to delinquency? The argument is that most status offenders have also committed delinquent acts (a favorite example is stealing small amounts of money prior to running away), and it would be a simple matter to charge the youth with theft if the police and the court really wanted to lock him or her up. Agency statistics would record the youth as a delinquent rather than as a status offender, and there would be formal compliance with the law. This is only one example of the difficulties of relying on agency-generated data. There are other illustrations that deal with potential racial bias, the characteristics of institutions, and other important issues. In some instances, we have been able to shed light on these issues through indirect evidence; in other instances, however, the questions raised by these issues remain unanswered.

Thus far, the study assumes the goals of deinstitutionalization. The problem of defining those goals from a policy perspective will be fully addressed in chapter 3. Later chapters also address the matter of how particular types of federal intervention can further the goals of deinstitutionalization. That is, assuming that we want to deinstitutionalize these juveniles and can agree on what this means, how can that goal be accomplished?

A further level of analysis poses a different question: Given what we know about the playing out of the policies and programs of deinstitutionalization thus far, should the policy of deinstitutionalization be pursued? This question, in turn, separates into two broader inquiries. The first concerns the limits of institutions, and society's capacities to direct and implement social change. For example, and by way of anticipating one of the major findings, it turns out that, for the most part, status offenders are being locked up less and less; in a sense, the first aspect of the deinstitutionalizaton mandate is being accomplished. However, there may be far less effort directed toward the second aspect of deinstitutionalization—that is, the provision of alternative services to these youth and their families within their communities. In some jurisdictions, little seems to be happening at all, at least insofar as the juvenile justice system is concerned; in others, there is a growth in private providership, particularly of a residential variety; in still others, a growth in foster care; and so forth. Given the coalitions that supported deinstitutionalization (including the fiscal conservatives) and the present posture of law enforcement personnel, is there ever likely to be much in the way of publicly provided or funded alternative services for status offenders? Some would favor no intervention at all, but is this sound policy?

Recent shifts of opinion and concern cast even more doubt on the provision of alternative services for status offenders. Historically, status offenders were considered a less serious problem than delinquents, but the two groups were treated in essentially the same ways until very recently. Following the enactment of the first CHINS legislation, there was concern about differentiating status offenders from delinquents and, as we shall see, considerable efforts were made on their behalf. But now attention seems to be turning again toward the delinquents. They are viewed as the serious problem, and this renewed concern is being expressed at both state and federal levels. Indeed, in its most recent reauthorization of the Juvenile Justice and Delinquency Prevention Act, Congress instructed the Office of Juvenile Justice and Delinquency Prevention to concentrate more of its attention on the serious youthful offender (U.S. Congress 1980b). In the states and local communities examined as part of this study, there is increased concern with controlling delinquency. What this means is that there may be even fewer resources devoted to noninstitutional services for status offenders; thus, there is even less likelihood that the second goal of deinstitutionalization will be accomplished. If this analysis is correct, then pursuing a policy of deinstitutionalization means a withdrawal of the state from the lives of these children and their families; it means that the families and the communities have to deal with these youth as best they can. Some who favor deinstitutionalization have always taken this position, but others believe in the necessity of providing services and alternative kinds of care.

The second aspect of the question of whether to pursue a policy of deinstitutionalization is more basic: How has deinstitutionalization affected the lives of the youth and their families, and has the impact been beneficial or harmful? This ultimately is what public policy is all about. The direct answer to this question is beyond the scope of this study, but it is an underlying normative concern that implicitly affects almost every question addressed here. Society looks at institutional settings in terms of "normalization" and assumes, implicitly or explicitly, that a "normal" environment is better for a particular youth than a "nonnormal" environment, which is usually taken to mean one that tends to resemble a prison. It is assumed that community-based care is better than noncommunity-based care, and so on, for almost all of the key issues in deinstitutionalization. Many of these value positions not only reflect considerable professional opinion about how these youth should be treated, but have also been legitimized by court decisions and statutes.[4] Nevertheless, they remain value positions that rely for their support more on basic feelings of humanity and social justice than on evidence.

In this research, we do not address directly the impact of policy changes on the lives of youth and families, let alone the question of whether these changes are good or bad. We note that in some jurisdictions status offenders are no longer dealt with at all by the police and juvenile courts. In other jurisdictions it appears that they are being referred to certain kinds of program settings, and we will discuss the characteristics of some of these settings later on. In still other jurisdictions they may be ignored altogether. But ultimately, it will be up to the reader (or further research) to decide whether these programs, or the lack thereof, are good or bad either for the youth in question or for society.

Our research explores the complexity and major configurations of the juvenile justice system as it relates to the deinstitutionalization of status offenders. It shows, at least in part, what is the most efficacious role of the federal government. Certain kinds of sanctions and incentives are effective and others are not. It shows the limited but special role of the federal government in stimulating change, principally by providing resources at discretionary points in the system.

The study also sheds light on implementation issues of a more general nature. The deinstitutionalization of status offenders is one example of many social welfare and education programs that share basic structural and organizational characteristics—namely, a federal-state, grant-in-aid relationship, with most power and discretion at the state and local levels. This study draws on the research and literature about those programs, and should increase our understanding of implementation issues in these fields. Our study hopes to make a contribution to the growing intellectual and scholarly concern with implementation analysis. This is an exceedingly complex subject, and little theoretical work has been done. Nevertheless, it has come to be recognized as a critical area of inquiry that is of basic importance in an interdependent society, and this study has been cast with these larger issues in mind.

ORGANIZATION OF THE REPORT

The report of this study is divided into two parts. Part I offers a historical overview of the treatment of status offenders and deinstitutionalization,

[4] In addition to the Juvenile Justice and Delinquency Prevention Act as amended (Notes 1 and 3 *supra*), see e.g., *Wyatt* v. *Stickney* 325 F. Supp. 781 (1971); *In re Gault* 387 U.S. 1 (1967).

lays out the major problems and issues associated with the policy, and describes the characteristics of the implementation system and the framework for analysis. It contains the principal findings from the seven state case studies, the analysis of a range of facilities in use for status offenders in several of these states, and the principal findings from the nine federal program analyses. Part I also presents the conclusions and recommendations of the Panel.

Part II presents most of the basic data of the study. It contains the state case studies and the federal program analyses as well as several commissioned papers on particular aspects of deinstitutionalization. It also presents the study's general research design, a discussion of the methods and problems encountered in collecting and analyzing the federal, state, and local data, and the instrument used in conducting the facilities analysis.

Problems and Issues in Deinstitutionalization: Historical Overview and Current Attitudes

2

JULIE ZATZ

INTRODUCTION

Deinstitutionalization of status offenders is a policy that serves a wide variety of interests. What those interests are, how they came to collaborate with one another under the general rubric of deinstitutionalization, and their current standing are the underlying themes of this chapter. In the next chapter, we examine how the laws, concepts, and policy goals reflect the coalescence and conflicts of those interests.

By way of introduction, we present a brief historical overview of attitudes and practices toward troubled youth. This story is but a small part of the history of the deinstitutionalization movement, which is itself a part of the larger debate over how best to deal with social deviance. The following is an overview of attitudes and practices directed at youth who commit status offenses. It begins in the early nineteenth century and focuses on events leading up to the establishment of the juvenile court. It goes on to trace the rise and diffusion of the juvenile court movement that ultimately resulted in modifications in the juvenile justice system such as deinstitutionalization. It concludes with a review of current social attitudes toward deinstitutionalization as it has affected status offenders.

14

ORIGINS OF PUBLIC RESPONSIBILITY AND CONCERN FOR JUVENILES

By the time the first juvenile court was established in 1899, laws punishing children for wayward behavior had been in effect for over 200 years. However, efforts to ferret out and redirect antisocial juvenile behavior intensified over the course of the nineteenth century. It was not so much the character of juvenile misconduct per se but the tendency to perceive it as part of a larger threat to social stability that differentiated nineteenth-century attitudes toward children from those held in earlier periods of our history. Laws providing for state intervention into the lives of disobedient children date back to the Massachusetts Bay Colony where, as early as 1654, disrespect for parents could be corrected by public flogging (Bremner 1971). Juveniles deemed to be disorderly, idle, vagrant, or given to gambling or fornication could also be punished. Although such behavior was punishable by law, colonial Americans depended, in the main, on informal mechanisms—the family, church, and community—to manage and resolve these problems (Morgan 1966, Rothman 1971). Deviance was accepted as an inevitable part of the human condition. Its root causes were perceived as residing in the individual; and while they could never be eradicated, they could be controlled.

By the beginning of the nineteenth century, this consensus had broken down. The importance of the community and the sense of personal and collective well-being associated with it collapsed under the weight of growing urbanization, industrialization, and corresponding increases in geographic and social mobility. Cities and factories were clogged with increasing numbers of people. The factory became the focus of family life, and men, women, and children were drawn into the swelling labor force. Primary control groups became ineffective as urban life was increasingly carried on among strangers, a problem exacerbated by the influx of immigrants. Social deviance was no longer perceived as an isolated condition, and traditional mechanisms of control quickly became outmoded. The entire social fabric was endangered by what was perceived to be the rise of a whole class of people given to chronic poverty and a life of crime.

Indeed, for nineteenth-century Americans, poverty and crime went hand in hand. It was believed that moral inferiority, environmental temptation, or some combination of the two led the poor to engage in idleness, drinking, gambling, and ultimately more serious forms of crime

(Rothman 1971). Believing that the situation called for strong measures, and driven by self-protective instincts, elite groups of the period began to agitate for more formal and effective means of social control. The problems that had once been the province of the family and the community became the occasion for the construction of institutions, asylums, and prisons. Those who could be "saved," would be; those who could not, would be restrained. In any case, society would be protected from the effects of deviant behavior.

Chief among those for whom rehabilitation was believed to be a meaningful possibility were the children of the poor. Like their parents, they were subject to the manifold temptations of urban ghetto existence. The only way to break the cycle of poverty and crime was to remove such children from their families. Child advocates of the period warned that because "poor blood, low moral culture, the pinch of poverty, [and] the habit of indulgence, predispose this class to early crime," there were "no dangers to the value of property or the permanency of our institutions, so great as those from the existence of such a class of vagabond, ignorant, ungoverned children" (Peirce 1869:249-50). Every effort was made to drain the city of these dangerous classes by sending them to live with farming families in the West (Garlock 1979), or by otherwise isolating them from the perverse influences of their immediate surroundings.

The first "houses of refuge" for deviant children were established in New York (1826) and Philadelphia (1829). Generally speaking, the children who were placed in these institutions were not hardened offenders but vagrant or wayward youth whose noncriminal misconduct could be rehabilitated. Over the course of the century, public attention was focused almost exclusively on those children who had yet to commit any serious crime, but whose life circumstances might eventually incline them in that direction. Indeed, some have argued that the juvenile court movement was the means used to implement the concerns of nineteenth-century "childsavers," who were more interested in curtailing juvenile noncriminal misconduct than punishing serious juvenile crime (Platt 1970). Others have cast the juvenile court movement in somewhat more positive terms and have accepted its claims to jurisdiction over non-criminal youth as a function of its humanitarian zeal (Folks 1902, Leiby 1978, Mennel 1973). Serious juvenile offenders were dealt with by the criminal system, while the petty offender was the focus of juvenile justice reform (Fox 1970). The theory was that by removing minor offenders— that is, idle, vagrant, deserted, or wayward children—from the setting that nurtured their depravity, and by placing them in surroundings that would instill the values of hard work, self-discipline, and obedience, the public safety as well as the best interests of such children would be served.

The spread of juvenile institutions and wayward-child laws, and the passage of various types of protectionist legislation (e.g., child labor laws, compulsory school attendance laws, the exclusion of children from particular types of settings and occupations) signaled a fundamental change in the status of children. Although this change was by no means complete until the early twentieth century, nineteenth-century child advocates were bent on differentiating childhood as a distinct developmental stage and on influencing its progression.

The salvational thrust of these efforts to instill proper moral values in the young paradoxically accounts, in large part, for many of the peculiarly punitive features of the system that emerged. Under the guise of reformation and salvation, life within the houses of refuge was harsh and unrelenting (Hawes 1971, Mennel 1973, Rothman 1971). Against charges that children were being committed without proof of crime or due process, institutional administrators argued that the goals of rehabilitation and education did not require such measures. Some officials openly acknowledged the punitive aspects of the system, but most were anxious to stress that restraint of liberty was a necessary condition of treatment and, ultimately, was in the best interests of all concerned. Thus, although there was a good deal of discussion as to the most appropriate form that public intervention should take, the question of *whether* to intervene in the lives of children who were perceived as a potential community crime problem never arose.

Institutions for wayward children spread beyond the eastern urban centers during the mid-1800s. As they did, efforts were made to differentiate between the kinds of children to be served as well as the kinds of treatment to be offered. Care within the early institutions had been essentially custodial, punitive, and undifferentiated. The families of the children in these institutions were believed to be the root causes of their depravity. Hence, institutional life made no attempt to mirror family life. By 1850 child advocates began to reassess this conclusion, at least as it applied to some children in care, which in turn led to a more differentiated series of institutional arrangements. The distinctions were still quite gross, with the only real agreement being that children whose destitution was the unlucky result of birth or parental misfortune and who tended to be quite young should be dealt with differently than the older, more willful offenders. Attempts were made to place destitute children in suitable foster families whenever possible, with institutional confinement to be reserved for criminal, wayward, and neglected children.

While the differences among many of those children deemed ripe for institutionalization were often blurred, there was consistency in the belief that noncriminal youth had to be restrained to be saved. However, the debate persisted over how best to accomplish this end. One of the grayest areas was on the question that also preoccupied a good deal of public attention, namely, what to do with wayward children. Some felt that such children were incipient offenders who, like their criminal counterparts, should be placed in institutional settings that were essentially correctional in nature. Others believed that wayward children were the products of the same kinds of physical and moral negligence that characterized neglected children. As such, both groups could profitably be mixed in institutions bent on their rehabilitation.

State statutes supporting both of these ends (i.e., punishment and rehabilitation) proliferated, and the lines demarcating wayward, neglected, destitute, and even criminal juvenile behavior were continually redefined but rarely clarified. Broader statutory bases for institutionalizing children were sought, and state legislatures and courts regularly complied. The passage in 1853 of the first compulsory school attendance laws that made truancy an offense (in New York), as well as the expansion of the definition of wayward behavior to include incorrigibility, stubbornness, ungovernability, and running away, increased the occasions for coercive state intervention into the lives of ever greater numbers of children. Massachusetts established the nation's first reform school in 1847; wayward, neglected, and criminal youth were often mixed. In an attempt to isolate destitute and neglected children, the state established its first primary school in 1866 for "dependent and neglected" children, whose previous lot had been the almshouse. However, milder cases of waywardness routinely were admitted, effectively blurring whatever original distinction had existed. Similarly, in New York a wayward child might be placed at the judge's discretion in the house of refuge with criminal offenders or in the juvenile asylum with neglected children.

In most jurisdictions, courts and legislatures worked concertedly to expand the grounds for commitment of wayward children. In those rare instances of discord in which the court either resisted institutionalizing incorrigible children at the behest of their parents or sought to limit the statutory parameters of wayward behavior, the legislature responded by circumventing the judicial process or by enacting new and more comprehensive statutes (Garlock 1979). The doctrine of *parens patriae* was steadily expanded to justify the power of the state to institutionalize children and youth who were unable to care for themselves, whose parents were either unwilling or unable to care for them properly, and who constituted not only a danger to themselves but a moral irritant to their communties as well (see e.g., *Ex parte Crouse*, 4 Whart. (Pa) 9 (1838)).

By 1870 at least 18 jurisdictions had made statutory provision for the institutionalization of youth engaged in wayward behavior, either by equating it with a criminal offense (e.g., Ohio, New Hampshire, Massachusetts) or by extending the grounds for commitment for noncriminal conduct (e.g., New York, Connecticut, Louisiana, Kentucky) (Garlock 1979). While the numbers of institutions as well as the numbers of children housed within them steadily increased, few challenges to either the nature or extent of state authority over such children were raised, and those objections focused principally on the lack of procedural due process. Such objections were generally denied (see e.g., *Ex parte Ah Peen*, 51 Cal. 280 (1876); *In the Matter of Ferrier*, 103 Ill. 367 (1882); *Angelo* v. *the People*, 96 Ill. 209 (1880)).

One interesting but limited exception was the ruling of the Illinois Supreme Court in the case of *The People ex. rel. O'Connell* v. *Turner* (55 Ill. 280 (1875)). The court questioned the salutary purpose of coercive state intervention in the lives of incorrigible children and ruled that a child's right to liberty could not be infringed upon for any reason without due process of law. In rejecting several of the bases for extending the power of the state over juveniles and their families, the ruling appeared to rely more heavily on appeal to passion than legal precedent. State attempts to dissolve poor families by prohibiting juvenile conduct that could be only vaguely described and by unreasonably intruding into family relations were persistently criticized. The court also held that the liberty of wayward children was every bit as precious and its deprivation as heinous as that of juvenile or adult criminal offenders. Therefore, guaranteed due process of law was equally important whether the objective of state incarceration was punishment for a crime or rehabilitation of a life of misfortune.

Although the court strongly contested the power of the state to substitute its judgment for that of parents in any determination of action to be taken in the best interests of their children, it neither obviated the doctrine of *parens patriae* nor gave parents complete authority to deal with their children as they saw fit. In spite of its rhetoric, the court objected more to the form of state intervention than to the fact itself: "Other means of a milder character; other influences of a more kindly nature; other law less in restraint of liberty, would better accomplish the reformation of the depraved, and infringe less upon inalienable rights" (55 Ill. at 287).

The Illinois ruling was limited in its impact on subsequent child reform developments. Although the child reform movement was fraught with internal contradictions, it had nevertheless achieved considerable momentum. Indeed, the last third of the nineteenth century was a particularly active period in the development of legal and social conventions directed at children. Major statutory developments reflected an intensified concern with child welfare and included age and hour limitations on child labor, restrictions on the types of occupations and activities in which children could engage, and further extensions of the wayward child jurisdiction. Legislation of the period was supportive of and in turn was supported by growth in the fields of social work, education, and child development, which were specifically devoted to the resolution of juvenile behavioral and emotional problems (Levine and Levine 1970). Societal explanations of individual maladjustment, which had sustained state intervention in the lives of children over the course of the century, were increasingly being supplemented by psychological explanations for juvenile misconduct (Levine and Levine 1970).

At the same time, theoretical justifications for state intervention were also developing and becoming more sophisticated and scientifically oriented. The complexities of childhood and adolescence as unique developmental stages were repeatedly stressed by scholars of the period, such as G. Stanley Hall, William Healy, and Adolph Meyer (Rothman 1980). Their writing greatly influenced professional and lay child advocates and reshaped public attitudes toward children of the middle class and poor alike. Groups such as the National Congress of Mothers (the forerunner of the Parent-Teacher Association) became a major lobbying force in child welfare measures. Leaders of the settlement house movement, such as Jane Addams and Julia Lathrop, were also active in working for programs that stressed the importance of individualized approaches to the problems of familial and social disorganization. Discordant children could not be dealt with uniformly. Once again, existing institutional arrangements for children were criticized for their homogeneous treatment strategies. A system was needed that was both capable of differentiated and preventive care and appreciative of the contributions to be made by psychologists, educators, social workers, and physicians (Hall 1904). This orientation stressed the value of professional expertise and the importance of preserving and extending the discretionary authority of the state (Rothman 1980). Its culmination was the establishment of the Illinois Juvenile Court in 1899 as the first in the nation.

THE GROWTH AND DIFFUSION OF THE JUVENILE COURT MOVEMENT

The founding of the juvenile court was a milestone in juvenile justice reform. It represented the culmination of a century-long effort to rehabilitate and protect dependent, neglected, incorrigible, and delinquent youth through the coercive intervention of the state for the purpose of instilling proper moral values. As such, the court became a vehicle for the child reform movement, of which the social worker, teacher, and psychologist were also now an integral part. Indeed, the first probation officers were settlement house workers who were members of the Juvenile Protective Association, a private lobby organization that actively sought to root out and correct the malevolent influences of urban life (e.g., curtailing alcohol and tobacco sales to minors; fostering community improvement programs, such as the construction of playgrounds and social centers) that helped to foster delinquent behavior. Its treatment philosophy was predicated on the assumption that children who appeared before the court were not inherently bad, but were in need of educative and purposeful activity. For those children who needed more intensive help, the first court clinic was established under the guidance of Dr. William Healy, a pediatric neurologist whose earlier writing had proved influential in establishing the court itself (Levine and Levine 1970).

The probation and clinical services of the court initially were privately supported; child advocates did not wish to submit troubled children to the supervision of public employees whose professional qualifications did not match the treatment needs of their clients. Although they were ultimately unsuccessful in their attempts to prevent the court from being staffed by public employees, the ties between the social service and mental health professions and the juvenile court remained strong.

The court persisted in its belief in the doctrine that wayward behavior was a precursor to criminality, and based its intervention in the lives of such children upon the now well-established principle of *parens patriae*. By separating juveniles from adult proceedings, establishing individuated case dispositions and remedies designed to be therapeutic rather than exclusively punitive, designating specialized police and social service units to deal with young people, and enacting statutory reforms that further enhanced its jurisdiction, the court set in place a system of considerable magnitude and power. Every young person in need of assistance was eligible for judicial attention. As Julian Mack, judge of the juvenile court in Chicago, stated the issue (1909:107):

Why is it not just and proper to treat these juvenile offenders as we deal with the neglected children, as a wise and merciful father handles his own child whose errors are not discovered by the authorities? Why is it not the duty of the state, instead of asking merely whether a boy or girl has committed a specific offense, to find out what he is, physically, mentally, and morally, and then if it learns that he is treading the path that leads to criminality, to take him in charge, not so much to punish as to reform, not to degrade but to uplift, not to crush but to develop, not to make him a criminal but a worthy citizen.

The jurisdiction of the court steadily expanded to include all children who violated state and local laws or who were morally or physically endangered or neglected. In spite of the fact that the causes of these behaviors ranged from parental failure to criminal intent (Teitelbaum and Harris 1977), they were perceived nonetheless as falling along a common continuum, the entire extent of which fell under the control of the court. Criminal and nonoffender youth often were categorized as delinquents. Although rudimentary distinctions were drawn between delinquent and neglected youth, in practice such distinctions were often collapsed (Lerman 1977).

By 1925 juvenile court statutes had been enacted in all but two states. The reform coalition had broadened considerably. The courts drew support from voluntary and philanthropic organizations, criminal justice and child welfare professionals, and child agency and institution administrators. Although each group had its own agenda, they all looked to the courts for legitimization and the further advancement of their interests. For their part, the courts drew support from these groups and continued to dismiss constitutional objections to the incarceration of children without due process of law. The most noteworthy decision of the period, *Commonwealth of Pennsylvania* v. *Fisher* (1905), repeated the arguments that were to carry the reform movement well into the twentieth century: (1) When the state's purpose is to rescue and rehabilitate the child, whatever means it must use to do so are justified; and (2) inasmuch as punishment is not the *object* of state action, procedural guarantees are both unnecessary and inappropriate.

Thus, by about 1925, following a century-long period of experimentation and debate over the best way to resolve the problems of troubled youth, a number of comprehensive juvenile justice reforms were in place. The major objective of these reforms was the rehabilitation of all juveniles who were deemed to be in need, whether they had actually violated state and local laws or, as a result of family circumstances, were morally or physically endangered or neglected. Whatever behavioral distinctions existed between these youth were collapsed in the interests of their common salvation. The juvenile court was at the center of that rehabilitative effort.

PROBLEMS WITH REFORM

In order to apply the principles of reform, new administrative networks had to be created and staffed, judges of adequate caliber and sufficient sensitivity had to be recruited, and treatment programs had to be set up and continued. Although by the early twentieth century there was an apparent ideological consensus among reformers as to how best to construe the problems of delinquent and predelinquent youth, in practice there was much less uniformity. While this was a period of relative stability in social policy for juveniles, the application of reform principles was not without its problems. Imprecise statutory language, the force of judicial personality, and the legislative desire to combine the functions of child welfare and juvenile justice in defining the court's appropriate role produced systems that varied tremendously across states. The duties, standard procedures, and preferred dispositions of the court differed markedly not only from state to state but within states as well. Early reformers had envisaged a juvenile court system comprising judges who would be sensitive to the different needs of individual youth, and who would work with highly trained court staffs that in turn would be guided by the principles of psychology and social work. Together and with the assistance of other child professionals, the judge and court staff would reform both minor offenders and delinquent youth through a variety of means, including institutionalization when necessary, and would sharply reduce juvenile crime.

Such was rarely the case. The judicial selection process was not geared to produce judges of such caliber or with such exclusivity of purpose. There were exceptions of course—Hoffman (Cincinnati), Baker (Boston), Mack and Pinckney (Chicago), and Hoyt (New York)—but these men were unique personalities who dominated their courts and defined the entire character of the system of which they were the most important part (Rothman 1980). More often than not, however, the judge was a man with other responsibilities as well, and did not place a high priority on his juvenile duties. His probation staff were often either inadequately trained, worked only part-time, or were altogether nonexistent. Probation services were entirely lacking in many rural communities. In the urban areas, heavy case loads and the political nature of the appointment process operated to the detriment of juvenile probation programs. Court staffs were often an extension of the judge's personality rather than equal partners in the process. The fate of the court clinics that were established to diagnose children and recommend treatment was not much brighter. Judges were often unwilling or unable to adhere to their recommendations. Unavailability of or lack of coordination of services was a standard problem (Levine and Levine 1970).

These difficulties were exacerbated by the fact that increasing amounts of court time were taken up by petty offenders and youth whose errant behavior defied precise description. Such youth were most often handled informally by court staff, a practice that spared exposure to the courtroom but also encouraged the use of the court as a first resort for the most minor of offenses. Although such intervention practices were quite consistent with the view of the juvenile court as a child-saving agency, they further extended the reach of the court into the family, school, and community. In addition, the informal nature of the process was often obscured by the possibility of the criminal arraignment that awaited youth who refused to accept the help that was offered. This underside of the juvenile justice system was most intensely felt by the children of the poor and foreign-born, who came to the attention of the court on a far more regular basis than did the children of the middle class (Bremner 1971). Such a bias was hardly surprising, nor was it unique to the juvenile justice system.

The lack of uniform procedures, the homogenization of treatment, the inadequately and insufficiently staffed programs, and the worsening plight of the children of the poor were all factors that undercut the success of the early juvenile justice reform efforts. However, they were only part of the cause for mounting concern about the suitability of the juvenile justice system, which had been created to serve the needs of children while securing the stability and safety of the community.

THE DIFFERENTIATION OF STATUS OFFENDERS AND THE POLICY OF DEINSTITUTIONALIZATION

As we have suggested, the reform coalition that originated in the nineteenth century to rehabilitate deviant children and that pushed for the creation of the juvenile court included diverse elements. Some of the supporters of the juvenile justice system believed that the court could rehabilitate children by performing as a child welfare agency. By working with professional specialists, such as social workers, psychologists, and psychiatrists, the court could serve more children in need through a wider range of correctional resources and instill in them respect for social institutions. Others believed that the court should place priority on the protection of the community by incarcerating juvenile offenders until they were reformed. Most child advocates fell somewhere in the middle of this continuum. By midcentury it had become clear that various elements of the coalition were reexamining the premises of the coalition itself.

The juvenile court was not much in the public eye, but it became increasingly apparent during the decades succeeding the court's establishment that all was not working out as expected. By the 1960s the contrast between expectation and practice was so great that the policies and practices of the juvenile court began to emerge as a national problem. Delinquency rates were climbing steadily—a trend that was in sharp contrast to the expectations underlying the juvenile justice system. Crimes of violence (murder, forcible rape, robbery, and aggravated assault) and crimes against property (burglary, larceny, and auto theft) had risen by more than 100 percent (Empey 1973). Juveniles figured prominently in these statistics. By middecade as many as 1.5 million persons under 18 were being arrested annually. Roughly one-half were being referred to court for formal processing.

Concern over these matters and general dissatisfaction with the way in which they were being handled eventually came to the attention of the federal government. The federal role in criminal and juvenile justice had been fairly passive; it rendered advice on technical matters and served as a kind of clearinghouse for information on state practices and juvenile crime rates in those jurisdictions that chose to report that information. The federal role, albeit limited, was largely one of encouraging public support for its reform principles. In 1909 the first decennial Conference on Children and Youth was held to promote a sense of national concern for the well-being of children and to lend legitimacy and support to the efforts of those working in the child welfare field.

Its Children's Bureau (established in 1912) undertook to provide technical support to the state juvenile court movement by promulgating standards for court procedures and by collecting and disseminating juvenile delinquency statistics from various jurisdictions across the country (Kobrin and Hellum 1981). By the 1960s, and beginning with the tenure of President Kennedy, the federal government began to take a more active role in juvenile justice matters (although that role was still quite limited in comparison to that of the states). In 1961 the Juvenile Delinquency and Youth Offenses Act was passed. It undertook to (1) coordinate all federal delinquency-related programs (i.e., principally those of the Departments of Labor, Justice, and Health, Education, and Welfare); (2) improve the economic and social lot of the disadvantaged; and (3) organize, at the local level, the various political, economic, social service, and educational insitutions that have some impact on the lives of troubled youth and their families. In pursuit of these objectives Congress appropriated the modest sum of $10 million for each of three years.

In 1967, with juvenile arrest rates surpassing those of adults, the President's Commission on Law Enforcement and Administration of Justice was formed. The commission had several related objectives, but the one cited as most literally in keeping with its mandate was to "inquire into the working of the existing system of juvenile justice and suggest methods of improving it" (President's Commission 1967b:xi). Noting that over 80 percent of all juvenile institutions were either at or in excess of capacity, that the population of institutionalized juveniles was steadily rising, that operating costs were increasing, that staff/client ratios were deplorable, and that trained caseworkers and psychologists were in short supply, the commission acknowledged that neither the interests of juveniles nor the interests of society were being well served. Of special concern was what the commission perceived as the excessive intrusiveness of the juvenile justice system into the lives of youth whose offenses were noncriminal in nature, and in its report it deplored this tendency.

The states were well aware of the problems of overcrowded reformatories and training schools, mounting institutional costs, and rising juvenile crime rates. The juvenile justice system had been under fire from groups concerned with what they perceived to be its leniency, as well as from groups objecting to the capriciousness of its actions. Many felt that the system's reach had diminished its effectiveness—that the use of a single label to define conduct ranging from curfew violations to aggravated assault was impracticable as well as unjust. Too much attention was being paid to lesser offenders while valuable resources were diverted from more serious cases. Of equal if not greater importance was the concern that juveniles who committed only minor offenses were being treated much too harshly. Youth who had run away from home, had repeatedly challenged parental authority, or were habitually truant were finding their way into the same correctional settings as delinquents and adult offenders. Throughout the nation, legal advocacy groups pressed for procedural regularities in the treatment of juveniles, particularly the lesser offender. Such considerations were thought to be no less important to the operations of the juvenile justice system than to the criminal justice and mental health systems in which due process and right-to-treatment reforms were already taking place. After more than a half century of experience, there could be little pretense that the juvenile justice system had become essentially punitive and adversarial in nature. In spite of its rhetoric, it too often resembled adult corrections.

The first break with the juvenile court's classificatory and treatment philosophy within the states began around 1960, when New York and California modified their juvenile statutes to differentiate between status offenders and delinquents (N.Y. Fam. Ct. Act Sec. 712(b) Consol. (McKinney 1976); Cal. Welf. and Inst. Code Sec. 600-602 (West 1972)). Variously referring to them as children, persons, juveniles, or minors in need of supervision (CHINS, PINS, JINS, MINS), the legislation established a separate jurisdictional classification for status offenders. Some states, like Massachusetts, forbade the commitment of status offenders to the state youth correctional agency, requiring instead that welfare or some other social service agency assume responsibility for them (Mass. Gen. Laws Ann. Ch. 119, Sec. 39G (1976)). It was hoped that by separately classifying status offenders, distinct dispositional and treatment arrangements would emerge as well. One particularly prominent expectation was that community-based programs would play a greater role in the rehabilitation of the status offender than had theretofore been the case.

In trying to determine the precise nature of the reform process and the influences on it that culminated in the national policy of deinstitutionalization, it is clear that many things were going on at once. The lobbying efforts of state and local interest groups stressed the necessity for due process and humanitarianism in juvenile proceedings as well as the cost-effectiveness and overall efficacy of community-based treatments. Legal activists, whose major concerns were with procedural reform and particularly with gatekeeping (i.e., divesting the juvenile justice system of status offenders and keeping potential entrants out), joined forces with fiscal conservatives, whose reasons for pushing for change were quite different. Convinced that the costs of care would remain fairly constant and could be shifted to the federal government through increased reliance on federal cash assistance and service programs, state agency administrators joined with legal advocacy groups in pressing the case for deinstitutionalization with the state legislature. With its supporters lodged both within and outside the system of which it was to become a prominent showpiece of reform, deinstitutionalization became not only politically feasible but politically advantageous.

Federal political and economic support also continued to be forthcoming. This support both reflected and reinforced state and local efforts to amend their juvenile systems. Federal court decisions, such as *Kent* v. *United States* (383 U.S. 541 (1966)), *In re Gault* (387 U.S. 1 1967)), and *Wyatt* v. *Stickney* (325 F. Supp. 781 (1971)), had the effect of legitimizing ongoing child advocacy activities at both the state and federal levels. The *Kent* case challenged juvenile court jurisdiction on due process grounds. The *Gault* decision questioned the rehabilitative facade of a juvenile justice system intent on punishment, and required that procedural guarantees be provided to youth who were subject to the juvenile court's commitment power. Indeed, the *Gault* ruling has proved a milestone in juvenile justice reform, for it pointed up the essential incompatibility between the goals of punishment and rehabilitation that the juvenile court embodied. Although the ruling did not definitively resolve this contradiction, it called attention to the problem as a matter of constitutional importance. Subsequently, in the *Stickney* decision, the federal district court made it quite clear that institutionalization without proper treatment was tantamount to incarceration, and as such was a denial of due process of law. Even though the issues in *Stickney* did not arise as a result of claims being brought on behalf of institutionalized youth per se, the results were broadly applied. Together these decisions helped to set the tone for the prisoner and patient reform movements, of which the juvenile justice reform effort was an integral part. Indeed, in terms of broadening the grounds on which recent juvenile litigation has been based, the impact of these decisions has been substantial. Litigants have used these precedents to (1) attack the extent of the juvenile court's jurisdiction over status offenders on grounds of vagueness and overbreadth; (2) insist on a juvenile's right to appropriate services in the least restrictive setting and to nonpunitive treatment; and (3) argue for procedural protections in status offense as well as delinquency proceedings.

A number of federal standard-setting groups and commissions were active during this period, including the Joint Commission on Juvenile Justice Standards of the Institute of Judicial Administration and the

American Bar Association (Standards Relating to Noncriminal Misbehavior), the National Council on Crime and Delinquency, the President's Commission on Law Enforcement and Administration of Justice
(Task Forces on Corrections and on Juvenile Delinquency and Youth
Crime), and the National Advisory Commission on Criminal Justice
Standards and Goals (Task Force on Juvenile Justice and Delinquency
Prevention). These groups focused their recommendations on reduction
or elimination of the juvenile court's status offense jurisdiction and
argued for increased reliance on voluntarily sought, community-based
services. Although differences existed between these groups as to the
extent of the reform sought and the best means by which to implement
it, all parties were anxious both to redress the inability of the juvenile
justice system to curtail juvenile crime and to redirect its attention
toward the more serious offender.

Federal legislation, such as the Omnibus Crime Control and Safe
Streets Act of 1968 (P.L. 90-351) as amended, the Juvenile Delinquency
Prevention and Control Act of 1968 (P.L. 90-445) as amended, and
ultimately, the Juvenile Justice and Delinquency Prevention Act of 1974
(P.L. 93-415) as amended, served to reinforce the legislative reform
efforts of state and local child advocates and to lend economic support
to a wide variety of demonstration projects aimed at preventing juvenile
crime and diverting juveniles from correctional processes. Indeed, in
several states, federal money supplemented and in some cases was the
sole source of initial support for the development of noninstitutional
alternatives.

The 1974 Juvenile Justice and Delinquency Prevention Act, which
committed the federal government for the first time to deinstitutionalization as a reform in the treatment of status offenders, mandated the
following: (1) imposing restrictions on the placement of status offenders
in juvenile detention or correctional facilities; (2) discouraging the practice of commingling status offenders and delinquents and, more generally, juveniles and adult criminal offenders; (3) favoring small, community-based, less restrictive programs as a preferred mode of service;
and (4) encouraging the diversion of status offenders from the juvenile
justice system whenever possible. The federal act stimulated and reinforced change by redirecting federal delinquency prevention programs,
encouraging the decriminalization of status offenses, and promoting
deinstitutionalization as a policy objective of state and federal practices.

THE CURRENT STATUS OF
DEINSTITUTIONALIZATION

After more than a century of experimentation and wrestling with the problem of how best to deal with a broad range of juvenile misconduct, it had become apparent that the results of juvenile justice reform efforts had proved to be largely unjust, costly, and ineffective. Deinstitutionalization held out the promise of improvement in various respects to several different constituencies and received their initial support for a variety of reasons. Thus, it is not suprising to find that there are fundamental discrepancies among the expectations of various constituencies of deinstitutionalization. A central concern that permeates the entire issue is how broadly or narrowly to construe the requirements of deinstitutionalization. One view stipulates only the removal of inappropriately institutionalized children; the other not only wants removal but also demands the provision of alternative services. The contrast is essentially between the objective of reducing occasions for intervention in the lives of these youth and the objective of modifying the form that such intervention should take.

The fact that deinstitutionalization means different things to different people naturally affects the range of reactions to it. Generally, responses to deinstitutionalization can be described in terms of the concerns of those who from the outset were intrigued by its prospects for increased humanitarianism and economization as well as in terms of professional and community resistance to the policy.

Deinstitutionalization was reform born primarily out of concern for the lack of due process and for humane treatment of juveniles, particularly those youth whose actions did not constitute a crime. State and local lobbying efforts focused on the necessity of removing these youth from secure detention and correctional settings, of divesting the juvenile justice system of such youth, and of keeping potential entrants out. The Juvenile Justice and Delinquency Prevention Act embodied these objectives by prohibiting the use of juvenile detention or correctional facilities for status offenders, by encouraging their diversion from the juvenile justice system whenever possible, and by promoting increased reliance on a wider variety of community-based services.

Today different aspects of deinstitutionalization appear to threaten the occupational and jurisdictional interests of juvenile justice professionals, to arouse the sensibilities and security concerns of certain segments of the community, and to raise questions regarding the overall cost-effectiveness of the policy. But what of the ramifications for youth?

In light of initial claims to its superior humanitarianism, what have been the general results of deinstitutionalization to date?

Although there is widespread concern over what are perceived as the humanitarian shortcomings of deinstitutionalization, there is little consistency in the criticism. For example, some argue that deinstitutionalization has resulted in a kind of benign neglect signified by the lack of community-based services sufficient to meet the demand of recently decarcerated and diverted juveniles (Scull 1977). Others point out a policy that, in seeking to reduce its grasp over youth, has generated "a system with even greater reach"—a widening of the net (Blomberg 1980, Klein 1979a:59). Far from reducing the number of juveniles identified for processing and treatment by the state, community-based services may further augment rather than supplant institutional care (Sarri and Vinter 1976, Morris 1974). Furthermore, deinstitutionalization and diversionary programs may not simply expand the numbers of youth in care (Pappenfort and Young 1977, Rutherford and Bengur 1976), but they may do so in ways that are both more subjective and less pervious to review and procedural control (Coates et al. 1978, Lerman 1975, Scull 1977, Spergel 1976).

A primary humanitarian objective of deinstitutionalization was the separation of status offenders from criminal youth. Yet there is continuing concern that status offenders are not being sufficiently differentiated from delinquents. Adjudicated status offenders, as well as those who are diverted from formal processing, often end up in facilities with delinquent youth and receive the same services. It is apparent that many state and local officials feel that the labels that distinguish status offenders from delinquents are artificial legal constructions used to draw behaviorally meaningless distinctions between essentially similar types of youth (Arthur D. Little 1977). Moreover, a number of recent studies seem to confirm this impression, noting the lack of evidence to suggest the existence of anything resembling a "pure" status offender (Erickson 1979, Kobrin and Klein 1981, Thomas 1976). The common link between those who eschew treating status offenders and delinquents in the same manner and those who eschew treating them differently is concern for the humanitarian quality of their care. Nevertheless, the appropriateness of that care is difficult to comment on in light of the more fundamental difference.

Additional concerns about the humanitarian failings of deinstitutionalization pertain to its potential sexist and racist biases. In the first instance, some have argued that there is evidence of sex-based discrimination in the application of the status offender jurisdiction to young women (Anderson 1976, Barton 1976, DeCrow 1975, Gold 1971, Riback 1971, Sussman 1977, Velimesis 1973). There is a tendency for women to be overrepresented in correctional statistics as a result of greater parental and community intolerance for certain behaviors when manifested by young women, and the types of dispositions that are available (Chesney-Lind 1977b, Teilmann and Landry 1981). It has been suggested that the variability and vagueness of status offender statutes, which enhance judicial discretion, also contribute to the overprocessing of female offenders, who tend to be viewed by the court as being in greater need of protection and care than their male counterparts (Sarri and Hasenfeld 1976). Hence, behavior such as loitering, which might be ignored in a young man, is perceived as sexual promiscuity in a young woman and becomes the occasion for court referral and processing.

There have been studies that suggest that young women are detained for longer periods as well as incarcerated more frequently than young men (Chesney-Lind 1977a). Other investigations have focused on sex-differentiated dispositions by type of offense, finding that girls are more often cited for running away than are boys (Mann 1979). Some states, such as New York, had made it a practice to draw a distinction in their juvenile codes between the sexes and, in so doing, to discriminate against young women in terms of the length of time during which the juvenile court would continue to have jurisdiction over their behavior. Although these statutes have been repealed, the biases that they conveyed most likely continue to influence the juvenile court in its dispositional choices for women (Sussman 1977).

In the second instance (i.e., race), there have been charges that preoccupation with the plight of the status offender occasioned by deinstitutionalization has diverted public attention and federal financial support away from the more pressing problems of minority youth. It has been suggested that such youth, and particularly blacks, tend to be charged and incarcerated as serious offenders more frequently than their white counterparts (Thornberry 1973). Although racial information on the bases for status offender and delinquency petitions is difficult to obtain, there is reason to suspect that race does exert an influence on both the construction of a given offense and on the severity of the eventual disposition. As a result, black offenders are more likely to be arrested, referred to intake, detained, and processed as delinquents than white youth who engage in the same behaviors (Liska and Taussig 1979).

A good deal of work has been done on the differential penetration of minority and nonminority youth into the juvenile justice system. While studies have examined samples of juvenile offenders and have found that race and socioeconomic status are important factors that influence the dispositional process (Arnold 1971, Axelrad 1952, Thornberry 1973), many of these studies have identified other variables as being of more critical importance. Factors such as severity of the offense, previous record, and age of the offender were seen to have as much influence as race, and perhaps more influence.

Although contemporary critics of juvenile justice reform have expressed concern over the prospect of racial discrimination, they are perhaps less concerned with how racial imbalance occurs than with what is being done to correct it. There is concern that the children who are being diverted to alternative treatment programs are, in the majority of cases, nonminority middle-class youth, while minority youth continue to be incarcerated. Once again, it is difficult to find reliable data that substantiate these charges. However, recent modifications in the reauthorization of the Juvenile Justice and Delinquency Prevention Act are specifically directed at resolving such issues.

Criticism of juvenile justice reform variously focuses on such issues as the absence of needed services or provision of the wrong kinds of services, widening of the net, nondifferentiation of status offenders from delinquents or overdifferentiation of the two groups, or discrimination in the identification and court processing of young women and black youth. Regardless of which issue is singled out, however, it is readily apparent that many of those who viewed deinstitutionalization as a means to improve the lot of juveniles now perceive that these interests have not been well served.

Although the thrust of reform efforts was to increase the prospects for the decent and judicious treatment of these children, there were those who joined in these efforts because they believed that the costs of these changes would remain fairly constant or could be shifted to federal or private sources and would thereby be reduced for state governments. However, another source of concern about the contemporary status of deinstitutionalization stems from its apparent lack of economy. Here again, the matter of how narrowly or broadly to construe the requirements of the policy is of critical importance to any evaluation of the results. For those who view deinstitutionalization as entailing no more than a substantial reduction in the size of the states' institutionalized populations with no significant subsequent provision of replacement services, the policy appears to have yielded some increment of cost savings. However, the realization that deinstitutionalization may be more and not less expensive than its institutional counterparts stems from a different reading of the policy—one that requires more than a simple reduction in the size of any given institutionalized population. It further entails the creation and maintenance of a system of noninstitutional alternatives (Arthur D. Little 1977; Peat, Marwick, Mitchell & Co. 1978).

One commentator has observed that, until recently, the assumption that community-based services would be cheaper by nature to provide than institutional care seemed to be largely supportable (Klein 1979a). The underlying premise was that a significant proportion of the institutionally confined could be treated more flexibly, less intensively, and less expensively within the community. By reducing the number of persons served within institutions, and by shifting the incidence or burden of providing particular services (e.g., food, shelter, education, medical care) to private or other public sources, states expected to be able to reduce their own expenditures. Although there is evidence to suggest that the comparative costs of community-based services can be less than those of institutionally based care (President's Commission 1967a, Empey 1973, Empey and Lubeck 1971), such comparisons can be quite misleading.

The first reason for caution in drawing the comparison is that any decline in the size of an institutional population may be offset by an increase in the number and types of juveniles served within the community. By generating what are presumably new types of services and by improving public access to them, more juveniles may be identified as being in need of those services. Even if one were to assume that the types of services offered and the costs of providing those services were no more expensive within a community setting, an increase in the demand for services as well as an increase in the average length of time over which those services are provided could easily eradicate any potential savings.

Second, cost comparisons are quite difficult to make in situations in which the types of services being compared are often dissimilar. The thrust of the community treatment movement, of which deinstitutionalization is a part, is to provide services that are noncustodial in nature. The costs of providing more innovative services may be more expensive both in and of themselves and when offered on a small-scale basis (Koshel 1973).

Third, a decline in the size of an institutional population with no subsequent increase in either the number of persons served or the costs of services provided in alternative settings may still not result in a net reduction of expenditures for the state because certain institutional costs, such as upkeep and maintenance of the physical plant and general overhead, are fixed. Nor can such expenditures be shifted to other public or private sources. Hence, they must be calculated into the total cost of service provision when drawing comparisons between institutionally based and community-based care.

Most institutional costs are not fixed. A reduction in state outlays may be realized if these costs can be effectively transferred to the private sector or are picked up by another source, such as the federal government. However, this is not always possible. For example, juveniles who live at home rather than in an institution may constitute a savings for the state because they are not under the constant supervision of paid staff (Koshel 1973). In this sense families may represent an important source of free labor. But when the families are either unwilling or unable to have their children live at home, and when other sources of support for their care are not forthcoming, the state must once again assume financial responsibility. As we have suggested, such costs will not necessarily be reduced in noninstitutional settings. In fact, quite apart from the inherent cost of the services in question, the transference of responsibility for providing those services from one state governmental department to another may actually result in an *increase* of total public outlays (Bachrach 1976).

Hence, any determination of the extent and degree of cost savings emanating from deinstitutionalization is a complicated matter. The types of alternatives employed, the numbers of persons served, and the degree to which certain costs can be reduced and others assumed by nonstate sources are just a few of the variables that will affect the outcome. While it is fair to assume that cost considerations such as these did not initially occupy the exclusive attention of deinstitutionalization advocates, such considerations have become increasingly important. Indeed, to a significant extent the variability of state responses to and interpretations of the deinstitutionalization mandate reflects a sober appreciation of some of the unanticipated costs of the policy.

A good deal of resistance to deinstitutionalization has come from within the juvenile justice system itself. Increasingly constrained by state statutory restrictions on the nature and range of permissible dispositions for status offenders, and generally frustrated by what they perceive as excessive limitations on judicial discretion, many juvenile justice professionals—including police, court intake and probation personnel, and juvenile court judges—have openly expressed dissatisfaction with such policies (Gill 1976, Isenstadt 1977, Tamilia 1976). Although they generally support the idea of diverting noncriminal offenders from the courts, juvenile justice professionals consistently have opposed attempts to delimit the extent of their protective authority over such children (Arthur 1975). Particularly relevant in this regard have been the attempts of legal advocacy groups as well as prominent bodies (e.g., the National Council on Crime and Delinquency, the National Advisory Commission on Criminal Justice Standards and Goals, the American Bar Association, the National Association of Counties, and the National Council of Jewish Women) to eliminate the jurisdiction of the juvenile court over status offenders as a part of the general deinstitutionalization thrust.

As one commentator has noted, the debate on the issue reflects different kinds of priorities: a protectionist agenda on the one hand and a civil rights agenda on the other (Klein 1979a). Juvenile justice personnel have long perceived themselves as ideally suited to determine what is best for young people whose errant behavior they construe as a cry for help. They further believe that the court is the best guarantor of the right of these youth to services, and are generally mistrustful of both the capacity and the inclination of social service agencies to provide these services. Some would go farther, arguing that needed services are seldom sought on a voluntary basis and that far from eliminating the authority of the court over status offenders, its reach in this area ought to be extended to a degree commensurate with its jurisdiction over more serious youthful offenders. This position is further supported by the view that there is little if any difference between the delinquent over whom the court has extant authority and the status offender whose needs are increasingly being defined as within the sole purview of social service agencies (Drake 1978).

On the other side, the case for removal of status offenders from court jurisdiction expands on the common themes raised by post-*Gault* juvenile justice reformers. There is concern for the lack of due process entailed by the overbreadth and vagueness of state statutes, and for the frequent lack of counsel in status offender dispositions. Those who favor limiting jursidiction also focus on the stigmatizing nature of the court process in which status offenders essentially stand accused by their parents and the presumption is ordinarily one of guilt rather than of innocence (Rubin 1976).

The importance of this debate to the current status of deinstitutionalization efforts is particularly telling when one considers the role of juvenile justice personnel, and especially the judge, in facilitating or impeding the implementation of the policy. The impact of court resistance on the implementation of deinstitutionalization is a topic that has been taken up by others (Arthur D. Little 1977), and is one that we address in subsequent chapters.

Deinstitutionalization represents a challenge to the status quo, in which juvenile justice professionals have long had a stake. Specifically, the removal of minor offenders from correctional facilities, the diversion of such youth from court processing, and the use of noninstitutional settings all threaten the hegemony of certain actors within the juvenile justice system. Much of the institutional control of correctional staff over status offenders has been displaced as a consequence of deinstitutionalization, and their reaction has been considerably less than positive. Indeed, in some locales the investment of these professionals in custodial practice and ideology has proved to be a significant source of resistance to the successful implementation of deinstitutionalization. Certainly this was the case in Massachusetts, where it has been suggested that the abrupt and radical nature of the deinstitutionalization effort was the direct result of two years of failed negotiations with institutional staffs who were resistant to suggested modifications in their correctional practices and resistant to plans to introduce treatment reforms (Miller et al. 1977).

According to the literature, the impact of professional resistance to deinstitutionalization on status offenders has been varied. In some localities, police and court intake staff who are aware of limitations upon their abilities to securely detain such youth have responded by ignoring status offenders altogether (Klein 1979a). Here the objective might be to prod communities into devising ways of dealing with such youth, or to resist diverting the court's resources away from juvenile offenders over whom control can still be effectively exerted, or some combination thereof. In other localities police, court staffs, and judges are continuing to find ways to exercise protective custody over status offenders (e.g., through increased use of detention, or by upgrading the offense) (Arthur D. Little 1977). In any case, and as we will discuss in subsequent chapters, it is clear that the position adopted by juvenile justice professionals is crucial to the manner and extent to which deinstitutionalization has been implemented.

A final source of resistance to deinstitutionalization originates within the communities to which recalcitrant youth are being returned or diverted. The trend toward community treatment of both juvenile delinquents and status offenders is part of a broader movement that disparages the use of institutional confinement for various kinds of noncriminal deviant behavior. The underlying principle of the community treatment movement is localism, which perceives the community as the nexus of rehabilitative and preventive treatment strategies (President's Commission 1967a). Accordingly, those closest to the source of the juvenile's problems are believed to be the most capable of identifying and resolving them. Indeed, federal deinstitutionalization efforts have concentrated on channeling assistance to the local level as a means of inducing communities to develop effective noninstitutional responses to the needs of troubled youth.

However, if an essential remedial objective of deinstitutionalization is to catalyze the creation of a network of informal, locally based services on which families and their children can rely for assistance, many communities have failed to heed the call. Indeed, some have purposely used restrictive zoning ordinances to forestall the establishment of alternative facilities as well as the placement into them of certain types of youth (Coates et al. 1978). To some extent the level of antipathy has varied with both the characteristics of the population to be served and the socioeconomic status of the community in question (Wolpert and Wolpert 1974). Indeed, one national study found that the status-related problems of juveniles tend to be defined by the schools and police as requiring court attention when such youth come from poorer families and when the communities in which they reside lack the commitment or resources to assist these families (Sarri and Hasenfeld 1976). In any case, it is clear that the community can directly and substantially influence the nature and extent of the services that are available to deal with juvenile and family problems.

Availability of community resources in turn exerts a powerful influence on the decisions undertaken not only by referral sources but by the court itself. It is difficult to make an appropriate (i.e., noninstitutional) disposition where no facilities, or very few, exist. Under such circumstances the range of decision choices is limited. The court can either return the child home and hope for the best, or redefine the child's problem in a manner that renders him or her eligible for an available placement. Consequently, the kind of system response that a child receives is more frequently determined by organizational or economic factors (of which resource availability is a prime example) than by the age, problem history, or specific behavior of the child (Sarri and Hasenfeld 1976, Spergel et al. 1980).

Community concerns about deinstitutionalization stem from more than a simple gut-level intolerance to deviance, although there is evidence that middle- and upper-income communities have vehemently resisted the establishment of alternative care facilities at least partially on this basis (Wolpert and Wolpert 1974, 1976). However, even communities that were initially receptive to the idea have become increasingly concerned about the viability of such programs, particularly with regard to their ability to control their juvenile populations. In light of the continuing escalation of youth crime, the voluntary character of such programs has given rise to serious misgivings about their capacity to rehabilitate the juveniles within their charge while protecting the community. These concerns are quite real, and in many cases they have led to a renewed call for the creation of secure facilities.

The literature would suggest that it is not altogether clear whether or not such concerns are well founded. To the extent that deinstitutionalization has meant foreclosure of the option of using secure placements for status offenders without a corresponding increase in viable alternatives, the policy may well have contributed to the state of community anxiety. Furthermore, claims to the effect that the deinstitutionalization and diversion of juveniles into community treatment programs have produced more efficacious results than their incarceration have gone substantially untested (Klein 1979a). What results there are, have been mixed (Coates et al. 1978, Lerman 1975, Palmer 1974). In any event, community resistance to deinstitutionalization has been a significant complicating factor in its effective implementation.

Added to the resistance and types of reservations cited above, it is evident that deinstitutionalization has proved so far to be something less, or at least something other than, all that was promised or expected. The discrepancies are reflected not only in the ambiguities of the basic legislation but also in the practice of deinstitutionalization to date. In subsequent chapters we will examine the promise and the practice of deinstitutionalization in the states included in this study.

CONCLUSION

Nineteenth-century child advocates focused their efforts on the rehabilitative potential of institutions and created a separate juvenile justice system to deal with the problems of recalcitrant youth. By the middle of the twentieth century, it was clear that this social experiment was not an overwhelming success—juvenile crime rates were on the rise and the rehabilitative potential of institutional confinement, especially for lesser offenders, was under scrutiny. A new coalition was formed at the state level between (a) legal advocacy groups concerned with the lack of procedural guarantees and the appropriate treatments that characterized the juvenile justice system, (b) law and order advocates, and (c) fiscal conservatives whose objective was cost savings through increased reliance on federally supported programs for children.

Deinstitutionalization was championed within the states and supported at the federal level as a mechanism with the potential to serve

several sets of interests. The arguments raised in behalf of deinstitutionalization focused on the essential injustice of incarcerating noncriminal youth, and expressed the hope that such youth could be handled
informally within their communities. As such, deinstitutionalization was
essentially a policy aimed at removing inappropriately institutionalized
youth and preventing new entrants from experiencing the same fate.

As was the case during the period immediately following the creation
of the juvenile court, the manner in which the principles of reform were
to be applied was left relatively unspecified. Nor was there much agreement on the key theoretical and administrative issues or policy goals of
deinstitutionalization. Consequently, the task of reformers has been
complicated once again by imprecise and at times conflicting definitions
of purpose, as well as by obscurities inherent in the major concepts of
deinstitutionalization.

3 Problems and Issues in Deinstitutionalization: Laws, Concepts, and Goals

JULIE ZATZ

INTRODUCTION

Deinstitutionalization is a composite reform, one that represents the convergence of a number of different but interrelated objectives. These include: (1) making existing ways of handling troubled youth more humane as well as more responsive to their needs; (2) decreasing the probability that status offenders will eventually become criminal offenders by separating them from youth who commit serious offenses; (3) focusing more resources on the problems of juveniles who commit crimes; (4) promoting recognition of the need for greater procedural and substantive regularity in state intervention in the lives of status offenders; (5) encouraging the diversion of such youth from the juvenile justice system; (6) promoting the growth and development of community-based services for noncriminal offenders; and (7) reducing the costs of care, or at least holding them constant. This list is by no means exhaustive, but it is suggestive of the range of issues raised by the policy.

The complexity of deinstitutionalization is partially attributable to the scope and diversity of its aims, but it is also important to note that none of its objectives has been defined or pursued in a particularly singular fashion. Among its adherents, there is a lack of agreement over what is to be accomplished as well as what has been achieved. The task of its detractors is equally complicated. The difficulty of evaluating results is directly related to the existence of imprecise and conflicting definitions of purpose.

41

This study does not attempt to deal directly with all of the issues raised by the policy of deinstitutionalization, to resolve the conceptual and practical tensions implicit in its several objectives, or to make a case for or advance the cause of one over another. However, in order to understand the impact that deinstitutionalization is having at state and local levels, the different concerns that have been expressed and initiatives that have been taken, and the nature of the federal influence on this process—all of which are subjects of this study—one must understand something of the larger picture. We are interested in knowing what is happening both to youth who were institutionalized as status offenders and to those who commit status offenses today. Have status offenders been removed from secure detention and correctional facilities? Are they being diverted from the juvenile justice system? Are they receiving alternative kinds of services? Are they being ignored altogether? These are the questions we will be answering further on. In this chapter, we briefly review the major concepts and goals of deinstitutionalization and begin to assess some of the considerable dilemmas posed for evaluation and measurement.

THE CONCEPTS AND GOALS OF DEINSTITUTIONALIZATION

Deinstitutionalization is neither a concept nor a process of federal invention. It is a composite of different objectives pursued by various groups at the state and local levels that ultimately found expression in federal legislation. As is often the case, however, the federal policy outcome is the sum of such a variety of initiatives that it is difficult to point with certainty to a single or predominant weave in the policy fabric. As a result, it should come as little surprise that there are gaps as well as genuine discrepancies between the avowed aims of deinstitutionalization and its application at state and local levels.

At the federal level, deinstitutionalization is a broad legislative mandate. Among other things it calls for a cessation of the use of "secure detention or correctional facilities" for "juveniles who are charged with or who have committed offenses that would not be criminal if committed by an adult," mandating instead reliance on "the least restrictive alternative" if such youth are to be placed in facilities at all (P.L. 93-415, Sec. 223). It further specifies that such alternatives be not simply "nonsecure" but wholly dissimilar, in terms of both size and function, from the institutional settings traditionally used to provide custodial care to juvenile offenders. To this end, the legislation recommends that services be "community-based" and "rehabilitative" in nature (P.L. 93-415, Sec. 223).

On first view, the primary emphases of the legislation appear to be both clear and reasonably narrow in scope: (1) to remove noncriminal youth from secure detention and correctional facilities and (2) to prevent the placement of these youth into such facilities in the future. On closer examination, however, the statute either fails to define key terms and goals or defines them ambiguously. The order and nature of the priorities established by the deinstitutionalization initiative are not altogether clear. In this section, we explore and clarify the parameters of the major concepts and goals ascribed to deinstitutionalization.

THE MAJOR CONCEPTS

When Congress identified the deinstitutionalization of status offenders as a major objective of the 1974 Juvenile Justice and Delinquency Prevention Act, it did not precisely define the meaning of the basic terms of its initiative. There was some concern that Congress not be perceived as rigid or inflexible in pursuit of its objective. Federal policymakers were no doubt aware of the magnitude of variation among states (and indeed within states) on such matters as the types of behaviors regarded as status offense violations, the range of settings considered to be of an institutional nature, and the dispositional alternatives to such settings that were available to juvenile justice professionals in their dealings with these youth. Such variations were not to be easily captured under a single definition of *status offense, deinstitutionalization, diversion, detention,* or *least restrictive alternative.* The lack of clarity insofar as the key concepts of this objective are concerned has posed considerable difficulty for those seeking to implement the deinstitutionalization initiative as well as for those intent on evaluating it.

Status Offender and Status Offense

The federal legislation and much of the professional testimony offered on behalf of its passage assumed the existence of a discrete entity known as a "status offender." The term was never precisely defined, but referred generally to "juveniles who are charged with or who have committed offenses that would not be criminal if committed by an adult" (Sec. 223(a)(12)(A)). In contrast to "such nonoffenders as dependent or neglected children" (Sec. 223(a)(12)(A)), to whom the federal proscription against incarceration and secure detention also applies, status offenders generally are not regarded as the passive victims of either their circumstances or the actions of others. Rather they are viewed as having engaged in some action that may be subject to some type of official response.

While not spelled out in the Juvenile Justice and Delinquency Prevention Act, these behaviors are subsumed in state statutes under such categories as truancy, incorrigibility, runaway, beyond control, and variations on the phrase "in need of supervision." However, the definitional task is compounded by several factors, including: (1) different jurisdictions join different actions under the rubric of a status offense; (2) many jurisdictions do not have a separate classification for youth who have committed status offenses, preferring to label them as delinquent, or dependent or neglected children; and (3) social science data and the experience of many juvenile justice professionals call into question the premise that the status offender is in real life any different from the delinquent offender. All of these matters serve to complicate the process of definition.

Although the intent of the federal legislation seems clear, a number of major problems surface in the course of trying to assess whether or not a given youth is in fact a status offender. Among the various states, as well as within them, young persons who engage in similar behaviors are often given different labels, while youth who engage in different behaviors may in fact receive the same label. Quite apart from the highly discretionary aspects of this process, which play a prominent part in determining any given outcome, the fact remains that there is little consistency in statutory definitions of a status offense. Some behaviors, such as running away or incorrigibility, generally obtain as status offenses across states, but others, such as truancy and habitual school offenses, appear to be selectively included. States may vary in their classifications of identical behaviors, as with the case of alcohol violations, which are handled either as delinquent offenses (e.g., in Utah and Arizona) or as status offenses (e.g., in Louisiana and Massachusetts).

Furthermore, even where consistency exists, the behavior in question may lack specification of the kinds of empirical referrants that would give the term meaning. For example, what are the particular characteristics of ungovernable behavior, and are they more a function of the level of parental and community tolerance than a child's actions? What to one family, neighbor, or classroom teacher might constitute disruptive behavior in need of attention could to another be symptomatic of normal adolescent growing pains. In many jurisdictions, there are occupations, conduct, environmental influences, and associations considered to be "injurious to children." What are these entities and do they obtain equally for all children? Indeed, the implicit subjectivity of the standards employed and the general vagueness and overbreadth of these kinds of statutory classifications have persistently given rise to constitutional challenges to their application (e.g., *Gesicki* v. *Oswald*, 336 F. Supp. 371, (S.D.N.Y. 1971) (three-judge court), affd. mem., 406 U.S. 913 (1972); *District of Columbia* v. *B.J.R.*, 332 A. 2d 58 (D.C. App.) 1975).

In many jurisdictions the youth who commits a status offense may not necessarily be labeled as a status offender. The trend in recent state legislation has been to divide juvenile court jurisdiction into three broad categories—delinquent, status offender, and dependent or neglected child—but such neat distinctions do not always apply in practice. The distinctions between a status offender and a delinquent or a dependent or neglected child, though possible to articulate in theory, may well become blurred in application.

The distinction between delinquents, status offenders, and dependent youth is further blurred by the Juvenile Justice and Delinquency Prevention Act. In several places in the federal act Congress makes reference to delinquents, delinquency, and programs designed to prevent and control delinquency. Nowhere does Congress specify a meaning for these terms, although presumably they are meant to apply at a minimum to those youth who commit criminal offenses. In addition, the federal legislation directs that delinquency prevention programs be used for "neglected, abandoned, or dependent youth" (Sec. 103(3)) as well as for "juveniles who are charged with or who have committed offenses that would not be criminal if committed by an adult" (Sec. 223(a)(12)(A)). This expansion of purpose appears to collapse the distinctions that were proposed between these various types of youth.

Further complicating the process of differentiation is the way in which state juvenile codes use these terms. As we have pointed out, a given state's definition of a delinquency offense is not always applied to acts that would be criminal if committed by an adult. Some noncriminal activities, such as curfew and alcohol violations, are classified as delinquency offenses irrespective of the existence of status offense laws (Council of State Governments 1977, Sarri and Hasenfeld 1976). Furthermore, several states are using the delinquency category to cover violations of court orders, such as those in which a child is remanded on his or her own volition into care as a status offender. Finally, many states simply subsume all status offenses under the delinquency heading (Hutzler and Sestak 1977). Taken together, such practices undermine whatever practical distinction exists between status offenders and delinquents.

If status offenders are frequently "confused" with delinquents, they fare no better in contradistinction to dependent or neglected youth. We have mentioned that the term *status offender* fails to appear as such either in the Juvenile Justice and Delinquency Prevention Act or in any state juvenile code. It is a term that derives its meaning by reference to a variety of substitute terms, which in turn are often classified under the statutory heading of dependency. The reasoning here is twofold. First, the desire to decarcerate status offenders and to remove them from the adversary processes of the juvenile justice system has often resulted in the transference of responsibility for such youth from state departments of correction to departments of social services (e.g., Massachusetts), family services (e.g., Utah), and the like. These divisions of state government have long had responsibility for the abused, dependent, or neglected child. Hence, states have simply expanded their definitions of such children to take into account various types of status offenders as well. Wisconsin, for example, categorizes juveniles either as delinquents or as children in need of services and protection. Included under the latter heading are abandoned, abused, and neglected children as well as truants, ungovernables, and runaways.

A second related reason for the collapse of the statutory distinction between status offenders and dependent or neglected children originates with the perception that both types of youth suffer from the same sorts of negative influences. Although status offenders may be theoretically or even behaviorally distinguishable from their dependent counterparts, their actions may be the result of the kinds of parental neglect that occasion the condition of dependency as well. Even though status offenders may not generally be perceived as the passive victims of their circumstances, their actions may well camouflage the fact that all is not well at home. Thus, in trying to take account of this fact, while at the same time attempting to distinguish status offenders procedurally from delinquents, some states have elected to label status offenders as a subcategory of dependency.

Of course, even if states uniformly employed the statutory classifications of status offender, delinquent, and dependent or neglected child, it is quite likely that vast differences would remain as to the kinds of behaviors and conditions to be grouped under each heading. For example, changes of these types have occurred in Pennsylvania three times in the past ten years. Prior to 1972, youth who committed criminal offenses, youth who committed petty offenses, and nonoffenders (i.e., dependent and neglected children), were grouped under two headings: *delinquent* or *deprived*. The delinquent category included all youth who committed offenses of any type, criminal or otherwise. The deprived category included all abandoned, abused, dependent, and neglected children. The juvenile court had exclusive jurisdiction over all delinquent youth, and the county child welfare agencies assumed responsibility for all youth classified as deprived. In 1975 all of these juveniles were reshuffled and categorized under the headings of *delinquent*, *deprived*, and *neglected*. The delinquent category now applied to youth who committed criminal offenses as well as youth who engaged in certain kinds of nuisance behavior, such as running away, incorrigibility, loitering, and the like. The deprived category encompassed youth who engaged in other kinds of lesser violations, particularly truancy and habitual school offenses. The neglected category now covered youth who had previously been labeled as deprived (i.e., abandoned, abused, etc.). The juvenile court continued to have jurisdiction over delinquents while county welfare maintained its responsibility for neglected youth. Responsibility for young people classified as deprived, however, was shared between the two systems, with welfare performing the intake functions and the court supervising all out-of-home placements. In 1978 the categories and their contents were rearranged once again. The headings that emerged this time were *delinquent* and *dependent*. The behaviors classified under the delinquent heading remained the same as they had been in 1975, but deprived and neglected youth were merged under the label of dependent. The juvenile court retained its primary jurisdiction over delinquents and continued to share jurisdiction for dependent children who were placed out of their homes. While the county welfare departments still retain primary responsibility for dependent youth, they do not distinguish youth who commit status offenses from other types of juveniles categorized under this heading for identification purposes. How, then, does one discern what proportion of dependent youth are status offenders? Moreover, since youth who committed status offenses have been continually reclassified, it is not easy to know what has been happening to these juveniles over time.

Furthermore, any theoretical distinctions that could be drawn might very well be undone in practice. Youth who commit identical acts may be consigned to one category or another as a result of the discretion of court personnel or the police. In the event that a youth commits multiple acts, such as running away after stealing money from his or her parents or skipping school to shoplift, the role played by discretion is even more pronounced. Labeling decisions are frequently but not always discretionary. For example, the age of the child is a common measure by which such decisions are made; truancy or running away carry different meanings when manifested by a teenager and by an 8-year-old child. Status offenders have come to be regarded de facto as older adolescents, even though their younger counterparts may well engage in identical kinds of activities. In some states (e.g., Arizona) the law recognizes this distinction by stipulating that very young children who commit status or delinquent offenses must be classified and served as dependent children. Given the fact that similar behaviors may evoke different policy responses on the basis of age alone, the need to probe the practical and jurisprudential consequences of dealing with youth of different ages who commit status offenses becomes all the more important.

Even if the classificatory headings had remained the same over time, if the behaviors grouped under them had been consistently included and defined, and if patterns of interagency responsibility had remained constant, it would still be a complex matter to account for any changes that might have ensued. One would need to consider a wide array of contributing factors in trying to account for changes in the size and rate of growth or decline of the status offender population. For example, if the overall juvenile population grew but the incidence of status offenses remained the same, this fact might be attributable to a decline in the rate of juvenile offenses generally, to changes in the referral practices and intake procedures of juvenile justice professionals, to a change in the level of community tolerance for nuisance behavior, to the numbers of available placements, or to some combination thereof. Although such epidemiological factors are beyond the scope of this study, they may be important determinants of change.

The difficulties implicit in the tasks of consistently categorizing those actions that constitute status offenses and of labeling the youth who commit such offenses as status offenders are quite real. These efforts are further complicated because the premises on which they depend appear to be increasingly open to question. Claims made on behalf of the deinstitutionalization of status offenders have relied on two related rationales. The first is that there is an identifiable population of youth whose behavior is of a noncriminal nature, whose secure confinement is both legally unjustifiable and morally reprehensible, and who require a different order of treatment than their young criminal counterparts. The second rationale is that status offenders are more likely to recidivate to careers of crime to the extent that they are either imbued by the labeling process with a deviant self-identity or commingled either in correctional or detention facilities with youth who have committed criminal offenses (Kobrin and Klein 1981).

Both assertions, particularly the claim that there is a discrete group of juveniles who commit only status offenses, have been challenged. Most studies, both the official and self-report varieties, have concluded that youth who commit status offenses and youth who commit criminal offenses are virtually impossible to differentiate (Erickson 1979, Klein 1971, Thomas 1976). Rather, it is the view of such studies that the actions of both groups of youth constitute a common offense pattern in which the differences are largely temporal and a matter of degree (Klein 1979a).

The latest empirical efforts to ascertain whether there are youth who confine their offense behavior exclusively to status violations has yielded a somewhat more mixed picture. In their recently completed evaluation of eight federally funded deinstitutionalization projects, Kobrin and Klein (1981) discovered that youth who were charged with having committed a status offense fell into two quite distinguishable groups. In the first and larger group, most youth had no official record of any type of prior offense. A minority had a prior record of status offenses only. Youth in this first group tended not to recidivate either to status or delinquent offenses over the course of a year. Of the youth in the second and smaller group, the records indicated a previous history of either delinquent offenses exclusively, or a mixed pattern of status and delinquent offenses. While noting that the evidence for progression from status offenses to delinquent offenses was debatable, the data seemed to suggest that youth who were only peripherally involved in status offense behavior bore the least likelihood of moving on to a career of delinquency and more serious crime. However, those youth for whom a prior record of status offenses already existed appeared more likely to become chronic offenders, as apt to commit subsequent status offenses as they were to commit criminal acts.

The Kobrin and Klein data appear to lend tentative support to the first premise of the status offender deinstitutionalization movement—namely, that there is a distinguishable group of youth whose offenses are principally confined to status violations, in virtue of which distinctive service approaches (or no services) may be required. However, there is little support for the notion that these youth ought to be accorded service on grounds of delinquency prevention, inasmuch as the data suggest no pattern of subsequent offenses, either of a status or delinquent variety. Furthermore, nothing in the data from that study substantiates the claim that traditional juvenile court processing heightens the likelihood of an escalation in the offense patterns for those youth who have no prior records of either status or delinquency violations.

To what extent debates in the literature over matters of this kind either condition or reflect the perceptions of youth practitioners toward status offenders is an interesting question. If in fact there is a clearly distinguishable group of youth who confine themselves to status offenses, is their existence attributable to overly zealous identification programs? Are the youth who are now being targeted for services the same youth who previously would have been institutionalized, or would they most likely have been ignored altogether? In other words, to what extent are the clients of diversion and deinstitutionalization programs *not* the same youth as those most directly suggested by the underlying rationales of these programs? It may well be that there are truly identifiable differences between status and other types of offenders that need to be better captured in statutory definition and practice. Or, the variance in both the classification of actions that constitute a status offense and the categorization of youth who commit such offenses may reflect fundamental empirical uncertainties as to the truly unique features of this class of offenses and offenders.

Deinstitutionalization and Diversion

Deinstitutionalization entails both the removal of status offenders from any type of secure custody—either detention or some postadjudicatory facility—and the prevention of subsequent placements of this type for such youth. It is this concern with the prevention of inappropriate placements that links deinstitutionalization to another strategy—diversion— which is aimed at reducing juvenile contact with formal system processing. Diversion shares with deinstitutionalization the common desire to minimize the intrusion of the state into the lives of juvenile offenders.

If diversion and deinstitutionalization call attention to the need to establish the appropriate parameters of state action, they certainly provide no clear-cut answers as to how this is to be done (Klein 1979b). There are at least three general variations on the diversion theme.

The first diversion strategy tries to find different ways to deal with status offenders under the aegis of the juvenile justice system; specifically, it tries to provide more limited forms of intervention than those measures associated with the use of secure detention or correctional placements. This strategy observes those limitations made explicit by the federal deinstitutionalization mandate on the authority of the the juvenile justice system generally to detain or to incarcerate youth who are alleged to have committed status offenses, either prior to or following their adjudication. However, it by no means seeks to restrict the jurisdiction of juvenile justice professionals over status offenders; instead, it contemplates increased use of supervisory probation or alternative forms of court-ordered or court-supervised services, or court referrals to other services.

A second diversion strategy seeks the removal of status offenders from the jurisdiction of the juvenile court. This strikes at the heart of the longstanding role of the juvenile court as the chief dispenser of justice for the child. As we noted in chapter 2, a number of groups have made this form of diversion or divestment of juvenile court authority the centerpiece of their reform efforts. There is both concern over the lack and abuse of due process inherent in the court's processing of status offenders and doubts concerning the ability of the juvenile justice system to find new and different ways to meet the needs of such youth. In this view, the most important element of reform is removal of status offenders from any contact whatsoever with the juvenile justice system; and if alternative services are to be forthcoming, they must not be initiated or controlled by constituent parts of the juvenile justice system (e.g., police, probation, etc.).

A third diversion strategy insists that status offenders not only be removed from juvenile justice processing but that they also be referred to some type of service alternative within the community. Most typically, such service takes the form of counseling or some type of therapy (Klein 1979b). This approach to diversion necessarily excludes nonservice as an option and can be understood either as (1) supporting the provisions of services to all youth formerly within the jurisdiction of the juvenile court, as well as to youth who would have been subject to its authority, or (2) supporting the provision of services only to those youth for whom they have been deemed appropriate. In theory, of course, there should be some practical distinction between these positions. However, regardless of any theoretical difference between the two—that is, to provide alternative services to all youth who commit status offenses or to provide such services only to those youth deemed in need of them—the practical result often may be the same. Furthermore, as we later discuss, regardless of what that result may appear to imply about public perceptions of status offenders and their needs, more often than not the programs for them will be a function of the availability of alternative service arrangements rather than of the problem histories or family circumstances of such youth.

Taken together, these three approaches to diversion—decarceration, divestment, and referral to community-based alternatives—overlap on some points but diverge on processes and outcomes. Federal efforts to deinstitutionalize these youth mainly concentrate on decarceration and referral to community-based alternatives. The Juvenile Justice and Delinquency Prevention Act emphasizes the removal (and the subsequent prohibition of placement) of status offenders from secure detention or correctional facilities as well as the use, if necessary, of the least restrictive alternative in providing services to these youth.

Divestment is a diversion strategy that is altogether missing from the federal legislation. Although a few states (e.g., Utah, Alaska, Maine, Washington) have elected to revise their statutes to bring about either partial or total divestment of juvenile court jurisdiction over status offenders (Kobrin and Hellum 1981), most have not gone this far. Indeed, efforts to achieve statutory divestment are being countered in several states by attempts to reinstitute the compulsory powers of the court over status offenders by means of "come back" provisions. Such provisions were used prior to deinstitutionalization reforms to make violation of a probation order a delinquent act. Today these provisions are being used to treat noncriminal acts in violation of a court order as delinquent offenses. Under such provisions, for example, a status offender who refuses to accept a court-authorized placement or who persists in running away from home can be brought back to court and detained and/or committed as a delinquent. Thus, instead of moving toward exerting less control over status offenders, some jurisdictions are moving back to more control.

However, while some states seem to be moving away from divestment as a diversion strategy, others appear to be practicing it, at least in a de facto sense. For example, when alternative service arrangements are either insufficient or altogether unavailable, youth who would have been diverted to community-based care may instead be ignored. This result is not necessarily at odds with the view of deinstitutionalization as the simple removal of status offenders from secure facilities. Indeed, some deinstitutionalization advocates of a radical noninterventionist type probably hoped that once these youth were decarcerated, nothing more would happen to them. In any case, as we shall illustrate further on, where alternative service arrangements are either unavailable or juvenile justice professionals refuse to use them, the diversion strategies of referral and decarceration really amount to a form of de facto divestment.

Detention

The difficulties associated with inferring the precise meanings of *status offender*, *status offense*, *deinstitutionalization*, and *diversion*, either from federal or state statutory sources, further complicate the task of determining the nature of both the preferred and prohibited placement alternatives for status offenders. The mandate to deinstitutionalize status offenders requires that states desist in the use of "juvenile detention or correctional facilities," relying if necessary on the "least restrictive alternative" of a "community-based" nature.

The emphasis of the federal effort has been on applying the criteria of security, size, and location to facilities in use for status offenders. Concern has focused on encouraging the use of nonsecure, smaller, community-based programs. However, while mandating the removal of status offenders from "detention or correctional facilities" and in proscribing such subsequent placements, Congress supplied few guidelines as to how these terms were to be defined. Until it was amended in 1980, the federal act provided no definition whatsoever of a detention facility. Recent changes now stress the physically secure aspects of this kind of confinement and permit its temporary use both for juveniles who are charged with having committed a delinquent act and for *any* juvenile charged with violating a valid court order. Similarly, the definition of a correctional facility has been changed from "any place for the confinement or rehabilitation of juvenile offenders or individuals charged with or convicted of criminal offenses" (Sec. 103(12)) to one that permits physically secure, postadjudicatory confinement for juveniles found to have committed an offense or to be in violation of a valid court order. While the original intent of the federal act appeared to be to prevent the use of the same facilities for serious juvenile offenders and for status offenders, this distinction has often been ignored in practice. The changes in the federal statute appear to be responsive to the fact that states and localities wished to retain secure confinement as an option for status offenders under certain circumstances.

The results of applying the original criteria had been mixed and widely criticized, for the criteria were perceived as being too vague to provide much useful guidance. For example, states varied widely in their detention practices. In the juvenile justice system, detention is commonly used both to ensure that no further offenses are committed pending disposition and to protect juveniles either from themselves or their environment. As such, both preventive and therapeutic detention are in use for status offenders (Teitelbaum and Harris 1977). The standards governing their application are neither uniform across or within states nor clearly articulated, raising concerns over the extent to which the due process guarantees of such children are in fact observed (Levin and Sarri 1974). It is by no means clear that the amended definition of detention and correctional facilities will help to resolve problems of this kind. On the contrary, it remains to be seen whether these problems will in fact be further exacerbated by the lack of specificity over the meaning of terms such as "valid court order" or "temporary."

It is widely suspected that status offenders as a group are more likely to be detained than delinquents, and various studies have endeavored to demonstrate this point (Ariessohn and Gonion 1973, Arthur D. Little 1977, Ferster 1969, National Council on Crime and Delinquency 1967, Sarri 1974). The difficulty in defending this conclusion is that while data are generally available on the total number of juveniles admitted to detention, data regarding the offenses of detained juveniles are either unavailable (e.g., NCCD 1967) or available on too small a scale to warrant making such a generalization (U.S. Department of Justice 1975, 1977). Furthermore, in those studies in which data on detention practices for status offenders are presented, the variance both across and within states in the application of the status offender label lessens the ability to make comparative statements or generalizations.

Without explicit delineation of standards by which to make and to assess detention decisions, it is likely that status offenders will continue to be at considerable risk (Arthur D. Little 1977, Pappenfort and Young 1977). The delineation of such standards, which would include specification of probable cause requirements, the evidentiary bases of court intervention, and regularization of procedures governing the delegation of decisionmaking authority, are unlikely to be forthcoming as a consequence of the federal mandate, which is itself entirely silent on these points.

If a broader view is taken of the federal statutory purpose than merely the prevention of the incarceration of status offenders, it is conceivable that state detention programs and facilities may operate in ways that comport with the more relaxed federal requirements, but nonetheless foster coercion. For example, the simple removal of locks from the doors and bars from the windows would not appear to convert a juvenile hall or training school into an acceptable nonsecure environment. This is especially true when facilities continue to use the same sorts of procedures during the admissions process or to impose punitive disciplinary measures (Chesney-Lind 1977b, Council of State Governments 1977). Similarly, the proscription against correctional placements may not be readily satisfied by reliance on the use of staff-secure therapeutic environments, such as public or private adolescent mental health facilities. These kinds of settings may in fact be less susceptible to scrutiny and more pervasive in their infringement on individual liberty than a secure correctional placement, where a juvenile's term of stay presumably is limited by court order. Although this study has not turned up evidence of a substitution of public mental health for correctional placements insofar as status offenders are concerned, other researchers suggest that evidence of such practices may already exist (Children's Defense Fund 1978, Lerman 1980).

Much of the ambiguity surrounding the nature, extent, and specific features of federal concern about the placement of status offenders in detention or correctional facilities can be better understood within the context of two broader concerns. The first concern is with the prevention of inappropriate institutionalization; the second is with the use, when necessary, of the least restrictive alternative in providing services to status offenders.

Although certain sections of the Juvenile Justice and Delinquency Prevention Act proscribe the use of secure detention or correctional facilities for status offenders, other sections take a broader view of this objective and seek to "reduce the number of commitments of juveniles to any form of juvenile facility . . ."(Sec. 223(a)(10)(H)). Congressional concern with the matter of inappropriate institutionalization is evident throughout the act. Indeed, in stipulating its purpose Congress cited the need ". . . to provide critically needed alternatives to institutionalization" (Sec. 102(b)) and mandated that states spend a certain proportion of their formula grant funds in pursuit of this end. Thus, it would appear that federal deinstitutionalization efforts were intended to discourage the use of a broader array of institutional arrangements than those specifically referred to as detention and correctional facilities. However, the federal act does not characterize the features of these institutional arrangements. Nor does it specify the criteria by which to evaluate the appropriateness of their use. There is great variance among the states both as to what is considered an institutional setting and as to what is regarded as an acceptable alternative. We take up these matters only in the most general terms at this juncture, reserving a more complete account of them for chapter 6, which assesses selected alternative facilities in use for status offenders in the states included in this study.

As noted earlier, an underlying premise of deinstitutionalization is that juveniles who are charged with or who have committed offenses that would not be criminal if committed by an adult should not be locked up, forcibly confined, or otherwise securely detained. Such responses have come to be regarded as both excessive and inappropriate in light of the nature of the offense and the underlying problem that the offense may conceal. However, as we have indicated, readily acceptable and agreed-upon definitions of the kinds of alternative settings that would be preferred have proved somewhat elusive. As is so frequently the case, it turns out to be easier to specify in general terms that which is to be avoided rather than that which is to be sought in developing alternatives to institutionalization.

Alternatives to Institutions

The cluster of characteristics generally associated with institutional settings is composed of a number of elements, including size, nature of the physical plant and degree of security, extent of isolation from family and community, length of stay, and nature of the services provided and activities available to the resident population. Although these elements are commonly emphasized both in the literature and in state and federal statutory provisions, their meaning varies. For example, what appears to one person to be a large, routinized setting may well strike another observer as being quite moderately sized and well disciplined. Or, what some would describe as an isolated and essentially custodial environment might be characterized by others as an integrated, rehabilitative setting.

Although individuals may differ on how to categorize and weigh the impacts of these elements when viewed as independent of one another, there is greater agreement on their collateral effects. For example, a large institution that has bars on the windows and locks on the doors, in which scores of children are confined for long periods of time and are regimented in their activities, and that is located in an area remote from their families and communities, is likely to be regarded *prima facie* as a hostile, depersonalizing, and generally inappropriate place for a child to reside. Accordingly, the alternative to be sought is once again very loosely characterized as one in which the fewest restrictions apply, in which the child is reintegrated into his or her community and depends on and uses its resources (e.g., schools, recreational facilties, employment opportunities, etc.), in which individualized attention and individuated services are forthcoming, and in which release from the program is the service goal.

The definitional dilemmas that we discussed above pertaining to the distinguishing behavioral features, if any, of a status offender do not improve the prospects for consensus in defining with greater specificity the necessary and sufficient characteristics of an appropriate alternative treatment setting. The federal act presses upon the states the need to develop and to use the least restrictive alternative for status offenders. However, the act does not define with any precision the hallmark features of such settings, except to urge that they be "in reasonable proximity" to a juvenile's family and home community, and that certain kinds of rehabilitative services (e.g., "medical, educational, vocational, social, and psychological guidance, training, counseling, alcoholism treatment, [and] drug treatment") be provided (Sec. 223(a) (12)(B); Sec. 103(1)).

The stipulation that the least restrictive alternative setting be community-based is a central precept of deinstitutionalization. In principle, "community-based" connotes a small, open setting in which residents have ready access to their families and the support services of the surrounding community. Conversely, the communities in which these facilities are located are encouraged to take a role in the planning, operation, and evaluation of the facilities' programs. Such settings are further differentiated from their institutional counterparts by the specialized attention and types of services that are available. From a federal perspective the goals of removing status offenders from isolated, secure, and depersonalizing environments and preventing subsequent placements of this kind are well served by the development of these types of alternative settings.

The ideal alternative setting, however, has proved to be difficult both to define and to make operational. For example, it is unclear what form such programs should take or what specifically they are to do for the juvenile. Are they to prevent and treat juvenile delinquency, strengthen the family unit, divert youth from the juvenile court, protect and advance the rights of youth involved with the juvenile justice system, provide alternative learning situations, supply work and recreational opportunities, or some combination thereof? All of these purposes are cited as appropriate targets for state action by the federal act (Sec. 223(a)(10)). Furthermore, are these objectives best accomplished by fostering particular types of programs to the exclusion of others? Are group homes and residential treatment centers a better investment of resources than short-term facilities, such as shelter care and emergency crisis centers? Are certain types of youth better served by certain types of alternatives? Are there instances in which the preference for alternative services should take precedence over the requirement that youth be treated within their communities?

Further difficulties arise because of different definitions among states. The federal act does not define terms such as *group home*, *shelter care*, *foster care*, and the like. Although certain gross distinctions can be drawn between such terms, these distinctions often break down when applied in a comparative context. Each term has been used in a variety of ways, and rigorous definitions of the characteristics of these settings are lacking (Children's Defense Fund 1978).

An illustration of definitional and operational difficulties inherent in the use of these terms is represented by the term *shelter care*. Historically, the term has had a reasonably circumscribed meaning. Most observers agree that it means short-term or temporary care of children in nonsecure settings pending adjudication or disposition by a juvenile court (Council of State Governments 1977). Although *temporary* and *nonsecure* are the adjectives most commonly used in connection with shelter care facilties, it is important to note that the facilities designated as shelter care settings frequently do not measure up to these standards. For example, the critical distinction between shelter care and detention—that is, the degree of physical security—may become blurred in practice. Or states may vary widely in their estimations of the temporary character of shelter care. For example, in Virginia the limit is 30 days whereas in Utah such facilities may only be used for up to 48 hours.

These kinds of differences complicate the tasks of evaluation and measurement and raise questions about the congruence between federal intentions and state practice. Where such intentions are not altogether clear or are contradictory, and where states diverge in their application of the concepts under discussion, it becomes more difficult to make causal statements about the impact of the federal deinstitutionalization

initiative on state action. We will have more to say about the characteristics of the implementation system as it affects the federal/state interaction in the next chapter. However, the definitional difficulties that
we have been discussing have an important bearing on policy outcomes
for status offenders. Having discussed some of the more common meanings ascribed to the major concepts associated with deinstitutionalization, we turn now to a discussion of some of its goals.

POLICY GOALS

From its origins as a reform movement sponsored at the state level by
coalitions of youth advocacy groups and political and fiscal conservatives, through its enhancement by federal judicial and legislative activity,
to its ultimate enactment as a national mandate, the policy of deinstitutionalization has embodied a number of diverse aims. As we suggested
at the outset, its goals range from improving, in a humane sense, the
character of the treatment of young people by releasing from secure
confinement youth who are neither criminal nor severely disturbed and
pressing for greater procedural regularity in their dealings with the juvenile justice system, to enhancing delinquency prevention techniques
and achieving greater cost efficiency in the design and delivery of youth
services.

These purposes are not necessarily incompatible, but they are diffuse.
The objectives that deinstitutionalization was intended to serve are neither uniformly defined nor clearly ordered. They can be translated into
a wide variety of program possibilities, the content and structural features of which have gone largely unspecified except in the most general
of terms—that is, the programs are to be "alternative" in nature. Furthermore, the difficulty of ordering the normative and operational priorities of deinstitutionalization is exacerbated by precisely the kinds of
underlying conceptual ambiguities and inconsistencies mentioned earlier. These definitional complexities have been cited as major impediments to successfully implementing deinstitutionalization (Klein 1979b).
Imprecision in specifying and ordering the policy goals and operational
objectives has led to the characterization of deinstitutionalization as "ad
hoc policymaking" by some (Rutherford and Bengur 1976) and as a
nonsystematic "strategy of activity" by others (Empey 1973).

One way of conducting an orderly investigation of these policy goals
is to identify the important underlying characteristics of the various goals
associated with deinstitutionalization and to determine how they have
been captured in the operational features of the policy. Clearly, the
major rationale for deinstitutionalization is one of finding ways to reduce

the extent of the coercive reach of law enforcement and juvenile justice agencies over youth whose conduct may pose a nuisance to parents and communities but is nevertheless without criminal content. As part of a broader wave of reform that emphasizes the punishment's fitting the crime rather than the criminal (Matza 1964, 1969), deinstitutionalization and diversion emphasize that juveniles who have not committed criminal offenses should not be treated, on the grounds of rehabilitation or delinquency prevention, as if they had done so. Indeed for some, deinstitutionalization represents an opportunity to place certain types of juvenile behavior completely off limits to state intervention (Schur 1973).

Inasmuch as the juvenile justice system and the larger law enforcement network of which it is a part are the traditional vehicles of social condemnation and punishment of deviant conduct, a consistent objective of deinstitutionalization advocates has been to try to divert youth who commit status offenses from these systems by means of a variety of diversion strategies. Each of these strategies—decarceration, divestment, referral to community-based alternatives—has achieved a certain amount of currency among those whose actions are most immediately affected by the deinstitutionalization mandate (i.e., law enforcement officers, judges and related court personnel, community service workers, etc.) as well as among social scientists and legal advocates for children. Furthermore, each view of the appropriate end of diversionary programs carries with it a different construction of both the problem to be resolved and the significance of the behavior of the youth in question, and the best means by which to address the needs of these youth and their families.

For example, if decarceration is the primary objective, then those who favor this end might be expected to resist the substitution of alternative types of services for these youth. Such a noninterventionist approach suggests that the problem to be resolved is one of securing the conditions for removal of these children and monitoring the placement system to prevent abuses of restrictions in the future. This approach also imparts a view of status offense behavior as an ordinary part of adolescent development—a stage through which all children pass on their own accord. It assumes that formal system intervention in the lives of children whose behavior is of the status offense variety is inappropriate, unwarranted, and potentially more harmful than simply doing nothing at all while waiting for time to pass (Schur 1973).

However, if the provision of an appropriate replacement service is the goal, then the problem to be resolved is cast in a somewhat different light. The tasks then become those of specifying the content and form of the nonjudicial alternatives to be used and of establishing the criteria for selecting those youth who are to receive services. This approach places a different construction on status offense behavior than that attributed by the view of deinstitutionalization as decarceration, for now the status offender is perceived as the object of unmet needs or faulty interpersonal relationships. The objective under these latter circumstances is to treat the child for some restorative or rehabilitative purpose in settings that are nonrestrictive and more humane than their institutional counterparts. Although this approach to deinstitutionalization is predicated on concerns about the efficacy of institutional settings similar to those held by adherents of deinstitutionalization as decarceration (or even deinstitutionalization as divestment), it perceives a problem in the child that stands in need of redress whereas the other approaches may perceive that, on balance, no such problem exists.

It seems clear that there is support for increasing the possibilities for nonjudicial handling of youth who commit status offenses. The claimed advantages of this approach are familiar. To some extent they are the outgrowth of efforts to impress the importance of due process considerations on the ways in which we have traditionally thought about the general problem of delinquency and the appropriate limits of state action. Nonjudicial handling holds out the promise of placing the status offender issue in a more proper context; youth who have done little or nothing to warrant the coercive intervention of the state will in turn receive less stringent attention. Nonjudicial processing, at least in theory, permits a more flexible response to juvenile misbehavior, one that will minimize the likelihood that what starts out to be a relatively trivial matter will end up being magnified in ways designed to accommodate the needs of the system rather than the needs of the child. Furthermore, the voluntary character of nonjudicial alternatives may serve to channel available services to those who are both most in need and most prepared to accept them, while reducing the tendencies toward overreach and overkill in a system in which services are both narrowly defined and forcibly imposed.

However, the fact that increased reliance on nonjudicial handling is a recognized policy goal of deinstitutionalization has not produced a similar consensus on how that goal is to be pursued. Just as diversion has proved capable of taking many forms, so too are the goals of alternative processing and alternative services susceptible to diverse interpretations and outcomes. As a result, the consequences of these reform efforts appear to have confounded the expectations of advocates and child professionals alike in a number of different respects. For example, there is mounting concern that instead of reducing the extent of formal intervention in the lives of aberrant children, the development and growth of alternative service arrangements may in fact lead to a more expanded processing of these children (Coates et al. 1978). Consequently, and contrary to expectation, more and not fewer young people may be getting caught up in the juvenile justice or social service system than was the case prior to deinstitutionalization (Lerman 1975, 1977; Scull 1980).

One explanation for the possible overprocessing of noncriminal youth may be that it is subject to the difficulties inherent in the task of what some have called "client targeting" (Klein 1979b). The federal deinstitutionalization legislation speaks of the need to "divert juveniles from the traditional juvenile justice system and to provide critically needed alternatives to institutionalization" (Sec. 102(b)), but it does not specify (1) who the targets of these services are to be, (2) how they are to be identified, and (3) under what circumstances they are to receive services. Presumably, the clients of these services are previously incarcerated status offenders *and* those youth who would have been institutionalized as such in the past. The problems, of course, come in knowing who would have been institutionalized in the past and in further determining whether such children would benefit by the provision of services today. For example, the fact that the states do not uniformly define the kinds of behaviors that previously would have rendered a child eligible for institutionalization makes it very difficult to assess whether the children who receive services today are in fact the same as those who would have been candidates for institutionalization in the past. The Kobrin and Klein data provide some basis for such a comparison because of their success in establishing an appropriate sample (Kobrin and Peterson 1981). For the most part, however, the state of the art and forces of circumstance make it impossible to know with certainty whether these children would *in fact* have been institutionalized or whether they will be any better off in an alternative setting than they would be if they were simply left alone. These kinds of questions will always be extremely difficult to answer. Nonetheless, without a clearer understanding of and greater agreement on the kinds of principles that should govern the development and use of nonjudicial alternatives, problems of this type will likely continue to confound deinstitutionalization efforts.

A related discontinuity between the policy goals and the policy outcomes of deinstitutionalization is suggested by the kinds of emphases placed by both the courts and social service agencies on "problemizing" the very juvenile behaviors that, in theory, the goals of deinstitutionalization seek to normalize. Indeed, part of the mystique of deinstitutionalization lies in its devotion to the principle of "normalization" (Rosenheim 1976a). Instead of incarcerating a juvenile for nuisance

behavior, society should instead reorient its thinking and alter its institutional reponses to reflect a greater tolerance of low-level deviancy.
Services will focus on helping youth through what is avowedly a turbulent
period for all young people while trying to ameliorate the most severe
differences that strain interactions among adolescents, their parents,
and their communities. Normalization, then, entails acceptance of the
fact that *some* deviance from parental and societal norms is a normal
part of growing up.

The difficulty may come when attempts are made to realize this policy
goal in the context of another—namely, the separation, for purposes of
identification and treatment, of youth who commit status offenses from
those who engage in more serious kinds of misconduct. To do so may
be to succumb to the fallacy of which we previously spoke—that is,
drawing a distinction between types of juveniles where none may exist.
More importantly, however, society may be encouraging the kind of
specialization of treatments and service procedures that will lead to a
greater "problemization" of status offender behavior. Consequently,
those who receive services for whatever reason automatically will be
perceived as "problem youth"; those who do not receive services may
be mistakenly assumed to be without need. Under these circumstances,
the efficacy of a program becomes a function of the numbers of children
that it serves and the degree to which it is successful in resolving their
problems. The measures chosen by which to make such evaluations are
likely to be inappropriate if the programs mistake their own purpose
and misperceive the needs of the youth whom they serve. Such inconsistencies result from a programmatic approach in which many objectives
are being pursued in many fashions. Once again, without a clearer
depiction of the objectives that deinstitutionalization is intended to serve
and of how those objectives are to be ordered, the task of the reformer
as well as the researcher is likely to be subverted.

CONSEQUENCES FOR EVALUATION

The obscurities and complexities inherent in the major concepts and
policy goals of deinstitutionalization are not accidental; rather, they
reflect the ambiguity and lack of agreement on who status offenders
are, how they got to be the way they are, and what if anything should
be done to or for them. We have spoken of the difficulties posed by
the ambiguities and inconsistencies inherent in the major concepts and
goals of deinstitutionalization for those who are trying both to implement
the policy and to live with it. These same difficulties also have conse-

quences for those who are interested in the study and evaluation of policy.

The federal deinstitutionalization legislation recognizes but does not elaborate on the behavioral distinction that it draws between status offenders and youth who commit delinquent offenses; nor does the act establish a classification scheme by which to determine the kinds of actions that uniformly constitute status offenses. At the state level, matters are frequently no more clear—different actions are often labeled the same, while identical actions are labeled differently. This is the case both within and across states. Furthermore, in practice the distinctions between a status offense and a delinquent offense, as well as between a status offender and a delinquent offender, are commonly blurred.

The lack of distinction in law and practice is troubling to those who work with these youth as well as to the youth themselves. In the absence of clear rules to govern the extent of intervention, discretion becomes an even more important tool in an already subjective process. Of course, discretion can cut both ways. While fewer rules may permit greater flexibility, their absence may also result in a myriad of practical dilemmas for those charged with responsibility for youth who engage in petty offenses. Whether and what to do for (or to) these youth are choices that may largely come down to the personal preferences and predilections of referral sources and key actors (e.g., intake personnel, judges, case workers, etc.). Dispositions become uncertain. Youth, who under a prior system might have received a stiffer disposition, could also be handled informally or diverted altogether. Under a more flexible, humane system, youth who commit minor offenses may be handled more harshly.

These kinds of disparities are also troublesome from a research and evaluation perspective. Determining who and how many status offenders there are, and whether and why there are more or fewer of them being identified and labeled as such today, is hazardous under circumstances in which the classificatory headings and the behaviors that are grouped under them vary so widely. These tasks are further complicated to the extent that the definitions of these children and their behaviors, as well as the state agencies that bear responsibility for their care, have fluctuated over time.

The problems associated with determining who status offenders are and what a status offense is, necessarily have implications for the tasks of discovering where status offenders have gone and what is happening to them. Have status offenders in fact been deinstitutionalized? Have they been removed from preadjudicatory and postadjudicatory detention, correction, and other kinds of secure facilities? Are they being diverted from the juvenile justice system to some other public system, such as welfare or social services? Or are they simply being diverted out of care altogether? These questions are addressed in some detail in the individual state case studies as well as in our overall findings and conclusions.

As we have suggested, the core of the deinstitutionalization mandate consists of the requirement that juveniles who are charged with or who have committed offenses that would not be criminal if committed by an adult be removed from secure detention and correction facilities. There is fairly consistent evidence to support the finding that such youth in the states that we have studied are being removed from postadjudicatory secure placements of the old stripe (training schools, jails, etc.), but that at least in some states, their places are being taken by delinquent youth (see chapter 5). The evidence is less clear, however, with regard to preadjudicatory detention facilities.

Interagency shifts in responsibility for youth who commit status offenses have been accompanied by seemingly significant changes in referral, intake, labeling, payment, and placement practices as well. Services and facilities that were traditionally reserved for treatment of one kind of child are being extended and adapted for use by another. One important example is the increased use of foster care for status offender youth. Traditionally, foster care has been used for a younger, less troublesome population. Today it is a prominent alternative placement for status offenders as well. Furthermore, the picture is in more or less constant flux as states continually modify and reorganize their public systems in response to factors that may have nothing directly to do with these juveniles but that may affect them nevertheless. New public officials are elected with different political priorities and different ideas about how state government should be structured and run. State and local court districts are redrawn; social service systems are made more centralized or are decentralized altogether. Such changes have consequences for youth as well as for the individuals who study them.

Changes of this type can complicate the task of determining where youth who commit status offenses have gone and what, if anything, is happening to them. Variance in the content and extent of diversion practices, in the availability of noninstitutional resources, and in the readiness of officials to push for the development and use of these resources are just some of the variables that may influence what happens to these youth as a consequence of deinstitutionalization. The manner in which such decisions are made and accounted for and the means employed to review and monitor the outcomes of these decisions in terms of their impact on youth are often fuzzy and eclectic. Why one youth and not another receives a particular disposition, and the character of the ensuing treatment, are questions that are made even more difficult to answer when labeling, dispositional, and oversight procedures are so highly variable, and the statutory guidelines that do exist are either so vague or so unpalatable as to go unobserved.

These are just some of the difficulties that policy goals and underlying concepts of deinstitutionalization pose for attempts at measurement and evaluation. They will be described and illustrated in more complete detail in the individual state studies of deinstitutionalization presented in Part II. As we have suggested, such difficulties have important consequences for youth and for those who work with them, and we have been concerned with these as well. The framework for analysis presented in the next chapter suggests the way in which we have gone about studying these consequences.

4 The Implementation System: Characteristics and Change

JOEL F. HANDLER *and* JULIE ZATZ

INTRODUCTION

What accounts for change in the process of the deinstitutionalization of status offenders? In this chapter we set forth a framework for organizing the data that were gathered on federal, state, and local programs over the course of our research. We first delineate the general characteristics of the implementing structures on which the success of any public program must, to some degree, rely. These structures comprise a decentralized system of relatively autonomous agencies that exercise a good deal of control over their own affairs. Decentralization is especially pronounced in the juvenile justice system, with its strong traditions of local control, independent courts, and associated social welfare agencies and service providers that have their own organizational needs and agendas. This implementation system is characterized by the reciprocity of relations between its component parts rather than by the exercise of control from above.

The second part of the chapter discusses theories of implementation. What variables are important when assessing the likelihood that programs will be implemented? In answering this question, our focus is on the characteristics and the processes of the implementing agencies and the relationships between them. The chapter concludes with a discussion of "backward mapping," a mode of analysis that starts at the ground level of implementation systems and focuses on the exercise of discretion. Backward mapping is both descriptive and normative. Here, it is

66

used descriptively. In chapter 9, in which we discuss principal findings and recommendations, we use backward mapping normatively to suggest how the federal government might better go about implementation.

THE CHARACTERISTICS OF THE IMPLEMENTING STRUCTURES

The federal policies and programs that are the subject of this study are addressed to the states, their courts, their political subdivisions, and their service providers. They are the organizations that will deliver the actual services. The characteristics of these organizations are important because the implementation of public policies is uncertain, particularly in the broad area of social welfare where there are multiple programs and where different jurisdictions and agencies, each with its own agenda, are called on to respond to these policy mandates. Programs get carried out, but to varying degrees and often in unintended ways (Bardach 1977, Berman 1978, Hargrove 1975, Nakamura and Smallwood 1980, Pressman and Wildavsky 1979, Sabatier and Mazmanian 1980, Williams 1980).

Something happens when programs enter the implementing structures. Mayer Zald, drawing on the literature on the implementation of public policy, posits (1980:20-21):

To the extent that the actual delivery of service, goods, contracts, behavior, depends upon an inter-connected, though not well integrated set of groups and authority, to the extent that the various components of the target system [the state and local governments as social systems] do not share the same goals, nor share the goals with the implementing agency, and to the extent that the components of the target system are not well coordinated and integrated, implementation will fall short of the mark and target systems will not deliver desired outputs. Where, on the other hand, the target objects [state systems] have unambiguous structures of coordination and well established procedures, or easily established procedures for monitoring actual progress and program compliance, implementation problems decline.

The basic relationship between the federal programs of this study and the states is the grant-in-aid. Under this arrangement, the federal government offers the states money that will pay for varying portions of the service to be delivered. The states are free to accept or reject the offer, but if they do accept, then they have to abide by certain conditions of the program. Most major social welfare programs have this relationship: health (Medicaid), income maintenance (AFDC and, until recently, adult categorical assistance), education, and social and child protection services. In some of these programs, the federal financial contribution is crucial (e.g., Medicaid, which is literally a creation of federal government). The federal contribution is almost as crucial with AFDC, although the state programs were in place and functioning long before the federal programs went into effect (Steiner 1966). In programs relating to education and to criminal justice administration, however, federal involvement is more recent and the proportion of federal dollars is much less than in the other areas.

The states are not, however, required to participate in grant-in-aid programs. Arizona, for example, has not joined the Medicaid program; but that is the only state which does not participate, and in all other major federal grant-in-aid programs in the social welfare field there is 100 percent state participation. Nevertheless, the situation is different with participation in the Juvenile Justice and Delinquency Prevention Act. It took several states (e.g., Utah and Louisiana) a long time to join; for what they were getting, they felt that they could well afford to wait.

State agreement to participate raises rather than settles the implementation issue. The degree of implementation of the program depends on the characteristics of the mandate (e.g., what the federal government wants the states to do), the funding, and the characteristics of the federal and state agencies as well as their environments—in short, the entire social system of the implementation structure. The federal programs in this study cut across several fields, including law enforcement and corrections, welfare, child protection, social services, health, and mental health. Each field has its own traditions and relationships, not only with the federal government but also within each of the states and their subdivisions and agencies. Although this makes generalization difficult, there are some basic characteristics that apply more or less generally across fields.

First, each of the fields has its own bureaucracy or system of agencies that delivers the services. In every state and local subdivision there are schools, courts, police departments, child protection agencies, social welfare departments, and quite often hospitals, clinics, public institutions, and networks of private providers. It is crucial to recognize that these are on-going agencies that have had a long and active life before the federal programs began, that these agencies have their own agendas and organizational needs, and that the significance of federal programs may vary among individual state and local agencies. In any event, deinstitutionalization is not of major significance for most of these agencies. The central mission of the schools is not to deal with status offenders. The same is true of welfare, social services, health, and mental health and, to a lesser extent, of police, juvenile courts, and child protection agencies.

The second point to note is that most agencies in the social welfare field are relatively autonomous from state government. Autonomy is a matter of degree; it is used here to indicate latitude of discretion. Some agencies have a great deal of autonomy as a matter of both historical tradition and of current structural arrangements. For example, there is very little state control over law enforcement and the juvenile courts. These local agencies have strong traditions of independence, few state requirements, and exercise a great deal of discretion. The same can fairly be said of education; the independent traditions of local school districts are quite strong, and usually resist state efforts for control (Murphy 1971). Social welfare and child protection agencies are under more state control but still retain a great deal of autonomy. Welfare functions traditionally were local, but over the years state governments have assumed more control. There is now a great deal of state-level control over local departments of welfare with regard to income maintenance, but there is less control over the more discretionary programs, such as social services and child protection, where the nature of the work makes supervision more difficult (Handler 1979, Lipsky 1980, Pesso 1978).[1] Within each state, the traditions and patterns of autonomy vary and there is variation for each of the substantive areas. The important fact, though, is that this autonomy does exist and it is significant. The problems of implementation that the federal government has with the states are the same problems that state governments have in dealing with their bureaucracies.[2]

A third factor that fosters autonomy is the purchase of services from private and nonprofit organizations. There has been a long tradition of public purchase of services from the private sector in the social services and child protection fields, and it seems to be an increasingly frequent practice as a result of deinstitutionalization of status offenders. States that choose to purchase rather than provide services to these youth contract with a variety of private organizations that offer an array of programs ranging from counseling and after-school recreation to residential facilities with on-site schooling. To the extent that these private organizations are used, they become part of the implementing structure; but they are loosely coupled and are difficult to coordinate. These organizations, in the course of time, become independent actors in the bureaucratic and political process; they fight for their prerogatives and

---

[1] In looking at two intake units of the Massachusetts Department of Public Welfare, Pesso draws the distinction between "soft areas," where a great deal of discretion is exercised, and eligibility determination, where the activity is highly formalistic, highly visible, and involves careful supervisory review.

[2] For a history of the struggle of the Wisconsin Department of Welfare to assert control over county departments of welfare, see Handler and Hollingsworth (1971).

their interests as they see them, not only within the implementation system but also at the political level. Their strength varies by state and by substantive area.

In most of the substantive areas, there are professional organizations and other interest groups (e.g., teachers, judges, police, social workers, health and mental health professionals, as well as citizen advocacy groups) that have varied and complicated relationships to state and local governments. These organizations take a keen interest in the work of the agencies and lobby at the executive and legislative levels for their programs. Depending on the issue and the degree of their strength and influence, they can either resist state efforts at control, thereby serving to increase local autonomy and discretion, or they can aid in efforts to curb local discretion. They are often an important component of the implementation process.[3]

In sum, despite the variation across substantive fields, it is probably accurate to say that within every state the relationship between the chief policymakers in the state (including the heads of the major departments) and the agencies that deliver the services is best characterized as decentralized, with loose chains of command and concomitant problems of communication, information gathering, and coordination. This overall characterization, of course, can vary in degree.

A similar analysis applies when one considers the relationship of the states to the federal government. In most of the substantive social welfare areas, history, tradition, power, and influence are weighed on the side of the states. Federal participation is in the form of the grant-in-aid accompanied with a range of federal requirements. The extent to which the federal requirements and money are successful in influencing state behavior depends on the level of funding, the characteristics of the requirements, and the willingness and ability of the federal government to monitor the programs and, if need be, insist on state compliance. There is great variance in all aspects of the federal-state relationship. In some programs, such as AFDC, there are federal conditions (e.g., basic eligibility) that are fairly clear-cut, but there also are large areas of the program that are left almost entirely to state discretion (e.g., the level of benefit). In other programs, such as Medicaid, the regulatory presence is heavy with a great many specific rules. In still others, federal requirements amount to little more than authorization to do things under vague standards.

---

[3] The more sophisticated implementation studies incorporate special interest groups as part of the implementation system rather than as forces outside the bureaucratic chain of command. For two of the best statements, see Lowi (1969) and Wilson (1973).

Federal enforcement is uneven. The enforcement machinery itself is weak and understaffed. Procedures are not well established and monitoring is difficult because of the inadequacies of the data-gathering systems (Kaufman 1973, Levitan and Wurzburg 1979). The politics of enforcement usually serve to weaken federal control. The major state bureaucracies are powerful forces within the states and, as such, usually have powerful friends in the Congress. After programs are enacted at the federal level, the interest of the Executive Office usually turns to other more pressing matters, and the implementing agency is left to contend with the states without much support from the White House. In really serious fights in which states feel that important interests are at stake, they and their allies can usually muster enough political strength in the Congress to force a federal agency to back down. This certainly has been the pattern in a fields of welfare, social services, and education. The federal cut-off of funds is an almost meaningless sanction (for welfare and social services, see Handler 1972 and Steiner 1966; for education, see Murphy 1971).

This is not to say that the federal government is without influence on state and local programs. Infusions of federal money have impact on the level of state programs and perhaps even their direction, although the latter is less clear. The availability of federal funds allows states to launch programs they otherwise could not afford, to expand existing programs, or to create new programs by substituting federal money for state money to pay for existing programs. Conversely, cutbacks in federal funding affect state and local programs, forcing cutbacks at these levels as well. In many programs the federal government pays a certain percentage of administrative costs; if that percentage is reduced, it almost invariably means that there is a reduction in the size of the state administrative force, which in turn means reduced delivery of services, inspection, or monitoring (Derthick 1975).

In addition, there is also the paperwork, formal compliance reporting, and a whole range of federal rules and requirements that do require some effort by the states. State and local officials feel the federal regulatory presence and complain. These requirements extend throughout the entire administrative process—deadlines for filing forms, accounting procedures, multiple forms, and reporting requirements. In some substantive areas, these requirements probably influence the delivery of services. Certain procedures may be avoided to lessen paperwork; others may be modified to facilitate compliance. Nevertheless, despite this overlay of paper and forms, the basic characteristics remain true over most of the important federal-state grant-in-aid programs. A great deal of discretion over substantive areas remains at the state level, and control and monitoring techniques and other forms of federal supervision are generally uncertain and weak.[4]

Decentralization, lack of federal control, and state and local discretion in these major social welfare programs have not come about by accident. These programs were originally state and local programs, and although the federal presence has grown enormously, consensus is still lacking as to the division of jurisdiction between the states and the federal government on most of these issues. Although, for example, such consensus has been reached on adult income maintenance programs, such is not the case to any significant extent for other major programs that deal with children and youth, the family, education, and criminal justice. States are willing to accept federal money, to be sure, but are less likely to accept federal control and direction.

The factors that lead to decentralization, lack of federal control and monitoring, and discretion at the state and local levels are powerful and perhaps even dominant in the federal-state exchange. Nevertheless, there are counterinfluences at the state and local levels as well. Some forces leading to change operate in the direction of the federal effort. Federal programs do not spring full-blown out of the minds and hearts of officials in Washington. Rather, by the time a program in the social welfare area is enacted into law, it has more often than not been debated and usually tried at state and local levels, often for considerable periods of time. Federal intervention is usually reactive, responsive to increasingly incessant demands arising out of the states and communities that, by the time they reach Washington, have extensive support. This is clearly true for programs that are finally enacted after long periods of gestation, debate, and argument. Even programs that seem to "slip through" the legislative process without much debate or other attention have had sponsorship and support. It is one thing to tack on a little-noticed rider; it is quite another to secure a meaningful appropriation.

What this means is that there are groups and interests at the state and local levels that agree with and support the federal initiative, just as at the local level there are groups and interests that support state-level efforts to direct the local delivery of services. These groups and interests support federal efforts and at the same time draw support from

---

[4] There will, of course, be disagreement with this conclusion. Some of the disagreement depends on one's perspective—lower-level officials feel the heavy hand of state and federal government; top-level officials think the field level is out of control. But there is also considerable conceptual and empirical difficulty in dealing with centralization versus decentralization in the federal-state relations. For a recent review and analysis of the "state of federalism," see Scheiber (1980).

federal initiatives. Sources of federal support are usually diverse, and vary as to form, content, and influence, depending on how hospitable the local environment is and the strength of the various interests that are allied with the federal initiative. One source of federal support is the mandates themselves—the legislation, the administrative regulations, the court decisions. How much voluntary obedience there is to the law is, of course, a much-debated issue, but there is ordinarily some, and it may be considerable if really vital interests or conflicts are not at stake.

Legal mandates also serve other functions. They legitimize the values of interest groups, give them moral support, and provide the bases for arguing their cause. The effects of legitimacy and moral persuasion are hard to specify, let alone quantify. Although the groups that are involved certainly think that legitimacy in the form of law is important, and that they are better off with a favorable court or legislative decision than without one, it cannot be said with any degree of confidence that a court ruling or a statute was crucial or even influential in any given conflict. Social change depends on many factors, including whether there are strong local groups and interests that are capable of drawing strength and support from the legal system. Some groups are quite strong and can even use the law to launch a major lawsuit to force compliance, but others may be weak and ineffectual. And there will also be states and local areas where there is no interest at all in taking up the federal initiative. In broader aspects of social change, it would seem that values affirmed by the legal system often influence the media and the opinions of elites, and help to change public opinion (Friedman 1975, Handler 1978, McCarthy and Zald 1977, Scheingold 1974).

Federal funding already has been mentioned as a source of control and direction. It need hardly be said that implementation is made easier when extra money is available and the state or local government does not have to use its own resources. Federal money is used either to add to state and local initiatives or, as sometimes happens, to allow the state and local governments to free up money to do something else. In either event, the carrot is no doubt far more significant than the stick in stimulating social change. One caveat must be added here. Although we certainly are aware of the near impossibility of forcing states and local governments to make changes that come directly out of their pockets, the converse is not that clear—that when money is available, change will be made, and in the desired directions and amounts. There are many ways in which money gets spent other than on what officials at the top policy level intended (Derthick 1975, Pressman and Wildavsky 1979).

Federal funding is usually thought of as supplying significant fractions of the costs of major program costs, such as foster care, AFDC, or Medicaid. In lesser but nonetheless important amounts are federal grants of a more discretionary, flexible nature that work on the edges of programs. As will be seen, these kinds of flexible grants have been important in the deinstitutionalization of status offenders and in other kinds of law enforcement activities. State councils of criminal justice, for example, can be staffed with federal money, and these councils in turn can fund demonstration projects (e.g., a group home or a diversion program) or special positions attached to existing agencies. In some important instances, grants have been given to citizen advocacy groups.[5] These kinds of federal grants are small, especially in comparison to big block grants that go to the states under the major programs. On the other hand, the large sums of money usually are committed and carry little capacity for flexibility. The more elastic features of the smaller federal grant may lead to its having considerable influence, for in a given situation it can be the type of money that a state agency or an interest groups really wants.

Another form of federal support is technical assistance. People in state and local government, as well as in interest groups and professional organizations, belong to networks that include federal officers at the national and regional level. These people exchange information and give assistance and support for programs and policies.

In sum, when we look at the basic general characteristics of the social system of the major social welfare programs that are involved in the deinstitutionalization of status offenders (i.e.,foster care, law enforcement and corrections, child protection, social services, health and mental health, and education), we find that each area is more accurately conceived of as a political or social arena rather than a well-defined, pyramid-shaped implementation structure (Elmore 1978, Hall 1977). Within each area, there are major governmental jurisdictions (federal, state, and local); there are major bureaucracies of long-standing historical importance; and there are often interest and advocacy groups and professional organizations. In Zald's characterization, the implementation "system" is loosely coupled, not well integrated, and often lacking in established procedures for information gathering and monitoring compliance.

---

[5] Some of the advocacy groups in deinstitutionalization efforts received federal grants. Other prominent examples are the National Welfare Rights Organization grant from the Department of Labor (Piven and Cloward 1977) as well as the funding of antipoverty groups during the War on Poverty (Kramer 1969, Moynihan 1969).

THE JUVENILE JUSTICE SYSTEM AS AN IMPLEMENTATION STRUCTURE

When we narrow our focus to the juvenile justice system, tendencies toward decentralization become even more pronounced. Of all of the substantive areas within the ambit of social welfare, crime and delinquency control have the strongest local traditions. In state governments, there are at least state departments of education that try to exercise some direction over local school boards, and there is a federal department of education. There is nothing at the state or federal level, however, that approaches these functions for delinquency and crime prevention.

The federal government's concern for juvenile delinquency, which dates back to the establishment of the Children's Bureau in 1912, has for the most part been slight, uncertain, and fractionalized among various agencies within the Department of Health, Education, and Welfare and the Department of Justice. At the time that the Law Enforcement Assistance Administration was established in 1968 (P.L. 90-351), HEW was given primary responsibility for juvenile justice by the Juvenile Delinquency Prevention Control Act (P.L. 90-445). Over the course of the next several years, competition over juvenile programs developed between these two agencies, although LEAA was not primarily concerned with juveniles. During this time, Congress began shifting responsibility away from HEW to LEAA and, at the same time, increased the pressure on LEAA to take juvenile programs more seriously. In 1973 LEAA finally established a separate unit for juveniles, but it had no authority over state comprehensive plans.

In 1974 the Juvenile Justice and Delinquency Prevention Act established the Office of Juvenile Justice and Delinquency Prevention (OJJDP) within LEAA (P.L. 93-415). However, that office was not allowed to assert even minimal authority over state planning agencies until 1977, and even then LEAA continued to downgrade the office. Under the new Justice System Improvement Act (P.L. 96-157), OJJDP became an independent office within the Department of Justice, reporting directly to the Attorney General, but, at least during the entire period of this research, OJJDP was never in a position to assert strong federal leadership. It operated in the shadows of LEAA, which basically was not interested in juvenile justice issues.

As noted in chapter 3, JJDPA itself is loosely drawn. The formula grants generally are tied to the state's commitment to deinstitutionalize status offenders and dependent and neglected children, but there is no requirement that formula grant funds be spent for this population. Moreover, there is nothing in the legislation that requires that discretionary funds be spent for status offenders. How funds will be spent is a matter of discretion to be worked out between the states, localities, and LEAA.

Federal monitoring procedures for LEAA grants and contracts are weak; monitoring consists primarily of written reports by the state planning agencies and individual grantees and contractors. There are no requirements for routine audits, and the practice has varied widely. LEAA has no state or local offices and has no systematic information on individual projects funded at the state level. The states send data on progress in complying with JJDPA, but there is no verification of the data; OJJDP does some monitoring of the state planning agencies but not of the subgrants within the states. The state planning agencies are required to keep detailed records of formula grant expenditures within the states, but under a ruling from the Office of Management and Budget they are not required to send this information to Washington, nor is Washington permitted to ask for it.

What we have at the top of the implementation system, then, is a broad, discretionary statute; a weak, subordinate administrative agency harried by a superior agency resistant to juvenile justice issues; and ineffective monitoring procedures. This is an organizational arrangement that yields only minimal federal control.

The most important organizational characteristic of the juvenile justice system is the autonomy of the juvenile court.[6] All local administering units of government within the system have some measure of autonomy. Autonomy, however, is a matter of degree, and there is variation. For example, local school districts are probably less subject to state-level coordination and control than are departments of welfare. If we look at the juvenile courts as part of an implementing social system, however, it is clear that the court is by far the most independent, the most autonomous of any of the agencies we are considering. Juvenile court judges are either elected or appointed officials; in either case, they are largely independent of the usual methods of coordination and control. They are, to some degree, controlled by their staffs, the police, other intake personnel, and the corrections system generally, of which the court is a part. But this environmental control is different from bureaucratic hierarchical control by top-level policymakers. Juvenile court judges are relatively immune from policy directives issued by executive departments. They are subject to legislative mandates in the form of

---

[6] For a general discussion of the characteristics of the juvenile justice system, see Rosenheim (1962, 1976b).

legislation, but for the most part the applicable laws are sufficiently vague to allow considerable discretion. As will be seen in the next chapter and in the state case studies themselves, the juvenile court judge has an enormous latitude of discretion. The posture that individual judges take toward deinstitutionalization is critical to the manner and extent of its implementation.

There are constraints on the judge; for example, the environmental context within which the court operates serves as a constraint. Although judges are powerful, the fact that they have little direct control over the availability of placements serves as a real constraint on their options. They have more control over their own immediate staffs, but even that control is far from complete. Judges have even less control over the police. Active and aggressive judges can overcome many of the formal or bureaucratic limitations on their authority and, through force of personality and public activity, can stimulate change far beyond their formal powers; however, comparatively few judges are charismatic leaders, even if they care deeply about the issues (Rosenheim 1962, 1976b).

There are other aspects of the environment that also impinge on the court and affect its position. We have mentioned the availability of placements, which is crucial and which depends on the activity and resources of other government agencies. The same is true for other programs that affect status offenders, such as welfare, social services, education, child protection, and private charity. All of these programs and bureaucracies can affect the flow of youth to the courts and the dispositional considerations of the court. The presence of a group home for runaway girls, which is sponsored and funded by local charity, can make an enormous difference in the treatment of this class of status offenders. Usually the presence of this kind of resource depends on the activities of actors outside the juvenile court. However, the judge is still an important figure who at times helps to generate these resources and, in other instances, becomes involved in blocking their creation.

The environmental constraints on the judge serve to further complicate if not fractionalize the implementation of policy. The judge is constrained because he or she has to bargain with other agencies. As powerful as the court is, it is only one of several agencies that have an impact on deinstitutionalization. This is the point made earlier about the autonomy and patterns of interaction between substantive agencies at the local level; they serve both to constrain the court and simultaneously to make coordination of implementation more difficult.

At the bottom of the structure is a provider system that further decentralizes the implementation structure, because it too is a separate, autonomous system serving its own organizational needs. Status offenders enter the provider system either from the court, through diversion programs (which may or may not be court-connected), or on their own. They are commingled with other youth, including delinquents, in the various out-of-home placements and service programs. Although some of these facilities are public, most are privately operated and are often sectarian. In either case, the facilities have their own organizational needs and agendas. Youth are classified and served according to treatment and service goals as defined by these organizations, and such goals may not coincide with the goals of the juvenile justice system. Most providers have a great deal of discretion over intake and can reject or expel troublesome youth. It is reported that foster homes and other agencies accustomed to handling younger dependent and neglected children resist handling older, more difficult-to-manage youth. Reimbursement formulas may also conflict with deinstitutionalization goals; for example, smaller facilities may be under strong financial incentives to keep beds occupied. Changing funding patterns can lead to changes in classifications, services, treatments, and the populations served. Fashions change in public programs. One year, mental retardation is in the public eye; the next year, physical disabilities, educational enrichment, or mental health.

The major point is that the service provider system is different from the juvenile justice system, and involves a different set of actors, organizations, and funding arrangements. It will treat its clients according to its own organizational needs—needs that may be different from the needs of the clients or the juvenile justice system (Lipsky 1980). Just as status offenders who enter the juvenile justice system are treated according to the needs of that system, so too when they enter the provider system are they treated according to the needs of that system.

Although the centrifugal forces in the deinstitutionalization process are strong, other forces unify the implementation structure in a manner that modifies the exercise of local discretion. An important source of conformity is the law itself. The influence of the law depends to a considerable extent on the characteristics of the mandate. The law, for example, can remove jurisdiction for certain categories of offenders or limit dispositional alternatives (e.g., status offenders cannot be placed in training schools). The law may prohibit certain coercive treatments, such as mental health commitments, unless specific procedural and substantive standards are met. These legal mandates are not foolproof, however; the police and the courts, for example, can relabel a status offender as a delinquent. But in the main, implementation issues are far less complicated when the mandate is clear and the results can be easily quantified (Lipsky 1980). As we will see, some of the rules dealing with juveniles who commit status offenses are of this character.

Other laws also have had an impact on the juvenile justice system, but these laws are less specific and express more general values and attitudes about how children and youth should be treated. Although their direct impact is difficult to trace, they nevertheless have contributed to the character and focus of the deinstitutionalization movement. These laws have redefined the legal position of children and youth and have called into question some of the central tenets of the original juvenile justice reforms that served to broaden the discretion of the state under the guise of treatment. Specifically, the *Gault* decision stripped away the facade of treatment and demanded procedural regularity for what the Supreme Court called a coercive system. A series of decisions developed the right to treatment, the right to the least restrictive alternatives, and the right to entitlements for social welfare benefits, as well as children's rights in a range of fields (Wald 1979). These legal developments lent support to those groups and individuals, including judges and court-related personnel, who were seeking changes in the treatment of status offenders.

Finally, public or community attitudes toward crime, delinquency, and other forms of deviant behavior have an impact on the juvenile court and other agencies within the juvenile justice system. Generally speaking, if there is really strong sentiment to put troublesome youth away, the courts or the local agencies will find the means to do so. Often, however, the views of what is to be done either conflict or are not held with great intensity, which in turn may allow more leeway for the exercise of discretion. Whatever their direction and intensity, public attitudes—especially if manifested by advocacy groups—are part of the implementing social system.

RECIPROCITY, NOT CONTROL

An implementation structure that is viewed as a social system is not a system in which influence, control, and direction flow from the top to the bottom. Rather, there is continual interaction and reciprocity (cf. Elmore 1978, 1979-80). The simplest reciprocity model is the relationship between the advocacy, grass roots interest, and professional groups and the federal sources of support. Federal changes are produced from political activity that arises out of the states and local communities. The federal response to these demands is never complete, in the sense of solving the problem; rather, the result is some form of compromise between conflicting demands. Funds are granted, requirements are vague; in short, the problem is only partially resolved. What remains to be sorted out is delegated back to the state and local levels for further working out of the value conflicts. It is at this juncture that the federal voice (and perhaps money) lends further support and legitimacy to the interest groups and organizations that are still pressing for change. There continue to be reciprocal demands and support between these two parts of the implementing social system.

The relationship between the grass roots organizations and the federal government varies, depending on the existence and strength of the groups in any given locality and the form and content of the federal policy at a particular time. Nevertheless, as is evident in the state case studies, in certain states and communities this relationship has been clear as well as important. Similar reciprocal relationships extend throughout the social system—between grass roots groups and professional organizations and local agencies (including the court), and between these and the state agencies. There are also regional and national networks. The relationships work both for and against deinstitutionalization; they vary in strength, influence, and intensity. The implementation system in these large social welfare programs is a highly complex, loose grouping of various political arenas in which there are elements of both control and conflict. Social welfare programs that rely on state and local delivery of services are thus highly discretionary at the field level, and vary greatly in implementation strategies.

A FRAMEWORK FOR ANALYSIS

How, then, does one account for change, given the complexity and diversity of an implementation system in which the states and local jurisdictions are dominant and the federal initiatives are weak, inconsistent, and only one among many forces for change. Mayer Zald (1980) sets forth a framework for explaining the deinstitutionalization of status offenders that addresses four issues. The first issue is concerned with institutionalization and deinstitutionalization as social movements set within broader trends in American society. He asks: How do these broader trends relate to beliefs and ideologies about the proper treatment of deviants in general and status offenders in particular?

There has been a growth in the symbolic climate that has turned against the use of institutions and is supported by such diverse groups as advocacy organizations, state and local officials, professionals, and reformers. Attitudes toward deinstitutionalization vary in terms of clients and interest groups (Lerman 1978). In some instances deinstitutionalization is pressed without alternatives; doing nothing is considered better than institutionalization. In other instances replacement services are sought, the objection being to the form and content of institutionally based treatments rather than to the notion of care itself. The carriers of the movement—the reform-minded middle class, professionals, and public officials—are widespread and diverse in their strength, composition, and influence.

The second issue concerns with how these ideas work themselves out at the state and local levels. States vary in terms of their structure and political culture and in terms of their ability to innovate. The literature that deals with state political culture and innovation classifies states as being "leaders," "laggards," or "nonadopters" (Downs 1976, Elazar 1970, Gray 1973, J. Walker 1969, 1975). Scholars stress the importance of the structure and the operation of what they call the "policy subsystem" within the state. This subsystem encompasses the major agencies involved in the particular substantive area and those responsible for the operation of the programs, including the executive, legislature, judiciary, and various interest groups that have a stake in the issue. Again, the characteristics of these policy subsystems vary. For example, in a situation in which the juvenile court judges have an active, systematic organization (as compared to a state in which communication between the component parts of that organization is weak and infrequent), we would expect the subsystem to play a more active role in the process of innovation (Becker 1970, Downs 1976).

The third issue addressed by Zald's framework concerns the interplay between federal programs and state policies and programs. He points out that federal programs can have important links to these state policy subsystems. Federal programs may operate as constraints or as opportunities for promoting different interests, and they may supply technical and staff contacts for these subsystems. Established consultative linkages have proved important for federal assistance. Moreover, in addition to federal connections, these subsystems can have regional contacts, such as associations of municipal and state officials, which can also affect the diffusion of innovation.

Summarizing the argument, Zald notes that even without federal intervention, the general trend toward deinstitutionalization of status offenders was linked to the even more general trend toward deinstitutionalization of other populations. Because of variations in the strength and intensity of the ideology, the existence and characteristics of the interest groups, the size and scope of the delinquency and status offender problem, and the structure and culture of the states, states vary in terms of both the content and rate of innovation.

Although these changes were occurring prior to federal intervention, the federal government did intervene to encourage deinsitutionalization. The fourth and final issue with which we must be concerned is how best to think about the impact of such an intervention. What is the range of outcomes that occurs during the implementation process? How do the line agencies cope with the various demands made upon them, and with what results for status offenders?

The federal government speaks in voices that both encourage and discourage states and localities with technical assistance, regulations, judicial opinions, and various other kinds of incentives and disincentives. Some federal initiatives are judged to be successfully carried out, others moderately so, and some fail. What accounts for the differences in impact? These questions have traditionally been addressed through impact analysis, a comparison of the outcomes with the legislative or policymakers' intent. More recently, impact analysis has been modified by what is called implementation analysis, which, although concerned with impact or outcomes, pays more attention to "the processes and factors that facilitate or inhibit the carrying out of legislative and policy mandates" (Zald 1980:17). Implementation analysis critically examines the explicit or implicit theory explaining the relationship between the policy or program and the expected outcome. As such, it is especially relevant when examining a policy carried out by multiple agents or jurisdictions that may have different conceptions of the program or different priorities, information, and resources.

While differing among themselves in emphasis, implementation theorists focus on the importance of the characteristics and processes of the implementing agencies and the relationships between them. Sabatier and Mazmanian (1980) have gone the farthest in specifying the relevant variables and hypotheses (see also Handler 1978, Wilson 1973). Summarizing the major points of their work, they note that problems differ in their solvability; some are far more tractable than others. In deinstitutionalization, it is far easier to close down certain types of institutions than to create suitable alternatives. Many statutes specify the problems that they are addressing and the desired outcomes, but they may fail to establish the structure of the implementation process, such as the machinery and necessary resources for participation by the actors both within and outside the process. These decisions about the structure of the implementation process will affect the program's success.

Lack of coherence in the causal theory underlying the statutes and conflicting or ambiguous policy objectives are often cited as major problems in implementation. Implementation success will be increased to the extent to which statutory objectives are clear and ranked in importance, thus serving as unambiguous directives. Clear objectives can also serve as a resource for those who challenge the agency on the grounds that performance does not match objectives.

All students of implementation emphasize the problems of coordination between implementing agencies. To the extent that these agencies are hierarchically integrated—that is, actions within and between them are coordinated—success is enhanced. When agencies are relatively autonomous, they are more likely to perceive statutory objectives in terms of their own organizational incentives. There are other factors internal to the structure of the implementation process that affect success. A crucial one, of course, is the availability of sufficient resources to carry out implementation objectives. Another may be rules for administrative decisions, which can hinder or help the implementation process. For example, the imposition of procedural rules for decisionmaking may unduly burden or clog the process.

Then there are important factors that are more or less external to the implementation structure. These include the extent to which actors external to the implementation process (e.g., target groups, constituency groups, or legislative, executive, and judicial officials) can and do participate in the process. Other external factors are more amorphous but nonetheless are likely to be critical. Most important programs, if they are to be implemented successfully, need political support—especially if implementation requires the cooperation of loosely integrated agencies. However, public and political support is variable, which makes support for implementation difficult to maintain. Changes in social, economic, and technological conditions affect both the sources of support and the perceptions about the seriousness of the problem. The media play an especially important role in shaping perceptions on the part of all of the relevant actors. Changes in the relative importance of the target or constituency groups also affect political support. Finally, variations in local social and economic conditions create pressure for "flexibility" in rules and administrative practices, thereby lessening chances for success in implementation.

Thus, factors such as tractability, lack of statutory coherence, imprecise ranking of objectives, poor coordination between and within implementing agencies, insufficient resources, lack of flexibility in decision rules and administrative practice, and variation in media attention and in public and political support for reform can affect the success of the implementation process. According to Sabatier and Mazmanian (1980), the variable most directly affecting the success of the implementing agencies is commitment of agency leaders to the statutory objectives and their skill in using available resources. However, what these officials think and are able to do is the necessary, but not the sufficient, condition of success.

While agreeing with the importance of this analysis, Zald would also emphasize two other factors that have special relevance to this study: the characteristics of the mandate and the implementing agency, and what he calls the target object as a social system. Concerning the characteristics of the mandate, Zald implicity distinguishes between a specific and clear statutory directive and a vague standard or goal as the stated objective. The operative statute—the Juvenile Justice and Delinquency Prevention Act of 1974 (as amended)—seems to speak in precise terms: A state cannot receive any money (under this program) if it has more than 25 percent of its status offenders in secure detention or correctional facilities three years after entering the program and, after two more years, *any* status offenders in such facilities. As was pointed out in the previous chapter, considerable ambiguities lurk in such terms as "status offenders" and "secure facilities"; nevertheless, as measured by many other statutes in the social welfare field, there is a high degree of precision here. The usual statute, for example, would read something like, "the states shall make all reasonable efforts to provide nonsecure alternative treatment facilities for status offenders." All other things being equal, it is far more difficult to implement the latter type of statute than the former (Lipsky 1980). Vagueness in statutory terms in effect creates discretion and invites conflicting, or at least nonconforming, definitions by lower-level officials. With a precise statute, lower-level officials may disagree with statutory objectives, but at least they know what is expected of them. Precision, however, is a matter of degree; it would be rare indeed for a statute to eliminate all ambiguity or discretion.

Even with a fairly precise statute, implementing machinery is still necessary. Zald asks: What precise mechanisms did the implementing agency, in this case LEAA, have for surveying performance? Did it rely exclusively or mostly on state self-reporting? Was there monitoring? Were credible attempts made to apply sanctions? Were waivers given?

Concerning the target objects as social systems, Zald draws the distinction implied earlier between (a) implementing systems (i.e., agencies) that have clear coordinating structures and well-established procedures, especially for monitoring actual progress and compliance, and (b) social systems that consist of loosely integrated agencies that do not necessarily share the same goals, that are not well coordinated, and that lack established procedures for the flow of information and for monitoring and compliance. In the latter, "implementation will fall short of the mark and target systems will not deliver desired outputs" (Zald 1980:21).

The subject of this research is the latter system, one in which state and local jurisdictions are not well integrated in any of the fields relevant to a federal mandate that is addressed to the system. Moreover, there is not one federal policy but several, some of which may be operating at cross-purposes to the deinstitutionalization mandate. How then does one account for change in this kind of an implementation system? We know that deinstitutionalization has progressed at different rates in different states and localities. Yet, all states and local areas share the same implementation characteristics.

Richard Elmore and other scholars argue that conventional implementation analysis is not capable of accounting for change in these types of social systems. Elmore draws a distinction between "forward mapping" and "backward mapping." Forward mapping is the conventional, commonsense approach—the approach one would ordinarily take in looking at what impact, if any, a particular policy change would have on the actual delivery of services. Forward mapping starts with an analysis of the policymakers' intent (in this case, the language of the federal statutes) and then examines each subsequent step in the implementation process (e.g., the intent of the administrative rules and guidelines, the structure of the organization). The main focus, however, is on identifying and measuring the outcomes and comparing those outcomes with the intent, as defined, at the top. As Elmore puts it, "the details of forward mapping are less important . . . than the underlying logic. It begins with an objective, it elaborates an increasingly specific set of steps for achieving that objective, and it states an outcome against which success or failure can be measured" (1978:603).

Backward mapping, as the name implies, starts from the opposite end; it is a bottoms-up approach. It shares the concern of conventional implementation analysis with outcomes, but starts with the field-level officials and agencies that are responsible for the actual delivery of services, and looks at the problem of trying to achieve changes in output from the point of view of those who have the responsibility for implementing the desired changes.

According to Elmore, the critical point of difference between forward mapping and backward mapping is an assessment or assumption concerning the ability of top-level policymakers to control the implementation process. If one assumes that this ability is fairly decisive in the process, then it is logical to engage in forward mapping. But if one assumes the opposite—that the efforts of policymakers are less than decisive, that they may only be one of several important factors (and may not even be the most important factor)—then to measure outcomes in terms of policymakers' intent may invariably result in research findings that indicate that implementation has failed. Indeed, this is what most implementation research does in fact find.

CONCLUSION

Backward mapping takes a wider look at the connections and relationships between the ground-level agencies and institutions that affect the deinstitutionalization of status offenders. Because of the importance of local discretion, backward mapping should more accurately describe the processes of change and should provide more explanatory power than conventional forward mapping.

On the other hand, local units of government do not work in a vacuum. Even in a decentralized system, state governments can influence the delivery of services by legally creating or foreclosing options and by controlling funding and creating incentives. The basic statutory framework, the bureaucratic organization, the funding patterns, and the availability of resources and placements set the parameters within which the local units of government exercise their discretion. For this reason, the design of our research combines forward mapping with backward mapping. This does not lessen the importance of examining local operations. Given the inevitable latitude of discretion always allowed in state legislation, and the history and politics of state-local relations—especially in the administration of juvenile justice—the local units still remain decisive in the implementation of policy, but that discretion is exercised within a state-level framework.

At the federal level the emphasis is more on backward mapping. Federal initiatives and support are important, and considerable research effort has gone into examining their structures and impact. Nevertheless, the most significant policy arena by far in juvenile justice and in the deinstitutionalization of status offenders is at the state and local levels. We first look at what has been happening at the state and local levels, and then see in what ways, if any, the federal initiatives have helped or hindered the process of deinstitutionalization.

The present division of power between the states and the federal government seems likely to continue. In the concluding chapter of this study we address the following normative question: In light of the characteristics of the implementing social system and the likely scope and character of future federal initiatives, in what ways can state and local agencies and actors be encouraged to pursue the goals of deinstitutionalization? The resulting analysis, in turn, will better frame the question raised in the introductory chapter: In view of the implementation structure and the prospects for producing changes in the system, should deinstitutionalization goals be pursued?

5 Deinstitutionalization in Seven States: Principal Findings

JOEL F. HANDLER, MICHAEL SOSIN,
JOHN A. STOOKEY, *and* JULIE ZATZ

INTRODUCTION

In order to examine the impact of deinstitutionalization efforts at the state and local levels, we selected seven states for study: Arizona, Louisiana, Massachusetts, Pennsylvania, Utah, Virginia, and Wisconsin. These states differed in a number of respects, including geographical distribution, urban-rural dimensions, socioeconomic characteristics, and historical response to youth who commit status offenses. Although each experienced a more or less intensive period of legislative activity that began somewhere between the late 1960s and mid-1970s, they took somewhat different approaches to deinstitutionalization. Despite these differences, certain important findings apply to all seven states and can be summarized as follows:

• The placement of adjudicated status offenders in secure public institutional facilities has been virtually eliminated. Judging from the experiences of the seven states, the most basic goal of deinstitutionalization—that status offenders no longer be sent to the large red-brick institutions—has been substantially accomplished. Moreover, there was evidence of relabeling (i.e., upgrading the status offender to a delinquent) in only one locality in one of the states.

• There has been a substantial reduction in the use of detention for preadjudicated status offenders. Accomplishing this objective has proved to be more controversial and troublesome than the prohibition of in-

88

carceration. In some jurisdictions, particularly in the rural areas, there are few if any alternative nonsecure facilities. In other jurisdictions there is sharp disagreement over whether eliminating detention is a sound policy. As will be discussed, considerable backlash on this issue has resulted in a strong movement to allow detention under limited conditions.

• There has been a decline in the number of youth who commit status offenses and who then enter the juvenile justice system. Although the federal mandate does not clearly state that diversion is necessary, there is a range of diversion activities in all of the states. In some, existing practices were codified (e.g., local police practices), but in others, more formal procedures were implemented. Data on diversion and alternative services are considerably less available and less reliable, but most officials and observers agree that fewer status offenders are being processed by the juvenile court.

• For those status offenders who are diverted to some other service system, the predominant forms of out-of-home care are group homes or foster care arrangements (the choice between the two often depends on the level of commitment and amount of resources that a state has to devote to the development of alternative types of facilities).

• It is unclear what is happening to youth who commit status offenses but do not enter the juvenile system or its closely related diversion programs. Are more of these youth being ignored altogether or are they entering other public or private systems? Most officials and observers in the seven states are of the opinion that the former rather than the latter is the case, but this study was not able to examine systematically other possible community settings (e.g., private hospitals, clinics, and schools) in which status offenders might be receiving services. Once out of the juvenile justice system, the status offender label often ceases to exist. Other public and private agencies use their own classifications, which may or may not be synonymous with the behavior associated with status offenses.

This chapter discusses the findings at the state and local levels. How did the states and local areas reach common results on some issues and different results on others? The first section begins with a brief historical overview of each state and then discusses the determinants of social change in deinstitutionalization at the state level. It discusses the sources of influence for social change, including the activities of various reform coalitions, and pays particular attention to the variety of sources of federal influence. The second section presents the findings from the local areas. As predicted, there is not only variety among the states but also within each state. This section analyzes processes of change at the local level, and discusses the relative importance of the local juvenile court judge, the availability of resources, and the local environment. It sets forth the various approaches or models that local agencies have taken with regard to deinstitutionalization, ranging from complete diversion to various court-controlled strategies. The principal finding is that regardless of what approach is taken, the role of the local juvenile court judge is crucial. That is the key discretionary point in the system.

STATE PROGRAMS

PROGRAM SUMMARIES

Massachusetts

From its earliest days, Massachusetts has taken an active, interventionist position toward children and youth and has been in the forefront of reform legislation and programs. For example, Massachusettes established the first state-funded reformatory (1847) and eventually developed a statewide system of training schools for status offenders and delinquents. Paralleling this development was the state's early and active concern with dependent children; here, though, the private sector played an important role in providing services. By the 1960s, Massachusetts not only had a long history of reform in child welfare, but also a wide variety of experienced and active religious and citizen groups, plus a solid private provider industry.

During the 1960s, the debate over children and youth policies intensified, and coalitions emerged on both sides of the reform issue. An articulate, bipartisan coalition, which included members of children's interest groups, legislators, and child care professionals, took an active stance in favor of reform. The opposing coalition was represented primarily by the entrenched bureaucracies, including the people who ran the institutions, as well as some judges, professional organizations, and their allied citizen groups. At this time, scandals within the institutions were uncovered and official investigations were launched; there was extensive media coverage of the entire affair.

A unique part of the Massachusetts story centers on Jerome Miller, the reformer who was brought in as Commissioner of Youth Services by a Republican governor strongly committed to reform. After initial frustrations, Miller simply closed the major institutions for delinquents by administrative fiat in 1972. Deinstitutionalization, at this level, was suddenly accomplished; and very soon thereafter the state began to fund private providers to develop services for this population, which included status offenders.

The reform groups next turned their attention to separating status offenders from delinquents. In 1973 legislation concerning children in need of supervision (CHINS) was passed that differentiated status offenders from delinquents, encouraged the diversion of status offenders from the courts, and transferred jurisdiction over them from the Department of Youth Services to the Department of Public Welfare. However, because the legislation made no provision for the detention of CHINS and the Department of Public Welfare had neither the funds nor the facilities to do so, status offenders still went to the Department of Youth Services for detention. Nevertheless, the use of community-based facilities instead of the old institutions was an important change. In 1977, under pressure from LEAA over the detention of status offenders, the Department of Public Welfare set up a CHINS unit to carry out the 1973 legislation. This unit emphasized early intervention, diversion, placement in the least restrictive alternative, and the use of short-term emergency shelters. These actions fully established the CHINS program at the state level. In 1980 the Department of Public Welfare was recast; a new Department of Social Services was created and given responsibility for CHINS.

CHINS—that is, runaways, incorrigibles, truants, and habitual school offenders—may either be brought before the juvenile court, which decides whether to divert them or how actively it will become involved in the service and placement process, or they may go directly to the Department of Social Services, bypassing the court altogether. When there is court involvement, the courts have wide latitude and there is great variation in their practices, even though they have no formal coercive powers over the social services agencies, the private care providers, or even over the CHINS: CHINS are free to refuse services and providers are free to reject any child.

If a CHINS is to be removed from home, a range of options is available that includes foster care, group homes (8-15 beds), boarding and special schools, but not the red-brick training schools. Usually it is the availability of the slot that determines placement. CHINS are frequently commingled with special education and Department of Youth Services adolescents in various programs, because providers often run multiple contracts and because officials believe that most youth are labeled for bureaucratic reasons (i.e., to take advantage of service placements) rather than on the basis of differences in behavioral or psychological characteristics.

The Department of Social Services provides casework, foster care, daycare facilities, long-term emergency residential care, group activities, and protective, adoption, homemaker, and information and referral services. In addition, several other state agencies offer services for children, but the provision of these services is seriously fragmented. Agencies fight over scarce resources and restrict use of their resources to carefully defined populations. School districts, for example, resist mandated duties to pay education costs, which are higher for children in some out-of-home placements and for "nonlocal children" in local foster homes. The Department of Mental Health has continued its long tradition of not serving youth; there has been no widening of the net here.

The distinguishing characteristic of the Massachusetts system is its network of private providers, which has always been the primary source of services for dependent children. When the state closed its training schools for delinquents and status offenders, it opted to use this system rather than to offer public services. The private provider system experienced a period of rapid growth—from $25 million in fiscal 1969 to $300 million in fiscal 1979—that raised a number of problems, some of which are also applicable to a public system but others of which are unique to private providership. There has been and continues to be community resistance to facilities in certain localities. Since private providers control the intake decision, they tend to exclude the more troublesome youth, and state agencies cooperate by sending those children with the greatest likelihood of being accepted. The state has never developed an effective system for monitoring the performance of the private providers, and it lacks even basic information on most aspects of the system. Another potential problem has been the consolidation of the private providers. After an initial outburst of numerous small, single-mission providers, the system is now becoming dominated by larger conglomerate service providers that have become an important lobbying group in the state. Reportedly, there has been a significant increase in the number of CHINS and dependent children in out-of-home placements. One possible explanation for this increase is that the net has widened to fill private provider slots.

Although there are more children in placement in Massachusetts than ever before, there have been significant changes in the type of placement. The children are most often placed in smaller facilities, such as group homes, or in foster homes. The oppressive large-scale institutions are gone.

Louisiana

Louisiana is at the opposite end of the spectrum from Massachusetts. It has only reluctantly followed national trends and has displayed relatively little commitment to reforming procedures for dealing with troubled youth. After the usual juvenile court reforms at the turn of the century, there was little further legislative activity until 1950, when neglected children were separated from delinquents. The former were considered to be in physical or moral danger; the latter included status offenders. As in other states at this time, however, no distinctions were made between neglected and delinquent children in terms of intake, processing, or disposition. The next significant change came in 1974, when Louisiana adopted its first major deinstitutionalization legislation stating that nondelinquents could be placed neither in secure detention nor in reform schools. Custody of status offenders was transferred from the Department of Corrections to the newly created Office of Youth Services, which later became the Division of Youth Services in the Department of Health and Human Resources. In 1975 the state applied for enrollment in JJDPA, thus committing itself to deinstitutionalization within three years. The 1974 statutes became legally effective in 1978, and with this Louisiana finally created the CHINS category. CHINS could be placed only in nonsecure detention, with a 10-day limit. Earlier mandates that prohibited commingling with delinquents and placement in secure facilities were continued.

The impetus for reform in Louisiana seems markedly different from that in Massachusetts. In Louisiana it appears that the issue of troubled youth, and especially status offenders, received little attention until the 1970s; and even then the issue was tangential to concern about a perceived rise in serious delinquency. To the extent that it existed, the reform effort for status offenders was a low-visibility, residual activity that was pushed by a few key legislators and citizen advocacy groups. Support for the 1974 deinstitutionalization legislation reflected commitment to the principle; little thought was given to the costs.

There was some federal impetus for these changes. Although the amount of money available from OJJDP was small, some in the state wanted it. In addition a 1976 federal court decision (*Gary W. v. State of Louisiana*), which granted the right to treatment and applied the principle of "least restrictive alternative" to mentally retarded, physically handicapped, and delinquent youth, lent support to those who argued for reforms for status offenders. Chronologically, Louisiana changed its law one year prior to applying for JJDPA funds, but the federal influence was probably already being felt.

In addition to the changes in the laws, there also has been some administrative reorganization. As noted, the Division of Youth Services was created to supervise programs for status offenders and delinquents. In addition regional boards have been created to review restrictive placements. Although these organizational changes are relatively recent, they seem to reflect cooperative efforts between the judges and the boards. There is an increasing professionalism in juvenile justice and youth services generally within the state that ties in with national trends.

Yet in Louisiana, as in the other states, there are counterforces. Within the ranks of the juvenile court judges and among certain elements of the police and probation workers, there is strong feeling that detention and secure facilities should be used for some categories of status offenders, particularly chronic runaways, truants, and ungovernables. At the same time, citizen group support on behalf of deinstitutionalization is waning. The most important group—Advocates for Juvenile Justice—ceased operations in 1979 after LEAA refused to fund it. Louisiana is still not in full compliance with the federal mandates (e.g., preadjudicated status offenders are still being held in secure detention), and the cost of complying is being increasingly viewed as prohibitive.

Although changes have been occurring in the direction of deinstitutionalization, these changes are small and must be viewed against the backdrop of little concern for status offenders. Prior to 1974, status offenders rarely were processed officially by the system; they were counseled and released, or were ignored altogether. This is still basically true today, although even fewer are arrested (and therefore detained) and the state claims that none are placed in secure facilities. At the same time, however, very little effort is going into providing services or alternative placements. The state has authorized the construction of shelter care facilities but has appropriated no funds. In short, status offenders are probably being ignored more than ever before.

Because of the rise in daytime burglary, some effort is now under way to deal with truancy in New Orleans. Schools are referring and police are escorting truants to truancy centers for counseling and referral to social service agencies. So far the courts have not been involved, but they may well become so if the voluntary program fails. Given the large number of truants, involvement by the judiciary could place an excessive burden on the courts.

Virginia

Virginia has been slow to implement state and federal policies. As in several of the other states, the move to rethink the organization of the juvenile court and its jurisdiction began with the *Gault* decision. The court system eventually was changed, and provisions were made for upgrading the role of the juvenile court judge. The state then began to consider the jurisdictional issues.

At this time the state planning agency—the Division of Justice and Crime Prevention—was staffed in large part by people who were paid out of LEAA funds and who thus had a vested interest in pushing reform. Citizen groups also took an interest, particularly women's groups. These groups became influential, enlisted the support of major political figures, and juvenile court reform became a political issue. Helping the reformers was the Department of Corrections, which could not handle the overcrowding and wanted to stem the flow of certain less troublesome youth into the system. The judges also complained of crowded dockets. In addition it was brought to light that a high proportion of children were being placed out-of-state, which was more expensive than in-state care, and this became an issue with fiscal conservatives.

Public hearings were held in 1975, and the following year a statute was passed creating three categories of juveniles: CHINS, delinquents, and dependent and neglected children. This constituted a major code revision. Intake services and diversion were encouraged for CHINS; court intervention was limited to cases in which there were clear dangers of serious harm. Detention of CHINS was also restricted to cases in which there was clear and substantial danger to the child or when necessary to ensure appearance in court. On a showing of good cause, CHINS could be detained for up to 72 hours (this is the only provision not in compliance with JJDPA). CHINS could not be committed to the Department of Corrections, and the juvenile court judges had the authority to order other agencies to provide services. The statute also authorized juvenile court funding for placement of status offenders in private facilities without requiring commitment to the Department of Corrections. The intent of that provision was to develop a network of local providers rather than having to rely on state care. The Department of Corrections itself encouraged deinstitutionalization by establishing prevention programs and developing detention and community residential alternatives. It provided technical assistance and block grants to local areas.

As in the other states, the success of the Virginia effort depended ultimately on the response of the juvenile court judges. Although it is expected that in the future more judges will be sympathetic, their response to date has been varied. The 1976 statute only requires that CHINS be diverted from the Department of Corrections, not that the court has to use community-based facilities. Reformers anticipated a significant drop in the youth populations of the state-run institutions, but the actual drop was much less than expected. According to information from the Department of Corrections that has been corroborated by other data, a considerable amount of relabeling is occurring in some of the juvenile courts; that is, status offenders are now petitioned as and adjudicated as minor delinquents (petitions and adjudications in this category have risen proportionately). Other courts, however, are refusing to take status offender petitions at all. Still others have embraced the new law and have given their staff wide discretion in diversion and referral.

Wisconsin

Wisconsin, like Massachusetts, is also an activist, interventionist state in terms of its children and youth policies. Prior to the reforms of the 1970s, however, it had the highest rate of detention of any state. By the close of the decade, policies toward status offenders and dependent and neglected children had been changed substantially. These changes came about incrementally through a series of reforms. Most of the changes were highly visible and were the result of intense interest group conflict among reformers, fiscal conservatives, professional organizations, and state and local officials. Federal influence was important at a variety of critical points.

The reforms of the 1970s originated in the previous decade. Through the War on Poverty, legal services offices were funded. Legal aid lawyers in turn established an effective, organized lobbying force for deinstitutionalization that drew support from federal court decisions (e.g., *Gault*) and the President's Commission on Law Enforcement and Administration of Justice. LEAA funded the Wisconsin Council on Criminal Justice (WCCJ), which picked up national trends concerning deinstitutionalization and became an important source of reform throughout the 1970s.

In 1971 the reform group introduced a far-reaching bill in the legislature. It was opposed by the Juvenile Court Judges' Association, police groups, correctional officials, and public social workers, but out of the defeat the category of CHINS emerged as a compromise. Runaways, truants, and youth who were beyond control could no longer be sent directly to correctional institutions (but could if they violated court probation even by committing another status offense). As a result of this experience, the reform groups sought to broaden their coalition, press for incremental reforms, and provide alternatives to institutional placements.

In that same year the age of majority was lowered to 18, and the jurisdiction of the juvenile court was changed accordingly. Within three years, this change alone probably was responsible for cutting the juvenile institutional population in half. Starting in 1972, WCCJ, using federal grants, began encouraging counties to build shelter care facilities and group homes as alternatives to institutional placements.

In 1973 a law was passed that prohibited the commitment of status offenders to state institutions, even if probation was violated. This was a major step forward in deinstitutionalization. The law was passed as a little-noticed item in the budget bill. Nevertheless, the passage of this bill did require the consent of key actors, including both reformers and fiscal conservatives. By this time, ex-WCCJ employees were working in the Department of Corrections and were sympathetic. The governor, who was a fiscal conservative, agreed with the principle of deinstitutionalization. He knew that the state paid for correctional placements, but not for local noninstitutional care. Both the governor and the Department of Administration were convinced that status offenders could be better served in the community. The juvenile court judges, who would have opposed the change, were unaware of the bill.

The state changed its funding arrangements with the counties in 1974, which gave additional impetus to deinstitutionalization. County social services budgets were now a sum-certain appropriation. Counties were charged for placements in state facilities and, because the costs of state facilities rose much higher than the cost of placement in local group homes, reformers hoped that this new funding procedure would serve as incentive for counties to limit their use of state facilities. In fact, the number of group homes rose from 41 in 1975, to 136 in 1976. Again, the alliance of reformers and the fiscal conservatives had effected change that furthered deinstitutionalization. Also in 1974, WCCJ financed studies about the conditions of detention that laid the groundwork for reforms in this area. During the following years the alliance continued its efforts to close state institutions. Status offenders could no longer be sent to these institutions, but reformers feared relabeling if space were available.

WCCJ funds were used by the Department of Health and Social Services to establish Juvenile Offender Review Boards, which reviewed cases of youth who were already in institutions to see if less restrictive placements would be more appropriate. The state enacted a shelter care reimbursement law that provided for 50 percent reimbursement of costs for shelter care but not for detention, which had the intended effect of making shelter care more economical for the counties.

Finally, in 1978 a new children's code was enacted that formalized the changes with regard to status offenders. CHINS were combined with dependent and neglected children, placement in correctional institutions was prohibited, and detention was effectively precluded for status offenders in most circumstances.

Other trends also were working to further the deinstitutionalization of status offenders during this decade. Two of the more important factors were (1) deinstitutionalization in the mental health field, which resulted both in the closing of many public facilities for youth and the establishment of restrictions on commitments, and (2) the economic crunch at the county level. All status offenders and most dependent and neglected children were under the jurisdiction (and budgets) of the county departments of social services. These agencies suffered losses in staff and increases in demands on their sum-certain budgets. Although there was great variation among the counties, generally the number of these youth in out-of-home placements decreased.

In terms of overall results, status offenders apparently are no longer being placed in correctional institutions; there also has been a sharp decline in treatment facility placements. Far fewer status offenders are in secure detention; more are in shelter care and group homes. Foster care has decreased, and group home placements have not made up for the reductions in other types of placements. There seems to be a lack of programs for in-home services for these youth. Perhaps it was inevitable that the reformers would align themselves with fiscal conservatives, but one of the costs of this alliance may be the lack of resources for status offender services. The counties are strapped for funds for staff, which results in a decline in foster home and group home placements and in provision of in-home services.

On the other hand, the total number of youth in correctional institutions and detention has not declined over this period. The admission of delinquents has increased, but there is little evidence that this change is the result of relabeling or an increase in crime. However, as in all of the state case studies, many of these trends may turn out to be temporary.

Pennsylvania

Prior to the reform period of the late 1960s and early 1970s, the Pennsylvania juvenile code included status offenders in the delinquency category under vague and broad terms. In some counties the probation staff expanded into full-fledged social service departments and handled all of the "difficult" children. The courts had wide detention powers. Although available data are unreliable, it seemed that significant numbers of status offenders were in secure facilities. In addition Pennsylvania, like Massachusetts, had a strong private provider system that was mainly sectarian and constituted a powerful and effective lobby in the state. Most long-term residential care facilities, for both delinquents and status offenders, were furnished by private providers.

The start of the reform period can be dated from the *Gault* decision in 1967. Interest groups that were supported in part by LEAA funds became active, especially the Philadelphia-based Juvenile Justice Center, which had close ties with the office of Senator Bayh, the sponsor of the Juvenile Justice and Delinquency Prevention Act. Their efforts resulted in the first legislative change in 1972, which created two categories of youth—delinquent and deprived. Truants were moved from the former to the latter; ungovernables and runaways remained delinquents. This was a modest change, but it did signal the start of the process of separating status offenders from delinquents. Changes also were made in detention practices. Deprived children could no longer be commingled with adults or delinquents and could only be placed in shelter care. The act also encouraged diversion (called "informal adjustment") and the use of "consent decrees," which could be entered into after proceedings had started.

Pennsylvania by this time had joined JJDPA but still was not in compliance. The money that could be lost through noncompliance was relatively small—$2 million out of $100 million. Though not an amount sufficient to force the state to change its policy, it was nevertheless large enough so that the state bureaucracy wanted to comply, especially in a time of fiscal stringency.

The next legislative reform, in 1976, encouraged the development of alternative facilities by establishing a sliding reimbursement schedule for alternative placements; incentives favored group homes, community-based facilities, and in-home services. Ninety percent funding was offered for new services; the lowest reimbursement percentage was offered for state placements.

The removal of status offenders from the delinquent category was completed the following year. There were now no distinctions drawn between status offenders and dependent and neglected children; all were called "dependent." The statute was not clear, however, as to whether the child welfare departments would have exclusive jurisdiction over dependent children or how much jurisdiction the courts would retain. Other provisions further restricted detention of these youth (and by 1979, they were not to be sent to jail under any circumstances), and required the counties to develop service plans and to codify the principle of the least restrictive alternative.

In the various legislative battles of the 1970s, several groups were especially active and influential both for and against deinstitutionalization. The Juvenile Justice Center was very effective in its pro-deinstitutionalization efforts. The Department of Public Welfare was committed to deinstitutionalization; it wanted to comply with JJDPA and retain the extra money. The Juvenile Court Judges Commission supported deinstitutionalization, but only if sufficient alternative facilities were available. Basically, the judges doubted that the child welfare departments could handle difficult status offenders, and they feared an upsurge of relabeling. Many child welfare workers were also opposed because they lacked the threat of secure detention; they felt that they were not only getting the more difficult cases but were also being denied access to the tools that the court had previously used in dealing with these youth. Private providers opposed the implementation of welfare department regulations. They wanted higher reimbursements for residential facilities and a loose definition of "community-based" so as to maximize the state reimbursement for placements.

One of the goals of the reformers was to shift status offenders from the juvenile courts to the county child welfare departments. The law, however, remained quite unclear on the last point, and judges have retained control over status offenders when they want it. Similarly, it was reported that several child welfare departments have experienced difficulties with this new and different case load, and have either dropped some status offenders or referred them to probation.

As to other outcomes, the one year of post-1977 data that is available indicates a significant drop in status offender referrals to the courts. Even before the change in the law, ungovernables were being diverted in some areas. However, it also seems that many status offenders are not being referred to the child welfare agencies; that is, they are dropping out of the system altogether. There does not seem to be much evidence to support the hypothesis of upgrading; most observers also seem to think that status offenders are not being held in secure detention.

Counties were quick to comply with the law for several reasons. First, they had advance notice of these changes. Second, the Department of Public Welfare required the development of county plans for shelter care and threatened loss of funds and the state takeover of child welfare functions. Third, state reimbursement for secure detention of dependent children was eliminated. Finally, status offender placements were monitored by interest groups and by the Governor's Justice Commission, which reported to LEAA.

Out-of-home placements of status offenders have not declined. Private providers furnish nearly all of the services in the state and the counties. These services are of three major types: group homes, facility-based institutions (more than 8 beds), and voluntary child care agencies (counseling, in-home services, supervision of independent living arrangements, and supervised foster care). There has been an increase in residential placements, which may indicate that although many status offenders are being diverted from the system, those that remain are more likely to receive residential placements than in-home services. The incentives to reduce placements may not, in fact, be that strong; some officials might not have faith in the efficacy of noninstitutional placements, and the cost-per-diem formulas may serve to prolong stays in the smaller group homes.

Although there is great variation among the counties in Pennsylvania, generalizations can be made. It seems safe to conclude (a) that status offenders have been removed from secure detention, separated from delinquents, and removed from secure residential care, and (b) that the formal role of the court has been reduced (though informally it remains extensive). There has been a noticeable shift in services toward smaller group homes and nonresidential forms of assistance, but institutional services have not been reduced. Diversion of status offenders seems to be taking hold, and many youth might not be receiving any services at all as a result. There is no information on what happens to youth who are diverted from the system altogether.

The federal effort in these developments was supportive but not determinative; it added legitimacy and some financial support to deinstitutionalization advocates. Federal legislation by itself did not place deinstitutionalization on the legislative agenda or contribute substantially to its passage. Federal funds did help to pay for services, but since these funds were combined with state funds in the form of reimbursement, they were not structured to generate change.

Arizona

Arizona has achieved considerable success in its deinstitutionalization efforts in the sense that there have been dramatic declines in the number of status offenders in secure detention and secure residential facilities, but it has effected this change with less state legislative or policy activity than was the case in the other six states. State-level activity, in fact, was relatively slight; progress toward deinstitutionalization more often was made through changes in attitudes and practices at the local level.

The first state-level efforts were by lobbying groups that formed in 1975 around the issue of whether the state should participate in JJDPA. It was felt at that time that the cost of complying was too high both in relation to the small amounts of federal money being offered and the commitments required by the federal government. In the following year the governor accepted JJDPA money for one year for planning and, in the next year, authorized full participation. All parties seemed to agree on the goal, and there was little formal opposition until implementing legislation was introduced.

In 1976 the first attempt to change the law failed. The legislation, which proposed removing incorrigibles from juvenile court jurisdiction and referring them instead to the Department of Economic Security (the state umbrella social welfare agency), was opposed by the department because it did not want to handle these youth. In the next year, however, the first and most significant piece of legislation was enacted. It barred commitment of the major categories of status offenders (i.e., runaways, truants, and ungovernables) to the Department of Corrections. Proposed legislation to also bar secure detention was killed. Juvenile court judges lobbied on both sides of these proposals; in general, the split was along urban-rural lines, with judges in rural areas opposing deinstitutionalization measures. Another significant item of legislation, enacted in 1978, allowed police to divert preadjudicated nondelinquent youth to nonsecure detention.

Other state-level activity also may have had some influence. The State Justice Planning Agency, which was charged with implementing and monitoring JJDPA, actively used LEAA funds for the development of alternative facilities, public education, training, staffing grants, and information systems. It kept looking over the shoulder of the juvenile court judges and prodded them toward JJDPA goals. LEAA funding was also used to create a Joint Juvenile Justice Committee in the legislature, which held hearings throughout the state and issued reports on status offenders. Interest groups also were active throughout the state during this period.

The change in Arizona's approach to status offenders was primarily due to changes at the local level; State and federal influence was not that great. As will be seen in the next section, it was basically changes in local culture and attitudes, with some prodding and stimulation by state and federal sources, that shaped Arizona's response to deinstitutionalization.

Utah

Utah agreed to participate in JJDPA very late (in 1978). Whereas late participation on the part of some states indicated reluctance either to deinstitutionalize or to become involved with the federal government, neither was the case with Utah. Since 1971 there has been an extensive and largely successful deinstitutionalization effort; moreover, it was aided by a variety of federal sources that were primarily of two kinds—information and ideology, and money to finance programs.

Impetus for change was first provided by the President's Commission on Law Enforcement and Administration of Justice. Utah officials and citizen groups began seriously to consider deinstitutionalization as conceptualized in the commission's 1967 report. In the next year Utah started obtaining a series of grants that were used to build programs. The first grants were from HEW under the Juvenile Delinquency Prevention and Control Act, which, with LEAA funds, began the first diversion efforts. HEW, at the state's invitation, studied the State Industrial School (now called the Youth Development Center) and recommended the removal of status offenders from juvenile court jurisdiction.

In 1971 the first legislative change was enacted. This law removed runaways and truants from the juvenile court but did not fix responsibility elsewhere. There was a lot of ensuing confusion and, on the part of law enforcement, considerable frustration. Law enforcement agencies also obtained LEAA funding to start their own diversion programs, called youth bureaus, which handled less serious cases through family crisis intervention, informal counseling, and referrals to nonjudicial agencies.

In 1973 and 1974 the Utah Department of Social Services began the Youth Services System, the start of the present diversion system in Utah. The major projects were in Weber County (Ogden) and Salt Lake County (Salt Lake City), with smaller projects in other parts of the state. These projects required the active cooperation of mental health, and law enforcement agencies, schools, social services, juvenile courts, local detention centers, and interest groups. The project was especially successful in Salt Lake County and built a firm institutional base there for future reform. Of particular importance was the Salt Lake County Commission on Youth, which was composed of representatives of the participating agencies plus community groups. The Commission served as a continuing, expert proponent of deinstitutionalization and was instrumental in passing the 1977 legislation on diversion.

The most important interest group was the Board of Juvenile Court Judges, an organization that was an early and sympathetic force for deinstitutionalization but for mixed reasons. The judges wanted to reserve scarce court time for serious delinquents, but they also believed in a family-centered approach to status offenders. The continued success of the Youth Services System with runaways and ungovernables served to broaden the base of support for deinstitutionalization. This expanding coalition was aided by the law enforcement diversion programs, the overcrowding of juvenile facilities, the belief that court contact had negative implications for nonoffenders, and the view that a family-centered approach would be more productive.

Despite the growing coalition of pro-deinstitutionalization forces, in 1975 the governor refused to participate in JJDPA. His reasons were not philosophical; rather, he perceived that the cost of complying was much higher than the amount of federal money being offered, and that Utah could not comply within the required time.

In 1977 new legislation was passed that transferred jurisdiction over runaway youth and youth beyond control of parents and school authorities to the Department of Family Services. These categories of status offenders could be referred to juvenile court only if counseling efforts failed or if there was a probation violation. Again the Board of Juvenile Court Judges was strongly in favor of this legislation.

By 1978 Utah was ready to join JJDPA. Under a special arrangement, the state was offered more money and was given more flexibility in meeting deadlines (that is, the state was allowed to use earlier baseline statistics).

During the 1970s, Utah's efforts were focused on diversion, and significant results were achieved. With the exception of tobacco and alcohol violations, far fewer status offenders were being referred to juvenile court. Although data on detention are much less accessible, there also seem to be fewer status offenders in secure detention. A major problem here, however, is the lack in rural areas of nonsecure facilities to be used in lieu of jails.

Utah seemed less concerned about postadjudication placement. During the decade, there was great concern about conditions in the Youth Development Center, and the state began to develop alternative placement facilities, some of which accepted status offenders. From time to time, federal grants were received for the building of these alternative facilities. Although state statistics do not separate out status offenders, some studies indicate (and state officials insist) that status offenders are no longer placed in the Youth Development Center (a state survey showed only two status offenders there in 1979, and the state said that they were not "pure" status offenders). However, status offenders may well be appearing in the State Hospital Youth Center—a program for psychotic and severely disturbed children with normal IQs. The program is considered quite successful, and its 50-bed capacity is always full. On the other hand, the training school for the mentally retarded receives very few children from the juvenile court. These are the only large (more than 12-bed) institutions in Utah. All other out-of-home placements are either in group homes or foster homes that are run by private providers. Foster homes are used mostly for dependent and neglected children, and the private provider system has not catered to status offenders. The best guess is that there has been a real decline in out-of-home placements for status offenders, rather than relocation into group homes.

Utah, then, has come close to reaching its deinstitutionalization goals. The federal influence was quite important, but it was not directly related to JJDPA. Rather, federal or national influence was important in this state in terms of ideology and seed money. The 1968 HEW grant was critically important as a catalyst; it brought citizens and agencies together to do something, and out of this union came the Youth Services System. Throughout the period, the federal government acted as a source of ideas and specific grants to start programs that, in turn, added to the support of deinstitutionalization efforts.

CONCLUSIONS AT THE STATE LEVEL

A large number of legal and policy changes have occurred at the state level. Moreover, they have occurred in a short period of time. Although there was some activity in the 1960s, most of the changes occurred during the decade of the 1970s, in disparate states. Deinstitutionalization with its myriad of meanings was a national movement whose time had come; it swept the country.

Decarceration

Deinstitutionalization, if it means nothing else, surely must mean that no more status offenders may be incarcerated in the large state red-brick institutions. This is one of the few JJDPA mandates. All of the states in this study appear to have accomplished this objective. Six have done so by specific legislation that prohibits incarceration, and the seventh (Utah) requires the diversion of status offenders from the juvenile justice system, except under fairly special circumstances.

The mandate prohibiting the incarceration of status offenders is an instance in which prospects are strongest for the implementation of state or federal policy. This is a clear statutory provision that lends itself to a certain level of monitoring and enforcement. Of course, there is still room for slippage; the police, court intake, and the judge can relabel or can upgrade the offense if there is some delinquency involved. This can be made easier or harder, depending on how the state statute distinguishes delinquency from status offenses. Nonetheless, a carefully drawn statute with a clear prohibition can influence considerably the exercise of local discretion.

In addition, there was more agreement on this mandate than on any other in the federal deinstitutionalization package. This is not to say that there was no opposition to decarceration. In several of the states, traditional bureaucracies (e.g., corrections, the juvenile courts, and law enforcement) opposed it; this was particularly true in Massachusetts. But this opposition was not solid. In some of the states, corrections and the courts no longer wanted to devote scarce resources to what they viewed as a much less serious deviancy problem. In Virginia, corrections staff were funded by LEAA and had a vested interest in reform. In Pennsylvania the bureaucracies were divided; the Department of Public Welfare was in favor of reform, but several of the child welfare offices were reluctant to take a new and more troublesome clientele.

Whereas the opposition to decarceration may have been divided, the reform groups and their allies were united on this issue. Fiscal conservatives as well as the full spectrum of advocacy groups opposed the continued placement of status offenders with delinquents in the large state institutions. It was on the subject of commingling that the arguments in favor of deinstitutionalization were strongest: It was unfair (status offenders had committed no crime); it was counterproductive (status offenders would become delinquent); and it was costly. Scandals and deplorable conditions (with attendant media coverage) were easier to uncover and demonstrate here. The goal was simply stated, the mandate was clear and, within limits, monitoring and implementation problems were relatively easy to overcome.

The reform coalitions apparently broke down on the question of what to do with status offenders once they were no longer to be incarcerated. It was four years between the passage of the Massachusetts' CHINS legislation in 1973 and the establishment of procedures for diverting CHINS and for placing them in less restrictive alternatives. These programs came into existence as a result of pressure from LEAA. Wisconsin and Louisiana set up boards to review placements of youth, but Louisiana apparently has done little to provide alternative treatment programs. There has been some development of alternative services (mainly group homes) in Virginia, Arizona, Utah, and Wisconsin, but these efforts have not run very deep and the number of placements is not significant. The favored approach is to obtain federal money to start projects and to give the counties incentives to use alternative placements. In some of the states, notably Wisconsin and Pennsylvania, these measures succeeded for a time. In Wisconsin over a three-year period the number of group homes tripled, but then the effort withered. The goal of the fiscal conservatives at the state level was to shift the costs from the state to the counties through the combination of the legal mandate, seed money, and variable reimbursement formulas. However, when the counties began to face an economic crunch and limited social services budgets, placements started to decline. In contrast, in Massachusetts and Pennsylvania—states with strong private provider industries—out-of-home placements reportedly have not declined and in fact may even be on the rise.

Faced with a mandate prohibiting incarceration and a lack of alternative placements, there is the prospect that officials will turn to relabeling or upgrading the offense. There is a noticeable rise in minor delinquency adjudications in Virginia, and some officials (especially those in the Department of Corrections) are convinced that the judges are engaging in this practice. Wisconsin took some active steps to try to prevent relabeling. Early on the law was changed to disallow the violation of a court order as grounds for upgrading the offense. Several state institutions were closed during this period, allaying fears that the pressure of empty beds would lead to more commitments. Although the questionable reliability of data warrants caution, there is no evidence in any of the other states that the courts or intake personnel are engaging in this practice.

It was also thought that status offenders would end up in other forms of secure institutions, most likely mental hospitals. It seems clear that a substantial population of children and youth are using mental health facilities (Lerman 1980), but on the basis of existing data and reported research it is difficult to know how this usage relates to issues of deinstitutionalization. Our research has yielded no evidence of an increased use of public mental health facilities by status offenders as a consequence of deinstitutionalization. Although we did not look at the usage rates of private mental health facilities, other research suggests that there has been an increase in the use of private outpatient services by a juvenile population that could well include status offenders (Sowder 1980). Whether they are in fact included and, if so, under what circumstances and with what results, are issues that clearly merit further investigation.

Detention

The response to detention may be contrasted with that to incarceration. The mandate of each is in similar form; that is, a negative prohibition for which implementation and monitoring are relatively straightforward—not completely without difficulty, but somewhat so. Yet detention has had a different history at the state level. Only four out of the seven states in our study forbid its use for status offenders. There was and still is decidedly less agreement about both the wisdom and the feasibility of abolishing secure detention for status offenders. There is a strong feeling, by no means restricted to law enforcement, that there must be a way to hold ungovernable and runaway youth—at least for a short period—until parents, courts, or some other agency can take over. This need is especially felt in the rural areas, where there are only jails and no other facilities, secure or nonsecure. There is a high level of frustration and strong feelings about this point in the process; bewildered, anxious, and angry parents call on the police for help and want them to respond. There is also the feeling that secure detention, as a short, snappy, informal punishment, is a needed sanction for troublesome youth. It is a good lesson of what the future holds if certain conduct continues. In all of the states we studied, there was a strong local feeling in favor of some form of secure detention for status offenders; this was clearly different from feelings about the wisdom of prohibiting incarceration. Detention is much closer to home than incarceration.

The experience in California is a good illustration of the conflicts over detention. In that state, the politics of deinstitutionalization was almost entirely confined to the struggle over what to do about detention (see Steinhart, appendix E). Prior to 1976, when the detention prohibition was enacted, California had substantial numbers of status offenders in secure detention. Moreover, there was a powerful array of forces in favor of this policy, including not only professional organizations and the bureaucracy that staffed the large network of facilities, but also some of the community-based youth service centers that felt that detention was necessary for intervention and treatment. There were strong law-and-order sentiments in California at this time, in part a reflection of the significant rise in serious and sensational crime in the 1960s. In fact, the 1976 detention prohibition was enacted under the guise of law and order; it was part of an overall retrenchment in the juvenile justice laws and was kept alive by the work of a few tenacious, reform-minded legislators, some advocacy groups, some compromises, and legislative fatigue at the eleventh hour.

The 1976 law had an impact. Although there may have been some relabeling, there was a swift and dramatic decline in status offender arrests and petitions; many police and probation departments refused to respond to runaways and beyond-control youth. But a backlash set in almost immediately. There was broadly based support to restore some form of limited detention; legislators heard from individuals, groups, and newspaper editorials, among others. A modification was proposed the following year to permit 48 judicial hours of secure detention to check on warrants or to arrange for a return home; longer periods could be imposed for youth who had previously fled a nonsecure facility in violation of a court order, or for youth found to be in danger because of drug, alcohol, medical, or mental problems. This provision was in conflict with JJDPA and, at the last minute, after the intervention of the governor's office, a compromise was enacted that conformed to JJDPA standards. The current California statute (1978) permits 12 hours of secure detention for a warrant check, 24 hours to return home, and

72 hours for out-of-state runaways. The longer holding periods were dropped and the controversy, at least at the state level, has subsided for the time being.

In most of the seven states in our study, it has been more difficult and has taken longer to enact the detention prohibition than the incarceration prohibition. Three of the states are not yet in full compliance with this JJDPA requirement; in Louisiana, if not in some other states, there is serious rethinking about whether the state will comply. As in California, the detention prohibition is likely to have more loopholes than the incarceration prohibition; in Virginia, for example, secure detention is allowed if there is a clear danger of substantial harm, or to ensure court appearance for up to 72 hours for good cause.

The incarceration prohibitions may have been more fully implemented than the detention prohibitions because they have been more absolute, more susceptible to effective monitoring and enforcement, and more acceptable to the states themselves. We may now be starting to see federal recognition of this fact in the recent changes incorporated into JJDPA. Although the statutory language of the act appeared to prohibit uncategorically the secure confinement of status offenders (Sec. 223(a)(12)), congressional intent was considerably more flexible. In its report on the JJDPA amendments of 1977, the Senate Judiciary Committee recognized that "there may be rare situations in some states where short-term secure custody of status offenders is justified" (U.S. Congress 1977:60). Two situations in which this might apply are (1) holding the youth in order to contact parents and to return him or her home and (2) arranging for a suitable out-of-home placement. The gap between statutory language and intention was resolved at least partially in favor of those pushing for reinstatement of secure detention for status offenders with the passage of the JJDPA amendments of 1980 (P.L. 96-509). Following a sustained lobbying effort on the part of such groups as the National Council of Juvenile and Family Court Judges, states may now use secure detention for status offenders who run away from a nonsecure placement in violation of a valid court order.

The development of shelter care as an alternative to detention has been uneven in the states, but in certain regards it did not differ from the general pattern of development of alternative placements. States that were interested in doing something used the familiar combination of seed money and reimbursement formulas. In Wisconsin the reform coalition, in anticipation of their legislative effort, encouraged the building of 28 shelter homes with LEAA money. After a considerable growth in shelter care, the law prohibiting secure detention was passed in 1978. Once the programs were in place, the state charged the reimbursement rates to the counties—50 percent for shelter care costs, and no reimbursement at all for secure detention. Pennsylvania and Massachusetts took a similar approach—some development through seed money and changes in the reimbursement rates. In Virginia the Department of Corrections developed some shelter care. Louisiana authorized the construction of shelter care but has not yet appropriated any money.

In California the legislature enacted only the prohibition on detention; it neither required alternative nonsecure facilities nor appropriated any money for this purpose. However, it did authorize probation departments to contract with public or private agencies for nonsecure shelter facilities and counseling programs for status offenders, and large amounts of LEAA funds were used to develop alternative facilities. Subsequently, some counties also were able to use state funds for this purpose.

Diversion

Diversion has become a key part of deinstitutionalization. As we have seen, diversion is an ambiguous part of the federal mandate; yet there has been considerable activity in all of the states except Louisiana. In some of the states, legislative activity may have been only a codification of local practice. The Arizona statute, for example, allows the police to divert status offenders to nonsecure detention. Pennsylvania and Wisconsin have codified their "informal adjustments" and also allow "consent decrees," which are informal adjustments after proceedings have started. Codification of existing practice is not that unusual in social welfare law, and it probably has some behavioral consequences in regularizing activity and encouraging change.

Other states have made more fundamental efforts toward diversion. The leader in these efforts is Utah, which early on effectively used federal grant money to start its programs. One of the most interesting aspects here was police-sponsored diversion, again using federal grants. As noted, Massachusetts, after some delay and some prodding by LEAA, set up a CHINS unit in its Department of Social Services that encourages diversion.

Activity has been slight in the area of service planning for status offenders, even though five of our states have made some move in this direction. Pennsylvania mandated planning on the part of the counties and threatened fund cutoffs and the state takeover of child welfare services. Apparently these threats, plus zero reimbursement for secure detention costs, had some influence in what observers feel is the successful implementation of the prohibition on secure detention there. But beyond this, efforts to encourage planning at the county level did not seem very important.

What can we say about the results of diversion, the prohibitions on secure detention and incarceration, and the apparent lack of development of alternative facilities? Evidence seems strongest for the proposition that fewer status offenders are entering the juvenile justice system. Most officials and observers in the states agree. The state data show that there are fewer status offender referrals to the juvenile court; in two of the states, status offender arrests are slightly up, but in the others they have declined. In the two states with the strongest private provider systems—Massachusetts and Pennsylvania—status offenders who get into the system are more likely to be placed out-of-home than they are in the other states. But the view still is that fewer status offenders are entering the juvenile justice system, even in these two states.

These same officials and observers in the states are also of the opinion that most status offenders are now being ignored altogether; that is, not only are they not entering the juvenile justice system, but they are not going into any other system either. Proof of this assertion, of course, is beyond the scope of this study. We have noted the possibility that status offenders are now receiving outpatient mental health services. There also may be other programs or systems that are dealing with significant numbers of status offenders. We do know, for example, that large numbers of shelter facilities have been funded under the Runaway Youth Act, and that many youth are using these shelters. But we have no systematic evidence of whether more sustained or different kinds of treatments are being received by status offenders in different kinds of settings or what the impact of these settings on status offenders has been. These are questions that have not been directly addressed in this research.

We see then at the state policy level a significant amount of legislative activity, but this activity is uneven in terms of pace, content, and depth of commitment. Policy is clearest on the incarceration prohibition; somewhat less clear, but still fairly consistent, on detention; but much weaker and inconsistent on the "second stage" of deinstitutionalization—that of providing alternative services and placements. What accounts for this trend?

In all of the states except Louisiana, deinstitutionalization seemed to be in the interest of a wide coalition. In most of the states, liberal reform groups started in the late 1960s, partly stimulated by the *Gault* decision and the President's Commission on Law Enforcement and Administration of Justice. However, these groups of liberals were roughly divided into two camps. One group not only wanted status offenders removed from secure facilities but also wanted alternative services and placements made available. Deinstitutionalization, to them, meant more appropriate services. The other group was more radical and felt that state intervention of any kind was not justified for status offense behavior.

Complicating the picture were other elements of the coalition. In most of these states the concern about crime had increased. Some felt that status offenders were taking up too many valuable court, law enforcement, and correctional resources. In just about every urban local area studied, concern was expressed that status offenders were time-consuming and not seriously delinquent. Dealing with status offenders detracted from dealing with serious delinquents; for this reason, at least, it would be advantageous to deinstitutionalize status offenders in order to get them out of the system. Deinstitutionalization was a way of reducing case loads, and these proponents were not interested in developing alternative services. Finally, there were the fiscal conservatives, who favored deinstitutionalization because they thought it would save the state money. When it became clear that providing alternative services and placements would also cost money and might be even more expensive, their interest in reform waned.

In any event, once the states passed the legislation to get status offenders out of correctional institutions and secure detention, the coalitions began to break down. There was a lack of interest or agreement on the part of most of the groups that advocated change, and this was clearly reflected in state-level policy. There were no state-level programs for status offenders, and few tangible resources.

Federal Sources of Influence

In order for social change to occur, ideas have to be born, and advocates have to come together to press for change and then carry through. Reform coalitions were influential in six of the seven states; they were weakest in Louisiana, the state with the poorest record of deinstitutionalization. In all of the states, including Louisiana, federal sources of influence were important to both the conceptual and mobilization efforts of these groups, although that influence was quite varied.

In broad social movements it is somewhat artificial but heuristically convenient to pinpoint specific sources and times for ideas. In six of the seven states, observers credit the *Gault* decision and the findings of the President's Commission on Law Enforcement and Administration of Justice. These statements fell on fertile ground and stirrings began among concerned groups. The procedural requirements that the U.S. Supreme

Court now demanded served as the occasion to think about other changes in the juvenile laws.

Laws are thought to serve a legitimizing, supportive function. One has to be cautious here; less is known than one might suppose about the legitimizing function of the law. It may be that values expressed in legal norms only confirm or strengthen views previously held, and that minds are not changed, at least on important issues, by changes in the law. But there is little doubt that Americans like to think that values expressed in the law are important. Certainly interest and advocacy groups have always laid great stress on the appropriation of their position by the legal system. Here, too, advocacy and interest groups did take heart from Supreme Court decisions, national commission reports, and other authoritative sources of support.

In Louisiana the federal judiciary also had an influence, but of a different sort. A federal court decision dealing with mental health commitments (right to treatment/least restrictive alternative) led some in that state to think that they had better start doing something about status offenders lest there be litigation and federal court interference (see *Gary W.* v. *State of Louisiana* 437 F. Supp. 1209 (1976)).

In Texas the federal court influence was more direct. As a result of law reform litigation, the U. S. District Court threw into question the entire operation of the juvenile justice system, which led to widespread reforms, including reforms for status offenders. After the initial shock of the litigation, the legislature and the Texas Youth Council took a lot of action on their own, but it clearly was in the shadow of the federal court (see Churgin, appendix G).

Once groups began to form, federal discretionary grants became quite important in building the institutional base for reform. In almost all of the states, federal money (primarily, but not exclusively from LEAA) was given to organizations for planning and for programs. Planning grants went to Jerome Miller of Massachusetts to blueprint his reforms; to the Wisconsin Council on Criminal Justice, which through the decade was the major reform organization in that state; to the Arizona Legislative Joint Juvenile Justice Committee, and to that state's juvenile justice planning agency, which used LEAA money for training, information, and education, as well as facility development; to the Virginia state planning agency; and to the Philadelphia-based Juvenile Justice Center, which was the single most important reform group in Pennsylvania. In a negative way the importance of federal money for these advocacy groups was best illustrated by the Louisiana experience. When LEAA declined to fund the principal advocacy group in that state, the group died shortly thereafter and with it the principal reform effort in that state.

The federal government gave grants to these groups for projects. The Wisconsin Council on Criminal Justice used this money to start group homes and shelter care. In Arizona the Pima County Juvenile Court used these funds to develop nonsecure facilities in the Tucson area; LEAA funds were used for a similar purpose in Maricopa County, and for the Children's Village in Yuma County. Federal funds played an important role in projects in Utah, in both the Youth Services System (initially funded by HEW) and the police diversion projects. In addition to helping to build new mechanisms for the delivery of services, these projects served the all-important function of institution building. In Utah, for example, the Salt Lake County Commission, which was created to supervise the youth services project, included representatives from education, law enforcement, social services, mental health, the juvenile court, and the community. This organization not only broadened the coalition, but became a continuing force for change within the state. The same happened in Wisconsin with the Council on Criminal Justice; ex-employees began to show up in other parts of state government and exercised influence there. In California substantial amounts of LEAA money were, for a crucial time, the exclusive resource for the development of alternatives to detention. The staff and organizations that developed from these projects were the most vocal, experienced groups in the fight to preserve deinstitutionalization gains.

Concerning the JJDPA block grant funds, observers in most of the states said that the amount of money was not significant enough to make a critical difference. It seems that the federal grant money may have been much more important to reform groups and for individual projects. On the other hand, in Pennsylvania the state Department of Public Welfare did not want to lose the JJDPA money, even though it was only $2 million out of a $100 million budget. In several of the other states, there also was some pressure not to lose this money. In California, federal legislation and money were not mentioned in the first legislative battle, but when it came time to defend the detention prohibition, the potential loss of federal funds was used, apparently with some effect, to reach a compromise in that state. In sum, where other conditions for change were present, the federal money helped but does not appear to have been crucial.

The conclusion about the relatively small importance of the direct JJDPA block grant funds does not apply, however, to the sum total of all of the federal influence. In some of the states the evidence is clearer than in others, and effects are more pronounced. In general, however, one can safely say that the variety of forms of federal support played a significant role in the process of change. This role served different functions: It stimulated thinking, it helped advocacy groups, it funded projects; and these activities combined to build the institutional base for change at the state level.

LOCAL PROGRAMS

The striking point about the operation of programs in local areas is the great variation even within states. In fact, it could be argued that there is more variation within each state than between states. What accounts for this variation?

Implementation of deinstitutionalization at the local level depends on the interaction of three factors. First, and by far the most important, is the attitude of the local juvenile court judge and his or her staff. This is the critical discretionary point in the system; how the judge views deinstitutionalization influences to a large degree whether there will be a program at all, and what kind of program there will be. The second factor is the availability of facilities at the local level—willing and able child welfare offices, group homes and shelter care, and other kinds of needed services. Unless alternatives are available, a sympathetic court can only do so much; and the presence of facilities can sometimes influence a court. The third factor, which is related to the second, is the local environment—that is, whether groups and interests in the community are supportive or not of deinstitutionalization. Judges often reflect community attitudes, and a supportive community environment often facilitates the development of alternative services.

Deinstitutionalization programs at the local level can take one of two basic approaches: a pure *diversion* approach in which status offenders completely bypass the court and enter the social service or some other system; or a *court-centered* approach in which, as the name implies, status offenders are handled by the court. Within the court-centered model, there are also two variations: in one—the *broker* approach—the court acts as a referral source for outside services; in the other—the *court-control* approach—the court takes a much more active role in orchestrating the service program itself.

Before drawing generalizations and implications from these various approaches, we will briefly illustrate the interaction of the three factors on which deinstitutionalization at the local level depends.

CONDITIONS FAVORABLE TO DEINSTITUTIONALIZATION

There are some local areas that we studied in which all three factors—
the court, available facilities, and local environment—were favorable
and deinstitutionalization policies worked smoothly. In Maricopa County,
Arizona, dramatic changes in local policies and administrative structures
accomplished significant deinstitutionalization. This was achieved primarily on the basis of broad commitments to the principle of deinstitutionalization on the part of the most significant local actors, namely,
the juvenile court judges, the probation officers, and the police. There
was some help from the federal government, but little from the state.
The local people accomplished deinstitutionalization pretty much on
their own. As early as the mid-1960s, the police began to question their
involvement with status offenders; they felt that the issues were more
of a family matter than a police matter, and besides, scarce resources
were better used for delinquency and crime. On the other hand, the
police were aware of what was happening at the federal level and wanted
to make changes of their own. By the mid-1970s, two of the Phoenix
area police departments established counseling units to deal with status
offenders. One of the units—the Crisis Intervention Unit—handles a
variety of juvenile-family matters. All runaway and incorrigible matters
are first referred there. Since 1975 the Phoenix police have not taken
runaways to court unless there was a warrant outstanding. The police
are opposed to removing all jurisdiction over status offenders; for example, they feel the need for curfew laws to prevent burglaries. Nevertheless, referrals have gone down sharply—by more than one-half between 1973 and 1977. In 1975 a nonsecure facility for runaways,
Tumbleweed, was established with an LEAA grant (it is now funded
through Title XX). However, this facility handles only a small number
of referrals from the police, and has not been a significant factor in the
reduction of status offender referrals to court.

The Maricopa court intake unit has 34 officers and 5 supervisors who
staff the Family Crisis Unit (established in 1976), which handles all
incorrigible and runaway cases and attempts to reduce the likelihood of
detention by seeking alternatives that are acceptable to the parents and
the youth. In 1977 the unit had contact with 1,444 incorrigible youth,
and only 154 went to detention. The juvenile court, by court rule (as
distinguished from state statute), narrowed the grounds for detention
to failure to appear at a hearing, and the likelihood of suicide or other
personal injury. In addition, three facilities for short-term shelter care
were established with state and JJDPA funds. Between 1974 and 1979

there was a significant drop in detention, even though during the same period status offender arrests went up slightly. The significant drop in referrals occurred before 1975 and leveled off thereafter, and the number of status offenders referred to the three LEAA-funded shelters was relatively small. In addition, and in keeping with trends during the entire decade, the use of the Department of Corrections for status offenders continued to decline.

Although the Maricopa experience illustrates the importance of the combined efforts of all of the relevant actors, the key is still the juvenile court judge. In Pima County, Arizona, the juvenile court judge who sat for most of the 1970s was an early and strong supporter of deinstitutionalization, and that court became a national leader even before JJDPA was passed. He began by stimulating the local community to develop private alternative placements. In 1976 the court was awarded a three-year grant of $1.9 million from LEAA to develop programs for preadjudicatory status offenders. This money was used for counseling and school programs, the development of three shelter homes, a loose confederation of foster shelter homes, and a mobile diversion unit within the juvenile court. The unit, which was staffed by 14 probation officers on a 24-hour basis, responded to incorrigibility complaints at the home or at the arrest site to counsel and to divert while still "in the field." By 1979 almost all of these innovations were permanently funded; for example, the shelter homes were carried by the Department of Economic Security (the umbrella welfare department), and much of the school program was assumed by the school district. In that year, however, the juvenile court judge was replaced by a judge with a completely different philosophy. She publicly renounced the deinstitutionalization policy; the mobile diversion unit was disbanded and replaced in probation intake by a family services unit with a much less activist diversion orientation. Within one year the detention rate for status offenders who were referred to the court increased from about 11 percent (1978) to over 30 percent. Pima County Juvenile Court is our most dramatic illustration of the importance of the position of the judge, a matter to which we will return.

Another locale in which deinstitutionalization ultimately worked smoothly is Salt Lake County, which is the home of a "model" status offender diversion program. We have previously mentioned the cooperative efforts of that community in establishing the Youth Services Center, which reflected not only the importance of relevant local agencies and actors but also the critically important supportive role of federal financing. Despite strong support from the community, the project was seriously underfunded; it stabilized only when JJDPA funds permitted the hiring of four professionals. Currently the budget is shared equally by the county, the state, Title XX, and JJDPA.

The turning point with the Youth Services Center in Utah was the attitude of the juvenile court in Salt Lake County. When the facility opened in 1974, the presiding judge ordered all law enforcement agencies to take runaway and ungovernable youth to the center, which he also declared to be a shelter facility. Initially, there was some resistance on the part of the police, who had their own diversion program—the youth bureaus—also funded in part from LEAA. After a relatively short period of time, law enforcement cooperated fully; in fact, in the following year the city police turned their diversion program over to the Youth Services Center (the county sheriff's office kept their own diversion program but also cooperated fully).

The results of the Salt Lake County diversion program have been significant. There have been substantial declines in the number of status offenders referred to the courts (e.g., a drop of 38 percent between 1974 and 1975), and there is no evidence of relabeling (criminal delinquency referrals also declined during this same period). In 1977 the success of the Salt Lake County program led the legislature to divert all runaways and ungovernables, and the Salt Lake program was implemented statewide. This change in the law further accelerated the decline in court referrals for these categories of status offenders; at the same time, there was a sharp rise in intake for this group at the Youth Services Center. In other words, more runaways and ungovernables are being apprehended by the police (the major source of referral in Utah). But this is not serving as a funnel to the court; rather, the Youth Services Center is the primary program for runaways and ungovernables in Salt Lake County.

Both secure detention and postadjudication placement of status offenders have dropped significantly in Salt Lake County. If there is to be an out-of-home placement, the most preferred alternative is the foster home, although there is difficulty in placing older or more troublesome youth. The use of foster homes as the preferred alternative is a reflection of the consistent family-centered philosophy of the Utah juvenile court judges.

CONDITIONS UNFAVORABLE TO DEINSTITUTIONALIZATION

As we noted earlier, Pima County, Arizona, under the new judge illustrates how a change in the juvenile court judge can kill a deinstitutionalization program even though the other factors were favorable.

Uintah County, Utah, represents a local area in which the court and the local community are in favor of deinstitutionalization but facilities are not available—a major problem in rural areas. This county contains only one percent of the state's population, but it is also the tenth most populous county in the state. Vernal is the county seat, with a chief probation officer who acts as intake officer and referee for minor offenses, two probation officers, and two support staff. The juvenile court is 100 miles away in Provo; the judge comes to Vernal on a biweekly basis. The court in this county is just as family-centered as the court in Salt Lake County but does not have access to the same range of facilities. When a youth is apprehended, there are only three alternatives: (1) release to parents, (2) shelter in foster homes, or (3) lockup in one of the two "juvenile detention" cells in the county jail. The shelter foster homes will not take older, out-of-state, or troublesome youth. Another possibility is to take the youth to the Youth Detention Home near Provo, a 155-mile trip. The same lack of facilities hampers postadjudication placements; if release to parents or foster homes cannot be worked out, then the youth is sent far away to other institutions.

Under the 1977 legislation, runaways and ungovernables have to be diverted to the Division of Family Services. The Vernal office of the division has a very meager budget and only one youth services worker. Three staff from child welfare services are on loan to maintain a 24-hour, on-call service for status offenders, but the police complain that the division workers are reluctant to respond promptly after hours, and the police resent the extra time and effort that it takes to handle status offenders themselves. The problem is easing somewhat with the addition of an LEAA-funded juvenile officer, who is available to transport youth to the Provo center, but it is mostly delinquents who are making the trip.

There has been a rise in the number of status offense referrals in Uintah County between 1973 and 1979. There also has been a growth in the population (including the youth population), a boomtown economy, and consequently more activity on the part of law enforcement. There has been some widening of the net as well with the advent of federally funded youth officers and the availability of the Division of Family Services as a referral agency. However, diversion has not taken hold because of the lack of alternative facilities to handle these youth. On the other hand, although statistics are hard to come by, respondents there report a drop in the use of secure detention. The judge has ordered much tighter restrictions on the use of jail for status offenders. Some effort has been made recently to build a shelter facility, but funding is hard to find. In this rural county, service alternatives are really thin. They have the deinstitutionalization philosophy but simply lack the ability to implement the 1977 legislation. This lack of facilities in the rural areas was one of the major reasons why Utah delayed in joining the JJDPA; the state felt that it just could not comply.

There are situations in which all three factors operate against deinstitutionalization: The judges are opposed, the local environments are opposed, and there is a lack of out-of-home residential facilities. One such example is Vernon Parish, Louisiana—a community known for holding high numbers of juveniles in jail. It has the reputation for attempting to develop counseling programs, but has relatively few facilities. Officials and other court personnel were nearly unanimous in their concern that deinstitutionalization not be used for all juvenile offenders. In their view, detention and postadjudication institutionalization were desirable alternatives for certain troublesome status offenders; they felt that the juvenile justice system had to have this flexibility.

Prior to 1978—the year in which Louisiana's deinstitutionalization statutes went into effect—there had been little movement toward achieving that goal in this parish. With the change in the law, there has been a start in developing some community resources (e.g., a mental health center and a youth counseling center) as well as a combination shelter-facility/group home. There also has been no evidence of law evasion after the change; that is, there does not seem to be relabeling, the use of contempt orders, or commitments to mental health facilities. It is probable that most status offenders are either warned and released, or are simply ignored altogether.

DEINSTITUTIONALIZATION MODELS

The data collected from the seven states suggest that there are at least two general models of deinstitutionalization, both of which focus on the extent to which the juvenile justice system is the center of activity vis-à-vis these youth. The first of these models, *diversion*, lodges primary responsibility for these youth with a system other than juvenile justice (e.g., welfare). The court's role is reduced to the extent that it becomes a mode of last resort rather than first resort. The second of these models, *court-centered*, focuses on the primacy of the juvenile court as either the sole source of authority over these youth or as the broker on their behalf for arranging the provision of needed services by other public or private systems (e.g., welfare, education, mental health, etc.). We discuss each of these models and their variations in turn.

Diversion Approach

Salt Lake County is the prime example of a diversion model. Here status offenders are initially processed not by the juvenile court but by the

Youth Services Center, a contract shelter facility that is funded by the Department of Social Services. Runaways and incorrigible youth do not find their way into the juvenile justice system unless they persist in their status offense activity while under the jurisdiction of the social services system. As a consequence of this arrangement, there has been a substantial decline in the number of status offenders referred to the courts and a significant drop in the use of detention for these youth.

Pennsylvania, where in 1977 all status offenders were placed in the dependent category, also could turn out to be an instance of the diversion model. The Pennsylvania statute, however, is not clear about whether the Department of Public Welfare is to have exclusive jurisdiction over all dependent children. In Philadelphia there is at present a division of responsibility that reflects local practices and attitudes. In that city there are a great many facilities for youth, including several private agencies that are under contract to the city. These agencies are often the first point of contact for many youth, including status offenders. With the change in the law, nondelinquents should be referred to the Department of Public Welfare, but the police and other referral sources lack faith in that department and are using the private providers instead. Although all cases that are sent to these agencies have to be approved by the welfare department, that department is apparently cooperating with the arrangement because prior approval only amounts to a technical formality. Runaways, however, have to go to the department if they are to be held in shelter care.

Another development in Philadelphia is the court-run counseling and referral service that serves both delinquents and nondelinquents. The service offers direct counseling as well as referral to private providers. It thus provides many of the same services as the child welfare departments. Although it is in fact a form of diversion, it still is an arm of the court; therefore, one cannot say that as a result of the change in the law, all status offenders now go to the child welfare agencies rather than to the court. But whatever the name on the agency door, in terms of results, status offenders are no longer incarcerated or placed in secure detention. On the other hand, there is much use of foster care and other types of out-of-home placements.

The Court-Centered Approach

If the court stays in the business of implementing deinstitutionalization, it may do so in one of two basic ways: court control or court brokering. We use as our main examples the courts in two Virginia counties, not only to illustrate the differences in approach, but also to reemphasize the importance of the court's discretion even within one state.

Court Control   The Richmond Juvenile and Domestic Relations Court, the court control example, did not regard the 1977 legislation that prohibited secure detention and commitment of CHINS as significantly altering court practice. That court has always handled a heavy case load of delinquents and status offenders, and had to struggle with the problems of placing the latter youth. The presiding judge views the court as a family court in the sense that all problems associated with the family, including the problems of children and youth, regardless of their source, are the legitimate concern of the court. The judge feels that the distinction between delinquents and status offenders is arbitrary; in his view, there is only one class of children.

The removal of the coercive sanction is not a serious problem for the court: Status offenders can be detained for up to 72 hours and the court has engaged in relabeling. The court services unit (CSU), which handles intake, strongly discourages parents from filing CHINS petitions, thereby communicating to them that the court is powerless to control CHINS; therefore, parents who want the court to take control of their children file minor delinquency petitions, which have increased here significantly. Those youth who do come in as CHINS are ordered by the court to seek services, with the clear warning that if they fail to cooperate they will eventually be back before the court on more serious charges. The court also will use contempt orders against the parents if their children disobey court orders. With this array of sanctions, the court takes an active role in the lives of the youth that come before it, and involves itself in the process of delivering services.

The court services unit is the first point of contact with CHINS. At first the CSU was reluctant to deal with status offenders; it still will not handle runaways, truants, or youth charged with possession of alcohol. Those status offenders who are handled are curfew violators (the police are the referral source here) or those youth who are habitually beyond parental control (habitually is defined as repeating the same behavior three or more times). Many beyond-control youth are considered to be the same as delinquents, reflecting the philosophy of the court. CSU provides its own services—a family counseling center and a group home that is used as a long-term placement. The group home receives both delinquents and status offenders but has had difficulties (it recently closed). CSU is reluctant to become an active service broker because so much of its time is spent trying to get youth to show up for programs.

In the private sector, the Youth Development Program (YDP) works closely with CSU and the court. The program was developed by the Youth Service Commission and reports directly to the city council. The commission is a large group of representatives from the legal, medical, and health professions, the juvenile justice system, and citizens' organizations. It views itself as an active advocacy group on behalf of children and youth. The YDP is the key service broker in the area and also runs a diagnostic referral program and an advocacy program for children and youth.

Two consequences of the combined activity of the court, the CSU, and the YDP are that there has not been much growth of private programs in the Richmond area, and that the existing private providers resist their policies. Direct private providers experience difficulty in raising funds because the CSU and the YDP also provide direct services. For example, it was reported that the CSU discouraged the Virginia Council of Churches from developing a residential program for CHINS on the grounds that it was not needed. As far as resistance is concerned, the Richmond Welfare Department is reluctant to accept CHINS into its foster care and other service programs, because CHINS are thought to need more "structure" than the department can offer. The school system is also resisting by tightening definitions of eligibility for special programs in order to exclude CHINS. Not surprisingly, tension has developed between the school system and the juvenile court. In general there are not many programs for CHINS outside of those offered by the court services unit and the Youth Development Program.

Court Brokering   The juvenile court in Charlottesville has a very different conception of its role and its reponse to status offenders. The juvenile court is seen as moving toward a "junior criminal court" that handles only delinquents, with status offenders completely removed from its jurisdiction. In the interim the sole function of the court is to provide needed services to CHINS. The view of the court is that the youth is almost always better off in the home and that parents have a right to noninterference from the state. Accordingly, the court is removing itself from functions that it previously performed; for example, it no longer considers itself to be responsible for safeguarding youth from promiscuity. Finally, the court believes that the best way to stimulate the development of public and private alternative services is for the court not to provide these services itself. This court and the CSU have never been interested in providing direct services; and there is little or no evidence of the use of minor delinquency petitions to gain control over troublesome children, as is the case in Richmond. Instead, the court wants the CSU to divert all youth except serious delinquents and to act as a broker for services. The court itself becomes active in CHINS cases when service is denied and will then chastise uncooperative agencies.

The CSU reflects the court's philosophy; its basic approach to families and their children is low-key. It is strongly oriented toward keeping children and youth in their homes, and it will seek out-of-home placements only when there is real distress. It acts as an advocate for the family in seeking services and will go to court only when parents are not cooperative. Its initial inquiry is always whether the family has first sought out assistance from the social services department, which is the CSU preference.

In Charlottesville, alternative service programs are well developed. This is due in part to the presence of the University of Virginia, but also is due to the court's efforts to involve the community in dealing with CHINS and delinquents. About one-half of the 60 or more programs are private, and the CSU diverts CHINS to public and private programs more or less equally. The social services department also shares the court's strong orientation about leaving children in their homes with a minimum amount of intervention. However, some pressure was required from the court before the schools stopped trying to use it as a first resort in their dealings with troublesome children.

CONCLUSIONS AT THE LOCAL LEVEL

In looking at the great variety in the local areas, we may perhaps be overemphasizing formal or structural characteristics in our efforts to impose some analytic order. Systems that are formally different may in fact be operating in a similar fashion; and the opposite may be true as well. For example, one distinction that has been made implicitly is the *location* of the diversion program. Salt Lake County is considered to be a pure diversion program in contrast to other counties because, in part, its program is formally separate from the juvenile court. Philadelphia is considered to be an example of incomplete diversion because part of the diversion program is the court referral service program, which is located outside the juvenile court system. One of the family crisis units in Maricopa County is operated by a police department. It may be, however, that this kind of classification scheme places too much emphasis on the *name* of the agency rather than on the actual *relationship* between the court and the diversion program and how youth are served.

The Charlottesville system may in operation be very close to Salt Lake County's Youth Services Program, even though the key agency is the Charlottesville court service unit. In that community, the court does not get involved with status offenders, and the CSU is active in promoting in-home and community services and alternatives. The treatment of these youth in Salt Lake County and Charlottesville may be very similar.

In Richmond the court is actively involved in the diversion and brokering process, works closely with the CSU and the principal private agency, and is willing and able to use its authority in the process. Even in Salt Lake the court could take more of an active role if it wanted to. The discretion and flexibility is there; the critical distinction is the posture of the juvenile court.

In all of the local areas examined, the conclusion about the importance of the judge stands. The power of the court and the intake staff over diversion is almost complete: They can make or break any facility or program that is established by other local actors. As discussed earlier, the incoming judge in Pima County dramatically reversed almost a decade of significant progress toward deinstitutionalization. One can also find the opposite case. A new juvenile court judge and sheriff in rural Wisconsin, in the course of one year, dropped the detention rate of status offenders by 65 percent (from 187 to 66), and they did this without the development of any truly alternative facilities. In several of the states there were major differences in deinsitutionalization between demographically similar areas—e.g., two rural counties (Arizona), and two medium-sized counties (Massachusetts, Wisconsin). In each case these differences could be accounted for by the philosophy of the court.

A potential limitation on the exercise of discretion by the judge is the role of the police. The police in several localities have set up their own diversion units; they can either divert status offenders on their own (under threat of court referral), or they can refuse to deal with status offenders at all. There has been some evidence that the police have acted inconsistently with the court, but the strongest evidence points to cooperative efforts between these two agents. Differences between the police and the court eventually get ironed out, with the police taking their cues from the court, at least insofar as status offenders are concerned. In short, there is reciprocity between law enforcement and the courts. As discussed earlier, the court services unit in Richmond refused to take status offender petitions for runaways, truants, and youth charged with alcohol possession, but would take curfew violators who were referred by the police.

Probation departments also may have some leeway, as was the case in three California counties. In Santa Cruz County, the probation department took the initiative and began referring all status offenders to a private community-based program that provided shelter and crisis care. The county obtained JJDPA funds for counseling, housing, and other services, and the transition to alternatives to detention seems to have worked smoothly. In contrast, implementation has not worked well in San Francisco (city and county) or in Santa Clara County. In the former, the probation department operates its own version of shelter care, a converted wing of the juvenile hall, which at various times has been locked at night, allegedly to keep out intruders. There has been little referral to other programs. The Santa Clara probation department has not yet developed clear policies on status offenders, and referrals to shelter care with counseling are sporadic. The exercise of discretion by probation departments is not inconsistent with the general finding of the importance of the juvenile court judge. The power of the judge depends on the ability and the willingness of that official to exercise that authority, and on his or her relationship with the probation department. Probation departments will tend to exercise more authority where turnover is higher among judges than among the probation staff, or where the judge lacks a clear position or is not all that interested, or where for other structural reasons (e.g., work load) the judge has to delegate authority.

The power of the court is much less telling when it comes to disposition. In all of the states the option of incarceration is closed; the court has no power to alter this unless it wants to upgrade the offense. The court's use of detention is also restricted, although here the statutes are more flexible or ambiguous. Moreover, the courts have no legal authority over service providers; however, this is not the same as saying that the courts are totally without influence. For example, when the judge takes an active interest in the disposition process, he or she often is able to exercise considerable influence. Such was the case in both Boston and Richmond.

The autonomy of the judge has important implications for implementation, a theme that will be developed more fully in the chapter containing our conclusions. At this point, though, it is important to recall the statement of the hypotheses concerning the chances of success for implementation. A critical factor is how well coordinated or integrated the implementing structure is; to the extent that the structure is not well integrated or is loosely coupled, implementation becomes more problematic. In view of the findings of this chapter, it is hard to conceive of a less well integrated or more loosely coupled implementing structure than the one called upon to effect deinstitutionalization policies. The key element in the process is the court, and it is hard to imagine a more independent unit. This, of course, is not to say that deinstitutionalization therefore will not be implemented. Indeed, as we have seen, there has been considerable implementation. But what it does point out is the great importance of local actors—in this case, the judges. Deinstitutionalization cannot proceed without their support.

Alternative Facilities for Youth in Trouble: Descriptive Analysis of a Strategically Selected Sample

6

JEAN ANN LINNEY

INTRODUCTION

The Juvenile Justice and Delinquency Prevention Act incorporates two primary prohibitions: removal of status offenders from correctional institutions, and an end to the use of secure detention. In addition the act calls for development of community-based facilities and alternative modes of services. Although there is a great deal of ambiguity as to what constitutes "community-based alternatives," there is an implicit presumption that they will differ in kind from institutional settings. To date, however, there has been little systematic assessment of how these facilities are different from the institutions they replace, what kinds of services are available for status offenders, and how these settings affect the lives of the participating youth. Certainly the ultimate impact of the policy should be felt by the youth involved in the system. However, without analysis of the facilities that are used as community-based alternatives, an understanding of how this policy has been implemented and translated at the level of the individual youth cannot be reached.

This facility analysis is designed to be a descriptive assessment of alternative residential facilities as out-of-home placements for status offenders. The assessment procedure is intended to (1) describe the range of alternatives available in a sample of facilities across program

The author gratefully acknowledges the research assistance of Mindy Rosenberg, Lisa W. Woody, Edward P. Mulvey, and Jamie S. Ross in preparing this paper.

types and geographic regions, (2) address the question of the degree to which these alternative treatment facilities are different from institutional settings, and (3) examine how the programs began and to what extent their evolution corresponds with legislative mandates.

Although the definition and attributes of "community-based" and "alternative services" are far from precise, advocates seem to agree that these settings should strive to replace the dehumanizing and depersonalizing nature of the institutional facility and instead should provide an environment that is more conducive to "normal" adolescent growth and development. Similar goals for alternative services can be found in the mental health field (Jones 1953, Roosens 1979) and in discussion of care for the mentally retarded (Baker et al. 1977, Wolfensberger 1972). Capsulizing this ideology, Wolfensberger defines the principles of "normalization" as the "utilization of means which are as culturally normative as possible, in order to establish and/or maintain personal behaviors and characteristics which are as culturally normative as possible" (1972:28), and "making available . . . patterns and conditions of everyday life which are as close as possible to the norms and patterns of the mainstream of society" (Nirje 1969:181). This philosophy of normalization forms the conceptual base for the assessment and analyses reported in this study.

PROCEDURES

We adopted an interview and observation methodology for this facility analysis. The assessment procedures and design provide a sample of facility case studies that allow for some comparison among four program types that were sampled from six cities in six states. These particular sites are not intended to represent the individual cities or states; rather, we consider the sample of programs as a whole to be illustrative of the range and diversity of out-of-home placements, other than foster care, that are available to youth. Foster care homes were not included because of the small number of youth who are placed in any single home, and because of the potential disruptiveness of the site-visit methodology to the foster family.

The data reported here were gathered during two-day site visits conducted by two female observers who are trained in interviewing and observation procedures. Although the specific format of each visit was flexible, uniform information was sought from each program regarding program goals, available services, admission/intake policies, the types of youth served, referral patterns both prior to and after placement, flexibility and individualization in program activities, family involvement, and community integration. The observers periodically recorded information from interviews and observation throughout their visit to each program.

FACILITIES AND PROGRAM TYPES

In order to provide data that are consistent with the larger study, we chose to focus on the states in which case studies were also completed. Given the concentration of services in urban areas, and the fact that most youth involved in the child-caring systems come from the urban centers, we felt that our resources could best be used by focusing on the metropolitan area that was studied within each state study. This narrowed the investigation to six cities: Boston, New Orleans, Philadelphia, Phoenix, Richmond (Va.), and Salt Lake City. (Since the major metropolitan area in Wisconsin had not been included in the study of that state, it was not included in the facility analysis.)

Facilities were selected in each city to obtain a cross section of program types, including secure and nonsecure facilities, small and large programs, and short- and long-term programs. Because individual states use different names for apparently similar facility types, four program types representing a range of residential services for youth were included in the analysis. These program types were operationally defined as follows:

1. *Secure detention facilities.* The primary criteria for a detention facility are that it be physically secure and serve the general metropolitan area.

2. *Nonsecure alternatives to detention.* The alternative to detention is defined as a nonsecure, relatively short-term alternative to locked detention, such as an emergency shelter.

3. *Group homes.* A group home is a residential facility serving 15 or fewer youth who attend local community schools.

4. *Residential treatment facilities.* Residential treatment facilities are those residential programs with a capacity greater than 15 youth, that operate a relatively self-contained program, and that typically provide an on-grounds school program for residents. Group homes and residential treatment facilities are usually longer term facilities than either detention or nonsecure alternatives to detention.

For each of the six cities, consultants who completed the state case study suggested five facilities to visit (one of each of the four specified program types and the facility considered by local officials to be a model program for the city, regardless of program type). These programs tended to be those that were frequently identified by state and local officials during the case study interviewing, or by specific recommendations from an individual in the provider system. This process of site selection has probably resulted in the identification of slightly "better" programs, that is, programs that are more stable or more visible than most in the larger provider system of each area. Taken together, the facilities probably represent "the best the area has to offer," except when there is just one facility of a particular type serving the area. For example, in four of the six cities the secure detention facility is the only such facility for the city. Similarly, the nonsecure shelter facilities were likely to be one of two or three available for the city. During the visits the observers were alert to the number of program options available in the area, and often directly questioned the staff and residents regarding other programs in the vicinity to determine the representativeness of the program selected.

The total sample included 30 facilities from six cities: six secure detention facilities, six nonsecure alternative facilities, six group homes, six residential treatment programs, and six identified model programs. Four of the model programs fall in the category of residential treatment programs, and the other two are group homes. This breakdown among the model programs is particularly interesting given that by definition the residential treatment facility is larger and less integrated within the community. Given the mandates of JJDPA, we had expected model programs to be the more short-term and community-integrated types. Because the model programs were not found to be significantly different along the dimensions assessed from the other program types, each was categorized as either a group home or residential treatment facility for the purposes of analysis. Thus, the findings of this study are drawn from the four defined program types.

Table 6-1 presents descriptive information for each of the facilities in the study. The majority of the programs (21 facilities) are considered private agencies due to their purchase-of-service financial arrangements and their direct control over admissions and dismissal. Only the detention facilities and one of the nonsecure alternative shelters are directly affiliated with the juvenile court and the department of corrections. The detention facility in New Orleans is under the jurisdiction of the department of social services, not the court.

In four of the religiously affiliated programs, clergy are actively involved as staff. The concentration of these programs in Boston and Philadelphia reflects the tradition of religious charities and the private provider systems in these localities. Thirty-seven percent of the programs are one facility within a larger "umbrella" provider organization. Again reflecting regional tradition, this arrangement is more common in the two northeastern cities. Two of the residential facilities are programs that are operated within a state psychiatric hospital. As a group the 30 facilities offer a cross section of programs with varying capacities, lengths of stay, organizational structures, and funding arrangements.

SITE VISITING ARRANGEMENTS

Program directors of each facility to be visited were contacted by telephone approximately one month in advance of the requested visiting date. During the telephone conversation, the National Academy of Sciences was identified, and the project was described as a study of the impact of changes in the juvenile code and policy on patterns of service to children and youth. A two-day visit to the facility was requested so that we could discuss with the director the ways in which legislative mandates and funding and policy changes had affected their service and the types of youth referred. In addition, we requested to meet informally with the staff, to eat at least one meal in the facility with the residents, to speak with the residents, and to participate in program activities whenever possible during the visit. Each facility director was informed that his or her program had been suggested to us by state and local officials and that no program would be identified by name. In five of the six localities, all directors agreed to participate. Once a visit had been scheduled, a follow-up letter was mailed to each facility director to confirm the details of the visit and to resummarize the purposes of the study.

The visits began June 1, 1980, and were completed by November 15, 1980. Most facilities indicated that they had not made any special arrangements or plans for the visit. In a few places the observers were carefully chaperoned through the facility and the residents apparently had been told to be on their best behavior. Overall, however, the visits occurred at flattering times for some programs and unflattering times for other programs. The visits seem to represent a cross section of the nature of activity and day-to-day operation in these program types.

A typical facility visit began with a semistructured interview with the program director (approximately two hours) that focused on program history and change, treatment philosophy, and program goals. This interview generally was followed by a tour of the facility during which the observers noted the physical layout and the general condition of the facility. For the remainder of the two days, the observers "moved with

TABLE 6-1 Descriptive Data for Facilities Visited

City	Program Type	Security Status		Residents			Average Percent Status Offender	Maximum Capacity	Part of Resident Census at Visit	Typical Length of Stay	Organization Status				Major Funding Source			
		Secure	Non-Secure	Males Only	Females Only	Co-ed					Private	Religiously Affiliated	Free-Standing	Umbrella Organization	Corrections	Mental Health	Social Services	Other
Phoenix, Ariz.	D[a]	X				X	7	101	107	14 days	X		X		X			
	S		X			X	95	9	3	5 days	X		X				X	
	GH		X	X			10	11	10	18 mos.			X				X	
	RT	X				X	35	23	23	6 mos.				X		X		
	M(RT)		X			X	5	63	63	12 mos.	X		X				X	
New Orleans, La.	D	X				X	0	50	50	23 days	X		X					X
	S		X			X	85	16	9	8 days	X			X				X
	GH		X	X			0	14	13	24 mos.	X			X			X	
	RT		X				10	60	51	12 mos.	X		X				X	
	M(GH)		X			X	25	15	11	11 mos.	X	X		X			X	
Boston, Mass.	D	X			X		0	12	10	30 days	X	X	X		X			
	S		X			X	20	12	7	7 days	X		X				X	
	GH		X			X	80	30	27	24 mos.	X						X	
	RT		X		X		50	60	49	16 mos.	X	X		X			X	
	M(RT)		X	X			50	18	16	10 mos.	X	X		X	X			

									Avg. stay							
Philadelphia, Pa.																
D	X				X	0	115	110	9 days	X			X		X	X
S	X	X			X	33	95	67	34 days		X				X	X
GH	X	X	X			5	13	14	30 mos.		X				X	X
RT	X	X			X	0	15	—	—	X	X					
M(GH)	X				X	0	15	14	54 mos.	X			X			
Salt Lake City, Utah																
D	X	X			X	15	40	36	10 days	X			X			X
S	X				X	92	10	6	2 days							
GH	X	X	X			99	60[b]	55	9 mos.		X		X		X	
RT	X			X	X	25	55	49	8 mos.				X			
M(RT)	X				X	25	30	26	9 mos.					X		X
Richmond, Va.																
D	X	X			X	2	22	22	21 days	X			X			
S	X	X			X	99	12	11	19 days			X				
GH	X	X		X	X	85	10	7	12 mos.		X		X		X	
RT	X	X			X	35	20	14	6 mos.				X		X	
M(RT)	X				X	20	63	41	12 mos.				X		X	
Total	21	5	22	4	8					7	21	19	11	8	2	18	2

[a] D—Detention
S—Shelter (nonsecure detention alternatives)
GH—Group home
RT—Residential treatment
M—Identified model program

[b] Includes 7 group homes

the flow" of the program, interacting informally with both residents and staff, and participating whenever possible in ongoing activities. The observers spent a minimum of 12 hours in each facility, with an average of 15 hours per program. The particular times of day that were spent in a facility varied with the activities and schedule of the program but always included mealtimes, bedtime, and changes of staff shifts, since these routine activities provide opportunities to observe the quality of resident-staff interaction, staff attitudes toward residents, and discipline procedures.

ASSESSMENT INSTRUMENTS

Specialized data recording forms were developed to ensure systematic information gathering across facilities (see appendix C) and are summarized as follows:

- *An Administrative Questionnaire* was completed by program directors. The questionnaire focused on demographic information for the populations of youth served by their facility, admission requirements, referral sources, length of stay in the program, services provided, and most common postplacement options.
- *The Program History Recording Form* provided the basis for a semistructured interview with the program directors. It focused on program evolution and the factors seen to be responsible for program formation and change. In addition, information regarding the reaction of the professional and nonprofessional communities to the program, funding sources, and future program directions was included.
- *The Program Variables Recording Form* included observable information on program activities; prevalent treatment model; rewards, punishments, and the use and type of disciplinary action; resident privileges and opportunities for privacy; independence and responsibility; and the degree of family involvement in the program. Any specific information that was not observed during the visit was requested from staff and residents.
- *The Location and Physical Plant Recording Form* was used to record information on the neighborhood context, the physical layout and resources available to a program, and community resources readily accessible to the facility.

At the conclusion of the two-day visit, modified forms of the following two standard assessment instruments were completed by the observers.

- *The Multiphasic Environmental Assessment Procedure* (MEAP) (Moos and Lemke 1979) measures both the overall social climate of a residential facility and the quality of the physical environment. The Physical and Architectural Features subscale of the MEAP was modified to be appropriate to the adolescent population of this study and focused on the condition of the neighborhood, the building itself and the interior furnishings, and the degree of variation in design and personalization in residential living spaces. The MEAP was completed independently by the two observers, with interrater reliability of 0.90.

• *The Program Analysis of Service Systems* (PASS-3) (Wolfensberger and Glenn 1975) measures "normalization" by assessing the following: the physical, social, and cultural integration of the program's facility with the surrounding community; age- and culture-appropriate activities and programming; the physical comfort of the setting; and an overall assessment of the degree to which the facility meets the normalization ideology. The PASS-3 was modified for the purposes of this study in two primary ways: (1) it was shortened from 50 items to 35 items, and (2) descriptors of item ratings were rewritten to be more relevant to the adolescent population being considered and the relatively shorter-term period of residence in the facilities. These modifications were based on the factor analytic work of Flynn and Heal (1980) and the specific purposes of the facility analysis (see appendix C for a more detailed description). The two raters completed the modified PASS independently, with calculated interrater reliability of 0.92. The two ratings per item were averaged, and total scores were calculated using the procedure described by Wolfensberger and Glenn (1975).

HISTORICAL DEVELOPMENT AND RESPONSE TO POLICY

PRECIPITATING FACTORS IN PROGRAM FORMATION

One-third of the facilities in our sample were established after 1974 (i.e., after the passage of the Juvenile Justice and Delinquency Prevention Act) (Table 6-2). Since this group includes two detention homes, only eight facilities in this sample are likely to have begun in response to the legislative mandate for community-based alternatives. Among the five facilities in the Boston area, two were begun before JJDPA, which suggests that Massachusetts' deinstitutionalization effort may have been instrumental in creating the need for its current program.

During the administrative interview regarding the history and development of each facility, only one program director (of an emergency shelter) specifically spoke of legislative mandates in the juvenile justice system as being causal in the development of the program. Two of the six emergency shelter facilities used funds provided through the Run-

TABLE 6-2   Breakdown of Program Types by Age of Facility

Program Type	Pre-1900	1900-1954	1955-1967	1968-1973	Post-1974	N
Detention	0	2	1	1	2	6
Shelter	0	0	1	2	3	6
Group home	1	0	1	3	3	8
Residential treatment	3	0	2	3	2	10
Total	4	2	5	9	10	30

away Youth Act, which suggests that this legislation may have been important in the development of shelters for runaway youth. The program director in one referral-based shelter facility reported that the facility was developed in response to legislative change at the behest of the juvenile court judge and the director of social services. In this locality the prohibition on placing status offenders in secure detention, and the passage of child abuse laws that allowed for the immediate removal of a child in physical jeopardy, created a serious need for temporary shelter for displaced children. In response the juvenile court and social service department jointly organized an emergency shelter.

Consistent with the diversion components of JJDPA, seven program directors identified keeping youth out of the juvenile justice system as an initial goal of their service. However, only one of these facilities was established after JJDPA. Four of these programs (begun prior to JJDPA), which focused primarily on youth with drug-related problems and school problems, sought to prevent the entry of these youth into the juvenile correctional system by providing an alternative placement. In contrast, staff in the Boston and Philadelphia areas, rather than seeking to reduce the youth's involvement in the court and correctional systems, indicated a desire to have more help from the court in asserting authority and ordering the acceptance of services.

Nearly 60 percent of the program directors (including only one detention home administrator) indicated that the primary factor responsible for the program's establishment was the number of unserved youth in the community (Table 6-3). Twenty percent of the facilities indicated that changing youth populations were responsible for their current program (e.g., the decline in unwed mothers needing out-of-home care). Seventeen percent of the programs (all secure facilities) cited the need for a secure residential facility as the primary factor precipitating program formation. Several directors cited secondary influences that contributed to the need for more residential placements, including the declining number of foster families and the particular difficulties in placing "troublesome adolescents" in foster homes. In describing a program's inception, staff and administrators perceive the growing numbers of children in need, inadequate services, and insufficient placement options as contributing to the need for additional services. Given the median age of these programs (10 years), these perceptions may be attributable to the national zeitgeist that recognizes the needs of youth in general and troublesome groups in particular, rather than to any specific policy or legislative changes.

The facilities in this study have come into existence through a variety of avenues. Thirty-three percent started as a result of the efforts of one individual, 30 percent from the efforts of a particular interest group, 17 percent through a coalition of community groups, and 20 percent as a result of the growth and modernization of an existing service or facility. As Table 6-3 illustrates, there is little correspondence between facility type and the organizing figure(s). However, there is an interesting relationship between the diversity of groups and individuals who initiate programs and their particular reasons for doing so. For example, a group home was begun by a social service caseworker who was frustrated by the unavailability of placements for adolescent females. A residential treatment facility began with the efforts of a high school guidance counselor who was upset at the handling of school youth with drug-related problems. Concerned with a similar group of young people, a court-based chaplain began a residential program for first offenders with school problems and a history of drug use. A family-based group home was begun when a foster parent couple gradually increased the number of youth they received into their home. Most of the individuals responsible for developing programs had been involved in some capacity with this population of youth, and through frustration, anger, or the desire for change had acted on the systemic needs they perceived.

The interest groups that were instrumental in program formation were almost exclusively nonprofessional groups, such as religious groups or philanthropic organizations. In contrast, the groups that formed a coalition to support a new service were more likely to be professional service groups. For example, corrections, law enforcement, and social service personnel coordinated efforts to support the construction of an adequate secure detention facility or an alternative to secure detention. The newer detention homes are almost exclusively the result of these coalitions.

In only one program was there mention of the local judge's direct role in the formulation of the program, although program staff often

TABLE 6-3 Breakdown of Program Types by Precipitating Factors

Program Type	Organizing Variable			Perceived Need				
	Identified Individual	Interest Groups	Coalition of Community Groups	Modernization of Existing Service	Number of Unserved Youth	Need for Secure Facility	Changing Populations	Response to Legislation
Detention	1	1	2	2	1	4	1	0
Shelter	2	1	2	1	4	0	1	1
Group home*	5	3	0	0	5	0	2	0
Residential treatment	2	4	1	3	7	1	2	0
Total	10	9	5	6	17	5	6	1

* One group home reported none of these perceived need factors. This home began as a foster home, and the houseparents cited their own satisfaction in providing child care as the reason for increasing the number of children served.

mentioned the judge's importance in providing support for referrals and in promoting good professional relations. Our impression, however, is that the local judges, the law enforcement system, and the court probation departments are more likely to be consumers of these services than initiators. We did not hear of any activity on the part of citizen advocacy groups, nor did respondents mention the presence of advisors from state and federal agencies.

ADMINISTRATIVE AWARENESS OF POLICY MANDATES

In arranging the visits to each facility, we discovered that the reactions of the program directors to the study provided an initial indication of the salience of policy change to program functions. In Richmond, New Orleans, and Salt Lake City, program directors were commonly unaware of recent policy changes that might affect their programs. In Boston and Philadelphia most program directors were quite aware of the specifics of the policy changes and how they affected service delivery. These administrators spontaneously offered their opinions during the telephone conversation regarding alternative directions and potential problems ensuing from the changes. In Phoenix the response was more diverse, but the reactions of directors who were aware of changing policies reflected the enthusiasm of a group recently experiencing change and enjoying its promise.

Generally, program directors were knowledgeable about JJDPA and state legislative policies only insofar as the changes directly affected their service. These effects were usually felt in the area of funding, either in terms of where monies were to come from or to whom and for what kind of service the monies could be used. Rather than being associated with a shift in the child care policy, these changes were more often than not seen as the results of budgetary cuts and the influence of special interest group representation in the legislative body.

There are a few notable exceptions to these generalities. A handful of program administrators (one each in Phoenix, Richmond, New Orleans, and Salt Lake City; two each in Boston and Philadelphia) were quite knowledgeable about policy and had been actively involved in the process of change, either as a member of an advocacy group or as a result of their position in the correctional system prior to the implementation of legislative mandates. For example, a Boston program director had been superintendent of a state training school prior to the 1971 deinstitutionalization order and had been actively involved in the planning commissions. Apart from these individuals, the program directors did not indicate involvement with advocacy groups, planning

TABLE 6-4 Breakdown of Program Types by Identified Goals and Change in Goals Since Program Inception

Program Type	Current Program Goal							Comparison of Current Program Goals with Initial Goals at Program Inception	
	Keep Youth out of the Juvenile Justice System	Shelter and Care	Individual Behavior Change	Provision of Secure Custody	Diagnosis and Referral	Preparation for Independent Living	Provision of Normal Home Life	Same	Different
Detention	0	0	0	6	0	0	0	6	0
Shelter	3	3	0	0	0	0	0	5	1
Group home	0	0	3	0	0	1	4	7	1
Residential treatment	0	1	5	0	1	0	3	7	3
Total	3 (10.0%)	4 (13.3%)	8 (26.7%)	6 (20.0%)	1 (3.3%)	1 (3.3%)	7 (23.3%)	25	5

commissions, or advisory bodies. In fact, one director commented that although it would be a good idea to have service providers on local planning bodies, such a move had never really been considered in that locality.

REPORTED PROGRAM CHANGES

Administrators and staff reported that a variety of changes had occurred within their programs since program inception. Specifically they mentioned rule changes; adoption of alternative treatment models; addition of new activities; changes in staffing patterns, staff training, program size, and in the physical plant; and changes in the population served. Overall, however, these reported changes do not reflect changes in the primary goals and philosophy of these facilities.

In the discussion of program formation, directors were asked to identify the original goals and purposes of the facility. Table 6-4 presents a summary of current goals by program type and a count of programs that reported change in their goals from the beginning of the program to the present. Only five programs report change in primary goals despite change in various other aspects of programming. The three residential programs in this group are older facilities, and they report changes from their initial goal of custodial shelter and care to current, more treatment-oriented goals. On the basis of interview data regarding historical evolution, it seems that staff and program attitudes toward youth in trouble have been modified only superficially. Generally, the youth continue to be seen by staff as in need of help and "on the road" to more serious problems. New attributions and causal patterns have been identified as contributing to the existing problem, such as family background and poor living environment. Despite the identification of these environmental causal factors, the youth continue to be seen as damaged and lacking in necessary skills. The basic notion of providing shelter, care, and a program of activities to repair the damages or teach skills, with the ultimate goal of changing the youth, remains as the overriding theme of these out-of-home placements. Across the majority of programs the youth is identified as the focus of change and in large part as the figure responsible for the presenting situation and difficulties.

Staff identified several factors as being responsible for the reported changes in facility operation. The four most commonly identified factors were (1) changes in legislation (e.g., status offenders can no longer be incarcerated), (2) changes in the type of youth referred (e.g., more disturbed youth, more serious offenders), (3) changes in funding patterns (e.g., funding formulas favoring short-term rather than long-term placement), and (4) changes in personnel (e.g., new director). The first three factors may be direct or indirect effects of JJDPA and corresponding state-level policy efforts at redefining both the types of youth served by the correctional system and the kind of service available. The information gathered here does not allow for more detailed analysis of the relationship between JJDPA and reported programmatic changes. It is apparent, however, that program staff do not report these programmatic changes as a part of a larger policy or directional change in service delivery. From the service provider's perspective, the more immediate issues to be dealt with are regulations, funding patterns, and local needs and the problems presented by area youth; as such, they seem to be primary in the historical reporting of events.

Overall, among the sample of facilities included in this study, factors that were tangential to JJDPA appear to be responsible for program initiation. Local actors who work primarily outside the juvenile court system seem prominent in program formulation. The histories of these 30 facilities seem to indicate that JJDPA may have served to trigger modifications in existing programs rather than the formation of new programs. Only a very small number of program directors reported that legislative mandates were instrumental in program design and subsequent change. Although JJDPA was not pinpointed by directors as a primary causal factor in program development, it may have had definite, albeit subtle, effects that may be masked by the post hoc, self-report methodology employed. While we are unable to assess how these stated perceptions match reality, it is apparent that program directors do not report legislative mandates as a primary causal factor in program development.

YOUTH IN RESIDENTIAL FACILITIES: DESCRIPTIVE CHARACTERISTICS AND REFERRAL PATTERNS

DEMOGRAPHIC CHARACTERISTICS

Youth in the 30 facilities range in age from 8 to 18 years, with an average age of 15.06 years. Table 6-5 shows the age distribution of typical populations by facility type. There is no significant difference in the age of the youth served by these four program types. There also are no significant differences in age between males and females in these out-of-home placements.

The majority of the youth in residence at these facilities are non-minority youth. Table 6-6 shows the racial composition by facility type for individual programs. The overall averages by facility type do not

TABLE 6-5   Average Age of Youth Served by Four Facility Types

Facility Type	Percentage of Typical Residents by Age Categories				N
	13 yrs. or younger	14-15 yrs.	16-17 yrs.	18 yrs. or older	
Detention	10.83	36.67	52.00	0.50	6
Shelter	20.17	48.50	31.17	0.16	6
Group home	13.88	44.75	34.62	6.62	8
Residential treatment	14.22	38.78	45.56	1.44	9*

*One facility did not provide this information.

necessarily indicate racial segregation in program placements; however, the racial composition of individual programs indicates that 22 of the programs serve a group of youth of whom more than 65 percent are of the same race. In the two western cities, Chicano and Native American youth constitute the majority of the nonwhite group served. The facilities in two cities appear to be racially segregated. Among all programs in the six cities, minority youth are somewhat disproportionately represented in the most restrictive placement option (i.e., detention) and are similarly underrepresented in the least restrictive setting, the shelter

TABLE 6-6   Facility Racial Composition (Percentage White) by Program Type and Locality

Locality	Program Type				Locality Average
	Detention	Shelter	Group Home	Residential Treatment	
Phoenix	55	75	80	60; 75*	(69.0)
New Orleans	6	71	54; 66*	83	(56.0)
Boston	65	76	35	86; 80*	(68.4)
Philadelphia	17	0	52; 25*	—	(23.5)
Salt Lake City	77	90	87	95; 83*	(86.4)
Richmond	80	63	35	75; 56*	(61.8)
Average	(50.0)	(62.5)	(54.2)	(77.0)	

Note: The numbers in the table are the percentage of the total population of each program type that is represented by white youth.

* This was the model program in the locality.

facility. Residential treatment facilities and shelter facilities, particularly the runaway drop-in shelter, seem to serve a predominantly white youth population. The interview data from one of these cities revealed that programs are informally identified in the service network as white or nonwhite facilities, and referrals are made accordingly—a practice that results in racially homogeneous facilities within program types. Across the entire sample of facilities, staff report that on the average, 4.4 percent of the youth are bilingual. Only Phoenix and Philadelphia programs reported percentages of bilingual youth that were greater than 10 percent.

The facilities included in this sample are all considered by service providers to be community-based; however, the youth in residence are not necessarily from the surrounding community. Table 6-7 indicates the geographic location of the typical population served by these facilities, presented by facility type. As an average across program types, just 55.2 percent of the youth served by this group of facilities reside in the city in which the program is located. Detention facilities are most likely to serve youth from the same city as the facility's location, although given the size of the cities visited this may not necessarily mean they are from the same community. The Boston detention facility serves the entire state. Shelter facilities serve a mobile population of youth, the majority of whom come from within 25 miles of the facility site. The residential treatment facilities appear to include the most geographically dispersed group. Just over one-third of the youth in these facilities come from a distance greater than 26 miles.

TABLE 6-7   Extent of Community-Based Service as Reflected in Distance from Facility to Youth's Homes

| Facility | Location of Youth's Home (Percentage of Typical Population Within Distance Category) | | | | |
	Same city	Within 25 miles	26-50 miles	More than 50 miles	N
Detention	78.2	4.6	12.6	4.6*	6
Shelter	47.8	39.3	8.5	4.1	6
Group home	66.7	17.0	8.3	7.0	8
Residential treatment	34.6	27.9	22.8	13.3	10
Average	55.2	22.4	13.7	7.8	30

* One facility accounts for this category.

Generally, the facilities included in this sample do not serve an exclusively local group of youth. Although some program staff pointed to several of the difficulties in accepting youth from outside the city, few seem to have any systematic priority for local youth. In fact, of the factors considered in admission, geographic location of the family was identified as a primary consideration by only one facility, a group home. Generally, the larger the capacity of the facility and the more long term and self-contained the program, the more likely it is that the facility serves a wide geographic region.

OBSERVATIONS AND IMPRESSIONS OF THE YOUTH

Qualitatively, the youth observed in the facilities varied from tough, street-wise kids, to seemingly all-American high school students. Generally they displayed normal adolescent behavior; that is, they were moody, rebellious, striving for independence, and sometimes shy or playful. We observed them testing the limits with staff and program rules, and heard about incidents like panty raids on the girls' residence. We also heard reports of more violent outbursts among the residents. When fights began between residents in the larger nonsecure facilities, staff reacted in a manner suggesting that these were normal occurrences among adolescents to be worked out among the youth. In most instances any child who is assaultive toward staff or residents will be moved to a secure facility, where these activities are more closely supervised and controlled. Consequently, the youth in the majority of facilities we visited did not display seriously disturbed behavior patterns.

Most of the youth placed in any of the facilities had had problems of one sort or another at school. Many had substantial academic deficiencies and attended special education classes, although they were not apparently mentally retarded or learning disabled. A significant number had been suspended from the public school because of their behavior and disruptiveness. A few were considered to be hyperactive, and this was identified as a causal factor in their poor school performance. Staff indicate that the typical youth does not use leisure time well and that few are skilled in athletic activities. On the bases of conversation with the youth and observation of their behavior, they seem to be bright and inquisitive. Two of the residential treatment programs received referrals from the forensic unit of the court and tended to have more violent and suicidal youth. One state hospital treatment program used psychotropic medications heavily, and the youth appeared to be quite seriously affected by the medication, looking dazed and sedated.

Youth in the detention facilities were generally more street wise and had a sophisticated working knowledge of the juvenile system. In several of the detention facilities, the youth were described as "slick" and the staff seemed somewhat afraid of them. In the two smallest detention facilities, the youth seemed very much like typical big-city high school students (i.e., less hardened to the system), although many had been in detention before. The youth were being detained on charges that most commonly included breaking and entering and petty theft as well as more serious felonies and property crimes. In Philadelphia, Phoenix, and Boston there seemed to be a large number of youth in facilities on drug-related charges.

Youth in the detention facilities and in the two referral-based emergency shelters projected a sense of "waiting for something to happen." In contrast, those at the drop-in shelters, most of whom were there because of family problems, displayed a mixed mood—anticipation with hesitation, excitement with anxiety. In the emergency shelter facilities, group homes, and residential treatment programs, the youth were quite articulate in explaining why they were in the program and what placement options were available to them following their current program. The majority of the youth in group homes and residential treatment facilities had been in other out-of-home placements prior to their current residence, most commonly foster homes. They told us either that foster parents didn't want them anymore or that they themselves did not like the foster home setting, ran away from the home, and subsequently were placed in a group facility. Hence the youth in these settings had experienced various aspects of the child-caring and court systems. The majority of the youth in group homes and residential treatment facilities had been involved with these systems for several years, which suggests that group placements are chosen after other kinds of placements have failed to work satisfactorily. Despite the fact that most of these youth had left home on their own or because parental custody has been restricted, almost all said they wanted to return home to live.

Program directors across facility types report that the sample of youth we observed is typical of their total population. In discussing the types of youth served over the years, there is an overwhelming sense among staff and administrators that those referred in recent years are more seriously disturbed and present more serious problems than the youth of five years ago. Although this particular study is unable to assess the factors underlying this perception, staff suggest that the changing moods of society are partially responsible. They further suggest that changes in policy (specifically, deinstitutionalization and diversion) have resulted in the delay of intervention so that by the time youth are referred to these facilities, problems have been left unattended and/or the youth has been "shuffled" through the system. Many staff believe that legislative and funding changes have made it more difficult to obtain services for troubled youth.

In summary, the youth currently served in the sample of facilities represent a diverse group. One commonality is the report of family problems and a marked incidence of school problems. The sample overall is approximately 60 percent white, with slightly more nonwhite youth in secure detention and more white youth in residential treatment facilities. The typical youth is 15 years old and his or her family lives within 25 miles of the facility. Approximately two-thirds of the youth, regardless of facility type, have had at least one other out-of-home placement prior to their current residence. The overwhelming majority are not classified psychiatrically and, because of facility admission procedures, youth with extreme acting-out, destructive, or withdrawn behavior are not included.

PROGRAM INTAKE POLICIES AND THE SEPARATION OF STATUS OFFENDERS

Implicit in the deinstitutionalization reform was the expectation of different services for status offenders and the separation of status offenders from delinquent youth. On the basis of the facilities that we visited, there is no indication that programs make distinctions between these statutory categories, except in secure detention. Three of the six detention homes included in the sample indicate that they do not accept status offenders; the other three do accept them. The latter three facilities additionally report that 2 percent, 7 percent, and 15 percent of their average population are status offenders. Some of these youth seem to be out-of-state runaways, while others are judged to be in danger of some kind (e.g., one 10-year old female was to testify against an adult male assailant and was being held in secure detention for her own protection). The facility that reported a status offender population of 15 percent also operates a nonsecure detention program on its grounds, as well as a home detention program. It is possible that the status offenders reported are participants in these nonsecure programs and have been included in the statistics of the total facility.

The nonsecure (i.e., not locked) shelter facility appears to be the only type in this study that might be viewed as an alternative service for status offenders. These facilities were established primarily as runaway drop-in shelters, and the majority of youth in these settings are status offenders. Of the four totally voluntary drop-in centers, program directors' reports indicate that 93 percent of the youth served might be classified as status offenders. It is important to note, however, that two of the nonsecure shelters operate in tandem with the juvenile court and public welfare departments and accept only youth referred by these agencies. In these two facilities, less than one-third of the youth are status offenders. Here, both delinquents and status offenders are detained in a "staff-secure" setting in which residents are not permitted to leave the premises and are closely supervised by staff members. In the drop-in shelters, youth who have also committed delinquent acts may be admitted, although the basis of their admission is most likely to be non-delinquent activity.

Status offenders and delinquents similarly commingle in group homes and residential treatment facilities. There is a tendency among the group homes in our sample to house either a predominantly status offender population (i.e., about 85 percent of the residents) or a non-status-offender group (i.e., only 20 percent are status offenders). The residential treatment facilities serve a population in which an average of 25 percent are status offenders. In both of these longer-term placements (i.e., group homes, residential treatment facilities) status offenders, delinquent youth, and dependent/neglected youth may be in residence.

Administrators were questioned specifically regarding the types of youth they accept in their program and the factors that bear on admissions decisions. Table 6-8 shows a summary of those responses by program type. Group homes and residential treatment facilities do not appear to make distinctions between types of youth on the basis of statutory categories (e.g., status offenders, delinquents). One-half of the detention centers do not detain postadjudicated youth or status

TABLE 6-8   Reported Intake Criteria for Four Facility Types

Percentage of Facilities Accepting:	Detention (N = 6)	Shelter (N = 6)	Group Home (N = 8)	Residential Treatment (N = 9)*
Preadjudicated youth	100	100	75	78
Postadjudicated youth	50	3	75	89
Violent youth	100	17	25	33
Repeat offenders	100	100	75	78
Court-ordered placements	83	50	100	89
Emotionally disturbed youth	83	67	100	89
Status offenders	50	100	12	89
Youth admitted before	100	100	100	89

NOTE: Data in the table are from the administrative questionnaire. For each category, the director indicated whether the program would accept youth.

* One facility did not provide this information.

offenders, and one-half of the shelter facilities do not accept court-ordered placements. Generally, however, these facilities do not identify their populations by legally defined categories. Instead, behavioral categories seem to be employed. As shown in Table 6-8, only the detention homes routinely accept violent youth. Less than one-quarter of the other programs accept this type of youth. Program directors report that the two factors that are most important in determining a youth's admission are (1) the referring source's recommendation and (2) the youth's agreement to voluntary participation.

Interview data also indicate that specific behaviors may preclude admission but that legal categories seem relatively unimportant. Of the 30 programs, only the detention homes accept arsonists. Most programs believe that they are not adequately equipped to handle psychotic or "seriously emotionally disturbed" youth, and they therefore do not accept youth with these diagnoses. All of the group homes and residential treatment facilities visited require psychological evaluations for admissions, which presumably are used to screen out serious behavior problems. Only one facility accepts pregnant adolescents, and several facilities indicate substantial reluctance to accept homosexual youth.

Table 6-9 shows the average percentage of referrals from a variety of potential referral sources by program type. The pattern of referrals indicates that for the facilities included in this sample, just over one-third of the youth who are admitted are referred from social service agencies. In most states this would include CHINS (status offenders) and other troubled youth. Detention homes are the only program type that takes a substantial portion of referrals from law enforcement personnel. There is some slight evidence that emergency shelters are used as a diversion alternative by the intake division of the juvenile court. Group homes and residential treatment facilities seem to receive occasional referrals from probation, and placement in a residential treatment facility as a disposition alternative is not uncommon. Certainly there does not appear to be a strong relationship between agents of the court system and nonsecure residential alternatives; however, the ties are not completely severed. Instead, the social service departments seem to be the most likely source of referrals for these programs.

Once youth have been admitted to a program (regardless of type), their treatment is differentiated only insofar as the program allows for individualization in programming. Generally, there are no discernible differences by legal status except when a court-related or legally based decision is necessary. Program staff do not seem to distinguish between status offenders and delinquents when considering either treatment or placement options, except when a particular label or classification is

TABLE 6-9   Source of Referral by Facility Type

Percentage of Referrals from:	Detention (N = 6)	Shelter (N = 6)	Group Home (N = 8)	Residential Treatment (N = 9)[a]
Public social service agency	35.0	29.3	50.0	30.3
Mental health agency	0.0	0.8	4.2	6.2
Police/sheriff department	53.7	16.0	0.0	0.0
Juvenile court intake	0.0	6.5	0.0	0.1
Juvenile court disposition	5.6	0.0	0.0	19.8
Juvenile court probation	0.0	7.5	7.5	2.5
Residential correctional facilities	0.3	0.0	4.2	4.0
Religious agencies[b]	0.0	0.0	15.8	0.0
Schools	0.3	1.7	3.3	3.5
Private social service agency	1.7	1.3	10.0	0.5
Self or family	1.7	20.2	0.0	6.1
Other[c]	0.0	11.5	0.0	28.7

NOTE: Percentages are based on director's estimates by category as reported in the administrative questionnaire. In some instances, directors reported actual percentages from their annual reports.

[a] One facility did not provide this information.

[b] These are religiously affiliated, multicomponent organizations that refer from one component to another.

[c] Includes other residential treatment facilities, state regional review committee, mixed private agencies.

necessary to obtain services. For example, one agency staff member in Boston, told us that there are more service options for CHINS than for delinquent youth, and as such they see a greater incidence of CHINS petitions. The opinion of several program directors is that these classifications make little difference. Many suggested that delinquents were probably also status offenders, and that status offenders may also commit delinquent acts. Program staff seem to think of youth as being in behavior categories (e.g., "troubled" or "emotionally disturbed") rather than in the statutory categories of status offender and delinquent. The definitional category "troubled youth" encompasses both those youth who are involved with the juvenile justice system and law enforcement and those with more diffuse family problems. Thus, the nondetention facilities seem to identify the troubled or emotionally disturbed youth as the appropriate target of their service. This alternative definition of populations (among other factors) has resulted both in the commingling of youth in various definitional categories, and in the use of these residential facilities by corrections, welfare, mental health, and education referring agencies.

The pattern of referrals, the commingling of status offender and delinquent youth, and the comments from service providers suggest a realignment among service systems such that status offenders are now handled primarily by the social service system. The extent to which there has been a complete transfer of certain classifications of youth from the juvenile correctional system to the social service system cannot be determined by this analysis. Nor can we estimate either the number of youth who are not included in these referral and service systems or the number of youth who are not involved in these systems but might have been previously. Service providers now receive referrals from a greater variety of sources, and the populations of youth in out-of-home placements reflect that diversity.

SERVICE PROVISION AND TREATMENT PHILOSOPHY AMONG THE FACILITIES VISITED

One apparent intention of the call for alternative facilities was the assumption of different "treatment" strategies and the provision of multiple services either within the context of a program or available to youth through community agencies. Table 6-10 summarizes the program directors' reports of services that are available within each program type.

COUNSELING SERVICES

All programs report that they offer individual counseling, and all but two indicate provision of group counseling. In over one-half of the programs, staff describe these forms of counseling as a critical component of their program. Just over one-half of the programs assign a staff member as primary counselor to each child. Most detention programs and many group homes relied on the court service unit worker or social service caseworker to provide counseling.

Our data from observations and interviews indicate that both the form and frequency of counseling varied tremendously. In some programs it seems that any kind of talking with the residents is considered to be counseling. In most detention facilities and in a few group homes and residential facilities, individual counseling sessions serve to get the youth accustomed to the facility. Once the youth has been acclimated, the individual sessions cease. In a few programs the residents did not know who their counselor was, which suggests that the frequency of contact with the counselor was low or that the content of discussion was indistinguishable from that with other staff. Resident and staff reports of

TABLE 6-10   Services Offered by Facility Type as Reported by
Program Administrator

| | Percentage Reporting Service Availability | | | |
| | Detention (N = 6) | Emergency Shelter (N = 6) | Group Home (N = 8) | Residential Treatment (N = 9)* |
Services				
Individual counseling	100	100	100	100
Family counseling	50	67	62	100
Group counseling	83	83	100	100
Peer counseling	33	50	87	89
Substance abuse counseling	33	33	50	67
Crisis intervention	83	100	50	55
Diagnostic and referral service	67	0	62	67
Recreation programs	100	50	100	100
Legal services	17	33	37	0
Advocacy	33	100	75	55
Education in local public schools	17	33	87	44
Facility-based educational program	100	33	12	89
Educational tutoring	50	0	75	78
Job/career counseling	50	17	100	67
Work placement	17	0	75	67
General supervision	100	100	0	100

* One facility did not provide this information.

counseling activities indicate that the content of these meetings varies
from preparing for a home visit to reviewing behavioral contracts and
weekly progress.

Similar diversity was reported and observed in group counseling.
Counseling meetings cover a range of subjects, including resident "gripe"
sessions, preparation for a group trip, staff "feedback" to residents,
discussion of special topics like desert survival techniques, and an invited
speaker's presentation. In all but five facilities, group counseling meetings are essentially business meetings or a group activity. Very skillfully
directed group therapy was observed in one facility, while another's
group session was seen as unproductive at best and potentially damaging
for the youth involved.

Peer counseling in these facilities might best be described as the friend-
ships and relationships that develop among the residents. In only one
residential treatment facility did the residents conduct regular group

meetings of staff and residents focusing on problems, disciplinary decisions, and resident behavior. In the same facility we observed a carefully executed system of peer helping, with the more advanced residents serving as guides, helpers, and friends to new residents. Substance abuse counseling also seems to be conducted in an informal manner, with most facilities using outside programs as needed. Counseling that is relevant to issues of substance abuse appears to be handled in the contexts of both group and individual counseling within each facility. All of the facilities except group homes indicate that they provide "general supervision." It is curious that none of the group homes report provision of general supervision, because all youngsters need supervision of some sort. This response pattern suggests that "general supervision" may have a unique meaning for group home staff, perhaps implying the absence of "treatment" or a close monitoring of youth behavior.

ALTERNATIVE SERVICES

A majority of facilities indicate provision of crisis intervention services. Shelter facilities clearly define their program as crisis intervention. Because of the 24-hour intake policy of detention homes, these too are classified as providing crisis intervention. From our observation, however, neither group homes nor residential treatment facilities provide crisis intervention except in handling crises that occur with their own residents. We saw no evidence of 24-hour emergency intake, telephone hot-line service, or diagnostic services. Diagnostic evaluations are subcontracted or are completed by a psychiatric or psychological consultant in several of the facilities that provide this service. Two-thirds of the facilities indicate advocacy as a service provided, although, as with counseling, the nature and intensity of this service varies widely. It is our impression that job and career counseling are considered as part of individual counseling within their respective programs. Vocational training was available to residents of group homes only to the extent that their school program offered such a curriculum. Three residential treatment facilities offered some vocational training courses as a part of their school program or as recreational activities.

TREATMENT PHILOSOPHY

Multiple treatment philosophies and strategies of intervention are evident in this sample of facilities, including behavior modification techniques, individual counseling, group milieu strategies, family systems models of intervention, and advocacy. A majority of the programs em-

ployed some form of behavior management using points, merits, de-
merits, or levels. However, the consistency of use and relationships
between points, rewards, levels, and discharge varied widely. For example, in four programs we were unable to determine how these components were used, how a youth moved up a level, or how discharge
was accomplished through the level and point system. Conversely, in a
group home setting, points and contracts were a well-integrated and
unobtrusive part of the daily routine leading systematically to progress
through the programs and eventual return home or placement in foster
care or independent living.

In one-third of the facilities there appeared to be no identifiable,
consistent treatment approach. The staff of these facilities frequently
indicated that the youth needed a "stable supportive environment,"
which seemed to be translated as "tender loving care" and was implemented in a variety of nonspecific ways. In some facilities this strategy
appeared to approximate a "normal" family living arrangement, while
in other facilities it seemed that little or nothing actively directed toward
support or change was occurring.

The particular treatment model and the specific services offered by
these facilities are not systematically correlated with program type or
with normalization as measured by the PASS, and there is no evidence
of new or different treatments or services. Much of what is offered within
these programs can also be found in programs for the retarded, psychiatric populations, and adult offenders. The definition of service clearly
varies from "three hots and a cot" in a shelter facility to in-depth analysis
and reevaluation of self through counseling in a residential treatment
facility. With only minor exceptions, these facilities provide for the basic
physical needs of the youth and provide a safe environment in which to
live. Of the 30 facilities we visited, only one was seen to be detrimental
to the well-being of the youth. It seemed so because of the lack of
activity and resources, the apparent overuse of behavior-controlling
medication, and the negative attitude of staff toward the residents. Four
were disconsolate places to be because of the dearth of physical resources
and activities. The remaining 25 facilities, however, were at least comfortable places to live and offered an alternative living arrangement for
displaced youth.

PHYSICAL PLANT AND ENVIRONMENTAL CONTEXT OF THE FACILITIES

Size, security, physical plant characteristics, and location are typially
referred to as salient features differentiating institutional from nonin-

stitutional or community-based settings. The noninstitutional settings are expected to be small, nonsecure, and located within the community to be served. These features do differentiate the program types included in this analysis, although considered singly they offer only minimal predictive and explanatory information.

PROGRAM CAPACITY

The maximum capacity of each facility was presented in Table 6-1 above. Detention and residential treatment facilities in our sample average 56 beds and 44 beds, respectively. Group homes and shelter facilities are smaller, averaging 11 beds and 25 beds, respectively. The voluntary drop-in emergency shelters are similar in size to group homes, with an average capacity of 12.

Residential treatment facilities have attempted to create smaller units within the larger facility by maximizing the physical separation afforded by the physical plant. For example, one facility has created individual units in each wing of a large building, and another operates programs like those in group homes in each of several smaller buildings or cottages on the campus of the facility. Though physically adjacent to and administratively part of an "institutional complex," these units operate autonomously while simultaneously sharing the activities and services of the larger facility.

Program directors stated repeatedly that it is becoming increasingly difficult to operate the small (i.e., 15 or fewer beds) independent facility. With the demands of economic inflation, increasingly stringent licensing requirements, administrative reporting demands, and ever-changing priorities and funding sources, the multiunit organization is seen to be the more viable arrangement for service provision. Among the facilities in this sample, 37 percent are operated under the auspices of such an umbrella or multiunit organization. Specific administrative features of these organizations appear to undermine the potential benefits of the small size of an individual unit or program, however. For example, some organizations apply a standard set of rules or program operations to all facilities that they administer rather than allowing individual determination of these rules within each site (which allows the flexibility necessary to match the needs of the particular youth in residence). Across the country we observed substantial tension between individual facility autonomy in programming and the demands of administrative standardization.

Program demands for autonomy versus administrative economy have additional implications for daily programming and opportunities for resident participation. In most group homes, for example, residents have some responsibility for meal preparation and at least some input into menu planning. In several multisite agencies, either menus were prepared by the food division and applied to all programs or residents ate in a central cafeteria or dining hall. Although such measures eliminate a time-consuming task for individual programs and provide opportunities to mingle with other populations and groups, the benefits are not always apparent. In one state hospital, for example, the youth ate in a hospital dining hall along with patients from all parts of the hospital, many of whom appeared to be quite "institutionalized." This arrangement was in sharp contrast to the overall program, which seemed to be a remarkably normalizing experience (given the secure state hospital setting) and well planned to match the developmental needs of adolescents.

In the northeastern cities the individual sites constituting a larger organization are most likely to be located throughout the city. In Philadelphia, for example, we visited two of six group homes that are run by a single organization. They were almost an hour's drive from each other, and both were located in residential neighborhoods. In contrast, a single agency in a western city operated seven group homes, three of which were immediately next to each other on the same street, with a shared parking area in front of the homes and a sign on the lawn indicating the name of the agency. With this latter arrangement, the beneficial effects and purposes of small size may be diminished by the visible identification and clustering of sites that resemble the larger child-caring institution.

The 30 facilities vary in size. The smaller facilities generally offer a more normalizing experience as measured by the PASS. Our observations indicate, however, that size is not always strongly correlated with program flexibility and individualization. Some of the larger facilities operated very individualized programs and were able to create an atmosphere resembling the warmth and fun of overnight camp or a boarding school. Conversely, a few small group homes were operated in a regimented and controlling manner.

SECURITY AND FREEDOM

All of the detention facilities visited and two of the residential treatment facilities were secure. Only three of these facilities had obvious surveillance equipment throughout the building. Most of the newer secure facilities employed a floor plan that allowed staff to view all communal parts of the building simultaneously, and they had audio contact with the residents' rooms and more remote parts of the building. Though not locked in, residents in 23 percent of the nonsecure facilities are not permitted to leave the premises without a staff member. In 41 percent of the nonsecure facilities, freedom to leave the premises is dependent on the residents' status or level within the program, which implies "good behavior." Residents may come and go as they choose in only 36 percent of the nonsecure programs (including shelters, group homes, and residential treatment facilities).

Program philosophy and goals seem to determine the nature of activity and the degree to which resident behavior is monitored within both the secure and nonsecure facilities that we visited. Most of the detention facilities perceive their mandate as one of secure custody. Correspondingly, little activity occurs except that required by law (e.g., some school activity), and the youth in residence spend large portions of time with little to do. Staff activity also appears to be directed toward monitoring and controlling behavior in an institutionlike manner. In sharp contrast, two of the secure facilities had strong change-oriented treatment programs. One of these programs offered the residents more opportunities for responsibility, self-governance, and leadership than most of the other facilities, regardless of type or security status. Although the differences are less extreme, several of the nonsecure facilities maintained significant control over youth behavior by limiting their freedom to leave the premises and by providing limited opportunities for activities within the building.

Overall, the secure facilities offer a less normalizing and often quite institutionlike experience; individual behavior is closely monitored and individual activity is restricted. The very fact that a facility is operated as a secure program implies some limitations on freedom. However, our observations indicate that the locked facility need not operate as a "total institution" (Goffman 1961); rather, it can operate as a self-contained facility in which there can be limited opportunities for personal autonomy. Similarly, the nonsecure facility that is based on the notion of behavior control may impose rules and restrictions that approach the limits on individual autonomy of the institutional setting (e.g., requiring that youth return to the facility immediately after school and remain on premises for scheduled activities). Our observations suggest that the ideology of secure custody and containment has been replicated in some unlocked facilities, with rules and restrictions replacing locked doors.

THE PHYSICAL PLANT AND FURNISHINGS

The physical building in which each program is located largely defines the parameters of privacy, flexibility, and normalization within the program. Within this sample, detention homes were the only program type to be housed in buildings constructed specifically for that purpose. Security arrangements and surveillance are a high priority in these settings, and there are few opportunities for privacy or relaxation. There are essentially no opportunities for personalizing surroundings, and residents' rooms are generally cold and sterile.

Among the eight secure facilities, there is great diversity in the overall atmosphere generated by the physical structure of the building. One older detention facility is very dark and dungeonlike; another employs a mazelike floor plan of narrow, crisscrossing hallways that created feelings of claustrophobia for the observers. In contrast, the newest detention facility was built with cathedral ceilings in the communal areas and large windows that look out on a playing field and wooded area, allowing for more light and a greater sense of open space.

Nearly 60 percent of the nonsecure facilities are located in large, single family houses, which physically maximize the normalizing aspects of living conditions. Over one-third of the facilities (across types) are part of an institutional complex of buildings (e.g., cottages on the grounds of a state hospital, orphanage, or boarding school). These buildings tend to be larger and older, typically with a dormitory area and "day room" layout.

The furniture and furnishings overall were clean and well kept. Of the 30 facilities, only one was considered dirty—unfortunately to such an extreme that the observers questioned whether the health department would approve the facility. Several of the older facilities were badly in need of repairs, and the lack of resources to cover these repairs was cited by administrators as a serious problem. Facilities generally seemed concerned about the physical surroundings; most buildings were painted in bright colors and residents were involved in house maintenance. The condition of the buildings and their furnishings is obviously related in part to the resources available to the facility, but this is especially true where capital improvements and major repairs are concerned. Beyond that, the condition of the furnishings seems to reflect programmatic concern for order and structure within the program, and a sense of responsibility and ownership of the program among both staff and residents. For example, the facilities in which staff either owned the building or lived there full-time tended to be better maintained.

The type of building in which each program is located tends to match both the expected resident capacity and the treatment philosophy of the program. Group homes that operate on the assumption of the need for a supportive, "normal" family environment are located in single-family homes. The larger, more self-contained residential treatment programs occupy an institutional complex that provides facilities for school, recreation, meal preparation, and so forth. Their philosophy of individual change and reeducation without the distractions of family, peers, and community is mirrored in the physical structure. At the same time, the physical structure places limits on certain activities and creates a need for specific kinds of programming. The most salient example is the group home that is located in a single-family dwelling. The size and space limit the number of residents, provide opportunities for shared living experiences, and increase the likelihood that community services and resources will be used.

LOCATION AND COMMUNITY INTEGRATION

The facilities included in this study occupy sites in the greater urban areas; 60 percent are within the highly urbanized areas of cities, and the remaining 40 percent are in surrounding suburban areas. The shelter facilities are all within the more centrally located areas of the cities in order to maximize availability to youth who are on the run or in need of emergency shelter. The detention facilities are located in suburban areas or near the edges of cities. One-fifth of the facilities (from all program types) are located in high-crime areas and in economically deteriorating city neighborhoods. In contrast, nearly 40 percent of the programs (across types) are situated in pleasant, tree-lined areas with easy access to parks and outdoor recreation. Two facilities are located on the edge of university campuses, one amidst a row of sorority houses. The variation in locations seems to result from the restrictiveness of zoning laws and the economic limits imposed by property values and rents.

Given the locations of these programs, a variety of community resources are within easy access of the facilities. With the exception of the less centrally located detention facilities, the programs are located within a mile of convenience and retail stores, churches, libraries, movie theatres, parks, and recreation centers. Many are located on public transportation routes.

Although the facilities in this sample are defined as community-based, this term seems to be used loosely and most accurately reflects an urban location. Implicit in the rhetoric of community-based facilities is an active integration of program activities and community resources, and of program residents and community members. For detention and residential treatment programs, there is essentially no community integration other than the use of professional services, such as the courts, the police, or medical clinics and hospitals. These programs usually are isolated from the community and remain relatively self-contained. Among group homes, "community-based" implies attendance at public school—either the public school attended prior to placement or the school that serves the program's locale.

Data from observations and interviews indicate that residents rarely participate in activities in the community other than attending public school. Staff indicate that the major obstacles to such involvement are the financial expense and transportation difficulties. Most nonsecure programs take advantage of free activities (e.g., concerts), but movies, skating, or bowling present prohibitive costs. In the few programs in which residents are free to leave the facility premises as they choose, the youth seem to be as involved in the surrounding neighborhood as adolescents who are in their natural home setting.

It should be noted, however, that the widespread geographic regions served by the facilities and the consequent number of youth from the immediate city further diminish the degree to which these programs can be truly community-based. Because the surrounding neighborhood and community are unfamiliar for a substantial number of residents, other residents become their friends and introduce them to the area.

Community resistance does not appear to be a major factor prohibiting community involvement. Administrative staff of only five programs (1 detention center, 2 group homes, 2 residential treatment facilities) reported current community opposition to their program. Generally, the surrounding neighborhoods accept the program's presence. The staffs of several of the group homes and of a few residential treatment facilities report that the neighbors know very little about the program and that some may not even be aware of its existence.

The facilities generally keep a low profile in the community, preferring to remain relatively anonymous. Apart from graduate student interns or fund-raising activities, the programs seldom seek involvement from community members and are seldom sought by community groups. There is surprisingly little volunteer involvement in these facilities, especially given the number of university students in the area. Only the detention facilities were likely to have any nonprofessional members of the community involved in activities (e.g., bingo, games, parties). For most programs, however, any participation in community activities provides a chance for the residents to get out of the facility and reduces the need for the program to organize in-house activities. In this sense many of these facilities provide experiences parallel to those of "normal" adolescence. The low visibility of the long-term residential facilities is more consistent with the normalization ideology, but for most of the programs isolation and lack of participation in community, school, and club activities appears to be the end product. It is not clear, however, that low visibility must mean lack of involvement in community activities. There is no apparent reason other than staff perception why individual youth from these facilities could not participate in community activities without stigmatization or drawing undue attention to the facility.

NORMALIZATION IN PROGRAM ACTIVITIES

Despite the great variations in size, physical buildings, location, and security status among the 30 facilities, the most obvious characteristics of the institutional setting are not present in this sample. With the exception of detention facilities, programs are small or have made attempts to create smaller living units. The physical surroundings are similar in many ways to a family living arrangement or school environment. Although these features set the limits for a normalizing experience, day-to-day activities, interaction patterns, and program operation are equally important in assessing normalization for this adolescent population. In this section we discuss the findings regarding normalization and the program structures and activities that promote a normalizing experience. Normalization is defined both quantitatively in terms of the PASS assessment and qualitatively in terms of expectations for a family living arrangement.

QUANTITATIVE ASSESSMENT OF NORMALIZATION: THE PASS

The items of the PASS are heavily focused toward the physical location of the facility, its accessibililty to the service region, the degree to which the facility stands out as deviant amidst its surroundings, the age-appropriateness of activities, and the extent to which it is possible to use community resources. Overall, the facilities rate well on the normalization dimension assessed by the PASS, with an average rating of 321.9. According to the scoring procedures of Wolfensberger and Glenn (1975), the possible scores range from -940 to $+1000$. Their work indicates that the typical setting (primarily those for retarded persons) rates about zero. Table 6-11 gives the PASS ratings for this sample of facilities by program type.

Substantial differences are apparent by program type, with the detention facilities providing the least normalizing setting and, as expected, the group homes on the average offering the most normalizing setting. The more important observation from these ratings, however, is reflected in the range of scores within each program type. The ranges indicate the diversity observed in the settings and suggest that program type alone does not ensure or preclude the features of normalization

TABLE 6-11   PASS Ratings by Program Type

Program Type	Average	Minimum Observed	Maximum Observed	Standard Deviation	Standard N
Detention	−98.2	−235	354	227.3	6
Shelter	381.2	−190	748	392.7	6
Group home	447.6	249	739	155.6	8
Residential treatment	364.1	−304	619	262.4	10
Overall Average	321.9				

assessed by the PASS. It is apparent that the specialized physical plant for detention facilities and the two secure residential treatment facilities substantially detracts from their normalizing features. Similarly, the names of these facilities connote some deviancy image, with most having the descriptor "detention," "home," or "hospital" in their name. Because of the secure nature of the detention facilities and the accompanying self-containment in programming for the residential treatment facilities, access to and use of community resources are severely restricted. Nevertheless, one secure detention facility should be highlighted for the degree of normalization that it has achieved even with these restrictions. This facility is small and is located in a family residence-like building. Although secure, program activities include almost daily excursions into the community, opportunities for individualization in programming, and staff-resident interactions that are characterized by warmth, spontaneity, and humor.

Within the category of shelter facility, two programs are referral-based shelters operated by the court and/or social service departments. The remaining four shelters are emergency drop-in facilities to which youth are voluntarily admitted and are often self-referred. The PASS ratings of these two forms of shelter indicate substantially different programs. For the drop-in shelters in this sample the average PASS score is 627.5; the referral-based shelters scored −111.5. The similarity in PASS scores between referral-based shelters and secure detention facilities suggests that these types of shelter do not offer a true alternative to secure detention in any fundamental way. Rather, it suggests their replication of detention in a "staff-secure" setting in which the residents are restricted to the premises, and in which there is essentially no community integration or individualization in programming.

Comparisons among the items of the PASS indicate that the facility types are most consistently differentiated by the degree of individualization, the quality of interaction, and overall adherence to the normalization principle. Detention facilities rate very low on the degree of individualization allowed within program operation. These facilities tend to be more regimented and, in order to maintain security, offer very few opportunities for individualized activities or treatment. Given the forced participation by residents in a detention facility, a somewhat antagonistic relationship between staff and residents is often prevalent and seriously affects the nature of interaction observed. Contact between residents and staff tends to be cool and professional rather than warm, supportive, and friendly (as is consistent with the normalization ideology). Many staff readily acknowledge that the detention facility is not intended to be "normal," and to some extent its potential effect lies in its deviance from normality. The drop-in shelters and group homes offer significant opportunities for individualization and close interpersonal contact, both in the context of counseling and in the overall functioning of the facility. Several of the group homes and residential treatment facilities identify as their goals (a) the provision of a supportive group atmosphere approximating normal family life and (b) preparation for independent living. These goals are highly consistent with the normalization philosophy. Similarly, the drop-in shelters are directed toward returning the youth to their families and facilitating a resolution of immediate difficulties. Hence, the goal of these shelters is, in a very real sense, establishing normalization in family life for the youth, with the shelter providing a transition toward that goal.

The external goals and service mandates that are placed on each facility type define limits on the degree of normalization that is possible in any given program. Within those limits, however, staff attitudes and program philosophy may magnify or minimize normalizing features and activities. From our observations it is apparent that one can establish a self-contained, isolated, and secure facility that within those boundaries provides a normalizing, growth-enhancing experience that offers some protection of individual autonomy and rights and makes allowances for individual responsibility and independence. It is also apparent that a group home, with its seeming openness and small size, may be operated in a restrictive and regimented fashion.

FAMILY INVOLVEMENT

One aspect of normalization is contact and involvement between the youth and his or her family. Family involvement is also cited as an intended component of alternative services. In this sample, 80 percent of the facilities indicate that they provide family counseling. An even greater proportion (84 percent) cite the family as the primary cause of the youth's problem behavior. In actuality, less than one-fifth of the programs involve families in any systematic way. Almost half have no consistent family involvement other than visiting hours for families and regular home visits for the youth (except those in detention). Only a small number of facilities target the family as part of the youth's service plan or make admission to the facility contingent on family cooperation. Many staff members (across program types) said that because the family was causal in the youth's problems, including it would be disruptive for the child. These staff believed that the youth was better off without the parent(s).

Staff uniformly report difficulty in getting families involved in counseling, which seems to be the primary mode of involvement and intervention. Most indicated that they made initial efforts that were not received well or were ignored, and they failed to follow up. Certainly the distances from the youth's family to the facility location may be one important factor that inhibits the amount of family involvement. In addition, the youth in group homes and residential treatment facilities tended to be those whose homes were seen as unsuitable placements and whose parents were unable to provide the structure and guidance deemed appropriate. Many had been in more than one placement before their current one, and it is reasonable to assume that parental involvement had diminished through these changes.

A common theme among residential treatment programs and group homes in particular is the assumption that the youth will not return home and that the goal of the facility's program is preparation for independent living. This implies not only an extended length of stay but also a "quasi-parent" role for the staff or houseparents. In at least two of the group homes, the houseparents (live-in) were unable to have children of their own and indicated that that was a primary reason for choosing this type of work (i.e., raising children). Although these parents seemed to have established uniquely caring relationships with the residents, such relationships also seemed to diminish the potential involvement of the natural family.

There generally is little or no family involvement across program types. Systematic family participation is clearly the exception in this sample. Detention facilities offer no vehicle for family involvement other than visiting hours. Residential treatment facilities and group homes typically provide periodic home visits for the youth. Only the drop-in shelter facilities as a group and individual group homes or residential treatment facilities actively solicit family contact.

The lack of family involvement lessens the normalization experience in these facilities by not providing continuing contact with a natural or surrogate parent and by not facilitating the return transition to their natural home or to independent living. Our observations suggest that familylike relationships and living conditions do not develop in out-of-home placement except when staff have made the time and emotional commitments that are usually required of parents or guardians, and when the youth expect to remain in the placement until the age of majority or whenever independent living is feasible. Under these circumstances, staff and resident expectations most closely parallel those of the natural family living arrangement.

PROGRAM STRUCTURE AND RULES

Every program that we visited had rules of some sort. Most commonly these included prohibitions on violence, weapons, stealing property, drug and alcohol use, homosexual or heterosexual activity on the premises, and being AWOL. Individual facilities added rules and expectations regarding completion of chores, privileges, use of free time, use of the telephone, home visits, and participation in activities. Rules and subsequent consequences for rule infraction serve as a primary mechanism for maintaining order and organization within the program. Each resident is instructed in the house rules at admission in every facility. Two-thirds of the facilities have some form of resident handbook that is made available to each resident, and over 40 percent have the rules posted on bulletin boards or in other prominent places.

Programs use a variety of incentives and consequences in conjunction with their rules. Incentives include (1) material goods and consumables, such as cigarettes, candy, soda, or money; (2) freedom or time away from the facility; (3) social activities, such as group outings, dances, or dating; and (4) status and responsibility (e.g., change in program status such as being named group leader, staff assistant, or resident of the week). The most common consequences involve a loss of freedom (e.g., room restriction, time-limited lockup in detention, or being grounded) and loss of a social activity (e.g., phone privileges, visitors, group activity or outing). School attendance was required in the majority of programs, but in a small number school attendance was considered a privilege and as such was something to be either earned or denied as a consequence for some infraction.

Almost all of the facilities permitted the residents to make telephone calls. In detention facilities these calls were typically limited to parents and caseworkers only, with some restrictions on the number of calls and the length of time on the phone. Only five facilities (16 percent) allowed unlimited use of the telephone, and these provided a pay telephone for the residents' use. One-half of the facilities provided a separate phone for the residents' use but maintained some time restrictions on its use. Two-thirds of the programs allowed residents to use the agency phone, again usually with time and location limits. In the majority of programs, use of the telephone is considered a privilege. As such it may be taken away, or additional time to use the phone can be earned.

We observed little evidence of the use of medication to control the behavior of the youth in residence. A few facilities report individual instances of psychotropic medication, but only one setting evidenced extensive use of medication that significantly depressed the level of activity of the residents. Generally, there was little concern among staff regarding violence or assaultive behavior among the residents. Almost one-half of the programs indicate that assaults on the staff never occur. The more serious concern among staff in over one-third of the facilities is assault and vandalism from the community. For facilities that are located in high-crime areas, the more prevalent danger is apparently on the street and not within the facility. Consequently, there is little indication of staff activity aimed at controlling violence, except in secure detention facilities.

Although there is little evidence of activities or structures to control overtly the behavior of residents, we found that the use of rules, rewards, and punishments frequently serves to maintain organizational control of the residents. In approximately one-half of the programs, rules function to control youth behavior and serve organizational purposes rather than individualized resident needs by (1) imposing negative sanctions (e.g., if you do not complete your chore you lose group activity privilege) to the exclusion of recognition, privilege, or reward for accomplishing an expected task; (2) administering rewards and punishments inconsistently; (3) threatening punishment or loss of a routine "privilege" for undesirable behavior; and (4) providing minimal variety in the types of rewards or punishments employed (e.g., lockup or restriction for all infractions). In contrast, some facilities have a system of incentives and consequences that is more clearly integrated with the overall treatment goals of the residents and seems to match more clearly the developmental needs of the youth for responsibility and individual choice. Settings in which such a system functions as just one component of the overall program and ethos of the facility, rather than as the overriding influence, appear to allow for individual development and a normalizing experience more similar to that of noninstitutional settings, such as a family or school.

PRIVACY AND PERSONALIZATION

The absence of or significant infringements on privacy are frequently cited in descriptions of institutional settings. Aside from detention, the facilities we visited offer the physical and structural necessities for privacy. In all but the detention facilities and one shelter facility, youth had a private place to store personal belongings. Unless overcrowded conditions prevailed, the residents were able to find privacy and places to be alone, which is quite similar to a family or school living arrangement. Privacy in the use of bathrooms was also available within the limits of sharing. In 70 percent of the facilities, one bathroom was shared by 10 or fewer persons, not too unlike a large family setting. In just over one-half of the facilities, there were locks on the bathroom doors so that an individual could maintain additional privacy. With the security and observation capabilities in detention, however, privacy is essentially eliminated.

Only in detention is there a routine search at the time of intake. Here the youth's clothes and personal belongings are confiscated, and the standard dress of the home is issued. In the nondetention facilities, youth maintained their own clothing and other personal belongings. Many of those in group homes and residential treatment facilities brought pictures, posters, and stuffed animals or other toys. Residents' rooms in these facilities tended to be personally decorated and quite individualized. The shelter facilities permitted the youth to bring personal items, but because of the short stay and crisis nature of the placement, the residents had few possessions with them. Consequently, rooms tended to be essentially undecorated and lacked the personalization of other longer-term residences.

In all but two facilities, residents' rooms were inspected "regularly" for cleanliness and/or contraband (e.g., drugs). Our impression is that these inspections are formal in only a minority of the programs. In some facilities we observed rooms with clothes and other paraphernalia strewn about, while other facilities required that residents' rooms be straightened to earn privileges.

Overall, the nondetention facilities allowed residents opportunities for privacy. Our observations suggest that the residents, as expected of adolescents, spent time with each other and sought privacy from staff but not necessarily from other residents. Only in detention were there infringements on the degree to which residents could personalize their living space. Many places involved the residents in redecoration efforts (e.g., painting) in an effort to enhance their sense of ownership and satisfaction with the physical surroundings.

RESIDENT RESPONSIBILITY AND INDIVIDUALIZATION

Several mechanisms to enhance individualization and resident responsibility in programming are common across facilities. In 63 percent of the programs, each resident chooses or is assigned a primary counselor who serves as an advocate for the youth within the program. Two-thirds of the facilities (primarily nondetention) formulate individual service plans detailing personalized goals as well as strategies for intervention. These plans and resident progress are reviewed periodically and necessary changes in a resident's program are discussed. One-third of the facilities (across types) have a formal grievance system that provides a mechanism for residents to assert their autonomy and appeal any disciplinary decisions. Most nondetention programs have a weekly meeting of all residents, providing a forum for their grievances.

Residents in all programs were responsible for some chores around the facility, including taking care of their immediate belongings, making their beds, and keeping their own rooms clean. Group homes and shelter facilities also involve the residents in house maintenance, cleaning communal areas, and meal preparation. Most nondetention facilities give residents some weekly allowance or spending money, with amounts varying from $2.00 to $12.00 per week. This money is rarely denied and is for the personal use of the resident.

Aside from these somewhat insignificant opportunities for responsibility, a small number of programs (across types) allow residents to leave the premises as they choose and to be responsible for their activities. A few programs offer opportunities for resident leadership, self-governance, and positions as staff assistants. Generally, however, the facilities allow only minimal personal responsibility and decisionmaking by the youth. It seems that rather than promote responsibility, the typical facility operates on the assumption that the lack of a sense of responsibility has gotten these youth in trouble and the "treatment," ironically, is to reduce the options for such activity. Facilities seem to define "taking responsibility for oneself" as staying out of trouble.

Although most programs provide mechanisms for individualization in programming, our observations indicate that individual resident programs generally are similar. These facilities seem to experience many of the same difficulties as other groups in balancing the perceptions of "fairness" and consistency in the treatment of group members, on the one hand, with the differing needs of individuals on the other. The resolution most commonly observed in these programs seems to be in favor of group consistency, as is often the case in family settings and other groups.

RECREATION ACTIVITIES

Every facility offers some opportunities for recreational activities and some form of unscheduled time. The program philosophy and the resources (i.e., materials, space, money) that are available to the facilities determine to some degree the nature and location of these activities. All of the programs had television sets and some athletic equipment, such as bats and balls or a volleyball set. Most had playing cards and a few games, magazines, and books; a Ping Pong, pool, or Foosball table; arts and crafts materials; and music equipment (radios and stereos). A few programs with more extensive grounds and resources also had tennis courts and a swimming pool. A few group homes and residential treatment facilities take overnight camping trips and annual vacations. Most group homes and residential treatment facilities had some weekly activity either on- or off-premises.

Our observations and data on weekly schedules indicate that residents have significant periods of time without scheduled activity, in many instances as much as 60 percent of their day—a situation perhaps comparable to agemates who live at home during the summer months. During the school year, school presumably would occupy a significant portion of this time. During our visits, residents spent most of this time watching television, smoking cigarettes, playing cards, and generally "hanging out."

In each program type there are a handful of facilities that offer fairly extensive recreation programs. Three programs in particular are notable for ways in which they have incorporated recreation activities with the treatment/change program. One residential program is rooted in some of the Eastern philosophies highlighting the importance of synchrony between the mind and the body. Their program includes counseling and physical activity in a unique "treatment" approach. Two secure facilities (one detention, one residential treatment program) use recreational activities to bolster self-esteem, to give youth a sense of accomplishment, and to provide opportunities for them to interact and work together productively.

The extent to which an organized recreation program is available in any facility does not appear to be related exclusively to resource availability; rather, it reflects the creativity and energy of the staff in using available resources for the residents and in encouraging productive use of leisure time. Additionally, how the facility interprets its mandate and how it perceives the needs of youth seem critically important in understanding the observed differences in the extent of available activities. For example, one referral-based shelter felt that its mandate was to provide productive things for youth to do during their stay, rather than to reform them. This facility had a variety of recreation options and in fact had a full-time recreation staff. Similarly, the superintendent of a detention facility has organized a program that includes five to six hours per day of organized and semiorganized recreation to provide an outlet for adolescent activity and the tension that is naturally generated in a locked facility.

The amount of unstructured time that is available to residents in these facilities is similar to that of adolescents who live at home. However, for youth in out-of-home placements there are significant limits on their freedom to pursue off-premises activities. Although a completely structured day does not parallel the "normal" experience of adolescents living at home, neither does the lack of opportunity to pursue activities. Only a small number of facilities in this sample provide optimally normalizing alternatives.

SUMMARY AND CONCLUSIONS

This study of alternative facilities for status offenders is based primarily on a case-study observation methodology. A sample of 30 facilities of four program types provides the data base. With the limited sample size, strategic sampling, and methodology, it is important to recognize clearly the limitations inherent in making conclusive generalizations from this set of case studies. Nevertheless, the sample seems to be representative of the "best available services" in the cities that we visited. Given this apparent sampling bias and the consistency between the observations of the facility analysis and the individual state case studies, the findings and conclusions suggested here are presented as independent findings supportive of the larger study of which this research is a part. Several exploratory hypotheses and areas of future inquiry are also suggested.

ISSUES RELEVANT TO THE SYSTEMATIC IMPLEMENTATION OF JJDPA

The historical evolution of the facilities that we visited supports the conclusion that few new programs or facilities were initiated by the mandates of JJDPA. Rather than precipitating new services, the act seems to have triggered modification and "modernization" in existing facilities. The program directors' reports of facility goals suggest that despite changes in terminology, rules, and treatment models, there has been only minimal change among these facilities in underlying philosophies, assumptions about youth in need of services, and overall "mission."

Local needs, not general direction-setting policy in service provision (such as JJDPA), appear to be the most salient factors in precipitating the development of new services and changes in existing facilities. These local needs may come to the forefront as a result of community pressures, changing mores, or changes in the youth population. Local actors who were involved in service provision in this sample seem to be responding to their perceptions of community needs rather than to state or federal policy. In fact, several of the new services were initiated as part of a strategy to handle *immediate* local needs. For example, a home-based detention program was begun by one detention facility because of severe overcrowding. More often than not the specific legislation stemming from state and federal policy is viewed by service providers as something to live with and adapt to. Consequently, we observed program features that on the surface are consistent with JJDPA expectations (e.g., changes in terminology for program identification and the labeling of services), but the providers do not seem to offer a fundamentally different type of program.

Referral patterns and funding sources suggest that the social service departments, not corrections, are largely responsible for services to status offenders. It appears that the disposition of status offenders has moved outside the correctional system into the social service system. However, the methodology of this study does not permit the extensive analysis of the impact of the referral system and diversion practices on patterns of service delivery.

EXPECTED SERVICE CHARACTERISTICS

There are a number of specific outcomes for service provision that are suggested or mandated by JJDPA. One of these expectations is the provision of alternative services for status offenders. Within this sample the only example of a service that is uniquely designed for status offenders is the runaway emergency shelter. All four of the program types accept both status offenders and delinquents, although the number of status offenders in secure detention is minimal. Our data suggests that service providers do not make distinctions between these legally defined categories either in intake policies or in programming, and both status offenders and delinquent youth are commingled in the out-of-home placements in this sample.

Service providers seem to perceive youth as "troubled" or "emotionally disturbed" and use behavior and attitude, rather than legally defined classifications, as placement criteria. The opinion that the youth referred to their facilities are more seriously disturbed than the youth of several years ago was widely held among these providers. The degree to which there are real differences between today's youth and those of a decade ago cannot be determined by this analysis; however, the implications for service provision may be significant. Several hypotheses for these changes were suggested by service providers, some of which identify perhaps unintended negative outcomes from the deinstitutionalization/ diversion policies (e.g., "it is harder to get service for youth now and hence the youth's situation deteriorates before service is available"; and "youth, particularly status offenders, know that nothing will happen to them, so the authority of the court and correctional systems serves only a minimal deterrence function").

The provisions of JJDPA called for community-based services. Within this sample of facilities there is minimal evidence of community integration, except in the use of the public school system among group home youth. As a group, detention facilities provide no options for community integration or the use of community resources. The remaining three program types examined here use professional services in the community on an as-needed basis, but they have few mechanisms for generating or maintaining community involvement in the program or resident involvement in the community. In an effort to maintain a low profile in the community, the facilities are functionally isolated from most typical community youth activities. Furthermore, the youth who are placed in the facilities are not necessarily from the immediate community, and in the long-term facilities youth may come from a broad geographic region.

Family involvement, an additional component called for by JJDPA is essentially absent from the programs of this sample of facilities. Although the family is viewed as a primary causal factor in the youth's problems across facility types, only a few programs include the family in any aspect of program or treatment activities. The distance from the youth's home and the lack of other community-based activities may limit the potential involvement of families.

PROGRAMMING AND NORMALIZATION

The most salient finding regarding the nature of programming and the quality of the settings is the variability and diversity evidenced in this sample. With only minor exceptions the long-term facilities offer safe, clean, and physically comfortable living space. Of the four program types, the detention facilities provide the minimum in comfort, but those in this sample would not be considered damaging or inhumane environments. Beyond these minimal requirements, however, there is as much variability within program types as among program types in the degree of normalization evident, the treatment models adopted, day-to-day programming, and the physical features of the setting.

There are no obvious differences in programming that are related to age, sex of the youth, or geographic locality. Rather, the diversity observed in the total sample extends across these variables. Our sample is not large enough or racially diverse enough to determine the degree to which the race of the youth is related to the quality of the setting. However, we have observed some evidence of referral preferences that are related to race. The degree to which services are differentiated by race is an issue in need of further study.

All of the facilities indicate that provision of treatment in the form of counseling is minimal. The site observations and interview data indicate that although activities may be labeled as treatment in many places, the reality of their occurrence and therapeutic significance is questionable. Again this may be evidence of a change in terminology without a concomitant change in philosophy and practice.

Under both quantitative and qualitative definitions of normalization, the nonsecure settings provide most of the physical and structural necessities for a normalizing setting. Certainly, natural families also show broad interfamilial variability; some provide minimal comfort, varying amounts of supervision and structured activity, and restrictions on youth mobility. For the sample of out-of-home placements included here, it is important to recognize that there is overlap between these facilities and the range of natural home-living conditions along these dimensions. However, the extent to which the out-of-home experience parallels that of home living is more formally restricted by (a) the degree of supervision of resident activity afforded by program rules, (b) the limits on the youth's freedom to leave the facility premises, and (c) the availability of opportunities to become involved in nonprogram activities. Most facilities maintain a "structured" program that has limitations on the youth's choice of activity and companions. The very existence of a program (i.e., rather than a family-living environment) renders these facilities at least marginally institutional, even though they do not have the blatantly depersonalizing and controlling features of the stereotypic institutional setting.

The few facilities that most closely approximate the family-living style seem to place less emphasis on programmed activities and treatment and place a premium on the development of close interpersonal relationships and individual decisionmaking in a group context. These facilities are characterized by extended emotional and time commitments from the staff, usually houseparents, and the youth's expectation to remain in the home for an indefinite time period.

CURRENT SERVICE PROBLEMS

Program administrators reported a variety of problems and issues facing them in their attempt to deliver services, and there is a discouraging sense of helplessness among them and their staffs. Administrators report massive funding cuts, retrenchment, and ever-increasing licensing requirements that drastically affect their program; at the same time, they feel they have no control over the direction of these changes. In order to keep some stability in the face of changing mandates, many programs want to develop into multiservice organizations that include diagnostic centers, group homes, shelter facilities, longer-term residential treatment programs, and aftercare services. The logic of this strategy is that "all bases are covered" and the organizations will be less vulnerable to changes in funding priorities.

Lack of resources, inadequate staff training, extensive staff turnover, and more difficult youth seem to be the primary explanations for less than complete success among larger programs. Smaller facilities complain of the lack of adequate postplacement transitional facilities and suggest that this constitutes a serious threat to whatever progress they may have been able to make. Directors of smaller facilities in group homes (in particular) report that community awareness of deinstitutionalization is resulting in growing community opposition. They suggest that such resistance, coupled with increasingly complex financial requirements and licensing provisions, makes it very difficult to continue to develop new and innovative small residential facilities.

The problems identified by providers seem to be more closely related to organizational needs than to the needs of the youth in placement. The solutions currently proposed—primarily the development of multipurpose and multiservice organizations—are similarly a response to organizational demands and, if accomplished, bear close resemblance to the larger institutional complexes that they were designed to replace.

DIRECTIONS AND IMPLICATIONS

The findings of this report suggest that the residential services available to youth generally offer comfortable living alternatives and provide a more normalizing experience than those reportedly found in institutional settings. Nevertheless, there are still substantial differences between the home-living arrangement and life within these settings. The ultimate question of the efficacy of these programs and their impact on the lives of youth cannot be addressed by this study; they remain as salient, unanswered questions. The decisionmaking processes and functioning of the referral system need further study to determine how placement decisions are made and why some youth enter the system and others do not. The current problems expressed by program administrators and their suggested solutions may result in a gradual return to the institutional system that deinstitutionalization was intended, in part, to replace.

The Role of Federal Programs in Efforts to Deinstitutionalize Status Offenders

7

SALLY A. KORNEGAY *and*
SUZANNE S. MAGNETTI

INTRODUCTION

There are two types of federal influence on state deinstitutionalization activities. First, there are federal policy sources that either speak directly to the juvenile justice system or are closely associated with the deinstitutionalization movement. One early example is the *Gault* decision, which specifically addressed questions concerning the rights of children processed by juvenile courts. Other examples include judicial decisions concerning the right to treatment and to the least restrictive setting for mental health patients, as well as the incorporation of such concepts into programs targeted at specific groups, such as the handicapped. Second, there are federal programs that provide funds that states can use in their efforts to deinstitutionalize status offenders. Some of these programs are concerned directly with alternative services for status offenders (e.g., the runaway youth program); other programs are more general in focus, but they certainly can be adapted by state and local governments to serve this population (e.g.,Title XX). In this chapter, we focus on the second type of federal influence.

Federal programs that provide support for efforts to deinstitutionalize status offenders can be divided into two categories. The first category includes federal laws and programs that directly address the issue of deinstitutionalization of status offenders. The most conspicuous of this form of federal leverage are grants available under the Juvenile Justice and Delinquency Prevention Act (Juvenile Justice Act). That act not

176

only expressed the basic federal mandate for the deinstitutionalization of status offenders and dependent and neglected children, but also provided funds that states could use to meet that mandate. In addition, Title III of that act, the Runaway Youth Act, provided funds and some limited guidance for programs that serve the "runaway" subgroup of status offenders.

The second category is made up of federal programs that are not aimed directly at status offenders but include those youth as part of their potential service population. These programs were designed to achieve purposes far broader than the deinstitutionalization of status offenders, but they do provide substantial sources of funds that states may tap in order to provide services to such youth. The coordination and use of these more general federal funding sources are more important in attempts to respond to the need for alternative services than to efforts to remove status offenders from institutional settings. Although the complexities and inconsistencies inherent in the intent, financing mechanisms, and administrative and regulatory structures of federal programs do contribute to the way that these programs affect these youth, it is the manner in which states interpret or use such provisions that actually determines the impact of these programs on status offenders. However, it should be remembered that in the states these federal programs fit into the larger scheme of social programs, and status offenders are at best only a small portion of the population that is served.

We examined nine federal programs to determine the extent to which such programs directly or indirectly assist or impede the process of implementing deinstitutionalization strategies: the Juvenile Justice Act grant programs, the runaway youth program, LEAA's grant programs, Title XX social service grants, Title IV-B child welfare services, foster care grants under the Aid to Families with Dependent Children program (AFDC), Medicaid, Title I of the Elementary and Secondary Education Act (ESEA), and the Education for All Handicapped Children Program (P.L. 94-142).

The purpose, structure, and potential effects of the federal programs were examined through data collected at both the federal and state levels. The state and local data collection was conducted between early 1979 and the spring of 1980, and the timing of the fieldwork should be considered relative to the findings emanating from certain of the programs investigated.*

---

* For example, on June 17, 1980, President Carter signed the Adoption Assistance and Child Welfare Act of 1980 (P.L. 96-272), which, if implemented, will substantially alter

This chapter is organized into three sections. The first section generally describes the origins and purposes of each of the programs, including a brief analysis of how each addresses status offenders, dependent and neglected children, and deinstitutionalization. The second section describes the manner in which the various federal programs affect the structure and content of services provided to status offenders, with special attention given to the seven states in this study. The third section consists of a short summary.

THE PROGRAMS STUDIED

The nine federal programs selected for study are administered at the state and local levels primarily through the justice, education, or social service systems. If status offenders or their families are served by those systems, they may receive services that draw on funds from these programs. Federal grants under one program—the runaway youth program—are received directly by providers who serve that population of youth. Two of the programs (LEAA and OJJDP grants) are administered through the juvenile or general justice systems, which identify status offenders as a target group. The other six federal programs are administered by state social service and education systems, and status offenders are only a minor part of the populations served by those systems. Several of the social service and education programs contain provisions that allow or even require that services be provided to dependent and neglected children; however, few references were found that directly addressed services for status offenders.

The following summaries of the nine federal programs highlight the purposes and structures of each. The manner, if any, by which each program's purpose and requirements relate to the deinstitutionalization of status offenders is also discussed here. Chapters 17 through 23 in Part II contain more detailed descriptions of the programs as well as the analyses of their effects on the deinstitutionalization of status offenders.

---

the AFDC-foster care program by changing the focus to reduced duration of care and more permanent placements (i.e., adoptions) instead of only financial support. Child welfare services under Title IV-B also will be changed to stress activities that would support the new foster care/adoption program. In addition, the act changes certain provisions of Title XX and Medicaid. Furthermore, the 1982 Reagan budget contains provisions that would change several of the programs by replacing them with block grants that cover general areas (e.g., social services).

OJJDP GRANTS

The Juvenile Justice and Delinquency Prevention Act of 1974 established the Office of Juvenile Justice and Delinquency Prevention (OJJDP) within the Law Enforcement Assistance Administration (LEAA). From its appropriations ($100 million annually for fiscal years 1978 through 1980) OJJDP could make grants in four areas: (1) formula grants to state planning agencies, (2) special emphasis grants, (3) grants from the National Institute for Juvenile Justice and Delinquency Prevention (primarily for evaluations, research, and demonstrations), and (4) the concentration of federal effort program. States primarily receive federal support from OJJDP through the first three types of grants.

The formula grants are dispersed to states that have made commitments to deinstitutionalize status offenders and dependent and neglected children, but the funds do not have to be spent for that purpose. Funds are allocated on the basis of a formula that considers the size of a state's population under the age of 18. The minimum state grant is $225,000.

The other two types of grants that are usually awarded to state and local governments and service agencies are for specific projects. However, this does not necessarily mean that they are one-time awards; many projects and demonstrations continue to receive funding for several years. These grants do not have to be used solely for projects that are connected with status offenders.

RUNAWAY YOUTH PROGRAM

Title III of the Juvenile Justice Act comprises a separate Runaway and Homeless Youth Act, which authorizes a program that is completely separate from those under the rest of the act. In fact, this program is administered by the Department of Health and Human Services, Youth Development Bureau, rather than by OJJDP. When first enacted, this program was unique in that it was designed specifically to serve one category of status offenders—runaways. Homeless youth were added to the program and the title of the act at a later date.

The program distributes approximately $11 million in grants annually. There are some national-level projects (e.g., a hotline that runaways can use to request assistance or to contact home), but most of the funds are awarded directly to centers that serve runaways and other youth (see e.g., D. Walker 1975). The grant recipients are supposed to use the federal funds to provide services and temporary shelter to youth in need of such services. These centers are required to be outside the law enforcement and juvenile justice systems, although coordination with these systems is expected.

LEAA GRANTS

Until recent program budget cutbacks, LEAA administered several different types of grants authorized by the Crime Control Act. Most LEAA funds are distributed to the states as block grants, including planning grants and action grants that can be used by the states to fund specific projects.

From 1974 to 1980, LEAA funding levels were considerably higher than those of the OJJDP programs. LEAA monies have been applied to a variety of purposes in the justice and law enforcement areas, only one of which is juvenile justice. However, because LEAA funding levels are so much larger than those of OJJDP, one of the requirements placed on the use of LEAA funds—the maintenance of effort clause—has had the potential for producing greater effects on state and local programs for juveniles than the OJJDP programs. The maintenance of effort clause requires that 19.15 percent of LEAA's funds be spent on programs or services that deal with juveniles. Projects that are specifically for juveniles as well as portions of projects that affect the general population associated with the criminal and law enforcement systems can be counted toward meeting this requirement. The maintenance of effort provision applies not only to the discretionary funds spent by LEAA but also to the block grants awarded to the states. These maintenance of effort funds do not have to be spent on programs involving status offenders.

TITLE XX

Title XX of the Social Security Act provides funds that states can use to provide social services to individuals and families. Although there are federally set goals, limits on eligibility, and prohibitions against certain services, considerable program responsibility and authority are delegated to the states. Until the 1980 legislative changes there was a $2.5 billion cap on federal funds available through Title XX; however, the funding level was increased to $2.7 billion in fiscal year 1980. The funds are distributed to states by formula grants that are based on population.

Title XX contains five goals for services that are provided with federal funds, and a state can provide any service that it decides will help a recipient attain at least one of those goals. The goals are: (1) achieving self-support; (2) achieving self-sufficiency; (3) preventing or remedying neglect, abuse, or exploitation; (4) preventing or remedying inappropriate institutionalization, and (5) achieving appropriate institutionalization. These goals are diverse and broad enough so that a state can justify almost any service it wants to provide.

It is important to note that Title XX funds are available for services to persons of all ages, and services for children and youth and those specifically for status offenders have to compete for the limited funds along with other age and special interest groups. The federal government has specified three categories of persons that can be eligible for services: (1) those eligible for federal cash assistance (AFDC or SSI); (2) those whose family income falls below the state limits, which cannot exceed 115 percent of a state's median income; and (3) those in need of certain services that can be made available without regard to income. This last category includes protective services for children.

Title XX contains no references to services that states might provide in pursuit of the goal to deinstitutionalize status offenders. Although this does not mean that status offenders are excluded from services under this program, it does mean that there is no federal requirement that Title XX funds must be used to serve such youth. Title XX funds can be used to provide both community-based and institutional services.

TITLE IV-B CHILD WELFARE SERVICES

The purpose of grants under Title IV-B of the Social Security Act is to encourage states to establish, extend, and strengthen child welfare services. Prior to the 1980 legislative changes, child welfare services were defined to include protective services, care of dependent and neglected children, care of children of working mothers, and any other services that promote the welfare of children. The definition contained in the 1980 legislation highlights protective services and services to prevent family dissolution and eliminates the reference to services to children of working mothers. The federal rules do not tie eligibility for Title IV-B services to any other programs or income levels; rather, they permit the funds to be used solely on the basis of need for child welfare services.

The amount of funds available through the federal child welfare program has always been considerably less than for other federal service programs. While the fiscal year 1980 program authorization was $266 million, the budget allocation was only $56.5 million, the same as it had been since fiscal year 1977. The 1980 legislation was expected to correct this large discrepancy between authorization and appropriation levels. However, although larger appropriations will be required to effect the

1980 legislated program, funding levels remain tied to the annual appropriations process (U.S. Congress 1980a).

The federal child welfare services program identified runaways and delinquents as target recipients for services. Title IV-B allowed federal funds to be used for the care of runaways in facilities for up to 15 days and covered the costs of their interstate transportation to return home. It also permitted the provision of services for "preventing, or remedying, or assisting in the solution of problems which may result in the . . . delinquency of children" (42 USC 625(1976)). The term delinquency was not defined and, depending on a state program's requirements and operational procedures, services to status offenders could have been included.

Title IV-A of the Social Security Act funds the Aid to Families with Dependent Children (AFDC) program, which was part of the Social Security Act as passed in 1935. It was not until 1961 that federal funds were available through this program to support children in foster care who otherwise would be eligible for AFDC. This is an entitlement program with no cap on the federal funds available. The federal government reimburses states for a portion of foster care maintenance payments for all eligible children and youth.

In order to receive a federal foster care payment, a child first must meet a state's definition of "dependent." Basically, the federal rules state that a dependent child is one who has been deprived of the support or care of at least one parent by reason of death, absence, or incapacity. A dependent child who was removed from his or her home "as a result of a judicial determination to the effect that continuation therein would be contrary to his welfare" is eligible for foster care payments under the AFDC program (42 USC 608(a)(1976)). As part of the new federal foster care program created by legislation passed in 1980, a child would have to meet the above eligibility criteria, and reasonable efforts must have been made to prevent the removal of the child from the home.

The AFDC-foster care program provides support for eligible children who are removed from their homes because of harmful conditions. Most state laws concerning dependent and neglected children define a variety of harmful conditions that would allow a ruling of dependency or neglect. Thus, a state may be able to receive some federal reimbursement for some dependent and neglected children removed from their homes by judicial determinations and placed in foster care. Eligibility, of course, would depend on whether the AFDC eligibility requirements were met.

One interpretation of the AFDC-foster care provisions is that a judicial determination that a child has committed a status offense also meets the federal requirements. If such a court finding causes a status offender to be placed in foster care because remaining at home is harmful for the youth, then federal reimbursement could be claimed (U.S. Congress 1979b).

AFDC-foster care funds can be used to support eligible children in both foster family homes and child-caring institutions, but the former is the predominant type of care. In November 1979, 86 percent of AFDC-foster care placements were in foster family homes (U.S. Department of Health and Human Services 1980). Program changes caused by the 1980 legislation encourage care, when necessary, in the least restrictive setting (U.S. Congress 1979a, 1979b, 45 Fed.Reg. 86836(1980)).

MEDICAID

The Medicaid program provides federal funds for medical services to the poor. The program provides federal funds to offset part of the costs that states incur when they furnish medical assistance to persons who are (a) members of families with dependent children, (b) age 65 or over, or (c) blind or disabled, and whose income and resources are not sufficient to meet the costs of necessary medical care. Subject to certain limited federal rules and regulations, the program is administered by each state according to its own rules and constraints.

In order for states to receive the federal program funds, certain services must be included in their programs. Medicaid also provides federal reimbursement for several other types of medical services if a state wants to provide them. The federal program allows a state both to define the specific medical items and procedures that will constitute the various types of services and to determine any limits on the amount or duration of offered services.

Federal Medicaid funding is open-ended; that is, there is no specific amount of federal funds available for reimbursement to the states, and all eligible claims will be reimbursed. The percentage of federal reimbursement is based on a formula that varies inversely with a state's per-capita income, but it cannot be less than 50 percent or more than 83 percent of the incurred expenses. In fiscal year 1978 the federal and state costs of the Medicaid program totaled $18.6 billion (U.S. Department of Health, Education, and Welfare 1980).

Medicaid contains no references to status offenders or dependent and neglected children. Such children and youth would have to be eligible for this program by meeting one of the more general eligibility requirements.

Medicaid funds can be used for services both in and out of institutions. The federal rules allow a state to provide several different types of institutional care, including services to residents in psychiatric facilities. However, a variety of ambulatory care services can also be provided; thus, many types of care may be provided without requiring institutionalization. Other Medicaid eligibility rules can extend eligibility to children and youth who are in certain types of nonmedical out-of-home placements, such as foster homes, group homes, or small nonsecure residential facilities.

TITLE I

The purpose of Title I of the Elementary and Secondary Education Act (ESEA) is to fund special compensatory programs to meet the specific educational problems of targeted groups of educationally deprived children. In particular, Title I authorizes financial assistance to programs that address the special educational needs ". . . of educationally deprived children . . . of children of certain migrant parents, of Indian children, and of handicapped, neglected and delinquent children" (20 USC 241a).

Title I is the largest federal program of assistance to elementary and secondary education. The total allocation for all Title I programs for fiscal year 1980 was more than $3 billion (U.S. Department of Health, Education, and Welfare 1979b). Grants to the states generally are based on the number of pupils from low-income families and the average per-pupil level of spending in the particular state. Portions of this money are then distributed by each state to state-run or state-supported residential institutions that educate children (in particular, state facilities that house neglected or delinquent children, and state schools for the handicapped) on the basis of the average pupil population of those facilities. The major part of the Title I grant, however, is allocated by the state among school districts in proportion to the number of eligible children in the district. School districts then supply the funds to individual schools based on their concentration of counted children.

Title I eligible children are children from low-income families, children receiving AFDC, or children in local institutional or foster care programs. The eligibility terminology, however, is somewhat deceiving. After the money has been allocated to the school districts and individual schools, any child who attends a school that offers a Title I program can be served by the program if that child is educationally disadvantaged, without regard to economic status.

Title I authorizes several programs, and we examined three. In each of these programs Title I funds can be used to provide educational services to status offenders, but all of the specific references to such children involve institutional placements. For example, compensatory educational programs funded under Title I can be used to provide services to children in institutions for neglected or delinquent children. Under these Title I programs status offenders are included in the definition of delinquents.

Title I also funds compensatory education in regular public schools, thereby serving children, including status offenders, who live at home or in foster care. Some children who reside in institutions also attend regular public schools and could be served by this Title I program. However, Title I funds can also be used for educational services in institutions for delinquent, dependent, or handicapped children. While there is no clear program preference for either the institutional or the community setting for the provision of compensatory educational services, most Title I funds are allocated through the local school districts to the regular public schools.

P.L. 94-142

The Education for All Handicapped Children Act of 1975 (often referred to as P.L. 94-142) both provides funding and sets out detailed requirements for state educational programs for handicapped children. The purpose of the legislation is to ensure that a free appropriate public education is available to all handicapped children. Services under P.L. 94-142 are provided without regard to income, and they must be provided to any handicapped child. The philosophy of P.L. 94-142 reflects some of the general goals of deinstitutionalization. Specifically, the act requires that placement of handicapped children, to the maximum extent possible and appropriate for the individual child, must be in the least restrictive setting. The law expresses definite preference for regular school placements when appropriate.

The fiscal year 1980 federal allocation for P.L. 94-142 was $804 million (U.S. Department of Health, Education, and Welfare 1979c). Since the law was never intended to supply more than 12 percent of the costs of educating handicapped children in the required programs, the actual costs of the special education programs mandated by P.L. 94-142 are considerable. All costs in excess of the funds provided by the federal government must be absorbed by state and local education agencies.

Status offenders are not as a group eligible for any services under P.L. 94-142. However, individual status offenders and dependent or neglected children who are handicapped, or who are treated as if they are handicapped, could receive special education in accordance with the law.

THE EFFECT OF FEDERAL PROGRAMS ON SERVICES FOR STATUS OFFENDERS

Although our research began with individual analyses of the different programs, it became obvious that across these programs there are common aspects that describe the relationship of the federal and related state programs to efforts to deinstitutionalize status offenders and dependent and neglected children. This section describes how implementation of the various federal programs has both contributed to and detracted from the achievement of the deinstitutionalization goals and requirements of the Juvenile Justice Act in the seven study states.

RELATIONSHIP BETWEEN FEDERAL AND STATE PROGRAMS

Most federal programs are integrated into state programs to such an extent that it is difficult to isolate the specific impacts of the federal versus state programs on services to status offenders. Except for Medicaid, Title I, and the runaway youth projects, the federal programs in this study are not administered as separate programs at the state and local levels. Federal funds and program requirements ordinarily are integrated into the state's juvenile justice, education, social services, or foster care programs, which for the most part were operating before the federal funding programs began. The impact of the federal policies is filtered through and adapted to state and local needs and policies.

As illustrated throughout this study, OJJDP and LEAA funds did have an important impact on state activities. In most cases, however, the impact was not one of getting states to do something (e.g., deinstitutionalize status offenders) but rather of assisting with their early or ongoing initiatives and programs. The OJJDP and LEAA grants have been used by the states as part of their juvenile and criminal justice programs. The largest share of these funds has been distributed to state planning agencies through block grants, and those monies then are distributed by these agencies in ways that will best meet their program objectives. Most states did not have these planning agencies prior to participation in the LEAA program, but many have integrated them into their existing justice and law enforcement systems.

The federal social service programs funded under Titles IV-B and XX and the AFDC-foster care program do not appear to have dramatically changed state programs. Among all of the programs examined, these three seem to have been substantially absorbed into existing state structures in most of the seven states. We were not surprised to discover that state laws, program policies, and traditional practices are the predominant controlling mechanisms for state social service and foster care programs.

Title XX imposes few requirements on program content. There is considerable latitude in federal program goals and objectives, so that most states can adapt the language of their service programs to meet Title XX requirements. While there is always a state Title XX planner or coordinator, the actual program that is implemented is a state social service program and not necessarily a separate Title XX program. This is more frequently true in states that have extensive social service funding. The state programs with lower levels of funding appear to be more identifiably Title XX programs, probably because Title XX and the state match constitute most, if not all, of the program's budget.

Title IV-B, the federal child welfare services program, has almost no controls on the types of services that states provide or the clients they serve. For the most part these federal funds are used by existing child welfare service programs along with funds from a variety of other sources.

In the seven states studied, state and local funds provide most foster care maintenance payments. State guidelines control the manner in which most foster care cases are handled. Those guidelines usually contain separate AFDC-foster care eligibility rules, but such rules are primarily used to identify which children already in the foster care system are eligible for federal benefits. The overall program operations seem to conform to state rules and practices regardless of whether the child is eligible for federal funds.

The two federal education programs (P.L. 94-142 and Title I) have had considerable impact on the growth of special services in state education programs. P.L. 94-142 greatly expanded special education programs for the handicapped, but it did not start a separate program at the state or local level. Some local areas were providing extensive special education programs in separate schools or in the regular public schools prior to the federal legislation (e.g., Massachusetts), but many states had very limited special education programs. P.L. 94-142 motivated considerable growth in special education programs and especially fostered the growth of special classes in community-based settings.

In contrast, funds from Title I actually did provide the impetus to establish compensatory education in most states. Many states now provide compensatory education programs for children who need special remediation. Unlike many other federal programs, Title I continues to operate as a distinct program in every state. Even though Title I services are provided within the larger framework of the state's education system, states that operate a state-funded compensatory education program are required to keep those programs distinct from Title I.

Medicaid appears to be the one major federal program that has not been absorbed into preexisting state programs. By and large the federal Medicaid program provides the basic structure for state medical assistance programs for the poor. Six of the states we studied participate in this program; Arizona is the one state in the country that does not participate. In those six states Medicaid is a separate, identifiable program that operates in response to the federal program and its requirements. Even Medicaid funds, however, go into state medical assistance programs that sometimes, although infrequently, include program components other than those directly associated with the federal program.

The runaway youth program is another exception among the federal programs studied. These funds are awarded by the federal government directly to the runaway centers themselves. Most of these centers are operated by private agencies and do not fall under the purview of any state bureaucracy, although some also receive funds distributed by state agencies (e.g., state funds, Title XX). These runaway and youth service centers have grown in number since the early 1970s when 60 centers were identified. By 1980 over 200 were known to exist, but not all were supported by funds through the runaway youth program. In 1979 one national study surveyed 212 centers, and only 66 percent (or 140 centers) reported that they received funds through the runaway youth program (National Youth Work Alliance 1979). Many of these centers have formed a strong national organization, the National Youth Work Alliance, that dispenses information and training to its members and also lobbies for services for youth at the national and state levels.

Because of the integration of most of these federal programs into state-administered programs, state officials frequently view the federal programs as a funding source, rather than as the major determinant of the types or content of the services provided. The states, in fact, control the actual methods of operations of these programs. This perception, and the organizational reality that lies behind it, further hampers efforts to determine the influence of federal programs on services to any particular group of youth, including status offenders.

Some federal programs do have provisions that specify how funds are to be used, thereby determining how states will operate their programs. Although the state programs must conform to the federal program requirements in order to qualify for funds, state implementation of federal requirements may yield results that were either unintended or unanticipated at the federal level. For example, the AFDC-foster care program requires a judicial determination within at least six months from the time of placement in foster care to the effect that the conditions in the natural home are harmful for the child in question. This requirement was intended to safeguard the rights of both parents and children by curbing the power of caseworkers, who in some states previously had had a relatively free hand in removing children from their homes. In fact, in many states this required review is merely pro forma and is viewed only as a rubber-stamping process in order to acquire federal funds. The court does not perform the gatekeeping function that was originally intended by the federal legislation (Children's Defense Fund 1978).

Other provisions of these federal programs allow or suggest that states should operate their programs in a certain manner, but because these provisions are not mandated, states are not required to comply. One example of this type of federal influence occurs under the Medicaid program, which allows states to provide coverage to all financially needy children. States not only can elect to provide or not to provide such coverage, but they can define exactly what the category "financially needy" means. As of January 1979 only 20 states covered the category of all financially needy children, while several other states covered some subgroups of such children (U.S. Department of Health, Education, and Welfare 1979a). Although we know how many states extend this coverage, we cannot identify which classes of children and youth fall under the individual state definitions. We do know, however, that in some instances foster children and status offenders are eligible for Medicaid based on this provision.

Several state program administrators said that their program decisions are based on the total amount of available funds and that they do not consider whether those monies are state or federal. Financial and budget staff provide the state program officials with overall figures of available service funds, all of which are spent operating the program under the state-specified guidelines, which may or may not include the same objectives as those of related federal programs. The budget of a particular program often comes from a combination of sources, and the program operating staff frequently are unaware of all those sources. After localities submit bills for services provided, state officials, frequently in the management and budget office, decide which charges to assess against which monies. The fungibility of the federal funds, the potential overlapping of services or service categories in many of these programs, and the fact that many different groups compete for a share of the state and federal service monies all contribute to the difficulty of tracking federal funds to the extent necessary to determine their individual or collateral effects on status offenders.

FEDERAL FUNDS AND STATE EFFORTS TO DEINSTITUTIONALIZE STATUS OFFENDERS

Even where federal programs have contributed to expanding the range of services available for children and youth, the types of juveniles served through state social service programs have not altered dramatically. Status offenders comprise only a limited portion of the children and youth who are reached by any expanded service network. Those status offenders affected by these services are generally found to be eligible on the basis of some other characteristic, such as family income.

In some states it was possible to identify increases in expenditures for services since 1974 as being attributable, at least in part, to the existence of certain federal programs. For example, federal social service expenditures under the programs later combined into Title XX were $1.6 billion in fiscal year 1974 (U.S. Congress 1974), while in fiscal year 1980 expenditures under Title XX had risen to $2.7 billion. Almost all states have witnessed increases in their Medicaid programs, with national expenditures rising from $9.7 billion in 1974 to an estimated $19.7 billion in 1979 (U.S. Department of Health, Education, and Welfare 1979a). Many of these federal programs have grown substantially in the past years, but it remains difficult to determine who has benefited from this growth. The manner in which program data are reported limits the ability to determine whether or not any of the recipients are status offenders or dependent and neglected youth.

Clearly, OJJDP and LEAA funds were the most obvious, though not the largest, source of federal support for state deinstitutionalization activities. In order for a state to receive a formula grant under the Juvenile Justice Act, it had to make a commitment to deinstitutionalize status offenders and then demonstrate progress toward meeting that goal. However, the funds available through such grants were not particularly large. The small size of the available funds, in fact, discouraged some states (e.g., Utah) from participating in the Juvenile Justice Act program for some years, even though they were in the process of deinstitutionalizing their status offender populations. Other states (e.g., Pennsylvania) viewed these funds, no matter how small, as a source of additional funding in times of increasing budgetary strains. Still other states (e.g., Virginia) did not wish to lose these funds once they had become accustomed to having them.

States did not have to use any of the OJJDP and LEAA funds to deinstitutionalize status offenders. In those states where these funds were used to deinstitutionalize status offenders, the principle of deinstitutionalization already had been accepted, or conditions were favorable to its acceptance. One report claimed that 59 percent of the 1979 formula grants were used by the states to deinstitutionalize status offenders and dependent and neglected youth (Schwartz 1980). In addition, we do know that some of the maintenance of effort funds were spent in ways that affected status offenders, such as funding for runaway centers, but we do not know the exact amounts of monies spent in this fashion.

Once states made the decision to deinstitutionalize status offenders, other federal programs became important sources of money for alternative services. Federal funds, both program funds and research and demonstration funds, have been used to initiate and to provide continuing support for services in noninstitutional settings. These service initiatives are only infrequently recognized as being for status offenders or previously institutionalized youth; by and large such services have been used for broader categories of children, which often include status offenders. Research on the seven states revealed that when status offenders are receiving services they frequently are provided by the social service systems. These systems rely heavily on the more general federal programs that fund social services. Federal programs can be and have been used to implement the policies of deinstitutionalization, but the degree to which these programs were relied upon varied among the different states and localities.

Runaway centers were started outside the formal juvenile justice and social service systems to provide alternative placements for these youth. Before the centers came into existence, runaways who came into contact with these formal systems were locked up or transported home. The centers encourage youth to contact and return home of their own volition, but they do not require them to do so, and runaways are always free to leave the centers.

A sizable number of youth come into these centers through formal referrals from the juvenile justice system. In fiscal year 1979, 27 percent of those who were served by federally financed runaway centers were referred by such sources as the police, court intake, probation, and other juvenile justice agencies (Swicord 1980). Thus, the juvenile justice system appears to be using these alternative facilities, at least to some degree, instead of incarcerating youth who run away.

Funds for projects under the Runaway Youth Act increased from $5 million in fiscal year 1975 to $11 million in fiscal year 1978 and have remained constant at that level ever since. In the first year, the federal funds were distributed to 65 centers that provided services to 32,000 runaways. The number of centers that are federally funded reached a high of 166 in fiscal year 1978 but dropped to 158 in 1980; however, the number of youth served increased slightly in each of those years, reaching 45,000 in 1980. The runaway youth program does provide funds for services to youth other than runaways (e.g., homeless youth). In fact, in 1979 only 42 percent of the clients were runaways.

We have a more difficult time determining whether the more general federal programs are used for alternative services for status offenders. For example, in fiscal year 1979, Title XX provided $2.7 billion to states for their social service programs. The Department of Health, Education, and Welfare estimated that $1.7 billion (or 62 percent) of those funds were spent on services to children and youth (Kilgore and Salmon 1979). But even this information is not very helpful. A diverse range of services is included in this estimate, and it is not possible to determine how many of the service recipients were status offenders.

For some types of services that federal social service money supports, it is unclear what the real purpose of the service is or who actually is the client. For example, is day care a service that is provided to meet the needs of the child or the needs of the parent? Other federally funded services that may be available for status offenders are included in categories of services that are provided to the general population of all ages. Many services, such as family counseling or case management (which refers to the work involved with keeping records, and planning and arranging services), fall into these general categories. Some of these general services are for youth, and some portion of those services are for status offenders. Other services appear to be more readily identifiable as services to troublesome youth or children deemed to be in need of services.

TYPES OF SERVICES AVAILABLE

Traditionally, public welfare and social service agencies provided services to poor children and their families, children in need of protection, and dependent and neglected children. In most cases public child welfare services did not include services to status offenders. One by-product of the deinstitutionalization movement in several states has been the tendency to transfer responsibility for serving status offenders from the juvenile justice system to the social service system. Although the characteristics and perhaps the needs of status offenders are likely to differ from more traditional juvenile clients, public social service agencies for children and youth have not dramatically changed in response to the new clientele. Where social service agencies have developed or adapted services for status offenders, such services generally are provided in limited number and as part of the existing program structure and delivery methods.

There has been some packaging of services specifically for status offenders, such as those delivered through special centers that provide services and training during the day. The number of group homes, which some consider to be more appropriate settings for adolescents than large institutions or foster family homes, has increased during the last decade. Review of the state service programs did show that the majority of publicly provided services for children and youth are for the more traditional types of clients (e.g., an abused or neglected child, or one needing day care to ameliorate his or her environment or to free an adult for work). Such services and methods of service provision may frequently be unrelated to the needs of status offenders.

This is one of the reasons that runaway centers were developed in the late 1960s and the 1970s. They were not part of either the existing juvenile justice system or the traditional social service delivery systems. These centers were located in places where runaways could most often be found and were extremely low-key in their orientation. Youth on the run tend to be very wary of authority. Frequently, for example, the way in which the police dealt with such youth was to lock them up or return them home, and neither outcome was particularly relished. Many of these alternative centers began before the Runaway Youth Act was passed, using primarily local and private funds, although federal funds from several sources were used, notably LEAA (often through the state planning agencies) and the National Institute of Mental Health. After the Runaway Youth Act legitimatized these types of service providers and made funds available specifically for their operation, the number of centers dramatically increased, although various funding sources continue to provide support.

Another factor restraining the potential expansion of the types of services available for status offenders is the current economic situation. Among close-ended federal grant programs, such as Title XX, almost all states are spending their entire allocations. In addition, several of the open-ended programs have experienced substantial increases in expenditures over the past several years. These higher levels of expenditures do not always reflect expanded service programs but can be the outcome of attempts to maintain existing levels of services. In fact, in some instances states have been cutting back on types of services that they offer even while incurring rising expenditures. For example, several states have eliminated certain optional medical services from their Medicaid programs. In other instances, states have responded to the lack of increased federal funding levels by enlarging the state and local funds used for those programs. In any event, states and local governments are finding it harder and harder to continue to raise funding levels.

SERVICES FOR STATUS OFFENDERS

Because status offenders are not identified as such in program data, we do not know the total amount of the federal funds that states use to provide services for these youth. There are no federal requirements that data be tabulated in a fashion that would reveal the amount expended on services for status offenders, so most states do not maintain such records. Although projects funded by the Runaway Youth Act are required to report the number of their clients who are runaways, they do not have to report either the number who are status offenders or how much of their funds are spent on such youth. We were able to identify some special services for status offenders that were federally funded; however, the diverse purposes and client populations of the state service programs limited our ability to define how the general federal social service programs affected services for status offenders.

Three of the states in our study—Louisiana, Massachusetts, and Pennsylvania—had established Title XX funded social service programs specifically for status offenders. The content of these programs varied by state, but they often included counseling, life skills education, and transportation. While the other four states did not package services for status offenders, they did identify such youth as potential clients for certain of their Title XX services, such as counseling or court processing services, and transportation specifically for runaways.

Under AFDC-foster care rules, states can receive partial federal reimbursement for the maintenance of status offenders who are placed in foster care and are eligible for AFDC. Even if a status offender does not qualify for AFDC-foster care, placement in a foster home or institution often allows the child to be eligible for services using funds from Title XX, Title IV-B, and Medicaid. All such eligibility rules are the prerogative of the state. In the past, when status offenders were placed in care under the auspices of the juvenile justice system, they frequently did not receive benefits from these federal sources because either the federal funds did not flow into that system or federal rules prevented coverage of "convicted" youth. In many states, foster care placements for status offenders are now administered by the social service agency, and thus the youth are more likely to be determined eligible for the various programs. Other states have developed interagency arrangements that prescribe procedures for determining when federal funds can be tapped.

Even programs that were originally targeted directly at status offenders have diversified their approach to juveniles. The runaway youth program originally made grants to centers to provide shelter and services to runaways. Eventually, more and different kinds of youth came into the facilities seeking assistance. Many are considered to be homeless; that is, they are youth who are not technically runaways, since they have parental permission to be away from home. Others who came to the centers, however, are still living at home (29 percent in fiscal year 1979). Many of the centers have become comprehensive centers that provide services to youth in general, not just to runaways. Data are not reported in such a way that we can determine how many of those served are status offenders, but it is likely that other youth as well as runaways, whether labeled as status offenders or not, are being served by these multiservice centers.

When states have decided to extend social and educational service coverage to status offenders, they have had to examine the federal eligibility rules, some of which are mandatory and very specific. For example, states must allow AFDC recipients to be eligible for Medicaid. Other federal eligibility rules may be optional or vague or left to the states to define. Where discretion is allowed, states have defined the federal criteria to fit their individual needs and programs. In some cases these interpretations allow program coverage of status offenders. The operative consideration for the availability of services to status offenders is not whether the federal rules allow coverage of status offenders but whether the state has the desire to interpret those rules to cover such youth.

For example, the federal Medicaid program allows the optional coverage of "financially needy children." While the Department of Health and Human Services has defined four groups of children who could be considered to fit into this category, states may define the category as they wish. States that elect to cover "financially needy children" frequently extend coverage to children in out-of-home placements, such as foster care, under the federally defined subgroup of children for whom a public agency is responsible. Under this subgroup states also can cover status offenders who are in foster care or small nonsecure residential facilities (U.S. Department of Health, Education, and Welfare 1978). However, only one state (Virginia) among the seven studied was found to use the federal provision in this way by specifically spelling out eligibility requirements for status offenders (Virginia Department of Health 1979).

Title XX allows states to specify eligibility rules in several different ways. For example, under the federal group eligibility rules, a state may offer some services to a specified group if 75 percent are members of families with incomes below 90 percent of the state's median income level. While several of the study states have made delinquents eligible on a group basis, only one (Louisiana) appears to include status offenders as a covered group (Louisiana Department of Health and Human Resources 1979).

Another federally allowed Title XX eligibility procedure is that states may provide protective services to all children in need of them, without regard to other eligibility criteria. Of the seven states studied, all but Arizona and Wisconsin include runaways among the types of juveniles who are eligible for protective services. Two of the seven states, Massachusetts and Utah, have provisions stating that status offenders are in need of such services (Massachusetts Department of Public Welfare 1977, 1978, 1979; Utah Department of Social Services 1979, no date). Under this type of provision, Title XX services may be provided to all status offenders, not just those who can meet the income requirements. In addition, foster children in all seven states were found to be eligible for all needed Title XX services through one provision or another. This includes children who were placed in foster care because they were found to be dependent and neglected, as well as status offenders or even delinquents, depending on state policy.

While some status offenders can be identified as part of the client population of the federal education programs—most notably the institutionalized children served under Title I—these programs for the most part do not connect eligibility for services to legal status. Eligiblity for service under Title I and P.L. 94-142 is based on need for that particular educational service, and only those status offenders who exhibit an educational problem would be eligible for help.

When states have decided to serve status offenders through their general social service systems, they often have found ways to define federal eligibility rules so as to provide program coverage to those youth. Some states do not have special provisions for status offenders; they simply treat them as they do any other children needing service. In such cases status offenders are screened by the general eligibility criteria. Other states, however, have sought ways to ensure coverage of status offenders and have developed special eligibility categories or refinements. This allows services to be available to the entire class of youth without excluding some because they do not meet such general eligibility criteria as income limits. Where special status offender provisions have been enacted, it is easier to provide services to these youth.

STATE INTERPRETATIONS OF FEDERAL PLACEMENT INCENTIVES

Even when federal programs contain incentives that might cause inappropriate placements, the manner in which states interpret or use such provisions actually determines their impact on status offenders. Certain provisions of federal programs allow for care in institutional settings. While such care is included to meet the purposes and goals of the programs, the existence of funds for institutional care is a possible inducement for placing youth in order for them to qualify for federal reimbursement as opposed to placing them in response to their needs. In these times of limited resources it is easy to imagine scenarios in which state and local officials encourage types of services and placements that allow funds from other sources to pick up a larger share of the tab. If a status offender must be served at all, then one option is to get that youth into a situation in which the services can be partially financed by sources other than state or local funds. Certain placements may allow a previously ineligible juvenile to become eligible for some federal program. For example, placement in foster care may allow a child to become eligible for Medicaid services. The youth may have already been eligible for other programs, but certain placements may qualify for a larger amount of federal reimbursement for the total costs of care.

Whether they are in family homes, group homes, or institutions, all foster children may be eligible for a variety of federally funded services even if they do not qualify for AFDC-foster care. Social service program structures have developed around foster care. Foster children not only receive financial support through foster care maintenance programs, but they can receive health services through Medicaid, and social services through Title XX and federal child welfare services. In addition, these children and youth may be eligible for an even wider range of services, such as Title I or special education programs. Even Arizona, which does not participate in the federal Medicaid program, operates a state-funded health program for children in foster care.

Medicaid pays both the medical and maintenance costs of care in medical institutions (i.e., general hospitals, skilled nursing facilities, intermediate care facilities, intermediate care facilities for the mentally retarded, and psychiatric facilities). The availability of this source of federal funds to cover maintenance costs may act as an incentive for placements in those types of institutions. Five of the six study states that participate in the Medicaid program have higher than national average rates of provision of certain types of institutional care to children under age 18. Due to the manner in which the data are reported, it is not possible to determine if possibly inappropriate placements or services to juvenile status offenders have any role in these service use patterns.

Title I operates under a multitiered funding and client-identification structure that may seem to create some incentives for out-of-home placements. Under Title I, a higher rate of federal funding generally is available for children in residential settings than for children living at home, for approximately the same service.

Even though there are inducements in some of these federal programs for making inappropriate placements, there is no evidence that states are using the provisions for such purposes. In addition, the program data do not identify whether those who are institutionalized through these programs are status offenders.

SUMMARY

An examination of the influence of these nine federal programs on the deinstitutionalization of status offenders must be considered within the broader context of federal activity. While the federal grant programs are an important factor contributing to the expression of federal policy in the states, other federal legislation (such as that in the areas of civil rights and welfare) and federal court decisions have also influenced state deinstitutionalization efforts. Many of these federal actions were reflections of national movements in the areas of children's rights and justice system reform. The specific programs studied here may have had limited impact on decisions to initiate the deinstitutionalization of status offenders, but the broader federal influences have been significant.

Once deinstitutionalization was adopted as a policy by the states, Juvenile Justice Act and LEAA monies were used to effect deinstitutionalization of status offenders, and the federal social service and education grant programs were used to reinforce the movement to deinstitutionalize by supporting alternative services. The decision to use these federal funds to deinstitutionalize and to provide services to status offenders was not made at the federal level; rather, state implementation of federal programs adapted them to respond to the new state policies. Both the officials who are involved in actual service delivery and the state financial staffs have manipulated federal funding sources to offset the costs of their program initiatives to deinstitutionalize status offenders.

Generally, the types of services available for status offenders are similar to those that are provided to the general social service clientele. With the two exceptions of shelters funded under the Runaway Youth Act program and isolated cases of specific packaging of services for status offenders, changes in service delivery to accommodate the needs of status offenders have not been dramatic. This is in part a response to tightening federal, state, and local budgets and in part a response to the fact that status offenders continue to comprise only a limited portion of the children and youth who are served by these social service systems. When states have decided to provide services to status offenders, they have often been able to adapt federal eligibility rules to provide coverage for this client group. Eligibility for one federal program, in addition to allowing payment for services covered by that program, often will have the collateral effect of opening up eligibility for a number of other federal programs.

8 Conclusions

We found on the basis of our state case studies that: (1) the vast majority of adjudicated status offenders have been removed from traditional institutional facilities; (2) there has been a decline in the use of preadjudicatory detention for youth who have been charged with status offenses; (3) fewer youth who are labeled as status offenders are entering the juvenile justice system; and (4) for those status offenders who are diverted to some other service system, the predominant forms of out-of-home care reportedly are group home and foster care arrangements (the choice between the two often depends on the level of commitment and the amount of resources that a state has to devote to the development of alternative types of facilities). It is unclear what is happening to youth who commit status offenses but who do not enter the juvenile court system or its closely related diversion programs. Many of the respondents in the state and local areas are of the opinion that these youth are being ignored altogether. There has been some suggestion that some status offenders are being treated in private mental health facilities, but this issue has not been systematically researched.

In the first part of this chapter, we discuss why the various goals of deinstitutionalization have been implemented differentially, and we review the theoretical determinants of this process. The second part of the chapter focuses on the conclusions to be drawn from our principal findings.

200

IMPLEMENTATION: THE POSSIBILITIES AND LIMITS OF FEDERAL ACTION

Based on our analysis of state and local deinstitutionalization programs, we may draw several conclusions about the implementation of federal policies. These conclusions apply not only to this particular policy but also to many other policies that share the structural characteristics outlined in chapter 4. We start with the assumption that the basic implementation framework is the federal-state-local, grant-in-aid structure. Certain modifications in that framework can be made and will be discussed, but the essential organizational structures and the means for distributing power will remain intact. We think that for social welfare programs like deinstitutionalization, this pattern will be in force for an extended time. Certainly for the short run there appears to be no shift in favor of more federal influence.

As noted in chapter 4, this complicated bureaucratic structure further complicates a difficult implementation task. Implementation, it will be recalled, depends on, among other things, the quality of leadership in the various bureaucratic units; the clarity, consistency, and agreement on goals; the solvability of the problem; the ability to coordinate and control subordinate units; the sufficiency of resources; and political support. These factors make implementation more difficult when the implementation system is decentralized and loosely coordinated, with faulty information and weak tools for control and compliance. Key agencies within the system have large amounts of autonomy, both from each other and from higher levels of authority, but there also are countervailing forces. Federal initiatives in the social welfare field are often responsive to pressures arising out of states and communities, and reciprocal supportive relationships are formed. Federal initiatives take a variety of forms, including the enactment of laws, rules, and policies, various kinds of funding arrangements, and technical assistance. The influence of these initiatives ultimately depends on the responsiveness of the local actors.

The juvenile justice system is probably even more decentralized than other social welfare programs in that there is a strong tradition of local control. The federal presence is of relatively recent origin and is slight compared to state and local influence. Most significant is the considerable autonomy of the juvenile court judge—the key discretionary point in the system. Other actors and agencies at the local level also serve to decentralize the system. These agencies are in other public fields, such as health, child welfare, social services, and education, and they have their own agendas and priorities. Youth who are labeled as status offenders by the juvenile justice system compete with the clientele of these systems for services. Moreover, youth who are referred to these other agencies are classified and served according to the terms of those agencies rather than the terms of the juvenile justice system. Autonomy is even more pronounced when the receiving agencies are private providers of service.

Because of the decentralization of authority and the latitude of discretion at the local level, our method of analysis was to start at the ground level—an approach called "backward mapping"—rather than at the top as with conventional implementation analysis, which tries to see to what extent initiatives from above are being carried out below. Backward mapping seemed more appropriate, given the working hypothesis of this study—that the most important centers of influence in the deinstitutionalization of status offenders operate at the local level—and given the characteristics of the implementation system. Federal influences are important, but it is local support, which will vary from community to community, that determines the type of influence and the nature of its effects.

DEINSTITUTIONALIZATION: A POSITIVE AND NEGATIVE MANDATE

If the goal of federal policy is to achieve relative uniformity in the change of behavior at the state and local levels, then implementation will succeed to the extent that the characteristics of the decarceration mandate can be replicated. The decarceration portion of the mandate required only the removal of status offenders from correctional facilities. The statement of the rule was relatively clear; it was a negative duty in that officials were told not to do something, rather than to take action. Monitoring compliance was not difficult technically; results could be measured or counted. The mandate prohibited the court from using the correctional system. It operated outside the control of the court, a key discretionary and autonomous part of the implementation structure. Most actors concurred with this portion of the mandate. There was some dissension to be sure—there always is on important matters of social policy—but compared to other goals of deinstitutionalization (e.g., the provision of alternative services), there was considerably more agreement on the decarceration requirement.

Of course, we are dealing here in matters of degree. No law or mandate is completely airtight. There may be definitional problems on the order of those discussed in chapter 3 (e.g., what is a status offender, or a secure facility, or a community-based facility). The autonomy of key actors may represent a powerful source of resistance to the mandate; a strong-willed judge, for instance, can evade the mandate by upgrading or relabeling the offense. Correctional or court statistics may mask the true nature of the case (e.g., data may not be organized in a manner conducive to monitoring compliance). But taking these factors into account, our data suggest that most adjudicated status offenders have been removed from and are no longer being sent to state correctional institutions. As far as this particular portion of the deinstitutionalization mandate is concerned, implementation seems to have been fairly successful. Moreover, we have detected no strong impulse to reconsider this part of the policy decision.

The prohibition on placing status offenders in secure detention is a somewhat different matter. This too is a relatively clear mandate and is more easily monitored, although there can be some slippage, particularly when detention is used as stopgap measure. For a variety of reasons, there is far less consensus on this requirement than on the prohibition of postadjudicatory incarceration. With the option of secure placements foreclosed, detention is perceived as the only available secure alternative. Those who perceive a need for a secure alternative have urged that detention be retained as a short-term option for status offenders. The police feel particularly strongly about this issue, as do a good many judges and their court staffs. In practically every state and local area that we investigated, there is strong sentiment for keeping or restoring some form of secure detention for status offenders (notably for runaways). In California a last-minute compromise saved the state from adopting a detention statute that would have been out of compliance with JJDPA. Now, the 1980 amendments to JJDPA reflect the widespread sentiment for detention for certain purposes. As a result of vigorous lobbying efforts from the National Council of Juvenile and Family Court Judges and other groups, states may now use detention for status offenders who run away from a nonsecure placement in violation of a court order. The prohibition on the use of detention is an instance in which a clear negative mandate may not continue to work in light of the growing opposition at the state and local levels. The decarceration prohibition was a negative mandate; but in contrast to the detention prohibition, it carried a higher degree of consensus on goals, there were fewer actors involved, monitoring was easier, and it was cheaper to implement.

Implementation is more problematic when state and local officials are mandated to do something, such as divert status offenders from the juvenile justice system or provide alternative services, than when they are told to refrain from doing something. Under present circumstances, there is very little that the federal or even state government can do about the autonomy of the juvenile court. Jurisdiction can be removed from the court, and the judge can be prohibited from taking any action on behalf of status offenders; but as long as the court does have jurisdiction, then the judges cannot be required to do things to or on behalf of these youth. We have seen judges refuse to have anything to do with status offenders (Louisiana); we have seen judges kill well-developed, functioning deinstitutionalization programs (Pima County, Arizona); we have seen them circumvent those programs altogether (Richmond, Virginia); and we have seen them play a crucial role in developing such programs (Maricopa County, Arizona). Unless the judge is willing to cooperate in promoting diversion, there is little real chance for success. This was even true in Salt Lake County, which had developed an extensive diversion program. Given the location and power of the court in the implementation structure, the federal and state governments will not be able to achieve uniformity in results. All else remaining equal, there will be variation for this reason alone.

THE ROLE OF OTHER ACTORS

If judges want to implement deinstitutionalization, there are certain things that they can do on their own: They can tighten up the use of detention, or they can refuse to send youth to certain kinds of facilities while encouraging the use of other types. However, there are limits. Judges cannot build alternative facilities or dictate that providers accept every child sent their way. Depending on the force of personality, a judge can cajole or even persuade agencies to provide services, but he or she ordinarily cannot compel them to do so.

Even with fairly clear mandates it is often difficult to achieve compliance on the part of autonomous agencies and programs, such as child protection services, welfare, mental health, education, and private providers, that have other agendas and responsibilities. For most if not all of these agencies, status offenders are not their major concern. Indeed, the assumption of responsibility for status offenders may be viewed as detrimental to their mission, and they may refuse to recognize these youth as part of their clientele, preferring to try to shift the burden of expense to some other agency. At a minimum, this older and more unruly clientele will cause more trouble. There have been reports of difficulties in placing these older youth in foster homes. We noted that in some of the states and local areas and facilities there was a tendency either to reject status offenders outright or to discharge them if they misbehaved.

DISAGREEMENT OVER ENDS AND MEANS

Implementation issues pass from the problematic to the acute when one tries to assess what happens to status offenders who are in alternative programs and placements. In part this type of problem arises from disagreement over policy goals. Problems of evaluating performance, of course, are not unique to the treatment of status offenders. Since there is disagreement on the best way to ameliorate the difficulties of many clients of human services agencies, on what to do to or for them, and on what success is and how best to evaluate it, it is not possible in any systematic or scientific way to assess what the impact of these policies has been. The best available observations, at present, are crude indicators or proxies of success—the youth stays in the foster home without running away for a certain period of time, or the youth seems "happy and reasonably adjusted" (whatever that means) in a group home, or the conditions in a setting approach some conception or a priori standard of "normal" and "humane" (e.g., individualized rooms, varying amounts of privacy and freedom to come and go, attendance in the regular schools). It may be that these are appropriate measures of successful implementation, and we will have more to say about this later. But the point here is that as long as there is no *official agreement* on the goals of the policy and the evaluative criteria, there is no way to decide whether the implementation of that policy has been successful. And that is the situation with most programs and services for status offenders.

Although there appears to be little agreement on what alternative placements for status offenders are supposed to do, the establishment of noninstitutional services and placements remains part of deinstitutionalization policy. We have seen from the state and local area studies, as well as from the facility analysis, that there are several situations in which alternative services and programs have been established and are being used. In other words, there has been some implementation not only of the decarceration and detention prohibitions, but also of the affirmative side of deinstitutionalization—diversion and the development of alternative services. Under what circumstances does this come about? The various theories of implementation that were discussed earlier shed light on this question.

USES OF IMPLEMENTATION THEORY

For analytic purposes, Zald (1980) presented a linear, sequential-sounding implementation scheme—the growth of ideas, the mobilization of social groups (the carriers of the ideas), the reception of the ideas at the state and local levels, the intervention of the federal government, and an analysis of the results of implementation. Although this simplified model is useful in identifying the major factors, the interaction between factors is more complicated than the model suggests. Instead of linearlike relations, most of the relations between the essential actors at various levels were reciprocal, and more often were simultaneous rather than sequential.

Ideas of deinstitutionalization took hold in various states and local areas at different times and were argued in terms of different issues. In some states, deinstitutionalization focused in large part on a single issue (e.g., prohibition of detention in California); in other states (Wisconsin, Pennsylvania) deinstitutionalization was a series of measures—a program that not only included prohibitions on detention and incarceration but also included separation of status offenders from delinquents, the provision of alternative placements and services to youth in need, and diversion. Sometimes the whole package was adopted by groups advocating deinstitutionalization, and was pressed forward as a unit; but more often the approach was incremental. When some of the goals of deinstitutionalization were realized, these groups and other actors would go on to the next step. In many states the growth and transformation of ideas was a continual process that evolved over a period of years. And, of course, the interaction among ideas, mobilization, and change becomes even more complicated when the deinstitutionalization of status offenders is considered as part of much broader currents, such as the deinstitutionalization of other populations, the legal rights and civil rights explosion, and the recognition of legal rights for children and youth.

Similarly, the impact of the federal government was complicated and diverse; it extended beyond the influence of the Juvenile Justice and Delinquency Prevention Act. The federal government was a source of financial support as well as of ideas and legitimacy well before JJDPA was enacted (e.g., President's Commission, the *Gault* decision). Discretionary funds were given for projects and advocacy groups, which generated more ideas and led to additional mobilization efforts. In some instances, federal efforts were instrumental in helping to change the political culture of the state and local areas. For example, staff paid for out of federal grants became employees of state and local agencies and argued from within for deinstitutionalization (as in Wisconsin).

The federal influence, in all of its diverse manifestations, varied in impact even where local environments were hospitable to deinstitutionalization. In Maricopa County, Arizona, for example, there was some downward flow of ideas, but essentially deinstitutionalization was a local effort that was largely independent of both state and federal government. In other local areas, of course, the federal influence was rejected altogether.

The picture that emerges, then, is one of great variety and complexity. Ideas circulated. Groups and agencies or parts of agencies, and various federal, state, and local officials interacted with each other, sometimes in a more or less sequential fashion but more often in reciprocal relationships. Mobilization of groups on the basis of ideas led to the enunciation of policies and the development of new projects, which mobilized more people, which led to more ideas, more mobilization efforts, and so forth. But why, then, did some ideas take and others not?

THE ROLE OF STATE AND LOCAL LEADERSHIP

The most important variable or factor, at least according to Sabatier and Mazmanian (1980), is leadership—the commitment and skill of the relevant actors. Clearly this was found to be true in this study. The most important leaders were the juvenile court judges. In at least one case, opposition of the local judge did not curtail the deinstitutionalization initiative because other key actors took up the cause (e.g., Winnebago County, Wisconsin). In the main, however, if the local judges were not sympathetic and were unwilling to act, it was less likely that alternative services would be provided. This general finding applied most clearly to those areas that were within the discretion of the court. In the case of the prohibition on secure confinement in institutions, however, the role of the judge was less significant, with one exception: if the judge was sufficiently opposed to the mandate so that he or she was willing to engage in relabeling, then decarceration could be partially curtailed, as was the situation in only one locality in our study (Richmond). In the absence of this condition, however, the more relevant actors for decarceration would be located in other parts of the implementation system—the legislature, the executive, the department of corrections, or wherever power resided for this particular issue.

TRACTABILITY OF THE PROBLEM

Leadership, though, is not enough for successful implementation. An important implementation factor is the tractability of the problem. The contrast is between prohibitions on incarceration and detention, on the one hand, and provision of alternative services and placements and diversion programs, on the other. It is clearly easier to implement a prohibition, a decision that says "no more"; both the goals and the evaluative criteria are relatively self-evident. For other reasons, it may be difficult to reach a decision on whether the command should be issued; in Massachusetts and California, for example, an enormous industry stood to lose a great deal if the mandate were issued (and implemented). But given the political will, the problem can be solved relatively easily.

The situation is different with other parts of deinstitutionalization. Tractability is related to other factors that affect implementation—the coherence or lack of coherence of the causal theory underlying the policy; or the clarity, consistency, and relative priorities of the policy's goals. These variables in turn affect issues of coordination and control within the implementation system. In other words, problems will also tend to be intractable (and chances of implementation success will decline) to the extent that the causal theory lacks coherence, or goals lack clarity, consistency, and priorities. Or tractability will decline to the extent that the implementation system lacks coordination and control; and lack of coordination and control will increase to the extent that goals lack coherence, clarity, consistency, and priorities.

In the provision of alternative services and programs for status offenders, there are conflicts over goals; goals are ambiguous, and there are differences in priorities. As noted in chapter 3, there are lively disputes as to what constitutes a status offender in actual behavioral terms, what these behaviors mean, and what, if anything, should be done about them. There appears to be little coherence in theories of rehabilitation of status offenders or crime prevention, little agreement on the order of priorities. When goals are ambiguous, or in conflict, or lack clear priorities, it is easier for autonomous agencies or parts of agencies to perceive the goals in terms of their own organizational needs, which may or may not be consistent with the perceptions of goals emanating from other units in the implementation system.

POLITICAL SUPPORT AND AVAILABILITY OF RESOURCES

Another cluster of factors involves political support, the participation of actors external (more or less) to the process, and the availability of resources. In all of the states, the deinstitutionalization coalitions tended to fall apart once detention and incarceration prohibitions were enacted and it came time to do something about alternative services and placements. Again, we note the differences between mandatory prohibitions and affirmative requirements. In most of the states, political support had to be rallied for the mandatory prohibitions; with few exceptions, these were highly visible struggles. But once enacted, a great deal of participation by other actors was not necessary; nor was it necessary to provide resources. In California, no state money was provided at all for alternatives to detention; yet the detention prohibition had a significant impact in that it was implemented. Creating new programs is a different story, however. Mobilization efforts have to continue, and resources have to be made available. In several instances we saw that this happened (e.g., the development of the Youth Services Program in Salt Lake County). Continual efforts and institution-building were required. But in other localities, there was a failure to implement this stage.

It is important to emphasize that lack of alternative programs for status offenders at the local level may well be attributable to insufficient resources rather than to deliberate resistance to the deinstitutionalization mandate. Local implementation efforts are frequently hampered by the inability of localities to extract money from the state or county for the development of needed services or even to reallocate funds previously committed. Deinstitutionalization was undertaken partially on the assumption that it would be less expensive (or at least no more expensive) to serve youth on a noninstitutional basis. This assumption is now proving to be doubtful, particularly from the perspective of local areas that are under considerable pressure from parents, police, school systems, and the like to provide services to youth who previously were either ignored or institutionalized at the state's expense. It is easy to understand why, caught in this dilemma, many localities have made little or no progress in developing noninstitutional services.

A final variable is the pressure for local variation. Here, we note the pressure on the detention prohibitions, most notably in California but also in Virginia, which arises from a number of sources. There may be disagreement over policies and programs, but there also may be considerable justification, in fact, for local variation. In certain substantive areas, such as family and youth policy, resistance to federal and state-level control may be very strong; it draws its strength from history and political theory, as well as from tradition.

The variables or factors shed light on what happened in the several states and local areas. At this stage of theory-building, there are no weights or agreement on the relative importance of factors other than the importance of leadership. There is no evidence as to which variable or combination of variables is crucial. Furthermore, the variables are not dichotomous. Leadership is essential, but how much leadership? For example, presumably really strong judicial leadership would lessen the importance of some of the other variables, as is the case with actors who are external to the implementation system, such as advocacy groups. Conversely, a somewhat weaker judge would be persuaded to go along if strong citizen groups could mobilize the resources for demonstration projects.

We sense from the local area studies that combinations of factors were necessary for implementation, although in varying degrees. Deinstitutionalization worked smoothly in Maricopa and Salt Lake Counties, where judicial leadership was supported by groups and agencies, resources, sustained public opinion, and agreement on certain goals. Where some of these variables subsided over time, such as public opinion or the availability of resources, progress toward deinstitutionalization became uncertain and faltered.

The lack of certainty or predictability of factors considered important for implementation comports with the reality of uncertainty and discretion found at the local level. The autonomy and critical role of the juvenile court judge alone guarantees uncertainty at this stage of the implementation system. Most of the other factors also contribute to the variability.

This basic fact of discretion at the local level has important policy implications. In chapter 4 the implementation analysis was described as backward mapping. Instead of assuming that policies emanating from the top influenced behavior below (that is, forward mapping), the approach was to examine how discretion was exercised at the bottom and then to see to what extent, if any, policies and rules affected the exercise of that discretion. The normative implications of this research are to accept the fact of discretion and variability, and to see to what extent and in what manner that discretion can be influenced. Richard Elmore (1979-1980:604) describes the analysis as follows:

[Backward mapping] begins with a statement of the specific behavior at the lowest level of the implementation process that generates the need for a policy. . . . Having established a relatively precise target at the lowest level of the system, the analysis backs up through the structure of implementing agencies, asking at each level two questions: What is the ability of this unit to affect the behavior that is the target of the policy? And what resources does this unit require in order to have that effect? In the final stage of analysis the analyst or policymaker describes a policy that directs resources at the organizational units likely to have the greatest effect.

In several of the states and local areas, the federal government generally followed the normative or prescriptive aspects of backward mapping. Discretion throughout this implementation system was accepted as a fact of life and one that the federal government not only had to live with, but also used to achieve its policy goals. Even with a willing judge, deinstitutionalization requires a supportive local environment and alternative facilities. Here, the federal government played a significant role.

THE ROLE OF THE FEDERAL GOVERNMENT

The federal government was a source of ideas, technical assistance, and financial support that allowed groups and organizations at state and local levels to mobilize resources necessary to effect deinstitutionalization of status offenders. Social reform groups and organizations needed these kinds of federal support to translate their ideas into action. By distributing grants to organizations for advocacy activities, by providing demonstration project funds, by providing general sources of funds that could be tapped, and by synthesizing and disseminating ideas and information, the federal government played a crucial part in the process of change.

We have previously discussed the role of the federal government as a source of ideas—how court decisions, commission reports, legislation, and rules helped to stimulate thinking about deinstitutionalization and the treatment of status offenders, and served to legitimize the activities of local people and organizations. There was also technical assistance. Prior to 1974, some federal funds had been used to explore different aspects of deinstitutionalization by supporting individual research efforts and disseminating the results; such efforts, however, were relatively minor. Most of these efforts have continued to originate with LEAA and the Department of Health and Human Services (especially through its administration of the Runaway Youth Act). Such information usually focused on the legal and service aspects of deinstitutionalization and helped states and local areas to mount their own deinstitutionalization efforts.

Federal financial support can be distinguished by the extent of its emphasis on serving status offenders. One category consists of programs that are specifically targeted, either totally or partially, for status offenders. Such programs include those that are funded through JJDPA and the Runaway Youth Act. How important have these various sources of federal funds been for the implementation of deinstitutionalization policies? Under the Runaway Youth Act, the federal government made direct grants to establish or continue operation of facilities that provide temporary shelter and counseling to runaway youth. The recipient facilities were required to be outside the juvenile justice system. At the present time, funds are provided directly to 164 local projects throughout the country, serving approximately 43,000 runaways annually. All of these facilities have other sources of funds. In fact, the runaway project funds are considered seed money, and projects are expected to obtain other replacement sources of funds over time. It appears as though this federal program has been important in assisting the development of continued funding for many locally based runaway centers.

The JJDPA formula grant carried a mandate to deinstitutionalize in order for states to receive funds, but it was not a large amount. Although it took some time, all states now participate in this program. In some states (e.g., Utah), it was thought that the costs of complying with the federal mandate exceeded the financial benefits of doing so. In other states (e.g., Pennsylvania), important actors wanted the relatively small amount of JJDPA money available, apparently to help them through a period of financial stringency. It was not so much the size of the federal funds compared to the state budget, but their marginal value. In California and Virginia, the potential loss of JJDPA funds was used as an argument for saving the detention prohibition in legislative battles to eliminate it. The most that can be said about the JJDPA money is that it helped when conditions were favorable. There was not much evidence (or at least few individuals at the state and local levels would admit to it) that JJDPA money was crucial in either placing deinstitutionalization on the agenda or in forcing its implementation.

Another category consists of programs that, though not directly associated with status offenders, can be used by federal agencies to serve such youth as part of their more broadly defined service population. These programs tend to be of much larger magnitude. Sometimes the recognition of status offenders as possible clients is only a minor element of the program, and there is no guarantee that funds actually will be spent on them. Some of the programs in this second category, while not targeted for status offenders, nonetheless have a historical affinity with those programs that are targeted to serve them (e.g., programs grouped under the Administration for Children, Youth and Families (ACYF), which, prior to the establishment of LEAA and OJJDP, were the responsibility of organizational units within HEW). These units were the forerunners of the Youth Development Bureau, which is now located in ACYF. A second example is the LEAA program. LEAA's participation in programs for status offenders is tangential to its broader concerns with delinquency prevention policies and with youth who are involved with the courts. Through the maintenance of effort provision, 19.15 percent of LEAA's funds were to be used for projects concerning juveniles. These funds have accounted for well over $100 million each year since the provision was enacted. For reasons discussed in chapter 4, we cannot determine how much of these LEAA funds have been targeted for or expended on status offenders, but at least some were.

The LEAA discretionary funds, both those used for projects funded directly by the federal agency and those distributed through the state planning agencies, have supported a wide range of deinstitutionalization projects.

Other federal programs in this second category include foster care, Medicaid, special education, and social services. These programs do not have any particular historical affinity with the programs targeted either directly or indirectly for status offenders.

In our opinion the discretionary funds administered primarily by LEAA and HEW were the most critical sources of support. Federal sources of financial support were most important when they aided those groups and organizations (both public and private) at the state and local levels that were actively pursuing deinstitutionalization goals. In most of the states and local areas in which deinstitutionalization projects were successful, some sort of LEAA or HEW discretionary money was provided. It may have funded a demonstration project, paid for some staff, assisted an advocacy group, or provided planning money. By itself it was never sufficient, but in many cases it was clearly important.

Local-level groups and organizations also have been able to obtain discretionary funding from the more general federal funding sources, that is, programs in the second category that do not mention status offenders but are broad enough to include them, particularly Title XX. The distribution of these federal funds is made at the state level. By approving grant applications, state agencies with no specific emphasis on status offenders acknowledged that these youth were included in their more generally defined target populations. In some communities, federal funds had a multiplier effect; that is, federal seed money was used to establish and prove the need for a certain service. If the locality recognized the usefulness of such a service, other funding sources were usually located to continue the facility's operation when the seed money was cut back or eliminated. These replacement funding sources often included state or local public funds or private funds (e.g., the United Way), but they also included more general federal funding sources (e.g., Title XX). As a case in point, the Salt Lake County Youth Services Program is now funded in part by Title XX money.

It is very difficult to make any judgment about the relative importance of the general programs in the second category. It is difficult to trace the impact of federal programs on status offenders when federal funds are allocated to states for broadly defined purposes and populations, and when states control their actual distribution. We found this to be true even with LEAA and OJJDP funds, partially due to the multiple-year funding, the amount of control and information available only at the state level, the method of recordkeeping (especially filing proce-dures), and staff turnover. When reviewing the more general federal programs, such as Title XX and education programs (e.g., P.L. 94-142 and Title I), it is often impossible to determine which services are being provided to status offenders, much less the impact of those services. Since these general programs are not targeted for status offenders, there is no reason why state and local agencies would keep the necessary records to identify which recipients were status offenders. Indeed, quite often the service agencies may intentionally avoid doing so. Philosoph-ically, the agency may disagree with the classification of status offenders; organizationally, there may be costs to providing information by such specific categories.

State and local budgetary practices make it difficult to trace federal funds. These practices serve to maximize the discretion of state gov-ernments. Generally, states inform counties how much money is avail-able for certain types of services or programs, and the local actors have only the vaguest idea of the sources of those funds. The counties claim reimbursement from the state for services that have been provided, by placing costs under the categories that the state has announced. Then state budgetary officers see which sources of federal funds can be used to help pay the bills. The budgetary practices are simply not structured to ensure that federally proposed initiatives are actually implemented. This may be intentional obscuring, but states do not see the point in having every federal program's funds handled in separate accounts all the way to the client level. From their perspective, such procedures are not cost-efficient.

Another state and local level practice that hinders the tracing of fed-eral impact is the substitutability of program funding. Because federal money is often used to replace state money, which in turn may be recommitted elsewhere, it is not always clear that federal funds increase the availability of services. For example, federal funds that are provided to a state for foster care may increase the number of foster children served in a state, but the state may also replace state foster care dollars with the federal funds and there consequently will be no net increase. The same is true with shelters for runaways that receive federal funds from the Runaway Youth Act. If there are no such facilities in the area, then the award of a grant will mean that at least that facility will begin operation; on the other hand, if a facility already exists prior to the grant award, then using federal funds to replace previous sources of support (state, local, private, or federal) can occur, and there may be no net increase in the availability of services.

The differential use of federal funding is in keeping with the major findings of this study concerning the importance of state and local influences and the special but limited role of the federal government. The federal government has not had a monopoly on the ideas and resources associated with deinstitutionalization; indeed, quite the opposite. In those areas where deinstitutionalization seemed to be implemented most successfully, the local climate was right: There were groups and organizations that were dissatisfied with prevailing policies on children and youth and that were in favor of deinstitutionalization programs for status offenders. This is often the pattern in the flow of ideas and programs in the social welfare field. More often than not, federal sources are reactive to the ferment present in the states and communities. Federal money has its greatest impact when it aids those actors who were predisposed toward deinstitutionalization.

If deinstitutionalization is to mean anything more than ignoring status offenders altogether, the role of federal resources in influencing and assisting the progress of social movements at the state and local levels is, in our opinion, second in importance to the role played by the juvenile court judge. If anything at all is to be done—even something as seemingly insignificant as opening a shelter home—then there has to be a force for social change somewhere in the system. The importance of the role of the federal government has been amply demonstrated in several of the local areas, but it is still dependent on the exercise of discretion at the state and local levels. The federal government can encourage, can stimulate, and can provide necessary resources, but only if conditions are favorable. States that disagree with the policy objective probably will not accept or apply for the federal funds.

As far as outcomes are concerned, the federal government can expect more uniformity only when the characteristics of the decarceration aspects of the mandate can be approximated. To the extent that those characteristics cannot be approximated (for example, the deinstitutionalization mandate cannot be made clear, or there is a great deal of conflict over goals), then uniformity cannot be achieved. The question, then, is how to stimulate or encourage the exercise of discretion in the desired channels, recognizing that there is going to be unevenness in administration and failures along with successes.

As we have suggested, one obvious route is the discretionary grant to groups and organizations, both public and private, that want to pursue the policy goals and need various kinds of resources. In some of the communities this was done by LEAA and HEW and was quite successful. In Elmore's terms, policymakers at the top looked to see what resources street-level actors needed to get the job done, and then provided those resources (1979-1980). As noted, these resources sometimes had a multiplier effect; state, local, or private funds were used after the federal seed money was spent. What this policy means, though, is that certain grants will not take. If the local judge cannot be persuaded to go along, or a new judge reverses the policy (as in Pima County), then the shelter home might close or the advocacy group might die. On such occasions, implementation will not succeed.

Barring either massive infusions of federal dollars or sharp departures in the character of federal-state relations, we do not see any real alternative to the discretionary grant approach. The federal government can make money available for specific projects only (e.g., shelter homes for runaways or other specifically defined groups). Such a program will be partially successful. In states that have no shelter homes but that choose to accept federal money, the chances are that such homes will be built; if the incentives are right, the eligibility criteria are carefully drawn, and the courts are willing to go along with the plan, the homes will probably be used for the intended purpose. However, if the states already have such homes and choose to accept federal money for this purpose, the chances are that there will be only a substitution of federal funds for state funds. Of course, this is not certain; there could still be an increase in alternative facilities, but this is not the prevailing pattern. And finally, states that disagree with the policy objective probably will not accept the funds. Can these recalcitrant states be coerced into building and using shelter homes? We think that the answer is a fairly clear *no*, for all of the reasons spelled out above. The courts cannot be required to use the homes, eligibility will be fudged, and special exceptions and discretionary excuses will inevitably creep back into whatever mandatory language there is.

Thus, unless the federal government is willing and able to establish specific targets, conditions, and effective monitoring procedures, the most viable strategy is to provide incentives and hope that they will take. In some states they will, and in other states they will not. If the state government is reluctant to go along with the federal policy, the federal government can bypass that level and directly fund local projects. This is the procedure under the Runaway Youth Act. But the same issues remain. Unless there are specific targets, conditions, and monitoring procedures, local conditions have to be favorable for the grants to succeed.

The politics of the federal system is to distribute money to all of the states on some kind of formula basis. What can be done under this system? One approach is revenue sharing or other funding mechanisms with fairly loose federal controls and guidelines (e.g., Title XX, which requires very little accountability or information about how the states are spending this money). There are arguments in favor of such an approach; since federal influence over the direction of the program is minimal anyway, the federal government might as well save administrative costs and anguish. Under Title XX, local groups and organizations have been successful in obtaining state funds. Therefore, even under this type of funding approach, the federal government should use its discretionary grants to assist the state and local groups, organizations, and officials in their efforts to effect change.

WHAT IS HAPPENING TO STATUS OFFENDERS?

In this section, we discuss the results of deinstitutionalization policies and draw conclusions from them. First we describe what is happening to status offenders who enter the juvenile justice system. Next we turn to those who do not. In the beginning of this chapter, we noted that status offenders have been largely removed from traditional facilities and that there has been a decline in their number in detention. We further observed that fewer status offenders are entering the juvenile justice system. Some of these youth are being diverted to other service systems, but many are reportedly being ignored altogether.

STATUS OFFENDERS WHO ENTER THE JUVENILE JUSTICE SYSTEM

Use of Detention

Detention is proving to be a difficult issue, far more difficult than the ban on commiting status offenders to state training schools. We have discussed the reasons for the lack of consensus on detention—the feeling on the part of many in law enforcement, the courts, and youth service agencies that a short stay is a good, quick, and effective treatment for a lot of youth; frustration on the part of law enforcement personnel who have no place to take status offenders and therefore hold them until others can take over; community pressure to handle certain kinds of status offenders, notably runaways; and lack of facilities, especially in rural areas. It is clear that there is growing pressure to relieve the states of this part of JJDPA. As a result of recent amendments to the act, juveniles who violate a court order may now be kept in secure detention or secure correctional facilities (P.L. 96-509, Sec. 11(a)(13)).

States and localities have taken different approaches to the problem of balancing these community and law enforcement concerns against the need to find alternatives to secure detention for status offenders.

Some localities (e.g., Philadelphia and Richmond) use emergency shelter care in ways that make it very similar to secure detention: Admission is not voluntary, youth are not free to come and go as they please and are simply awaiting a court date or subsequent out-of-home placement, and facilities house delinquent youth as well as status offenders.

Other localities (e.g., Phoenix, Salt Lake City, Boston, New Orleans) have chosen nonsecure alternatives by establishing facilities that resemble emergency drop-in centers. Although such facilities are more clearly distinguishable from their secure counterparts, they appear to have some difficulty in gaining the confidence of the local police departments and the surrounding community. Typically, the youth in residence are there on their own accord (most are runaways); they are for all practical purposes free to come and go at will; and because of the voluntary aspect of their admission, there are no identified delinquents. The average stay in the drop-in center is much shorter than in secure shelter care (3 to 4 days as compared to 30), and the usual outcome is returning home.

Some localities reportedly continue to use secure detention for status offenders, but on a much reduced basis and only under certain circumstances. For example, youth who have run from either of the nonsecure options may be picked up by the police and returned to detention. Or runaways from out of state may end up in detention until arrangements can be made for their return. For the most part, the localities we visited have negotiated the "secure detention issue" by resorting to one of the two approaches described.

The controversy surrounding secure detention is troublesome. Do nonsecure detention facilities work; that is, do they serve a sufficient number of status offenders in a manner that satisfies law enforcement, the courts, and the community (e.g., can they "control" but not physically intimidate these youth)? If so, then the creation of additional nonsecure facilities may relieve some of the pressure caused by demand for services, except in the minds of those who believe in the intrinsic value of a harsher setting. And if there is a return to or simply a more open use of detention, under what sorts of circumstances might this occur (e.g., to prevent crime or to protect the child against doing harm to himself or herself)? How has secure detention worked in those states that have these restrictions?

The experience of social welfare programs is that if enough states feel very strongly about a key issue, they eventually get at least some of what they want. If enough communities press for a return to the use of secure detention for status offenders, the best policy for deinstitutionalization advocates may be to pursue a combination of statutes that restrict detention (with careful attention to the difficulty of monitoring such a provision) and incentives to encourage the use of nonsecure detention and diversion programs whenever possible.

Placements and Services

For those status offenders who enter the system, the dominant mode of service in most of our states seems based on a strategy of minimum intervention. There is no evidence that large sums of money and amounts of energy are going into in-home services. There are counseling programs connected with diversion, but, again, significant amounts of resources do not seem to be going into these efforts.

Concerning out-of-home placements, there is of course the very significant drop in commitments to state training schools. However, we are much less certain about other kinds of out-of-home placements. In states with strong traditions of private providership (e.g., Massachusetts, Pennsylvania), there seems to be a greater commitment to the fostering and use of alternatives. Respondents in the different states perceive fluctuations in the rates and types of out-of-home placements, but no really consistent pattern emerges. In some areas the increased use of diversion coupled with the scarcity of available alternatives seems to have produced an overall decline in the total number of youth placed out of their homes (e.g., Louisiana). In other states, the tendency appears to run in the other direction (e.g, Massachusetts).

The character of the typical out-of-home placement varies both across and within states, but generally speaking the predominant types are group homes and foster family homes. Some states seem to prefer foster home placements for status offenders because they are less expensive than other out-of-home alternatives. However, not much is known about the life of status offenders in foster homes. Although there is considerable research on foster care (and much of it is ambiguous), it tends to focus on younger children or, in a very few cases, younger adolescents (see e.g., Fanshel and Shinn 1978, Wald 1980). But there is no research to speak of that deals with juveniles who enter foster care at the age most typical of status offenders (i.e., 12 to 16).

Foster home care for children has been persistently and severely criticized: Children go from home to home, foster parents are not well qualified, there is not much nurturing, homes are overcrowded, there is minimal public supervision (see, e.g., Goldstein et al. 1979). These are arguable propositions (Wald 1976, 1979, 1980; Mnookin 1973; Symposium 1972). However, the alleged deficiencies in foster care for younger children may not be that relevant or serious for status offenders. One cannot be sure about assuming that the characteristics of foster care for young children are the same as for older children, but what is worth examining is whether foster care is desirable for older juveniles.

For many status offenders, the most significant problem is their home life. The preferred course may be to provide services to the family as a whole in order to keep it intact and to get at some of the core difficulties. Some of these preventive services are already in place (e.g., family counseling), and more needs to be known about how such services are working. But inasmuch as this is a far from ideal world, appropriate services may not be forthcoming for families who need them, and it is not entirely clear to the professional community which services are necessary or most effective. Faced with this situation, a foster home placement may be a tolerable solution; it allows the status offender not only to leave home but provides a place for the youth to live. Those who are identified as status offenders are older and do not need the same kind of parental bonding that presumably an infant or a small child needs. In a relatively short time the status offender will attain the age of majority and leave the foster home. Thus, the lack of continuity that is commonly complained of in foster placements may not be a serious problem. In sum, the foster home has been criticized for failure to conform to the medical or treatment model, but this may be an inappropriate model. Many status offenders may only want (and need) a parent (natural or otherwise), and a foster home placement would be successful to the extent that it replicated an adequate home—that is, a home not staffed by professional houseparents or trained counselors but rather by parents who talk to their children about their problems in the course of other activities instead of in "counseling" sessions.

Several years ago, Margaret Rosenheim argued for "normalization" instead of "problemization" in the treatment of what she referred to as "juvenile nuisances" (1969, 1976a:44,52). In her opinion much of the behavior of the juveniles who came into contact with official agencies was normal in the sense that a great many youth did the same things, but that only certain ones found their way into an official system: They could have been unlucky in getting caught by the police; some parents tolerate some behavior that others do not; different referral sources have varying criteria. Referral, in other words, is not necessarily rationally related to behavior.

If one is confronted with a normal range of behavior in status offenders, then a normalization or minimum intervention strategy may be called for rather than problemizing status offense behaviors, which many professionals tend to do. This does not necessarily mean that minimum intervention means doing nothing; rather it means doing as little as possible that will disrupt normal adolescent development. Most of the youth we saw in out-of-home placements in our very limited sample were veterans of the system. This was usually because other approaches had been tried and had failed (e.g., the youth had run from several placements, in-home counseling had proved unsuccessful). Applying Rosenheim's analysis, it could be that the minimal custodial arrangement, such as a foster home, is not only the best that we can hope for under the present climate, but may even be a desirable alternative.

Within our sample of out-of-home placements, neither the quality of the setting nor the nature of the resident's activities was predictable by program types. Overall, among the four types of facilities visited there was as much diversity within program type as between program types in the degree of normalization evident, the service model adopted, day-to-day programming, and the physical features of the setting. Generally, there was minimal evidence of community integration except in the use of public schools by group homes, and there was little or no family involvement in residential life. With only minor exceptions the facilities appeared to provide a safe, clean, and physically comfortable living environment. However, the extent to which the experience parallels a family living arrangement is diminished by the degree of supervision of resident activity, restrictive rules, and the limits on the youth's freedom to leave the premises and/or become involved in nonprogram community or school activities. The few facilities that most closely approximated the family living environment seemed to place a premium on developing close interpersonal relationships and individual decisionmaking in a group context, rather than on directing attention to carefully programmed activities and monitoring of resident behavior.

As we have pointed out, our sample was deliberately small and selected, and our observations were conducted over a two-day period. Although the results are limited in their generalizability, they nevertheless raise some important issues and questions for further research. The variability and diversity within the sample was not predictable by program type or size of the facility, which suggests that mandates that reduce size and create specific program types may not be sufficient to accomplish the goals desired in alternative services. The desire expressed by many program directors—to develop into multiservice organizations—also may run counter to the goal of creating small, noninstitutional settings. Furthermore, future research is necessary to determine whether these facilities make a difference in the lives of the youth. What happens to the youth after leaving the facility? Which youth are not being placed and what is happening to them? What events and decisions lead to placement in any particular facility?

For example, the nonsecure facilities served a predominantly nonminority population. There may be a pattern of racial bias in placement as a result of the tendency of facilities to exercise their prerogative to refuse certain youth. As Testa's paper points out (appendix F), when facilities do accept minority youth, these juveniles face a greater likelihood of being expelled and ending up in correctional facilities or some other type of private restrictive placement. Speaking more generally, one-half of the facilities in our sample report said that they accept less than 75 percent of those youth referred to them; one-third accept less than 50 percent. The reasons vary and are not terribly specific, ranging from a preference for "nonviolent, nonpsychotic, cooperative" youth, to a reluctance to work with recalcitrant families. Ironically, very few of the facilities in our sample were full (except for the detention centers), yet law enforcement and social services personnel alike complain of the shortage of nonsecure, long-term alternatives.

A different issue is presented by the service response of other agencies in the community. There is evidence that some social service, mental health, and education agencies are resisting status offenders. With mental health, resistance might be a blessing; it was feared that when the option of incarceration was removed, reinstitutionalization in a mental health facility might follow. This does not seem to have happened, at least to any significant extent. On the other hand, status offenders as well as others often need mental health services. We noted that through 1975 there had been a large increase in the number of youth being served by private mental health facilities, mostly on an outpatient basis. We do not know, however, who these youth are (i.e., whether they are status offenders), the circumstances of their admission, or the consequences of their care.

What to do about agencies who decline either to serve status offenders at all or to serve them satisfactorily is a difficult matter. We do not think that commands will work; if the agencies are truly resistant, they will either find a way to avoid taking these clients or will serve them in ways that may be more harmful than not serving them at all. A more sensible approach would be the use of simple incentives such as funding additional positions and programs. In certain agencies—the recalcitrant ones—there will be no applications for grants, but status offenders will be no worse off than they are now, and some money will be saved. In some agencies there will be a substitution of federal funds for agency funds, but in other agencies new programs will be added. In other words, resources will be directed toward those actors who want to work along desired paths. The more difficult task will be deciding which kinds of services and programs are desirable.

The Purchase-of-Services System

The states in this study vary in the manner in which services are provided to juveniles. In some of the states, most services are publicly provided. Other states prefer instead to enter into purchase-of-service arrangements with private providers. The purchase-of-services system is often cited as permitting greater flexibility, innovation, and freedom from bureaucratic encumbrance than its public counterpart. In addition, it is frequently easier to obtain funding for publicly purchased private services than to expand public personnel rolls as a means of providing them. Similarly, purchased services may enjoy a level of political support that public services may have greater difficulty mustering. The disadvantages of private production have received less attention but include the difficulty of controlling quality and monitoring provider activities, and the increased possibilities for suspension of operations; or, conversely, retention of youth after the providers' services are no longer needed. At the service level, different kinds of juveniles are often mixed together in the same facility and given undifferentiated care. The facility analysis has uncovered no unique status offender "treatments" and only one unique status offender setting (i.e., runaway shelters); as a result, status offenders are either assimilated into these facilities or ignored altogether. Recent changes in the Runaway Youth Act that target services to "homeless" youth may result in a repetition of these patterns. Inasmuch as runaways comprise only a part of this homeless population, these shelters will have to serve a broader range of youth and attract multiple sources of funding in order to survive.

As Pollak points out in his paper (appendix H), increased state reliance on the private sector has pointed up the difficulties of structuring and managing publicly purchased but privately provided services. Several reasons account for this problem. First, states have yet to work out adequate procedures to monitor and evaluate performance. They often lack the information necessary for effective planning and monitoring, such as numbers and types of children served, the kinds of services provided, and the methods of cost allocation. Second, state agencies often lack the political support necessary to assert control over private agencies, a problem not uncommon to publicly provided services as well. In fact, state agencies may even need the support, resources, and services of the providers to help fight for programs at the political level. With funding becoming more scarce and funding priorities themselves being reexamined, we have found that many of these providers are exploring ways to retain their foothold with the state. There have been instances in Cook County, Illinois, and in Massachusetts in which providers have successfully fought off the attempts of public agencies to renegotiate or cancel their contracts altogether. Other providers have sought to convert themselves into multipurpose centers that provide on-site shelter care, diagnostic services, education, day programs, aftercare services, and so forth.

Furthermore, as previously indicated, the tendency of many of these facilities is to accept only those youth who are likely to succeed and/or are the least troublesome to the provider as well as to the community. Indeed, some communities have passed (or tried to pass) restrictive zoning ordinances and have pressured their state legislators to ensure that certain types of youth are not served within these boundaries, as a part of a more general effort to keep deviants out. Of course, community resistance can occur regardless of whether a facility is publicly or privately administered. However, at least insofar as the facilities are concerned, there is little that a state agency or court can do to make private providers, who may be taking their cues from their communities, accept these youth.

As we have indicated, the most important determinant of the delivery of services to status offenders is not the federal dollars but the needs of the providers and of the state and local agencies themselves. If in fact, as we believe, status offenders are not being dumped into public mental hospitals as a result of deinstitutionalization, it may well be because the mental health system does not want to accept them; the few remaining slots appear to be used for children whose problems are much more severe. Alternatively, if the schools have historically tried to dump habitual school offenders onto the court, it is because school personnel believe themselves to be incapable of dealing with these youth, or because they are unwilling to deal with them, or because they lack the resources to do so. The same point applies to the providers of service. Local discretion, not federal money, is the most important variable.

STATUS OFFENDERS WHO DO NOT ENTER THE JUVENILE
JUSTICE SYSTEM

Fewer youth who are charged with status offenses are being referred to court or to court-related diversion programs. Of course, this finding is subject to exception: In certain cases, there was some widening of the net (e.g., Uintah County's LEAA-funded juvenile officer was coming into contact with more status offenders than the police had been; in other locations, diversion programs were handling some status offenders with whom the overburdened court and law enforcement system would not have bothered). But on the whole, one result of deinstitutionalization is that fewer status offenders are coming into contact with the system.

It is not clear from the evidence what is happening to these youth. Our research has not investigated all of the possible public or private systems that could be treating some of these youth. We have mentioned the large increase in the number of young people going to outpatient private mental health facilities, and clearly this is an issue that should be looked into. Some communities have established shelters for runaways, and such shelters may provide the stopgap, normalizing, nonprofessional, low-key kind of service that Rosenheim and others have called for. Similarly, there may be other kinds of facilities and programs serving youth. Some research has been done, but more must be learned about these projects, the circumstances under which they are used, and what the results have been (Berkeley Planning Associates 1980, Brennan et al. 1978, Opinion Research Corporation 1976, Walker 1975).

Many of the respondents in the states and local areas think that nothing is happening, that status offenders are being increasingly ignored, that they are not coming into contact with any system, that public agencies are telling the families and the youth to work out their problems on their own. If this is in fact happening, it could be that community and parental attitudes are changing, that there is more acceptance of (or resignation to) drug use, promiscuity, or youth who are on their own. Maybe there have been changes in culture, or maybe the lack of response on the part of the police and the courts, many of whom perceive themselves as powerless to compel status offenders to obey their orders, has led parents and other sources of referral to give up as well. It is equally possible that status offenders are being ignored because authorities have chosen to focus their energies on the more serious offender, or because there is no place to send them.

If this finding is true, why should it be a matter of concern for public policy? We noted in chapter 3 that some people think the state has no business intervening in the lives of families and youth when crimes have not been committed. We feel that this position rests on philosophical or value foundations beyond the purview of this study.

There are, however, important empirical questions about how these youth are faring as a result of nonintervention. Those who express concern that such youth are "falling through the cracks" worry that many who are in genuine need of services are being denied help as a partial consequence of deinstitutionalization. Is there real suffering; if so, how extensive is it and what can be done about it? As stated in chapter 1, this study was not able to address these very important issues, but they clearly call for research. The choice has been a policy of deinstitutionalization, and whatever the original or current position of the various proponents (e.g., deinstitutionalization as simple removal, deinstitutionalization as removal plus replacement services), it may be that many youth are no longer entering any part of the system. If true, this may be good or it may be bad, but it seems to us that it is clearly a matter of social responsibility to at least try to find out what has happened to youth in the wake of this policy choice.

If significant numbers of status offenders are no longer being handled by any system, then who is getting left out and who is being taken in? The most probable answer is that those youth who best fit organizational needs are being handled by the system. Those who might benefit most from services, but who for one reason or another do not match organizational requirements, may have been excluded. For example, the courts may handle certain juveniles and not others in response to perceptions by the police that certain kinds of status offenses are more directly related to the commission of crime. Thus, in one of the court intake units, the staff refused to take status offenders who were runaways or ungovernables but would take curfew violators. Why? The police view curfew violators as potential burglars and want them off the streets. In New Orleans the police are indifferent to most types of status offenders but have recently started picking up truants and taking them to holding centers. There has been a rise in daytime burglaries, and it is thought that truants may be responsible. In either example there is no reason to assume that whatever program or service the community has to offer would be successful with curfew violators and truants but not with runaways and ungovernables; clearly, there were other factors affecting the choice of whom to serve.

In a society that values the importance of equality before the law, it is a matter of concern that the juvenile justice process is differentially enforced (e.g., youth who engage in substantially different acts are treated the same, youth who engage in substantially similar acts are treated differently). But having said that, what can be done? Differential enforcement of the law has always been a troublesome characteristic of our system, especially given the coercive features of the juvenile justice system. But how would one go about *requiring* the local police and juvenile courts to administer the laws applying to status offenders in a more uniform manner? As pointed out in our discussions of the prohibition on incarceration, specific mandates can be effective under certain conditions. In the absence of these conditions another viable strategy would be to provide incentives to encourage different directions in law enforcement—for example, funding for specially trained juvenile officers to work with runaways or ungovernables or any other class of status offenders who are perceived as needing special attention. No doubt some of these grants would be wasted, but others would take and would produce the desired results.

The differential administration of the law not only means discrimination in coercive interventions but also in the distribution of benefits. Youth who are ignored may not be getting help that is needed. This too is a serious and complex concern, raising important value and empirical questions. Even if it can be established that there are youth who are in need of services and are not receiving them, it is not self-evident that public policy (e.g., the federal government) should respond to this need. This depends, of course, on other priorities. In a world of scarce resources, where the claims of children and youth are competing against the claims of other populations and, moreover, where the claims of status offenders are competing against the claims of other children and youth in need (i.e., delinquents, the physically and mentally handicapped, those who need special education), it may be that those scarce resources should be spent elsewhere.

Today, as in the past, there is a body of opinion that maintains that prevention is more economical than cure and that well-directed efforts to prevent status offenders from crossing the line into delinquency would be a prudent use of scarce resources (Bremner 1956). This research takes no position on this issue; our charge has been to examine policies of deinstitutionalization of status offenders. We have something to say about how those policies have been implemented, not whether status offenders are more deserving of support than others.

We have stressed throughout that agencies tend to deliver services more in terms of their organizational needs than the needs of the youth. While we have not conducted systematic research on the provider system in each locality of our study, we have uncovered some evidence of racial discrimination. In addition, there is evidence that providers will not take more troublesome youth, and that the stay of some youth is prolonged to avoid empty beds. The providers have a great latitude in choosing whom they will take. As previously noted, given the characteristics of the provider system, it is very difficult to control and redirect this discretion. Clearly, much more systematic attention has to be paid to the potential for race and sex discrimination; and to the extent that such discrimination is uncovered, combinations of negative and positive sanctions must be rigorously applied. In addition, as with law enforcement, incentives should be provided to agencies to encourage them to handle those youth who now have difficulty in entering and remaining in more normalized settings.

A Final Note

What brings about social change? What does this study tell us about social change? As with much social research, this study no doubt raises more questions than it answers; it certainly presents a complex picture. At the macrolevel, it is said that significant social change comes about through cataclysmic events, such as wars, serious depressions, plagues, significant charismatic leaders, or the gradual change in public opinion. The deinstitutionalization of status offenders probably fits the last. It had its roots in a time when children and youth began to be differentiated from adults, and public concern focused increasingly on the nonconforming aspects of the behavior of older adolescents. More recently it grew out of the civil rights era, the growing disenchantment with the juvenile court, changing beliefs in the efficacy of mental health treatments, special education programs, the War on Poverty, and the legal rights explosion. The deinstitutionalization of this population was woven out of the same cloth as the deinstitutionalization of other populations and the concern about the loss of liberty and the imposition of coercion under the guise of treatment. It was a broad social movement, and this was seen in several of the states that were studied. In some instances deinstitutionalization was an active idea, program, or trend well before the federal government made known its interest. There had been changes in public opinion and there was activity. In some communities deinstitutionalization had been accomplished with minimal federal influence.

Does this lead to the conclusion that the federal government was unnecessary or irrelevant, that deinstitutionalization would have occurred anyway, especially in view of our conclusion that the federal government cannot bring about deinstitutionalization unless local actors are willing to go along? We do not think so. Although we cannot recreate the world as if the federal government had not intervened, we can point to many instances in our research in which the federal government played an important if not critical role in helping the process along. Social change, at least in broad, locally based movements, proceeds at an uneven pace. One could say that deinstitutionalization was an idea whose time had come, and that it swept the country in a relatively short period of time. But it didn't sweep all of the country, and it didn't complete its sweeping before the federal government enacted the Juvenile Justice and Delinquency Prevention Act. Furthermore, it swept the country only on the legislative and policy levels, and in terms of the decarceration mandate. Other parts of deinstitutionalization still remained to be implemented in various states and localities.

We found the federal government taking an active, creative role in the process of implementing this movement. There were many instances in which it made the difference in particular local programs. And, of course, there were also instances in which lack of federal support had serious negative consequences. Federal support, as was pointed out, was varied and flexible—the kind of thing that was needed at particular times. It demonstrated, at least to us, that in the day-to-day business of social change, the federal government made a significant difference in many communities.

9 Recommendations

The recommendations that flow out of this study depend in large part on what the federal government wants to do about deinstitutionalization. The Panel was charged with examining the effects of federal efforts on this endeavor. It was an analysis of implementation; it was not a study of whether deinstitutionalization was a good or bad policy, either in conceptualization or in fact. However, recommendations as to what the federal government *should* do have to be based on a judgment as to whether deinstitutionalization should be pursued or not.

We noted in chapter 1 that the answer to this question is not easy. There is probably substantial agreement on decarceration; there is less agreement on detention. On the issues of diversion and alternative placements and services, however, there is disagreement on every aspect. What should be done, for whom, to what extent, and for what purposes? In addition, we are not unmindful of the fact that there is now a real question as to how to allocate scarce resources.

If it is decided that deinstitutionalization is a desirable policy and that the federal government will continue its efforts, then we do have a set of recommendations that we feel will make those efforts more effective. If it is decided, for whatever reasons, that the federal government will no longer pursue deinstitutionalization (or will reduce its efforts), there are still certain things that should be done. Our first set of recommendations is based on the assumption that the federal government will continue to pursue deinstitutionalization.

THE FEDERAL ROLE IN SUPPORTING DEINSTITUTIONALIZATION

1. *The federal government should continue to enunciate standards and policy.* The federal government should continue to support the goals of deinstitutionalization in a highly visible manner. It was clear to us that the federal government's enunciation of standards and policy was important. Except for decarceration, the goals of deinstitutionalization have not been substantially accomplished and the situation is in flux. These goals need continued visible policy support to lend legitimacy and to stimulate activity at the state and local levels.

2. *The approach of the federal government to implementation should vary in terms of the different goals of deinstitutionalization.* Some goals call for substantial uniformity of implementation. This was the case with the prohibition on incarceration in state correctional institutions. In this type of situation, there has to be agreement on the standards, and the standards have to be stated in terms of outcomes that are easily measured. The measure of performance, in fact, should be the goal, not a proxy. For example, the goal of decarceration should be stated and evaluated in terms of the decrease in the number of status offenders in state correctional institutions rather than in terms of crime prevention or rehabilitation. And there has to be a clear, agreed-upon sanction that is specifically tailored to the goal.

Another example would be a standard for secure detention. The pressure to make exceptions has resulted in recent changes in the law that permit the secure detention of any juvenile, including status offenders who allegedly violate a valid court order. These terms need to be stated much more specifically; a number of points remain unclear, such as what constitutes a valid court order and how long a young person can be held. Although no rule can be airtight, the pressure for the use of secure detention except in very limited cases will need to be resisted.

The question of sanctions is difficult. If the sanction is too severe (e.g., the total withdrawal of substantial amounts of federal funds), then the sanction will not be applied. If the sanction is too narrow or small, then it may not be effective. Will threats of taking money away result in compliance or in a state's refusal to participate in federal programs? Sanctions and benefits should be balanced. In pursuing detention goals, the federal government can supply funds for alternatives and staff. Not only are such incentives potentially powerful, but they also make retreat more difficult.

The goal of alternative responses by the states, such as diversion programs and services, with some exceptions are not subject to uniform implementation. Here, the federal government should accept and encourage local variation and discretion along the lines discussed below. The exceptions relate to cross-cutting issues, such as race and sex discrimination or other legal requirements, and on these issues, the federal government must insist on uniform adherence to national policies.

3. *The federal government should promote a variety of activities encompassing all of the goals of deinstitutionalization.* As noted, implementation of the goals of deinstitutionalization has varied from substantial compliance to almost no progress. Nevertheless, circumstances change, and we think that the federal government should be prepared to support activities that encompass the full range of deinstitutionalization goals subject to the qualifications discussed below. Specifically, the federal government should be responsive to local groups, organizations, agencies, or individuals that are interested in pursuing deinstitutionalization goals. Responsiveness can be demonstrated by providing grants for specific projects (e.g., shelters, group homes), program development and staff positions, technical assistance, education, and the gathering and dissemination of information. To the extent that these grants succeed, the projects will not only provide specific benefits, but also will help to bring together and stabilize groups and organizations that are interested in furthering deinstitutionalization goals. These organizations serve a number of functions that are critical to the implementation process. In some instances they perform important monitoring functions and encourage the exercise of discretion in desired directions. In other instances they serve as spokespersons for the cause of this class of youth. They press their demands for resources at all levels of government. In most of the localities that we studied, there was strong local group activity that either developed out of or was aided by federal grants to a variety of projects.

We found that much of what HEW and LEAA did was in the right direction: They took a flexible approach in supporting local efforts where there were local actors who were interested in pursuing deinstitutionalization objectives. Such an approach requires a willingness to make grants available to citizen advocacy groups, community groups, courts and probation staff, state agencies, private providers—in short, wherever local support can be found. We found that grants were in fact given to these different actors and, it would appear, with considerable success. Because one cannot predict which local combinations will succeed, different combinations must be tried.

Certain steps can be taken, however, to increase the likelihood for success. The chances of success are greater to the extent that more of the important relevant local actors join in the endeavor. Thus, if the court as well as community leaders and agency heads join in a proposal for a diversion project or a shelter care network, results would appear to be promising. It does not necessarily follow, however, that if these other important actors do not join, projects are not worth funding. It depends on the nature and intensity of the opposition, and small grants to get things going may serve to persuade officials who have adopted a "wait and see" attitude.

4. *Within the range of deinstitutionalization goals, we think that the most important problem now is detention and that the federal government should concentrate its efforts here.* At the present time most controversy centers on detention. This is an issue on which opinions differ sharply. It is also an area that is difficult to monitor and is subject to abuse. The federal mandate concerning detention has been important in stimulating change. Nevertheless, detention is still being used for status offenders, and there seems to be a considerable backlash on this issue. Whether recent changes in JJDPA on this score will stem this tide or open the floodgates is unclear. As noted above, there are combinations of measures that the federal government can take. It can have clear mandates that are easily monitored; but it also should provide discretionary funds to build alternatives.

5. *Problems associated with funding alternative programs for status offenders deserve more attention.* The funding of alternative programs is an area fraught with problems. Care must be taken to avoid building alternatives that widen the net too much; but how much is too much? Can there be agreement on minimum alternative placements (e.g., every community should have a place for runaways to go, and more foster care should be available for these youth)? There are very difficult issues with providers, both public and private, who respond to funding incentives by redefining their mission or relabeling their populations. We hesitate to recommend that the federal government should cease support in the funding of alternatives, because of the lack of theory, information, and monitoring ability. On the other hand, the problem is not only the waste of scarce resources but also the harmful consequences for the youth in question.

Problems cannot be approached in a wholesale manner. For example, a policy that emphasizes group homes that approach a "normal" home in terms of freedom of movement can be agreed upon for a great many status offenders but may serve to eliminate troubled youth who need somewhat more structure; and when the latter are rejected, they may end up in far worse settings (e.g., state institutions). It should also be recognized that services for status offenders need not be confined to traditional family counseling, group homes, foster homes, or other out-of-home placements. For example, programs that use or strengthen both existing networks of available community services (e.g., drop-in centers, neighborhood health clinics, after-school and recreational programs, job opportunities) and the natural support system of friends, family, and neighbors—and do so in a voluntary, noncoercive, and nonstigmatizing fashion—should also be considered in planning services for status offenders. The federal government must proceed cautiously, must try to obtain agreement on certain minimum standards for services and facilities, and must improve dramatically its sources of information as to what is going on in these places.

6. *Seed-money programs should be encouraged.* We noted that building on local discretion requires not only flexibility but also patience. On occasion, seed money operates as the name implies; it gets things going, which then attracts other sources of support, and the federal government is no longer needed. But there are other important examples of projects that have been started with state or local money and have then faltered. The Salt Lake County Youth Services Project was one such example. After it was started, federal funds helped stabilize it (in midstream) and it then was able to continue on its own. Traditionally, seed-money projects are evaluated in terms of how much community support the project has been able to attract. In the present economic situation, local sources of support may be withdrawn for projects that are worthwhile. In such cases the federal government has to consider saving projects that previously looked solid.

7. *The federal supervisory role has to be strengthened.* While we did not extensively examine the organization and operation of LEAA, it became apparent that the federal government had trouble coming to grips with deinstitutionalization. Understandably, there is conflict as to how resources should be divided among adult criminals, delinquents, status offenders, and dependent and neglected children. These conflicts were never satisfactorily resolved and are still subject to the pull-and-haul of politics. We fully expect that this conflict will continue for some time. It is therefore somewhat sanctimonious to admonish the federal government to administer the deinstitutionalization program in a consistent, coherent manner, since society itself lacks a consistent, coherent view as to what should be done. Nevertheless, the federal government has to try. There are many things in this program that LEAA and OJJDP did that we think were right. But there was also a considerable amount of uncertainty on their part that hampered state and local efforts. Implementation would be improved to the extent that the federal agencies involved can sort out their difficulties and agree on an administrative plan.

One way to facilitate implementation would be to establish data collection guidelines for states and localities. A persistent problem encountered in this study has been the lack of data and the inconsistencies and low quality of the data that do exist. This is more than a mere research problem. For example, the current diversity of data collection approaches makes the task of monitoring compliance almost impossible. However, even if the federal government decides not to actively assume this role, federally devised standards for data collection would still be useful. Consistent and complete data would allow the federal government to take advantage of the natural experimental situation that arises from the fact that various states and localities take different approaches to deinstitutionalization. One could determine which approaches appear to work best under particular circumstances; these approaches could then be encouraged through further funding. Additionally, the data that are made available would serve as a solid base for local decisionmakers and interest groups to evaluate more systematically the performance of their policies and programs, and thereby assess with greater confidence the need for change.

THE FEDERAL ROLE IF DEINSTITUTIONALIZATION IS NO LONGER SUPPORTED

If the federal government decides to reduce its efforts in deinstitutionalization or to get out of the business altogether, there are certain things that it still should do.

1. *The federal government should find out what has happened to youth as a result of deinstitutionalization.* We feel most strongly that, at the very least, the federal government has the responsibility to find out what has happened as a result of its efforts. This study examined the extent to which the policy has been implemented and the determinants of implementation. It did not look at what is happening to the youth in question and their families. Are they being ignored altogether? Are they being served by other agencies in the community? Are they being relabeled? And what are the consequences of these various dispositions?

It is rare that social problems disappear. Status offenders have been trouble to society for centuries. Society's definitions of and tolerance for trouble may vary, as well as its response; but just as social conditions change, so too will attitudes and responses toward these youth. At the minimum, the effects of the present policy should be understood, both for the sake of clients of the system and for the sake of policy choices that are now being made and that will be made in the future.

2. *The federal government should be selective in its withdrawal.* It may be that the federal government will decide to reduce its efforts on the affirmative side of deinstitutionalization and decrease its funding of alternative services. It could take this position for reasons of economy or because of disagreement on goals or on knowledge. But it does not necessarily follow that it should abandon its efforts on other aspects of deinstitutionalization. Although resources are important, the federal government still plays an important role as a source of ideas and as a supplier of technical assistance. Legislation, regulations, court cases, and studies and reports have been important in the past, and should remain so in the future.

STATE AND LOCAL RECOMMENDATIONS

Recommendations directed at states and local communities mirror the recommendations for the federal government. If states elect to continue to pursue deinstitutionalization, they should adopt a role essentially similar to that of the federal government. Recognizing the importance of local actors, agencies, and interest groups, states should be prepared to fund a variety of programs at the local level. Funds can be supplied either through general purpose monies, or, as is more likely the case, through formula or block grant revenue-sharing funds from the federal government (e.g., Title XX social services). To the extent that more discretion over funds is delegated to the states, they have the opportunity to assume a more influential role, and they should employ the full range of techniques that the federal government has used.

We saw that various strategies were used at the local level to bring about social change. In different localities different roles were played by judges, agencies, providers, interest groups, and individuals. They sought technical assistance, discretionary funds, and local support to organize, build projects, and institute programs. Whether it is funded by states or the federal government, this kind of activity has to continue if deinstitutionalization programs are to be implemented and maintained.

If states decide to reduce or eliminate their deinstitutionalization efforts, they can still fulfill important responsibilities. Many states have expended considerable time and resources on deinsitutionalization, particularly through the use of private purchase-of-service arrangements. How have these arrangements benefited status offenders, if at all, and at what cost? Are these experiences transferable to other populations in need? What are the implications for public management of human services in general? In addition, by now a considerable body of expertise has been built up in the various states and localities, and states and local governments ought to establish procedures for gathering and disseminating this information. Technical assistance supplied by the federal government proved valuable, and other agencies should continue these efforts.

In the next section we discuss recommendations for research, but we emphasize here that states and local agencies are much closer to the ground level than the federal government, and they have a more important responsibility and opportunity to investigate the issues raised in providing alternative care, particularly the operations and activities of private providers and foster care.

RESEARCH ISSUES

1. *Who is being served and who is being ignored?* There are several questions that in one way or another are raised but not resolved by this study. The most conspicuous of these questions focuses on what is actually happening to young people who commit status offenses but who can no longer be institutionalized as a consequence of deinstitutionalization. We know that most status offenders have been removed from traditional state correctional facilities, that fewer of these youth are entering the juvenile justice system, and that many of these young people may be diverted to some other service system. However, we know very little about exactly how many are being served alternatively and to what effect. Furthermore, we know almost nothing at all about the fate of those youth who are ignored altogether.

2. *What is the structure and organization of services?* Our assessment of facilities, though limited in scope, was intended in part to point up the need for such knowledge as part of a broader awareness of the impact and nuances of the implementation process. But as we indicated, such an assessment raises as many questions as it attempts to answer. We need to know much more about the range of facilities in use for status offenders as well as the kinds of youth who are to be found there. How do particular youth come to be singled out for service and placed in particular facilities while others are passed over altogether? Are those who receive services, for whatever reason, left any better off than those who do not, and by what account? We have postulated that the most important determinant of which youth get served and in what manner is not the needs of the youth but the needs of providers, communities, and the state and local agencies. If this is true, if local discretion and organizational requirements are the key variables, then what are the consequences for these young people?

As we have indicated, there is great diversity of opinion regarding what is best for these youth. We find little evidence of coherence in these matters; thus, it is not surprising that state and local practices are as idiosyncratic as they are, or that there is as much variability as there is insofar as the dispositions and programming for these youth are concerned. At the present time it seems as though the level of supply is a more important influence on the use of services than the needs of these youth. While it would be naive to assume that the organizational requirements of the system will lessen in importance, one might hope that a better balance could be struck between the needs of these youth and the needs of the systems that are responsible for serving them.

3. *Are status offenders being reinstitutionalized by the private sector?* This study did not make the individual its unit of analysis for reasons stated earlier. Ours was an institutional analysis and one that focused on public systems that serve status offenders. We are not unmindful of the fact that status offenders who are not being served by the juvenile justice, welfare, social services, or mental health systems may be finding their way into private systems. For example, and as we have noted, there has been an increase in the number of youth being served by private mental health facilities, particularly on an outpatient basis. What accounts for this increase is not clear, nor is the increase in and of itself necessarily a cause for concern. What may be a more serious matter, however, is the fact that the recently revised major diagnostic classifications (e.g., "oppositional disorder," "identity disorder") that are used by these settings may still be vague enough to encompass the kinds of behavior that are classically considered to be status offenses. It would be important to know what these classifications mean and how they are being applied in order to guard against a situation in which the private sector reinstitutionalizes the juveniles that many have labored to remove from secure public settings.

4. *What are the possibilities for discrimination as a result of differential use of services?* A different but related issue is raised by the prospect that youth who engage in essentially similar behavior and who are singled out for services may experience radically different outcomes. Differential treatment may be due to the availability of resources, but there is concern that racial, sexual, or social-class biases—or some combination thereof—are at work here. We have some evidence that there have been instances of racial discrimination (appendix F; chapter 6). We have not systematically researched these possibilities, but this by no means diminishes the importance of such an analysis of their effects. If deinstitutionalization is a policy that was designed in part to promote greater equity and equal protection of the law insofar as youth are

concerned, then it is essential to be sure that some youth are not being made to suffer more as a consequence of these kinds of biases.

5. *What kinds of practices will further the goals of normalization?* Finally, it may be inevitable that categorical programs single out groups for special attention, and that such programs separate people from society and from one another. Although any service or special assistance program can have these tendencies, those that focus on deviant behavior are particularly susceptible. Given this fact, careful attention should be paid to the extent to which status offenders are really that different from young people as a whole, for whom adolescence is not a particularly easy time. Whatever can be done to ease the transition of these youth into adulthood, to reintegrate them into society, and to treat them as if their problems are not stigmatic but manageable may be an important first step in strengthening the family and encouraging the integration of these youth into society.

References

Anderson, E.A. (1976) The 'Chivalrous' Treatment of the Female Offender in the Arms of the Criminal Justice System: A Review of the Literature. *Social Problems* 23(3):350-357.

Ariessohn, Richard M., and Gonion, Gordon (1973) Reducing the Juvenile Detention Rate. *Juvenile Justice* 24(May):28-33.

Arnold, William R. (1971) Race and Ethnicity Relative to Other Factors in Juvenile Court Dispositions. *American Journal of Sociology* 77:211-227.

Arthur D. Little, Inc. (1977) *Responses to Angry Youth: Cost and Service Impacts of the Deinstitutionalization of Status Offenders in Ten States*. Washington, D.C.: Arthur D. Little, Inc.

Arthur, Lindsay G. (1975) Status Offenders Need Help Too. *Juvenile Justice* 26(February):3-7.

Axelrad, S. (1952) Negro and White Institutionalized Delinquents. *American Journal of Sociology* 57:569-574.

Bachrach, Leona (1976) *Deinstitutionalization: An Analytical Review and Sociological Perspective*. Washington, D.C.: U. S. Government Printing Office.

Baker, Bruce L., Seltzer, G.B., and Seltzer, Marsha M. (1977) *As Close as Possible: Community Residences for Retarded Adults*. Boston: Little, Brown.

Baradach, Eugene (1977) *The Implementation Game*. Cambridge, Mass.: MIT Press.

Barton, W.H. (1976) Discretionary Decisionmaking in Juvenile Justice. *Crime and Delinquency* 22(4):470-480.

Becker, Marshall (1970) Sociometric Location and Innovativeness: Reformulation and Extension of the Diffusion Model. *American Sociological Review* 35(April):267-282.

Berkeley Planning Associates (1980) *National Evaluation of the Runaway Youth Program: Final Report and Summary Findings*. Washington, D.C.: Department of Health and Human Services.

Berman, Paul (1978) The Study of Macro- and Micro-Implementation. *Public Policy* 26(Spring):157-184.

240

Blomberg, Thomas G. (1980) Widening the Net: An Anomaly in the Evaluation of Diversion Programs. Chap. 23 in Malcolm Klein and Katherine H. Teilmann, eds., *Handbook of Criminal Justice Evaluation*. Beverly Hills, Calif.: Sage Publications.

Blum, G. S. (1969) *Prepuberty and Adolescence*. 2nd ed. Toronto: MacMillian.

Bremner, Robert (1956) *From the Depths: The Discovery of Poverty in the United States*. New York: New York University Press.

Bremner, Robert, ed. (1971) *Children and Youth in America: A Documentary History*. Cambridge, Mass.: Harvard University Press.

Brennan, Tim, Huizinga, David, and Elliott, Delbert (1978) *The Social Psychology of Runaways*. Lexington, Mass.: Lexington Books.

Chesney-Lind, Meda (1977a) Judicial Enforcement of the Female Sex Role: The Family Court and the Female Delinquent. *Issues in Criminology* 8(Fall):51-69.

―――――(1977b) Judicial Paternalism and the Female Status Offender. *Crime and Delinquency* 23:121-130.

Children's Defense Fund (1978) *Children Without Homes: An Examination of Public Responsibility to Children in Out of Home Care*. Washington, D.C.: Children's Defense Fund.

Coates, Robert B., Miller, Alden D., and Ohlin, Lloyd E. (1978) *Diversity in a Youth Correctional System: Handling Delinquents in Massachusetts*. Cambridge, Mass.: Ballinger.

Council of State Governments (1977) *Juvenile Facilities: Functional Criteria*. Lexington, Ky.: Council of State Governments.

Daedalus (1971) Twelve to Sixteen: Early Adolescence (Special Issue) *Daedalus* 100(4).

DeCrow, Karen (1975) *Sexist Justice*. New York: Vintage Books.

Derthick, Martha (1975) *Uncontrollable Spending for Social Services Grants*. Washington, D.C.: The Brookings Institution.

Downs, George W., Jr., (1976) *Bureaucracy, Innovation and Public Policy*. Lexington, Mass.: D. C. Heath.

Drake, Robert L. (1978) Elimination of Status Offenses: The Myth, Fallacies and More Juvenile Crime. *Juvenile and Family Court Journal* 29(May):33-40.

Elazar, Daniel J. (1970) The States and the Political Setting. Pp. 171-185 in Ira Sharkansky, ed., *Policy Analysis in Political Science*. Chicago, Ill.: Markham Books.

Elmore, Richard (1978) Organizational Models of Social Program Implementation. *Public Policy* 26(Spring):185-228.

―――――― (1979-1980) Backward Mapping: Implementation Research and Policy Decisions. *Political Science Quarterly* 94(Winter):601-616.

Empey, LaMar T. (1973) Juvenile Justice Reform: Diversion, Due Process and Deinstitutionalization. Pp. 13-48 in Lloyd E. Ohlin, ed., *Prisoners in America*. Englewood Cliffs, N.J.:Prentice-Hall.

Empey, LaMar T., and Lubeck, S.G. (1971) *The Silverlake Experiment: Testing Delinquency Theory and Community Intervention*. Chicago: Aldine.

Erickson, Maynard L. (1979) Some Empirical Questions Concerning the Current Revolution in Juvenile Justice. Pp. 277-311 in LaMar T. Empey, ed., *The Future of Childhood and Juvenile Justice*. Charlottesville, Va.: University of Virginia Press.

Erikson, Erik H. (1959) Identity and the Life Cycle. *Psychological Issues* 1(1):1-171.

―――――― (1965) *The Challenge of Youth*. Garden City, N.Y.: Doubleday.

―――――― (1968) *Identity: Youth and Crisis*. New York: W.W. Norton.

Fanshel, David, and Shinn, Eugene (1978) *Children in Foster Care: A Longitudinal Investigation*. New York: Columbia University Press.

Ferster, Elyce Z., Snethen, Edith N., and Courtless, Thomas F. (1969) Juvenile Detention:

Protection, Prevention or Punishment? *Fordham Law Review* 38(December):161-196.

Flynn, Robert J., and Heal, L.W. (1980) A Short Form of PASS-3 for Assessing Normalization: Structure, Interrater Reliability and Validity. Unpublished manuscript, Purdue University School of Science at Indianapolis.

Folks, Homer (1902) *The Care of Destitute, Neglected and Delinquent Children.* New York: MacMillan.

Fox, Sanford (1970) Juvenile Justice Reform: An Historical Perspective. *Stanford Law Review* 22(June):1187-1239.

Freud, Anna (1962) Adolescence. In Judy Rosenblith and Wesley Allinsmith, eds., *The Causes of Behavior.* Boston: Allyn and Bacon.

Friedman, Lawrence (1975) *The Legal System.* New York: Russell Sage Foundation.

Garlock, Peter D. (1979) Wayward Children and the Law, 1820-1900: The Genesis of the Status Offense Jurisdiction of the Juvenile Court. *Georgia Law Review* 13:341-447.

Gill, Thomas D. (1976) The Status Offender. *Juvenile Justice* 27(August):3-10.

Goffman, Erving (1961) *Asylums: Essays on the Social Situation of Mental Patients and Other Inmates.* Garden City, N.Y.: Anchor Books.

Gold, S. (1971) Equal Protection for Juvenile Girls in Need of Supervision in New York State. *New York Law Forum* 17(2):570-598.

Goldstein, Joseph, Freud, Anna, and Solnit, Albert J. (1979) *Before the Best Interests of the Child.* New York: The Free Press.

Gray, Virginia (1973) Innovation in the States: A Diffusion Study. *American Political Science Review* 67(December):1174-1185.

Group for the Advancement of Psychiatry (1968) *Normal Adolescence: Its Dynamics and Impact.* New York: Charles Scribner.

Hall, Granville Stanley (1904) *Adolescence.* New York: D. Appleton.

Hall, Richard (1977) *Organization, Structure, and Process.* Englewood Cliffs, N.J.: Prentice-Hall.

Handler, Joel (1972) *Reforming The Poor.* New York: Basic Books.

———— (1978) *Social Movements and the Legal System.* New York: Academic Press.

———— (1979) *Protecting the Social Service Client: Legal and Structural Controls on Official Discretion.* New York: Academic Press.

Handler, Joel, and Hollingsworth, Ellen (1971) *The "Deserving Poor": A Study of Welfare Administration.* New York: Academic Press.

Hargrove, Erwin C. (1975) *The Missing Link: The Study of the Implementation of Social Policy.* An Urban Institute paper (797-1), July 1975. Washington, D.C.: The Urban Institute.

Hawes, J. (1971) *Children in Urban Society: Juvenile Delinquency in Nineteenth-Century America.* New York: Oxford University Press.

Hutzler, J.L., and Sestak, R.M.O. (1977) *Juvenile Court Jurisdiction over Children's Conduct: A Statutes Analyses.* Washington, D.C.: National Center for Juvenile Justice.

Isenstadt, Paul M. (1977) An Overview of Status Offenders in the Juvenile Justice System. Pp. 298-320 in Paul F. Cromwell et al., eds., *Introduction to Juvenile Delinquency.* St. Paul, Minn.: West Publishing Co.

Jones, Maxwell (1953) *The Therapeutic Community.* New York: Basic Books.

Juvenile Justice Standards Project (1980) *Juvenile Justice Standards: Rights of Minors.* Institute of Judicial Administration/American Bar Association. Cambridge, Mass.: Ballinger.

Kaufman, Herbert (1973) *Administrative Feedback: Monitoring Subordinates' Behavior.* Washington, D.C.: The Brookings Institution.

Kilgore, Gloria, and Salmon, Gabriel (1979) *Technical Notes, Summaries and Characteristics of States' Title XX Social Services Plans for Fiscal Year 1979.* Office of the Assistant

Secretary for Planning and Evaluation. Washington, D.C.: U. S. Department of Health, Education, and Welfare.

Klein, Malcolm (1971) *Street Gangs and Street Workers*. Englewood Cliffs, N.J.: Prentice-Hall.

———— (1979a) Juvenile Justice: Trends, Assumptions and Data. Unpublished manuscript prepared for the Regional Institute in Law and Mental Health.

———— (1979b) Deinstitutionalization and Diversion of Status Offenders: A Litany of Impediments. Chap. 5 in Norval Morris and Michael Tonry, eds., *Crime and Justice: An Annual Review of Research*. Vol. I. Chicago: University of Chicago Press.

Klein, Malcolm W., and Peterson, John (1981) Comparison of Program and Pre-Program Youth. Chap. 15 in Solomon Kobrin and Malcolm W. Klein, eds., *National Evaluation of the Deinstitutionalization of Status Offender Programs*. Vol. I. National Institute for Juvenile Justice and Delinquency Prevention. Washington, D.C.: U.S. Department of Justice.

Kobrin, Solomon, and Hellum, Frank R. (1981) Deinstitutionalization of Status Offenders: The Legislative Mandate. Chap. 1 in Solomon Kobrin and Malcolm W. Klein, eds., *National Evaluation of the Deinstitutionalization of Status Offender Programs*. Vol. I. National Institute for Juvenile Justice and Delinquency Prevention. Washington, D.C.: U. S. Department of Justice.

Kobrin, Solomon, and Klein, Malcolm W., eds. (1981) *National Evaluation of the Deinstitutionalization of Status Offender Programs*. Vols. I and II. National Institute for Juvenile Justice and Delinquency Prevention. Washington, D.C.: U. S. Department of Justice.

Koshel, Jeffrey (1973) *Deinstitutionalization—Delinquent Children*. Washington, D.C.: The Urban Institute.

Kramer, Ralph (1969) *Participation of the Poor*. Englewood Cliffs, N.J.: Prentice-Hall.

Leiby, James (1978) *A History of Social Welfare and Social Work in the United States*. New York: Columbia University Press.

Lerman, Paul (1975) *Community Treatment and Social Control*. Chicago: University of Chicago Press.

———— (1977) Delinquency and Social Policy: A Historical Perspective. *Crime and Delinquency* 23(October):383-393.

———— (1978) Deinstitutionalization in America: An Assessment of Trends and Issues in the Fields of Mental Illness and Retardation, Aging, Child Welfare and Delinquency. Prepared as a research contract for the National Institute of Mental Health, Division of Special Mental Health Programs, Contract No. 278-76-0087, September 1978, Rockville, Md.

———— (1980) Trends and Issues in the Deinstitutionalization of Youth in Trouble. *Crime and Delinquency* 26(July):281-298.

Levin, Mark, and Sarri, Rosemary (1974) *Juvenile Delinquency Assessment: A Comparative Analysis of Legal Codes in the United States*. National Institute of Juvenile Corrections. Ann Arbor, Mich.: University of Michigan.

Levine, Murray, and Levine, Adeline (1970) *A Social History of the Helping Services: Clinic, Court, School and Community*. New York: Appleton-Century-Crofts.

Levitan, Sar, and Wurzburg, Gregory (1979) *Evaluating Federal Social Programs*. Kalamazoo, Mich.: Upjohn Institute for Employment Research.

Lipsky, Michael (1980) *Street-Level Bureaucracy*. New York: Russell Sage Foundation.

Liska, Allen E., and Taussig, Mark (1979) Theoretical Interpretations of Social Class and Racial Differentials in Legal Decision-Making for Juveniles. *The Sociological Quarterly* 20(2):197-207.

Louisiana Department of Health and Human Resources (1979) *Final Comprehensive Annual Services Program Plan* (July 1, 1979 - June 30, 1980). Baton Rouge, La.: Department of Health and Human Resources.

Lowi, Theodore (1969) *The End of Liberalism*. New York: W.W. Norton.

Mack, Julian W. (1909) The Juvenile Court. *Harvard Law Review* 23:104-122.

Mann, C. (1979) The Differential Treatment Between Runaway Boys and Girls in Juvenile Court. *Juvenile and Family Court Journal* 30(May):37-48.

Massachusetts Department of Public Welfare (1977) Federal Eligibility Codes for CHINS Referrals. Memorandum dated August 19, 1977. Department of Public Welfare, Boston, Mass.

————— (1978) *Social Services Policy Manual*. Boston: Department of Public Welfare.

————— (1979) *Fifth Comprehensive Annual Social Service Plan for the Commonwealth of Massachusetts* (for fiscal year 1980). Boston: Department of Public Welfare.

Matza, David (1964) *Delinquency and Drift*. New York: John Wiley and Sons.

————— (1969) *Becoming Deviant*. Englewood Cliffs, N.J.: Prentice-Hall.

McCarthy, John, and Zald, Mayer (1977) Resource Mobilization and Social Movements: A Partial Theory. *American Journal of Sociology* 82(6):1212-1241.

Mennel, R. (1973) *Thorns and Thistles: Juvenile Delinquents in the United States 1825-1940*. Hanover, N.H.: University Press of New England.

Miller, Alden D., Ohlin, Lloyd E., and Coates, Robert B. (1977) *A Theory of Social Reform: Correctional Change Processes in Two States*. Cambridge, Mass.: Ballinger.

Mnookin, Robert (1973) Foster Care—In Whose Best Interest? *Harvard Educational Review* 43(4):599-638.

Moos, Rudolf, and Lemke, S. (1979) *Multiphasic Environmental Assessment Procedures*. Palo Alto, Calif.: Social Ecology Laboratory.

Morgan, E.S. (1966) *The Puritan Family: Religion and Domestic Relations in Seventeenth-Century New England*. New York: Harper and Row.

Morris, Norval (1974) *The Future of Imprisonment*. Chicago: University of Chicago Press.

Moynihan, Daniel P. (1969) *Maximum Feasible Misunderstanding*. New York: The Free Press.

Nakamura, Robert T., and Smallwood, Frank (1980) *The Politics of Policy Implementation*. New York: St. Martin's Press Inc.

National Advisory Commission on Criminal Standards and Goals (1973) Working papers prepared for the National Conference on Criminal Justice, held January 23-26, 1973.

National Advisory Commission on Juvenile Justice and Delinquency Prevention (1980) *Standards for the Administration of Juvenile Justice*. Washington, D.C.: U. S. Government Printing Office.

National Council on Crime and Delinquency (1967) Corrections in the United States. Pp. 115-213 in Appendix A of the President's Commission on Law Enforcement and Administration of Justice, *Task Force Report: Corrections*. Washington, D.C.: U. S. Government Printing Office.

National Youth Work Alliance (1979) *National Directory of Runaway Programs*. 4th ed. Washington, D.C.: National Youth Work Alliance.

Nirje, Bengt (1969) The Normalization Principle and Its Human Management Implications. Pp. 179-195 in Robert Kugel and Wolf Wolfensberger, eds., *Changing Patterns in Residential Services for the Mentally Retarded*. President's Committee on Mental Retardation, National Institute on Child Health and Human Development, U. S. Department of Health, Education, and Welfare, Washington, D.C.

Opinion Research Corporation (1976) *National Statistical Survey of Runaway Youth*. Princeton, N.J.: Opinion Research Corporation.

Palmer, Ted (1974) The Youth Authority's Community Treatment Project. *Federal Probation* 38(1):3-14.

Pappenfort, Donnell M., and Young, Thomas M. (1977) *The Secure Detention of Juveniles and Alternatives to its Use.* Washington, D.C.: U. S. Government Printing Office.

Peat, Marwick, Mitchell & Co. (1978) *Comparative Cost Analyses of the Deinstitutionalization of Status Offender Programs.* Washington, D.C.: Peat, Marwick, Mitchell.

Peirce, Bradford K. (1869) *A Half Century with Juvenile Delinquents.* New York: Appleton.

Pesso, Tana (1978) Local Welfare Offices: Managing the Intake Process. *Public Policy* 26(Spring):305-330.

Piven, Frances, and Cloward, Richard (1977) *Poor People's Movements.* New York: Pantheon.

Platt, Anthony (1977) *The Child Savers: The Invention of Delinquency.* Chicago: University of Chicago Press.

President's Commission on Law Enforcement and Administration of Justice (1967a) *Task Force Report: Corrections.* Washington, D.C.: U. S. Government Printing Office.

——— (1967b) *Task Force Report: Juvenile Delinquency and Youth Crime.* Washington, D.C.: U. S. Government Printing Office.

——— (1967c) *The Challenge of Crime in a Free Society.* Washington, D.C.: U. S. Government Printing Office.

President's Science Advisory Committee (1973) *Youth: Transition to Adulthood.* Panel on Youth. Washington, D.C.: U. S. Government Printing Office.

Pressman, Jeffrey, and Wildavsky, Aaron (1979) *Implementation.* 2nd ed., rev. Berkeley, Calif.: University of California Press.

Riback, L. (1971) Juvenile Delinquency Laws: Juvenile Women and the Double Standard of Morality. *UCLA Law Review* 19(2):313-342.

Roosens, Eugeen (1979) *Mental Patients in Town Life: Geel—Europe's First Therapeutic Community.* Beverly Hills, Calif.: Sage Publications.

Rosenheim, Margaret K. (1962) *Justice for the Child: The Juvenile Court in Transition.* Chicago: University of Chicago Press.

——— (1969) Youth Service Bureaus: A Concept in Search of a Definition. *Juvenile Court Judges Journal* 20(1):69-74.

——— (1976a) Notes on Helping Juvenile Nuisances. Pp. 43-66 in Margaret K. Rosenheim, ed., *Pursuing Justice for the Child.* Chicago: University of Chicago Press.

——— ed. (1976b) *Pursuing Justice for the Child.* Chicago: University of Chicago Press.

Rothman, David (1971) *The Discovery of the Asylum: Social Order and Disorder in the New Republic.* Boston: Little, Brown.

——— (1980) *Conscience and Convenience: The Asylum and its Alternatives in Progressive America.* Boston: Little, Brown.

Rubin, Ted. H. (1976) The Eye of the Juvenile Court Judge: A One-Step-Up View of the Juvenile Justice System. In Malcolm Klein, ed., *The Juvenile Justice System.* Beverly Hills, Calif.: Sage Publications.

Rutherford, Andrew, and Bengur, Osman (1976) *Community-Based Alternatives to Juvenile Incarceration.* Washington, D.C.: National Institute of Law Enforcement and Criminal Justice.

Rutherford, Andrew, and McDermott, Robert (1976) *Juvenile Diversion.* Washington, D.C.: National Institute of Law Enforcement and Criminal Justice.

Rutter, Michael, Graham, Phillip, Chadwick, O.F.D., and Yale, W. (1976) Adolescent Turmoil: Fact or Fiction. *Journal of Psychology and Psychiatry* 17:35-56.

Sabatier, Paul, and Mazmanian, Daniel (1980) The Implementation of Public Policy: A Framework for Analysis. *Policy Studies Journal* 8(Special Issue 2, 4):538-560.

Sarri, Rosemary (1974) *Under Lock and Key: Juveniles in Jails and Detention.* National Assessment of Juvenile Corrections. Ann Arbor, Mich.: University of Michigan.

Sarri, Rosemary, and Hassenfeld, Yeheskel, eds. (1976) *Brought to Justice? Juveniles, the Courts, and the Law.* National Assessment of Juvenile Corrections. Ann Arbor, Mich.: University of Michigan.

Sarri, Rosemary, and Vinter, Robert (1976) Justice for Whom? Varieties of Juvenile Correctional Approaches. Pp. 161-200 in Malcolm Klein, ed., *The Juvenile Justice System.* Beverly Hills, Calif.: Sage.

Scheiber, Harry (1980) Federalism and Legal Process: Historical and Contemporary Analysis of the American System. *Law and Society Review* 14(Spring):663-722.

Scheingold, Stuart (1974) *The Politics of Rights.* New Haven, Conn.: Yale University Press.

Schwartz, Ira (1980) *Juvenile Justice Amendments of 1980.* Testimony in U. S. Congress, hearing on March 19, 1980, by the House Committee on Education and Labor, Subcommittee on Human Resources. 96th Congress, 2nd Session. Washington, D.C.: U. S. Government Printing Office.

Schur, Edwin M. (1973) *Radical Non-Intervention: Rethinking the Delinquency Problem.* Englewood Cliffs, N.J.: Prentice-Hall.

Scull, Andrew (1977) *Decarceration: Community Treatment and the Deviant—A Radical View.* Englewood Cliffs, N.J.: Prentice-Hall.

Sosin, Michael (1981) Models of Organization and Commitment: Rates in Juvenile Courts. *Journal of Social Services Research.* (June).

Sowder, Barbara J., Burt, Maura R., Rosenstein, Marilyn J., and Milazzo-Sayre, Laura J. (1980) *Utilization of Psychiatric Facilities by Children and Youth.* Bethesda, Md.: Burt Associates.

Spergel, Irving (1976) Interactions Between Community Structure, Delinquency and Social Policy in the Inner City. Pp. 55-99 in Malcolm Klein, ed., *The Juvenile Justice System.* Beverly Hills, Calif.: Sage.

Spergel, Irving, Lynch, James P., and Korbelik, John (1980) Deinstitutionalization in Illinois: The Case for Removal of Status Offenses from Court Processing. Unpublished paper prepared for the Panel on Deinstitutionalization of Children and Youth, National Academy of Sciences, Washington, D.C.

Steiner, Gilbert (1966) *Social Insecurity: The Politics of Welfare.* Chicago: Rand McNally.

Sussman, Alan (1977) Sex-Based Descrimination and PINS Jurisdiction. Pp. 179-199 in Lee Teitelbaum and Aidan Gough, eds., *Beyond Control: Status Offenders in the Juvenile Court.* Cambridge, Mass.: Ballinger.

Swicord, Donald (1980) Characteristics of Youth Served. Youth Development Bureau, U. S. Department of Health and Human Services, Washington, D.C.

Symposium (1972) The Relationship Between Promise and Performance in State Intervention in Family Life. *Columbia Journal of Law and Social Problems* 9:28-62.

Tamilia, Patrick (1976) Toward a More Credible Juvenile Justice System in the United States. *Juvenile Justice* 27(2):3-11.

Teilmann, Katherine S., and Landry, Pierre H., Jr. (1981) Gender Bias in Juvenile Justice. *Crime and Delinquency* 18(1):47-80.

Teitelbaum, Lee, and Harris, Leslie J. (1977) Some Historical Perspectives on Governmental Regulations of Children and Parents. Pp. 1-44 in Lee Teitelbaum and Aidan Gough, eds. *Beyond Control: Status Offenders in the Juvenile Court.* Cambridge, Mass.: Ballinger.

Thomas, Charles W. (1976) Are Status Offenders Really So Different? *Crime and Delinquency* 22(4):438-455.

Thornberry, Jerome P. (1973) Race, Socioeconomic Status and Sentencing in the Juvenile Justice System. *Journal of Criminology and Political Science* 64(March):9^-98.

U.S. Congress (1974) *Staff Data and Materials on Social Services.* Senate Committee on Finance. 93rd Congress, 2nd Session. Washington, D.C.: U. S. Government Printing Office.

———— (1977) *Juvenile Justice Amendments of 1977.* Senate report 95-165. Committee on the Judiciary. 95th Congress, 1st Session. Washington, D.C.: U. S. Government Printing Office.

———— (1979a) *Adoption Assistance and Child Welfare Act of 1979.* Senate Report 96-336. Committee on Finance. 96th Congress, 1st Session. Washington, D.C.: U. S. Government Printing Office.

———— (1979b) *Social Services and Child Welfare Amendments of 1979.* House report 96-136. Committee on Ways and Means. 96th Congress, 1st Session. Washington, D.C.: U. S. Government Printing Office.

———— (1980a) *Adoption Assistance, Child Welfare, and Social Services.* House report 96-900. Conference Report. 96th Congress, 2nd Session. Washington, D.C.: U. S. Government Printing Office.

———— (1980b) *Juvenile Justice Amendments of 1980.* Hearings before the House of Representatives, Subcommittee on Human Resources, March 19, 1980, Washington, D.C.

U. S. Department of Health and Human Services (1980) *Public Assistance Statistics, November 1979.* ORS report A-2 (11/79). Washington, D.C.: Social Security Administration.

U. S. Department of Health, Education, and Welfare (1978) Application of Regulations Concerning the Exclusion of "Inmates of Public Institutions" from Medicaid Coverage to Certain Juveniles in the Custody of the Commonwealth of Virginia's Department of Corrections. Memorandum dated November 9, 1978, from Galen D. Powers, Assistant General Counsel, HEW, to Alwyn Carty, Jr., Regional Medicaid Director, Washington, D.C.

———— (1979a) *Data of the Medicaid Program: Eligibility, Services, Expenditures.* Health Care Financing Administration. Washington, D.C.: U. S. Department of Health, Education, and Welfare.

———— (1979b) Elementary and Secondary Education Act of 1965, P. L. 89-10 as Amended Title I, Assistance for Educationally Deprived Children Allotments for Fiscal Year 1980. Table dated March 30, 1979. Office of Education, Washington, D.C.

———— (1979c) *Progress Toward a Free Appropriate Public Education: A Report to Congress on the Implementation of Public Law 94-142, The Education for All Handicapped Children Act.* Interim Report. Office of Education. Washington, D.C.: U. S. Department of Health, Education, and Welfare.

———— (1980) *Preliminary National Medicaid Statistics: Fiscal Year 1978.* Washington, D.C.: Health Care Financing Administration.

U. S. Department of Justice (1975) *Children in Custody: Advance Report on the Juvenile Detention and Correctional Facility Census 1972-1973.* National Criminal Justice Information and Statistics Service, Law Enforcement Assistance Administration. Washington, D.C.: U. S. Government Printing Office.

Utah Department of Social Service (1979) *Final Title XX Plan, Utah Comprehensive Annual Service Program Plan for FY 1980.* Salt Lake City, Utah: Department of Social Service.

_____ (no date) *Family Service Manual*. Division of Family Services. Salt Lake City, Utah: Department of Social Services.

Velimesis, M.L. (1975) The Female Offender. *Crime and Delinquency Literature* 7(1):94-112.

Virginia Department of Health (1979) *Medicaid Manual*. Medicaid Transaction 25, dated October 1979. Richmond, Va.: Department of Health.

Wald, Michael (1976) State Intervention on Behalf of "Neglected" Children: A Search for Realistic Standards. Pp. 246-278 in Margaret K. Rosenheim, ed., *Pursuing Justice for the Child*. Chicago: University of Chicago Press.

_____ (1979) Children's Rights: A Framework for Analysis. *UC Davis Law Review* 12(Summer):255-282.

_____ (1980) Thinking About Public Policy Toward Abuse and Neglect of Children: A Review of *Before the Best Interests of the Child*. *University of Michigan Law Review* 78(5):645-693.

Walker, Deborah Klein (1975) *Runaway Youth: Annotated Bibliography and Literature Overview*. Washington, D.C.: Department of Health, Education, and Welfare.

Walker, Jack (1969) The Diffusion of Innovation Among the American States. *American Political Review* 63(September):880-899.

_____ (1975) The Diffusion of Knowledge and Policy Change: Toward a Theory of Agenda Setting. Paper delivered at the annual meeting of the American Political Science Association, Chicago, Ill., 1975.

Weiner, Irving B. (1970) *Psychological Disturbance in Adolescence*. New York: John Wiley.

Williams, Walter (1980) *The Implementation Perspective: A Guide for Managing Social Science Delivery Systems*. Berkeley, Calif.: University of California Press.

Wilson, James Q. (1973) *Political Organizations*. New York: Basic Books.

Wolfensberger, Wolf (1972) *The Principle of Normalization in Human Services*. Toronto: National Institute on Mental Retardation.

Wolfensberger, Wolf, and Glenn, Laura (1975) *PASS 3, A Method for the Quantitative Evaluation of Human Services*. Toronto: National Institute on Mental Retardation.

Wolpert, Julian, and Wolpert, Eileen (1974) From Asylum to Ghetto. *Antipode* 6(3):1-14.

_____ (1976) Relocation of Released Mental Hospital Patients into Residential Communities. *Policy Sciences* 7(1):31-51.

Zald, Mayer N. (1980) The Federal Impact on the Deinstitutionalization of Status Offenders: A Framework. Working paper commissioned by the Panel on Deinstitutionalization of Children and Youth, Assembly of Behavioral and Social Sciences, National Research Council, June 1980, Washington, D.C.

PART II

Overview

The materials contained in this part constitute the basic data of this study. As we stated at the outset, this study was charged with examining the effects of federal efforts on deinstitutionalization of status offenders in several states. It was an analysis of implementation; it was not a study of whether deinstitutionalization was a good or bad policy, either in concept or in fact. The themes and implementation theory developed in Part I are borne out in the ensuing chapters, and the findings and conclusions as well as the recommendations that we have made are based on what follows. These materials are important because they describe in detail the richness and complexity of the deinstitutionalization policies that have been implemented in the seven states under study.

The general thrust of deinstitutionalization as it applies to status offenders has been to separate these youth from delinquents and to keep them out of secure detention or correctional facilities. Those who have supported deinstitutionalization efforts at the state and local levels have not always agreed on their reasons for doing so, and the same can be said of those who have opposed such efforts. These forces and interests have had different motives even when allied on the same side, and their strength and intensity has varied both across and within states. Nor has there been much consistency in the cast of key actors. In some localities, for example, the juvenile court judge may favor deinstitutionalization; in

251

other localities--even within the same state--judges may
be in vigorous opposition. In some communities citizen
groups may press for deinstitutionalization; in others,
there may be no such activity, or the most influential
constituency may support institutionalization.

What should be done to or for these youth, to what extent, and for what purposes are unsettled questions.
There are those who argue that status offenders have done
nothing to warrant public reprobation and that their behavior is a matter to be worked out within the confines
of the family. Others, however, feel that even though
status offenders have not committed crimes, they are still
youth in trouble and in need of services. It is not
enough merely to remove them from secure facilities; they
should be provided with replacement services of a noninstitutional, community-based nature as well. Thus, the
deinstitutionalization initiative can be viewed as potentially having two parts: the removal of status offenders
from secure facilities, and the provision of alternative
kinds of services.

States and local areas have varied greatly in their
deinstitutionalization practices. This practical level
is where issues are being fought out: Judges are defending their jurisdictions, legislators and state agency
personnel are trying to economize, children's advocacy
groups are pressing for reform, and parents are demanding
help with their recalcitrant youth. It is against this
background that the federal government has asserted its
role. Federal intervention with regard to status offenders was not nearly so dramatic in its effect as it has
been in other social welfare areas. It was not a catalyst
of change and was in fact dependent on state and local
developments for its expression. Nevertheless, as both
the state case studies and the federal program analyses
attest, the federal effort was multiple and varied in its
impact both as to timing and to substance. In some
states, for example, citizen advocacy groups were influential, and they received important support from court
decisions and from LEAA grants. In other states these
groups were not as important, but the federal influence
was felt in other ways, such as through funds for state
and local agencies to use in rendering noninstitutional
services to status offenders.

Briefly stated, our theoretical framework is as
follows. There are variations across states in the types
and intensity of attitudes toward deinstitutionalization
of status offenders, in the characteristics and types of

interest group activities, in the size and scope of the status offender problem, and in the rates and kinds of innovation. In describing and accounting for these variations we stress a mode of implementation analysis known as backward mapping, which we feel is particularly well suited to studying the types of changes that have occurred in implementing the policy of deinstitutionalization.

Conventional implementation analysis starts with an assessment of the policymakers' intent and then examines each subsequent step in the implementation process to identify and compare outcomes with that intent as defined at the top. This type of analysis, or forward mapping, assumes that the closer one is to the source of the policy the greater the ability to influence it. Backward mapping, as the name implies, starts at the opposite end. It shares the concern of conventional implementation analysis with outcomes, but starts with the field-level officials and agencies that are responsible for the actual delivery of services. It looks at the problem of trying to achieve changes in output from the point of view of those who have the responsibility for implementing the desired changes. It assumes that the closer one is to the source of the problem, the greater the ability to resolve it. Although we did find federal sources of influence to be important, the most significant determinants of social change were at the state and local levels.

We found on the basis of our state case studies that (1) most adjudicated status offenders have been removed from traditional institutional facilities; (2) there has been a decline in the use of preadjudicatory detention for youth who have been charged with status offenses; (3) fewer youth who are labeled as status offenders are entering the juvenile justice system; and (4) for those status offenders who are diverted to some other service system, the predominant forms of out-of-home care reportedly are group home and foster care arrangements (the choice between the two often depends on the level of commitment and the extent of the resources that a state has to devote to the development of alternative types of facilities). It is unclear what happens to youth who commit status offenses but who do not enter the juvenile justice system or its closely related diversion programs. Many of the respondents in the state and local areas believe that these youth are being ignored altogether.

The recommendations that result from this study depend in large part on what the federal government wants to do about deinstitutionalization. If the federal government

chooses to continue its efforts, there are several steps
it can take to make these efforts more effective. Briefly
stated, these steps include: (1) continuing to declare
standards and policy; (2) tailoring its approach to implementation according to the different goals of deinstitutionalization; (3) promoting a variety of activities
encompassing all of the goals of deinstitutionalization;
(4) concentrating its attention on the most controversial
deinstutionalization goal--that of preventing detention
of status offenders; (5) focusing in a more systematic
fashion on the problems associated with funding alternative programs for status offenders; (6) continuing to
provide seed money to those local programs that it wishes
to encourage; and (7) finding ways to strengthen its monitoring and oversight capabilities. If the federal
government chooses to discontinue its support of deinstitutionalization, we recommend that it make every effort
to find out what has happened to these youth as a result
of its efforts and to be selective in its withdrawal of
support. The recommendations that we directed at the
states and localities mirror the recommendations for the
federal government. All these recommendations, along with
those that present important issues for future research,
have been spelled out in Part I.

10 Deinstitutionalization of Status Offenders in Arizona: State and Local Initiators of Policy Change

TIMOTHY MACK C. *and*
JOHN A. STOOKEY

APPROACH

A major task of this study is to determine the impact of the Juvenile Justice and Delinquency Prevention Act (JJDPA) of 1979. The focus of our study will be the state of Arizona.

The Office of Juvenile Justice and Delinquency Prevention (OJJDP) acknowledged in a letter to the Arizona Justice Planning Agency in July 1979 that Arizona had met the compliance requirements of JJDPA. That is, Arizona had reduced the number of status offenders in secure facilities by 75 percent (specifically, 75.2 percent) within three years. We attempt to determine if this dramatic decrease in the number of detained status offenders can be associated with passage of JJDPA. This attempt involves an examination of pre-JJDPA trends in the treatment of status offenders in Arizona, coupled with projections of these trends into the post-JJDPA period. We assess the relative importance of JJDPA, other federal legislation, and state and local initiatives in explaining any change in the treatment of status offenders since 1974.

Treatment of status offenders is broadly defined in this paper. JJDPA focuses on the placement of status offenders in secure settings. It is logically possible, however, that movement of status offenders out of those secure settings might represent instead the retention of the same population under different classifications (re-

labeling) or the transfer to other noncorrectional but no
less secure settings (e.g., a mental health facility).
Our examination of treatment, therefore, also includes
reference to patterns within delinquency and mental health
populations as well as placement policies generally.

This report is divided into three sections. The first,
on state policy, is a historical case study describing the
growth of concern over status offenders in Arizona, particularly during the period 1975-1978. We investigate
four statewide systems--juvenile justice, social services,
mental health, and corrections--and look closely at the
role they played in effecting deinstitutionalization in
Arizona. The discussion of the juvenile justice system
centers upon changes in Arizona legislation and the actors
who were responsible for those changes, while the social
services discussion examines the growth of mechanisms for
out-of-home placement in nonsecure settings. This placement focus is continued in the discussion of mental health
and corrections systems and the possibility of their use
for status offenders. Attention is given to whether deinstitutionalization can be ascribed to legislative action, administrative action, local court initiative, provider lobbies, public interest groups, or some combination
thereof.

The second section focuses on two Arizona localities
and their treatment of status offenders. One is the urban
area surrounding Phoenix in central Arizona (Maricopa
County), and the other is in the largely rural area along
the state's western border (Yuma and Mohave counties).
Other areas in the state are mentioned to illustrate specific points, when appropriate. The local section also
employs a case study approach, but in addition actively
pursues a quantified analysis of change. We show that
although anecdotal evidence is available indicating that
JJDPA created new programs and policies within the local
areas studied, long-term numerical trends appear not to
support this hypothesis. That is, neither JJDPA nor the
local programs born out of it appear to be the causal
factor in Arizona's deinstitutionalization. Rather, any
change that has occurred seems largely a result of influences within the state, (e.g., local decisionmakers, such
as judges or police departments). In the final section
of the paper we identify pervasive themes and draw conclusions based on our findings.

STATEWIDE SYSTEMS

Juvenile Justice System

The trial-court system in Arizona is organized by county. This means that each county funds its own court administration, secure facilities, and probation system. Since the passage of the 1907 Juvenile Court Act by the Territorial Legislature, the juvenile court in Arizona has been the superior court when it exercised its jurisdiction over juveniles.

The juvenile court is responsible for intake, adjudication, placement, and treatment of all children under 18 years of age who fall into one of three statutory categories--dependent, delinquent, or incorrigible (Arizona Revised Statute (ARS) 8-201 (1956), as amended 1980). A dependent child in Arizona is any child who has been neglected, abandoned, or abused. This category also includes any child under eight years of age who has committed an act that would have resulted in a finding of delinquency or incorrigibility if committed by an older child. A delinquent child is one who commits either an act that would be a public offense if committed by an adult or an act that would constitute a public offense that could only be committed by a child or minor (e.g., violations of Arizona's alcohol, tobacco, and curfew laws, the latter most often being a local ordinance). Also considered a delinquent is any juvenile who fails to obey a lawful order of the juvenile court. An incorrigible child is one who refuses to obey his or her parent, guardian, or custodian and is beyond control. This category also includes runaways, truants, and children who endanger the morals or health of themselves or others. As we shall see, the category into which a child is placed largely determines the type of treatment he or she will receive.

Most county juvenile courts in Arizona have consisted of a single superior court judge who sat part-time. The remainder of that judge's time was devoted to other judicial business in the county. The time of the county probation staff was often split in a similar manner between juvenile and adult probation duties. Decisions concerning this division of labor remained a matter of local discretion. Only the most urbanized counties had judges who spent their full time on juvenile matters, and this remains the case today. As Arizona's population grew and began to concentrate in urban areas, the structure of those urban juvenile courts also began to change. The history of the urban courts is one of constant adjustment to population growth and attendant changes in demands for services.

The Arizona court system is decentralized; from their inception the 14 superior courts have had some discretion concerning local practices and policies. According to observers within the juvenile court system, prior to 1970 each court had a different set of procedures for processing juveniles. In 1970, however, the supreme court instituted rules of procedure for juvenile courts in response to In re Gault (387 U.S. (1967))--which initially was an Arizona case--and its progeny. These rules provided a uniform set of procedures for handling children who come in contact with the juvenile court, regardless of county. The new rules of procedure were an amalgam of procedures from several counties and the new U.S. Supreme Court standards (e.g., a right to notice, counsel, and a hearing with all parties present) established in the Gault case.

The administrative authority of the state supreme court over the superior courts is broad but has been exercised only occasionally--for example, when a uniform set of rules of procedures became necessary. The supreme court is the official governing body for the state court system, but it was not perceived as a strong leader by the local court staff we interviewed. Although the supreme court is now beginning to assert more authority over local expenditure and policy, most changes in juvenile court policies and practices between 1970 and 1978 were not a result of supreme court initiative. Other actors, including the local courts, took the lead, and the major arena of change was the state legislature.

The most significant change pertaining to status offenders involved those who were held in secure facilities--either in the detention facilities run by each county or in those operated by the Arizona Department of Corrections. In August 1975 there were 339 status offenders being held in county detention and 110 in secure state-run facilities. By August 1978 these figures had fallen to 76 and 10, respectively--a reduction of 81 percent over the three-year period (Higgins et al. 1979). We attribute this dramatic decline to a number of factors--lobby efforts, local support, federal funds--that are discussed in detail later in this paper.

It is evident in Arizona that significant changes occurred around the time that the Juvenile Justice and De-

linquency Prevention Act was passed, and that changes in
state policy occurred subsequent to Arizona's decision to
participate in the act. Beginning in 1975 an Arizona
lobby began to form around the issue of state participation in JJDPA. As in other states, the act in its original form aroused the concern of state officials. Many
were concerned about the lack of nonsecure residential or
temporary shelter care centers that would serve as an alternative to county detention centers. The governor of
Arizona expressed reservations about fiscal liabilities
that the state might incur through participation. This
latter concern specifically involved the limited funding
initially available to Arizona under the act in contrast
to the cost of deinstitutionalizing status offenders,
which was estimated by the Arizona State Juvenile Justice
Advisory Council to be as much as $5 million (Higgins et
al. 1979). Additionally, the governor was concerned both
about the legal and administrative changes that the act
might require and about whether the Office of Juvenile
Justice and Delinquency Prevention might demand return of
federal funds should attempts to make these changes prove
unsuccessful. Largely in response to these reservations,
a number of public hearings to discuss the implications
of participation in JJDPA were held beginning in August
1975. These hearings involved legislators, law enforcement officials, juvenile courts, and interest groups such
as the Arizona chapter of the League of Women Voters. The
strongest advocates for participation in the act were the
interest groups and the Pima County Juvenile Court. As a
result of their advocacy and of OJJDP assurances that good
faith efforts would be sufficient for Arizona to qualify
for federal funds, the governor agreed to accept limited
participation in the act for one year (November 1975-
November 1976). Under this arrangement the state accepted only enough funding to allow the writing of a plan for
1976. At the end of that year the governor authorized
full participation in the act to begin in December 1976.
Although some reservations concerning the act had been
expressed at the public hearings (largely by juvenile
probation departments in rural counties, whose reservations focused on the mixed benefits of the act and the
federal seed money concept), little opposition was expressed to the goals of that act or to the deinstitutionalization effort in general. Opposition began to build
only when proposed legislation suggested that total deinstitutionalization was at hand.

During the 1976 legislative session, a bill designated SB 1038 was introduced in the Arizona Senate that would remove incorrigibility from juvenile court jurisdiction; that is, it would no longer be possible to bring juveniles before the juvenile court for running away, ungovernability, or truancy. Persons interviewed who were involved in drafting this bill indicated that their intention was to have the social services system accept those incorrigibles in need of services as dependent children. This suggestion, however, was not well received at the state social services agency, the Department of Economic Security (DES). DES staff whom we interviewed estimated that up to 9,000 additional cases per year would have become the department's responsibility, and they stated that the agency had neither funds nor staff to handle this influx. Juvenile court personnel asserted that this reluctance was part of a long-time lack of interest by DES in dealing with incorrigible youth. Some court staff asserted that the department had often refused to take custody of dependent children after they reached the age of 12, and would have those already in their custody declared incorrigible (and therefore transferred to the jurisdiction of the juvenile court) at the first sign of difficulty.

Although DES resistance served to undermine the success of SB 1038, its death knell was sounded by party politics. Originally a Democratic bill, it passed the Democratic senate and then moved over to the Republican house, where it promptly died in the judiciary committee.

In early 1977 two new proposals were introduced in a legislative package designated HB 2080.[1] The first of these prohibited the commitment of incorrigible youth (runaways, truants, and ungovernables) to the Department of Corrections. The practical effect was to prohibit long-term postadjudicatory placement of these youth in secure facilities. Because it only affected incorrigibles, however, placement options for other status offenders (e.g., alcohol, curfew, and tobacco violators) were not changed, and these offenses remained delinquencies under Arizona law. The second proposal went even further by prohibiting the preadjudicatory secure detention of incorrigibles.

---

[1]Ironically, the numerical designation HB 2080 was also assigned in two subsequent years to bills pertaining to juvenile justice issues. To distinguish among these bills, the year is added in the text (e.g., HB 2080 (1977).

Response to these initiatives appears to be distributed along urban/rural lines, with the most active lobbyists on both sides of the issue being the juvenile courts. The urban courts largely favored the initiatives, while rural courts did not. In this instance the rural courts prevailed, with neither of the proposals passing in their original forms. The prohibition on commitment to the Department of Corrections was eventually passed during the last days of the 1977 session as part of a less controversial foster care bill (SB 1356).

The unconditional prohibition on the use of detention for incorrigibles aroused a fatal opposition from the rural courts. The Coconino County Juvenile Court was the most active, not only rallying the surrounding rural courts against the bill but also sending its probation staff to testify at the legislative hearings. Interviews with the Coconino County court staff indicated that their opposition was based on the belief that certain status offenders, especially out-of-county runaways, would not remain in any but secure facilities while efforts were being made to return them home. It was also this court's conviction that juveniles under the influence of alcohol needed to be kept in secure facilities until they were sober and presumably less likely to commit alcohol-related crimes. This appeared especially necessary to them in cases involving youth from Indian reservations because long distances and poor communications made it difficult to contact parents within the 48 hours before a detention hearing was required. It was therefore the case in Coconino County that "youth are rarely released at the detention hearing" (Willett 1979:30).

A number of groups in addition to the urban courts lobbied in favor of the bill, including the Justice for Children Coalition, a private group that had a role in drafting the legislation. This coalition had also been active in the effort to bring about Arizona's participation in JJDPA. Founded in the mid-1970s under the sponsorship of the Arizona chapter of the National Council of Jewish Women, it soon became the focal point of a number of activist organizations, including Arizona chapters of the National Women's Club and the League of Women Voters. Together these groups ran conferences throughout the state promoting deinstitutionalization goals. Although their commitment to the concept of deinstitutionalization appears to be based on their acceptance of the doctrines expressed in JJDPA, it also appears to have predated that act. It is probably more accurate to say that the groups

were involved in the national movement toward deinstitutionalization of status offenders, of which JJDPA was a
part.

Another major leader in the deinstitutionalization
movement was the Pima County Juvenile Court, which had
been an active supporter of state participation in JJDPA
and had been intimately involved in deinstitutionalization
efforts. Before the state became a full participant in
JJDPA, this court had actively sought out discretionary
funds from the Law Enforcement Assistance Administration
(LEAA) for deinstitutionalization of status offenders.
With a $1.6 million grant they began developing nonsecure
facilities in the Tucson area in 1976, using the funds for
start-up costs. The court was convinced that a community-
alternative emphasis would be beneficial to the entire
state, and Pima County court staff were active legislative
lobbyists for several years. These lobbying efforts
ceased in January 1979, however, with the appointment of
a presiding judge who was not as sympathetic to deinstitutionalization efforts.

The 1978 session passed HB 2080 (1978), which allowed
police officers to divert preadjudicated, nondelinquent
youth directly to a nonsecure placement. In that year a
Joint Juvenile Justice Committee had been created with
LEAA funding. Designed as a "neutral" resource on children's issues, it was staffed out of the bipartisan Office
of Legislative Counsel and contained three members from
each house. During its first year the committee held a
series of public hearings in various parts of the state
concerning juvenile justice issues and JJDPA. Prior to
the hearings, the committee circulated an issue paper that
summarized arguments for and against full state compliance, reviewed the findings of various juvenile justice
standards groups, and highlighted the experience of other
states with JJDPA. A number of juvenile court staff and
law enforcement personnel spoke against compliance, while
providers and citizen groups spoke in favor of it. About
this same time the committee also conducted studies of
group care financing, juvenile court use of referees, and
costs of bringing shelter care into compliance with JJDPA.
In 1979 the committee proposed no legislation, in part
because of members' perceptions of the tone of the 1978
hearings--that is, that legislative positions on many
issues remained unresolved. Committee staff instead issued three further studies concerning (a) recommendations
for child care policy and financing, (b) recommendations
on revised placement procedures for children's and

adolescents' mental health facilities, and (c) recommendations about present juvenile court procedures. Fifty additional bills related to children and youth were introduced in the Arizona legislature during the 1980 session. Many concerned issues such as child health and safety that were unrelated to the deinstitutionalization of status offenders, but they were perceived nonetheless as the product of a concern for juvenile issues that had been spawned by the joint committee.

The agency charged with the implementation and monitoring of JJDPA in Arizona was the State Justice Planning Agency. Originally created under the Omnibus Crime Bill and Safe Streets Act of 1968, this agency has had a definite impact on the course of state deinstitutionalization policy. Legislation prohibiting the secure detention and commitment of status offenders to long-term secure facilities was a priority of the planning agency as early as 1976. Another target for change was the lack of nonsecure shelter and foster care available as alternatives to incarceration. To remedy the situation, the agency used LEAA discretionary funds to develop new facilities, to supply local training in fund-raising techniques, and to design statewide public education programs. Finally, the agency addressed the issues of the lack of intake personnel to divert status offenders, the lack of staff expertise in handling status offenders, and the lack of uniformity in deinstitutionalization policies throughout the state. They did this by funding staffing grants, training programs, and the development of information systems to aid monitoring and local decisionmaking. The Justice Planning Agency has been the most comprehensive source of information on status offenders within the state since 1975, and their data have been used by Arizona deinstitutionalization advocates, service providers, and the Joint Juvenile Justice Committee to support proposals and initiatives.

In conclusion, the changes wrought at the state level by the 1974 Juvenile Justice and Delinquency Prevention Act are fairly evident. New legislation, increased technical assistance to a number of local courts, and formal compliance with the deinstitutionalization mandate are the most obvious. More subtle is an apparent increase in concern with juvenile justice issues at both the legislative and local court levels. The impact that those changes in the juvenile justice system have had on other statewide systems and the impact statewide changes have had on local systems and the juveniles served by them are discussed in later sections.

TABLE 10-1 Arizona Juvenile Court Use of Out-of-Home Placements, 1969-1979

Years (January Count)	Total Children in Arizona Foster Care	Number of Children Placed by Juvenile Court in Foster Care	Percentage of all Arizona Foster Children Placed in Care by the Juvenile Court	Monthly Cost per Juvenile Court Placement ($)	Total Monthly Cost for Juvenile Court Placements ($)
1969	2,325	48	2	78.15	3,751
1970	2,314	143	6	76.06	10,877
1971	2,458	261	11	194.84	50,852
1972	2,355	267	11	229.45	61,262
1973	2,508	401	16	276.20	110,758
1974	2,727	448	16	360.37	161,446
1975	3,032	526	17	457.64	240,720
1976	2,942	483	16	502.40	242,658
1977	2,843	424	15	669.72	283,963
1978	2,577	518	20	698.80	361,980
1979	2,566	431*	17	932.08	401,730

*Approximately 50 of the 431 were status offenders.

Source: Unpublished data provided for this study by the Arizona Department of Economic Security, Administration for Children, Youth and Families, Phoenix, Arizona.

Social Services System

The Department of Economic Security is the largest of
Arizona's executive agencies. Its responsibilities encompass not only dependent children in need of protective
services, but children in foster care, mentally retarded
children, and children for whom assistance payments are
made. The department monitors the almost entirely private
system of residential care used by Arizona agencies and
courts and is also responsible for the administration of
the comprehensive medical and dental program, which is
state-funded care providing Medicaid-type (the state has
no Medicaid program) assistance to children in foster care
(ARS 8-512 (1956), as amended 1977).

Both the juvenile court and the Department of Economic
Security use foster care placements of all types. As a
practical matter this means that children who are adjudicated delinquent, dependent, or incorrigible may be placed
in the same facility. According to statistics provided
by DES for 1979, the majority of dependent placements are
in foster home settings while the majority of delinquent
placements are in larger (over five children) facilities.
Incorrigibles showed no definite placement pattern, but
this is not surprising as they seldom accounted for more
than 2 or 3 percent of the 1979 foster care population in
any given month, while delinquents account for around 14
or 15 percent. Data on status offender populations in
foster care are not available before 1979, but Table 10-1
shows an 11-year pattern for all juvenile court placements, based on a January count. All foster care placements, including placements made by juvenile court probation, are paid for out of the DES budget.

Upon further examination, it is apparent that despite
their reliance on DES funding, the Arizona juvenile courts
have remarkable independence in setting their placement
policies--an independence that has developed historically. In January 1969 the Arizona legislature decreed that
juvenile probation could draw whatever funds it needed for
foster care placements from the DES foster care line item.
At first this open draft made little impression on foster
care funds. For example, in January 1969 the cost of
foster care placements made by the juvenile probation office consisted of $3,750 for 48 children out of a total
of $166,610 for 2,325 children (see Table 10-1). Accord-
ing to juvenile court staff, there were only three commonly used dispositions in 1969--adjustment; probation
commitment to the Department of Corrections; and placement

in the one major alternative, the Arizona Boys Ranch. With apparently unlimited funds available, however, things began to change. As entrepreneurs developed services for the juvenile court population (which included status offenders), the foster care line item began to show the effects. By 1977 the "take what you need" approach had become impractical. Therefore, all parties sat down and developed a schedule for determining how this money was to be divided. The courts relied on historical usage as a guide, both as to how much the juvenile courts should receive out of the total, and also as to how it would be divided among the 14 individual courts. At the same time, an interagency task force of DES and all placement agencies was formed to participate in setting provider rates and in monitoring procedures. This task force lasted little more than a year, however, because of the inability of the parties to agree on standards.

The courts generally have abided by these self-imposed subdivisions, but each year more of the juvenile courts overspend. Court staff interviewed in Yuma County, for example, indicated that their fiscal 1980 allocation was spent before the end of calendar 1979. The staff said that this had never happened before. Although the actual number of children in juvenile probation placements dropped in 1980, the total cost of placements has continued to climb. This is in part the result of a steady increase in the cost of alternative care and in part a result of the growing willingness of courts to place children in more sophisticated and therefore more expensive placements.

Although placements to secure facilities within the state do not draw on this DES fund, the fiscal motivations that might in other states influence the increased use of secure facilities do not seem to apply to incorrigibles in Arizona. Arizona courts have not yet been pinched for placement dollars. Because at least some juvenile courts underspent, those more active consumers of placement dollars can draw on the surplus of other counties.

Arizona's juvenile justice system showed much more radical change in the treatment of status offenders. This change involved the state-mandated prohibition on the placement of status offenders in secure settings, which appeared to coincide with the timetable of JJDPA. Change in nonsecure placements, in contrast, has been much less marked and less obviously connected with JJDPA. This suggests that relabeling of status offenders as neglected or dependent children did not occur to any significant

extent. The figures in Table 10-1 do seem to be associated, however, because both figures decline gradually after 1975. In addition to a specific statutory constraint
(HB 2080 (1977)) on placement of incorrigibles with the
Department of Corrections, case law and policy have begun
to restrict the use of other systems (such as mental
health).

Mental Health System

The Department of Health Services was created in 1974 (HR
2004) by drawing together the existing Department of
Health and all public boards, homes, and hospitals that
provide health services within the state. Among these
facilities was the state mental hospital, which was incorporated into a division designated Behavioral Health
Services. Except for community placements, provided by
some Title XX funds from DES, public mental health services for children in Arizona have been limited to the
children's ward at the hospital, now called the Children's and Adolescents' Unit.

Children's mental health facilities began to develop
in private hospitals in the Phoenix and Tucson areas as
entrepreneurs became aware of the market presented by offender and nonoffender populations. Private facilities
large and small were quick to note the possibilities provided by the family counseling program and the apparent
ease with which juveniles could be committed or sent for
evaluation to a mental health facility. Because of this
growth in the more expensive private placements without a
corresponding growth in public placements (and, in fact,
a shrinkage as the hospital gradually dropped in population during the deinstitutionalization period of the early
1970s), many placing agencies became concerned. By 1979,
30 percent of expenditures by the DES comprehensive medical and dental program were for inpatient psychiatric
care. In January 1979 an ad hoc task force of state
agencies and juvenile probation departments began meeting
to discuss the possibility of expanding the Children's and
Adolescents' Unit at the Arizona State Hospital. At the
same time, however, concern was growing in other circles
that too many juveniles were being sent to this and all
other Arizona mental health hospitals.

In Arizona, offenders and nonoffenders could enter the
mental health system in a variety of ways. Under ARS
8-242 (1956, as amended 1972), if evidence at the dis-

positional hearing of a child adjudicated delinquent, dependent, or incorrigible indicated that the child could be suffering from mental illness, the juvenile court could order a psychiatric study and report. If it was found that the child could be committed under the laws of the state, the court could order commitment to an appropriate institution. This same provision could be used to assign a mentally retarded juvenile to the Department of Economic Security. ARS 36-518 of the Mental Health Services Act outlined those procedural protections to be afforded to a minor during admission to a mental health facility. This 1974 statute laid out the procedure for voluntary commitment and specifically stated that a minor 14 years or older must request commitment in writing for it to be considered voluntary. Without that voluntary status, the full investigation and hearing process was to be accorded the child. In 1980 this procedure was made even more rigorous, and a provision was added for a review of the case every 10 days (ARS 8-518.01 (198)).

In September 1979 a report issued by the Joint Juvenile Justice Committee of the Arizona Legislative Council charged that in many cases existing procedures were not being observed. The report cited instances in which the Departments of Economic Security and Corrections were placing juveniles who were under their jurisdiction in mental health facilities without a court hearing. The report also stated that juveniles were being sent for evaluations prior to adjudication and that such evaluations were allowed to go on for as long as 60 to 90 days. According to the report, "these admissions are most often based on the discretion of the individual judges, social workers, and staff involved, and vary from agency to agency, from court to court, and from county to county" (Arizona Legislative Council 1979:1).

Judicial interviews confirmed the report's findings. This situation had occurred, it was felt, as the result of two considerations. The first was that the Arizona commitment statutes were unwieldy and time-consuming. Second, the Children's and Adolescents' Unit was the only secure mental health treatment center in the state. Many Arizona judges felt that the unit would not take court referrals unless placed under duress, and that even then they would release the youth prematurely. From that perception developed a practice of keeping the child in the unit for a fixed period of time, regardless of hospital assertions that the child was ready for release. The paucity of appropriate services for disturbed children other than the Children's and Adolescents' Unit was one of the major concerns of the Joint Juvenile Justice Committee's report.

Although it is difficult to document the possible use of mental health facilities as a substitute for secure detention of status offenders, we do not imply that it did not occur. Prior to the joint Committee's report on these practices, it is extremely likely that it occurred more often. In December 1979, for example, a special action in Division Two of the Arizona Court of Appeals found that the Pima County Juvenile Court had exceeded its authority by committing to the Arizona State Hospital a juvenile who had not been adjudicated (Dandoy v. Fisher, 2 Ct. App. 79-3477). The special action was filed by the Arizona State Hospital (in the person of the director of the Department of Health Services) in regard to a female who had been committed for a 30-day evaluation. At a review the juvenile court found that she was still dangerous to herself and to others and ordered that she remain at the Children's and Adolescents' Unit until further notice. The juvenile, however, had not been adjudicated dependent, delinquent, or incorrigible, and so the hospital argued that it had no legal justification to keep her, since they deemed it clinically inappropriate to do so. In addition, the state hospital argued that the juvenile court had not complied with the commitment procedures of the Mental Health Services Act, and the commitment was therefore invalid on a third ground. The Arizona Court of Appeals agreed with the state hospital, finding that the juvenile court must follow these procedures for commitment, that the state hospital does have the authority to discharge patients who do not require in-hospital care, and that the juvenile court may only commit adjudicated youth. It is evident that while some growth in the placement of juveniles within Arizona mental health facilities occurred over the last few years, there is much to suggest that this system will be used less in the future, in part as a result of subsequent additions to the juvenile commitment statute (ARS 8-242.01 (1980)). Insufficient data are available to substantiate prior relabeling of status offenders as residents of the mental health system. The Arizona mental health system provides an additional instance in which federal legislation has directly changed state policy through the funding of agents responsible for the change.

Corrections Systems

Created in 1968, the Department of Corrections provided
an administrative structure for what had previously been
a series of largely independent institutions and parole
functions. Department data make it evident that while
referrals to the juvenile court were increasing over this
period, commitments to corrections were beginning to decrease. In 1969, for example, there were 36,069 referrals to the courts from all sources and 1,024 commitments
to corrections. By 1972 the total referrals to juvenile
court had climbed to 40,250 annually, but commitments had
dropped to 535.

Although no referral data are available in Arizona for
the period 1973-1979, Table 10-2 shows the number of commitments to the Department of Corrections over the last
11 years by type of offense. These data are open to numerous interpretations, but the analyses center upon two
issues. The first issue is the impact of JJDPA on commitment policies. Although there has been a tremendous
drop in the number of status offenders sent to corrections, that decrease seems to have started considerably
before the passage of the act in 1974. This is fairly

TABLE 10-2 Commitments to the Arizona Department of
Corrections by Offense, 1969-1979

Year	Status Offense	Violent	Property	Drug
1969	460	78	330	82
1970	383	74	351	96
1971	352	84	288	96
1972	205	55	198	55
1973	156	38	175	33
1974	174	61	207	36
1975	134	92	249	37
1976	87	40	173	21
1977	104	79	169	25
1978	61	103	233	20
1979	56	128	223	17

Source: Unpublished data provided for this study by the
Arizona Department of Corrections.

TABLE 10-3   Status Offense Arrests
in Arizona, 1975-1978

Year	Status Offense Arrests
1975	8,339
1976	8,554
1977	8,908
1978	9,041

Source: Higgins et al. (1979:31).

consistent with commitments during the same pre-1974 period for drug, violent, and property offenses. It should be noted that during the last two years (1978 and 1979) there has been an increase in violent and property offense commitments, an increase that has not occurred in status offense commitments. This may reflect the dampening effect of HB 2080 (1977) on status offender commitments.

One possible explanation for this drop in status offense commitments would be that overall status offense arrests decreased during this period, but available data show that this is not the case. Data on juvenile crime levels are not available for the entire 11-year period, but we do have arrest levels for 1975 to 1978. As is clear when comparing Table 10-2 with Table 10-3, which shows the number of commitments to corrections from 1975 to 1978, there is no concomitant decrease in status offense arrests during this period. This explanation for the reduced number of commitments to the Department of Corrections must thus be rejected.

The most significant aspect of these data is that the trend toward reduced use of the Department of Corrections began at least six years before JJDPA was introduced into the state and eight years before HB 2080 was passed in 1977. Thus, if the commitment rates between 1969 and 1974 were used to define a trend, it would have been possible to predict the continuing drop of commitments to corrections without knowing that JJDPA and HB 2080 were to come to pass. This leads to the conclusion that, at least with regard to the deinstitutionalization of status offenders from long-term secure facilities, policies were developing before any formal federal or state legislative actions were taken.

Few definite conclusions, however, can be made by comparing Tables 10-1 and 10-2. Although some inverse relationship is evident between the drop in secure commitments and the rise in nonsecure placements, the populations are essentially different. Available data indicate that status offenders constituted only 15 percent of nonsecure placements in 1979, while percentages for earlier years are unavailable. In addition a major variable--the availability of nonsecure placements after the 11-year period--remains unaccounted for. Reliable indicators, such as those discussed in the conclusion in reference to Pima County, imply that availability grew substantially over this period, and thus the principle of supply and demand alone might account for much of the increase in placements. Also difficult to account for is the impact of placement funding, as was discussed in the section on social service systems. It must be concluded, therefore, that the question of the relationship between the decline of placements in secure facilities and the growth of placements in nonsecure facilities cannot be effectively addressed at this time. It remains, however, a critical issue that might profitably be addressed by researchers with access to more complete data.

A secondary issue raised by Table 10-2 concerns the use of data generally. While the data supplied by the Department of Corrections show a significant decrease in status commitments over the past decade, the 1979 levels shown in Table 10-2 remain well above those figures cited by state officials and reported to OJJDP. According to corrections administrators and the Justice Planning Agency staff, this anomaly results from the use of committing offense rather than adjudicated offense as the system denominator. To illustrate the distinction, a juvenile who had been adjudicated a delinquent and put in a community placement or on probation could be committed to the Department of Corrections as an incorrigible for running away from that placement or for any status offense that violated the terms of probation. According to a survey done by the department in December 1979, a maximum of three so-called pure status offenders were committed in 1979 (versus the 56 shown by the department's computer). Two of the three status offenders were reportedly delinquents under Arizona law, which from 1977 to 1980 barred commitment of adjudicated incorrigibles but not of alcohol or curfew violators. The third was a runaway who had also stolen a car but was charged for the lesser offense. While the survey was accomplished by informally polling youth-hearing officers who review the records of each committed juvenile, it appears to indicate that present status offender commitments to corrections are in fact minimal. It also points up the necessity of closely examining Arizona's often misleading statistics.

We now proceed to the local area studies in which we describe local systems, detail changes that occurred in them over time, and speculate concerning possible relationships between state and federal initiatives and local outcomes.

LOCAL AREAS

In order to examine in detail the impact of state and federal initiatives on local service systems, we looked at one urban and two rural counties. The urban county is Maricopa County, the most populous in the state. As of July 1979 it contained 55.6 percent of all Arizona residents under 18 years of age. Because Maricopa County also contains the state capital and the majority of the state's out-of-home placements, it is an ideal site at which to observe the workings of many actors within a single area and to observe the influence of local government and private providers on state policymaking (and vice versa).

The second local area is a planning region that contains two rural counties, Yuma and Mohave. The decision to use a planning district rather than a single county did not affect comparisons with Maricopa County, which also constitutes a planning district (Region I). The regional structure also has characteristics that make it more attractive than a county as the unit of analysis. Most federal funding, including Title XX and JJDPA funding, is distributed by region. Social services are delivered through a DES district structure that, in rural areas, usually includes more than one county.

The rural area chosen was Region IV, whose two counties account for the entire western border of the state. As opposed to Maricopa County, which has one large city (Phoenix) surrounded by a number of small satellite cities, each of the Region IV counties has one small city (Yuma and Kingman) surrounded by vast areas that are very sparsely inhabited. Both counties together contain only 4.8 percent of the state's total population and only 5.3 percent of all Arizona residents under 18 years of age (as of July 1, 1979).

Local Area Design

Although this study attempts to determine the current treatment of all status offenders in Arizona, its primary goal is to assess the impact of the Juvenile Justice and Delinquency Prevention Act on Arizona and its constituent counties. In order to accomplish this, our analysis of the nonoffender systems in the three selected counties will examine the following issues:

1. Have the structures and/or procedures for dealing with status offenders changed during the last 10 years? If they have, in what ways?
2. To what extent are changes in structures and/or procedures a result of JJDPA?
3. If there were changes in structures and/or procedures, to what extent did they result in the deinstitutionalization of status offenders?

County Status Offender Systems

The hub of the status offender system in each county is the juvenile court. Rather than considering the counties individually, we will compare them with regard to specific court processes--court referral, court intake, detention, and disposition.

Court Referral   Status offenders are referred to the court from one of five sources: a social service agency, most often the Department of Economic Security (DES); police; family; school; or probation officer. The source of referral for status offenders depends on the type of offense. For example, in Maricopa County during 1977, 70 percent of the incorrigibility referrals to the court came from the family, while 87 percent of the truancy referrals came from the schools. Over 90 percent of the other categories of status offenses (i.e., curfew and liquor violations and running away) were from the police.

Under HB 2080 (1978), the police in Arizona have the option to refer status offenders to nonsecure facilities without taking them first to juvenile court. Facilities have been established in two of the three counties (Maricopa and Yuma) specifically for this purpose. Tumbleweed, a nonsecure facility for runaways, was established in Maricopa County in October 1975 with an LEAA grant. Upon the expiration of that grant in 1979, Tumbleweed re-

ceived $88,000 of Title XX funding from DES to continue
its services. According to a recent study conducted between July 1977 and March 1979, Tumbleweed received 64
(20 percent) of its 324 referrals directly from the police
(Associates for Youths Department 1980).

Also in Maricopa County, the Scottsdale and Chandler
Police Departments have attempted to deal with status offenders by setting up counseling units within the department for these youth. The Chandler program was started
in late 1979, but the Scottsdale Crisis Intervention Unit
has been operational since 1974. The role of the unit is
to respond to family fights, cases of child abuse, sexual
assaults, and other crisis situations. The majority of
situations involve juvenile and family-related crises.
When parents file a runaway or incorrigibility report to
the Scottsdale Police Department, it goes directly to the
crisis intervention unit for investigation. For the
quarter July to September 1978 the crisis intervention
teams handled 319 juvenile cases, primarily first-time
offenders and status offenders.

Another diversion program that police can use in lieu
of juvenile court detention is Children's Village in Yuma.
Originally conceived by a local citizens organization
(Yuma County Child Abuse and Neglect, Inc.) as a home for
neglected and dependent children, Children's Village has
now become a short-term residential facility for status
offenders as well. This 13-bed facility opened in July
1979 and has been operating at or near capacity ever
since. The creation of this facility provides an example
of a multiplicity of actors coming together to develop a
new community placement. Initial investigations by Yuma
County Child Abuse and Neglect Inc. indicated that the
dependent child case load in Yuma County would be insufficient by itself to justify the development and support
of a shelter care center. These original supporters
therefore formed a coalition with the county juvenile
court and the Yuma County Association for Behavioral
Health Services, Inc.--a mental health services conglomerate that had an LEAA grant and supplied counseling services to the juvenile court under the Arizona Supreme
Court's family counseling program. Much of the early
planning was done by a member of the probation staff who
was funded by the state Justice Planning Agency (with
JJDPA monies) to provide services to status offenders; the
salary for the director of the new facility came out of
the LEAA grant to Yuma County Association for Behavioral
Health Services, Inc. Funding for the first quarter came

relatively equally from city, county, and state (DES),
while the referrals were fairly evenly distributed between
dependent children from DES and status offenders from the
Yuma County Juvenile Court Center. According to the first
quarter report, more than 60 percent of its referrals returned home upon leaving Children's Village, while approximately 15 percent went to other nonsecure out-of-home
placements and 10 percent returned to secure detention.

Mohave County attempted to support an emergency foster
care receiving home for status offenders, but consistently
had troubles with retaining reliable foster home parents
in that rural setting. Part of the problem appeared to
be an unwillingness by local government in Mohave County
to make the sort of financial commitment necessary to ensure permanent facilities.

Discussions with police departments from all three
counties revealed a consensus on the issue of the total
removal of status offenses from the books; the police were
uniformly against such a step. They seemed to feel that
status offense laws were a necessary tool that allowed
them to apprehend or detain youth before they could get
into worse trouble. A Phoenix police officer gave the
example of using curfew violations as a way of preventing
a youth from committing a more serious offense, such as
burglary. Another Phoenix police officer attributed the
drop in status offense referrals to the futility of making
such a referral. He said that street officers know that
if they take a status offender to the juvenile court, the
youth "will be home before the officer." It appears that
court policies with regard to status offenders have an
anticipatory effect on police referrals.

Despite their general opposition to removing these offenses from the books, the police did indicate that they
were referring fewer and fewer status offenders to court.
This statement is supported by the official complaint
data. For example, in Maricopa County there was a 57
percent decrease in status offense complaints between 1973
and 1977.

Probably a more significant factor in explaining the
drop in referrals in Maricopa County was a new policy on
processing many of the complaints involving children that
was instituted by the Phoenix Police Department in January
1975. This new policy changed the treatment of runaways
and the use of paper referrals. Runaways were no longer
to be taken to court unless there was an outstanding warrant and no alternative disposition could be arranged.
Additionally, the Phoenix police stopped using paper re-

ferrals--a process in which the complaint is sent to the court even though the youth is not physically taken there.

As can be seen in Table 10-4, which gives the number of court referrals of status offenders in Maricopa County, between 1974 and 1975 the number of referrals was cut in half, while in the following years the level remained about constant. Runaways, for example, experienced a 62 prcent drop in referrals from 1974 to 1975, but a drop of only 17 percent in 1975-76 and 10 percent in 1976-77.

This change in policy, with concomitant reduction in the potential pool of detainees, would seem to be an important step toward the deinstitutionalization of status offenders. Similarly, given that this change happened before Arizona entered the act, we might conclude that the impetus for this step was totally local in origin. An interview with a Phoenix police official who was involved in the policy change, however, suggests what might be called an anticipatory impact of JJDPA. According to this official, there was a feeling among some members of the police department as early as 1964 that the force should be less involved with status offenses. This feeling was based on two convictions: (1) status offenses are family matters and should not, except in rare instances, be dealt with by the police; and (2) the police and courts are overcrowded and all of their available time should be devoted to serious juvenile offenses. A large segment of

TABLE 10-4 Court Referrals of Status Offenders in Maricopa County, 1973-1977

Reason for Referral	1973	1974	1975	1976	1977
Incorrigibility (ungovernable behavior)	1,538	1,910	942	582	1,023
Runaway	4,308	4,220	1,611	1,331	1,199
Runaway from other jurisdictions	316	299	197	254	411
Truancy	249	233	107	85	118
Total	6,411	6,662	2,857	2,252	2,751

Source: Unpublished data provided for this study by the research department of the Maricopa County Juvenile Court Center.

the police department, however, was opposed to any changes
in the police officers' options with regard to status offenders. The turning point, according to this official,
was an LEAA meeting on JJDPA that was held in Washington,
D.C., in 1974. Attendees came back to Phoenix with the
message that the deinstitutionalization of status offenders was a "wave from the East" that would soon reach Arizona in the form of federal mandates. Police officials
became convinced that it was better to take steps toward
deinstitutionalization now on their own than be forced
into it later. The police official whom we interviewed
asserted that "it is hard to get the attention of a conservative state like Arizona" on a matter like this, and
the "threat" of federal action was necessary to achieve
the policy at that time. The official also opined that
change would have occurred eventually, because of the
growing work load of the police and court system.

Court Intake   If the youth is referred to the county juvenile court rather than released or diverted, he or she
is first processed by the court intake unit. In Maricopa
County there is an intake unit of 34 probation officers
and five section supervisors who review all police requests for detention, screen all nondetention referrals,
and staff the family crisis unit. This unit was set up
as part of the intake unit in January 1976, and it provides a means of informal adjustment within the court
itself. It handles all incorrigible and runaway cases,
and attempts to reduce the likelihood of detention by
providing family counseling. The family crisis unit pursues this goal by (1) working exclusively with runaway and
incorrigible cases; (2) carrying all cases through disposition; (3) looking at problems from a family perspective (i.e., the child is not the exclusive focus); (4)
working in two-person teams of probation officers; (5)
offering counseling services to families for up to six
weeks; and (6) having the petition process initiated by
parents, not the probation officer or county attorney.
The unit's orientation toward detention in cases of running away or incorrigibility is first to minimize the use
of detention and then to seek out alternatives that are
acceptable to the parents and the youth. As an indication
of the success of their efforts, in 1977 the family crisis
unit had 1,444 contacts with incorrigible youth, 154 of
which resulted in detention.
     The history of the family crisis unit is much more
complicated than a simple response to a deinstitutionali-

zation initiative; the juvenile court in Maricopa County contained a diversion unit long before the creation of the family crisis unit. Initially designated the Adolescent Offenses Unit, its diversion role was even more radical than the family crisis unit, for it was designed to screen the maximum number of incorrigibles out of the court system entirely. According to the judge who presided over the juvenile court at the time, it was the role of the diversion unit to convince as many parents as possible that the juvenile court was the wrong place for their child. This unit, however, was not set up to provide alternatives or counseling, which gradually came to be seen as a basic flaw in its design. The presiding judge began to feel that aggravated situations were thus worsened and that for want of appropriate services, juveniles who could not appropriately be turned away all too often were placed in detention. So when the family crisis unit was established in 1976, it was designed to screen juveniles into the system and to provide services, not to screen them out as the diversion unit had done. One might say, therefore, that in creating the family crisis unit the presiding judge was reacting to an _excess_ of diversion.

In addition to the family crisis unit, the Maricopa intake unit has three shelter care facilities that can be used for short-term crisis housing of status offenders. They are Family Villas, Tumbleweed, and Pre-Hab of Mesa, all of which are funded by both DES and JJDPA.

Through the process of administrative rule-making, the Maricopa County Juvenile Court has limited the number of situations in which the intake unit can decide to place a youth in detention. Unlike the broader statewide standards, detention is allowable only in two instances: (1) when the youth has failed to appear at an appointed hearing in the past, and (2) when suicide or personal injury is likely if the youth is released. This avoids the potentially muddy areas of the interest of the public and the possibility of additional offenses, both of which are contained in the 1970 Rules of Procedure.

In Yuma County, intake is handled by three juvenile probation officers. One officer spends two days a week in Parker, Arizona, holding hearings and adjusting cases in this outlying area when possible. In addition to detention, Yuma intake has two major options: short-term placement in Children's Village and nonresidential counseling by Yuma County Association for Behavioral Health Services, Inc., which has a contract with the court to handle counseling of youth.

In Mohave County the intake process is handled by a full-time juvenile probation officer or youth services coordinator who specializes in status offenders and who has been operative since 1978 under an LEAA grant. Like all intake workers, this coordinator has full discretion in each case. In addition to the detention option, the Mohave juvenile probation officer may provide counseling to status offenders and their families directly, or may informally adjust the case by referring the youth to Mohave Behavioral Health, Inc., which provides counseling services to the court under contract. A less dependable option is to place the youth in the four-bed emergency foster care receiving home. The undependability of this option arises from a problem endemic to rural areas, namely, the difficulty of recruiting and retaining foster parents who are willing to work long hours with difficult youth for low wages. This sort of problem appears endemic to Arizona's rural areas, and suggests that infusion of outside monies into underdeveloped areas may leave unaffected those services that are not directly funded.

A recurring theme in both Yuma and Mohave Counties concerning intake was the ambiguity of the jurisdiction between the Department of Economic Security and the juvenile court in handling some status offenders. On the one hand, the court intake staff felt that DES was unwilling to take any youth who might be incorrigible, even if that youth was neglected or abused. On the other hand, DES said that the court intake unit attempted to send to them the children with behavioral problems—that is, children with whom their child protective services unit was not capable of dealing.

Detention Maricopa County has a unified juvenile court center, which means that the juvenile court, juvenile probation, and the detention center are all in the same complex. These units were centralized in 1970 and have a detention capacity of 101 juveniles. In Yuma the current detention center was constructed in 1970 and has 25 beds. The Mohave detention center was also completed in 1970 and has 12 beds. Construction in all three counties was aided by LEAA funding.

A look at the detention statistics gathered by the Justice Planning Agency to monitor compliance with JJDPA (as shown in Table 10-5) indicates a distinct drop in the number of status offenders detained (Higgins et al. 1979). Although these data reflect a downward trend in the use of detention facilities since Arizona began to participate

TABLE 10-5   Status Offenders in Detention for More than 24
Hours During August 1975-1979

County	August 1975	August 1977	August 1978	August 1979
Maricopa	103	n.a.*	32	13
Yuma	34	25	6	6
Mohave	6	3	1	2

*Not available.

Source: Higgins et al. (1979:15); Arizona State Justice
Plans (1977, 1979).

in JJDPA in 1975, we cannot assume that that act was the
only cause of the drop. For example, it is possible that
a reduction in crime levels during this period resulted
in a reduction in the potential pool of detainees.   One
indirect way of addressing that possibility is to look at
the arrest levels for that period. As revealed in Table
10-6, the level of status offense arrests was consistent
in Maricopa and Mohave Counties and increased slightly in
Yuma County over the period 1975 to 1979, and therefore
did not contribute to the reduction in detention rates.
   Similarly, changes in referral behavior do not seem to
explain adequately the drop in the level of detention, at
least with regard to Maricopa County. After a drop in
referrals between 1974 and 1975, as we saw in Table 10-4,
the referral of incorrigibles stabilized in Maricopa
County at the lower level.
   Another indicator of the importance of JJDPA to the
reduction in detention levels would be the point at which
the drop in such levels began. If the levels were fairly

TABLE 10-6   Status Offender Arrests by County, 1975-1979

County	1975	1976	1977	1978	1979
Maricopa	3,466	3,810	3,916	3,698	3,933
Yuma	263	267	399	474	542
Mohave	129	108	116	125	119

Source: Higgins et al. (1979:29-31).

constant or rising until Arizona entered the act in 1975
and then began to drop, this would provide strong evidence
for the importance of the act. However, if a downward
trend in detention levels existed before 1975, this would
indicate the importance of other factors. Detention
levels by year for Yuma and Mohave Counties are presented
in Table 10-7. Before we can draw any conclusions concerning the impact of JJDPA on detention practices in
these counties, however, it is necessary to issue several
caveats concerning the data in Table 10-7. First, data
from as far back as 1969 are (according to staff in all
three of the counties) very poor in terms of completeness
and accuracy. In fact, Maricopa County officials refused
to release detention data for years preceding 1977 because
they felt such data would be so inaccurate as to be
meaningless. Thus, we must consider the data presented
in Table 10-7 as illustrative at best.

A second factor to be kept in mind when examining this
table is that these data represent the total number of
youth who were admitted to detention. This is a different
measure of institutionalization than that mandated by the

TABLE 10-7   Status Offenders Detained in Yuma and
Mohave Counties, 1969-1979

Year	Yuma	Mohave
1969	310	n.a.*
1970	293	n.a.*
1971	308	n.a.*
1972	423	n.a.*
1973	407	266
1974	405	148
1975	362	164
1976	391	143
1977	428	122
1978	401	110
1979	398	74

Note: Figures represent the number of status offenders
officially registered as having been placed in detention.

*Not available.

Source: Official detention statistics compiled for this study
by detention facility staff.

LEAA and used by the Justice Planning Agency. The federal guidelines deal with detention of status offenders for a period of over 24 hours, whereas the data presented here include all youth placed in detention, no matter how long they stayed. Although these data were used because detailed information on length of stay was not available, we believe that insights into the attitudes of a county toward deinstitutionalization can be gained by looking at gross detention figures. We would argue that if a county is committed to deinstitutionalization, it will attempt to reduce the number of status offenders placed in detention for any length of time.

With these caveats in mind, we can see that the number of youth who were placed in detention for status offenses in Yuma County over the period 1969 to 1979 has remained constant. In Mohave County, however, we see that the detention level does consistently decline from 1973 to 1979. Thus we can say that, to the extent that these data are accurate, no change caused by JJDPA is apparent in either area. In Yuma County there is no drop in detention level, and in Mohave County the downward trend appears to have begun before the act was passed.

Although we do not have data on detention rates in Maricopa County for the period preceding JJDPA, we do have detailed data by month for the period 1977 to 1979. In Table 10-8 we see that there has been a trend away from the use of detention for status offenders. Again this table reports detention, regardless of length of stay, but these results are consistent with those found by the Justice Planning Agency using the greater-than-24-hour criterion. In summary, we have seen that Mohave and Maricopa Counties show a drop in the use of detention for status offenders since the act. This finding is supported by both the planning agency data and the data gathered specifically for this study.

In both counties, however, there are some indications that the downward trend may have begun before JJDPA was passed. In Mohave, for example, we have demonstrated a drop in detention levels beginning in 1973, two years before Arizona entered the act. Although the data does not permit us to delineate trends in Maricopa County before JJDPA was passed, interviews indicated that there was a movement toward deinstitutionalization before 1974. The presiding Maricopa County juvenile judge at the time said that the move toward deinstitutionalization in that county grew out of dissatisfaction with the previous policy and had "zero" to do with the act. He said that when the

TABLE 10-8   Status Offenders Detained in Maricopa
County, July 1977 to June 1979

Month/Year	Youth Detained on Status Offense Complaints*
July 1977	143
August 1977	171
September 1977	153
October 1977	134
November 1977	110
December 1977	76
January 1978	116
February 1978	93
March 1978	70
April 1978	86
May 1978	81
June 1978	58
July 1978	45
August 1978	68
September 1978	75
October 1978	51
November 1978	43
December 1978	28
January 1979	59
February 1979	45
March 1979	53
April 1979	48
May 1979	60
June 1979	43

*Number of status offenders officially registered
as having been placed in detention.

Source: Unpublished data provided for this study
by the research department of the Maricopa County
Juvenile Court Center.

court began to look at potential changes in the treatment
of status offenders, JJDPA was "never even heard of" in
Maricopa County.

Thus we can conclude that in Maricopa and Mohave Counties the seeds of change were present before JJDPA. Furthermore, at least in Maricopa County, the funds provided
by the act do not seem to have been crucial to the deinstitutionalization effort. For example, the number of
youth referred from the court to the three LEAA-funded

shelter care facilities in Maricopa County (as shown in Table 10-9) is relatively small in comparison to the drop in detention level (as shown in Table 10-8). This suggests that the creation of these alternatives was not a necessary condition for deinstitutionalization in most cases. Even when the police and court referrals are added together, the total impact of the LEAA-funded shelter care facilities on deinstitutionalization has been small in Maricopa County. In Mohave County, however, LEAA funding in the form of a salary for a special juvenile probation officer does seem to be affecting deinstitutionalization rates. In Yuma County the partially LEAA-funded Children's Village was also an important step toward deinstitutionalization. As we have seen from the Yuma data, however, the establishment of this facility did not precipitate a significant increase in deinstitutionalization of status offenders in that county. Although more data are necessary, the most plausible explanation of the difference in result lies in the fact that although Yuma County expanded its placement options, the policies governing intake and referral, and the personnel interpreting those policies, remained unchanged. In both Maricopa and Mohave Counties changes did occur.

Dispositions   As we mentioned above, there has been a general statewide decrease in the number of adjudicated status offenders who are referred to the Department of Corrections. That observation is specified in Table 10-10 with regard to the three counties under consideration. Maricopa County shows a consistently downward trend in the use of the Department of Corrections for status offenders over the decade of the 1970s. Similarly, while starting from a small base, Yuma County also has consistently reduced its number of commitments to corrections. Finally, status offender commitments to corrections from Mohave County have been so small throughout the study period as to prevent the delineation of any trends. It should be reemphasized that the number of status offenders placed in any out-of-home placement is extremely small. Of the 542 status offenders referred in 1979 to the Yuma County Juvenile Court, for example, only two were actually placed outside the home. Although comparative data were unavailable for the other two counties, interviews with juvenile justice decisionmakers in Maricopa and Mohave lead us to deduce that in those counties too, the majority of status offenders who are referred are diverted, and the majority of those petitioned are placed on probation.

TABLE 10-9   Police and Court Referrals to LEAA-
Funded Shelter Care Facilities in Maricopa County,
July 1977 through March 1979

Source of Referral	Pre-Hab of Mesa	Family Villas	Tumbleweed
Court	6	20	77
Police	4	11	64
Total	10	31	141

Source: Associates for Youths Departments (1980).

CONCLUSIONS

We have seen indications of at least some degree of deinstitutionalization in all three counties. The change has
been most dramatic in Maricopa County. Yuma and Mohave
have experienced less change in detention behavior, with
Mohave County showing the greater change of the two.

The changes in policy and structure have been dramatic
in Maricopa County and much smaller in Yuma and Mohave
Counties. In Maricopa County the changes most related to
deinstitutionalization are the change in policy, the addition of the family crisis unit, and, most fundamentally,
the change in standards for detaining status offenders.
The availability of nonsecure facilities, however, appears
to have contributed to deinstitutionalization in only a
minor way.

In Yuma and Mohave Counties the changes have been the
addition of nonsecure alternatives in Yuma and of a special probation officer in Kingman who is concerned with
the diversion of status offenders. Of these changes, the
special probation officer appears to have contributed more
to the relatively minor change in institutionalization
patterns in these two counties.

Our final question concerns the extent to which these
structural and procedural changes that resulted in deinstitutionalization were the result of the Juvenile Justice
and Delinquency Prevention Act. In Maricopa County the
change in police screening policy seems to be at least
partially, though not directly, a result of JJDPA. The
establishment of the family crisis unit and the change in
the standards for detention appear to have been locally
motivated and have little to do with the act. The establishment of the three nonsecure facilities was directly a
result of JJDPA. This evidence leads us to conclude that

TABLE 10-10 Status Offenders Sent to the Department of Corrections in Maricopa, Yuma, and Mohave Counties, 1969-1979

County	1969	1970	1971	1972	1973	1974	1975	1976	1977	1978	1979
Maricopa	243	198	185	198	80	117	98	62	75	47	39
Yuma	13	15	8	5	7	6	4	1	6	0	0
Mohave	3	4	5	9	12	6	4	0	0	1	0

Source: Unpublished data provided for this study by the Arizona Department of Corrections.

although JJDPA facilitated deinstitutionalization efforts in Maricopa County, it neither provided the initial impetus nor was the continuing driving force.

The picture of the impact of JJDPA in Yuma County is less clear. According to the Justice Planning Agency statistics, Yuma has reduced its levels of detention for status offenders. However, additional data presented here would cast some doubt on that finding, at least as it relates to the use of 24-hour holds for status offenders. Even if some deinstitutionalization has been accomplished, there is little evidence of procedural changes in the handling of status offenders. Children's Village appears to be the only step taken in that direction, and although this project is certainly important, there is little indication that broad change has occurred in Yuma County since the act's passage.

Mohave County has demonstrated a drop in detention levels of status offenders as reflected both in the planning agency data and in those data presented here. This downward trend, however, seems to have begun before the act. The only direct impact that the act seems to have had is the creation of a status offense probation officer. As in Yuma County, deinstitutionalization appears to be very gradually moving forward, but the act is not the most important force in the movement.

The most important factors in predicting deinstitutionalization appear to be the interest of the local officials and their commitment to that end. Maricopa County's dramatic changes in structures and procedures and the concomitant reduction in detention levels are the result of the interests and beliefs of the juvenile judges, juvenile probation officers, and police officials. Only a broad commitment of local decisionmakers appears to result in the coordinated changes in policy, personnel, and available facilities that we have found to be connected with significant reform.

The most impressive data supporting this analysis has yet to be presented. Pima County, which was not one of the three counties selected for special consideration, was a national leader in the deinstitutionalization of status offenders even before JJDPA was passed. This local commitment was primarily the result of the views of the juvenile judge who sat in Pima County for most of the 1970s. According to a colleague, this judge "was committed to deinstitutionalization long before JJDPA, and it [JJDPA] just gave him some money to implement that commitment."

Although the judge had successfully stimulated the local community to develop a number of alternative private placements, these were largely alternatives to the Department of Corrections and therefore were designed to accept only adjudicated offenders. When the federal RFP for the Deinstitutionalization of Status Offenders (DSO) action grant program was circulated in 1975, the Pima County Juvenile Court applied for a grant that would address the needs of preadjudicatory status offenders. In January 1976 the court was awarded $1.6 million for two years, which was later extended to three years (with an additional $275,000).[2] In addition to providing counseling and school programs, the funds stimulated the development of three group shelter care homes and a loose confederation of foster shelter homes designed for preadjudicatory status offenders. The grant also funded the creation within the juvenile court of a mobile diversion unit. Staffed by 14 probation officers on a 24-hour basis, this unit responded to incorrigibility complaints by traveling to the home or arrest site and attempting to counsel or divert the juvenile while still in the field.

These programs continued under the grant until 1979, at which point permanent funding sources were found in nearly all instances. All the shelter care programs were continued under funding from the Department of Economic Security, and much of the school program was absorbed by the school district. The mobile diversion unit, however, was disbanded soon after a new juvenile court judge assumed office. This unit was replaced in probation intake by a family services unit, and although this new unit practiced a much less active form of diversion, its focus remained on status offenders.

As mentioned above, a new juvenile court judge assumed office in Pima County in 1979. The new judge publicly renounced the deinstitutionalization policy--a move that was reflected in subsequent detention levels. As shown in Table 10-11, the detention rate in Pima County had been

---

[2]This grant appears to have served a double purpose at the federal level. First, it provided the early introduction of diversion models into a local community. Second, it was an ultimately successful project that could be pointed to in an analysis by Peat, Marwick, Mitchell & Co. (1978) as demonstrating that the unit cost of serving a status offender in social services verses juvenile justice programs was lower, at least in 1977.

TABLE 10-11   Detention Levels and Rates for Status
Offenders in Pima County, January 1978 to February 1980

Month/Year	Number of Youth Referred to the Court for Status Offenses (a)	Number of Youth Referred for a Status Offense Who Were Detained* (b)	Detention Rate (%) (b/a)
January 1978	126	15	11.9
February 1978	115	13	11.3
March 1978	100	9	9.0
April 1978	142	13	9.2
May 1978	121	13	10.7
June 1978	74	8	10.8
July 1978	104	9	8.7
August 1978	98	5	5.1
September 1978	92	2	2.2
October 1978	156	7	4.5
November 1978	96	4	4.2
December 1978	93	11	11.8
January 1979	106	11	10.4
February 1979	93	22	23.7
March 1979	141	32	22.7
April 1979	141	42	29.8
May 1979	142	43	30.3
June 1979	125	38	30.4
July 1979	139	36	25.9
August 1979	130	36	27.7
September 1979	119	37	31.1
October 1979	146	62	42.5
November 1979	105	35	33.4
December 1979	102	37	36.3
January 1980	123	37	30.1
February 1980	139	53	38.1

*Number of status offenders officially registered as having
been placed in detention.

Source: Unpublished data provided for this study by the
research department of the Pima County Juvenile Court.

less than 10 percent during much of 1978. In January 1979 however--the month in which the new judge took office--the detention rate more than doubled despite the availability of continued funding for local placement options.

The Pima County example further demonstrates the importance of local officials in changing deinstitutionalization policy. In Maricopa County, and in Pima County until January 1979, the juvenile judge appears to have been crucial to the achievement of deinstitutionalization, and the differences in the judges' attitudes toward deinstitutionalization correlate with the number of status offenders detained in each county (see Table 10-12). Since January 1979 the Pima County judge has been equally influential in reestablishing the use of detention for status offenders.

TABLE 10-12   Status Offenders Detained in Pima and Maricopa Counties, January 1978 to June 1979

Month/Year	Pima County	Maricopa County
January 1978	15	116
February 1978	13	93
March 1978	9	70
April 1978	13	86
May 1978	13	81
June 1978	8	58
July 1978	9	45
August 1978	5	68
September 1978	2	75
October 1978	7	51
November 1978	4	43
December 1978	11	28
January 1979	11	59
February 1979	22	45
March 1979	32	53
April 1979	42	48
May 1979	43	60
June 1979	38	43

Note: Figures represent the number of status offenders officially registered as having been placed in detention.

Source: Unpublished data provided for this study by the research departments of the Pima County and Maricopa County juvenile courts.

This interpretation is also consistent with findings for Yuma and Mohave Counties. In neither instance has there been a great change in detention levels, and in neither instance has the juvenile judge shown great interest or commitment to deinstitutionalization. While this may be due to several factors, one common perception in Arizona is that because rural juvenile judges handle the job part-time, they are therefore not as likely to get as involved in issues (such as deinstitutionalization) as are the urban judges who devote all their time to juvenile matters. This is also true of juvenile court staff, who in urban areas are not required to share time between juvenile court and adult court duties.

It should be noted, however, that committed juvenile court judges and committed juvenile court staff may not necessarily be committed to identical goals. A sophisticated court administration could tend to either lessen or increase the influence of the judge. In the two most urbanized areas of Arizona (Maricopa and Pima Counties), the turnover of juvenile court judges is high in comparison to the rural areas. The urban court staff, however, retain relative continuity and therefore provide more uniform policy contributions over time. In the rural areas judge and staff are subject to similar long-term influences and present a more united front in policy making.

REFERENCES

Arizona Legislative Council (1979) Mental Health
    Commitments of Children in Custody. Joint Juvenile
    Justice Committee. Phoenix, Ariz.: Legislative Coun-
    cil.
Associates for Youths Department (1980) Three Shelter
    Care Alternatives: An Empirical Assessment. Prepared
    for the Maricopa Council of Governments.
Higgins, Joe, Krieg, Terrie L., and Johnson, Jan (1979)
    Implementation of the Juvenile Justice and Delinquency
    Prevention Act in Arizona. Prepared under LEAA grant
    78-680-0JJDP. Phoenix, Ariz.: Arizona State Justice
    Planning Agency.
Peat, Marwick, Mitchell & Co. (1978) Comparative Cost
    Analysis of the Deinstitutionalization of Status Of-
    fender Program. Prepared for the Social Science Re-
    search Institute, University of Southern California,
    Los Angeles, Calif.

Willett, Martin (1979)   A Review and Analysis of Juvenile
    Court Process in Arizona.   Unpublished paper written
    for the Arizona Joint Juvenile Justice Committee,
    Phoenix, Ariz.

OFFICIALS INTERVIEWED

Dr. Randall Adams, Research, Behavioral Health Services,
    Department of Health Services
Captain Thomas Agnos, Phoenix Police Department
Norman Bann, Director, Yuma Behavioral Health, Inc.
Virginia Bryant, Liaison with Department of Economic
    Security, Department of Corrections
Joyce Constanza, Family Crisis Unit, Probation Intake,
    Maricopa County Juvenile Court
Diane Cunningham, Navaho Youth Services, Window Rock
Noel Dessant, Administrator, Arizona Supreme Court
Robert Doherty, Probation Placement, Maricopa County
    Juvenile Court, Phoenix
Boyd Dover, Special Consultant on Foster Care, Department
    of Economic Security
Sue Elliot, Division of Developmental Disabilities, and
    Mental Retardation, Department of Economic Security
Jeanne Englund, Administration for Children, Youth and
    Families, Department of Economic Security
Dr. B. Fine, Children's and Adolescents' Unit, Arizona
    State Hospital
William Flirth, Finance, Department of Economic Security
Peter Francis, Staff, Joint Juvenile Justice Committee,
    Arizona State Legislature
Ernesto Garcia, Director of Court Services, Maricopa
    County Juvenile Court, Phoenix
John Giovando, Administrator, Coconino County Juvenile
    Court, Flagstaff
Jim Galliher, Research, Maricopa County Juvenile Court
Commander M.G. Gannon, Scottsdale Police Department
Lt. Harris, Family Services Bureau, Chandler Police
    Department
Eunice Hays, Director of Probation, Yuma County Juvenile
    Court
Sharon Hekman, Deputy Director Program Services, Pima
    County Juvenile Court, Tucson
Dorothy Heitel, Child Protective Services, Dist. 1--
    Phoenix, Department of Economic Security
Joe Higgins, Juvenile Specialist, Arizona State Justice
    Planning Agency

Maria Hoffman, Chairperson, Justice for Children
    Coalition, Tumbleweed (Runaway House), Phoenix
Mary Lou Kaelke, Police Crisis Intervention Service,
    Scottsdale Police Department
Don Kearns, Supervisor, Elementary and Secondary
    Education Act, Department of Education
William Kleine, Assistant Chief Patrol Agent, U.S. Border
    Patrol, Yuma
Damien Kirwan, Staff, Foster Care Review Board
Judge Langford, Mohave County Superior Court
Rod Marquart, Chief Probation Officer, Mohave County
    Superior Court, Kingman
Bill McCarthy, Research Director, Maricopa County
    Juvenile Court
John McFarlin, Deputy Director, Department of Corrections
Alice McLain, Executive Staff Assistant to Dr. Carol
    Kamin, Department of Economic Security
Linda Moore, Data Processing, Department of Economic
    Security
Paul Mulleux, Chief, Buckeye Police Department
Judge William Nabours, Yuma County Superior Court
Jeanne Occino, Community Service, Division of Behavioral
    Health Services, Department of Health Services
Diane Peterson, Supervisor, Division of Special
    Education, Department of Education
Ron Peterson, President, Arizona Council of Child Care
    Agencies, Phoenix
Lt. Phipps, Yuma County Sheriff's Office
Lynn Progreba, Division of Statistics, Department of
    Education
Lillian Reed, Special Education, Federal Programs,
    Department of Education
Jim Riggs, Research, Department of Corrections
Julian Rodela, Office of Elementary and Secondary
    Education Act, Arizona Department of Education
Judge Kimball Rose, Chief Judge, Maricopa County Juvenile
    Court, Phoenix
Terry Schlage, Juvenile Specialist, Northern Arizona
    Council of Governments, Flagstaff
Carolyn Schooler, Title XX Specialist, Department of
    Economic Security
Bernard Schwartz, Financial Consultant to Dr. Kamin,
    Administration for Children, Youth and Families, De-
    partment of Economic Security
Murl Shaver, Mohave County Sheriff, Kingman
Virginia Skinner, Title XX Planner, Maricopa Association
    of Governments

Lt. George Smith, Phoenix Police Department
Representative Jackie Steiner, Arizona House of
    Representatives
Pam Stewart, Records, Yuma County Juvenile Court
B. J. Tatro, Division of Developmental Disabilities and
    Mental Retardation, Department of Economic Security
Bonnie Tomlin, Status Offender Specialist, Mohave County
    Superior Court, Kingman
John Valasquez, Gila Bend Police Department
Senator Steve Vukavitch, Arizona State Senate

11 Deinstitutionalization Efforts in Louisiana

JOSEPH F. SHELEY *and*
STEVEN L. NOCK

INTRODUCTION

The claim is often made that Louisiana has not been kind to juveniles entering its legal system. This portrait of the state's handling of children is painted not by outside observers, but by persons currently working in Louisiana's juvenile justice system, and refers not to the distant past but to recent state juvenile justice history.

Louisiana has been known to jail juveniles with every type of adult offender for extended periods of time without due process. Status offenders have been committed to reformatories for longer periods of time than delinquents who commit serious offenses. Indeed, juvenile court judges have been so unconstrained in sentencing that juveniles could literally be treated according to the judge's whim, anger, righteousness, or interpretation of parens patriae, with little or no reference to law.

The situation has been exacerbated by the lack of alternatives available to judges dealing with juveniles. Essentially, a judge could either incarcerate or release a child; for either disposition, there was little available in the way of treatment services. It is not surprising even today to encounter judges in rural areas who speak of "raising" an entire family of black youth in a state reformatory.

It is with this reputation in mind that we examine Louisiana's response to recent national trends toward the deinstitutionalization of status offenders. The state's reputation suggests that Herculean efforts would be necessary to accomplish deinstitutionalization goals, and we cannot fully assess either the strength or success of Louisiana's efforts. As this paper will demonstrate, the state is actually several years behind most others in addressing the deinstitutionalization issue. The question of the impact of the movement in Louisiana therefore is less one of "What has happened?" or "What success has been achieved?" than of "What is happening?" and, perhaps, "What success might be expected in coming years?" Furthermore, deinstitutionalization efforts simply are not well enough established to have produced hard data sufficient to assess the direction of these efforts--especially in a state that is not oriented toward data collection and analysis. This paper relies primarily on material generated through interviews with state and local officials and workers who are connected with the Louisiana juvenile justice system; secondarily, it relies on documents, reports, and statistics. We feel, however, that reliance on softer data does not preclude firm conclusions. Although the findings reported in this paper would surely be bolstered by reliable statistics, we are confident that the thorough and critical nature of the interviews, coupled with information contained in the documents at hand, has produced an analysis capable of standing on its own.

LOUISIANA: AN ECONOMIC, DEMOGRAPHIC, AND POLITICAL PROFILE

By way of setting the stage for analysis of Louisiana's deinstitutionalization efforts, some mention should be made of Louisiana's economic, demographic, and political characteristics. It is a predominantly rural state that depends on agriculture and oil for its livelihood. Taxes are low--a response both to its rural poverty and a historical reluctance to tax its citizens. Since the 1950s Louisiana's population has shifted considerably from the rural north to the rapidly urbanizing south. Immigration into the state from northern states has primarily affected southern Louisiana. Contrasts between rural and urban areas are becoming more pronounced. Public services and the demand for them are concentrated more than ever in urban areas.

The United States Census estimates that the state's population in 1979 was approximately 4,026,000 (U.S. Department of Commerce 1981). More important than its overall size, however, is the fact that its age-dependent population (i.e., those under 18 years of age) is declining. Paralleling the generally lower fertility trends for the nation as a whole, the age-dependent population in Louisiana has declined from 1,394,000 in 1970 to 1,300,000 in 1979 (U.S. Department of Commerce 1981), a decline most noticeable in urban areas. It is clear that legislators are aware of the decline. Demands for more extensive and costly services to a dwindling group of nonvoters are becoming less persuasive than comparable cries for services to more politically attractive and growing populations, such as the elderly, who compete for scarce social service dollars. One legislator whom we interviewed remarked that, considering the lack of political punch on the part of the juvenile population, it is surprising that any beneficial legislation has been directed toward it.

The number of adjudicated juvenile delinquents acknowledged by state officials in 1979 is relatively small, about 4,000.[1] Police records from New Orleans, the state's largest city, show fewer than 450 status offender arrests per year in 1976 through 1978, and state probation records show fewer than 400 status offender cases screened in 1979 in all but two of Louisiana's juvenile courts. Louisiana juvenile justice system personnel do not view status offenders as a numerical problem. The statement made almost universally by our respondents was: "Louisiana does not have a status offender problem; it has a problem with the treatment of its status offenders."

Finally, it is important to understand the political climate of Louisiana. Both state and local governments demonstrate an intense desire for autonomy. Some local communities are funding their own mental health centers rather than risk putting themselves under obligation by

---

[1]This figure represents an estimate provided by respondents willing to hazard a guess, since court statistics are not accessible. The estimate seems to be in line with the figures for commitments in fiscal 1978-79 by major Louisiana parishes to reform schools (1,236) and for 1979 active cases on local probation in Louisiana courts in major parishes (2,594--not including status, neglect, and traffic cases), which together total 3,830 (Louisiana Commission on Law Enforcement 1980).

accepting state funds. Other communities accept state
funds but do so without any intention of yielding to state
control. Antifederalism is very strong at the state level, primarily because of recent federal attempts to tap
Louisiana oil and natural gas resources and to store nu-
clear waste in the state's salt domes, and the current
resentment has merely magnified a traditional resistance
to federal influence. Louisiana has long been known for
its powerful legislators in Washington who have been able
to deflect much federal "interference" away from the state
while still obtaining considerable federal funding.

THE HISTORY OF LAWS GOVERNING JUVENILES IN LOUISIANA

A search of historical documents indicates that a traditional concern among social reformers for child welfare
in Louisiana has not always been reflected in the state's
treatment of its juveniles. A study commissioned by the
New Orleans Board of Prisons and Asylums in 1916 (Slingerland 1916) chastised institutions for dependent children (primarily orphans) in New Orleans as crude and outmoded. It also condemned "the provision made for custodial care of delinquents in the city of New Orleans and
the State of Louisiana [as] confessedly inadequate and
unsatisfactory" (Slingerland 1916:27). The study argued
for better temporary care of delinquent boys, noted that
little is done for "defectives" (the feeble-minded and
epileptics), and defined the juvenile court and detention
buildings as outdated. It criticized Louisiana as "almost
alone among the states in not having a well organized and
equipped child-placing agency, state-wide in its field,
and devoted to securing good family homes for needy
children" (Slingerland 1916:33). Notably, the report
classified New Orleans as the most progressive area in the
state.

The Louisiana Children's Code Committee, in its Compilation of Louisiana Statutes Affecting Child Welfare,
suggested in 1933 that state laws regarding children
should require alignment "with the more responsible and
humane trend of society and government in these matters"
(Daggett 1933:i). The report also suggested that the
children's statutes were not being faithfully administered, and called for responsible state agencies to offset the "greed, depravity, heartlessness or indifference
of individuals and groups" (p. ii).

A 1948 state report by the Juvenile Court Commission described the lack of adequate resources available to the courts in dealing with children and also expressed the opinion that children who were not hardcore delinquents should be kept in their homes and communities rather than be put in a state institution. A 1950 report by the Louisiana Interdepartmental Committee, which lists available services for children, was able to list only "Department of Public Welfare" for delinquency and neglect cases, and commented simply that private resources must be used.

Juvenile Laws Prior to 1950

Despite its reputation, Louisiana has not been without laws concerning the treatment of juveniles. Indeed, the state has a history of juvenile law that dates back to the turn of the century. According to Pugh's history of Louisiana juvenile laws (1957), the first state legislation that pertained to the trial of minors was Act 136 of 1902. The act essentially required that a person under the age of 16 be given a preliminary hearing upon arrest, a trial within three days of the hearing, and a court-appointed representative. Furthermore, the minor was to be segregated from adult prisoners, and his or her trial was to be kept separate from trials that pertained to nonjuvenile matters.

Act 82 of 1906 conferred jurisdiction upon district courts in cases involving dependent, neglected, incorrigible, and delinquent children under the age of 16. The same act authorized district court judges to compel the appearance of children and their parents before the court, and authorized the appointment of probation officers for juvenile cases. Children could be placed in the custody of their parents subject to supervision by a probation officer, or they could be placed in a suitable institution or with a responsible citizen. Pending a hearing, the child could not be confined in a jail, a police station, or any other institution to which adult offenders were sentenced. A neglected or dependent child could not be placed in an institution for delinquent children, and delinquent children could not be placed in institutions for dependent and neglected children.

According to Pugh (1957), Louisiana's first actual juvenile court system was established by Act 83 of 1908. The act provided for a juvenile court and judge in Orleans Parish and mandated that district courts in the state,

when hearing cases concerning juveniles, be known as juvenile courts and that their sessions and records must be
kept separate from other district court matters. Subsequent acts and appeals court rulings through 1950 specified jurisidiction and, more importantly, affirmed that
court handling of juveniles was a <u>noncriminal</u> proceeding,
thereby giving judges considerable latitude and juveniles
relatively few procedural rights.

Legal definitions of delinquent and neglected children
remained relatively consistent and specific from 1908
(Act 83) through 1950 (i.e., through subsequent acts,
namely, 83 of 1921, 126 of 1921, 119 of 1922, 30 of 1924,
and 169 of 1944). During this period a delinquent child
was defined as one who, among other specific behavioral
characteristics, visits saloons, wanders around railroad
tracks, or uses vile language (Act 119 of 1922). Act 169
of 1944, however, broadened the definition of delinquents
to refer to any child who violates state or local laws or
ordinances or is uncontrollable, habitually truant, or in
physical or moral danger. The neglected child was one who
is abandoned or without proper custody, does not receive
proper sustenance, associates with immoral persons, or is
in a physically or morally injurious environment.

In short, Louisiana law through 1950 displayed the same
basic concern for juvenile justice and child welfare apparent in any legal system subscribing to <u>parens</u> <u>patriae</u>
ideology. An attempt was made to segregate juvenile cases
from adult cases, to distinguish delinquent from neglected children, and to place powers in the hands of judges.

The state's negative reputation for the treatment of
status offenders and abused and neglected children indicates what has essentially become a criminal justice system maxim: Legislation and law enforcement are rarely in
harmony when the legislation is designed to constrain
rather than to broaden the powers of the criminal justice
system. The apparently constraining and benevolent intent of law in segregating juvenile from adult cases and
delinquent from neglect cases seems by most accounts to
have been ignored by the administrators of the law.

Juvenile laws themselves contributed in part to this
conflict between intent and practice. The legal definition of delinquent was so broad as to cover nearly any
child's behavior, and the overlap between definitions of
delinquent and neglected children was sufficient to provide judges with the discretion to institutionalize some
neglected children and to treat some obvious delinquents
rather gingerly. Within statutes, qualifications that

amounted to legal loopholes were apparent in the consistent use of such phrases as "unless it is impracticable," "which the Court in its discretion may deem proper," and "whenever, in the Court's judgement, the best interests of the child will be served."

According to our sources, state legislation lacked teeth because of tremendous local autonomy, and because judges used legal loopholes and not infrequently acted counter to law. Within local communities, especially rural areas, judges were extremely powerful both socially and politically, often through their related positions in the community economic hierarchy. They were socially respected, and their decisions were generally unchallenged.

One respondent noted that the rural courts in the 1940s were very much intertwined with a Baptist world view, which held that troublesome youth represented a problem of evil rather than of sickness. Judges, like other citizens, were indignant over the actions of the troublemaker. Indeed, delinquency, drunkenness, and sin were viewed as the rural community's greatest social problems. Our informant noted that "delinquents were a big deal in most farm towns. They gave a judge a chance to be a judge. Since there were few real criminals around, delinquents really upset people, and judges treated them like big-time crooks. It seemed like everybody went to an LTI [a reformatory]." It is against this background that recent attempts to change the juvenile justice system in Louisiana should be considered.

Revised Statutes of 1950

In 1950 Louisiana made its first attempt to coordinate and centralize its laws. This attempt resulted in the Revised Statutes of Louisiana, which were adopted in 1950 and which included a chapter devoted exclusively to juvenile courts (Pugh 1957). Chapter 6, Title 13 of the revised statutes was divided into three sections; one pertained to all parishes other than Caddo (rural) and Orleans, and one section each pertained to these two parishes. Definitions of neglected and delinquent children and their rights were uniform throughout the three parts. The revised statutes repealed all previous laws pertaining to juveniles.

Immediately noticeable in the revisions were changes in the definitions of neglected and delinquent children. Neglected children were those who were not receiving proper care or whose situations were viewed as injurious to their welfare. Delinquents were children who ran away from home, were ungovernable or habitually truant, or violated any legal statutes. Thus, the definition of neglected children was broadened somewhat, permitting the court even greater latitude in defining a child's situation as injurious, and the definition of delinquent was narrowed to exclude children who were in physical or moral danger. It was no longer possible to label an endangered child as either delinquent or neglected; the two types of children were now legally distinct. The new law, however, made absolutely no distinction between neglected and delinquent children in terms of the treatment and disposition of their cases. Both were subject to identical processing. Absent from the 1950 statutes was the former mandate that neglected and dependent children not be institutionalized with delinquents.

The prospect of like treatment for all children before the court was surpassed in importance only by the greatly increased powers assigned to law enforcement agencies and judges by the 1950 statutes. The basic tone and language of these laws differed from those of previous laws. The qualifying remarks were broader (e.g., "unless it is impracticable or inadvisable or has been otherwise ordered by the court"). Although the statutes mandated that, unless impracticable, children taken into detention shall (rather than may) be released to their parents (Sec. 177), the same laws specifically retained the provision from previous acts that "nothing in this act shall be construed as forbidding any peace officer from immediately detaining any child" found violating a law or in any danger (Sec. 1577). The only limitation placed on police officers in this regard was the requirement that all detentions should be reported to the court or probation officer within 24 hours. Children generally were not to be confined in police stations, prisons, or jails, but children 15 years of age and older could be placed in a jail or other adult detention center if they were kept in rooms entirely separate from adults. For the first time, Louisiana law went beyond forbidding detention in adult facilities and mandated that temporary detention of children be provided. This could occur in the form of placement in a detention home, a private home supervised by the court, or any institution or agency designated by the court (Sec. 1578).

Although neglected children were definitionally distinct from delinquents under the revised statutes, the two categories were in effect one, given the options for dis-

position that the new law gave to judges. After finding
a child neglected or delinquent, a judge could a) place
the child on probation, under supervision in the child's
own home, or in the custody of a suitable person; b) assign custody of the child to a public or private institution or agency, or place the child in a private home; c)
place the child in a public mental hospital or institution
for the mentally defective, if deemed necessary; or d)
dismiss the case. Furthermore, no attempt was made in the
1950 revisions to distinguish status offenders from delinquents. Although the law mandated, rather than merely
allowed, that initial preadjudication custody be with the
parents "unless impracticable," the language of the law
was very much detention-oriented.

Louisiana law seems to have taken a conservative turn
in 1950. If so, we can only hypothesize reasons for the
shift, since no written historical analyses exist, and
since knowledge of the system is beyond the recall or
years of service of system incumbents. We feel that the
following four hypotheses, though not thoroughly spelled
out, deserve special mention here.

(1) What happened in Louisiana in 1950 may only have
reflected nationwide trends of the time. The trend toward
institutionalization of both adult and juvenile offenders
was informed by a trust in the rehabilitative capabilities
of institutions structured around a medical rather than a
punitive philosophy. Although it is generally conceded
now that the institutional rehabilitative model was a
failure, in its day it was viewed as progressive.

(2) It is possible that the revision of Louisiana statutes in 1950 coincided with a popular or, at least, legislative perception of and concern over high delinquency
rates, which in turn led to a move toward greater control
over juveniles coming before the courts.

(3) Pugh's summaries (1957) of appellate decisions
pertaining to juvenile courts prior to 1950 suggest great
concern among juvenile and nonjuvenile court judges with
the jurisdiction of those courts. It is possible that by
1950 juvenile court judges were sufficiently powerful and
their domain sufficiently legitimate that they were able
to affect the legislative process in ways that broadened
their powers and offered them a greater monopoly over the
juvenile justice system.

(4) Perhaps by 1950 the judges' freedom to act contrary
to the law--by commingling neglected and delinquent
children, for example--was meeting with more frequent le-

gal challenges. Judges may have been sufficiently powerful to persuade the legislature to restructure the law to
avoid such challenges.

The Revised Statutes of 1950 constituted Louisiana
juvenile law until their repeal in 1979 in favor of the
Louisiana Code of Juvenile Procedure. Little change occurred in the statutes from 1950 to 1975, when reforms
that led to construction of the 1979 code began.

Reform in the 1970s

From 1950 to the mid-1970s the number of juveniles who
might have been labeled as either status offenders or neglected children remained relatively small. Most of these
youth were ignored by the system, either at the initial
point of contact or at ensuing points. The problems that
reform efforts sought to address were (1) what to do about
providing services for the juveniles who were being ignored, and (2) what to do about the quality of treatment
given those few who were not ignored. Regarding the latter, the Louisiana juvenile justice system appears to have
been quick to securely detain nonadjudicated juvenile
nonoffenders (i.e., status offenders and neglected children) seen as problems, and to institutionalize this same
population after adjudication.
    Between 1974 and 1975 the Louisiana legislature passed
acts prohibiting both the secure detention of nondelinquents and the placement of nondelinquents in Department
of Corrections facilities (reform schools) as of July 1,
1976 (a deadline later extended to July 1, 1978). For the
first time, nonoffenders who were not neglected children
(i.e., status offenders) were not defined as delinquent.
Custody of status offenders was transferred from the Department of Corrections to the Office of Youth Services,
an agency created in 1974, and now the Division of Youth
Services within the Office of Human Development of the
Department of Health and Human Resources. This agency
supplies screening and probation services and purchases
postadjudication services for the majority of Louisiana
courts.
    In August 1975 Louisiana applied for enrollment in the
Juvenile Justice and Delinquency Prevention Act (JJDPA)
of 1974, a move that committed the state to prohibiting
the placement of nonoffenders in juvenile detention or
correctional facilities within three years.

After several delays that were largely due to confusion
over the exact meaning of the federal act, Louisiana deinstitutionalization laws took full effect July 1, 1978.
It was assumed that at this point, no further confusion
as to the meaning of the laws could be claimed, and no
excuses for lack of compliance were accepted. In essence,
this is Louisiana's official deinstitutionalization date.

On January 1, 1979, Louisiana's Code of Juvenile Procedure (HB 288, Act No. 172) became effective. The code
had both bureaucratic and symbolic content. From a bureaucratic standpoint it consolidated juvenile justice
laws, specifying clearly the separate procedures to be
followed in the apprehension, disposition, and treatment
of cases involving delinquents, children in need of supervision (status offenders), and children in need of care
(abused and neglected children). The law was symbolic in
that it became the focal point of all efforts toward and
criticisms concerning the deinstitutionalization movement.

The code established three categories of juveniles:
(1) delinquents (children who violate criminal statutes),
(2) children in need of supervision, and (3) children in
need of care. Chapter 1, Article 13 (13) defines children in need of supervision as those who need care or rehabilitation because they are habitual truants, ungovernables, or runaways, because they attempt to purchase al-
coholic beverages, because they either engage in conduct
or exist in a situation injurious to their welfare, or
because they violate laws applicable only to children.
In essence, then, the children in need of supervision are
the traditional status offenders. Article 13 (Sec. 14)
defines children in need of care as those who are physically, sexually, or mentally abused by their parents;
whose welfare is endangered through the negligence of a
parent; or who are abandoned or without parents. Thus,
children in need of care are the traditional neglected or
dependent children.

The code did little to change the process by which
children first enter the juvenile justice system. Basically, any peace officer or probation worker can take a
child into custody if he or she appears to be a truant, a
runaway, or in some form of danger. The officer who takes
the child into custody must counsel and release the child
to his or her parents. If release is inappropriate, the
child alleged to be in need of supervision or care must
be taken to a temporary nonsecure shelter care facility,
not to a detention center for delinquents. Parents must
be notified, a report must be submitted by police to the

court within 24 hours, and a hearing must be held within 72 hours. The child may be detained for no more than 10 days while continuance hearings are being held and various petitions are being filed.

The child adjudicated in need of supervision may be placed in parental custody, placed on probation, assigned to a public or private institution or agency, or, if found mentally defective, committed to a public or private mental institution. The child in need of care is subject to the same dispositions, with the exception of placement on probation. The law strongly suggests, though it does not absolutely require, assignment of the least restrictive disposition in each case. Placement of nonoffenders in secure facilities is not permitted, and placements in mental institutions must be based on psychological or psychiatric evaluations.

SOURCES OF CHANGE IN THE 1970s

In this section, we are concerned with legislation in the mid-1970s. More precisely, the question here is "What caused deinstitutionalization laws to be enacted?" We assume, for reasons that become obvious below, that the forces for enactment of the laws and those for preservation of the laws are distinct.

It is difficult to sort out and assign relative importance to the various forces that coalesced in the mid-1970s to initiate Louisiana's deinstitutionalization legislation. A climate for juvenile justice reform seems to have been fostered within the state by a growing number of professional juvenile justice and social service workers during the late 1960s and early 1970s. According to State Senator Nat Kiefer--a major force in juvenile justice legislation during that period--state system workers were no longer defining their roles simply within traditional parameters but were modifying their services in response to contemporary national trends toward reform. It was this linkage with the national network that provided the ideas for directions that reforms might take.

National trends that influenced the Louisiana juvenile justice system were best embodied in the landmark case of In re Gault (387 U.S. 1 (1967)) in which the U.S. Supreme Court held that the Constitution requires "fundamental fairness" in delinquency proceedings. This and other decisions--for instance, Kent v. United States (383 U.S. 541 (1966)) and In re Winship (397 U.S. 358 (1970))--

by which juvenile procedural rights were further specified
influenced Louisiana courts and their associated systems
at least to the degree that they affected most other
states.   While some in the Louisiana system championed
them, others were clearly threatened and outraged.   Above
all else, these landmark decisions served notice that
state juvenile justice systems were being evaluated at
the national level, and they provided a national trend to
which those pushing for change in Louisiana could anchor
their appeals.

A general social and political climate conducive to
reform existed in Louisiana in the early 1970s.   Although
this climate could hardly produce legislative changes by
itself, it did serve to intensify the statewide perception
that Louisiana had an increasing juvenile delinquency
problem (again, a national concern as well) that could not
be addressed by its current legal system.   Louisiana responded to its perceived delinquency problem by establishing a combined house-senate committee, the Joint Committee on Juvenile Justice.   The key figures in the legislature who were charged with investigating and providing
recommendations to address the deliquency problem were
Senator Kiefer and Representative Charles Grisbaum, co-
chairmen of the committee.

In Kiefer's view, the formation of the joint committee
in 1974 initiated a process that led to most of the legislative changes in evidence today.   In that year, for
example, the Office of Youth Services was established and
given jurisdiction over nonoffender cases.   Also, Louisiana's criminal and juvenile justice standards were developed through an effort that began in May 1974 and culminated a year later in the publication of the standards for
juvenile justice and crime prevention that guided legislation for several years thereafter.

Senator Kiefer is careful to note that changes since
1974 in the state's posture regarding juvenile nonoffenders are primarily an indirect result of legislative concern for delinquency prevention.   In Kiefer's opinion,
questions concerning the handling of status offenders are
bound to arise during discussions of delinquency prevention and treatment, and status offender legislation always
follows delinquency legislation.   Kiefer argues that no
thought would have been given to the problems of children
in need of supervision or care if state legislators had
not perceived Louisiana as having a severe delinquency
problem.

Given the options facing the legislature in dealing
with status offenders (i.e., taking no action, some action, or much action), it is important to know what forces
determined the course of Louisiana's legislation. As we
noted above, the state's concern with serious juvenile
crime served as a prime motivating force. Beyond this,
three other important forces that must be considered are
economic incentives, the influence of advocates, and federal influence.

Economic Incentives

Surprisingly, the economics of dealing with status offenders did not seem to be a major issue during initial
legislative efforts directed at juvenile justice reform.
That is, there was no lengthy discussion of reducing the
costs of housing status offenders in correctional facilities and detention centers. Legislative approval of deinstitutionalization seems to have been based primarily
on principle, without serious consideration of costs or
savings to the state--with the possible exception of anticipated federal dollars (see "Federal Influence," below). The Joint Committee on Juvenile Justice was seen
by many as one of the hardest working and most respected
committees in the legislature, and its recommendations met
with almost no resistance from legislators.

The Influence of Advocates

Juvenile justice advocates seem to have had a measurable
impact on the specific forms of legislation aimed at juvenile nonoffenders. Advocacy has not been particularly
well organized in Louisiana. Most advocacy efforts have
been relatively ad hoc in nature, conducted by temporary
coalitions of liberal individuals who are connected in one
way or another with the juvenile justice system. For example, advocacy efforts often are carried out by Catholic
clergy in charge of diocesan social services, including
services for abused and neglected children. One organized
advocacy group, however, did appear to be influential in
the formation of juvenile law in the mid-1970s. This
group was Advocates for Juvenile Justice in New Orleans.
This and other less organized advocacy efforts served to
link state legislation with national efforts to upgrade
juvenile justice programs and to provide better services
for status offenders.

An important function of the advocate groups was to mitigate conservative forces in the state. One instance in which these groups were particularly effective concerns the drafting of the new juvenile code. In 1976 the executive office established the Governor's Conference on Juvenile Justice. Following this forum on the legal rights of juveniles, the Louisiana Commission on Law Enforcement (LCLE, the state planning agency) funded the Criminal Justice Institute to develop a code of juvenile procedure. The code was drafted by an interdisciplinary steering committee composed of judges, legislators, youth advocates, and representatives from nonprofit community service, law enforcement, and prosecutors' organizations.

It appears that Advocates for Juvenile Justice had a considerable liberalizing effect on steering committee members who, though favoring deinstitutionalization efforts, were fairly conservative in their approach to structuring those efforts. This particular advocacy group seemed especially influential when the steering committee's recommendations were put before the Joint Committee on Juvenile Justice. Forming an alliance with the senator, the advocates were able to persuade the committee to include within the code provisions that (a) allowed status offenders to have legal counsel, (b) specified standards for psychiatric evaluations, (c) restricted the state in terms of the time periods allowed to elapse between various hearings, and (d) placed a 15-day restriction on the commitment of a status offender for a contempt citation. It should be noted, however, that inclusion of these provisions in the code did not ensure their implementation, because economic problems limited their use.

Federal Influence

Louisiana entered into participation in the Juvenile Justice and Delinquency Prevention Act (JJDPA) in August 1975. Most respondents at the state level pointed with considerable pride to the fact that many legislative changes in Louisiana were initiated in 1974 _prior_ to participation in JJDPA. Nearly everyone we spoke with agreed that most of the changes that have occurred in the state would have happened without federal dollars. Yet, there is disagreement among the same persons concerning the extent of federal influence on the speed and direction of the changes.

Traditionally Louisiana politicians and officials are likely to dismiss entirely the role of the federal government in the development of Louisiana juvenile law. However, Senator Kiefer, whose position as cochairman of the joint legislative committee involves oversight of federal programs, argues that federal influence, in terms of both guidance and finances, was extremely important to the development of Louisiana's juvenile code.

It does appear that many of the 1974 changes in Louisiana juvenile law were made in anticipation of federal funding, and that little thought was given to eventual state cost. In fact, given current state bitterness about how little money can be obtained through JJDPA participation and the problems encountered in attempted compliance with JJDPA requirements, we feel safe in hypothesizing that the state's basic commitment to juvenile justice reform was furthered considerably by the erroneous notion that federal funds could be had without extensive state expenditure. Several respondents employed the same analogy in reconstructing the situation: "The government held out a carrot on a stick and then when we went for it, there was really nothing there."

In sum, we feel that Louisiana was essentially ripe for juvenile justice reform in the mid-1970s and that the federal government supplied some, though not major, impetus for the direction taken in legislative changes. It also appears that without the contribution of advocacy efforts, such as those of Advocates for Juvenile Justice, the Louisiana Code of Juvenile Procedure would be considerably less constrictive of state powers.

SUSTAINING THE MOVEMENT

As noted earlier, we do not assume that the same forces that fostered deinstitutionalization legislation now operate to prevent repeal of the new laws. Indeed, initiating those laws seems to have been less problematic than sustaining them. Most opposition to the laws has followed rather than preceded their passage.

There is still commitment to the principle of deinstitutionalization of status offenders, but there is also considerable sentiment for altering the law to allow secure detention and commitment of certain kinds of status offenders, notably, habitual runaways and ungovernables. The moving force behind this sentiment exists <u>within</u> the juvenile justice system. Judges express frustration that

they no longer have a means of coercing status offenders
to act in accordance with the law and that there are no
suitable alternatives to confinement for dealing with
these youth. Pessimistic about the development of such
resources, they argue for less rigid restrictions regarding secure confinement of nonoffenders. In similar fashion, local peace officers complain that the new code in-
capacitates the police, fosters a lack of respect for the
law among status offenders, and places officers in the
position of "turning youngsters back into the streets
without care." Probation officers assigned to status offender cases complain that these cases, always difficult,
have now been made nearly impossible to manage.

Although the wisdom or accuracy of these statements may
be questionable, it is worth noting that they are made
sincerely and vociferously. Legislators have not yet had
to contend with an organized lobbying effort, but they are
becoming attentive to juvenile justice functionaries and
are considering legal changes, especially on the issue of
the detention of status offenders.

In short, the period since the initiation of the deinstitutionalization laws has been one of ongoing tension
as some factions (e.g., legislators who structured the
code) struggle to maintian the juvenile justice code and
others (e.g., select judges) challenge it. The tenure of
the code surely is not secure. We are concerned here with
identifying the forces that have been working--with various degrees of success--to ensure that the provisions of
the code remain intact and honored.

Fading Advocacy

The ability of organized juvenile justice advocacy groups
to effect change in the treatment of nonoffenders in Louisiana has waned in the last few years. Advocates for
Juvenile Justice, which had a strong hand in the creation
of the code, took an equally strong adversary approach in
protecting children from state under and overreaction to
the provisions of the code. In this capacity a 1978 grant
application for $360,000 in JJDPA special emphasis funds
was submitted to promote the rights of juveniles, charging
that Louisiana "exemplifies the resistance and affirmative
opposition to implementation of numerous federal acts designed to promote adequate and appropriate services to
children." Furthermore, the construction of what was
viewed as unneeded psychiatric facilities for children was

vociferously opposed. Through such efforts the advocates alienated the governor, LCLE, the State Juvenile Justice Advisory Board, and the governor's steering committee for the code.

LCLE, in particular, opposed the advocacy stance. Although the JJDPA special emphasis grant proposal was approved by the administrator of the Office of Juvenile Justice and Delinquency Prevention, John Rector, it was ultimately denied by the acting administrator of the Law Enforcement Assistance Administration, Henry Dogin. Dogin's decision was based in large part on a letter from LCLE, which questioned the intentions of the advocates. He concluded that the advocacy agency did not display sufficient "good faith" in the state system and would "start the project off on a bad footing with the very group which must be influenced by the project activities." Without funds, Advocates for Juvenile Justice ceased operations in January 1979, raising questions concerning the future of state or federally funded advocacy efforts (Youth Alternatives 1979).

Advocacy of a less adversarial nature still exists in Louisiana. Individuals, often persons connected with organized religions, still work to better juvenile justice conditions at the local level. Only one semiadvocacy group now appears to be working at the state level. That group, the Juvenile Justice Project, has recently been established within the state legislature. The project is funded through OJJDP, private funds, and legislative funds; project coordinators are officially employed by the Center for Legislative Improvement in Englewood, Colorado. Project coordinators serve as special legislative advisors to house and senate committees on the status of juveniles. In essence, the project helps to write bills and to shepherd them through the legislature. It is generally credited with having increased greatly the awareness of state legislators concerning problems of juveniles in the legal system.

Declining Federal Influence

Federal influence now seems to be of less importance than it was during the initiation of juvenile justice legislation. Louisiana is not yet in full compliance with JJDPA requirements and does not expect to be in the near future. The extent to which this concerns state public officials varies. On the one hand, it is clear that most officials would like to keep federal funds. On the other hand, antifederalism is so strong in the state that many would rather forfeit funding than comply with the requirements. Furthermore, public officials view JJDPA funds as so meager that their loss is preferable to the costs of compliance with the federal requirements.

Thus the economic aspects of deinstitutionalization in Louisiana have taken on an importance that was clearly not present during initiation of the legal measures, and deinstitutionalization is now viewed as being extremely costly. It seems that the state might be willing to meet these costs slowly, but only if deinstitutionalization efforts appeared as being state initiated rather than as being part of a federal mandate. The widespread belief that the federal government is forcing these costs up, however, seems counterproductive to JJDPA goals. Legislators now seem particularly combative, talking in terms of conflict models of lawmaking. Some argue that they voted for deinstitutionalization laws but against the funding necessary for alternative services in order to force a crisis in the juvenile justice system and hasten the revolt against federal dependence.

In the past year and a half, Louisiana's approach to compliance with JJDPA mandates at the state level has been characterized by respondents as halfhearted. Some accuse former governor Edwin Edwards (in office at the time of JJDPA enrollment) of initially supporting participation in JJDPA in order to procure funds for the construction of facilities rather than to provide community services in the spirit of deinstitutionalization. Some also feel that LCLE, the state planning agency, has defined its major task as raising funds rather than as acting to ensure deinstitutionalization.

In fairness to LCLE, that agency has no legal clout and can accomplish the goals it sets for itself only by informally influencing legislators and, because it screens and evaluates all requests for LEAA funds, by gaining concessions from local planning agencies that are seeking such monies. Whether or not the state's failure to comply with JJDPA requirements is due to LCLE's inaction or to its relative lack of power cannot be determined at present.

Two other factors seem to lessen federal influence on juvenile justice programs in Louisiana. First, state officials view federal monitoring of programs as ineffective. That is, beyond demanding minimal satisfaction of JJDPA requirements, the federal government is viewed as "inactive" in terms of forcing compliance. Second, public officials refer to an "ace in the hole." They feel that the state's traditional power in the U.S. legislature will serve to neutralize any federal agency attempts to withhold funds.

In addition to the forces of advocacy and federal influence, two other forces operate to promote deinstitutionalization efforts. They are (1) the 1976 case of Gary W. v. State of Louisiana (437 F. Supp. 1209 (1976)), in which a federal court ruled that the state could not formulate its child treatment policies without regard to laws concerning the institutionalization of certain categories of juveniles, and (2) the recent (mid-1970s) reorganization of state agencies that has facilitated both monitoring at the state level and the interagency sharing of resources.

The Gary W. Case In 1976 there was a scandal involving the treatment of mentally retarded, physically handicapped, and delinquent children who had been placed in institutions in Texas by the state of Louisiana. In response to claims that these children were being given substandard and sometimes abusive care, private advocates, the Children's Defense Fund, and the federal government brought suit against the state of Louisiana to prohibit unnecessary out-of-state placements of children. The case of Gary W. v. State of Louisiana produced a ruling stating that mentally retarded, physically handicapped, and delinquent children had a right to treatment if taken out of their homes and that they must be placed in the least restrictive setting possible. The state was forced to create individual treatment plans for the children, to bring most back into the state, and to justify each out-of-state placement it made.

Although the federal court ruling did not pertain specifically to children in need of supervision or care, it held a certain symbolic significance for the Louisiana juvenile justice system. System functionaries resent the coercive nature of the decision, but they also seem to fear a similar ruling pertaining to treatment in the least restrictive setting for status offenders and neglected children. Yet even here, deinstitutionalization through court-inspired fear has its limits. Four years after the court ruling, not all of the children involved have been returned to Louisiana. In 1979 the federal court appointed a special master to force the state to comply.

State Reorganization Also important to maintaining deinstitutionalization legislation was the reorganization
of state government agencies during the mid-1970s. Governor Edwin Edwards consolidated the many decentralized
social service agencies in the state under a large umbrella agency called the Department of Health and Human
Resources. The department oversees virtually all aspects
of human service delivery (e.g., hospitals, mental health,
welfare, protective services, licensing, vocational rehabilitation). No new services were provided as a result
of this reorganization, but the various agencies have become easier to monitor at the state level and, more importantly, can share resources more easily.

The Division of Youth Services within the Department
of Health and Human Resources is a key agency in terms of
the deinstitutionalization of status offenders. Its importance lies in the fact that since 1974, when it was
known as the Office of Youth Services, the agency has assumed responsibility from the Department of Corrections
for both status offenders and delinquents on probation
(though not on parole). The division is responsible for
coordinating the placement of all adjudicated delinquents
and children in need of supervision. What is important
here is that it has a stronger and more specific interest
in the treatment and control of nonoffenders than did the
Department of Corrections, whose main focus has always
been on delinquents in reform school. Thus, the Division
of Youth Services could act, in some ways, as a lobbyist
for status offender interests. (It should be noted that
youth services officials and employees do not display total commitment to deinstitutionalization of status offenders. Many favor secure detention of "problem" status
offenders. Nevertheless, the division affirms deinstitutionalization in principle and has encouraged the state--
unsuccessfully thus far--to provide alternative services.)

An important aspect of the consolidation of social
services within the Department of Health and Human Resources is the creation of regional review boards to
oversee restrictive placements of delinquents and children
in need of supervision or care. By state law, children
who are to be placed in group homes or more restrictive
facilities (not including delinquents assigned to reform
schools) must receive medical and psychological evaluations, and their cases must be reviewed by a regional
board composed of social service workers, mental health
specialists, and supervisors from the department. Although the regional review board generally seeks the ap-

propriate placement for the category that has been assigned by the judge who heard the case, the board may recommend to the judge that the type of placement he or she
seeks is inappropriate.

While there was for a short while confusion regarding
whether or not the court or the Department of Health and
Human Resources possessed ultimate placement authority, a
1980 appeals court decision has resolved the issue. The
Court of Appeals of Louisiana, Fourth Circuit, consolidated two cases, State of Louisiana in the Interest of
Robin Sapia (387 So. 2d 689) and State of Louisiana in the
Interest of Tod Reddicks (387 So. 2d 41), both of which
concerned judges' decisions to place children in need of
care or supervision in private facilities without reference to the department's placement mechanisms. The judges
had ordered the department to pay for treatment of the
juveniles, and the department had refused, arguing that
it had final placement authority and would only pay costs
related to its decisions. The appeals court ruled against
the department, stating that the juvenile court had ultimate placement authority, and that the department must
assume placement costs.

Despite the fact that juvenile court judges have final
placement authority, it is important to note that they no
longer must make placement decisions single-handedly. The
regional review board mechanism serves to encourage them
to avoid hair-trigger decisions to place children in settings that are more restrictive than is necessary. Perhaps because the review boards must share responsibility
for placement errors with judges, judges seem to view them
in a positive light, complaining only that they are too
slow in reviewing cases. Thus, the deinstitutionalization
movement has coincided with government reorganization to
produce a mechanism that encourages fewer institutional
placements. Of course, the review board, like the judge,
could be influenced in its decisions by such practical
factors as bedspace requirements. That is, empty beds in
an institution may structure decisions as much as do a
child's needs.

In sum, it appears to us that deinstitutionalization
measures were initiated in Louisiana without full awareness of their potential costs and without a commitment to
total deinstitutionalization of nonoffenders. Key factors
behind the passage of deinstitutionalization laws were a
legislative view of delinquency as a major social problem
and an ensuing interest in the treatment of status offenders, an increasing professionalism among state social

service personnel (which served to link the state to national trends in deinstitutionalization), some strong advocacy efforts, and some (apparently overestimated) financial gains from the federal government.

It seems reasonable to assume that deinstitutionalization laws will be modified in the near future to include
provisions for the secure detention of children in need
of supervision who are ungovernables, runaways, and
chronic truants. The forces pushing the state in this
direction seem to outnumber those attempting to hold the
line. Federal and advocacy influence on juvenile justice
practices has weakened. The costs of compliance with
JJDPA requirements and the provision of alternative services for nonoffenders are increasingly viewed as prohibitive. Local-level juvenile justice officials and workers
are becoming more vocal in their opposition to the concept
of total deinstitutionalization. The only factors that
seem to work against modification of the laws are the
state bureaucracy, which has been geared toward deinstitutionalization and is somewhat committed to the concept,
and the fact that Louisiana has recently been startled by
a federal court decision directed specifically at the
state's provision of services for children. These factors have resulted in a hesitancy on the state's part to
move too quickly away from treatment of nonoffenders in
the least restrictive setting.

OUTCOMES OF CHANGE

It is difficult to evaluate the progress of Louisiana's
deinstitutionalization efforts to date because the state's
formal program has only been in effect since mid-1978.
Similarly the Code of Juvenile Procedures, which has
served as the focal point of arguments both for and a-
gainst deinstitutionalization, did not become effective
until 1979. Nonetheless, despite the recency of the
state's formal efforts, deinstitutionalization efforts
actually have existed in Louisiana since 1974, and we do
note apparent changes in awareness of the special problems of nonoffenders in the juvenile justice system. In
an effort to determine whether or not the deinstitutionalization movement has made a tangible difference in the
handling of juvenile nonoffenders since 1974, we have explored three indices: (1) changes in the state's handling of juvenile nonoffenders, (2) differences in the
handling of juveniles at the local level, and (3) evidence

of relabeling practices by judges (i.e., the labeling of status offenders as delinquents to enable them to be confined).

State Response

Analysis of the few statistics available relating to status offenders in the juvenile justice system provides a muddled picture of deinstitutionalization efforts in Louisiana. The primary goal of these efforts is, of course, to remove juveniles from adult facilities and to remove nonoffenders from secure facilities. Although Louisiana's prohibition of these confinement practices did not legally take effect until July 1978, the deinstitutionalization movement and its companion legislation began in 1974. We would, therefore, expect some changes in the numbers of youth at various points in the juvenile justice system between 1974 and 1978.

Between September 1, 1977 and August 31, 1978, a total of 1,250 juveniles were held in adult incarceration facilities for more than 24 hours. Of this number, 386 (31 percent) were status offenders and 11 (1 percent) were children in need of care. Another 364 children in need of supervision (29 percent) were held in secure facilities (but away from adults) during that same year. These are fairly substantial numbers, yet the state claims that they reflect large reductions in the number of wrongly institutionalized juveniles. This claim is based on the results of a monitoring study that estimates the average daily populations of various facilities in which juveniles might be held (Louisiana Commission on Law Enforcement 1978). The average was computed from yearly figures provided by local jails and from juvenile justice facility figures for 21 randomly selected days from the study years in question (i.e., fiscal years 1975-76 and 1977-78).

As the data in Tables 11-1 and 11-2 indicate, the number of nonadjudicated nonoffenders in detention centers and in jails decreased by 52 percent and 74 percent, respectively, over the two years of the study. The number of adjudicated nonoffenders in reform schools decreased by 92 percent during the same period, and the number of these youth in private facilities increased by 20 percent. By the state's own admission, however, these data are suspect (Louisiana Commission on Law Enforcement 1978). Records have not been kept in standardized fashion by all facilities and therefore are of uneven quality; some have

TABLE 11-1 Average Daily Population of Nonadjudicated
Juvenile Nonoffenders by Type of Facility: Fiscal
Years 1975-1976, 1977-1978

Facility	Average Daily Population 1975-1976	Average Daily Population 1977-1978	Percentage Change
Juvenile detention homes	27	13	-52
Local jails	19	5	-74
Reform schools	0	0	0
Private facilities	0	0	0

Source: Louisiana Commission on Law Enforcement (1978).

been destroyed or lost. In addition, the monitoring
method (i.e., daily tallies) could not account for persons
who were on leave or who escaped from the institutions.
Discrepancies even appeared in separate lists from the
same institution (e.g., the cook's list and the master
list would account for different numbers of inmates on a
given day). Most importantly, there was often no distinction made between delinquents and children in need of
supervision or between accused and adjudicated juveniles.
    Despite the apparent decrease in the use of institu-
tionalization to deal with children in need of supervision

TABLE 11-2 Average Daily Population of Adjudicated
Juvenile Nonoffenders by Type of Facility: Fiscal Years
1975-1976, 1977-1978

Facility	Average Daily Population 1975-1976	Average Daily Population 1977-1978	Percentage Change
Juvenile detention home	0	0	0
Local jails	0	0	0
Reform schools	74	6	-92
Private facilities	30	36	+20

Source: Louisiana Commission on Law Enforcement (1978).

or care, data provided by the Division of Youth Services
concerning their supervised probation cases indicate case
loads of 2,004 in 1976; 1,810 in 1977; 2,049 in 1978; and
1,768 in 1979. At least some small increase in probation
cases was expected if the juvenile justice system was in
fact being made to accommodate juveniles who could no
longer be incarcerated. Yet, we see a small decrease in
probation cases. We can only surmise that more juveniles
are being ignored or diverted at the preadjudication level, are being released by judges without official probation status at the adjudication level, or are in fact
still being institutionalized despite the apparent changes
reflected in Tables 11-1 and 11-2.

Finally, we might gauge Louisiana's response to the
deinstitutionalization movement in terms of its expansion
of alternative services. We were told by persons within
and outside the mental health system that referrals to
mental health and family counseling centers are higher
than ever, although statistical evidence is not available.
While the licensing office of the Department of Health and
Human Resources stated that, in general, the number of
private provider programs is increasing rapidly, we were
told by a Division of Youth Services official that, in
fact, there has not been a significant growth in the private provider industry in recent years. In 1978 four
programs were closed while one was initiated. Some new
programs have been developed, but, more often, already
established programs have received state funds in place
of support from charitable organizations. Available lists
of out-of-home facilities in the state from 1975 on indicate little year-to-year variation in number. Because of
these discrepant estimates, it would seem wise to assume
only minor growth in the private provider industry and
relative stability in the number of programs in recent
years.

Local Response

State and local officials have claimed that the deinstitutionalization movement in Louisiana has had an effect
on local law enforcement practices. In order to determine
whether or not state legislative measures have been reflected in local police and judicial actions, we interviewed criminal justice officials and personnel in Orleans
Parish and Vernon Parish. Orleans Parish was selected
primarily for its size and dominant political posture in

Louisiana. Functionally it is equivalent to the city of
New Orleans and currently accounts for approximately
one-sixth of the state's population. Furthermore, it has
some of the more developed programs for juveniles in the
state, many of which existed before the deinstitutionalization movement formally began in 1974. In contrast,
Vernon Parish is a large but relatively sparsely populated area located on the Louisiana-Texas border. Mostly
rural, it contains one small city, Leesville, and a military base, Fort Polk. The parish was selected for study
on the advice of knowledgeable informants who noted that
it would reflect the problems of a steadily growing rural
area. Although the presence of Fort Polk has increased
the size of Vernon Parish's juvenile case load relative
to other rural areas--a fact that makes the parish somewhat atypical--we believe it is more apppropriate for
study than other rural parishes, because the others simply
do not possess sufficient official nonoffender cases to
permit conclusions about juvenile justice reforms in rural
areas. In addition, the parish has traditionally held
significant numbers of juveniles in jail. In 1978, for
example, it was eighth among the 64 Louisiana parishes in
number of status offenders held in adult facilities.
Nonetheless, Vernon Parish reputedly has (or is forming)
a great many programs for juveniles and also has extremely
well coordinated social services. These apparent contradictions also make the parish attractive for study.

New Orleans and Vernon Parish have responded somewhat
differently to deinstitutionalization laws. New Orleans
is accustomed to dealing with a large number of juveniles
and over the years has developed a range of alternative
placement options to accommodate its large population of
juvenile offenders. Implementing the deinstitutionalization laws has involved little more than shifting the nonoffender segment of the juvenile population from one existing location (i.e., the city's juvenile detention center) to other, legally acceptable locations (e.g., nonsecure juvenile homes, walk-in counseling centers).

Data from the city of New Orleans indicate that the
number of youth held in the juvenile detention facility
has dropped from a high of 946 in 1973 to a low of 604 in
1978. Furthermore, as Table 11-3 indicates, the percentage of arrestees detained by the New Orleans police (as
opposed to those who were released to their parents) also
has dropped somewhat since 1973. The number of placements
in Greenhouse, a temporary crisis center for runaways and
troubled children, has fluctuated since 1973 but jumped

TABLE 11-3   Number of Juvenile Arrests and Case
Dispositions in New Orleans, 1970-1978

Year	Status Offender Arrests	Delinquency Arrests	Percentage of Arrestees Detained	Placements in Crisis Center (Greenhouse)
1970	828	4,507	17	0
1971	951	4,731	14	0
1972	889	4,794	17	2
1973	663	4,768	24	38
1974	624	4,513	21	76
1975	502	4,657	18	56
1976	384	4,586	16	41
1977	380	4,708	18	26
1978	430	4,758	16	72

Source: New Orleans Police Department.

dramatically in 1978 over the previous year.   Most importantly, status offender arrests have steadily decreased
since the early 1970s, although they have risen again in
1978.   Against this trend, we note the relative stability
of New Orleans delinquency arrest figures.

Vernon Parish has never developed alternative placement
options, both because of its relatively small juvenile
population and because officials of the juvenile justice
system apparently were comfortable with existing resources
(e.g., secure detention facilities or adult facilities).
Knowing that they would have to develop such options if
they were to comply with the law, parish officials resisted joining the deinstitutionalization movement until
forced to do so in order to meet the July 1978 deadline.
Since that time, greater reliance on existing community
resources (e.g., the mental health center and a youth
counseling center) and the development of a group home in
Leesville represent the extent of the system's response
to deinstitutionalization.   The home will also act as a
shelter facility.   In addition, Vernon Parish and Fort
Polk have intensified social service ties in an effort to
address juvenile problems at earlier stages of development.

Officials and personnel in the two juvenile justice
systems are nearly unanimous in their condemnation of to-

tal deinstitutionalization of status offenders. Although they are not wholly against deinstitutionalization, they clearly feel that there are some status offenders who should be put in secure detention, and they would like to have the flexibility to make such a decision. Both areas display high levels of compliance with the code, but Vernon Parish, which joined the deinstitutionalization movement as recently as 1978, cannot be fully evaluated for a few more years.

Although members of the juvenile justice system in both Orleans and Vernon parishes are against total deinstitutionalization, their reasons differ. In New Orleans, officials and personnel tend to view deinstitutionalization as a numerical problem; that is, there are now more juveniles on the streets for police to handle, more probation cases to be overseen, and more juveniles who are beyond the control of judges in that they can no longer be threatened with confinement. In contrast, Vernon Parish officials and personnel do not have to deal with large numbers of juveniles, and have focused their discontent on the fact that institutionalization is now denied to those juveniles whom they feel would benefit more from that experience than from any other available treatment option. This discontent stems from their view of institutionalization as an acceptable treatment alternative rather than as a control mechanism, and from a firm belief that each case is unique and that deinstitutionalization is not necessarily the best treatment for all status offenders. Overall, the Vernon Parish juvenile justice system seems more opposed to the recent changes in deinstitutionalization laws than does its counterpart in New Orleans.

The magnitude of the numerical problem that New Orleans faces deserves further mention here. A good illustration of the implications of deinstitutionalizing large numbers of juveniles is the problem of truancy, a status offense traditionally ignored in that city. Truancy is suddenly receiving considerable attention as a correlate of daytime burglaries, and the police and the local school board have joined forces to deal with the problem. In their efforts to curb truancy they have established centers to which truants may be brought by police for evaluation, counseling, and referral to social service agencies. The intention is to redirect truants back to school. Yet the fear expressed by court staff is that in order to enforce the program, its administrators will begin to rely on courts by filing petitions for truancy when chronic truants refuse to participate voluntarily in the program. Since truants number in the thousands in New Orleans, it is possible that their refusal to cooperate could explosively increase the population of status offenders to glut an already overburdened system.

Relabeling Possibilities

Given that the law now prohibits the institutionalization of status offenders, an option once very popular among judges, one might expect that juvenile justice officials will discover other means to accomplish this end. The most obvious method by which this can be done is relabel-ing, the placement of the status offender in a legal ca-tegory that permits secure confinement. This section discusses the three methods that can be used by judges in Louisiana to relabel status offenders and the extent to which these practices seem to occur. The three methods are (1) elevating the charge, (2) charging the youth with contempt, and (3) committing a youth to a mental health facility.

Elevating the Charge Children who have committed what is basically a status offense may be treated as delinquents if some aspects of their behavior can be construed as a violation of a law pertaining to adults. For example, children who run away from home may be dealt with as thieves because they stole $5.00 from their mother's purse in the process of fleeing.

The judges whom we interviewed denied that they prac-ticed such relabeling, but they did allow that some judges might practice it. Demonstrating that relabeling occurs is quite difficult. One indicator may be an increase in delinquency cases. But available evidence indicates that delinquency arrests, active delinquency probation cases, and juvenile admissions to reform schools decreased be-tween 1977 and 1979, suggesting that judges are not ele-vating charges in substantial numbers.

Contempt Charges As previously noted, one source of re-sistance to deinstitutionalization efforts is the juvenile court judges' fear of losing control over juveniles. There is no specific provision within the code to ensure that children will avail themselves of the services or-dered by the court. In order to maintain a coercive ele-ment in the judicial process, the code allows the court to find a child adjudicated in need of supervision in constructive contempt if he or she violates the court's orders. In such cases, the child may be sentenced to a maximum of 15 days' detention in a state reformatory.

Although nearly every judge with whom we spoke advocated a contempt clause, none admitted to using it. Most referred to the contempt citation as a threat by which to bring a recalcitrant status offender into line. Yet, many respondents argued that contempt charges have been used liberally, and state data on admissions to reform schools for violation of probation terms show a marked increase between 1977 and 1979 (Louisiana Commission on Law Enforcement 1980). At present, there is considerable debate concerning the constitutionality of the contempt clause, and both judges and juvenile justice advocates expect the matter to move into appeals courts.

Mental Health Commitments   The code defines emotionally or mentally disturbed children as children in need of supervision and permits their commitment, following particular guidelines, to mental health facilities. The extent to which such placements occur as a method of confining status offenders is open to question. The judges whom we interviewed vehemently denied that they or their colleagues engaged in this practice. By way of supporting the judges' claim, mental health officials note that Louisiana's mental health facilities have been overcrowded for so long that it would be impossible to fill them suddenly with status offenders.

There is concern, especially among juvenile justice advocates, about potential misuse of a number of psychiatric treatment facilties for adolescents that are scheduled to be built by the state in coming years.[2]   The

---

[2]There appears to be considerable confusion throughout the state concerning plans for building new psychiatric facilities for juveniles. Legislation was passed four years ago that permits the building of five such units throughout the state for diagnosis and short- and immediate-term care of juvenile delinquents who have mental and emotional problems. The facilities are to be built with state funds and operated through a combination of state and federal funds. To date, money has been set aside for only one unit, which is to be built in New Orleans. However, as of 1980, planning and construction of this facility had not yet begun. We have been told by

first is to be built in New Orleans. Some fear that facilities like these, with large bedspace capacities, will
encourage the juvenile justice system to produce patients
to fill the beds, and that a likely pool of patients is
the status offender population. Those who support the
treatment facility concept argue, however, that regional
review boards will not permit the improper commitment of
juveniles to these facilities and that competent, professional staff will prevent improper emergency placements
in the wards.

Although there is no evidence of overt use of mental
health commitments in order to confine status offenders,
we wonder whether restricting institutional alternatives
for status offenders has not caused some judges to consider juveniles as mental health problems more readily
than in the past. Sufficient ambiguity exists in the
definition of incorrigibility, for example, to view it
either as a juvenile offense or as being symptomatic of
deeper psychological problems. Prior to 1974 judges
clearly were more inclined to conceive of a juvenile offense in legal terms. Perhaps now the deinstitutionalization movement has forced them to deal with juvenile offenses in medical/mental health terms. This could result
in the improper treatment of status offenders or, conversely, more appropriate treatment of mentally disturbed
youth.

In short, the prospects for relabeling are obviously
recognized by Louisiana officials; yet we have found no
strong evidence of relabeling. The judges whom we interviewed seemed disinclined to relabel status offenders as
either delinquent or mentally ill. Ironically, they
seemed more inclined to relabel in the opposite direction,
that is, to categorize delinquents as status offenders.
This practice has occurred for many years throughout the
country for certain selected populations, particularly
middle-class youth. It represented an attempt to soften

---

some sources that the units will not house status offenders, by others that they surely will house status offenders, and by still others that status offenders will be
treated as outpatients. Bedspace estimates have ranged
from 75 to 300 per unit. The only thing we can be certain of is that no one really seems to know exactly what
will happen. Several respondents suggested that, given
current construction costs, no facilities will ever be
built.

the stigma associated with juvenile delinquency. In Louisiana today, however, the motive for such relabeling appears to be different. The deinsitutionalization movement
has resulted in improved group home programs, and judges
report that relabeling (or delabeling) delinquents as
children in need of supervision permits access to more of
these programs. Some facilities, for example, do not wish
to receive delinquents but are willing to accept status
offenders. This is the case with most shelter care homes
for neglected children. Furthermore, adjudication as a
child in need of supervision permits a "sentence" of indeterminate length, while adjudication as a delinquent
usually carries a sentence of specified duration. Thus,
as one judge noted, the relabeling of the delinquent as a
child in need of supervision allows the judge to maintain
supervisory control over the child for a longer period of
time.

Outcomes Evaluated

To recapitulate, the outcomes of deinstitutionalization
efforts in Louisiana, given the short life of those efforts, are not easily discerned. Services to juveniles
have improved but not markedly. The private provider
system has grown very little, and shelter care facilities
still are desperately needed. Statistical evidence of
change is either questionable or inconsistent, but data
collected from the state and from New Orleans (Tables
11-1 and 11-3) do indicate that considerably fewer status
offenders are being arrested and/or securely detained
prior to adjudication. Similarly, state reports argue
persuasively that no (or perhaps few) adjudicated children in need of supervision are being placed in reformatories (see Table 11-2). We find no evidence of large-
scale relabeling practices.

Our impression is that, overall, the treatment of status offenders in Louisiana today differs little from their
treatment a decade ago. Most status offenders in the past
were warned and released by the juvenile justice system;
most receive the same response today. In short, most
status offenders are simply ignored.

Some critics of deinstitutionalization laws in the
state assert that the situation of the typical status offender has actually worsened through well-intentioned deinstitutionalizaton efforts. Without asking whether status offenders should in fact receive services, we note

only that some who may have received services in the past
are not receiving them now. (Of course, some who were
institutionalized in the past are no longer institutionalized.) Law enforcement officers, judges, and court
staff now argue that their hands are tied, and they are
increasingly reluctant to have any involvement with status offenders. Indeed, one rural sheriff interpreted the
code in such a literal manner that he forbade his officers
to place status offenders in police cars. This, he said,
represented secure detention.

SUMMARY AND CONCLUSIONS

Conclusions based on the findings presented in this report
are necessarily tempered by an appreciation of the uneven
quality of information. We place dubious faith in many
of the statistical reports we have seen.

We have characterized Louisiana's deinstitutionalization efforts as recent (that is, dating from 1978). Although the origins of these efforts can be traced back to
events in 1974, deinstitutionalization laws did not actually take full effect in the state until July 1978, and
the full significance of those laws was not appreciated
until the Code of Juvenile Procedure became effective in
January 1979. It is difficult, therefore, to analyze
Louisiana's deinstitutionalization efforts in terms of
success or failure. This will not be possible for at
least three years.

In our opinion, the state entered into participation
in JJDPA, and into deinstitutionalization generally,
without fully comprehending the implications of its decisions. Chief among the forces leading to deinstitutionalization laws were a concern with juvenile crime, advocacy efforts, and perceived financial benefits from
alignment with federal efforts. Today, only a concern
with juvenile crime remains an effective force; advocacy
has weakened, antifederalism is high, and the state is
beginning to view deinstitutionalization as very costly.
Furthermore, judges, probation workers, and law enforcement agencies argue that they have lost control of status
offenders and are calling for the ability to securely
detain status offenders in cases in which they deem institutionalization to be the most appropriate treatment
option. We anticipate at least some modification of the
code in this regard.

Despite the forces that are working against deinstitutionalization, compliance with deinstitutionalization laws
seems high in Louisiana. Local governments appear con-
sciously to avoid violation of these laws. The state has
reorganized its machinery to facilitate the delivery of
alternative services and has approved construction of
shelter care facilities. Despite these good intentions,
however, it is not yet clear whether alternative services
or shelter care facilities will actually materialize.

It is obvious that the new code produced changes in the
treatment of juveniles by the juvenile justice system.
According to the people we interviewed and to scattered
documentary evidence, fewer status offenders are now being
institutionalized. However, the deinstitutionalization
goal has yet to be fully met. Some status offenders continue to be held in secure environments, if only for short
periods of time.

Perhaps as important, fewer status offenders may be
receiving services than in the past. If the intention of
the JJDPA mandate was to remove status offenders from the
courts, then we may say that this goal soon may be
achieved in Louisiana. Fewer status offenders seem to be
moving beyond initial police contact to the courts, and
judges seem to be becoming more frustrated with the cases
that do reach them. The judges whom we interviewed perceive their role as that of matching the needs of a client
population ("kids in trouble") with available resources.
They feel that some juveniles require institutionalization
while some do not, and that they are unable to employ institutionalization as a legitimate service for certain
status offender cases. It is our impression that by
drawing a distinction between status offenders and delinquents, deinstitutionalization laws have forced judges to
acknowledge a dichotomy they feel is more artificial than
real.

We necessarily view the problem of deinstitutionalization in Louisiana as one of resources. The state is
frustrated by the costs of alternative services, and
planners are perplexed by a dearth of specific plans for
creating those alternatives. And, lacking alternatives,
the juvenile justice system is likely to be unable to
serve a growing number of juveniles. We consider this to
be an undesirable consequence of deinstitutionalization
efforts, since many status offenders do, in fact, need
services. If the state were able to provide a greater
range of alternative services (e.g., a more inventive and
attractive shelter care service), judges clearly would be
more willing to deal with status offenders.

The fact that the general political climate and the attitudes of the juvenile justice system in Louisiana are constantly changing complicates the issue immensely, of course. Increased concern with delinquency seems to influence concern with status offenders. At present, following some recent sensational homicides by juveniles in New Orleans, the issue of violent youth has dwarfed all others. Local officials are calling for incarceration of career delinquents and for the immediate construction of a juvenile psychiatric facility that has been promised by the state.

Exactly what is, or has been, the federal government's role in this changing scene is still uncertain. If the federal government's goal was to accomplish total deinstitutionalization of nonoffenders and the provision of replacement services, it has failed in Louisiana and undoubtedly will continue to fail. If, however, the government wished to inject into a stagnant and recalcitrant juvenile justice system the kind of conflict that produces some results in terms of decreasing the number of securely confined nonoffenders, it has met with success.

REFERENCES

Daggett, H. S. (1933) A Compilation of Louisiana Statutes Affecting Child Welfare. Baton Rouge, La.: Louisiana State University Press.

Juvenile Court Commission for the State of Louisiana (1948) Report of the Juvenile Court Commission of the State of Louisiana. Baton Rouge, La.: Juvenile Court Commission for the State of Louisiana.

Louisiana Commission on Law Enforcement (1978) State Monitoring Report. Baton Rouge, La.: Louisiana Commission on Law Enforcement.

Louisiana Commission on Law Enforcement (1980) Juvenile Justice Data Book. Vol. III. Baton Rouge, La.: Louisiana Commission on Law Enforcement.

Louisiana Interdepartmental Committee (1950) State Service for Louisiana Children. Baton Rouge, La.: Louisiana Interdepartmental Committee.

Pugh, R. G. (1957) Juvenile Laws of Louisiana. Baton Rouge, La.: Thomas J. Moran's Sons.

Slingerland, W. H. (1916) A Constructive Program of Organized Child Welfare Work for New Orleans and Louisiana. New York: Russell Sage.

U.S. Department of Commerce (1981) State and Metropolitan
    Area Data Book, 1979. Bureau of the Census.
    Washington, D.C.: U.S. Government Printing Office.
Youth Alternatives (1979) Louisiana Blocks Federal Funds
    for Advocacy Group. Youth Alternatives 6(February).

ACKNOWLEDGEMENTS

We gratefully acknowledge the following persons for the
cooperation and assistance they offered us in researching
deinstitutionalization efforts in Louisiana.

Judge Anthony J. Graphia, Nineteenth Judicial District,
    Baton Rouge
Judge Thomas W. Tanner, Twenty-Second Judicial District,
    Covington
Judge Theodore R. Broyles, Thirteenth Judicial District,
    Leesville
Judge Salvadore T. Mule, Orleans Parish Juvenile Court,
    New Orleans
Judge Chris Smith III, City Court, Leesville
Senator Nat Kiefer, Second Senatorial District, New
    Orleans
Kerry Williamson, Committee Resource Coordinator,
    Juvenile Justice Project, Louisiana State Legislature,
    Baton Rouge
Daniel Lombardo, Committee Resource Coordinator, Juvenile
    Justice Project, Louisiana State Legislature, Baton
    Rouge
Brad Gater, Juvenile Law Clinic, Tulane University Law
    School, New Orleans
Holly Ackerman, Juvenile Law Clinic, Tulane University
    Law School, New Orleans
Robert Rochester, Deputy Assistant Secretary, Office of
    Human Development, Baton Rouge
Don Fuller, Director, Division of Evaluation and
    Services, Baton Rouge
Jeanette Hendricks, Protective Service Specialist,
    Division of Evaluation and Services, Baton Rouge
Maxine Hanks, Foster Care Specialist, Division of
    Evaluation and Services, Baton Rouge
Thomas A. Jenkins, Coordinator of Services, Division of
    Youth Services, Baton Rouge
Donald Wydra, Assistant Secretary, Office of Juvenile
    Services, Department of Corrections, Baton Rouge

John Futrell, Regional Director, Office of Human
Development, New Orleans

Dolores Kozloski, The Louisiana Commission on Law
Enforcement, Baton Rouge

Steve Phillips, Supervisor of Licensing and
Certification, Division of Licensing and
Certification, Baton Rouge

Sally Hubbard, Children's Program Coordinator, Baton
Rouge Mental Health Center, Baton Rouge

Valerie Woznick Lorio, Children's Program Coordinator,
New Orleans Mental Health Center, New Orleans

Jack Fontaine, Executive Director, Youth Alternatives,
Inc., New Orleans

Ed Berns, Executive Assistant III, Division of Youth
Services, New Orleans

Edward J. Parrino, Sr., Community Technician II, Division
of Youth Services, New Orleans

Janet Dauphin, Intake Worker, City Probation Office, New
Orleans

Francis Antille, State Superintendent, Child Welfare and
Attendance, Department of Education, Baton Rouge

Dennis Nugent, Supervisor of Discipline, Department of
Education, Baton Rouge

Sara Foulks, Director, School Social Work Services,
Orleans Parish School Board, New Orleans

Frank Serpas, Jr., Director, Criminal Justice
Coordinating Council, New Orleans

Harry Hull, Chief Assistant Director Attorney, Juvenile
Division, Orleans Parish District Attorney's Office,
New Orleans

Patsy Greer, Chief, Resource Development Unit, Division
of Technical Services, Office of Human Development,
Baton Rouge

Mary Jane Patten, Planning Officer, Division of Technical
Assistance, Office of Human Development, Baton Rouge

Elizabeth Brown, Administrative Social Worker III,
Department of Health and Human Resources, Baton Rouge

Richard Winder, Superintendent, Milne Boys Home, New
Orleans

James Williams, Director, Youth Study Center, New Orleans

Capt. Kenneth Dupaquier, Commander, Juvenile Division,
New Orleans Police Department, New Orleans

Gilbert Jeane, Assistant Chief, Leesville Police
Department, Leesville

Lt. Arthur Perrot, Assistant Commander, Juvenile
Division, New Orleans Police Department, New Orleans

Susan Dowden, Juvenile Officer, Vernon Parish Sheriff's
    Office, Leesville
Georgia West, Supervisor, Division of Evaluation
    Services, Office of Human Development, Leesville
Fr. Joseph Montalbano, Leesville
Col. Gerald E. Russell, Chief, Social Work
    Services/MEDDAC, Ft. Polk
Maj. Herman Martin, Social Work Officer, Social Work
    Services/MEDDAC, Ft. Polk
W. W. Parker, Supervisor of Child Welfare, Attendance,
    and Special Services, Vernon Parish School Board,
    Leesville
E. Wayne Parker, Acting Administrator, Leesville Mental
    Health Center, Leesville
Ray Slayter, Community Services Technician, Division of
    Youth Services, Alexandria
A.C. Dowdand, Leesville

The Deinstitutionalization of Status Offenders in Massachusetts: The Role of the Private Sector

12

JOANNE A. ARNAUD *and*
TIMOTHY C. MACK

INTRODUCTION

Public concern over children in trouble is longstanding in Massachusetts. Since the mid-seventeenth century, questions regarding the most appropriate settings and services for such children have been matters of vociferous public discussion. It is understandable, therefore, that Massachusetts should have been the scene of vigorous debate over policies of deinstitutionalization--the removal of status offenders and delinquents from traditional institutions associated with the correctional system, to be followed where necessary by their placement in less restrictive community-based programs.

The purpose of this paper is to assess the impact of the 1974 Juvenile Justice and Delinquency Prevention Act (JJDPA) on the process of deinstitutionalization in Massachusetts. This impact will be analyzed in terms of the relative effect of federal, state, and local influences on the inception and implementation of deinstitutionalization policies. These influences will be traced through analysis of (a) events leading up to deinstitutionalization, (b) the reactions of the state bureaucracy and local political settings to deinstitutionalization, and (c) the growth of the private provider system as one of the consequences of deinstitutionalization.

During the 1970s deinstitutionalization emerged as a major thrust of children and family policy within the

335

state. Several trends were evident during this period,
including a radical shift in the balance between public
and private sector service arrangements, an increase in
the use of voluntary commitments as a form of diversion
from the juvenile court, and a definitional separation of
status offenses from delinquent behavior. Implementation
of these new policies was not without difficulties. Insufficient funds, inadequate planning and evaluation, the
absence of an adequate transition period, the lack of a
unified and accurate data system, and a maze of children's
service systems without common aim all stood in the path
of change.

Few states have put the ideals of deinstitutionalization into practice as completely as Massachusetts. The
training schools and locked red-brick institutions are
gone, and a range of alternative nonsecure settings has
taken their place. New legislation provides that status
offenders cannot be compelled to accept services, and they
are increasingly diverted from the adversary process altogether. Nonetheless, problems have emerged during the
implementation of deinstitutionalization. Officials in
juvenile courts and social service agencies are frustrated
by their lack of control over status offenders and are
confused as to who has the actual authority to make decisions concerning these youth. Current methods of recording and analyzing state data have been seen as unsatisfactory by a number of state officials, who were also
concerned about the growing system of private providership
and the lack of systematic planning for the future. Finally, as the state's children's service system becomes
more decentralized, there is concern within the state bureaucracy over the increasing discretion exercised at the
local level.

A HISTORY OF CHANGE

Early Policies and the Growing Use of Private Providers

Interest in deinstitutionalizing juveniles in Massachusetts began in the 1960s, a period marked by a growing
nationwide concern for the rights of incarcerated populations and a desire to use the least restrictive alternative on their behalf. The definition of deinstitutionalization and the political struggle surrounding its implementation took place against this background. In advocating deinstitutionalization, liberals whose concerns

centered on more humane treatment of juveniles joined forces with conservatives who were ready to adopt a policy that they believed might reduce spending and juvenile crime. Research on recidivism rates among training school graduates suggested the failure of large institutions to stem growing crime (Lerman 1968, Vorenberg and Vorenberg 1973), and questions were being raised regarding the efficacy of therapeutic treatment within a community setting (President's Commission on Law Enforcement 1967). In this context, deinstitutionalization in Massachusetts was pursued with optimism.

Advocates of deinstitutionalization received broad federal cultivation of their efforts. One of the most important sources of ideological support was the Task Force Report: Juvenile Delinquency and Youth Crime, which was issued by the President's Commission on Law Enforcement and Administration of Justice in 1967. This report was often cited as being well known to Massachusetts activists (Bakal 1973, Ohlin et al. 1977). Fresh support for reform was added by In re Gault (387 U.S. 1 (1967)), a U. S. Supreme Court decision that specified that institutions restricted liberty and that any young person in jeopardy of commitment was therefore entitled to due process of law. The Gault decision was critical of the tradition of parens patriae, and limitations on parens patriae were incorporated into Massachusetts' subsequent status offender legislation.

Although federal research efforts, federal policies, and federal court decisions reinforced the efforts of state actors, many Massachusetts reforms were linked to its own tradition of progressive social policy in the area of child welfare. For example, in addition to providing leadership on issues of child welfare, the 1972 Massachusetts law on special education (Chapter 766) was both more comprehensive in its mandate and more rigorous in its civil rights provisions than the federal legislation enacted in 1975 (P.L. 94-142). It shifted a significant portion of the fiscal responsibility for broadly defined educational services to local government, and greatly expanded the population that could expect to receive these services.

Beginning in the 1960s, concerned groups, such as the League of Women Voters, who published a report on the conditions in the training schools, succeeded in directing public attention toward the treatment of delinquents (Spangenberg et al. 1977). The number of people who were committed to change grew, and by the end of the decade an

articulate, organized coalition of children's interest
groups, legislators, local politicians, and child care
professionals had emerged.

Allegations of brutality at the state training schools
were reported by the press in the early 1960s, and reformers called for an investigation. Partly in response
to their demands, John Volpe, the Republican governor,
brought in a panel from the U. S. Department of Health,
Education, and Welfare in 1965 . This panel ultimately
charged that the Massachusetts system was primarily punitive and custodial in its focus and that it was neither
diagnosing nor treating adolescents' problems (U. S. Department of Health, Education, and Welfare 1966). A subsequent state study, led by Martha Elliot, a former director of HEW's Children's Bureau and the chair of the
influential Massachusetts Coalition on Children and Youth,
confirmed these findings (Spangenberg and Studen 1977).
Further investigations were undertaken in Massachusetts
by the attorney general's office and the state senate.

Public reactions to this disclosure of severe physical
abuse in state training schools brought about the resignation of the head of the Department of Youth Services
(DYS), the agency responsible for running the schools.
Despite the tremendous effort exerted by the reform coalition, however, major deinstitutionalization did not
really occur until changes were made in the policies and
practices of the state agencies themselves. These changes
were set in motion by the appointment of Dr. Jerome Miller
as Commissioner of the Department of Youth Services in
1969. Miller was appointed by Volpe's successor, Francis
Sargent, a Republican who was a strong supporter of reform.

Miller found out early in his tenure that his power was
not coterminous with his authority. Only the top of the
hierarchy could be easily altered; the base was still
staffed by people who were largely opposed to change.
Funds for new hiring were limited and staffing was controlled by a Civil Service Commission that gave jobs to
political proteges. Unable to get additional funds in the
short-run from Massachusetts' complex budgetary process,
Miller turned to federal funding sources (e.g., direct
grants from the Law Enforcement Assistance Administration
(LEAA), from Title I of the Elementary and Secondary Education Act, and from Title IV of the Office of Manpower
Development and Training) for high-level planning staff
and for experimental programs. By early 1971 the planning
group hired with these funds had developed an outline for
reform to guide the state through a transition period.

Almost from the beginning, Miller began to make changes within the juvenile institutions. He abolished inmates' uniforms, the practice of marching in silent formation, and the use of physical abuse and isolation as punishment. Massachusetts' juvenile institutions historically had been allowed a great deal of autonomy. As conflicts developed in response to Miller's reforms, those staff who were opposed to change began to ally themselves with sympathetic outsiders, and a conservative coalition slowly took form. Although never as organized as the reform coalition, its core consisted of conservative legislators (both Democrats and Republicans), former staff members of the institutions, and citizens who were concerned about taxes and crime in the streets. The conservative coalition sent letters to newspapers to publicize the dangers of placing out-of-control juveniles back on the streets and began to lobby the legislature (Scull 1977). Stories of loss of control within the institutions were broadcast, and many judges, probation officers, and police officers who initially had been sympathetic to the idea of reform began to oppose it (Ohlin et al. 1977), thereby threatening the future of Miller's deinstitutionalization efforts.

As the struggle for reform began to take shape, the governor, legislative appropriations committees, and individual legislators took active and frequently conflicting stances. During the legislative recess in January 1972, Miller suddenly closed all juvenile institutions. Within one month, the youth had been relocated and staff were either reassigned or kept on temporarily as guards for empty institutions. Swift implementation may have been intended to forestall growing public opposition and legislative action, but the means for carrying out this mandate had not yet been established. No alternative placements were available for most of the youth suddenly decarcerated, and makeshift settings had to be rapidly created. Private providers responded quickly; contracts were signed, and Massachusetts' purchase-of-services system began its rapid expansion. Thus, Miller's decisions led not only to deinstitutionalization but also to the growth of privately provided services. Once set in motion, however, deinstitutionalization led to increased opposition to Miller and his policies.

The new community-based approach worried some reformers who saw the development of these facilities as totally unplanned entrepreneurship that would result in an overconcentration of providers in some parts of the state and their total absence in others. Other reformers began to worry that the new facilities were not actively using community services, providing sufficient treatment, or focusing on returning children to their families at the earliest opportunity. The most radical reformers were afraid that the humane elements of the new system might encourage the use of substitute care. Other members of the reform coalition began to feel that community placement only commingled status offenders and "hard core" delinquents.

These growing concerns tended to weaken and diffuse the once powerful reform coalition. At the same time, the conservative view of the private provider system as nonpunitive, poorly managed, too expensive, and insufficiently controlled was gaining currency. Some went so far as to advocate a return to state-run training schools.

These defections from the reform coalition and the consolidation of a conservative opposition appear to have contributed to Miller's decision to resign in January 1973, one year after he closed down the institutions. The growth of the private provider system that began during his administration continued after him, however, and brought about far-reaching changes in Massachusetts' provision of services to status offenders. The implications of these changes will be addressed in the subsequent section on the outcomes of change.

While Miller was deinstitutionalizing the juvenile offender population as a whole, efforts to alter the treatment of status offenders specifically were also increasing. In contrast to Miller's sudden administrative changes, these efforts were largely legislative in focus and had been under way for a number of years. The Massachusetts reform coalition had long worked for legislative changes to improve the treatment of status offenders without relinquishing the state's right to intervene in their lives. This general strategy involved separating status offenders from delinquents, diverting status offenders from the courts, and providing them with special services.

Among the initial legislation introduced in 1971 was HB 6226, which had been approved by Governor Sargent. It introduced the term <u>child in need of supervision</u> (later to become children in need of services, or CHINS) and provided that status offenders could no longer be committed to facilities for delinquent children. This bill, however, caused open conflict within the reform coalition. One of the strongest deinstitutionalization advocates, the Massachusetts Committee on Children and Youth, strongly

opposed the bill because it insufficiently detailed both
the mechanisms of diversion and the services available to
these children. These objections ultimately shaped the
successful 1973 legislation (Chapter 1073).

With reform advocates split and many legislators and
the general public undecided, the proposals languished in
committee. In 1972 additional legislation was introduced
that prohibited, among other things, the classification
of status offenders as criminals and regarded them instead
as youth with unmet social, psychological, and educational
needs. For a variety of reasons, however--ranging from
belief in the efficacy of punitive measures to fear of
increased expenditures--many citizens and politicians
joined forces to oppose this legislation. Several judges
also opposed the 1972 legislation because they saw it as
an encroachment on their authority over status offenders,
and this judicial criticism reinforced the arguments of
the conservatives. Finally, the defection of those reformers who favored complete decriminalization assured the
bill's defeat.

New legislation was again introduced by Governor Sargent and others in 1973, but this time it was supported
by the House Speaker and Senate Whip. This support was
largely the result of a series of compromises that had
occurred during committee (Spangenberg and Studen 1977).
As the bill evolved, however, the reform coalition again
split. The Massachusetts Advocacy Center felt that such
a bill was merely creating a new category of crime, and
they were especially concerned about the use of bail and
detention for status offenders. Even after the bill's
passage in the legislature, the Massachusetts Office for
Children lobbied against the governor's signing it
(Spangenberg and Studen 1977). Little criticism was
forthcoming, however, from the conservative coalition--
not because they favored the provisions of the bill, but
rather because their energies were now focused on another
issue, namely, racial imbalance in the public schools.
The 1973 bill (Chapter 1073) was passed largely because
of their lack of opposition. Status offenders were thus
legally differentiated from delinquents, and they would
be diverted from the court to the Department of Public
Welfare prior to adjudication whenever possible. Although
the law also stated that status offenders could no longer
be detained in facilities run by the Department of Youth
Services, that department in fact continued to be responsible for the detention of status offenders until alternative structures were available. In this regard, treat-

ment of status offenders, or CHINS, was not measurably
different despite the passage of the CHINS legislation.

Two years later, in 1975, the Department of Public
Welfare (DPW) applied to LEAA for a grant to develop services for CHINS, but the application was rejected on the
grounds that Massachusetts was too far along in the deinstitutionalization process to be eligible. Ironically,
impetus for that department to assume full responsibility
for CHINS increased after Massachusetts received a memo
in 1976 from the regional office of LEAA threatening the
loss of federal funds if Massachusetts did not comply with
federal regulations forbidding detention of status offenders in Department of Youth Services facilities. Massachusetts was given two years to comply, but agreement
was reached after only six months to gradually transfer
CHINS to the Department of Public Welfare. Thus, it was
really not until 1977 that DPW accepted responsibility for
carrying out the 1973 mandate.

According to persons interviewed, many DPW staff felt
that the populations they served were very different from
the status offenders whom they were scheduled to receive
from the Department of Youth Services. Informants told
us that the welfare staff felt that they had dealt only
with orphans and "nice kids," and therefore did not have
the staff complement, training, facilities, nor inclination to handle these troubled youth. In addition to the
fact that the Department of Public Welfare had not been
appropriated additional new funds to carry out its new
responsibilities, it was also being asked to perform in
an unfamiliar role, one different from the traditional,
surrogate-parent role for neglected, dependent, or abandoned children (or care and protection children as they
are called in Massachusetts). It was not until 1977 that
the agencies were able to secure additional funds specifically for the development of CHINS programs.

From its inception the CHINS unit in DPW emphasized
early intervention, diversion of children from the court
system, and placement in the least restrictive alternative. Although DPW administrators felt that detention
seemed to be antithetical to the objectives of a social
service agency, the legislature passed a bill specifically
ordering that agency to develop some kind of detention
capability. In response, DPW developed several emergency
shelters with a staff-to-youth ratio sufficient to provide
functional as opposed to physical security. Officials
interviewed at the Massachusetts Committee on Criminal
Justice (the state justice planning agency) held that

placement of status offenders in these emergency shelters did not violate the detention provisions of JJDPA. Massachusetts was found to be in compliance with that act, having achieved a 94 percent reduction in the secure detention (over 24 hours) of status offenders and dependent and neglected children between 1975 and 1978 (Massachusetts Committee on Criminal Justice 1979). In addition, juveniles have not been placed in adult facilities under state law since 1969.

OUTCOMES OF CHANGE

The CHINS System

The CHINS category includes runaway, stubborn, and truant youth. Prior to 1973 such youth were classified as delinquents. The 1973 CHINS legislation held that these youth could no longer be committed to either a county training school or an institution for adjudicated delinquents (although a group home or foster home used for delinquents was acceptable). Under Chapter 1073 of the Acts of 1973, CHINS may be referred to any one of four Massachusetts juvenile courts (Boston, Bristol, Springfield, or Worcester) or to one of the 72 district courts that have juvenile sessions. These referrals may be made by a parent or guardian, a police officer, or a school official (for either truancy or school disobedience).

In order to illustrate the number of CHINS relative to the other categories of juveniles who are referred to the Massachusetts court system, referral figures for the years 1969 to 1979 are shown in Table 12-1. Interestingly enough, several respondents perceived the choice of whether to place a juvenile in the dependent or status offender category to be a function of age rather than behavior. Thus, identical acts engaged in by a 9- and a 12-year-old could result in the classification of the younger child as dependent and the older child as a status offender.

There are a number of possible dispositions for a CHINS case that has been referred to the court: (1) dismissal without a petition; (2) informal assistance by juvenile probation; (3) referral to some other agency for processing, such as social services; and (4) issuance of a petition on the merits. Upon adjudication of the youth as a CHINS, the court's options under the 1973 act include either leaving the CHINS with his or her parents or

TABLE 12-1   Number of Children Brought into
Contact with the Juvenile Justice System in
Massachusetts, 1969-1979

Year	Delinquents	CHINS	Care and Protection Children	Total
1969	19,301	0	922	20,223
1970	28,486	0	544	29,030
1971	33,018	0	718	33,736
1972	32,663	0	844	33,507
1973	26,297	0	826	27,123
1974	25,723	1,686	1,338	28,747
1975	24,950	2,396	1,394	28,740
1976	22,689	2,692	1,643	27,024
1977	23,112	3,652	2,600	29,364
1978	24,958	4,052	3,479	32,489
1979	27,244	4,708	2,409	34,361

Source: Annual Reports of the Office of the Commissioner of
Probation (1969-1979).

placement with another adult, a private agency, or the
Department of Public Welfare.

Three critical provisions of the CHINS statute proved
to be the phrase that held that all dispositional options
were also "subject to any conditions and limitations as
the court may prescribe," the prohibition of secure
placements for CHINS, and the selection of the Department
of Public Welfare as the agency responsible for services
to CHINS. The first provision gave the courts potential
influence over agencies that provided services to status
offenders, while the second gave these same courts relatively less leverage over the children themselves. With
nonsecure group homes and foster care as the most predominant placement options, treatment assumed a highly voluntary nature. Status offenders could leave the placement
at will, without the possibility of receiving further or
more severe sanctions from the court.

The third element involved the department's approach
to CHINS services. Supervised by a state-level CHINS coordinator and six regional coordinators, the DPW system
involved a network of 40 CHINS court-liaison social workers who were assigned to a specific court or courts within
a region. Despite insufficient funding, CHINS workers
were able to develop innovative counseling and tracking
programs. A low staff/client ratio seemed to foster open

communication and a sense of responsibility. Based on interviews with CHINS workers in selected locations and with other DPW personnel, it appears that their direct accountability to the courts, which necessitated careful recordkeeping and periodic case reviews, also contributed to the CHINS workers' having a clearer sense of their responsibility for the progress of the youth under their purview. The fact that staff turnover among CHINS workers is lower than in other parts of the Department of Public Welfare may reflect a greater sense of professionalism and stronger group identification on the part of people who like their work and are clear about the program mission.

Placement Options   If a decision is made to place a CHINS outside the home, there are two types of placement options—group care and foster care. Group care includes: (a) specialized foster care, (b) group homes in a residential setting for 8 to 15 children, (c) residential treatment facilities with on-grounds schools and services, (d) boarding schools with a residential learning center but no social services, (e) special schools for the mentally retarded, and (f) special schools for the physically handicapped. According to respondents, adolescents most frequently are found in group homes rather than in foster care because they are less easy to place in foster homes than younger children, they are less in need of parental protection, and many adolescents resent the substitute parenting found in foster care. Youth in group homes attend the regular public schools whenever possible to avoid the problem of cost-sharing between the Department of Public Welfare and the local school system.

Ideally the selection of a placement is made according to the specific treatment or care needs of the child. Respondents often admitted, however, that availability plays a large role in placement. The scarcity of slots and the fact that courts frequently order that a child be placed quickly often force the group care unit to use whatever is available. Once a youth has been referred to group care, responsibility for the child is shared by the state group care unit in Boston and the child's local social worker—a practice that some respondents felt dissipated responsibility for the child.

The second residential placement option for both CHINS and dependent and neglected children is foster care. The Department of Public Welfare currently uses 3,500 foster homes. Department officials involved with foster care admitted that serious problems exist in attracting and keeping adequate numbers of qualified foster parents, largely because of lack of training and support services.

Although foster care is the least restrictive alternative available in Massachusetts, several respondents spoke of the following problems with its use:

1. It may be an inappropriate placement for adolescents who are rebelling against their own family relationships.

2. It may be used as a dumping ground for younger children whose needs are then neglected.

3. Many Massachusetts foster homes are overcrowded.

4. Little training or support is given to foster parents and, as a partial result,

5. The overall quality of Massachusetts foster parents is low.

Criticisms of the System   Both DPW personnel and private child welfare professionals stated that CHINS frequently are commingled with special education children and Department of Youth Services delinquents in treatment and in residential programs. Few officials seemed hesitant about this commingling of youth, however, because many in the Department of Public Welfare believe that children are labeled primarily to allow them to flow into the bureaucratic channels where service and placement possibilities exist. The availability of a program slot and its organizational location are critical determinants of whether a youth ends the intake journey as a CHINS or as a Department of Youth Services client.

Some respondents attributed the consistent increase in the number of CHINS entering the system since 1974 (as shown in Table 12-1) to the common belief that the CHINS program provides services for needy adolescents not available elsewhere (i.e., emergency short-term shelter, counseling, and residential placement). The availability of these services and of state special education monies apparently has encouraged use of the CHINS program. But even with these existing services, more emergency shelters (there are only 46 in the whole state) where counseling and diagnosis can occur are needed. Emotional and psychological counseling for children and adolescents are rare because the Department of Mental Health does not make its professional staff available for these purposes. It has waiting lists of one month at its mental health outpatient clinics and uses slots for youth (577 direct services; 3,174 privately provided) for its own clients in that age group.

Many saw the lack of enforcement provisions as the focal point of problems with the CHINS program. Parents cannot be compelled to accept help nor are they called upon to contribute financially to their childrens' care and treatment. As for the youth themselves, CHINS can "vote with their feet" against any placement that they do not like, since there are no enforcement provisions to require CHINS to accept any given social service plan. In addition, providers are free to refuse services to any young person whom they do not wish to accept into their program.

Department of Public Welfare officials and private child welfare professionals agreed that there are problems with the state's use of substitute care in foster or group homes for both dependent children and CHINS. Many asserted that the quality of the substitute care system is not uniformly acceptable in any of the possible settings. Almost no systematic evaluation or monitoring of foster homes is done, and training of foster parents has begun only recently; monitoring of group homes is spotty and sporadic. Many officials wondered whether displaced children and youth would ever be returned home or at least provided with a stable, long-term living arrangement.

Almost all court personnel who were interviewed felt that the 1973 legislation increased their responsibility for CHINS, but also restricted their power in dealing with them. For example, many felt that the law made it impossible to hold a young person in one place long enough to provide services, and that this situation ultimately weakens the youth's respect for the legal process. There was also general agreement that (a) the state must monitor its service contracts more effectively; (b) acceptance of services by these youth should be mandatory; (c) providers must be forced to accept a wider spectrum of children; (d) a wider array of services is needed to help these young people; and (e) some sort of secure placement option, preferably detention, is needed.

Finally, a number of respondents desired some secure, locked detention, coupled with the ability of judges to classify chronic runaways as delinquents. Events in Massachusetts subsequent to our research indicate that change in this direction may occur.

Future Prospects There are great differences of opinion about deinstitutionalization in Massachusetts--whether it is better than its institutional predecessor, whether it has improved the lives of young people, and whether its objectives have been realized. There also are significant gaps in knowledge about the impact of deinstitutionalization on children. In a partial attempt to address this problem, a DPW-sponsored Children's Information System (CIS) was implemented in 1978, and CHINS data were added to it starting in 1979. In 1980, however, the CIS ceased to function for a number of reasons, including dissatisfaction with the contractor and a desire to remodel old DPW programs, and was not expected to resume operation until late 1981.

In July 1980 the Department of Public Welfare was reorganized into two departments--the Department of Public Welfare (DPW) and the Department of Social Services (DSS). DPW retained the income and health maintenance programs and the old name; DSS assumed responsibility for social services (including children's services). Both were cabinet-level departments. In addition to suspending the Children's Information Service, DSS has given indications that general policies toward CHINS are in transition. Their operation has become more decentralized, and the regions and 40 local service areas now have the option to choose among administrative structures. For example, since July 1980 a number of service areas have chosen to discontinue the CHINS worker approach and have returned to a pool of social workers who respond to CHINS cases as one of several types in their case load. In addition, the department shows signs of changing CHINS programs from a budget line item to an element of the more generalized "Children in Crisis" account.

While these changes may signal a decrease in services available to the CHINS population or even a possible change in the law, one respondent pointed out that deemphasis might now, in fact, be the appropriate response to a pioneering effort that has largely achieved its goals. With CHINS now established as a recognized population, it might be time to shift the focus to new areas.

The Purchase-of-Services System

An intrinsic part of Massachusetts' present children's services system is its philosophical and programmatic commitment to the public purchase of privately provided services. Local school systems and state agencies serving children and youth have come to depend on the private sector to meet their expanding needs. This section describes how the state uses and evaluates private service

providers, and summarizes concerns surrounding the purchase-of-services system.

While the needs of dependent children historically have
been privately met, the majority of services to youth who
were involved with the court have been provided by state-
run systems. In 1967 and 1968, for example, there were
only nine Massachusetts programs available for court-
involved youth, and all of these were run by the now
defunct Division of Youth Services. During the 1960s administrators came to believe that privately provided service arrangements would offer more efficient, effective,
and economical services to these youth. As a matter of
policy the state began in 1969 to phase out its role as
direct service provider and to assume instead the position
of manager, regulator, and monitor of these privately
provided services.

Until the abrupt and rapid deinstitutionalization
movement, the state still owned and operated facilities
for the detention, long-term incarceration, and treatment
of juvenile delinquents. Status offenders, who were
categorized as delinquent youth until 1973, had been
housed in these state institutions. The switch to a
private purchase-of-service system was not a logically
necessary result of the decision to close large, geographically segregated institutions, since the state could
have developed its own community-based, decentralized
system of care. Once the decision to use private sources
of care was made, however, scores of programs opened in
response. The rapidity of this conversion for the state
as a whole is shown by the rise in Massachusetts' spending
for privately purchased human services in all categories,
from $25 million in fiscal 1969 to $300 million in fiscal
1981 (Massachusetts Taxpayers Foundation, Inc. 1980).
More specifically, by 1975 the total number of residential
programs for court-involved youth had climbed from 9 to
95, 93 percent of which were privately run. By 1978 the
figure had risen to 138 (92 percent private), and by 1980
the Massachusetts Committee on Criminal Justice reported
164 programs serving court-involved youth. Many of these
programs serve both CHINS and delinquents, but the Department of Social Services reports that in fiscal 1980, 68
programs were funded for CHINS alone (46 emergency shelter
contracts and 22 foster care contracts). Of these 68, 45
were closed-referral contracts that served only DSS-
referred CHINS. In addition, there were 43 CHINS
counseling contracts. CHINS are also served by larger
residential facilities, but these slots are not a CHINS

budget item per se. Data on contracts specifically serving CHINS were not collected in any aggregate form before
fiscal 1980, but the general growth trends are evident.

Several factors prompted Massachusetts to encourage the
growth of a purchase-of-services system. The 1967 and
1974 amendments to the Social Security Act provided federal funding mechanisms that promoted purchase-of-service
arrangements. It was also believed that specialized services could be developed and provided more effectively by
the private sector. Attracting new, highly qualified
personnel or retraining state institutional staffs would
have been difficult given Massachusetts' civil service
laws and its strong civil service employees' union. In
addition, a movement developed within the state under
Governor Michael Dukakis to reduce the public payrolls.
Operation within a purchase-of-services framework avoided
the need to pay the salaries of possibly superfluous but
entrenched state employees. Finally, under state law, the
initial capital costs of new programs would be absorbed
by the providers themselves.

Many state officials supported the purchase-of-services
system because they believed that innovation and experimentation in program development could not be accomplished
by a system of publicly provided services. Even if state
workers were willing to adapt, the expense of retraining
them would have been prohibitive. Furthermore, once large
sums of state money were spent on an experimental program,
the state would own it, like it or not, for years. One
perceived advantage of the purchase-of-services system was
that programs would be more likely to endure because of
their inherent worth and success with the youth that they
served rather than because the state had made an irre-
versible investment. Flexibility, these officials argued,
could be attained and retained better through a privately
purchased system of care. But this approach may not have
sufficiently accounted for the possibility that the state
would have less quality control over the services for
which it contracted than might have been the case if those
services had been publicly provided.

Criticisms of the System Three types of problems are most
often noted in critiques of the purchase-of-service system
and its role in deinstitutionalization: (1) community
resistance to deinstitutionalization, (2) the quality of
the state's management of its purchase-of-services system,
and (3) the ability of the state to control the growth of
this system.

The first problem concerns the extent of community resistance to deinstitutionalization. It is true that community resistance can occur with both publicly and privately operated programs, but the particular problems of private providers appear to have exacerbated resistance. For example, in the early 1970s many inexperienced providers were unable simultaneously to sustain their operations, produce innovative programs, and control their clientele. As a result, communities that initially were receptive to the prospect of community-based programs became wary of them. Some of this resistance was a reaction to the programs' failure to control their clients, but there was also a reluctance to have children's programs as neighbors. An ad hoc "spectrum of noxiousness"* developed, with mentally retarded children as the most unwelcome. Some service providers were willing to lose lucrative contracts, if necessary, to retain control of their own intake decisions. In fact the children's services providers whom we interviewed all asserted that providers prefer empty beds to accepting into their program a child whom they do not want. Although the desire to be autonomous and to work with a more responsive population of youth is understandable, it created problems of proper placement for young people judged unacceptable by most host communities.

This situation is exacerbated because apparently a greater number of children are being served now than before deinstitutionalization. A sample of CHINS shelter care populations taken by the Massachusetts Committee on Criminal Justice for the second quarter of 1975 showed 160 CHINS and care and protection children (plus 10 additional CHINS in the more structured shelter facilities). By the second quarter of 1978, there were 487 CHINS and care and protection children (while CHINS in DYS shelter care dropped to only three). Over the same general period, the committee's publication, Residential Programs for Court Involved Youth in Massachusetts (1979), estimated that the number of CHINS and nonoffenders in group homes jumped from 303 in 1975 to 525 in 1978. Analyses of this phenomenon were varied. Some of those interviewed speculated that the net had widened to provide

---

*The phrase "spectrum of noxiousness" was coined by a respondent with varied experience as a direct care staff member, director of a group home, and as a representative of human service providers.

the clients needed to fill private providers' slots; others asserted that the increase involved youth who had needed help before but had not received it.

The second general type of difficulty relates to the way Massachusetts has managed its purchase-of-services system. After 1969 the state human service agencies gradually took on the responsibilities of financing and managing their private service providers. This new role included cost accounting, cost-benefit analysis, monitoring program performance, and evaluating program services. It is generally accepted in Massachusetts that the state agencies have not developed adequate capabilities to carry out their new responsibilities, in part because a constitutional prohibition of state-funded capital costs has prevented them from setting up the necessary mechanisms to do so. While the present study cannot confirm this conclusion because of its limited on-site observations, there does appear to be support for these kinds of criticisms of the state's performance as a manager (Contract Research Corp. 1978, Institute for Government Service 1977, Massachusetts Taxpayers Foundation, Inc. 1980, Spangenberg and Studen 1977).

Monitoring and evaluating privately provided services necessitate knowledge of the kinds of services that these programs are delivering to children, the quality of the services, and what the daily life of children in the programs is like in terms of some set of operationally definable variables. Officials whom we interviewed seemed to feel that the state did not have the requisite information to evaluate program performance and that their personnel had not been adequately trained for their new roles as service brokers. The Office for Children, which functions independently of any other state agency and operates both as a public advocacy organization for children and youth and as the state licensing authority, does require a service plan as part of its initial licensing procedure. Review of the content of that plan, however, is left to the contracting agencies. Few on-site reviews of programs and their services are provided by the procedures of either the group care unit or the Office for Children. In addition, the purchase-of-service unit in DPW has insufficient staff to conduct such visits (Massachusetts Taxpayers Foundation, Inc. 1980). As a result, after initial licensing a program is visited only for two days or so at eighteen-month intervals.

Under a grant from HEW, the Office for Children has addressed this lack of consistent, periodic, on-site re-

views. In each service region it has trained teams of
citizens in evaluation techniques that use questionnaires
developed by outside consultants.   Once trained, these
regional teams are responsible for conducting frequent,
structured, on-site monitoring of program performance.
Without consistent and continued evaluation, however, it
will remain impossible for the state to ensure that the
quality of services purchased for its youth is maintained
and improved.

When the purchase-of-services system first began providing services to youth in Massachusetts, the system was
characterized by small, independent, low-budget operations
that provided community-based programs.   This is no longer
the case, however. DARE, Inc., for example, which opened
the first group home for adolescents in Massachusetts at
the beginning of the 1970s, now provides services to
court-involved youth through 12 separate programs across
the state.   In addition, this conglomerate has branched
out into services to the mentally retarded and even to
adult mental health populations, and now contracts with
four different agencies (Departments of Youth Services,
Social Services, Mental Retardation, and Mental Health).
The Massachusetts Taxpayers Foundation (1980) estimated
that these contracts totaled $3 million annually by 1979.
Several respondents criticized the mixing of such diverse
populations within the facilities, and further questioned
the ability of a single private provider to manage such a
wide range of programs effectively.

The growth of large providers with statewide programs
raises a third problem directly related to the increased
use of private providers. Many respondents asserted that
private providers have developed sufficient influence with
the state legislature to block attempts by DPW to cancel
existing contracts or to award new contracts to other
programs.   The Massachusetts Taxpayers Foundation noted
that contract negotiations were often conducted between
the experienced contract lawyers of the providers and the
comparatively inexperienced contract specialists of the
agency (1980).   Additionally, some respondents believe
that even well-run, professional, large-scale providers
are threats to the goal of community-controlled, community-based programs and to the need for experimentation
and flexibility in program development.

In rebuttal the representatives of one large provider
network pointed out that large corporations are necessary
to provide the financial resources needed to start new
programs. Both start-up costs and cash reserves are es-

sential when state disbursement procedures delay payments, and they argue that these costs can be absorbed only by corporate providers. They also pointed to the wide variety of services, program sizes, service patterns, and type of youth they serve as proof that flexibility is possible within a large, centralized provider system.

After a decade of experience, there is little argument that the state needs to be more effective at purchasing, monitoring, and evaluating services. Several factors were suggested as to why the state has not developed these capabilities, including (a) agency failure to determine what is necessary for an effective community system, (b) continuing interagency competition (in spite of common management needs and objectives), and (c) agency resistance to the transfer of contracting responsibilities to a central office, such as the Massachusetts Rate Setting Commission. One observer felt that the failure of top management within state agencies to realize the fiscal and administrative implications of their policies represented a critical lapse in program administration.

LOCAL POLICY IMPLEMENTATION

Policy formulated at the state level must be interpreted and implemented at the local level. Examination of local areas provides information regarding this phase of policymaking and the influence of federal policy on local patterns of policy adaptation. In particular, insight can be gained into the following aspects of local policy implementation:

1. How much information about state policies do local actors possess?
2. What is the level of awareness of federal policies and funding patterns?
3. Is there empirical evidence of local adaptation of deinstitutionalization policies?
4. If so, what options have been chosen by the primary local actors?

Before these questions can be addressed effectively, it is first necessary to gain some understanding of Massachusetts' organization and demographics at the local level.

A Flow of CHINS Through the System

The Massachusetts courts have no legal control over the
social service agencies, the direct care providers, or
CHINS. The courts, however, do control much of the intake process and exert a great deal of influence over the
processes of placement and service. The extent of influence often varies with the personal or political power of
the judge. Individual judges can and do issue subpoenas
for the appearance and testimony of any person connected
with the provision of services--from commissioner to service provider--to show cause as to why the court's recommendations are not being followed. Some courts, for example, have succeeded in ordering the Department of Public
Welfare to pay for unappropriated services or to compromise in situations in which the department would ordinarily take a firm stand. A struggle continues between the
courts and the social service agencies as to which is in
the better position to determine what is in the best interests of children and youth.

The compromises in the CHINS legislation, which were
necessary to gain its passage, continue to complicate its
implementation. Key elements of the 1973 act were couched
vaguely and have led to wide variations in statutory interpretation. As we shall see below, individual personalities and varying judicial philosophies are often more
significant than mandated procedures in the outcome of a
given case. The discussion that follows supplements the
initial outline of the CHINS process with the details of
actual practice and local variance.

Intake--CHINS   Historically, the most common referral
source at intake has been parents, primarily because the
police were reluctant to initiate action, usually returning youth to their homes and referring parents seeking
help to the courts or to a CHINS worker. Several respondents, however, asserted that because of changes in the
Massachusetts special education law one of the major initial referral sources for CHINS was the schools. In the
first few years following the passage of Chapter 766 in
1972, many young people whose behavior was of a status
offense variety were brought to the attention of the
school system by their parents, who felt that they were
entitled to an educational needs assessment. The schools
in turn attempted to pass as many of these youth as possible on to the juvenile court. As the local school systems gained experience with the 766 process, however, they

were better able to distinguish those youth whose difficulties were more exclusively education-related. In addition, the juvenile court began to insist that schools
perform Chapter 766 evaluations before referral.

Most courts help the family find services before they
sign an application for a CHINS petition. This assistance
involves either immediate diversion of the case to the
Department of Public Welfare or supervisory retention of
the case while providing counseling and educational and
psychological testing and evaluation. A number of judges
and probation officers believe that the court is not the
proper forum for solving certain interpersonal problems
because the adversary system exacerbates these problems
and isolates the youth. Some court personnel feel that
the goal of decriminalizing status offenses may be jeopardized by resort to the formal judicial process. Many
feel, however, that court supervision, court recordkeeping, and hearings before judges are essential elements of
the judicial process that guarantee young people both
equal protection and due process of law.

Diversion practices vary sharply from court to court.
Since no court keeps records on the number of youth diverted or on their age, sex, race, or alleged offenses,
only rough estimates of the extent and impact of diversion
are possible. Many courts are committed to diverting as
many youth as possible to the Department of Public Welfare
or to private agencies for service, but other courts do
not have such a standing policy. Sometimes it is the
clerk or the probation officer who may decide to divert,
but there are no generalizable criteria that these intake
workers follow in making their decisions. A youth's
chance of being diverted may depend less on the merits of
the parents' case than on which intake person first con-
fronts the child.

The hearing on the merits of the case seldom questions
whether the child actually is a stubborn child, a runaway,
or a truant. Rather, the real controversy concerns the
service plan. Judges differ in the degree of their personal involvement in shaping the placement and service
plans. Some try to dictate to the Department of Public
Welfare, while others defer to its judgment. In any case,
the youth is seldom consulted and the youth's lawyer usually accepts the recommendation of the court or DPW. Few
appeals have been made from CHINS adjudications because
youth who are dissatisfied with their situation simply
leave their placement or stop going to receive services.

Bail and detention also involve the enforcement powers of the courts. Bail can be imposed only on CHINS who the court feels will fail to respond to a hearing or who have already failed to do so. Judges, probation officers, and police resent these limitations on imposing bail. Judges interviewed feel that these legislative restrictions on the use of bail impede their ability to act effectively. In addition, some complain that the lack of secure facilities for detention of CHINS leaves the process vulnerable to abuse and disrespect. Child advocates, however, decry any use of bail in a noncriminal system, and assert that detention criminalizes the CHINS process and therefore abrogates the civil rights of CHINS.

Many of these controversial practices--restrictions on the use of secure placements for CHINS, the completely voluntary nature of the process, the inability of the court to enforce its recommendations--may be radically modified in light of the 1980 amendments to the federal Juvenile Justice and Delinquency Prevention Act. For example, states now will be able to detain securely or incarcerate any juvenile who is charged with or found to be in violation of a valid court order. It remains to be seen what impact this relaxation of the prohibition on use of secure facilities for status offenders will have in Massachusetts.

Local Areas

To find out how deinstitutionalization has been implemented at the local level, we visited three locations--the city of Boston and two counties in western Massachusetts. Selection of these areas was based on several factors. First, Boston is the largest urban center in the state and the site of one of the four Massachusetts juvenile courts. Second, Massachusetts' highly centralized system of social services is characterized by some friction among the agencies that share responsibility for the care of status offenders. According to DPW administrators, the degree of cooperation among agencies is inversely related to the proximity of their social service region to the main office in Boston. To capture this variance, we visited Franklin and Hampshire counties--adjacent counties in western Massachusetts that are geographically distant from Boston and demographically distinguishable from each other. The seat of Franklin County's court and welfare office is an economically depressed urban area surrounded

by smaller mill towns and rural hill areas. Hampshire
County, however, is a community of the affluent and educated. Professors, prosperous merchants, and professional
people live and work here. Small farms, rural villages,
and a few old pockets of industry—many now abandoned—
complete the Hampshire County court's jurisdiction.

Local Actors

Administrative policies and personal views of judicial and
social services personnel at the local level naturally
affect the way in which deinstitutionalization has been
implemented. The reaction of local area administrators
to new procedures and regulations is a decided factor in
their actual impact on the youth served by these systems.

Franklin County Local judicial discretion in interpreting the CHINS statute is substantial, and personal predilections play a critical role. The judge in Franklin
County had strong reservations about the CHINS legislation
and deinstitutionalization. He asserted that CHINS should
be merged with all juveniles into a single intake system
and be channeled through the court. Other judicial personnel in Franklin County were concerned that a lack of
court control allowed private providers to be irrespon-
sible and far too selective about the clients they would
take.
    The judge and his staff were not very interested in
federal policy or funding. The level of government that
they perceived as having the power to effect change and
that they wished to influence was state government—in
particular, the legislature. The judge, his probation
officer, the Franklin County CHINS worker, and the juvenile officer in the Greenfield Police Department have all
lobbied the legislature and the governor to reopen secure
public institutions in Franklin County. The judge was
adamant on two points: (1) the need for secure preadjudicatory detention to prevent juveniles from taking advantage of the system by running from their placements,
and (2) the need for secure postadjudicatory placement to
provide CHINS with treatment in a structured, disciplined
setting.
    Records of the Franklin County court show that the
judge regularly reviewed the progress of individual CHINS
cases, that he often continued cases, and that he regularly placed CHINS under the supervision of his probation

officer for up to a year. Diversion is rarely used in Franklin County, but it should also be noted that there are few programs to which a status offender can be diverted.

The CHINS worker in Franklin County was in charge of all the county's status offenders. By refusing to accept any voluntary placements, he shared the Franklin County court's general perception of itself as the necessary first stop for all youth charged with committing status offenses. He was critical of the CHINS legislation and the manner in which it has been implemented. Dissatisfied with many aspects of deinstitutionalization, he felt that centralized group care was functioning inefficiently. The CHINS worker favored the return of publicly run placements and stressed the need for secure detention.

Hampshire County Hampshire County's judge liked the part of the CHINS legislation that removed status offenders from the justice system, but he thought that its essential failure was the inability of state agencies to deal effectively with what he felt was a familiar problem. The judge would have liked to see more authority given to the agencies to help families. Because he felt the parents were often responsible for their children's problems, he favored mandatory parental contributions for their children's support in an out-of-home placement. He would have liked to see the 1973 act expanded to include provisions for family counseling and services.

The Hampshire County judge approved of deinstitutionalization, but he felt that the Department of Public Welfare should have enforcement power to make private providers take the youth the providers often reject. While believing that secure facilities are necessary for CHINS who run, he felt that the private sector could provide this type of placement more effectively than the state. He felt that decisions to use secure facilities should be made only by the Department of Public Welfare, subject to judicial review.

The judge and court staff in Hampshire County were very critical of the performance of the DPW bureaucracy. They were impressed, however, with the local CHINS worker, with whom they had a close working relationship. Unlike the Franklin County CHINS worker, the Hampshire County worker encouraged troubled adolescents to come to him voluntarily and then labeled them CHINS so that, without formal adjudication, CHINS money could be used to provide them with services. This practice, and the extensive court use of

diversion to the Department of Public Welfare, resulted
in relatively few court appearances for CHINS.

The Hampshire County CHINS worker was more positive
about the CHINS program than anyone else we interviewed.
He believed it had several advantages over other youth
programs in that it was a program with clear responsibility for a specific population and, more importantly, that
the CHINS program was accountable to the courts for those
youth. He believed that rebellious adolescents need as
flexible a response as possible, and he advocated non-
intervention whenever possible. Satisfied with the purchase-of-services system, he was opposed to secure facilities for noncriminal youth. His experience with private
providers had been positive, and he found that he could
convince them to accept his clients if they had a vacancy.
He was familiar with many programs personally and had
strong opinions about their quality. Of the local area
respondents, the Hampshire County CHINS worker was clearly
the best informed about federal funding patterns and
policies.

Boston The Boston Juvenile Court has jurisdiction over
all CHINS and care and protection cases in the city of
Boston. Its chief justice also serves as administrative
justice for all four juvenile courts in the state. The
chief justice, who was one of the authors of the original
CHINS legislation, felt that the law had been weakened by
the compromise that involved the removal of almost all of
its coercive aspects. Secure facilities were essential,
in his view, to enhance the court's ability to deal with
youth who refuse services, and he looked foward to modifications in the state law in response to his lobbying
efforts.

Deinstitutionalization created many good programs, he
said, but he felt it went too far in closing all large
institutions. While admitting that some training schools
were physically deteriorated and had no provisions for
therapeutic treatment, the judge felt several were well
run and were beneficial for certain types of youth.
Another problem with deinstitutionalization, in his view,
was that private providers never want to run the secure
facilities that are an essential part of a juvenile justice system.

The Boston judge was extremely critical of the performance and attitudes of DPW workers and administrators.
He thought that courts had the inherent authority both to
order that department to act and to specify the disposi-

tion of youth for whom it was responsible. The judge tried to get a test case to establish that authority, but each time DPW capitulated to him--a move that he thought DPW had made to avoid the possibility of an adverse ruling.

Using his authority, the judge often ordered services for CHINS without concern for budgetary limits, and he often referred CHINS directly to private providers. He wanted complete court involvement, and his large probation staff were involved not only with youth who remained at home under informal court supervision, but also with youth who needed out-of-home placement. The staff often referred such young people directly to private providers or private service agencies and were knowledgeable about the relative strengths of some programs.

There are 16 different service areas in the Boston region, and there is little opportunity for an individual CHINS worker to influence regional CHINS policy. In fact, the Boston region was often cited in interviews as one in which the juvenile court exercised much more exclusive influence over the CHINS process than was the case with courts in other parts of the state.

New CHINS entering the system for the first time were assigned to either a CHINS worker or a probation officer at the Boston Juvenile Court. However, any young person brought to court as a status offender whose family was already being served by the Department of Public Welfare or Social Services was not recorded as a CHINS but could in fact receive the same services. This explains the remarkably low number of CHINS reported by the Boston region. According to the regional CHINS coordinator, in 1978 Boston had 173 CHINS out of a state total of 2,351; in 1979 the CHINS unit recorded 225 CHINS. The Boston CHINS coordinator believed that perhaps 300 to 400 additional adolescents were diverted by the courts directly to local social services offices, where their services were at least partially paid for by CHINS funds. This sort of problem suggests the need to be cautious in interpreting detailed data on CHINS.

CONCLUSIONS

Local Policy Implementation and Adaptation

Based on our research in Boston and in Franklin and Hampshire Counties, we are able to draw the following general

conclusions about how local areas in Massachusetts have
responded to state and federal policies on deinstitutionalization.

Awareness of State Policies   Local actors in the three
areas were aware of the substance of state policies, even
when they decided to implement those policies according
to their own standards (e.g., accepting only court-adjudicated CHINS, encouraging adolescents to come to the Department of Public Welfare instead of the court, keeping
CHINS cases for a year, or commingling different categories of children in the same facility).

Awareness of Federal Policies and Funding Patterns   Court
personnel, in general, were not interested in details of
federal policy or funding. Most, however, were alert to
the current federal positions on topics such as detention
and diversion, and were aware of federal research on
broader issues such as delinquency, status offenders, and
deinstitutionalization.

Other local area actors were familiar with federal
policies and federal programs dealing with children.
Private child welfare agencies, program providers, and
some DPW workers could trace their funding back to its
federal sources. Only private agencies attempted to develop new programs purposely tailored to fit federal requirements in order to receive federal funds.

Local Adaptation to Deinstitutionalization   We found a
great deal of variation in implementation of CHINS legislation among the local areas studied. Personal views and
the location of specific local actors within the organization were critical elements in shaping adaptations of
state and federal policies. Implementation in Hampshire
County essentially followed the outline of the 1973 CHINS
legislation, and substantial effort was expended to support the local CHINS system. Franklin County, in contrast, had a CHINS system with far less flexibility and
internal support. Finally, in Boston the juvenile court--
the most prominent actor in the system--worked hard to
modify the CHINS legislation both in terms of the court's
interpretations of the statute and its lobbying efforts
at the state level.

The Impact of Primary Local Actors on Deinstitutionalization Personal discretion prevails over state statutes and
departmental regulations in terms of their relative in-

fluence on the handling of CHINS by the juvenile justice
and social services systems. The autonomy of local judges
and probation staffs is almost absolute in intake and diversion, but they have limited ability to compel other
actors (i.e., DPW, private providers, parents, and youth)
to accept their placement or service decisions. The force
of individual personality appears to explain how, despite
a lack of formal power, some judges maintained control
over CHINS cases while others deferred to the jurisdiction
of the Department of Public Welfare.

To some extent, local DPW workers also had considerable
latitude in interpreting CHINS policy. They could refuse
voluntary commitments or seek them out; they established
their own working relationships with the local courts;
they played a large role in deciding whether children
should receive in-home or out-of-home placements; and they
often chose the service plans and placements for the
youth, thereby indirectly affecting the utilization patterns of private providers. Private providers, however,
had total discretion in deciding which youth to accept
into their programs.

The absence of established administrative precedents
and longitudinal data appeared to leave individuals in the
system free to act, unburdened by the weight of accumu-
lated knowledge. For example, there is no longitudinal
data on case histories of CHINS before and after decriminalization. Massachusetts courts do not keep records on
diversions to the Department of Public Welfare, and
therefore no distinctions can be made between adjudicated
CHINS and diverted status offenders. No consistent system for periodic, on-site evaluation or monitoring of
private providers has been instituted in any of the three
local areas. Local actors do have impressions about the
quality of some providers based on personal knowledge or
reputation which could produce problems if the reputation
of a program is not well grounded in fact.

The comparative patterns of activity suggest that individual initiative and personal discretion of those in
the local power structure are central to the actual implementation of social policy at the local level. While
not unaware of federal policies, local actors did not
perceive them as significant in their day-to-day functioning. Local influences appear to predominate over
centrally established state directives.

Reactions to Reform

Most state and local respondents viewed deinstitutionalization as an accepted part of the change that has occurred
in services to children and youth. There were, however,
several recurring criticisms. The variance in these
criticisms reflects the complexity of both the policy of
deinstitutionalization and the character of resistance to
it.

The first set of criticisms are system-specific in the
sense that their proponents, while accepting the broad
outlines of deinstitutionalization, want to improve its
functioning according to their own views. Changes of this
sort include the following: (a) integrating facilities
more fully into their communities, (b) improving state
monitoring and evaluation of programs, (c) making the decisions of the juvenile court compulsory, (d) restoring
secure detention, and (e) allocating more funds for group
facilities, especially for emergency shelters. Proximity
of a facility to the natural home and community of the
CHINS has been used by the Office of Juvenile Justice and
Delinquency Prevention as a measure of success in deinstitutionalization, but as with many other states, Massachusetts has had difficulty achieving this goal.

Many state and local respondents felt that deinstitutionalization in Massachusetts focused too narrowly on
relatively nonsecure, small facilities that emphasize
counseling. They asserted that certain types of youth
could benefit most from larger, secure facilities with
strict discipline and a high degree of internal structure.
A large contingent reported that, in their view, the CHINS
classification was an artificial distinction, and that
status offenders, delinquents, and dependent and neglected
children were all part of a juvenile population in need
of attention. This contingent argued that the categorical
distinctions and the dispositional options permissible for
each group under the current legislation meant that some
youth were either inappropriately or inadequately treated.
Only a very small minority of respondents, however, were
so disaffected as a result of their experiences with deinstitutionalization that they wanted to move back to a
fully state-run system of institutions.

A second set of criticisms stems from legal advocates
and child welfare professionals. Deinstitutionalization,
in their opinion, has not been effective enough in improving the quality of life or quality of services that
young people receive. Referring to new placement settings

as alternative facilities instead of institutions, they claim, has not necessarily purged them of their negative characteristics. Many of the advocates interviewed felt that youth were being institutionalized under new, more inclusive categories, that increased capacity has led to increased use. A greater emphasis on family-centered services was the main improvement that child advocates recommended, although a small minority wanted to adopt a policy of radical nonintervention.

Few of the state-level actors who were interviewed were well informed about how reforms were working at the local level. Even fewer had any idea of how important the personal discretion of local personnel was in shaping the way in which deinstitutionalization had been implemented. Many local actors were critical of the effectiveness and responsiveness of the state bureaucracy.

Many respondents at both state and local levels felt that the CHINS program was worthwhile and wanted to improve it. Increased funding, strengthening enforcement powers over children and parents, and coercing service providers to provide a broader array of services (particularly counseling and psychological testing) were all mentioned as possible reforms.

More extreme solutions were pressed by some groups of respondents. Police, most judges, and some child welfare professionals wanted increased secure detention and placement options; some wanted secure detention as a preventive measure while others wanted it for punitive purposes. Preventive detention was perceived by the former as being a crucial part of the treatment plan for runaways with serious problems. The latter group felt that punitive detention is required to teach youth to respect the law. Very few respondents wanted to recriminalize status offenses completely, although several spoke of the need to reclassify chronic status offenders--particularly runaways--as delinquents in order to deal more firmly with their problems.

One group of state and local child welfare workers wanted to focus on the family for diagnosing and treating problems of status offenders. They felt that the point of entry into the child welfare system was largely a matter of accident or of arbitrary factors unrelated to the problems of the youth, and that giving youth particular labels may have lasting consequences on how they will be treated and viewed by others as well as by themselves. The solution that these workers suggested was to abolish the CHINS classification and create a program for all young people who are in need of services. This appears, in fact, to be the goal of current DSS policy.

Federal, State, and Local Influences on
Deinstitutionalization

In Massachusetts, federal, state, and local influences have had their greatest effects at different stages of the reform process. The periods leading up to change and reform show the clearest imprint of federal influences. During the birth of reform coalitions and the legislative proposals, state actors became more central, and their importance remained paramount during the administrative reorganizations that followed passage of substantive reforms. Finally, local influences predominated during the implementation phase of deinstitutionalization reform.

Throughout the period of deinstitutionalization and CHINS reform, state actors were aware of the position of the federal government, largely through federal research activity. State reformers looked at times to federal statements and policy recommendations as guidelines for their own policy goals, and federal statements, decisions, and money helped to build support within the state for reforms. But aside from a few instances in which a federal grant or regulation directly influenced a policy result (e.g., the 1970 grants to Jerome Miller for staff development, and the 1976 LEAA memo to Massachusetts regarding detention of CHINS in DYS facilities), federal influence in Massachusetts served mainly to reinforce a preexisting determination to deinstitutionalize.

Some federal grants have been efficacious at the local as well as at the state level in Massachusetts. For example, the Office for Children received two federal grants that provided in part for the direct participation of local citizens in program monitoring and advocacy activities. This type of grant ties together all levels of government, with a state agency receiving federal funds to develop and direct local interest in children's welfare.

State influence on the process of deinstitutionalization was most marked during the period of legislative reform activity in the 1970s. The state government has ongoing control over the budgets, administrative regulations, and staffing policies; thus, the contribution of state-level actors—both governmental and private—was most effective during the period of struggles for reform.

Members of executive commissions, the state legislature, and lobbying groups, and prominent individual state actors helped to transform the existing system and conceptualized the new forms of change.

While less important during the period of state legislative reform, local influence was prominent in shaping the implementation of those reforms once they became state policy. Local actors and coalitions became involved pragmatically and philosophically when faced with the responsibilities for putting policies into practice. This local involvement included influence over the way changes relating to deinstitutionalization were actually carried out in various communities and influence at the state level by means of lobbying activities designed to secure modifications in the legislation.

The important point here is that the federal-state-local interaction is a dynamic one. State and federal actors were aware of their local constituents, and many prominent local actors participated in research sponsored by state and federal agencies. Together these influences alerted people to the need for change, shaped the form that change was to take in Massachusetts, and affected the implementation of changes at the local level. While the results are open to differing interpretations, it is clear that in Massachusetts deinstitutionalization has created a wide range of privately provided services and less restrictive placement settings for status offenders.

REFERENCES

Bakal, Yitzhak, ed. (1973) Closing Correctional Institutions. Lexington, Mass.: D.C. Heath.
Contract Research Corporation (1976) Client Flow and Information Collection in Massachusetts' Juvenile Justice System. Boston: Massachusetts Committee on Criminal Justice.
Institute for Government Service (1977) The Children's Puzzle. Boston: Institute for Government Service.
Lerman, Paul (1968) Evaluation Studies of Institutions for Delinquents: Implications for Research and Social Policy. Social Work (July): 55-64.
Massachusetts Committee on Criminal Justice (1979) Residential Program for Court-Involved Youth in Massachusetts. Boston: Massachusetts Committee on Criminal Justice.

Massachusetts Taxpayers Foundation, Inc. (1980) Purchase
     of Services: Can State Government Gain Control?
     Boston: Massachusetts Taxpayers Foundation, Inc.
Ohlin, Lloyd, Miller, Alden, and Coates, Robert (1977)
     Juvenile Correctional Reform in Massachusetts.
     Washington, D.C.: National Institute for Juvenile
     Justice and Delinquency Prevention.
President's Commission on Law Enforcement and
     Administration of Justice (1967) Task Force Report:
     Juvenile Delinquency and Youth Crime. Washington,
     D.C.: U.S. Government Printing Office.
Scull, Andrew T. (1977) Decarceration--Community
     Treatment and the Deviant: A Radical View. Englewood
     Cliffs, N.J.: Prentice-Hall.
Spangenberg, Robert, and Studen, Laura (1977) History of
     CHINS Program. Prepared for the Massachusetts
     Committee on Criminal Justice by Abt Associates,
     Cambridge, Mass.
Vorenberg, Elizabeth, and Vorenberg, James (1973) Early
     Diversion from the Criminal Justice System: Practice
     in Search of a Theory. In Lloyd E. Ohlin, ed.
     Prisoners in America. Englewood Cliffs, N.J.:
     Prentice-Hall.
U.S. Department of Health, Education, and Welfare (1966)
     A Study of the Division of Youth Services and Youth
     Service Boards: Commonwealth of Massachusetts.
     Children's Bureau. Washington, D.C.: U.S. Government
     Printing Office.

BIBLIOGRAPHY

Aber, Larry (1978) Survey of Health Care Facilities on
     Management of Services to Children at Risk. Boston:
     Massachusetts Office for Children.
Arthur Young and Company (1980) CHINS Program/Contracted
     Services: Boston and Springfield Regions. Report for
     the Department of Social Services. Boston:
     Department of Social Services.
Boisvert, Maurice, and Wells, Robert (1978) CHINS,
     Deviancy and the Law. Boston: Youth Opportunity
     Unlimited, Inc.
Bremner, Robert, ed. (1971) Children and Youth in
     America's Documentary History. 2 vols. Cambridge,
     Mass.: Harvard University Press.
Coates, Robert, Miller, Alden, and Ohlin, Lloyd (1978)
     Diversity in a Youth Correctional System. Cambridge,
     Mass.: Ballinger.

Fay, Juliette (1978) 1978 Monitoring Report:
   Massachusetts' Compliance with the Deinstitu-
   tionalization and Separation Mandates of JJDPA.
   Report for the Massachusetts Committee on Criminal
   Justice. Boston: Massachusetts Committee on Criminal
   Justice.
Miller, Alden, Ohlin, Lloyd, and Coates, Robert (1977) A
   Theory of Social Reform. Cambridge, Mass.: Ballinger.
Spangenberg, Robert, and Studen, Laura (1977) Diagnostic
   Study of Massachusetts' CHINS Program. Prepared for
   the Massachusetts Committee on Criminal Justice by Abt
   Associates, Cambridge, Mass.
Vasaly, Shirley (1976) Foster Care in Five States: A
   Synthesis and Analysis from Arizona, California, Iowa,
   Massachusetts, and Vermont. Washington, D.C.: U.S.
   Department of Health, Education and Welfare.

PERSONS INTERVIEWED

Diane Anderson, Director, Group Care Unit, Massachusetts
   Department of Public Welfare
Gregory Anrig, Massachusetts Commissioner of Education
Diane Ansiana, CHINS Worker, Holyoke
Doug Baird, Massachusetts Council of Human Service
   Providers
Jackie Blasi, Juvenile Justice Specialist, Massachusetts
   Committee on Criminal Justice
Maurice Boisvert, Director, Youth Opportunity Unlimited,
   Inc.
Don Bovere, Director, Community Services Association,
   Northampton
Kevin Brown, Information System Data Analyst,
   Massachusetts Department of Public Welfare
Ed Budleman, Coordinator of Children's Service,
   Massachusetts Department of Mental Health
Michael Carey, Probation Officer, Northampton
Nancy Carmel, Boston Children's Services
Pat Cavanero, Regional CHINS Supervisor, Springfield
Jim Colgan, Probation Officer, Greenfield
Christina Crow, former Deputy Assistant Commissioner for
   Social Services, Massachusetts Department of Public
   Welfare
Marsha Defazio, Probation Officer, Northampton
Judy DeWitt, Child Protective Services, Greenfield
Russ Dunning, Director, Greater Boston Legal Services
Mary Jane England, Commissioner, Massachusetts Department
   of Social Services

Julie Fay, Planning Specialist, Massachusetts Committee
    on Criminal Justice
Doris Fraser, Administration and Finance, Massachusetts
    Executive Office of Human Services
Robert Fusco, CHINS worker, Northampton
Joyce Gevirtzman, Purchase of Services Contracting,
    Massachusetts Department of Social Services
Mel Green, Educational and Social Services, Massachusetts
    Rate Setting Commission
Gailanne Healy, former Budget Analyst, Massachusetts
    Executive Office of Human Services
Robert Hernandez, Title XX Coordinator, Massachusetts
    Department of Public Welfare
Roberta Hershhorn, Director, Foster Care, Massachusetts
    Department of Public Welfare
Jeff Howe, Assistant Regional Manager, Department of
    Public Welfare, Springfield
John Isaacson, Director, Massachusetts Office for Children
Elyse Jacobs, former Welfare Budget Analyst,
    Massachusetts House Ways and Means Committee
Chip Jones, leader of DARE, Mentor, Cambridge
Jeff Justen, Contract Research Corporation, Belmont
Harvey Kramer, Judge, Greenfield
Joseph LaChance, Juvenile Officer, Greenfield Police
    Department
John Ladd, Probation Officer, Orange
Robert Law, CHINS Worker, Northampton
Bambi Levine, Director Special Education, Massachusetts
    Department of Education
Kevin Lucy, Probation Officer, Northampton
Lou Maglio, Director of Probation, Boston Juvenile Court
Pat Malone, CHINS Coordinator, Massachusetts Department
    of Public Welfare
Betty McGuire, Director, Roxbury Crossing Community
    Service Association
John McManus, former Commissioner of Social Services,
    Massachusetts Department of Public Welfare
Rose Mary McCron, Children's Information Services,
    Massachusetts Department of Public Welfare
Alden Miller, Center for Criminal Justice, Harvard
    University
Manuel Moutinho, Deputy Commissioner of Probation,
    Springfield
Paul Murphy, Licensing Division, Massachusetts Office for
    Children
Morse, Judge, Northampton

Brian Mulvey, Regional Coordinator, CHINS, Boston,
    Massachusetts Department of Public Welfare
Thomas Nicols, Care and Protection Worker, Greenfield
Joseph O'Reilly, Probation Officer, Boston Juvenile
    Court, CHINS
Ellen Pataschnich, Regional Director, Care and Protection
    Worker, Springfield
Francis Poitrast, Chief Juvenile Judge of Massachusetts
Dorothy Parks, Probation Officer, Boston Juvenile Court
Jane Provost, Head Supervisor of caseworkers, Department
    of Public Welfare, Springfield
George Reichert, Pioneer Valley Child Services, Holyoke
Marge Roy, Director of Research, Office of Commissioner
    of Probation
Joy Saunders, Program Planning, Department of Education
David Seagel, Planning and Research, Massachusetts
    Department of Youth Services
Susan Sherman, Foster Care Coordinator, Northampton
Robert Spangenburg, Abt Associates, Cambridge
Marty Stiles, Greenfield Commuity Services Area
Joyce Strom, former Director, Massachusetts Office for
    Children
Laura Studen, Abt Associates, Cambridge
Greg Torres, Program Analyst, Massachusetts Committee on
    Criminal Justice, Boston
Barbara Trevetts, Public Information Officer,
    Massachusetts Department of Youth Services
Robert Troope, Office of Finance, Massachusetts
    Department of Public Welfare
Elizabeth Vorenberg, former CHINS Coordinator,
    Massachusetts Department of Public Welfare
John Wassner, Director, Roxbury Crossing Child Protective
    Services
Robert Weaver, Lawyer at Greater Boston Legal Services
John York, Commissioner of Social Services, Massachusetts
    Department of Public Welfare

13 The Deinstitutionalization of Status Offenders in Pennsylvania

STANLEY FELDMAN

INTRODUCTION

The past ten years have witnessed the persistent efforts of deinstitutionalization forces in Pennsylvania to alter the manner in which status offenders are treated. In a number of respects these efforts have produced concrete and significant results. Status offenders are no longer detained for extended periods in jails or in secure detention with alleged delinquents; they may no longer be placed in state-operated or private delinquency institutions; nonresidential services and group homes are used more than previously; and the role of the courts in the intake and supervision of status offenders has been reduced. At the same time, the process of change has not been problem-free. Entrenched systems do not give way easily, tools for inducing change are not always available or practical, and the implementation of legislative mandate typically is far from straightforward.

This paper reports on the Pennsylvania experience with deinstitutionalization, with respect to changes both in juvenile justice legislation and in the actual delivery of children's services. We will first look at the statutory changes that occurred in the 1970s and the role of various interest groups in the process. We will then turn to the juvenile justice system as it affects status offenders. Available data will be used to illustrate the magnitude of actual changes at the state level and in two selected counties. However, it is first necessary to set out the context in which the deinstitutionalization forces were required to operate.

According to the 1970 census, Pennsylvania has a population of almost 12 million people, approximately 4 million of whom are under 18 years of age. The population, however, is far from evenly distributed among the state's 67 counties. Although Pennsylvania is the third most populous state, only five of its cities have more than 100,000 people. Almost one-third of the children under 18 live in Philadelphia or Allegheny County (Pittsburgh), whereas Cameron, Forest, Pike, and Sullivan counties each contain less than one-tenth of one percent of the state's children. These extreme differences in population density and other population characteristics (e.g., age distribution) mean that the problems encountered in the delivery of children's services vary drastically across counties.

A major characteristic of Pennsylvania's political system is its decentralized organizational framework. Local governments do not merely carry out the mandates of the state government but instead have a considerable degree of control over the organization, funding, and delivery of social services. In fact, the state has only a very limited role in the delivery of these services. In the area of children's services, each county has its own autonomous public child welfare agency that is completely county-run and has jurisdiction over runaways, truants, incorrigibles, and neglected and abused children. There is no mandated organizational structure for these agencies (frequently referred to as children and youth agencies), and aside from required child abuse services that each county must submit to the state for approval, the counties may organize these agencies in any manner desired.

This decentralization extends beyond the child welfare system. The juvenile court system is also organized on a county basis, except for some of the smaller counties which are combined into single judicial districts (there are 59 judicial districts for 67 counties). A significant degree of local discretion is evident in administrative and staffing matters, particularly in the use of the probation staff. The effect of this discretion is potentially great, since the probation staff is permitted by law to handle cases on the basis of informal adjustments, thus avoiding formal court action in many cases.

Similarly, the delivery of mental health/mental retardation and drug and alcohol services is organized on a county basis. Each county is required to submit annual

plans to the state that describe in detail the services
and funding available in each of these program areas.
Although there is some standardization of intake procedures in the mental health system, the provision of various types of services (for example, inpatient or outpatient) and the development of programs for different age
groups are decisions that each county is largely free to
make for itself.

This system of local autonomy results in a great deal
of variability in the treatment of juveniles across counties. Not only are different mixes of services available
in different counties, but they may be provided by different local agencies and with different patterns of reliance on private providers. Furthermore, since in many
cases some combination of services will be required, this
system results in different patterns of interaction between local agencies and different degrees of coordination
of services.

Another important aspect of the Pennsylvania system is
the widespread use of private providers approved and reimbursed by the state. Rather than permitting state
agencies to provide services themselves, Pennsylvania has
chosen to contract out many services to private, usually
nonprofit, providers. For example, the state operates
only nine residential facilities, and all nondelinquent
youth in residences for long-term care are in privately
owned and operated facilities. The state has a large
number of private residential facilities, some of which
have been in existence for a long time. These private
providers constitute a vocal and powerful lobby, which is
active in a number of matters affecting child care. Many
of the private providers are religiously based, administered by the Catholic Church and other denominations.

THE STATUTORY CLASSIFICATION OF STATUS OFFENDERS
PRIOR TO 1972

Until the passage of new legislation in 1972, Pennsylvania's juvenile justice system was governed by the 1933
Juvenile Court Act, which had remained essentially unchanged since the 1933 revision of the state code. This
legislation was vague in many respects; it left open the
responsibility for long and unwarranted detention of juveniles in secure facilities, offered few guidelines for
placement, and provided few due process protections for
children and youth. The Juvenile Court Act defined three

categories of children under the age of 16: delinquent, neglected, and dependent. A _delinquent child_ was (a) one who violated any law or ordinance, (b) a status offender (i.e., truant, runaway, or a habitually disobedient or uncontrollable child), or (c) "a child who habitually deports himself or herself as to injure or endanger the morals or health of himself, herself or others" (Sec. 1(4)). The category of _neglected child_ referred to (a) a child who was either abandoned by parents or guardians or whose parents or guardians refused to provide the care "necessary for his or her health, morals, or well being"; (b) "a child who is found in a disreputable place or associated with vagrant, vicious or immoral persons"; or (c) "a child who engages in an occupation, or in a situation, dangerous to life or limb, or injurious to the health or morals of himself, herself or others" (Sec. 1 (5)). Finally, the category of _dependent child_ included those who were not receiving proper care through no fault of their parents or guardians.

The effect of such language was to give the juvenile court a great deal of power and discretion in both offender and nonoffender cases. Status offenses were explicitly defined as delinquent acts, and this category was further expanded by vague wording that made it possible to attach the delinquency label to an unusually large number of juveniles. For example, the wording of the neglected child definition allowed the adjudication of many cases as either delinquent or neglected, since the law left so much room for interpretation. The juvenile court thus had formal jurisdiction over many nondelinquents, who would in turn be supervised by the court's probation staff. In some counties this resulted in the rapid expansion of the juvenile court probation staff, which took on many of the characteristics of a full-fledged social service agency. In addition to the court's jurisdiction over those children defined as delinquent, it also had the final say in any neglect or dependent cases in which out-of-home placement was deemed necessary. The latter cases typically would be supervised by the county child welfare (or children and youth) agency, which in most respects took a back seat to the county juvenile court. The pattern, then, was for the court to handle all aspects of the more difficult juvenile cases, while the children and youth agency was left to supervise abuse and neglect cases, with court approval needed for residential placements.

The 1933 Juvenile Court Act also gave the court the ability to place a child in detention pending final disposition of the case. A child could be detained regardless of whether the case was considered as delinquent, neglected, or dependent. The only restriction the law made in such cases was that the child could not be held in a facility with adults. It was not entirely clear, however, that a separate building was needed for juveniles, since the law only required that each county "shall provide, furnish, and heat a separate room or rooms, or a suitable building" (Sec. 6) to be used for juvenile detention. There was no mention of whether this was to be a secure or nonsecure setting. The law said nothing about the issue of detention hearings nor about the length of time a child might be kept in detention. Although data for the period prior to 1972 are generally unavailable, it is clear that a large number of status offenders were detained in secure facilities and, in many cases, in facilities with adult criminal offenders. As late as 1975, 42 percent of status offenders were detained for some length of time (approximately 25 percent of all those detained were status offenders) and there were 53 facilities used for both juvenile and adult detention (Pennsylvania Governor's Justice Commission 1978).

Finally, the only restriction the law made concerning placement was that a neglected or dependent child who is not delinquent could not be placed in an institution that received delinquent children. Beyond this, a judge could place a child--whether delinquent, status offender, neglected, or dependent--in a suitable public or private institution, foster home, or an incorporated association or society, one of whose objects was the care, guidance, and control of delinquent, dependent, and neglected children (Sec. 8). The counties paid for such placements and were then reimbursed by the state for approximately 50 percent of the cost. The major exceptions were placements at the state-operated youth development centers and youth forestry camps for delinquents, which were free to the counties. As might be expected, the counties took advantage of these free placements, and they were usually filled to capacity despite frequent allegations of poor conditions.

THE PROCESSES OF CHANGE, 1972-1980

Major Legislative Changes

The decision to rewrite the state's juvenile justice legislation was primarily a response to the growing concern
for the lack of due process protection of children and
youth. The U.S. Supreme Court decision in the <u>Gault</u> case
(387 U.S. 1 (1967)) stands out clearly in this respect.
Although the state had decided to rewrite the 1933 juvenile justice legislation for the purpose of increasing due
process protection and to make other changes, the question
of what direction those changes should take seems to have
received little attention from state officials. This
created an opportunity for interested persons or groups
to step in and play a major role in drafting the new legislation. More or less coincidentally, this period in the
early 1970s witnessed a growing number of people in Pennsylvania who were committed to the principles of deinstitutionalization. Although direct causality is difficult
to assess in such cases, this trend appears to be both
somewhat independent of, and at the same time encouraged
by, national movement in this direction.
     Most prominent in the deinstitutionalization forces was
and is the Philadelphia-based Juvenile Justice Center and
its founder and director, Barbara Fruchter. The Juvenile
Justice Center was started in the spring of 1971 as a
coalition of various citizen groups concerned with the
condition and treatment of delinquents, status offenders,
and dependent and neglected youth. Fruchter was clearly
the driving force behind the center, organizing and serving as the spokesperson for the coalition. Respondents
in Pennsylvania were unanimous in attributing to Fruchter
a critical role in the state's deinstitutionalization effort. The Juvenile Justice Center was supported in part
by grants from the Law Enforcement Assistance Administration, and Fruchter spent some time in the Washington office of Senator Birch Bayh studying juvenile justice legislation. She met frequently with the head of Pennsylvania's Intergovernmental Commission, which was in charge
of writing the new legislation, and she had a major role
in drafting it. The combination of Fruchter's direct efforts in writing the new legislation and the pressure her
citizen group was able to place on the legislature significantly influenced the direction of the new legislation.

The Juvenile Justice Act of 1972   The Juvenile Justice Act
(Act 333) was enacted by the legislature in November 1972,
and brought about a number of nonincremental changes in
Pennsylvania's legal code.   Some compromises were necessary to obtain legislative approval, but an increased
concern for due process protection, deinstitutionalization, and the treatment of status offenders and dependent
children is quite evident.   The new legislation defined
two categories of juveniles--delinquent and deprived.   In
a major compromise truancy was placed in the deprived
(nondelinquent) category, and habitual disobedience (ungovernability) and running way remained delinquent acts.
The broad and ambiguous wording of the previous juvenile
act was completely eliminated.   Summary offenses (e.g.,
minor theft and vandalism) were also removed from the delinquency category unless the fine levied was not paid.
The category of deprived child combined the old deprived
and neglect categories and was defined as a child who
(a) is without proper parental care or control, subsis-
tence, or education;   (b) has been placed for care or
adoption in violation of the law;   (c) has been abandoned
by parents or guardians;   (d) is without a parent or
guardian;   or (e) is legally truant from school.   The
elimination of truancy as a delinquent act is significant
as it was the start of a process to separate status offenders from delinquent youth and consequently to remove
them from supervision by the court to supervision by the
local children and youth agency.

Another area in which the new law made significant
changes was pretrial detention.   The old law placed virtually no restrictions on detention, but Act 333 explicitly states that a child should not be detained or placed
in shelter care unless it "is required to protect the
person or property of others or of the child or because
he has no parent, guardian, or custodian or other person
able to provide supervision and care for him and return
him to court when required" (Sec. 12).   The law also requires that an informal hearing to determine if detention
or shelter care is needed must be held by the court within
72 hours of the time the child was placed in detention.
A child alleged to be deprived may only be detained in
shelter care (i.e., in physically unrestricted settings)
and may not be kept in any jail or facility with adults
or in a facility for delinquent children.   A child alleged
to be delinquent may be placed in an adult facility only
if there is no other appropriate facility available and
if the child is kept apart from the adults.   Such detention cannot exceed five days.

Act 333 also added two new alternatives to adjudication—informal adjustments and consent decrees—which were intended to increase the possibilities for diversion and to avoid, if possible, attaching a label to the child. Informal adjustment is a process in which, prior to filing a petition for delinquency or deprived child status, the probation officer may advise the child and parents and/or refer them to some other social agency for counseling and advice. Such advice and counseling may extend for a period of up to nine months. This process can only be used with the consent of the child and parents or guardians and is not obligatory. A consent decree may be used any time following the filing of a petition and before an adjudication order. It enables the judge to suspend the proceedings and continue the child under supervision in the child's own home. The terms of the supervision are worked out with the juvenile probation services and agreed to by all parties. The consent decree remains in effect for six months and may be extended for an additional six-month period. During the period of the consent decree, if the child fails to fulfill the terms of the decree or if another petition is filed, the original petition may be reinstated and proceedings resumed. If the period of the consent decree expires, or if the child is discharged by juvenile probation, no further action may be taken on the original petition or with regard to the conduct cited in the petition.

Act 333 was the first step in the deinstitutionalization forces' efforts to change Pennsylvania's juvenile justice system. The immediate goals were to eliminate the detention of juveniles in adult facilities, to get nondelinquent youth out of secure facilities, to transfer jurisdiction over status offenders from the court to the children and youth agencies, and to encourage the use of group homes and nonresidential services. Within two years of its passage, efforts were under way to extend the changes that Act 333 introduced. The major force behind this was again the citizen lobbies led by the Juvenile Justice Center. These groups worked with sympathetic members of the legislature to prepare and push new legislation addressing the issues of funding, how to handle status offenders, and the use of jails for detention. They also sought to bring the state into compliance with the requirements of the 1974 Juvenile Justice and Delinquency Prevention Act (JJDPA), which was sponsored by Senator Birch Bayh. Compliance with federal regulations was clearly a significant factor in the push to draft new legislation, but its importance should not be exaggerated. The money attached to these regulations made up only about $2 million of the approximately $100 million of funding that went into children's services in Pennsylvania. The amount was substantial enough that the state preferred not to lose it, but it was not large enough to force the state into actions opposed by political leaders.

Act 148 of 1976   In order to secure passage of legislation that would require further deinstitutionalization of juveniles, reformers sought first to enact legislation to encourage through financial incentives the development and use of alternatives to institutional care. As a result of their efforts the legislature passed Act 148 in July 1976. This act significantly reorganized Pennsylvania's funding of youth services. Prior to Act 148 the state reimbursed the counties at a 50 percent rate for most services (it provided 100 percent funding of the state-operated delinquency institutions). The act combined various funding sources (state funds plus some money from Titles IV-A and XX of the Social Security Act) and set up a new reimbursement schedule that provided financial incentives for certain youth services purchased by the counties. Instead of the across-the-board 50 percent reimbursement previously given, services to children in their own home, in foster care and group homes, and in community-based facilities (e.g., for counseling and intervention) were now reimbursed at the 75 percent level. The reimbursement rate for institutional care (defined as more than eight children served in a single setting) for both delinquent and nondelinquent children was 50 percent; for shelter care in group homes or foster family settings, 90 percent; for shelter care in larger facilities, 75 percent; and for secure detention, 50 percent. The legislation also provided 90 percent funding for new services (i.e., start-up costs) for up to three years. This was intended to help counties that did not have existing services for children. Act 148 was also designed to avoid costing the counties any more than the previous funding system. This did not cover, however, the few counties that had sent large numbers of juveniles to state delinquency facilities, because state funding of these facilities was reduced from 100 percent to 50 percent. For example, Act 148 initially cost Allegheny County (Pittsburgh) over $1 million because the county had placed so many children in state facilities. As a result, some legislators from Allegheny County were opposed to the act.

Aside from this opposition, Act 148 was not particularly controversial. The resulting regulations published by the Pennsylvania Department of Public Welfare, on the other hand, raised a great deal of continuing controversy.

Act 41 of 1977 In 1977 the legislature passed Act 41, an amendment to the 1972 Juvenile Justice Act. This legislation continued the changes in the treatment of status offenders and the conditions of detention. The two legal categories of juveniles were changed to dependent (formerly deprived) and delinquent, and all the remaining status offenses (i.e., ungovernability and running away) were eliminated as delinquent acts. The dependency category now included all cases of neglect, abandonment, abuse, truancy, and habitual disobedience. This completed the process of taking status offenses out of the delinquency category that began when the 1972 Juvenile Justice Act took truancy out and added it to the deprived (now dependent) category. No special designation was created for status offenders, and they currently are indistinguishable under Pennsylvania law from all others in the dependency category (i.e., neglected, abandoned, and abused children). This holds for all aspects of the treatment of these children and youth; no special provisions are made for handling status offender cases. Act 41 also provided that a child under 10 years of age could not be alleged or adjudicated delinquent. Even when charged with a delinquent act, the juvenile could only be adjudicated dependent. Also, if a child who has been adjudicated dependent and who has been placed by the court then runs away or commits some other ungovernable act, that child is by law still dependent and cannot be adjudicated delinquent.

The intent of these changes was twofold. First, removing status offenders from the delinquency category would, in effect, eliminate the option of placing them in secure facilities. Only adjudicated delinquents could be placed in secure facilities, which include all of the state-operated youth development centers and youth forestry camps. Second, it was expected that status offenders, who legally were now dependent children, would fall under the jurisdiction of the local children and youth agency instead of the court, thereby taking the probation staff out of the business of supervising status offenders. It is significant that the law does not explicitly forbid the court from taking on such cases and that certain features of the law may be interpreted as encouraging such a practice. In any event the court must become involved in dependency cases that require a change of custody or out-of-home placement. We will return shortly to the problems induced by ambiguities in the law.

The conditions under which a juvenile could be held in detention or shelter care were tightened considerably by the new law. The Juvenile Justice Act of 1972 permitted children to be held in jails for up to five days if there were no alternatives available. Through a compromise, Act 41 permitted this to continue until December 31, 1979, only if (a) there was no appropriate facility available in the county or within a reasonable distance or in a neighboring county; (b) the jail had been inspected and approved by the Department of Public Welfare; (c) it could be shown that jailing was necessary for public safety; (d) the child was held in an appropriate room; and (e) there was adequate supervision for the child. After that date, a child could not be held in a jail under any circumstances.

The 1977 legislation also specified that a child could not be held in detention or shelter care for more than 24 hours unless a petition of delinquency or dependency was filed. In addition to the informal hearing required within 72 hours of the initial confinement, it is now necessary that a juvenile in detention or shelter care be given a full adjudicatory hearing within 10 days. These provisions are designed to reduce both the amount of time a child is kept in detention or shelter care and the child's uncertainty about the future. Detention or shelter care is not supposed to continue for more than 30 days, and state regulations associated with Act 148 forbid reimbursement of costs for any period longer than 30 days.

Two other mandates of Act 41 should be noted here. The first requires each county to develop concrete plans for short-term care of children held under dependency petitions. Such shelter care programs may make use of short-term foster care, group homes, or institutions. Counties that use smaller program settings benefit the most from state funding assistance. While shelter care programs are required under the law, mandatory detention programs are not. A county may detain alleged delinquents in shelter care (i.e., a nonsecure setting), but those held under dependency petitions may not be kept in detention (secure setting). Second, the principle of the least restrictive alternative is codified here and specifies that "when confinement is necessary, the court shall impose the minimum amount of confinement that is consistent with the protection of the public and the rehabilitation needs of the child" (Sec. 25).

Before moving on, we should mention one other piece of legislation--the Child Protective Services Law passed in 1975, which was concerned with the handling of child abuse cases. It set up new procedures for reporting abuse cases, investigating allegations of abuse, and taking such children into custody when necessary. More specifically, it required various agencies and officials to report abuse cases, it created a 24-hour hotline to facilitate reporting, and it required that investigations of abuse be started within 24 hours of the initial report and completed within 30 days. The responsibility for abuse cases was clearly given to the county child welfare agencies, which were required to set up a separate division for child protective services. The overall handling of these cases is still governed by the 1972 Juvenile Justice Act and the amendments contained in Act 41.

Positions of the Organized Interests

As in any case of legislative action that involves an important issue like deinstitutionalization, several observable interests in Pennsylvania adopted fairly clear positions on various aspects of the reform legislation of the 1970s. The organized citizen lobbies, led by the Juvenile Justice Center, were strongly for deinstitutionalization. They fought hard for this entire legislative package and were effective in putting direct pressure on legislators and in using the media to mobilize support for the legislation. Their efforts are impressive in the context of other public and political pressures that were building for reversing the more liberal trends in the treatment of status offenders. In this section we discuss the various groups that exerted pressure both for and against deinstitutionalization, namely, the Pennsylvania Department of Public Welfare (DPW), juvenile court judges, and private providers.

The Pennsylvania Department of Public Welfare played an important role in the process of change because the intent of the legislation, especially the reimbursement program of Act 148, was consistent with its own philosophy. DPW used this legislation to actively support and implement the program of reform. Two reasons for this action can be cited: (1) the department's commitment to

the principles of deinstitutionalization, and (2) its desire to bring the state into compliance with the guidelines of the Office of Juvenile Justice and Delinquency
Prevention in order to take advantage of the federal funds
that that office distributes. As was pointed out above,
this money makes up a small portion of Pennsylvania's
funding for youth services, and the state would be far
from crippled if this source were cut off. However, the
DPW would prefer not to lose this funding, which it considers a significant amount relative to its total budget.
In addition, the availability of federal money gives DPW
some leverage in an era of budget tightening, because it
can use the existence of this funding as an argument in
support of its drafting of reform regulations.

As a group, juvenile court judges in Pennsylvania feel
particularly affected by the changes in the juvenile justice system. Although it is impossible to say there is
consensus among the judges on these issues, some very
clear and articulate positions have emerged during this
period of change, and considerable pressure has been exerted on some matters. The Juvenile Court Judges Commission, the organization that represents the juvenile
judges, was established in 1959 to develop standards of
court practice and to make recommendations for the improvement of the juvenile court system. In addition the
commission distributes some funds to local court districts
for probation services.

Pennsylvania juvenile court judges basically supported
Act 333 and were in general agreement with the goals of
Act 148. As a group, judges have supported deinstitutionalization when alternative treatment programs were
available, and they felt that Act 148 would help to create
the programs needed to remove children from large institutions. The judges would have preferred, however, a
somewhat less graduated reimbursement schedule so as to
maintain as much placement flexibility as possible. Where
their objections really emerged was in regard to the DPW's
Act 148 regulations. When the various funding streams
were combined in the legislation, DPW used the new regulations to specify exactly which services could not be
covered by the state as Act 148 reimbursements. These
services included mental health or mental retardation
programs, drug and alcohol abuse programs, education programs, and the costs of the county probation staff, juvenile court staff, and court social service staff that were
not part of the county children and youth agency.

The Department of Public Welfare's denial of funding for court services reflects its view that the courts should function only as judicial bodies and not as providers of social services. Judges who were interviewed labeled this a narrow view of the juvenile court process and the role of probation. They argued that the courts often developed their own services where none had existed before, that Act 333 provided for informal adjustment by the probation staff, and that the probation staff were well trained and experienced in dealing with difficult children. Many judges displayed a low regard for the county children and youth offices and staffs. They believed that their own probation staffs were better able to deal with the more difficult cases. The judges would like to see a system in which services for children are funded regardless of which agency provides them. Ideally, they would prefer a system that allowed the probation and court staffs as much flexibility as possible in making placements and providing services. They are thus trying to modify the regulations and, failing this, would seek either to amend Act 148 or to challenge the regulations in court.

The juvenile court judges were also vocal in their opposition to Act 41, the 1977 amendment that completed the elimination of all status offenses from the delinquency category. Although they do support the principle of deinstitutionalizing status offenders, they question whether existing services are adequate to accomplish this end. They are also concerned that many of the more difficult status offenders will now be the responsibility of child welfare case workers who have little experience with such children. They fear that many status offenders will not get adequate supervision and that the absence of court authority will prevent them from being kept in one place long enough to be helped. Under these circumstances, the judges argue, there may be an incentive to upgrade the seriousness of the offense. As evidence they note that when truancy was removed from the delinquency category in 1972, the total number of court referrals should have declined. That it did not was attributed by the judges to the upgrading of truancy to incorrigibility.

Child welfare directors also had reservations about this aspect of Act 41, not because they felt they did not have the training to deal with status offenders, but because they lacked the threat of secure detention. When status offenders could be adjudicated delinquent, it was argued, child welfare staff knew that if juveniles ran away from a nonsecure setting they could then be placed in a secure facility. Because such placement is no longer possible, the child welfare directors claim that they cannot hold many status offenders in treatment facilities long enough for them to receive the services they need.

Thus, for different reasons both juvenile court judges and child welfare directors oppose the continuing shift of status offenders from the delinquency category to dependent child status. The judges feel that they and the probation staff are better able to deal with such children effectively than the local children and youth agencies. Some judges, in fact, feel the child welfare people are not even competent to handle cases of abuse and neglect. The child welfare directors, however, feel that the shift of status offenders to dependency status not only has given them more difficult cases but has also deprived them of the tools the court previously had to deal with these children. These attitudes reflect deep-seated differences between the child welfare staff and the courts that will be discussed in detail in the next section.

Another interest group deeply involved in juvenile justice issues is the large number of private service providers represented by the Pennsylvania Council of Voluntary Child Care Agencies. These private providers did not actively oppose the legislation, but they did protest the DPW regulations. They wanted all residential placements to be reimbursed at the 75 percent level. When they failed to get this through the legislature, they focused on the DPW regulations for community-based facilities, which would receive 75 percent reimbursement as opposed to the 50 percent reimbursement for residential-based facilities.

The private providers sought a loose definition of community-based so that their institutions could qualify. They also sought a liberal definition of which expenses the state should pay. They were disappointed with the proposed DPW regulations that defined community-based facilities as those, regardless of size, that house children reasonably near their families (i.e., in the same counties) and that do not restrict access to the community any more than a family setting would. Furthermore, the proposed regulations limited reimbursements to only those expenses incurred for food, shelter, and social services staff. As a result the facilities would not provide additional services for which they could not be reimbursed. An additional problem for the providers was that under the proposed regulations a residential-based facility would have to be used completely for either dependent children or delinquent children, whereas larger facilities for dependent children could accept some delinquent children.

The controversy generated by the private providers' protests led DPW to withdraw the regulations pertaining to community-based facilities. This left two classes of residential facilities—residential-based, which may house nine or more children, and group homes, which may house no more than eight. The latter are reimbursed at 75 percent, the former at 50 percent. It is interesting to note that when the provision for community-based facilities was written into Act 148, it was seen by the legislative staff as a residual category for small programs, such as crash pads for runaways. Because the regulations for these facilities have now been withdrawn to be rewritten, it seems likely to remain a small residual category.

Some large private providers also opposed the DPW regulations that forbade Act 148 money to be used to pay for educational programs. Although most of the residential facilities arranged for education through the local school district or the Pennsylvania Department of Education, a few large facilities do run their own schools. The cost for this was then included in the per diem charged to the counties. With the new regulations the counties could, and did, refuse to pay for these facility-run schools. The institutions in turn refused to give up their own educational programs. This has created a controversy which is yet to be satisfactorily settled. An interesting issue here is that some of these facilities either have strong religious affiliations or are run by the church directly, which brings up the broader question of the possible use of public funds for religious instruction.

In summary, the 1970s were a decade of significant legislative changes in the treatment of status offenders in Pennsylvania. Children were no longer allowed to share jails with adults, status offenders were removed from the delinquency category, and financial incentives were enacted to encourage county officials not to institutionalize children. Proponents of deinstitutionalization have been successful in bringing about the passage of legislation designed to remove status offenders from long-term residence in large institutions. Whether deinstitutionalization has indeed been a direct consequence of this legislation is a different question, one that cannot be answered by reading the laws or by inquiring into the intentions of the legislators. Rather, the answer can be found by examining the current treatment of status offenders in Pennsylvania, and it is to this task that we now turn.

THE DELIVERY OF SERVICES TO STATUS OFFENDERS
AND DEPENDENT YOUTH

The goals of the statutory changes summarized above were basically threefold: (1) to remove status offenders and dependent youth from jails and secure detention, (2) to increase the use of group homes and nonresidential treatment options, and (3) to transfer status offenders from the custody and supervision of the court probation staff to the county child welfare office. This third change is critical to the operation of the new system but also has created the most problems. We will therefore begin our examination of the current system of juvenile services by looking at the relationship between the courts and the county children and youth agencies.

Prior to 1978 the juvenile court assumed full responsibility for the care of status offenders because they were legally considered delinquents (with the exception of truants, who were removed from the delinquency category in 1972). The court probation staff was in charge of intake, supervision, and recommendations for services for both status offenders and delinquent youth. The juvenile court judge had the final say in cases of residential placements and was the only public official who was able to order services in all cases. Nondelinquency cases (i.e., neglect and abuse) could be supervised by the county child welfare office, but mandated services and residential placements still needed the court's approval.

The intention of deinstitutionalization forces was to take the court out of the business of providing social services and to remove status offenders and dependent youth from the court system. The intake and supervision functions for these children would be assumed by the children and youth agencies. The law, however, is quite vague in this respect. It is clear only that the court retains the sole right to require services and to make residential placements, a right that in turn derives directly from the court's power to make dependency adjudications. The law does not explicitly forbid the probation staff's involvement in the intake of dependent children and even appears to encourage the staff to supervise dependent children through the practice of informal adjustment. This permits the probation staff to provide assistance to, or divert children from, formal court proceedings before a petition has been filed. The legal ambiguity surrounding the jurisdiction over dependent children has exacerbated the problems involved in adapting to the new system.

As the system is now supposed to work, all dependent children, including status offenders, should be referred to the county children and youth agency for intake and investigation. If nonresidential services are deemed necessary and all parties agree, no further action is needed. If the parties cannot agree, or residential services are required, a dependency petition must be presented to the court. If the child is adjudicated dependent, the judge has several options. The court could approve a recommendation for services if presented with the petition. Alternatively, the judge could give custody of the child to the children and youth agency and require them to come back with a package of services for court approval. The judge could also directly mandate that certain services be provided either without the suggestion of child welfare staff, or contrary to their advice. There is no challenge to the authority of the court in this respect, although the spirit of the legislative changes would require it to defer to the children and youth agency in the matter of services. Thus, it is well within the ability of the court to maintain full control over status offenders and other dependent children if the administrative judge so desires.

There are two basic reasons why the courts are reluctant to transfer responsibility for dependent children to the children and youth agencies. First, the court believes that these agencies are inexperienced in dealing with the more difficult cases they now encounter. Prior to the recent series of changes in Pennsylvania's juvenile justice legislation, the child welfare agencies had responsibility only for cases of neglect, abandonment, lack of parental care, and child abuse; the children they dealt with were deprived but not difficult to handle. Acts 333 and 41 not only increased the case loads of these agencies, but also introduced a whole new group of children with whom these agencies had little or no experience (e.g., older youth who manifest antisocial behavior). Many respondents reported that they doubted the ability of the agencies to deal effectively with these children. This accounts in large part for the reluctance of some judges to involve children and youth agencies in providing services to status offenders and other dependent children.

In fact, it is not only the child welfare agencies that have had to adapt in order to learn how to provide services to status offenders, but the entire system of public and private agencies has had to confront this new class of client. Respondents frequently described this as a ripple effect; that is, as more difficult cases make their way through public and private providers, their presence forces changes to be made at all levels.

The second reason the role of child welfare agencies has been limited is that patterns of interagency cooperation and referral had developed under the pre-1972 legislation. Efforts to remove status offenders from their traditional agencies encountered entrenched procedures and biases. Merely because the county children and youth agency now had responsibility for status offenders did not necessarily mean that traditional patterns of services would be altered. Interagency patterns, once formed, do not change quickly.

In summary, change has been slowed by a combination of institutional inertia and the belief that child welfare agencies are incapable of dealing with the more difficult cases they now face. This belief in the limitations of the child welfare agencies may be rooted in reality or may be completely contrary to the performance of these agencies. Nevertheless, the views are prevalent among police and court officials, and serve to divert status offenders from the child welfare system.

Not surprisingly, directors of children and youth agencies see themselves as quite capable of dealing with status offenders, although they do admit to having more difficulty with their new clientele. They cite three reasons for these problems. First, many of these children are simply difficult for social workers to handle. For example, runaways often cannot be kept in one place long enough to be helped. Second, there frequently is a lack of adequate services and placements for these cases. This is the result both of the lack of services for certain types of children (e.g., gay incorrigibles) in some counties and of the fact that private providers can refuse to accept certain cases if they wish. Third, it is often argued that the new legislation makes it difficult to deal with status offenders, since it removes the possibility of a delinquency adjudication and the threat of secure detention. According to this argument, many children learn that they cannot be kept in one place if they resist treatment. Several respondents reported that child welfare agencies in some counties either drop the more difficult status offender cases or turn them over to the probation office for supervision, although we could not confirm this practice.

It is impossible to describe a single or even a typical pattern of the organization and delivery of children's services in Pennsylvania because of the many variations that are possible in the relationships among the courts, the children and youth agencies, and other public and private agencies, and because of the large number of counties (67). How children's services are organized and delivered in any county depends on a number of factors, including the attitudes, philosophy, and structure of the court; the influence of the child welfare agency; the number and nature of private providers in the county; and the pattern of interaction and referrals among these and other county agencies, such as the schools, police, and community mental health clinics. In a later section we look at how these services have developed in two very different counties. We now examine some evidence on the effect of the recent legislative changes on the treatment of dependent children at the state level.

Patterns of Treatment of Dependent Children

If some caution is exercised, it is possible to use data collected by the Juvenile Court Judges Commission and the Pennsylvania Department of Public Welfare to examine some aspects of the treatment of dependent youth. One of the most important issues with respect to the changes that have occurred in Pennsylvania's juvenile justice and child welfare systems is the effect that Act 41 has had on the ways in which status offenders are handled. This is crucial, since Act 41 changed most status offenses from the delinquency to the dependency category and, thus, from the supervision of the courts to the child welfare agencies. Unfortunately, the data now available in the state are inadequate to permit a thorough analysis of this issue. Such an analysis would require detailed case histories of all or a representative sample of status offenders taken before and after the passage of Act 41 in August 1977. The only data available are aggregated statistics in very grossly defined categories with virtually no way to cross-tabulate important characteristics of the cases. We use these data here to illustrate some of the gross changes that have occurred and to suggest some plausible inferences. In many cases, however, several conflicting interpretations may be supported by the statistics at hand, without our having any means of deciding among them.

One of the problems in evaluating the impact of Act 41 is that data are currently available only through 1978. Since Act 41 became effective in August 1977, that year's data reflect a transition period; that is, pre- and post-August data cannot be distinguished. Thus, while we have data for several years prior to the change, there is really only one full year's data after, and estimates of long-term trends are thus tenuous at best.

One obvious indicator of the impact of Act 41 should be the number of dependency referrals to juvenile court as given in the yearly court statistics. According to the guidelines for preparing these data, the figures should reflect the number of dependency cases that originate in the probation office. Prior to Act 41 this should have included almost all status offender cases and, after its passage in August 1977, virtually none. In practice, however, the source of origin requirement appears not to have been uniformly followed by the local courts in reporting the data. Table 13-1 shows the number of dependency referrals and their proportion of total referrals for 1974 through 1978. To permit comparisons over time, the neglected and status categories prior to 1978 were combined under the current dependency label. As is readily apparent, the figures for 1978 show a sharp break from the pattern of the previous four years. The number of dependency referrals for 1974 through 1977 averaged 8,461 (18.7 percent of total referrals). In 1978 these figures

TABLE 13-1 Number and Percentage of Dependency Referrals Originating in the Probation Office, 1974-1978

Year	Total Referrals	Dependency Referrals	Percentage of Dependency Referrals
1974	44,169	8,409	19.0
1975	48,074	9,073	18.9
1976	45,511	8,092	17.8
1977	41,527	8,269	19.2
1978	40,529	3,548	8.8

Source: Pennsylvania Department of Justice (1974-1978).

fell to 3,548 and 8.8 percent, respectively. By any standard this is a significant drop.

An interesting feature of these data is that while the number of dependency referrals fell by 4,721 between 1977 and 1978, the total number of referrals declined by only 998 over this same period. Figures like these have led some deinstitutionalization advocates in Pennsylvania to argue that some local officials are relabeling status offenders as delinquents in order to keep them under the jurisdiction of the court and to continue the threat of secure detention. This suspicion is not based on concrete data, however, and much more detailed information is needed before this hypothesis can be tested in any reasonably rigorous manner. The data we have seen cannot settle the issue. The Juvenile Court Judges Commission recently issued an analytical report (1979) that attempted, among other things, to use aggregate data to determine the extent of relabeling. The report concluded that relabeling was not occurring in significant numbers across the state. Two indirect tests were used to support this conclusion. First, delinquency referrals per juvenile arrest did not increase in 1978 over the prior four years, and an increase would be expected if relabeling were prevalent. Second, by using DPW data on the number of cases initiated by the county children and youth agency and adding that figure to the number of court-initiated dependency referrals, a total dependency case load can be computed and compared with delinquency referrals. This is shown in Table 13-2. The study concluded that although the percentage of dependency referrals did decline between 1977 and 1978, the 1978 figure was not far from the mean for the period 1974 to 1977, and therefore the 1978 figure was not unusually low. This conclusion must be viewed with caution, since it is based on only a single data point after the new legislation; an analysis like this will require several more years of data before more substantial inferences about trends can be drawn.

Another way to look at the issue of relabeling is to examine the statewide DPW figures on the numbers of cases that were initiated in 1977 and 1978. If status offenders are in fact being diverted from the court to the child welfare agencies, the numbers of cases initiated by those agencies should increase. As Table 13-3 shows, however, the opposite has happened. Overall, 3.6 percent fewer cases were initiated in 1978 than in 1977. The number of services provided to children who had not been seen before declined by 8.1 percent, while there was an increase of

TABLE 13-2   Dependency and Delinquency Cases: Total
Originating in Probation Offices and in Children and
Youth Agencies, 1974-1978

Year	Delinquency Referrals	Dependency Referrals	Percentage of Dependency Referrals
1974	35,760	41,197	53.5
1975	39,001	47,390	54.9
1976	37,419	46,703	55.5
1977	33,258	46,341	58.2
1978	36,981	41,979	53.2
Mean	36,484	44,722	55.1

Source: Pennsylvania Juvenile Court Judges Commission (1979).

19.5 percent in services to children who had been seen
previously during the year.   Thus, it would appear as if
status offenders were either being relabeled as delinquents or were being diverted from the court but not directly to the county child welfare agency.   A study of
status offenders in Philadelphia done by the Youth Services Coordinating Office (1978) tends to support the
latter conclusion.   This study found that case loads of
private providers who offer counseling and other nonresidential services increased significantly after the passage
of Act 41.   They also found no evidence that relabeling

TABLE 13-3   Cases Initiated at County Child Welfare
Agencies, 1977 and 1978

Year	Cases Initiated	Services to New Clients	New Services to Previous Clients
1977	46,598	39,074	7,524
1978	44,909	35,921	8,988
1977-1978	-1,689	-3,153	+1,464
% change	-3.6	-8.1	+19.5

Source: Pennsylvania Department of Public Welfare (1978).

had been a problem in Philadelphia in the year after the
act was passed.

One other bit of statewide data supports the conclusion
that Act 41 has removed many status offenders from the
court system, but has not directed all of them to the local child welfare agency. DPW data provide figures for
the number of cases initiated through court commitments
of delinquency and dependency. The number committed to
the child welfare agencies as delinquents declined from
2,147 in 1977 to 341 in 1978, a difference of 1,806 cases
(Pennsylvania Department of Public Welfare 1978). Because
it is safe to assume that prior to Act 41 most delinquency
cases referred to the child welfare agencies were status
offenders, this sharp drop-off is consistent with the absence of relabeling, since relabeling would have caused
an increase in delinquency commitments. On the other
hand, the cases committed to the child welfare agencies
as dependent increased only by 112 (from 6,025 to 6,137)
(Pennsylvania Department of Public Welfare 1978). If we
assume for the moment that the number of status offenders
in Pennsylvania remained approximately constant from 1977
to 1978, then a simple change of adjudicatory status would
increase the number of dependency commitments by an amount
similar to the decline in delinquency commitments. Since
this did not happen, one conclusion is that many children
who were adjudicated delinquent on status charges are no
longer receiving any form of adjudication.

A great deal of caution must be used in interpreting
an analysis like this. Although the data do support the
hypothesis that Act 41 did divert many status offenders
out of the court system and, in fact, out of the entire
formal juvenile services system, this outcome could simply
be an artifact of the highly aggregated data. An adequate
test of this hypothesis would require detailed case histories of similar types of children drawn before and after
the passage of this law. Anything less will always result
in tentative conclusions.

An alternative way to examine the possible effects of
Act 41 is to consider whether the nature of the children
and youth receiving services has changed. Before looking
directly at this question, it should be noted that the
nature of status offenses in the court system had been
changing even before new legislation was passed. Specifically, from 1972 to 1976 court referrals for runaways
increased from approximately 2,200 to 2,600; at the same
time, referrals for ungovernability declined from approximately 2,500 to 1,650 (Pennsylvania Department of Justice

1976). Thus, even before legislative changes were introduced, ungovernables were being diverted out of the system, most likely by a number of private organizations in
large counties like Philadelphia. These data also show
that the decline was not due to the drop in the problem
population, nor in the total number of status offender
cases.

The information we have on the nature of dependency
cases and the impact of Act 41 comes from various studies
of Philadelphia, with nothing comparable available for the
state as a whole. This fact necessarily restricts the
scope of the conclusions that may be drawn but, on the
other hand, Philadelphia does account for a large percentage of the state's dependency cases.

The 1978 study by the Youth Services Coordinating Office in Philadelphia showed an amazing reduction of 91
percent between the number of status offenders processed
through the juvenile court in the first six months of 1977
(589) and the corresponding period in 1978 (51). In 1977
status offenders all were processed as delinquents, and
in 1978, as dependent children. This change in jurisdiction is consistent with Act 41, although the study did not
investigate what was happening to those who were being
diverted out of the court system altogether. Another
study of status offenders supported the conclusion that
these children were being diverted from the court system
and, when processed, were being dealt with in dependent
court (Freedman 1979). This study compared random samples of 65 status offenders drawn from those in the system
before and after the passage of Act 41. Some interesting
differences emerged from this comparison. While the
pre-Act 41 sample appeared in court largely on runaway
petitions (58 of 65), the post-Act 41 children were
largely seen on incorrigibility petitions (61 of 65).
This shift is statistically significant at well beyond the
.01 level. Furthermore, 51 percent of the post-Act 41
sample received adjudications as opposed to 41 percent of
the pre-Act 41 sample, and the former were also more
likely to receive placements by the Philadelphia DPW than
were the pre-Act 41 group.

Some additional information on the nature of dependency
cases in Philadelphia can be obtained from the family
court statistics compiled for 1978. Table 13-4 shows the
breakdown of the 1,583 dependency cases seen by the court
(i.e., new charges) by the reason for referral. These
figures seem to confirm the conclusions of the studies
discussed above, as they show that only 21.4 percent of

TABLE 13-4   Philadelphia Dependency Cases by Nature of
Charge, 1978

Type of Case	Number	Percentage of Total
Inadequate care	467	29.5
No parent	40	2.5
Neglect	336	21.2
Abuse	235	14.8
Abandonment	35	2.2
Mental/physical health	80	5.1
Delinquent case referral	137	8.7 ⎫
Truancy	89	5.6 ⎬ 21.4
Incorrigibility	112	7.1 ⎭
Others	52	3.3
Total	1,583	100.0

Source: The Court of Common Pleas of Philadelphia (1978).

the 1,583 cases were for possible status offenses.   The
remainder were basically cases of abuse, neglect, abandonment, and inadequate care.   As might be expected, the
age distributions for these two groups were very different.   Almost 64 percent of the latter cases were children
under 12, while 95 percent of the status offender group
were over 12 years old.

Some interesting information on the source of referral
for different types of dependency cases and the disposition of the cases is presented in Tables 13-5 and 13-6.
Looking first at Table 13-5, we see that only about one-
third (580) of the cases are referred to the court by DPW.
The other two-thirds are referred by schools, parents, or
the court itself.   This shows quite clearly that even after the passage of Act 41, many status offenders are still
not being referred directly to child welfare agencies, at
least in Philadelphia.   This conclusion is reinforced by
looking at school authorities, who were responsible for
referring 22 percent of the outside total apparently directly to the courts rather than to DPW.   It should be
noted that the court itself was the source of referral for
a significant number of cases other than status offenses.

Finally, as is indicated in Table 13-6, 408 of the
cases (26 percent) were either dismissed or discharged

TABLE 13-5 Referrals to Court in Dependency Cases in Philadelphia, 1978

Reason for Referral to Court	Source of Referral							
	Parent	Rela-tive	Other Indi-vidual	Dept. of Public Welfare	School Author-ities	Court	Other	Total
Inadequate care	6	40	5	161	208	46	1	467
No parent	—	—	—	32	2	6	—	40
Neglect	6	31	5	182	59	53	—	336
Abuse	7	4	1	145	—	77	1	235
Abandonment	—	4	2	20	—	7	2	35
Mental/physical health	—	—	5	25	1	49	—	80
Delinquent case referral	—	—	—	—	2	135	—	137
Truancy	2	—	2	4	79	2	—	89
Incorrigibility	103	8	1	—	—	—	—	112
Others	5	1	16	11	—	18	1	52
Total cases	129	88	37	580	351	393	5	1,583

TABLE 13-6 Reason for Referral in Dependency Cases in Philadelphia, 1978

Case Disposition	Inadequate Care[a]	Neglect[b]	Delinquent Case Referral	Others[c]	Total
Dismissed or discharged	79	71	3	68	221
Petition withdrawn	69	59	6	53	187
Protective supervision	116	151	14	85	366
Placed in custody of:					
Parent	11	14	2	7	34
Relative	35	87	1	8	131
Other individual	12	7	3	7	29
Committed to:					
Dept. of Public Welfare	179	204	97	64	544
Private agency	1	2	5	8	16
Mental health facility	1	1	--	24	36
Others	4	10	6	9	29
Total cases	507	606	137	133	1,583

[a] Includes no parent.
[b] Includes abuse and abandonment.
[c] Includes mental/physical health, truancy, and incorrigibility.

(221) or the petition was withdrawn (187). Of the remaining cases, most were either placed under protective
supervision or committed to DPW for services and placement. Overall, 74 percent of the cases committed to DPW
were for inadequate care, abuse, and neglect.

Although any conclusions from the data examined here
must be considered tentative, the following inferences can
be made:

1.   Act 41 appears to have been successful in moving
status offender cases from the delinquent to the dependent
categorization.
2.   There is little evidence of systematic, widespread
upgrading of status charges to delinquency offenses.
3.   Many status offenders seem to have been diverted
out of the formal juvenile services system entirely, as
not all of these children and youth appear to be referred
to county child welfare agencies.
4.   The remaining status offender cases seem to be in
court for more serious charges.
5.   A majority of the dependency cases seem to be under
consideration for reasons of abuse, neglect, and inadequate care.

Services to Status Offender and Nonoffender Youth

The legislative changes of the 1970s were intended to do
more than just decrease the juvenile court's role in the
care of nondelinquent youth; these children were also to
be removed from detention in adult or other secure facilities, and a greater use of nonresidential and group home
treatment options was expected. The data already examined
provide evidence on the first of these matters. In the
absence of widespread relabeling of dependent children,
the observed changeover of status offenders from delinquent to dependent youth seems to indicate that they have
been removed from secure detention in delinquency facilities. The law now explicitly prohibits holding juveniles
in adult facilities and holding dependent children in secure detention. All the interviews suggested that the
changes required by the law had been almost fully realized
and only a few exceptions were mentioned. A 1978 report
by the Governor's Justice Commission in Pennsylvania documents these changes well. In 1975 and 1976 an average
of 2,496 status offenders were detained. This was almost
42 percent of all status cases seen by the courts and ap-

proximately 25 percent of all detentions. Act 41 became effective on August 3, 1977, and the figures for that year reflect the drop in that only 1,639 status offenders (24 percent) were detained as opposed to the 42 percent who were detained in 1975 and 1976. Figures for the first half of 1978 showed that only 60 status offenders were detained (only 1.5 percent of all detentions). Officials now indicate that there is almost full compliance with the law.

Several reasons may be suggested for the counties' quick compliance. First, they were given advance notice that the change was coming. The 1972 Juvenile Justice Act removed truants from the delinquency category and placed strict limits on the use of jails for detaining juveniles. State DPW regulations also speeded up compliance by requiring the counties to develop plans for shelter care in their annual reports. Failure to do so carried the threat of either loss of funding or assumption by DPW of control over children's services in the county. Counties could also no longer get state reimbursement for the cost of dependent children who are held in secure detention. Finally, the counties' compliance with the law was carefully monitored by a number of groups, including the Juvenile Justice Center and the Governor's Justice Commission. The commission was responsible for reporting to LEAA the state's compliance with JJDPA.

Although statistics documenting the actual services provided to children and youth in Pennsylvania do not contain a great deal of detailed information, the aggregate data from DPW do show general patterns of services and suggest changes that occurred as a result of the deinstitutionalization effort. Before looking at the number of children being served, we will briefly discuss the private provider system and how it works. Most services for children and youth in Pennsylvania are provided by private agencies that are approved by the state DPW and contracted out by the counties. The counties are free to negotiate with any approved provider and can set payments at any level. The providers are free to accept or reject any cases they wish. There currently are three major categories of private providers in Pennsylvania: (1) group homes, (2) facility-based institutions, and (3) voluntary child care agencies. The latter may offer counseling and in-home services, supervise independent living arrangements, or provide supervised foster care. Facility-based institutions (more than eight children) may be approved for the care of delinquent or dependent chil-

dren; delinquency institutions may not accept dependent
children although dependency facilities may accept delinquents.

According to the state's list of approved private providers, as of May 1979 there were 125 group homes, 77
residential facilities for dependent children, and 75
voluntary agencies. As Table 13-7 shows, these providers
are far from equally distributed among the counties. This
is especially true for group homes. Fully one-third of
the 125 group homes are located in one county (Philadelphia), and five of the 67 counties account for two-thirds
of all group homes. More than one-half of the counties
(36) have no group homes and must send children to facilities in other counties if such placements are desired.

Table 13-8 shows the number of dependent children who
received services in 1977 and 1978. The children are
categorized according to the type of service they received. Almost three-fourths of the services either provided or purchased by county child welfare agencies are
in-home services or supervised independent living, and
over 70 percent of those services provided in homes or in
independent living arrangements are protective services
specifically for neglected and abused children. A majority of the out-of-home placements are foster care settings. While the percentage of services provided in group
homes and residential facilities was only 4.2 percent in
1977, it was 5.9 percent in 1978. This increase is interesting in two respects. First, the increase in the
number of group home placements from 1977 to 1978 is significantly greater than the increase in residential facility placements (58 percent and 29 percent, respectively) for the same period. This is in line with the state's
desire to increase reliance on group homes and is probably
due in part to the financial incentives for group home
placements written into Act 148. Also of interest is the
overall 35 percent increase in total residential placements (i.e., groups homes and residential facilities).
While this appears to be inconsistent with the philosophy
of deinstitutionalization, it does fit with earlier conclusions that post-Act 41 status offense cases are of a
more difficult nature. These new data would seem to indicate that although many status offenders are being diverted from the system, the ones that remain are somewhat
more likely to receive residential placements.

Although the data in Table 13-8 show that institutional
care is not used in most of the dependency cases handled
by public agencies in Pennsylvania, it is also clear that

TABLE 13-7 Group Homes, Residential Facilities, and
Voluntary Agencies in Each County (as of May 1979)

County	Group Homes	Residential Facilities	Voluntary Agencies
Adams	0	1	0
Allegheny	10	9	4
Armstrong	0	0	1
Beaver	1	2	3
Bedford	0	0	0
Berks	1	3	2
Blair	0	1	3
Bradford	1	0	0
Bucks	2	5	2
Butler	0	2	1
Cambria	1	1	1
Cameron	2	0	0
Carbon	0	0	0
Centre	0	0	1
Chester	4	2	2
Clarion	0	0	0
Clearfield	0	1	0
Clinton	0	1	0
Columbia	0	0	0
Crawford	0	0	0
Cumberland	0	1	1
Dauphin	1	1	4
Delaware	3	3	1
Elk	0	0	0
Erie	13	3	3
Fayette	2	1	1
Forest	0	0	0
Franklin	2	1	1
Fulton	0	0	0
Greene	0	0	1
Huntingdon	0	0	0
Indiana	1	0	1
Jefferson	0	0	0
Juniata	0	0	0
Lackawanna	2	2	3
Lancaster	1	5	2
Lawrence	0	0	2
Lebanon	1	1	0
Lehigh	3	1	3
Luzerne	3	1	1
Lycoming	0	0	0
McKean	0	1	0
Mercer	1	1	1
Mifflin	1	1	0

TABLE 13-7 (Continued)

County	Group Homes	Residential Facilities	Voluntary Agencies
Monroe	0	0	0
Montgomery	8	5	3
Montour	0	0	1
Northampton	1	1	1
Northumberland	0	0	0
Perry	0	0	0
Philadelphia	40	14	14
Pike	0	0	0
Potter	0	1	0
Schuylkill	0	0	2
Snyder	0	0	0
Somerset	10	0	2
Sullivan	0	0	0
Susquehanna	0	0	0
Tioga	0	0	1
Union	0	0	0
Venango	0	0	1
Warren	0	2	0
Washington	2	0	1
Wayne	1	0	0
Westmoreland	1	0	3
Wyoming	0	1	0
York	6	2	1
State totals	125	77	75

Source: Department of Public Welfare, Approved Children's
Service Agencies and Facilities (March 1979).

use of such care is not being significantly reduced by the
financial incentives now in place. The slow progress in
this area appears due to several factors. The first is
the lack of faith that some officials have in the ability
of noninstitutional programs to care successfully for
certain children, especially older youth and adolescents.
A subtle factor here may be the difficulty involved in
supervising children in more open settings; officials may
feel that it is easier in many respects to use larger,
more restrictive residential facilities. A second possible factor inhibiting deinstitutionalizaton is that the
financial incentives may be insufficient inducements. It
is also questionable whether those incentives always make

TABLE 13-8 Services to Dependent Children in Pennsylvania, 1977 and 1978

Type of service	1977 Number	1977 Percentage	1978 Number	1978 Percentage
In homes of parents, relatives, or in independent living arrangements	41,810	74.9	40,201	73.3
(For protective services)	(29,813)	(53.4)	(29,175)	(53.2)
Adoptive homes	722	1.3	703	1.3
Foster care	10,910	19.5	10,719	19.5
Group homes	469	.8	741	1.4
Residential facilities	1,922	3.4	2,479	4.5
Total	55,833	100.0	54,843	100.0

Note: Figures represent the number of children receiving each service.

Source: Pennsylvania Department of Public Welfare (1978).

the institutional alternative the more expensive choice
for the county. If the extra 25 percent reimbursement
given to the group homes and community-based services is
to bring about their increased use, the cost to the county
per child serviced must be no more than for residential
care in institutions. But in many cases the community-
based care costs sufficiently more than residential institutional care, so that even with the additional 25
percent reimbursement, the county's net cost per child may
be about the same. The effect may simply be to keep the
counties' costs for group home placements at about the
same level as residential facility care.

A final problem inhibiting deinstitutionalization is
the payment for children's services on a per-diem basis.
This has less impact on the larger facilities because the
loss of income associated with the turnover of a few
children is not severely damaging to the overall financial
situation of the institution. In a group home with a capacity of only six or eight, however, the loss of income
for two children for a period of time could be a financial
burden that the facility might not be able to handle. A
number of group homes have failed for exactly this reason,
and many of the more successful group home programs have
been developed as a series of financially linked facilities to attempt to overcome this problem.

A COMPARISON OF TWO COUNTIES

A description of children's services at the state level
is of limited use in Pennsylvania because of the wide
variation across the 67 counties. In this section we will
look in more detail at the organization and pattern of
services in two very different counties. Philadelphia
County is functionally equivalent to the city, a large
metropolitan center in the southeastern corner of the
state. Cambria County, with less than 200,000 citizens,
is an Appalachian area in the center of the state with
high unemployment and a declining population. Its largest
city, Johnstown, is still recovering from the most recent
in a series of devastating floods. One of the differences
between the two counties in the delivery of services obviously will be in overall scale. A related factor is
that Cambria has fewer financial resources than Philadelphia.

As the previous section showed, there is a significant
difference in the number of private providers in each

county. Philadelphia County has 14 institutions for dependent children, 40 group homes, and 14 voluntary agencies; Cambria County has one of each. Of these three private agencies, the group home only provides shelter care, not long-term care, and the voluntary agency is an adoption service.

The disparity in the number of private providers, even relative to their different populations, has several important implications. First, the children and youth agency in Cambria provides more services directly than does the Philadelphia DPW. With the availability of providers in Philadelphia, intake units of DPW are able to refer clients to appropriate services in the private sector; Cambria intake units are much more likely to provide services themselves, most often in the form of family counseling. Another consequence of the absence of private providers in Cambria County is that certain services are simply not available. In the case of residential services, particularly group homes, the children and youth agency is forced to send children out of the county, usually a fairly long distance. In Philadelphia, however, there is little problem in finding local programs.

One important effect of the disparity in the number and kind of private providers is that the Cambria children and youth agency is almost invariably the initial point of contact for children who need services. Once the court probation staff ceased to accept status offender cases, referral had to go directly to the children and youth agency. In Philadelphia, however, there are a number of private agencies offering counseling services that may be the first point of contact with the system. These agencies require state approval and may be funded from a number of sources including the Philadelphia DPW, the local school department, or private charities. Technically, all cases they initiate must be cleared with the intake unit of DPW, but this appears to be little more than a formality. DPW could probably require all such cases to go directly to their own intake unit first, but doing so would vastly increase their case loads.

The presence of these private providers has significantly affected the way Philadelphia has adapted to the legislation that classified status offenders as dependent children. Prior to this change, status offenders were referred directly to the court by police, schools, or parents, and the probation staff handled intake. This change should have sent status offenders directly to the Philadelphia welfare department, but the lack of faith that many, especially the police, have in that department has caused these children to be sent instead to various private providers for initial counseling. The major exception to this is runaways, who must be sent to the welfare department if they are to be held in shelter care.

Another alternative to the child welfare department in Philadelphia is the court-run Counseling and Referral Service (CRS). This service deals with juveniles, both alleged delinquent and nondelinquent, who are referred to it by the probation staff, police, private providers, or individuals. CRS offers direct counseling and also makes referrals to private providers for further intervention. After monitoring the child's progress, CRS may terminate aid, refer to probation for delinquency charges, refer to the child welfare department in dependency cases, or prepare a dependency petition for direct submission to the court. CRS therefore performs many of the same duties that the child welfare department might take on in its absence. In this case, however, the established links are much stronger with the court (under whose control it falls) than with child welfare. Aggregate data from CRS show that most of its services are provided for juveniles who would generally be classified as status offenders (Youth Services Coordinating Office 1978). CRS has provided an option in Philadelphia for the police juvenile aid officers, who used to refer status offenders directly to the court probation staff. These cases are now sent to CRS, and they might not come to the attention of child welfare until a dependency petition has been filed with the court. This pattern reflects both the previous ties that the police had with the court and the negative attitudes of police juvenile aid officers toward the child welfare staff. Such relationships and attitudes, once formed, do not change quickly even after major statutory changes. Thus, while Act 41 has been successful in Philadelphia in stopping delinquency adjudications for status offenses and in reducing the roles of the probation staff, not all of these cases have gone to the child welfare agency (Philadelphia DPW), and in many instances they are handled by another arm of the court. This option is not available in counties like Cambria; if the probation staff there refuses to supervise dependent children, they are likely to be transferred to child welfare. In other counties, the probation staff continues to accept dependency cases. It was reported that one juvenile judge even directs the probation staff to supervise abuse cases, because of his low regard for the county child welfare

agency. The law does not forbid this, and local philosophies and attitudes are likely to have a critical influence on how this works in practice.

One other way in which the procedures in Philadelphia
and Cambria have differed is the role of the court in
making residential placements. As we mentioned earlier,
there are currently only two legally recognized categories
for children and youth who come under the jurisdiction of
the formal juvenile justice system. According to Pennsylvania law, if a child is either delinquent or dependent, a residential placement cannot be made unless an
adjudication order is issued by the court. The court thus
has final say in any decision to remove a child from the
home, even in nondelinquent cases. The only major exception to this rule has been a system operating in Philadelphia in which a voluntary agreement between the city
welfare department and the parents was used to permit the
placement of a child in a residential facility or in foster care. The agreement was then certified by the juvenile court without a formal hearing or adjudication order.
While an ambiguity in the juvenile justice act apparently
permitted this process to go on for a number of years, the
state DPW regulations for Act 148 have now put an end to
the practice of making placements without adjudications.
Since the new regulations require that all reimbursements
for residential care be made only after a court adjudication order has been issued, Philadelphia would have to
assume full financial responsibility for all of these
cases at a substantial cost to the county. This new cost
factor and the question of the legal rights of the parents
have led Philadelphia to revise this system to increase
the role of the court in the placement decision. The new
agreement procedures are currently being worked out by the
child welfare department and the juvenile court.

Some data are available to help illustrate the differences between these two counties, both directly and
with respect to their adaptation to the 1977 legislative
changes. Since the counties are far from uniform in the
way in which they report data on juveniles, some caution
will be required in making direct comparisons between
them. Contrasts between 1977 and 1978 data within each
county should be more reliable, since county idiosyncra-
cies in reporting data are likely to be relatively stable
over time.

First, juvenile court data show that both counties have
been completely successful in removing status offenders
from secure detention. In 1976 Cambria detained 46.2

TABLE 13-9 Cases Initiated by County Child Welfare Agency
in Philadelphia and Cambria Counties, 1977 and 1978

| | Philadelphia | | Cambria | |
Type of Case	1977	1978	1977	1978
Court-committed dependent	126	106	309	34
Court-committed delinquent	0	0	0	2
Not court-committed	8,038	8,698	46	310
Total	8,164	8,804	355	346

Source: Pennsylvania Department of Public Welfare (1978).

percent of its status offenders and Philadelphia 53.7
percent (Pennsylvania Department of Justice 1976). In
1978 records show that neither county had detained any
dependent children (Pennsylvania Department of Justice
1978). In Philadelphia such youth are placed in the
county-run shelter care facility or in one of a few community-based options. In Cambria a privately run group
home is used for shelter care.

Given the differences between these two counties, it
is interesting to look at how they responded to the shift
of status offenders from the delinquency to dependency
category. Table 13-9 shows comparative data for Cambria
and Philadelphia on cases initiated by the county child
welfare agency in 1977 and 1978. The total is broken down
into those cases that were court-committed as dependent
or delinquent and those that were initiated directly by
the child welfare agency. Looking first at Philadelphia,
virtually no change can be seen aside from a slight decline in cases processed as dependent by the court relative to a small increase in total cases. This lack of
real change is consistent with our earlier observation
that new status offender cases were more likely to go to
the court CRS or to private providers than to the county
child welfare agency. The child welfare case load increased somewhat, but not in relation to court referrals.

The situation is very different for Cambria. Although
the total number of cases initiated did not change significantly, the source of those cases changed dramatically. In 1977, 87 percent of all new cases were court-

committed dependent, but in 1978 only 10 percent came from this source. Thus in 1977 most dependency cases came to the child welfare agency only _after_ some experience with the court. Act 41 brought about a swift change by making the child welfare agency in Cambria the major intake point for dependent children. Unlike Philadelphia with its large private provider network, in Cambria these cases had nowhere else to go after the probation staff stopped handling them.

Another way to look at these changes is through court statistics on delinquency and dependency cases that originate with the probation office. One problem with these data, which are shown in Table 13-10, is that Philadelphia reports a large number of dependency cases, many of which clearly were not handled directly by the probation staff (see Tables 13-5 and 13-6). Nevertheless, the patterns are interesting. Philadelphia showed a one-year drop of 980 dependency cases. Thus, a number of dependency cases appear to have been diverted from the court, although they also appear not to have gone directly to child welfare intake. Cambria, on the other hand, again shows a significant change from 1977 to 1978. In 1977, 119 of the 419 court cases (28 percent) were dependent children; only 1 of 322 cases was a dependent child in 1978. This finding is consistent with the data in Table 13-9 and shows that the juvenile court in Cambria, once active in the supervision of dependent children, has responded to Act 41 by diverting these children directly to the county child welfare agency.

TABLE 13-10 Cases Initiated by Court Probation Office in Philadelphia and Cambria Counties, 1977 and 1978

Type of Case	Philadelphia		Cambria	
	1977	1978	1977	1978
Delinquency cases	10,982	12,568	300	321
Dependency cases	2,563	1,583	119	1
Total	13,545	14,151	419	322

Source: Pennsylvania Department of Justice (1977, 1978).

Table 13-11 shows the services that the child welfare
agencies in Philadelphia and Cambria provided to dependent
children in 1977 and 1978. The most obvious feature of
these data is that despite all the other changes occurring
at this time, the relative mix of services in these two
counties was virtually unchanged. This is significant
because it suggests that in both counties decisions about
services are largely unaffected by the process of diverting dependent children from the court system. There are,
however, substantial differences in the types of services
provided by the two counties. Approximately 80 percent
of Cambria's services are nonresidential as opposed to 61
percent in Philadelphia. Philadelphia is more likely to
use foster care (27 percent) and institutions (10 percent) than Cambria (13 percent and 6 percent, respectively). Although it is impossible to determine the exact
reason for such differences with a base of just two counties, there are four factors that likely contribute.
First, as discussed earlier, Cambria does not have the
placement options that Philadelphia has; children must
travel great distances, and the placement options therefore reflect the available services. A second factor may
be the philosophies of the local officials. Although officials in both counties seem to accept the principles of
deinstitutionalization, this acceptance may be put into

TABLE 13-11   Services Provided to Dependent Children in
Philadelphia and Cambria Counties, 1977 and 1978

	Philadelphia		Cambria	
Type of Service	1977	1978	1977	1978
Nonresidential (i.e., in homes of parents, relatives, or in independent living arrangements)	7,584	7,507	411	459
Foster care*	3,329	3,346	66	82
Adoptive homes	183	180	0	1
Residential facilities	1,314	1,242	36	35
Total	12,410	12,275	513	587

*Includes group homes.

Source: Pennsylvania Department of Public Welfare (1978).

practice more effectively in Cambria. A third possibility
is that there may be proportionally more difficult children in Philadelphia than Cambria, and this could account
for the greater use of residential services and foster
care in Philadelphia. (In these figures, group home
placements are counted as foster care.) Finally, a major
factor is likely to be financial considerations. Since
the counties must pay 50 percent of residential placement
costs of each institutional placement, Cambria may find
it too much of a financial burden to place many children
this way. The director of the Cambria children and youth
agency explicitly mentioned that he would like to spend
less on residential placements and use the money to support more nonresidential services. Since these factors
all point in the same direction, there is unfortunately
no way to determine which accounts for the intercounty
differences. Most likely all contribute in some way.

CONCLUSIONS

In the last eight years, Pennsylvania has made a concerted
attempt to change its system of juvenile justice and
children's services to emphasize the goals of minimal
confinement and the provision of community-based and in-
home services. Much of this effort has led to significant
and often nonincremental changes in the state's juvenile
justice legislation. At the same time, because services
are organized and delivered at the county level, state
policy must be directed through 67 local political units.
Each of these counties has developed its own pattern of
youth services, influenced in part by the philosophies and
attitudes of its officials, its demographic characteristics, the availability and nature of private providers,
and the mix of county-provided or county-purchased services.

In a decentralized system like Pennsylvania's, the
state can influence the delivery of services at the local
level either by controlling funding to create financial
incentives or by legally creating or closing certain options for dealing with children and youth through the
formal juvenile justice-child welfare system. Given the
latitude of discretion written into the state legislation,
uniform or smooth implementation of state policy across
counties cannot be expected and has not occurred. This
is not peculiar to the delivery of children's services,
but it is a characteristic of this form of state and local
government.

Despite the intercounty variations, some general conclusions may be drawn about the success of the legislation to date. First, although it has taken a number of
years, dependent youth have been effectively removed from
all forms of secure detention, including county jails and
other adult facilities. Status offenses are no longer
categorized as delinquent acts; thus, the delinquency
label has been eliminated, thereby removing the possibility of residential care in secure facilities and reducing
the role of the juvenile court system in the intake and
treatment of these youth. As we saw in Philadelphia,
however, the role of the court in dealing with these youth
is still extensive in many areas.

There has also been a noticeable shift in the provision
of services toward smaller group homes for residential
care and an increased use of nonresidential forms of assistance. While fairly rapid change has been exhibited
in some areas, progress in the changing of services has
been slow due to several complicating factors, including
the philosophies and attitudes of local officials and the
lack of substantial financial incentives to overcome previous service delivery patterns. It seems clear that much
more must be done if the use of institutional services is
to be significantly reduced in Pennsylvania. This is one
area in which the efforts of the deinstitutionalization
advocates have not met with a great deal of success.

In the past decade advocates of deinstitutionalization
in Pennsylvania have called for greater diversion of dependent children from the formal juvenile justice system.
Our study has found that the passage of Act 41 in 1977
furthered considerably the progress made in this direction. The data available do not allow precise estimates
of the magnitude of this trend, and although some may argue that it has not gone far enough, many children who
would have come in contact with the formal juvenile service system several years ago are apparently now being
diverted from it. This raises the question of whether
these children are now receiving the help they need to
deal with their problems? There are no data to answer
this question, but it clearly deserves to be the focus of
further research. It is easy to see how this could be a
major problem in some areas of the state. As shown here,
both public and private services are distributed very un-
evenly across the state, and new services designed for
helping children in their homes or community settings are
slow in developing. A philosophy of deinstitutionalization cannot work in practice if suitable alternatives are

not available. The major problems we now see in Pennsylvania relate to questions of the availability and effectiveness of services, not to the overinstitutionalization
of status offenders.

Finally, conspicuous by its absence from this report
has been lengthy discussion of the impact of the policies
of the national government on deinstitutionalization in
Pennsylvania. None of the respondents felt that federal
policies were a determining factor in bringing about
changes in legislation and practices. Federal deinstitutionalization efforts supported change in Pennsylvania by
legitimizing the process of change, and at times by providing financial support for deinstitutionalization advocates in the states. However, federal legislation did not
by itself place the issue of deinstitutionalization on the
legislative agenda in Pennsylvania, nor did federal activity contribute significantly to the passage of state
legislation. Federal funds do help to provide both residential and nonresidential services to children in Pennsylvania, but since they are combined with state funds in
the form of reimbursements, the funds are not structured
to generate change. The overall conclusion must be,
therefore, that the driving forces for change were within
the state and that deinstitutionalization was and is a
function of these local efforts and not of federal policies or regulations.

REFERENCES

Court of Common Pleas of Philadelphia (1978) Annual
    Report. Family Court Division. Philadelphia, Pa.:
    Court of Common Pleas.
Freedman, Carol (1979) Study of the Impact of Act 41 on
    the Status Offender Referred to Court. Unpublished
    M.S. thesis, Graduate School of Hahneman Medical
    College.
Pennsylvania Department of Justice (1974-1978)
    Pennsylvania Juvenile Court Dispositions 1978 (and
    earlier years). Annual report. Harrisburg, Pa.:
    Department of Justice.
Pennsylvania Department of Public Welfare (1978) Annual
    Statistical Report, 1977-78. Harrisburg, Pa.:
    Department of Public Welfare.
Pennsylvania Governor's Justice Commission (1978)
    Inspection and Monitoring Report for Pennsylvania.
    Harrisburg, Pa.: Governor's Justice Commission.

Pennsylvania Juvenile Court Judges Commission (1979)
    Juvenile Court Analytical Report, 1978. Harrisburg,
    Pa.: Juvenile Court Judges Commission.
Philadelphia Youth Services Coordinating Office (1978) A
    Descriptive Study of Status Offenders in Philadelphia.
    Philadelphia, Pa.: Youth Services Coordinating Office.

OFFICIALS INTERVIEWED

These officials are listed in the order in which they were
interviewed. When more than one respondent was in the
room, we list only the most senior official. The first
interview was held on July 9, 1979; the final one was on
December 12, 1979.

Robert H. Sobolevitch, Bureau of Youth Services, Office
    of Children and Youth, Department of Public Welfare,
    Commonwealth of Pennsylvania
David McCorkle, Pennsylvania Joint Council on Criminal
    Justice
Anne DeMuro, Juvenile Justice Planner, Governor's Justice
    Commission
John Pierce, Pennsylvania Association of Voluntary
    Institutions
Chrysandra Gantt, Office of Children and Youth,
    Department of Public Welfare, Commonwealth of
    Pennsylvania
Ron Sharp, Juvenile Court Judges Commission
Park P. Bierbower, Children and Youth Services, Office of
    Mental Health, Department of Public Welfare,
    Commonwealth of Pennsylvania
Linda Hicks, Juvenile Court Judges Commission
Samual Yeaghley, Director, Children and Youth Services of
    Dauphin County
William Ohrtman, Bureau of Special Education, Department
    of Education, Commonwealth of Pennsylvania
Biagio Mustro, Guidance and Counseling Section, Division
    of Pupil Personnel Services, Bureau of Instructional
    Support Services, Department of Education,
    Commonwealth of Pennsylvania
William Mader, Correction Education, Department of
    Education, Commonwealth of Pennsylvania
Herbert C. Witmer, Social Services of the Central Region,
    Department of Public Welfare, Commonwealth of
    Pennsylvania
Kenneth Chilsen, Juvenile Court Judges Commission

Connie Dellmeth, Bureau of Social Services Policy and
    Planning, Department of Public Welfare, Commonwealth
    of Pennsylvania
William Logan, Student Services, Department of Education,
    Commonwealth of Pennsylvania
Marjorie Rynk, Cash Assistance, Program and Policy
    Division, Department of Public Welfare, Commonwealth
    of Pennsylvania
Clyde Weidner, Division of Contracts, Department of
    Education, Commonwealth of Pennsylvania
April McClane, Senate Democratic Research Staff
Michael McCarthy, Senate Democratic Research Staff
Kenneth Adami, House Democratic Research Staff
John Alzamore, Legal Division, Department of Education,
    Commonwealth of Pennsylvania
Richard Jamison, Office of Children and Youth, Department
    of Public Welfare, Commonwealth of Pennsylvania
Antoinette Chavius Chapman, Right to Education Division,
    Department of Education, Commonwealth of Pennsylvania
Steven Abram, Bureau of Management Information Systems,
    Governor's Council on Drug and Alcohol Abuse
Clarice Kendall, Office of Non-Public Schools, Division
    of Private Academic Schools, Department of Education,
    Commonwealth of Pennsylvania
David Feinberg, Bureau of Policy and Planning, Office of
    Medical Systems, Department of Public Welfare,
    Commonwealth of Pennsylvania
Barbara Fruchter, Director, Juvenile Justice Center
Marsha Levick, Juvenile Law Center
Walter Duron, Mentor Program, Juvenile Justice Center
Steven Burgh, Baptist Children's Home of Philadelphia
James E. Rowley, Youth Services Coordinating Office,
    Office of the Managing Director, City of Philadelphia
Rodney P. Lane, Government Studies and Systems
Debra Stone, Public Information Office, Special
    Education, Board of Education of Philadelphia
Malcolm Amos, Youth Studies Center, Philadelphia
Kenneth Hale, Juvenile Court Probation Staff, Philadelphia
Thomas M. Roselli, Juvenile Aid Division, Philadelphia
    Police Department
Richard J. Cohen, Coordinating Office for Drug and
    Alcohol Abuse Programs, City of Philadelphia
Daniel Falko, Rites of Passage, Philadelphia
Frank Jost, Counseling and Information, Office of Mental
    Health and Mental Retardation, Philadelphia
Wetonah Jones, Children's Service, Inc., Philadelphia

Stephanie Reynolds, Office of Mental Health and Mental
    Retardation, Philadelphia
Barbara A. Lloyd, Stenton Child Center, Emergency
    Services Division, Children and Youth Agency,
    Philadelphia Department of Public Welfare
Augustus Keirans, Community Based Emergency Shelter
    Program, Emergency Services Division, Children and
    Youth Agency, Philadelphia Department of Public Welfare
Judge William Lederer, Family Court, Courts of Common
    Pleas of Philadelphia
Theodore Levine, Youth Services, Inc., Philadelphia
Rocco Donatelli, Juvenile Branch, Family Court, Courts of
    Common Pleas of Philadelphia
Sister M. Charity Kohl, CORA (Counseling or Referral
    Assistance) Services Inc., Philadelphia
Herbert C. Boykin, Children and Youth Agency,
    Philadelphia Department of Public Welfare
Jake Armstrong, Youth Services Coordinating Office, City
    of Philadelphia
Isabelle Ginsberg, Intake Division, Children and Youth
    Agency, Philadelphia Department of Public Welfare
Palaka Fatah, House of Umoja, Philadelphia
Reverend Edward P. Cullen, Catholic Social Services,
    Philadelphia
Gary Estadt, Westmont Hilltop School District, Johnstown,
    Pennsylvania
Jerry Clauser, Juvenile Division, Office of Probation,
    Court of Common Pleas of Cambria County
James L. Drapchak, Office of Children and Youth,
    Department of Public Welfare of Cambria County
Elton Atwater, Pennsylvania Association for Retarded
    Citizens

14 Deinstitutionalization in Utah: A Study of Contrasts and Contradictions

RICHARD E. JOHNSON *and*
TIMOTHY C. MACK

INTRODUCTION

In our analysis of Utah's handling of status offenders, we will develop the themes of contrast and apparent contradiction. The most critical contradiction is Utah's long delay in participating in the Juvenile Justice and Delinquency Prevention Act of 1974 (JJDPA), despite early and effective state action consistent with the philosophy espoused by that act. We will look not only at changes since the 1974 passage of JJDPA but also at forces in operation before 1974, and will argue that state-level deinstitutionalization began before the 1974 act, and that the impact of JJDPA has largely been supportive of previously developed programs rather than provocative of new ones.

Most of the earlier deinstitutionalization programs in Utah were aimed at diverting status offenders from juvenile court. Until the late 1970s no significant efforts were made to alter the out-of-home placement patterns of those juveniles who had been processed by the court. Utah's liberal diversion of status offenders from the juvenile court has always been intermixed with a contrasting conservative desire to protect the public from serious delinquents. One perceived benefit of diverting status offenders was the resulting opportunity to devote more court time and resources to dealing with criminal offenders. In short, early (pre-1974) federal diversion efforts

419

appealed to Utah actors as a possible way to improve both
their assistance to status offenders and their control
over criminal juveniles.

It is impossible to separate the issue of control over
serious delinquents from the philosophy of diversion and
deinstitutionalization of status offenders in Utah. The
federally espoused concepts of diversion and deinstitutionalization were reinforced throughout the 1970s by the
recommendations of several research groups who examined
Utah's justice system (Council of State Governments 1975,
John Howard Association 1976, Miller 1977, Utah State
Legislature 1978). A major stimulus to continuing study
was local concern over the State Industrial School (now
the Youth Development Center), which was viewed as being
too institutional and impersonal for less serious offenders and at the same time too lax for the serious offenders, who easily escaped. Concern for controlling hardcore delinquents therefore appears to have helped to sol-
idify a commitment to diversion and deinstitutionalization
of nonoffenders.

Philosophies, however, do not automatically produce
funded programs. The contrast between philosophies and
funding will be highlighted as another central feature of
Utah's experience. In fact, both Utah's delay in participating in JJDPA and that act's impact on the state can
more accurately be viewed in financial rather than philosophical terms. Utah refused to participate in the 1974
act primarily because it did not appear to be financially
advantageous. There was little quarrel with the philosophy, and their concerns about compliance centered around
the lack of rural detention facilities. Those concerns,
in turn, were not characterized by a desire to keep juveniles in jails but rather by distress over the cost of
providing approved facilities.

By 1977, when the state passed major diversion legislation (HB 340), Utah was clearly in the national forefront in diverting and deinstitutionalizing status offenders. Yet it was one of only a few states not participating in the 1974 JJDPA. Many Utah actors remained
convinced that the incoming funds would not equal the
financial costs incurred to meet compliance. Because of
increased JJDPA funding levels, changes in key state personnel, and relaxed compliance terms, Utah finally joined
the act in late 1978.

The infusion of OJJDP funds did improve the financial
position of the state's major diversion program--the Salt
Lake County Youth Services Center (YSC)--and also stimu-

lated the development of alternatives to the Youth Development Center. Gradual reduction of the center's population virtually eliminated the placement of status offenders there, continuing an already existing decline in its status offender population.

Another impact of JJDPA was on Utah's rural detention. Utah was a pioneer in making the jailing of juveniles illegal, yet because of the lack of alternative facilities in rural areas it still occurs. It is not merely fiscal conservatism that is responsible for a dearth of approved juvenile detention facilities, alternatives, or youth services in rural areas. It is a financial reality that the cost per individual for rural facilities and services is much higher than in urban areas, and is sometimes beyond rural capabilities. JJDPA compliance requirements that prohibit the detention of status offenders have forced the issue into the open. Within the state, there is the feeling that "this is good for us," or that "maybe now we'll finally get something done," but there is also tremendous frustration over what is perceived to be inflexibility on the part of the Office of Juvenile Justice and Delinquency Prevention. The situations in urban and rural Utah are seen as so divergent that there is little patience with the imposition of a single set of guidelines for all locations.

Influencing all juvenile justice policy in Utah are the state's juvenile court judges. This influence derives from Utah's intertwining of juvenile justice and social service responsibilities. With status offender cases that involve at some point both court and social services, the judge nearly always has a stake in what occurs. The judge can and does influence policies at every point, from police encounters (e.g., by developing procedures favoring citation versus apprehension) to placements (e.g., by requiring periodic progress reports). Much of this power derives from the autonomous and unified structure of the Utah juvenile court. On juvenile matters the governing Board of Juvenile Court Judges answers only to itself. Because of the above-mentioned intertwining of the systems, it presently sets most of the policy regarding juvenile justice and much that deals with juvenile social services. Moreover, the board has also been an active and persuasive lobbying force in debates over such issues as diversion legislation and Youth Development Center alternatives. Its influence therefore goes well beyond its extensive legal mandate.

This discussion will examine these themes in terms of legal and administrative practices governing the disposition of Utah's delinquents and status offenders. It will first examine the forces that led to change and the outcomes of those changes, with particular attention to the federal role in those developments. Detail will be provided through an examination of two local areas--an urban and a rural setting.

HISTORY OF THE UTAH JUVENILE COURT

One striking aspect of the Utah juvenile court is its relatively nonjudicial history. From 1907 to 1965 the court was administered under the executive and not the judicial branch. In 1963 this unusual arrangement was held by the Utah Supreme Court to violate the separation of powers clause of the Utah State Constitution (In re Woodward, 384 P2d 1 (1963)). The juvenile court's separation from the Utah Department of Welfare in 1965 was a political as well as legal decision, the result of eight years of lobbying on the part of juvenile court judges. The 1965 Juvenile Court Act (78-32-1 through 62 UCA) established the nation's first statewide integrated juvenile court system and gave the court a modern and consolidated code. Under the new arrangement the juvenile court was given equal status with the district courts.

The state was divided into five judicial districts designed so that rural districts covered several counties while urban districts covered only one or two. With Utah's demographics the courts in the more populous Wasatch Front areas (Ogden, Salt Lake City, and Provo) have two, three, and two judges respectively, while the rural districts have one each. In the geographically larger rural districts the judges must become circuit riders, holding court in every county seat on scheduled days of the month. Because of this statewide structure the juvenile court in Utah is very centralized, with relatively uniform policies throughout the state. In comparison with other states the quality of available data concerning most court activities over the last 10 years is very good. Complete court records go back to 1967, when the first computer system was installed. We will use those records as the basis for charting statistical trends later in the paper.

FORCES OF CHANGE: A STUDY OF CONTRASTS AND CONTRADICTIONS

The decade of the 1970s was marked by sharp changes in
Utah's handling of youthful nonoffenders. At the most
general level, the force that pervaded all changes was the
Mormon influence, with its dual emphasis on the eternal
importance of the family and on the spirit of community
involvement and cooperation. It is therefore no surprise
to find early acceptance of deinstitutionalization as well
as interorganizational cooperation in its implementation.
The major counterforce to this effort was fiscal conservatism, which also has a strong tradition in Utah.

The 1967 report of the President's Commission on Law
Enforcement and Administration of Justice marked the first
major identifiable force in the direction of diversion and
deinstitutionalization of nonoffenders. Utah officials
seriously considered that report's concept of youth services bureaus as an alternative approach to the traditional judicial processing of those kinds of cases.

Utah relied heavily on federal funds to initiate its
diversion programs. The first grants came from HEW under
the authority of the Juvenile Delinquency Prevention and
Control Act of 1968. Another source of funds was the Law
Enforcement Assistance Administration (LEAA). Both types
of funds initially were channeled through Utah's law enforcement planning agency, the Utah Council on Criminal
Justice Administration (UCCJA). In 1970 Utah received
$100,000 from HEW for a statewide delinquency prevention
program, which was funded again in 1971. While work began on those programs, related events in Utah were beginning to directly and indirectly influence the handling of
nonoffenders.

An area of great concern in Utah was youth corrections.
The State Industrial School, renamed the Youth Development
Center in 1977, had long been criticized for its overcrowding and high escape rates. In 1970 the Utah governor
requested that HEW's Youth Development and Delinquency
Prevention Administration investigate the Youth Development Center and study the Utah juvenile justice system
(Wheeler and Malmstrom 1978). Among its findings were a
number involving status offenders, including a recommendation that they be removed from the jurisdiction of the
juvenile court.

Also in 1971 the Utah legislature passed SB 73, which
removed runaways from the jurisdiction of the juvenile
court. Part of the reasoning behind this was that large
numbers of pre-1971 cases had involved single episodes of

running away or disobedience, and the court did not have time or staff to involve itself in nonchronic problems (Utah Board of Juvenile Court Judges 1977). SB 73 amended what was then 55-10-77 (2) (b) UCA 1953, which gave the juvenile court jurisdiction over any child who "is habitually truant from school or who has run away from his home or is otherwise beyond the control of his parents, custodian or school authorities." SB 73 deleted the portion in brackets and substituted instead "who is beyond the control of his parent, guardian or other lawful custodian to the point that this behavior or condition is such as to endanger his own welfare or the welfare of others." This officially removed from court jurisdiction not only runaways but children beyond the control of school authorities. In addition it placed limitations on what constituted an ungovernable child.

Unfortunately, the legislature at the time did not assign responsibility for runaways to any other agency, nor did it appropriate funds to provide services to runaways and their families. The result was confusion, anger, and frustration--followed by apathy--on the part of law enforcement and social services personnel. The traditional social services agencies were not interested in providing services to runaways, were not prepared to handle such youth, and had no funds allocated to them for such services. Several observers felt that law enforcement, frustrated by its inability to deal effectively with runaway referrals, began to relabel runaways as ungovernables and to refer them to the juvenile court under that heading (Wheeler and Malmstrom 1978). While some relabeling is evident statewide, we found that the total number of runaways and ungovernables actually dropped for a period following the passage of SB 73.

The issue of juvenile court jurisdiction had long been debated in Utah. It was an attempt to remove traffic offenses from its jurisdiction in 1957 that sparked the juvenile court's initial efforts toward independence. In 1971 the Utah Board of Juvenile Court Judges supported the diversion of juveniles, but it counseled the governor to take time to develop alternatives. The 1971 initiative was ultimately the product of the executive and legislature, and did not include the judicially recommended development of alternative resources.

Law enforcement agencies had also become involved in youth diversion in the early 1970s. Using LEAA funds, several departments organized youth bureau units whose duties included handling as many of the less serious cases

as possible through family crisis intervention and informal counseling or through referral to nonjudicial agencies. These units seem to have been set up in response
to frustration over the state's jurisdictional confusion
and the lack of alternatives for nonoffender treatment,
as well as from a readiness to use the available federal
money.

In 1972 the Juvenile Delinquency Prevention and Control
Act of 1968 was amended to limit HEW to funding only those
programs administered outside the juvenile justice system.
In accordance with these amendments the governor of Utah
placed the primary responsibility for the administration
of all delinquency prevention funds, regardless of source,
with the Utah Department of Social Services (DSS) as opposed to the state justice planning agency (UCCJA). Under
this administrative arrangement, delinquency prevention
in Utah came to be treated largely as a social service.
During 1973 and 1974 DSS received $325,000 in HEW delin-
quency prevention funds that were used to begin the Youth
Service System/Youth Development Project. This project
developed the pilot plans for Utah's present diversion
system and laid much of the groundwork for the 1977 act
(HB 340) that in effect removed ungovernable and runaway
youth from Utah's juvenile justice system. The philosophy
of the youth services system was that agencies should be
interdependent, with a focus on the coordination and cooperation of all agencies that deal with the problems of
youth. Mental health, law enforcement, local schools,
social services, juvenile courts, the local detention
center, county human services (where they existed), and
local civic and community groups would ideally work together for common goals.

This philosophy closely followed the youth service bureau model detailed in the 1967 report of the President's
Commission. The youth services movement in Utah had actually begun in 1972, when the system's funds were still
being distributed by UCCJA. The two major projects, however, did not begin until 1973 in Weber County (Ogden) and
1974 in Salt Lake County. Both were funded primarily by
HEW's Office of Youth Development until 1976, when the
Weber County project was discontinued and the Salt Lake
County Youth Services Center had its funding picked up on
a shared basis by Salt Lake County and the Utah Department
of Social Services. Smaller projects throughout the
state, some funded by HEW and some by LEAA, met with
varying degrees of success. The success of local youth
services diversion programs was dependent on the willing-

ness of local agencies and interest groups to work together. Many respondents contrasted the cooperative
spirit shown in Salt Lake County with a great deal of in-
terest-group fighting over jurisdictional territory in
Weber County.

In the same year that the Youth Services Center opened
(1974), Congress passed the Juvenile Justice and Delinquency Prevention Act, which offered federal funds to
states willing to participate in the diversion and deinstitutionalization of juvenile nonoffenders. Even though
the state was moving rapidly in the direction espoused by
JJDPA, Utah did not view the act as a viable means of addressing the issue. In 1975 Governor Calvin Rampton made
an executive decision that Utah ought not to participate
in JJDPA for three reasons: (1) the cost of implementation would be more than monies received through participation, (2) sufficient state-match funds were not available, and (3) the state could not make assurances that
deinstitutionalization would be completed within the initial guideline of two years. Regardless of the validity
of these arguments (largely provided by UCCJA), they were
accepted by the governor and he acted accordingly. There
was no movement toward JJDPA participation until after the
election of a new governor in 1976 and amendments to JJDPA
in 1977. In the meantime state diversion programs were
continuing, independent of act participation.

By the fall of 1976 the Salt Lake County Youth Services
Center (along with several of UCCJA's youth service bureaus) was working successfully with ungovernable and
runaway youth outside the juvenile court. Juvenile judges
backed and supported this effort because it cleared court
time for dealing with more serious offenders and was consistent with the judges' family orientation. In addition
a wide coalition had formed under the auspices of the
youth services system project to work on legislation aimed
at clearing up the status offender jurisdictional gap
created by SB 73 back in 1971.

The process of preparing and introducing the youth
services legislation (HB 340, which became law on May 10,
1977) was a prolonged and complex one involving a large
number of actors from both the state and local levels.
Their efforts were furthered by a number of influential
studies, several of which have already been mentioned.
Both the 1967 President's Commission on Law Enforcement
and Administration of Justice and the 1973 National Advisory Commission on Criminal Justice Standards and Goals
had recommended status offender diversion. In 1974 the

National Council on Crime and Delinquency recommended complete removal of status offenders from juvenile court jurisdiction. Local informants felt that these studies had great influence in Utah. In addition Utah's juvenile justice system had drawn the attention of such national advocates for the deinstitutionalization of juveniles as Kenneth Wooden in Weeping in the Playtime of Others (1976).

The most influential study done in Utah prior to the passage of HB 340 was published in 1976 by the John Howard Association of Chicago. While the overall emphasis of this study was on unified corrections, its juvenile services section touched on juvenile justice as well as corrections. The study made a number of recommendations concerning the juvenile courts, including the removal of jurisdiction over status offenders.[1]

HB 340 gave the Division of Family Services primary responsibility for the provision of services, directly or by contract, over three categories of status offenders: (1) runaway children, (2) children beyond the control of lawful custodians (including parents and guardians), and (3) children beyond the control of school authorities. It also limited juvenile court jurisdiction over those three categories to individuals who are transferred to the court by the Division of Family Services or its contracting agencies (public or private), unless the youth's actions constitute a probation violation (thereby allowing the court to assume immediate jurisdiction). Prior to transfer to the juvenile court, the division or its contracting agency must have made "earnest and persistent" efforts in dealing with the behavioral problems of the youth. Even in the face of such efforts, the youth must have run away again or demonstrated continuing behavior that threatens to endanger his or her welfare or the welfare of others to be transferred to juvenile court. It is interesting to note that in light of the 1971 law (SB 73), this conditional jurisdiction over runaways and school ungovernables represents an expansion of jurisdiction for the juvenile court, which between 1971 and 1977 had no jurisdiction in these areas.

---

[1]The impact of these recommendations is apparent in the work of the 1976 Legislative Interim Study Committee on Social Services. The concerns communicated to that committee (which did the ultimate drafting of HB 340) are summed up by Wheeler and Malmstrom (1978:21).

The system and statistics that resulted from HB 340 will be examined in the next section. We should note here, however, that the only significant resistance to HB 340 came from law enforcement agencies. Many officers feared that troublesome youth would simply be turned loose by social services personnel after the officers went to the trouble of apprehending them. As the diversion programs developed records of success, however, law enforcement agencies became more supportive of the new approach.

The strong support of the Board of Juvenile Court Judges for the diversion effort made it almost impossible for law enforcement to resist effectively. Judges were simply not going to allow their courts and detention centers to be crowded with nonoffender cases. Evidence of the judges' determination along these lines, as well as an indication of their power in status offender cases, is provided by their 1977 ruling that curfew and tobacco violations could and should be handled with a citation and forfeiture of bail. This same procedure, which requires no appearance in court if guilt is admitted, was extended in 1979 to include first-offense alcohol possession or consumption.

By 1977 Utah was ready to seriously consider JJDPA participation--a move that was supported by both the new governor and his new director of the Department of Social Services. In addition, many of the objections to the costs of participation expressed in 1975 and 1976 were rendered moot by 1977 JJDPA amendments, which increased both the amount of money available and the length of time in which to comply. Finally, the position of UCCJA had changed. UCCJA concluded in 1978 that Utah had come far in altering its status offender policies and that compliance would therefore be an achievable goal. Interviews with UCCJA staff indicated that the major motives for entering the act were the 1977 amendments and "changes in administration and policy" that appeared to be coming in OJJDP. In August 1978, when the state entered the act, a bargain was struck with OJJDP in which Utah received both 1978 and 1979 funds totaling $800,000. For the next two years the state would receive $400,000 annually, and had until August 1981 to comply fully.

The attitude toward JJDPA in Utah appears to emphasize maximum benefit with minimum risk. In addition to their 1981 deadline to reach full compliance (plus two additional years of funding if an extension was granted), Utah requested 1975 as the statistical base year for Salt Lake County and 1976 for the rest of the state, an approach that would assure the maximum statistical drop in status offender institutionalization.

It is difficult to analyze the role that UCCJA has played in implementing the Juvenile Justice and Delinquency Prevention Act. An observer receives the impression that UCCJA's espousal of the act has been less than spirited. Although lauded by many for its deinstitutionalization efforts in distributing funds and convening forums, UCCJA was accused by others of being initially unsympathetic with the goals of the act. As support for this assertion they noted that since 1978 only one state plan has been written and monitoring has been spotty.

One clear conclusion at this point is that research ought not to focus only on JJDPA and its impact in order to understand what has happened to nonoffender policies in Utah. In fact, many of Utah's efforts in this area were only indirectly connected with the act, in part because of the late date at which the state began participation. This is not to say that change was not a product of a larger trend of which JJDPA was also a part. Over the last decade Utah has been the scene of a number of state and national efforts to change juvenile justice policies. It is important to note, however, that many of these efforts had only an indirect effect on nonoffenders. Efforts directed primarily at nonoffenders have focused almost entirely on the issue of precourt diversion. In the area of placement after adjudication, almost all of the attention has centered on criminal offenders and Utah's Youth Development Center.

The Youth Development Center has always had an effect on status offender placement policies in Utah. The Youth Development Center, formerly the State Industrial School, has long been the target of criticism both from inside and outside the state, and this has brought attention to the juvenile justice system in general. The previously noted Utah juvenile justice studies of the early 1970s were largely responses to perceived problems within the Utah youth corrections system. Following the passage of HB 340, a study by Jerome Miller (1977) and one by the Utah state legislature (1978) also made a number of recommendations for change in the system.

Another problem has involved the specific issue of alternatives to the center, that is, the development of smaller out-of-home placements within the state. According to the 1976 John Howard study, the 22 group homes in Utah at that time had all been developed as alternatives to the Youth Development Center. Since that time a num-

ber of new facilities have been created with state and
federal funds under a project designated Community Alternatives for Troubled Youth (CATY). These facilities have
the specified goal of providing alternatives to the center. Although these programs were originally designed to
serve serious delinquents, many have subsequently accepted
status offenders as well, becoming part of a growing number of residential placements available to nonoffenders.
Funded with Part E monies under JJDPA, the CATY programs
included seven residential treatment facilities of group
home size. As designed, the program was intended to serve
property offenders with six or more offenses on their record (i.e., juveniles who were chronic offenders but did
not have a history of violence). Some effort has been
expended to discover what in fact has been the impact of
these programs, but little is evident yet. It is clear
that federal funds stimulated the growth of alternatives
within the state, and that subsequent project evaluations
are claiming reduced recidivism rates. Persons outside
the program complained during interviews that the alternatives were very similar to traditional group homes but
were more expensive; several of these informants, however,
were competing providers.

The CATY grant was applied for and managed by the Utah
Council on Criminal Justice Administration. At the same
time, the Department of Social Services was pursuing more
general funding for development of alternatives that could
be used both for serious offenders and for nonoffenders.
In late 1978 the Office of Juvenile Justice and Delinquency Prevention awarded Utah an $800,000 grant for the
development of alternatives, to be administered by the
Department of Social Services and not UCCJA. This unusual
arrangement was perceived to have come about for a number
of reasons, the most critical one being a clash of personalities between key personnel in OJJDP and UCCJA. In
any event, the monies were used for a number of projects,
including proctor advocate (full-time, one-on-one) and
tracker (part-time, case loads of three or four) programs
and one delinquent group home for the mentally retarded.
Although most agree that these programs would not have
come into existence without this funding, it is difficult
in Utah to trace specific funds to specific facilities and
say "this caused that." This inability is largely due to
an "open pot" philosophy in Utah social services budgeting, the basic idea being to "help yourself until the
money is gone and then make the figures match."

The federal role in these events has been largely indirect. The President's Commission, HEW, and OJJDP have all presented a consistent deinstitutionalization-of-nonoffenders message from Washington that quickly made a favorable impression on Utah actors and has not been seriously challenged since. Utah actors were therefore amenable to deinstitutionalization programs throughout the 1970s. If left to their own resources (or to their willingness to spend those resources), however, it is doubtful that meaningful alternatives to traditional juvenile justice processing would have developed. The only major effort that did not involve federal funding was SB 73 in 1971, and it created frustration and confusion because of that very lack of funded alternatives.

It can be argued that of all of the federal legislation, the 1968 Juvenile Delinquency Prevention and Control Act administered by HEW had the greatest impact on deinstitutionalization of status offenders in Utah. This act pushed the state into the business of seriously doing something about status offenders, a movement that was self-propelled thereafter. Perhaps its major effect was to provide the opportunity for local citizen groups to form, work with diverse public agencies, and address the issue of nonoffenders. The citizen groups and interaction machinery that was created as part of the early youth services system project became key elements in the two central events in Utah's deinstitutionalization experience—the formation of the model Salt Lake County Youth Services Center in 1974 and the passage of HB 340 in 1977.

State and local people were not going to be told what to do by policymakers in Washington, as evidenced by Utah's refusal to participate in the 1974 JJDPA. But when the "strings attached" were perceived to be minimal compared to the financial incentive, federal money was readily accepted to support existing local programs and goals. Utah wants to do things its own way, but it seems to wait until federal funding consistent with its goals comes along before it does anything. Utah's "own way," in turn, has definitely been influenced by federal policy.

In the day-to-day debates over nonoffender policies, one interest group that seems to stand out as especially influential is the Board of Juvenile Court Judges, the virtually autonomous "board of experts" on juvenile matters. Its consistent concern over ensuring adequate court time for, and sufficient community protection from, serious delinquents, and its conviction that the family is the best setting within which to solve less serious problems,

TABLE 14-1 Reported Status and Criminal Offenses in Utah, 1968-1979

Year	Ungov-ernable	Runaway	Transient Runaway	Possession of Alcohol	Minor in Tavern	Possession of Tobacco	Habitual Truancy	Curfew	Total Status	Status Offenses per 1,000 School Students	Total Criminal	Criminal Offenses per 1,000 School Students
1979	884		287	3,025	24	1,660	687	1,112	7,679	--	19,564	--
1978	933		295	2,769	45	1,531	859	1,187	7,619	50	17,346	114
1977	1,670		345	2,707	51	1,248	507	929	7,457	49	18,558	121
1976	2,911		*	2,421	33	1,238	496	739	7,837	52	17,394	116
1975	1,658	1,195	334	2,569	50	908	551	700	7,965	53	16,788	111
1974	1,615	1,703	501	2,709	63	1,199	608	920	9,518	64	17,315	116
1973	1,764	1,669	443	2,284	56	1,405	444	775	8,830	61	13,453	93
1972	1,358	1,905	539	1,777	77	1,383	445	948	8,432	58	11,870	82
1971	1,051	2,791	612	1,860	60	1,421	390	1,064	9,249	66	12,271	88
1970	1,147	2,550	573	1,630	--	1,363	650	1,146	9,059	65	11,421	82
1969	1,207	2,332	507	1,644	--	984	938	1,265	8,877	66	10,640	79
1968	961	1,931	490	1,523	66	747	736	1,557	8,009	62	9,680	74

Note: 1976-1979 combines ungovernable and runaway; 1969-1970 combines possession of alcohol and minor in tavern.

*In 1976 the category of transient or out-of-state runaway was not used.

Source: Juvenile Court for the State of Utah (1968-1979) and Utah State Board of Education (1968-1978). Data were compiled by the authors from these annual reports.

have often placed it in the forefront of nonoffender diversion movements.

In this respect the judges reflect the state's family-centered orientation, which in turn stems from Mormon influence. It is very difficult to gauge the impact of the Church of Jesus Christ of Latter-Day Saints (Mormons) on state policies in general. Most of those administrators interviewed in Utah's social services and juvenile justice systems are members of the Mormon Church. While few were definite about what influence membership might have on decisionmaking, unique characteristics of Utah intake data suggest that such influences might be significant. In light of the church's stance against the use of alcohol and tobacco, it is interesting to note that both judges and law enforcement officials stressed their efforts to curb alcohol and tobacco violations. Stakeouts and the use of police agents were mentioned as law enforcement techniques. This enthusiasm may account for the extraordinarily high number of reported alcohol and tobacco violations compared with other states studied in which tobacco violations, for example, were negligible (see Table 14-1).

Apart from specific policy choices, the church's influence may extend to the willingness to cooperate in decisionmaking in the first place. With most members of interest groups seeing themselves as "brothers and sisters" in the church, it is reasonable to speculate that the church would be an intangible but significant influence on the amount of cooperation that occurred.

With few forces resisting the movement toward the diversion and deinstitutionalization of nonoffenders (except those of inertia and fiscal constraint), we would expect to find great changes through the 1970s in Utah's handling of these youth. In the next section we examine the degree to which those changes have actually occurred.

OUTCOMES OF CHANGE

Our approach to measuring change in the processing of nonoffenders will be to describe the system as it has been conceptualized, and then compare it with actual numerical and policy trends in court referrals, detention, and judicial dispositions.

As indicated in the previous section, HB 340 (1977) was intended to divert local runaways and ungovernables from the juvenile court to youth services programs that were

run or contracted by the Division of Family Services.
Other status offenders, and even those committing lesser
criminal offenses, may find their way into these programs,
but there is no legal mandate to divert them from judicial
action.

From the juvenile court's point of view (as presented
by the presiding judge at that time) the implementation
of this new law presented three problems of interpretation: (1) What in fact constituted "earnest and persistent" efforts by Division of Family Services or the contracting agency in working with the status offender before
referring the matter to court? (2) What degree of aggravated behavior should exist before the juvenile court can
accept jurisdiction? (3) What, if any, limitation would
be placed on a court's action concerning juveniles referred under HB 340 (Utah Board of Juvenile Court Judges
1977). These issues were discussed among the various
participants in the new system that was set up by HB 340
(i.e., juvenile court, Division of Family Services and its
contractors, and Utah law enforcement agencies). Guidelines were developed by the juvenile court to answer these
questions and were issued as part of the Utah juvenile
court's Guidelines for Practice and Procedure (J2-1 to
2-9).

The judges dealt with the first problem, the attempt
to define earnest and persistent efforts, as a matter requiring detailed substantiation. Each petition for juvenile court jurisdiction must be accompanied by a statement
containing the following information: (a) dates when services were initiated; (b) names of caseworkers on the
case; (c) contacts with the child and parents; (d) descriptions of all services, programs, and therapy provided;
(e) times and descriptions of the child's out-of-control
behavior since services were initiated; (f) an explanation
of why the Department of Social Services has been unable
to correct the problem and why court action should be
taken; (g) what court action they recommend, why it would
be in the best interests of the child and the public, and
why it cannot be achieved without court action; and (h)
if a change of custody is recommended, an additional
statement specifically stating why the child's continuing
in the custody of parents would endanger the child or
others.

The judges' reaction to the behavior of the child was
left largely to individual discretion, but the guidelines
specify that the reactions be to "something more aggravated than the usual or typical runaway or out of control

situations." The third issue, disposition, was dealt with by a detailed series of considerations, which essentially stated that special emphasis should be placed on family ties and reconciliation, with the court recommending against accomplishing by force of law what could not be done by the persuasion of social services.[2]

We now turn to a quantitative analysis of the outcome of these policies. Table 14-1 shows an overall decrease in both the actual numbers and the rates of status offenses reported to juvenile court between 1968 and 1979. During the same period, the numbers and rates of criminal offenses have risen significantly. Figure 14-1 shows the rates for both status and criminal offenses reported. This graph further indicates that status offenses make up a decreasing proportion of the total delinquency (i.e., status and criminal) case load. Taken together, these data clearly show that changes have occurred in the pre-adjudicatory handling of status offenders (and, perhaps, criminal offenders).

It is often asserted in Utah that under SB 73, which mandated the diversion of runaways but provided no alternatives, most diverted runaways were simply relabeled as ungovernables and reported as usual to juvenile court. In 1972, the year after SB 73 was passed, there was in fact a dramatic drop of 886 (32 percent) in the number of runaway cases (from 2,791 in 1971 to 1,905 in 1972, followed by a 12 percent, 236-case drop the next year). Between 1971 and 1972 the increase of 307 ungovernable cases (up 29 percent) did not approach "canceling out" the 886-case runaway decline. And while the number of ungovernable cases rose again in 1973 (for the last time), the sum of runaway and ungovernable cases has never since approached the 1971 peak. This is especially significant in view of the fact that the juvenile population-at-risk has been increasing throughout the years reported in Table 14-1 (from 130,116 in 1968 to 151,492 in 1978, up 16.4 percent).

Data on referral rates for the years immediately following the passage of SB 73 reflect a combination of some relabeling and even more true diversion of runaways, and that diversion seems to have taken two forms. First, a number of police youth bureaus were handling some of these

---

[2]These considerations are discussed in detail in the Utah juvenile court manual, Guidelines for Practices and Procedures.

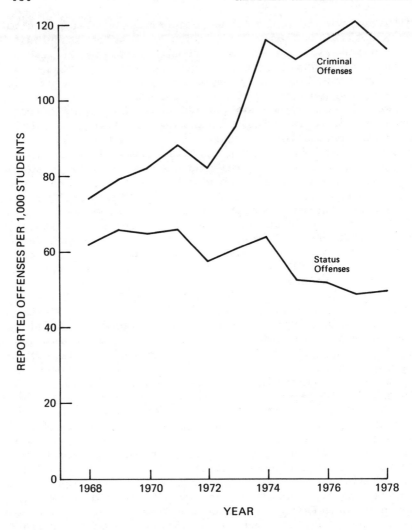

FIGURE 14-1 Utah Juvenile Court Offense Rate Per 1,000
Students in Grades 7-12, 1968-1978.

Source: Juvenile Court of the State of Utah (1968-1978)
and Utah State Board of Education (1968-1978). Data were
compiled by the authors from these annual reports.

cases informally with the families. Second, runaways were simply being ignored in many areas. Most observers feel that the latter was the most common diversion result of SB 73. In contrast, data related to the passage of HB 340, which did provide alternatives, show a different profile. Taking 1976 and 1978, the years before and after the passage of HB 340, we see a 68 percent drop (from 2,911 to 993) in runaway/ungovernable offenses reported to the court--a decline that continued in 1979 (see Table 14-1). The state's youth services approach has clearly resulted in significant diversion of at least some kinds of status offenders from juvenile court.

Statewide data that reflect long-term trends in numbers of status offender detentions are not available. A nearly universal perception, however, is that in the early 1970s about one-half of all youth in detention in Utah were status offenders. A study done in Utah by the Council of State Governments (1975) found that across a random sample of 30 days in 1974, 40 percent of the 3,874 "instances of detention" (the same youth could be counted again on different days) were preadjudicated status offenders. Similarly, the John Howard Association study (1976) found that among those youth detained in the Salt Lake County Detention Center in 1975, 46 percent were status offenders, while of those detained at Moweda (near Ogden) in 1975, 53 percent were status offenders. Where figures are available, the numbers and percentages of detainees who were status offenders have dropped since HB 340 passage in mid 1977, so that fewer than 20 percent were status offenders in 1979.

Looking at the impact of HB 340 from another angle, 11.6 percent of all known nonoffender cases between May 1, 1977, and April 30, 1978, involved the use of detention, according to the 1979 delinquency prevention plan of the Utah Council on Criminal Justice Administration. This was acclaimed as a major decrease from the (there unspecified) high percentages in the past. All evidence indicates that for the state as a whole, detention now is used much less often for nonoffenders, in accord with the desires of those who supported HB 340. A persisting problem, however, is the lack of alternatives to detention (or jail) in rural areas. The John Howard report estimated that as many as 1,100 youth were held, primarily in rural local jails, as recently as 1975. Current comparative estimates, however, are lacking.

It is even more difficult to verify patterns in judicial dispositions of nonoffender cases numerically. Utah

data on juvenile justice dispositions are generally complete; but although each disposition is listed separately,
these categories are not broken out by criminal versus
status offenders. The data therefore are useful only in
noting general dispositional trends, from which only indirect information on nonoffender dispositions can be ex-
tracted. For example, there are only three institutions
with more than 12 beds (i.e., institutions larger than
group homes) that are used by the juvenile court in Utah
(there is an out-of-state placement used infrequently for
placing a criminal offender). These three are the correctional Youth Development Center, the mental health
State Hospital Youth Center, and the mental retardation
State Training School. A total of 541 commitments, 1.9
percent of all dispositions, were made to these institutions in 1978. By comparison, in 1967 the three institutions (mainly the Youth Development Center) were sent 208
youth, or 2.2 percent of the total. The missing detail
in data for both years is the number of those who were
nonoffenders. All we can say is that for juveniles as a
whole, there apparently was not much of a shift in large
institutional placement tendencies between 1967 and 1978.
However, there are some noticeable patterns within this
aggregate picture of stability.

First, the daily population of the Youth Development
Center has gradually declined from about 500 in 1970 to
about 100 in 1979. This phenomenon apparently was the
result of two changes in judicial sentencing patterns, as
shown in Figure 14-2. These changes are (1) the relatively sharp decrease in regular commitments, beginning
in 1970, and (2) the trend toward the use of short-term
commitments of 60 to 90 days that began in the same year.
Some Utah observers asserted that those "diagnostic" periods of short-term observation were in fact used by a few
judges for "therapy" or even punishment, thus producing
increased use of the Youth Development Center in combination with a declining total population. As is evident
from Figure 14-2, this situation has developed over the
last 10 years, and therefore substantially predates the
1974 JJDPA.

Second, the proportion of Youth Development Center
placements that are nonoffenders appears to have dropped
tremendously in the late 1970s. The John Howard study
reported 85 status offender commitments to the center in
1975, while Division of Youth Services data in 1979 showed
only two (and state officials claimed that those two must
not be "pure" status offenders because the official poli-

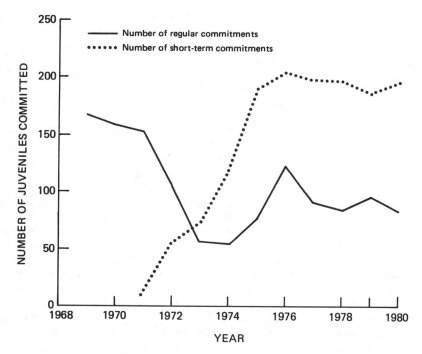

FIGURE 14-2 Juvenile Commitments to the Utah Youth Development Center, 1968-1979.

Source: Juvenile Court for the State of Utah (1968-1979).

cy, primarily developed in the aftermath of HB 340, is to use the center only for criminal offenders).

A noticeable pattern in institutional placements has been the increase in the use of the State Hospital Youth Center. The youth center (for ages 13 to 17) began in conjunction with the children's center (ages 5 to 12) in 1964, but they became separate programs in 1969. Before 1964 youth were housed with adult patients. The children's center has a capacity for 25 but is never filled, while the youth center can serve 25 males and 25 females and always has a waiting list. Both centers are officially intended to provide care and treatment for the psychotic or severely disturbed child whose IQ is within the norm. Clearly, some status offenders might qualify as appropriate candidates for these programs.

In 1967 there were seven juvenile court commitments to the state hospital, compared to 54 in 1978. The youth center program is considered innovative and successful, and there would undoubtedly be more commitments if space were available. Referrals have rapidly outpaced available space, so much so that of the 260 referrals made to the youth center in 1979, only 97 could be accommodated. Youth center staff estimated that about 75 percent of these referrals had had previous court contact, but that this court contact was sometimes only of a nonoffender nature. Mental health administrators felt that because of the limited number of alternatives in Utah the young criminal offender was often crowding the psychotic out of mental health bed space. Youth center staff indicated that their program only occasionally handles nonpsychotic behavior problems, and that those are cases of a chronic nature. In fact, a consistent lament throughout the juvenile justice, social services, and mental health systems is that Utah has a great shortage of treatment facilities for youth (offenders and nonoffenders) who exhibit serious emotional disturbance; inadequate funding is again a key factor in this shortage.

The third institution, the State Training School, receives very few placements through the juvenile court, in some years none at all. While training school records did not indicate the percentage of these placements that might be status offenders, staff members indicated that the numbers were negligible.

Utah's noninstitutional out-of-home placement of status offenders consists almost entirely of group home and foster home care contracted with private providers. The size of the private provider system relative to the juvenile population appears to have remained fairly stable over the last decade, with the exception of a jump in 1978-79 in new alternatives to the Youth Development Center (the CATY program).

Data on status offenders in out-of-home placements are very sketchy. Although deeply involved in deinstitutionalizing these youth through initial diversion, Utah remains largely unaware of what happens to status offenders in out-of-home placements (with the exception of recent efforts to remove them from the Youth Development Center). This is another ironic contrast in Utah's deinstitutionalization experience.

Status offenders apparently have been placed more often in group homes than in foster homes (the latter placement primarily receives dependent or neglected children). In 1976, for example, the Department of Social Services estimated that of 144 juveniles in group homes

per average month, 102 were status offenders while only
29 were dependent or neglected youth and 13 were criminal
offenders. There is the possibility, too recent to verify, that more status offenders are now finding their way
into group homes by entering the CATY homes, which were
set up with federal money (discussed in the previous section) in 1978-79 as alternatives to the Youth Development
Center for its less dangerous <u>criminal</u> offenders. For
example, January 1980 data from the Department of Social
Services showed 203 juveniles in group homes, compared to
the 1976 estimate of between 140 and 150. The most reasonable estimate, based on interviews and sketchy institutional and group home data, is that for status offenders
per se there has been a real decline in total out-of-home
placements in the late 1970s.

LOCAL AREAS

Within the general pattern of Utah's status offender
practices, there are significant variations among local
areas. These variations reflect differences in population
density and service resources rather than divergent philosophies for dealing with status offenders. Nearly everyone in Utah's youth-serving systems speaks of being
committed to diversion and deinstitutinalization for nonoffenders. Translating ideals into action continues to
pose problems, however, especially in sparsely populated
rural areas.

Approximately 65 percent of Utah's population resides
in four adjacent counties along the west side of the Wasatch Mountains in northcentral Utah. The principal cities in the so-called Wasatch Front area are Salt Lake
City, Ogden, and Provo. Although there are variations
among these and other Wasatch Front locations in terms of
status offender practices, these areas have much more in
common with one another than with the remainder of the
state. Consequently, we decided to compare and contrast
one urban Wasatch Front locale with one relatively distant
and rural area. This approach provides a closer look at
the types of practices and problems unique to these two
categories of Utah localities.

The most obvious choice of a local area is Salt Lake
County. It includes all of Salt Lake City--the urban
center of the state--and several surrounding suburbs, and
it contains approximately 40 percent of Utah's population.
This county, which is the heart of the juvenile court's

Second District, is also the location of the "model" non-offender diversion program, a separate social services district, one of the three full-service detention centers in the state, and most of the state's providers of services to nonoffender youth. In short, Salt Lake County contains almost every type of service found in Utah and in many respects serves as a model for the rest of the state. It is the best single location in which to view Utah's philosophy of handling status offenders in action.

The choice of a contrasting local area was not so clear-cut. We selected Uintah County, which was consistently mentioned by state-system people as being actively involved with deinstitutionalizaton problems. Located in northern Utah along the eastern border, it contains only one percent of the state's population but is the tenth most populous of Utah's 29 counties and ranks sixth in juvenile court referrals. We found Uintah County to have enough people and services to be of interest, yet distant and different enough from Salt Lake County to highlight the contrasting status offender systems in urban and rural Utah.

Referral

In all areas of Utah the juvenile court is central to the handling of status offenders. The proximity and extent of actual court services, however, varies tremendously. For example, Salt Lake County essentially is the juvenile court Second District. The Second District in 1978 was staffed by three full-time judges and a referee, and received 11,817 referrals. Uintah County, on the other hand, is served by a juvenile court headquartered over 100 miles away in Provo. Uintah currently is one of eight counties in the juvenile court's Third District. The entire Third District in 1978 was staffed by one judge and one referee (a second judge was added late in 1979), and received 1,034 (11 percent) of its 9,490 referrals from Uintah County. The juvenile court branch office is in Vernal, the major town and county seat, and it is staffed by a chief probation officer (who acts as intake officer and referee for minor offenses), two probation officers, and two support personnel. For formal court hearings, one of the judges travels from Provo to Vernal on a biweekly basis.

Trends in the number of criminal and status offense referrals in Salt Lake and Uintah Counties are shown in

Tables 14-2 and 14-3. Beginning in 1973 data are available by county and by category of offense. Prior to 1973 the percentages of reported delinquency offenses that were status or criminal are available only for Salt Lake County. Table 14-2 reveals a trend in Salt Lake County that parallels the statewide pattern of an overall decrease through the 1970s in the numbers and rates of status offenders, as well as in the proportion of status offenders among all delinquency referrals to the court. Salt Lake County now has one of the state's lowest proportions of status offenders in court. The most significant drop in the rate, proportion, and number of status offense referrals came between 1974 and 1975. That was undoubtedly due in large part to the opening of the Youth Services Center diversion program in September 1974. The next largest decrease in the rate and the number of status offense referrals came in 1977, the year of diversion legislation HB 340. We will discuss in greater detail the local dynamics of the center and HB 340 shortly. The earlier (1968-72) data on reported offenses indicate a major decline in the number and rate of status offenses following passage of SB 73 in 1971. It is important to note that criminal offense rates did not rise when status offense rates dropped in 1971-72 and 1974-75, which seems to indicate that the decline of the latter cannot be attributed solely to the practice of relabeling.

As shown in Table 14-3, the trends in Uintah County are quite different. Since 1973 the trend has been a rise in the number, rate, and proportion of status offenses, contrary to statewide trends. Even more surprising, the biggest jump occurred in 1977, the year of diversion legislation HB 340. There are several possible reasons for this unexpected finding. Some respondents referred to the Vernal area as a boomtown--the center of a recent flurry of oil and gas-related developments. In fact, Uintah County's secondary school population increased 29 percent between 1968 and 1978 (compared to only a 16 percent growth in Salt Lake County and in the state as a whole). Not only are there suddenly more juveniles, but many coming into the area are perceived to be from transient, unstable families. The rates of criminal referrals have just kept pace with population changes, but status offense referrals have doubled relative to the juvenile population between 1973 and 1978. Additionally, the implementation of the mandate in HB 340 to handle all runaways and ungovernables within the Division of Family Services has been slow to develop in Uintah County. The division of-

TABLE 14-2 Salt Lake County Juvenile Court Delinquency Referrals (1973-1978) and Reported Offenses (1968-1972)

Year	Criminal Offenses	Status Offenses	Total Offenses	Criminal Offenses per 1,000 Students Grades 7-12	Status Offenses per 1,000 Students Grades 7-12	Total Offenses per 1,000 Students Grades 7-12
1979	7,453 (77)	2,250 (23)	9,703	--	--	--
1978	7,122 (77)	2,138 (23)	9,260	113	34	147
1977	6,779 (76)	2,112 (24)	8,891	107	33	140
1976	6,198 (72)	2,465 (28)	8,663	101	40	141
1975	6,423 (73)	2,350 (27)	8,773	103	38	141
1974	7,081 (65)	3,763 (35)	10,844	116	62	178
1973	5,552 (59)	3,889 (41)	9,441	94	66	160
1972	4,668 (59)	3,244 (41)	7,912	79	55	134
1971	5,083 (57)	3,835 (43)	8,918	89	67	156
1970	4,741 (54)	4,038 (46)	8,779	83	70	153
1969	4,101 (52)	3,786 (48)	7,887	74	68	142
1968	3,603 (50)	3,602 (50)	7,205	67	66	133

Note: Numbers in parentheses represent percentage of total.

Source: Juvenile Court for the State of Utah (1968-1979) and Utah State Board of Education (1968-1978).

TABLE 14-3 Uintah County Juvenile Court Delinquency Referrals, 1973-1978

Year	Criminal Offenses	Status Offenses	Total Offenses	Criminal Offenses per 1,000 Students Grades 7-12	Status Offenses per 1,000 Students Grades 7-12	Total Offenses per 1,000 Students Grades 7-12
1979	209 (52)	194 (48)	403	--	--	--
1978	227 (53)	201 (47)	428	93	82	175
1977	246 (64)	141 (36)	387	104	60	164
1976	188 (75)	64 (25)	252	80	27	107
1975	193 (68)	91 (32)	284	86	41	127
1974	184 (68)	87 (32)	271	84	40	124
1973	208 (73)	77 (27)	285	96	36	132

Note: Number in parentheses represents percentage of total offenses.

Source: Juvenile Court for the State of Utah (1973-1979) and Utah State Board of Education (1973-1978).

fices in rural areas are small and have had neither the facilities nor the staff necessary to relieve the court of these cases quickly and efficiently. In fact, high status-to-criminal referral ratios are quite common among rural counties in Utah, even after HB 340. So the delay and difficulty involved in putting the 1977 diversion mandate into operation in Uintah County might lead us to expect a slower drop in the rate and proportion of status referrals than that which occurred in Salt Lake County, where the Youth Services Center (the contracting county diversion agency) was fully operational and prepared to implement HB 340. But that still would not explain an actual increase in status offense activity in juvenile court.

It is reasonable to speculate that the combination of population growth, renewed attention given to status offenders in the last three years, and/or boomtown fears (valid or not) of more and more youth getting out of hand have affected the way in which Uintah officials respond to status offenders. For example, local law enforcement efforts against juvenile alcohol and tobacco violations appear particularly zealous. And local schools have recently begun a concentrated effort to curb truancy, including the use of court referral on a third offense. Runaways and ungovernables who might have been handled informally in the past can now be taken to family services (and then perhaps on to juvenile court after "earnest and persistent" efforts). Unfortunately, data on specific types of status offense referrals in Uintah County over the last three years are not presently available, making it difficult to choose among these (or other) explanations. Our educated guess is that the pattern of increasing numbers, rates, and proportion of status offense referrals in Uintah County is attributable in part to all of the above-mentioned factors. One juvenile court administrator said that in rural areas served by circuit-riding judges, local officials refer more minor offenses to court to give the judge something on the calendar when he comes to town.

The source of the greatest number of status offender referrals to juvenile court in Utah has always been police agencies. The complexity of law enforcement agencies in Salt Lake and Uintah Counties differs significantly. In Salt Lake County nine city police departments, in addition to the county sheriff and state highway patrol, refer status offenders to the Second District Juvenile Court. Most of the law enforcement referrals come from the Salt

Lake City Police Department and the Salt Lake County Sheriff's Office. By contrast, in Uintah County there is just the sheriff's office, the Vernal City Police Department, and the highway patrol.

Before SB 73's passage in 1971 Salt Lake County law enforcement agencies were almost the sole source of referrals to juvenile court. In 1970 they provided 95 percent of all delinquency referrals (criminal and status) and 77 percent of dependency and neglect referrals; about one-half of all delinquency offenses reported were status offenses. Then in the early 1970s there was an increase in the in-house diversionary activities of the major law enforcement agencies in Salt Lake County (county sheriff and Salt Lake City police). The police department formed a new youth bureau at this time; but respondents described it as cumbersome, and the department seemed quite pleased to turn over status offender diversion to the Youth Services Center when it became fully operational in 1975. While Salt Lake City's police youth bureau began and ended rather quickly, the county sheriff's office took a more steady course of gradually expanding the diversionary duties of their longstanding juvenile division.

The post-1971 reduction in Salt Lake County status offense referrals seems to have been the result both of (a) police simply ignoring more status offenders, especially runaways, and (b) police in-house diversion efforts. These efforts were in turn spawned by early national diversion philosophy statements, Utah's tradition of preserving family unity, a temporary jurisdictional and service gap created by SB 73, and the availability of LEAA grant money for police projects.

The use of LEAA money was also noticeable in the rural areas. In 1975 Uintah County entered an arrangement with two neighboring counties to share a special juvenile officer. Since 1977 (except for a 10-month funding loss), the county sheriff has employed a federally funded deputy assigned solely to juvenile matters. However, the specific impact of this program and the results of Utah's 1971 SB 73 diversion bill are difficult to ascertain in rural Uintah County. The only information we have for specific offenses during the 1968-1977 period is the recollection of the county sheriff. He cited much greater involvement of law enforcement officials in truancy referrals in the pre-1977 era. He also said that before HB 340, the county locked up runaways and ungovernables and routinely referred them to juvenile court. Our best guess is that HB 340 in 1977 was the first event that had any major impact on

police practices regarding court referrals of status offenders in Uintah County, and that SB 73 in 1971 was
largely ignored in rural areas.

There was a particularly significant event in Salt Lake
County between the 1971 (SB 73) and 1977 (HB 340) legislative efforts regarding status offenders. That was the
opening of the Salt Lake County Youth Services Center
(YSC) in September 1974. The YSC is an excellent example
of the impact that federal philosophies and grants have
had on Utah's status offender services system. With the
diversion and deinstitutionalization thrust of the 1967
report of the President's Commission and the grant-pro-
vision structure set up by the 1968 Juvenile Delinquency
Prevention and Control Act as amended in 1972, the state
was set for implementation of the youth services center
concept in Salt Lake County. Initially funded by HEW
through the Utah Department of Social Services, the Salt
Lake County Youth Services Center proved to be the most
successful youth services system project in the state.

The Salt Lake County YSC was developed through the cooperative efforts of the juvenile court, Division of
Family Services, local schools, mental health and law
enforcement agencies, the detention center, and civic
groups. Virtually everyone involved recalls that teamwork
and the nearly unanimous commitment to diversion saved
what was initially an underfunded experimental program.
The original design of the center included professional
staff loaned from family services and mental health, along
with MSW students from the University of Utah. That arrangement could not last indefinitely, and the center was
in danger of losing its professional staff because of
budget constraints between 1976 and 1978. Utah's 1978
entrance into the 1974 JJDPA stabilized the center's budget by providing funding for four professionals. At the
end of 1980 the budget for the center was supplied one-
quarter each by county, state, Title XX, and OJJDP funds.

The success of the Youth Services Center was assured
by a combination of strong support from the County Commission on Youth (formed with the Juvenile Delinquency
Prevention and Control Act money) and from juvenile court.
When it opened in 1974, the local presiding judge issued
an order to all law enforcement agencies in the county to
take status offenders to the center. He also declared the
center a place of shelter. While this order was of questionable legality, it has been credited by Utah observers
with ensuring the success of YSC: "The Youth Services
Center would never have opened its doors or succeeded

without the Court's support and the specific order of the Judge" (Wheeler and Malmstrom 1978:1).

Even though there was some initial reluctance on the part of law enforcement to support the nonsecure facility, they did not substantially resist the judge's order to use it. Most police administrators now congratulate the center for a job well done, and most officers consistently take status offenders, along with some lesser criminal offenders, to the center rather than to court. The number of juvenile court status offense referrals in Salt Lake County dropped 38 percent (from 3,763 to 2,350) between 1974 and 1975 (see Table 14-2). Because criminal delinquency referrals also declined by 9 percent (from 7,081 to 6,423) during the same period, we can assume that the drop was not merely due to relabeling.

The success that the Youth Services Center exhibited between 1974 and 1977 undoubtedly influenced the legislature's willingness to divert all runaways and ungovernables by passing HB 340 in May 1977; that bill can be viewed as a mandate to implement the Salt Lake County YSC model statewide. This law certainly accelerated the diversion of status offenders in Salt Lake County. In spite of increasing population, the total number of Salt Lake County status offense referrals to juvenile court declined slightly in the 1977-79 period from the already low figure in 1976 (see Table 14-2). Even more specifically, Figure 14-3 shows that a sharp _rise_ in the center's runaway/ungovernable intakes from 1976 to mid-1980 is paralleled by a sharp _decline_ in local runaway/ungovernable court referrals held in detention during that period. The Salt Lake County Sheriff's Office apprehended 136 percent more runaways in 1977 than in 1976 (946 and 401, respectively) and 62 percent more ungovernables (202 and 125). This supports the view that many status offenders were still being ignored in 1976 as a result of SB 73. It also shows that the increase in police activity did not spill over into the court. The Youth Services Center prepared a breakdown of its population for the first half of 1979: 85 percent of the center's 180 cases per month (average) were runaways or ungovernables, 1 percent were dependent or neglected, and 14 percent were "other." Only 10 cases per month (or 6 percent) were sent to detention and four (2 percent) were petitioned to juvenile court. In sum, the Youth Services Center serves primarily as _the_ program for status offenders in Salt Lake County, and very minimally as a funnel into juvenile court.

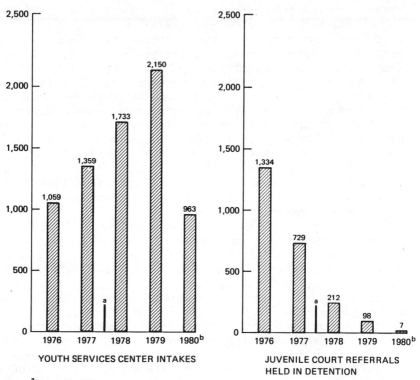

YOUTH SERVICES CENTER INTAKES

JUVENILE COURT REFERRALS
HELD IN DETENTION

[a]Passage of HB 340.
[b]Totals through May 1980.

FIGURE 14-3   Runaway/Ungovernable Status Offender in Salt
Lake County, 1976-1980.

Source: Juvenile Court for the State of Utah (1976-1979)
and unpublished data provided for this study by the Salt
Lake County Detention Center.

The youth services situation in Uintah County is quite
different.   Instead of a full-service, professionally
staffed, independent youth services center, youth services
are the responsibility of the Vernal office of the Division of Family Services.   The funding given to the division in 1977 to implement youth services programs was
woefully inadequate.   The only way they could provide diversionary services in rural areas was to turn to the
UCCJA for grant money.   Consequently, with passage of HB
340 in May 1977, the Vernal youth services program was

funded through UCCJA. Funding for that program was picked up by the division in 1980.

A primary objective of the Vernal youth services program is to maintain a 24-hour, seven-days-a-week intake process. Because this is almost impossible with only one youth services worker, an arrangement has been made for the three staff members in child protective services to work with the youth services worker so that one of them is on call at all times. Any police officer who encounters a local runaway or ungovernable is supposed to be able to reach the youth services program through the already-existing protective services 24-hour crisis line. But a common complaint throughout rural Utah concerns reluctance by Division of Family Services personnel to respond promptly after working hours. And some police officers resent the extra time and effort that they are required to spend with a youth whom they would have simply locked up before HB 340. Use of an electronic paging system in Vernal, however, seems to have made the system as efficient as it can be under the circumstances.

All respondents reported that juvenile court referrals in Uintah County for runaway/ungovernable behavior have decreased as a result of the youth services program. Statistical verification of diversion from juvenile court, however, is difficult to obtain. As mentioned earlier and as shown in Table 14-3, both the number and proportion of status offenses referred to court from Uintah County have increased since HB 340.

Rough figures from the Vernal office of the Division of Family Services indicate that during September and October 1978 they received 73 youth services referrals. Of these, apparently 23 were runaways/ungovernables who were handled without court referral, 35 were truancy cases who were handled in the truancy program, and 15 of unlisted type who were referred to juvenile court. Although it seems that at least some diversion of status offenders, especially runaways and ungovernables, is occurring, it is difficult to ascertain the overall impact of the Vernal youth services program, because it also seems that many truants, who may have simply been handled informally before the diversion program was started, are now finding their way into the program. And once in the division's program, they become candidates for court referral.

The policy toward truancy remains in a state of flux in Utah. It is expected that a bill to add truancy and curfew violations to the HB 340 mandate will be presented during the 1981 legislative session. In the meantime,

schools seem to be paying greater attention to this kind
of behavior than in the past, especially in cooperative
arrangements with the new youth services programs. Utah
schools have largely been left holding the bag as law enforcement agencies in general have become increasingly
reluctant to occupy themselves with truancy. In both Salt
Lake and Uintah Counties, officers referred to truancy as
"the school's problem these days."

In Uintah County most schools have developed a truancy
policy that includes a parent conference for the first
offense, suspension and a parent conference for the second
offense, and suspension and referral to a youth services
program for the third offense. If the Division of Family
Services is convinced that the school has put forth "earnest and persistent" efforts to solve the problem, they
in turn will attempt "earnest and persistent" efforts
themselves. Only if the division's efforts fail will the
case be referred to juvenile court. Still, an unspecified
number of truancy referrals do make it to court via this
route.

Truancy is not the only example of increased attention
given to status offenders in Uintah County in recent
years. Federally funded juvenile officer programs, which
began to reach full force in the area at about the same
time as HB 340 was passed (1977), have along with the
truancy programs promoted a potential widening of the net
of official attention given to status offenders in Uintah
County. These factors may have contributed to the increase in status offender referrals in that area since
1977.

Net-widening is also evident in urban Salt Lake County,
but its impact has been reduced there by the dominant
posture of the Salt Lake County Youth Services Center.
The center has become the place to which officers take
status offenders and even less serious offenders. While
Salt Lake County schools are also taking a greater role
in truancy problems, several are developing that role in
cooperation with the center, and the center seldom refers
these cases on to juvenile court.

Judges in both local areas report that curfew or tobacco cases seldom reach the courtroom itself. This observation, combined with the increasing numbers of juvenile court referrals for these offenses, indicates the
near exclusive use of the citation technique for handling
these types of offenders.

Detention

The statewide detention policies and practices (outlined
above) largely describe the situation in Salt Lake County.
There is a 40-bed detention facility located adjacent to
the juvenile court offices that includes educational and
some recreational facilities. Detention in Utah is restricted to predispositional processing of cases and
pending placement. The law emphatically provides that
detention will not be used if it is safe to release the
child to parental custody. Detention center and probation
intake staff have a great deal of authority over whom they
will admit.

As noted above, Salt Lake County detained many status
offenders, about one-half of all detainees in the county,
during the early and mid-1970s (John Howard Association
1976). Figures on the numbers and proportions of status
offenders who were detained in Salt Lake County from 1977
to 1979 (figures for 1979 are for January through June,
doubled) are presented in Table 14-4. They show a significant (50 percent) reduction from 1977 to 1978 in the
number of local runaways and ungovernables who were detained. This reflects the considerable impact of HB 340
(May 1977). The 1979 totals do show some bouncing back
in runaway and ungovernable detentions, but those totals
still represent a net decrease of 98 cases (32 percent)
from the 1977 figures. For other categories of status
offenders, HB 340 did not seem to have much of an impact.
The number of youth who were detained for these offenses
remained quite stable, although their percentage of all
detentions declined from 9 percent in 1977 to 7 percent
in 1979, suggesting that runaways and ungovernables are
not being detained under other labels within the larger
status offense category.

The existence of several local alternatives to detention make it comparatively easy for Salt Lake County officials to handle status offenders in other ways. These
nonsecure alternatives include shelter homes, a "home detention" program, and a county-owned shelter facility adjacent to the detention center. The shelter facility is
used to keep older status offenders (and less serious
criminal offenders) out of detention. Private shelter
homes often refuse to take older youth because Utah will
not accept liability for damage to shelter homes that is
caused by the clients.

It is precisely the absence of such alternatives that
makes the detention situation so different in rural Uintah

TABLE 14-4   Status Offenders Detained in Salt Lake County, 1977-1979

Offense	1977	1978	1979*
Local runaway	179	90	110
Ungovernable	127	62	98
Transient runaway	114	74	98
Minor in a tavern	2	3	6
Possession of alcohol	28	48	44
Possession of tobacco	0	1	6
Curfew violation	25	14	16
Total status offenders	475	292	378
(with percentage of	(24% of	(13% of	(16% of
all detainees)	1,983)	2,194)	2,400)
Local runaway/ungovern-able subtotal (with percentage of all detainees)	306 (15%)	152 (7%)	208 (9%)
Other status offense subtotal (with percent-age of all detainees)	169 (9%)	140 (6%)	170 (7%)

Note: These figures are only for those who were detained more than 8 hours. The figures for the other "quick release" closely parallel these, with the number of quick releases averaging about 40 percent of the number of regular detentions for every category.

*Figures were only available for the first half of 1979. The figures shown here were obtained by doubling those half-year figures.

Source: Unpublished data provided for this study by the Salt Lake County Detention Center.

County. When official reaction to juvenile misbehavior is deemed necessary in Uintah County, the only local op-tions available for temporary care have been (a) release to parents, (b) placement in a private shelter or emer-gency foster home, or (c) lockup in one of two "juvenile detention" cells in the county jail. And while the four shelter/foster homes in Uintah County are adequate for serving younger and milder youth, very seldom will any of them accept older, out-of-state, or more troublesome juveniles.

There is very little statistical information available on Uintah County juvenile jailings. The Uintah County sheriff and the local juvenile court chief intake officer, however, have each served in the area for many years, and both report a great decrease in the use of the jail for status offenders, especially since HB 340 was passed in 1977. The judge in Provo issued an order in 1978 that no juvenile could be held in the county jail for more than 48 hours. An additional judicial statement in 1980 has essentially closed the jail to all types of juvenile offenders.

In the absence of suitable local options in Uintah County, the alternative to jail detention is transporting the youth about 155 miles to the nearest detention center, the Utah County Youth Home near Provo. This places a tremendous time, expense, and manpower burden on the sheriff's office. It is not as inconvenient now as it was before the sheriff had the services of the LEAA-funded juvenile officer (who handles the transporting), but it is still a burden. Nonetheless, most juveniles are now transferred to the Utah County Youth Home, whereas until early 1980 some simply "sat it out" in the county jail.

An examination of all detention admissions to the Utah County Youth Home from 1971 through 1979 reveals only limited use of that facility by Uintah County. It is only in the last two years (1978-79) that a significant number (mostly criminal delinquents) have been transported. For our purposes, it is interesting to note that HB 340 in 1977 did not reduce the number of runaway/ungovernable official detentions transported from Uintah County. The numbers are too small to be the basis of firm conclusions, but they are consistent with the overall picture that the Vernal youth services program has limited facilities and nonsecure alternatives. Plans are underway to alleviate this situation, but they are largely dependent on the availability of funding. UCCJA has held out some hope for the possible funding of a shelter home and perhaps even a second transportation officer. Federal funding for improvement in the detention situation is definitely not forthcoming, however, due to an OJJDP decision that their funds may not be used for the construction of any sort of secure facility, regardless of local need. The county itself is now moving toward a shared-cost arrangement with the state that may result in a viable detention facility for Uintah County.

Disposition

Judges from both Salt Lake and Uintah Counties responded similarly to questions about the out-of-home placement of status offenders. They have always preferred to keep status offenders in the home and are more committed to that goal now than in the past. The judges who were interviewed claimed that "very few" status offenders get placed, and that the number has been decreasing. They backed off, however, from a "100 percent deinstitutionalization" stance and freely admitted the use of institutions as a last resort for status offenders with long histories of troublesome behavior (often including criminal acts, they point out). It is therefore safe to assume that a small number of status offenders are still being placed out-of-home from both local areas, especially if they repeatedly refuse to stay at home.

Types of placement and alternatives to placement vary greatly by location. In Uintah County the only residential care available is foster care; there are no group homes or larger institutions within 100 miles. Local officials therefore are reluctant to recommend more than foster care, as that means removing the juvenile from his or her community. One of the 80 foster care homes in the area is usually tried first, but those homes cannot be coerced into taking (or keeping) older or difficult youth, and there may be no alternative to a distant group home.

The specific placement decision does not belong to the judge in Utah. The judge grants custody to the Division of Family Services, which officially handles placement. However, a great deal of behind-the-scenes influence can be exerted by judges or court staff. The ultimate placement decision is usually the result of a cooperative effort by both family services and court staff who feel they have a stake in the case. The juvenile court then requires frequent progress reports on the child from the division, and can rule division workers in contempt of court if they do not seem to be following the prearranged treatment plan.

A family-centered philosophy is present in both Uintah and Salt Lake Counties. In situations in which Salt Lake County juvenile court or Division of Family Services personnel feel constrained to use an out-of-home placement,

however, they have many more local alternatives from which
to choose. Some elements of the foster care situation are
similar to Uintah County's in that there are in general
an adequate number of homes, foster homes are the most
preferred and most often used type of residential placement, and there can be difficulty in placing older, more
troublesome youth. But there the similarities with Uintah
County end.

SUMMARY AND CONCLUSIONS

Several themes stand out in Utah's experience with the
deinstitutionalization of status offenders since the late
1960s. One is that federal influence has been significant
throughout this period, with a noticeable movement toward
deinstitutionalization as the result. This has not been
a simple process of Washington's making policies and
Utah's carrying them out. Rather, three stages of primarily local activity are identifiable in the evolution
of deinstitutionalization policy, each of which was aug-
mented by federal influence. First was the period of
consciousness-raising concerning alternative approaches
to nonoffenders, lasting from about 1965 to 1970. Utah's
family-centered ethos was amenable to deinstitutionalization programs, but stability takes less energy than
change, and change always contains an element of expense.
It was the report of the President's Commission in 1967
and the Juvenile Delinquency Prevention and Control Act
of 1968 that lent legitimacy and plausibility to the deinstitutionalization philosophy.

Once the issue had been raised, the second stage began.
It was a period of serious debate among local interest and
advocacy groups and agencies, at its most intense between
1970 and 1974, but still continuing. Salt Lake County
witnessed the most extensive and consequential discussion,
partly because of its position as the demographic and
governmental center of the state. The seed money from HEW
under the 1968 act, which spawned the youth services program and designated Salt Lake County as a pilot area, made
possible a heightened degree of local interaction. It
also created the County Commission on Youth, which included representatives from education, law enforcement,
social services, mental health, juvenile court, and the
community at large. Not only did this commission create
a forum for discussion of youth issues, but it probably
ranks second behind the Board of Juvenile Court Judges in

overall influence on deinstitutionalization developments,
especially in lobbying for legislative change.

The third stage of local activity was the implementation of funded alternatives to detention, adjudication,
and institutional corrections. It began in earnest with
the opening of the Salt Lake County Youth Services Center
in September 1974. This event too bears the stamp of
federal influence. The center came about as a result of
the youth services system grant and the activity of the
commission on youth previously mentioned. In the meantime, several smaller but similar diversion programs in
both social service and law enforcement agencies were receiving initial funds from another federal source, the Law
Enforcement Assistance Administration. It is very unlikely that Utah would have been able to implement the
youth services diversion system in 1977 (under HB 340)
without this federal funding. It was precisely the lack
of funding, in fact, that scuttled Utah's initial diversion effort in 1971 (i.e., SB 73). Similarly, at the
placement end of the system, Utah only began developing
alternatives to institutions with the receipt of a good
financial package from OJJDP in 1978. In short, the process seems to be: (a) become aware of the problem, (b)
reach agreement through discussion that something should
be done about the problem, and (c) accept federal programs
that will fund alternatives when the money-to-restrictions
ratio becomes appealing.

Within this general scenario, several specific themes
also appear in Utah's experience. Fiscal conservatism
toward spending state and local funds is clearly an element of the overall picture. But so is "law and order"
conservatism toward serious juvenile criminal offenders.
Concern over community protection against these youth has
been very evident throughout this period, especially among
the juvenile court judges. And with the judges as the
most influential of all local actors (another theme), the
issue has had a great impact. Diversion of status offenders not only saves juveniles from negative labeling
and gets their families involved in handling family difficulties, but it clears court calendars for ever increasing numbers of criminal cases.

The deinstitutionalization of status offenders also
makes room for criminal offenders in expensive secure facilities. When the institutional population is exclusively criminal, increased attention can be paid to security and community protection. In short, fiscal and
judicial conservatism (relative to criminal offenders)

have complemented a genuine commitment to status offender
deinstitutionalization.

The role of law enforcement youth programs in Utah is
also important. Many agencies began diversionary youth
bureaus in the early 1970s. When the unfunded 1971 SB 73
created a services gap, law enforcement agencies established their own approaches to status offenders. This
they did with LEAA grant money. Some of these programs
still operate, but do so within the confines of HB 340 and
subsequent policy statements by the Board of Juvenile
Court Judges. Others let the HB 340 youth-services-
approach replace their youth bureaus.

At the same time, many law enforcement agencies received (and still receive) LEAA money for specialist juvenile officers. Some of these programs have had contradictory implications for nonoffenders. With more time
available to pay attention to juvenile matters, more juvenile acts of all kinds are detected. Some of this increased detection involves status offenses--especially
alcohol and, to a lesser extent, tobacco violations. So
the net has widened, especially in rural areas where personnel shortages precluded this kind of attention before.
On the other hand, the agency now has the capability to
transport the juvenile in lieu of temporary jail custody.
As a result, juveniles are placed in rural Utah jails much
less often than in the past, partly because of juvenile
officer programs.

Before leaving the subject of alcohol and tobacco violations, we should again note that in Utah these status
offenses have not undergone the same diversionary changes
in jurisdiction as have running away and ungovernable
behavior. Even though they remain under the juvenile
court's primary jurisdiction, and even though some law
enforcement agencies exert relatively strenuous efforts
to apprehend them, tobacco and first-offense alcohol violators are still less likely to be institutionalized than
in the past. Citation and forfeiture of bail, which recently has been implemented and widely used, effectively
diverts most of these youth from detention. Others are
diverted to the runaway/ungovernable youth services programs. In terms of correctional institutional placement,
these offenders have rarely been handled in that manner
anyway. So although Utah has not deinstitutionalized
alcohol/tobacco offenders in as complete a manner as runaways and ungovernables, movement in that direction is
real. Moreover, in the next few years we may well see
first-offense alcohol, tobacco, and/or curfew violations
included in the HB 340 diversion mandate.

This brings us to our final theme--the dichotomy between urban and rural Utah. Blanket policies are almost
never applicable to both areas. As a matter of fact, the
perceived inapplicability to rural Utah of the guidelines
in the 1974 JJDPA was a major reason for Utah's long delay
in participation. Resources and populations are simply
too diverse across Utah to allow uniform policy implementation.

Utah's nonoffender services programs generally have
begun in Salt Lake County, then have spread to other urban
areas, and finally have been incompletely copied in rural
locations. As they spread, they become thinner. Salt
Lake County's full range of youth services and placement
options are contrasted with Uintah County's one youth
services worker, a few foster/shelter homes, and a
jail--and many counties have less. Virtually all of Utah
seems to embrace a philosophy of deinstitutionalization,
but there is tremendous disparity in the abilities of
various areas to implement that philosophy.

REFERENCES

Council of State Governments (1975) Status Offenders: A
    Working Definition. Lexington, Ky.: Council of State
    Governments.
John Howard Association (1976) Unified Corrections Study
    for the State of Utah. Chicago: John Howard
    Association.
Juvenile Court for the State of Utah (1976-1980)
    Guidelines for Practice and Procedure. Manual with
    updates. Salt Lake City, Utah: Administrative Office
    of the Juvenile Court.
Juvenile Court for the State of Utah (1968-1979). Annual
    Reports. Salt Lake City, Utah: Administrative Office
    of the Juvenile Court.
Miller, Jerome (1977) Report on Technical Assistance on
    Consultation on Developing and Implementing a
    Continuum of Services to Troubled Youth in Utah to the
    Division of Family Services. Washington, D.C.:
    Arthur D. Little Inc.
National Advisory Commission on Criminal Justice
    Standards and Goals (1973) Police. Washington, D.C.:
    U.S. Government Printing Office.
National Council on Crime and Delinquency (1974)
    Jurisdiction over Status Offenders Should be Removed
    from the Juvenile Court: A Policy Statement.

Hackensack, N.J.: National Council on Crime and
Delinquency.
President's Commission on Law Enforcement and
Administration of Justice (1967) Task Force Report:
Juvenile Delinquency and Youth Crime. Washington,
D.C.: U.S. Government Printing Office.
Utah Board of Juvenile Court Judges (1977) Juvenile Court
Discussion Statement on Status Offenders Under SB
340. Memorandum by Paul C. Keller, Presiding Judge.
Utah State Board of Education (1966-1978) Annual Reports
of the State Superintendent of Public Instruction.
Utah Public School System, Salt Lake City, Utah.
Utah State Legislature (1978) Final Report of the Blue
Ribbon Task Force on Corrections. Salt Lake City,
Utah: Office of Legislative Research.
Wheeler, James, and Malmstrom, Willard (1978) The State
of Utah's Effort Toward Diverting Status Offenders
from the Juvenile Justice System. Division of Family
Services. Salt Lake City, Utah: Department of Social
Services.
Wooden, Kenneth (1976) Weeping in the Playtime of
Others. New York: McGraw-Hill.

OFFICIALS INTERVIEWED

Mark Alred, Data Specialist, Division of Youth
Corrections, Department of Social Services
Lt. Atkinson, Salt Lake City Police Department, Youth Unit
David Attridge, Juvenile Justice Specialist, Utah Council
on Criminal Justice Administration
Douglas Bates, Offender Education Program, State Board of
Education
Max Beatty, Director of Guidance, Intermountain Indian
School, Bureau of Indian Affairs
John Billings, Director, Division of Family Services,
Youth Corrections, Department of Social Services
Darrell Bingham, Youth Corrections, District 2B,
Department of Social Services
Joseph Boren, Youth Officer, Vernal Police Department
James Brady, Director, Salt Lake County Alcohol School
Barbara Burnett, Chairperson, Utah Juvenile Justice
Advisory Board
Kent Christiansen, Administrator, Substitute Care and
Protective Services, District 3, Department of Social
Services

Shirley Cox, former Director, Children Youth and
   Families, Department of Social Services
Paul Dean, Supervisor, Youth Diversion and Family
   Functioning Project, District 3, Department of Social
   Services
Don Dixon, Director, Utah State Hospital Youth Center
Malcolm Evans, Director, Utah County Youth Home
William Evans, Probation Officer, District 1, Utah
   Juvenile Court
LaMar Eyre, Director, Salt Lake County Youth Services
   Center
Representative Francis Farley, Utah State Legislature
Thomas Freestone, Administrator, District 3, Juvenile
   Court, Vernal Office
Doug Gale, Supervisor, District 5, Department of Social
   Services
Judge Regnal W. Garff, Jr., District 2, Utah Juvenile
   Court
Ralph Garn, Former Director, Youth Development Center
Lt. Joe Gee, Salt Lake County Sheriff, School Project
Kathryn Getz, Director, Catholic Charities
Cindy Haag, Medical Assistance, Department of Social
   Services
Richard Hanks, Medical Assistance, Department of Social
   Services
Cathy Hardy, Juvenile Specialist, Utah Council on
   Criminal Justice Administration
Lt. Ray Haueter, Salt Lake County Sheriff, Youth Bureau
Officer Henchcliff, Youth Officer, Sandy Police Department
Judge Merrill Hermansen, District 3, Utah Juvenile Court
Representative Stephen Holbrook, Utah State Legislature
Tim Holm, Director, District 2A, Department of Social
   Services
Elizabeth Hunter, Field Services, Title XX Specialist,
   Department of Social Services
Warner Klem, Data Specialist, District 2B, Department of
   Social Services
Judge John Farr Larson, District 2, Juvenile Court
Mary Lines, Adoption Specialist, Department of Social
   Services
William Low, Protective Services Specialist, Department
   of Social Services
Willard Malmstrom, Detention Specialist, Division of
   Youth Corrections, Department of Social Services
Randall McCathern, Director, CYCIS-DATA Project,
   Washington, D.C.
Heber Mehr, Permanent Planning Specialist, Department of
   Social Services
Frank Mendez, Staff, Adolescent Residential Treatment and
   Education Center

Jerome Miller, National Institute for Corrections Alternatives Washington, D.C.

Anthony Mitchell, Director, Utah Department of Social Services

Morris Neilson, Chief Intake Officer, District 2, Juvenile Court

William Nelson, Group Care Specialist, Division of Family Services, Youth Corrections Department of Social Services

Dr. Elwood Pace, Director Special Education Program, Utah Board of Education

Elaine Pachecco, Youth Services, District 5, Department of Social Services

Charles Patterson, Deputy Director, Division of Mental Health, Department of Social Services

Sally Patterson, Foster Care Specialist, Department of Social Services

Mauray Payne, LDS Social Services, Provo

Doug Peterson, Fiscal Specialist, Department of Social Services

Michael Phillips, Deputy Administrator, Utah Juvenile Court

Nancy Plant, Staff, Salt Lake County Commission on Youth

Melvin Sawyer, Administrator, District 3, Utah Juvenile Court

Meredith Simmons, Data Specialist, Department of Social Services

Veon Smith, Former Youth Services Specialist, Department of Social Services

Mark Soler, Attorney, Youth Law Center, San Francisco, California

Arden Steward, Uintah County Sheriff

Scott Surrey, National Institute for Corrections Alternatives, Washington, D.C.

Mae Taylor, Special Education, Utah Board of Education

Heber Tibbits, former Alternatives Specialist, Division of Youth Corrections, Department of Social Services

James Walker, Director, Salt Lake County Detention Center

James Wallis, Assistant Director, Child Welfare, District 2B, Department of Social Services

William Walsh, Church of Jesus Christ of Latter-day Saints

William Ward, Administrator, Division of Family Services, Department of Social Services

Sharon Wasek, Medical Assistance, Department of Social Services

Norma Webb, Social Services, Utah State Training School

Richard Wheelock, Computer Specialist, Division of Family Services, Department of Social Services

Kent Worthington, ESEA Title I, Utah Board of Education

Competing Definitions of Troublesome Children and Youth in Virginia

15

STEVEN L. NOCK *and*
WAYNE M. ALVES

INTRODUCTION

A central theme in the deinstitutionalization of "troublesome children" in Virginia has involved the use of alternative definitions of "status offenders" and "delinquents" so that certain types of children no longer fall within the jurisdiction of some or all of Virginia's juvenile justice system. Relabeling of children as a response to the national deinstitutionalization movement has occurred both formally (via legal codification) and informally (via local response of judges, service providers, and other professionals dealing with juveniles) in Virginia. On the formal side, state law relating to troublesome children has been successively refined to sharply distinguish juvenile delinquents from children in need of services (CHINS), Virginia's current label for status offenders. Concomitant with this shift in legal definitions has been the restriction of the juvenile court's ability to commit CHINS to the Virginia Board of Corrections. Informally, the deinstitutionalization of youth in Virginia has been played out in local areas of the state, where this process has hinged on the judicial philosophy of local juvenile and domestic relations court judges. In this study we look at how deinstitutionalization has been effected in Richmond and Charlottesville.

464

We use the term CHINS or status offender to refer to a child adjudicated guilty of some offense applicable only to juveniles. We refer to troublesome children to mean those juveniles with behavior problems that some would call status offenses or delinquencies. CHINS is a judicial determination; troublesome is not.

Two essentially different judicial philosophies regarding CHINS are operative in Virginia, both relating to the appropriate role of juvenile and domestic relations courts in CHINS cases. One view holds that the court should become actively involved in mediating the problems of troublesome children and their families. Underlying this view is the presumption that the court is best able to decide what is best for the CHINS. The other view stresses the right of children and parents to noninterference from the court when a child or his or her family is denied help to which they are legally entitled.

Informal relabeling occurs at the local level as these alternative philosophies are translated into operating policies. The particular model of CHINS versus other children in trouble that is held by the local juvenile and domestic relations court judge influences most of those who deal with children in the community. We will describe three views (or models) of CHINS in a later section. Briefly, the first sees CHINS as being no different from other children in trouble. The second view acknowledges some, albeit minimal, differences between CHINS and other children in trouble. The third view stresses the unique needs of CHINS apart from those of other children. These views determine the operating practices of the court and its staff, especially the patterns of diversion and disposition of troublesome children. Such practices, in turn, influence the perception of local service providers as to what constitutes "appropriate" diversion and disposition strategies.

In this study we examine the history and organization of juvenile justice in Virginia as it pertains to status offenders, especially those forces that led to formal manipulation of labels for troublesome children. We then look at the handling of status offenders (or CHINS) in two local areas of Virginia--Richmond and Charlottesville. In the local area portion of the study we focus on the local judicial philosophies, how they determine the operative models of CHINS, and how these models affect the delivery of services by local providers.

HISTORY OF JUVENILE JUSTICE IN VIRGINIA

The juvenile court system in Virginia is predicated on the English chancery concept of parens patriae. As such, the state has always assumed a benevolent posture vis-à-vis its children as surrogate parent with responsibility for their care and development. There were no "bad" children as such, only those in need of attention and guidance. The child was seen as malleable and influenced by his or her environment; if surroundings were changed, the child would change too. The welfare of children, not their actions, counted most in adjudicatory or dispositional processes. Judges were allowed considerable discretion in determining what was in a child's best interests and were given broad powers to remove children from undesirable environments.

Removing children from their surroundings, however, often meant that they were confined with the poor, the mentally ill, or adult felons with whom they shared filthy, crowded, and unhealthy institutional environments, or even a cell in the local jail. Efforts to alter this situation began in 1890 with legislation that allowed a child to be committed to the Prison Association of Virginia for treatment at Laurel Reformatory, the state's first institution for children. Troublesome children, however, continued to be sent to local jails (Curtis 1973). Pressure from reform groups resulted in the 1910 Juvenile Session Legislation, which provided that juvenile cases should be heard by special sessions of the regular courts (Virginia State Board of Charities and Corrections 1909). The state legislature then began considering the proper jurisdiction of Virginia juvenile courts. This question has been addressed many times in the state's history, and reflects the competing views on the nature of troublesome children. On the one hand, all children have been seen as basically "good," with invidious distinctions to be avoided lest children be stigmatized. On the other hand, many have claimed that some children were clearly "bad" and should be dealt with accordingly by the courts.

This "good-bad" child dilemma was first resolved in 1918 by giving juvenile judges jurisdiction over all children. Distinctly anti-institutional in the early period of juvenile justice history, the Virginia juvenile court relied heavily on probation and placement in "good homes" as its primary adjudicatory disposition. The benevolent mercy of the courts, however, was not widely ap-

preciated by the public. Growing numbers of troublesome
children contributed to the belief that there clearly were
children in need of more control, particularly in urban
areas. The courts were called upon to develop more effective means of handling this problem.

Virginia's long series of reform attempts culminated
in 1946 with the establishment of the Virginia Council for
Juvenile Court Judges, which began seeking the unification
of juvenile court judges and the development of an autonomous juvenile court system. The catalyst for significant
change was the 1940 case of Joseph R. Mickens, a black
teenager who confessed to the rape of a white woman in
rural Virginia. Tried in circuit court and convicted of
rape, Mickens was sentenced to be electrocuted. In appeals Mickens claimed that the exclusive original jurisdiction of the juvenile court had been violated and that
his case should have been heard first in juvenile court.
In upholding the lower court's decision the superior court
held that the trial and punishment of children who have
committed grave offenses should remain in the hands of the
criminal court. In effect, juvenile courts were held to
be civil in nature and hence not empowered to convict a
child of any crime.

The question of jurisdiction was now open to public
debate. The appropriateness of leaving sole jurisdiction
over children charged with committing very serious offenses with the juvenile courts proved difficult to resolve. Following an investigation of statutes relating
to the juvenile courts, the legislature revised the Virginia Code in 1950 to specify that all juveniles (under
18) be tried in juvenile court except in the case of offenses that might result in the death penalty or in confinement in a penitentiary for a period of 20 years or
more, including a life sentence (Virginia General Assembly 1950).

Virginia's juvenile statutes changed little following
the 1950 revision until In re Gault (1967), the U.S. Supreme Court decision requiring constitutional due process
in juvenile proceedings. The implementation of such a
provision was viewed as potentially difficult in Virginia,
given the fragmented structure of its courts. Virginia
had four types of courts that took juvenile cases (county,
city, town, and juvenile and domestic relations). None
of these were courts of record, and each had different
procedures and degrees of state supervision. From 1968
to 1971 the Virginia Court System Study Commission reviewed the entire court structure of Virginia (Virginia

House of Delegates 1971). In its final report, the commission recommended that courts that were not of record
should be organized into a unified district court system
of both juvenile courts and general district courts, and
that such courts should be supervised by the state's supreme court and staffed with state employees. The commission also proposed that judges should hold law degrees
and serve full time. These recommendations were enacted
into law in 1973.

Court reorganization, by itself, did not satisfy the
demands of Gault. The 1950 Virginia Code revision had not
provided a consistent or unified set of juvenile laws.
Further amendments that were enacted following the Gault
decision merely added to the disarray of the fragmented
code. For example, jurisdiction for the juvenile court
covered all persons under 18 in many diverse situations,
including (a) those dependent without parental support;
(b) those abused, neglected, or abandoned; (c) delinquents
and status offenders; (d) those for whom custody was in
dispute; (e) the mentally defective; (f) those needing
work permits or wishing to marry or join the armed forces;
and (g) those needing medical help for whom parental consent could not be obtained. Additionally, certain adults
who were charged with abandoning a child or who committed
acts contributing to the disruption of the family were
within the jurisdiction of the juvenile court. This
rather broad jurisdiction, coupled with growing pressures
from reform groups (e.g., League of Women Voters), indicated to many the need for a wholesale revision of juvenile law.

Pressures for substantial revisions of the Virginia
Code relating to minors came from numerous sources. To
begin, there was a perceived federal fiscal incentive in
that Virginia was participating in programs of the Law
Enforcement Assistance Administration (LEAA) and hence
subject to P.L. 93-415, Section 223, which required 75
percent deinstitutionalization of nonoffender youth in
order to continue receiving certain funds from the Office
of Juvenile Justice and Delinquency Prevention (OJJDP).
Furthermore, the state planning agency for LEAA--the Division of Justice and Crime Prevention--was staffed in
large part with employees funded with LEAA money who thus
represented a vested interest group in pushing for reforms. Civic groups, particularly local women's groups,
joined forces with legislators, child-care professionals,
and concerned citizens in calling for reform of juvenile
statutes, and they secured the commitments of several lo-

cally influential persons throughout the state. Such efforts became campaign issues for a number of state and
local politicians, most notably State Senator Frank Slayton, who joined forces with the director of the Division
of Youth Services within the Department of Corrections.
Juvenile justice presented an attractive and timely campaign issue, because the existing correctional facilities
for juveniles were not adequate to meet the demand for
services and placements. As one official noted, "We simply couldn't handle all the kids . . . something had to
be done at the front end of the process to cut down the
number of children sent to us."

In addition to emerging political pressures, court
dockets were crowded and judges complained that many
frivolous and unnecessary petitions reached their courts.
The 1950 code revision had specified that all complaints
be initiated by petition, and had noted the need for court
intervention. Anyone (with a few exceptions) could file
a complaint, and court staff were bound to process it
(Virginia General Assembly 1950). Children taken into
custody could be held in detention if ordered by a judge.
If the court was closed, the officer taking custody could
place the child in a separate section of a jail (if the
child was over 15) after obtaining a criminal warrant that
could be authorized by a judge, a clerk of a juvenile and
domestic relations court, or a judge or clerk of a court
of record.

Finally, attention was drawn to the fact that significant numbers of Virginia's youth were being placed in
out-of-state facilities, presumably because appropriate
in-state programs were unavailable. In 1974, for example,
959 children were placed in state, while 431 were placed
out of state, with the cost of the latter greatly exceeding the costs of the former (Virginia House of Delegates
1977). This concerned both fiscally conservative legislators and private providers who were facing dwindling
populations of juveniles in need of their services.

1977 Revisions to the Virginia Code

Following a series of public hearings in 1975, Senate
committee recommendations for broad changes in Virginia's
juvenile code were formalized and presented to the 1976
session of the General Assembly (Virginia Advisory Legislative Council 1976). The bill was carried over to the
next year, when a revised code was adopted effective July

1, 1977. In large part the revised code reflects the concerns of those individuals and agencies who pushed for its adoption. Several changes are particularly worth noting. Most generally the emphasis of the new law is on the family rather than on the juvenile. "Parents must become more accountable for the acts of their children and take a more active role in the modification of the behavior of any member of the family which is unacceptable to the community" (Virginia Advisory Legislative Council 1976:7). Additionally, the law stresses alternatives to traditional dispositions, the most important of which is diversion. Finally, the new law gives judges the power to require rehabilitative treatment, reparation, restitution, or "any other condition of behavior necessary to protect the community from dangerous citizens" (Virginia General Assembly 1977:7).

The revised statutes eliminated the cumbersome jurisdictional section of the 1950 code and established three categories of juveniles: (1) the delinquent, (2) the abused or neglected child, and (3) the child in need of services (CHINS). A CHINS is a child who is habitually truant, is disobedient, remains away from home, deserts or abandons his or her family, or violates any law applicable only to juveniles. The juvenile court has exclusive original jurisdiction for persons less than 18 years of age for matters of custody, visitation, support, control, and disposition.

The law requires that court intervention on behalf of CHINS be limited to cases in which a clear and present threat to the life or health of the child and/or the child's family exists. The tightened definitional categories and restrictions on court intervention represent a compromise between the force that perceived status offenders as predelinquent or otherwise troublesome children in need of court involvement and the force that perceived status offenders as being outside the purview of the court.

Additional restrictions are placed on detention, in that a CHINS may be detained only when there is a clear and substantial danger to the child or when detention is necessary to ensure an appearance before the court. Such a determination must be accompanied by a petition authorized by an officer of the court. The law allows CHINS to be held, for good cause, in secure detention for up to 72 hours prior to a detention hearing. This is the sole provision in the Virginia Code that is not in compliance with the Juvenile Justice and Delinquency Prevention Act of 1974 (JJDPA).

Perhaps the most important procedural change contained in the new code is the requirement of continuous intake services and the associated proviso that the intake officer may refuse petitions for cases of abuse and/or neglect of CHINS as well as for cases involving certain minor delinquencies. This provision is intended to discourage unnecessary petitions and encourage diversion. If a complaint is refused, the decision may be appealed to the supervisor of the court staff.

An appropriate set of dispositional alternatives for each category of juvenile within the court's jurisdiction is set forth in Section 16.1-279 of the code. Children who are adjudicated CHINS may (a) be remanded to their parents, subject to court orders; (b) be placed on probation under conditions and limitations of the court; (c) be excused from mandatory school attendance; (d) be given a work permit; or (e) have custody transferred to another individual, a child welfare agency, or the local board of public welfare. Furthermore, the judge may order agencies or programs to deliver appropriate services to the child. CHINS may not be committed to the Department of Corrections. A CHINS found to be abused and/or neglected may (a) remain with his or her parents subject to court order; (b) have custody transferred; (c) be ordered to services by local agencies; or (d) have parental rights terminated. Section 16.1-278 of the code states: "The judge may order, after notice and opportunity to be heard, any state, county or municipal officer or employee or any governmental institution to render only such information, assistance, services, and cooperation as may be provided for by State or federal law or an ordinance of any city, county, or town." Hence, the judge is given the mechanism to require that services be delivered by responsible public employees or agencies.

Since under the new law the court may not commit a CHINS to the Board of Corrections (and its associated secure facilities), a mechanism to provide alternative nonsecure placements was needed. Section 16.1-286 authorizes placement in an approved private facility when it is determined that the child cannot be dealt with in his or her locality. For example, a child who was found to be in need of services and whom the court believed to be mentally ill could be committed by the judge to a mental hospital, although the child could not be held in a maximum security unit in which adults reside. The cost of such placements is borne by the state, and such placements are reviewed annually.

An illustration of the need for alternative nonsecure placements before the code was revised concerns children who were either retarded or emotionally disturbed. The Department of Corrections reported that in 1975, 48 percent of the children held in secure state correctional facilities were either retarded or emotionally disturbed. During this period, one-third of the juvenile correctional population consisted of status offenders (Virginia Department of Corrections 1975b). State mental hospitals lacked programs for adolescents and hence refused to accept them. However, the Department of Corrections could not refuse them, notwithstanding the fact that they offered marginal, if any, mental health services (Hopper and Slayton 1978). In describing the provision of the new code, legislative attorney Lelia Hopper and Senator Slayton noted that "too often, the placement of a child depended upon the availability of public funds while appropriate treatment in the proper facility was a secondary consideration" (Hopper and Slayton 1978:47).

ORGANIZATION OF JUVENILE JUSTICE

Virginia is divided into 32 judicial districts served by 61 judges. Within each district the chief judge establishes and maintains his or her own rules and procedures regarding court operations. The staff of the courts are typically state employees who constitute a court service unit (CSU), which consists of probation workers and administrative staff. These units are administered by the Department of Corrections and regulated by minimum standards promulgated by the state Board of Corrections. The political culture of Virginia stresses local autonomy, and local areas are free to opt out of the state-administered CSU system. In 1980 court staff in approximately one-third of the judicial districts were local employees.

All court service units provide certain mandated services (Virginia Department of Corrections 1976). These include, but are not limited to, the following:

• <u>Intake services</u>. These services operate 24 hours a day, every day of the year. Intake staff receive complaints and are authorized to file or refuse to file petitions (within legal limits) at their discretion.

• <u>Social studies</u>. These are prepared by CSU staff for each case that is under their active supervision.

• __Probation supervision.__ All cases under supervision are followed according to a service plan and are reviewed every three months.
• __Residential care supervision.__ This covers all youth placed in postdisposition residential care facilities.
• __Case records.__ These are maintained for each youth handled, and exist in addition to those records kept by the court.

Court service units have a legislative mandate to divert children from the system. The implementation of diversionary programs is a __local__ initiative, however, and most units lack developed programs or standards for determining when a case should be diverted. The beginnings of a formal diversion policy, however, can be found in some large units. Alternative programs most commonly offered by court staff include the following:

• __Family counseling.__ CSU staff in many localities are trained to provide family counseling. In one area studied, the court runs its own program located in a separate building. Families are referred from intake.
• __Unofficial probation.__ This is the most common type of diversion and requires that a youth agree to a period of supervision by the probation staff. There is no formal disposition involved, nor is the juvenile brought before the judge in many cases.
• __Work programs.__ Youngsters are allowed to perform a community service by working with a local agency for a certain number of hours per week. Jobs typically involve unskilled, menial sorts of labor.

The intake officer has the responsibility to decide who will supervise the child prior to a court proceeding. If it is not feasible to release the child to his or her parents, some form of detention is required. Detention of CHINS varies from court to court. Not surprisingly, districts with easy access to detention facilities have higher rates of detention than those districts with few if any detention facilities. To encourage the development of nonsecure detention facilities, the Department of Corrections reimburses localities for two-thirds of the salaries of approved staff, all operating and maintenance costs, and one-half of the cost of construction. One reason for the continued use of secure detention is a lack of uniform criteria for determining when it is warranted (although the department cites as exemplary the detention standards of LEAA [1976] and the California Department of Youth Authority [1975]).

Despite the legislative changes in Virginia relating to troublesome youth and the formation of public interest and child advocacy groups, the juvenile judge is still perceived by many as the most important factor in establishing the philosophy and practices of juvenile courts. Wide disparity in judicial philosophy and court practice makes any attempt to characterize Virginia's juvenile judges difficult. Not only are there clear differences among the judges in different judicial districts, but there is also considerable disagreement among judges within the same district. Although the actual practices among Virginia courts differ considerably, they differ within a range of options and alternatives established by legislative action that permits us to describe typical patterns.

Through the System: From Referral to Disposition

Juveniles first come into contact with the system by referrals to the intake staff of court service units. Our interviews indicated that typical referral sources include parents (most often), school officials, hospital staff, or other social service agencies (e.g., local welfare departments). Figures drawn from Department of Corrections publications (Virginia Department of Corrections 1975a, 1976, 1978a; Virginia Division of Justice and Crime Prevention 1977, 1978) reveal that complaints have increased steadily since 1974 (see Table 15-1). Complaints refer to all requests for court intervention (covering both delinquency and nondelinquency).

TABLE 15-1 Total Complaints at Intake

Fiscal Year	Number of Complaints	Rate of Increase (%)
1974	53,556	--
1975	58,253	8.8
1976	62,337	7.0
1977	72,905	16.9
1978	90,951	25.0

The relative increases seen year to year indicate that while complaints at intake in 1977 were almost 17 percent greater than the previous year, there was an even greater increase (25 percent) in 1978. Much of this increase occured because prior to 1978 intake officers did not receive all complaints. In 1978 intake officers began to see virtually every complaint brought to the court service unit, thereby increasing the importance of intake in the juvenile justice system.

Before we examine statistics regarding the number of children, types of complaints, and modes of detention (secure and nonsecure) in the years immediately prior to and following the revisions of 1976, it will be helpful to look at some general trends in the handling of CHINS in Virginia related to the new code. The proportion of CHINS committed to the Virginia Department of Corrections as a percentage of all juvenile commitments declined considerably between 1976, in which 23 percent of all commitments to corrections were CHINS, and fiscal 1979, in which only 0.1 percent of all such commitments were CHINS. Table 15-2 presents a more detailed breakdown of this trend. A similar pattern can be found by examining the available information on children and youth committed to Virginia jails. The proportion of children coming into

TABLE 15-2 Children Committed to the Virginia
Department of Corrections, 1976-1979

	1976	1977	1978	1979
Number of commitments	1,411	1,370	1,216	1,306
Single commitments (%)[a]	78.6	83.6	81.8	83.5
Two or more commitments (%)[b]	21.4	16.4	18.2	16.5
Number of CHINS committed	328	125	25	1
As percentage of all commitments	23.2	9.1	2.1	0.1

[a]Refers to proportion of all commitments that represent child's or youth's first and only commitment for year of interest.
[b]Refers to proportion of all commitments that represent a child or youth having more than one commitment for year of interest.

Source: Virginia Department of Corrections (1976-1979).

contact with the Virginia juvenile justice system who were
subsequently jailed declined 50 percent between 1973 (4.6
percent of children being jailed) and 1979 (2.3 percent).
More dramatically, especially for the present study with
its focus on CHINS, the use of the category "wayward or
other delinquent child," the only category other than
specific crimes by which the number and proportion of
jailed children is reported, declined considerably after
the implementation of the new code (see Table 15-3). Our
research indicates a decline in the use of labels appropriate to CHINS who might be jailed, and later we present
data indicating that the decline in the use of the "wayward child" category results in an increase in the use of
minor delinquency labels. With these general trends as a
backdrop, we now look at some selected statistics on types
of complaints and number of children detained in both secure and nonsecure settings during fiscal 1977 and 1978,
the years immediately prior to and following the implementation of the new code (see Table 15-4).

In 1977, 62,547 children and youth came to the attention of the juvenile justice system; in 1978, 79,445
children made such contact. We also found that there was
a slight increase in the proportion of children or youth
who were diverted from the courts (from 30.4 percent in
1977 to 32.9 percent in 1978). If a complaint results in
a petition's being filed with the court, the alleged offender is often released to the custody of his or her
parents. This occurs in about 45 percent of all cases
involving petitions (Virginia Division of Justice and
Crime Prevention 1978). If the alleged offender is to be
detained, a detention order must be issued by the judge,
clerk, deputy clerk, or other court personnel with delegated authority. In 1977 roughly 30 percent of children
who were referred to the courts were detained in either
secure or nonsecure settings (12,863 of 43,540), while in
1978 roughly 22 percent of such children were similarly
detained (11,597 of 53,269). Although not sufficient to
establish any trend, these figures suggest a decrease in
the use of secure detention. Such a change would be consistent with the provisions of the revised code.

After a preliminary hearing a few cases are dismissed,
withdrawn, or nol-prossed, but most return to the courts
for adjudication. Those found innocent then exit the
system, and those found not innocent must return for sentencing and disposition. If a guilty verdict is rendered,
a background investigation is usually conducted prior to
disposition of the case. The court must then determine

TABLE 15-3   Selected Statistics on Children and Youth Committed to Virginia Jails, 1973-1979

Year	State of Virginia				Charlottesville		Richmond	
	Number Committed	Percentage of Total	Wayward or Delinquent[a]	Net Change[b]	Number Committed	Percentage of Total	Number Committed	Percentage of Total
1973	6,295	4.6	929	-1,110	119	7.1	201	4.1
1974	6,017	4.3	1,492	+ 563	76	4.1	174	3.5
1975	6,573	4.4	1,600	+ 108	60	3.3	167	2.5
1976	5,361	3.9	1,241	- 359	76	3.6	183	2.9
1977	4,557	3.2	897	- 344	31	1.4	209	3.4
1978	3,749	2.5	75	- 822	30	1.3	133	2.2
1979	3,956	2.3	49	- 26	22	0.9	134	0.8

[a] Number of youth committed as "wayward or delinquent child" during year.
[b] Absolute change in number committed as wayward or delinquent.

Source: Virginia Department of Corrections (1973-1979).

TABLE 15-4 Selected Statistics on Number of Children, Types of Complaints, and Children Detained in Secure and Nonsecure Facilities in Virginia, 1977 and 1978.

Number of Children and Intake Decision	Year	Number Diverted[a]	Number Referred to Court	Total Children
	1977	19,007 (30.4%)	43,540 (69.6%)	62,547 (100.0%)
	1978	26,176 (32.9%)	53,269 (67.1%)	79,445 (100.0%)

	Year	CHINS	Delinquent	Custody/Child Welfare	Total
Complaints Intake	1977	15,869 (21.8%)	43,024 (59.0%)	14,012 (19.2%)	72,905 (100.0%)
	1978	13,751 (15.1%)	57,924 (63.7%)	19,276 (21.2%)	90,951 (100.0%)
	Net Change	-2,118 (-13.3%)	+14,900 (34.6%)	+5,264 (37.6%)	+18,046 (24.8%)
Children Detained in Secure Detention Facility[b]	1977	4,528 (42.3%)	5,930 (55.3%)	254 (2.4%)	10,712 (100.0%)
	As Percentage of Category Detained	83.5	84.6	58.5	83.3
	1978	1,427 (16.4%)	7,169 (82.4%)	107 (1.2%)	8,703 (100.0%)
	As Percentage of Category Detained	63.5	79.8	28.8	75.0

Children Detained in Less Secure Detention Facility				
1977	173 (36.4%)	287 (60.4%)	15 (3.2%)	475 (100.0%)
As Percentage of Category Detained	3.2	4.1	3.6	3.7
1978	201 (35.3%)	349 (61.2%)	20 (3.5%)	570 (100.0%)
As Percentage of Category Detained	8.9	3.9	5.4	4.9
Children Detained in Outreach Detention				
1977	90 (46.3%)	333 (53.1%)	4 (0.6%)	627 (100.0%)
As Percentage of Category Detained	5.3	4.8	0.9	4.9
1978	275 (33.3%)	544 (66.0%)	6 (0.7%)	825 (100.0%)
As Percentage of Category Detained	12.2	6.1	1.6	7.1
Children Detained in Crisis Detention Facility				
1977	431 (41.1%)	457 (43.6%)	161 (15.3%)	1,049 (100.0%)
As Percentage of Category Detained	7.9	6.5	37.1	8.2
1978	344 (22.9%)	917 (61.2%)	238 (15.9%)	1,499 (100.0%)
As Percentage of Category Detained	15.3	10.2	64.2	12.9

TABLE 15-4 (continued)

	Year	Number Diverted[a]	Number Referred to Court	Total Children
Number of Children and Intake Decision	1977	19,007 (30.4%)	43,540 (69.6%)	62,547 (100.0%)
	1978	26,176 (32.9%)	53,269 (67.1%)	79,445 (100.0%)

	Year	CHINS	Delinquent	Custody/ Child Welfare	Total
Total Detained	1977	5,422 (42.2%)	7,007 (54.5%)	434 (3.4%)	12,863 (100.0%)
	1978	2,247 (19.4%)	8,979 (77.4%)	371 (3.2%)	11,597 (100.0%)
	Net Change	-3,175 (-58.6%)	+1,972 (28.1%)	-63 (-14.5%)	-1,266 (-9.8%)

a"Diverted" refers to any case in which a petition was not filed. The child or youth may still have received unofficial services, been referred to another agency, or received other dispositions. Tabulations of the number of children handled in these alternative ways were not available.
bSee text for description of secure and nonsecure detention facilities.

Source: Virginia Department of Corrections (1978b).

how best to meet the security needs of the community and the individual needs of the offender.

Turning to Table 15-4, we note that the number of CHINS complaints decreased 13.3 percent between fiscal 1977 and fiscal 1978, with delinquent complaints increasing 34.6 percent and custody/child welfare complaints increasing 37.6 percent. Since CHINS may not be held more than 72 hours in secure detention, the Department of Corrections has encouraged the development of various nonsecure detention facilities. In the year following the implementation of the new juvenile code there was a 58 percent decline in the number of CHINS detained. The likelihood that a CHINS, if detained, would be held in secure detention still remained fairly high (dropping from 83.5 percent in 1977 to 63.5 percent in 1978). This may simply indicate the lack of alternative detention facilities in the state, and we do find that the likelihood of a detained CHINS being held in facilities other than secure detention increases slightly for each category of detention. The same pattern is evident in the detention of delinquent children and youth, which might be expected if more "less serious" delinquency complaints were used in cases formerly considered as CHINS. Indeed, overall there was almost a 10 percent decrease in the number of children who were detained. To anticipate later discussion, the data we can find is at least consistent with the relabeling process that we note in this study.

The Department of Corrections exerts influence on the juvenile court process in several ways. The department certifies detention homes as being in compliance with minimum standards set by the Board of Corrections. Juvenile detention centers, however, are administered on a local level by the juvenile courts, local boards, city managers, or directors of public welfare responsible to the Board of Corrections (Department of Corrections 1974). In addition to secure detention, three programs of nonsecure detention exist:

(1) Crisis/runaway centers. There are six such centers in the state; they simulate a home environment and offer counseling and planned activities.

(2) Less secure detention facilities. There are three facilities that provide 24-hour supervision, but are not locked.

(3) Outreach detention programs. These programs maintain daily contact with the child and attempt to integrate the child into group activities. There are no

current reliable estimates of the number of such programs in the state.

The Department of Corrections is also responsible for providing court services through the court service unit. Minimum standards for these units produce some consistency throughout the state in that all are certified biannually by a unit of the department. The department is also responsible for a number of residential programs, such as community youth homes or group homes, which were developed as alternatives to incarceration. There are now 20 such homes, four of which are state owned. The others are operated by local governments. Fourteen community homes serve males, five serve females, and one has a coeducational population. These facilities housed 457 juveniles in 1977 and 614 in 1978. The average population of group homes is 12 to 15 residents, whose ages range from 8 to 18 (Virginia Department of Corrections 1976, 1978a). The homes are administered through the Department of Corrections, and programs are developed through a sharing of responsibility among local courts, community representatives, and the department. These programs typically serve a mix of children that includes both delinquents and status offenders.

Family-oriented group homes (FOG homes) are community-based private family dwellings that are contractually affiliated with a local jurisdiction and the Department of Corrections. FOG homes serve no more than four children between 10 and 18 years old, in either pre- or postadjudicatory status. They are designed to deal with the "acting out" child and are basically foster homes operated by the corrections department. FOG homes are supervised regionally by corrections employees to ensure compliance with minimum standards passed in 1978. Families are paid a daily rate ranging from $8.00 to $13.50 per child, depending on the parents' qualifications and length of time the parents have been with the program. The state reimburses localities for all costs except one-third of the salary of a FOG supervisor (if such a position is needed). There is no accurate count of such programs, although corrections staff indicate the number is probably under 40.

IMPLEMENTING CHANGE: DEINSTITUTIONALIZATION, CORRECTIONS,
AND THE COURTS

Several forces have operated either independently or in
concert to change the system of juvenile justice in Virginia. It would be facile to argue that legislative initiatives produced immediately observable results. But in
Virginia the legislative reforms interacted in subtle ways
with a constellation of actors standing in different positions with respect to troublesome youth. In this section we focus on forces operating within the Department
of Corrections and local juvenile courts and their associated staff. It is within these two major components of
Virginia's juvenile justice system that deinstitutionalization of troublesome children has been played out.

Corrections has become increasingly removed from the
direct provision of care to status offenders or CHINS because this group may no longer be committed to the state
Board of Corrections. Before the 1977 revision of the
juvenile code, the 1976 General Assembly implemented
amendments to existing laws to allow juvenile courts
funding for placements of status offenders in private facilities approved by the state Board of Corrections without requiring the commitment of children to the board.
The development of such facilities, however, has been
slow, although the intent of the legislature--to encourage
use of local providers in lieu of state care--is clear.
The Department of Corrections is most involved in encouraging deinstitutionalization in three ways--detention alternatives, prevention programs, and alternative community
residential program development. We have described detention alternatives in an earlier section.

During the 1979 session of the General Assembly, HB
1020 authorized approximately $750,000 for delinquency
prevention services. The Department of Corrections draws
on these resources to offer technical assistance through
its regional offices in planning delinquency prevention
programs. Additionally, block grants are available to
localities for such programs. In the past, television
commercials, cooperative task forces, and training packages for delinquency prevention programs have been provided by Corrections' Juvenile Delinquency Prevention
Service.

The nominal goal of Corrections is ". . . to develop
and help coordinate a full range of community program alternatives which serve to minimize the number of juveniles
committed to state care" (Virginia Department of Correc-

tions 1978a:137). Ninety-four percent of the existing
family-oriented group homes and community youth homes
(group homes) have been opened within the past five years.
Such alternative programs benefit from generous funding
by corrections. Localities are reimbursed for 67 percent
of the salaries of approved staff, 100 percent of operating and maintenance costs, and 50 percent of construction
costs. Furthermore, Section 16.1-286 of the code of Virginia allows a judge to use other types of public and
private child-caring facilities that may exist either
within or outside the locality. The department pays 100
percent of the expenses for this kind of placement, up to
the average cost of providing needed services to a state
ward in a learning center (what was once called a reformatory).

Community-based programs developed and financed by the
Department of Corrections operate under minimum standards
approved by the Board of Corrections. While these efforts
appear generous enough, there is nothing inherently attractive in them to induce judges to rely on community-
based programs. And nothing in the code requires non-
serious offenders to be handled first in a community-
based program.

The code does, of course, prohibit the commitment of
CHINS to corrections. Status offenders constituted about
25 percent of state learning center clients prior to the
passage of the code revision, and one would expect that
prohibiting the confinement of CHINS in these facilities
would produce a similar reduction in their populations.
In fact, following the code revision the populations of
learning centers dropped only 12 percent. This was due
in part to the practice of charging troublesome youth with
delinquency for offenses that would probably have been
entered as status offenses prior to the code revision,
solely for the purpose of securing institutional placement. The Department of Corrections acknowledges that the
less-than-expected drop in learning center populations
reflects judicial relabeling of status offenders (Virginia Department of Corrections 1978b).

Although the definition of a status offense is clearly
stated in the present code and carries with it defined
allowable dispositions, this has not been the case in the
past. Corrections officials note that before 1977 status
offenders were committed to the Board of Corrections and
were institutionalized, in many cases, longer than their
delinquent counterparts. While there was a general understanding of what constituted a status offense, deter-

minations of incorrigibility or truancy were sometimes
arbitrary in that they did not reflect the behaviors that
brought the juvenile before the court in the first place.
In some instances status offense dispositions appear to
have been used as a less serious outcome for cases that
might otherwise have been handled as delinquencies.
Finding a child to be a status offender was one way to
bring the force of the court to bear without the stigmatizing effects of a delinquency charge. Anecdotal comments from persons interviewed in this study suggest that
middle-class youngsters were likely to be found status
offenders rather than delinquents. By means of such
charges parents used the court's power to deal with their
troublesome children; little else was available to them
as sanction or incentive to ensure their children's compliance.

Several individuals whom we interviewed indicated that
many judges are not qualified, or willing, to deal with
the subtle problems of the children they see. Whereas
they would once dispose of cases by committing the youth
to state learning centers, under the new law these judges
are required to provide alternative treatments and services in lieu of institutionalization. Certainly not all
judges in Virginia embrace the philosophy of state law as
revised in 1977. As a matter of fact, most judges appear
to disagree with its provisions. We found three noteworthy responses to the new juvenile code.

First, many judges circumvent the new law by relabeling
juveniles so as to permit commitments. Juveniles brought
before them for habitually running away from home, for
example, may be dealt with as delinquents. The process
is rather simple, since most troublesome youth engage in
a number of troublesome behaviors, some of which may carry
delinquency charges. Running away from home may involve
a child's taking a parent's car or perhaps some money.
Rather than deal with the child as a status offender, a
judge may choose to consider the delinquent offense--
stealing the car or the money. In the past such problems
would likely have been dealt with as status offenses. But
as the director of intake of one large court service unit
told us, "kids are now being dealt with according to their
actual offenses. Many delinquents in the past were called
status offenders. Now they are called what they are, delinquents."

The practice of elevating the offense to allow for the
institutionalization of juveniles continues because many
judges believe that the best solution to troublesome be-

havior is a "structured environment," by which they mean
an institution. The practice also reflects an underlying
definition of status offenses as predelinquent acts. In
several interviews we discovered that the respondent used
the term "status offense" to mean "predelinquent." Judges
interviewed also felt that many status offenders go on to
become delinquents, and while a distinction was always
drawn between the two types of children, the distinction
was sometimes more apparent than real. When a judge orders a CHINS to receive some service, there now are no
legal mechanisms to enforce that order. Should a CHINS
refuse to take advantage of such services, the only re-
course the judge has is to find the parents in contempt
of court. Our observations indicate that such a practice
is rare, and most judges complain that they have "lost the
clout of the court" in dealing with status offenders.
However, as one judge told us, this is not really a problem, because if a child is ordered to services and that
child does not go, "I will remind the kid when he comes
before me on a more serious charge that he did not go to
services as I ordered." Some judges, in effect, see status offenders as likely to return to court on delinquency
charges.

Table 15-5 shows statewide figures for less serious
delinquent complaints relative to all complaints received
at intake. As the data indicate, there was often an increase in the use of various less serious delinquent categories following the implementation of the new juvenile
code, even though each category of offense remained in
the same rank relative to all other complaints filed in a
given year. Although it was not possible to obtain comparable figures for earlier years, it is worth noting
that the Department of Corrections interprets this same
data to indicate the relabeling phenomenon described in
this study. Our interviews convince us that the relabeling practice occurs, and the data in Table 15-2 are at
least consistent with such an interpretation. We do not
have comparable data on increases or declines in other
categories of delinquency, but we would not expect more
serious offenses to be reduced to the status of "less
serious delinquency," especially at the intake point.

A second noteworthy response to the new law is a de
facto change in the court's jurisdiction by some judges.
Although the law clearly stipulates that a judge may order
services for CHINS from any public or private program or
facility, some judges have interpreted the prohibition
against commitment and the corresponding lack of provi-

TABLE 15-5 Selected Statistics on Less Serious Delinquent Offenses in Virginia, 1977 and 1978

Offense	1977 Complaints	1977 Percentage of Total Complaints	1978 Complaints	1978 Percentage of Total Complaints	Percentage Increase
Simple assault	2,860	4.3	3,415	4.3	19.4
Break and enter	3,335	5.1	4,267	5.4	27.9
Petty larceny	4,029	6.1	4,685	6.0	16.3
Shoplifting	2,787	4.2	3,016	3.8	8.2
Unauthorized use of auto	347	0.5	554	0.7	59.7
Tampering with auto	236	0.4	397	0.5	68.2
Bad checks	71	0.1	149	0.2	109.8
Vandalism	1,861	2.8	2,536	3.2	36.3
Vandalism/destroying public property	342	0.5	479	0.6	40.0
Trespassing	2,295	3.5	2,732	3.5	19.0
Check forgery	325	0.5	474	1.0	45.8
Disorderly conduct	492	0.7	722	0.9	46.7
Cursing, obscenity	732	1.1	1,062	1.4	45.1
Drinking in public	258	0.4	419	0.5	62.4
Littering	55	0.1	76	0.1	38.2
Telephone misuse	93	0.1	138	0.2	48.4
Other offense against morality, decency, and peace	174	0.3	294	0.4	69.0
Contempt of court	118	0.2	169	0.2	43.2
Illegal possession of liquor	505	0.8	601	0.8	19.0
Other offense against public justice, policy, and property	1,427	2.2	4,080	5.2	185.9

Source: Virginia Department of Corrections (1978b).

sions for enforcement of court orders to mean "we can't do anything for status offenders." In short, some judges have defined status offenders as being outside the court's ability to offer assistance.

Like relabeling, redefining jurisdiction is a rather simple process, because the judge has direct influence over which cases the intake staff will pursue through a petition and which cases the staff will divert. If a judge instructs the intake staff to refuse petitions for status offenses, that judge effectively keeps such cases from coming before the court. Only by appeal to the CSU director can such a decision be reversed (for CHINS offenses); and the same force (i.e., the judge) that influences the intake staff is well understood by the CSU director.

If the child and his or her family were diverted to agencies and programs outside the court in such circumstances, there would be little need for concern. However, we have seen instances in which diversion of such cases means telling the complainant, either directly or over the telephone, "I'm sorry, there is little this court can do for you with this problem. Why don't you call (see) . . . ." As one judge indicated, "if a judge can't do what he wants with these cases, he may refuse to see them."

Finally, the most progressive response to the new law is found in districts in which intake staff are given considerable authority in deciding how to handle complaints. Their authority derives from the judge, who delegates responsibility to the CSU staff in making diversion decisions and deciding on appropriate referrals. In one area we studied, CSU staff regularly met with their judge (often sharing brown-bag lunches) to discuss problems encountered in deciding how to handle complaints. In short, CSU staff provide either direct services (e.g., counseling) or referral services to children and families with CHINS complaints, and the court is only very rarely involved.

This practice reflects a judicial belief that CHINS are best left out of the juvenile court system and that court staff are capable brokers (or, in some cases, providers) of needed services for CHINS. To be effective in securing services for children outside the court process, the court staff must be well trained in diversion, well informed about community programs, and must be given considerable discretion over how best to handle complaints. Unfortunately, this is not often the case. It requires close communication between CSU staff and the judge, and not all judges wish to delegate so much authority. The CSU staff are more or less bound by the wishes of the judge in whose court they serve. In fact, the judge is empowered to transfer a member of the court unit staff to another unit for good cause. Thus, an interesting relationship between judges and staff develops, for the staff are also employees of the Department of Corrections and are thus subject to rules and standards of that department. There have been reported incidents of conflicting interpretations of law between judges and CSU staff. This is most likely when disposition of a minor offense is viewed by staff as unnecessarily harsh. In such instances the court staff are in a difficult position, for while they may understand and agree with what they see as the law, they are obviously subject to the wishes of their judge. Furthermore, in some districts in which more than one judge presides, different philosophies among judges place court staff in a similarly awkward position. Living under what may be two or more sets of rules, the court service unit may operate in a different way for each judge.

Although there continue to be reports of commitments of CHINS by judges, or reports of cases in which the judge's orders violate minimum standards for programs and facilities, such practices in our opinion are more the exception than the rule. Nonetheless, the revised law will not be fully implemented while judges who are accustomed to radically different notions of juvenile justice continue to preside. Even when the CSU staff become better trained and more familiar with the new law, judicial prerogative will still prevail. And should that prerogative be in conflict with the philosophy of deinstitutionalization, we must expect to see incidents of institutionalization that might be unnecessary by the standards of those who revised the law. However, the trend in Virginia is toward a general upgrading of the juvenile court, of its structure and position within the state judiciary as well as of the position and qualifications of the juvenile judge. The impression of judges with whom we spoke is that the younger and better-trained judges tend to embrace the philosophy of Virginia's law concerning juveniles.

In sum, it is the philosophy and practices of local judges that set the general tone of juvenile justice in Virginia localities; and the service providers, police, and other professionals must learn quickly to work within the boundaries set by the court. Although pressure from the community might produce a different set of court practices, this appears to be very unlikely in Virginia because the philosophy of the judge will obviously determine how the court is seen by members of the local community, service providers, police, and all others who seek the services of the court. The judge appears able unilaterally to determine when and how the court will be used (i.e., which sorts of complaints will eventuate in petitions, which complaints will be diverted, and so on). This situation was brought home most forcefully in interviews with local education professionals and welfare administrators, who lamented the direction the court had taken concerning their type of clients. These individuals indicated that they were "forced" to deal with children without being able to rely upon the courts for help. The judge in the particular locale had recently changed the operating philosophy of the court and the CSU by refusing to deal with truants and certain other juveniles who had what the judge viewed as minor behavior problems. This suggests that the local juvenile judge in Virginia has the ability to influence the entire nature of services for status offenders within his or her community. It is in local areas, then, that deinstitutionalization of troublesome children is fully played out.

LOCAL COURTS AND THE TROUBLESOME CHILD

In the following section we describe the operations of two local juvenile and domestic relations courts (Richmond and Charlottesville). The two courts differ radically in their orientations toward CHINS, and the judges hold radically different views about the role of the court in the lives of young persons. Briefly, the Richmond court takes an aggressive stand and is actively involved in the lives of many youngsters. The Charlottesville court is considerably less directly involved in minors' lives and operates under the presumption that the child is best off in his or her home and that parents have a right to non-interference.

We describe three views of CHINS that appear to explain, in large measure, the differences found among juvenile courts. We argue that the operating practices of each court reflect the particular view of CHINS held by the presiding judge in that court. Judges who adhere to a view of CHINS as fundamentally different from other troublesome children (e.g., delinquents) will prescribe

treatment for them that departs from that ordinarily given
to troublesome juveniles. Those who hold that CHINS are
actually no different from other troublesome children will
make few, if any, distinctions in their handling of the
different types of children brought before them or their
court service unit. The third view acknowledges that
CHINS are different from other children in trouble, although the extent of such difference is minimal.

We do not suggest that judges in Virginia hold tena-
ciously to stereotypical views of their charges. Rather,
we posit these models of CHINS as general types that guide
judicial practice. Our observations suggest that juvenile
judges in Virginia are quite concerned about the idiosyncratic problems and needs of the children they see. Yet
we also have discerned that there are clear differences
among judges as to their notions about sources and consequences of troublesome behavior patterns.

Our interviews with the chief judge of the Richmond
court (one of the few black judges in Virginia) and those
with associated CSU staff form the basis for the discussion of the first local area. Following this, we present
our impressions of the Charlottesville court, based on
interviews with the chief judge and CSU staff there. We
conclude with a description of the three different models
of CHINS revealed by these interviews as well as those
with service providers in these areas.

Judicial Philosophy

Richmond Richmond's juvenile and domestic relations court
judges do not perceive Virginia's approach to deinstitutionalization of children and youth as having a significant impact on their court policies and practices. They
do not view the 1977 code revision as "drastic," but they
do consider the prohibition of detention and the commitment of status offenders as lessening the clout of the
court, thereby reducing its effectiveness in dealing with
some children. Certain categories of CHINS still routinely appear in court, but others are routinely diverted.
This is a noteworthy change because, according to Richmond's Chief Judge Willard Douglas, prior to 1977 all
children were regarded as being within the purview of the
juvenile and domestic relations court (except in some
cases involving serious felonies). Because most complaints resulted in petitions being filed with the court,
Richmond's juvenile judges were confronted with a fairly

large intake group. The Richmond court had to "wrestle" with the problems associated with the placement of CHINS more often than with delinquents during this period, because many more or less criminal activities were simply regarded as status offenses (i.e., minor delinquents were relabeled as status offenders). Parents frequently sought assistance from the court in controlling their children. However, they were reluctant to press issues to the point of having their child sent to a learning center. The status offense category served these parents well because it enabled the court to enforce discipline by threatening children with commitment if problems persisted. Now, of course, the court is prohibited from committing status offenders (CHINS), and some court officials feel that the removal of this threat has reduced their ability to help these parents.

Since 1977 Richmond's judges have seen an increased willingness on the part of parents to bring delinquency complaints against their children. Parents are more willing to bring delinquency charges once they understand that the force of the law is no longer behind the court insofar as the handling of CHINS is concerned. Additionally, part of this tendency may be attributed to the policies of the Richmond court service unit, which strongly discourage CHINS complaints. Legal prohibitions relating to the handling of CHINS have convinced some CSU staff that in such cases the court is powerless--a belief openly communicated to parents. In order to ensure court control of their troublesome children, parents file more serious complaints. What has evolved in Richmond, as a consequence of Virginia's deinstitutionalization efforts, is an agreement among court officials and parents to use the category "minor delinquent" rather than "CHINS" to effect control.

The data presented in Table 15-6 are from the Virginia Juvenile Justice Information System (VAJJIS) and show the number of complaints, petitions filed, and court dispositions for the Richmond Juvenile and Domestic Relations Court from fiscal 1977 to fiscal 1979. VAJJIS data are at best illustrative and should be interpreted with caution. The year following the implementation of the new code (fiscal 1978) saw a 38 percent increase in the absolute number of complaints, most the result of increases in the "delinquent" and "custody/welfare" categories. Complaints alleging status offenses declined as a proportion of all complaints. The court disposed of relatively fewer status offenders and relatively more delinquents

TABLE 15-6 Summary Statistics for the Richmond Juvenile
and Domestic Relations Court, Fiscal 1977-1979

Actions	Fiscal 1977	Fiscal 1978	Fiscal 1979
Total number			
of complaints	3,578	4,962	4,015
Delinquents	2,579	3,674	2,787
Status offense	350	351	308
Custody/welfare	610	838	840
Other	39	99	80
Petitions filed			
Petition filed	1,600	2,419	2,111
Case diverted	1,691	2,132	1,530
Court disposition			
Status offense	149	85	75
Delinquent	965	1,310	1,451
Child welfare	519	587	613

Source: Virginia Juvenile Justice Information System,
Department of Corrections (provided by the Richmond Court
Service Unit upon request).

than in the previous year. In short, the increased
number of complaints following the code revision was
accompanied by an increase in the number of delinquency
dispositions. As a consequence, while the number of CHINS
complaints remained constant during the year following the
code revision, the number of CHINS dispositions declined
relative to total complaints. This, of course, is consistent with any tendency to elevate what once would have
been status offenses to delinquencies.

The following year (fiscal 1979) saw a decline in the
number of complaints alleging delinquencies as well as of
those alleging status offenses. During this period, however, proportionately more complaints resulted in petitions than in either two previous fiscal years, and the
relative number of dispositions for status offenses
declined even further. The Richmond court, in sum, accepted fewer complaints for status offenses and delinquencies, filed fewer petitions, and made fewer CHINS
determinations and more delinquency determinations in

fiscal 1979 than it had made in each of the two years
previously.

As previously mentioned, the Richmond court is actively
involved in the lives of many children brought before it.
The appropriate function of the juvenile and domestic
relations court, according to Richmond's chief judge, is
that of a family court; any (and implicitly all) problems
associated with family life are viewed as being within its
jurisdiction. As such, Richmond judges feel that proper
jurisdiction extends to all children regardless of the
source of their problems. The judicial philosophy of the
judges considers CHINS and delinquents as one class of
children who experience similar problems. The court's
policy in all cases involving children is simply to find
out what's bothering the young person. As Judge Douglas
noted, it makes little, if any, sense to force a more or
less arbitrary distinction between CHINS and delinquent
youth at the court, since a similar distinction doesn't
exist in the community.

The chief judge does not lament the code revision.
While acknowledging that the revisions have prompted some
changes, most are relatively minor by his account. For
example, despite new statutes governing allowable detention, CHINS may still be detained for up to 72 hours under
the revised code. More importantly, although CHINS may
not be detained for a longer period, they may still be
ordered to seek certain services or be placed on probation. The chief judge feels that the court should not
resist making such orders, even if the youth do not avail
themselves of ordered services. Judge Douglas believes
that he and his colleagues have an indirect sanction anyway. He believes that children who do not participate in
ordered services will likely return to court, at which
time the judge may impress the child with the seriousness
of earlier court orders. The judicial philosophy of
Richmond's judges does not seem to be overly concerned
with commonsense notions of "success" or "failure" in
handling CHINS. Judge Douglas pointed out that being
successful requires getting at the underlying causes of
children's problems, and since in time many children will
be seen again on more serious charges, it is not at all
difficult to work within the current juvenile code provision to make use of whatever treatment and caring facilities are available. The Richmond judges feel that they
see the same type of children now as they always have, and
tend to see the code revision as nothing more than a name
change. As a consequence, the judicial philosophy in

Richmond is that the court should have some control over the process that channels children into various service alternatives.

Judge Douglas expressed concern that the intake process of the court service unit results in an understatement to parents of what the court can do in terms of ordering troublesome children into treatment services. He believes it is important to impress on parents that although the court cannot detain or commit CHINS, judges do maintain effective control over the handling of these youth. The court operates on the idea that it can best decide optimal placement of troublesome youth, especially in those cases in which appropriate placement is less than obvious. Douglas noted, for example, that he sometimes places boys in a military academy rather than entrusting them to state care. Yet where direct private placement has been worked out in advance by parents or other agents for the child, the court apparently goes along with the plan and orders that placement.

To ensure control over the placement of CHINS, the judge uses contempt charges against parents whose children disobey his orders. Richmond's court has been moving toward diversion for some time, including diversion of entire families. Implicit in the judge's current philo-sophy and practice is the notion that the court is capable of dealing with a wide variety of problems _if_ service programs are available. The court's placement strategy seems to be to find out what is bothering troublesome children and then direct them to an appropriate service program. The court can then deal with any complications raised by the current code.

Charlottesville Whereas the Richmond Juvenile and Domes-tic Relations Court appears actively involved in the lives of many youngsters, the philosophy of Charlottesville's court is that the child is best off in his or her home, and that parents have a right to noninterference. The sole function of the juvenile and domestic relations court is seen as ensuring that CHINS receive needed services. Charlottesville's Chief Judge Ralph Zehler asserts that his court is not a "big stick" to enforce parental disci-plinary prerogatives, and he believes that the court should remove itself from many issues and problems that it once routinely considered. For example, it is not considered the court's responsibility to safeguard a juvenile, or her family, against promiscuity. This is best left to others, especially the family. According to

Judge Zehler, CHINS are a class of children entirely different from delinquents, and the muscle power of the court is not required in handling their problems. The source of this philosophy lies in his belief that the trend in juvenile and domestic relations courts is in the direction of functioning as "junior criminal courts" from which status offenders would be removed entirely.

Judge Zehler believes that so long as the court remains involved in providing services to CHINS, public and private service providers will not become involved, particularly those whose mandate is to provide the types of services needed by CHINS (e.g., schools or social services agencies). In fact, the judicial practice of Charlottesville's court reflects an underlying commitment to the belief that status offenders should be entirely removed from the court's jurisidiction, which is in sharp contrast to the practice of the Richmond court.

Charlottesville's chief judge will deal most vigorously with cases in which CHINS are denied services (e.g., those who have tried to seek services from the schools or welfare and have been unable to get them). Rather than to haul troublesome children before the court, the operative philosophy in Charlottesville is to examine each case and ask why the child is not receiving services appropriate to the problem at hand. The two possible reasons are that the agencies are not providing the services or that the parents are not making sure that their child is cooperating with the providers. To resolve the problem the court chastises the agencies who are supposed to be providing those services. Judge Zehler would like to have the CSU staff act as brokers for services, diverting all children except in cases of serious delinquency or greater charges. CHINS, and presumably their parents, would appear before the court only when parents refuse to cooperate in programs worked out by CSU intake staff. The desired effect is to remove from the court those children whose parents merely view the court as an instrument of discipline.

Judge Zehler's belief that CHINS are quite different from delinquents stems from his view that status offenders are not necessarily predelinquents. In fact, he feels that most CHINS will grow up to become "normal" adolescents and adults and do not require any involvement with the court. Judge Zehler believes that alternative services for CHINS won't appear unless the court gets out of direct services, a belief that is founded on his observation that as his court has become less involved with children, the community resources for dealing with children have expanded.

Children typically do not want to go to residential facilities, and with CHINS there is little the court can do to make them. Unlike Richmond's court, the Charlottesville court has never been interested in providing services directly through its associated court service unit. Furthermore, there was little indication that officials and parents have tacitly agreed to use minor delinquency charges either as a mechanism for ensuring control over troublesome children or as a means of ensuring that they will receive needed services.

Table 15-7 presents information taken from VAJJIS for Charlottesville. Several points are noteworthy. The number of complaints received at intake has remained fairly constant across the time period represented in these data. At the same time, there has been an increase in the number of petitions filed with the court and a decrease in the number of cases referred elsewhere. This trend reflects the growing number of delinquencies seen

TABLE 15-7   Summary Statistics for the Charlottesville Juvenile and Domestic Relations Court, 1976-1979

	1976	1977	1978	1979
Total number				
of complaints	1,069	908	1,080	1,098
Delinquent*	567	546	665	803
Status offense	153	140	111	80
Custody/welfare	349	222	304	215
Petitions and				
diversions	982	796	935	940
Petition filed	245	257	490	479
Case diverted	737	539	445	461
Court disposition	479	298	423	340
Status offense	64	32	29	12
Delinquent	240	203	240	219
Child welfare	175	63	154	109

*This category includes "other" complaints or dispositions as well, 95 percent of which are traffic-related offenses.

Source: Virginia Juvenile Justice Information System, Department of Corrections (provided by Charlottesville Court Service Unit on request).

by the court each year. Delinquents represent a growing
proportion of all cases seen by the court and seen at
intake. The number of status offense complaints was
almost halved from 1975 to 1979, reflecting the court's
philosophy of noninvolvement concerning status offenders.
This philosophy is most clearly reflected in the almost
fourfold drop in the number of CHINS dispositions during
this time.

We must urge that caution be exercised in considering
these data. The Department of Corrections admits that
VAJJIS figures are not very trustworthy, and the CSU
director who provided these figures said that they are
only about 75 percent correct. Nonetheless, we are willing to accept these figures as indicating a noticeable
trend toward dealing more with delinquents at intake and
less with status offenders both at intake and in court.
Status offenders have been almost completely removed from
the court in Charlottesville. The trend, which is evident
in several other courts, to elevate the offense with
status offenders in order to deal with them as delinquents
is not found in this court. While complaints of delinquency have increased significantly, dispositions have
declined for this category as well as for status offenses.

Implementing Judicial Philosophy: The Court Service Unit

The central importance of the court service unit in the
handling of CHINS was illustrated earlier in this paper.
It is at the court service unit that CHINS first come into
contact with the court, and it is through this unit that
the court's philosophy and practices regarding CHINS cases
are played out. In this section we examine the operating
policies of court service units in Richmond and Charlottesville and how local judicial philosophy influences
the ways in which CHINS are either diverted from the court
or handled after adjudication.

Richmond   The Richmond court service unit's initial
response to deinstitutionalization was a general reluctance to get involved in status offense cases. This was
reflected in a policy of categorically refusing petitions
for certain types of status offenses. The data in Table
15-8 reflect the unit's reluctance to supervise these
youth. The unit appears to have become somewhat hesitant
to use probation supervision options, especially unofficial supervision of children, which dropped from 645 cases
in fiscal 1978 to 164 cases in fiscal 1979.

TABLE 15-8   Children Under Supervision in Richmond and
Charlottesville, 1978 and 1979

Action	1978	1979
Richmond		
Intake referrals	4,520	4,420
Placed on probation supervision	957	449
Official	(312)	(285)
Unofficial	(645)	(164)
Children released from		
aftercare supervision		
Direct state care	63	19
Community care	103	61
Other services		
Social history reports	613	588
Other reports	1,333	638
Family counseling	242	319
Charlottesville		
Intake referrals	936	940
Placed on probation supervision	37	54
Official	(37)	(54)
Unofficial	(0)	(0)
Children released from		
aftercare supervision		
Direct state care	5	4
Community care	10	8
Other services		
Social history reports	65	42
Other reports	148	60
Family counseling	10	7

Source: Virginia Department of Corrections (1978, 1979).

Although some of this early reluctance still remains,
Richmond's court service unit has more recently adopted a
policy of "absorbing" youth by making use of the probation
(both formal and informal) and direct service placement
powers of the court.   The rule in handling troublesome
children is "do not detain," although it was admitted that
this practice took some time to implement fully, since
there was some confusion among the staff regarding legislative intention relating to the 72-hour detention provision of the new code.   In any case, their policy now
interprets the code as allowing the court to circumvent

the usual child-placing and child-caring bureaucracy and order local public service institutions to provide services. It is still too early to tell what will be the results of this policy of absorbing children and youth through use of probation (especially unofficial supervision).

A key word in the legal definition of CHINS is "habitual," for only chronic troublesome behaviors justify court intervention. For purposes of filing petitions, Richmond's court service unit defines a habitual offender as a child who has committed the same offense three or more times. However, the unit categorically refuses petitions for runaways, truants, and those charged with possession of alcohol. Petitions are filed for curfew violations (with the police typically the complainant) and for children alleged to be beyond parental control, if such behavior is habitual. CSU staff in Richmond find CHINS harder to handle than delinquents, the former being seen as somewhat "headstrong." Finding them more "antisocial" and "arrogant," they now treat children "beyond parental control" the same as delinquents, pressing charges as far as they can go. By CSU staff accounts, the idea is to treat such children as what they actually are--"delinquents." CSU staff indicated that the label "incorrigible" is never used when the behavior is a "delinquency." As mentioned before, the Richmond court feels that CHINS and delinquents are not different in terms of their needs, and that CHINS are really predelinquents anyway and should be treated as such. The Richmond CSU staff attributed the decline in the number of CHINS petitions and simultaneous increase in delinquency petitions to parents who felt that the court could do little in CHINS cases. An alternative explanation, however, would assign that responsibility to the CSU staff, who held much the same belief they attributed to parents.

The guiding question of the Richmond court service unit's diversion policy is whether, for any juvenile, out-of-home placement is necessary. When deciding that it is, in some cases CSU strategy has been to set up its own direct services programs. In part this stems from a belief that if CHINS were simply put on probation, much probation staff time would be devoted to service brokering and trying to get children to show up--a belief that reflects the experiences of the CSU staff in handling CHINS. The court's inclination to involve the families of the youth prompted the establishment of a family counseling center. CSU response to the lack of residential

programs for CHINS led to the establishment of a group
home intended as a long-term facility for diverting CHINS
as well as for placing adjudicated children.

The court service unit has had little success in operating its own residential facility for troublesome youth.
A consequence of the tendency of the Richmond court to
view CHINS and delinquents as a single class of children
led to a placement pattern that did not distinguish among
the children placed in the facility. The mix of children
placed was untenable from the point of view of managing
the residential program and resulted in the temporary
closing of the home not long before we visited the city.
Now the unit's philosophy is that only minor delinquents
(most likely CHINS) should be placed in the facility. In
any case, CSU staff are reluctant to act as service brokers and would prefer to rely on other agencies to find
appropriate placement for troublesome children.

Charlottesville In sharp contrast to Richmond, the Charlottesville court service unit has adopted the role of
service broker, preferring to have some control over
referral of CHINS to appropriate community alternatives
rather than providing those services themselves. A close
working relationship between the judges and CSU staff has
enabled them jointly to establish a more or less consistent diversion strategy. The unit's basic approach is to
be "low key" in encounters with parents and children,
treating such encounters as work sessions in which it acts
as a mediator between parent and child. The CSU staff act
as advocates of the child, and seek court action only in
cases in which parents do not cooperate with the plan laid
out by the staff. Only in cases in which "distress" is
obvious (on either the child's or parents' part) is some
sort of nonsecure out-of-home placement sought.

All children are handled as CHINS unless they are involved in something more than a minor delinquency. CSU
staff feel that many parents attempt to use the court as
a threat, bringing children in when their own disciplinary
efforts fail. Hence, the current policy is to force parents to deal with disciplinary issues, and the court
intervenes only when parents or children are unsuccessful
in obtaining desired services. In fact, the first question parents are asked when they approach the court service unit is whether they have sought help from the welfare department. CSU staff preference is to use locally
available social services to meet most of the service
needs of CHINS. When this strategy was first implemented,

there apparently was a concerted effort to describe status
offenders as "neglected" children simply to secure appropriate services from the social services department. Now,
however, that department simply offers counseling or voluntary participation in whatever programs it has available
at the time. Consistent with local judicial philosophy,
the Charlottesville CSU policy is, in effect, to work most
vigorously with those parents and children who were denied
services in the past (i.e., prior to revision of the
juvenile code).

Data presented in Table 15-8 on children under supervision of the Charlottesville court service unit appear
consistent with the findings mentioned above, in that more
youth have been brought under some sort of supervision.
However, the data are far too sketchy to be definitive.

Local Services and the Troublesome Child

When local children who were once handled by the court are
turned over to other service providers, the sudden demand
for alternative programs prompts public and private providers to develop them. In some cases, of course, these
providers may try to manipulate the demand by seeking to
develop programs that "fill in the gaps" in the service
delivery system.

Richmond Few alternative programs for CHINS were developed in Richmond as a response to efforts directed at
deinstitutionalization. Some of this lack of response on
the part of direct service providers stems from the fact
that the court and the court service unit were involved
in developing their own direct service programs and, in
some cases, actively discouraged others from doing the
same. One informant indicated that when the Virginia
Council of Churches became interested in developing a
residential program for CHINS in Richmond, it was convinced by CSU staff that it was not needed. But more
important to understanding the lack of program development
in Richmond is the response of service providers to local
judicial philosophy and subsequent policies relating to
CHINS. Service providers in Richmond resist relabeling
children whom they have historically found to be very
difficult to handle. In effect, they see CHINS as being
quite different from the sort of children their programs
are designed for, and they strongly believe that these
differences should be recognized when handling CHINS.

Providers are likely, however, to find all types of children being diverted to their programs. This is in large part due to the operating policy of the key service broker in Richmond, the Youth Development Program.

The Youth Development Program is a diagnostic, referral, and advocacy program that takes an active role in seeking services for CHINS. It was developed in 1977 by the Richmond Youth Services Commission, a very active public youth advocacy group consisting of 105 persons representing the legal, medical, and educational professions, the juvenile justice system, private citizens, and youth. Originally operating out of the Richmond city manager's office, the Youth Services Commission now has more or less independent status and reports directly to the Richmond city council. The Youth Development Program represents the commission's major effort relating to services for CHINS. At first all CHINS referrals to the program came from the court and the court service unit. The program has recently begun to accept referrals from agencies and individuals outside the court. In addition, while it used to focus solely on status offenders, the program recently has expanded to include juvenile delinquents. The rationale for the expansion is that delinquents often exhibit behaviors more appropriately labeled "status offenses," while status offenders commit "delinquent" acts. Program staff do not, however, go so far as saying that the two categories of troublesome youth are really one. Rather, they recognize that there are some legitimate differences between the two groups of children, although it is not clear that those differences should be emphasized when placing them in various treatment programs.

Service providers in Richmond find that the operating policies of the court, the court service unit, and the Youth Development Program result in a placement pattern that the providers would rather avoid. For example, the main program thrust of Richmond's welfare department is foster care services. Welfare staff, however, view CHINS as a difficult group of children to handle and, therefore, as unsuitable for foster care settings. The few foster care units that do exist are seen as able to provide only a small number of the services needed for CHINS, and welfare staff see the court as unable or unwilling to do anything about this shortage. Prior to the code revision the welfare department would petition the court to commit some children in their custody to the Department of Corrections, ostensibly to give them the "structure" they

needed. Since the code revision, however, welfare staff
feel that some children who really need more secure
placements no longer even appear before the court. Welfare officials feel that an unintended consequence of the
changes in the code has been to prevent them from filing
petitions as a third party. Yet welfare staff often are
unable to find anyone who is willing or available to take
CHINS in as foster children; to force the issue might
jeopardize the entire foster care program by making persons less willing to be foster parents. Although welfare
officials admit it was difficult to ensure that even
children who were committed to corrections would receive
needed services, some staff claim that some CHINS are so
desperate for the "structure" afforded by a secure setting
that they deliberately commit delinquent acts.

Welfare department officials also indicated that they
have had to respond to problems in placing troublesome
children. For example, some providers demand that the
children indicate a "commitment to getting better" as
requisite to participation in the program, and some CHINS
simply refuse to go to treatment programs. Welfare staff
see programs for CHINS dwindling because, they believe,
CHINS are so difficult to deal with. In addition, some
of these children are seen by providers as "dangerous" or
as "major delinquents."

Resistance to changes brought about by the code revision is also found in the Richmond school system. The
schools have had little history of involvement in services
for CHINS. Tension now exists between the court and the
school system, with the court having difficulty ordering
CHINS into special education programs. School officials
have tightened their definitions of children who are eligible to receive special education services in order to
exclude CHINS. School officials even now see CHINS as
merely having "a hard time learning," and this alone does
not qualify them for special education programs. At the
same time, school officials feel that the court is pres-
suring them to develop programs for CHINS, and they feel
compelled to comply. There seem to be several education
programs being developed that could benefit CHINS, although there is little evidence that the court directly
orders CHINS to these programs. Most such programs are
oriented toward high school completion (or General Education Diploma [GED] equivalency), job training, in-school
suspension programs, and various counseling programs for
youth returning from corrections institutions or truancy.
The most recent is a centralized diagnostic and prescrip-

tion program operated through the schools and using staff
from various local agencies involved in services that
could benefit CHINS. The Youth Development Program is
also part of this new program. Richmond's judges express
some doubt that such a program will be of any use to
CHINS, since it does not involve any direct services.

Private providers have never gained a strong foothold
in Richmond, mainly because public service brokers operate
within the context of the public institutional framework.
Service providers in the private sector claim that it is
difficult to find the funds to start up programs. Given
the fact that the court service unit is also in the business of providing direct services, and therefore competes
for available funds, private providers are struggling to
stay alive. Those private providers that do get referrals
are finding CHINS difficult to handle and often must turn
to the welfare department for advice on dealing with them.
Some private providers argue, however, that they alone
have facilities resilient enough to accommodate CHINS,
and that they should be given funds to develop the
services that can fill the gaps in the delivery system
for services to CHINS.

Charlottesville   Unlike Richmond, Charlottesville has not
lacked programs oriented toward CHINS. A strong residential program has developed, owing in part to the court's
efforts to involve the community in dealing with CHINS and
delinquents. In addition, about one-half of the approximately 60 programs serving CHINS are private. A large
professional population (due mainly to the presence of the
University of Virginia), along with the impetus provided
by Judge Zehler, appears to be the reason for the abun-
dance of programs. The court service unit diverts CHINS
more or less equally to public and private programs. CSU
staff tend to view CHINS who come into contact with the
unit as those who have already exhausted most public
sources of services available to them. Both public and
private providers of services to CHINS in Charlottesville
see these children as predelinquents, and many state that
if services do not reach them as CHINS they eventually
will show up as delinquents. This perception contradicts
the view taken by the court.

The direct service providers' belief that CHINS are
really not different from delinquents stems from their
early experiences with residentially based care. The
pioneer residential programs endorsed by the court were
given little direction from either the court or the CSU

staff, and they offered little in the way of treatment. In addition, the parties involved could not agree on what sort of children should be sent to these programs. The first such program, the Community Attention Home for Boys, originally received both CHINS and "difficult offenders" on referral from the court service unit. This proved to be an untenable mix of children from a control point of view, and the enterprise was considered a failure. Eventually the entire program became a Charlottesville city department, and admission criteria were developed that acknowledged that not all children could be helped by such programs. The current policy is to seek a "workable mix" of children, although apparently fewer status offenders now appear in these programs. The court uses a "suspended commitment" procedure to ensure that the child agrees to go to the Community Attention Home.

Charlottesville's social services department (i.e., the local welfare department) has adopted the court's policy of noninterference--that is, leaving children in the home--even when it senses community pressure to remove the child. Although social services officials still view the court as an instrument for achieving service ends, the thrust of policy is toward voluntary placement. The schools also view the court as an instrument to be used only when school counselors have exhausted available school resources. CSU staff point out, however, that in their experience the schools use the court as a first resort rather than a last resort. As the court removes itself from the business of handling CHINS, the schools feel increasingly pressured to deal with these children directly. School officials also acknowledge a sense of frustration because they cannot turn to the court for help with truancy problems. In response, the schools have placed less emphasis on trying to force children to attend school and more on making school a more attractive place to be.

In sum, direct service providers both in Charlottesville and in Richmond are sensitive to the philosophy and operating policies of their respective court and court service unit, although the nature of the providers' response differs in the two cities.

SUMMARY AND CONCLUSION

In our study of local areas we detected three competing models of CHINS as perceived by various actors in the juvenile justice system. These models draw varying distinction between CHINS, delinquents, and the "proper clients" of service agencies. In each local area the following three models of CHINS were present:

1. The no-difference model, in which CHINS are seen as being no different from any other child, regardless of what label is applied. All children experience more or less the same problems, with the same prognosis.

2. The minimal-difference model, in which differences between CHINS and other children are acknowledged to exist but the differences are seen as fuzzy at best, and differential consequences in terms of placement and treatment strategies are not at all obvious.

3. The greatest-difference model, in which CHINS are seen as a unique class of children, often exhibiting more problematic behaviors than other children, and presenting more difficult social control problems. CHINS are not viewed as either delinquent or predelinquent.

Our experience in the local areas indicates that these competing models of status offenders or CHINS rendered initial attempts to deal with deinstitutionalization of troublesome children problematic. Initially, considerable ambiguity and confusion existed regarding who was to be responsible for what type of child. In response to this situation, service providers typically tightened their definitions of clients such that CHINS were excluded. As it became clear that the local courts would ensure proactive solutions to handling CHINS, local officials were forced to reconsider their respective operating definitions if alternative service programs for CHINS were to be locally available.

We found that the finer details of how the relabeling of CHINS occurs in local areas differed in the two cities studied, mainly due to the philosophies of the juvenile and domestic relations court judges in each area. Further, which model of CHINS was adhered to by various persons representing the essential components of the local juvenile justice system varied systematically with the person's position in the system. For example, in Richmond the more removed that persons were from direct services contact with CHINS, the less likely they were to adhere to the greatest-difference model, while in Charlottesville the opposite was true. The judges in each city took contrasting positions regarding CHINS and other troublesome children. In Richmond all troublesome children were seen as identical by local judges (the no-difference model), while in Charlottesville CHINS were seen as being uniquely different from other troublesome children (the greatest-difference model).

The competing models adhered to by the judges in the two localities make good sense from their views of the appropriate role of the court in CHINS cases. In Charlottesville, Judge Zehler sees his court moving in the direction of a "junior criminal court" in which there is no place for CHINS because criminal proceedings are inappropriate for CHINS offenses. Judge Douglas in Richmond, however, views his court as a "family court" with jurisdiction over all children, including CHINS and delinquents. Since judicial philosophy influences the pattern of diversion and disposition at the court service unit level, we would expect that similar types of children would receive different types of treatment depending on which city they reside in. In turn, the type of children served by providers will influence the model of CHINS that the CSU staff view as appropriate for their own programs because children labeled CHINS present quite different problems from "usual" clients.

Direct service providers in the two localities adhere to opposite models of CHINS compared to their respective judges. Service providers in Richmond appear to have experienced an unworkable mix of CHINS and delinquents (stemming from the no-difference model of the court) and, as a consequence, they tend to resist relabeling and to stress or accentuate the differences between CHINS and delinquents and their "appropriate clients." In Charlottesville, however, providers apparently have seen the same sort of children over and over again and have experienced some managerial problems. Charlottesville providers believe that a firm hand is needed to regain control over CHINS before they show up again as delinquent offenders and, in effect, that CHINS should be treated the same as delinquents (the no-difference model). Our observations lead us to believe that it is the existence of these competing models of CHINS that account for the problems we have seen in implementing change in the way in which services are provided to CHINS.

Finally, it appears as though the system based on non-involvement of the court generates local responses by way of developing alternatives for handling troublesome children outside the court. The system based on the concept of active involvement of the court generates similar response, but within the structure of the court and its staff. Whether there are noticeable differences in terms of the consequences for children cannot be determined from our investigations. To make such a determination would require careful consideration of children and their cases, an approach we purposely did not take.

REFERENCES

Curtis, George B. (1973) The Juvenile Court Movement in Virginia. Unpublished PhD dissertation, Department of History, University of Virginia.

Hopper, Lelia B., and Slayton, Frank (1978) The Revision of Virginia's Juvenile Court Law. Unpublished paper. Division of Legislative Services, Richmond, Va.

Law Enforcement Assistance Administration (1976) Report of the Advisory Committee to the Administration on Standards for the Administration of Juvenile Justice. September 30, 1976.

Saleebey, George (1975) Hidden Closets: A Study of Detention Practices in California. Prepared for the California Department of Youth Authority, Sacramento, Calif.

Virginia Advisory Legislative Council (1976) Services to Youthful Offenders, Revision of the Juvenile Code. Report to the Governor and the General Assembly of Virginia. Senate document 19. Richmond, Va.

Virginia Department of Corrections (1973-1979) Commitments to Jails, 1979 (and earlier years). Annual report. Richmond, Va.: Department of Corrections.

_____ (1974) Minimum Standards for Secure Juvenile Detention Homes Financed by or Affiliated with the Department of Corrections, Division of Youth Services. Richmond, Va.: Department of Corrections.

_____ (1975a) Characteristics of Children Committed in 1974 as Assessed by the Mobile Psychiatric Unit. Program Evaluation Unit, Division of Youth Services. Richmond, Va.: Department of Corrections.

_____ (1975b) An Insight to Corrections, 1975-1976. Richmond, Va.: Department of Corrections.

_____ (1976) Minimum Standards for Court Services in Juvenile and Domestic Relations Court. Richmond, Va.: Department of Corrections.

_____ (1976-1979) Characteristics of Children Committed to the Virginia Department of

Corrections in 1979 (and earlier years). Annual
report. Richmond, Va.: Department of Corrections.
_____ (1978a) Corrections Options for the
Eighties. Richmond, Va.: Virginia Department of
Corrections.
_____ (1978b) Impacts: The First Year.
Richmond, Va.: Department of Corrections.
_____ (1978 and 1979) Adults and Children
Under Community Supervision, 1979 (1978). Richmond,
Va.: Department of Corrections.
Virginia Division of Justice and Crime Prevention (1977)
First Quarterly Data Monitoring Report. Council on
Criminal Justice. Richmond, Va.: Division of Justice
and Crime Prevention.
_____ (1978) Annual State Comprehensive
Plan for Criminal Justice. Council on Criminal
Justice. Richmond, Va.: Division of Justice and
Crime Prevention.
Virginia General Assembly (1950) Acts of the General
Assembly 1950. Title 16.1, Chapter 8. Richmond, Va.:
Department of Purchases and Supply.
_____ (1977) Acts of the General Assembly
1977. Chapter 559 at 839. Richmond, Va.
Virginia House of Delegates (1971) Report of the Court
System Study Commission to the Governor and the
General Assembly of Virginia. House document 6.
Richmond, Va.
_____ (1977) Report to the Governor and the
General Assembly of Virginia. Subcommittee on the
Placement of Children, Committee on Health, Welfare,
and Institutions. House document 16. Richmond, Va.
Virginia State Board of Charities and Corrections (1909)
First Annual Report.

OFFICIALS INTERVIEWED

We would like to thank the following individuals for
providing assistance and information:

Lt. G. Carlton Baird, Chief, Youth Division,
    Charlottesville Police Department
Prince Brailey, Counselor, Outreach Counseling Services,
    Inc., Charlottesville
Phillis Bridenbaugh, Chief, Child Protective Services,
    Virginia Department of Public Welfare

Sally Cecil, Chief, Foster Care Program, Child Services
Division, Richmond Welfare Department
Ann Cook, Chief Social Worker, Children and Youth
Project, Secretary, Thomas Jefferson Child Advocacy
Group, Charlottesville
Richard DiMurro, Chief Intake Officer, Charlottesville
Juvenile and Domestic Relations Court Service Unit
Judge Willard H. Douglas, Jr., Chief Judge, Richmond
Juvenile and Domestic Relations Court
Gary Duncan, Director, Adventure Bound School,
Charlottesville
John Eberhard, Assistant Superintendent for Curriculum
and Instruction, Charlottesville School Board
Ann Emmons, Chief, Child Services Division, Richmond
Welfare Department
David Fitch, Director of Child Mental Health Services,
Virginia Department of Mental Health and Mental
Retardation
Cynthia Gadsbury, Director of Research and Community
Planning, United Way of Greater Richmond
Jack Gallagher, Director, Attention Home for Boys,
Charlottesville
Cathy Godsey, Counselor, Outreach Counseling Services,
Inc., Charlottesville
Lou Hall, Chief, Intake Unit, Child Services Division,
Richmond Welfare Department
Jim Jones, Division of Program Evaluation and Monitoring,
Virginia Department of Corrections
Joan Kammire, Protective Service Supervisor,
Charlottesville Department of Welfare
Daniel R. Kitchen, Director, Community Attention,
Charlottesville
Dianne M. LaMountain, Executive Director, Greater
Richmond Child Advocacy Office
Ella Lankford, Director, Oasis House, Richmond
Lt. Gordon Maddox, Juvenile Division, Richmond Police
Department
Linda Mansfield, Coordinator of Mental Health Services,
Richmond Department of Mental Health and Mental
Retardation
Cathy Mays, Virginia State Crime Commission, Richmond
Alick Moody, Chief Probation Supervision Unit, Richmond
Juvenile and Domestic Relations Court Service Unit
Sidney G. Morton, Intake Supervisor, Richmond Juvenile
and Domestic Relations Court Service Unit
Ed Mulvey, Department of Psychology, University of
Virginia

Stuart Napier, Program Developer, Division of Program
    Development and Evaluation, Virginia Department of
    Corrections
Ray Pardue, Director, St. Joseph's Villa, Richmond
Will Paulsen, Director and Senior Counselor, Outreach
    Counseling Services Inc., Charlottesville
Kitty Parks, Division of Program Evaluation and
    Monitoring, Virginia Department of Corrections
Ray D. Pethtel, Joint Legislative and Audit Review
    Commission, Richmond
Mary Saunders, M.D., Assistant Director for Medical Care,
    Richmond Health Department
M. H. ("Cookie") Scott, Director, Juvenile and Domestic
    Relations Court Service Unit, Charlottesville
Mary Secret, Director, Youth Development Program, Richmond
Fred Smith, Director of Pupil Placement, Richmond City
    Schools
Robert Shepphard, Professor of Law, T.C. Williams Law
    School, Richmond
Robert Smith, Director, Providence Forge-Williamsburg
    Court Service Unit, Providence Forge
William ("Chico") Smith, Administrator, Youth Services
    Commission, Richmond
Carolyn Stevens, Division of Program Evaluation and
    Monitoring, Virginia Department of Corrections
Clinton Strane, Coordinator of Child Protective Services,
    Richmond Department of Welfare, Richmond
Sue Urofsky, Joint Legislative and Audit Review
    Commission, Richmond
Charles Weston, Staff Attorney, Division for Children,
    Richmond
Porty Weston, Division of Justice and Crime Prevention,
    Richmond
Professor Charles Whitebread, University of Virginia,
    School of Law
Grace Williams, M.S.W., Chief Medical Social Worker,
    Richmond Health Department
Judge Ralph Zehler, Chief Judge, Charlottesville Juvenile
    and Domestic Relations Court
Jay Ziel, Administrative Supervisor, Juvenile and
    Domestic Relations Court Service Unit, Charlottesville

16

Deinstitutionalization of Status Offenders and Dependent and Neglected Youth in Wisconsin

MICHAEL SOSIN

INTRODUCTION

Wisconsin experienced a number of changes in juvenile justice policy during the 1970s, many of which were aimed at deinstitutionalizing status offenders and dependent and neglected children. A new legal code limited the types of facilities to which these youth could be sent, some institutions were closed, and financial policies encouraged alternate forms of intervention. Because these reforms began in 1971, three years before the passage of the Juvenile Justice and Delinquency Prevention Act, Wisconsin can be viewed as one of the states in which, at the policy level, deinstitutionalization began earliest and progressed farthest. An analysis of the Wisconsin experience is useful in determining the forces that may give rise to deinstitutionalization policies, and in assessing the manner in which some types of new policies affect services to children.

Some of the characteristics of the system of services to youth before 1970 must be kept in mind in looking at the Wisconsin experience. Before this time, deinstitutionalization was decidedly not state policy. Rather, Wisconsin policies were consistent with the most progressive philosophy at the time, an interpretation of <u>parens patriae</u> that encouraged high levels of intervention and an informal mode of handling youth. Wisconsin operated under a 1955 children's code that sanctioned intervention

513

into the lives of both status offenders and delinquents
without many due process guarantees. Because of this code
and a willingness of all levels of government to provide
for facilities, Wisconsin had a high level of out-of-home
placements. For example, before reforms occurred in
detention practices in the mid-1970s, the state had the
highest rate of detention for children in the country
(Sarri 1975). These beliefs and practices were clear
barriers to deinstitutionalization.

Barriers also arose because extensive alternate care
facilities did not exist in Wisconsin before 1970. Many
judges, legislators, and state officials were not convinced that the deinstitutionalization of status offenders
could be accomplished without a great reduction in care
and a consequent neglect of troubled children and youth.
Resistance was also strong even after legal changes were
enacted. As in other states, Wisconsin judges are quite
autonomous, and their behavior is difficult to control.
Many of them believed that deinstitutionalization was a
threat to their power and opposed any change that would
remove status offenders from their jurisdiction. Powerful
local social service departments also had reservations
about deinstitutionalization. These units could limit
the effectiveness of legal changes due to their role in
recommending dispositions to judges, along with their
historical tradition of providing a considerable number
of local out-of-home placements (Giles 1883).

By 1970, however, other conditions had arisen that
created an atmosphere in which some changes in policy and
practices might be possible. The progressive tradition
itself encouraged a willingness to consider the new,
deinstitutionalization-oriented suggestions emanating from
national sources at the end of the 1960s. Increased centralization of institutional placements also gave the
state government some important leverage in altering local
policies as many of the placement facilities controlled
by local governments were closed down. In addition, as
the services budget expanded during the years of the War
on Poverty, the state government, which dispensed these
funds, gained financial control; a strong state apparatus
came to counterbalance local service networks. Ironically, while the state took control of institutional
placements and thus could work to limit them, it could
legitimatize the deinstitutionalization effort partly in
terms of the traditional ability of local areas to provide
social services to youth. Thus, the state government used
the nationwide call for decentralization to legitimate

decisions that forced local governments to find alternatives to institutionalization in dealing with children.

This tension among federal, state, and local governments, between the old and new philosophy, between resistance to and desires for progress, and between centralization and decentralization led to a complicated pattern
of change. As will be seen, a group of reformers relying
on the changing context built a coalition to help overcome
resistance and achieve a series of incremental reforms
aimed at altering policies. After the changes were enacted, their effects interacted with local patterns of
organization, needs, and desires. In understanding the
patterns and effectiveness of reform even in a progressive
context, it is thus useful to analyze both the legislative
history of the deinstitutionalization movement in this
state and the effect of new policies on services to youth.

LEGISLATION

There is no written history of the deinstitutionalization
movement in Wisconsin, and even coverage by the press has
been limited. An understanding of the deinstitutionalization movement must therefore rely on other types of
evidence. Proposed and enacted legal changes are in
written form, as are a series of studies written by those
who wanted to call the practices of serving youth into
question. In addition, we interviewed a great many individuals who generally were considered to be important in
the deinstitutionalization movement. A large part of the
evidence is based on such interviews.

Status Offenders

According to informants, the legal changes during the
1970s that involved dependent and neglected youth were
largely a product of new directives within the state
welfare bureaucracy, whereas the policies that involved
status offenders were a matter of public debate. For
status offenders the deinstitutionalization movement of
the 1970s was actually a result of the social reform of
the previous decade. War on Poverty support encouraged
the establishment of legal aid offices throughout the
state. Legal aid workers in the two largest cities, Milwaukee and Madison, soon began to lobby for deinstitutionalization. The leaders of these two agencies were

directed toward children's issues partly by two other sets
of federal suggestions. The Gault decision (387 U.S. 1
(1967)) noted that the traditional discretion granted to
juvenile courts was often abused, and the President's
Commission on Law Enforcement and Administration of Justice (1967) set out policies for youth that advocated
differential treatment for status offenders. With the
perspective laid out by these federal sources in mind, the
Wisconsin attorneys began lobbying for a new children's
code that would reflect Gault and some of the other new
ideas concerning deinstitutionalization.

The national trend toward deinstitutionalization also
affected other professions. Many social workers, in particular, embraced deinstitutionalization and played crucial roles in the Wisconsin Council on Criminal Justice
(WCCJ), the planning agency formed under the Law Enforcement Assistance Administration (LEAA), an agency which
itself was established in response to federal commissions.
Within the context of Wisconsin's progressive tradition,
WCCJ was heavily oriented toward altering policies toward
youth.

In 1971 the legal aid attorneys and their allies, asserting that reforms were necessary to comply with Gault,
introduced a far-reaching revision of the 1955 children's
code into the state legislature. This bill, AB 510,
reflected Gault guarantees, proposed to deinstitutionalize
status offenders, and attempted to add legal safeguards
to other systems of services to youth. It was countered
by SB 99, the Juvenile Court Judges' Association's attempt
to restrict reforms to the minimum mandated by the U.S.
Supreme Court. Based on our interviews, it appears that
the existence of two bills, and the opposition of many
law enforcement officials, correctional officials, and
social workers from the local departments of social services to AB 510 resulted in the failure of both.

Although AB 510 was defeated, the legislature did pass
one component of the desired change in 1971. A new category, "child in need of supervision," was established for
youth who committed those status offenses mentioned in
the 1955 code--running away from home, truancy, and being
beyond the control of parents. Youth in the new category
could not be directly committed to a correctional institution. However, if these youth were placed on probation
and then violated its terms by committing another status
offense, they could then be committed. This legislation
thus directly affected only those youth who were brought
to court for the first time on a status offense.

To the reformers the 1971 change was only a modest first step. They desired a very broad alteration in the children's code that would take deinstitutionalization of status offenders much further at the postadjudication stage, remove these youth from detention facilities, and greatly increase procedural protections during hearings. After failing to obtain a completely revised children's code, the reformers realized that a sophisticated strategy was needed in order to reach their goals. First, they had to broaden their base by building a children's rights coalition that would include citizens' groups such as the League of Women Voters, members of other government agencies, and some local departments of social services. Second, they had to institute a number of reforms that would allow local alternative services to develop, thereby countering the argument that deinstitutionalization was impossible due to a lack of such services. In short, the legislative thrust for a new code, a thrust that was successful by 1978, became an exercise in incremental reform and in coalition building. Four separate components of change resulted from their efforts:

1. New laws forbidding the commitment of any status offenders to state institutions were passed in 1973.

2. Policies were promulgated throughout the reform period that were aimed at reducing the use of treatment facilities while encouraging the use of more "normalized" group homes.

3. State institutions were closed in 1975 and 1976.

4. Provision for services as alternatives to detention, along with laws forbidding the detention of status offenders, were included in the 1978 children's code. Each of these changes is discussed separately below.

Commitment of Status Offenders   In 1973, only two years after the first bill relating to deinstitutionalization was passed, a key legislative change was enacted. A small, unpublicized item in the budget bill removed status offenders from the list of those juveniles who could be committed to state institutions, even when the status offense was a violation of the conditions of probation for a youth who had been found to be a child in need of supervision. By this one-line change, a major component of deinstitutionalization for status offenders was accomplished.

This quiet amendment represents a case study in behind-the-scenes bargaining, and even with information

from a wide range of informants, some of the details of
the process are obscure. But it is clear that this legislative change was partly due to the continued efforts
of the legal reformers, and that these reformers were
joined by pro-deinstitutionalization advocates within the
Department of Corrections. For the most part the advocates from corrections were ex-WCCJ employees who had
filtered throughout the corrections community. These two
groups suggested the amendment directly to the Department
of Administration--the unit of government that wrote the
budget bill, and whose approval was therefore needed.

The two sets of reformers apparently convinced Department of Administration officials that status offenders
could be better served in the community. As evidence,
they pointed to a few group homes recently funded by WCCJ.
Governor Patrick Lucey, who had recently adopted a fiscally conservative stance, was consulted and apparently
was convinced by the arguments of state officials that
deinstitutionalization would save money because the state
paid for correctional placements but not for local noninstitutional care. He also seems to have approved of the
philosophy behind the deinstitutionalization movement.
With the support of the governor and the sponsoring government agency, the bill, with its one-line item on deinstitutionalization, was passed.

Many judges probably would have opposed the change,
but they were unaware of the bill. Most did not find out
about it until a conference held a year later. By then
it was too late to present a counteroffensive; and by 1974
the state legislature was in the hands of Democrats, many
of whom supported Lucey's pro-deinstitutionalization
position.

Service Priorities In bringing about the change in laws
involving the commitment of status offenders, reformers
noted the possible use of group homes--small, familylike
five- to eight-bed facilities--as an alternative to institutions. Throughout the entire reform period, WCCJ made
an active effort to build such alternatives. Partly with
WCCJ funding, partly as a response to WCCJ publicity, and
partly because of local changes in attitudes, many new
group homes were established. According to sources at
the Wisconsin Department of Health and Social Services,
45 group homes were established by 1973, most of them
located in the large and medium-size cities, such as Milwaukee, Madison, and Oshkosh.

Reformers considered the group homes an acceptable alternative to correctional placements, but they soon noted the importance of a second and, to them, unacceptable alternative--treatment facilities. These privately run large facilities generally are not locked, but they are otherwise quite like correctional facilities. Traditionally, they housed many status offenders, and the reformers feared that the new legal changes would result in an increased use in treatment facility placements rather than in the use of group homes.

Fiscal policies interacted with reformers' attempts to reduce the use of treatment facilities. Because Wisconsin does not rely on Medicaid funds for placement in out-of-home facilities for any but the most medically needy cases, the main public sources of support for placement and services in treatment facilities are the general services funds under Title XX, foster care funds under Title IV, and state funds (Hamilton 1979). Although the counties place youth, the historical pattern was for the state to pay the bill; counties rarely had a clear idea of which pool of funds was used to pay for which placement or even of how much services cost. In short, there were few fiscal incentives for counties to restrict the number of placements.

All of this began to change in 1974 when Governor Lucey and the state legislature instituted a new funding procedure. Counties were restricted to the limits of a state-mandated social services budget and would be charged for each placement into a treatment facility or group home (Hamilton 1979). The counties were (and are) still unaware of which pool of funds the money came from, but the state set a sum-certain appropriation for each county based on an estimate of how much Title XX, Title IV, and state services money would be available. The appropriation was given to counties on the basis of population and past spending. Counties had only one choice; they could expand the pot by 8 percent with matching local dollars.

Currently Wisconsin has reached its federal social service limit, so that the state's total service budget is not open to much yearly expansion. All mandated social services, including services to welfare mothers and mental health services, must be provided by dividing up this limited source of funds. Because services to the mentally ill have been expanded (for reasons that will be detailed below), there are fewer resources available for treatment facility placements.

The reformers hoped that these fiscal incentives would result in fewer placements to treatment facilities. This possibility was made more certain when policies that would make the cost of treatment facilities rise were instituted. The state issued new regulations that required more staff for treatment facilities, and this drove costs up. In addition, although counties had once negotiated costs directly with facilities, rates were now to be set directly by the Wisconsin Division of Management Services. Rates are high; for example, they averaged $2,100 per child per month by 1979 (Hamilton 1979).

Central government also set rates for group homes, but this type of facility has slightly different state-mandated requirements, and the average cost therefore is much lower--about $1,100 per child per month in 1979 (Hamilton 1979). Consequently there has been tremendous growth in the number of group homes. According to unpublished statistics of the Department of Health and Social Services, there were 41 county-funded group homes in 1975 (a few less than in 1973) but 136 just one year later in 1976.

Once again reformers and fiscal conservatives had formed a coalition. Apparently the reformers convinced the governor's office that group homes could appropriately serve youth and that the cost of treatment facilities should be allowed to rise. These changes were especially effective when services were placed within budgetary limits that discouraged expensive treatment facilities.

Institutional Closings Deinstitutionalization seemed to promise some drop in the juvenile population in state institutions, but an even more powerful force was also working in this direction. As a response to the change in the voting age, the age of majority was lowered from 21 to 18 in 1971. To be consistent with this change, the maximum age of juvenile court jurisdiction was also lowered to extend only to a child's eighteenth birthday. As a result, the juvenile institutional population was cut in half within three years. In 1970, 1,801 boys and 458 girls were admitted to the state institutions. By 1972 the total admissions were 879 and 230 respectively (Mitchell and Ziegler 1978).

Advocates for deinstitutionalization viewed this decrease as a means of solidifying gains in policies toward status offenders and delinquent youth. They reasoned that if the institutions were closed, there would be fewer possible placements and thus fewer commitments. They also

were able to convince members of the administration that
an expected decrease in the number of children in the
state, along with the lowering of the age of majority,
implied that fewer placements would be made in the future
and that therefore fewer facilities would be needed. The
reformers who favored deinstitutionalization and the state
officials who desired to save money were again in alliance, this time to close facilities. One of the boys'
schools, Kettle Morraine, was closed in 1975. The Wisconsin School for Girls was closed in 1976, and one of the
remaining boys' schools, Lincoln Hills, was made coeducational. Some of the smaller correctional camps were
closed at about the same time. The closing of the Wisconsin School for Girls was especially important to certain advocates, because one-half of the inmates reportedly
were black, a figure out of proportion to the small percentage of minority group members in the state. The fight
against institutionalization was viewed by some as a battle against racism and sexism.

Because status offenders and dependent and neglected
youth could not be placed in correctional facilities after
1973, the closing of institutions was not directly aimed
at this group. Nevertheless, some feared that status
offenders might be institutionalized under other labels,
and the reduction in the number of facilities was viewed
as one means of guarding against this possibility. Other
policies were also initiated to keep the institutional
population low. With WCCJ funding, the Department of
Health and Social Services established the Juvenile Offender Review Board in 1977. This board reviews case
folders of youth who are held in institutions in order to
determine if other, less restrictive alternatives would
be more appropriate. The board's establishment was a
reflection of the fact that many state officials had come
to accept deinstitutionalization as a worthy goal.

Reformers originally hoped that the review board would
place such youth back into county-run group homes. However, over time the Division of Corrections developed its
own system of group homes, with some WCCJ (and, thus,
LEAA) funding. The use of group homes by the Division of
Corrections expanded tenfold in two years to 160 placements in 1978 (Wisconsin Council on Criminal Justice
1979). Group homes actually helped to offset the reduction in institutional capacity, because children held in
correctional institutions for a few months were moved out
to group homes as newcomers arrived.

Detention and the New Children's Code   After 1974 the
provision of alternatives to detention and the promulgation of legislation that forbade the use of detention
facilities for status offenders became high priorities of
the legal reformers. They hoped that the latter provision
would be included in a new children's code. Part of their
strategy involved a new federal law, the 1974 Juvenile
Justice and Delinquency Prevention Act (JJDPA). This act
mandated the separation of status offenders and dependent
and neglected youth from delinquents at prehearing and
posthearing placements.

This does not imply that JJDPA was solely or even
largely responsible for either the changes in detention
or the final adoption of a new children's code. The code
had been a goal of reformers since 1971; even before the
enactment of the JJDPA the reformers were attempting to
alter detention practices. One important component of
the reform attempt was the promulgation of reports and
other means of publicity in support of changes. These
efforts seemed to be financed almost entirely by WCCJ,
although other agencies carried them out. For example,
juveniles in Wisconsin were most often detained in county
jails that also housed adults, because only the three
largest counties (Milwaukee, Racine, and Dane) maintained
separate facilities. As part of the reform effort, WCCJ
granted funds to the Division of Corrections in 1974 to
increase the number of jail inspectors from three to five.
The inspectors were exacting in their demands that jail
standards be met, and they also documented some problems.
Accordingly, immediate improvements were made, and the
necessity for further changes was made evident. WCCJ also
funded a number of studies that seemed to provide momentum
for changes in detention and for a new children's code
(League of Women Voters 1976, Special Study Committee on
Criminal Justice Standards and Goals 1975, Wisconsin Department of Health and Social Services 1974, 1976).

Despite the past efforts of the reformers, some may
argue that because JJDPA provided loss-of-funding penalties for noncompliance, the new Wisconsin children's code
would not have passed without this federal legislation.
But this does not seem to be true. Informants told us
that the threat of a loss of funds was not a powerful
instrument of change in Wisconsin, as the amount of money
involved was simply too small a part of the total correctional budget. Attempts to place the need for legislative
change in financial terms were often countered by the
suggestion that it was children, not dollars, that should

be the central issue. In fact, even if some legislators desired to retain the federal funding, opponents of the legal changes did not; the federal funds were committed to programs that supported deinstitutionalization, and those who opposed meeting JJDPA standards therefore did not find the jeopardized funds a benefit.

Thus, at most it can be said that the funds provided by JJDPA were incorporated into the existing reform movement and helped bring about the changes in the treatment of status offenders that many desired anyway. JJDPA funds were also useful in providing an institutional base from which reforms might occur. They supported some employees of WCCJ--which handled all LEAA funds, including JJDPA money--and this funding link served to commit the council to the legal changes even more completely. In addition, JJDPA funds were used to start the Youth Policy and Law Center. Headed by a former-legal aid attorney, Richard Phelps, this state agency became the umbrella under which the coalition for further legal changes gathered. Legal reformers began the agency and were employed by it, and some social service staff were added later on. In general the agency became the primary interest group for children's rights in Wisconsin.

The reformers realized that, as in the case of reforms concerning correctional institutions, the proposed reforms in detention practices had to deal with the objection that few alternatives were available to this prehearing option. WCCJ funds were used to help provide alternatives, and JJDPA money was added to the effort. In particular, counties began to adopt shelter care facilities, that is, nonsecure alternatives to detention in which status offenders could be placed. The first shelter care facility opened in 1972, and 28 were in operation with WCCJ funds before the new code was adopted (Hamilton and Kosteckey 1978). It was possible to claim that, because of the new facilities, laws mandating the restriction of detention would not necessarily result in the complete abandonment of status offenders.

One problem with this funding was that it was seed money that would run out after three years. Some members of the reform movement feared that the lack of funds would restrict the use of the alternatives, resulting in a renewed upsurge in the use of detention. Accordingly, a Shelter Care Reimbursement Act was passed in 1977. This law provided a 50 percent reimbursement for the costs of care for children (but only for 20 days). Shelter care became economically more rational than detention, because only the former was reimbursed by the state. The main economic problem now was building shelter care facilities in counties that had not received federal funds through WCCJ.

With the efforts of the Youth Policy and Law Center, past incremental changes, the momentum implied in the wide range of studies, the perceived need to make statutes consistent with U.S. Supreme Court decisions, the new alternatives, and the growing coalition in government, many opponents as well as supporters of change believed that a new code was inevitable. This perception resulted in some bargaining between proponents and those who had previously opposed the code because opponents believed that it was best to gain some concessions from the reform coalition. Such bargaining led to more support for the changes. For example, judges received some expansion of their power to determine the length of stay in institutions, social workers managed to increase their role in the process, and police officers were pleased with provisions mandating formal detention hearings within 24 hours of arrest. Some members of all three groups lobbied for the new code.

The new children's code passed unanimously, was signed by Acting Governor Schreiber in May 1978, and became effective in November of the same year (although few counties complied with all of its provisions for another full year). The code mandated a wide range of changes in practices. It brought the law into conformity with U.S. Supreme Court decisions, and it mandated formal procedures for detention and disposition. In addition, the code mandated that the "least restrictive alternative" be used for juveniles, and that institutionalization could only occur for an offense that, had it been committed by an adult, could result in a six-month prison term.

The code also formalized existing changes concerning status offenders. It created a "children in need of protection and services" category that combined status offenders with dependent and neglected youth, and it prohibited the institutionalization of these youth in correctional facilities. The code set up procedures and safeguards for the use of alternate care facilities, carefully mandating formal hearings whenever changes of placement were contemplated for any youth.

Most significantly for present purposes, the code altered detention practices. It established a presumption of release of a child to the parent, guardian, or legal custodian, and it established specific criteria for de-

tention. These criteria effectively precluded the detention of status offenders and dependent and neglected youth
under most circumstances. Individuals in need of protection and services could only be placed in a secure facility if they were fugitives from another state, runaways
from local nonsecure custody, or fugitives from another
Wisconsin county who had been alleged to be adjudicated
delinquents. In other cases, shelter care could be used
as an alternative to detention. In the absence of shelter
care facilities, youth could be placed in receiving homes,
the traditional alternative for children awaiting foster
care placement.

Complementary Systems

In Wisconsin, policies toward status offenders overlapped
with policies toward other youth. For example, treatment
centers and group homes could house youth traditionally
described as dependent and neglected as well as status
offenders (and some delinquents), because both sets of
youth were officially placed by local departments of
social services. Another overlap occurs because it is
possible that reform in laws relating to status offenders
might result in increased institutionalization in another
context, such as in mental health.
     Pro-deinstitutionalization   changes   were   occurring
simultaneously for dependent and neglected youth and for
youth with mental health problems. While each set of
reforms involves a complicated and separate historical
pattern, it is important to note briefly some of the
trends toward deinstitutionalization.

Foster Care and Protective Services Even though overlap
exists between placement alternatives for status offenders
and for dependent and neglected youth, the two have somewhat independent histories. The trend for dealing with
dependent and neglected youth seems to have been somewhat
circular over the past 100 years. The effort was almost
entirely a local one in the nineteenth century, but the
state took an increasing part of the responsibility
through World War II. The state took custody and guardianship of children in need of protective services, placing
some in foster care and others in the Wisconsin Children's
Center. This center was the only state-operated institution for dependent and neglected youth. It provided
placements for up to 700 children.

After World War II, local areas were again given more responsibilities. The 1955 children's code required that each county must provide its own child welfare services through the local department of social services. However, the state agency continued to provide services for children with special needs, and it maintained adoptive services. The state agency also began to rely more on private treatment facilities and foster homes. According to state officials, the population of the children's center had declined to 150 by 1975.

The decision concerning whether a child would be served by the county or the state demanded much discretion by courts and local departments of social services, and the percentage of youth handled each way changed over time. In an effort to save money after the funding limits, counties began to refer more youth to the state agency. But the state was becoming fiscally conservative, and the central social services agency had to cut its own costs. Accordingly, in 1975 the Wisconsin Children's Center was closed, and it was expected that less expensive group homes and treatment facilities would take up the slack. A 1977 law that amended child welfare services reversed the trend toward state involvement in foster care. The legislation, which apparently was put forward by the Wisconsin Department of Health and Social Services, separated custody from guardianship and thus made it possible for counties to retain custody (and thus the cost of care) even if the court declares the state agency as guardian. The number of youth handled directly by the state agency was reduced, because counties knew that the change in guardianship might not transfer costs. State costs were clearly cut; foster care staff were reduced from 150 to 75 between 1975 and 1979. By 1979 counties handled 85 percent of the children, and paid the costs of placement services from the local services fund. (The state has retained control only in adoption cases, under the assumption that it is desirable to place youth outside the original community. Milwaukee County, which is large enough to provide placements in alternate communities within its boundaries, is the exception.)

The local department of social services had always completed placements for status offenders, dependent and neglected youth, and delinquents. This agency obviously was affected by the changing financial policies and the pressures to provide more of the services for dependent and neglected youth. Even though the total social services budget has increased somewhat over the last few

years, counties have been under much pressure to use the
additional money to deal with adult mental health deinstitutionalization. The funds spent on children's welfare
services therefore could not keep pace with inflation.
For example, Wisconsin's 1974-1976 biannual budget included $39.5 million for treatment facilities, while the
1976-1978 budget included only $37.5 million. Similarly,
the foster care budget, which also includes group homes,
declined from $18 million to $15.8 million. Deinstitutionalization had thus become an economic necessity.

Another effect of the budget changes was the reduction
in local social services staff. Exact breakdowns are not
available, but local officials in two counties said that
the overall decrease has averaged about 10 percent.
Visits to local areas also suggest that outreach services
were reduced most, and that as a result it became more
difficult to recruit foster parents. There have been a
few recent studies that point up a lack of coordination
among services (Becker 1978, Johnson et al. 1978), and it
appears that the problem is partly a result of inadequate
staff and funds.

Mental Health A common fear is that deinstitutionalization of status offenders and dependent and neglected youth
can lead to their reinstitutionalization in mental health
facilities, but this was not possible in Wisconsin. The
1972 state supreme court Lessard v. Schmidt decision (94
Sup. 713 (1974)), like Gault, restricted grounds for commitment and was a first step in reducing institutionalization. The decision noted that commitment to a mental
health facility could only occur if an individual is dangerous to self or others.

As in the case of status offenders, reformers dealing
with mental health issues worked to ensure that alternatives to commitment would exist. In 1973 the state legislature mandated so-called 51.42 boards (named after the
legislation) in each county. The boards were mandated to
coordinate local services for individuals with mental
health problems and to help provide alternatives to institutionalization. Funds for the new services were to
come from the county social services sum-certain appropriation; in fact, large increases in the local mental
health budget followed this mandate.

The most important legislative action was the revision
of the mental health code in 1976. The new code was consistent with Lessard, but it went much further. For
juveniles who are 14 to 18 years old, the code mandated

that even voluntary admissions require written consent of
the child and a review by the juvenile court. Judicial
review was also necessary for youth under 14. The code
also mandated that transfer from a correctional institution to a mental health facility required a hearing.

After 1976, mental health facilities began to close
down wings and refuse cases that did not meet the legal
standards of Lessard and of the new code. For children,
the result of the changes in policy was dramatic. The
largest mental health center, Mendota State Hospital, had
eight children's wards before the legal changes; it now
has only one. According to unpublished figures, 120 youth
under the control of either state or local departments of
social services were placed in mental health institutions
in 1973, but only 63 were placed in 1977 (the last year
in which figures were available). Many adults were also
filtered back to local communities. Given funding limits,
counties had all they could handle in dealing with deinstitutionalized adults and children from mental facilities. There simply were not enough facilities to
allow any large-scale reinstitutionalization of status
offenders and dependent and neglected youth in local mental hospitals.

PATTERNS OF SERVICE

Legal impact literature points out that legal reforms
often meet unexpected resistance at the implementation
stage, and that this resistance is likely to be stronger
when the target of change has some independent power
(Sosin 1979a). Laws relating to deinstitutionalization
in Wisconsin seem to exemplify this possibility. Judges
in Wisconsin are organizationally separate from the local
departments of social services, and the budgetary reforms
have only affected the latter; it is possible that court
decisions might not reflect the difficulties faced by
social service agencies, so that patterns of placement
might not change. The local departments of social services themselves might resist some of the state reforms.
Wisconsin is state supervised but county administered, and
the local agency has some leeway in establishing policy.

Resistance is also likely to be strong when laws are
not popular, and this was true of certain aspects of the
deinstitutionalization laws. To be sure, in our interviews few challenged the legitimacy of the new statutes,
and there was general agreement around the state that most

status offenders should not be sent to state institutions. In fact, judges who were interviewed claimed that few such youth had been institutionalized even before the reforms took effect, and, in addition, local departments of social services did not indicate much resistance on their part to the general philosophy of local control. However, judges seemed to believe that the threat of institutionalization was necessary to control status offenders with whom the court dealt, and they were particularly adamant in their desire to use detention as a way of controlling youthful problems. Local departments of social services were quite upset about the loss of funds and placements, and generally did not see a reduction in the use of treatment facilities as desirable.

The changes in policy had some internal limits that might also affect the patterns of reform. For example, laws forbidding the institutionalization of status offenders leave some room for maneuvering because categories of conduct are not always clear, and status offenders might be reinstitutionalized under different labels. More important, the reform movement was the result of political compromises and, as such, deinstitutionalization was combined with other reform measures that might lead to unanticipated consequences. For example, the alliance between reformers and fiscal conservatives helped to close institutions and restrict the use of treatment facilities, but it coincided with an overall reduction in the budget that might affect the provision of local, nonrestrictive alternatives. Furthermore, the reformers created grants for group homes and shelter facilities, hoping to convince legislators that deinstitutionalization was feasible, but there was no guarantee that these facilities would be used as intended. Some counties might perceive the new facilities as supplements to institutions and not as alternatives. Given these possibilities, it is important to review patterns of services during the reform years.

Restricting the Commitment of Status Offenders, 1970-1972

The first attempt to deinstitutionalize status offenders occurred in 1971, when it became illegal for these youth to be committed to correctional institutions unless they had already been placed on probation. Although the factors mentioned above must have played some role in the local response to this state-level change, a thorough investigation of the matter is not possible. The age of

majority changed at the same time as policies toward
status offenders, and it is difficult to disentangle the
effects of two simultaneous changes. In addition, data
on the use of alternate care facilities, such as foster
homes, treatment facilities, or group homes, does not
exist for that period. It cannot be ascertained whether
these placements were substituted for correctional care.

Nevertheless, data concerning correctional placements
exist and can be used to gauge some effects of the legal
change. In looking at legal impact, patterns of placement
for 1970 and 1972 can be compared. This avoids calcula-
tions involving 1971, the year in which a transition was
occurring. Table 16-1 reports the number of admissions
to correctional facilities in these two years.

It is clear from Table 16-1 that the number of youth
admitted to correctional facilities decreased greatly
between 1970 and 1972, and that admissions of all kinds
were more than halved during this period. The change occurred both in the readmission of youth who had been in
correctional facilities before and in first admissions.
But the causes of the decline must be analyzed separately
for the two types of admissions.

Readmissions The change in the pattern of readmissions
cannot be attributed to new laws involving status offenders, because the legal change did not affect youth who
were on parole. Thus, one might suspect that the change
in the age of majority is the explanatory factor, as older

TABLE 16-1 Admissions to Wisconsin Correctional
Institutions, 1970 and 1972

Admissions	1970	1972
Total admissions	2,526	1,109
Readmissions from parole	1,172	382
New admissions	1,087	602
Miscellaneous (e.g., returns from other facilities)	267	125
Status offenders only:		
Readmissions from parole for status offenders under 18 (estimates)	424	135
New admissions of status offenders under 18 (estimated for 1970)	393	115

Source: Wisconsin Division of Corrections (1971a, 1973a).

youth could no longer be committed. To some small extent this seems to directly explain the change; that is, fewer readmissions occurred because older youth could not be committed. However, the decrease in readmissions occurred even among those youth who were under 18 and could still be committed. Thus, according to age breakdowns provided in documents (Wisconsin Division of Corrections 1971a, 1973a) but not in Table 16-1, readmissions decreased from 1,023 to 337 among youth under 18 years of age between 1970 and 1972.

Certainly some may claim that the change occurred because judges, realizing that the institutions would have to release youth at age 18, reduced the number of 17-year-olds whom they committed. But the same pattern holds up for youth under 17; readmissions dropped from 684 to 215. The reason for decreases, according to some of the individuals we interviewed, is indirectly tied to the age of majority. As the age of majority was altered, the state parole office decided to reduce efforts to recommit youth who once had been in an institution.

New Admissions   The drop in readmissions among status offenders simply reflects this general decline and is proportioned to it. But the number of youth who were admitted for the first time due to a status offense decreased by an unusually large amount. The existing data do not separate out new admissions by both age and offense simultaneously, but assuming that status offenses are evenly distributed across age categories, the best estimate is that the number of new admissions of status offenders under 18 decreased by 273, or about 70 percent. In fact, figures for delinquents remained about constant; the reduction in the institutionalization of status offenders accounts for most of the overall decrease in new admissions during the period. This reflects the fact that few new admissions involved youth over 17. Thus, the new law seems to have had a profound effect on new admissions of status offenders.

Summary   It can be said that the 1971 legislative change accomplished some of the goals of those who favored deinstitutionalization. After 1970, status offenders were committed to institutions less often than before. Insofar as new admissions are concerned, this change is clearly attributable to the new status offender law. Indeed, the reduction in the commitment of status offenders was not a continuation of a trend that had been occurring otherwise;

the percentage of all new admissions who had been committed for a status offense remained about constant between 1965 and 1970 (Wisconsin Division of Corrections
1966a-1971a). The legal change seemed to begin an entirely new trend.

Little is known about whether other treatment possibilities took up the slack for the loss of correctional
placements. Therefore, it is unclear whether status offenders were dealt with by other programs as their numbers
in correctional facilities decreased or whether they were
simply turned out of the system. But it is known that no
new treatment facilities were built after 1971 and that
only a handful of group homes existed at this time. It
thus seems likely that an increasing number of status
offenders were not placed at all. Nevertheless, accurate
figures do not exist; it is possible that the use of foster care increased, that the existing treatment facilities
became more populated, or that status offenders replaced
other youth in existing facilities.

Patterns of Change, 1973-1977

The bulk of the changes in policy occurred after 1972.
There is a large amount of data for the period 1973
through 1977, and they are summarized in Table 16-2. The
table reports the number of youth found in each of the

TABLE 16-2   Out-of-Home Placements of Juveniles in
Wisconsin, 1973-1977

Placement	1973	1974	1975	1976	1977
Foster care	6,457	6,236	6,264	6,045	6,039
Group homes	333	373	419	522	493
Treatment facilities	1,613	1,524	1,528	1,112	1,075
Correctional institutions (new admissions)	942	926	833	1,023	982
Total	9,345	9,059	9,044	8,702	8,589
Rate per 1,000 juveniles	5.69	5.51	5.55	5.35	5.23

Source: Wisconsin Department of Health and Social Services
(1974, 1976) and Division of Corrections (1974a-1978a).

four postadjudication placement settings that we believe
are used for status offenders and dependent and neglected
youth in Wisconsin. They are: (1) foster care homes,
which may house up to four children; (2) group homes,
which may serve up to eight; (3) treatment facilities,
serving at least eight youth, but possibly over one hun-
dred; and (4) state correctional facilities. Figures
regarding the first three placement settings come from
internal population data provided by officials in the
Wisconsin Department of Health and Social Services. Correctional placements are reported each year (Wisconsin
Division of Corrections 1974a-1978a), but in the form of
yearly admissions. Because the average length of stay in
state correctional facilities was slightly under a year
for most of the period (according to officials), the correctional data are roughly comparable to the internal
population data. For the correctional data, we chose to
concentrate on new admissions only. For those who are
interested, it might be noted that readmissions dropped
during the period, from 282 in 1973 to 235 in 1977. However, much of this drop occurred in 1974 and seems to
reflect the continuation of the trends relating to the
change in the age of majority mentioned in the last section. In 1974 there were 241 readmissions. Readmissions
do not appear to be directly relevant to the discussion
of status offenders. It is best to examine the data by
dividing the pattern into two periods, 1973-1975 and
1975-1977.

1973-1975 The period from 1973 to 1975 is characterized
by a number of legislative reforms. The possibility of
committing status offenders on a violation of probation
charge if that violation is another status offense was
eliminated, some group homes were developed, and the sum-
certain social services appropriation was instituted.
During this period the total number of out-of-home placements for the four types of facilities was reduced by 3
percent (301 youth). Foster care placements decreased by
193, treatment facilities by 85, and correctional placements by 109. The group home population increased by 86
youth.
     These changes represent a fairly small percentage drop,
and do not indicate radical changes in services. Nevertheless, the trends are quite consistent with the policy
reforms of the period. Financial incentives were meant
to reduce the use of treatment facilities and increase
the number of youth in group homes, and this occurred.

In fact, the decrease in the number of youth in the former
is nearly exactly offset by the increase in the latter
(85 and 86 respectively).

The impact of new laws that restricted the commitment
of status offenders is also reflected in the change in
the number of new admissions to correctional facilities.
Although this change was only slightly more than 10 percent, it is just about what one would expect if counties
simply stopped committing status offenders and changed no
other policies. Thus, Table 16-3 presents the number of
new admissions to state facilities in 1973 broken down by
the most serious offense. The potential effect of reform
on total admissions is indicated by the number of status
offenders—truants, runaways, and uncontrollable youth—
who were in the system in this pre-reform year. These
youth (boys and girls) totaled 115 admissions in 1973,
nearly identical to the 109 drop in overall institutional
admissions (see Table 16-2) over the course of the 1973-
1975 period. The drop is 11.3 percent.* For example,
status offenders represent 52 percent of all new female
commitments in 1973, and the reduction in new female admissions was 53 percent during the period (Wisconsin
Division of Corrections 1974a, 1976a).

It might be noted that, as a result of the decrease in
the use of treatment facilities and the almost identical
increase in the use of group homes, along with the decrease in correctional placements, the total number of
youth in these three facilities decreased during the period by about 4 percent. There was also a small reduction
in the use of foster care facilities. The decreases are
small and may be indicative of nothing more than year-
by-year random fluctuations. Nonetheless, local social
service workers insist that financial problems are often
dealt with by an immediate decrease in outreach staff,

_____

*A second source of data supports the validity of this
figure. Based on 1965 data, a Wisconsin dissertation
(Sharon 1977) reported the offense patterns of committed
males at this prepolicy change time, although new admissions and readmissions are not distinguished. The dissertation finds that only 18 percent of youth in institutions were committed for a status offense (although when
"near" status offenses, such as joyriding, are added, the
figure doubles). Given the decrease between 1965 and
1973, it appears that the 11.3 percent figure is not too
far off.

TABLE 16-3   New Admissions to Wisconsin Correctional
Facilities in 1973 by Most Serious Offense at Admission

Offense	Boys (N = 559)	Girls (N = 101)
Criminal Offense		
Aggravated assault	17 (3.0)*	5 (5.0)
Sex misconduct	12 (2.2)	3 (3.0)
Auto theft	113 (20.2)	6 (5.9)
Burglary, illegal entry	184 (32.9)	5 (5.0)
Vandalism	9 (1.6)	0
Other theft	48 (8.6)	12 (11.9)
Status offense		
Uncontrollable youth	23 (4.1)	16 (15.8)
Truant	12 (2.2)	11 (10.9)
Runaway	28 (5.0)	25 (24.7)
Drinking	7 (1.2)	5 (5.0)
Carelessness or misconduct	1 (0.2)	0
All other offenses	105 (18.8)	13 (12.8)
None recorded	0	0

Note: A small number (32) of new admissions come from state
probation. These admissions are not included in Table 16-3 or
16-4, and they do not significantly alter the distribution.

*Numbers in parentheses are the percentage of N.

Source: Wisconsin Division of Corrections (1974a).

which in the long run might reduce the number of families
who will accept foster care children.   And by 1975 the
sum-certain appropriation certainly limited funds available for both outreach and for placement of youth in noncorrectional, out-of-home facilities.   Thus, a causal
relationship is possible.

1975-1977   Further policy changes occurred between 1975
and 1977.   Attempts were made to limit correctional
placements by closing some institutions and by forming
the Juvenile Offenders Review Board.   In addition, the
Wisconsin Children's Center was closed in 1975.   Finally,
while the cost of operating treatment facilities skyrock-
eted, the sum-certain appropriation formula effectively
reduced funding for children's out-of-home placements
because the total services ceiling was met.

What are the effects of the changes? According to
Table 16-2, there was a reduction of 455 placements during
this period, or 5 percent. As was true in the 1973-1975
period, the number of foster care placements decreased
and the number of group home placements increased. The
trend in correctional placements between 1975 and 1977,
however, reversed the earlier changes; the number of admissions to these facilities increased by 149, to about
where it stood in 1973. The decrease in the number of
treatment facility placements is particularly large, as
is the percentage of change in the use of group homes over
the entire 1973-1977 period.

How do these changes relate to the alterations in
policy? Three of them seem consistent. First, by the
changes in funding and the closing of the Wisconsin Children's Center (a treatment facility, technically),
reformers hoped to reduce the enrollment in treatment
facilities. This occurred, although probably in a complicated manner. Officials claim that many youth who had
been in the Children's Center were moved to other treatment facilities; thus it seems that more youth than one
might expect, who were traditionally held in private facilities, were no longer placed.

Second and third, budgeting reforms were expected to
facilitate the use of groups homes and perhaps decrease
the use of out-of-home foster care placements. Cause and
effect are difficult to determine, but a decrease in the
use of foster care and an increase in the use of group
homes did occur. However, the group home total did not
completely compensate for the reduction in care in treatment facilities. There is a possibility that more youth
were simply left alone.

Correctional Admissions   One change is unexpected--the
substantial increase in correctional admissions. The
number of admissions had returned to the 1973 level by
1977 (see Table 16-2).

One possible explanation for the increase after the
reform is that judges learned how to circumvent the new
laws that banned the commitment of status offenders on a
violation of probation charge. It can be argued that they
found new ways of classifying youth who previously would
have been committed as status offenders, so that after a
small lag during which legal impact was maximized, these
youth then were committed under different labels. However, available evidence does not support the existence
of extensive relabeling. First, the local officials whom

we interviewed were quite adamant in their claims that there was no relabeling of youth. Second, while the decreases in the earlier period (1973-1975) occurred largely with respect to girls, the increases occurred among males (Wisconsin Division of Corrections 1974a, 1978a). Thus, it is clear that relabeling girls could not have occurred to a great extent. In addition, there were more boys in custody in 1977 than in 1973, making it unlikely that the increase was related only to status offenders (particularly as policy documents reveal no large alteration in the percentage of apprehensions involving a status offense during the period, as reported below).

Perhaps the most convincing argument against relabeling is presented in Tables 16-4 and 16-5, which present offender patterns for youth who were committed in 1973 and 1977. To make the figures comparable, status offenders were eliminated from the 1973 figures. If relabeling oc-

TABLE 16-4   New Admissions to Wisconsin Correctional Facilities in 1973 by Most Serious Offense at Admission

Offense	Boys (N = 496)* (%)	Girls (N = 49)* (%)
Aggravated assault	3.4	10.3
Sex misconduct	2.4	6.2
Auto theft	22.8	12.1
Burglary, illegal entry	37.1	10.3
Vandalism	1.8	0
Other theft	9.7	24.5
Drinking	1.4	10.3
Malicious mischief	0.2	0
All other offenses	21.2	26.3
None recorded	0	0
Total	100.0	100.0

Note: The order of listed offenses is that of the Division of Corrections, with the offenses presumed to be most serious listed first. For each individual, only the most serious offense is listed.

*Total excludes status offenders.

Source: Wisconsin Division of Corrections (1974a).

TABLE 16-5   New Admissions to Wisconsin Correctional
Facilities in 1977 by Most Serious Offense at Admission

Offense	Boys (N = 759) (%)	Girls (N = 95) (%)
Murder	0.3	1.1
Endangering safety, reckless use of weapons	0.3	0
Assault/battery	5.9	11.6
Rape	0.3	0
Robbery (armed)	5.4	0
Robbery (unarmed)	0.7	0
Carrying a concealed weapon	0.8	0
Burglary	44.1	12.6
Auto theft	19.1	10.5
Other theft	12.6	21.0
Receiving stolen property	0.9	0
Forgery/fraud, extortion	1.4	4.2
Arson	0.3	2.1
Malicious destruction of property	2.0	7.4
Drug offenses	0.5	3.2
Other sex offenses	1.1	2.1
Prostitution	0	7.4
Disorderly conduct	0.8	2.1
Resisting arrest	0.3	0
Trespassing	0.3	0
Traffic offenses	0.3	0
Bank threats	0.1	0
All other offenses	2.5	14.7
Total	100.0	100.0

Source: Wisconsin Division of Corrections (1978a).

curred, one might expect to find increases in admissions
among offenses that are most similar to status offenses.
For example, one might expect increases in sex offenses,
prostitution, or assault (uncontrollability, in theory,
can often be relabeled as assault against parents). Even
though the list of offenses was altered somewhat between
the years 1973 to 1977 (informants told us the alteration
was meant to reduce the "other" category, and the reader
may compare the two lists to gain some idea of what was
included in "other" in 1973), it is apparent that few such
decreases occurred. To be sure, for boys there are some

increases in the percentage of youth incarcerated for
assault, from 3.4 percent of new admissions in 1973 to
5.9 percent in 1977. Assaults are also up slightly as a
proportion for girls, from 10.3 percent of new admissions
in 1973 to 11.6 percent in 1977. For girls, sex offenses
and prostitution also increased as a proportion of all
offenses, constituting 6.2 percent of new admissions in
1973 and 9.5 percent in 1977.

These increases are too slight to imply a widespread
practice of relabeling. At best, they can account for 10
percent of the increase in commitment for these offenses.
One might claim that status offenders who also committed
more serious offenses were committed as status offenders
in 1973 and as delinquents in 1977, but this is unlikely;
the corrections figures report the most serious offense,
using a scale on which status offenses are at the bottom.
The largest increase in absolute numbers occurs in burglary, an offense that seems to be quite distant from
running away from home, uncontrollability, or truancy.

A second explanation for the return to the 1973 level
of correctional admissions by 1977 is that there was an
increased concern over crime in the years after 1975,
which in turn led to a desire to commit more children.
But it is not likely that the new crime control trend
accounts for all of the change. For example, one might
expect a crime control trend to affect police arrest and
referral rates as much as it affected courts, yet police
conduct changed little. The number of juvenile arrests
decreased slightly, from 89,586 in 1975 to 85,583 in 1977,
and the percentage of referrals to courts increased only
slightly, from 45.9 percent of all arrests to 47.0 percent
(Wisconsin Department of Justice 1976, 1978). In fact,
multiplying the two statistics, there was a small overall
decrease in the number of referrals to courts over the
period. If judges changed their commitment rate only to
the same extent to which the police changed their arrest
or even referral rate, the large changes in admissions
data would not have occurred.

One also might argue that judges were faced with more
seriously delinquent youth in the later period because
police officers refrained from referring status offenders
to court, but this does not seem to be the case. The
percentage of all arrests for status offenses actually
increased slightly during the period (Wisconsin Department
of Justice 1976, 1978). In sum, while it must be stressed
that the argument concerning an increased concern for
crime cannot be discounted completely, this view is not
supported by data.

A third explanation, one that also cannot be proved completely, does seem to make sense. Sosin (1979b) argues that the commitment rate is nearly a constant and is affected more by the judge's opinion of how many youth should be committed in proportion to referred cases than by the average seriousness of the offense. The rate at which judges commit youth is independent of the crime rate in the community. Furthermore, judges commit a proportion of youth that does not decrease significantly with the extent of intake screening, even though such screening may remove the less serious offenders. In short, the rate of commitment in juvenile courts might be so well established that it is somewhat immune from changes in the type of offenses that may result in commitment. It is possible that, after a short-run reduction in the number of commitments when the 1973 law created some uncertainty, judges reverted to previous behavior; that is, they re-placed status offenders with other youth in their commitment decisions, simply sending more burglars, for example, to institutions instead.

It is possible that all three explanations have some validity, but the last two seem most likely. It may even be argued that the 1973-77 fluctuations are random. But, given the efforts of the Juvenile Offenders Review Board to reduce the institutional population, and the limitations in the number of facilities, one might wonder how the population could possibly have increased. The most direct answer is that there are too many decisionmaking points for these policies to control. For example, while the review board may remove youth from institutions, it cannot forbid the original commitment. Judges apparently did not respond to any potential placements the board might have made. In addition, the expansion of group home placements by the Division of Corrections acts as a "safety valve" for the institutions, so that review board placements to group homes may simply make more room in the institutions for newcomers. In short, judicial behavior apparently did not need to change as a result of the size of facilities; rather, the institutions had to adapt.

Some County Differences

The patterns of change are not uniform around Wisconsin. Counties have different interests and backgrounds that shape their responses to laws. As part of this research, two counties were visited--Winnebago and Rock counties.

Both had cities of about 100,000, an important criterion because this seemed to be the most common size for cities in the state. While some observations on behavior in Milwaukee will be reported in this paper, the research focused on middle-sized cities that represent the modal pattern.

The number of commitments to correctional facilities for the years 1973 to 1977 in Winnebago County is shown in Table 16-6. In keeping with the statewide trends, commitments decreased in the years after the 1973 mandates involving status offenders were instituted (i.e., 1973-1975). Yet Winnebago County did not experience the statewide increase from 1975 to 1977. Instead, according to information provided, the number of youth in group homes increased by 17 while the number sent to treatment institutions decreased from five to two. The pattern in this county is thus consistent with an attempt to substitute group home placements for institutional placements in keeping with the new state policies. The reductions in out-of-home placements characterizing the state as a whole did not occur here.

Table 16-7 presents the same data for Rock County. This county is about the same size as Winnebago, but has almost double the rate of referrals to juvenile court. According to one judge, despite the large case load few status offenders were ever referred to court. Interestingly, in the first few years after 1973 there were some

TABLE 16-6   Juvenile Commitments to Correctional Institutions in Winnebago County, 1973-1977

Commitments	1973	1974	1975	1976	1977
Boys					
New admissions	15	13	9	13	11
Readmissions	13	8	7	8	4
Girls					
New admissions	2	0	2	0	0
Readmissions	4	3	2	3	0
Total	34	24	20	24	15

Source: Wisconsin Division of Corrections (1974a-1978a).

TABLE 16-7   Juvenile Commitments to Correctional
Institutions in Rock County, 1973-1977

Commitments	1973	1974	1975	1976	1977
Boys					
New admissions	25	35	28	35	38
Readmissions	7	19	13	16	26
Girls					
New admissions	10	5	6	3	3
Readmissions	5	7	7	6	3
Total	47	66	54	60	70

Source: Wisconsin Division of Corrections (1974a-1978a).

decreases in the commitment of girls, which might indicate
that the new law did have an impact.   (Perhaps many girls
who were committed before 1973 had been charged with a
status offense.)   Yet, for boys, the trend was upward
throughout the period.   In one of the two major cities in
the county (Beloit) a new judge was installed who favored
higher commitment rates.   But the upward trend began in
the entire county even before his installation.   (The
slight decrease in 1975 may represent a response to the
law forbidding institutionalization of a status offender
for violation of probation, but commitments had increased
even beyond the 1974 rate by 1977.)   In addition, officials said that treatment facilities in Janesville—the
other major city—continued to be used as heavily as
before.   We were told by local officials that there was
some decrease in the number of suggestions from the department of health and social services staff for treatment
placement for dependent and neglected youth because the
department had some control over this matter and it desired to keep within the sum-certain budget.   However,
there was a judicial desire to continue to use placement
resources for status offenders.   Thus, the changes in Rock
County did not occur as the legal reformers had wanted
them to.   Commitments increased and treatment facilities
continued to be heavily used.
    While these two counties differ to some degree from
the statewide pattern in which services were reduced but
commitments were stable, other individual counties cer-

tainly do fall into line. The trend in Milwaukee County, and in all counties taken together, exactly matches the pattern outlined for the entire state (Wisconsin Division of Corrections, 1974a-1978a). The most important point is that the great autonomy of counties can result in many different patterns.

Categories of Children

This report centers on youth who are not delinquent, although data do not always make such distinctions. Estimates, however, can be made of the changes in the number of status offenders and dependent and neglected youth placed over the 1973-1977 period. This may be accomplished for each option:

1. Placement in correctional facilities for status offenders included 115 status offenders in 1973 (Wisconsin Division of Corrections 1974a) and, assuming that no relabeling occurred, zero in 1977. The drop was thus 115.
2. There were 160 more placements in group homes and, according to studies of a subset of these facilities (Wisconsin Council on Criminal Justice 1978), 75 percent of group home youth are status offenders and dependent and neglected youth. The increase in such placements in these facilities is thus about 120.
3. Foster care placements dropped by 396 youth, and nearly all youth in these facilities were status offenders or dependent and neglected youth. However, since 1977, there is said to have been an increase in the use of foster care for delinquents. We will use the estimate of a decline of 396 status offenders and dependent and neglected youth.
4. According to Table 16-2, the number of youth in treatment facilities declined from 1,613 to 1,075 between 1973 and 1975. We do not know exactly how many of these youth were status offenders and dependent and neglected youth, but estimates are possible. Let us assume that the closing of the Wisconsin Children's Center in 1975 resulted in a decrease of 150 placements for such youth (officials reported that there were about that many youth in the facility when it closed). A survey of facilities conducted by the Wisconsin Council on Criminal Justice (1978) helps estimate the number of other such youth in treatment programs, assuming that the percentage did not alter dramatically over time. This survey (the raw data,

minus the names of the facilities, were made available)
asked facilities to report the total enrollment, the
number of available beds, and the percentage of status
offenders and dependent and neglected youth in residence
on a given day. If the facility mixed these youth with
delinquent youth, all the data were reported; if the facility did not mix delinquent and nondelinquent youth,
only the number of available beds was reported. In the
latter cases we know if delinquents of nondelinquents are
placed, but we must estimate the number of placements by
assuming that these facilities had the same percentage of
potential capacity (87 percent) used as did other facilities (this is calculated by dividing enrollments by beds).
Averaging the actual percentages and the estimates, when
needed, our estimate suggests that 77 percent of youth in
treatment facilities are status offenders and dependent
and neglected youth as of 1978. Assuming that the percentage had not changed substantially over time, and dis-
counting the Children's Center cases, it appears that
there was a drop of 376 in the number of these youth in
treatment facilities. Adding the decrease caused by
closing the Wisconsin Children's Center (160), the total
decrease is 536.

Summary Taking all these estimates together, it seems
that status offenders and dependent and neglected youth
were placed much less often in 1977 than in 1973. The
estimated drop is 839 youth, or 11 percent. If we assume
that the pattern of the decrease for dependent and neglected youth is closest to that represented by foster
care, while status offenders are more likely to be placed
in the other alternatives, the decline may be slightly
under 10 percent for dependent and neglected youth and
closer to 20 percent for status offenders. Of course,
all of these statistics are merely estimates, but it would
take counterintuitive assumptions to demonstrate anything
other than a large decrease in placements for these youth.
     Once again, it is important to note that these declines
are not only in the less restrictive alternatives. Foster
care, the least restrictive placement, demonstrates large
declines in absolute numbers, while the increase in group
home placements is not as great in absolute terms. In
absolute numbers the reduction in placements is similar
in the two least restrictive alternatives as compared with
the two more restrictive alternatives. In percentage
terms the change in the use of correctional institutions,
treatment facilities, and group homes is much more substantial than that in foster care.

Court Variation Officials in Winnebago and Rock Counties
agree that these decreases in placements have occurred.
They also claim that the decrease in out-of-home placements for status offenders and dependent and neglected
youth was not completely counterbalanced by an increase
in local community services. Most of the expansion in
services to children involved new outpatient psychiatric
facilities that were meant to compensate for the changes
in the mental health code. Because of new federal laws,
special school programs were also instituted in both
counties, but local officials made it clear that status
offenders were not enrolled in these programs and would
not be welcome. Many of the programs dealt only with
youth who are at least 18 years old. Court personnel in
these counties were particularly concerned by the lack of
programs that could deal with drug and alcohol problems.
In fact, although it is hard to prove, county officials
felt that there was a growing number of status offenders
who knew that they could not be institutionalized and who
lived on the fringe of the law, ignored by school, court,
and community.

The overall picture of services must vary by county,
and our sample of two is not sufficient to discern all
patterns. Both counties seemed to have maintained a
higher level of out-of-home placements than is true
throughout the state; Winnebago County increased the use
of group homes while Rock County continued to commit many
youth to state facilities and treatment programs. Our
general sense is that the most severe problems occur in
the smaller counties that do not have the resources needed to create new alternatives, and perhaps in Milwaukee.

Delinquents While the number of status offenders and
dependent and neglected youth receiving services may have
declined between 1973 and 1977, the number of delinquent
youth may have increased slightly. Comparing overall
changes in Table 16-2 to estimates for status offenders
developed above, there were 155 more offenders in correctional institutions, 40 more in group homes, and 97 fewer
in treatment facilities. In sum, the estimates indicate
that 98 more delinquents were in out-of-home placements
at the end of the period than at the beginning. The
increase is most apparent in correctional institutions.
Consistent with the possibilities of a growing concern
about crime and a constant judicial commitment rate, less
intervention in the lives of status offenders coincided
with increased intervention in the lives of delinquents.

However, the change for delinquents, even if estimates are accurate, is quite small in percentage terms.

<u>Patterns of Change: 1978-1979</u>   What has been occurring since the new children's code was passed in 1978?   Statistics involving all of the alternatives could not be located, but Wisconsin Division of Corrections (1979a) reports concerning correctional facilities are available. According to these documents, the number of new admissions in 1978 declined somewhat from 1977 admissions, standing at 778.   Monthly reports for 1979 suggest that admissions decreased by another 100.   In 1978 a new juvenile code, which was meant to reduce institutional confinements, was passed, and the results are consistent with the intended change--perhaps even reversing the trend toward increases in the commitment of other types of offenders as status offenders leave the correctional system.   Nevertheless, one should not make too much of the results.   Officials believe that correctional commitments and stays in detention have increased dramatically in 1980.   This would repeat the pattern suggested for 1973 and 1977, in which a decrease in the number of commitments in response to a new law was followed by a return to an earlier high level of commitment.

Some evidence suggests that as Wisconsin's financial problems are increasing, the number of alternative placements is declining.   According to internal documents, there were 136 group homes in 1976 but only 115 in 1979. Given this decrease we cannot be sure whether alternative placements are being provided for many status offenders or for delinquents who would have been placed in correctional facilities under previous policies.

Detention and Shelter Care

Reformers attempted to alter patterns of care in detention as well as in postadjudication placements, and a number of strategies were involved.   These strategies included:

   • The deinstitutionalization of status offenders from correctional facilities in 1973.   Many officials feared that the lack of the institutional disposition would result in an attempt to use detention as a punishment for status offenders.
   • The growth of shelter care facilities, encouraged by WCCJ funds and policies in an effort to replace more restrictive facilities with less restrictive ones.

* The new children's code, which virtually eliminated legal detention of status offenders.

The third issue must be dealt with separately, because less data exist for the post-1978 period. The actual patterns of change in response to the first two, however, can be gauged from detention admissions data for the 1973-1977 period, as reported in Table 16-8. The table separates prehearing stays in detention facilities from stays in county jails. In Wisconsin only the three largest counties (Dane, Milwaukee, and Racine) have separate facilities, and the jail figures represent patterns of detention in the rest of the state. Once again, it is useful to divide the trends into two periods. The analysis must begin in 1973 in order to avoid changes involving the age of majority (detention was not a matter of major concern to reformers before 1973). For comparative purposes it is interesting to note that the number of youth in detention increased slightly in the two years before 1973.

1973-1975 Even though the total number of youth in detention remained nearly constant between 1973 and 1975, there are a number of countertrends. For example, the number of detained youth increased between 1973 and 1974 (the 1972 totals were a bit higher than those of 1973), and decreased slightly after that. Furthermore, the pattern varies across counties. In the separate detention facilities the number of youth remained constant between 1973 and 1974, and then decreased; in county jails the number of detentions increased in the first two years and remained constant in 1975.

The various trends may represent differential responses to the changing policies relating to status offenders. WCCJ officials believe that as lobbying efforts increased, and as WCCJ began its campaign to deinstitutionalize status offenders, the judicial philosophy of the three counties with detention facilities altered in response. These counties also had large case loads and viewed status offenders as their least serious problem. Even without any formal change in the law, judges in the three counties therefore were receptive to the new ways of handling certain types of juveniles.

Other counties apparently did not share this philosophy. Rather, after the 1973 law prohibited the commitment of status offenders, these counties apparently responded by increasing detention rates. For example, in both Win-

TABLE 16-8 Wisconsin County Jails' and Detention Facilities' Detention Rate of Juvenile Confinements to County Juvenile Population, 1973-1977

Detaining Facility	1973			1974			1975			1976			1977		
	Number of Juvenile Confinements (Total)	County Juvenile Population (Total)	Detention Rate Per 1000	Number of Juvenile Confinements (Total)	County Juvenile Population (Total)	Detention Rate Per 1000	Number of Juvenile Confinements (Total)	County Juvenile Population (Total)	Detention Rate Per 1000	Number of Juvenile Confinements (Total)	County Juvenile Population (Total)	Detention Rate Per 1000	Number of Juvenile Confinements (Total)	County Juvenile Population (Total)	Detention Rate Per 1000
Grand Total	17,789	1,641,326	10.84	18,486	1,643,694	11.25	17,543	1,629,846	10.76	15,836	1,626,048	9.74	15,730	1,642,443	9.58
Detention Facility Total	7,521	524,783	14.33	7,625	514,478	14.82	6,712	500,655	13.41	5,382	485,556	11.08	4,971	481,744	10.32
Dane County Det. Ctr.	1,444	102,837	14.04	1,607	98,819	15.25	1,559	96,900	16.09	1,355	96,957	13.98	957	98,291	9.74
Milwaukee Co. Det. Ctr.	5,131	353,463	14.52	5,131	347,183	14.78	4,160	323,725	12.85	3,116	319,082	9.77	3,348	313,682	10.67
Racine Co. Det. Ctr.	946	68,483	13.81	987	68,476	14.41	992	69,914	14.19	911	69,517	13.10	666	69,771	9.55
County Jail Total	10,268	1,641,326	6.26	10,861	1,643,694	6.61	10,831	1,629,846	6.65	10,454	1,626,048	6.43	10,759	1,642,443	6.55

Source: Wisconsin Division of Corrections (1978b).

nebago and Rock counties the judges claimed that they
liked to use a one- or two-day stay in detention in order
to make status offenders realize that even without the
threat of institutionalization the court "meant business."
As one statewide report completed during this period notes
(Hamilton and Kosteckey 1978):

> The use of detention is one of the primary
> methods, if not the primary method, of dealing
> with status offenders in Wisconsin. As such,
> secure detention is a form of treatment. The
> youth is placed in jail to "think it over."
> The belief in its value has been summarized by
> one Juvenile Court Judge: "Detention has a
> tremendously favorable therapeutic . . .
> value." It is not uncommon for this judge to
> sentence status offenders to the county jail,
> sometimes explicitly and often more implicitly.

The leveling off of detentions in 1975 might simply indicate that the reaction to the legal change was complete.

1975-1977 There was an overall reduction in the use of
detention in this later period, and the change follows
the patterns noted above. There were continued, even ac-
celerating, reductions in the counties with separate detention facilities, while the jail population remained
rather stable.

Because the number of shelter care facilities increased
dramatically during this period, it might seem surprising
that this new alternative did not help ease the pressure
on county jails. Apparently many counties (other than of
the three largest ones) viewed shelter care facilities as
a means of supplementing, not replacing, jail detentions.
The total number of youth in custody in counties that
maintained both jails and shelter care facilities increased from 11,450 in 1974 to 14,282 in 1978--the two
years for which statistics are available (Wisconsin Council on Criminal Justice 1979).

At the same time some of the counties that relied on
jails experienced a decrease in detention rates. Simply
put, the new philosophies that caused the larger counties
to change also were adopted in some of the counties that
relied on jails. A WCCJ report (1978:34,36) notes that
these changes could be accomplished with nonfunded alternatives:

In 1975 there was a new Juvenile Court Judge installed in Polk County, as well as a new sheriff. The philosophies of each regarding the use of secure detention differed from their predecessors. In 1974 there had been a total of 187 secure detentions, but in 1975 this was reduced to 66. The 65% reduction occurred without the development of any real new alternatives. . . .

Primary goals of WCCJ-funded juvenile officer projects . . . include increasing the number of juveniles diverted from formal involvement with the juvenile justice system. . . . We have gathered data on the impact juvenile officers have had in reducing secure status detentions in Chippewa and Pierce Counties. During the project's first full year of operation, secure status detention dropped by 46.8% in Chippewa County and 31.6% in Pierce County. . . .

In short, the trends in detention were to a large degree based on an interaction of local values with the new philosophies. Grant support could result either in an increase in total placements (in counties with jails and shelter care facilities) or in a decrease.

Out-of-Home Placements: 1973-1977 A number of new shelter care facilities were built during the reform period, and one key question might be how the total number of preadjudication placements changed in response to all the trends. According to best estimates (Miller 1977), about 2,600 youth were placed in shelter care facilities in 1977, there were virtually no youth in shelter care in 1973. Because the total number of detained youth decreased by about 2,000, overall detentions and shelter care placements rose slightly. Thus, if reformers attempted to decrease total placements, they did not succeed through 1977.

Of course, the average restrictiveness of care decreased during the period because shelter care placements are less restrictive than jails. Furthermore, actual decreases probably occurred in those three counties with separate detention facilities. Thus, the general level of care decreased, as the reformers desired, even if total placements did not.

Types of Offenders: 1973-1977   There apparently were some
alterations in the composition of temporary placements.
A WCCJ study (1979) compares detention figures for 1974
and mid-1978, separating out status offenders from other
detainees. According to the statistics, there was a 33
percent decline in the detention of status offenders in
jails and detention facilities (about 2,600 out of 8,200
status offenders in the period). Shelter care placements
rose 2,000 (from near zero). Other WCCJ studies (1978)
suggest that half of those placed in shelter care are
status offenders; thus, the decrease in the use of jail
detention is somewhat offset by the use of less restrictive alternatives. But even compensating for shelter care
placements of status offenders (about 1,300), there was a
17 percent decrease in the preadjudication custody of
these youth. The decline was about twice as large for
counties without shelter care facilities as for those
with such placement alternatives. In sum, fewer status
offenders were detained at the end of the reform period
compared to the beginning, and those who were detained
were more often placed in less restrictive facilities.

However, detention of delinquents seemed to increase
during the period. Subtracting the number of status
offenders in the system from the 1973 and 1977 total number of youth in the system, one finds 600 more delinquent
youth in jails and detention facilities and about 800 more
in shelter care facilities at the end of the period. This
represents an overall increase of 1,400 (13 percent).

Once again, one might suspect that the pattern of handling delinquents reflects local responses to the trends
in care. Perhaps status offenders were relabeled as
delinquents in some counties. In others perhaps an increased concern about crime led to a higher detention
rate. In still others judges might have had an unchanging
sense of how many youth should be committed, and they
might have replaced status offenders with delinquent
youth. Finally, in some counties detention of status offenders decreased, with no corresponding increases in the
detention of delinquents.

As these hypotheses suggest, county variation in detention policies and practices is large. For example, in
one of the two counties visited, Winnebago, detentions
increased throughout the period as a response to the lack
of an institutional alternative. In the other, Rock, an
increase in the early years was countered by a decrease
in the later years. Although Rock County had a shelter
care facility, it appears that the total temporary place-

ment rate declined as a result of both the predilections
of the judge and some pressure from local child advocates.

The New Code   The new children's code was meant to greatly
reduce the detention of alleged status offenders and alleged delinquent youth.   The code forbids the detention
of most status offenders in locked facilities and limits
conditions under which alleged delinquents can be detained.   In assessing the effect of the new code, we may rely
on the raw data from which the WCCJ makes its yearly report to the Office of Juvenile Justice and Delinquency
Prevention.

According to this data, the use of detention had declined by 1979.   The 1978 statistics include 18,602 detentions, while the 1979 total of detained youth stands
at 11,519 (8,978 alleged delinquents; 1,220 alleged status
offenders, and 1,321 others).   Between 1978 and 1979 the
number of status offenders who were detained decreased by
4,370 while the number of delinquents declined by 1,690.
Compared to the base year of 1974 that WCCJ uses for its
statistics, the number of status offenders had declined
85 percent by 1979.   This is in keeping with OJJDP compliance standards.

Once again, the changes in detention are not uniform
across the state.   According to the figures, the detention
of alleged status offenders was reduced greatly in the
counties with separate detention facilities before the end
of 1978.   After 1978 virtually all of the decrease in the
detention of this group is due to changes in statistics
involving the counties that rely on jails.   Thus, the
counties without detention facilities were clearly influenced by the new code.   However, most of the decrease in
the detention of alleged delinquents since the new code
was implemented has occurred in the three counties with
detention facilities.   Detention of delinquents in these
counties decreased by 1,176 between 1978 and 1979.   Little
change occurred elsewhere.   Interestingly, compared to
1974 there were 1,325 fewer alleged delinquents held in
the three counties with separate detention facilities by
1979, and 571 more alleged delinquents held in other
counties.

At least as far as detention is concerned, the new code
clearly helped to reduce the number of status offenders
who were institutionalized.   Apparently it also resulted
in a decrease in the use of detention for delinquent
youth, particularly in the cities with separate detention
facilities.   But we do not know how fast the use of shel-

ter care facilities has grown over the last two years. The total number of youth in preadjudicatory care is thus unclear. Furthermore, it is important to note that despite some recent reductions, the number of delinquent youth detained in county jails is higher in 1979 than in 1974. A final caveat is that one must be wary of making too much of short-term trends. Officials have told us they believe the 1980 figures will demonstrate an increase in the use of detention for delinquents and, perhaps, even for status offenders.

THE FUTURE OF REFORM

Most of the changes outlined above are undramatic, but they are consistent with some of the most important goals of the reform movement. Youth who have committed a status offense but no other illegal act currently are not being placed in correctional institutions, and the number of these youth placed in treatment facilities has also apparently declined. A less restrictive alternative, group homes, is used more often. In addition, far fewer status offenders are placed in detention facilities and more are placed in shelter care. Apparently there are even some reductions in the use of treatment facilities to house dependent and neglected youth.

Despite progress in these areas, however, there are a number of continuing difficulties from the perspective of those who desired the changes in policies and services. For example, the number of youth in foster care has decreased since 1973. Furthermore, group home placements have not completely compensated for reductions in other areas. Some reformers may approve of these trends, claiming that all out-of-home placements should be reduced. Or they may rightly point out that the changes generally represent small percentages of youth. However, most agree that there is a lack of local programs to provide in-home services to status offenders, and some also may desire further reductions in the use of treatment facilities.

There are also some concerns over what might be a higher level of intervention in the lives of delinquents. While the trend may have reversed over the last two years, between 1973 and 1977 it appears that as status offenders left the correctional system, some delinquents replaced them. Many believe that post-1977 reversals of this pattern are temporary.

The number of youth detained in county jails increased over most of the reform years. Some counties even used new shelter care facilities to supplement jails. As a result, even though the detention of status offenders decreased overall and the detention of delinquents decreased in some counties, the total number of delinquents held in care across the state probably increased. The recent decrease in the detention of delinquents in the largest counties does not completely offset the trend, and may also be temporary.

Can these difficulties be addressed by future reforms? In dealing with the issue, it is important to note that some of the limits stem from key traits of the reform movement. The reforms linked changes in services to fiscal issues, and this coalition seems to be partly responsible for some of the other trends. Counties could not afford many group home placements nor could they provide extensive in-home supports, partly because of the funding limitations that were closely tied to the service reforms. Fewer staff were available to deal with the increasing county foster care case load. The limits on expenditures certainly had to affect services, especially considering the pressures caused by deinstitutionalization in mental health.

The strategies of coalition formation also seem to be implicated in the expansion of detention placements in some counties. The reformers believed that it was necessary to ease concern over the availability of alternative placements for children. The short-range strategy thus entailed encouraging the use of shelter care facilities. Apparently, reformers either were not concerned about the resulting increases in preadjudication placements in some counties, or they believed that the trends were necessary to solve short-run political problems.

The limits of change are as much a product of local conditions as of state policies. For example, the increase in detention in some counties occurred not only because WCCJ funds existed, but also because the counties chose to increase their level of intervention. Many counties must have looked at shelter care and detention as a means of circumventing the status offender amendments. The increased rate of correctional intervention for delinquents represents a further local strategy, whether it is due to reinstitutionalization, an increased concern about crime, or a constant judicial rate of intervention. Finally, counties so far have resisted any efforts to increase the use of foster care or treatment facilities.

It is also possible to argue that local predilections are implicated in the slow growth of less restrictive programs. Local officials had to decide whether to use the limited state funds for children's services or for other purposes, and in many counties other purposes took precedence. In Rock County the lack of in-home services was due in part to the judge's desire to limit his involvement with status offenses. This judge used the 1973 law and the new code as a means of protecting himself from objections to deinstitutionalization from the police and schools. In Winnebago County the new code convinced one judge that status offenders were too difficult to handle. He simply did not consider group homes to be a viable alternative.

To be fair, local discretion often worked to support changes that might not have occurred otherwise. Detention of status offenders decreased in some counties because officials believed that preadjudication control should be reduced. Reinstitutionalization might be minimal because judges respected the law. Some new services were provided by local communities, and both group home and shelter care facilities gained some voluntary acceptance. Similarly, the reduction in the use of treatment facilities was at least partly due to a local decision that the costs of placement were too high. A formula for reducing local discretion could thus eliminate some of the desired changes that have taken place.

In sum, many of the limits of reform appear to arise from compelling forces. Those limits that stem from reform strategies seem almost unavoidable in Wisconsin. Without the fiscal issues, the reformers might have been unable to make their case. The lack of funds might be a price reformers had to pay. Similarly, the necessity of providing alternatives made it difficult to avoid the use of shelter care as a supplement to detention.

Those limits that arise from local predilections also seem quite difficult to eradicate, given traditional limits of state laws concerning children. Judges and local social services departments have their own sources of power and their own agendas. Change will naturally vary to the extent to which the local communities differ in orientation. In Wisconsin those differences are great.

Such strong forces cannot easily be altered. Yet there is a continuing effort in Wisconsin to help ease some of the perceived difficulties. One result of federal funding and of the reform effort itself is the institutionalization of advocacy efforts. The Youth Policy and Law Cen-

ter, and to some extent, WCCJ (whose future is in some
doubt, due to changing federal policies) continue to
search for ways of dealing with some of the problems. The
new children's code, for example, attempts to control the
level of commitment of delinquents both by limiting the
type of offenses that can result in commitment and by
mandating the use of the least restrictive alternative.
It also attempts to alter detention practices. Similarly,
the recently passed "Youth Aids Formula" encourages counties to commit fewer youth and to spend more on local
services. It provides counties with a sum-certain appropriation that is reduced in accordance with the commitment rate.

In the short run, it appears that the new code has
temporarily reduced overall detention rates and commitments, demonstrating some possible effects of the continuing reform effort. It is important to avoid assuming
that the new code will result in long-lasting changes,
however; officials warn that 1980 may witness some reversals. Because financial incentives are not always a high
judicial priority, it is also possible that the Youth Aids
Formula might fail.

The success of the new reforms is thus still in doubt.
However, if these initiatives are not successful, others
may be attempted. Reform in Wisconsin continues, and the
reverberations of the deinstitutionalizaton movement are
not yet finished.

REFERENCES

Becker, Michael C, assisted by Grace Frudden (1978) The
    Organization and Administration of Children's Services
    in the Department of Health and Social Services:
    Problems and Proposals. Division of Policy and
    Budget. Madison, Wis.: Department of Health and
    Social Services.
Giles, H.H. (1883) County Care of Paupers. Proceedings
    of the Ninth Annual Conference on Charities. Madison,
    Wis.
Hamilton, Thomas (1979) Discussion of the Community
    Youth and Family Aides Proposal. Division of Policy
    and Budget. Madison, Wis.: Department of Health and
    Social Services.
Hamilton, Thomas, and Kosteckey, Ruth (1978) Changing
    Detention Practices in Wisconsin. Madison, Wis.:
    Wisconsin Council on Criminal Justice.

Johnson, Nellie, Imlen, Jeff, and Rosenhaum, Steve
    (1978) Children Services Study. Madison, Wis.:
    Wisconsin State Budget Office, Department of
    Administration.

League of Women Voters (1976) "In the Interests of . . ."
    Juvenile Justice in Wisconsin. Madison, Wis.: League
    of Women Voters.

Miller, Jill (1977) Shelter Care Reimbursement. Madison,
    Wis.: Youth Policy and Law Center.

Mitchell, Mark S., and Ziegler, Robert (1978) A Ten-Year
    Perspective of Juveniles Under Care and Supervision of
    Wisconsin Division of Corrections--Fiscal Year
    1968-1977. Office of Systems and Evaluations.
    Madison, Wis.: Division of Corrections.

President's Commission on Law Enforcement and
    Administration of Justice (1967) The Challenge of
    Crime in a Free Society. Washington, D.C.: U.S.
    Government Printing Office.

Sarri, Rosemary (1975) Under Lock and Key. Ann Arbor,
    Mich.: Center for Continuing Education.

Sharon, Nachman (1977) Juvenile Institutionalization and
    Adult Criminal Career. Unpublished Ph.D.
    dissertation, School of Social Work, University of
    Wisconsin.

Sosin, Michael (1979a) Social Work Advocacy and the
    Implementation of Legal Mandates. Social Casework
    60(5):265-273.

_____(1979b) Juvenile Court Commitment Rates:
    The National Picture. Discussion paper. Institution
    for Research on Poverty, University of Wisconsin,
    Madison.

Special Study Committee on Criminal Justice Standards and
    Goals (1975) Juvenile Justice Standards and Goals
    Report. Madison, Wis.: Wisconsin Council on Criminal
    Justice.

Wisconsin Council on Criminal Justice (1978) Funded
    Shelter Care Projects: A Program Assessment.
    Madison, Wis.: Wisconsin Council on Criminal Justice.

_____ (1979) Wisconsin's 1978 Monitoring
    Report on the Juvenile Justice and Delinquency
    Prevention Act. Madison, Wis.: Wisconsin Council on
    Criminal Justice.

Wisconsin Department of Health and Social Services
    (1974) Profiles of Juveniles in Wisconsin. Madison,
    Wis.: Department of Health and Social Services.

_____(1976) Juvenile Detention in
    Wisconsin. Madison, Wis.: Department of Health and
    Social Services.

Wisconsin Department of Justice (1976, 1978) <u>Wisconsin Criminal Justice Information: Crime and Arrests 1975</u> (and 1977). Annual report. Madison, Wisc.: Department of Justice.

Wisconsin Division of Corrections (1966a-1980a) <u>Admissions to Juvenile Institutions, 1980</u> (and earlier years). Bureau of Planning Development and Research. Madison, Wis.: Department of Health and Social Services.

_____ (1973b-1978b) <u>Jail and County Detention Facility Report, 1978</u> (and earlier years). Annual report. Madison, Wis.: Department of Health and Social Services.

OFFICIALS INTERVIEWED

Janet Anderson, Rock County Department of Social Services

Margaret Antes, Child Welfare Unit, Rock County Department of Social Service

Severa Austin, Bureau of Alternate Care, Department of Health and Social Services

Michael Becker, Division of Policy and Budget, Department of Health and Social Services

Jan Benda, Wisconsin Council on Criminal Justice

George Benz, Parkview Mental Health Clinic, Winnebago County

Ronald Blascoe, Division of Community Services, Department of Health and Social Services

Dr. Richard Brukenbacher, Mendota State Hospital

Mary Convoy, Bureau of Mental Health, Department of Health and Social Services

Robert Conway, Rock County Health Care Center

Patrick Devitt, State Public Defender, Rock County

Thomas Dickson, Youth Policy and Law Center

John Flanagan, School of Social Work, University of Wisconsin, Madison

Representative Richard Flintrop

Terry Footit, Winnebago County Sheriff's Department

Barbara Franks, Wisconsin Council on Criminal Justice

John Grace, Association of Wisconsin Child Care Institutions

Thomas Hamilton, Bureau of Alternate Care, Department of Health and Social Services

Paul Harris, Division of Community Services, Department of Health and Social Services

Dr. Robert Heintz, Winnebago County Mental Health Institute

David Heitzlinger, Janesville Public Schools
Audrey Hinegan, Division of Community Services,
    Department of Health and Social Services
Richard Hoetschl, Winnebago County Mental Health Institute
Wayne Hyler, Beloit Probation Department
Ray Jabloski, Rock County Juvenile Prosecutor's Office
Silvia Jackson, Office of Planning and Budget, Department
    of Health and Social Services
Daryl Jensen, State Public Defender, Rock County
John Juknailis, Winnebago County Court Intake Unit
Judy Kamarath, Winnebago Department of Social Services
Cheryl Kestly, Winnebago Department of Social Services
Richard Kiley, Division of Community Services, Department
    of Health and Social Services
Steven Krontzer, Division of Corrections, Department of
    Health and Social Service
Mary Kuhnen, Division of Economic Assistance, Department
    of Health and Social Services
Michael Lytowitzch, Winnebago County 51.42 Board
Jerry Majerus, Division of Community Services, Department
    of Health and Social Services
Christoper Marceil, Division of Community Services,
    Department of Health and Social Services
Donna McCleod, League of Women Voters
John Meltz, Winnebago County, Division of Community
    Services
Gene Messina, Private Attorney
Jill Miller, Youth Policy and Law Center, School of
    Social Work, University of Wisconsin, Madison
Dennis Mortiearty, Division of Corrections, Department of
    Health and Social Services
Patricia Nash, Child Welfare Unit, Rock County Department
    of Social Services
Karen Oghalai, Division of Community Services, Department
    of Health and Social Services
Richard Phelps, Youth Policy and Law Center
Judge Sverre Roang, Rock County Court
Susan Robillard, Division of Economic Assistance
Roland Robusen, Wisconsin Council on Criminal Justice
Judge J. G. Sarres, Winnebago County Court
Donald Schmidt, Juvenile Offender Review Board
Edward Schultz, Janesville Probation Department
Guy Schultz, Pathways Group Home, Janesville
John Scott, Rock County Sheriff's Office
Richard Shepard, Winnebago County Department of Social
    Services
Judy Steinbicer, Rock County Department of Social Services

Kenneth Tanner, Rock County Youth Homes
Lance Taylor, Oshkosh Public Schools
Mary Ann Test, School of Social Work, University of
    Wisconsin, Madison
Rowland Todd, Wisconsin Council of Human Concerns
Maureen Torphy, Dane County Juvenile Court
Robert Vanderloop, Private Attorney, Oshkosh
Sandy Venner, Youth Policy and Law Center
John Vick, Division of Community Services

Services for Status Offenders Under the LEAA, OJJDP, and Runaway Youth Programs

17

SALLY A. KORNEGAY *and*
JOAN L. WOLFLE

INTRODUCTION

The Juvenile Justice and Delinquency Prevention Act was passed in 1974 and created two new programs that focused specifically on status offenders or included them within their purview. The act created the Office of Juvenile Justice and Delinquency Prevention (OJJDP) within the Department of Justice's Law Enforcement Assistance Administration (LEAA) to provide direction and technical and financial assistance to states in juvenile delinquency matters. Included in the congressional direction of that program were the goals of deinstitutionalizing status offenders and dependent and neglected children, and separating juveniles from adults in detention and correctional facilities. In order to receive formula grant funds from OJJDP, states had to make a commitment to and then show progress toward meeting those goals. The second new program created by this act was a grant program for runaway centers to be administered by the Department of Health, Education, and Welfare (HEW, currently the Department of Health and Human Services). These programs are described here primarily from the federal perspective. Each program was found to have affected the deinstitutionalization movement by providing legitimization as well as funds for state and local initiatives; these activities are addressed in the state case studies.

Before the passage of the Juvenile Justice Act, federal responsibility for juvenile delinquency matters (which included status offenders) was shared by various agencies but primarily by LEAA and HEW. The net effect of this diffusion of responsibility was that no clear direction was given by the federal level for state or local levels. There was no consistent definition of federal policy concerning the control and treatment of juvenile delinquents and no recognizable focal point of federal leadership. The lack of consistent policy and leadership, combined with relatively small financial resources, created confusion at all levels of government.

Because the changing federal role regarding juvenile delinquency (and thereby status offenders) was an important issue in the history of deinstitutionalization at state and local levels, this paper begins by briefly discussing the development of that role. Next we describe the LEAA programs authorized by the Omnibus Crime Control and Safe Streets Act of 1968 (the Safe Streets or Crime Control Act) and the maintenance of effort requirements concerning the use of those funds for programs in the juvenile justice area. Since funding levels under the Crime Control Act were considerably higher than under the Juvenile Justice Act, LEAA grants had a greater potential for affecting state and local programs for juveniles than grants available from OJJDP. Finally, the OJJDP and runaway youth grant programs are described.

FEDERAL CONCERN FOR STATUS OFFENDERS

The first formal demonstration of federal concern about juvenile delinquency occurred when the Children's Bureau was established in 1912. Congress assigned the bureau a wide range of issues to study, including the functioning of juvenile courts, which around that time had been experiencing rapid growth (U.S. Congress 1980b). Over time, federal involvement in juvenile delinquency issues proved to be limited as well as scattered throughout many different agencies. The next major development occurred in 1961 when the Juvenile Delinquency and Youth Offenses Control Act (P.L. 87-274) was passed. This act authorized HEW to award grants for pilot projects that demonstrated new techniques for preventing or controlling juvenile delinquency. Authority for the program ended in 1967, and the decision about its reauthorization became involved with the broader issues of the federal role in crime control that were under consideration by Congress at that time.

In 1968 Congress produced two pieces of legislation that were related to the control and prevention of juvenile delinquency. One was the Juvenile Delinquency Prevention and Control Act (P.L. 90-445), which gave HEW primary federal authority for addressing problems associated with juvenile delinquency. Although the previous HEW program had consisted of demonstration projects, this new legislation mandated HEW to develop a national approach to juvenile delinquency and to provide federal funds to states to strengthen their activities in the juvenile justice area. The other piece of legislation was the Crime Control Act (P.L. 90-351), which established LEAA within the Department of Justice. That act made no mention of juveniles or delinquency. LEAA was intended by Congress to address the problem of crime and the overall improvements needed in the administration of criminal justice. It was expected that LEAA's concern about juveniles would be restricted to young people who had committed offenses that would be considered crimes if committed by adults and/or those who had come into formal contact with traditional law enforcement and criminal justice agencies.

From 1968 to 1974 the lack of federal leadership felt at the state level in the area of juvenile delinquency prevention and control was due in part to the confusion concerning which federal agency was responsible for providing that leadership. The problem was that although in theory both HEW and LEAA were assigned certain areas of responsibility, in practice these areas often overlapped. HEW was supposed to have overall direction for policies concerning juvenile delinquency, but LEAA had overall responsibility for assistance in the criminal justice area, including juvenile criminal behavior. In terms of prevention HEW had responsibility for what was called primary prevention, that is, for supporting general child and youth development programs to prevent juveniles from having initial contact with the formal justice system; LEAA had responsibility for sponsoring programs to prevent juveniles who had had contact with the justice system from having further and more serious formal involvement. This distinction in authority was not drawn clearly in either of the 1968 pieces of legislation, but the related congressional discussions had addressed the issue (Peskoe 1973). Within a few years the distinction between the responsibilities of HEW and LEAA had become blurred, and both were accused of duplication and lack of coordination with regard to programs for juveniles (U.S. Congress 1972, 1973a).

The lack of clarity between the functional limits of LEAA and HEW was in part due to the types of agencies that received funds under both programs. One of the reasons HEW was given program responsibility for the Juvenile Delinquency Prevention and Control Act was its supposed expertise with service systems that were not part of the criminal justice system. Juvenile delinquency by and large was regarded as a social problem rather than a criminal justice or law enforcement problem. It was hoped that HEW could help states to develop prevention and treatment programs that might be outside traditional juvenile justice systems, or at least help them to develop alternative methods within those systems (U.S. Congress 1977). The Crime Control Act specified that the federal funds were to be used for a range of activities (e.g., prevention) that were not necessarily viewed as the responsibility of the existing criminal justice system. Therefore LEAA, like HEW, accepted applications from a broad range of nontraditional law enforcement and community service organizations that chose to operate their programs independently of the juvenile and criminal justice systems.

The difference in levels of financial support for projects that focused on the problems of juvenile delinquency added to the confusion about which federal agency really had the leadership role in this area. LEAA's support of programs aimed at juveniles grew over the years and, because of its greater resources, accounted for larger expenditures than were available through HEW. In fiscal year 1970, for example, almost 12 percent ($32 million) of LEAA's appropriations was spent on programs for juveniles. Under the Juvenile Delinquency Prevention and Control Act, HEW had spent only $15 million that year (U.S. Congress 1977).

In an effort to clarify the situation, the Secretary of HEW and the Attorney General exchanged letters in May 1971 that formally delineated the juvenile delinquency responsibilities of their respective departments. HEW was to be responsible for prevention up to the point of formal contact with the juvenile or criminal justice system, and LEAA was to be responsible for programs to assist juveniles under the jurisdiction of the juvenile or criminal justice system (U.S. Congress 1972). While these letters may have defined the program responsibilities for the

federal agencies, they did not entirely clarify the areas
of responsibility and authority for program participants
at the state and local levels. The types of projects and
organizations funded by the two federal agencies in many
instances continued to be similar.

Amendments to the Crime Control Act in 1971 (P.L.
91-644) resulted in further confusion. The definition of
law enforcement and criminal justice was expanded to include programs to prevent, control, or reduce juvenile
delinquency, and LEAA's state planning agencies were authorized to include in their comprehensive plans community-based prevention and correctional programs for
preconviction or postconviction referral of offenders as
well as community service centers for repeat youthful
offenders.

Congress attempted to resolve the problem of overlap
in 1972 by passing amendments to the Juvenile Delinquency
Prevention and Control Act (P.L. 92-381) that specifically
limited HEW to sponsoring programs outside the juvenile
justice system. However, no amendments were made to the
Crime Control Act to limit activities or agencies that
LEAA could fund.

In addressing these jurisdictional issues, a later
report by the Senate Committee on the Judiciary asserted
that the existence of LEAA was largely responsible for
HEW's failure to become dominant in the field of juvenile
delinquency (U.S. Congress 1977). The report held that
LEAA had become the dominant federal force in the juvenile
field because of its leadership role in the overall criminal justice area and because its resources were greater
than those of the HEW program. The state justice and law
enforcement entities did not really look to HEW for guidance or assistance in the justice area; that federal department was not viewed as part of their system. Even the
funds distributed by HEW frequently found their way into
the state justice systems rather than the social service
agencies that were more closely aligned with other HEW
programs. By 1971 over 40 state criminal justice planning
agencies--the ones that administered the LEAA grants--were
also administering Juvenile Delinquency Prevention and
Control Act funds from HEW (U.S. Congress 1977). So even
though LEAA did not assume the leadership role for planning programs in the area of juvenile delinquency, neither
did HEW do so effectively. Congress added to the confusion during this period by assigning LEAA more and more
responsibilities in that area.

Among the 1973 amendments to the Crime Control Act
(P.L. 93-83) was the requirement that LEAA place greater
emphasis on juvenile justice and delinquency prevention.
LEAA thereafter was prohibited from approving any state
plan for the use of Crime Control Act funds unless the
plan included "a comprehensive program . . . for the improvement of juvenile justice" (Sec. 303(a)).   Such a
state program was not required to use Crime Control Act
funds, but it could use funds from other sources either
partially or entirely. In response to the amendment, LEAA
for the first time established a separate unit, the Juvenile Justice Division, to handle programs for juveniles.
That unit, however, was part of LEAA's Office of National
Priority Programs, which was responsible for LEAA's discretionary grant programs and not for those programs
funded under the comprehensive state plans. As a result,
there was little interaction between the Juvenile Justice
Division and the agencies that received and spent LEAA
block grants.

Between the passage of the Crime Control Act in 1968
and the passage of the Juvenile Justice Act in 1974 Congress neither required nor encouraged LEAA to provide
services specifically to status offenders and dependent
and neglected children. Until 1974 both the Congress and
the various administrations directed LEAA to address the
problems of juvenile delinquency, but they made no distinction between status offenders and more serious juvenile offenders. If anything, the prevailing attitude
appeared to be that status offenders and dependent and
neglected children were more appropriately the concern of
HEW.

With the passage of the Juvenile Justice Act in 1974
(P.L. 93-415), LEAA and its newly created subunit, OJJDP,
were assigned primary federal responsibility for policies
and programs pertaining to juvenile delinquency. While
HEW retained a grant program for runaway centers, the
focal point for federal concern about status offenders was
lodged with OJJDP. The Juvenile Justice Act gave OJJDP
lead authority for all federal policy and assistance in
the area of juvenile justice, but its two major program
goals were to assist with the separation of juveniles from
adults in detention and correctional facilities and the
deinstitutionalization of status offenders. In fact, the
receipt of formula grant funds by states was made contingent on meeting these goals. Thus, LEAA was mandated responsibility for the implementation of federal policy for
status offenders.

In an effort to mesh the Crime Control Act and Juvenile Justice Act programs, and perhaps in anticipation of LEAA's reluctance to give greater priority to juvenile delinquency concerns, Congress passed two conforming amendments to the Crime Control Act as part of the Juvenile Justice Act (P.L. 93-415). First, in order for a state to receive a Juvenile Justice Act formula grant, its Crime Control Act plan was required to include an additional plan for carrying out the purposes of the Juvenile Justice Act (Sec. 223). Specifically this included the mandates (1) that status offenders and dependent and neglected children be removed from detention and correctional facilities and (2) that juveniles alleged to be or found to be delinquent be separated from adults who had been convicted of a crime or were awaiting trial on criminal charges. Second, LEAA was required to expend the same level of its Crime Control Act funds (exclusive of administration) on juvenile delinquency programs as it had in fiscal year 1972 (Sec. 261). This provision, known as the maintenance of effort clause, was intended to prevent LEAA from supplanting Crime Control Act funds with Juvenile Justice Act funds and thus decreasing, or at least not increasing, its actual expenditures on juvenile delinquency programs. Partially due to changing appropriation levels and accounting difficulties, the maintenance of effort provision was changed in 1977 to a fixed percentage, 19.15 percent (P.L. 94-503, Subsec. (b)). The 19.15 percent figure was based on LEAA's own calculation of the amount of Crime Control Act block grant funds that it obligated in fiscal year 1972 for programs affecting juveniles.

Status offenders and dependent and neglected children were separated from the broader juvenile delinquency population when Congress was considering the Juvenile Justice Act. These youth may have been served with LEAA dollars during the 1968-1974 period, but only as part of general delinquency prevention or juvenile corrections programs. There is no evidence that status offenders were singled out in any way for special treatment, and there still is no requirement that LEAA's Crime Control Act funds be expended on programs for that population. The prevailing attitude at LEAA, at least through mid-1980, appeared to be that OJJDP resources might be applied to the status offender and dependent and neglected child population, but that LEAA's other resources should be used for adjudicated delinquents and, in particular, serious and/or violent juvenile offenders. This attitude was further strengthened by the most recent revision to the maintenance of effort requirement enacted as part of the Justice System Improvement Act (P.L. 96-157, Sec. 1002). The new legislation directs that emphasis be placed on the use of funds for programs directed toward juveniles who have been either convicted of criminal offenses or adjudicated delinquent.

LEAA PROGRAMS

Although it has been amended five times, the original Crime Control Act's major provisions were still in effect through the time of this study, 1979-1980. The specific purposes of the legislation were to (1) encourage states and units of local government to develop and adopt comprehensive plans based on their evaluation of state and local problems of law enforcement and criminal justice; (2) authorize grants to states and units of local government in order to improve and strengthen law enforcement and criminal justice; and (3) encourage research and development directed toward the improvement of law enforcement and criminal justice and the development of new methods for the prevention of crime and the detection, apprehension, and rehabilitation of criminals.

LEAA was given responsibility for administering several different types of grants under the Crime Control Act. These included planning grants; grants for law enforcement purposes (often called action grants); training, education, demonstration, and special grants; grants for correctional institutions and facilities; community anticrime funds; and public safety officers' death benefit payments. LEAA funds, with the exception of the officers' death benefit payments, some fellowships for individuals, and administrative funds, were expended through grants and contracts with public and private organizations. Most LEAA funds were distributed to the states as block grants, with each state getting a fixed amount for planning activities and a varying share of the remainder, based on population. The rest of the funds were discretionary and were awarded directly by LEAA for specific projects.

Crime Control Act planning grants were available to states that had designated state planning agencies to develop and administer plans to use LEAA block grant funds. Each state got a minimum of $250,000 per year. These federal planning grants could cover up to 90 percent of the expenses of the state planning agencies.

The action grants under the Crime Control Act accounted for the largest amount of LEAA funds, and most of these (85 percent) were allocated to the states as block grants. The remaining 15 percent of the action grant funds were discretionary and were distributed directly by LEAA to states, units of local government, or nonprofit organizations. Action grants were used for projects to improve and strengthen law enforcement and criminal justice. One of the 14 categories of eligible programs included projects concerned with juvenile justice and delinquency prevention. Federal funds could cover up to 90 percent of the cost of all action grant projects except for construction, which was limited to 50 percent.

LEAA's National Institute of Law Enforcement and Criminal Justice (now the National Institute of Justice) awarded grants and contracts for research, demonstrations, evaluation, and information dissemination. These federal funds could provide up to 100 percent of the costs of eligible projects. In the past this category of LEAA grants also included grants and loans for educational assistance in the areas of law enforcement and criminal justice. This program was transferred to the Department of Education when it was established in 1980, but funds were not appropriated for it after that time.

The grant program for correctional institutions and facilities began in 1971. These grants were provided to improve and upgrade correctional programs and facilities. One-half of these funds were available as block grants to state planning agencies, and one-half were distributed by LEAA on a discretionary basis. The federal funds could provide up to 90 percent of the project costs.

Community anticrime grants were available from LEAA to community and citizen groups and nonprofit organizations. Grants of up to 100 percent of the project costs were made for crime prevention, detention, deterrence, and apprehension activities that had a predominant focus on urban areas.

Crime Control Act block grant funds were awarded annually to state planning agencies. The state planning agencies in turn awarded subgrants and subcontracts to public and private agencies to conduct individual projects. Congressional appropriations under this act were available until expended (Sec. 520(a)); however, LEAA established a three-year restriction on expenditures whereby funds could be expended at any time up to three years after the end of the fiscal year in which they were appropriated.

The state planning agencies had no authority over the awarding of discretionary funds by LEAA in Washington. As a courtesy, however, and to prevent duplication of effort, each state planning agency director was given an opportunity to review applications received in Washington for projects planned for operation in his or her state. A state planning agency director could recommend that a discretionary grant application be rejected, but the final decision was made by the LEAA administrator.

LEAA itself had no state or local offices; the state planning agencies were state administered. Ten federal regional offices were established, but these offices were closed at the end of fiscal year 1977. With the exception of some auditing responsibilities, all federal program responsibilities were assumed by LEAA in Washington. Five regional audit offices were retained and were responsible for conducting audits of state planning agency block and formula grant disbursements and individual discretionary grant and contract expenditures. LEAA had no other federal field offices.

Although LEAA did have the power to ensure that states adhered to their plans, the administration had no policy or program control over state planning agency subgrant and subcontract decisions. The state planning agencies were required to maintain detailed program and financial records on each subgrant and subcontract awarded out of Crime Control Act block grant funds, but LEAA was prohibited by the federal Office of Management and Budget from requiring state planning agencies to submit copies of the records to Washington. This also applied to Juvenile Justice Act formula funds. LEAA does have a computerized program and project information system called PROFILE. The system, however, does not contain any information on individual projects funded at the state level unless a state wishes to supply it. We found that at least during the period covered by this research, few of the states that were included in the study supplied any information, and those that did appeared to do so for only some of their projects.

The Maintenance of Effort Provision

The maintenance of effort provision was potentially one of the most important legislative requirements enacted to ensure that funding for juvenile delinquency programs increased as a result of the Juvenile Justice Act. During

the mid-1970s when LEAA's budget was at its peak and
OJJDP's funding was just beginning, the funds required for
juvenile delinquency programs under the terms of the
maintenance of effort provision were considerably more
than the total annual OJJDP appropriation. For example,
in the first year after the Juvenile Justice Act (fiscal
year 1975), LEAA received $895 million as its appropria-
tion. The maintenance of effort provision required that
at least $112 million be spent on juvenile programs in a
year when OJJDP's entire appropriation was only $14.5
million. In fiscal year 1977 LEAA was appropriated more
than $750 million, which should have fixed the maintenance
of effort level at more than $140 million; OJJDP's total
appropriation that year was only $75 million (U.S. De-
partment of Justice 1978b).

Policy interpretations of the maintenance of effort
provisions and the accounting procedures used to document
funding levels have changed since the enactment of the
provision. Unfortunately, the varied nature of LEAA
grants combined with the multiyear expenditure period
prevent LEAA from determining precise annual maintenance
of effort expenditures. Reports of maintenance of effort
funding levels have been prepared on the basis of obligations rather than actual expenditures and by attributing
portions of general criminal justice grant and contract
awards to juvenile delinquency on the premise that if a
project serves an undefined population, or makes overall
improvements to the administration of justice, then a
portion of the award dollars can be counted as juvenile
delinquency funds. In addition, some maintenance of effort reports were prepared by budget officers who had
limited knowledge of what individual projects were intended to accomplish.

In its interpretation of the maintenance of effort
clause, LEAA determined that the requirements of the provision applied to block grants that were awarded to the
states as well as to the discretionary funds awarded by
LEAA itself (Madden 1975, U.S. Department of Justice
1976). This meant that through their subgrants and subcontracts states had to spend at least 19.15 percent of
their block grants on projects concerned with juveniles.
Through 1978 this requirement was applied to the aggregate
program funds, but beginning in fiscal year 1979 each
state was required to meet the 19.15 percent level for its
grant award (U.S. Department of Justice 1978a).

As can be seen from the amounts included in Table 17-1,
the funds reportedly allocated by the seven study states

TABLE 17-1 LEAA Funds Allocated to Juvenile Programs in Order to Meet the Maintenance of Effort Requirement, Fiscal Years 1975-1979

State	FY 1975 ($)	FY 1976 ($)	FY 1977 ($)	FY 1978 ($)	FY 1979 ($)
Arizona	958,923	747,460	931,131	655,745	833,404
Louisiana	1,517,114	2,701,720	1,466,240	997,244	1,042,798
Massachusetts	3,652,442	2,539,290	1,671,278	1,540,925	1,666,138
Pennsylvania	7,786,019	8,249,580	5,483,467	4,751,741	3,371,340
Utah	624,743	562,780	841,734	655,662	674,622
Virginia	1,768,869	2,994,720	2,440,792	1,411,602	1,648,560
Wisconsin	2,365,170	3,971,880	1,044,000	2,135,472	2,512,615

Source: Law Enforcement Assistance Administration (1978, 1979, no date).

for projects related to juvenile justice have not been inconsequential. According to data supplied by OJJDP, the maintenance of effort funding levels have, in most cases, exceeded the state allocations under the Juvenile Justice Act. This is not true for all seven states in all years, and the gap appears to have narrowed since LEAA appropriations have been reduced. For the most part the states reportedly have met their required maintenance of effort levels (especially since 1978), and in fact several have surpassed their quotas (see Table 17-2). This may or may not be reflected in increased obligations. For example, even though Utah only allocated about 20 percent of its funds to juvenile-related projects in the first year, approximately the same level of reported planned obligations represented about 35 to 40 percent of that state's Crime Control Act funds for the years 1978 and 1979.

There is no simple, single explanation as to why there is so much variation in the amounts reported in Table 17-1. Due to the sources of information (e.g., state plans, estimates), the reports cannot be interpreted as reflecting actual expenditures for activities focused on juveniles. The staff preparing the reports may have used slightly different procedures each year or made different decisions concerning the prorating of general project funds. The reported amounts also might reflect either the 1977 change in the maintenance of effort provision from an overall dollar amount to the percentage requirement, or the change from applying the provision to the aggregate amount to each state's grant. Once states became aware that LEAA would hold them accountable for the maintenance of effort allocations in their plans, they may have responded by assuring that an adequate level of obligations was indeed planned. This may be reflected in the fact that it was only in 1978 and 1979 that all seven states were reportedly over the 19.15 percent level. The fluctuations might also reflect changes in state and local priorities. Potentially one of the most important influences on these funding patterns has been the level of funds available from LEAA to the states each year. In fiscal year 1975 LEAA received its largest appropriation of $895 million, and $591.5 million of those funds were awarded to the state planning agencies. In each succeeding year the budget shrank. The combined impact of all these factors, possibly coupled with others we have not mentioned, may have led to the varying levels reported.

Whether LEAA maintenance of effort funds were used to assist in achieving the goals of the Juvenile Justice Act,

574

TABLE 17-2 Percentage of LEAA Grants Allocated to Juvenile
Programs and Counted for the Maintenance of Effort Requirement,
Fiscal Years 1975-1979

	Maintenance of Effort Percentage				
State	FY 1975	FY 1976	FY 1977	FY 1978	FY 1979
Arizona	19.23	14.0	26.44	21.87	27.28
Louisiana	15.98	28.0	23.90	19.33	19.18
Massachusetts	24.81	17.0	17.68	19.55	21.61
Pennsylvania	25.74	27.0	28.41	29.55	21.00
Utah	21.82	19.0	43.79	40.20	40.30
Virginia	14.61	24.0	30.49	20.90	24.00
Wisconsin	20.57	34.0	14.02	34.32	40.08

or at least were not inconsistent with that act, is an
issue separate from whether they were allocated. The LEAA
maintenance of effort funds were never required to be used
for efforts to deinstitutionalize status offenders and
dependent and neglected youth. In fact, it was theoretically possible for LEAA maintenance of effort dollars to
have been spent for the construction of juvenile institutions while Juvenile Justice Act dollars were being used
to remove status offenders from those same institutions.
Viewing the matter strictly from the perspective of financial resources, the maintenance of effort provision
alone gave LEAA greater ability to effect changes in the
juvenile justice system than OJJDP, and LEAA could use its
authority toward ends that, though consistent with the
Juvenile Justice Act, may not have supported its deinstitutionalization and diversion goals.

The New Federal Structure

Setting aside the fact that Congress in essence voted to
close down LEAA by virtually eliminating its appropriation, the Justice System Improvement Act (P.L. 96-157),
which was signed into law by President Carter on December
27, 1979, made fundamental changes in the structure and
function of LEAA. The act radically reorganized the assistance, research, and information functions of the
Department of Justice. It permitted the statistical
functions previously conducted by Main Justice (e.g., the
FBI's uniform crime reporting program) to be combined with
functions formerly performed by LEAA (e.g., victimization
studies) under the Office of Justice Assistance, Research,
and Statistics (OJARS). Services to state and local government would have remained with LEAA, separate from the
research and reporting functions, if funding for these
programs was continued.
    OJARS serves as an umbrella agency responsible for co-
ordination and support services. It consists of three
separate bureaus. The Bureau of Justice Statistics con-
solidates statistical functions. The National Institute
of Justice encompasses the research, evaluation, and program development responsibilities. The third bureau is
LEAA, which was to continue to administer the state and
local financial and technical assistance and community
anticrime programs. In effect, LEAA was to retain its
previous assistance functions, but it was to be stripped
of most of its research and information collection and

dissemination functions. OJJDP was removed from the LEAA but not entirely from the OJARS structure by the 1980 amendments to the Juvenile Justice Act.

The maintenance of effort provision was continued under the new legislation. The Senate Committee on the Judiciary had wanted to waive the requirement when the total appropriations for the grant programs under the Crime Control Act fell below $150 million during any fiscal year (U.S. Congress 1980c), but this provision was not contained in the legislation that passed. Some of the same influences that in 1980 caused the Juvenile Justice Act to focus on serious offenders also were evident in the Justice System Improvement Act of 1979. The newly worded maintenance of effort clause indicates that the funds should be expended "with primary emphasis on programs for juveniles convicted of criminal offenses or adjudicated delinquent on the basis of an act which would be a criminal offense if committed by an adult" (Sec. 1002).

OJJDP PROGRAMS

As previously stated, from its creation in 1968 until 1974 LEAA had been steadily, albeit reluctantly, gaining responsibility for juvenile delinquency programs. LEAA was created largely in response to the urban unrest and fear of rising crime rates in the 1960s. Juvenile delinquents, including status offenders, were not LEAA's primary concern. LEAA's original mandate was limited to addressing the problems of adult crime and overall improvements to the criminal justice system.

With the passage of the Juvenile Justice Act, Congress identified LEAA as the federal agency with primary responsibility for juvenile delinquency programs. Funds provided through the new legislation were to be used for juvenile delinquency programs that were in addition to, not in place of, those that were receiving LEAA support through the Crime Control Act. The Juvenile Justice Act not only established OJJDP as a quasi-independent unit within LEAA with its own appropriation, but it also mandated that all programs related to juvenile delinquency administered by LEAA were to be administered by, or subject to, the policy direction of OJJDP. This last, very important provision was intended to provide for uniformity in LEAA juvenile delinquency policy and program directions. Unfortunately, OJJDP made little progress in implementing it.

Congress' intent to force LEAA into a role of federal juvenile delinquency leadership by finally establishing OJJDP with clear policy and programming authority and direction as well as separate funding mechanisms was never fulfilled. Rather than accept its leadership position, LEAA chose to exert its authority in other directions by continually checking OJJDP's independence and attempting to force OJJDP into the LEAA traditional law enforcement and criminal justice orientation (U.S. Congress 1977). Congressional commitment to OJJDP's role of leadership in federal juvenile delinquency efforts and recognition of LEAA's failure is evidenced by the newly reauthorized Juvenile Justice Act. The 1980 amendments elevate OJJDP to a separate agency within the Department of Justice that is completely separate from LEAA. Under this new arrangement, OJJDP is under the general authority of the Attorney General (P.L. 96-509, Sec. 6(a)), with the OJJDP administrator having full administrative and operational authority. OJARS is to provide coordination and support services but has no policy control over OJJDP (U.S. Congress 1980b).

Appropriations for OJJDP increased in the first years of operation from $14.5 million in fiscal year 1975 to $75 million in 1977, and since fiscal year 1978 they have been at the $100 million level. From these funds OJJDP is authorized to make grants under four program areas. These are the formula grants to state planning agencies, special emphasis prevention and treatment grants, grants from the National Institute for Juvenile Justice and Delinquency Prevention, and the concentration of federal effort program.

Award of formula grants has been tied to a state's commitment to deinstitutionalize status offenders and dependent and neglected children, but there is no requirement that formula grant funds be spent for that purpose. Through fiscal year 1979, to be eligible for a Juvenile Justice Act formula grant, a state was to submit an annual plan for carrying out the purposes of the act in accordance both with Section 223, including the deinstitutionalization and separation mandates, and with the comprehensive planning requirements of the Crime Control Act.

All states and territories with duly established state planning agencies (now referred to as state criminal justice councils) are eligible for funds allocated on the basis of relative population under the age of 18. The minimum state grant is $225,000; the minimum territorial grant is $56,250.

Under the special emphasis prevention and treatment program, public and private agencies, organizations, institutions, or individuals are eligible for funds (on a discretionary basis) according to regulations established by the OJJDP administrator. Up to 100 percent of total project costs may be federal funds. Most of the funds have been distributed on the basis of national initiatives that are announced with separate guidelines during the course of each fiscal year. These programs have been a major source of funding for private nonprofit groups, both local and national.

Public or private agencies, organizations, or individuals are eligible to receive grants or contracts from the National Institute for Juvenile Justice and Delinquency Prevention. Again, funding may be up to 100 percent of project costs, and awards are made on a discretionary basis. Institute funding has been primarily for research, evaluation, information collection and dissemination activities, and evaluations of the national initiatives of the special emphasis prevention and treatment programs.

Under the concentration of federal effort program, any public or private agency, organization, institution, individual, or agency of the federal government is eligible for funds to carry out the purposes of the Juvenile Justice Act. Funds may be provided through grants, contracts, and interagency agreements for up to 100 percent of total project costs. Projects must in some way demonstrate or contribute to coordination of federal juvenile delinquency policies and programs.

One of the purposes of the Juvenile Justice Act was to encourage states to deinstitutionalize status offenders and dependent and neglected youth. The encouragement, however, was tied solely to the availability of formula grants for the states. In order to get and keep its allotted funds from OJJDP, a state had to demonstrate its progress toward implementing the deinstitutionalization and separation goals of the act. A state did not have to use its Juvenile Justice Act funds for these purposes; however, in testimony before the House Subcommittee on Human Resources in 1980, Ira Schwartz, then director of OJJDP, said that states did use a large portion of their funds in a manner consistent with the goals. He reported that 59 percent of the 1979 formula grants were allocated by the states to programs to deinstitutionalize status offenders and dependent and neglected youth. The levels varied by state, of course, but all states except New Jersey, the District of Columbia, and the Trust Territor-

ies did allocate some of their Juvenile Justice Act formula grant funds for deinstitutionalization activities
(U.S. Congress 1980a).

There is nothing in the Juvenile Justice Act that requires OJJDP to expend its discretionary funds on status
offenders. Discretionary funds, which have accounted for
approximately 35 percent of the annual OJJDP appropriation, plus formula grant funds reverted from previous
years, are awarded through OJJDP's special emphasis prevention and treatment programs, the National Institute for
Juvenile Justice and Delinquency Prevention, and the concentration of federal effort program.

Under the special emphasis prevention and treatment
programs, one of the 11 purposes established by Congress
for which grants can be awarded is to "develop and implement community-based alternatives to traditional forms of
institutionalization" (Sec. 224(a)(2)). However, it does
not specify what population these alternative programs are
to serve. Since 1974 only one special emphasis national
initiative has directly addressed the issue of deinstitutionalization of status offenders and dependent and neglected youth.

Similarly, OJJDP's National Institute for Juvenile
Justice and Delinquency Prevention is authorized by Congress to expend its research, demonstration, and evaluation funds on seven types of activities, none of which
directly identifies status offenders or the issue of deinstitutionalization. However, since 1975 the National
Institute for Juvenile Justice and Delinquency Prevention
has expended a considerable share of its budget on projects under its deinstitutionalization of status offenders
program initiative (Kobrin and Hellum 1981).

The purpose of the concentration of federal effort
program was to encourage coordination of federal juvenile
delinquency programs among federal departments and agencies. The emphasis is on coordination, not on what the
programs are designed to accomplish or who they serve.
Some of the activities of the National Advisory Committee
on Juvenile Justice and Delinquency Prevention and of the
Coordinating Council on Juvenile Justice and Delinquency
Prevention (both of which were established as part of the
concentration of federal effort program) have addressed
deinstitutionalization as a policy concern, but none of
these activities could be said to have directly contributed to deinstitutionalization at the state and local
levels.

With regard to the juvenile justice formula grant, OJJDP is responsible for determining state compliance with the deinstitutionalization and separation provisions. If OJJDP determined that a state was not in compliance, however, only the LEAA administrator—unless he chose to officially delegate authority—was authorized to place special conditions on the state's grant or terminate the grant and order that all funds be repaid. This is no longer true under the new legislation that, for the first time, grants this authority to the administrator of OJJDP.

Juvenile Justice Act formula grant funds are awarded annually to state planning agencies. The discretionary funds are expended through direct grants and contracts with public and private agencies. Juvenile Justice Act appropriations, like those under the Crime Control Act, are "no year" funds. Although there are restrictions governing obligation and expenditure of formula grant funds by states, Juvenile Justice Act discretionary funds and reverted formula funds are available to OJJDP until obligated and expended. This is in marked contrast to other federal assistance programs that are required to obligate (through grant and contract awards) or expend funds by the end of the fiscal year for which they have been appropriated.

Another feature of Juvenile Justice Act funds through fiscal year 1980 was the provision that "programs funded . . . shall continue to receive financial assistance providing that the yearly evaluation of such programs is satisfactory" (Sec. 228(a)). Some federal demonstration grant programs restrict funding to a maximum period of from one to three, and in a few cases, five years of federal funding, usually with the federal share declining each succeeding year. OJJDP could continue to provide funding on a nondeclining federal share and noncompetitive basis for as long as a project received a positive evaluation. During the reauthorization process, an amendment to the Juvenile Justice Act was passed that deleted the continuation funding language but did not preclude the possibility of unlimited continuation funding of projects. Under the current legislation, applications for continuation funding will be considered but only on a competitive basis with new applications.

As with LEAA, OJJDP has no program control over state planning agency subgrant and subcontract decisions. In terms of the Juvenile Justice Act formula grant funds, states supply data to OJJDP on progress in complying with the deinstitutionalization and separation requirements.

OJJDP does not verify, and from a practical standpoint cannot verify, the data. For several years it has contracted with a private nonprofit group for technical assistance in reviewing the reports submitted by the states and in determining on the basis of the state-supplied data whether or not individual states are in compliance. The contractor also has been available to assist states in their data collection efforts and in interpreting the rules and regulations. OJJDP prepared a detailed manual for use by states in monitoring compliance, and it has held a series of regional training sessions to which state representatives, including members of the state juvenile justice and delinquency advisory groups, were invited.

Within OJJDP itself, individual staff members from the Formula Grants and Technical Assistance Division have been assigned to a small number of states. Each staff member is reponsible for reviewing the annual plans for those states, handling their requests for grant modifications and waivers, and, in general, monitoring their activities. Staff members do conduct site visits to and maintain relatively close telephone contact with state planning agencies. Monitoring state compliance with the deinstitutionalization and separation requirements of the Juvenile Justice Act, however, is for the most part handled separately by other staff members of the division. None of the staff from the Formula Grants and Technical Assistance Division is responsible for monitoring individual projects (subgrants) at the state level. Their monitoring responsibilities extend only to the state planning agencies, not to the individuals and organizations with which the state planning agencies work and to whom they provide funds.

SUMMARY OF LEAA AND OJJDP ACTIVITIES

The various national, state, and local movements to deinstitutionalize status offenders occurred in an environment that included considerable confusion about the federal government's position on or role in such activities. In 1974 LEAA and its subunit, OJJDP, became responsible for federal direction and oversight concerning status offenders. The legislation made the federal position clear. In order to receive formula grant funds under the new Juvenile Justice Act, states had to make a commitment to deinstitutionalize status offenders. However, this mandate and the creation of OJJDP did not end the confusion

surrounding the federal role. Even within LEAA there were
conflicting messages given to states concerning that
agency's support of often opposing positions or activities
within the juvenile justice system. For example, Juvenile
Justice Act funds were used to develop community-based
services while money from the Crime Control Act supported
the construction of juvenile correctional facilities. Our
analysis has identified three major factors that have
contributed to the confusion concerning LEAA's and OJJDP's
support of deinstitutionalization activities--the ambig-
uousness of the legislation, the lack of clear administrative responsibility, and the lack of monitoring capabilities.

Although formula grants to states under the Juvenile
Justice Act are tied to the state's commitment to deinstitutionalize status offenders and dependent and neglected children, there is no requirement that the funds
must be used for that purpose. Furthermore, the discretionary grants awarded directly by OJJDP do not have to
be spent on programs for status offenders. The same is
true of the Crime Control Act funds counted under the
maintenance of effort requirements, whether they are dispensed directly by LEAA or by the state planning agencies.
The funds can be used for any projects as long as they are
not inconsistent with the deinstitutionalization or separation mandates. Thus, during the period of this study,
the funds distributed under the Juvenile Justice Act did
not directly have to support the act's goals with respect
to the deinstitutionalization of status offenders. Until
the 1980 changes gave increased focus to "more serious
offenders," the deinstitutionalization and separation
provisions were the emphasized, but not the exclusive
purposes of the act and thereby of the grant programs.
While the act retains the requirements that states deinstitutionalize status offenders and separate juveniles
from adults in detention and correctional facilities, the
1980 amendments make it clear that future federal resources are to have an increased focus on the more serious
juvenile offenders.

In 1974 the Juvenile Justice Act established OJJDP and
gave it responsibility for policy direction over all programs related to juvenile delinquency that were administered by LEAA. This authority was intended to ensure
uniformity in LEAA's juvenile delinquency policy and program directions, especially those not specifically administered by OJJDP. In reality OJJDP was able to assert
only minimal authority over LEAA's discretionary grant

awards and especially over the activities of the state
planning agencies. OJJDP was never able to influence
LEAA's basic involvement with criminal justice issues,
even as those issues related to juveniles. LEAA appeared
to operate under the premise that OJJDP could devote time
and money to projects for status offenders, but LEAA continued to concentrate on adults and the more serious
juvenile offenders. The administrative structure that had
OJJDP as a subunit of LEAA was in effect throughout the
period of this study; however, the 1980 amendments eleva-
ted OJJDP to an independent agency within the Department
of Justice, completely separate from LEAA. On the one
hand, its new administrative position may provide leverage
for greater authority and influence over programs for
juveniles, including status offenders, within the entire
Department of Justice. On the other hand, removal from
the LEAA structure might result in even less influence
over how the remaining funds--especially assistance provided directly to the states--are spent.

Finally, the monitoring practices of both LEAA and
OJJDP have been ineffective, consisting primarily of requiring written reports from state planning agencies and
individual grantees and contractors. The five field offices that perform audits have no requirement to monitor
routinely all grants and contracts, and in fact some projects have never been audited. The Office of Management
and Budget's ruling that LEAA cannot request information
from state planning agencies on subgrants and subcontracts
severely limited LEAA's monitoring capabilities. A main
source of the information that LEAA had on state activities was the comprehensive plans, and those plans may not
have accurately reflected the scope and content of projects when they were actually funded and operating.
Moreover, states supply data to OJJDP on their progress
in complying with the deinstitutionalization and separation mandates of the Juvenile Justice Act, but OJJDP has
not verified and really cannot verify those reports. It
should be noted that although OJJDP is the focal point for
federal juvenile delinquency programs, it is primarily a
grant-making not a regulatory agency. Its monitoring
authority and capability therefore are limited.

RUNAWAY AND HOMELESS YOUTH ACT

Title III of the Juvenile Justice Act constitutes a separate Runaway and Homeless Youth Act that authorizes a

self-contained program completely separate from those
operated under the rest of the act. Among all federal
programs studied, this program was an exception when first
enacted because its target population consisted solely of
one category of status offenders--runaways. When first
passed, the act did not identify homeless youth as a group
needing services under the act. The title was not changed
until 1980, even though the term homeless youth had been
added to several of the act's provisions in 1977.
Throughout this section we refer to this act by the
shorter title, Runaway Youth Act; however, it should be
remembered that the program is no longer limited only to
runaways or youth who have come in contact with the juvenile justice system.

Although runaways are by no means a recent phenomenon,
the 1960s witnessed a dramatic increase in their number.
Many young people left their homes across the nation and
traveled to large urban centers recognized for their alternative lifestyles, such as Haight-Ashbury in San Francisco and the East Village in New York (National Youth
Alternatives Project 1976). There were frequent stories
of young girls being trapped into prostitution and of
teenagers dying of drug overdoses once they arrived in the
"big city." A particularly gruesome story that received
national coverage involved the brutal murders of a large
number of runaways who had migrated to the Houston area
(Time 1973, Newsweek 1973). Many individuals, whether
personally affected by such occurrences or not, were hor-
rified by the stories.

In areas where large numbers of runaways began to congregate, communities had to cope with the fact that most
of the youth in need of services were opposed to the traditional methods of assistance, especially those of large
bureaucratic systems. In order to serve these youth,
small nontraditional facilities such as "free clinics" and
"crash pads," which operated outside the existing structure of social and medical service systems, were developed. Small houses were opened as refuges for youth and
were aimed at meeting the immediate needs of runaways.
When the centers first opened they were usually operated
by volunteers or by staff receiving minimum wages, and
were supported by private sources such as churches or
local charities. Over time the runaway houses became more
sophisticated and permanent providers of service. As
their range of services expanded they sought additional
sources of support (Berkeley Planning Associates 1979).
Their numbers also grew, and in 1972 HEW, through its

Youth Development and Delinquency Prevention Administration, funded a national conference that was attended by
representatives from 60 runaway centers (National Youth
Alternatives Project 1976).

The growing network of runaway centers was seen as a
way to divert runaways from the criminal justice system.
This diversion was considered desirable not only by the
youth and those operating the new centers but also by some
members of the law enforcement system. When the Senate
Committee on the Judiciary held hearings on the runaway
problem in 1972, several representatives from police
departments testified. They explained that runaways
required significant amounts of police time and that police could only return the youth home because they were
not equipped to provide needed counseling and services
(U.S. Congress 1973).

Growing pressure from these sources made the runaway
problem an unavoidable topic for Congress in the early
1970s. The publicity, resultant citizen outcry, pressure
from the new provider network, and police support caused
members of Congress to consider a possible federal response. Congress was able to justify its involvement in
the runaway area because of the interstate nature of the
problem at that time. Although there had been congressional reports on runaways as early as 1955, earnest consideration of proposed legislation began in 1971 and was
discussed from then until 1974, when it became part of the
Juvenile Justice Act.

As previously mentioned, prior to the 1974 passage of
the Juvenile Justice Act HEW had more or less been assigned responsibility for noncriminal youth who were involved with the juvenile justice system. Although the
Juvenile Justice Act assigned most federal responsibility
for juvenile delinquents and status offenders to the Department of Justice, specifically OJJDP, the program for
runaways was assigned to HEW for several reasons. First,
Congress specified in the act that one of the reasons
separate legislation was required for this group was that
runaways should not be the responsibility of the juvenile
justice system. The existing providers of services for
runaways had developed outside most traditional service
networks and were more likely to fit within the social
services system rather than the juvenile justice system.
Under the previous juvenile delinquency legislation, HEW
had been responsible for the more nontraditional diversionary types of programs, and it was thought that that
department would be better able to administer the runaway

program and keep it separate from the juvenile justice
system. Second, in 1974 HEW had an existing bureaucratic
structure pertaining to youth, and it has been suggested
that Congress simply wanted to leave some program operations lodged within that structure. If Congress took away
all of HEW's program responsibility for youth, there would
be no justification for the department to maintain an office concerned with the problems of youth. So although
HEW officials testified that they did not think a separate
program was necessary to provide funds to runaway centers
(U.S. Congress 1973), Congress mandated that department
to administer the new program. In HEW (currently the Department of Health and Human Services) the program is
operated by the Youth Development Bureau within the Administration for Children, Youth, and Families.

Federal Grants for Centers

The Runaway Youth Act authorizes a grant program to fund
"local facilities to deal primarily with the immediate
needs of runaway youth and otherwise homeless youth"
(Sec. 311). The federal regulations define a runaway as
a person who is less than 18 and is absent from home or
legal residence without permission. A homeless youth is
simply one without shelter, which includes supervision and
care (45 CFR 1351.1). Organizations that are eligible to
apply for the federal grants to care for these children
have to be locally based facilities capable of providing
temporary shelter and counseling services.
    One of the unique aspects of this program is that it
does not involve state-level agencies. The program consists of federal discretionary funds that are awarded
directly to the projects by HEW. It is true that states
are eligible to apply for these grants, but the facilities
must be community-based and most appear to be locally run.
In the first year of operation (1975) the program funded
65 centers (U.S. Department of Health, Education, and
Welfare 1976); in fiscal year 1978, 166 centers received
funds (National Youth Work Alliance 1979); but by fiscal
year 1980 the Director of the Division of Runaway Youth
Programs reported that the number of centers receiving
funds had dropped to 158. Since fiscal year 1978 the
funding for grants through the Youth Development Bureau
has remained the same (which in reality constitutes a cut,
due to inflation). Fewer centers have been funded each
year (Dye 1979), even though the number of youth served

has increased from 32,000 in 1978 (National Youth Work
Alliance 1979) to 45,000 in 1980 (U.S. Department of
Health and Human Services, no date). Of course, not all
of these youth were served only through the bureau's
grants, since centers receive funds from a variety of
sources.

In addition to funding individual runaway centers, the
Youth Development Bureau funds a 24-hour nationwide
telephone system. The toll-free number can be used by
runaways who need assistance, as well as by those who wish
to contact their parents. Even though this switchboard
system has been funded by HEW since 1973 and has used
Runaway Youth Act funds since 1975 (National Youth Alternatives Project 1976), it was not until 1980 that the
act was amended to grant statutory authority for this
activity (U.S. Congress 1980c). Although the national
switchboard is considered an integral part of services to
runaways, funding the individual centers remains the primary focus of the runaway youth program.

In order to receive a grant from the Youth Development
Bureau, runaway centers have to meet a few requirements
laid down either by the act or by regulations issued by
HEW. The 1974 act specified that facilities receiving
these funds were to be outside the law enforcement and
juvenile justice systems. Although coordination with
these systems is expected in order for runaway centers to
operate within their communities, there were pressures
from the federal as well as project and community levels
to keep the centers as separate systems of service. If a
center provides temporary shelter, the federal rules state
that a stay in the shelter is to be limited to 15 days.
Also, the capacity of the facilities is limited to 20
youth. The federal agency requires that the centers contact the parents within 72 hours. It is reported that
"if a runaway does not wish to contact his parents, he
either leaves on his own or is referred to a crash pad
where he can find overnight housing" (National Youth Alternatives Project 1976:9).

Congress has specified various levels of grant requests
that are to be given priority. In 1974 priority was specified for maximum grants of $75,000 to projects with
total budgets of no more than $100,000. In 1977 the pri-
ority grant level was raised to $100,000 for projects with
total budgets under $150,000. Finally, in 1980 the pre-
ferred grant limit was raised to $150,000 and the total
project budget limit was eliminated. The increase in grant
limits reflects not only the effects of inflation but also

the change in the character of the centers. In 1974 the centers were still mainly independent separate facilities. They have since become larger and more complex service centers. Now it is not uncommon for a number of small facilities to be combined into a single operating agency that has bureaucratized services as well as administrative and fund-raising duties. Moreover, these providers have expanded in order to offer a variety of services, partly because they have recognized the need for such services by the population that comes into the centers and partly to tap a variety of funding sources.

The act also specifies that priority shall be given to those private agencies that have had past experience in dealing with runaway or otherwise homeless youth. This by no means excludes public agencies, but it does reflect the fact that the network of runaway centers throughout the country is largely made up of private organizations. These private providers have formed a strong national coalition, the National Youth Work Alliance, that not only dispenses information and provides training to its members but has become a strong lobbying organization specifically concerned with youth.

As with many federal programs, although the appropriation levels for the runaway youth grant program have increased each year, they have never met the authorization level. The authorization for each fiscal year from 1975 to 1977 was $10 million; from 1978 to 1980, $25 million; and for 1981 to 1985, it is currently set at $25 million. The appropriations were $5 million in fiscal year 1975, $7 million in 1976, $9 million in 1977, and $11 million in each year thereafter (U.S. Congress 1977, Office of Management and Budget 1978, 1979, 1980).

The federal grants to projects can be used for up to 90 percent of the project costs. Eligible costs include but are not limited to temporary shelter, referral services, counseling services, aftercare services, and staff training. Costs associated with the acquisition and renovation of existing structures are limited to 15 percent of the grant amount; however, this limitation may be waived. The federal runaway youth project grants may not be used to cover the cost of constructing a new facility.

Runaway centers have tended to use a variety of funding sources either at different times or in various combinations. Prior to 1974, 11 runaway centers reportedly received LEAA funds through the state planning agencies. In fiscal year 1974, as part of an HEW department initiative, the National Institute of Mental Health (NIMH) awarded demonstration grants to 32 runaway centers. In its first year of operating the runaway youth program, HEW awarded approximately $4 million to 65 centers, including most of the NIMH demonstration centers (U.S. Department of Health, Education, and Welfare 1976). In 1975 the National Youth Alternatives Project (now the National Youth Work Alliance) conducted a survey of 125 runaway centers operating around the country, and in 1979 that survey was repeated, with 212 centers reporting. Table 17-3 shows the percentage of centers surveyed that received funding from each source in those years. In addition, in 1979 OJJDP joined with the Department of Labor's Office of Youth Programs to transfer an additional $3 million to the Youth Development Bureau to fund special

TABLE 17-3   Percentage of Runaway Centers Surveyed Receiving Funds from Various Sources in 1975 and 1979

Funding Source	1975 (N = 125) (%)	1979 (N = 212) (%)
Runaway youth program	52	66
LEAA and OJJDP, including funds from state planning agencies	20	30
National Institute of Mental Health	7	0
National Institute on Drug Abuse	4	2
General revenue sharing	8	9
CETA	4	24
Title XX	2	19
VISTA	1	0
Other federal	4	--[a]
USDA		5
DOL		3
HUD		
State funds	32	1
City funds	22	33
County funds	35	36[b]

[a]Data reported as "other federal" sources in 1975 were reported by more specific categories in 1979.
[b]City and county funds were reported together in 1979.

Source: National Youth Alternatives Project (1976:10) and National Youth Work Alliance (1979:26).

projects and services in the centers. These additional funds are not reflected either in Table 17-3 or in the annual congressional appropriations for the bureau.

There have been some important changes in support patterns of the runaway centers since funding began under the Runaway Youth Act. First, there has been an increase in the number of centers receiving Runaway Youth Act funds, from 65 in 1975 to 164 in 1979. As funds from certain federal sources (e.g., NIMH) have been decreased or eliminated, a number of centers have increased their use of other sources. For example, the proportion of centers receiving Title XX funds increased from 2 percent in 1975 to 19 percent in 1979, and while CETA funds were received by only 4 percent of the centers in 1975, 24 percent used such funds in 1979. Private sources of funds have been important to runaway centers since they began. These data were not reported in 1975, but the 1979 report indicates that centers were still receiving these types of funds from such sources as United Way (34 percent) and fees for services (15 percent) (National Youth Work Alliance 1979).

The Runaway Youth Act as passed in 1974 did not address the issue of geographic distribution of projects that were awarded grants; rather, projects were to be funded throughout the country in areas where runaways seemed to congregate. The 1980 amendments added the restriction that grants were to be made "equitably among the States based upon their respective populations of youth under 18 years of age" (P.L. 96-509, Sec. 18(b)). In its report, the House Committee on Education and Labor gave two reasons for this additional requirement (U.S. Congress 1980b). The first was to have the manner in which the Title III (Runaway Youth Act) funds were distributed conform with the procedures used under the rest of the act for programs administered by OJJDP. The second reason was based on evidence examined by the committee that runaways appeared to remain in their own communities rather than travel across the country. It was therefore felt that assistance was probably needed by communities nationwide.

Data from the Projects

In 1974 the Runaway Youth Act included the statement that usable data on the runaway population was nonexistent. Part of the response to this problem was the requirement that projects receiving funds under the act maintain adequate statistical records of the youth they serve. These

records are part of the national base operated by the
Youth Development Bureau, and those files provide some of
the best data on services to runaways. The describe the
youth served, the services provided, and the outcomes of
the youth's stay at the center. The most recent data
available to this study are for fiscal year 1979.

It is interesting to note that this program does not
serve runaways only. The Youth Development Bureau reports
on six categories of youth served by their projects: (1)
runaways, (2) pushed-out youth (those who leave home with
parental encouragement or direction), (3) mutual agreement
departures, (4) potential runaways (those considering
leaving home without permission), (5) nonrunaway crisis
youth (those who live in an unstable or critical situation
but who are not planning to depart), and (6) other youth
who come to the center for services. Of the 43,000 youth
served by runaway centers funded by the Youth Development
Bureau in fiscal year 1979, the data system indicated the
following distribution by types of youth: runaways, 42
percent; pushed-out youth, 12 percent; mutual agreement
departures, 16 percent; potential runaways, 4 percent;
nonrunaway crisis, 20 percent; and other, 5 percent (Swicord 1980).

Because of the manner in which the records are kept,
the 43,000 youth served during 1979 may not be 43,000
separate individuals. The data are maintained for each
youth who comes into a center and gets more than a simple
referral. A data file includes all services and activities provided through the center until the youth leaves
the center's care, even if he or she never received shelter but, say, only counseling. A youth could show up
several times a year at the same or different facilities
and would be a separate case each time.

The distribution of the served population by sex is
also reported for the six types of youth. In fiscal year
1979, 42 percent of the total youth population served were
males and 58 percent were females. Females constituted a
larger percentage of the runaway population (65.5 precent)
and those youth who are potential runaways (69 percent)
than the other categories. For only one group do females
represent less than one-half (47 percent) of the served
population and that is for the pushed-out youth (Swicord
1980). Opinion Research Corporation (1976) conducted a
survey on the runaway population that found that 53 percent of runaways were male and 47 percent were female.
The discrepancy between the sex distribution of the run-

away population and of those served at the centers may indicate that girls are more likely to seek assistance.

The age and race distributions of the clients of runaway centers have remained fairly constant. Most of the youth served by the centers were between the ages of 14 and 17. This age representation has held constant between fiscal year 1978, when 84 percent fell between these ages, and 1979, when 83 percent were aged 14 to 17. By far the most common racial group served by the centers was white youth (72 percent of the cases). This was followed by blacks, who represented 16 percent of the total client group in fiscal year 1979 (a slight increase from previous years). Hispanics represented 6 percent; American Indians, 2 percent; and Asian/Pacific Islanders, 1 percent (Swicord 1980). Race data were not recorded for the other clients.

The Youth Development Bureau data report the source of referrals for the centers, and it appears as though the most common single method of referral is youth who come into the centers on their own (19 percent). However, when the reported juvenile and criminal justice system components are considered together, they represent a larger portion of referrals (27 percent). In fiscal year 1979, 12 percent of the referrals came from the police, 9 percent from court intake, 1 percent from court hearings, 2 percent from probation supervision, and 3 percent from other juvenile justice agencies (Swicord 1980). Although the network of runaway centers is outside the juvenile justice system, the two appear to be coordinating their activities.

Among the runaways who come into the shelters, 82 percent were living at home with their parents or legal guardian prior to the runaway episode. According to the federal data system, 43 percent of the runaway youth who had received temporary shelter returned home when they left the center. The next highest category (12 percent), however, was runaways who left the centers to go "on the road/street" (Swicord 1980). A national evaluation of the runaway program in 1978 attempted some follow-up interviews with clients five weeks after they had left the shelter's care (Berkeley Planning Associates 1979). Obviously, these interviews could only have been conducted with clients who left the centers for some known address, thus eliminating those youth who continued to run away. Of those contacted, 79 percent had not run away again, but one-half of those interviewed said they might run away if future problems got "too bad."

Of all the youth who came into the centers, 73 percent were provided temporary shelter (Swicord 1980). Although the Youth Development Bureau places a 15-day limit on the provision of temporary shelter, the bureau does not tabulate the average length of stay as part of its management information system. The 1976 National Youth Alternatives Project's survey results reported that the length of stay at the centers varied from three days to two weeks. For 1978 the national evaluation reported that "large numbers" of youth were receiving shelter from the federally supported runaway centers for more than one or two weeks (Berkeley Planning Associates 1979). That report suggested that a possible explanation for the long length of stay in the centers might be the characteristics of the clients; that is, with the growth of the number of youth who are pushed out of their homes, the centers have to find more out-of-home placements. If it is determined that returning home is not a possibility, then it probably takes more time to find a suitable, more permanent placement.

There appears to be great diversity among the centers nationwide concerning the services they provide. Some provide only shelter with limited counseling activities, while others have become multipurpose youth agencies that provide a wide range of services (Berkeley Planning Associates 1979). The national client data system only reports the number of youth who have received certain services, not how many centers provide or contract for each type of service. After shelter, the most frequently provided service is counseling. Among those youth receiving shelter, 33 percent receive individual counseling, 20 percent receive group counseling, and 13 percent are provided family counseling. For nonsheltered youth the percentages are individual (46 percent), group (5 percent), and family counseling (28 percent). The next most frequently provided service is transportation, but some centers also provide living arrangements, medical services, education, employment services, financial support, legal services, and psychological services (Swicord 1980).

Summary of the Runaway Youth Act Program

When it began in 1975, the runaway youth program was the one federal program created solely to serve the status offender population, albeit only a part of that population. The focus of the program, however, has expanded to include other youth (i.e., homeless youth) who cannot be considered runaways or who are unlikely to have had contact with the juvenile justice system. Inclusion of these other categories of youth as part of the centers' clientele has occured as a response to the changing needs of the youth population, the changing characters of the centers themselves, and the nature of the federal leadership provided to this program by HEW.

First, the expansion of the target population to include homeless youth in addition to runaways was partially a response to the changing needs of youth between 1970 and 1980. In the late 1960s and early 1970s the population to be served was primarily runaways, and the centers were designed to meet their immediate needs with the understanding that the youth eventually would return to their families or find a place to live. More recently, however, an increasing number of youth with family or living problems technically may not be runaways, because they leave home with their parents' permission or, in some cases, may not leave home at all.

Second, what began as small alternative runaway shelters have developed, in many cases, into multipurpose service centers for youth. A more diverse and complete package of services could be offered as both funding and staff increased and became permanent and bureaucratic. As the character of the centers and their services changed, they attracted youth who had problems other than having run away from home. In addition, as a method of curbing the number of youth who actually leave home, some facilities specifically developed programs to assist youth with their problems while they remained at home or at least in the community.

A final reason for the change in program focus concerns the administrative location of the program within HEW instead of with another federal agency, such as OJJDP. It could be assumed that HEW, the federal administrating agency, was receptive to such changes in program orientation because of its concern with the overall social welfare needs of youth in general, and not just with status offenders or runaways. Thus, expanding the scope of the program was in all probability easier because it was administered by a federal department that was not concerned primarily with juvenile justice issues.

Although this program does collect considerable data on both the services provided and youth served, it is difficult to determine the actual effect of the program on the runaway population. The only recidivism data was

collected in 1978 on a very small number of clients (101
youth), and the follow-up period was only five weeks after
they had left the shelters. Runaway centers by and large
have not provided follow-up and aftercare services (Berkeley Planning Associates 1979). In short, we do not know
how many runaways have their problems solved--or at least
receive a plan for resolution--through their contact with
the runaway centers. Although previously served youth may
return to the centers rather than run away when they once
again are faced with problems, we do not know if or how
frequently this occurs. With the above-mentioned change
in the characteristics of the target population, it may
become even more difficult to determine the impact of this
program on the runaway problem.

little follow up

REFERENCES

Berkeley Planning Associates (1979) <u>National Evaluation
of the Runaway Youth Program</u>. Prepared for the Youth
Development Bureau. Berkeley, Calif.: Berkeley
Planning Associates.
Dye, Larry (1979) Director of the Youth Development
Bureau, interviewed in <u>Youth Alternatives</u> 6(7):2.
Kobrin, Solomon, and Hellum, Frank R. (1981) The
Deinstitutionalization Program Initiative. In Solomon
Kobrin and Malcolm W. Klein, <u>National Evaluation of
the Deinstitutionalization of Status Offenders
Program</u>. Vol. I. Washington, D.C.: National
Institute for Juvenile Justice and Delinquency
Prevention.
Law Enforcement Assistance Administration (1978) Mainten-
ance of Effort Report for 1974, 1975, 1976, and 1977.
Budget Division, Office of the Comptroller. Law
Enforcement Assistance Administration, Washington, D.C.
_____ (1979) Maintenance of Effort Report
for fiscal year 1978. Prepared by the OJJDP
Maintenance of Effort Task Force. Law Enforcement
Assistance Administration, Washington, D.C.
_____ (no date) Preliminary estimates of
Maintenance of Effort Report for fiscal year 1979.
Office of Juvenile Justice and Delinquency
Prevention. Law Enforcement Assistance
Administration, Washington, D.C.
Madden, Thomas (1975) Legal Opinion 75-17--LEAA's
Juvenile Delinquency Program Funding Requirements

Under the Juvenile Justice and Delinquency Prevention
Act of 1974. Draft memorandum. Law Enforcement
Assistance Administration, Washington, D.C.

National Youth Alternatives Project (1976) National
Directory of Runaway Programs. Washington, D.C.:
National Youth Alternatives Project.

National Youth Work Alliance (1979) National Directory of
Runaway Programs. 4th ed. Washington, D.C.:
National Youth Work Alliance.

Newsweek (1973)   Nicest Person; Murder of Teenage Boys
Near Houston, Texas. 83:32, August 20, 1973.

Office of Management and Budget (1978) Appendix to the
United States Budget, FY 1979. Washington, D.C.:
U.S. Government Printing Office.

_____ (1979) Appendix to the United States
Budget, FY 1980. Washington, D.C.: U.S. Government
Printing Office.

_____ (1980) Appendix to the United States
Budget, FY 1981. Washington, D.C.: U.S. Government
Printing Office.

Opinion Research Corporation (1976) National Statistical
Survey on Runaway Youth. Prepared for the Office of
Youth Development. Princeton, N.J.: Opinion Research
Corporation.

Peskoe, Howard (1973) The 1968 Safe Streets Act:
Congressional Response to the Growing Crime Problem.
Columbia Human Rights Law Review. 5(1):69–116.

Swicord, Donald (1980) Characteristics of Youth Served.
Youth Development Bureau, Washington, D.C.

Time (1973)   Houston Horrors; Sexual Abuse and Killing of
Teenage Boys. 102:24, August 20, 1973.

U.S. Congress (1972) Juvenile Delinquency Prevention
Act. Senate report 92-1003. Committee on the
Judiciary. 92nd Congress, 2nd Session. Washington,
D.C.: U.S. Government Printing Office.

_____ (1973a) Departments of Labor, and
Health, Education, and Welfare, and Related Agencies
Appropriations Bill, 1974. Senate report 93–414.
Committee on Appropriations. 93rd Congress, 1st
Session. Washington, D.C.: U.S. Government Printing
Office.

_____ (1973b) The Runaway Youth Act.
Senate report 93-191. Committee on the Judiciary.
93rd Congress, 1st Session. Washington, D.C.: U.S.
Government Printing Office.

_____ (1977) Juvenile Justice Amendments
of 1977. Senate report 95-165. Committee on the

Judiciary. 95th Congress, 1st Session. Washington, D.C.: U.S. Government Printing Office.

_____ (1980a) _Juvenile Justice Amendments of 1980._ Hearings on March 19, 1980 by the House Subcommittee on Education and Labor, Subcommittee on Human Resources. 96th Congress, 2nd Session. Washington, D.C.: U.S. Government Printing Office.

_____ (1980b) _Juvenile Justice Amendments of 1980._ House report 96-946. Committee on Education and Labor. 96th Congress, 2nd Session. Washington, D.C.: U.S. Government Printing Office.

_____ (1980c) _Juvenile Justice and Delinquency Prevention Act Amendments of 1980._ Senate report 96-705. Committee on the Judiciary. 96th Congress, 2nd Session. Washington, D.C.: U.S. Government Printing Office.

U.S. Department of Health and Human Services (no date) Unpublished data from the Youth Development Bureau's Management Information System. Computer printout tabulations of the Intake and Service Summary Form. Youth Development Bureau, Washington, D.C.

U.S. Department of Health, Education, and Welfare (1976) _Runaway Youth: A Status Report and Summary of Projects._ Prepared by the Intra-Departmental Committee on Runaway Youth. Washington, D.C.: Office of Human Development Services.

U.S. Department of Justice (1976) Reauthorization Meeting Issue Papers, Crime Control Act of 1976, P.L. 94-503, October 15, 1976, Law Enforcement Assistance Administration, Department of Justice, Washington, D.C.

_____ (1978a) Change to the _Guide for State Planning Agency Grants._ M4100.IF Change 3. Issued by the Law Enforcement Assistance Administration, July 25, 1978, Washington, D.C.

_____ (1978b) _Ninth Annual Report, FY 1977._ Law Enforcement Assistance Administration. Washington, D.C.: Department of Justice.

18
Title XX and Social Services for Status Offenders

SALLY A. KORNEGAY

Title XX of the Social Security Act provides up to $2.5 billion in federal funds that are allocated to states on the basis of population. A state can use these funds to meet the social service needs of its population, including status offenders. Title XX is very similar to a block grant program with only a few federal program requirements. There are limits on eligibility, prohibitions against certain services, and goals for the services provided under the program. As with a block grant, however, considerable program responsibility and authority are delegated to the states, and no prior federal approval of state plans is required. How a state chooses to implement Title XX is the critical factor in determining the program's impact on services for status offenders.

The three major program decisions that govern whether and how Title XX affects social services available to status offenders are: (1) the eligibility requirements, (2) the types of services offered, and (3) the target populations designated to receive services. Within the broad federal guidelines, states (and sometimes localities) define income limits for eligibility, proportion of services that will be provided to persons who are not public assistance recipients, location of services within the state, whether and what services will be purchased from private vendors or public agencies, and what priorities will be given to services for special groups.

Our examination of the effect of Title XX on efforts to deinstitutionalize status offenders and to provide them with alternative services is presented in four sections. First is a description of the federal requirements for state Title XX programs. The second section discusses how the program operates at the state level, highlighting its implementation in the seven states studied. Next we present the effects that Title XX has had on services provided to status offenders as well as to dependent and neglected children. Services to this latter group of children and youth were reviewed because they are included in the deinstitutionalization mandate of the Juvenile Justice and Delinquency Prevention Act, and are served for the most part by the state agencies that administer Title XX. Furthermore, services to dependent and neglected youth sometimes overlap with services to status offenders. The concluding section summarizes the effects of Title XX on services for status offenders.

THE FEDERAL PROGRAM

Title XX of the Social Security Act authorizes a program of grants to states to provide social services to individuals and families (P.L. 93-647 codified at 42 USC 1397-1397f and 45 CFR Part 228), and the program is administered by the Office of Human Development Services in the Department of Health and Human Services, formerly the Department of Health, Education, and Welfare. The program began in fiscal year 1975, replacing two previous federal programs that had funded services since 1956. Federal funds for social services had been provided through Title IV-A for children and adults who were eligible for Aid to Families with Dependent Children (AFDC) and through Title VI for aged, blind, or disabled persons who were eligible for the Supplemental Security Income (SSI) program. Persons eligible for services under both of those programs had to meet the eligibility criteria used for the public cash assistance programs, and both programs delivered services that were considered appropriate to alleviate the problems that assistance recipients were thought to have. Title XX gives states more discretion over program content and expands the types of individuals who can be eligible and the types of services that can be provided. Now only 50 percent of the case load must be recipients of public assistance, and this permits states to provide services to juveniles other than those from welfare households.

The five program goals specified in the federal law are aimed at the provision of services that will help (1) achieve or maintain a client's economic self-support; (2) achieve or maintain a client's self-sufficiency; (3) prevent or remedy neglect, abuse, or exploitation of children and adults, or preserve, rehabilitate, or reunite families; (4) prevent or reduce inappropriate institutional care; and (5) secure referral or admission for institutional care when appropriate, or provide services to individuals in institutions. The goals are diverse and vague enough so that almost any social service can be provided with Title XX funds if a state uses the appropriate language and key terms to describe it.

There are only a few federal requirements concerning the types of services offered through the program. A state's program must provide at least one service directed toward each of the goals. There are no federal requirements that any specific services must be provided, and there are no required definitions of what constitutes a specific service. Although HEW made several attempts to develop common definitions of social services, these are used mainly to facilitate reporting (Mott-McDonald Associates, Inc. 1976; U.S. Department of Health and Human Services 1980b).

It is important to note that Title XX funds are available for services to all age groups. Services for children and youth, including those specifically targeted for status offenders, have to compete for the limited funds along with other age and special interest groups. The federal program specifies three categories of persons who are eligible to receive Title XX financed services. The first category, categorical eligibles, includes individuals who are eligible for federal cash assistance (AFDC or SSI) and/or state supplementary payments. A state must provide some services to this group. The second category, income eligibles, includes individuals and members of families whose monthly gross income meets the state-set limits. These limits cannot exceed 115 percent of the state's median income, adjusted for family size. Under certain conditions a state may make services available to a group of income eligibles without individual income determinations; this subcategory of income eligibility is called group eligibility. The third Title XX eligibility category is based on certain services that may be provided to all persons in need without regard to their income, often called universal services. Under this provision, information and referral services, protective services for children and adults, and family planning services may be provided to anyone who needs them.

In 1972 Congress placed a ceiling of $2.5 billion on the previously open-ended federal funds available under Titles IV-A and VI (P.L. 92-512, Sec. 301(b)(1)). This ceiling was applied to the Title XX program when it was enacted, with specific additional funds being appropriated for certain fiscal years, usually earmarked for day care. After years of complaints that the ceiling level prevented adequate service provision, legislation in 1980 allows increases in the program's cap up to a maximum of $3.3 billion (P.L. 96-272, Sec. 201).

Title XX funds are distributed to states in amounts based on their population. Each state has a ceiling on the amount of federal funds it receives each year. The federal funds are available to pay for 90 percent of family planning services and 75 percent of all other allowable expenditures, and the state is required to pay the remaining percentage as its "match." If a state does not match its full allotment, it forfeits all unmatched federal funds. Although a state may spend more than its federal allotment plus the required state match on services, it will not receive any federal reimbursement over its ceiling.

While not mandating them, Title XX certainly encourages services to children who could be considered at least potentially dependent and neglected. Most state laws define dependent and neglected children as those who are abused, exploited, or neglected, and one of the goals of Title XX is the provision of services to prevent or remedy those situations. Over the last couple of years, increased attention about abuse and neglect issues has resulted in the growth of protective services for children. Protective services frequently are provided in lieu of or before an actual determination of dependency or neglect, partially to avoid the formal court process of assigning blame to the parent or other custodian of the child. Frequently, a formal finding of dependency or neglect requires that the child be removed from the home; protective services can be provided with or without that removal. Under Title XX, protective services may be provided to all children and youth in need, without regard to income.

Title XX funds can be used to provide services aimed at avoiding the institutionalization or deinstitutionalization of some clients, while at the same time services can be provided to institutionalized persons. In the first instance the services relate to the federal program goal to prevent or reduce "inappropriate institutional care by providing for community-based care, home-based care, or other forms of less intensive care" (42 USC 1397). This goal encourages recent deinstitutionalization efforts for a variety of populations, including mental health clients, the elderly, and status offenders. For example, in order to meet this goal states could use Title XX funds to provide alternative services for status offenders. On the other hand, another Title XX goal is to provide services to assist with the admission of individuals to institutions when such care is appropriate and to provide social services within institutions.

STATE PROGRAM OPERATIONS

Title XX allows states to decide which agency will administer the program. Nationally, the majority of social service programs are administered by a state agency rather than local (county or city) governments, and the same pattern holds true for our seven study states. Only two of them, Virginia and Wisconsin, have state-supervised but locally administered service programs (U.S. Department of Health and Human Services 1980a), and even they retain some service responsibility at the state level--that is, some aspects of adoption and permanent placement in Wisconsin and some child protection service functions in Virginia (Wisconsin Department of Health and Social Services 1980; Virginia Department of Welfare, no date). The remaining five states have state-administered programs in which the supervision of program operations is predominantly accomplished in local or district offices. The employees of these locally based offices are responsible to state officials and mandates. Decisions concerning actual content of services are made at these district offices, but the central state office retains final control of program operations. Some states handle certain service functions at the state or regional office level, such as group care placements in Massachusetts.

Among the states studied, the most complicated form of program administration occurs in Pennsylvania. Social services had been operated by county agencies until a move over five years ago to change to centralized state administration. However, certain county agencies still exist, notably the children and youth agencies. In essence, the Pennsylvania Department of Public Welfare (which administers Title XX) contracts with the county children and youth agencies for the provision of child development and child welfare services. Therefore, these services are greatly influenced by those local agencies. Moreover, some Title XX funded services to status offenders (called dependents in Pennsylvania) are available through local offices of the state's Division of Youth Services (Pennsylvania Department of Public Welfare 1979).

The federal Title XX funds available to states require a 25 percent match that may come from state and/or local sources. The state and local composition of the required Title XX match varies among the states in our study. Although which political jurisdiction provides the required matching funds may not determine program planning or administrative control, it does indicate fiscal responsibility for services, and those who pay for services usually like to make decisions about them.

We were able to identify which jurisdictions were responsible for providing the 25 percent matching funds in five states (all but Wisconsin and Massachusetts), and we found that the financial burden was split between state and local sources. In Arizona, state funds were reportedly insufficient to meet the federal matching requirements, and local resources were necessary to match a "considerable portion" of the federal allocation (Arizona Department of Economic Security 1979). Virginia, which has a locally administered program, passes the major burden for meeting the matching requirements to the local areas, and withdraws all state funds if local donations are available to cover what would have been the state's share (Virginia Department of Welfare, no date). Louisiana and Utah, both state-administered programs, use state funds to meet 80 percent of the matching requirements (Louisiana Department of Health and Human Resources 1979, Utah Department of Social Services 1979).

The state/local match requirements of Pennsylvania offer an interesting picture of how the federal funds are often incorporated into state service programs. According to the aggregate state budget figures, the match seems to be 15 percent from state funds and 10 percent from local funds—a 60-40 split of the nonfederal share. However, Pennsylvania has instituted a sliding reimbursement scale so that counties can receive from the state anywhere from 50 percent to 90 percent of the costs of different services. The reimbursement schedule was enacted by the state to encourage the development of community-based services by arranging for those types of services to receive higher rates of state reimbursement. According to

the state's Social Service Manual, shelter care is the
only service reimbursed at a 90 percent rate and adoption
services are the only ones that carry an 80 percent state
reimbursement rate. Almost all other services (i.e.,
those specified in the Title XX plan) carry a 75 percent
state reimbursement rate. The services that only provide
50 percent state compensation are both secure and nonsecure placements and services for delinquents that are
primarily funded by sources other than Title XX (Pennsylvania Department of Public Welfare, no date). Therefore, with the exception of shelter care and adoption
services, counties in Pennsylvania may be required to
provide the entire match for federal Title XX funds. Once
in the state, the federal funds are identified only as
part of the state service expenditures.

All seven states provide services directly as well as
through purchase agreements with both public and private
providers. The U.S. Department of Health and Human Services reports that nationally in 1980 "purchase of services is clearly the predominant mode . . . at least three
of every five dollars expended under Title XX is used to
pay other public and private agencies for providing services to clients" (U.S. Department of Health, Education,
and Welfare, 1980a:77). The most recent state data we
reviewed were for fiscal year 1978 and are displayed in
Table 18-1. The U.S. totals show that 46 percent of the
services were provided directly by the Title XX agencies,
21 percent were purchased from other public agencies, and

TABLE 18-1 Title XX Costs by Method of Service
Provisions, Fiscal Year 1978

State	Direct Services (%)	Public Purchase (%)	Private Purchase (%)
Arizona	30	10	60
Louisiana	48	23	29
Massachusetts	23	33	44
Pennsylvania	10	61	29
Utah	35	15	49
Virginia	57	13	30
Wisconsin	61	0	39
Total U.S.	46	21	33

Source: U.S. Department of Health and Human Services
(1980a:33, 85).

33 percent were purchased from private providers. One of our states, Pennsylvania, has a noticeably lower direct service rate and a higher public purchase rate than other states. This adds further weight to the assertion made above that although it is a state-administered program, much of the actual operation and the day-to-day program decisions have been contracted away (e.g., to the public county children and youth agencies). Three states (Arizona, Massachusetts, and Utah) have rates of services purchased from private providers that are higher than the overall national rates--a reflection of the traditional service delivery systems in these states. It is interesting to note that our locally administered states, Virginia and Wisonsin, have the highest rates of direct service provision.

EFFECTS ON SERVICES TO STATUS OFFENDERS

Title XX attempted to place the decisionmaking responsibility for services provided under that program at the state and local levels. When the program was developed, federal dictates concerning state program procedures centered upon requirements for a planning process that was based on the determination of service needs and public input. Although the federal program contains goals and eligibility rules, most aspects of program design and implementation are left to the states. That aspect of the program has only made it easier for states to incorporate the federal program into their state and local social service programs. Because the federal program makes no mention of services for status offenders (except for runaways), it is state implementation that controls the impact that Title XX may have on services for these youth.

Title XX and State Service Programs

One reason it is so difficult to determine the effects of the federal program on services to status offenders is that Title XX imposes few requirements on state program content. There is sufficient latitude in the federal program's goals and objectives so that most states can adapt the language of their service programs to meet Title XX's requirements. There is always a state Title XX planner or coordinator, but in some states the federal Title XX funds are absorbed into a broader state social

service program, while in others the state programs'
characteristics are limited almost entirely to those of
the federal program. States that have larger budgets
appear more often to consider Title XX as a source of
funds for their state social service programs; states with
lower levels of service funding appear to have programs
that are more closely aligned with the federal Title XX
program (probably because in each of these states Title XX
funds and the state/local match comprise the entire, or
almost the entire, budget).

Although Title XX allowed for the expansion of a
state's coverage of services and population, it did not
increase the federal funds available for social services.
Even before the passage of Title XX, several states were
spending their entire social services allocation (Benton
et al. 1978, U.S. Department of Health, Education, and
Welfare 1980a). Not surprisingly, all 50 states at least
planned to spend their entire federal allotment for fiscal
year 1980. Table 18-2 shows the amount of their federal
share that each of the seven study states has spent for

TABLE 18-2 Percentage of Federal Title XX Allocation
Used by States, Fiscal Years 1976-1980

State	1976	1977	1978	1979	Planned 1980
Arizona	26	51	88	79	100
Louisiana	70	79	97	91	100
Massachusetts	89	100	100	100	100
Pennsylvania	100	100	100	100	100
Utah	78	100	100	100	100
Virginia	66	90	100	100	100
Wisconsin	100	100	100	100	100
Total U.S.	87	94	98	100	100

Note: All of the above data are as of September 1, 1979,
except the 1979 numbers, which were updated in the spring of
1980. At the time the data were tabulated, states could still
continue to submit bills for services that were delivered in
1978 and 1979, so data for those years were not closed out at
that time.

Source: U.S. Department of Health and Human Services (no date).

the federal funding years 1976 to 1980. In the first year of Title XX (fiscal year 1976) two study states, Pennsylvania and Wisconsin, spent all of their federal allocation, and in the second year Utah and Massachusetts joined them. What this has meant for those states is that any increases in services has required increased funding from state and local sources or other federal sources, such as demonstration funds. It is possible that this lack of increased availability of federal Title XX funds has served to limit growth in the area of new and different types of services.

One effect of the Title XX ceiling and the fact that states are using their entire allocations is the implementation of substate ceilings on service funds. States such as Arizona and Wisconsin have placed limits on substate reimbursements for services (U.S. Department of Health, Education, and Welfare 1980a). Wisconsin was drawing its entire allocation in fiscal year 1973, the first year the federal ceiling was imposed on social service expenditures. In 1974 the state changed its method of distributing service funds to the counties and cities from reimbursement for all allowed expenditures (i.e., sum-sufficient funding) to reimbursement only up to predetermined ceilings (i.e., sum-certain funding). These substate ceilings were cited several times by state and local officials in Wisconsin as a major influence on service provision, especially on limiting the expansion of types of services and clients.

Services Provided

Although Title XX provided the opportunity to expand the types of services available, for the most part states have continued to provide the same types of services under their social service programs. There have been some changes and new services developed, but mostly these have been adjustments and adaptations within the context and pattern of service delivery as it existed before 1975. When they began, the two federal social service programs (Title IV-A and Title VI) that preceded Title XX were associated with the cash assistance programs and provided services that were designed primarily to meet the needs of welfare recipients. Prior to the early 1970s, when many state efforts to deinstitutionalize status offenders began, the state social service agencies that were receiving federal service funds did not provide services to

such youth. Some state welfare agencies were responsible
for evaluating and reporting certain psychological and
social conditions for juveniles involved with court cases,
but not all did so. Furthermore, prior to Title XX such
activities generally were not reimbursable under the federal service programs, except those involved in dependency
and neglect cases for eligible clients. Status offenders
were most often "treated" by the juvenile justice system.
On the other hand, protective services for abused and neglected children have been considered "traditional" social
services. In fact, protective services had been one of
the services mandated by the federal programs replaced by
Title XX.

One result of the deinstitutionalization movement in
some states has been the transferral of responsibility for
status offenders from the court to the social service
agency, which has caused to a more general change in the
characteristics of clients in the social service systems.
However, the social services available through that system
to children and youth have not changed dramatically in
response to the needs of these different clients. Changes
that have occurred in service delivery have been fragmented and have not always been a direct or rational response to the needs of the new clients. However, there
has been some isolated packaging of alternative services
for status offenders, such as those services delivered
through special centers that provide services and training
during the day. In addition, the past decade has witnessed a growth in the number of group homes (Shyne and
Schroeder 1978), which some deem more appropriate settings
for adolescents than either large institutions or foster
family homes (Children's Defense Fund 1978, Nemy 1975,
Scher 1958). Both youth service centers and group homes
have developed in limited numbers and as parts of existing
program structure and delivery methods. Several studies
have reported that the traditional types of services and
demographic characteristics of the clients have continued
unchanged under Title XX (Turem et al. 1976, U.S. Commission on Civil Rights 1979, U.S. Department of Health,
Education, and Welfare 1980a).

Although there is no evidence that Title XX encouraged
states to deinstitutionalize status offenders, several
states have used these funds to effect such a strategy.
Once a state decided to deinstitutionalize status offenders, Title XX became an important source of money for
alternative services both for status offenders and for
dependent and neglected children. Federal funds, both

program and research grants, have been used in a variety of ways to start and/or provide services in noninstitutional settings. In the seven states under study, a great deal of responsibility for status offenders has been shifted to the state social service system. As a result, services are now being provided to status offenders with funds that are tapped by the social service system, and Title XX is a major source of these funds.

The decision as to which services a state will actually provide with Title XX funds is a critical factor in determining how the program affects status offenders. In order for Title XX to be useful to such youth the services offered have to be appropriate to the problems and needs of status offenders or dependent and neglected children, and they have to be available through the network that serves those populations. Also, if Title XX is to assist with efforts to deinstitutionalize these children and youth, the services must be available through community-based providers and not limited to institutional locations. In all these regards the services provided by the seven study states vary immensely.

There are two ways in which Title XX services can be made available to status offenders. First, these youth may be served by general categories of services, such as family counseling, day care, and homemakers or case management services. In most states, however, we could not determine the extent to which such services were received by status offenders because information is not reported by client category. Once a status offender is determined eligible and in need of a service offered to the general population, it is simply reported that a child was a recipient of that particular kind of service.

The other way in which Title XX services are available to status offenders is through services that are provided by the state specifically for them. Some states have targeted certain services for youth who might be considered status offenders, and there are two ways in which this has been done in the seven study states. First, certain services are offered specifically for status offenders. Second, some services that are available to a wide range of individuals contain objectives that target portions of the services for status offenders or other relevant classifications of youth. In states in which services are not necessarily targeted for status offenders, certain services may still be identified as parts of grants or contracts with other agencies or service providers.

Three of the seven study states--Louisiana, Pennsylvania, and Massachusetts--identify specific social service programs for status offenders. In Louisiana status offenders receive three Title XX reimbursed services on the basis of group eligibility: (1) counseling, (2) education and training, and (3) health-related services that include psychotherapy (Louisiana Department of Health and Human Resources 1979). The state's Title XX planner informed us that status offenders were also eligible for protective services.

In Pennsylvania 2.4 percent of the state's 1980 Title XX funds reportedly was allocated to the Division of Youth Services. That division is in the Department of Public Welfare and serves both delinquent and dependent children and youth (which in Pennsylvania includes status offenders). Only delinquents are supposed to be served in the state and private institutions funded by the division, but no differentiation is made between delinquents and dependents as recipients of the division's nonresidential services. About 60 percent of the Title XX allocation to the division is spent for noninstitutional services, which include counseling, employment services, life skills education, service planning and case management, social and recreational services, and transportation. Figures for fiscal year 1979 indicate that Title XX funds accounted for 30 percent of the division's total institutional and community services budget (Pennsylvania Department of Public Welfare 1979).

Massachusetts provides social services through its 17 "programs," each of which is aimed at a specific population or designed to treat a certain problem. Once an individual meets the eligibility criteria for a particular program, all services included as part of that program are available as needed. Each program uses a variety of specific services that are deemed necessary to deal with the identified problem.

Three of the service programs in Massachusetts relate to status offenders. First, there is the Program for CHINS, which includes camping, case management, community residence, emergency shelter care, life education and counseling, information and referral, placement, and specialized foster care. Massachusetts also has a Program for Adolescents in Need of Care, which is a package of services aimed at serving children aged 13 to 20 who are considered predelinquents or pre-CHINS, or are unwed parents, individuals discharged from the custody of the Department of Public Welfare before they are determined to be ready, or adolescents with other social or behavior impairments. The services that are available through this program include all those available to CHINS, except for emergency shelter care. The third relevant services package is the Program for Children in Need of Care, which serves 10- to 12-year-olds who exhibit CHINS or delinquent behavior or whose parents are unable to care for them. Like the similar program for adolescents, this program contains the same services available through the Program for CHINS, except for emergency shelter care. In addition, this last program includes chore and homemaker services (Massachusetts Department of Public Welfare 1979). However, we were unable to determine from available data the percentage either of these programs or of these services that are provided to status offenders and reimbursed by Title XX.

In the other four states some services have components that are related specifically to status offenders. For example, transportation services are often identified for Title XX reimbursement, and the return of runaways is often identified as a component of such services. In addition to Pennsylvania, mentioned above, Arizona, Louisiana, Utah, and Virginia also provide this Title XX service for runaways (Arizona Department of Economic Security 1979; Louisiana Department of Health and Human Resources 1979; Utah Department of Social Services, no date; Virginia Department of Welfare 1979).

Another service that can be used for status offenders and that often uses Title XX funding is counseling, which is sometimes identified as a separate service but also can be included in other services, such as social development or crisis intervention. In addition to the three states with packages for status offenders, Arizona and Utah also identify status offenders among the recipients of counseling services that use Title XX funds. Status offenders are sometimes specifically mentioned (e.g., for receipt of crisis counseling and intervention services in Arizona); at other times, more general characteristics are used to describe the eligible population--for instance, children with behavioral problems or children not functioning at an adequate social level (Arizona Department of Economic Security 1979, 1980; Utah Department of Social Services, no date). In the remaining two states--Virginia and Wisconsin--there is no specific mention of status offenders, although counseling services are availabile in both states.

A final relevant service category that was identified
is "court services." These services are defined in Virginia and Wisconsin as activities not covered by other
service categories (i.e., court-related work involved with
child protection or adoption cases). In Virginia this
service is available on a universal basis, and no eligibility determinations are required. The Title XX plan
specifies that the services are to be provided by the Department of Welfare in domestic relations, child custody
related to divorce, and status offense cases (Virginia
Department of Welfare 1979). Wisconsin's court services
include activities associated with status offense cases
in addition to other areas, such as delinquency and termination of parental rights (Wisconsin Department of
Health and Social Services 1976, 1979).

In several of the seven states the Title XX agency was
found to have grants or contracts with agencies or specific service providers to purchase services for status
offenders. For example, both Louisiana and Pennsylvania
have made grant awards to the youth services agencies for
a package of services for status offenders. Arizona officials provided us with two examples of ways in which
Title XX funds could be used to provide services to status
offenders. First, there was some joint funding of status
offender services under an arrangement between the Title
XX agency and the Arizona Justice Planning Agency.
Through that agreement federal funds from the Office of
Juvenile Justice and Delinquency Prevention (OJJDP) actually were used as the required state matching money for
the federal Title XX funds. (According to David West,
Acting Administrator of OJJDP, up to 25 percent of a
state's formula grant can be used as a match for other
federal programs.) Arizona officials claimed that their
use of OJJDP monies as matching funds allowed more projects to be funded at higher levels. It is therefore
likely that the OJJDP funds freed up by this infusion of
Title XX money had been used to provide the same types of
services. This would result in increased availability of
relevant services. Arizona also provided a second example
of the use of Title XX funds. It was discovered that
Title XX money--in the form of a grant made directly to
the provider--has been used to finance a runaway center
following the expiration of other funding grants for that
facility.

Special Interpretations of Eligibility Rules

States have used eligibility categories that are federally
specified or allowed to make Title XX services available
to status offenders and dependent and neglected children.
There are several ways in which a state can design its
social services program so that such youth are eligible
for appropriate services. One way is to make status offenders eligible on a group basis; but only one state,
Louisiana, defined a group for Title XX eligibility specifically to include status offenders. Of all of the
states studied Louisiana has used the group eligibility
provision to the greatest extent. In their 1980 Title XX
plan, 23 individual groups were defined. One of those
groups consists of all clients of the state's Division of
Youth Services, which includes "children adjudicated delinquent and/or in need of supervision by the court and
placed under supervision of the Division of Youth Services. In addition, their families are eligible for
Title XX services on a group basis" (Louisiana Department
of Health and Human Resources 1979:11).
  Another way in which Title XX services are made available to status offenders is by making such youth eligible
for child protective services. The seven states studied
have adapted the federal rules in several different ways
in order to provide such eligibility. In some cases the
states have made only one category of status offenders--
runaways--eligible for protective services, while other
states have defined eligibility to include the entire
category of status offenders.
  Five of the states studied, all but Arizona and Wisconsin, include runaways among those eligible for child
protective services. The federal Title XX rules allow
even easier coverage of runaways than other types of
children. Although such services may be provided to all
children in need without regard to income, federal regulations require that the need for those services must be
documented in each individual case except for runaways,
who can be presumed to be harmed or threatened with harm.
Runaways are the only federally specified group that is
exempt from the requirement for an individual determination of need. States do not have to use the more lenient
eligibility rules for runaways, and we found only two
states, Louisiana and Pennsylvania, whose written program
guidelines exempt runaways from the documentation requirement (Louisiana Department of Health and Human
Resources, no date; Pennsylvania Department of Public
Welfare, no date).

Although federal regulations specify that juvenile delinquents cannot be presumed to be in need of protective
services, status offenders per se are not mentioned. Two
of the states, Utah and Massachusetts, have been creative
in their interpretation and definition of protection cases
so that they extend coverage to status offenders.

The Utah Family Service Manual (Utah Department of
Social Services, no date) notes that court-adjudicated
youth are to be considered "universally eligible," a
Title XX term. It also states that universal eligibility
applies only to two services—information and referral,
and protective services. Although the manual does not
directly tie court-adjudicated youth to protective services, these two statements allow such an interpretation.
Another section of the Utah manual states that ungovernable youth shall be treated as protective services referrals and that an immediate investigation shall be conducted to determine if there has been any abuse, neglect,
or exploitation. This section does not automatically turn
ungovernable children into protection cases, but it does
indicate that the policy allows either a service worker
to consider such a decision or the financial office to
claim Title XX reimbursement for services in such cases.
The manual continues with the statement that if a runaway
or ungovernable child has been referred for services and
the parents will not "get involved, the youth shall be
considered to be [a] neglected and dependent child . . ."
(Sec. VYS 200). Moreover, in Utah's Title XX plan protective services are defined as including "rehabilitative
services to children served by the Youth Services continuum . . ." that handles both status offenders and delinquents (Utah Department of Social Services 1979:28).

In Massachusetts the Social Services Policy Manual
(Massachusetts Department of Public Welfare 1978) states
that children who need foster care, group care, or residential, protective, or adoption services shall be considered to be children in need of services and will have
those services provided without regard to income. This
provision applies to the state program, but separate provisions had to be made in order to claim Title XX reimbursement for these services. For example, the state's
Title XX plan indicates that "services provided under [the
CHINS program] are given as protection services upon determination by a social worker or court adjudication that
the child is subject to or at risk of abuse, neglect, or
exploitation" (Massachusetts Department of Public Welfare
1979:A-3). A Department of Public Welfare memorandum

dated August 29, 1977, claims that the state considers CHINS to be eligible for Title XX services without regard to income because the needed services are protective services. That memorandum goes on to state that protective services are needed because CHINS have a "deteriorated family situation or other living problems [that] require such services to avoid physical or psychological harm" (p. 1).

Still another way in which states have made Title XX services available for status offenders is based on how they define "family" for eligibility purposes. Title XX allows eligibility to be determined on the basis of family income. The federal regulations define family as follows (45 CFR 228.1):

> . . . one or more adults and children, if any, related by blood, or law, and residing in the same household. . . . Emancipated minors and children living under the care of individuals not legally responsible for that care may be considered one person families by the state.

Depending on a state's definition of family, certain youth can become eligible for Title XX services. If a state defines certain categories of youth as one-person families, then only a youth's income, not that of the entire family, is considered for eligibility purposes. This provision may allow youth who are not eligible for Title XX while at home to become eligible when removed from their homes and placed in foster care or in an institutional setting.

In all seven states some categories of children outside their natural homes have been identified as one-person families, and this includes coverage for children and youth in foster care. Arizona has attempted to provide Title XX coverage to as many foster children as possible. That state's policy is that a foster child is considered either as a member of his or her family or as a one-person family, whichever allows the child to qualify for services (Arizona Department of Economic Security 1975). None of the seven states limits the services available to foster children to those that are called foster care services (i.e., case management, review, and other services related to the placement of the child in foster care). Rather, foster children can receive any services they need that are made available under a state's Title XX program once they are determined eligible. In Virginia, when a child or youth is returned home from foster care, the local welfare board can retain custody and thereby continue Title XX eligibility. In such cases the child can continue to receive supervision and other direct services until custody is relinquished, and can receive any needed services that are purchased from other providers for up to three months (Virginia Department of Welfare, no date).

In some states other groups of children have been identified as one-person families, and some of these groups may include status offenders. Louisiana's Policy and Procedure Manual states that minors, including students, not living at home may be considered as one-person families (Louisiana Department of Health and Human Resources, no date). This allows coverage of children in institutions and other out-of-home placements who might not be eligible if left at home. In Pennsylvania, children who live in residential facilities—including those for both dependent and delinquent children—are considered to be individuals for Title XX income eligibility purposes (Pennsylvania Department of Public Welfare 1979). Under this provision, only those dependent children (including status offenders) who are removed from their homes are favored with the less stringent income eligibility test. Those who remain at home may or may not be eligible for the same services, depending on the family's circumstances.

We do not know what effect, if any, these eligibility definitions have on service provision to status offenders. The major problem is that data are not collected or recorded in such a way that allows determination of how many, if any, of the youth who meet these eligibility rules are actually served. Status offenders often lose that label and become labeled by their Title XX eligibility category. There is little need to continue using the status offender label since Title XX accounting procedures tend to blend all children under age 18 together or, at most, separate them by whether they are categorical or income eligibles or are receiving services without regard to income (U.S Department of Health and Human Services 1980b).

SUMMARY

Title XX is a federal program that provides funds to states to support the delivery of social services. A range of services and clients can be covered by Title XX through the state service programs, and some of those services can be provided to status offenders. Such service delivery can occur either because the services are targeted toward status offenders or because such youth are part of the identified client group. In either case it is primarily state decisions that influence the potential Title XX coverage.

Analysis of the seven state programs has uncovered a variety of methods for providing coverage for status offenders and dependent and neglected children. However, it has been state initiatives rather than influences from the federal Title XX program managers that have caused changes in the state social services programs that affect these youth.

Services to status offenders have not been a focus of previous federal service programs, and they have not become one under Title XX. Title XX's requirements are vague enough that it could cover services to status offenders, but there are no specific provisions that would encourage inclusion of such services. Title XX is a federal program with relatively few restrictions on the design of state programs that use its funds. Most of the federal restrictions pertain to procedures for planning and public review rather than to specification of services or clients. States that want to use Title XX to fund services for status offenders have been able to.

Although many services may not have been specifically identified for status offenders, such youth are probably being served through Title XX more frequently than can be identified. More and more often status offenders are being referred to state and local social service agencies, and these agencies frequently are required by state law to serve these youth. Our field work has shown that the responses of service agencies to this new client group range from ignoring them to instituting complete packages of services for them. When services are provided or purchased by public service agencies, status offenders are served through the agencies' general service programs that are funded through a variety of federal, state, local, and private sources. Title XX is only one of the funding sources and is probably used on a case-by-case basis when the client (status offender or not) meets the eligibility requirements. Federal and state data simply do not allow for the identification of client characteristics other than the reason for eligibility.

States do not change their programs merely because the federal government sets up a new program (Benton et al.

1978, Derthick 1975, Turem et al. 1976). Instead state
bureaucracies maintain their own structure, objectives,
and programs, while they identify and use federal funding
sources to support their existing programs. By and large
this is what has happened with Title XX and services to
status offenders.

REFERENCES

Arizona Department of Economic Security (1975)
     Administrative Rules and Regulations. Includes
     revisions through July 1, 1980. Phoenix, Ariz.:
     Department of State.
     _____ (1979) 1979-1980 Title Twenty Comprehensive
     Annual Service Program Plan. Phoenix, Ariz.:
     Department of Economic Security.
     _____ (1980) Amendment to the 1979-1980 Title Twenty
     Comprehensive Annual Service Program Plan. Dated
     February 20, 1980. Department of Economic Security,
     Phoenix, Ariz.
Benton, Bill, Feild, Tracey, and Millar, Rhona (1978)
     Social Services: Federal Legislation vs. State
     Implementation. Washington, D.C.: The Urban
     Institute.
Children's Defense Fund (1978) Children Without Homes,
     An Examination of Public Responsibility to Children in
     Out of Home Care. Washington, D.C.: Children's
     Defense Fund.
Derthick, Martha (1975) Uncontrollable Spending for
     Social Services Grants. Washington, D.C.: The
     Brookings Institution.
Louisiana Department of Health and Human Resources (1979)
     Final Comprehensive Annual Services Program Plan (for
     July 1, 1979 to June 30, 1980). Baton Rouge, La.:
     Department of Health and Human Resources.
     _____ (no date) Policy and Procedure Manual. Baton
     Rouge, La.: Department of Health and Human Resources.
Massachusetts Department of Public Welfare (1977) Federal
     Eligibility Codes for CHINS Referrals. Memorandum
     dated August 29, 1977. Department of Public Welfare,
     Boston.
     _____ (1978) Social Services Policy Manual. Boston:
     Department of Public Welfare.
     _____ (1979) Fifth Comprehensive Annual Social
     Service Plan for the Commonwealth of Massachusetts
     (for fiscal year 1980). Boston: Department of Public
     Welfare.

Mott-McDonald Associates, Inc. (1976) Taxonomy of Title
    XX Social Services. Prepared for the National
    Conference on Social Welfare. Washington, D.C.: U.S.
    Department of Health, Education, and Welfare.
Nemy, Enid (1975) Agencies Unprepared for Soaring
    Numbers of Adolescents in Need. New York Times,
    January 3, 1975.
Pennsylvania Department of Public Welfare (1979)
    Comprehensive Annual Services Program Plan for
    1979/1980. Pennsylvania Bulletin 9(25): 1969-2113.
    Harrisburg, Pa.: Commonwealth of Pennsylvania,
    Legislative Reference Bureau.
_____ (no date) Social Services Manual. Includes
    revisions through January 1979. Harrisburg, Pa.:
    Department of Public Welfare.
Scher, Bernhard (1958) Specialized Group Care for
    Adolescents. Child Welfare 27(2):12-17.
Shyne, Ann, and Schroeder, Anita (1978) National Study of
    Social Services to Children and Their Families.
    Prepared for U.S. Department of Health, Education, and
    Welfare, Children's Bureau. Rockville, Md.: Westat,
    Inc.
Turem, Jerry, Benton, Bill, Millar, Rhona, and Woolsey,
    Suzanne (1976) The Implementation of Title XX: The
    First Year's Experience. Working paper. Washington,
    D.C.: The Urban Institute.
U.S. Commission on Civil Rights (1979) The Age
    Discrimination Study, Part II. Washington, D.C.:
    U.S. Government Printing Office.
U.S. Department of Health and Human Services (1980a)
    Annual Report to the Congress on Title XX of the
    Social Security Act, Fiscal Year 1979. Office of
    Human Development Services. Washington, D.C.: U.S.
    Government Printing Office.
_____ (1980b) Social Services U.S.A. Annual
    summary, October 1977-September 1978. Washington,
    D.C.: Office of Human Development Services.
_____ (no date) Actual use reports. Administration
    for Public Services, Washington, D.C.
U.S. Department of Health, Education, and Welfare (1980)
    Implementation of Title XX Social Services Programs:
    A Report to Congress. Draft dated April 1980. Office
    of Human Development Services, Administration for
    Public Services, Washington, D.C.
Utah Department of Social Services (1979) Final Title XX
    Plan, Utah Comprehensive Annual Service Program Plan
    for FY 1980. Salt Lake City, Utah: Department of
    Social Services.

_____ (no date) Family Service Manual. Division of
    Family Services. Salt Lake City, Utah: Department of
    Social Services.
Virginia Department of Welfare (1979) Comprehensive
    Annual Plan for Social Services (July 1, 1979 - June
    30, 1980) Under Title XX of the National Social
    Security Act. Richmond, Va.: Department of Welfare.
    _____ (no date) Manual of Policy and Procedures for
    Local Welfare Departments, Social Services. Vol.
    VII-A, with revisions. Richmond, Va.: Department of
    Welfare.
Wisconsin Department of Health and Social Services (1976)
    Social Services Manual. Includes revisions. Madison,
    Wis.: Department of Health and Social Services.
    _____ (1979) Final Comprehensive Annual Services
    Program Plan. Dated July 1, 1979. Madison, Wis.:
    Department of Health and Social Services.
    _____ (1980) Final Comprehensive Annual Services
    Plan (Title XX). Amended date January 1, 1980.
    Madison, Wis.: Department of Health and Social
    Services.

Federal Child Welfare Funds and Services for Status Offenders

19

SALLY A. KORNEGAY

Federal grants for child welfare services were included in the Social Security Act in 1935, and since 1968 those grants have been authorized under Title IV-B of the act. Compared to the Title XX social service program, federal support for child welfare services has never been substantial. Title IV-B funds are meant primarily to encourage the expansion of existing state service programs, especially in geographic areas with limited private as well as public services for children. Since status offenders may be served by child welfare agencies that use these funds, the program is relevant to our investigation.

The purpose of this paper is to describe the use of the federal child welfare service program and its effects on the provision of services to status offenders. When status offenders are served by child welfare services programs, they often are labeled as dependent and neglected youth or, more generally, youth in need of services. We first describe the federal child welfare program and the relationship of the program's provisions to status offenders and dependent and neglected children. Second, we discuss the relationship of the federal program to the organization and delivery of child welfare services in the states. Third, we examine the various ways in which the federal program affects the structure and content of services for status offenders. The final section summarizes the discussion of the federal child welfare services program and services for status offenders.

621

As with the AFDC-foster care program, which is discussed in chapter 20, the Adoption Assistance and Child Welfare Act of 1980 (P.L. 96-272) has the potential to affect our findings. That act repeals the child welfare services program that was in effect during our study and replaces it with a new program that will be closely aligned with the foster care program. In fact, federal child welfare services funds are to be used in tandem with the federal foster care maintenance grants to provide services to discourage placements, reunite families, or place children in adoptive homes. At the time of our study, the new law had not been implemented.

THE FEDERAL PROGRAM

The purpose of the Title IV-B program is to encourage states to establish, extend, and strengthen child welfare services (P.L. 90-248, as amended, codified at 42 USC 620-626 (1976), amended by P.L. 96-272 and 45 CFR Part 220 with proposed changes 45 Fed. Reg. 86812-86852 (1980)). Prior to the 1980 legislative changes, child welfare services were defined to include protective services, care of dependent and neglected children, care of children of working mothers, and any other services that promote the welfare of children. The definition contained in the 1980 legislation highlights protective services and services to prevent family dissolution, and eliminates the reference to services to children of working mothers.

The federal child welfare services program is administered by the U.S. Department of Health and Human Services, formerly the Department of Health, Education, and Welfare. The program's operations are handled specifically by the Children's Bureau, which is part of the Administration for Children, Youth, and Families.

The amount of federal funds that have been available under Title IV-B has always been small, especially when compared to some of the other federal service programs. Although the program authorization in fiscal year 1980 was $266 million, the budget allocation was $56.6 million, the same as it had been since 1977. It was anticipated that the Adoption Assistance and Child Welfare Act of 1980 would correct this discrepancy between authorization and appropriation levels. However, even though larger appropriations will be required to implement the program authorized by the 1980 legislation, funding levels remain tied to the annual appropriation process (U.S. Congress

1980). States would not have to meet the new program requirements unless funding for Title IV-B reaches $163.5 million in fiscal year 1981 and increases annually to $266 million by fiscal year 1983. Congress did appropriate the 1981 target amount as a supplemental appropriation (P.L. 96-536).

After each state receives a base amount of $70,000, the remaining Title IV-B funds are distributed by means of a formula based on a state's per capita income level and population under 21 years of age. Furthermore, federal and state matching rates are determined by a state's per capita income level, so that a "poorer" state has to put up a smaller share of state funds in order to receive federal funds. The federal share can range from 33-1/3 percent to 66-2/3 percent. In 1977 the federal matching rates for the seven states in our study varied from a high of 60.85 percent for Louisiana to a low of 46.96 percent for Massachusetts (U.S. Department of Health, Education, and Welfare 1976c).

States may use federal child welfare services funds to provide any services deemed appropriate to meet the needs of any child and thereby to improve the welfare of that child. The statutory definition of child welfare services identifies some specific services that may be provided, including services for dependent and neglected children, runaways, and delinquents. Status offenders per se are not mentioned in the legislation.

Although such coverage is not mandated, Title IV-B mentions the use of funds for services to one particular group of status offenders, runaways. The law specifically says that states may use federal child welfare services funds to return runaways under the age of 18 to their own communities in another state, but Title IV-B funds cannot be used to return a runaway within the same state. The federal program further allows states to pay the maintenance costs of runaways for up to 15 days prior to their return home. The language does not preclude other services for them, such as counseling parents in order to facilitate reunification.

Title IV-B also includes services for delinquents in its definition of child welfare services. Eligible services include those that are provided to prevent, remedy, or assist "in the solution of problems which may result in the . . . delinquency of children" (42 USC 625 (1976)). The term delinquency is not defined more specifically in either the law or the regulations. To the extent that a state chooses to view status offenses as predelinquent acts, services to status offenders may be covered.

The federal definition of child welfare services includes services designed to prevent or remedy situations
of neglect, abuse, or exploitation. These can cover a
wide range of more distinct services, such as the investigation of reports of abuse, homemaker services, day
care, and foster care. Such services often are used to
assist children who might be considered dependent or neglected, but for whom formal labeling, usually requiring
court involvement, has not occurred. In some cases, even
after the formal labeling, services continue to be called
protective services. Protective services also may be
provided to status offenders if they are considered in
jeopardy of harm, but such coverage depends on state program implementation.

Eligibility for some other federal programs (e.g.,
Title XX) may be associated with a person's income or
receipt of cash assistance, but eligibility for federal
child welfare services has no such requirements. Federal
regulations allow child welfare services that use Title
IV-B funds to be available solely on the basis of need for
such services.

STATE PROGRAM OPERATIONS

Although child welfare service programs vary across
states, all of these state programs include some services
provided with funds other than those received through
Title IV-B. The services most often identified as child
welfare services are day care, foster care, adoption services, and protective services.

Public child welfare services have been delivered
through a variety of state and local systems. In many
states prior to 1972 one state unit administered the child
welfare services program to the general child population
while another unit administered services to children who
were recipients of cash assistance. In 1972 new federal
rules required states to separate the administration of
services from cash assistance and to have one state agency
administering all social services. During the 1970s numerous states instituted massive reorganizations of their
welfare and service programs. The result is that child
welfare services now are usually delivered as a part of
more general social service organizational units (Austin
1978, Benton 1980, Oliphant 1974).

THE EFFECTS ON SERVICES TO STATUS OFFENDERS

The federal child welfare services program is filtered through state programs, which operate with funds from a variety of state and federal sources. Since these other funding sources may also influence the state child welfare programs, the job of sorting out the effects of this particular program is made all the more difficult. The locus of control over how this federal program is implemented and the extent to which it affects service delivery to status offenders lies at the state and local levels. How states interpret the federal requirements and operate their own programs determines the overall effect of the federal program.

Types of Services Available

In the past most federal child welfare funds reportedly were used to support staff and subsidize their training (Steiner 1981). However, more recently the majority of federal dollars for child welfare services has been spent on foster care. These expenditures include services to foster children, staff expenses incurred with the processing and review of cases, and actual maintenance payments (U.S. Congress 1979b). The 1980 legislation would reinforce these patterns of use. The goals of the new federal foster care maintenance and child welfare services programs are to prevent foster care placements whenever possible and, when children must be placed in foster care, to return them to their natural homes or to place them in a permanent home as quickly as possible. In accordance with these goals federal Title IV-B funds are to be used (a) for services designed to forestall removal, (b) for services to the families of foster children, (c) for monitoring children in foster placements so that they do not get lost in the system, and (d) for services to assist with adoptions.

Data on child welfare services have often been criticized as being incomplete or of variable quality (Kirst et al. 1980, Mott 1975, Shyne and Schroeder 1978, Steiner 1981). In order to get some picture of the types of services provided, we reviewed three sources of national-level data collected for the years 1961, 1977, and 1979 (Jeter 1963; Shyne and Schroeder 1978; U.S. Department of Health and Human Services, no date). The reports do not focus on Title IV-B expenditures alone; they often include

funds from a variety of sources. The two earlier surveys
(i.e., Jeter, and Shyne and Schroeder) report the number
of children who receive different types of services; that
is, one child could be reported more than once if he or
she received multiple services. However, the 1979 data
from the Children's Bureau are tabulations of money spent,
not the number of children receiving service. Although
less than ideal for purposes of comparison, these three
sources provide the best data available.

In 1961 a national survey was conducted that, among
other things, identified child welfare services provided
by both public and private agencies. In that year most
publicly supported services were provided directly by the
public agencies. The public purchase of services from
private providers did not become a major factor in service
delivery until the following decade (Derthick 1975,
Edwards et al. 1978). The 1961 survey asked service
agencies to identify the three most important services
provided to each client. In cases in which a child received more than three different types of services, only
the three thought to be the most important in meeting the
needs of that child were tabulated. The results of this
survey indicated that the four most prevalent services
provided by public agencies were as follows: foster care
services (40 percent), casework related to problems with
the child's adjustment (28 percent), protective services,
which primarily included casework and counseling (16 percent), and adoption services (11 percent) (Jeter 1963).

Another nationwide survey of services to children was
conducted in 1977. At that time protective services were
found to be the largest category of child welfare services, reportedly supplied to 33 percent of the children
who were receiving services. The other major service
categories were health services (26 percent), foster family care (25 percent), counseling (24 percent), day care
(16 percent), transportation (11 percent), educational
services (11 percent), and mental health services (10
percent) (Shyne and Schroeder 1978).

The Children's Bureau annually requests data from the
states concerning the distribution of the total funds used
by each state for child welfare services. The most recent
data made available to us are for fiscal year 1979. These
data are tabulations of child welfare service funds, not
the number of children who received a service. The distributions for the seven study states are shown in Table
19-1.

TABLE 19-1 Percentages of Estimated Child Welfare
Services Expenditures by Type of Services, Fiscal
Year 1979

State	Adoption	Day Care	Foster Care	Protective Services	Other
Arizona	2.1	0.0	83.3	0.0	14.6
Louisiana	0.0	2.3	97.7	0.0	--
Massachusetts	2.2	0.0	90.2	6.8	0.8
Pennsylvania	1.2	4.5	74.4	15.2	4.6
Utah	0.0	0.0	100.0	0.0	0.0
Virginia	1.1	1.2	91.3	6.0	0.4
Wisconsin*	0.0	0.0	91.6	0.0	8.4
Entire U.S.	3.3	8.5	73.4	8.2	6.7

Note: All figures in table are percentages, and each state's total
is 100 percent.

*Wisconsin only reports Title IV-B and state and local match.

Source: U.S. Department of Health and Human Services (no date).

Exactly which funds are reported in the Children's
Bureau's data varies a great deal by state. For instance,
Wisconsin only reported the use of Title IV-B funds while
Arizona appears to have reported all funds spent serving
children, including state and local foster care maintenance payments. Even with all their variations, the data
provide the most recent national-level statistics available. In fiscal year 1979 most child welfare services
expenditures were for foster care (73 percent), day care
(8.5 percent), and protective services (8 percent).

Through our fieldwork we were able to obtain some information from the seven states about the way in which
federal Title IV-B funds were spent. Except for Utah the
data were for 1979. Several of the states used the federal funds largely for their state and local agencies'
administrative costs. For example, an official of Arizona's Department of Economic Security reported that
one-half of their Title IV-B grant was used to pay the
salaries of the state's foster care workers. State officials in Massachusetts reported that all of their federal funds were allocated to salaries of child welfare
staff, and Pennsylvania officials said that about 60 percent was spent on the administration of the child welfare

services program. Three states reported that a large portion of their federal Title IV-B grant was spent on foster care services, but we could not determine if the funds were allocated to administrative expenses or direct services. These states were Arizona, which spent 47 percent (in addition to the 50 percent for salaries) on foster care services (Arizona Department of Economic Security 1979b); Utah, which used 42 percent of the Title IV-B allocation in 1978 for foster care services (Utah Department of Social Services 1978); and Wisconsin, which allocated all of its federal grant to foster care services (Wisconsin Department of Health and Social Services 1979). Louisiana used $1 million of its $1.3 million 1979 Title IV-B grant for maintenance payments for foster children, according to an official in their state foster care unit. Only Virginia did not spend the majority of its federal grant for administrative costs or foster care services. Instead the state reportedly spent its federal funds on a wide variety of services, with the top two categories of expenditures being adoption and court-related services. Court-related services include investigating and processing cases for status offenders, among other groups of clients (Virginia Department of Welfare 1979a, 1979b).

Thus, it appears that state Title IV-B grants provide funds for a variety of services, but the most frequently provided are often referred to as core services. The four services that are cited by the Children's Bureau as child welfare core services are (1) foster care, (2) day care, (3) protective services, and (4) adoption services. The majority of Title IV-B funds in four of the states (Arizona, Louisiana, Utah, and Wisconsin) are used for foster care. National reports throughout the 1970s also noted the predominant use of Title IV-B funds for foster care services (Mott 1975, U.S. Congress 1975, 1979a, 1979b). Funds allocated to foster care include payment for public agency staff, foster care maintenance payments, and services to foster children. We cannot be sure how these activities have affected services for status offenders because status offenders are not identified as such in the data on program recipients.

Relationship Between Federal and State Programs

For the most part, Title IV-B is integrated into state child welfare services programs that use funds from a variety of federal as well as state sources. This makes

it difficult to identify specific effects of this particular federal program on any specific group of children or
youth, including status offenders. Since the purpose of
the federal child welfare program is to enhance state
child welfare programs, it offers a ready source of federal funds to the states without requiring changes to
their programs. Most federal mandates that specify either
services or administrative structures are contained in
other programs, such as Title XX or AFDC.

Most states appear to consider Title IV-B as a source
of funds rather than as a federal mandate on the types or
context of child welfare services. One factor that hampered our determination of Title IV-B's impact is that
these federal funds go into a general pool of state and
federal funds that are expended for child welfare services. This is due in part to the nearly nonexistent
federal restrictions on the use of Title IV-B funds and
in part to the relatively low level of the federal grants.
State officials in several states said that Title IV-B
funds simply became part of the money available to the
local service units. Several policy and procedure service
manuals substantiated these claims, in that they contained
no separate eligibility criteria or other differences in
service provision (Peat, Marwick, Mitchell & Co. 1976b,
1976d).

Size of Title IV-B Grants

One aspect that limits the effect of this federal program
on state operations has been the level of Title IV-B
funding. The Administration for Children, Youth, and
Families estimates that states are spending over \$1 bil-
lion providing child welfare services, and the \$56.6 mil-
lion that has been available through Title IV-B is thereby
only a minor source of funding. Furthermore, state Title
IV-B grants are small compared to other federal or state
allocations for child welfare services. For example,
while Title XX funds do provide services to all age
groups, the federal funds available under that program are
50 times greater than the federal child welfare grants.
The smaller the amount of available funds, the less a
state is willing to make changes in its service programs
in order to obtain these funds. This is especially true
of changes in program design or methods of operation.

To get some idea of the potential impact of federal
child welfare funds, we estimated for each of the seven

states the percentage of total reported child welfare expenditures that come from Title IV-B. Our estimates are based on the Title IV-B state allocations combined with estimates of the required state and local matching funds, the sum of which was then calculated as a percentage of the total state expenditures for child welfare services. The state expenditure estimates are based on data collected by the Children's Bureau (U.S. Department of Health and Human Services, no date). Of the seven states, only Wisconsin did not report combined total state and federal child welfare expenditures.

The estimates of the federal Title IV-B grant amounts compared to total state program expenditures are presented in Table 19-2. Although these estimates obviously represent higher federal program expenditures than would similar determinations that were based only on the federal Title IV-B funds, they allow an examination of Title IV-B as if it were a separate program. As seen in Table 19-2, funds associated with the federal program represent a small portion of total state child welfare expenditures. Nationally, the federal and required state child welfare funds are less than 15 percent of reported expenditures for services to children. In Arizona, Massachusetts, and

TABLE 19-2 Estimated Percentage of Funds Spent on State-Reported Child Welfare Services That Are Title IV-B Plus Required State and Local Match, Fiscal Years 1976-1980

State	FY 1976[a]	FY 1977	FY 1978	FY 1979	FY 1980
Arizona	11.9	5.0	7.7	5.3	5.5
Louisiana	33.1	34.7	29.2	27.8	--[b]
Massachusetts	6.5	7.1	7.1	7.6	--[b]
Pennsylvania	11.6	8.9	4.9	5.1	4.3
Utah	21.8	75.1	45.3	53.7	36.5
Virginia	24.8	25.7	24.0	22.6	20.6
Entire U.S.	12.7	16.0	16.1	14.3	--[b]

[a]Includes funds used in the transition quarter.
[b]Not all states had submitted their budget documents by the date the data were tabulated.

Source: U.S. Department of Health, Education, and Welfare (1975, 1976b, 1976c) and U.S. Department of Health and Human Services (no date).

TABLE 19-3   Estimated Percentage of State-Reported Child
Welfare Expenditures that are Title IV-B, Fiscal Years
1976-1980

State	FY 1976[a]	FY 1977	FY 1978	FY 1979	FY 1980
Arizona	5.1	2.7	4.1	2.8	2.9
Louisiana	16.3	21.1	16.8	16.9	--[b]
Massachusetts	2.5	3.3	3.4	3.6	--[b]
Pennsylvania	4.7	4.5	2.5	2.6	2.2
Utah	10.4	44.5	26.8	31.7	21.4
Virginia	10.4	13.3	12.4	11.7	10.7
Entire U.S.	5.2	8.1	8.2	7.3	--[b]

[a]Includes funds used in the transition quarter.
[b]Not all states had submitted their budget documents by the date
the data were tabulated.

Source: U.S. Department of Health, Education, and Welfare
(1975, 1976b, 1976c) and U.S. Department of Health and Human
Services (no date).

Pennsylvania the Title IV-B rates are considerably lower
than the national average, while in Louisiana, Utah, and
Virginia the Title IV-B program funds represent a higher
than average percentage of expenditures. These last three
states report lower total funding levels for services to
children than the other states studied, and this may explain why the federal funds are a higher than average
percentage of their total service budgets.   It is also
questionable whether all child day care costs, especially
those funded by Title XX, have been included by the six
states in their reports of expenditures by service type.
Differences in reporting this service could greatly skew
the comparisons.   The importance of the federal funds
compared to all state funds is demonstrated in Table 19-3,
which shows the amount of the federal Title IV-B grants
as a percentage of the reported total state child welfare
expenditures.
     It should be noted that the figures shown in Table
19-2 differ substantially from those reported in the HEW
report, Child Welfare in 25 States (1976a).   In that study
the computations were based only on the federal Title IV-B
funds and on figures obtained by the contractor directly

from the states. However, the figures also differ with
those reported in Table 19-3, which are based only on the
federal Title IV-B funds. The data in the 1976 HEW report
were collected at the end of 1975 just after Title XX was
implemented. In that study the ratios of the federal
child welfare grants to total child welfare services funds
reported by the seven states in the present study as of
December 1975 were as follows: Louisiana, 9 percent;
Massachusetts, 2 percent; Pennsylvania, 3 percent; Utah,
5 percent; Virginia, 3 percent; and Wisconsin, 2 percent
(Peat, Marwick, Mitchell & Co. 1976a-f). Arizona was not
part of the HEW study. The differences in the reported
data in Tables 19-2 and 19-3, which are presented for
fiscal years 1976 through 1980, could represent either
changes over the time period or different data collection
methods.

Although the rates vary by reporting source and by
year, it appears that grants under Title IV-B are not the
major funding source for child welfare services in the
seven states that we studied. This finding was confirmed
by respondents in many states. They claimed that Title
IV-B had had little influence on the composition of state
social services programs in general and child welfare
services in particular because of the relatively low
levels of federal funding that were involved (Peat, Marwick, Mitchell & Co. 1976b; Pennsylvania Department of
Public Welfare 1979).

Services to Status Offenders

We could not find conclusive evidence to the effect that
Title IV-B either encouraged or discouraged the deinstitutionalization of status offenders. Moreover, this federal program does not appear to have provided the funds
necessary for implementation of such a strategy; the federal child welfare services program apparently has had
less of an effect on services to status offenders than
other programs. For example, Title XX seems to have
picked up a large share of expenses for the protection
services used to investigate reports and treat potential
and actual dependent and neglected children as well as
some status offenders. States do use Title IV-B grants
for foster care, which is frequently provided to dependent
and neglected children and sometimes to status offenders,
but we do not know to what extent Title IV-B funds provide
services to status offenders because they are not identified as such in the program data.

State Eligibility Requirements

Most states do not have separate eligibility criteria for child welfare services, much less specifically for Title IV-B services. All seven states in this study have special eligibility criteria that make services available to potential and actual dependent and neglected children through child protection and foster care programs, and status offenders can be eligible for such programs. Receipt of services other than those offered through protection programs often depends on the ability of a child to meet the general eligiblity tests (e.g., income) for public social service programs. Separate eligibility criteria for child welfare services are interesting to note because such criteria often allow coverage of both dependent and neglected children and status offenders.

In all seven states we found some eligibility provisions for the various child welfare services that were based on need, the only eligibility requirement in the federal program. Four states (Massachusetts, Arizona, Louisiana, and Utah) make certain specific services available to all children who need them. Two states (Pennsylvania and Wisconsin) make certain types of children eligible for all needed services. In only one state (Virginia) were we able to locate any eligibility rules related specifically to Title IV-B.

In Massachusetts, children are eligible for certain services without meeting the general service eligibility criteria if they are identified by the Department of Public Welfare or the court to be in need of those services. The state's Social Services Policy Manual lists the services available to such children; they include foster care, group care, residential care and treatment, adoption, and protective services (Massachusetts Department of Public Welfare 1978). All but one of the covered services are out-of-home, and all of those services have been used as part of traditional programs for dependent and neglected children. These services also are now being used as part of Massachusetts' program of services for status offenders. The department has responsibility for serving status offenders and classifies those youth as eligible for the protective services provided to all children and youth who need them (Massachusetts Department of Public Welfare 1977, 1979).

Arizona also makes certain services available to children who need them, even when they do not meet the eligibility requirements for the state's social service

program. In Arizona the first criterion for receipt of
public services is a demonstrated need for the particular
service. The second criterion focuses on categorical and
income requirements set by the state and associated with
the federal Title XX and WIN programs. According to the
state's Administrative Rules and Regulations, there is one
additional eligibility group that makes certain services
available to persons who are determined to be in need of
them, but "who have been found ineligible . . . by Title
XX criteria" (Arizona Department of Economic Security
1975:Sec. R6-5-2105). The specific services that can be
provided under this category are foster care, day treatment for children in foster care, adoption services (including subsidies), social problem-solving for children
and for families with children, family planning for youth
in foster care, and child protective services. Because
many of these services are limited to foster children, and
because Arizona allows foster children to be considered
as one-person families for Title XX eligibility (Arizona
Department of Economic Security 1979a), this provision
does not greatly expand the population that is already
eligible for services. It does, however, increase the
likelihood that children who receive these services will
qualify for at least some public support, including Title
IV-B.

The most recently published information for Louisiana
was from December 1975, but no subsequent changes were
identified during our field research. In 1975 certain
services were available to children who demonstrated a
need for such services. Most of the services covered by
this provision were out-of-home or were associated with
the permanent removal of a child from his or her family
(i.e., adoption, foster family care, group home care,
institutional care, residential treatment, and shelter
care). The only other service provided to all children
in need was protective services (Peat, Marwick, Mitchell
& Co. 1976a). Because need for services was the only
eligibility requirement for any of these services, they
could be provided to dependent and neglected children or
status offenders.

Utah also provides certain specified child welfare
services to all who need them. The state's Social Services Manual (Utah Department of Social Services, no date)
includes a section titled "Child Welfare Eligibility" that
indicates that in some situations the Division of Family
Services can serve people who are not eligible for Title
XX but who require specific child welfare services. One

service covered by this provision that might be particularly applicable to status offenders is voluntary foster care.

Two other states make a range of child welfare services available to certain children. Pennsylvania state statutes make child welfare services available to all children who need care and protection (Peat, Marwick, Mitchell & Co. 1976c). Although this provision was reported in 1975, it is apparently still in effect. In Pennsylvania, status offenders have joined dependent and neglected children in the category called dependents, and such youth are considered to be in need of care and protection. Under Wisconsin's social service program, child welfare services reportedly are available for "care and protection of dependent, neglected and delinquent children" (Peat, Marwick, Mitchell & Co. 1976f:20). It is not known exactly how status offenders fit into these eligibility categories, which are based solely on need, because data are not reported on status offenders or on services provided to them under these specific state provisions.

In these six states the services that are available without regard to income are mentioned as part of state child welfare services and not specifically as requirements related to the federal Title IV-B program. In all cases the provisions appear to account for services that are provided to children who might not meet the eligibility rules governing larger general public service programs, such as AFDC. Under such conditions federal child welfare services funds could be used as reimbursement for some of the services provided by the states' general public service programs, or the funds could come from some other source. The federal child welfare program is merely one source of funds, and while the existence of such funds might be welcomed by the states, it cannot be claimed as the only, and certainly not the major, cause of the availability of child welfare services.

The one state that specifically identifies Title IV-B eligibility is Virginia. Federal child welfare funds are reportedly used for several services, but the Virginia social service manual (Virginia Department of Welfare, no date) contains special Title IV-B eligibility procedures only for foster care services. For most services offered by the Department of Welfare, the eligibility criteria parallel those specified by the federal Title XX program (e.g., categorical eligibles, income eligibles, and universal services). The exception is foster care services. The first group of criteria for those services is based

on Title XX eligibility; however, the second group of
criteria includes "children determined ineligible for
Title XX." The manual states that such children are eligible for "child welfare services (Title IV-B)" coverage
for foster care services provided directly by the department (Sec. 5510). The manual goes on to note that any
purchased services for children who are ineligible for
Title XX would have to be provided entirely with local
funds. Some status offenders and dependent and neglected
children are placed in foster care in Virginia, and
through these provisions even those with too much income
for Title XX eligibility can receive services provided
with federal funds.

The eligibility rules in all these states potentially
could provide Title IV-B coverage for status offenders.
Such coverage, however, depends on whether or not state
policies and procedures for handling status offenders
provide these youth with the opportunity to come in contact with the state social service programs and the particular services offered. It was not possible in any of
the states we studied to identify how many children and
youth were provided services because of any one of the
described special eligibility rules, much less to determine how many were status offenders.

SUMMARY

Title IV-B provides federal grants to states for the provision of child welfare services. There are no federal
controls concerning exactly how the funds are to be used,
which services are to be provided, or which types of
children are to be served. It is possible that services
provided through this program may be used by status offenders, but it is state and local implementation, rather
than federal guidelines, that control such usage.

Review of the seven state programs reveals that established types and patterns of services offered and clients
served by Title IV-B have continued at least over the last
10 years. Since the mid-1970s Title IV-B grants have paid
for similar activities in several of the states, primarily
for administrative costs and foster care services. Any
increased expenditures for services seem to be used for
the same activities and types of services.

It appears that child welfare services have continued
to focus on foster care even though there has been a lot
of rhetoric advocating permanent placements and leaving

children at home whenever possible. Although identifying the use of Title IV-B funds is more difficult than identifying child welfare services in general, reports in several of the states we studied indicate that federal funds are frequently used for services to children and youth in foster care.

When implemented, the Adoption Assistance and Child Welfare Act of 1980 will require states to use their Title IV-B funds to develop data systems that will allow the tracking of individual foster children. This was included in the new legislation to overcome the problem of children who drift through foster care for most of their childhood. It is possible that such state data systems eventually might include the legal reason each child is in foster care, which would then allow the identification of status offenders, or at least those youth who are labeled as such. At this time, however, the existing state data do not allow us to determine how many, if any, status offenders are in fact receiving services through the Title IV-B program.

REFERENCES

Arizona Department of Economic Security (1975)
   Administrative Rules and Regulations. Includes
   revisions through July 1, 1980. Phoenix, Ariz.:
   Department of State.
   _____ (1979a) 1979-1980 Title Twenty Comprehensive
   Annual Service Program Plan. Phoenix, Ariz.:
   Department of Economic Security.
   _____ (1979b) Quarterly Report to HEW, Form 2D, for
   quarter ending March 1979. Department of Economic
   Security, Phoenix, Ariz.
Austin, David (1978) Consolidation and Integration.
   Public Welfare 36(3):20-28.
Benton, Bill (1980) Separation Revisited. Public Welfare
   38(2):15-21.
Derthick, Martha (1975) Uncontrollable Spending for
   Social Services Grants. Washington, D.C.: The
   Brookings Institution.
Edwards, Sam, Benton, Bill, Feild, Tracey, and Millar,
   Rhona (1978) The Purchase of Service and Title XX.
   Working paper. Washington, D.C.: The Urban Institute.
Jeter, Helen (1963) Children, Problems, and Services in
   Child Welfare Programs. U.S. Department of Health,
   Education, and Welfare, Children's Bureau. Washington,
   D.C.: U.S. Government Printing Office.

Kirst, Michael, Garms, Walter, and Oppermann, Theo (1980)
    State Services for Children: An Exploration of Who
    Benefits, Who Governs. Program report 80-B8. Palo
    Alto, Cal.: Institute for Research on Educational
    Finance and Governance.
Massachusetts Department of Public Welfare (1977) Federal
    Eligibility Codes for CHINS Referrals. Memorandum
    dated August 29, 1977, Department of Public Welfare,
    Boston.
_____ (1978) Social Services Policy Manual.
    Boston: Department of Public Welfare.
_____ (1979) Fifth Comprehensive Annual Social
    Service Plan for the Commonwealth of Massachusetts
    (for fiscal year 1980). Boston: Department of Public
    Welfare.
Mott, Paul (1975) Foster Care and Adoption: Some Key
    Policy Issues. Prepared for the U.S. Congress, Senate
    Committee on Labor and Public Welfare, Subcommittee on
    Children and Youth. 94th Congress, 1st Session.
    Washington, D.C.: U.S. Government Printing Office.
Oliphant, Winford (1974) Observations on Administration
    of Social Services in the States. Child Welfare
    53(5):279-285.
Peat, Marwick, Mitchell & Co. and the Child Welfare
    League of America (1976a) Profile of Louisiana's Child
    Welfare Delivery System as of December 1975. Prepared
    for the U.S. Department of Health, Education, and
    Welfare, Children's Bureau.
_____ (1976b) Profile of Massachusetts' Child
    Welfare Delivery System as of December 1975. Prepared
    for the U.S. Department of Health, Education, and
    Welfare, Children's Bureau.
_____ (1976c) Profile of Pennsylvania's Child
    Welfare Delivery System as of December 1975. Prepared
    for the U.S. Department of Health, Education, and
    Welfare, Children's Bureau.
_____ (1976d) Profile of Utah's Child Welfare
    Delivery System as of December 1975. Prepared for the
    U.S. Department of Health, Education, and Welfare,
    Children's Bureau.
_____ (1976e) Profile of Virginia's Child
    Welfare Delivery System as of December 1975. Prepared
    for the U.S. Department of Health, Education, and
    Welfare, Children's Bureau.
_____ (1976f) Profile of Wiconsin's Child
    Welfare Delivery System as of December 1975. Prepared
    for the U.S. Department of Health, Education, and
    Welfare, Children's Bureau.

Pennsylvania Department of Public Welfare (1979)
    Comprehensive Annual Services Program Plan for
    1979/1980. Pennsylvania Bulletin 9(25):1969-2113.
    Harrisburg, Pa.: Commonwealth of Pennsylvania,
    Legislative Reference Bureau.
Shyne, Ann, and Schroeder, Anita (1978) National Study of
    Social Services to Children and Their Families
    Overview. Prepared for U.S. Department of Health,
    Education, and Welfare, Children's Bureau. Rockville,
    Md: Westat, Inc.
Steiner, Gilbert (1981) The Futility of Family Policy.
    Washington, D.C.,: The Brookings Institution.
U.S. Congress (1975) Foster Care: Problems and Issues.
    Part I of the hearings before the Senate Committee on
    Labor and Public Welfare, Subcommittee on Children and
    Youth and the House Committee on Education, and Labor,
    Subcommittee on Select Education. 94th Congress, 1st
    Session. Washington, D.C.: U.S. Government Printing
    Office.
_____ (1979a) Adoption Assistance and Child
    Welfare Act of 1979. Senate Report 96-336. Committee
    on Finance. 96th Congress, 1st Session. Washington,
    D.C.: U.S. Government Printing Office.
_____ (1979b) Social Services and Child Welfare
    Amendments of 1979. House report 96-136. Committee
    on Ways and Means. 96th Congress, 1st Session.
    Washington, D.C.: U.S. Government Printing Office.
_____ (1980) Adoption Asistance, Child Welfare,
    and Social Services. House Report 96-900. Conference
    Report. 96th Congress, 2nd Session. Washington,
    D.C.: U.S. Government Printing Office.
U.S. Department of Health and Human Services (no date)
    Unpublished data collected by the Children's Bureau on
    the distribution of the total funds used by each state
    for child welfare services and on federal allotments
    on state and local matching rates for fiscal years
    1978-1980. Washington, D.C.
U.S. Department of Health, Education, and Welfare (1975)
    Federal Apportionment, Minimum State and Local
    Matching, and Federal Share Percent for Child Welfare
    Services Under Title IV, Part B of the Social Security
    Act, as Amended for Fiscal Year 1975. Program
    Instruction CSA-PI-75-7. Memorandum dated March 24,
    from John C. Young, Washington, D.C.
_____ (1976a) Child Welfare in 25 States--An
    Overview. Prepared by Peat, Marwick, Mitchell & Co.
    and the Child Welfare League of America for the

Children's Bureau. Washington, D.C.: U.S. Government
Printing Office.
_____ (1976b) Federal Apportionment, Minimum State
and Local Matching, and Federal Share Percent for
Child Welfare Services Under Title IV, Part B of the
Social Security Act, as Amended for Fiscal Year 1976
and the Transition Quarter, July 1, 1976 to September
30, 1976. Program Instruction, SRS-AT-76-29(PSA).
Memorandum dated February 20, 1976, from Michio
Suzuki, Washington, D.C.
_____ (1976c) Federal Apportionment, Minimum State
and Local Matching, and Federal Share Percent for
Child Welfare Services Under Title IV, Part B of the
Social Security Act, as Amended for Fiscal Year 1977.
Program Instruction, SRS-AT-76-167 (PSA). Memorandum
dated November 10, 1976, from Carolyn Betts,
Washington, D.C.
Utah Department of Social Services (1978) Quarterly
Report to HEW, Form 2D, for quarter ending September
1978. Department of Social Services, Salt Lake City,
Utah.
_____ (no date) Social Services Manual. Division of
Family Services. Salt Lake City, Utah: Department of
Social Services.
Virginia Department of Welfare (1979a) Comprehensive
Annual Plan for Social Services (July 1, 1979 - June
30, 1980) Under Title XX of the National Social
Security Act. Richmond, Va.: Department of Welfare.
_____ (1979b) Annual Report to HEW, Form 2D, for
year ending June 1979. Department of Welfare,
Richmond, Va.
_____ (no date) Manual of Policy and Procedures for
Local Welfare Departments, Social Services. Vol.
VII-A, with revisions. Richmond, Va.: Department of
Welfare.
Wisconsin Department of Health and Social Services
(1979) Quarterly Report to HEW, Form 2D, for quarter
ending March 1979. Department of Health and Social
Services, Madison, Wis.

20

State Use of the AFDC-Foster Care Program for Status Offenders

SALLY A. KORNEGAY

The primary purpose of Title IV-A of the Social Security Act is to provide federal funds for the public assistance program called Aid to Families with Dependent Children (AFDC). One component of that program makes federal funds available to reimburse states for part of the support costs for eligible children who are placed in foster care (P.L. 87-31, Sec. 2, codified at 42 USC 608). This aspect of the program, which we refer to as AFDC-foster care, is reviewed here because status offenders as well as dependent and neglected children often are served in foster care. Inasmuch as it has been alleged that the availability of federal AFDC funds for children placed in foster care facilitates unnecessary placement of children and youth outside their own homes (Children's Defense Fund 1978), we were interested in the impact of these funds on placement decisions that affect status offenders and dependent and neglected children.

The Adoption Assistance and Child Welfare Act (P.L. 96-272), which was passed after the completion of our research, will dramatically alter the program of federal assistance in the area of foster care, if and when implemented. In fact, that law schedules the phaseout of reimbursements under Title IV-A by September 30, 1982, to be replaced by a program authorized by a new Title IV-E. The purpose of this new federal foster care program is twofold: (1) to make removal from the home much more an option of last resort, and (2) if children are placed in

641

foster care, to return them home or place them in a permanent adoptive home as quickly as possible. We have tried, whenever possible, to take account of the changes that might be brought about by this new legislation.

This paper describes the effect of the AFDC-foster care program on the placement of status offenders and dependent and neglected children. The first section describes the federal program, including those aspects that pertain to the status offender and dependent and neglected child populations. The second section explains how the AFDC-foster care program interacts with state foster care programs. The third section focuses on the ways in which status offenders and dependent and neglected children were found to be eligible for AFDC-foster care. The final section summarizes how AFDC-foster care was found to affect the placement of status offenders and dependent and neglected children.

THE FEDERAL PROGRAM

Congress enacted the AFDC program as Title IV-A of the original Social Security Act in 1935. Under that program federal funds are available to states for cash assistance payments "for the purpose of encouraging the care of dependent children in their own homes or in the homes of relatives by enabling each state to furnish financial assistance . . . (and) to help maintain and strengthen family life . . ." (42 USC 601).

In order to qualify, a child has to meet the AFDC program's definition of a dependent child, which may be different than that used when defining a dependent and neglected child. The federal program defines a dependent child as one "who has been deprived of support or care" of at least one parent by reason of death, absence, or incapacity. The child also has to be under age 18 and living with any of a number of specified relatives ranging from the mother to a first cousin or even a niece. At the state's option a child may be covered up to age 21, if in school (42 USC 606(a)). The federal government also allows a state to extend its definition of a dependent child to one who is "deprived of parental support or care by reason of unemployment . . . of his father" (42 USC 607(a)).

Although the AFDC program began in 1935, the foster care component of the program is of relatively recent origin. Originally the Social Security Act did not include a provision for federally supported foster care, and the AFDC program emphasized the importance of supporting poor children in their own homes. AFDC payments were terminated if a child was removed and placed in foster care, and no federal program was available specifically to reimburse the state for the costs of care of such children. Amendments to the act in 1961, however, changed this policy and began foster care coverage under the program (P.L. 87-31).

The 1961 foster care provisions allowed federal reimbursement to continue for children who had been receiving AFDC payments in their own homes if they were removed from their homes "as a result of a judicial determination to the effect that continuation therein would be contrary to [their] welfare" (Sec. 2). In 1968 eligibility for the AFDC-foster care program was extended to children who were not actually AFDC recipients but who would have been found to be eligible if application had been made before they were removed from their homes (P.L. 90-248). Beginning in 1969 states had to include coverage of foster children in their AFDC programs. If a child meets the eligibility requirements, then the federal government reimburses the state for a share of the costs to support the child in foster care. As part of the new federal foster care program created by the 1980 legislation, a child would have to meet the same eligibility criteria, and the state agency also would have to ensure that reasonable efforts have been made to prevent the removal of the child.

Although the stated purpose of the AFDC-foster care program is to fund out-of-home placements, the program is part of the total AFDC program. The objective of the overall program is to maintain dependent children in their own homes and to assist parents with the care of their children. In fiscal year 1979 only 1.4 percent of all children who were recipients of AFDC payments were included in the foster care segment of the program, and only 3.8 percent of the federal and state program expenditures supported children in foster placements (U.S. Department of Health and Human Services, no date).

The AFDC-foster care program has been administered by the Department of Health and Human Services, formerly Health, Education, and Welfare, as part of its AFDC program. Within the department the program has been administered by various agencies, including the Social Security Administration, which was responsible for the program at the time of this study. At various times there have been greater or lesser amounts of policy input from the federal government concerning program operations. However, the major federal role, especially that concerning the foster care segment of AFDC, has been one of disbursing federal funds and ensuring that the federal eligibility requirements have been met.

The AFDC program (and thereby its foster care component) is a federal entitlement program. This means that there is no limit on the funds available; Congress must appropriate sums sufficient to meet the total bills submitted by the states. States are entitled to claim reimbursement for all individuals found to be eligible and to whom the state provides financial assistance. The federal government then provides funds to cover a share of the state payment. States may claim reimbursements using either the formula contained in Title IV-A (but only four do) or the formula associated with the Medicaid program. The federal share produced by the latter formula varies inversely with a state's per capita income but cannot be less than 50 percent or more than 83 percent. In 1977 the average federal share for AFDC-foster care payments for all states was about 52 percent (U.S. Congress 1979b). The costs of the foster care segment of AFDC were $410 million in fiscal year 1979 (U.S. Department of Health and Human Services, no date).

The AFDC-foster care program provides support payments for AFDC eligible children who have been removed from their homes because of exposure to harmful conditions. While the program does not require an actual determination of dependency or neglect under state laws, it is frequently interpreted and implemented at the state and local levels to mean as much. Most state laws concerning dependent and neglected children define a variety of harmful conditions that could result in a ruling of dependency or neglect. While the language is somewhat different, the intention is the same. A state may be able to receive partial federal reimbursement for some dependent and neglected children who are removed from their homes by judicial determinations and placed in foster care. Receipt of such funds, of course, would depend on whether the child for whom reimbursement is claimed meets the other AFDC eligibility requirements.

A judicial determination that a youth has committed a status offense would meet the federal requirements of the AFDC-foster care program. If a court finding causes a status offender to be removed from the home and placed in foster care because remaining at home is harmful for the child, then federal reimbursement could be claimed (U.S.

Congress 1979b). Not all states appear to be aware of or to have implemented this interpretation of eligibility. For example, as recently as October 1980 a report by an Arizona state agency included a statement that children adjudicated as incorrigible were not eligible for AFDC-foster care coverage (Arizona Office of the Auditor General 1980).

AFDC-foster care funds can be used to support eligible children in foster family homes and child-caring institutions. It appears that the predominant type of care under AFDC-foster care is in foster family homes. In November 1979, 86 percent of AFDC-foster care placements were in foster family homes (U.S. Department of Health and Human Services 1980). The congressional committee reports pertaining to the 1980 legislation frequently mention that when out-of-home care is necessary under the new program, the goal should be to find a placement in the least restrictive setting (U.S. Congress 1979a, 1979b). The Department of Health and Human Services issued proposed regulations that would require a child to be placed in the least restrictive (i.e., most familylike) setting available. Potential settings listed in order of preference are "placement with relative(s), tribal member(s), foster family care, group home care and institutional care " (45 Fed. Reg. 86836 (1980)).

STATE PROGRAM OPERATION

States must designate a single agency to administer the AFDC program; however, the foster care segment is usually handled by two offices. The management of cases (e.g., placement, review) is usually done by a foster care office that also oversees children in care under the state foster care program. If a determination is made that a foster child is eligible for federal reimbursement, then the financial aspects of the case usually are referred to the state public assistance office that administers the overall AFDC program. All required reports and claims for reimbursement usually are submitted to the federal government by the AFDC office.

The operation of the AFDC program is not standard across the country. One of the program's options concerns which of the optional parts of the definition of a dependent child will be used in determining eligibility. A state's choices are limited to deciding if it will include either (a) youth aged 18 to 21 who are in school or (b)

children whose fathers are unemployed. Among our study
states all but Wisconsin cover children up to 21 when they
are still in school (U.S. Department of Health, Education,
and Welfare 1977a). The second option allows coverage of
children who live in intact families, and four of the
seven states we studied--Massachusetts, Pennsylvania, Utah
and Wisconsin--include this option in their AFDC programs
(U.S. Department of Health and Human Services 1980).
Whether a state elects either of these options influences
the foster care segment, because by expanding the definition of dependent child they increase the population potentially eligible.

     States also set their payment levels for all AFDC com-
ponents that they operate. Table 20-1 presents the average AFDC grant level per recipient (including adults and
children) and the average AFDC-foster care payment per
child for the nation, as well as for each of our seven
states. The AFDC-foster care grant levels are consistently higher than those under the entire AFDC program.
It has been suggested that the larger payment levels
available through the program's foster care segment have
encouraged the out-of-home placement of AFDC children
because the basic grant amount is inadequate to meet the
needs of raising a child (Children's Defense Fund 1978,

TABLE 20-1 Size of Average AFDC and AFDC-Foster Care
Payments by State, November 1979

State	Amount of Average AFDC Payment per Recipient ($)	Amount of Average AFDC- Foster Care Payment per Child ($)
Arizona	60.17	306.36
Louisiana	45.02	202.60
Massachusetts	115.86	261.40
Pennsylvania	95.58	243.68
Utah	94.29	166.32
Virginia	74.95	143.93
Wisconsin	125.60	361.56
Entire U.S.	92.83	354.21

Source: U.S. Department of Health and Human Services (1980),
Tables 4 and 7.

Mott 1975, National Commission on Children in Need of Parents 1979).

THE EFFECT OF THE AFDC-FOSTER CARE PROGRAM
ON SERVICES FOR STATUS OFFENDERS

Since the foster care segment of AFDC is usually administered as part of the state foster care program under state AFDC guidelines, status offenders are affected differently depending on the state in which they reside. The major factors controlling how the program affects status offenders are the manner in which states interpret the rules and the ways in which they operate their programs. The federal program does not specify that status offenders per se are eligible; instead the program is designed to support children who are exposed to harmful conditions in their own homes. There has been little direction from the federal level that states should or could seek federal reimbursement for foster care for eligible status offenders under this program. At the state level the operation of the AFDC-foster care program is blended with the state- and locally financed foster care program. Thus, status offenders are included in the federal program to the degree that they fit into the state program. Although they usually are not separately identified as such within the recipient data, it can be safely assumed that status offenders constitute only a small portion of the foster care segment of the AFDC program.

The Foster Care Population

Within the last two decades there has been a dramatic increase in the number of children reported to be in foster care. In 1960, 241,900 children were said to be living in foster family homes and child-caring institutions, and that number grew slowly but steadily over the next several years--an increase that happened to coincide with the introduction of foster care provisions into the AFDC program (U.S. Department of Health, Education, and Welfare 1966). By 1971 the total foster care population had increased to 359,894 (U.S. Department of Health, Education, and Welfare 1973). By 1977 the total number of children in foster care reportedly had risen to 502,000 (Shyne and Schroeder 1978). These same patterns of growth have not held true for the foster care population under

the AFDC program. Since states began participating in the
foster care segment of the AFDC program, they have not
reported dramatic increases in that program's population
(Oliphant 1974, U.S. Congress 1979b). In fact, some years
have witnessed a decline.

Recently there has been a growing number of assertions
that the average age of the foster care population is
getting older and that more teenagers are entering care.
There is little national data that would allow the necessary comparisons over time, and most data used in support
of this assertion have reported on the New York City foster care population. New York City has collected foster
care statistics with age breakdowns at least since 1960.
In that city, children over the age of 12 accounted for
30 percent of the foster care population in 1960 and 42
percent in 1974 (Bernstein et al. 1975). Analysis of
these statistics does not indicate, however, whether these
children came into care at an older age or just grew up
in the foster care system. Although there were no data
presented, the 1974 review of the national AFDC-foster
care program by the Child Welfare League of America noted
that the overall foster care population was getting older,
that "there has been a sharp increase of older children,
many self-referred and seeking care because of a breakdown
in parent-child relationships" (Oliphant 1974:23).

A 1977 national survey of children's services reported
the following age distributions for the foster care population: children under 1 year (5 percent), aged 1 to 3
(16 percent), aged 4 to 6 (18 percent), aged 7 to 10 (19
percent), aged 11 to 14 (22 percent), and aged 15 to 17
(19 percent) (Shyne and Schroeder 1978). These age distributions did not vary much when compared with the total
U.S. population under age 18 in 1977. If anything, the
representation of children aged 15 to 17 in the foster
care population was close to that of the total population,
while the middle age groups were underrepresented and
children under 6 were somewhat overrepresented in the
foster care population (U.S. Department of Commerce 1978).

When the 1977 data are examined from another angle, it
appears as though foster care may be the service provided
more frequently for teenagers with problems than for
younger children. The purpose of the 1977 national survey
was to determine the types of social services provided to
or purchased for children and their families who use public funds. A review of the data on where the children
lived compared to their ages yielded some interesting
results. The percentage of children living in foster care

rises by age. Of the total population of children receiving public social services, 28 percent live in foster
care. This percentage representation is lowest for children under 1 year of age (17 percent), aged 1 to 3 (18
percent), and aged 4 to 6 (19 percent). The proportion
in foster care then jumps to 28 percent for children aged
7 to 10, 39 percent for children aged 11 to 14, and 36
percent for the oldest group aged 15 to 17 (Shyne and
Schroeder 1978).

One interpretation of these data suggests that when
social service agencies are confronted with older children
having problems at home, they more often recommend foster
care as a possible solution. Some might be inclined to
suggest, however, that the data may simply indicate that
social service systems avoid serving older children unless
they already have some ongoing responsibility for them,
as in the case of youth who have previously entered foster
care. One difficulty with this argument, however, is that
too many youth between the ages of 10 and 17 are served
for this conclusion to ring true. The proportion of these
youth receiving services is approximately the same as
their proportion in the total population (Shyne and
Schroeder 1978, U.S. Department of Commerce 1978). If
agencies provided services only to those youth already in
their care (i.e., foster children), it is more likely that
this age group would comprise a smaller proportion of
those served than they do in the total population.

Relationship Between Federal and State Programs

Respondents frequently reported that foster care programs
are predominantly state supported; it was therefore maintained that foster care programs are state designed and
operated. Programs providing foster care with state and
local funds were in existence prior to the enactment of
the AFDC program's foster care provisions. Both the predominance of state funding and the prior existence of
state programs would seem to minimize the possible effects of AFDC-foster care on state foster care programs.
The AFDC-foster care program component provides coverage
to a child when certain conditions are met: (a) the child
meets the state's AFDC eligibility rules prior to foster
placement, (b) a court determines that remaining in the
home would be harmful to the child, and (c) the child is
placed in a foster family home or private child-caring
institution. Other rules that control foster care place-

ments of AFDC eligibles are governed by the state and
local foster care programs.

State officials whom we interviewed in the seven states
indicated that federal funds were a minor part of the
total foster care programs. When the Child Welfare League
of America reviewed the AFDC-foster care program in 1974,
they conducted a survey in 11 states. They reported that
"a very wide variation in proportion of AFDC foster care
children to total in foster care exists, from a low of 7%
to a high of 62%" (Oliphant 1974:8). Across the board for
their 11 states, the average representation was 33 percent. They also found that the AFDC share of the total
state foster care costs varied considerably. The average
was 17 percent with a range of 5 to 27 percent.

In 1977 there were reportedly 502,000 children and
youth in foster care in the United States (Shyne and
Schroeder 1978). For that same year the national AFDC
statistics reported an average monthly case load of
111,022 children in foster care (U.S. Department of Health
and Human Services, no date). This would mean that 22
percent of the estimated total foster care population was
supported through the federal program. For those children
covered by AFDC-foster care, federal funds accounted for
about 52 percent of the maintenance payments (U.S. Congress 1979b). Although such support, approximately $213
million, is not superfluous, it does not diminish the
claims of state predominance in this area. Other federal
funds, such as Title XX or child welfare services monies,
are also used to maintain children in foster care, but
state and to some extent local programs appear to account
for the majority of support for children in foster care.

The percentage of foster care children covered by the
AFDC program varies across states, and for the seven
states whose programs we reviewed, the range of federal
coverage was quite wide. One state, Arizona, reported
that only 3 percent of their foster children were receiving AFDC payments in 1979 (Arizona Department of Economic
Security 1979, Arizona Office of the Auditor General
1980). Virginia, which had a computerized tracking system
for foster children, reported that 9,852 children were in
care in June 1979, and that about 23 percent of those
children were classified as eligible for AFDC-foster care
payments (Virginia Department of Public Welfare 1979).

The remaining five states had higher rates of foster
children receiving AFDC than our estimated national average of 22 percent. Annual data for 1979 were available
for four of the states and were compared to federal re-

ports for that year (U.S. Department of Health and Human Services, no date). In Utah an official with the state's Division of Family Services reported that there were about 900 foster children in that state. If that was the case, then approximately 30 percent of the state's foster care population was receiving AFDC support that year. A state official in Massachusetts estimated that in 1979, approximately 7,000 children were in foster care. This would mean that roughly 35 percent of those children were receiving AFDC-foster care support, since the Social Security Administration reported that the federal program financed an average monthly case load of 2,473 in Massachusetts for that year. Of the foster care population in Louisiana in 1979, approximately 43 percent were receiving federal support from the AFDC program (Louisiana Department of Health and Human Resources, no date). Wisconsin also had an estimated 43 percent of its foster care children supported by AFDC in 1979 (Wisconsin Department of Health and Social Services 1980). The fifth state--Pennsylvania--had data on foster care placements for December 1978. At that time 41 percent of their foster children received AFDC support (Pennsylvania Department of Public Welfare 1979; U.S. Department of Health, Education, and Welfare 1979).

Under the AFDC program, states are reimbursed by the federal government for part of the costs of providing public assistance. In 1977 the national average federal matching rate was reported to be 52 percent of the payments for children eligible for AFDC support. The rates varied by state, and the federal matching rates for the seven states were as follows: Arizona (44.6 percent), Louisiana (72.4 percent), Massachusetts (50 percent), Pennsylvania (55.4 percent), Utah (70 percent), Virginia (58.3 percent), and Wisconsin (59.9 percent) (U.S. Congress 1979b). Arizona is the only state in our study that uses the AFDC formula, which reimburses portions of various increments of the payment levels, rather than the Medicaid formula, which cannot produce a federal share below 50 percent. Nationwide only four states use the AFDC formula, and Arizona probably does so because it does not participate in the Medicaid program.

We compared foster care rates under both the state and local programs and the AFDC-foster care program to see if the AFDC-foster care payments were higher. Because states are reimbursed for part of the cost for children who are eligible for AFDC-foster care, they might provide higher support payments for children who are eligible for the

federal program. From the information available from our
seven states, it appears that the AFDC-foster care grant
levels are usually set at the same level as the state and
local foster care payments. This lends credence to the
claim by several respondents that foster care is a state
program, controlled by state laws and rules. If the state
can get reimbursed for some of this care from federal
funds, such reimbursement usually is considered after the
child is placed.

The Federal Requirement for Court Processing

As we have noted, the AFDC-foster care program component
provides coverage to a child when certain conditions are
met; that is, the child meets the state's AFDC eligibility
rules prior to removal from the home and is placed in a
foster family home or child-caring institution as a result
of a court determination that remaining in the home would
be harmful. The requirement of a formal judicial determination was originally enacted to provide a check on
social worker discretion (Oliphant 1974, Young 1975). The
federal requirement has been increasingly criticized as
"an anachronism and excessively encumbering" (Mott
1975:19). In its 1978 study of out-of-home placements
the Children's Defense Fund claimed that this provision
has created "little more than a rubber stamp process in
which all children are funneled through the courts to increase the pool of children eligible for reimbursement
under the AFDC foster care program" (Children's Defense
Fund 1978:126).

Critics object to the federal requirement of judicial
determination, partly because it requires states to process foster children through the court for financial reasons without regard to the sensitivities of children or
their families. It has been suggested that the very fact
of requiring court processing may place unnecessary barriers in the way of achieving rapport and cooperation with
a child's natural family (Oliphant 1974, Caulfield 1978).

In all of the states studied except Massachusetts,
state foster care requirements mandate some form of court
processing for children placed in foster care. There are
no data available from Massachusetts that indicate that
the lack of a requirement for judicial processing has reduced the number of foster care placements, the duration
of those placements, or increased the numbers of children
returned to their own homes. In 1976 the U.S. Department

of Health, Education, and Welfare (1978) audited several
state AFDC-foster care programs, including Massachusetts.
Many of Massachusetts' claims for reimbursement under the
AFDC-foster care program for the time period covered by
the audit were disallowed because they had not involved
court determinations (U.S. Department of Health, Education, and Welfare 1977b). Massachusetts continues to
claim and receive federal reimbursement under the AFDC-
foster care program for approximately one-third of its
foster care population. It is not known if all their
current claims meet the requirement for court involvement
or if Massachusetts is ignoring that aspect of the program
when making their claims for reimbursement. One state
official reported that reimbursement for all potentially
AFDC eligible foster children was not being claimed because children were not always being processed through the
courts.

In the other six states children can be placed voluntarily in foster care by their parents or guardians for
some period of time without court involvement, but most
states set limits on such placements. If the child does
not return to the parents at the end of the specified
time, court proceedings usually are begun to continue
placement. Under the federal program as it operated during our study, as long as the court proceedings are held
within six months from the time that the child is removed
from the home, AFDC-foster care eligibility requirements
can be met. The child is covered by the state/local program until the court determination.

Under the Adoption Assistance and Child Welfare Act of
1980, federal foster care payments will be made for AFDC
eligible children placed in foster care by voluntary
agreements. Federal payments will be available for no
more than 180 days before a judicial determination has to
be made for continuation of care. Although this provision
conforms to the previous federal requirements for court
processing within six months, it now allows states to
claim federal reimbursement from the start of even voluntary foster care placements for eligible children. Many
status offenders currently are being diverted from the
juvenile justice system to the social service system, and
voluntarily are being placed in foster care, at least for
the short term, without court review. This new provision
of federal program coverage of children who are voluntarily placed in care is not likely to encourage more foster
care placements for status offenders, but it might allow
more youth to meet the eligibility requirements for federal support.

State Use of the Federal Program

State laws, program policies, and practices seem to be the
dominant factors in shaping the operation of foster care
programs within the states. In the seven states studied,
most funds for foster care payments come from state and
local funds as opposed to federal sources. State guidelines appear to control the manner in which foster care
cases are handled. The AFDC-foster care eligibility rules
ordinarily are separately identifiable aspects of the
overall foster care programs and primarily pertain to
reimbursement claims. In all other respects the program
operations seem to conform to state rules and practices.

In most of the states studied, officials expressed the
opinion that AFDC-foster care did not influence whether
children were put in foster care, where they were placed,
or how long they stayed. Instead, AFDC-foster care was
viewed strictly as a source of funds with little or no
influence on program content--the judicial review requirement being the major exception. Foster care officials claimed that state laws and policies required that
children in certain circumstances be placed in foster care
whether or not they would receive any federal support for
that care. These statements were similar to those described in the review of this program by the Child Welfare
League of America (Oliphant 1974).

A review of state social service policy and procedure
manuals backed up these assertions. The manuals usually
contained separate subsections related to the AFDC program
within the overall sections on foster care. The AFDC
subsections described the program's eligibility rules,
which were to be applied after a child was already accepted for foster care, and procedures to be followed to
claim reimbursement, usually referral of the case to the
state public assistance agency that administers AFDC. It
appears that the AFDC program becomes a factor in a foster
care case after the decision to place the child or youth
has been made. When the state is determining how to pay
for the foster placement, all potential sources are considered, including AFDC. As mentioned before, the program's aspect that is most often cited as influencing this
determination is the required involvement of the court.
Several state manuals directed the caseworker to be sure
to schedule a judicial review within six months if a child
is thought to be potentially eligible for AFDC reimbursement. This was the only instruction we found that indicated there might be differential treatment for those
children for whom states claim AFDC reimbursement.

Services for Status Offenders

As we discussed previously, there are no national data that identify the number or proportion of children in foster care or AFDC-foster care who are status offenders or dependent and neglected children. The 1977 national survey of services to children, however, did report the primary reason for placement by the types of placements.

In 1977 foster children who were in residential treatment centers had a median age of 13.3 years. Among those youth, 30 percent were in the centers reportedly due to an emotional problem, 11 percent because of a parent-child conflict of some kind, 5 percent were labeled as status offenders, and 5 percent were delinquents.

The median age of foster children living in group homes was approximately 13.5 years. Reasons given for placement for these children included emotional problems of the child (20 percent), parent-child conflict (9 percent), status offenses (7 percent), and delinquency (5 percent).

The median age of children in foster family homes was only 9.7 years, much lower than the median age of youth in other out-of-home placements. Moreover, none of the aforementioned reasons—emotional problems, parent-child conflict, or commission of a status offense or delinquent act—accounted for as much as 5 percent of the placements in foster family homes (Shyne and Schroeder 1978). We do not know the extent to which these reasons may have accounted for foster home placements because data were not reported by reason of placement if that category accounted for less than 5 percent. Further complicating the entire issue is that the reasons for out-of-home placement (irrespective of type of placement or age of the child) are not mutually exclusive. For instance, some youth who are placed because of parent-child conflicts might, under different circumstances, be labeled as status offenders.

In our seven study states we found one extensive information system that was used to define and manage a foster care program. While other states had data files and systems of varying degrees of complexity, only the foster care information system (FOCIS) in Virginia collected and tabulated data that were adequate to identify status offenders by some of their program-related characteristics, such as source of support funds. The state provided us with special computer tabulations using data for the three-month period of July to September 1979. Among other things, their data showed that 12.9 percent of the children in foster care were there because they

were status offenders. Although approximately 24 percent
of the total Virginia foster care population receives
AFDC-foster care payments, only 17 percent of the status
offenders in foster placements receive them. The percentage of status offenders (70 percent) that are provided
foster care solely with state and local funds is higher
than that of the overall foster care population (64 percent).

State Interpretation of Federal Placement Rules

If the AFDC-foster care program has any effect on where
children are placed, it most likely encourages care in
foster family homes. The AFDC-foster care program currently provides federal reimbursement for an eligible
child who has been placed in a foster family home or private child-caring institution. The statute defines a
foster family home as one that has been licensed by the
state. Such homes could be private or public. A child-
caring institution is defined as being licensed, private,
and nonprofit. Group homes fall somewhere in between and
probably are reported as institutions as often as they are
reported as foster homes. When group homes are considered
institutions, the youth in public homes often are not
considered eligible for AFDC-foster care. The 1980 legislative changes would allow federal foster care coverage
of children in some public group homes.

    There are no data collected or reported at the federal
level that allow AFDC foster children to be classified by
any more discrete categories of placement than foster
family homes and child-caring institutions. Table 20-2
presents the federal placement statistics available for
November 1979. They show that the predominant placement
for AFDC foster children is in foster family homes. In
fact, all five of our states that reported these data had
rates of foster home placements for AFDC-foster care
children higher than the national average. We do not know
whether any of the reported placement locations were in
group homes. In 1977, 5 percent of the total number of
foster children were in private group homes and 2 percent
were in public group homes (Shyne and Schroeder 1978).

    For the most part, state placement data did not present
AFDC-foster care children as a separate category. This
hampered comparisons between AFDC-foster care and state/
local foster children that might demonstrate whether the
federal requirements affected placement decisions. Once

TABLE 20-2 Percentage of Children Receiving AFDC-Foster
Care Payments by Location in Foster Family Homes or
Child-Caring Institutions, November 1979

State	Percentage in Foster Family Homes	Percentage in Child-Caring Institutions
Arizona	91.5	8.5
Louisiana	95.7	4.3
Massachusetts	92.0	8.0
Pennsylvania*	--	--
Utah*	--	--
Virginia	95.0	5.0
Wisconsin	88.6	11.4
Entire U. S.	85.9	14.1

*State did not report the data.

Source: U.S. Department of Health and Human Services (1980),
Table 7.

again the one exception was the Virginia data system.
Data from that information system show that approximately
the same percentage of AFDC-foster care and state/local
foster children are placed in group homes (2.3 and 2 percent, respectively). The same consistency is exhibited
for placements in child-caring institutions: 2 percent
of all AFDC-foster care children and 1.7 percent of the
state/local foster children are in such placements. The
major difference in placement by type of foster care coverage is in the category of foster family homes. This
placement is provided to 63 percent of Virginia's AFDC-
foster care children while only 48 percent of the foster
children in the state/local program are in homes. It appears, then, that in Virginia the types of placement for
AFDC-foster care children are at least consistent with the
federal requirements. More foster children are placed in
residential treatment centers or other types of institutional care under the state/local program than under the
AFDC-foster care program. Among out-of-home placements,
foster family homes are considered the least restrictive.
Thus, in Virginia the AFDC-foster care placement rules
seem to encourage less restrictive placements for children
who have been removed from their homes.

One issue in the use of foster care for status offenders concerns the most appropriate type of placement for such youth. Some contend that the best compromise for teenagers is the group home, which is less restrictive than institutions and requires less interpersonal involvement than foster homes (Children's Defense Fund 1978, Nemy 1975, Scher 1958). Group homes do seem to be the type of placement used most frequently for older children. In 1977 the median age of children in foster family homes was 9.7, while the median age of public group home residents was 13.4 and that of private group homes was 13.8. The residents in the various types of residential institutions had median ages of from 13.1 to 13.7 (Shyne and Schroeder 1978).

Care in group homes has been allowed under AFDC at least since 1967, and if the 1980 program changes are enacted, the rules concerning such care will be more lenient in that they would allow coverage of placements in public group homes for 25 or fewer children. Placements in group homes that are used primarily for delinquents would be excluded from this new provision. To the extent that status offenders are placed in group homes, those new rules should make the receipt of federal support easier to obtain for eligible youth.

SUMMARY

The federal foster care program per se does not appear to promote placement of status offenders (or other groups of children) in out-of-home placements. Instead, the program has been absorbed into existing state foster care programs, and children and youth affected by the federal program usually are treated and processed the same as state-supported foster children. The overall package of federal and state benefits for foster children, however, provides a slightly different picture. Although we did not locate any hard data to suggest that the availability of various types of services for children and youth in foster care influenced placements for status offenders, we were told that the total federal support package did on occasion affect placement decisions for some children. The opinion has been expressed that children and youth who needed services, but whose families could neither afford them nor qualify for publicly supported services, were sometimes placed in foster care (Calhoun 1980, Children's Defense Fund 1978). Placement of these children and youth outside the home could provide the eligibility credentials necessary for many publicly provided services (see the chapters on Title XX, Title IV-B, and Medicaid).

As we have suggested, the Adoption Assistance and Child Welfare Act of 1980 was intended to make foster care placement a solution of last resort, and it pushes in the direction of permanency planning for youth who are placed in foster care. The act is scheduled to be implemented by September 30, 1982, and we cannot anticipate whether or how these provisions will alter state foster care programs. Their effects presumably will be tempered by the fact that these requirements apply only to federally supported foster children and are already a part of many state foster care programs.

To the extent that the federal program may make a difference to the operation of state foster care programs, it is important to note that these new modifications may not be very responsive to the needs of older adolescents who are increasingly finding their way into the foster care system. For example, the new program specifies a goal of an average length of stay of two years or less for children and youth in foster care. Whereas placements in excess of two years may be inappropriate to the needs of the younger child, a foster placement of longer duration for the older adolescent in need of a place to await the age of majority may be a tolerable solution. As states come to use foster care as an appropriate placement for status offenders who are older adolescents, the purposes of that system will need to be reconsidered and state and federal program operations modified to reflect this usage.

REFERENCES

Arizona Department of Economic Security (1979)
    Unpublished data from the Foster Care Information
    System. Computer printout dated September 17, 1979.
    Department of Economic Security, Phoenix, Ariz.
Arizona Office of the Auditor General (1980) A
    Performance Audit of the Department of Economic
    Security Foster Care Program. Report 80-5. Phoenix,
    Ariz.: Office of the Auditor General.
Bernstein, Blanche, Snider, Donald, and Meezan, William
    (1975) Foster Care Needs and Alternatives to
    Placement: A Projection for 1975-1985. New York
    City: New York State Board of Social Welfare.

Calhoun, John (1980) Remarks at his swearing in as
    Commissioner of the U.S. Administration of Children,
    Youth, and Families, as reported in Youth
    Alternatives 7(3):4.
Caulfield, Barbara (1978) The Legal Aspects of Protective
    Services for Abused and Neglected Children. Prepared
    for U.S. Department of Health, Education, and Welfare,
    Office of Human Development Services. Washington,
    D.C.: U.S. Government Printing Office.
Children's Defense Fund (1978) Children Without Homes, An
    Examination of Public Responsibility to Children in
    Out of Home Care. Washington, D.C.: Children's
    Defense Fund.
Louisiana Department of Health and Human Resources (no
    date) Annual Report, July 1, 1978-June 30, 1979.
    Baton Rouge, La.: Department of Health and Human
    Resources.
Mott, Paul (1975) Foster Care and Adoption: Some Key
    Policy Issues. Prepared for the U.S. Congress, Senate
    Committee on Labor and Public Welfare, Subcommittee on
    Children and Youth. 94th Congress, 1st Session.
    Washington, D.C.: U.S. Government Printing Office.
National Commission on Children in Need of Parents (1979)
    Who Knows? Who Cares? Forgotten Children in Care.
    New York: Institute of Public Affairs and the Child
    Welfare League of America.
Nemy, Enid (1975) Agencies Unprepared for Soaring Number
    of Adolescents in Need. New York Times, January 3,
    1975.
Oliphant, Winford (1974) AFDC Foster Care: Problems and
    Recommendations. New York: Child Welfare League of
    America.
Pennsylvania Department of Public Welfare (1979) Annual
    Statistical Report--1978; Public and Voluntary Child
    Caring Agencies. Data from form CY28. Division of
    Data Support. Department of Public Welfare,
    Harrisburg, Pa.
Scher, Bernhard (1958) Specialized Group Care for
    Adolescents. Child Welfare 27(2):12-17.
Shyne, Ann, and Schroeder, Anita (1978) National Study of
    Social Services to Children and Their Families.
    Prepared for U.S. Department of Health, Education, and
    Welfare, Children's Bureau. Rockville, Md.: Westat,
    Inc.
U.S. Congress (1979a) Adoption Assistance and Child
    Welfare Act of 1979. Senate Report 96-336. Committee
    on Finance. 96th Congress, 1st Session. Washington,
    D.C.: U.S. Government Printing Office.

_____ (1979b) Social Services and Child Welfare Amendments of 1979. House Report 96-136. Committee on Ways and Means. 96th Congress, 1st Session. Washington, D.C.: U.S. Government Printing Office.

U.S. Department of Commerce (1978) Estimates of the Population of the U.S. By Age, Sex and Race: 1970-1977. Report P-25, No. 721. Washington, D.C.: Bureau of Census.

U.S. Department of Health and Human Services (1980) Public Assistance Statistics, November 1979. ORS Report A-2 (11/79). Washington, D.C.: Social Security Administration.

_____ (no date) Unpublished advance data for fiscal year 1979 on public assistance recipients. Social Security Administration, Washington, D.C.

U.S. Department of Health, Education, and Welfare (1966) Foster Care of Children: Major National Trends and Prospects. Children's Bureau. Washington, D.C.: U.S. Government Printing Office.

_____ (1973) Children Served by Public Welfare Agencies and Voluntary Child Welfare Agencies and Institutions. NCSS Report E-9 National Center for Social Statistics, Washington, D.C.

_____ (1977a) Characteristics of State Plans for Aid to Families with Dependent Children Under the Social Security Act Title IV-A. Social Security Administration. Washington, D.C.: U.S. Government Printing Office.

_____ (1977b) Review of AFDC-FC, Commonwealth of Massachusetts. Boston: Audit Agency, Region I Office.

_____ (1978) Summary Report on Aid to Families with Dependent Children Foster Care Program. Washington, D.C.: Office of the Inspector General.

_____ (1979) Public Assistance Statistics, December 1978. ORS Report A-2 (12/78). Washington, D.C.: Social Security Administration.

Virginia Department of Welfare (1979) Report to the National Research Council. Computer printout dated December 21, 1979. Unpublished data from the Foster Care Information System (FOCIS) for June 1979. Department of Public Welfare, Richmond, Va.

Wisconsin Department of Health and Social Services (1980) County of Court by Legal Status of Children. Computer printout dated January 1, 1980. Division of Community Services. Department of Health and Social Services, Madison, Wis.

Young, John (1975) <u>Foster Care: Problems and Issues</u>.
    Testimony in hearings before U.S. Congress, Senate
    Committee on Labor and Public Welfare, Subcommittee on
    Children and Youth, and House Committee on Education
    and Labor, Subcommittee on Select Education. 94th
    Congress, 1st Session. Washington, D.C.: U.S.
    Government Printing Office.

21

Impact of the Medicaid Program on the Treatment of Status Offenders

SUZANNE S. MAGNETTI

The Medicaid program provides federal funds to the states so that they can offer needed medical services to persons who otherwise would be unable to pay for such services. Essentially each state develops, within certain limits, its own program; states may select many of the services they will provide and many of the groups of individuals eligible for those services.

This paper examines the impact of the Medicaid program on status offenders. As we will show, the program has the potential to affect where status offenders will be placed and the services they can receive. In most cases status offenders are determined eligible for Medicaid coverage on an individual basis, although states can choose to develop eligibility groups that can cover all such youth. Children eligible for Medicaid may face the chance of being institutionalized solely because the federal program reimburses maintenance and service costs for many institutional placements. Or they may be placed in an institutional facility covered by Medicaid when another placement might be more appropriate for the child's needs. Medicaid eligibility is based on both ability to pay and placement. Since a child in a Medicaid-eligible placement will frequently be eligible for many other social service programs simply because he or she has become Medicaid eligible, Medicaid eligibility may open the door to other cost-reimbursement programs as well, increasing the financial incentive to place a child in a covered institution.

663

The discussion of the effects of the Medicaid program on status offenders is divided into four sections. The first presents a brief review of the organization and requirements of the federal program. The second examines how states can shape their medical assistance programs in ways that influence the treatment of status offenders. The next section explores which status offender youth can be eligible for Medicaid services and discusses the major issues concerning Medicaid and its effects on the dein-stitutionalization of status offenders. The final section summarizes how Medicaid affects the placement and treatment of status offenders.

THE FEDERAL PROGRAM

Congress enacted the Medicaid program, Title XIX of the Social Security Act (P.L. 89-97, Social Security Amendments of 1965, 79 Stat. 286 [codified at 42 USC 139 (1976)] "Grants to States for Medical Assistance Programs")[1] in 1965 to supply partial federal funding to the states for the costs of providing medical services to the poor. The statute provides federal funds to offset the costs to the states of furnishing medical assistance to persons who are members of families with dependent children, or age 65 or over, or blind or disabled, and whose income and resources are not sufficient to meet the costs of necessary medical care. Subject to certain limited federal rules and regulations, the program is administered independently by each state, and each state defines the limits of its individual program.

States who wish to participate in this program (only Arizona does not participate) are required to develop and adopt a medical assistance plan that must set forth the services covered and the groups of individuals eligible for these benefits. The following eight "mandatory" services must be covered by every participating state: (1) inpatient hospital services, (2) outpatient hospital services, (3) rural health clinic services, (4) laboratory and x-ray services, (5) skilled nursing facility services for persons 21 or over, (6) family planning services, (7) early periodic screening and diagnostic services for children under 21, and (8) physicians' services. A par-

---

[1] Federal regulations concerning the Medicaid program are found at 45 CFR 435 et seq.

ticipating state must also provide home health care to all individuals who are eligible for care in skilled nursing facilities.

The federal law also allows coverage of several other categories at the state's option. These include, but are not limited to, inpatient psychiatric services for individuals under 21, home health care, intermediate care facility services, and services in intermediate care facilities for the mentally retarded. A state may define the specific medical items and procedures that will be covered in each of these categories and may impose limits on the quantity of service available to individual recipients.

The states also are required to specify the categories of individuals who will be eligible for specific types of benefits. Participating states must provide at least the eight mandatory services to certain categories of individuals, namely, persons who receive or who are eligible to receive public assistance who are age 65 or over, blind or disabled, or members of families with dependent children. These individuals are known as the categorically needy. States may also elect to cover persons who are medically needy--persons who would be eligible for public assistance except that their income is too high, but whose incomes are not sufficient to pay for their needed medical care. Other eligibility groups, as defined by the individual state, may also be covered at the state's option.

The federal Medicaid program is administered by the Health Care Financing Administration of the Department of Health and Human Services. This agency's primarily responsibility for the Medicaid program is to disburse federal funds to participating states. Federal Medicaid funding is open-ended; there is no cap or ceiling level. Participating states are partially reimbursed for all costs associated with the provision of services under their plan. The percentage of federal reimbursement is based on a formula that varies inversely with a state's per capita income but cannot be less than 50 percent or more than 83 percent of the costs of services. The national average reimbursement rate is about 55 percent. Table 21-1 shows the Medicaid reimbursement rates for the six participating states in the study. For fiscal year 1977, the most recent year for which data are available, the federal share of Medicaid expenditures was $9.18 billion.

TABLE 21-1 Federally Promulgated Medical Assistance Percentages
(January 1, 1966 through September 30, 1981)

State	Jan 1, 1966– June 30, 1967	July, 1969– June 30, 1971	July 1, 1971– June 30, 1973	July 1, 1973– June 30, 1975	July 1, 1975– Sept 30, 1977	Oct 1, 1977– Sept 30, 1979	Oct 1, 1979– Sept 30 1981,
Louisiana	76.41	73.57	73.49	72.80	72.41	70.45	68.82
Massachusetts	50.00	50.00	50.00	50.00	50.00	51.62	51.75
Pennsylvania	54.38	54.60	55.45	55.14	55.39	55.11	55.14
Utah	66.30	68.23	69.88	69.95	70.04	68.98	68.07
Virginia	66.96	65.04	64.03	61.58	58.34	57.01	56.54
Wisconsin	57.60	55.21	56.28	60.02	59.91	58.53	57.95

Source: U.S. Department of Health, Education, and Welfare (1979).

STATE PROGRAM OPERATION

States are required in their medical assistance plan to designate a single state agency to administer the program; all administration functions, with the exception of eligibility determinations, must remain with that agency. Eligibility determinations can be made by the state or local agencies that administer the Aid to Families with Dependent Children program (AFDC) and/or the Supplemental Security Income program (SSI). Although large amounts of federal money are channeled into these state medical assistance programs, the federal program requirements establish only the programs' frameworks.

Within those loose federal limits, the states individually establish the eligibility groups that will be covered, the types and range of services covered, the methods of service delivery, and administrative and operating procedures. In essence each state is operating a unique medical assistance program.

Several aspects of the programs that do differ across states can affect the deinstitutionalization of status offenders. First, states may elect to cover various types of institutional services that could be used for eligible status offenders. Second, states may by their selection and definition of the optional eligibility groups, increase or decrease the use of medical assistance payments for status offenders. To a large extent, because states can vary many of the services provided and expand or limit the eligible groups covered, it is the particular characteristics of the state medical assistance plan that determine the impact of the federal money on status offenders.

Medicaid requires that states provide certain mandated services. For persons under 21, the only federally mandated institutional service is general hospital care. However, states may decide to cover other types of institutional services in their medical assistance program, including (a) skilled nursing facility services (SNF), (b) intermediate care facility services for general care (ICF), or (c) services specifically for the mentally retarded (ICF-MR), and (d) psychiatric facility services (PF). Of course many other covered Medicaid services (e.g., physicians' services) can be provided to children who are living in various types of child-caring institutions. Both the specifically institution-based and the more generally accessible services are available without regard to the reason the child is institutionalized.

States also have the ability, through their selection
and definition of operational eligibility groups, to regulate certain categories of children eligible for medical
assistance payments, and thus affect the number of children eligible under the program. The way in which a state
chooses to frame an optional eligibility group may mean
that some children can only be covered under the medical
assistance program if they are first removed from their
homes. A state's selection and application of certain
optional eligibility groups--in particular, the state's
decision to cover the eligibility group of "all financially needy children" and its definition of that cate-
gory--can greatly expand the potential use of medical
assistance payments for status offenders.

THE EFFECT OF THE MEDICAID PROGRAM ON
DEINSTITUTIONALIZATION OF STATUS OFFENDERS

Because Medicaid is such a state-oriented, state-developed
and state-run program, status offenders will be affected
differently by it across the states. Although the federal
Medicaid program contains no specific references to status
offenders, the program in its application has the potential to affect where such youth will be placed and the
services that they might receive. The range of status
offenders affected by the availability of covered medical
services will therefore vary across the states.
     In general the manner in which a state chooses to de-
fine and operate its medical assistance program determines
how the federal funds will affect status offenders. For
example, the flexibility that the federal program allows
the states permits them to select services and eligibility
groups that may encourage inappropriate institutional
placements for status offenders. In addition, the way
in which a state develops and implements its particular
medical assistance program may directly affect where
children are placed. Another aspect of the Medicaid program that may affect where status offenders are placed is
how and to what extent the state is prepared to continue
financial outlays to cover its share of the costs of this
program.

Determining Eligibility of Status Offenders

The eligibility of status offenders for Medicaid coverage
is usually determined on an individual basis of where the

individual child is placed and what his or her income level is. Many status offenders will be eligible for medical assistance payments because they are members of the categorically needy groups for whom the federal program mandates coverage (e.g., AFDC children or SSI recipients); other children may be eligible for coverage because they are medically needy. States can also choose to develop eligibility criteria that may cover other subgroups of the status offender population. Many status offenders are eligible as members of categorical groups (e.g., financially needy children or children for whom a public agency is assuming at least some financial responsibility) that the state has elected to cover.

Of particular importance in determining which status offenders will be covered by Medicaid is whether the state chooses to cover the optional category "all financially needy children." If a state includes this eligibility group, it may cover children in a variety of placements outside their homes. States may elect to cover all financially needy children, reasonable subgroups of financially needy children that it specifies for itself, or any of the four subgroups defined by federal regulations (i.e., (1) children for whom a public agency is assuming some financial responsibility and who are in foster homes, private institutions, and private foster homes; (2) children in subsidized adoptions; (3) children in intermediate care facilities; and (4) children in psychiatric facilities). The election to cover any of these optional groups permits the eligibility of some children who otherwise would not be eligible for medical assistance payments if they reside in certain out-of-home placements. Table 21-2 displays the optional eligibility groups covered by each state in this study.

Four of the states in this study provide medical assistance coverage to all financially needy children (Massachusetts, Pennsylvania, Utah, and Wisconsin). Each of these states appears to have defined the term to be coextensive with the four federally established subgroups. The other two states, Louisiana and Virginia, only cover some of the federal subgroups. Since these subgroups allow the provision of Medicaid services to children in out-of-home or institutional settings, foster care, intermediate care, and psychiatric facilities, the financially needy child category can be implemented so as to invite unnecessary institutional use. Children covered under this category often are not eligible for Medicaid unless they are removed from their home. Even where

TABLE 21-2   Optional Eligibility Groups Covered

State	Financially Eligible Children	All Individuals Under 21	Unborn	Subgroups
Louisiana				X^1
Massachusetts	X	X	X	
Pennsylvania	X	X	X	
Utah	X	X	X	
Wisconsin	X	X	X	
Virginia				X^2

Note: Massachusetts, Pennsylvania, Utah, and Wisconsin appear
to cover all financially eligible children. Louisiana and
Virginia have elected to cover only some of the federally
defined subgroups.

[1]Louisiana Subgroups
        • children for whom a public agency is assuming
        at least partial financial responsibility
        • children in foster homes or private
        child-caring institutions
        • children in ICFs
        • children in psychiatric facilities

[2]Virginia Subgroups
        • children for whom a public agency is assuming
        at least partial financial responsibility
        • children in foster homes or private
        child-caring institutions and in subsidized
        adoptions
        • children in ICFs

Source: Information obtained through a review of each state's
Medical Assistance Program Plan, updated through 1979.

needed medical services are available in the community,
it might be necessary to remove a child from home in order
to secure Medicaid coverage. This may be especially true
for children with obviously severe medical needs. At
least one state respondent indicated that for other children the removal decision may be influenced not just by
the availability of Medicaid coverage but by the whole
range of federal benefits (Medicaid, Title XX, and Title
IV) available to children who are placed out-of-home.
Another consideration for the states in deciding whether

to institutionalize a child is that Medicaid reimburses maintenance as well as medical service costs for institutional placements.

The impact on the category of financially needy children may also be affected by each state's decision on how to determine financial need. The income levels under "financially needy children" are tied to other public assistance levels, but the issue here is whose income the state considers--the income of the child or of the child's family. In all of the six states in this study, children who are not living with their parents are considered to be single-member families for the purpose of income eligibility. For example, in Massachusetts all children in out-of-home placements are determined eligible under this category on the basis of their income alone. This policy may encourage out-of-home placements to secure services for children whose families have income above the established levels. Some states, however, seem to have attempted to limit this practice. In Utah only the child's income is considered for eligibility purposes when the child has been removed from home by court order or has been voluntarily relinquished for adoption; but when the child has been voluntarily placed in foster care, eligibility rests on the income level of the family (State of Utah 1979). Other states interpret this provision to achieve the maximum program flexibility. In Virginia, for example, medical assistance eligibility can continue for up to three months after the child returns home from a foster care arrangement (with eligibility based on the income of the child alone) if the local welfare unit maintains custody for that trial period (Virginia Department of Welfare 1979).

Another aspect of Medicaid eligibility that affects status offenders is whether state medical assistance programs have developed specific provisions concerning these youth. Under the Medicaid program, inmates of secure public institutions (not including medical facilities) generally are not eligible for coverage, and status offenders were considered a part of the population that could not receive Medicaid services. But in 1978 HEW's Office of General Counsel issued an opinion (1978a) holding that status offenders were eligible for Medicaid as long as they had not achieved inmate status as a result of that offense (i.e., they had not been placed in a jail, detention center, or other secure facility, or in a residential facility that housed more than 16 children). The decision was issued in response to a request for clarification initiated by persons in Virginia, and Virginia appears to be the only state in this study that has specifically acted to include status offenders among those eligible for Medicaid coverage under the optional coverage group, financially needy children. They are now eligible as children for whom some public agency is taking financial responsibility (Virginia Department of Health 1979). Once children become eligible under the category, they remain eligible as long as some public agency maintains responsibility for them, even if they return home and the agency has only supervisory responsibility. But according to an official in the Department of Health in Virginia, which was asked by the General Assembly to keep tabs on the number of children who are affected by this provision, only those status offenders with serious and therefore costly health problems were actually referred for Medicaid coverage, even though all status offenders in eligible settings could be covered. From a broad viewpoint the availability of Medicaid coverage for these children may have a positive effect on status offender deinstitutionalization, because the Medicaid-eligible placements are less restrictive than the noneligible placements.

Services Available to Status Offenders

As mentioned above, states are required to provide general hospital care but can also elect to cover four other types of institutional care (i.e., services in skilled nursing facilities, general intermediate care facilities, intermediate care facilities for the mentally retarded, and psychiatric facilities) in their medical assistance program for persons under age 21. These five types of care constitute the institutional services that can be covered under Medicaid. Although other Medicaid-funded services may be available to institutionalized children who are not in these Medicaid-covered institutions, medical assistance programs will frequently cover both the needed services and the maintenance costs of keeping a child in these five types of institutions. The availability of funds that can be used to cover maintenance costs may act as an incentive to place a child in one of the types of institutions covered under the state's medical assistance program. When other services or treatments are not available, the implications of the availability of Medicaid services for status offenders may be most pronounced.

States are required to report in their Medical Assistance Program Plans the services that are covered under their plan. States also report to the federal government the number of individuals who are served in the various institutional facilities (U.S. Department of Health, Education, and Welfare 1978c:83, 86), but there appears to be no way to determine how many children and youth served in these facilities are status offenders. Nor can we determine if the institutional services that are provided are medically necessary or if the treatment setting is the least restrictive necessary to treat the individual child. Reported figures are also of limited use in assessing the impact of Medicaid on status offenders because the states report only the numbers actually served by the program and do not compare "use" figures to the number who are eligible for these services.

States are not only free to select whether and which optional services they will cover, but they can also shape their plan by imposing certain limits on the extent of those services. In many cases these limitations are attempts to secure appropriate use of covered services. For example, in Pennsylvania skilled nursing facility care for individuals under 21 is only covered in certain preapproved facilities. The state medical assistance program will only reimburse skilled nursing facility services for persons under 16 when the placement has been approved by the state Standard Setting Authority (Commonwealth of Pennsylvania 1979). In Massachusetts an institutional review team of the Department of Public Health reviews each intermediate care facility placement for persons under 21, and if it recommends a lower level of care, the child must be moved (Commonwealth of Massachusetts 1979). Each of these provisions are in addition to the general state procedures for review of all institutional services for Medicaid recipients of all ages.

Although the selection of services to be provided and the limitations imposed on those services in part reflect state policies and the need to ensure appropriate use of covered services, the limitations imposed on service use may also result from the need to curb state expenditures (Finley 1978). Medicaid funding from the federal government is in the form of unlimited reimbursement at set matching rates, but tightening state budgets force states to limit what they spend on medical assistance programs. In some states the use of Title XX funds for some aspects of medical care is also decreasing, as those federal funds are the subject of intense competition among various social service agencies in the states. For example, program officials in Virginia indicated that after 1979 medical services would be funded only with the most appropriate federal money rather than with Title XX money. For 1980 Utah established state funding limits for medical assistance programs. In Virginia the 1980 state funding level for the medical assistance program was lower than the previous year's expenditures.

One way that states hold down Medicaid expenditures is by limiting the number of facilities in which services can be provided. For instance, Utah limits the number of institutions that can serve Medicaid-eligible children to a few state-run facilities; psychiatric facility care for children is only reimbursable when provided at the Utah State Hospital (State of Utah 1979). In Massachusetts ICF-MR care is only covered in public institutions (Commonwealth of Massachusetts 1979). States are also meeting these financial constraints by limiting the extent of institutional service that will be covered. Even the medical appropriateness review teams can be seen as a means of restricting expenses.

Although all of the states under review do offer some institutional services that can be used as federally financed placements for some status offenders, it is not possible to determine how many such youth are placed in these institutions or how many of these placements are not inappropriate for the child's medical needs. As mentioned above, some states are attempting to ensure appropriate placements through prior approvals or use review boards. In response to growing costs and tight budgets, states are constricting the extent of institutional services and limiting the facilities in which these services are covered. In most states there appears to be little room for expanding the use of Medicaid eligible institutions to house nonoffenders.

The Use of Institutional Services

The purpose of the Medicaid program is to provide funds for medical services to the poor. Since the program began in 1965, there have been changes concerning allowable services, but its focus has not been dramatically altered by any of the refinements in the scope of eligible medical services. However, several changes have been made relative to the types of institutional care for which the federal government will provide reimbursement, and these

have the potential to affect the provision of services to
status offenders. As states administered the Medicaid
program, they began to recognize the impact of the federal
restrictions, requirements, and rules. Intensive lobbying
efforts were begun by state organizations, individual
states, and persons in the health services field. These
efforts were aimed at increasing the types and locations
of federally covered services. Among other changes obtained through these efforts was Medicaid coverage of
intermediate care facilities and psychiatric facilities
for those under 21.

Intermediate care facilities are not considered to be
"real medical care" by some persons in the health field.
According to the federal regulations dealing with Medicaid, the only medical staff requirement for an ICF is
that there must be a registered nurse or a licensed practical or vocational nurse on the day shift seven days a
week. A physician is only required to see an ICF resident
"once every 60 days unless the physician decides that this
frequency is unnecessary and records the reasons for that
decision" (42 CFR 442.346). These limited medical requirements prompt some to question the legitimacy of ICFs
as medical care covered by Medicaid. Nevertheless, beginning in 1969 care in ICFs (including those for the
mentally retarded) was allowed by Medicaid. ICFs were
promoted as a form of less expensive care for persons who
no longer required hospital or skilled nursing facility
care but who still needed some observation. Care in psychiatric facilities for persons under the age of 21 was
added by the 1972 amendments. Care in state mental hospitals or other facilities had previously been provided
with private family funds or state support, and the states
were anxious to get federal reimbursement for such care
(Lerman 1978).

Currently, the types of institutional care covered by
Medicaid include inpatient care in general hospitals, in
psychiatric facilities, in skilled nursing facilities, and
in intermediate care facilities either for general care
or specifically for the mentally retarded. Only general
hospital care is a federally required service and is covered by all 49 states and four territories; the other
types of care are optional. Inpatient care for persons
under 21 in psychiatric facilities is covered by 31 to 35
states; 42 or 43 states cover skilled nursing care for
those under 21; general intermediate care facilities are
covered by 49 states (all participating states except for
the territories); and care in intermediate care facili-

ties for the mentally retarded is covered in 45 to 48 states.[2] Sources differed as to which institutional services were covered by the states. Table 21-3 lists the types of institutional services covered by the six states in this study for the categorically and medically needy, and indicates where there are limitations on the services available.

It is clear that some states do make greater use of these institutional services than do others, but it does not appear possible to tie these service use patterns to the status offender population in particular. For 1976, the latest year for which data are available, five of the six study states that offer a medical assistance program have higher than national average rates of service provision to children in certain types of institutional facilities. Louisiana has a higher than average rate of use for intermediate care for the mentally retarded for 6- to 20-year-olds. Massachusetts has a higher rate for intermediate care facilities for the mentally retarded for all children, skilled nursing facilities for all children, and general ICF for children under 6. Pennsylvania exhibits higher than national average use of skilled nursing facilities and intermediate care facilities for the mentally retarded for 6- to 20-year-olds. Virginia has a higher average rate of use of intermediate care facilities for the mentally retarded for 6- to 20-year-olds, and Wisconsin has a higher usage rate for psychiatric facilities for that same age group.[3] However, these rates may have nothing to do with our target population or with the medical needs of that population. It is not possible to quantify on the basis of this data how the availability of institutional services affects the placement of status offenders.

In fiscal year 1976, the most recent year for which there are complete data, approximately 24.7 million per-

---

[2]These figures are based on information contained in "Medicaid Services by State" and Medicaid State Tables, Fiscal Year 1976 (U.S. Department of Health, Education, and Welfare 1978b and 1978c).

[3]These figures are from the Medicaid State Tables, Fiscal Year 1976 (U.S. Department of Health, Education, and Welfare 1978c), Table 30, p. 83, and Table 31, p. 86. This is the most timely data available on the use of covered services.

TABLE 21-3   Covered Institutional Services by State

State	Psychiatric Facility (PF)	Skilled Nursing Facility (SNF)	Intermediate Care Facility (ICF)	Intermediate Care Facility Mentally Retarded (ICF-MR)
Louisiana[a]	Yes	Limits	Yes	Yes
Massachusetts[b]	No	Limits	Limits	Yes
Pennsylvania[c]	Yes	Limits	Yes	Yes
Utah[d]	Limits	Yes	Yes	Yes
Wisconsin[e]	Yes	Yes	Yes	Yes
Virginia[f]	No	Yes	Yes	Yes

[a]Louisiana PF: No limits for categorically needy; not provided to medically needy. SNF: For categorically needy, limited to AFDC children for up to three months; not provided to medically needy.
ICF: No limits for categorically needy; not provided to medically needy.
ICF-MR: No limits for categorically needy; not provided to medically needy.

[b]Massachusetts PF: Not provided. SNF: Limited to cases approved by Department of Public Health Review Team. ICF: Institutional review team may recommend lower level of care; such recommendations must be followed.
ICF-MR: Only available in public institutions.

[c]Pennsylvania PF: No limits. SNF: Limited to approved facilities; under 16 requires permission of Standard Setting Authority. ICF: No limits.
ICF-MR: No limits.

[d]Utah PF: Reimbursable only when provided at Utah State Hospital; must obtain a certificate of need for inpatient care, which requires statement that active treatment is essential to reasonably improve the patient. SNF: No limits. ICF: No limits. ICF-MR: No limits.

[e]Wisconsin PF: No limits. SNF: Requires independent medical review.
ICF: Requires plan of care and independent professional review.
ICF-MR: Only reimbursable in public institutions.

[f]Virginia PF: Not provided. SNF: No limits. ICF: No limits.
ICF-MR: No limits.

Source: Information obtained through a review of each state's Medical Assistance Program Plan, updated through 1979.

sons received medical services through the Medicaid program and the federal and state governments made payments
amounting to over $14 billion (U.S. Department of Health,
Education, and Welfare 1978c). Data are only available
for recipients, not for those who are eligible but do not
obtain any service during the year. Unfortunately, age
is not reported for all recipients; in fact, over 4 million recipients are dropped from the reports when age is
tabulated.

SUMMARY

The Medicaid program can affect status offenders in a
variety of settings, but its most pronounced effect appears to be on those status offenders who have been removed from their homes. Medicaid rules frequently require
that children must be living out of their homes to be
eligible for medical assistance payments, although this
varies according to the financial situation of the child
and his or her family and how the state implements certain
of the eligibility rules. To the extent each state's
medical assistance program requires that status offenders
must be removed from their homes to be eligible for service, the program may foster inappropriate institutionalization.

    Because the federal program allows the states to es-
tablish their own service coverages and eligibility
groups, there are numerous program differences across the
states. A service such as care in psychiatric facilities
may be covered in one state but not in another. The
effect of Medicaid on status offenders is not uniform
throughout the country.

    Some of the program requirements of the federal statute
may in themselves have some impact on the placement of
status offenders; that is, the availability of partial
funding for certain institutional services may promote
their use. Medicaid frequently will cover the maintenance
costs of institutional placements but not of more independent living arrangements, and this funding may continue
the use of such institutions when other less restrictive
but currently unfunded facilities would be more appropriate (Ewing 1979).

    States can determine not only the services covered
under Medicaid, but also the groups eligible for those
services. To some extent special eligibility groups,
especially the group "financially needy children," may

encourage the placement of children who are in need of
medical services in out-of-home situations. However, the
degree to which this occurs seems to depend on how the
individual state interprets and develops these eligibility
groups. There is some evidence that states may be restricting covered services and eligible groups as a means
of reducing their costs for medical assistance programs.

REFERENCES

Commonwealth of Massachusetts (1979) State Plan for
    Medical Assistance Under Title XIX of the Social
    Security Act. Includes revisions through 1979.
    Boston: Department of Public Welfare.
Commonwealth of Pennsylvania (1979) Medical Assistance
    Program Plan. Includes revisions through 1979.
    Harrisburg, Pa.: Department of Public Welfare.
Commonwealth of Virginia (1979) Medical Assistance
    Program Plan. Includes revisions through 1979.
    Richmond, Va.: Department of Health.
Ewing, Margaret F. (1979) Health Planning and
    Deinstitutionalization: Advocacy Within the
    Administrative Process. Stanford Law Review
    31(April):679.
Finley, Lucinda M. (1978) State Restrictions on Medicaid
    Coverage of Medically Necessary Services. Columbia
    Law Review 78(November):1491-1516.
Lerman, Paul (1978) Deinstitutionalization in America:
    An Assessment of Trends and Issues in the Fields of
    Mental Illness and Retardation, Aging, Child Welfare,
    and Delinquency. Prepared under a research contract
    for the National Institute of Mental Health, Division
    of Special Mental Health Programs, Contract No.
    278-76-0087, September, 1978, Rockville, Md.
State of Louisiana (1979) Medical Assistance Program
    Plan. Includes revisions through September 1979.
    Baton Rouge, La.: Department of Health and Human
    Resources.
State of Utah (1979) Utah Medical Assistance Plan.
    Includes revisions through 1979. Utah State
    Department of Social Services, Assistance Payments
    Administration. Salt Lake City, Utah: Department of
    Social Services.
State of Wisconsin (1978) State Plan Under Title XIX of
    the Social Security Act Medical Assistance Program.
    Includes revisions through 1978. Madison, Wis.:
    Department of Health and Social Services.

U.S. Department of Health, Education, and Welfare (1978a)
    Application of Regulations Concerning the Exclusion of
    "Inmates of Public Institutions" from Medicaid
    Coverage to Certain Juveniles in the Custody of the
    Commonwealth of Virginia's Department of Corrections.
    Memorandum dated November 9, 1978, from Galen D.
    Powers, Assistant General Counsel, HEW, to Alwyn
    Carty, Jr., Regional Medicaid Director, Washington,
    D.C.
    _____ (1978b) Medicaid Services by State.
    Health Care Financing Administration, June 1, 1978,
    Washington, D.C.
    _____ (1978c) Medicaid State Tables, Fiscal Year
    1976. Health Care Financing Administration.
    Washington, D.C.: Department of Health, Education,
    and Welfare.
    _____ (1979) Data on the Medicaid Program:
    Eligibility, Services, Expenditures. Health Care
    Financing Administration. Washington, D.C.:
    Department of Health, Education, and Welfare.
Virginia Department of Health (1979) Medicaid Manual.
    Richmond, Va.: Department of Health.
Virginia Department of Welfare (1979) Manual of Policy
    and Procedures for Local Welfare Departments. (Social
    services manual), Sec. 5264.B.2, with revisions
    through 1979. Richmond, Va.: Department of Welfare.

Title I of the Elementary and Secondary Education Act: Implications for the Deinstitutionalization of Status Offenders

22

SUZANNE S. MAGNETTI

Title I of the Elementary and Secondary Education Act (ESEA) (codified at 20 USC 241a et seq.) was enacted to provide special compensatory education to educationally deprived children. The size of Title I grants is based on a count of children from low-income families and of children in various out-of-home placements. The services provided under Title I are directed at children who reside in Title I eligible institutions or in specific state-selected target areas, which must have a high incidence of low-income families. However, Title I services are not tied to an individual determination of economic need. Within these geographic areas of impact any educationally deprived child is eligible for Title I services.

Status offenders may figure into the count for determining the size of the grant if they are from low-income families, are in foster care, or reside in child-caring facilities. Because the federal formula for calculating grant size places greater weight on children in out-of-home placements than on children who reside at home, it seems to offer some incentives for removing children from their homes. Although various aspects of Title I services and program operation and of the interaction of Title I and other education programs may affect how individual status offenders are treated after placement, Title I appears to have very little impact on where children are actually placed.

681

The purpose of this paper is to examine the ways in which Title I affects the placement and treatment of status offenders. The first section reviews the organization and purpose of the three Title I programs that appear to particularly affect status offenders. The second section explores state implementation of Title I programs. The third section offers an analysis of which status offenders may be affected by Title I and a discussion of the issues concerning Title I and the deinstitutionalization of status offenders. The final section summarizes the impacts of Title I on the placement of these youth.

THE FEDERAL PROGRAM

Title I is the largest federal program of assistance to elementary and secondary education. The total allocation for all Title I programs for fiscal year 1980 (school year 1979-1980) is more than $3 billion. The allocation amounts for each Title I program in each of the seven study states are shown in Table 22-1.

Title I is designed to fund special compensatory programs to meet the specific educational problems of targeted groups of educationally deprived children, including children in institutions for neglected or delinquent children and in state schools for handicapped children. In particular, Title I authorizes financial assistance to programs that address the special educational needs of ". . . educationally deprived children . . . children of certain migrant parents, of Indian children, and of handicapped, neglected and delinquent children" (P.L. 95-561, Sec. 101, codified at 20 USC 241a).

Grants to the states generally are based on the number of pupils from low-income families and the average per-pupil level of spending in the particular state. Portions of this money are then distributed by each state to state-run or state-supported residential institutions that educate children--in particular, state facilities housing neglected or delinquent children and state schools for the handicapped--on the basis of the average pupil population of those facilities. The major part of the Title I grant, however, is allocated by the state among the school districts in proportion to the number of eligible children in the district. Eligible children are those from low-income families, the children of AFDC recipients, children in local institutional programs, and other children clas-

TABLE 22-1 Allocation of Title I Funding by Program in Each of the Seven Study States, Fiscal Year 1980

State	Local Educational Agencies ($)	Handicapped ($)	Juvenile Delinquents ($)	Adult Correctional Institutions ($)	Neglected ($)	Migrant* ($)	State Administration ($)	Total ($)
Arizona	26,132,065	682,769	254,283	87,442	--	5,698,724	492,829	33,348,112
Louisiana	77,730,112	2,985,631	420,596	34,966	--	3,083,537	1,263,822	85,518,664
Massachusetts	50,639,608	10,307,096	325,113	309,453	--	4,227,438	987,130	66,795,838
Pennsylvania	120,932,276	10,589,423	646,310	465,812	257,759	2,147,282	2,025,582	137,064,444
Utah	8,576,677	553,468	90,928	6,692	--	338,175	225,000	9,790,940
Virginia	60,678,141	1,970,399	508,034	338,518	--	778,917	964,110	65,238,119
Wisconsin	43,380,423	2,469,370	548,921	185,908	--	1,193,336	716,669	48,494,627
Total U.S.	2,630,022,667	143,459,588	20,675,515	10,703,079	1,803,613	209,593,746	46,417,792	3,078,382,000

*State entitlements are subject to adjustment for funding of the Migrant Student Record Transfer System.

Source: U.S. Department of Health, Education, and Welfare (1979).

sified by certain gross criteria (e.g., low income).[1]
School districts then apply the funds to Title I target
schools, that is, schools with high concentrations of
eligible children.

Title I is subdivided into several programs directed
at particular target groups of children. Three of these
programs can affect status offenders:

1. The local educational agency (LEA) program that
provides financial assistance to these agencies (school
districts) for supplementary education of educationally
deprived children. It includes coverage of children who
are supported in foster care with public funds and children who live in locally run institutions for neglected
or delinquent children (20 USC 241a-m, 45 CFR 116a).

2. The program that provides grants to state agencies
to meet the supplementary special educational needs of
children in state institutions for neglected or delinquent
youth. This program is specifically for institutions that
are run either by a state agency or under a contractual
arrangement with a state agency, as opposed to those run
or supported privately or by local agencies (e.g., a
county orphanage or a city-run group home) (20 USC 241c-3,
45 CFR 116c). Allocations under this program are represented in Table 22-1 under both the "Juvenile Delinquents"
and "Neglected" headings.

3. The program for handicapped children that provides
grants to state-operated or state-supported schools for
these children. Typical acceptable schools are state-run
residential school programs, state-run day school programs, and some programs in private schools under contract
with a state agency. Children who have been covered by
the program in any of these situations and who then return
to their local school to complete their education may
continue to receive supplemental assistance under this
program (20 USC 241c-1, 45 CFR 116b).

Two other programs, which serve the adult correctional
institutions and migrants populations, also are included

---

[1]This eligibility terminology is somewhat deceiving in
that after the money has been allocated to the school
districts and individual schools, any child attending a
school that offers a Title I program can be served by the
program without regard to economic status if he or she is
educationally disadvantaged (20 USC 241 (c3).

within Title 1. We did not examine the effect of these programs on the deinstitutionalization of status offenders because all evidence from the seven states we studied indicated that no status offenders were in adult correctional facilities and migrant children were not seen to be a significant part of the status offender population.

STATE PROGRAM OPERATION

Title I is a distinct program operated by each state but funded with federal money. Each state's program must meet the requirements of the federal statute. Generally the state's Title I program is administered by an office of the state education agency created specifically for that purpose. This office acts as the state program liaison with the federal government; it processes grants through to eligible programs and collects and reports required compliance and eligibility data to the federal government. Money for state administration of the Title I programs is calculated as a part of every Title I grant.

States are required to demonstrate to the federal government that funds available under a Title I grant are spent to provide supplementary services to eligible children. The requirement that Title I services be supplemental to the education provided by the state has meant that Title I remains a distinct federal program even in states that also operate a state-funded compensatory education program. The states also are required to demonstrate the success of the program by reporting information related to participants' educational achievement.

All seven states in our study had Title I programs in most of their school districts. In fact in Louisiana, Virginia, and Pennsylvania, every school district in the state was eligible to participate in a Title I program. This does not mean that every school in those districts had a Title I program or that every district chose to participate, but rather that at least one target school in each participating district had such a program.

As a compensatory education program, Title I instruction emphasizes reading and basic mathematics, although this emphasis is not dictated by federal requirements. Most of the children who participate in Title I programs are in grades 1 through 6.[2] Title I administrators in

---

[2] In Massachusetts, children in grades 7 through 12 were only 9.3 percent of all those served by Title 1. In

the states surmise that older children are no longer in
need of compensatory education programs, that they have
"outgrown" their educational deprivation, either because
they had been recipients of special assistance when they
were younger or because of some other less explicable
reasons. It may be that the educational difficulties of
older children are either ignored or dealt with under some
alternative education program. For example, the child may
be placed in a low-achievement track or may be labeled
handicapped and served under a different special program.
Since most status offenders are beyond the sixth grade,
either because of academic achievement or age, Title I
appears to have less impact on these children than the
size of the program would indicate.

THE EFFECT OF TITLE I

Services

Title I provides funding for compensatory education services directed at educationally deprived children. As an
educational funding program it is not concerned with the
relationship of the children it serves to the juvenile
justice system. Little information collected in conformity with the requirements of this program would indicate
whether a child is a status offender. The lack of data
on the relationship of the status offender population to
the population affected by Title I makes it quite difficult to determine the impact of Title I on the deinstitutionalization of status offenders.

The problem of tracking Title I funds to this population is further intensified because what little categorical data that are collected and reported to the federal
government relate to the population counted to determine
the size of the Title I grant, and not to the children who
actually are served by the program. The grant to each
state for the largest Title I program (i.e., assistance
to local educational agencies (LEA)) is based on a count
of children from low-income families, children in foster

Louisiana 30 percent of the Title I children were in
grades 7 through 12. In Virginia the large majority of
children served were below grade 7. In Wisconsin, there
are eight times as many eligible elementary schools as
there are eligible junior and senior high schools.

care, and children in locally run or supported institutions for neglected or delinquent children. The funding level for the Title I program in state-run or state-supported institutions for neglected or delinquent children is based on a count of children in those institutions. Title I assistance to state-run or state-supported schools for the handicapped is calculated on the number of children in those schools and the number of children who have left those schools to return to their local schools. While the grant for Title I funds is based on counts of these categories of children, the services provided under Title I are directed toward a separate category, educationally deprived children. Children counted as the basis for the grant and educationally deprived children served by Title I can and, to some acknowledged but undefined extent, do overlap, but they are not entirely coextensive. Some children who receive Title I services because of their educational need may not fit into the category on which the count is based. Thus, because the children who are counted are not labeled in a way that would indicate whether they were status offenders, and because the children counted may not be the children served, it is not possible to make affirmative statements about the number of status offenders affected by Title I.

Furthermore, although Title I does serve large numbers of educationally needy children, it does not reach all potential Title I students because it has never been fully funded at the federal level. In Louisiana Title I program officials estimated that the state's Title I grant allows only about 50 percent of the educationally deprived to be served. A similar proportion of the population of educationally needy children is served by the federal program in other states. The problem of unserved children appears to be even greater in the state-run institutional programs for neglected and delinquent children, where even larger proportions of students might be educationally deprived. The federal funding structure does favor these institutional programs in that they currently receive more money per counted child than the LEA programs. Nonetheless, although institutional grants are based on a count of the average daily attendance of the institutional school, many of the children whom the program was intended to help are not being served because of insufficient funding.

Status offenders who receive Title I services can be living in a number of settings. The following discussion focuses on how each of these three Title I programs can affect these youth.

The LEA Program   In terms of money and number of children served, the largest Title I program by far is that for educationally disadvantaged children in local educational agencies (see Table 22-1). The budget allocation for the LEA program also includes a separate allocation earmarked for children in locally run or supported institutions for neglected or delinquent children. Because most status offenders in our seven-state study are found either in the community or in small residential facilities, this grant has the greatest impact on these children.

The largest part of each LEA allocation is based on a count of children who live in the community and attend local schools. Most of this grant is spent to provide services to similarly situated, educationally deprived children. Potentially served status offenders could be living at home with their parents, with or without court or social service agency supervision. Children in foster homes in Title I school districts could also be included in this program.

A smaller portion of the LEA grant is earmarked for children in eligible locally run or supported institutions for neglected or delinquent children (as defined in 45 CFR 116a.2). Children who live in these institutions may receive Title I services either in the institution in which they reside or in the local school. In most of the seven states relatively few of the local institutions applied for this special Title I status. This may be either because the institution does not fulfill all of the federal requirements for eligibility or because institution officials did not see any particular benefit in securing Title I funds. Children in other noneligible or nonparticipating local institutions are not specially counted, and therefore do not have Title I funds tagged for themselves or for other children in the facility. However, children in these institutions may still be eligible for Title I services if they attend a Title I school in the local school district.

Title I is essentially blind to the place of residence of children who participate in the LEA program, at least at the state and federal levels.[3] There is no federally

---

[3]At the district level, however, there must be some accounting for the money attributable to children from eligible local institutions. There is also frequently some informal knowledge that a "few kids from that group" are Title I students.

required administrative breakout of the part of the grant spent on children who live in the community as opposed to those who live in some residential facility. States do not attempt to catalogue or even to determine the amounts of an LEA grant attributable to children by the type of placement they occupy, nor do they account for the way the grant is spent by type of placement of served children.

In each of the seven states under review, status offenders are either returned to their home or placed in foster care or some community-based facility after court or social service agency involvement. In Massachusetts, status offenders can only be returned home or placed in foster care or a nonsecure group setting. Status offenders in Virginia are to receive treatment in community-based programs. In Arizona and Utah few if any children who are labeled as status offenders are sent to state-run secure facilities. Status offenders in Louisiana may not be placed in the care of the Department of Corrections, which operates all the state institutions for delinquent children. Status offenders in Wisconsin and Pennsylvania may not be placed in secure facilities. Obviously the LEA program, which serves children in the community, has a greater potential for reaching status offenders in all of these states than do the other two programs.

Program for Children in State Institutions for Neglected or Delinquent Children The state-run facilities for delinquent children in all seven states were larger and more secure than most of the locally run institutions, and were generally considered to be potential placements for more serious juvenile offenders. In these seven states status offender children do not appear in large numbers in state facilities, at least when labeled as status offenders. However, some status offenders may be classified as delinquents and placed in state-run institutions. Frequently the distinction between a status offender label and a minor delinquent label is, in practice, a matter of the discretion of the actors in the adjudication process.

Status offenders in state-run institutions for neglected or delinquent children may receive compensatory education through the Title I program directed at those institutions. Only one of the states we looked at, Pennsylvania, has even one state-run institution for neglected children (U.S. Department of Health, Education, and Welfare 1979). In short, this program does not have a large effect on status offenders in these states.

Program for the Handicapped (P.L. 89-313)   Still other
status offenders may be affected by Title I because they
are in state-run or state-supported schools for the handicapped. Children in these schools, and children who have
been in these schools and who then return to their local
school, may receive compensatory education services under
the Title I program known as the P.L. 89-313 program.
Officials in several states indicated that although status
offenders may be part of the institutionalized population
of handicapped children, especially in such ambiguous
categories as mildly mentally retarded and emotionally
disturbed children, they are seldom labeled as such.

Effects on Status Offenders

On the basis of currently available information, it is
very difficult to quantify the impact of Title I on the
status offender population. This difficulty is largely
due to the fact that Title I services are not directed at
children who have come to the attention of the courts or
of social service agencies (numbers of which are identifiable) but at children who are educationally deprived.
Although the statutory framework of Title I recognizes
that children in facilities for "problem" children (neglected, delinquent, or handicapped) and children in
low-income families and those supported by public funds
may have a high incidence of special educational needs,
the actual program delivery is based on the individual
child's educational need and not on whether or how the
child fits into any of these categories.

     Several aspects of the Title I programs appear to have
some impact on the institutionalization and deinstitutionalization of status offenders. Title I may seem to
make institutional placements more financially attractive
than community placements. However, while Title I services and program operations may directly affect an individual status offender, the effect of the potential
availability of some Title I services in a placement appears to be only remotely determinative of the choice of
that placement, as we discuss below.

     The apparent availability and use of Title I services
for children in the nonoffender class is the most immediate impact that this program has on status offenders.
Title I services are available to these children in a wide
range of placements, but, as previously suggested, these
same services are potentially available to every child.

Only the indication that status offenders are more likely to be in certain out-of-home placements that enjoy an enhanced Title I status implies that Title I may have certain relatively unique impacts on these children. The majority of status offenders affected by Title I services reside in community facilities or at home (rather than in an institution) and receive Title I services in the local schools.

The three Title I programs under review count children differently when computing the size of their Title I grant. Each program is separately funded, and the differences in the funding structures make it apparent that certain placements generate more federal Title I money than do others. Children in out-of-home placements generally will produce more Title I money for a state or locality than will children who live at home. Children in foster care are always counted as eligible for purposes of determining the size of a Title I grant, while children at home may or may not be counted, depending on family income levels. Children who live in Title I eligible local institutions or in foster care may be fully counted. Furthermore, children in eligible local facilities are guaranteed that some Title I services will be provided to them while children not in these institutions (whether at home, in foster care, or in other noneligible institutions) must live in the proper target area of a Title I program to be even potentially served by Title I.

Title I programs in state-run or state-supported institutions (both for neglected or delinquent children and state schools for the handicapped) are assured a certain funding-level advantage over the programs that are available at local institutions or in the local schools. A considerably larger amount per counted child is available for the state institution programs ($500-$700 per counted child) than for local programs ($200-$400).

The current federal funding arrangement, however, will not continue to support this disparate level of Title I funding for state programs over the local programs if state institutionalization increases. If the number of children institutionalized at the state level were to increase significantly, the size of the Title I grant per child at the state level would decrease. One principal reason for this complex funding scheme seems to be that Title I has never been fully funded at the federal level. Many more children display the kind of educational need that could benefit from Title I services than are ever served. Congress enacted an 85 percent hold-harmless provision whereby state programs get at least 85 percent of the money that was available to them the year before, even if their child count on a strict formula allocation is too low to support that level of funding. But this also means that at some level below last year's child count, the financial advantages of institutionalizing or counting more children taper off.

Title I does appear to offer support for the practice of inappropriately institutionalizing children. To some extent the funding structure actually seems to encourage more restrictive placements. While these rather broad effects appear obvious, it is much more difficult to determine that Title I directly affects the choice of a placement for any child. The restrictions imposed on the use of Title I funds make it difficult to use them for maintenance costs or for any other costs necessary to the care of institutionalized children. In addition, the placing authority is usually divorced from any institutional knowledge about the funds available through Title I, and most placement decisions seem unaffected by the availability of Title I services. Only one of the seven states, Pennsylvania, has a state-run facility for neglected children. If the larger grant-per-child figure actually was an inducement for institutionalization, it would seem that more states would have such facilities. Instead, other state policy decisions have limited this type of institutionalization.

All seven states operate institutions for delinquent children. For the most part, however, other state decisions have established that status offenders will not be committed to the states' secure facilities. With relatively few exceptions, in all seven states status offender children who are served by Title I receive these services either in their local school system or in small community-based institutions. This is true despite the greater financial support for Title I programs to children in state-run institutions. The implication is that Title I funding is simply not an important determinant of placement. There are a number of reasons why this seems to be true. First, state departments of education, which in all states administer Title I programs, appear to be isolated from placement and educational program decisions. Second, coordination and cooperation between education agencies and other social service offices in which institutional decisions are made is seldom noteworthy. Third, the funds made available through Title I must be used for compensatory education programs. Title I funds cannot be used to pay the costs of a child's placement. Furthermore, the services provided by Title I are not services that the state is required to provide to children in its care as, for example, medical services may be.

Other aspects of the Title I programs may also affect the deinstitutionalizaton of status offenders. For example, length-of-stay requirements in Title I may serve to increase the time a child spends in an institution, even though the requirements were intended to ensure that the Title I funds were used to the child's educational advantage. Under federal regulations, children in local institutions may be counted as eligible for Title I programs only if they have resided in the institution for some set amount of time. State institutions must have an average length of stay greater than 30 days to be eligible for Title I funding. The purpose of these regulations is not to lengthen the stay of any child in an institution but to make certain that the institution applying for aid under this statute can ensure some degree of educational continuity for participating children. It may be best for an individual child to move quickly through an institutional facility, but it may not be helpful to his or her education.

Other Title I regulations seem to work at cross purposes to the goals of the deinstitutionalization mandate by allowing for the commingling of status offenders and delinquents, and of juveniles and adults. The way in which Title I regulations define "institutions for delinquents" does not prevent the inclusion of status offenders in these settings. Title I is concerned not with the type of offense with which any child is charged but with providing services to ameliorate educational deprivation. Because Title I seeks to cover the largest possible number of children, it will not deny services to children who have been inappropriately placed.

Commingling of status offenders and delinquents appears to be a problem in several states. Instead of operating public facilities to care for status offenders, Massachusetts purchases services from private providers. Under this purchase-of-services arrangement, several different agencies may buy slots in the same facility. It is quite possible that delinquent children in the care of one agency, the Department of Youth Services, are in the same facility as status offenders in the care of another agency, the Department of Public Welfare. None of the children's service agencies in Massachusetts like to make exclusive contracts with private providers for fear they

will not use all of the available space they purchase.
The frequent result is that several agencies, with different client populations, have children in the same facility. Similarly, in Louisiana one agency, the Division
of Youth Services, has the ability to place both status
offenders and delinquents, and it may be placing both
populations in the same facilities.

There is also the nearly universal but subtle problem
of relabeling or misclassifying children in order to place
a child in a specific facility or to provide a specific
array of services. In some locations status offenders
may be purposely mislabeled as delinquents so that they
can be committed to a secure facility in circumvention of
state law. In other areas delinquents may be relabeled
as status offenders, because superior treatment services
may be available to children in the care of a social service agency. In these situations it is not that populations with different labels are mixed but that populations
whose actual underlying behavior patterns are dissimilar
have been tagged or labeled alike. Children whose behavior is borderline status offender or delinquent or is a
mixture of both present even more complex problems of
labeling and placement.

However, Title I does not seem to be a major factor
contributing to these results. We have found no evidence
that a particular placement was selected over another because of the availability of Title I services. Although
Title I does countenance mixed population placements by
providing services whether or not the facility houses a
mixed population. there is little to indicate that the
availability of Title I services affected placement decisions. Title I is not concerned with the nature of a
child's involvement with the juvenile justice system, nor
does it attempt to require independent judgments on whether a child is placed appropriately.

Some aspects of the Title I program may have deleteri-
ous effects on those status offenders who are institutionalized. In particular the lack of adequate transition
services for children who are leaving institutions to re-
enter local schools may reduce any educational gains resulting from Title I in the institution. This problem is
particularly acute when, as in many states, the educational program in institutions for neglected and delinquent children is operated by the agency responsible for
the institution and not by the education department. The
administrative distance between an education agency and
the corrections department, for example, may intensify

readjustment problems for released children who are placed in a class that is their age-grade equivalent but far beyond their actual abilities, or in which they are required to repeat material already learned.

In 1979 Congress recognized the need for transition services and authorized a program to develop links between institutional schools and local school districts, but this program was never funded. Nonetheless, some states are moving to improve the coordination of services between institutions and local schools. For example, Virginia has recently instituted a program of record transfers and has opened avenues of communication between community schools and the institutional schools run by the Department of Corrections.

Some status offenders may be receiving educational services under Title I as handicapped children. The P.L. 89-313 program can affect two separate populations of status offenders: (1) children with actual, perhaps severe, handicaps who have been abandoned by their families, and (2) children who may have been labeled handicapped as a means of securing a particular type of treatment for them. Several of the statutory handicapping conditions covered by P.L. 89-313, especially mental retardation and emotional disturbance, are not clearly defined or easily observable conditions and may be subject to a range of interpretations. It is particularly in these categories of institutionalized handicapped children that we could expect to find status offenders.

Money from P.L. 89-313 is only available for children who are in or who have been in a state-run school for the handicapped. Most frequently these schools are attached to residential programs for specific populations of handicapped children (e.g., schools for the deaf and blind); some states may offer a few day programs. It is important to note that P.L. 89-313 funds are used only for children who at one time have been isolated from regular school programs. To this extent it can be interpreted as encouraging institutionalization.

Handicapped children may be counted as eligible either under the P.L. 89-313 program under Title I or under the P.L. 94-142 program for handicapped children, but not under both. There would seem to be a larger federal financial incentive to keep a certain number of children in the P.L. 89-313 program, because its federal funding is substantially greater per child (about $750) than under P.L. 94-142 (about $175), and because P.L. 89-313 is covered by the 85 percent hold-harmless provision mentioned

above. However, because of this hold-harmless provision,
some states have found that it may be more financially
advantageous to reduce the number of children counted
under P.L. 89-313 and count more children under P.L.
94-142, because this maximizes both the number of children
eligible for and the size of federal aid to special education. Because children can be eligible for either of
these programs whether or not they are in institutions,
this sort of financial juggling will seldom affect where
a child actually will be placed. In other instances, when
P.L. 89-313 funds are passed through directly to localities, states may be less concerned with how much money per
child is collected from the federal government. For example, in Virginia, children who have been in P.L. 89-313
programs in state institutions and who then return to
local schools are frequently dropped from the P.L. 89-313
count and are included under the P.L. 94-142 program because of the administrative difficulties of setting up,
operating, and reporting on a special education program
for only a few children.

SUMMARY

Although Title I funds can provide supplemental services
for children who are in institutions, there is little
evidence to support assumptions that the availability of
Title I funds actually influences placement decisions.
Title I does provide funds for children in institutional
placements, but the use of these funds is limited to specific compensatory education programs. At the same time,
several aspects of the program do influence the kinds of
services provided to status offenders. Title I does differentiate between children on the basis of placement in
that institutionalized children seem to receive more advantageous treatment under Title I than children in the
community.
    Several reasons have been suggested as to why Title I
has such little effect on where children are placed. Most
obviously, placement policies for status offenders are the
result of state responses to issues that are only remotely
related to the question of where a child will be educated.
State decisions on the issue of institutionalization are
responses to many competing factors, and compensatory education programs are a minor concern at best in the debate
over deinstitutionalization.

Second, the financial incentives to place status offender children in restrictive environments under Title I are not obvious to placement decisionmakers. In almost every instance, placements are determined by judicial staff or social service agencies; education services and funding are seldom considered.

A third reason for the weak effect of Title I on placement decisions may be that the services available through Title I, wherever the child is placed, are not services that the state must provide to any child. The compensatory education services funded by Title I are supplemental to a normal educational program; they are not services that must be offered. Furthermore, the Title I grant can only be spent to provide those supplemental services. Under Title I grants, which have been characterized as "differential add-on grants" (Feldstein 1978), states must demonstrate both that Title I represents a real difference in the amount of money spent on Title I children and that this difference is the amount of the Title I grant. States must also show that the programs reflect a significant educational achievement gain for participating children. There is little opportunity to divert these funds to supply basic support services.

Finally, the educational organization represents a completely different system of classifying and treating children than those used by the juvenile justice system and social service providers. While responding to the needs of the same child, these three systems evaluate the child in terms of completely different theoretical conceptions. Children identified as status offenders under the juvenile justice system may be foster children in terms of social services and educationally deprived children for educational purposes. Because these separate classification systems have little common reference, it is also very difficult to identify how children classified in terms of these other systems are affected by compensatory education programs.

REFERENCES

Feldstein, Martin (1978) The Effect of a Differential Add-on Grant: Title I and Local Education Spending. The Journal of Human Resources 13(4):443-458.
U.S. Department of Health, Education, and Welfare (1979) Elementary and Secondary Education Act of 1965, P.L.

89-10 as Amended Title I, Assistance for Educationally
Deprived Children Allotments for Fiscal Year 1980.
Table dated March 30, 1979. Office of Education, U.S.
Department of Health, Education, and Welfare,
Washington, D.C.
_____(1980) State Agencies Directly Responsible for
Free Public Education of Children in Institutions for
Neglected or Delinquent Children and Eligible for
Grants Under Title I, P.L. 89-10 as Amended Fiscal
Year 1980. Unpublished tally sheets. Office of
Education, U.S. Department of Health, Education, and
Welfare, Washington, D.C.

Effects of the Education for All Handicapped Children Act on the Deinstitutionalization of Status Offenders

23

SUZANNE S. MAGNETTI

The Education for All Handicapped Children Act is designed to assure that all handicapped children in the country are provided a free appropriate public education. Contrary to most of the other federal programs examined in this study, which were shaped to serve the poor and the disadvantaged, P.L. 94-142 is universally applicable without regard to placement or income. Any child found to be handicapped and in need of special education must be provided the services required under the terms of the statute.

Status offenders are not as a group eligible for any services under P.L. 94-142. Rather, eligibility is based on the recognition that a particular child is handicapped. Individual status offenders who are handicapped or who are treated as if they are handicapped, should receive special education in accordance with P.L. 94-142. This program, therefore, potentially influences where such children are placed and what services will be offered in that placement.

Although P.L. 94-142 sets up a well-defined federal program, its effects on status offenders do vary across states. In general, these effects appear to result from three sources. First, program requirements established by the federal statute may themselves have some impact on where a child is placed and the services available to that child. Second, the requirements of P.L. 94-142 seem to interact with state and local policies, with the

699

result that similar children may be treated differently in different localities. Finally, the interplay of P.L. 94-142 and other special needs education programs may affect service use in the school systems.

In this paper we examine those effects and what they imply for the treatment of status offenders. The first section briefly reviews the organization and requirements of the federal program. The second section analyzes how state special education programs adapt the federal requirements. The third section discusses of the ways in which aspects of the federal law itself, the interaction of P.L. 94-142 and state and local programs and policies, and the interplay of P.L. 94-142 and other policy directives affect services and placement of status offenders.

THE FEDERAL PROGRAM

The Education for All Handicapped Children Act of 1975 (P.L. 94-142 codified at 20 USC 1401 et seq.) provides funding and sets out detailed requirements for state educational programs for handicapped children. The purpose of the legislation is to make available to all handicapped children "a free appropriate public education which emphasizes special education and related services designed to meet their unique needs" (P.L. 94-142, Congressional Statement of Findings and Purpose). This statute has the potential to directly affect up to 12 percent of all school-aged children in the United States.[1]

In order to be eligible to receive federal funds for the costs of educating handicapped children, the states and localities are required to establish a special education program that incorporates several key provisions. All potentially handicapped children in the jurisdiction must be identified and evaluated. The jurisdiction must develop and implement an individual education program for each handicapped child. Placement of handicapped children, to the maximum extent possible and appropriate for the individual child, must be in the least restrictive

---

[1]Congress imposed a 12 percent ceiling on the number of children that could be served by P.L. 94-142 based on estimates developed for the Bureau of Education for the Handicapped (BEH) of prevalence rates of handicaps in this country.

setting. School districts also are required to establish an extensive and specific system of procedural safeguards particularly designed to protect the child in the identification, placement, and program development processes.

The fiscal year 1980 allocation for P.L. 94-142 was $804 million (U.S. Department of Health, Education, and Welfare 1979b). Based on a count of 3,709,639 handicapped children participating nationwide, the federal contribution to special education programs under P.L. 94-142 for that year breaks out to about $217 per child. P.L. 94-142 supplied only about 12 percent of the costs of educating handicapped children in the required programs; the actual costs of the special education programs mandated by that law are considerably in excess of the federal allocation. All costs in excess of the funds provided by the federal government must be absorbed by state and local educational agencies. The relative amounts of the costs of special education contributed by federal and state sources are listed in Table 23-1. Table 23-2 demonstrates the growth of federal funding for special education programs through P.L. 94-142 for fiscal years 1977 through 1980.

STATE SPECIAL EDUCATION PROGRAMS

At the state level, P.L. 94-142 is administered not as a separate federal program but as an integrated part of the state's special education program. Although P.L. 94-142 does provide some funding, its greatest impact is through the mandated requirements for state special education plans. Each state is free to develop a special education program that best responds to state needs and policies, but such a program must comply with the provisions of P.L. 94-142. In essence this means that an individual state's special education program must fit within the framework of principles established by the federal law: state programs may differ somewhat, but these elements must be contained in every state's program.

To demonstrate adequate implementation of the federal program, states are required to submit annual P.L. 94-142 program plans to the Office of Special Education (formerly Bureau of Education for the Handicapped) in the Department of Education. That office reviews the state's plan to determine whether the written requirements of the special education program conform with the federal requirements. The Office of Special Education also con-

TABLE 23-1 Contributions of Part B Funds Relative to State Funds for Education of Handicapped Children

State	State Special Education Revenue FY 1976 ($)	FY 1978 Allocation (Actual) ($)	Combined ($)	Federal Contribution as a Percentage of Combined ($)
Arizona	20,500,000	2,537,384	23,037,384	11
Louisiana	44,474,500	5,860,310	50,334,810	12
Massachusetts	132,900,000	8,442,257	141,342,257	6
Pennsylvania	180,000,000	13,808,578	193,806,578	7
Utah	19,215,000	2,057,060	21,272,060	10
Virginia	25,990,400	5,296,653	31,287,053	17
Wisconsin	48,833,700	4,348,328	53,182,028	8
Total U.S.	2,477,955,000	245,775,773	2,723,730,773	9

Note: Part B refers to those sections of the Education of the Handicapped Act that deal with providing a free, appropriate public education to handicapped children through states and localities.

Source: U.S. Department of Health, Education, and Welfare (1979a).

TABLE 23-2 State Grant Awards Under P. L. 94-142 by State, Fiscal Years 1977-1980

State	FY 1977 Allocation (Hold harmless) ($)	FY 1978 Allocation (Formula-based) ($)	FY 1979 Allocation (Actual) ($)	FY 1980 Allocation (Estimated) ($)
Arizona	1,921,124	2,537,384	6,318,460	9,480,689
Louisiana	3,775,472	5,860,310	12,809,566	18,697,367
Massachusetts	5,212,919	8,442,257	19,103,830	27,132,919
Pennsylvania	10,378,532	13,806,578	26,303,162	36,715,448
Utah	1,213,009	2,057,060	5,485,978	7,307,831
Virginia	4,561,746	5,296,653	12,178,610	17,937,636
Wisconsin	4,348,328	3,868,986	8,772,508	12,368,991
Total U.S.	200,000,000	249,386,974	563,874,752	804,000,000

Source (FY 1977-1979): U.S. Department of Health, Education, and Welfare (1979a).

Source (FY 1980): U.S. Department of Health, Education, and Welfare (1979b).

ducts on-site monitoring. The focus of on-site monitoring visits, which are conducted in a state only every
other year (U.S. Department of Health, Education, and
Welfare 1979a), has been primarily directed toward formal
compliance with written federal requirements. In the
past the Office of Special Education has been less involved with monitoring the actual implementation of federal requirements or the effect of that implementation on
handicapped children. In the face of growing controversy
and criticism of the federal monitoring of the implementation of P.L. 94-142 (Children's Defense Fund 1980), the
U.S. Department of Education has initiated several efforts
aimed at increasing its effectiveness in monitoring state
implementation (1980).

Several aspects of state programs (e.g., definitions
of particular handicaps) that do differ across states may
particularly affect status offenders. Because these
state definitions may be more or less inclusive, or may
cover different behaviors under one label across states,
how a state defines a particular handicap may affect the
number of status offenders served by special education
programs.

P.L. 94-142 mandates that all handicapped children in
the country be provided an appropriate education. The
statute lists specific covered categories that are further defined by regulation (45 CFR 121 2.5). States are
required to cover all children in those categories.
Within these limits, states can redefine what will be
recognized as a particular categorical handicap and thus
expand or contract the potential population of handicapped children.

States are also free to include as part of their
special education population children who do not have
federally recognized handicaps. Wisconsin, for example,
includes children who are pregnant in its category of
children with "exceptional educational needs," which is
equivalent to the special education population (Wisconsin
Department of Public Instruction 1979). Children who
receive special education services but are not included
in the scope of the federal initiative should not be
eligible for federal assistance. However, they may
receive special education services from the state that
would not have been available without P.L. 94-142. One
state, Massachusetts, has abandoned completely the categorical approach and has adopted a functional definition
of a handicapped child so as to cover the widest possible
number of children; any child who "is unable to progress

effectively in a regular school program" for whatever reasons is eligible for special education (Commonwealth of Massachusetts 1972). Massachusetts' proportional count of handicapped children who were eligible for P.L. 94-142 assistance in 1979-1980 is the highest in the country.

In addition, state funding mechanisms for special education can affect service provision by regulating the amount of state support available for specified services. States have adopted various methods of paying for the services required by P.L. 94-142. Because the federal law requires that expensive special services be provided to large numbers of children but only funds a small portion of the costs of those services, state and local governments have had to absorb the large costs associated with expanded special education services. The differential cost usually is made up by a combination of state and local money. Although the patterns and levels of state funding for special education services vary across states, the amount of state aid to local educational agencies frequently is determined by some formula based on the number of special education children in the district. The state seldom pays the entire costs of special education services. This split funding may affect where children in out-of-home placements outside their home school district are placed and what services are provided. School districts often are reluctant to pay for educational services for children who are not a part of its tax base.

States have chosen to approach special education funding for children in out-of-home placements in a variety of ways. Some have organized, routinized methods of arranging payments across district lines; some have assumed state responsibility for children in at least a few specific placements; and others have made no arrangements for special education services for children placed out of district. The extent to which financial responsibility is prearranged and formalized can affect substantially both the extent of services and how soon they may be provided. The variety of potential approaches to this issue is apparent in our study states. Arizona, for example, has a system of three types of educational vouchers that accounts for all types of possible placements: (1) certificates of educational convenience, which reimburse school districts when a child is placed out of home by a public agency; (2) special education vouchers, which reimburse special education costs when a child is placed

in a private institution by the Department of Economic
Security, the Department of Corrections, or juvenile probation; and (3) institutional vouchers, which reimburse
the costs of education in the three state mental retardation training institutions (Arizona State Board of Education, Regulation R 7-2-404). A portion of the costs of
these vouchers is reimbursed to the state by the home
district of the child. Virginia's education department
has instituted a system of tuition grants for children in
private special education facilities through which the
state pays a portion of the costs when the local district
is unable to provide the necessary educational program
and state facilities are not available (Virginia House of
Delegates 1977). Use of these tuition grants, however,
is regulated by the education system alone. If the welfare department were to apply for a tuition grant as a
means of offsetting costs for a child it had placed, the
special education division could refuse the grant and
refer the child to programs in the local school systems
that could meet that child's needs (Virginia House of
Delegates 1977). A state respondent in Massachusetts
indicated that children there may be moved from placement
to placement to find a school district that will pay the
educational costs of a residential placement, and the
result may be delays or actual denial of special education services for children in out-of-home placements.

THE EFFECT OF P.L. 94-142

Potentially every handicapped or arguably handicapped
child in the country will be affected by P.L. 94-142, and
some of these children will be status offenders. We have
not found, however, any reliable data that would indicate
how many of the children affected by P.L. 94-142 are
status offenders. The education system is simply not
required to collect information in terms that answer the
categories of other social service systems. Even where
some information exists it is very subjective, incidental,
and incomplete; that is, a local school district administrator knows that some troublesome children are placed in
special education classes, or a social worker may recognize that a few institutionalized children may be hard-
to-place handicapped children. Because it is so difficult to know on the basis of currently collected information how many status offenders are served under P.L.
94-142, it is also very difficult to quantify the effects
of P.L. 94-142 on the status offender population.

Essentially two types of status offenders may be served under P.L. 94-142. Some may have actual, easily identified handicaps, the nature and extent of which will affect where each child will be placed. Other status offenders may be affected by P.L. 94-142, not because whatever handicap they may have is easily identifiable or clearly defined, but because the conforming P.L. 94-142 special education programs offer a potential treatment or service for problem or troublesome children.

Children in the status offender category who are receiving special education services that are required and partially funded by P.L. 94-142 may be living in a wide variety of settings. Many will be at home, as when, for example, a special education referral is used as a diversionary technique. Others may be in foster homes or group homes in which special education services are provided by the local school system. Still others may be in residential schools and institutions, and the placement may be either the result of the particular handicapping condition or the result of court or social service agency involvement.

For these reasons it is difficult to know why, where, or how many status offenders are served by P.L. 94-142. Its impact on these youth, however, is potentially large. The federal government estimates that 12 percent of the school-aged population is handicapped, and P.L. 94-142 incorporates this 12 percent figure as the level of full implementation of the act. This figure is noted not only as a limit to the number of children who can be served under P.L. 94-142 but also as a goal to be reached by each state's special education program. For 1979-1980 only one state's child count, Massachusetts', approached that ceiling. In most of the states in our study, the child count was substantially less than 10 percent of all school-aged children (U.S. Department of Health, Education, and Welfare 1979a). Although it may be to a state's financial advantage not to identify all handicapped children, there exists considerable controversy surrounding the reliability and accuracy of original estimates of the incidences of the handicapping conditions (U.S. Department of Health, Education, and Welfare 1979a). Most of the states claim that the 12 percent figure is too high. Only Massachusetts expects to reach the 12 percent goal in fiscal year 1980 (Commonwealth of Massachusetts 1979). It has been argued that Massachusetts nominally has reached this goal by lowering the standards used to determine whether a child is handicapped. Massachusetts employs a functional definition as the rule to gauge whether a child needs special education, and it thereby has widened the scope of its services to include children who, although they individually might benefit from special services, would not in other states be considered handicapped.

While this dispute over the child count continues, some populations may not be served at all. Massachusetts notes that it may be underserving the children with the most difficult needs--young persons in institutions, those with severe special needs in Boston, and adolescents in many areas of the state who could benefit from vocational education (Commonwealth of Massachusetts 1979). In Virginia the Department of Education recognizes that severely emotionally disturbed children are not served (1979). Louisiana continues to identify previously unserved children (Louisiana Department of Education 1979). Until the 1979-1980 school year children in Louisiana Department of Corrections facilities had not even been evaluated for special education. This information seems to indicate that the most difficult to serve, or the most expensive to serve, may still lack the services guaranteed by P.L. 94-142. However, because the number of status offenders affected by the law is not known, it is quite difficult to draw conclusions about how these service gaps affect them.

In general, P.L. 94-142's requirements have enlarged the special education system in this country, touching many children not previously served and creating numerous programs to provide special education services. New special education programs are available, and most of these are directed at integrating handicapped children into the regular school atmosphere as closely as possible. To the extent that the reality is in keeping with the philosophy of P.L. 94-142--that each child is educated in the least restrictive setting appropriate for the child-- the law can be said to have a widespread deinstitutionalizing effect. For example, in Virginia for school year 1977-1978, 2,463 children received special education services in institutions; 11,086 from clinics; and 8,929 in juvenile detention homes. A total of 92,410 children were served in the public school system. Of those educated in public schools, nearly three times as many were taught by itinerant resource teachers as were educated in self-contained environments (Virginia Board of Education 1978). Although we have no longitudinal data to indicate trends over time, these figures indicate that the great majority of special education students in Virginia are educated in a normal school environment.

State policy appears to play some part in the extent of deinstitutionalization that may result from P.L. 94-142. For example, Massachusetts' special education law, chapter 766, was developed at a time when broadly based deinstitutionalization efforts were reducing the populations of many state institutions. The philosophy of deinstitutionalization also affected the composition of the state's special education system. State education officials told us that after the passage of chapter 766, the number of children in state institutions decreased from 2,200 in 1974 to 1,600 in 1979. Even many children who reside in state institutions are now educated in community-based programs (Massachusetts Board of Education 1978). In school year 1977-1978, 154,000 special education children were educated in local school districts. One percent of the special education count was in residential placements and of these, 3 percent received their education in special day programs (Massachusetts Board of Education 1978). Where the state impetus to deinstitutionalize is not as clearly defined as it is in Massachusetts, proportionally greater numbers of children may be left in and placed in institutions.

The federal law identified 11 specific handicapping conditions: mental retardation, hard-of-hearing, deaf, speech-impaired, visually handicapped, seriously emotionally disturbed, orthopedically impaired, deaf-blind, multihandicapped, other health-impaired, and specific learning disability. Several of these categories, especially those in which no specific handicap is readily apparent, are vaguely defined and may be subject to a range of interpretations. In some cases special education may be used to isolate certain "undesirable" populations from a normal school curriculum. Preliminary data compiled by the Office of Civil Rights of HEW, for example, indicates that black children are substantially overrepresented in classes for the mildly mentally retarded and that this overrepresentation does not appear to be educationally justified (Chatham 1979). Recent court cases in several states indicate that special education services are in some instances used to separate certain children from the normal education process (Lora v. Board of Educ. 1978 [N.Y.], Larry P. v. Riles 1979 [Cal.], Mattie v. Holliday 1979 [Miss.], PASE v. Hannon 1980 [Ill.]).

The focus of these cases most frequently is on black children or other high-visibility minority children, but

some elements of this problem indicate that status offenders also may be particularly vulnerable to this type
of misclassification. At the heart of the safeguard procedures for P.L. 94-142 is a rather elaborate parental
oversight and complaint process that depends on interested
and knowledgeable parents or surrogates to protect their
child's educational rights. But even involved and informed parents may defer without question to the expressed
expertise of the labeling educators, and poorer, less well
educated parents are even less likely to understand the
issues involved in labeling and placement (Note 1979).
By the nature of the category, status offenders in particular generally lack effective parental advocates who
would inspect and raise objections to the procedures used
to identify the child as handicapped. Children in out-of-
home placements usually do not have parents available who
can put into motion the procedural safeguards designed to
protect against misclassification. To the extent that
special education is used to isolate children who perform
poorly on standardized tests or who are referred by classroom teachers because they have behavior problems, it may
have a heavy and perhaps unjustified impact on the status
offender population. If special education is used to
sequester children who are troublesome from the normal
educational process, then status offenders may be particularly subject to such misclassification (O'Neill 1977).
Not only will misclassification give these children a
label that will effectively follow them throughout life,
but it frequently means that the education they do receive
is a restricted curriculum at a much slower pace and, as
a result, the classification seems to be a self-fulfilling
prophecy.

Federal policy may be intensifying this problem. P.L.
94-142 established an estimate that 12 percent of all
school-aged children in the country are handicapped and
in need of special services. The Office of Special Education points to the 12 percent figure cited in the legislation as the goal of full identification of all handicapped children. However, few states have yet identified
more than 7 or 8 percent of their school-aged population
as handicapped. Most of the states in this study objected that the 12 percent figure was just too high.
Although state special education departments are certainly
not disinterested parties in this dispute, there is some
question as to whether the estimate was ever accurate,
and some claims have been made that it was originally
inflated, or that it is now outdated (U.S. Department of
Health, Education, and Welfare 1979a).

There are two opposite and competing risks in this child identification policy. On the one hand, if the program pushes too hard to identify large numbers of children as handicapped, the risk is that children who are not handicapped may be labeled as such. On the other hand, if the child identification effort is weak or lax, the risk is that special education programs may bypass children who are handicapped and who could benefit from special education (U.S. Department of Health, Education, and Welfare 1979a). This mislabeling, in either direction, is a serious problem in the new special education laws; while it is difficult to document, there is some evidence that both possibilities are occurring simultaneously.

The Office of Special Education continues to encourage states to identify more handicapped children. It looks for the largest gains in the national child count to be in the categories of emotionally disturbed, mentally retarded, learning-disabled, and speech-impaired (U.S. Department of Health, Education, and Welfare 1979a), categories in which definitions and standards of identification may be subjective or indistinct. This emphasis may result in what one state special education officer called "manufactured" handicaps that disappear when a child reaches high school age.

As noted above, only Massachusetts closely approaches the federally imposed 12 percent limit on special education services. Massachusetts, however, offers a rather unique case among the states reviewed in this report, because it refuses to categorize children by handicap, using instead a functional definition of handicapped that appears to encompass more children than could otherwise be accounted for. Because of this nonlabeling approach it is difficult to tell what problems these children have.

At the same time as they object to the level of the estimates of expected handicaps, the states are willing to admit that certain populations may be underrepresented in the child count. In Virginia, state administrators indicated that local school administrators, particularly in rural and low-income areas, did not look very thoroughly for children with handicapping conditions, because they were cautious of the money and effort they would have to exert for those special services. In Louisiana many institutionalized children were not served. This phenomenon is relatively difficult to document, because presumably if a state knew of an unserved population, it would attempt to extend services to those children. However, if the federal estimates are in fact accurate, then there may still be numerous unserved children.

P.L. 94-142 actually incorporates the idea of deinstitutionalization into the concept of the program. A central principle to the law is that to the maximum extent possible, handicapped children should be educated with nonhandicapped children. This policy requires the cooperation and acceptance of the educational community, the parents of handicapped children, and the agencies that control institutionalized children. To a degree, each of these groups may contribute a counterforce to the deinstitutionalizing principle expressed in the statute.

The principle of integrating handicapped children into the regular school program requires teachers to face new demands and respond to a more varied class population. To some extent the adjustments necessary to deal with handicapped children reduce teacher time for "regular" students. Children who exhibit behavior difficulties and who are likely to be disruptive in class are particularly unwelcome. Since most special education placements appear to originate with teacher referrals (U.S. Department of Health, Education, and Welfare 1979c), some teachers actually may use the special education system to purge difficult or problem children from the regular school environment.

Parents also may inhibit the provision of special education in the least restrictive setting. They may feel that an institutional setting best protects their child from the violence and exploitation of the world (Lowenbraun and Afflect 1978). They may not want to accept the burdens of caring for a previously institutionalized child, or they may believe that the best treatment and learning experience for the child is in a special program (Note 1979). In any case, parents who are involved in the educational decisions made about their child have the opportunity under the law to affect the decision in a number of ways. In Massachusetts the majority of procedural safeguard hearings conducted under P.L. 94-142 are brought by parents who are protesting the potential change of placement of their child out of a residential facility (U.S. Department of Health, Education, and Welfare 1979b). One state official categorized this phenomenon as "middle-class abuse" of the special education laws. Parents now can return the costs of educating handicapped children to the public education system; in the past, however, parents or often some third party bore the costs of that education. They can use the procedural safeguards written into the P.L. 94-142 system to continue more restrictive and more costly placements than the school divisions feel are appropriate for the child. Parents who know how to manipulate the system can often find and push through outside special placements. This may present a serious problem in locations where the public education system is very poor, or where the special education programs in the public schools are clearly inferior.

Another impediment to the adoption of the least restrictive educational environment for each child is that in the absence of clear state directives there is little cooperation between agencies with responsibilities for children in institutions and educational units. Handicapped children in institutions and programs run by government agencies other than the state educational agency are particularly affected by this problem. Conflicting lines of responsibility for the education of these children seem to confuse the authority of the federal mandates. For example, in Virginia the responsibility for the education of children in institutions rests on the agency that runs that institution (Commonwealth of Virginia 1979). These other agencies have the authority to decide to educate children in their facilities or to make arrangements with local school boards for their education outside the institution. The regulations implementing Virginia's special education program indicate that the financial responsibility for special education of children in these institutions is generally shared by the state special education budget and the local school division that the child care is from (Virginia Department of Education 1978). School districts, however, can refuse to pay for placements that were not generated by the special education program when they feel there are educational alternatives within the community to care for these children. Rather than offering a clear system of who is responsible for what, these confusing arrangements may prevent children from receiving special education in the least restrictive setting.

When states have moved to provide educational services in the least restrictive setting to institutionalized children, it frequently has been the result of strong pressures from advocacy groups to enforce the federal mandates.[2] Witness the litigation of the Gary W. case

---

[2]The ongoing resolution of the PARC case (Pennsylvania Association For Retarded Citizens v. Commonwealth of

(1976) in Louisiana, in which a class of more than 400 handicapped children complained that their placement in institutions outside the state of Louisiana violated their rights to an education in the least restrictive setting. State officials indicate that since that suit there have been at least two large statewide efforts to move children out of private facilities, where they were supported with state funds, into placements closer to their homes or, in many cases, into the local schools.

While the costs of national compliance with the requirements of P.L. 94-142 have not been fully calculated (Bernstein et al. 1976), the available evidence suggests that these costs will be substantial. Since P.L. 94-142 was intended to fund only a small part of special education costs (probably not more than 12 percent), the large excess costs must be absorbed by state and local educational agencies. The way in which these costs are allocated among federal, state, and local sectors can influence the location and type of services that are provided to handicapped children.

The federal funding formula is based on a percentage of the average national per pupil costs in elementary and secondary schools and the number of children who are receiving special education services in the state. This type of funding (unit funding) may create disincentives for the operation of more expensive programs, and could support the misclassification of children into handicapping categories that require less intensive special education services and, within handicapping categories, into the less expensive programs (Gallagher et al. 1975). To counter this tendency, however, the federal law does require that federal funds go primarily to children who are not served and to children who receive an inadequate education. Because so little cost analysis information is available, it is difficult to estimate the actual effect of the P.L. 94-142 funding arrangement on placement and services for handicapped children.

The excess costs of P.L. 94-142 generally are met by some combination of state and local funds. State funding formulas for special education, therefore, can also influence placement and services. Because placement and program decisions are almost always made at the local

---

Pennsylvania, 343 F. Supp. 279 [E.D. Pa. 1971]) indicates that this is often a long, involved method of resolving education problems.

level, they may be influenced by the degree of support available from the state for any particular placement or program.

State funding formulas support the placement of children in the most normal environment in some states, while in other states the local agencies actually may benefit from restrictive placements for handicapped children (Simons and Dwyer 1978). Two of our study states provide interesting examples. The state-local funding arrangement in Massachusetts seems to encourage the deinstitutionalization of many handicapped children. Local school districts have spent considerable amounts of money developing a special education curriculum that allows a child to remain in the local school whenever possible. They are therefore most reluctant to pay for the educational costs for a child in a residential placement when the school district has adequate means to serve the child in the community. In all cases in which the local education agency is responsible for the costs of a child's education, they also have a say in where the child will be placed. State education money is only available to children in the care of the Department of Youth Services, the Department of Corrections, and to a few children who were institutionalized before 1972. The Department of Education will reimburse for education outside the public school only when the education program required for the child dictates a residential placement. This very restrictive funding arrangement means that almost all handicapped children in the state are educated in the local school system, including children who are otherwise institutionalized or isolated from the normal population.

A second case is that of Virginia, which appears to assume the costs of education for children in state-run facilities for handicapped individuals. The state also will reimburse school districts for 60 percent of the costs of placing handicapped children in private programs, either day or residential (Virginia House of Delegates 1977). This type of funding arrangement is to some extent supportive of increased institutionalization. State policy on educational placement, which in light of this funding arrangement can be seen as cost-conscious, indicates that private placements can only be effected after a determination has been made that no public day program or state facility is appropriate to meet the educational needs of the child (Virginia House of Delegates 1978). This policy may limit the number of private placements that are educationally motivated, but because it continues state financial support for the education of children placed in state facilities, it may provide some encouragement for institutionalization.

The federal categorical education programs in general are individually administered and funded as if each particular target group were an independent population with discrete characteristics. In reality there appears to be considerable overlap between various special needs populations, but the extent of these overlaps is as yet undetermined. Many children in those ambiguous handicapping categories (i.e., emotionally disturbed, learning-disabled, speech-impaired, and educable mentally retarded) who are served under P.L. 94-142 also could, for example, be considered educationally deprived under Title I. These children could be served under both programs if they live in Title I eligible attendance areas.[3] As a result, some special needs children, who are theoretically educated in the regular school environment, could spend substantial portions of their school day isolated from regular children. Take, for example, a child who is classified as educable mentally retarded and provided special education services in a separate resource room in the regular local school for about four hours per day. A special education review might well consider that child to be placed in the least restrictive environment appropriate. However if the child also receives other special needs services in "pullout" programs such as Title I and is out of the regular class for up to two more hours per day, then in reality that child is segregated from normal children for most of the school day.

These program and service overlaps seem to have several policy implications. First, the mutable characteristics of special needs populations may indicate that estimates of handicapped children need further evaluation. Second, the overlaps also raise questions about how, under existing programs, to allocate limited funds and services. Should each special needs child be eligible for only one service and, if so, what should guide that selection decision? Or should services be rationed independently, with the known result that some children will receive several services and others none (Berke and Demarest 1978)?

---

[3]Children who are served under the P.L. 89-313 program of Title I may not also receive services under P.L. 94-142; all other Title I children may also be eligible for P.L. 94-142.

Program distinctions are also blurred by the multitude of funding sources available to any local school district. School districts may have between 15 and 100 different sources of funding; the number is usually a function of district size (Berke and Demarest 1978). Much of the available funding is tagged with requirements responding to federal, state, and local policy pronouncements. In response to those competing demands, local school districts seem to engage in multi-pocketed budgeting; that is, while symbolically accounting for the requirements established by funding sources, they actually create and fund programs that respond to local needs and priorities (Porter et al. 1973).

To some extent P.L. 94-142 may be susceptible to these pressures. Although the federal program does require that states institute conforming state special education programs, most of the substance of what the program actually will look like, within the limits of the federal requirements, is left to state and local administrators. Since almost every decision about where a child will be placed and what services will be provided is made on the basis of localized responses to the individual child, local attitudes and available resources will shape that special education program.

SUMMARY

P.L. 94-142 can affect the placement of and the provision of services to at least some status offenders. Since the program potentially covers all handicapped children in the country, the special education services mandated by the federal statute may be available to children in every possible institutional and noninstitutional setting. In that the statute fundamentally espouses the principle that all children should be educated in the least restrictive setting appropriate to their particular needs, P.L. 94-142 actually adopts the idea of deinstitutionalization. However, various aspects of the program itself and of its interaction with other policy directives may militate against this express deinstitutionalizing position.

Although some potential effects of federally mandated special education on status offenders can be specified, the extent of these effects remains difficult to evaluate. There seem to be three primary reasons why little information evaluating the effects of 94-142 on status offenders is available. First, P.L. 94-142 focuses on the category of handicapped children. While there may well be overlaps between the handicapped children served under P.L. 94-142 and status offenders, these overlaps are not obvious and are not of particular interest to special education administrators.

Second, P.L. 94-142 is a relatively new program, and not much data are available on the effects of any particular program requirement on the placement or provision of services to handicapped children. Such basic questions as the costs of full implementation of the program have yet to be completely addressed. Conflicts over the accuracy of and the weight to be placed on estimates of potentially affected children based on incidence rates of particular handicaps are not resolved.

Third, education traditionally has been and continues to be very much a locally administered program. Because they remain responsive to local needs and priorities, education programs may differ substantially across jurisdictions. Placement and program decisions in special education almost always are made at the local level, and these decisions are only compared across districts and states in very gross terms.

P.L. 94-142 may affect status offenders in several different ways. The program requirements of the federal statute may in themselves have some impact on placement and provision of services to status offenders. Although some of these effects appear positive, some children may be inappropriately placed or underserved. Integrating handicapped children into regular school environments is stressed under P.L. 94-142 and, as a result of the statute, many children who previously would have been institutionalized receive at least part of their education in a local classroom. However, the need to identify and classify handicapped children as required by the federal statute may actually encourage some inappropriate institutionalization.

State and local program and policy considerations also affect how P.L. 94-142 is implemented. Education remains fundamentally responsive to local priorities and goals. Because most of the essential decisions concerning a child's educational placement and the services provided to that child are made at the local level, similar children may be treated differently depending on their school district. State and local funding of special education may make it more or less desirable to place children in restrictive educational environments.

Finally, the interaction of P.L. 94-142 and other special needs education programs may affect the ways in which
special education services are used in schools. To the
extent that the client populations of special needs programs for handicapped, bilingual, or educationally deprived children overlap, these children effectively may
be isolated from a regular school environment by a daily
succession of pullout programs. Although most of these
programs were designed to meet the needs of children within a normal school environment, the potential for their
inappropriate use does exist. Decisions on how these programs are coordinated and organized, and on which children are served, are usually made at the district or even
local school level.

REFERENCES

Berke, Joel S., and Demarest, Elizabeth J. (1978)
    Alternatives for Future Federal Programs. In M. F.
    Williams, ed., Government in the Classroom: Dollars
    and Power in Education. Academy of Political Science
    Proceedings 33(2):1-156.
Bernstein, Charles D., Kirst, Michael W., Hartman,
    William J., and Marshall, Rudolph S. (1976) Financing
    Educational Services for the Handicapped. Reston,
    Va.: Council for Exceptional Children.
Chatham, Wilbert A. (1979) Testimony of the Deputy
    Director, Office of Civil Rights, U.S. Department of
    Health, Education, and Welfare, to the U.S. House of
    Representatives, Committee on Education and Labor,
    Subcommittee on Select Education, October 24, 1979.
Children's Defense Fund (1980) Report by the Education
    Advocates Coalition on Federal Compliance Activities
    to Implement the Education for All Handicapped
    Children Act (P.L. 94-142). Education Advocates
    Coalition, Children's Defense Fund, Washington, D.C.,
    April 1980.
Commonwealth of Massachusetts (1972) Chapter 766 of The
    Acts of 1972. Codified at Massachusetts General Laws,
    Chapter 71B.
    _____ (1979) Fiscal Year 1980 Annual Program Plan.
    Division of Education, Department of Special
    Education, Boston.
Commonwealth of Virginia (1979) Virginia Code Ann.
    22-9.1:04 (Cumulative Supp. 1979).

Gallagher, James T., Forsythe, Patrice, Ringelheim,
    Daniel, and Weintraub, Frederick J. (1975) Funding
    Patterns and Labeling. In N. Hobbs, ed., Issues in
    the Classification of Children. Vol. 2. San Francisco,
    Calif.: Jossey-Bass.
Gary W. v. State of Louisiana, 437 F. Supp. 1209 (E.D.
    La. 1976).
Larry P. v. Riles, 343 F. Supp. 1306 (N.D. Cal. 1972)
    (order granting preliminary injunction) aff'd. 502 F.
    2d 963 (9th Cir. 1974), 495 F. Supp. 926 (N.D. Cal.
    1979) (decision on merits) appeal docketed, No.
    80-4027 (9th Cir., Jan. 15, 1980).
Lora v. Board of Education, 456 F. Supp. 1211 (E.D. N. Y.
    1978).
Louisiana Department of Education (1979) Louisiana Annual
    Program Plan, Fiscal Year 1979. Baton Rouge, La.:
    Department of Education.
Lowenbraun, Sheila, and Afflect, James Q. (1978) Least
    Restrictive Environment. Pp. 30-34 in Office of
    Education, Developing Criteria for the Evaluation of
    the Least Restrictive Environment Provision.
    Washington, D.C.: Bureau of Education for the
    Handicapped.
Massachusetts Board of Education (1979) Annual Report
    1977-1978. Bureau of Educational Information
    Services. Boston: Department of Education.
Mattie T. v. Holliday, Civil Action No. DC 75-31-5 (N.D.
    Miss., July 28, 1977, February 22, 1979).
Note (1979) Enforcing the Right to an Appropriate
    Education: The Education for All Handicapped Children
    Act of 1975. Harvard Law Review 92(March):1110-1112.
O'Neill, Dave M. (1976) Discrimination Against
    Handicapped Persons: The Cost Benefits and Economic
    Impact of Implementing Section 504 of the
    Rehabilitation Act of 1973 Covering Recipients of HEW
    Financial Assistance. Prepared by the Public Research
    Institute, Arlington, Va., for the Office of Civil
    Rights, HEW Order SA-4141-76, Washington, D.C.
PASE v. Hannon, No. 74-C-3586 (N.D. Ill., July 16, 1980).
Porter, David O., Warner, David C., and Porter, Teddie W.
    (1973) The Politics of Budgetary Federal Aid:
    Resource Mobilization by Local School Districts.
    Beverly Hills, Calif.: Sage.
Simons, Janet M. and Dwyer, Barbara (1978) Education for
    the Handicapped. In M.F. Williams, ed., Government in
    the Classroom: Dollars and Power in Education.
    Academy of Political Science Proceedings 33(2): 1-156.

U.S. Department of Education (1980) Final Report of The
Secretary of the Task Force on Equal Educational
Opportunity for Handicapped Children. Washington,
D.C.: Department of Education.

U.S. Department of Health, Education, and Welfare
(1979a) Progress Toward A Free Appropriate Public
Education: A Report to Congress on the Implementation
of Public Law 94-142, The Education for All
Handicapped Children Act. Office of Education.
Washington, D.C.: Department of Health, Education,
and Welfare.

_____(1979b) Progress Toward a Free
Appropriate Public Education: A Report to Congress on
the Implementation of Public Law 94-142, The Education
for All Handicapped Children Act. Interim report of
the Office of Education, August 1979. Washington,
D.C.: U.S. Department of Health, Education, and
Welfare.

_____(1979c) Service Delivery Assessment:
Education for the Handicapped. Unpublished report
dated April 1979, from the Inspector General's Office,
U.S. Department of Health, Education, and Welfare,
Washington, D.C.

Virginia Board of Education (1978) 1977-78 Report on
Public Education in Virginia. Richmond, Va.: Board
of Education.

Virginia Department of Education (1978) The Regulations
and Administrative Requirements for the Operation of
Special Education Programs in Virginia. Chapter Six,
effective September 1, 1978. Division of Special
Education Support Services. Richmond, Va.:
Department of Education.

_____(1979) Annual Report 1977-1978.
Superintendent of Public Instruction. Richmond, Va.:
Department of Education.

Virginia House of Delegates (1977) Report to the Governor
and the General Assembly of Virginia. House Document
16. Subcommittee on the Placement of Children,
Committee on Health, Welfare, and Institutions.
Richmond, Va.: Department of Purchases and Supply.

Wisconsin Department of Public Instruction (1979)
Wisconsin Annual 94-142 Program Plan, Appendix B.
Madison, Wis.: Department of Public Instruction.

A Research Design

The research design of this study was multifaceted and consisted of three major, interrelated components: federal program analyses, state case studies, and analyses of a range of facilities serving status offenders in the states included in this study. The following is a brief discussion of these three components, the sampling criteria involved, and the procedures employed in carrying out the analysis.

STATE CASE STUDIES

Selection Criteria

Seven states were selected for intensive study: Arizona, Louisiana, Massachusetts, Pennsylvania, Utah, Virginia, and Wisconsin. The process of state selection involved three steps:

1. All states were arrayed along a continuum of high to low rates of growth in public and private juvenile institutions for the time period 1970 to 1974.
2. Each state was then assigned to one of four cells representing public and private institutional growth rates (i.e., High-High, High-Low, Low-High, Low-Low).
3. Within each category, states were ranked according to how well they conformed to the category label.

723

A fifth category was subsequently added to accommodate states with very little change during the period. Ultimately, our choices were made from states that fell within the interquartile range of each category. While the overriding objective was to make final choices that would maximize variance in the kinds of placement alternatives among states, given the pre-Juvenile Justice and Delinquency Prevention Act data base, factors such as geographic region, urban/rural composition, and presence of diverse and significant minority populations were relevant as well.

It was assumed throughout that data on institutional populations of juveniles give a good indication of the comparable situation of status offenders. Prior to 1974, data on juveniles in public institutions were not typically reported by offense type. We focused on changes in the populations of juveniles in different institutional arrangements because we felt that this was the best single indicator of statewide changes in the treatment of juveniles. We had also explored the relationship between deinstitutionalization rates and such factors as delinquency rates, state per-capita income, portion of the state budget spent on juvenile institutions, median education of the population at large, and several other socioeconomic variables. However, the relationships between deinstitutionalization rates and such variables generally were found to be quite small.

The years 1970 to 1974 were chosen as a baseline period. The choice of this period has several attractive features. In contrast to a single time point, the four-year period establishes a trend and is hence much less subject to historically idiosyncratic fluctuations. The U.S. Census (decennial) provides reliable population counts for the 1970 period. Furthermore, the Law Enforcement Assistance Administration (LEAA) census of juveniles in custody as of 1974 was conducted by the U.S. Census Bureau using comparable sampling strategies, definitions, and time-frame references, thus providing comparability in the design of the data-gathering effort.

State-Based Research

The state-based component of the study proceeded in three stages. In each of the seven states the first stage involved providing a comprehensive description of the public systems that serve status offenders and their relationship to federal programs and policies; the second stage focused on comparing two regional or local areas within the state in order to uncover intrastate variations in the intake, processing, placement, and services for these youth; the third stage involved visiting a select number of programs representing a range of placement alternatives. In each state, primary attention focused on youth who commit status offenses in several interrelated categories and contexts:

- Formally adjudicated and/or referred youth who are either processed by the juvenile court or are diverted to some other public or private social service agency for services and/or placement.
- Youth who have not come into contact with the juvenile court because they go (or are brought) directly to the departments of public welfare, education, mental health, and/or corrections.
- Youth whose initial contact is with a provider and who subsequently are formally (or informally) referred back to the juvenile court or the aforementioned agencies (e.g., for purposes of authorization of payment).

The scope of the inquiry was guided by our estimates of the most likely sources of available data on these youth, as well as by our reluctance to regard the juvenile justice system as the sole source of their disposition. By extending the analysis to include state and local welfare, corrections, mental health, and education systems, we hoped to describe the flow of children both within and across these systems as well as appraise the factors contributing to the rate and direction of that flow. This type of analysis de-emphasizes strict reliance on the labels per se that are attached to these children, recognizing that children with different behaviors are often given the same labels while, conversely, children with similar behaviors are frequently labeled differently.

The research consisted of semistructured interviews conducted with welfare, mental health, education, corrections, legislative, juvenile court, children's advocacy, licensing, and rate-setting personnel within each state at both state and selected local levels. Within each state, between 30 and 50 interviews were conducted (exclusive of program site visits). Persons to be interviewed were selected by identifying key agency personnel through use of state organizational charts and directories and follow-up conversations confirming their appropriateness,

as well as leads from local researchers, state justice
planning agencies, local interest groups, state legislative staffs, and so forth.

The questions posed by our two-person teams of state
investigators were designed to elicit information about
the intake, processing, placement, payment, and service
outcomes for status offenders at both the state and local
levels. Generally, we were interested in learning how
terms such as "status offender," "status offense," "diversion," "deinstitutionalization," and "detention" were
being used; how status offenders came to the attention of
the authorities; what the range of dispositions for such
youth were; who entered into the disposition decision; the
types of factors that influence that decision; how long
these procedures have been in place; the nature of the
relationship between different systems with responsibility
for these youth; the sources of payment for services rendered to status offenders; and any particular administrative, statutory, or regulatory problems posed by existing
systems of intake, processing, placement, and care for
such youth. A more extended discussion of the data collection and analysis methods used to measure the outcomes
of state deinstitutionalization activities is contained
in appendix B.

The second stage of research in each state focused on
two regional or local areas within the state in order to
round out the state-level description and document any
intrastate variations. Persons with the welfare, education, mental health, corrections, and juvenile justice
systems in positions analogous to those at the state level
were identified and interviewed along the same lines as
previously described. In addition, police, probation,
court intake, and other line personnel were sought out
and interviewed.

Selection of local areas was predicated on the same
bases as our initial state selections, that is, maximization of inter- and intrastate variation. Principal among
these bases was the rate of institutional population
growth and decline. Other important considerations included urban/rural contrasts, variations in types of court
organization and jurisdiction, concentrations of noninstitutional service arrangements, and concentrations of
status offenders. In all cases, selections were purposive, matching as closely as possible the themes and
trends that had emerged as most salient within each state.

FEDERAL PROGRAM ANALYSES

Selection Criteria

Nine federal programs were chosen for study: Title XX
social services, Title IV-B child welfare services, Title
IV-A foster care grants under AFDC, Medicaid, Title I of
the Elementary and Secondary Education Act (ESEA), and the
Education to All Handicapped Children Program (referred
to as P.L. 94-142); the study also reviewed the Runaway
Youth Act and selected programs operating out of LEAA that
dealt with juveniles. These program choices were consistent with the objective of assessing the impact of a wide
range of federal programs with different but substantial
actual or potential effects on status offenders and those
dependent and neglected children who were or would have
been confined in juvenile detention and correctional
facilities.

In general, criteria for selection of federal programs
for analysis included (1) the potential impact on these
youth, (2) the amount of money appropriated and/or spent
on them, (3) the comparative size of the population actually or potentially affected by the program, and (4) diversity in the types of services and the contexts within
which they could be provided to these youth.

Federal Program Research

Research on federal programs was conducted more or less
simultaneously at the federal and state levels. In making
the data collection efforts parallel, the objective was
to gain as complete an understanding as possible of both
the structure and function of these programs as well as
the diversified nature of their impacts.

At the federal level the research focused on gathering
general background information on the legislative intent
and origins of each program, and their respective administrative and regulatory procedures and effects.   The
sources of information reviewed included federal statutes
and regulations, congressional hearings and reports, policy issuances, statistical reports, federally sponsored
audits and evaluations, and the general literature of
federal policy implementation. Interviews were also conducted with federal program staff.

At the state level we were concerned with general program operation (e.g., program size, purpose, methods of

administration, monitoring, and compliance), the degree
to which the purposes and procedures of the program were
consistent with the deinstitutionalization mandate, the
manner in which the programs were implemented and used at
the state and local levels, the degree and manner in which
the programs had been adapted for use for status offenders, and the types of structural, regulatory, and/or administrative impediments posed by the programs themselves
to states and localities seeking to comply with the deinstitutionalization mandate.

Interviews were conducted in each state with state
personnel involved directly with the federal program, as
well as with those responsible for the administration of
service programs that use those federal funds. One of the
purposes of these interviews was to clarify and supplement
information beyond that provided in various public documents concerning program operations. These documents
included federally specified state plans, state laws and
regulations, policy and administrative manuals, statistical and fiscal reports, and legislative and administrative
evaluation reports. A second purpose of these interviews
was to discover any formal or informal program interactions with services for status offenders.

FACILITY ANALYSES

Selection Criteria

Thirty facilities across six of the seven states included
in the study constituted the sample. Given the concentration of services in urban areas and the number of urban
youth placed in these facilities, the decision was made
to concentrate on a range of programs located in the major
metropolitan areas of the states studied. Because the
Wisconsin study did not include the major metropolitan
area of the state (Milwaukee), it was not a part of this
particular analysis.

To obtain a cross section of types of facilities and
to allow for comparison across states, four program types
representing a range of residential services for youth
were specified a priori as facility types to be included
in the analyses: (1) a secure detention facility serving
the metropolitan area; (2) an alternative to detention,
typically an emergency shelter care facility or nonsecure
detention center; (3) a group home; and (4) a residential
treatment facility.

Across the states there are varying definitional categories for facilities such that there was often little consistency. Hence, operational definitions were adopted for each facility type to maximize comparability across cities. The primary criterion for a detention facility was that it be physically secure, while a shelter facility was defined as a nonsecure alternative to detention. Group homes and residential treatment programs were distinguished primarily by size and secondarily by degree of community integration. Thus, a group home was defined as a facility serving 15 or fewer youth and using community schools; a residential treatment program was defined in terms of its capacity to serve 15 or more youth in a relatively self-contained way (e.g., typically providing an on-grounds school program for residents). Both group homes and residential treatment programs typically offered longer-term programs (i.e., six months or more) to the youth involved, while detention and shelter facilities were typically expected to be short-term (i.e., 30 days or less).

In each metropolitan area (Phoenix, Salt Lake City, New Orleans, Philadelphia, Boston, and Richmond), one of each of these four types of facilities was visited. In addition, a program considered to be a model facility, irrespective of program type, consitituted a fifth site visited in each city. Thus, the total sample of 30 facilities included six detention centers, six shelter facilities, six group homes, six residential treatment programs, and six identified model programs (two group homes and four residential treatment facilities). The particular programs were chosen on the basis of the recommendations of the state-based investigators who in turn were reporting the programs most frequently identified by state and local officials over the course of their interviews. In addition, specific suggestions were sought from persons in each state who were more directly involved in the child care system. This process of site selection probably resulted in the identification of slightly "better" programs—more stable or more visible programs in the larger service network of each area—and as such has implications for the generalizability of the observations.

Facility-Based Research

The facility analyses were based on a modified assessment strategy designed to allow for a qualitative and quantita-

tive evaluation of a sample of placement facilities along
the dimension defined by "institutional" at one extreme
and "normal" at the other. In the absence of a longitudinal analysis of changes in the nature of these facilities,
two theoretical models were adopted by which to characterize these extremes: Erving Goffman's definitional characteristics of total institutions (1961), and Wolf Wolfensberger's "normalization" schema (1972).

Elaborating on the operational definitions that stem
from these models, a multilevel, ecological model of program evaluation was developed. The program settings were
assessed in terms of the following general categories: (1)
the extent to which the facilities were integrated within
their community systems and maintain or promote healthy
liaisons with residents' families, as opposed to remaining
isolated and being viewed as rehabilitative/treatment
facilities for the deviant; (2) the amount of autonomy and
responsibility afforded residents; (3) the degree of flexibility in individual programming; (4) the resident and
staff sense of efficacy regarding program and individual
concerns; (5) the quality of resident/staff interaction;
(6) program goals, philosophy, and source of financial
sponsorship; and (7) formal rules and policies regarding
admission, programming, and discharge. Information was
also collected on resident/staff characteristics and the
history and intent of the programs.

Although the specific format of each visit was flexible, every effort was made to keep the time actually spent
in each facility comparable. Similarly, uniform information was sought from each program. Additionally, the
Program Analysis of Service Systems (PASS) (Wolfensberger
and Glenn 1975) was modified and employed as a standard
"normalization" measure in each facility (see appendix C).
The primary questions addressed in the data analysis concern the degree to which these settings provide an alternative to institutional settings and are consistent with
the intentions of the Juvenile Justice and Delinquency
Prevention Act.

Program visits took place over the course of the summer
and fall of 1980. All visits were made by the same team
of trained observers. The team was occasionally joined
by the principal investigator of the facility-based research as a means of assessing the reliability of the data
being recorded. Each visit was scheduled to last two full
days. A typical visit began with a 2- to 3-hour interview
with the program director that focused on program history,
philosophy, current operations, goals, and future direc-

tions. The director and supervisory staff reviewed the scheduled activities with the observer team whose own schedule was then set to include staff meetings or briefings, group resident activities (recreation, eating, counseling sessions, etc.), and a wide range of informal interactions with both residents and staff. Most facilities indicated that they had not made any special arrangements or plans for the visits. These comments were frequently corroborated by the staff's unawareness of the visit, or by information from the residents. Of course, there were exceptions. Overall, however, the visits and the observations seemed to represent a good cross section of the nature of the activity and the day-to-day operations in these program types during the time that they were visited (e.g., summer, rather than school term).

REFERENCES

Goffman, Erving (1961) Asylums: Essays on the Social Situation of Mental Patients and Other Inmates Garden City, N.Y.: Anchor Books.
Wolfensberger, Wolf (1972) The Principle of Normalization in Human Services. Toronto: National Institute on Mental Retardation.
Wolfensberger, Wolf, and Glenn, Laura (1975) PASS 3, A Method for the Quantitative Evaluation of Human Services. Toronto: National Institute on Mental Retardation.

Data Analysis:
APPENDIX
B Methods and Problems in the State Case Studies

INTRODUCTION

This project has three major components: federal program analyses, state case studies, and facility analyses. We are concerned here with evaluating the data collection and analysis methods used in the state case studies to measure the outcomes of efforts to deinstitutionalize status offenders (chapters 10 through 16). Special consideration is given to these particular data for two reasons. First, the state and local outcomes of deinstitutionalization efforts are the primary variables that we have tried to measure and explain. This is consistent with the backward mapping approach outlined in chapter 1 and elaborated in chapter 4. Second, data necessary to measure these outcomes were often not available or were of questionable quality, forcing modifications in our planned design. Thus, we think it is important to discuss how we dealt with these problems and arrived at our general conclusions about the outcomes of deinstitutionalization in chapter 5. We hope this discussion not only will assist the reader in interpreting and evaluating our findings and conclusions, but also will prove helpful to future scholarly attempts to measure the outcomes of deinstitutionalization efforts.

732

FRAMEWORK FOR EVALUATION OF DATA AND DATA INTERPRETATION

Efforts to deinstitutionalize status offenders have at least four potential outcomes, which are reflected in the following research questions:

1. To what extent has the secure placement of adjudicated status offenders been reduced?
2. To what extent has the detention of preadjudicated status offenders been reduced?
3. To what extent have status offenders been diverted from the juvenile justice system?
4. Where are status offenders going who are not being securely detained or confined?

Data to address each of these questions were gathered and analyzed for each of our seven states and fourteen local areas and then aggregated in chapter 5 to formulate the generalized answers to the questions. Therefore, the credibility of our general conclusions depends on the validity of the state and local data.

In order to assess that validity, the four research questions will be considered seriatim. After restating each question, we present a summary of the data drawn from each of the state case studies (including the data from the local areas in that state) to answer the question. Those data are then evaluated in terms of the following three criteria:

Suitability and consistency of empirical indicators. Included in each question is one or more key concepts, such as diversion or secure detention, that requires delineation of empirical indicators by which it can be measured. We evaluate the rationale for the selection of a particular indicator, and judge the advantages and disadvantages associated with that selection. Second, we examine the consistency of indicators across states and within states (in some instances the same indicator was not available in all locations, which led to problems of comparability and interpretation).

Data availability. We discuss the extent to which appropriate data were available for the needed time periods.

Data quality. This dimension of evaluation concerns how much confidence we can have in the accuracy of the data used.

EVALUATION OF DATA AND DATA INTERPRETATION

Question 1: To what extent has the secure placement of adjudicated status offenders been reduced?

A. Relevant data from the case studies:
    Arizona, Tables 10-2 and 10-11
    Louisiana, Table 11-2
    Massachusetts, pp. 335-336
    Pennsylvania, pp. 380-381
    Utah, Figure 14-2, pp. 438-439
    Virginia, Table 15-2
    Wisconsin, Table 16-3, pp. 533-536

B. Evaluation of data:
    Suitability and consistency of empirical indicators.
Postadjudicatory secure placement has been defined as placement in the traditional red-brick reformatories, and an adjudicated status offender was defined as a youth who was sent to such an institution by a court for a status offense. As was pointed out by some of the key informants in our states, there is a potential problem in using this indicator. Although the committing offense may have been a status offense, sometimes the youth was actually guilty of a delinquent offense but had the charge reduced. It was contended that some youth who were labeled status offenders and placed in secure facilities were not "pure" status offenders, and that their placement therefore was not inappropriate. Similarly, there appears to be some inconsistency in how a youth who was charged with a status offense, and then violated probation, should be labeled. Is the youth still a status offender, or is he or she a delinquent for having violated probation?
    Data availability. Again, data appear to be generally available to answer this question because of federal mandates to collect such data. Also as before, there is normally only one before-and-after data point, not more extensive time-series data.
    An additional problem is demonstrated in Pennsylvania, where changes in law caused changes in data recording and, therefore, in the ability to conduct research. In 1977 that state transferred status offenders to a category labeled dependent, which includes all cases of neglect, abandonment, abuse, truancy, and habitual disobedience. No special designation was created for status offenders, and they are currently indistinguishable under Pennsylvania law from all others in the dependency category.

This also led to the disappearance of status offenses as a separate statistical category. Therefore, it became impossible to trace directly the changing patterns of status offender placement.

Data quality. The data to answer this question seem to be of the highest quality encountered in the study, resulting from the fact that it is relatively easy to determine how many and what type of children are located in secure facilities for adjudicated youth. As we will see, it is much more difficult to determine how many children are in less secure private facilities.

Question 2: To what extent has the detention of preadjudicated status offenders been reduced?

A.   Relevant data from the case studies:
     Arizona, Table 10-5
     Louisiana, Table 11-1
     Massachusetts, pp. 340-343
     Pennsylvania, pp. 400-401
     Utah, Table 14-4
     Virginia, Table 15-3
     Wisconsin, pp. 552-553

B.   Evaluation of data:
     Suitability and consistency of empirical indicators. The key concepts in this question are detention and preadjudicated status offender. The indicator used in all states was the number of youth accused of a status offense as their highest offense, and who were detained in a secure facility during a specified period of time (month, year). We were not concerned with length of stay, although all of the states appear to record only those youth who were detained for more than 24 hours. The meaning of secure detention was consistent across states because a single definition was mandated by the OJJDP.
     Data availability. There were data available for addressing this question in all seven states. This appears to be due to the fact that such data were required by the OJJDP for monitoring purposes. In fact, we found that throughout the study the best data were always those required by some agency, either federal or state, for monitoring purposes. Data were available for all seven states, but tended to be appropriate for only simple before-and-after research designs. In other words data were available on secure detention of status offenders for one or two time points before the state entered the JJDPA

and for a few points after. This type of data is appropriate for the monitoring purposes of the JJDPA, but frus-
trates any efforts to determine whether the observed
changes were a direct result of the act or reflected a
preexisting trend.

    Data quality. The major problem of data quality is
that all of our statistics were gathered by the relevant
agencies themselves. For example, it was the local county
court that determined the number of accused status offenders detained. This creates the possibility of systematic
relabeling or mislabeling of youth. This possibility
appears to be greatest in Richmond, Virginia, where,
concomitant with the reduction in the number of status
offenders at various points in the system, there was an
increase in the number of minor delinquents. This
suggests that some youth may have been labeled delinquent
to avoid the detention prohibition of the OJJDP for status
offenders. However, with the exception of Virginia, data
and expert opinion appear not to point toward that conclusion.

Question 3:   To what extent have status offenders been
diverted from the juvenile justice system?

A.   Relevant data from the case studies:
     Arizona, Table 10-4
     Louisiana, Table 11-3
     Massachusetts, pp. 355-357
     Pennsylvania, Tables 13-1, 13-2. p. 393
     Utah, pp. Table 14-1, pp. 435-437
     Virginia, Tables 15-3, 15-6, 15-7
     Wisconsin, Table 16-5, pp. 537-539

B.   Evaluation of data:
     Suitability and consistency of empirical indicators.
This question presented us with the problem of determining
an appropriate empirical indicator of diversion. Before
doing that, however, it was necessary to examine the competing conceptualizations of that term. Two were considered. The first defined diversion as a process that
prevents an accused status offender from entering the
juvenile justice system; the second also would include a
process that allows status offenders to enter the juvenile
court system briefly, if they were then referred elsewhere. We saw no theoretically justifiable reason to
select one or the other of these conceptualizations and
therefore examined both.

In terms of selecting empirical indicators, differentiating between the two conceptualizations of diversion became a moot issue because of data availability problems. Arrest and referral rates for status offenders were the only available data that were relevant to diversion. We used these measures on the grounds that a reduction in either would reflect a drop in the number of youth entering the juvenile justice system, and therefore would also imply an increase in diversion. This limited data did not allow us, however, to measure the second conceptualization of diversion, namely, the number of youth who enter the juvenile court and are referred elsewhere.

The major problem associated with these measures is the lack of consistent data across states. We could not obtain data for a single indicator from all seven states; consequently, it was necessary to examine this question with arrest data from some states and referral data from others. While we realize the potential problems associated with this inconsistency, we feel that an adequate general picture is presented of changes in diversion.

Data availability. As we have just discussed, the major problem of data availability was the lack of consistency in types of data for all states. Additionally, data were only available for relatively short time periods.

Data quality. These data seem to be reliable, subject to the problems of self-labeling noted with regard to Questions 1 and 2.

Question 4: Where are status offenders, who are not being securely detained, going now (both pre- and postadjudication)?

A. Relevant data from the case studies:
    Arizona, Tables 10-9 and 10-10, pp. 284-286
    Louisiana, p. 321
    Massachusetts, pp. 345-346
    Pennsylvania, Table 13-8
    Utah, pp. 440-441
    Virginia, Table 15-5
    Wisconsin, pp. 543-544

B. Evaluation of data:
    Suitability and consistency of empirical indicators. Our primary concern here was to determine where pre- and postadjudicated status offenders are now being placed, given the decreased use of secure placements. Of partic-

ular concern was the degree to which in-home services had
increased and the relative use of foster care, group
homes, and institutions for out-of-home placements.

    Data availability. Data to answer this question were
almost nonexistent in all states, which appears to be due
to three factors. First, OJJDP mandated that certain
types of youth could not be placed in secure facilities,
and this was monitored to demonstrate compliance. OJJDP
did not, however, mandate what must consequently be done
with these youth, and therefore no such data collection
occurred. Second, although it is relatively easy to
determine the population of secure state facilities, it
is very difficult to determine the populations of the
numerous public and private nonsecure facilities in the
social service system to which status offenders might be
referred. Therefore, while our research efforts were
equally concerned with the corrections, juvenile justice,
and social service systems, the first two had consistently
more and better data than the latter. Thus, we were able
to answer Questions 1 through 3, but were unable adequately to answer Question 4.

    Finally, when we talk about where these status of-
fenders are now going, we are confronted with the fact
that youth are often moving back and forth between the
juvenile justice and social service systems. This causes
severe data problems because these systems tend to have
distinctly different data collection procedures and do not
have tracking systems that allow tracing the movement of
youth from one system to another. Utah is attempting to
overcome this problem by establishing a uniform tracking
system, but it generally remains difficult to determine
where these youth are now going. Clearly, this is a question that must be addressed further with another research
design.

CONCLUSIONS

We have tried to present the reader with an explicit overview of the data problems we encountered in this study.
We believe that most of these problems are endemic to this
type of research, and that our design has handled them in
the most appropriate manner possible. For example, the
following data problems have been isolated:

    1. Lack of time-series data.
    2. Labeling procedures by the agencies themselves,

resulting in idiosyncratic reporting and potential biases (e.g., mislabeling or relabeling).

    3.   Inconsistent data available across locations.

    4.   The problems of inconsistent data when dealing with two separate systems, such as the juvenile justice system and the social service system.

Given our research purposes, none of these problems seems to be amenable to correction through a different design.

    Finally, it should be kept in mind that in this appendix we have only considered one part of the two-part research procedure used in the state case studies. In addition to the data reviewed here, each of the studies contained information gathered through in-depth interviews with key actors in the youth social service and justice systems. Our findings and conclusions are based on both of these sources of information.

APPENDIX
C

Multicomponent Assessment of Residential Services for Youth (MARSY)

JEAN ANN LINNEY

Various assessment materials were used to gather information on the services provided to youth in out-of-home placements. The Administrative Questionnaire, the Program History Recording Form, the Program Variables Recording Form, and Location and Physical Plant Recording Form were developed to assess programmatic, organizational, and environmental variables in each facility. The Post-Observation Ratings are drawn from the Multiphasic Environmental Assessment Procedures (Moos and Lemke 1979). The PASS-3 (Wolfensberger and Glenn 1975) was modified to apply to residential settings for youth; it assesses the degree to which each setting is consistent with the "normalization" ideology. Facscimiles of all recording forms appear at the end of this appendix.

PASS-JM

The PASS-3 (Wolfensberger and Glenn 1975) was modified for use in residential facilities for children and youth in two primary ways: (1) it was shortened from 50 items to 35 items, and (2) descriptors of item ratings were modified to be more relevant to an adolescent population. The factor analytic work of Flynn and Heal (1980) suggested retention of 18 items from the PASS-3. These items and an additional 17 items most relevant to normalization in out-of-home placements for youth are included in this modified version of the PASS-3.

The following are item descriptors for the 35 items constituting the PASS-JM. The user should refer to Wolfensberger and Glenn's (1975) description of the PASS-3 procedures and become familiar with the normalization ideology before using this shortened version of the PASS. The ratings are similar in basic content and ideology to those of the PASS-3, with descriptor examples for juvenile facilities. The PASS-3 field manual should also be consulted in the completion of these ratings. The scoring procedure described is based on the prorating method presented in Wolfensberger and Glenn (1975) and allows for comparison of PASS-JM scores with norms for the PASS-3.

Local Proximity

1. Facility is physically remote from any population cluster e.g, a residential treatment facility in a rural area 10 miles from the nearest town.

2. Facility close to but not in a population cluster, e.g., an emergency shelter on the outskirts of town.

3. Facility located within a population cluster but with improvements possible, e.g., detention facility located within city (population cluster) but not at center.

4. Optimal location at center of population cluster.

Regional Proximity

1. Facility located on edge of or outside of its catchment area or defined service region, and majority of clients come from another community e.g., detention facility serving city population located in the suburban area.

2. Less severe dislocations, but substantial distance from facility location and regional populations distribution.

3. Moderate dislocation, e.g., a diagnostic center at the geographic center of the region, but population scattered in northeastern area of region.

4. Distinct but minor dislocation of facility site relative to regional population.

5. Location at center of region's population distribution being centrally located for almost all of facility's potential population.

Access

Use rating table from PASS-3 to rate speed and convenience of access considering routes of access, variety in
means of access, facility proximity to these routes and
safety for families, local and regional clientele, and the
public.

Physical Resources

1. Facility located in setting without resources for
social integration (e.g., restaurants, parks, shopping
facilities, library, movie theater) or these physical
resources are too far or too difficult to reach by residents.
2. Physical resources seriously limited in number and
variety, or difficult to assess (e.g., require long walk
or use of irregular public transportation system).
3. Physical resources accessible with relative ease,
but variety and number available somewhat limited (e.g.,
group home located two blocks from drug store and small
reraurant, but not near recreational or educational resources).
4. Acceptable number of socially integrative resources
available for facility.
5. Optimal availability of physical resources in both
number and variety.

Note: Include only relevant resources and rate presence
of resources, not utilization by residents.

Program-Neighborhood Harmony

1. Program grossly inappropriate to the general neighborhood context, its presence highly nonnormative and
draws undue attention or strong deviancy image to residents and programs (e.g., runaway shelter located on state
hospital grounds, group home located in decaying, industrial area of town).
2. Location inappropriate although not so grossly as
in Level 1, but differentness implies deviancy image,
(e.g., emergency shelter adjacent to adult jail complex).
3. Location inappropriate although not so grossly as
in Level 1; differentness apt to draw undue attention
rather than deviancy image, (e.g., emergency shelter facility in a professional building).

4. Facility within the range of normative matching with the ambience of the neighborhood.

5. Optimal location in neighborhood matching facility type and enhancing the status of residents, (e.g., group home located among fraternity houses on college campus).

Congregation and Assimilation Potential

Use rating table from the PASS-3 to rate the potential for neighborhood assimilation of facility residents. The rating is primarily concerned with the size of the facility population and the relationship between this number and the number of community systems capable of integrating these individuals.

Program Name

1. Program name (or part of name) is extremely detrimental to a nondeviant perception and/or apt to set up barriers to social integration (e.g., "institution," "hospital," "detention," "asylum," or inclusion of term "juvenile delinquency").

2. Program name inappropriate in unnecessarily suggesting deviancy or impairment, but not apt to constitute significant barrier to social integration (e.g., "rehab center"; "halfway house"; names suggesting pity, charity, or dependency, including "home," "haven," "hope" (as in Hope House), "shelter").

3. Program name does not suggest deviancy but is operated by an agency with a clearly deviancy-associated name (e.g., Association for Retarded Citizens), or the name suggests deviancy because other facilities nearby are not named (e.g., a group home in a residential neighborhood with a sign identifying it as "Gemini House").

4. Name and labels do not suggest deviancy, but no effort taken to pursue even more favorable labels.

5. Favorable program name which enhances image of clients (e.g., vocational program named "Futuristic Industries").

Function-Congruity Image

1. Facility building appearance grossly incongruent with program type such that community's perception of the

residents would seriously inhibit social integration
(e.g., a runaway shelter in a former jail).

2. Mild to moderate incongruity (e.g., a group home
in a hospital building, a residential treatment program
in a factory building).

3. Facility adequately within the range of normative
building function images, but minor discrepancies exist
(e.g., building atypically large or small for the type of
service).

4. Function-congruity image optimal both in size and
design (e.g., a group home in an average sized family home
building).

Building-Neighborhood Harmony

1. Building clashes with neighborhood surroundings and
strongly suggests deviancy (e.g., a group home in a residential neighborhood with a security-type fence when no
other house has one; house in need of building repairs so
as to appear grossly neglected in contrast to rest of
neighborhood, parking area substituted for front yard area
to accommodate staff parking).

2. Minor disharmony (e.g., broken screens or broken
furniture kept on the house porch, absence of yard landscaping when other buildings are well landscaped).

3. Harmony between building and neighborhood; facility
not distinguishable from other buildings surrounding it.

4. Building blends perfectly with neighborhood and
continuous efforts to normalize physical aspects of the
facility are apparent (e.g., painting exteriors, decorating for Christmas).

Deviancy Image Juxtaposition

1. Any imagery, symbolism, or history that reinforces
strong deviancy image, such as subhumanity, criminality,
corruption, disease, or worthlessness (e.g, a group home
for females housed in a building that was formerly a house
of ill repute).

2. Level 1 conditions are present, but not to an extreme degree (e.g., a funding source is deviancy labeled,
a runaway shelter is housed in the Salvation Army mission
building).

3. Deviancy image juxtaposition may exist, but is
minor or relatively invisible (e.g, a group home shares
recreation facilities on the state hospital grounds).

4. No discernable deviancy image juxtaposition.

5. No deviancy image juxtaposition; instead positive, status-enhancing image juxtaposition exists (e.g., vocational development program for juvenile offenders shares building with Junior Achievement).

Deviancy Program Juxtaposition

1. Devastating and extremely injurious juxtaposition of facility and other deviancy program(s)--group home for youth adjacent to a halfway house for alcoholics; a juvenile detention facility adjacent to an adult maximum security prison (while two deviancy programs are involved, the severe deviancy of the adult facility spills over affecting the less deviant juvenile facility).

2. Level 1 conditions present to a less serious degree.

3. Minor deviancy program juxtaposition exists.

4. No discernable deviancy program juxtaposition.

5. Appropriate program juxtaposition and efforts apparent to locate facility to enhance positive and valued program juxtaposition (e.g, emergency shelter placed near YMCA or 4-H office).

Deviant Staff Juxtaposition

1. 30 percent or more of the staff consists of rehabilitated deviant persons or persons generally viewed by the community as dropouts or undesirables (e.g., ex-felons, former drug addicts. Include consideration of style of dress and general appearance in context of community norms).

2. 5-30 percent of the staff are perceived as deviant.

3. Project is virtually devoid of deviant workers or type of differentness present is not highly devalued.

4. No transferable staff deviancy, and staff tend to have high status in the public eye (e.g., shelter facility operated by University divinity students).

Deviant Client & Other Juxtaposition

1. Juxtaposition of residents and other clients or persons characterized by different types of deviance to such an extent that strong deviancy image transfer or

generalization is likely (e.g., a shelter facility for runaways also provides shelter for prostitutes).

2. Level 1 conditions exist but to a lesser degree or deviancy involved is less severe.

3. Deviant juxtaposition exists to only a minor degree (e.g., residents of a group home for status offenders and a group home for psychiatric outpatients meet weekly for a recreational program).

4. No deviant client juxtaposition exists.

5. No deviant juxtaposition exists and program has succeeded in accomplishing client/other juxtapositions that enhance, generalize, or transfer status.

Socially Integrative Social Activities

1. Few or no feasible structures and/or activities exist to promote involvement of residents in culturally normative integrative activities. Contact with "ordinary" citizens in culturally typical activities is extremely limited or nonexistent. "Secure" facilities and totally self-contained programs would be rated Level 1.

2. Some integrative social activities occur, but quantity or quality is limited (e.g., residents of a residential school go bowling in community facility but only in large, segregated group).

3. Moderate degree of integrative activity occurs (e.g., residents attend public school but are transported by facility and are not permitted to remain at school after closing).

4. Extensive provisions are made for integrative activities but some segregation exists (e.g., youth attend local concerts and dances but early curfew necessitates leaving before the end).

5. Maximum efforts to integrate residents in culturally normative community activities so that assimilation is maximized.
(See Table in PASS-3 materials for areas and degree of integration.)

Age-Appropriate Facilities

1. Gross incongruities between appearance and design of building and life-age of residents.

2. Distinct and major incongruities exist, but are not as extreme as Level 1.

3. Minor and subtle incongruities exist (e.g., pictures and decor in a group home for adolescents are suggestive of young childhood).

4. No age incongruities exist.

5. No age incongruities and positive efforts to appropriately match age of residents.
(It is expected that most facilities will be level 4; however facilities changing populations may display incongruities.)

Age-Appropriate Activities

1. Grossly inappropriate activities and routines for age group of residents; note curfews, bedtimes recreational activities, school schedule, etc.

2. Activities and routines are inappropriate for age group but inconsistency not as severe as Level 1.

3. Only minor incongruities exist (e.g., recess or break periods during an educational program are long or quite frequent, suggesting play atmosphere or underdeveloped attention span for adolescents).

4. Activities within the normative range

5. Activities culturally normative and systematic, and staff are acutely sensitive to the issues involved so as to maintain appropriate developmental match.

Age-Appropriate Labels & Forms of Address

1. Staff use highly age-inappropriate forms of address in speaking to or about clients, either implying younger or older age and competence.

2. Effort at age-appropriate address apparent, but limited by lack of commitment from staff. Note consistency between forms of address and labels employed when staff speak about residents and speak directly to residents.

3. Age-appropriate address with only minor deviations (e.g., condescending tones of voice or gestures).

4. Labels used are age-appropriate.

5. Staff "bend over backward" to use forms of address that are age appropriate and status enhancing. Staff commitment may be evidenced in verbal and nonverbal ways.

Age-Appropriate Autonomy & Rights

1. Little or no concern for age-appropriate legal and human rights of residents; residents may be given no choice in activites or no independence of movement.
2. Significant infringement exists, but not as extreme as Level 1.
3. Apparent, overt expectations regarding autonomy and rights are met, but staff lack awareness and/or commitment to these issues (e.g., residents may choose recreational activities but have no method for appealing staff decisions).
4. Staff display desired commitment, and allow for resident autonomy in most instances. Some shortcomings exist, perhaps related to staff belief that certain rights and autonomy should not be afforded the residents.
5. Program continuously encourages resident autonomy and protects age-appropriate rights.

Age-Appropriate Possessions

1. Possessions are grossly inappropriate in regard to the age differential they imply.
2. Moderate age inappropriateness, (e.g., adolescents having possessions suggestive of mature adulthood or childhood).
3. Only minor inappropriateness apparent.
4. Age inappropriateness in possession is virtually absent and staff are sensitive to these issues.

Age-Appropriate Sex Behavior

1. Grossly inappropriate practices (e.g., no opportunities for heterosexual interaction or socialization).
2. Significant but not gross shortcomings (e.g., residents may interact with members of the opposite sex, but no dating is allowed).
3. Residents may engage in age-appropriate socialization with members of both sexes and are supported in such activities (e.g., dating allowed, may be alone in some parts of the facility with a friend).
4. Extensive support and guidance in areas related to appropriate sexual behavior, (e.g., sex education provided, appropriate role models available).
5. Program so advanced, it constitutes a model for others.

Culture-Appropriate Internal Design (internal function congruity image)

1. Role image of the residents is diminished by gross incongruities between program function and internal decor (e.g., treatment facility for juveniles housed in a building formerly a state hospital, with barred windows and locked doors still apparent).

2. Some loss of resident image due to culturally inappropriate internal designs.

3. Consistent internal decor and program function.

Culture-Appropriate Personal Appearance

1. Grossly culture-inappropriate personal appearance of residents marking them as deviant (e.g., donated, culturally inappropriate clothing distributed to residents).

2. Shortcomings less extreme than Level 1, but a significant projection of deviancy still exists (e.g., hairstyles, personal grooming, mannerisms).

3. Adequate attention paid to most salient aspects of culturally appropriate appearance, but attention necessary to minor, more subtle features that detract from personal appearance and make residents look odd or marginal (e.g., clothing too large or too small for residents).

4. Positive attention paid to normative aspects of appearance, few shortcomings.

5. Staff acutely aware of maximizing culturally normative personal appearance for residents and go to considerable personal and programmatic extent to accomplish these goals.

Culture-Appropriate Labels and Forms of Address

1. Demeaning or devaluing labels used by staff in reference to residents (e.g., terms labeling clients as objects, like "clinical material", referring to clients by diagnostic category such as "schizo," "ED," "JD"; or the use of stigmatizing or derogatory terms, such as "brats," "junior cons").

2. Level 1 labelling may be observed, but some effort made by agency staff to remedy the situation; or, labels or nicknames used are less demeaning than Level 1 (e.g., "fatso").

3. Staff make efforts to address residents in appropriate, courteous, and respectful manner, although underlying tone or gestures from staff suggest that residents are deviant; or manner of addressing residents indicates lack of sensitivity by staff to the individuality of the residents (e.g., addressing youth by last name only).

4. Appropriate labeling and forms of addresses are used by almost all staff most of the time. Minor shortcomings may be observed, but these are judged to be the result of changing attitudes or changing terminology in the field.

5. Staff consistently use labels and forms of address that promote and enhance the status of the residents.

Culture-Appropriate Rights

1. Little or no concern exists for the culture-appropriate legal and human rights of residents, (e.g., no provision for privacy or personal space exists).

2. Significant infringement apparent but less extreme than Level 1.

3. Overt expectations for culture-appropriate rights are met, but rather than staff commitment to these issues, only superficial compliance is evident or staff are responding to external forces such as regulations or minimum standards.

4. Staff display acceptable commitment to culture-appropriate rights but minor limitations exist, primarily in staff lack of aggressive advocacy of these issues.

5. Residents afforded culture-appropriate rights, and staff assertively encourage expression of these.

Model Coherency

This rating assesses the degree to which several program variables combine coherently and harmoniously and are consistent with the normalization ideology. The factors to be considered are client grouping by cultural norms (age, sex, etc.) and age-appropriate behavior, the human management model, manpower, program content, and program process.

1. Factors combined in grossly inappropriate manner detrimental to the needs or image of the residents (e.g., program for delinquent and dependent youth operates a

high-security and surveillance program in which program content and process are inappropriate for one or both groups of youth).

2. Two or more factors are inconsistent, but project not grossly inappropriate (e.g., program for adolescent males with some aspects of program content that are developmentally inappropriate).

3. Most facets of program combine appropriately, but some shortcomings exist (e.g., overuse of medical personnel in facility for status offenders, or counseling program for status offenders where youth are referred to as patients, or insufficient staff for size of resident groupings).

4. All variables related to model coherency combine appropriately.

5. Components so well integrated that improvements cannot be identified; program serves as a model on this dimension.

Physical Overprotection

1. For residential programs where the physical environment is protected from the residents and the residents are protected from the environment to such an extreme as to imply deficiency, irresponsibility, or lack of trust in the residents (e.g., bars on the windows, windows too small to jump from, water controls in the showers not operative by residents).

2. Nonresidential programs with Level 1 features, or residential facilities with one very definitely overprotective feature built into the environment (e.g., furniture bolted to floor or walls).

3. Only minor and tolerable overprotective features designed to reduce normative risks.

4. No unnecessary physical overprotection features; environment allows normal risks and adaptation by residents.

Social Overprotection

1. For residential programs, extreme social control and management measures present that impair dignity and status of residents; may be in the form of rules, medication, surveillance or use of special equipment (e.g., use of plastic utensils, restrictions on carrying of lighters

or matches). Need to distinguish between controls that insure reasonable protection and those of overprotection (e.g, in high crime area residents are not permitted outside facility alone to reduce risk of assault).

2. Level 1 conditions in a nonresidential program; or definite overprotective measures, but not as overpowering or extreme as Level 1.

3. Moderate overprotective social controls in only one aspect of the program.

4. No nonnormative social controls; program improvements in this area difficult to specify.

Physical Comfort

1. Absence of physical comfort perceived as intolerable by majority of residents. Note comfort in furnishings, cleanliness, temperature and light control, noise levels, quality of food, crowding, etc.

2. Shortcomings apparent but would not be considered intolerable (e.g., drafty hallways and absence of carpeting; shortage of clean comfortable clothing for residents).

3. Setting would be considered physically comfortable by majority of individuals.

4. Requirements for physical comfort met and program makes extensive efforts to provide for resident comfort.

Environmental Beauty

1. Little or no attention paid to appearance and beauty of the setting's internal environment; appears drab, barren and unattractive. Note color, decorations, arrangements, and furniture.

2. Some attempts at beautification made, but only the most obvious and superficial. Environment not unpleasant or ugly, but neither is it aesthetically appealing.

3. Obvious efforts made to enhance environmental beauty, but minor shortcomings exist (e.g., some lights do not have covers or shades; color schemes mismatched).

4. Thoughtful and appropriate beautification.

5. Great efforts made in enhancing environmental beauty, facility serves as a model.

(Note: Monetary resources may influence this rating; however, raters should bear in mind that a great deal of beautification can be achieved at little or no cost given the ideological commitment of staff.)

Individualization

1. Residential programs demonstrating total disregard for client individuality through excessive regimentation, elimination of resident choices and opportunities to personalize living space, humiliating or depersonalizing staff attitudes and program routines. Note intake procedures, programming and treatment models employed for residents.

2. Nonresidential programs having Level 1 characteristics, or presence of uniform practices or routines that minimize individualization (e.g, prohibition on decorating personal living space).

3. No obvious routines or practices that deny individuality, but neither is there support or encouragement for individualization and personalization.

4. Program permits resident individualization, but improvements possible.

5. Program allows for extensive individualization, and staff are committed to providing for and enhancing individual differences.

Interactions

Five ratings from PASS-3 assessing the quality of (1) client-staff interactions, (2) attention paid by staff to developing appropriate interactions among residents and (3) between residents and public, (4) staff-staff interactions, and (5) staff-public interactions.

Ties to Academia

1. No contact with academic center or personnel, and such contact unlikely to develop.

2. Some contact with academic centers exist (e.g., setting is practicum site, staff take courses at the college, a staff member teaches a course at the college, or concrete plans exist to restablish some relationship with academia).

3. Program maintains several signficant ties to academia (e.g., consultant or in-service training regularly occurring; ties with academia for evaluation.

4. Evidence of strong and effective ties to academia through several different means.

5. Imaginative, far-reaching relationships with academic center.

Staff Development

1. Provisions for staff development and training nonexistent.

2. Provisions for staff development are minor and appear to have minimal impact upon services (e.g., notices of outside training workshops put on bulletin board, quarterly in-service training of short duration and addressing significant isues).

3. Staff development activities appear adequate for service type but are sporadic, vary in quality and intensity, or must be sought out by staff rather than integrated into program.

4. Reasonably extensive staff development exists and is integrated into regular programming; includes orientation and ongoing supervision.

5. Near-optimal methods for staff development; program actively, provides and encourages staff to pursue multiple training and development activities, including attendance at conferences and workshops, pursuit of advanced degree, ongoing supervision, release time for staff development, payment of training expenses by program, etc.

Administrative Control and Structures

Same as PASS-3.

Program Evaluation and Renewal Mechanisms

Use tables from PASS-3 to assess awareness and frequency of evaluation measures both internal to the program and from external sources.

ADMINISTRATIVE QUESTIONNAIRE

Population served:

1. What is the <u>maximum</u> capacity of your facility? _____ residents
   What is the <u>usual</u> number of residents in your facility?
   _____ residents

2. How many residents are currently living in your facility?
   _____ residents
   How many are male?   _____
   How many are female? _____

3. What percent of your residents fall in these age categories?

   Your current residents: Your typical population:

   13 years or younger _____%   13 years or younger _____%
   14 or 15 years old   _____%   14 or 15 years old   _____%
   16 or 17 years old   _____%   16 or 17 years old   _____%
   18 or older   _____%   18 or older   _____%

4. What percent of the residents are:

   Your current residents: Your typical population:

   American Indian   _____%   American Indian   _____%
   Asian American   _____%   Asian American   _____%
   Black   _____%   Black   _____%
   Chicano/Hispanic   _____%   Chicano/Hispanic   _____%
   White   _____%   White   _____%
   Other (_____)   _____%   Other (_____)   _____%

5. What percent of the residents are fluent in a language other than
   English?
   Of your current residents: _____% What languages? _____
   Of your typical population: _____% What languages? _____

6. What percent of the resident's families live:

   Your current residents: Your typical population:

   In the same city as your   In the same city as your
   facility?   _____%   facility?   _____%
   Within 25 miles   _____%   Within 25 miles   _____%
   Within 26 to 50 miles _____%   Within 26 to 50 miles _____%
   More than 50 miles away _____%   More than 50 miles away _____%

7. Thinking about your current residents, how typical of the population
   you serve is this group?

   _____ much easier to deal with

   _____ somewhat easier to deal with

_____ quite typical

_____ a bit more difficult than average

_____ very much more difficult than average

8. How would you say your current residents compare with the typical population you serve? (Fill in the descriptive word)

More _____ Less _____

9. Do you accept: (Circle the appropriate)

Pre adjudicated youth	YES	NO
Post adjudicated youth	YES	NO
Violent youth	YES	NO
Repeat offenders	YES	NO
Court-ordered placements	YES	NO
Emotionally disturbed youth	YES	NO
Status offenders	YES	NO
Youth who have been previously admitted to your facility	YES	NO
Males	YES	NO
Females	YES	NO

Do you require:

Voluntary participation by youth	YES	NO
Family cooperation	YES	NO
Post placement arrangements prior to admission	YES	NO
Psychological evaluations	YES	NO

10. What is the <u>minimum age</u> for admission to your facility? _____ years

   What is the <u>maximum age</u> for admission to your facility? _____ years

   What is the <u>average age</u> of the residents you accept? _____ years

11. What percentage of those referred to your facility are actually admitted to the program?

   _____ less than 25%

   _____ 25 to 50%

   _____ 50 to 75%

   _____ 75 to 99%

   _____ 100%

12. Do you currently have a waiting list for admission? YES _____ NO _____

13. On the average what percentage of your residents are status offenders? _____ %

14. From the list below, choose che 3 which are most important to your admission decisions. Place a <u>1</u> next to the most important, a <u>2</u> next to the second most important, and a <u>3</u> next to the third most important.

_____ Geographical location of the youth's family

_____ Funding considerations and source of payment for the services

_____ Youth's agreement of voluntary participation

_____ Family's involvement and agreement to cooperate

_____ Post placement options

_____ Past criminal record

_____ Referring source's recommendation

_____ Other (please specify): _____

_____

_____

15. Please indicate where referrals for your facility come from by placing a 1 next to the source accounting for the largest number of referrals, a 2 next to the second most frequent referring source, and so on indicating the five (5) most common referral sources. For each of these referring sources, on the average what percentage of your referrals come from the 5 sources indicated?

_____ _____% public social service/public welfare departments

_____ _____% mental health agencies

_____ _____% police/sheriff's department

_____ _____% juvenile court intake

_____ _____% juvenile court disposition

_____ _____% juvenile court probation

_____ _____% residential juvenile correctional facilities

_____ _____% religiously affiliated agencies

_____ _____% schools or educational institutions

_____ _____% private service agencies

_____ _____% self referrals/family referrals

_____ _____% other _____

16. What is the minimum length of residence expected in your facility?

_____

What is the maximum length of residence permitted? _____

What is the average length of stay? _____

17. In the past year how many residents have completed their program and left the facility? _____

18. In the past year how many residents have been referred elsewhere prior to completion of their program in your facility? _____

19. In the past year how many residents have left the program without program approval? _____

20. Who decides when a resident is ready to move out of the facility? (Check all that apply, and place a * next to the most influential)

_____ Facility director

____ Facility staff

____ Resident's counselor

____ Resident's probation officer

____ The resident

____ Other residents

____ Other professionals, e.g., social worker, psychologist.

____ Other (please specify) _____

21. Of the following which most accurately describes your facility?
    Place a 1 next to your choice:

    ____ A supportive group atmosphere

    ____ Training in work skills

    ____ Training in social skills

    ____ Counseling for personal adjustment

    ____ An education program

    ____ A transitional facility

    ____ General supervision

    ____ Other _____

    Which of the above least accurately describes your facility? Place a
    0 next to that descriptor.

22. Which of the services below are provided as part of your program?
    (Check all that apply)

    ____ Crisis intervention

    ____ Diagnostic services

    ____ Individual counseling

    ____ Family counseling

    ____ Group counseling

    ____ Peer counseling

    ____ Substance abuse counseling

    ____ Recreation programs

    ____ Legal services

    ____ Advocacy

    ____ Education in local public schools

    ____ Facility based educational program

    ____ Educational tutoring, individual instruction on site

    ____ Job counseling, career counseling

    ____ Work placement

    ____ Employment agency referrals

    ____ General supervision

    ____ Other: _____

23. The residents of this facility need:
    (Check the three most important)

    ____ supervision

    ____ education

    ____ confidence

    ____ friends

    ____ exposure to new experiences

    ____ structure

    ____ guidance

    ____ support

    ____ responsibility

    ____ counseling

    ____ discipline

    ____ protection

24. What do you see as the primary program goals for residents?

25. Post-program options: Place a <u>1</u> next to the most common post-placement option for residents, a <u>2</u> next to the second most common, and a <u>3</u> next to the third most common option.

    _____ Return to court

    _____ Return home

    _____ Independent living

    _____ Foster home placement

    _____ Other residential facility

    _____ Nonresidential community-based program

    _____ Other: _____

26. Is there a follow-up or after-care program for residents leaving the facility?

    YES _____   NO _____

    If YES, for how long? _____

    What is the nature of the follow-up?

Staffing:

How many total staff are employed by this facility?   _____

How many are: professional, consulting staff? . . . . _____

                  line staff? . . . . _____

                  part time? . . . . _____

                  full time? . . . . _____

                  American Indian? . . . . _____

                  Asian American? . . . . _____

                  Black? . . . . _____

                  Chicano/Hispanic? . . . . _____

                  White? . . . . _____

Male, 18 to 30 years old . . . . ____

Male, 31 to 45 years old . . . . ____

Male, over 45 years? . . . . ____

Female, 18 to 30 years? . . . . ____

Female, 31 to 45 years? . . . . ____

Female, over 45 years? . . . . ____

College graduates? . . . . ____

Master's level? . . . . ____

live-in staff? . . . . ____

How many of your staff have been working here less than 6 months?   ____

. . . working here 6 to 18 months?   ____

. . . working here more than 18 months?   ____

How many of the staff are bilingual? ____

How many of the staff are CETA employees? ____

How many are non-paid or volunteer staff? ____

What is the typical staff resident ratio during the evening hours
(6 - 11 p.m.)?

staff _____   # residents _____

Thank you.

Facility: _____

Code: _____

Date: _____

Observer: _____

PROGRAM HISTORY

Date of the facility's opening?   _____

Where did the primary impetus come to form the facility?

Who was the primary figure responsible for starting the program/unit?

What was his/her position in the service delivery network?

Did this facility grow out of any other service?

What factors or perceived needs were responsible for the program's beginnings?

Legislation?

Innovative leadership?

Change in number of children needing placements?

Perceived need from local agency?

What rationale and set of values were presented for initially forming the facility?

What were the initial goals and expected outcomes?

What are they now?

Are they the same?

Was there opposition to forming the facility? If so, what was the nature?

From the professional community?

From the nonprofessional community?

What is the community perception of the agency now?

Professional community perception?

Nonprofessional community perception?

How and in what ways has the program changed since its inception?

What factors have been responsible for those changes?

Determine "golden years" beliefs if any.

Have there been radical changes in the sources of funding since the program's beginning?

How many of the original staff or core group are still with the agency?

Is the program better now than 5 years ago?

Where does the staff and administration see the program moving?

Facility: _____

Code: _____

Date: _____

Observer: _____

PROGRAM VARIABLES

What is the primary model of behavior change in this facility?

_____ Behavior modification

_____ Cognitive behavioral approaches

_____ "Outward Bound" - self sufficiency model

_____ Group process/milieu model

_____ Isolation/time-out

_____ Advocacy

_____ Family systems models

_____ Communications enhancement

_____ Counseling, individual therapeutic model

_____ Other: _____

Describe the general program philosophy and treatment orientation.

Do the residents have chores or duties which they perform? . . . . YES   NO

If yes, check those included:

_____ make bed

_____ clean own room

_____ do laundry (own _____ house _____)

_____ do food shopping

_____ clean communal areas, bathrooms, lounge, recreation areas

_____ set table

_____ fix meals, assist in meal preparation

_____ wash dishes/clean up following meals

_____ yard work, general maintenance, i.e., lawn mowing and leaf raking

_____ other: _____

What are the rewards for doing these chores?

Are these tasks performed by the residents only, in place of a designated staff person or custodian?

How many of the residents have a <u>paying job outside</u> of the facility? _____

How many of the residents have a <u>paying job inside</u> the facility? _____

Are residents permitted to leave the premises? . . . . YES   NO

   When?   What conditions?

Are residents permitted in staff offices? . . . . YES   NO

   Any restrictions?

Is there evidence of the use of medication for the residents? . . YES   NO

   What type?

What is the nature of the evidence observed?

   _____ medication distributed before or after meals, bedtimes, etc.

   _____ medication distribution included in the schedule or handled at a regularly scheduled time

   _____ staff or residents mention use of medication

   _____ administration or staff indicate medication prescribed for some residents

What are the meal time/eating arrangements?

   _____ residents eat in their rooms   _____ residents eat in shifts

   _____ residents eat together at large   _____ residents eat together at
         tables   small tables

   _____ other:

Do staff eat with residents?

   _____ Yes, eat at the same time but in a different room

   _____ Yes, at different tables

   _____ Yes, everyone eats together

   _____ No

Are there any differences in eating patterns by staff position?

15. What are the 4 most coveted resident privileges?
    How are they earned or awarded?

16. Who has the authority to impose immediate discipline?

        _____ volunteers

        _____ all counselors/line staff

_____ supervisors only

_____ residents

_____ other:

17. How are disciplinary decisions made regarding more serious infractions, e.g., AWOL, destruction of property, drugs in the house?

_____ group process (staff & residents)

_____ established rules

_____ staff discussion

_____ resident discussion

_____ individual contract, between resident and staff member

_____ other:

18. How are disciplinary actions recorded?

19. What types of disciplinary action are utilized? (Check those that apply)

_____ early bedtime

_____ room restriction

_____ loss of visitors

_____ loss of points/demerits

_____ loss of privileges (e.g., _____)

_____ added chores

_____ physical demands (e.g., exercises)

_____ retribution

_____ other:

20. If log recordings available, note:

disciplinary actions per week _____

disciplinary actions per resident in last week: _____ _____
                                                    min   max

average length of time per restriction: _____

21. How often are there assaults on staff?
Is this something the staff are worried about?

22. Do residents have a specifically designated counselor? . . . YES NO

Is this person an advocate for the resident
within the program? . . . . YES NO

23. How is information conveyed to residents?

_____ central bulletin board

_____ individual notification

_____ mailbox

_____ group meeting

_____ individual verbal message

_____ other:

24. Are the "house rules" and regulations posted in a
    convenient public location? . . . . YES   NO

25. At admission are there any special routines that
    serve a kind of initiation routine, e.g., strip
    search, isolation, clothing . . . . YES   NO

26. Are residents instructed in house rules upon admission? . . . YES   NO

27. Is there a resident handbook? . . . . YES   NO

28. Is there a handbook for staff? . . . . YES   NO

    Does the handbook include policies, operating
    procedures and treatment approaches? . . . . YES   NO

29. Is there a separate phone for residents' use? . . . . YES   NO

    Can residents use agency phone? . . . . YES   NO

    Is there provision for privacy in making phone calls for residents?

        _____ private booth

        _____ small room where door can be closed

        _____ phone is in public place

    When and under what conditions may residents use the phone?

30. What are the restrictions surrounding resident "free time"?

31. Is there a set time for "wake up" in the morning? . . . . . . YES   NO

    What is the time?

    How is wake-up accomplished?

32. What restrictions surround bedtime?   and curfews?

    Times?

33. Is there a resident grievance system? . . . . YES   NO

    What do staff think about the system?

    What do residents think about the system?

    How often is it used?

34. Are the residents' rooms inspected regularly . . . . YES   NO

    If so, for what reason?

35. Can residents entertain nonresidents of the opposite sex in the house?

    _____ only in certain areas of the house

    _____ during certain hours

    _____ yes, no restrictions

    _____ no

    _____ no policy

36. Is church attendance required? . . . . YES   NO

Indicate the community services utilized by this facility?

    _____ sheriff/police dept.   _____ religious organizations

    _____ local schools   _____ family services groups/
                                                  agencies
    _____ youth organizations, e.g.,
          YMCA, youth services bureau   _____ employment agencies

    _____ recreation facilities   _____ substance abuse programs

    _____ community mental health   _____ hospital, clinic
          center

What variables if any, prevent or inhibit the use of community services
and resources? Rank order the top three.

    _____ competition with other agencies   _____ expense

    _____ transportation   _____ distance

    _____ community attitudes   _____ program philosophy

    _____ lack of resident interest   _____ lack of staff interest

    _____ other:

How does the community view the residence?

1	2	3	4	5	6	7
resistance			toleration			acceptance

Rate program philosophy and programmatic support for community liason:

    _____ (1) avoidance of outside facility services, seen as detrimental,
              temptation for residents, or interfering in some way with
              the goals of the facility

    _____ (2) outside facilities used only on occasional basis (e.g.,
              special events, resident seeks out service on own)

    _____ (3) use of community resources appears to be incidental to
              program operation

    _____ (4) outside facilities seen as helpful in supporting program
              functions

    _____ (5) utilization of services and resources seen as crucial to
              program operation and the process of change, e.g., par-
              ticipation in work placement, public school attendance.

To what extent are families actually involved in this program?

1	2	3	4	5	6	7
none			some			a lot

Indicate what programmatic activities are included with the intention of changing or enhancing family-child relationships?

_____ home visiting by the residents

_____ provision for staff liason to family

_____ family visiting the facility

_____ family meetings/counseling with families

_____ regular report to families regarding resident progress

_____ special events, e.g., dinners for families

_____ other:

How many regular visiting hours per week are available to residents? _____

In general, what is the role of the family in this facility's operation?

Rate program philosophy on family involvement and family support:

_____ (1) avoidance of family involvement, seen as detrimental, interfering

_____ (2) family involvement is tolerated but incidental to program operation

_____ (3) family involvement is planned for but not targeted in programming

_____ (4) family involvement is viewed as one important component of program operation

_____ (5) family involvement seen as crucial to program and the process of change.

Briefly describe any programmatic differences in activities by time of year, e.g., school year schedules as compared with summertime schedules.

Facility: _____

Code: _____

Date: _____

Observer: _____

LOCATION AND PHYSICAL PLANT

Is the facility all in one building? . . . . YES   NO

     If not, explain:

How old is the building? _____ years

In what type of building is the agency housed?

    _____ ex-apartment building   _____ ex-hospital, jail or training school

    _____ big old house   _____ farm or ranch

    _____ big new house   _____ former school

    _____ other:

Is the neighborhood primarily: _____ urban   _____ suburban   _____ rural

    If rural, how far to the nearest town? _____ miles

What type of neighborhood is the facility in?

    _____ one family or low-rise apartment residential

    _____ high-rise apartment residential

    _____ business

    _____ business and residential

    _____ other:

Comment on the neighborhood context, surroundings, and building:

Is there a bell or call system for entry into the building? . . . YES   NO

Is this a secure facility . . . . YES   NO

Is there any surveillance or security equipment in view? . . . . YES   NO

    If so, please describe:

Check the community resources which are within walking distance (i.e.,
1 mile or less) of the facility:

	on premises	walking distance	more than a mile	not available
Drug store or grocery store				
Movie theatre				
Church				
Public library				
Park				
Recreation center or gym				
Public transportation system				
School				
Shopping district, mall				
A local "hangout" (e.g., pinball, pizza shop)				
Other? _____				

Check the recreational options available on premises:

_____ ping pong   _____ T.V.

_____ pool table   _____ music equipment, stereo, radio

_____ basketball court, yard area

_____ sports equipment (balls, bats, etc.)   _____ books

                                     _____ shop, woodworking tools

_____ weights   _____ other: _____

_____ games, cards, etc.   _____ crafts

Indicate the floorplan of the facility below:

Room	#	floor	if locked, when?
single bedrooms			
double bedrooms			
triple bedrooms			
other bedrooms (indicate sizes: _____)			
recreation area			
kitchen			
living room			
dining room			
offices for administrative staff (# staff per office)			
offices for professional adjunct staff (# staff per office)			
other: _____			

Describe any distinguishing feature about the room arrangements, particular advantages or disadvantages, ways in which the layout may enhance
the program, etc. Note options for privacy

What is the largest number of residents who share one bathroom area? _____

Are there locks on all bathroom doors? . . . . YES NO

Do residents have a place for their own personal property,
i.e., books, clothing, radio, etc.? . . . . YES NO

     Please describe the nature of the space:

To what extent are the rooms and facilities kept locked?

Who has access to the keys? Where are they kept?

Facility: _____

Code: _____

Date: _____

Observer: _____

POST-OBSERVATION RATINGS

1. Rate the appropriateness of the program size to physical space available:

____ (1) more space than currently utilized, large rooms not used very often, residents could easily "get lost" in the facility

____ (2) optimal match, no evidence of crowding or underutilization of space

____ (3) a bit crowded, observe people getting in each other's way at meals, morning and bed times for example, few communal spaces given the number of residents

____ (4) severely overcrowded, crammed living space and overuse of common living areas, no opportunities for privacy or being alone.

2. Rate the salience of the treatment model in programming:

____ (1) no treatment approach is apparent

____ (2) less than half of the program activities appear to be focused and consistent with treatment philosophy

____ (3) approximately half of the activities appear to be consistent with treatment goals, but much of what occurs has no apparent treatment consistency or is actually in opposition to the model

____ (4) program activities reflect goals and treatment philosophy but consistency and intensity is less than ideal

____ (5) programming seems totally and actively consistent with treatment model, program goals and process of change are apparent to observer.

3. Rate the degree of individualization and flexibility in programming:

____ (1) total disregard for resident individuality

____ (2) program imposes uniform practices such that only moderate degree of autonomy and individuality is possible

____ (3) no obvious restrictions, but staff attitudes and programs not supportive and encouraging of maintaining individualization

____ (4) program permits, supports and frequently encourages individualization

____ (5) ceaseless, systematic efforts to elicit and support individual, personalized programming.

SECTION I   RATINGS OF THE OVERALL SITE (Check the appropriate box)

4. As a <u>neighborhood</u> for living, how does the area around this site look?

☐ (3) Very pleasant and attractive

☐ (2) Mildly pleasant and attractive

☐ (1) Ordinary, perhaps even slightly unattractive

☐ (0) Unattractive, slum-like

5. How attractive are the site <u>grounds</u>?

☐ (3) Very attractive   landscaping or very attractive natural growth; well maintained; no litter or weeds, clean paths, neatly trimmed

☐ (2) Somewhat attractive   show signs of care and frequent maintenance

☐ (1) Ordinary   somewhat attractive but poorly maintained or ordinary looking: little landscaping, some weeds or litter

☐ (0) Unattractive   no grounds, sidewalks only; show little or no maintenance

6. How attractive are the site <u>buildings</u>?

☐ (3) Very attractive   unique and attractive design, excellent maintenance

☐ (2) Somewhat attractive   may show some deterioration on close inspection, or design is adequate but not unusually attractive

☐ (1) Ordinary   buildings are somewhat attractive but poorly maintained, or are not notable in either design or maintenance

☐ (0) Unattractive   buildings are deteriorated or unattractive

SECTION II   RATINGS OF ENVIRONMENTAL CHARACTERISTICS

PART I   RATINGS OF FOUR MAJOR LIVING AREAS

     a. Lounge, commons room, living room

     b. Dining room

c. Residents' bedrooms (or individual apartments)

d. Hallways

<u>Directions</u>: Rate each of these four areas and enter your rating (0, 1, 2, 3) in the appropriate space.

7. NOISE LEVEL

(3) Very quiet   noticeable absence of sounds, even when area is being used by many residents

(2) Quiet   some sounds present, but reading would be easy

(1) Somewhat noisy   many sounds present or occasional loud interruptions; a conversation is possible but reading or sustained concentration would be difficult

(0) Very noisy   sounds are loud and distracting, e.g., sustained noise from buzzers, cleaning equipment, etc.

____ Lounge   ____ Dining room   ____ Bedrooms   ____ Hallways
4   5   6   7

                                                                  Evening,
____ Morning   ____ Afternoon   ____ Before Dinner   ____ Before Bedtime

8. ODORS

(3) Fresh   living spaces have pleasantly fresh odor

(2) No odors   nothing noticeable about the air, "normal"

(1) Slightly objectionable   air is slightly tainted in some way; stale, close, musty, medicinal

(0) Distinctly objectionable   unpleasant odors are apparent

____ Lounge   ____ Dining room   ____ Bedrooms   ____ Hallways
8   9   10   11

9. LEVEL OF ILLUMINATION

(3) Ample lighting   brightly illuminated, but without glare; reading would be easy in all areas of the room

(2) Good lighting   lighting is basically good, but may be low, uneven, or glaring in some areas; reading would be easy in most areas of the room

(1) Barely adequate   lighting is low, uneven, or glaring; reading is difficult or possible in only certain areas of the room

(0) Inadequate lighting   illumination very low or very glaring in most areas of the room; reading would be difficult or impossible

____ Lounge   ____ Dining room   ____ Bedrooms   ____ Hallways
12   13   14   15

10. ORDERLINESS/CLUTTER

    (3) Neat   living spaces are very orderly; there seems to be a "place for everything, and everything is in its place"

    (2) Some disarray   looks "lived in"; some furniture moved around, magazines lying around, etc.

    (1) Cluttered   living spaces are somewhat disorganized and messy; some objects lying about; area seems crowded

    (0) Very cluttered   furniture and other objects are in disarray; floor area has objects to maneuver around

___ Lounge	___ Dining room	___ Bedrooms	___ Hallways
16	17	18	19

11. CLEANLINESS OF WALLS AND FLOORS (OR RUGS)

    (3) Very clean   both walls and floors are kept very clean, spotless; floors are polished

    (2) Clean   both walls and floors are cleaned regularly; some dust in corners, fingerprints on walls

    (1) Somewhat dirty   either walls or floors need cleaning; considerable dust, fingerprints or stains

    (0) Very dirty   both walls and floors need a major cleaning; surfaces stained, scuff marks, surfaces dirty to the touch

___ Lounge	___ Dining room	___ Bedrooms	___ Hallways
20	21	22	23

12. CONDITIONS OF WALLS AND FLOORS (OR RUGS)

    (3) Like new   both walls and floors are new looking; appear to be recently installed or painted

    (2) Good condition   good condition, but either walls or floors show some wear on close examination

    (1) Fair condition   walls or floors show wear, but only in heavily used areas

    (0) Poor condition   walls or floors show evident wear; worn spots, cracks, peeling, faded paint or colors

___ Lounge	___ Dining room	___ Bedrooms	___ Hallways
24	25	26	27

13. CONDITION OF FURNITURE

    (3) Excellent condition   like new; well kept, spotless, highly polished or without stains

    (2) Good condition   not new, but in good condition; slightly worn, small scratches, dusty, a few stains, some dirt in creases

(1) Fair condition older, but still structurally sound and kept moderately clean

(0) Deteriorated old and in poor repair; some tears, stains, dirt or dust; may be structurally unsound or dangerous

____ Lounge ____ Dining room ____ Bedrooms
28   29   30

14. WINDOW AREAS

(3) Many windows living space has large window areas which give an open feeling

(2) Adequate windows windows are sufficient to allow good light; there is no closed in feeling

(1) Few windows room tends to be dark, even on sunny days; there is a feeling of being closed in

(0) No windows there are no windows, or the windows are nonfunctional

____ Lounge ____ Dining room ____ Bedrooms
31   32   33

15. VIEW FROM WINDOWS -- INTEREST

(3) Very interesting view overlooks very interesting and continuous activities, e.g., children playing

(2) Interesting view overlooks some activities which draw mild attention, e.g., pedestrians or cars passing

(1) Lacks interest view is fairly dull or only rarely captures interest

(0) No interest basically nothing happening; looking outside is boring

____ Lounge ____ Dining room ____ Bedrooms
34   35   36

PART II RATINGS OF RESIDENTS' BEDROOMS OR APARTMENTS (Check appropriate box)

16. VARIATION IN DESIGN OF RESIDENTS' ROOMS (APTS)

☐ (3) Distinct variation as if effort was made to vary style and decor from room to room

☐ (2) Moderate variation rooms (apartments) are distinct, but there is a general decor throughout

☐ (1) Nearly identical some variation in size, shape, or furniture arrangement; variation is not noticeable unless looked for

☐ (0) identical   no variation except for decorational detail such as paint or rug color

17. PERSONALIZATION OF RESIDENTS' ROOMS (APTS)

☐ (3) Much personalization   most of the furnishings and objects in the room belong to the individual; time and energy have been spent in personalizing the rooms

☐ (2) Some personalization   residents have added personal objects such as rugs, pictures, chairs, favorite objects

☐ (1) Little personalization   some family pictures or personal articles, but room does not seem to "belong" to an individual

☐ (0) No personalization is evident

PART III   RATING THE FACILITY AS A WHOLE (Check the appropriate box)

18. DISTINCTIVENESS OF ALL LIVING SPACES

☐ (3) Much distinctiveness   a concerted effort has been made to vary the decor from room to room

☐ (2) Moderate distinctiveness   furnishings vary from room to room, but the overall room design is the same; wall texture and floor coverings show little variation

☐ (1) Some distinctiveness   very little variation, even in furnishings; somewhat institutional, but some areas are distinct such as the lounge or lobby (e.g., floor coverings vary, pictures, signs)

☐ (0) Little distinctiveness   Institutional appearances; most areas are quite similar, as in a hospital (without furniture, all rooms look about the same)

19. OVERALL PLEASANTNESS OF THE FACILITY

☐ (3) Quite pleasant   "I would feel good about placing a person in this housing."

☐ (2) Pleasant   "I would not feel badly about placing a person in this housing if they were in some way limited to this choice (financial, closeness to friends, etc.)"

☐ (1) Somewhat unpleasant   "I would feel uneasy about placing a person here."

☐ (0) Distinctly unpleasant   "I would not place a person here."

20. OVERALL ATTRACTIVENESS OF THE FACILITY

☐ (3) Highly appealing — attractive enough to be desirable for one's own home

☐ (2) Appealing — overall effect is favorable; fairly comfortable, although there may be some drawbacks (old furnishings, inconvenient)

☐ (1) Neutral — neither positive nor negative features especially stand out; ordinary

☐ (0) Unattractive — physical plant is unattractive or unappealing; it may be cold or somewhat sterile; arouses negative feelings

SECTION IV   RATINGS OF STAFF

21. QUALITY OF INTERACTION

☐ (3) Personal interaction — staff interact with residents in a warm, personal manner

☐ (2) Warm professional interaction — much of the staff's contact occurs as a part of their duties, but contact is personalized and informal

☐ (1) Formal professional interaction — most contact is formal and relates mainly to duties

☐ (0) Stern professional interaction — contact is formal or abrupt; some condescension may be evident

22. STAFF CONFLICT

☐ (3) No conflict — detected no evidence of conflict among staff members; staff members show signs of friendliness toward one another

☐ (2) Mild conflict — mild uneasiness or tension observed in some staff interactions

☐ (1) Moderate conflict — some problems observed in staff interactions (e.g., some critical or disparaging comments may occur)

☐ (0) Considerable conflict — staff observed complaining to or about one another; some harshness, anger, or bad temper observed

23. ORGANIZATION

☐ (3) Very well
organized

facility is very well organized; staff members perform duties efficiently and on time;
residents' needs are met promptly

☐ (2) Fairly well
organized

facility is generally well organized, but
some confusion or inefficiency is evident in
procedures or handling of residents' needs

☐ (1) Somewhat
disorganized

facility is somewhat disorganized; residents'
basic needs are met, but residents may experience long delays in daily routines; some
tasks may remain undone

☐ (0) Very
disorganized

facility appears quite disorganized and confusing; residents' basic needs may be poorly
met

Data Issues and Problems in the Federal Program Analyses

APPENDIX

D

Soon after we began this study we realized that among the most difficult tasks in evaluating the effects of federal programs on the congressional mandate to deinstitutionalize status offenders and dependent and neglected children would be quantifying the actual number or potential number of such children and youth touched by these programs and identifying the amount of federal funds supporting programs and services that do or could affect them. We were successful in these tasks only in the broadest sense. Data on the number of status offenders and dependent and neglected children served by these federal programs either do not exist or do not exist in a useful form. Information concerning the amount of federal money from a particular federal program or even the general amount of federal support for a service or program affecting status offenders is confounded beyond recognition at the state level. State budgetary reports generally display the total amount of money to be expended in a particular service area, and lump all state and federal funds available for that purpose together as one sum. When federal funds are identified, the program that provides them usually is not named. Local officials reported that they had only the vaguest idea of which federal program or programs support the services they offer.

Three factors appeared to contribute to our difficulties in assessing the effects of various federal programs in terms of the numbers of status offender and dependent

and neglected children affected or the amount of federal
money expended on them. First, service program officials
often do not know whether or how many status offenders and
dependent and neglected children they serve.   Second,
status offenders are not a specific target group for many
of the federal social service or education programs we
studied.   Third, state budgeting practices obscure how
federal money, even categorical money, is used.

Except for some grants from LEAA and the runaway youth
program, most of the state program data systems are not
designed to specify the reasons why clients are eligible
for services in the detail necessary to identify youth who
are status offenders or dependent and neglected children.
Several reasons may account for this fact. Because most
of these more general federal programs are aimed at more
broadly defined populations, their eligibility categories
are defined in terms of economic, social, or educational
needs.   Data are usually collected and categorized by a
program's own eligibility criteria, and the federal agencies have little incentive to request information from the
states that would yield more refined client profiles.
States also have little use for particularized information
beyond that necessary to identify the youth as part of the
broadly defined clientele of a program. Few of the seven
states had reporting systems that supplied more information than that necessary to fulfill minimal federal reporting requirements and their own state client tracking
and financial management functions. Virginia, however,
has developed a rather sophisticated computerized data
system under a demonstration grant from the federal government. This system collects and records client characteristic information for Virginia's foster care system.
Under the new Adoption Assistance and Child Welfare Act,
funds are supposed to be available to states to develop
federally mandated information systems for foster children, but only data on children who are eligible for federal foster care payments will be required as part of
those systems. Furthermore, it is unlikely that this data
will identify status offenders.

State social service officials suggested that additional information on client characteristics, though interesting, would be costly both in terms of money and in terms
of the additional staff time required to collect it. Even
if additional data collection and analysis were undertaken by the social services and educational systems, the
identification of which clients were status offenders and
dependent and neglected children arguably would not be of
the highest priority.

In addition, social work professionals do not always recognize the distinctions between status offenders and the other children and youth they serve. Once in the social service system, status offenders often lose the status offender tag because social workers view them as children or youth in need of services, just like all of the others served through the agency. Agency administrators and workers see little reason to explain all of the circumstances that could result in a child's eligibility, because that process would create additional labels for the child as well as decrease the time available to meet the child's service needs. Furthermore, workers appear to think that any increase in data reporting requirements will have a snowball effect on the demand for information.

Another factor contributing to the difficulty of determining the number of status offenders and dependent and neglected children served under various federal programs is that such children and youth are not specific target groups for many of these programs. Most status offenders become eligible for a particular service not because they are status offenders but because they fit eligibility requirements that are defined in terms of economic, social, or educational needs.

State budgeting and accounting practices also contribute to the difficulties of obtaining accurate data on the effect of federal programs on status offender and dependent and neglected children because they frequently do not differentiate between state and federal funds. In addition, some state accounting procedures effectively conceal from local-level administrators the sources of the funds that sponsor their programs. As a result, there appears to be little evidence to directly tie changing patterns of service for status offenders and dependent and neglected children to increases and decreases in the funding of federal programs.

In many states the budget offices seem to lump together all of the money available from a variety of sources for social service and education programs, and then allocate an aggregate sum to various specific programs. Local officials are given a total budget amount to be spent for a category of services or certain state programs. After the localities submit bills for that amount, state officials decide which charges to assess against which funds. Local decisionmakers frequently claim that they have relatively little knowledge about which federal or state programs fund the services they provide. The essential fungibility of the federal funds, the potential overlapping

of services or service categories in many of these programs, and the fact that many different groups compete for
a share of state and federal service monies all contribute to the difficulty of tracking federal funds to the
extent necessary to determine their individual or collateral effects on this group of children and youth.

The Politics of Status Offender Deinstitutionalization in California

DAVID STEINHART

INTRODUCTION

The purpose of this paper is to review the political factors leading to the adoption of the California law prohibiting secure detention of status offenders--the runaways, truants, and "beyond control" minors who are processed through the juvenile justice system even though they have committed no crime. It also explores the impact on California law of the federal requirement, enunciated in the Juvenile Justice and Delinquency Prevention Act of 1974 (JJDPA), that states receiving federal funds must deinstitutionalize status offenders by removing them from secure detention facilities. Both purposes or themes are addressed in the legislative history constituting the main body of this work. The paper concludes with a section assessing the role played by the federal requirements.

Much of California's progress toward deinstitutionalization has been accomplished through the expenditure of funds for that purpose. However, the full impact of federal funding cannot be evaluated in the absence of a comprehensive study or count of California's nonsecure facilities and programs for status offenders. No statewide study of this sort has been done to date, and such an effort would be far beyond the resources of this project. Similarly, an evaluation of whether the status offender problem in California has been solved by efforts at deinstutionalization is beyond the scope of this paper.

There is a brief review of postreform changes in arrest and detention rates. For a more thorough review the reader is referred to studies that are now tracking the justice system's response to deinstitutionalization mandates. No study on record yet provides an answer to the question of whether California status offenders are being adequately cared for in deinstitutionalized settings.

Finally, the discussion is limited to status offenders. In 1977 Congress added "such non-offenders as dependent or neglected children" to JJDPA deinstitutionalization requirements already in effect for status offenders. California had, 16 years earlier, adopted a policy of segregating dependent and neglected children from offenders in the juvenile justice system, and by 1977 had transferred intake jurisdiction over most dependent and neglected children from probation to social service departments.[1] The real battle over deinstitutionalization and compliance with JJDPA occurred in relation to status offenders, who were still being incarcerated in massive numbers in California when JJDPA became law. That battle, as it emerged in the legislature, was a display of conflicting political attitudes about the need for justice system intervention in noncriminal cases. It was also a test of the state's willingness to conform its juvenile justice policies to the funding requirements of the federal government.

OVERVIEW OF CALIFORNIA DETENTION PRACTICES PRIOR TO 1976

In 1976 California passed legislation prohibiting all secure detention of status offenders--the runaways, truants, and "beyond control" minors subjected to the jurisdiction of the juvenile court under Section 601 of the Welfare and Institutions Code (W&I), even though they are not accused of havihg committed any crime.

---

[1]Until 1978 California law did not prohibit the secure detention of dependent and neglected children. In 1978 the legislature prohibited secure detention of all dependent/neglected minors except those covered by Welfare and Institutions Code Sec. 300 (c), referring to minors who are "physically dangerous to the public because of mental or physical deficiency, disorder or abnormality." The 1978 change is codified at W&I Sec. 206.

Prior to 1976 California was incarcerating large numbers of status offenders in locked facilities. In that
period the state applied the same initial detention criteria to W&I Section 601 status offenders as it did to W&I
Section 602 criminal offenders. Both classes of juvenile
offenders could, under prior law, be sentenced to secure
facilities in the court's dispositional order, with the
single exception that status offenders could not be committed to the California Youth Authority unless they had
also been adjudicated wards on the basis of a criminal
offense.

The years 1973 to 1975 were high-water marks for the
secure detention of status offenders in California. Table
E-1 gives a picture of the California practice in these
years.

In the years before 1976 the public and its policymakers were largely ignorant of these high detention
levels and rates for status offenders. Few persons outside the juvenile court and probation communities were
even aware of the distinction between a Section 601 status
offender and a Section 602 criminal offender. Practices
and levels of secure detention of status offenders varied
from county to county. Some probation departments experi-
mented in the early 1970s with alternative-to-detention

TABLE E-1   California Status Offender Arrests and
Juvenile Hall Admissions

Arrests and Admissions	1973	1974	1975
Total statewide arrests for status offenses	103,057	107,898	86,137
Percent of total juvenile arrests	(28.4)	(26.4)	(23.2)
Total admissions of status offenders to juvenile halls	51,753	50,406	41,202
Percent of total juvenile hall admissions	(34.9)	(32.6)	(29.6)

Source: Data derived from the California Bureau of Criminal
Statistics and from the 1977 California State Plan for Criminal
Justice, Office of Criminal Justice Planning, Sacramento,
Calif. Prior to 1974, the bureau's data category for 601
offenses included some minor criminal offenses.

programs, and adopted diversion and detention control
policies that reduced Section 601 detention levels.[2]
But in general, before 1976 the California juvenile justice system lacked any serious challenge to its tradition
of detention and was entrenched in the practice of using
locked facilities as a primary means of coping with the
status offender population.

THE ROOTS OF CALIFORNIA'S PRO-DETENTION POLICY

Why, prior to 1976, were California's juvenile justice
authorities locking up so many status offenders? The
forces underlying the California policy and practice of
detention are relevant to an understanding of the political battle that later surfaced as a legislative debate
over deinstitionalization. These pro-detention forces
took time to dismantle. They have also displayed a stubborn tendency to reemerge. To this day pro-detention
forces stir beneath the surface of the current policy of
deinstitutionalization.

Roots in the Interventionist Tradition
Underlying the Juvenile Court Law

The juvenile court law in California, like that of other
states, was founded on the parens patriae notion that care
and treatment should be provided to reform minors in
trouble. To facilitate this notion, California's early
jurisdictional statutes were broad grants of authority
over minors, blurring the distinction between criminal and
noncriminal behavior. Between 1937 and 1961 Welfare and
Institutions Code Sec. 700 was the basic jurisdictional
statute for all classes of juveniles, and even brought

---

[2]Sacramento, Santa Clara, and San Diego Counties, for
example, had early programs for the police and probation
diversion of status offenders to counseling and community-
based programs. The Sacramento 601 Project constituted a
model for others; results of that program are reviewed in
Roger Baron and Floyd Feeney, "Preventing Delinquency
Through Diversion, The Sacramento County Probation Department 601 Diversion Project," A Second Year Report, Center
on the Administration of Justice, University of California
at Davis, July 1973.

within its reach minors who habitually visited public
billiard rooms or habitually smoked cigarettes. Court
decisions emphasizing due process rights had led to some
shrinkage of this jurisdiction and to changes in juvenile
court procedure. Nevertheless, the interventionist,
child-saving tradition was and is very much alive in
California. To many police, probation officers, and
judges, secure detention is simply a tool that allows intervention and treatment to occur. Even among community-
based, youth-serving agencies--the dependable foes of
detention--it is possible to find advocates of secure detention as a means of getting the minor's attention and
imposing treatment.[3] The goals of care and rehabilitation are sometimes pursued at the cost of personal
liberty.

California's Juvenile Institutions, and their
Pro-Detention Constituency

At the state level the California Youth Authority operates
secure facilities for approximately 5,000 young people,
and has about 4,400 employees. In 40 of California's 58
counties, there are 45 juvenile halls for the secure detention of minors. There are also 74 camps, ranches, or
schools for the custody of juveniles at the county level.
These county facilities have a combined capacity of more
than 8,000 beds. It takes about 3,000 probation personnel
assigned to juvenile divisions to operate these facilities
and to perform collateral intake, court, and supervision
duties. There are more than 1,700 juvenile police officers in the state. There is a juvenile court in each
county, and more than one in large counties such as Los
Angeles, which has five juvenile court judges and 24 com-
missioners.[4]

---

[3]For a statement of the interventionists' case, see
Martin and Snyder "Jurisdiction Over Status Offenses
Should Not be Removed From The Juvenile Court," Crime and
Delinquency, January 1976, pp. 44-47. This article is
reprinted in a good anthology on status offender issues
by Richard Allinson, ed. (1978) Status Offenders and the
Juvenile Justice System, An Anthology. Hackensack, N.J.:
National Council on Crime and Delinquency.

[4]All figures in this paragraph are from the 1979 California State Plan for Criminal Justice, Office of Criminal

As these facts indicate, California has made a huge
investment in public institutions for the processing and
detention of minors. The mere existence of all of these
facilities exerts a pressure to use them. Additionally,
thousands of Californians are employed in juvenile police,
probation, court, and corrections operations. These employees are a ready-made constituency for support of the
system in which they work. They often belong to professional organizations, some of which hire directors or
lobbyists to represent them before the legislature in
Sacramento. The California Probation, Parole and Correctional Association, the Probation Chiefs' Association, the
California Peace Officers' Association, the Juvenile Officers' Association, the California Association of District
Attorneys, and numerous judges, boards of supervisors, and
Juvenile Justice and Delinquency Prevention Commissions
have gone on record at one time or another in support of
secure detention of status offenders.

The Meager Development of Community-Based Agencies in
California, and their Correspondingly Small Constituency

California's public institutions for minors are not matched in size, wealth, or political strength by private
sector programs serving young people. Although community-
based agencies do exist and do accept referrals from public institutions, they have never developed in to the extent visible in some other states.[5] This has been
blamed, in turn, on the lack of a church and parish tradition in the state; on the wealth of the state in its

---

Justice Planning, Sacramento, California, pp. V-J-28 to
V-J-42. The figure for juvenile probation personnel has
been revised according to an estimate furnished by the
California Probation, Parole and Correctional Association.

[5] In the city and county of San Francisco, for example,
there is only one privately run, community-based facility
for status offenders; it has an eight-bed capacity. This
is the case in a county with a population of 650,000 that
is also a historically favored destination for runaways.
Other counties, such as Los Angeles, have a more widely
developed private agency system, but those agencies generally suffer from the economic ills described in the
text.

growth years, making possible huge investments in public
institutions; and on the state's emphasis on strong county
governments with their own institutions doing local work.
Whatever the cause, community-based agencies have not developed in sufficient numbers to absorb a status offender
population displaced by a policy of deinstitutionalization. Where community-based agencies do exist, they are
often struggling, financially insecure organizations, with
lower salaries and higher turnover rates than their public
counterparts. Their political clout is minimal compared
to that of the public institutions.

Dominant Public Attitudes Favoring Lockup of Offenders

In the 1960s Californians witnessed an alarming increase
in highly publicized incidents of crime. Near the end of
the decade the state developed a reputation as the home
of cult slayings, mass murders, political assassinations,
ghetto riots, and juvenile gang wars. The public and its
lawmakers reacted severely, and sometimes irrationally.
Citizens began to arm themselves. Law-and-order candidates were elected to clean up crime. New laws emerged
in the 1970s; the death penalty was reinstated, mandatory
state prison terms were imposed for serious crimes, and
the indeterminate sentence system was scrapped in favor
of a punishment-based system of fixed terms. The seepage
of these attitudes and developments into the juvenile
court law has been substantial. Despite due process standards imposed by state and federal courts, legislators
worked to toughen the juvenile justice system and orient
it toward punishment. In their push for anticrime measures, lawmakers did not often acknowledge the distinction
between status offenders and criminal offenders. It is
not surprising that in this atmosphere secure detention
levels for status offenders crested in the years 1973-
1975. Only later did lawmakers begin to distinguish between classes of offenders and withdraw their support for
lockup as a means of controlling noncriminal minors.

CALIFORNIA REACTION TO THE JUVENILE JUSTICE AND
DELINQUENCY PREVENTION ACT OF 1974

The Juvenile Justice and Delinquency Prevention Act of
1974 (JJDPA) was signed by President Ford on September 7,
1974. In order to qualify for federal funds authorized

by the act, each participating state had to submit an approved juvenile justice plan promising to comply with federal requirements affecting state and local juvenile justice systems. One of these requirements, Section 223 (a) (12), was that the state juvenile justice plan must

> provide that within two years after submission of the plan that juveniles who are charged with or who have committed offenses that would not be criminal if committed by an adult shall not be placed in juvenile detention or correctional facilities, but must be placed in shelter facilities. . . .

In 1974, when the act was signed, California was eagerly incarcerating status offenders at record levels. It was clear to most observers that California law permitting secure detention of status offenders would have to be changed if the state were to comply with the federal act.

JJDPA itself proposed no specific means for conforming state law to federal juvenile justice policy. The act did, in several sections, establish funding criteria that emphasized community-based diversion, and prevention programs affecting status offenders.[6] These funding preferences, as will be seen, did have an eventual impact on the development of alternatives to detention.

Governor Ronald Reagan endorsed JJDPA, and his appointees at the state planning agency made preparations in 1974 to accept and administer juvenile justice funds. The federal money was welcomed in California, even though unmet conditions were attached.

Any elation the state planning agency may have felt at the prospect of new funds was dissipated by the change in governors that occurred when Edmund G. Brown, Jr., took office in 1975. Brown's view of LEAA was that it was a bloated, inefficient bureaucracy that wasted money while failing to accomplish its stated goals of crime prevention (Maslow 1976). By July 1975 Brown had cut the staff of the state planning agency from 220 to 46, and had transformed its supervising board (the California Council on

---

[6]Section 223 (a) (10), regarding spending preferences for "advanced techniques" from the state formula grant share, and Section 224, regarding criteria for spending from "special emphasis" funds awarded directly by the Office of Juvenile Justice and Delinquency Prevention.

Criminal Justice) with new appointments.[7] His skepticism extended to the Juvenile Justice Advisory Group, whose appointment was required by JJDPA. He waited more than a year to appoint its members.

It is tempting to characterize Brown's reconstruction of the state planning agency as a revolt against the concept of federal assistance. To some extent this is true, and it is an attitude that would later be reiterated by legislators who were hostile to the notion of changing state laws in order to qualify for federal funds. But there is no evidence that Brown disputed the specific goals and reforms enunciated in JJDPA. His challenge was based on his own concept of fiscal integrity, not on a defense of California's existing juvenile justice system.

When Congress reauthorized JJDPA in 1977, amendments were added to Section 223 (a) (12) and the other sections of the act affecting status offenders. In the same year, LEAA adopted guidelines that redefined detention and correctional facilities in a manner that reclassified many state and local facilities previously thought to be non-secure. These changes came after California adopted its primary deinstitutionalization statute in 1976, but were a concern during the 1977-78 legislative attempt to restore secure detention of status offenders. The 1977 changes will be discussed in that context later.

THE POLITICAL BATTLE IN THE CALIFORNIA LEGISLATURE OVER
THE REFORM OF LAWS RELATING TO STATUS OFFENDERS

The political battle over secure detention of status offenders in California divides into three main stages: (1) the years 1970 to 1975, when legislators considered the status offender issue but did not act; (2) the year 1976, when AB 3121 prohibiting secure detention was passed; and (3) the years 1977 and 1978, when a backlash movement succeeded in reversing, to a limited extent, the status offender provisions of the 1976 bill. For reasons discussed below, the impact of the federal funding requirements on state status offender law is most apparent in the 1977-78 backlash period.

---

[7] Information and data from interview with Douglas Cunningham, Director, Office of Criminal Justice Planning, Sacramento, California, on January 28, 1980.

1970 to 1975: Stirrings of a Reform Movement

The political mood in California during the early 1970s
has already been described in relation to the roots of
California's detention practice. That mood favored criminal justice legislation emphasizing the protection of
society and punishment for crime. It was a mood hostile
to legislative reforms promising prevention, diversion,
or rehabilitation of offenders.

There were, nevertheless, early advocates of deinstitutionalization of status offenders. Some citizen groups,
such as the National Council of Jewish Women, urged deinstitutionalization of status offenders in California in
the early 1970s.[8] Public interest lawyers, funded
through Office of Economic Opportunity (OEO) programs,
challenged California's status offender jurisdiction
statutes in 1971.[9] Some probation personnel, working
in experimental programs such as the Sacramento 601 diversion project, were supportive of changes in status offender policy.

In 1970 the Assembly Criminal Procedure Committee of
the California Legislature held interim hearings on the
juvenile court process. The report that emerged from the
hearings was a stinging indictment of California's treatment of status offenders. "The single greatest thing
wrong with Section 601," the report said, "is that it uses
criminal procedures and institutions to control noncriminal behavior" (California Legislature 1970:12). The
committee concluded that juvenile court intervention in
Section 601 cases was ineffective, and recommended the
repeal of Section 601 and the development of alternative-
to-detention services (California Legislature 1970).

---

[8] See testimony of Flora Rothman, National Council of
Jewish Women, in Hearings, Senate Subcommittee to Investigate Juvenile Delinquency, (92d, 93d Congress), on Sec.
3148 and Sec. 821, May, June 1972; February, March, June
1973; at p.443.

[9] Attorneys at the San Francisco Neighborhood Legal Assistance Foundation, funded by OEO, represented the plaintiffs in Gonzales v. Mailliard (U.S.D.C. No. Cal. No.
50425, 1971, 1975), voiding portions of the California
status offender jurisdictional statute covering minors in
danger of leading an "idle, lewd, dissolute or immoral
life."

Unfortunately, the report's conclusions reflected the then-liberal tone of the committee more than the sense of the legislature or the mood of the public. The committee's recommendations were not even introduced as a bill.

Other legislative groups considered the status offender problem prior to 1974. In 1973 the Assembly Symposium on Services to Children and Youth was convened, drawing together legislators, institutional officials, youth-service agency representatives, and concerned citizens. In 1974 the symposium issued a set of legislative recommendations, including specific proposals to prohibit secure detention of status offenders or the escalation of Section 601 offenses into Section 602 criminal offenses on grounds of failure to obey a court order (California Legislature 1974b:Sec. II). Like the 1970 Criminal Procedure Committee report, these recommendations were largely ignored by the 1974 legislature that received them.

Multiple proposals to revamp the juvenile court law in ways that would satisfy demands for crime control were introduced in the 1973 and 1974 legislative sessions. Many of these bills were stopped in the liberal-minded Assembly Criminal Justice Committee. In 1974 that committee was joined by Assemblyman Julian Dixon (D-Los Angeles), a black legislator with close ties to the Los Angeles law enforcement community. It was rumored that Dixon's appointment was intended to add pro-law-enforcement balance to the committee. In any event Dixon was probably unaware at the time that he would soon become the primary author and architect of juvenile justice reform legislation in California, and of laws deinstitutionalizing status offenders.

In 1974 Dixon chaired an Assembly Select Committee on Juvenile Violence. That committee's report was sympathetic to status offenders, assessing the justice system's handling of Section 601s as "a major intrusion on the rights of young people" (California Legislature 1974a:56). The report also referred to JJDPA, which had been signed two months before the report was issued. The report recommended that the legislature support statewide community-based juvenile diversion programs, which should "facilitate the implementation of the Federal Juvenile Justice and Delinquency Prevention Act of 1974" (California Legislature 1974a:80). In the 1974 session Dixon introduced legislation embracing the committee's findings on status offenders. His bill (AB 4120) generally prohibited secure detention of Section 601s, but allowed detention of status offenders who fled a nonsecure facility or disobeyed a court order. The bill passed the Assembly in 1974 but was held in committee in the Senate.

Because so many legislators were introducing piecemeal reforms of the juvenile court law, the Assembly Criminal Justice Committee took on the task of drafting a comprehensive juvenile justice reform bill in 1974. Using his prerogative as chairman of the committee, Assemblyman Alan Sieroty (D-Beverly Hills) hired two consultants to draft the legislation. Sieroty himself was an advocate of personal and civil liberties, and he happened to hire as consultants two defense attorneys with long experience defending juvenile offenders and status offenders in California courts. Their bias in draftsmanship was distinctly liberal, favoring diversion, deinstitutionalization, and the delivery of services to all classes of offenders.

The Assembly Criminal Justice Committee, in its efforts to prepare a comprehensive juvenile court reform bill, held interim hearings in 1974. The case for adoption of the JJDPA's provisions in California was presented at one of these hearings by John M. Rector, then Chief Counsel to Senator Birch Bayh's U.S. Senate Subcommittee to Investigate Juvenile Delinquency. Rector explained at length how federal funds would be used to establish justice system alternatives in California. Another witness, representing the state planning agency, was asked by Sieroty to submit a list of the law changes that would be necessary to bring California into compliance with JJDPA.[10]

Sieroty introduced his consultant-drafted juvenile bill in the 1975 legislative session. The bill, AB 1819, turned out to be something of a reformer's pipe dream. It would have created, at state expense, a Community Youth Board in each school district. The boards would accept referrals of minors with various problems, including law violators. Section 601 of the Welfare and Institutions Code would be repealed. "Beyond control" minors could not be referred to the juvenile court until conciliation had been attempted through the Community Youth Board. Runaways could choose to stay for seven days in a runaway house, without parental consent, while counseling services

---

[10]Transcript of hearings on the Juvenile Justice System Assembly Committee on Criminal Justice, California Legislature, in San Francisco, October 25, 1974 (unedited, unnumbered pages).

were offered. The court's secure detention options were severely limited for all status offenders.

AB 1819 clearly would not satisfy the demands of more conservative legislators for law and order measures. The bill never made it out of the Assembly Criminal Justice Committee. In June, Sieroty modified and reintroduced AB 1819 with a new number (AB 2385), but this bill also failed to clear the committee.

The 1975 legislature did amend Section 601 in two respects. Subdivision (b) was added, restoring court jurisdiction over truants (accidentally deleted in the previous year), but limiting removal from parental custody to school hours. The legislature also deleted Section 601 jurisdiction based on "danger of leading an idle, dissolute, lewd or immoral life." The latter amendment conformed statutory law to the decision in Gonzales v. Mailliard, the U.S. District Court decision holding the deleted language to be unconstitutionally vague.[11] These changes limited police, court, and probation intervention in Section 601 cases, but did not attack the mass of arrests and prosecutions for Section 601 offenses.

During the debates over AB 1819 and AB 2385, there is no evidence that the state planning agency intervened to assist Sieroty or to promote compliance with JJDPA, which was then in effect. The 1976 Juvenile Justice Supplement to the State Plan promised to study means of compliance with the federal law, but outlined no specific approach and made no reference to legislative changes that might be necessary.[12] In fairness it should be noted that the state planning agency was still reeling in 1975 from the massive displacements ordered by Governor Brown, and was probably not ready to implement JJDPA in a full and effective manner. The agency did allocate its full share of 1975 JJDPA formula grant funds to projects for the deinstitutionalization of status offenders. It also began

---

[11]Gonzales v. Mailliard, U.S.D.C. No. Cal. No. 50424, 1971, reaffirmed 1975. For a review of the vagueness doctrine as applied to status offender jurisdiction statutes, see M. West, "Juvenile Court Jurisdiction Over 'Immoral' Youth in California," 24 Stanford Law Review 568, 1972.

[12]1976 Juvenile Justice Supplement to the 1976 California State Plan for Criminal Justice, Office of Criminal Justice Planning, Sacramento, California.

to administer two special emphasis grants coming directly
from LEAA for status offender deinstitutionalization programs in Alameda County ($1.5 million) and South Lake
Tahoe ($175,000).

While the legislature debated and the state planning
agency spent for deinstitutionalization, the Director of
the California Youth Authority, Allen Breed, assigned
Deputy Director George Saleebey and a full-time staff to
study California secure detention practices. The conclusions of the study were issued in January 1975 in a
report titled Hidden Closets. The report was an authoritative denunciation of California detention practices.
It was widely circulated among legislators and policymakers, and probably had an impact on the status offender
reforms that eventually emerged in 1976. Hidden Closets
noted, among other facts, that status offenders accounted
for 35 percent of all juvenile hall detentions in 1973,
but for only 28 percent of all juvenile arrests. In its
conclusions the report (Saleebey 1975:3) made the following recommendations:

1. A moratorium should be declared on new juvenile hall construction. The only construction
justified at the present time is that which replaced outmoded and unsafe buildings.

2. An immediate goal for all juvenile halls should
be the achievement of a 75% reduction in resident
population from existing levels. Savings generated
from this reduction should be diverted into . . .
alternative-to-detention programs.

1976: The Legislature Passes a Deinstitutionalization
Statute

Four days after the 1975 legislature adjourned, Lynette
"Squeaky" Fromme, an avowed member of the Charles Manson
clan, held a pistol two feet away from President Gerald
Ford at the State Capitol in Sacramento. Two weeks later
Sara Jane Moore fired at the President in San Francisco.
In the same month Patty Hearst was arrested, and her trial
in San Francisco on federal bank robbery charges gave rise
to speculation that she would be acquitted because she had
an expensive lawyer. The Marin County trial of the San
Quentin Six, accused in the prison shootout that left
George Jackson and five others dead, dragged into its

ninth month in January 1976, raising questions about the
delay and the costs for elaborate courtroom security. At
the U.S. Supreme Court, arguments were scheduled in death
penalty appeals that had brought executions to a halt
across the country.

Legislators returning to Sacramento in this atmosphere
were besieged with complaints about the ineffectiveness
of the criminal justice system. Their top criminal justice priority in 1976 was Senate Bill 42, which would
repeal the indeterminate sentence in California and restore fixed or "determinate" sentences for offenders.
Juvenile justice reform was also a priority. Senators and
assemblymen introduced competing versions of juvenile justice bills designed to demonstrate tough postures toward
crime and delinquency. They were backed by strong lobbies representing law enforcement organizations and citizen groups demanding action.

At least four major bills introduced in 1976 sought
comprehensive changes in the juvenile justice system.
Assemblyman Julian Dixon introduced AB 3121, drafted by
the Los Angeles district attorney's office. AB 3121 proposed new standards for the trial of 16- and 17-year-olds
as adults, changes in the "purpose" section of the juvenile court law emphasizing the safety and protection of
the public, and changes in juvenile court procedures that
would reduce the role of the probation officer while increasing the role of the district attorney. A nearly
identical measure was introduced by Senator Alan Robbins
(D-Los Angeles) on the Senate side (SB 1598). Assemblyman
Art Torres (D-Los Angeles) carried AB 2672 for probation
employees, also proposing to increase the number of juveniles tried as adults and to bring the DA into juvenile
court, but with added emphasis on probation services and
nonsecure detention for status offenders. Assemblyman
Alister McAlister (D-San Jose) introduced his version of
juvenile justice reform, requiring mandatory state prison
sentences for minors convicted of serious crimes in adult
court (AB 3001).

Into this armada of law and order proposals, Alan
Sieroty reintroduced the liberal, service-oriented reforms
that had failed to move out of committee the previous
year. This time Sieroty tried a new tactic: He broke his
comprehensive juvenile justice bill into six smaller,
separate bills to increase the chances that one or more
might succeed. One bill gave minors accused of crimes the
right to trial by jury, another established Community
Youth Boards, and so on. AB 3894 reintroduced the status

offender reforms previously contained in AB 1819 and AB 2385, with separate sections for runaways, minors in need of placement, truants, and emancipated minors.

What finally emerged from this flurry of competing juvenile justice proposals in 1976 was a single compromise measure that incorporated bits and pieces of all of the major juvenile justice bills introduced in that session. One of the pieces that survived was the prohibition of secure detention of status offenders, drawn from Sieroty's AB 3894.

How did this relatively unpopular reform of status offender law become part of the final compromise? In all of the public hearings on the 1976 juvenile bills, the issue of compliance with federal law was never raised. The state planning agency and the Juvenile Justice Advisory Group remained mute. Nor did the federal requirements or concern for federal funds appear to play a significant role in the private discussions and bartering sessions that took place during the heat of the controversy over AB 3121. Allen Breed, then Director of the Youth Authority, and next to Sieroty and Dixon the person most responsible for maintaining the status offender provisions of AB 3121, says that in the strategic maneuvering that led to the compromise of 1976, JJDPA was "never even mentioned."[13] Survival of the prohibition of status offender detention can be attributed to the tenacity of a few reform-oriented policymakers, to some legislative horse-trading, and to the fatigue and confusion that traditionally surround the last two or three days of each legislative session.

The horse-trading began early, in Criminal Justice Committee hearings. Alan Sieroty, chairman of the six-member committee, insisted that his AB 3894 be included in any juvenile justice compromise that was reached in that session. As leverage, he had enough liberal votes in committee to kill the tough anticrime bills.

In two hearings on April 28 and May 20, 1976, the Assembly Criminal Justice Committee heard lengthy, heated arguments on all of the juvenile justice bills from district attorneys, police, judges, probation officers, public defenders, civil libertarians, bar associations, community and youth service organizations, parents, children, and

---

[13] Interview, Allen Breed, Director, National Institute of Corrections, Washington, D.C., and former Director, California Youth Authority, on January 8, 1980.

others. Fatigued by the advocacy pro and con, Sieroty, Dixon, and other committee members retreated to lunch where they pared their concerns down to a list of 11 essential points. After lunch the committee returned to the hearing room and voted on each of the 11 points, one of which was the whole of AB 3894. Each point that received four of the six members' votes became part of the committee bill. At the end of the day they had a bill merged under one number, AB 3121. The bill went through the Assembly, and arrived at the Senate Judiciary Committee. At that point it was 78 pages long, including the hardline adult court and district attorney provisions of AB 3121, the probation service expansions of AB 2672, and the status offender provisions of AB 3894.

The California legislature is an "open" forum in which the public is allowed to testify for and against bills that come before it. The rules of legislative procedure, though largely unwritten, have developed over time as matters of custom and tradition. One such tradition is that the chairman of a committee may, depending on the individual's standing and personality, wield almost complete control over the conduct of the committee.

On August 16, 1976, AB 3121 was "heard" in the Senate Judiciary Committee. The committee had a reputation for conservatism in criminal justice matters, and for killing bills sent in by the more liberal Assembly. On this day, the committee lacked a quorum much of the time, but its chairman, Senator Alfred Song (D-Monterey Park), was there. When AB 3121 was called, he discarded the normal rule of public comment. After Dixon presented the bill, Chairman Song accepted amendments prepared by the presiding juvenile court judge from Los Angeles and then choked off debate. These amendments removed the status offender reforms and left intact the tough law and order provisions relating to adult court, district attorneys, and other procedural matters. For the moment, Sieroty's status offender reforms appeared to be doomed.

Julian Dixon, author of the Assembly compromise, could have cried foul, but chose not to. First of all, he knew that the substantial amendments imposed by the Senate committee would throw the bill into a conference committee, where a new compromise would have to be reached. Second, the broad range of services included in the Sieroty portion of his bill had run into trouble with the Department of Finance, which had placed a $75 million price tag on these services. Dixon had already agreed, back in the Assembly Criminal Justice Committee, to stand

behind the compromise, including the status offender reforms. He would make good his word later, in conference
committee.

In the two-week space between the Senate Judiciary
Committee hearing and the conference committee hearing,
advocates of deinstitutionalization worked to restore the
provisions deleted by the Senate committee. Sieroty's
aides launched a scathing attack on the Department of
Finance, and Sieroty himself wrote the venerable head of
that department a letter in which he accused the sup-
posedly neutral department of playing politics with his
bill. More importantly, a series of meetings took place
between the government principals who had a direct interest in the outcome of AB 3121. These principals included,
at various times, the authors of the bills merged into AB
3121, representatives of the California Youth Authority
and of the governor's office, the director of the California Probation, Parole and Correctional Association, and
the lobbyist-attorney for the Los Angeles district attorney, who occupied a special role in all proceedings on AB
3121 as legal advisor to Assemblyman Dixon. The discussions centered on standards for the removal of minors from
juvenile to adult court, and on the role of the prosecutor
in juvenile court proceedings. Breed and Sieroty continued to insist on status offender reforms. They eventually won the support of the governor's office for an essential minimum reform in relation to Section 601s: The
secure detention of status offenders would be prohibited,
and the costly services mandated by the original Sieroty
bill would be scratched.

On August 30, 1976, Dixon's office prepared a mock-up
of the final compromise to be presented to the six-member
conference committee. That mock-up included a simple prohibition of secure detention of Section 601 minors, and
allowed probation departments to contract with public or
private agencies for nonsecure facilities for them. The
conference committee, meeting in the harried, confused
atmosphere of the last days of the session, stormily debated the adult court provisions of the compromise, but
quietly agreed to the status offender provisions.

As approved by the conference committee, AB 3121 was
an immensely complex set of reforms of juvenile justice
substance and procedure. In the crush of legislation moving through floor votes prior to the midnight August 31
deadline, legislators had no chance to weigh the merits
of the compromise that had been reached just hours earlier. They approved AB 3121 based on its acceptance by

committees and on its public relations value as a bill
that appeared to deal harshly with juvenile crime. More
than one observer close to the legislature has commented
that relatively few of the assemblymen and senators participating in the floor vote on the last night of the
session knew that, beneath the law and order provisions
of AB 3121, they had deinstitutionalized status offenders
in California.[14]

1977 and 1978: A Legislative Backlash Leads to the Partial Restoration of Secure Detention

The 1976 law deinstitutionalizing status offenders in
California crept quietly through the legislature, under
the cover of more popular law and order reforms; the real
battle lay ahead. In 1977 a backlash movement to restore
secure detention took hold in the legislature and was not
resolved until AB 958, which restored limited detention,
became law two years later. It is in this period--the
legislative sessions of 1977 and 1978--that the impact of
federal funding requirements on state law can best be
demonstrated. In fact the backlash movement was to some
extent a test of California's willingness to conform its
law to federal mandates. The outcome was compatible with
federal requirements, but it was a close call.

   In the fall of 1976 legislators began to receive letters complaining about AB 3121. Some were from outraged
parents relating horror stories about children who had run
away and were beyond the reach of the law. Others were
more reasoned statements about the loss of public authority and control over status offenders, or about the inability of probation officers and service providers to
deliver counseling or reunite runaways with their parents.

   Taking his cue from constituents, Assemblyman Alister
McAlister (D-San Jose), author of death penalty legislation and a conservative in criminal justice matters, introduced AB 706, proposing to reverse completely the deinstitutionalization provisions of AB 3121. Julian Dixon

---

[14] The provisions of AB 3121 prohibiting secure detention
of status offenders are at Welfare and Institutions Code
Sec. 207 (b). The bill amended the W&I Code in other
respects affecting status offenders, especially at Sec.
731, removing the secure disposition option, and at Sec.
654, describing nonsecure alternatives to detention.

viewed this development with alarm. Dixon was committed
to preserving the compromise reached the previous year,
including the status offender provisions. In March 1977
he wrote to the entire Assembly Criminal Justice Committee, asking them to hold McAlister's bill and to await his
own version of a status offender bill that would satisfy
the public demand for partial restoration of detention
while preserving a basic policy of deinstitutionalization.
In his letter, Dixon used the federal funding argument to
support his position:

> The federal Juvenile Delinquency Act of 1974 speci-
> fically notes that states are expected to provide
> shelter-type facilities for status offenders and
> (that they) are not to be placed in juvenile deten-
> tion or correctional facilities. This was also the
> philosophy embraced by the Committee last year and
> approved by both houses.
>
> . . . we have taken great care to communicate our
> intention to the federal Law Enforcement Assistance
> Administration in order not to endanger the federal
> funding received as a result of the federal legis-
> lation for programs developed in our state both
> before and after implementation of AB 3121.
> Establishing a blanket lock-up once again for
> status offenders will endanger those funds and put
> California in direct conflict with federal law in
> this area.

On March 16, 1977, Dixon introduced AB 958, his own
bill modifying AB 3121 and restoring secure detention.
Dixon's bill permitted 48 judicial hours of secure detention of 601s to check for outstanding warrants or to
arrange a return of the minor to his or her parents.[15]
It opened the way to long holding periods ("until the
court orders the minor otherwise placed") for 601s who had
previously fled a nonsecure facility in violation of a

---

[15]A good portion of the debate centered on the use of
"judicial hours" as a standard for length of detention.
"Forty-eight judicial hours" means 48 hours, excluding
weekends and judicial holidays. In effect, this would
mean that a minor detained on a Friday night could be held
legally until the following Tuesday night, a four-day
period.

court order. Long detention periods were also allowed for
minors found by the juvenile court to be dangerous to
themselves because of drug, alcohol, medical, or mental
problems. The bill also required that Section 601s detained under its provisions be held in facilities separate
from Section 602 (criminal) minors.

As introduced, AB 958 was obviously in conflict with
Section 223 (a) (12) of JJDPA, with which Dixon professed
to be concerned. The extent of the conflict may not have
been apparent to Dixon or to other observers who had questions about the status offender requirements of the federal law. It was rumored in California that although
Section 223 (a) (12) was a "no exceptions" statement prohibiting secure detention of noncriminal minors, LEAA
guidelines permitted states to use short-term, 24-hour
secure detention periods without penalty. Further confusion arose from the fact that, at the time, Congress was
considering amendments to Section 223 (a) (12) and Section
223 (c) of JJDPA that would reduce the levels of deinstitutionalization necessary for compliance and extend the
deadlines for compliance.

In April, Dixon wrote to LEAA, asking for clarification
of its position on exceptions to the rule of no detention
for status offenders. The juvenile justice planner at the
state planning agency, George Howard, also wrote to LEAA
asking for guidance. Both received letters from the LEAA
Office of Counsel, advising them that AB 958 would "raise
substantial barriers to California's compliance with the
deinstitutionalization requirement," and would threaten
California's future eligibility for juvenile justice
funds.[16] The LEAA Counsel's Office explained that "for
compliance monitoring purposes" LEAA would continue to
fund states that held status offenders for 24 hours or
less, exclusive of nonjudicial days. No other exceptions,
LEAA stated, were acceptable. Furthermore, LEAA said in
its letter to Dixon, California would be out of compliance
if it adopted a law permitting judges to escalate Section
601 offenses into Section 602 (criminal) offenses or to

---

[16]Letter, April 29, 1977, to George Howard, Juvenile
Justice Planner, Office of Criminal Justice Planning,
Sacramento, California, from Thomas J. Madden, Assistant
Administrator, General Counsel, LEAA; and Letter, May 25,
1977, to Assemblyman Julian C. Dixon, State Capitol,
Sacramento, California, from John H. Wilson, Attorney-
Advisor, Office of General Counsel, LEAA.

issue contempt citations for fleeing a nonsecure facility or violating a court order; bootstrapping the status offense behavior into jurisdiction categories for which secure detention was allowed would violate the terms of the federal act and LEAA guidelines defining status offenders.

AB 958 had its first hearing of the Assembly Criminal Justice Committee on April 28, 1977, before either Dixon or Howard (at the Office of Criminal Justice Planning) had their replies from LEAA in hand. For the occasion, opponents of secure detention had prepared presentations from 10 or 12 persons representing youth service agencies, public defenders, sympathetic probation officers, civil liberties organizations, and the California Youth Authority. Two young people who had been locked up as runaways also testified. Dixon's supporting witnesses for AB 958 included judges from the Los Angeles County Superior and Juvenile Courts, a representative of the Los Angeles District Attorney, the California Peace Officers Association, and other law enforcement personnel. Interestingly, the California Probation, Parole and Correctional Association, largest of the probation organizations, had split on AB 958 and did not take sides.

The Assembly Criminal Justice Committee hearing on AB 958 was interesting because, unlike the hearings on AB 3121, this debate was focused entirely on the issue of status offender detention. The exchange between Mark Savage, director of the Pacifica Youth Service Bureau, and Jack Knox (D-Richmond), speaker pro tem of the Assembly, vividly demonstrated what legislators were worried about. Savage made a statement about the damage done by incarcerating young people who ran away or were thrown out of their homes. He was suddenly interrupted by Assemblyman Knox. "I'm a practical man," Knox said, "and you tell me, how can I run for office in my district if I vote against the bill?" "I can't tell you how to get reelected," Savage replied, "but I can ask you, how would you feel if your father tried to beat you up and you ran away and were locked in a cell for three or four days while your parents decided whether to come down and pick you up? I suggest that you would feel bitter and hostile toward a system that treated you like that."[17] Knox, ordinarily an

---

[17]Quotations in from this and the following anecdote are taken from the author's notes of the Assembly Criminal Justice Committee hearings on AB 3121, April-May 1976.

advocate of individual liberties, was not persuaded and
voted for AB 958.

At the same hearing, I testified against AB 958 on behalf of the California Child, Youth and Family Coalition
and the San Francisco Bar Association. I was the only
speaker to mention that AB 958 threatened the future of
about $4 million per year then being received in federal
juvenile justice funds. Ken Maddy (R-Fresno), who had
replaced Sieroty as chairman of the committee, stopped me
in midsentence. "We don't care what the federal government says, and we don't care about federal funds. We're
concerned here with what's right for California, and you
should restrict your comments to that issue." In the exchange that followed, the name of Birch Bayh, Senate
author of JJDPA, was mentioned, provoking an angry response from Maddy. "I don't like Birch Bayh. I never
liked Birch Bayh, and I don't care what he would have to
say about this bill." That, for the time being, took the
wind from the sails of the federal funding argument.

When AB 958 was approved by the Criminal Justice Committee, advocates of deinstitutionalization began to feel
grim about the chances of holding the gains realized
through AB 3121. Legislators seemed eager to correct what
they perceived to be the excesses of AB 3121 in regard to
runaways and "beyond control" minors. Mail continued to
pour into Dixon's office demanding new holding periods for
601s. Editorials appeared in the press in support of AB
958. For example, in a June 7, 1977 editorial titled "For
Runaways Who Run Again" (p. 5), the Los Angeles Times
said:

> . . . legislators [have] overlooked the problem
> that many youngsters who run away from home and are
> picked up and placed in a county facility will run
> away from county custody, too, and be back on the
> streets, unsupervised and often committing crimes
> just to survive. . . . Dixon's bill would allow for
> placing status offenders who run away from unlocked
> facilities in locked detention (not jails), away
> from youths charged with crimes. The lockups would
> be for their temporary protection--not punishment.
> This bill deserves support.

In August the Los Angeles County Grand Jury called on
the legislature to pass AB 958. The Juvenile Justice
Committee Chair of the Grand Jury explained that, "unless
the law is amended as AB 958 calls for, these kids can

make a mockery of the system."[18]   The district attorney
in Los Angeles, John Van de Kamp, was quoted often in the
press and elsewhere saying that restoration of detention
for status offenders was badly needed.

There is some question at this point about Dixon's
commitment to the preservation of federal funds.   By
August 9, when the bill was scheduled for hearing in the
Senate Judiciary Committee, Dixon had had ample time to
digest the letters from LEAA informing him that a bill
allowing more than 24 hours of detention would not be
acceptable to LEAA.   Dixon did bring author's amendments
reducing the holding periods into Senate Judiciary Committee, but he left intact the long detention periods for
minors who failed to appear at a hearing, or fled a nonsecure facility in violation of a court order, or were
thought by the court to be dangerous to themselves.

In this period Dixon appeared to be struggling for a
compromise that would satisfy competing interests.   He was
under pressure from the presiding juvenile court judge and
the district attorney in Los Angeles, and from the California Peace Officers' Association, to extend detention
limits.   On the other side, youth service agencies, civil
liberties advocates, public defenders, and mental health
professionals were urging Dixon to stand by the commitments he had made the previous year to maintain a policy
of deinstitutionalization.   He was constantly besieged
with demands to move both ways on the bill, and tempers
sometimes flared as proponents of amendments failed to get
their way.

As the bill came up for hearing in the Senate Finance
Committee in late August, advocates of deinstitutionalization began to dig deeply for tactics and arguments that
would slow its progress.   Since the arguments against the
policy of secure detention were not working well, these
advocates began to emphasize the fiscal problems that the
bill would create.

Their efforts received a welcome boost from a Department of Finance report estimating that AB 958 would cost
counties more than $10 million in the first year alone to
process and detain the new load of 601s in separate facilities from Section 602s.   The projected cost of segregated
detention already had been a cause of concern to many
boards of supervisors, and county boards were either split
or opposed to AB 958 on the cost issue.

---

[18]Grand Jury Asks Juvenile Law Changes.   Los Angeles
Times. August 19, 1977.

In spite of these distressing cost factors, the passage
of AB 958 through the Senate Finance Committee and the
Senate floor seemed to be a foregone conclusion. Two
weeks before the committee hearing Dixon received a memo
from the state planning agency containing language that,
the memo said, would "protect the LEAA fund flow." This
proposed amendment was a somewhat garbled evasion of LEAA
policy, equating detention of Section 601s to "alternatives for responding to like circumstances created by the
actions of an adult."[19] Although the suggested amendment was not an acceptable solution, according to the
opinions on record from LEAA, Dixon could go to the Finance Committee armed with language that had been furnished by the state planning agency to protect juvenile justice funds.

AB 958 ground to a halt for the 1977 session in the
Senate Finance Committee. Like many events in the legislature, its defeat was something of an accident. The
committee, meeting only two days before the legislature's
adjournment, was short several of its more conservative
members. The liberal senators who did show up were opposed to the detention bill more on principle than for its
cost. The bill simply failed to get the necessary votes,
although it was granted reconsideration for the 1978 session. Opponents were thus given a reprieve in which to
shore up their position. They knew that AB 958's chances
would be good before a full committee next year.

---

[19]Memorandum, August 17, 1977, to Assemblyman Julian
Dixon from Douglas Cunningham, Director, Office of Criminal Justice Planning. The full text of the memo and the
amendment are: "Subject: AB 958. Here is the amendment
to protect the LEAA fund flow: 'Sec. 5. In enacting subdivisions (c) (4), (5), (6), and (7), the Legislature in-
tends to establish the statutory jurisdictional basis,
separate and apart from Section 601 of such Code, for the
secure detention of minors under the limited circumstances
set forth therein. The purpose of such statutory jurisdictional basis for detention is to provide the court and
other authorities with alternatives for responding to circumstances created by the actions of the minor that are,
to the extent appropriate, comparable to alternatives for
responding to like circumstances created by the actions
of an adult.'" This language was amended into the September 6, 1977, version of AB 958 and was later deleted.

In the meantime JJDPA was amended by Congress. The 1977 amendments extended the time in which states had to comply with Section 223 (a) (12) to three years from the date of plan submission, and added "such non-offenders as dependent or neglected children" to the class of minors not subject to secure detention. In Section 223 (c) Congress softened the deinstitutionalization requirement by permitting states to continue to receive funds if they achieved a 75 percent level of deinstitutionalization within the three years and demonstrated, "through appropriate executive or legislative action, an unequivocal commitment to achieving full compliance within a reasonable time not exceeding two additional years."

During the interim and into the next legislative year, the opponents of AB 958 leaned on the federal funding argument. This tactic was a risky one, since some legislators welcomed the opportunity to say they did not want to be pushed around by the federal government. The 1977 JJDPA amendments extending the compliance deadline probably helped the opposition more than they hurt, because of the insistence that participating states demonstrate an "unequivocal commitment" to full compliance through legislation or executive action. AB 958 could hardly be described as legislative action demonstrating an unequivocal commitment to full compliance.

Proponents of the federal funding argument finally found a friend in the governor's office. The governor's legal affairs advisor, J. Anthony Kline, often spoke for the governor on criminal and juvenile justice matters. His leverage over legislators who were unwilling to make compromises was the constant threat of a governor's veto. Kline also had a background in public interest advocacy, and was somewhat sympathetic to the antidetention position. As AB 958 was about to be reheard in Senate Finance Committee, Kline called the principals together and told them to draft a compromise that would, in fact, reduce the detention periods to a level consistent with JJDPA standards. Dixon, acknowledging the importance of the governor's position and looking for a compromise that would work, accepted Kline's suggestion.

On August 21, 1978, Dixon presented an attenuated version of AB 958 to the Senate Finance Committee. It permitted 12 hours of secure detention of status offenders to check on warrants, 24 hours for the purpose of returning the minor to parents, and 72 hours to hold out-of-state runaways. The longer holding periods, based on fleeing a nonsecure facility, violating a court order, and

the mental condition of the minor, were dropped. There
was little doubt that this bill would comply with federal
requirements. Dixon, addressing the committee, acknowledged that he could not please everybody. He told the
committee that he had a bill that would repair the essential problems created by AB 3121 while maintaining federal
funds through JJDAA. It would be up to the committee, he
said, to accept or reject amendments sought by proponents
for more or less detention. The California Peace Officers' Association was anxious to testify for amendments
extending the holding periods. The opponents of detention
had turned out in large numbers to counter the amendments
sought by law enforcement. After a brief debate the committee approved AB 958 in the form Dixon had offered,
without new amendments. The bill passed its Senate floor
vote and was signed by the Governor in September.[20]

The Period Since 1978

The passage of AB 958 in the 1978 legislature seemed to
satisfy most of the demands for a restoration of secure
detention of status offenders, and appeared for the time
being to settle California law in this area. Although
there was a dispute over California's compliance with
Section 223 (a) (13) of the act (in regard to the mixing
of juveniles and young adults in the California Youth
Authority), LEAA has not taken exception to California's
policy, or practice in relation to status offender detention.

     In the two legislative years after AB 958, two legis-
lators introduced bills to expand the use of detention for
status offenders (AB 1650--Chappie, R-Yuba City; AB 1761--
McVittie, D-Chino), but without success. They basically
lacked the public support necessary to legislate further
detention. Police and probation departments who previously backed bills restoring detention had begun to
adapt to the deinstitutionalization requirement of AB
3121, and many lost their enthusiasm for secure detention.
Some probation departments even joined the constituency
supporting deinstitutionalization. The Monterey County
probation department, for example, publicly endorsed the

---

[20] The provisions added by AB 958, restoring secure detention, can be found at Welfare and Institutions Code
Sec. 207 (c) through (f).

policy of referring status offenders to community-based agencies and opposed legislative attempts to restore secure detention. Many of the police and probation and court officials who backed AB 958 appeared to be satisfied with the 12- and 24-hour holding periods made possible by its enactment.

THE IMPACT OF STATE LAW CHANGES ON STATUS OFFENDER DEINSTITUTIONALIZATION IN CALIFORNIA

A number of studies have been conducted to determine the impact of changes in law that in 1976 prohibited all secure detention of status offenders and in 1978 restored secure detention on a limited basis.[21] Data on AB 958 are scarce, since the bill has only been in effect for little over a year. But there is no doubt that AB 3121 had a significant impact on reducing Section 601 case loads, and on forcing the development of nonsecure alternatives to detention for those Section 601s who were still being processed through the juvenile justice system.

According to data from the California Bureau of Criminal Statistics, in 1977, the first year that AB 3121 was in effect, there was a dramatic decline in Section 601 arrests, to 41,939 from 80,762 in the previous year. This 1977 figure is down from the all-time high of 107,898 in 1974. The number of petitions filed to establish juvenile court jurisdiction in Section 601 cases dropped by approximately 50 percent between 1976 and 1977. Statewide admissions to juvenile halls for status offenses in 1977 numbered 607, down from a staggering 33,344 in 1976. These 607 youth, who could not legally be detained on the

---

[21]The Youth Authority has issued a major study of the impact of AB 3121 in five northern and three southern counties: AB 3121 Impact Evaluation: Final Report, California Youth Authority, Sacramento, California, January 1980. Individual counties (e.g., Alameda, Contra Costa, and Santa Clara) have conducted their own evaluations of the impact of AB 3121. The Youth Authority is about to issue a further report on the impact of AB 958. For comparisons of California's deinstitutionalization efforts with those of other states, see "Cost and Service Impacts of Deinstitutionalization of Status Offenders in Ten States," Responses to Angry Youth, Arthur D. Little, Inc., Washington, D.C., October 1977.

basis of a status offense alone, were in most cases previously adjudicated Section 602 minors detained for probation violations that were Section 601 offenses.

There was speculation in 1977, when AB 3121 first went
into effect, that some Section 601 status offenders who
could no longer be detained would resurface in the juvenile justice system as Section 602 criminal offenders.
This was based in part on suspicion that probation personnel, threatened with budget and job losses by the decline in Section 601 case loads, would endeavor to fill
empty juvenile hall spaces. There was also speculation
that minors apprehended for a variety of conducts would
no longer receive the benefit of admission to detention
on the "soft" Section 601 charge, but would more often be
labeled with the Section 602 criminal charge.

The California Youth Authority's study of the impact
of AB 3121 does not substantiate this speculation. The
report shows a decline in total Section 602 arrests for
each of the years 1974 through 1978 (California Youth
Authority 1980:77). An increase does appear in the number of Section 602 petitions filed in 1977; statewide
(excluding Los Angeles County), Section 602 petitions increased 18 percent in 1977 over 1976, but in Los Angeles
County, representing one-third of the state's juvenile
population, such petitions declined by 5 percent over the
same period (California Youth Authority 1980:110,113).

The available data therefore give mixed results in the
attempt to discern a trend of relabeling Section 601s as
Section 602s. Even the 18 percent increase in Section 602
petitions for 1977 that appeared in the statewide average,
excluding Los Angeles, may not have been caused by the
prohibition on further detention of Section 601s, but may
be due instead to the requirement of AB 3121 that the
district attorney, instead of the probation officer, make
the decision to file a Section 602 petition in juvenile
court.

It is clear from the data available that Section 601
arrests and detentions dropped substantially after AB
3121. However, it is a different matter to determine
whether the status offender problem in California has been
solved by the changes in law limiting secure detention.
Many police and probation departments across the state
reacted to AB 3121 by refusing to intervene in cases involving runaways or beyond-control minors. Some police
officers were accused of telling parents whose children
had run away to "go talk to your legislator." Concern has
been voiced that, although California has discarded an
inappropriate solution, the problem still exists.

In theory status offenders needing shelter or treatment were supposed to be referred to nonsecure facilities after the passage of AB 3121. This was also the intent of the federal act, which stated, before amendment in 1977, that status offenders shall not be placed in detention or correctional facilities, "but must be placed in shelter facilities."

One problem in California is that the law prohibiting the secure detention of status offenders did not require or pay for the establishment of alternative nonsecure facilities for runaways, beyond-control minors, and others in need of placement or treatment. Amendments to Section 654 of the Welfare and Institutions Code, contained in AB 3121, allowed probation departments to contract with public or private agencies for nonsecure shelter facilities and counseling programs for status offenders, but this language was permissive, not mandatory. Legislators who were willing to outlaw secure detention were not willing to impose the cost of mandated nonsecure facilities on state or county governments. In discussions with legislators and others who helped steer AB 3121 through to its conclusion, the apology is frequently voiced that it was better to end the practice of detention and hope that alternatives would develop, than to refuse to support a bill that was flawed because it failed to appropriate funds for those alternatives.

In subsequent legislation funds to reimburse the state-mandated costs of AB 3121 were appropriated, and a portion of this amount was used by some counties to fund alternative-to-detention programs for status offenders.[22] Substantial funding for nonsecure facilities and programs came from federal sources, and the impact of these funds is dicussed in the following section.

---

[22]AB 90 (Dixon), passed by the 1977 California legislature, replaced the California probation subsidy program with the County Justice System Subvention Program, establishing fiscal incentives for the retention of offenders in local facilities and programs. Funds to pay for the state-mandated costs of AB 3121 were appropriated through AB 90 at an annual $18 million level. The costs of AB 3121 include district attorneys' salaries, costs of trying minors as adults, costs of switching from secure to nonsecure detention of status offenders, and other costs.

THE IMPACT OF FEDERAL EXPENDITURES ON STATUS OFFENDER
DEINSTITUTIONALIZATION IN CALIFORNIA

It is beyond the scope of this paper to assess the degree
to which community-based alternatives to secure detention
have in fact developed in California in the wake of legislation deinstitutionalizing status offenders. Nevertheless, a brief review of the efforts made with federal
funds to achieve deinstitutionalization of these youth in
California will add some perspective to the political
story of how the law was changed. Outside the legislative and political arenas, much of California's progress
toward deinstitutionalization of status offenders has
been accomplished by funding alternatives to detention.

Unfortunately, there exists no accurate statewide count
or assessment of programs and facilities for status
offenders. The California Office of Criminal Justice
Planning (OCJP)--the state planning agency that administers JJDPA in California--is charged with monitoring the
state's compliance with the status offender mandates of
the act. Nevertheless, OCJP does not have an adequate
administrative budget for the massive job of counting and
evaluating each California program that uses JJDPA funds
for status offenders.[23]

OCJP does record total federal dollars expended for a
category that covers both diversion and deinstitutionalization of juvenile offenders and status offenders. It
also monitors data collected by the California Bureau of
Criminal Statistics on arrests, outside referrals, and
dispositions of Section 601s by local police, probation
departments, and courts. By funding deinstitutionalization projects in target areas where Section 601 case loads
are high, OCJP has attempted to move California toward

---

[23]OCJP must depend on reports from 25 local and regional
planning units (RPUs) for its information on the development of alternative programs for status offenders.
Problems arise here because the RPUs fund multiservice
programs, of which only one component may be a status
offender program. Sometimes a local status offender program is partially funded with JJDPA funds and is also
supported by non-JJDPA sources. Given the limitations of
its administrative budget, it is difficult for OCJP to
trace exactly how federal funds moving through it, and
through the RPUs, are ultimately used at the local level
for alternative-to-detention projects.

full compliance with the status offender deinstitutionalization requirements of JJDPA.

In 1975 and 1976 the entire local share of the state
JJDPA formula grant (about $2.4 million out of a $3.3
million total of JJDPA money) went to fund alternative-to-
detention projects for status offenders in 20 California
counties. These counties, by OCJP count, were responsible at the time for 75 percent of all status offender admissions to secure detention. Prior to the passage of AB
3121, OCJP estimated that by re-funding the existing deinstitutionalization projects in 1977 and by adding funds
for projects in nine more counties, California would have
achieved a 92.6 percent deinstitutionalization level by
August 1, 1977, without the law changes prohibiting secure
detention that passed in 1976.[24]

After AB 3121 became law, about $3.4 million in 1977
JJDPA funds were made available to counties for purposes
of implementing it. A substantial portion of this (OCJP
estimates 75 percent) went to community-based alternative
programs for all classes of juvenile offenders.[25]

JJDPA funds represent only a portion of the federal
money being spent on California deinstitutionalization
projects. Maintenance of effort funds--the 19.15 percent
of the state share of Crime Control funds that must be
spent on juvenile justice and delinquency prevention pro-
jects--have been expended on status offender deinstitutionalization and offender diversion projects at levels
exceeding JJDPA expenditures for these purposes in some
years. Special emphasis funds coming directly from the
Office of Juvenile Justice and Delinquency Prevention in
Washington have supported deinstitutionalization projects
in Alameda County and South Lake Tahoe, as well as other
projects for the delivery of technical assistance to counties coping with deinstitutionalization requirements. The
Runaway Youth Act, created through JJDPA but administered
by HEW, has established 20 programs in California for the
shelter care of runaways.

---

[24] OCJP funding levels and compliance projects are from
the 1978 California State Plan For Criminal Justice, Juvenile Justice Section, Office of Criminal Justice Planning,
Sacramento, California, at VII-17.

[25] 1977 figures from an interview with George Howard,
Juvenile Justice Planner, Office of Criminal Justice
Planning, Sacramento, California, on January 28, 1980.

These references to gross expenditure levels do not reveal much about the character or number of local and community-based alternatives to detention for status offenders. Again there is no reliable statewide assessment of such alternatives. Lacking such an assessment, it is nevertheless possible within the framework of this paper to describe in general terms how three counties have used JJDPA funds to respond to the status offender mandates of federal and state law.

In Santa Cruz County (population 178,000) the probation department decided shortly after AB 3121 became law to refer all Section 601 cases to a private community-based program providing shelter and crisis care for status offenders and other youth. The county contracted with the Santa Cruz Community Counseling Center, and sought and obtained JJDPA funds from its regional planning unit to pay for counseling, housing, and other services for status offenders referred to the Youth Services program of the center. Santa Cruz Youth Services is now delivering shelter and crisis care to approximately 100 status offenders referred by probation each year, and both public and private agency personnel seem satisfied with the alternative-to-detention system that has developed in that county.[26]

In the city and county of San Francisco, status offender problems have not been so easily resolved. After AB 3121, JJDPA funds were allocated to an eight-bed shelter care facility for runaways and other status offenders. This is the only privately operated, community-based facility for status offenders in a county with a population of 650,000 that is a historic haven for runaways. The probation department operates its own version of a shelter care facility for status offenders, which is a converted wing of the juvenile hall. At various times this juvenile hall unit has been locked at night for the alleged purpose of keeping intruders out. The San Francisco probation department has drawn criticism, not only for locking the "nonsecure" unit, but also for resisting the more complete development of a system for the referral of status of-

---

[26]Information regarding the Santa Cruz County referral system was provided by Terry Moriarty, Director, Santa Cruz Community Counseling Center, and Jim Solomon, Chief Probation Officer, Santa Cruz County.

fenders to nonsecure facilities providing shelter care and treatment in community-based settings.[27]

Like San Francisco, Santa Clara County (population 1.25 million) has used federal funds for alternative programs for status offenders, but seems to lack a clear policy for the referral of status offenders to community-based agencies. There are two JJDPA-funded shelter and crisis care programs in the county, with a combined 12-bed capacity. Both programs are open 24 hours a day and offer family counseling designed to resolve behavior problems. The relationship of these JJDPA-funded programs to the probation department is shaky, at best. The probation department sporadically refers status offenders to these agencies, but also refers status offenders to one of about 40 foster homes, where treatment is not provided. In the four years since AB 3121, private agencies and public officials have discussed converting to a system for the referral of all Section 601s to community-based agencies providing shelter and crisis care, but no such policy has yet been adopted. Meanwhile, the JJDPA-funded programs for status offenders have suffered from a lack of public support, and from reductions in the levels of JJDPA funds available through their region.[28]

It is evident from these three examples that counties have responded differently to status offender law changes and to the availability of federal funds to establish status offender alternatives. Some counties have made smooth conversions to a system for the referral of status offenders to community-based agencies funded with JJDPA or Runaway Youth Act funds. In other counties public officials have resisted such a conversion, even though federal funds for alternatives have been made available. Clearly, federal expenditures have made full deinstitutionalization possible in some counties. In others the impact of federal expenditures on the development of al-

---

[27] Information regarding the San Francisco status offender situation was provided by Brian Slattery, Director of Youth Advocates, the agency which operates Rafiki Masada, the shelter care facility referred to in the text, and by other public and private sources.

[28] Observations regarding the Santa Clara County status offender situation are based on information supplied by Ray Gertler, Director, CASA SAY, Mountain View, California, and from other probation and private sector sources.

ternative-to-detention systems cannot be adequately assessed in the absence of a comprehensive study.

ASSESSMENT OF THE IMPACT OF FEDERAL FUNDING REQUIREMENTS
ON THE REFORM OF CALIFORNIA LAW

The influence of the federal act was practically nil in
bringing about the California statute that deinstitutionalized status offenders in 1976. Prior to 1976 only a few
contacts between federal and state policymakers on the
status offender issue can be traced, such as the appearance of the U.S. Senate Juvenile Delinquency Subcommittee
Counsel before the California Assembly Criminal Justice
Committee interim hearing in October 1974.

After 1976 the number of contacts between state and
federal officials on the status offender issue increased.
Faced with a backlash movement to restore secure detention
in California, advocates of deinstitutionalization emphasized the federal funding argument in an attempt to
maintain the policy of deinstitutionalization established
by AB 3121. The argument appeared to work only moderately
well. Many legislators resisted being told what to do by
the federal government, even if nonconformity meant the
loss of millions of federal dollars. In the end, when a
bill restoring secure detention became law, the fact that
the law was in compliance with federal standards was only
partly the result of efforts to mold it to federal requirements. The outcome in 1978 was a compromise devised
to satisfy competing interests within the state, and the
federal standard provided a line along which the compromise could conveniently be drawn. Certain other conclusions emerge from a review of the interplay between the
federal and state laws on detention of status offenders.

   1. LEAA's state planning agency in California kept its
distance on the issue and was not an active supporter of
federal policy. California's state planning agency made
no contribution to the 1976 status offender reform law,
and played the role of cautious and neutral advisor during the 1977-78 legislative debate that threatened to
throw California out of compliance with JJDPA. The aloof-
ness of the state planning agency may be explained in part
by the competing interests it serves as a funding agency
for law enforcement programs as well as for diversion,
prevention, and deinstitutionalization programs. Its
character is also stamped by the governor, who appoints

its board and its staff; in this case the governor was only mildly interested in the status offender detention issue, and was on record as being skeptical of the LEAA bureaucracy in general.

The authority of any state planning agency to implement JJDPA is certainly questionable. The LEAA Office of General Counsel at one point issued a legal opinion stating that the act does not give the state planning agency authority to implement a state plan, but that such authority must derive from a source within the state.[29] Since different states establish these agencies under different arms or branches of government, their authority varies from state to state. In California it is clear that the agency had a limited role as administrator of LEAA funds and was responsible to the governor for its activity, if any, in support of changes in juvenile justice law or policy.

2. The Juvenile Justice Advisory Group, charged with advising on juvenile justice matters within the state, failed to participate in the legislative debate over status offender detention. The Juvenile Justice Advisory Group must be appointed by the governor, must advise the SPA and, as of 1977, may advise the legislature and the governor on juvenile justice matters. Except for one letter of opposition from the chair of the JJDPA Advisory Group on AB 958, which was mailed in the second year of the debate, the Advisory Group did not participate in the development of status offender reform legislation. In this respect JJDPA was denied a ready-made advocate for its implementation in California.

3. The political temperament of the governor significantly affected implementation of LEAA policies in California. Under the Omnibus Crime Control Act of 1968,

---

[29]Legal opinion summarized in Removing Status Offenders from Secure Facilities: Federal Leadership and Guidance Are Needed, Report to the Congress by the Comptroller General, General Accounting Office, June 5, 1978, pp. 11–12. Section 223 (a) (2) of JJDPA requires the state plan to "contain satisfactory evidence" that the state planning agency "has, or will have authority, by legislation if necessary, to implement such plan." The California statutes establishing the staff and supervisory board of the state planning agency in California (Penal Code Sec. 13810 through 13825) make no reference to such authority.

Section 203(42 USC 3723), and the Juvenile Justice and
Delinquency Prevention Act of 1974, Section 223, the governor of a participating state is responsible for making
appointments to the state planning agency, its supervisory
board, and the JJDPA Advisory Group. By failing to make
appointments, as Governor Brown threatened to do in 1975,
a governor can thwart the intent and effect of the federal
act. By appointing persons who are insensitive to the
policies of JJDPA, the governor can temporarily maximize
the flow of funds while minimizing their impact. In California's case the governor holding office since JJDPA took
effect in 1975 has been only moderately supportive of deinstitutionalization and has adopted law enforcement positions on many criminal justice issues, probably out of
political necessity. The federal acts' deference to the
gubernatorial appointment power makes their impact dependent on the politics of the governor in question.

    4. Federal policy in relation to status offender de-
tention, though clearly stated in JJDPA, was confused by
monitoring guidelines constituting exceptions to the act,
by amendments to the act in 1977, and perhaps by a lack
of broad support within the federal government for the
policy of deinstitutionalization. Legislators and others
complained during the AB 958 debate about the lack of
clarity in federal policy. LEAA letters responding to
inquiries about that policy were fairly clear, but were
soon muddled by amendments to JJDPA adopted in the same
year. The state planning agency was itself unclear in its
communications with the author of AB 958 as to how the
federal fund flow could be maintained, and at one point
the agency's director offered an amendment purporting to
guarantee fund flow that was wholly inadequate for that
purpose. The potential influence that the federal government might have had was stifled by the manner in which
LEAA, including the state planning agency, communicated
with Californians who were in a position to reform state
law and policy.

    Internal confusion at the Office of Juvenile Justice
and Delinquency Prevention during 1977 and 1978 may have
been responsible for the lack of clarity in communications
with California. In June 1978 the General Accounting
Office of the Comptroller General issued a report titled
Removing Status Offenders from Secure Facilities: Federal
Leadership and Guidance Are Needed. The report criticized
OJJDP and the Associate Administrator for Juvenile Justice
for failing to take into account states' problems in meeting the deinstitutionalization mandates of JJDPA (General

Accounting Office 1978:12-13). The report also accused OJJDP of failing to identify nonconforming practices within participating states and of failing to encourage the leadership role of state planning agencies as implementation resources in nonconforming states (General Accounting Office 1978:13-14). The response of the Department of Justice to these charges is appended to the report and casts doubt on some of the accusations made by the GAO (1978: Appendix III). Nevertheless, it is clear that OJJDP had its own troubles in administering the nationwide mandate of deinstitutionalization of status offenders. Matters were complicated further by the fact that John Rector, the Associate Administrator for Juvenile Justice was, during 1977 and 1978, constantly under attack for his management of OJJDP.

OJJDP may have lacked broad support in the federal government for the policy of status offender deinstitutionalization mandated by JJDPA. Rector recalls the unpopularity of mandatory status offender deinstitutionalization in the House version of the bill that later was merged into JJDPA.[30] This sentiment returned to haunt Rector in House oversight hearings on the act in 1978, when one of the committee members accused OJJDP of concentrating on status offenders to the exclusion of other important problems, such as serious juvenile offenders. "Deinstitutionalization," the congressman admonished, "isn't the only flag this ship flies."[31]

5. Even where federal policy was clearly articulated, the outcomes of legislative debates over detention were determined primarily by factors other than federal policy or federal dollars. The legislative outcomes on status offender issues in California were primarily the results of compromises reached between competing interests within the state. Sometimes chance or accident determined short-term outcomes, as when AB 958 was held in committee because only a few of the more liberal members were in

---

[30] Interview with John Rector, Department of Justice, Washington, D.C., on January 9, 1980.

[31] Statement of Representative Ike Andrews (D-North Carolina), Chairman, House Subcommittee on Economic Opportunity, in oversight hearings on the JJDPA on June 27, 1978, quoted in Youth Alternatives, monthly publication of the National Youth Alternatives Project (now, National Youth Work Alliance), Washington, D.C., July 1978, p. 2.

attendance. The role of federal dollars and federal policy is necessarily limited in any debate involving intrastate policy and interest groups. Even where there is an interest in preserving federal funds, if the federal dollar amounts are low relative to the costs of the state systems they effect, the influence of federal dollar-related policies may also be low.

6. **JJDPA funds did contribute to the legislative compromise ultimately reached in California.** On a more positive note, JJDPA did have some impact on the outcome of AB 958. Though not the primary force determining outcome, JJDPA funds were emphasized at key points in the debate and did raise some concerns about their potential loss. The LEAA 24-hour monitoring guideline for secure detention of status offenders provided an external standard or line along which a suitable legislative compromise could ultimately be drawn.

7. **The most vocal advocates of status offender deinstitutionalization came from JJDPA-funded projects within the state.** Many of the witnesses who appeared in hearings to support the deinstitutionalization provisions of AB 3121, and to oppose the restoration of detention through AB 958, were youth service counselors and advocates whose projects were funded through JJDPA grants. The experience they collected through operation of alternative-to-detention projects was useful to legislators attempting to devise a statewide policy on status offender detention. At times, these advocates exerted behind-the-scenes pressure that helped move deinstitutionalization bills and slowed or modified pro-detention bills. Their presence and vigilance at legislative hearings were extremely important in keeping the pro-detention forces aware that the opposition was ready and able to counter the arguments in favor of secure detention. By supporting local advocates of reform, the act was effective in preserving a basic policy of deinstitutionalization.

8. **The act has had a vitally important effect on the achievement of de facto deinstitutionalization in California through the allocation of funds to nonsecure, alternative-to-detention programs.** By injecting millions of dollars into status offender programs at the local level, JJDPA has had a significant impact on deinstitutionalization in California. The dimensions of the alternative-to-detention system that has developed have not been accurately measured, in terms of either the number of status offenders receiving services or the quality of services delivered. Nevertheless, OCJP has estimated

that even without the passage of AB 3121, JJDPA-funded programs for status offenders would have led to a 92 percent level of deinstitutionalization by the end of the two-year period for compliance stated in JJDPA. Subsequent developments, such as the OJJDP change in the definition of detention and correctional facilities, and the addition of nonoffenders to the class that must be deinstitutionalized, have probably reduced that projected compliance level. Yet it is fair to state that the act has, at least in some California counties, contributed significantly to the development of alternative-to-detention systems through the expenditure of program funds for that purpose.

REFERENCES

California Legislature (1970) Report on the Juvenile Court Process. Assembly Interim Committee on Criminal Procedure. Sacramento, Calif.
_____ (1974a) Juvenile Violence: What it is, Why it is, How it stops. Report of the Assembly Select Committee on Juvenile Violence. Sacramento, Calif.
_____ (1974b) Legislative Proposals. California Assembly Symposium on Services to Children and Youth, Assembly Office of Research. Sacramento, Calif.
California Youth Authority (1980) AB 3121 Impact Evaluation: Final Report. Sacramento, Calif.: California Youth Authority.
General Accounting Office (1978) Removing Status Offenders from Secure Facilities: Federal Leadership and Guidance are Needed. Washington, D.C.: General Accounting Office.
Maslow, Jonathan Evan (1976) LEAA's Great Hardware Handout. Juris Doctor 6(February):23-34.
Saleebey, George (1975) Hidden Closets: A Study of Detention Practices in California. Prepared for the California Youth Authority, Sacramento, Calif.

PERSONS CONSULTED OR INTERVIEWED

Allen Breed, Director, National Institute of Corrections, Washington, D.C. former Director, California Youth Authority.
Peter Bull, Director, National Center for Youth Law, San Francisco.

Douglas Cunningham, Director, California Office of
    Criminal Justice Planning, Sacramento.
Dr. Timothy Fitzharris, Director, California Parole,
    Probation and Correctional Association, Sacramento.
Ray Gertler, Director, CASA SAY, Mountain View,
    California.
Ronald Hayes, Director of Field Services, California
    Youth Authority, Sacramento.
George Howard, Juvenile Justice Planner, Office of
    Criminal Justice Planning, Sacramento.
Richard Lew, Legislative Liaison, California Youth
    Authority, Sacramento.
Leonard Lloyd, Director, California Status Offender
    Deinstutionalization Training and Technical Assistance
    Project, San Francisco.
Douglas McKee, Assistant District Attorney (and
    legislative liaison), Los Angeles County.
Terry Moriarty, Director, Santa Cruz Community Counseling
    Center, Santa Cruz.
John Rector, former Associate Adminstrator of LEAA for
    the Office of Juvenile Justice and Delinquency
    Prevention, Washington, D.C.
Hon. Alan Sieroty, State Senator (D-Los Angeles),
    Sacramento.
Brian Slattery, Director, Youth Advocates, San Francisco.
Lawrence Smith, Deputy State Public Defender, Sacramento.
James Solomon, Chief Probation Officer, Santa Cruz County.
Michael Ullman, Chief Consultant, Assembly Criminal
    Justice Committee, Sacramento.
Michael Wald, Professor of Law, Stanford University,
    Stanford.
John Wilson, Attorney, Office of General Counsel, Law
    Enforcement Assistance Adminstration, Department of
    Justice, Washington, D.C.
Files, maintained in Sacramento, of Hon. Julian C. Dixon,
    United States Representative (D-Los Angeles),
    Washington, D.C., former California State Assemblyman.

Child Placement and Deinstitutionalization: A Case Study of Social Reform in Illinois

APPENDIX

F

MARK TESTA

INTRODUCTION

Child placement laws in the United States traditionally allowed broad discretionary powers to juvenile court judges and social workers in the placement of children who were adjudicated neglected, in need of supervision, or delinquent.[1] The purpose of these laws was to permit government officials and professionals an expanded viewpoint in tailoring placement decisions to a child's individual needs and circumstances. The goal was one of individualized justice; but litigation and social scientific research frequently showed actual practice to be overly punitive, racially biased, and generally abusive of the

---

[1] My use of the term "child placement" is the same as that of Goldstein et al. (1973:5): "Child placement, for our purposes, is a term which encompasses all legislative, judicial, and executive decisions generally or specifically concerned with establishing, administering, or rearranging parent-child relationships. The term covers a wide range of variously labeled legal procedures for deciding who should be assigned or expected to seize the task of being 'parent' to a child. These procedures include birth certification, neglect, abandonment, battered child, foster care, adoption, delinquency, youth offender, as well as custody in annulment, separation, and divorce."

legal rights of children and their parents (Matza 1966, Murphy 1973, Rosenheim 1966, Schur 1973).

In response, a reform movement arose to reduce discretion and flexibility in child placement in order to promote greater equity in these decisions. Two results of this movement were the strengthening of procedural safeguards for the legal rights of minors (i.e., due process) and the establishing of formal restrictions on the placement of children in correctional facilities, child care institutions, and mental hospitals (i.e., deinstitutionalization).

This paper examines the growth of the reform movement in Illinois and analyzes the major judicial, legislative, and administrative developments that increased the legal autonomy of minors and subsequently gave rise to the state's deinstitutionalization of children in public custody. It concentrates on the conflict between moderate and radical advocates of deinstitutionalizing status offenders and neglected children under the legal guardianship of the state department of child welfare. The moderates advocated the exclusion of young children and status offenders from "punitive" institutions but favored their placement in "benign" group quarters, such as group homes, child care institutions, and residential treatment centers.[2] The radicals sought to curtail the institutionalization of children altogether.

At the center of the conflict was a dispute over the value of professionalism in child placement. The moderates favored a stronger professional orientation that emphasized the caseworker's clinical judgment of the child's best interests both in the selection of foster placements and in the development of service plans. Institutional care was conceived as one of a range of placement options that a caseworker might choose. In the treatment of a neglected child traumatized by physical or sexual abuse or in the supervision of a runaway adjudicated ungovernable, for example, institutional care might be the placement of choice. The assumption was that such children required insulation from their social environments in order to restore stability to their lives before

---

[2] The old distinction between dependency institutions and institutions for disturbed children is thought by some to be no longer valid (Mayer et al. 1977:51). Throughout this paper the term "child care institution" will be used to describe both types of children's institutions.

they could successfully rejoin their families or the larger community (Bettelheim 1974, Mayer et al. 1977).
Almost all aspects of the placement process were left
indeterminate, including length of stay and geographical
distance from the parent's home, in order to permit the
caseworker the flexibility to individualize care and
treatment.

In contrast, the radicals opposed the individualized
approach to child placement. They viewed the role of the
helping professions in child placement as essentially repressive and as focusing attention on the individual child
and thereby diverting attention from the nonpsychological
causes of family disorganization, such as poverty, racial
discrimination, and neighborhood instability (Miller
1973). Because the child care institution was the primary
medium through which "scapegoating" was alleged to occur,
the radicals sought to curtail children's placements in
these facilities. Although the radicals failed to achieve
massive deinstitutionalization in child placement, many
of the reforms they sought eventually were established on
a lesser scale; caseworkers' discretion in the selection
of foster placements became more limited, and departmental
practices gradually turned from the flexible use of child
care institutions as an intervention option of choice toward a more restrictive use as the placement of last
resort.

The radicals' efforts to limit caseworker discretion
in the use of institutions speaks to a fundamental dilemma
inherent in many public policies on children: To what
degree should administrative discretion in child placement
be narrowed by formal standards and rules of procedure?
Lawyers and social scientists have long recognized that
the substitution of rules for discretion introduces
greater efficiency and procedural regularity into the
administrative process, but often does so at the risk of
a diminished capacity for the achievement of substantial
policy goals (Handler 1979, Janowitz 1978, Mnookin 1976,
Mouzelis 1971). The risk is one of legalism, as explained
by Nonet and Selznick (1978:64):

> A focus on rules tends to narrow the range of
> legally relevant facts thereby detaching legal
> thought from social reality. The result is legal-
> ism, a disposition to rely on legal authority to
> the detriment of practical problem solving. The
> application of rules ceases to be informed by a
> regard for purposes, needs, and consequences.

Legalism is costly, partly because of the rigid-
ities it imposes, but also because rules construed
in abstracto are too easily satisfied by a formal
observance that conceals substantive evasions of
public policy.

This paper examines the issue by analyzing some of the
consequences for children of the shift from indeterminate
to determinate standards of child placement through the
principle of institutionalization as a last resort. It
argues that the shift entailed a fundamental reordering
of administrative priorities concerning the evaluation of
the relative harms of institutionalization. The basic
assumption of deinstitutionalization was that the unnecessary institutionalization of children was more to be
avoided than their inadequate institutionalization. One
important risk of a liberal application of the concept of
institutionalization as a last resort is that it may involve substantial errors of the latter sort. For example,
the defense of the flexible use of institutions as an intervention option of choice assumes that significantly
higher rates of placement discontinuity (e.g., runaways,
repeated placements) are associated with delayed institutionalization; such discontinuity, it is argued, is contrary to the psychological and social well-being of the
child (Bowlby 1977, Goldstein et al. 1973). On the other
hand, the argument for institutionalization as a last
resort assumes either that placement continuity is unaffected or that the effects of discontinuity are negligible. Available data on child placements will be used
below to assess both viewpoints.
  A second issue is the radicals' claim that administrative discretion in child placement allowed racially biased
placement patterns to persist. A lawsuit brought against
the Illinois Department of Children and Family Services
by Chicago Legal Aid in 1973 charged racial bias on the
part of voluntary child placement agencies that provided
child care services under contract with the state. The
suit alleged that the racial biases of voluntary agencies
resulted in the inappropriate placement of minority group
children in state mental hospitals, county detention
homes, and substandard institutions located out of state
(Murphy 1974). The radicals cited these allegations to
justify the diversion of state wards from voluntary agencies and to support the provision of state funds to establish community-based programs to serve black and brown
youth. Available data on placements therefore will be

analyzed for evidence of biased treatment of minority children by voluntary agencies.

The first part of this paper provides a background for the analysis of these issues by tracing the major judicial, legislative, and administrative developments in Illinois child placement policy that preceded the conflict over deinstitutionalization. The spokesperson for the radicals' cause was Jerome Miller, D.S.W., who had been appointed director of the Illinois Department of Children and Family Services in January 1973. Prior to his coming to Illinois, Miller had attained national prominence as a proponent of deinstitutionalization while serving as Commissioner of Youth Services in Massachusetts. Almost overnight he had closed down virtually all of the correctional institutions for juveniles in that state. It was one of the first major efforts in the nation to deinstitutionalize delinquent youth (Bakal and Polsky 1979, Ohlin et al. 1977). Miller's efforts to accomplish the same with status offenders and neglected children in Illinois is the main focus of this paper.[3] The following section begins with case load statistics on the deinstitutionalization of children under the guardianship of the Department of Children and Family Services during Miller's first full program year as director.

DEINSTITUTIONALIZATION IN CHILD PLACEMENT: FISCAL 1974

Between May 1973 and June 1974 the number of institutionalized children in publicly subsidized foster care in Illinois dropped by 34 percent, from 3,160 residents to 2,078 residents.[4] This drop was due largely to the child placement policies inaugurated by Jerome Miller during his tenure as director of the Illinois Department of Children and Family Services. It marked the first significant decline in the size of the child welfare population in institutions since the department's establishment in 1964.

---

[3]Most of the program statistics were obtained directly from the relevant state departments serving children and youth. Statistics obtained from published sources are cited in the text.

[4]These figures exclude young women in maternity homes and children and youth in group homes, detention facilities, training schools, and mental hospitals.

Miller came to Illinois in January 1973 to serve in the administration of Democratic Governor Daniel Walker. Although the governor was elected on a "new populist" platform of fiscal conservatism, he had proposed liberal reforms in the areas of social welfare and criminal justice. Miller was brought to Illinois largely on the basis of the reputation he had earned in Massachusetts as an activist in the deinstitutionalization movement. At the time of his arrival there were 3,100 children under public supervision in child care institutions. Less than 10 percent of those children were housed in state-run institutions. The remainder lived in publicly subsidized placements in institutions operated by voluntary child welfare agencies under purchase-of-services contracts.[5]

In the spring of 1973 the Illinois press published allegations of brutality in several Texas wilderness camps that were eventually named in a lawsuit on behalf of Illinois wards who had been placed there by the child welfare department. Brutality charges included children's being confined to their tents for long stretches of time, being made to stand in tubs of cold water for hours as punishment, and having their heads shaved for offenses such as smoking (Murphy 1974). None of these wards had been adjudicated delinquent because of criminal acts; rather, all had been entrusted to state care because of dependency, parental neglect, truancy, running away, or incorrigibility. These allegations and the lawsuit prompted Miller to review all out-of-state placements, and shortly thereafter he ordered the return of some 500 children from out-of-state institutions.

In line with Miller's new policy on institutional placements, most of the returned children were not reinstitutionalized but instead were put into foster homes, placed in apartments, or released to the custody of their parents. As illustrated in Figure F-1, it was primarily

---

[5]In 1973 the state held purchase-of-service contracts with over 100 different voluntary agencies that operated a total of 190 child care institutions and group homes in Illinois. Many of these agencies had religious affiliations, such as Catholic Charities of the Archdiocese of Chicago, Lutheran Welfare Services, and the Jewish Children's Bureau. The sizes of these institutions ranged from an average residency of 30 children up to a high of 280 children in the case of Catholic Charities' Maryville Academy.

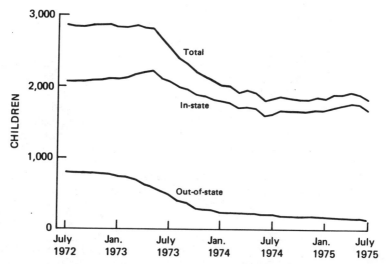

FIGURE F-1 Children in Publicly Subsidized Institutional
Foster Care Administered by Voluntary Child Welfare
Agencies, End of Year, July 1972 to July 1975.

the deinstitutionalization of these children from out-of-
state placements that resulted in the initial drop in the
size of the institutional case load in the spring of 1973.
Miller's restrictions on out-of-state placements did lead
to a short-term increase in the number of children in in-
state institutions, but by the summer of 1973 his policies
also began to decrease the number of paid referrals to
voluntary child welfare agencies.   It was largely these
policies on child placement, as well as his actions to
reorganize the child welfare bureaucracy, that brought
Miller into sharp conflict with the established voluntary
agencies and professional groups.   Because of the voluntary sector's large investment in institutional care and
treatment, these agencies and their professional affili-
ates stood to lose the most from deinstitutionalization.
Both groups intensely lobbied the governor's office and
the Illinois legislature for Miller's prompt dismissal and
a reversal of his policies.[6]   Partially as a result of
these political pressures Miller tendered his resignation
in August 1974.

---

[6]In May 1974 the Illinois chapter of the National Association of Social Workers distributed a letter addressed

ANTECEDENTS OF DEINSTITUTIONALIZATION

Miller's efforts to deinstitutionalize neglected children
in fiscal 1974 were not totally at odds with prevailing
thinking on child placement. Support for noninstitutional
foster care dates back to the 1909 White House Conference
on Children (Mayer et al. 1977). The conference recommended placement in the foster home as the best substitute
for a child's natural home. At that time the vast majority of children in foster care lived in child care institutions.[7] In the years following the conference's
recommendations, the institutionalization rate for foster
children gradually declined as federal cash assistance

---

to state legislators that denounced the policies and actions of the director. The letter (dated May 14, 1974)
reprinted the findings from a Massachusetts management
audit critical of Miller's administration of youth services, and asked legislators to halt Miller's reform efforts. It read: "In a word, this committee (an Illinois
review group composed of child welfare professionals)
found devastating and tragic parallels between the Massachusetts experience under Dr. Jerome Miller's administration (October 28, 1969 to January 1973) and what is happening in Illinois since he took over the Department of
Children and Family Services in January 1973. In consideration of your pressurized schedules, we are submit-
ting, for your careful review, the attached summary of the
report provided by the Commonwealth of Massachusetts rather than the 230 plus pages of the full report. We believe
you will want to read this material very carefully to obtain a picture of the destructive actions of the Miller
administration in Massachusetts which, in the main, are
being repeated in Illinois. You will be particularly interested in the same unplanned shot-gun approach to programming; the same fragmentation and lack of services; the
same disregard of legislative intent, constraints and
directives; the same questionable fiscal management; and
the same abuses of the state's civil service system and
personnel standards and practices."

[7]According to Hopkirk (1944), the percentage of institutionalized children in foster care was 69 percent in
1911.

became available to more families with dependent children and as foster homes increasingly became the placement option of choice. Few new institutions were constructed, and many of the older facilities were converted from custodial institutions into residential treatment centers to serve children diagnosed as emotionally disturbed. During the 1960s the institutionalization rate stabilized nationally for neglected and emotionally disturbed children at approximately 1 per 1,000 children under 18 years of age (National Association of Social Workers 1973). It was not until the early 1970s that the proponents of deinstitutionalization became activists in their efforts to close down all institutions for children throughout the country.

The reasons for the increased activism on behalf of deinstitutionalization in both Illinois and elsewhere can be tied to several changes that occurred nationwide in the administration of child welfare services during the 1960s. One was the growth of state government as a major benefactor of voluntary social service agencies. Steady erosion of agency endowments by inflation and static levels of both state reimbursement rates and voluntary contributions led these agencies to seek increased government subsidization of their child care institutions. As the voluntary agencies began to rely more heavily on government subsidization, these programs became increasingly vulnerable to spending cutbacks aimed at controlling public outlays in the early 1970s.

The evolution of children's legal and social rights gave additional momentum to deinstitutionalization. Children's institutions, along with governmental social service bureaucracies and juvenile courts, became major targets of suits by child rights defenders during the 1960s. This was largely because commitment procedures routinely denied children the same due process guaranteed to adults. In addition, commitment to an institution did not automatically guarantee children the requisite care and treatment, and it sometimes exposed them to harms that were disproportionate to the severity of their misconduct or emotional problems. The effect of such suits was to hasten deinstitutionalization both by exposing the gross abuses attending children's confinement in institutions and by reducing the options of judges and government social workers for institutionalization of children in the first place.

Finally, there was the spillover effect from efforts related to deinstitutionalization in the areas of mental health and corrections. Massive deinstitutionalization in these areas set a precedent for other areas of social service and also helped to discredit the concept of total institutions as a form of care and service. As a result of judicial and legislative restrictions on the incarceration of children in correctional institutions and their hospitalization in state mental institutions, the institutionalization rate for children in secure facilities in Illinois fell from 87 per 100,000 children under 18 years of age in 1971 to 56 per 100,000 in 1973.[8] Consequently, at the time of Jerome Miller's arrival in Illinois in 1973, state policy was already predisposed toward the deinstitutionalization of juvenile nonoffenders from correctional institutions and state mental hospitals.

Despite this shift in emphasis from institutional to community-based mental health and correctional services, state policymakers continued to recommend an expansion of residential services for mentally ill and emotionally disturbed children (State of Illinois 1969). The perceived shortage of facilities at the time was not confined to Illinois, but was national in scope (Joint Commission on the Mental Health of Children 1970). However, confusion over the respective responsibilities of the three major state departments that serve youth--mental health, child welfare, and juvenile corrections--with regard to the provision of services to children with emotional or conduct disorders stymied the development of a coordinated and comprehensive state program for these children, and children continued to be placed inappropriately in state mental institutions. To halt this practice, a series of court orders was issued in 1972 that

---

[8]Secure facilities include detention homes, juvenile correctional institutions, and state and county mental hospitals. As of June 30, 1971, there were 2,575 children under 18 years of age in detention homes and juvenile correctional institutions, and 708 children under 18 years of age in state and county mental hospitals. Two years later, as of June 30, there were 1,691 children in detention homes and juvenile correctional institutions, and 360 children in state and county mental hospitals (Illinois Department of Mental Health and Developmental Disabilities 1971, 1973; U.S. Department of Justice 1977). For these dates, the numbers of children in child care institutions (including maternity homes) were 4,152 and 3,640, respectively (Illinois Department of Children and Family Services, unpublished data).

limited state administrative powers to confine children involuntarily in mental institutions.

At the same time that concern was rising with respect to the inappropriate placement of children deemed in need of residential treatment, efforts were under way to enact state legislation that would prohibit the incarceration of children adjudicated minors in need of supervision (MINS) or delinquents younger than 13 years of age. As recently as 1973 the interpretation of "best interests" by the courts and by child welfare bureaucracies could extend to the commitment of children to juvenile correctional facilities because they were truants, runaways, or otherwise beyond the control of parents.[9]

Challenges to the constitutionality of the state's law allowing the correctional commitment of incorrigible youth had been repeatedly rejected by the Illinois courts. In People v. Presley (47 Ill. 2^{d}50), the court upheld the statutory powers of the state to commit an adolescent who had run away from the home of his foster parents (Murphy 1974:17-18):

> We perceive no consitutional infirmity in legislation allowing the adjudication of delinquency and commitment of minors to the custody of the Youth Commission [now Department of Corrections] for misconduct which does not amount to a criminal offense. To hold otherwise would substantially thwart one of the salutory purposes of the Juvenile Court Act, to provide for the rehabilitation of delinquent minors at a stage before they have embarked upon the commission of substantive criminal offenses. The state as parens patriae, clearly has an interest in safeguarding the lives of delinquent minors, as well as preserving an orderly society,

---

[9]Technically, only status offenders who had violated probation could be adjudicated delinquent and committed to juvenile correctional institutions. The 1965 amendments to the Illinois Juvenile Court Act prohibited the incarceration of first-time status offenders. The amendments withdrew from the category of delinquent and characterized as "minor otherwise in need of supervision" (MINS) persons under 18 years of age who were beyond the control of parents, guardians, or custodians, or who, if subject to compulsory school attendance, were habitually truant from school.

and it would be largely hamstrung if it were precluded from depriving incorrigible minors of their
liberty in the absence of the proof of their commission of substantive crimes.

The conservative thrust of the Illinois Supreme Court's
affirmation of the state's parens patriae powers, however,
ran counter to the liberal momentum that had been building
since the U.S. Supreme Court's decision in In re Gault
(387 U.S. 1(1967)). That ruling posed the first serious
legal challenge to the legitimacy of states' denying
children ordinary liberty rights in the name of protecting
their custody interests. The Court held that constitutional guarantees of due process of law were applicable
to the adjudicatory phase of delinquency proceedings. As
a result of this decision, the conservative opinion rendered in People v. Presley fast became the minority view
within legal circles in Illinois.

CHILD RIGHTS MOVEMENT IN ILLINOIS

The majority view, which came to dominate child advocacy
opinions in the early 1970s, was that the ideal of the
juvenile court's founders to create a truly rehabilitative
juvenile justice administration had remained an unfulfil-
led dream, a dream that concealed harshly punitive realities. The legal status of the child under Illinois law
continued to be defined to a large extent by the
nineteenth-century proposition that a child, unlike an
adult, had a right "not to liberty but to custody."[10]

---

[10] This view was described in the opinion delivered by
Mr. Justice Fortas in In re Gault, as follows: "The right
of the state, as parens patriae, to deny the child procedural rights available to his elders was elaborated by the
assertion that a child, unlike an adult, has a right 'not
to liberty but to custody.' He can be made to attorn to
his parents, to go to school, etc. If his parents default
in effectively performing their custodial functions--that
is, if the child is 'delinquent'--the state may intervene.
In doing so, it does not deprive the child of any rights,
because he has none. It merely provides the 'custody' to
which the child is entitled. On this basis, proceedings
involving juveniles were described as 'civil' not 'criminal' and therefore not subject to the requirements which

The assumption was that children lacked the physical and psychological maturity to act independently in their own best interests, and the state therefore was justified in denying them certain political and civil liberties ordinarily guaranteed to adults, in favor of granting them special social rights, such as exclusion from criminal prosecution, exemption from certain civil law liabilities, and entitlement to financial support by parents or guardians. Because it was the custody interests of children rather than their liberty interests that were presumed to be ultimately at stake, Illinois' early child placement laws allowed the courts to dispense with procedural due process and to make commitment decisions on the basis of what judges and social workers determined to be in the best interests of the child.[11]

Critics of the status quo argued that the balance juvenile court founders intended to strike between children's losses in liberty rights and their gains in social rights had become too heavily weighted on the losses' side. The gradual easing of adult criminal penalties had reduced the severity of punishments meted out in criminal courts, resulting in children's exposure to harms that sometimes exceeded those for adults convicted of similar crimes. Additionally, the development of the American welfare state had extended financial assistance and social services to families with dependent children, making the out-of-home placement of children less valuable and less necessary as a means of securing government aid. To re-strike the balance, therefore, required either lessening children's liberty losses or increasing their social gains.

---

restrict the state when it seeks to deprive a person of his liberty" (reprinted in Mnookin 1978:84-85).

[11]This exact language or a close variation, such as "welfare of the minor" or placement "best suited to protect the welfare of the child," is written into the dispositional provisions of 23 states' child protection laws (Mnookin 1976:243). The language of the Illinois Juvenile Court Act reads as follows: "to secure for each minor . . . such care and guidance, preferably in his own home, as will serve the moral, emotional, mental, and physical welfare of the minor and the best interests of the community" (Ill. Rev. Stat., Ch. 37, Sec. 701.2).

This sense of an imbalance between the legal and social aspects of the child placement process was one of the primary motivations behind the 1965 amendments to the Illinois Juvenile Court Act (Trumball 1965). The legislation was promulgated by a coalition of citizen and lawyer groups that relied on work completed by the National Council on Crime and Delinquency in 1963.[12] The basic policy assumption of the amended legislation was expressed in a publication of the council (1962:viii):

> Gradually with more intensive and critical observation and analysis of the work of the juvenile court, it became clear that the delicate balance between the social aspects of the court and the legal principles which should guide it was overweighted on the side of informality of procedure, with resulting injustices and violations of the basic rights of parents and children.

The 1965 amendments sought to restrike a balance primarily by improving procedural safeguards of the legal rights of children and parents and by narrowing judicial discretion to commit children to juvenile correctional facilities. The latter was accomplished by excluding from the category of delinquency the violations of traffic, boating, fish, and game laws; violation of these laws then became subject to criminal prosecution. In addition, the vague violation of "local laws or municipal ordinances which do not involve conduct detrimental to the social or moral standards of the community" was also excluded.[13]

---

[12]The council's report, titled "The Cook County Family (Juvenile) Court and Arthur J. Audy Home: An Appraisal and Recommendations for the Citizens Committee on the Family Court," was adopted by the Citizens Committee appointed by the Circuit Court of Cook County. The report recommended that the Illinois Family Court Act be completely revised to reflect current thinking in juvenile court legislation. Well in advance of the publication of the report, work on a thorough revision of the act had been commenced by the Chicago Bar Association and by a committee convened by the Illinois Commission on Children (Trumball 1965).

[13]Family Court Act, Sec. 1, Ill. Rev. Stat., Ch. 23, par. 2001 (1963). Cited in Trumball (1965:612).

The amended legislation also withdrew from the category of delinquents those juveniles who were beyond the control of parents, guardians, or custodians, or who, if subject to compulsory school attendance, were habitually truant from school. These youth were now categorized as "minors otherwise in need of supervision" (MINS). Because only adjudicated delinquents could be committed to juvenile correctional institutions, the aim of these legal changes was to narrow the range of juvenile behaviors that the courts could potentially sanction by committing a child to a correctional institution. Although the creation of the MINS category was a departure from the belief that adjudicated delinquents were not criminally guilty and that their placement in correctional institutions was rehabilitative rather than punitive, the supporters of the amended legislation defended the change as affording better protection to youthful offenders, particularly to younger children who might be inappropriately incarcerated under a broader definition of delinquency (Trumball 1965). This acceptance of juvenile correctional placements as fundamentally punitive subsequently gave a very explicit focus to the deinstitutionalization movement in Illinois, which began to work for the total exclusion of young children and status offenders from the juvenile correctional system.

DECARCERATION OF DELINQUENT CHILDREN AND STATUS OFFENDERS

In November 1970 the Illinois Commission on Children, a policy arm of the state legislature, issued a report advocating a change in the Juvenile Court Act that would prohibit the commitment of children under 13 years of age to the state's corrections department. As of February 1, 1970, there were 124 children aged 12 years or younger in state correctional institutions or on parole (Illinois Commission on Children 1970). Nearly all of the children were males, and approximately 20 percent had been committed for status offenses. (Under the 1965 amendments, children still could be committed to the corrections department for status offenses that violated the terms of probation set following a previous MINS adjudication.) Even though the Illinois Supreme Court had upheld the constitutionality of the correctional commitment of incorrigible youth in People v. Presley, pressures to decarcerate status offenders and young children continued to mount.

In 1970 the Chicago Legal Aid Society brought a series
of lawsuits against the state on behalf of incarcerated
status offenders. One case involved the commitment of a
girl whom the court had adjudicated delinquent because she
had violated her probation by running away from a foster
home. The Illinois Supreme Court again affirmed the
girl's commitment and upheld the constitutionality of the
MINS provision, ruling as they did in People v. Presley
"that the state should not be limited in its power to
discipline children for noncriminal acts" (Murphy
1974:23). Another case involved a civil rights suit filed
in federal court, alleging that the incarceration of three
girls for running away constituted "cruel and unusual
punishment" (Murphy 1974:29). An appeal to the U. S.
Court of Appeals for the Seventh Circuit on a technical
issue resulted in the court's holding that institutionalization could be considered unconstitutional if the placement "provided a punishment unequal to the gravity of the
so-called offense" (Murphy 1974:30).

The Chicago Legal Aid Society did not have to pursue
this line of argument because judicial and legislative
policy had already begun to change in response to the
publicity surrounding the lawsuits. The new presiding
judge of the Cook County Juvenile Court gradually began
to commit fewer status offenders to the corrections department. Then in 1972 the Illinois General Assembly
passed legislation that prohibited the correctional commitment of adjudicated delinquents under 13 years of age
(effective July 1, 1973) and of adjudicated MINS who violated a lawful court order (effective January 1, 1974).
With these legislative changes, a partial balance was restruck between the legal and social activities of the
court by imposing specific limitations on judicial discretion to institutionalize children. From 1973 to 1974
correctional commitments declined by 19 percent, and from
1974 to 1975 by another 16 percent.[14]

The obvious problem of how to dispose of these cases
still remained. One solution suggested the commitment of
these children to the state child welfare department for
placement in foster homes, group homes, or residential
treatment centers, and this disposition was written into
the statute by the 1972 amendments.

---

[14]Illinois Law Enforcement Commission, Fiscal Year 1979
State Plan, Table 39, p. I-123.

A major proponent of this point of view was the Illinois Commission on Children, whose position was strengthened by lawsuits initiated by the Chicago Legal Aid Society to establish a "right to treatment" for children in institutional care. Ironically, the respondent in these lawsuits was the state child welfare department, which was charged for inappropriately placing some of its wards in state mental hospitals, homes for the retarded, and in substandard institutions located out of state. The court orders from these lawsuits imposed formal restrictions on the placement of state wards in psychiatric hospitals, appointed the Legal Aid office to serve as attorney for all state wards in mental health facilities, and required that specific screening procedures be followed in transferring state wards to secure hospitals (Murphy, 1974). In short, these orders admonished the department to live up to its statutory duties to provide adequate care and treatment for neglected or abused children, with the judge noting that "governmental neglect and inadequacies are no more sacred or legally justifiable than parental neglect and inadequacies when they jeopardize the health and welfare of the child" (Murphy 1974:122).

The state's dereliction of duty in caring for its wards was perceived by the Illinois Commission on Children (1973), and to a lesser extent by the Legal Aid lawyers, as essentially a resource problem. There were not enough residential placement slots in the state child welfare system to care for rebellious or emotionally disturbed adolescents, and this necessitated either exporting them to out-of-state institutions or placing them in state mental hospitals. The judicially imposed restrictions on the hospitalization of state wards promised to exacerbate the resource crunch, as did the 1972 amendments to the Juvenile Court Act, which transferred to the child welfare department the responsibilities for delinquents under 13 and MINS who were formerly incarcerated in juvenile correctional institutions.

In anticipation of these mounting pressures the commission issued its agenda for the reform of children's services, placing heavy emphasis on expanding the residential placement capacity of the state's child welfare system to serve a new target group of "emotionally disturbed" children (Illinois Commission on Children 1973:7,17):

When the option for commitment to the [corrections] Department is removed . . . for [children under 13

and MINS] . . . the [child welfare] Department will
have additional placement dilemmas--for these children primarily are the same kinds of children [who
were hospitalized for emotional disturbance] . . .
but they happened to get caught in a delinquent
act, the institutions of the community (school,
police agencies) were less tolerant of their dis-
turbing and disrupting behavior, or the court chose
the corrections dispositions option either because
of a punitive reason or because the judge believed
the child would have a better chance of receiving
needed services.

With the necessity of finding more suitable placement resources for the children out of state, the
cases which by . . . Court order, should be removed
from State hospitals, and those which the amendments to the Juvenile Court Act will add to the
(child welfare) Department's caseload, it is estimated that Illinois needs 1,620 residential group
care beds to care for the children who are presently inappropriately or inadequately served.

The commission was quick to add that the term group care
did not necessarily imply institutional care.   In fact,
the budget worked up for the proposal called for adding
only 486 institutional beds to existing capacity, claiming
that the remaining 1,134 children could be placed in regular and specialized foster homes and in independent living arrangements (Illinois Commission on Children 1973).
Still, the commission's assumption was that approximately
20 percent of the department's case load would require
institutional or group home placement, which in 1973 translated into approximately 6,000 beds.
    The balance that the commission sought to strike be-
tween the new guard advocates of children's rights and the
old guard defenders of parens patriae was nonetheless a
precarious one, founded on the premise that decarcerated
youth were emotionally disturbed and in need of treat-
ment--a premise that was to be strongly challenged in the
coming months by the newly appointed child welfare director, Jerome Miller. Miller's perspective on child welfare
was a radical one that questioned the value of the prevailing professional orientation toward the care and
treatment of delinquent children and youth deemed beyond
the control of parents. There was a logical continuity
between Miller's perspective and the legal arguments

brought by Chicago Legal Aid against the state on behalf
of institutionalized children. Legal Aid's lawsuits had
focused attention on the broad discretionary powers of
juvenile court judges and government social workers and
psychiatrists to institutionalize children in the name of
"best interests." Miller's stance against broad professional discretion in child placement helped to direct
the momentum in favor of due process built up in the federal courts into the state's administration of juvenile
corrections and child welfare services. The overall effect of Miller's reforms was to bring the administrative
process for the residential placement and treatment of
children into stricter compliance with a more legalistic
model of decisionmaking and risk-taking.

THE LEGAL MODEL OF CHILD PLACEMENT

Prior to Miller, placement practice had been organized
around the clinical concept of institutionalization as the
initial intervention, to be followed by placement back
home, in a foster home, or in an apartment. Deinstitutionalization entailed a radical revision of this intervention sequence by locating institutional placement at
the opposite end of the service continuum. The child care
institution became the last refuge for children unable to
adjust to noninstitutional settings. The use of institutional placements became reoriented toward a "placement
of last resort" rather than an "intervention option of
choice." This reorientation of placement practice was in
many respects an administrative parallel to Legal Aid's
efforts in the courts to move decisionmaking on residential commitment and treatment away from a medical model
of best interests toward a legal model that emphasized the
least restrictive alternative.

Social workers and juvenile court judges long sought
to model their professional roles after the role of the
medical profession (Lubove 1975). As a result, they came
to share the medical profession's bias toward therapeutic
intervention. This bias helped to encourage the use of
institutional care as being in the best interests of the
child. It was a bias that was sharply at variance with
the lawyers' preference for minimal intervention. Thomas
Scheff (1966) has explained the basic differences between
doctors' and lawyers' respective approaches toward risk-
taking in terms of the distinction between type 2 and type
1 errors of statistical inference.

A type 2 error of statistical inference refers to the presumption that something is true when in fact it is false. Examples of a type 2 error include finding an innocent man guilty, treating a healthy man for an illness, and touching a hot iron that is believed to be cool. Scheff suggests that legal norms of decisionmaking tend toward avoiding type 2 errors, as suggested by such legal maxims as "innocent until proven guilty" and "beyond a reasonable doubt" (1966:107). In contrast, Scheff contends that medical norms of decisionmaking tend toward avoiding type 1 errors. In statistical terms a type 1 error refers to the presumption that something is false when in fact it is true. Examples include letting a sick man go untreated, acquitting a guilty man of a crime, and adding sugar to an already sweetened cup of coffee. Scheff notes that most medical doctors continue to suspect illness and administer treatment until illness is definitely ruled out and, hence, presumably strive to avoid type 1 errors.

Scheff points out that the logic of this bias of medical diagnosis toward type 1 errors (i.e., judging a sick person well, type 2, is more to be avoided than judging a well person sick, type 1) presupposes both that prognosis is highly predictable and that the effects of an incorrect diagnosis are inconsequential. He argues that neither presupposition is very well supported by medical evidence, and is supported even less so by psychiatric evidence. He concludes that the medical profession's bias toward type 1 errors results in more unnecessary impairment and incapacity than is generally accounted for in the everyday prevention and treatment of disease.

Jerome Miller shared a similar viewpoint with respect to child placement (1973). Social workers' and juvenile court judges' preferences for institutional care as a therapeutic option also meant that some children were unnecessarily involved in residential treatment (type 2 errors). He attacked the two basic assumptions of predictability and inconsequentiality that would justify taking those risks. First, the rehabilitative effects of institutional treatment in juvenile corrections were not predictable, as evidenced by high recidivism rates. He cited FBI statistics that 74 percent of adults imprisoned return within five years. He claimed that the same pattern could be found among juveniles (Miller 1973). If the presumed purpose of institutionalizing juvenile delinquents was rehabilitation, the low determinacy of this outcome therefore vitiated the rationality of this ap-

proach. The second assumption--that the harms of inadequate institutionalization (type 2 error) are greater than
those of unnecessary institutionalization (type 1 error)--
was also rejected. On this point Miller was adamant:
"The injustices of our correctional system by far outweigh
the injustices perpetrated upon society by the inmates"
(Miller 1973:3).

Miller did not restrict this characterization to juvenile corrections alone, but extended it to all helping
professions that adhere to a clinical model of diagnosis
and treatment in the management of deviant persons or
groups (1973:5):

> In much the same way as administrators, the helping
> professions are caught up in the social processes
> of subjugation and scapegoating. By their very
> existence, the professions came to assume latent
> functions of social control. The practice set-
> tings, roles, and skills of the helping professions
> are part of the social processes of control. In
> this sense, they represent a response to belief
> systems (families, communities, societies) and to
> definitions made by those systems. . . . The diag-
> nosis relieves strain on the system by allowing
> focus on the deviant who is in large part a product
> of the inconsistencies in the system.

This perspective on professionalism in the human services gave a very explicit focus to Miller's reform efforts in Illinois. Reform, as he saw it, was not to break
out of old labels, such as "delinquents," to more up-to-
date labels, such as "MINS" or "emotionally disturbed."
Rather it was to "(1) effectively break the vicious circle
of definitions calling for institutional arrangements
which, in turn, revalidate the definitions and; (2) build
into new definitions (since they will come) enough categories that show the social and psychological strengths
and the life-space of those defined as delinquent or criminal" (1973:61).

It is within this larger context of a reaction against
labeling that Miller's initiatives on the deinstitutionalization of foster children in Illinois should be understood. His concept of deinstitutionalization was not to
exclude certain children from one institutional arrangement termed "punitive" in order to include them in another
institutional arrangement believed "benign," as proposed
by the Illinois Commission on Children. Rather, his goal

was to reorient child placement policy away from the use
of institutions altogether in order to reduce abuses of
labeling, which he viewed to be inherent in the role of
the helping professions. Miller interpreted these abuses
as unintended consequences of the helping professional's
belief in the capacity of clinical judgment to serve the
best interests of delinquent and neglected children. His
argument was essentially that the medical model was mis-
applied in child placement--first, because it was founded
on an inadequate therapeutic knowledge base, as evidenced
by high recidivism rates, and second, because it discounted the harms of institutionalization, producing far too
much unnecessary impairment and incapacity. To correct
these abuses he felt it was necessary to shift decisionmaking in child placement from a medical model (institutionalization as an intervention option of choice) toward
a legal model (institutionalization as a last resort).

EMPIRICAL ANALYSIS

The effects of this shift can be seen in the data presented in Table F-1, which show a steady decline in the
number and percentage of institutionalized children with
no previous placements with relatives or in foster homes.
   As of June 30, 1975, approximately 59 percent of the
children in institutional care were placed there as their

TABLE F-1   Number and Percentage of Institutionalized
Children With No Preinstitutional Placements as of
June 30, 1975 to June 30, 1978

Year	Total	One or More Preinstitutional Placements		No Preinstitutional Placements	
		Number	Percentage	Number	Percentage
1975	2,296	941	41	1,355	59
1976	2,365	1,277	54	1,088	46
1977	2,282	1,506	66	776	34
1978	2,184	1,638	75	546	25

Source: Unpublished data tabulated for this study by the Illinois
Department of Children and Family Services.

initial placement. By June 30, 1978, however, only 25 percent were put in institutions as their initial placement; the remaining 75 percent were institutionalized following a prior placement with relatives or in a foster home. This trend reflects the policy of the Illinois Department of Children and Family Services to forestall children's institutionalization until after all noninstitutional options had been exhausted.

One infrequently examined consequence of this reorientation is the effect that "failure" in preinstitutional placements has on the custody interests of the child (which the placement process is supposed to protect), including the child's safety, need for continuity of relationships, and opportunity to forge new primary group attachments. The fact that a substantial number of children under departmental guardianship experienced failures in noninstitutional placements may be inferred from Table F-1. Even though the number of children placed initially in noninstitutional settings increased as a percentage of the institutional case load, the size of the total institutional case load remained relatively unchanged. If diversion into noninstitutional placements had worked as expected, there should have been an eventual drop in the size of the total institutional case load. Instead the case load remained approximately constant. One inference that can be drawn is that after 1975 more and more children were admitted to institutions following an unsuccessful preinstitutional placement.

Longitudinal data are not available to measure changes in placement continuity during this period or to assess the effects. However, data collected for a cohort of children institutionalized for the first time in fiscal 1974 in Illinois contain some relevant information that permits a preliminary examination of the effects of delayed institutionalization on placement stability. The data were drawn from a retrospective three-year study conducted by the State of Illinois on foster children placed in institutions operated under voluntary and local government agencies. The purpose of the Illinois study was to evaluate the effects of different organizational patterns of residential care and treatment on the subsequent adjustment of children released and placed in foster homes or back with their parents (Walsh et al. 1979). The total sample size is 471 children.[15]

_____

[15] The study originally called for the collection of data on a population of 680 children placed into residential

Fiscal 1974 was Miller's first full program year as director of the Department of Children and Family Services. One-half of the sampled cohort of children placed into institutional foster care for the first time in fiscal 1974 had experienced at least one noninstitutional placement prior to their commitment. The remainder had had no prior foster care experience. Information culled from the case records of these children showed no appreciably large differences in the characteristics of the two groups, with the exception of age at institutionalization. Children with no prior foster placement were, on average, 10 months younger than the children with previous placements. However, the average age (13 years) of the children at the time they initially came under the supervision of the department was approximately the same for both groups.

Two-thirds of both groups were males and one-third were either black or Hispanic. The most frequently recorded reason for case opening was "family conflict," followed

foster care for the first time during the fiscal year beginning July 1, 1973 and ending June 30, 1974. The data-gathering also was to include information on all prior and subsequent placements through June 30, 1976. All information was to be obtained from case records maintained by the Illinois Department of Children and Family Services and from a survey of 56 residential facilities throughout the state. The 56 residential facilities provided care and treatment to 527 of the original 680 children selected for the study.

Each of the remaining 153 children had received services in one of 49 facilities operated by 23 different voluntary agencies that failed to respond to the survey. Three of these 23 agencies had closed down and were unable to comply with the request. Another 14 agencies requested to drop out of the study because only one or two children in their programs appeared in the original sample. The remaining six agencies lacked the technical capacity or information to supply the requested data. Therefore, the final sample of 527 children was not totally representative of children placed by the state in smaller residential facilities. For purposes of this analysis, an additional 56 children were dropped from this sample because their placement was in detention homes operated by county governments, which did not qualify as institutional foster care.

by "uncontrollable child" and "runaway." Together these reasons accounted for one-half of the case openings. The remaining one-half were divided evenly between dependency, abuse, and neglect on the one hand, and psychiatric problems, and assaultive or criminal behaviors on the other. Again there were no significant differences by reason for case opening between children with prior placements and children without prior placements.

Although the differences between the two groups with respect to the frequency of arrests, episodes of running away, and other problem behaviors prior to case opening were small, the magnitude of the differences indicated that the group institutionalized after a prior placement was slightly more troublesome, on average, than the group institutionalized immediately. Obviously, initial placement in a noninstitutional setting functioned like a sieve that the difficult-to-control children "fell through" and eventually became institutionalized. These children constitute type 1 errors according to Scheff's scheme. These are placement errors made on the assumption that noninstitutional placement was adequate. The aim of this strategy is to minimize type 2 placement errors, i.e., children's unnecessary placement in institutions. The logic of this strategy, of course, depends on the costs of "falling through" not greatly exceeding the costs of unnecessary institutionalization.

There are no firmly accepted criteria other than strictly economic ones for gauging the quality of foster care for purposes of tallying the relative social costs of type 1 and type 2 placement errors. Institutional foster care is six times more costly in the short run than foster home care. Considering only these economic costs, the strategy of risking type 1 placement errors seems well worth the gamble. However, there are other noneconomic costs associated with placement errors that also should be taken into account, including the effects on children's safety, the need for continuity of relationships, and the ability to forge new primary group attachments.

Continuity of care and permanency of living arrangements have emerged recently as important criteria for gauging the quality of child care (Fanshel and Shinn 1978). One line of thought in child development theory holds that continuity of relationships to care givers is essential to a child's capacity to establish and maintain future personal and group ties (Bowlby 1977, Goldstein et al., 1973). According to this hypothesis, disruptions of relationships diminish this capacity and increase the

likelihood of future disruptions and the possibility of
the child's eventual withdrawal. Children in foster care
already have experienced a profound disruption in the continuity of their surroundings and relationships. Goldstein, Freud, and Solnit (1973) argue that foster placement should not compound the discontinuity by the repeated
movement of a child between residences, even if the apparent cause for movement was at the child's initiation
(e.g., a runaway). Placement ideally should be oriented
toward restoring the child's relationship to his or her
parents or, lacking this alternative, toward freeing the
younger child for adoption and preparing the older child
for independence.

The measures of continuity employed in the Illinois
study were of two types: (1) a planned versus unplanned
transfer between residences and (2) a stable versus unstable placement of children returned to parents. The
study's design called for the coding of each child's
transfer between residences as either planned or unplanned. A planned transfer was defined as one made as a
result of a child's completing a full term of care and
treatment or being transferred in accordance with a service plan. An unplanned transfer was defined as one made
as a result of a custodian's refusing to retain custody
of a child or as a result of a child's running away or
being transferred on an emergency basis (e.g., in the case
of attempted suicide). A child's placement with parents
was considered stable if it resulted in a case closing by
the department after a period of supervision or if it remained unchanged for a period of a year or more. Conversely, a child's placement was considered unstable if
it resulted in the parent's refusing to retain custody or
if it resulted in a child's running away or being removed
on an emergency basis.

The relationships of interest with respect to these
measures of continuity of care concern the effects of preinstitutional placements on the probability of a planned
release from institutional care and the effects of a planned release on the stability of a subsequent placement
with parents.[16] Two expectations emerge from theories

---

[16] Seventy-four percent of the sampled children institutionalized for the first time in fiscal 1974 were out
of the institution in less than one year. After three
years' time only 18 children or 5 percent of the original
sample were still living in the same institution. Of the

of continuity of care: (1) preinstitutional placements
should negatively affect the probability of a planned release, since they typically involve some disruption of
care; and (2) planned release from institutional care
should positively affect the probability of a stable home
placement.

The cross-tabulation of planned and unplanned releases
by the occurrence of preinstitutional placements lends
preliminary support to the continuity-of-care hypothesis.
The data suggest that children with no preinstitutional
placements were more likely to experience a planned release from institutional care (64.0 percent) than were
children with one or more preinstitutional placements
(44.3 percent). The model of no association between preinstitutional placements and planned release was rejected
at the .01 significance level (Yule's Q = -0.3821 and
Pearson's r = -0.1979). Therefore, one cannot safely conclude that release patterns were unrelated to prior placement experience. The cross-tabulation of planned and
unplanned releases by the stability of placement with
parents also supports the hypothesis.[17]   The data suggest that children who were returned home in accordance
with a plan were more likely to remain home (61.4 percent)
than were children returned home for unplanned reasons
(26.0 percent). The model of no association between the
two factors was rejected at the 0.01 significance level.

One must be cautious, however, not to infer that release patterns directly influence placement stability or
that preinstitutional placements directly influence release patterns. The zero-order association between release and preinstitutional placements and the zero-order
association between release and placement stability may

---

95 percent that were out in less than three years, only
54 percent were planned releases; the other 46 percent
either ran away, were expelled, or were discharged for
other unplanned reasons.

[17]Among children released in accordance with a plan, 40
percent were returned to parents, 30 percent were placed
in foster homes, and 27 percent were transferred to
another institution. Among children released for unplanned reasons, 30 percent were returned to parents, 20
percent were placed in foster homes, and 50 percent were
reinstitutionalized in detention centers, child care institutions, or mental hospitals.

be confounded with other relevant factors, such as the age of the child, race or ethnicity, and the perceived difficulty of controlling the child. Although case records showed no large differences with respect to the frequency of arrests, episodes of running away, and other problem behaviors between children with preinstitutionalized placements and children with no previous placements, the magnitude of the differences indicated that the former group was slightly more troublesome than the latter. Additionally, children who were institutionalized immediately were ten months younger, on average, than the children with previous placements. It is possible, therefore, that the negative association between planned release and preinstitutional placements and the positive association between placement stability and planned release are both spurious and that outcomes are primarily dependent on these additional factors.

In order to examine this issue, a series of logit models were fitted to a multidimensional cross-classification of data to test the significance of the partial effects of preinstitutional placement and planned release on the expected outcomes of institutionalization and home placement while controlling for relevant confounding factors. (These procedures are described in the "Methodological Note" at the end of this paper.) The first set of data analyzed is the cross-classification of children by release, preinstitutional placement, age at institutionalization, problem behaviors, and minority group status.[18] This latter variable was included to test for evidence of bias against black and Hispanic children in the discharge practices of voluntary child placement agencies.

The model that best fits the cross-classification is diagrammed in Figure F-2 and is presented in Table F-3 at the end of this paper. Preinstitutional placements, a record of problem behaviors, and racial or ethnic minority

---

[18]The variables are as follows: the planned or unplanned release of a child from residential care [C_i where i = (0) unplanned, (1) planned], the presence or absence of prior noninstitutional placements [P_k where K = (0) none, (1) one or more], the age of the child at institutionalization [A_j where j = (1) under 13 years old, (2) 13 to 15 years old, (3) 16 to 20 years old], a prior record of problem behaviors [B_l where l = (0) no, (1) yes], and the race of the child [R_m where m = (0) white, (1) other].

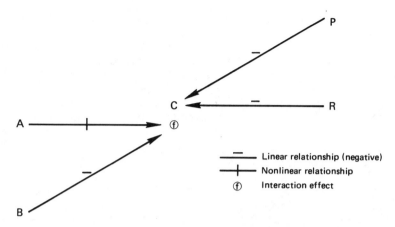

FIGURE F-2 Effects of Age (A), Preinstitutional Placements (P), Problem Behaviors (B), and Race (R) on the Odds of a Planned Release (C) from Institutional Foster Care.

each show a significant negative relation to planned release, irrespective of the levels of the other variables. In addition, age at institutionalization is shown to have a curvilinear relationship to planned release. Children aged 13 to 15 at the time of institutionalization were less likely to experience a planned release from institutional care than both children under 13 years of age and children aged 16 to 19. Additionally, the data reveal an interaction effect between age and problem behaviors; the negative effect of problem behaviors on planned release was amplified for children under 13 years of age, while it was diminished for youth over 16.

There are several important inferences that one may draw from this analysis. First, the occurrence of a placement prior to institutionalization did have a net negative effect on the probability of a planned release from institutional care beyond the effects of age, problem behaviors, and minority-group status. For example, minority children aged 13 to 15 with a prior record of problem behaviors faced a higher probability (38 percent) of planned release if institutionalization occurred immediately than if institutionalization occurred following a noninstitutional placement (28 percent) (see "Methodological Note" for details).

Second, the age of the child at the time of institutionalization had the largest net effect on planned re-

lease. Nearly 43 percent of the total association between
release and its explanatory factors could be accounted for
by the main effects of age. For example, a white child
under 13 years of age with no preinstitutional placements
or record of problem behaviors ran a 95 percent probability of experiencing a planned release from institutional
care. The probability declined to 62 percent if the child
with these same characteristics was between 13 and 15
years of age; if the child of this age with the same
characteristics was either black or Hispanic, the probability declined to 47 percent.

Third, this important statistical difference in the
probability of a planned release for minority group children compared to white children of similar age, placement
experience, and problem behaviors provides some evidence
of a pattern of racial bias by voluntary agencies.

The finding of possible racial bias adds an important
dimension to one's understanding of the issues surrounding
Miller's deinstitutionalization of foster children in
1974. The statistical evidence suggests that some of the
alleged abuses in child placement that prompted deinstitutionalization (e.g., the inappropriate placement of
foster children in correctional institutions and mental
hospitals or their exportation to out-of-state facilities)
might not have been due solely to an absence of resources,
as suggested by the Illinois Commission on Children.
Racially biased practices by voluntary agencies also might
have contributed to the state's practice of "dumping"
children into custodial institutions. This was essentially the premise of Chicago Legal Aid's lawsuit against
the child welfare department.

The Legal Aid lawyers also charged that voluntary agencies engaged in unfair practices in the care and treatment
of older youth with behavioral problems, irrespective of
their race or ethnicity (Murphy 1974). The frequent trad-
ing of MINS or emotionally disturbed youth by these agencies for younger dependent and neglected children also was
alleged to account for the inappropriate placement of
adolescents (Murphy 1974, Young 1976). The sharp decline
in the probability of a planned release for adolescents
aged 13-15, irrespective of race or ethnicity, lends additional credence to the charge of unfair practices toward
older children. Interestingly, the decline was not as
sharp for youths above 16 years of age.

Several directors who operated child care institutions
during Miller's administration have suggested that it was
not unfair practices that accounted for low rates of plan-

ned releases among older problem children during this period, but rather that it was the state's assigning them children who once had been eligible for commitment to corrections but who now were too difficult or too disturbed for their programs to manage. Indeed, the data show that the least successful placements occurred among the two new categories of children that the 1972 child welfare amendments made responsibilities of the child welfare department—delinquents under 13 and status offenders. Children who entered foster care with a record of problem behaviors, such as criminal mischief, running away, or chronic truancy, ran a lower chance of a planned release than children without such a record. In addition, the existence of an interaction effect between age and problem behavior underscores the system's difficulty in handling younger children who were not solely dependent or neglected.

These findings help to demonstrate the complexities of child placement. The deinstitutionalization of young children and status offenders in correctional institutions and their transfer to child welfare created an additional set of placement problems. Child care institutions that were geared primarily to the care of young dependent or neglected children were unsuccessful in caring for older children and children with problem behaviors. As a consequence, these children were placed inappropriately in mental institutions or detention homes or were sent to out-of-state facilities.

Jerome Miller's response to this state of affairs was to use institutional placement only as a last resort. However, the negative effect of prior placement on planned release from institutional care does raise some questions about this placement strategy. Does postponed institutionalization simply trade one problem for another by increasing the likelihood of failures in foster placements and thus heightening the risk of the child's estrangement from parental or substitute care?

The mechanism by which preinstitutional placement becomes translated into a lowered probability of planned release need not be psychological, as posited by theories of continuity of care. Equally plausible is an interpretation derived from labeling theory, which is that preinstitutional placements contribute to a child's becoming labeled a hard case by administrators, which in turn encourages his or her expulsion from institutional care at the slightest provocation. If this latter interpretation is indeed more consistent with the facts, then one should expect very little direct translation of the negative effects of preinstitutional placement to the stability of placements made outside the system of substitute care.

The zero-order associational measures of the relationship among preinstitutional placement, planned release, and stable home suggested evidence of at least an indirect effect through preinstitutional placement's negative association with planned release. To test for evidence of a direct effect on the stability of a child's placement back with his or her parents, a series of logit models was fitted to a set of data that cross-tabulated planned release and placement stability with preinstitutional placement. To facilitate comparison, the table was subdivided between children who were returned to parents and children who were placed in foster homes. Because of the small number of cases in several table cells, additional subdivisions of the data by age, problem behaviors, and minority group status could not be made. Therefore, the model fitted to these data should be seen as predictive rather than causal since there may be other important factors omitted from the model that may account for the coordination between these variables.

The model that best fits this cross-classification is presented in Table F-5 at the end of this paper. Consistent with the continuity-of-care hypothesis, the main effects of both planned release and no preinstitutional placements were positively related to stable home placements both in foster and natural families. The positive effects of the former were also enhanced by the placement of the child back with his or her parents, as indicated by the statistical interaction between planned released and the stability of placement with parents. However, there are also aspects to Table F-5 that suggest important modifications to the continuity-of-care hypothesis.

First, the largest effect is the positive interaction with respect to stability between preinstitutional placement and placement back with parents. The interaction means that the effect of a preinstitutional placement remained negatively associated with home stability if and only if the postinstitutional placement was in a foster home. The effect became positive if the postinstitutional placement was back with parents; that is, the probability of a stable placement with parents was higher if the child had experienced a placement prior to institutionalization. Second, the probability of a stable placement with parents was also increased if the release from institutional care was planned. These important findings suggest that much of the negative effect of disruptions in foster placements (especially preinstitutional ones) on future stability may be internal to the foster care system. The negative effect, with the exception of unplanned release from institutional care, does not carry over to the child's placement back with his or her parents.

One interpretation of these findings is that disruptions of preinstitutional foster placements may reflect a specific reaction by some children against forming new relationships with a set of surrogate parents rather than a generalized reaction against social control. The data show that children who went fro. a prior home placement to an institution achieved a stable postinstitutional home placement an estimated 68 percent of the time if the discharge was planned and only 47 percent if the discharge was unplanned. In contrast, if the postinstitutional placement was in a foster home, the probability for this same category of children was only 36 percent if the discharge was planned, but increased to 57 percent if the discharge was unplanned.

These findings should not be pushed too far without additional information and some replication. Nonetheless, the data point to a diversity of responses by foster children to different placement settings (e.g., foster homes, child care institutions) that are not adequately taken into account by the general principle of institutionalization as a last resort. In certain cases initial placement of a child in a foster home (which did not succeed) followed by institutionalization (which did succeed) was more highly associated with instability than an unplanned discharge either to a foster home or back to parents.

DISCUSSION: LIBERTY RIGHTS VS. SOCIAL RIGHTS

The majority of recent reforms proposed for the administration of juvenile justice and child protection laws in the United States have been aimed toward limiting the discretionary powers of government officials in child placement (Goldstein et al. 1973, Mnookin 1973, 1976, Wald 1975). Lawyers have been especially critical of the "best interests" standard of child placement that allows juvenile court judges and social workers broad discretion in tailoring placement decisions to a child's individual circumstances. It is argued that indeterminate standards, although they permit flexibility, are difficult to apply equitably, fairly, or consistently. In the language of

Gault, juvenile court history has demonstrated that "unbridled discretion, however benevolently motivated, is frequently a poor substitute for principle and procedure."

Many of the changes in the child placement process since Gault have occurred at the adjudicatory stage and have involved the extension of due process protections to children at risk of incarceration or separation from parents. In Illinois a sense of an imbalance between the legal and social aspects of the child placement process was a primary motivation behind these changes. The balance that was restruck by the 1965 and 1972 amendments to the Illinois Juvenile Court Act involved the expansion of the scope of children's liberty interests that were deemed protected under the law. Besides mandating due process at the adjudicatory stage by excluding status offenses from the definition of delinquency, the laws limited state powers to infringe on children's liberty rights. By contrast, very little in the way of substantive social rights was obtained either judicially or legislatively for delinquents, status offenders, or neglected children.

Changes in the dispositional stage of the child placement process have had a similar focus. The judicial standard of "least restrictive alternative" and its administrative analogue of "placement of last resort" function mainly to safeguard children's liberties, sometimes at the expense of the substantive rights and interests that the placement process is supposed to protect. Use of the substantive standard of continuity of care to evaluate the placements of children institutionalized for the first time in fiscal 1974 yielded mixed results concerning the principle of last resort. Immediate institutionalization in the sample of neglected children, controlling for age, problem behaviors, and minority group status, was found to increase significantly the expectation of a planned release from institutional care, which in turn was found to be positively associated with stable placements either in foster homes or back with parents. Conversely, institutionalization following a prior home placement was found to decrease significantly the expectation of a planned release, which was found to be negatively associated with stable placements only in foster homes. The major exception to the finding of a negative association between continuity of care and preinstitutional placements was among children returned to the custody of their parents. This observation suggests either that these children should never have been removed from their parents in the first place or that much of the long-term benefits of continuity of care across placements may be internal to the foster care system.

The implications of the above findings are that procedural safeguards alone are not sufficient to regulate the child placement process, and that strict adherence to a single procedure of placement, such as placement of last resort, can subvert the accomplishment of the substantive goals of child protection laws. An additional implication is that discretion is necessary in the selection of foster placements. However, this again raises the possibility of inequity, unfairness, and inconsistency. Analysis of the data on the sample of institutionalized children revealed evidence of a pattern of discrimination by voluntary child welfare agencies in their discharge of minority group children from child care institutions.

One alternative to the swings back and forth between a highly determinate legal model and a highly discretionary medical model of child placement is to develop an informational strategy of accountability. Such a strategy would allow broad discretionary powers to government officials but would continually monitor their behavior with performance indicators stored and updated for each case as part of an automated system. Length of stay, number of movements, parent visits, and so forth could be monitored for deviations from prescribed tolerance limits. Even the admissions and discharge practices of voluntary agencies could be monitored for discriminatory patterns. Public disclosure can sometimes be as powerful a regulatory mechanism as law enforcement. Of course, quality control checks would need to be built into the system to ensure the integrity of the information. The value of such a strategy would be to orient official behavior toward the achievement of substantive goals rather than toward an automatic adherence to rules, and to focus attention on correcting unresponsive rules and abuses of discretion.

CONCLUSION

The purpose of this paper has been to trace the major judicial, legislative, and administrative developments in Illinois that gave rise to the deinstitutionalization movement in child placement, and to examine the issue of how far formal standards and rules of procedure should be applied to limit discretion in the placement process. The

first part of this paper described the following three
major changes that occurred in the organization of governmental and voluntary social services and helped to predispose Illinois policymakers toward the deinstitutionalization of children: (1) the increased public subsidization of the voluntary sector, (2) the spillover effect
from massive deinstitutionalization in mental health and
corrections, and (3) the evolution of children's legal and
social rights.   The latter two changes gave momentum to
the state's decarceration of young children and status
offenders who formerly were housed in correctional institutions.   Responsibility for these wards was transferred
to the state department of child welfare.

The proposed response of child welfare groups and professionals to the department's new changes was to expand
the residential care and treatment capacity of the public
and voluntary sectors.   However, data analyzed in the
second part of this paper revealed serious shortcomings
in the capability of the child welfare system to care for
this target population composed primarily of adolescents
with problem behaviors.   Only about 50 percent of all institutional placements in fiscal 1974 were successful in
the sense that they terminated in the child's planned release from institutional care.   Most success was obtained
among the child welfare system's traditional service population of dependent children under 13 years of age; least
success was obtained among the new populations of delinquent children under 13 and adolescents between 13 and 15.
Additionally, the differential handling of minority group
children by voluntary agencies contributed to lower success rates among blacks and Hispanics than among white
children.   As a result, the children who were rejected by
the voluntary child care institutions (primarily adolescents with problem behaviors and minority group children)
were subsequently inappropriately placed in state mental
hospitals, detention homes, or substandard institutions
located out-of-state.

This was essentially the situation that Jerome Miller
confronted when he became child welfare director in January 1973.   Some of Miller's notions about the repressive
qualities of the child placement process hence were confirmed.   However, instead of holding the voluntary sector
accountable to some substantive standards of care and
treatment (e.g., continuity of care and equal protection),
Miller's approach was to limit the intervention of voluntary child welfare agencies into children's lives.   He

attempted this by adapting the judicial standard of least restrictive alternative to the child placement process, which reoriented casework away from the use of institutions as an intervention option of choice and toward their use as a placement of last resort. Analysis of the placement of children who were institutionalized after a prior foster placement, however, suggested that the strategy of last resort created additional problems such as placement instability, although much of the instability appeared to be internal to the foster care system.

This paper's findings of a possible pattern of racial bias by voluntary child care institutions against minority group children and of the success of voluntary agencies and professional groups in resisting policy change by state administrative agencies suggest the need for greater accountability to public institutions and to substantive goals of child placement. Analysis of the association of last resort and continuity of care suggests that procedural limitations on administrative discretion are only partially successful in assuring accountability. An informational strategy that monitors official behavior by reference to prescribed performance standards may offer one way of expanding discretion while controlling its abuse.

METHODOLOGICAL NOTE

This section describes the methods used to obtain the multivariate estimates of the relationships between the probability of continuity-of-care and child characteristics and placement patterns, which were discussed in the text. The estimates were derived using Goodman's (1972) techniques of log-linear analysis for the estimation of probability models where the dependent variables take on only discrete values. With these techniques one can assess the goodness-of-fit between a hypothesized model and the observed data, and examine the significance and magnitude of the partial effect of predictor variables on the probability of an expected outcome. In this study both dependent variables are dichotomies, and log-linear analysis is well suited to the task of analyzing discrete data. Regression analysis and other forms of the general linear model cannot be readily applied to these data because the statistical assumptions of unrestricted range and homoscedasticity are violated when the dependent variable is a dichotomy.[19]

The procedures followed in the analysis include: (1) testing the fit of a series of logit models to observed data to see if any explanatory factors can be discounted as having a significant effect on outcome, (2) assessing the net contribution of each significant factor to the total association, and (3) estimating the effect parameters that indicate both the direction and magnitude of relationships between explanatory factors and outcome.

The analysis proceeds by classifying subjects on a variety of characteristics, which together form a multidimensional cross-classification or contingency table. In this study the subjects first were classified by age at institutionalization, minority group status, problem behaviors, and prior foster care experience. The result is a contingency table composed of cell counts of subjects who all share similar characteristics. These observed cell counts of frequencies can be manipulated to form cell odds or probabilities. The goal of log-linear analysis is to find the appropriate population model that could account for variation in observed cell probabilities with the least complexity and least discrepancy between expected and observed data. If the observed cross-classification was indeed drawn from a population described by a given model, then any discrepancies between the expected and observed data should be due to sampling or measurement error. Appropriate statistics for testing this hypothesis are the familiar goodness-of-fit chi-

---

[19]For example, scoring a dichotomy 0 or 1 and regressing explanatory variables against it will sometimes yield estimates that are outside this range, which makes probabilistic interpretations difficult. Additionally, because the variance of a dichotomy is a function of cell proportions, its variance typically changes with different levels of the joint explanatory variables, which violates the assumption of homoscedasticity. No such assumption is necessary in the use of log-linear techniques, and the assumption of unrestricted range is not a problem because the dependent variable is not a dummy variable but is either the frequency of a response, the odds of a response, or the natural log of one or the other of these. Nevertheless, there are certain conditions under which regression analysis can be used to approximate the results obtained with log-linear analysis (Goodman 1975).

square (x^2) and the likelihood ratio chi-square (G^2), both of which compare expected and observed frequencies.

The first set of data analyzed is the cross-classification of children on variables pertaining to the planned or unplanned release of a child from residential care [Ci where i = (0) unplanned, (1) planned] as well as to the age of the child at institutionalization [A where j = (1) under 13 years old, (2) 13 to 15 years old, (3) 16 to 20 years old], the presence or absence of prior non-institutional placements [Pk where k = (0) none, (1) one or more], a prior record of problem behaviors [Bl where l = (0) no, (1) yes], and the race of the child [Rm where m = (0) white, (1) other].

Appendix Table F-2 lists several models that might account for the observed data. The first model (M1) listed in the table is that of independence between the response variables (C) and the joint explanatory variable ($APBR$). This model states that the effect on the expected odds pertaining to the response variable is equal to the general mean of the response variable and also that the main and interaction effects of the explanatory variables are nil. This is equivalent to saying that the expected odds of a planned release from institutional care are the same for all foster children regardless of their age, minority group membership, prior foster placements, or record of problem behaviors. Clearly this model does not fit the observed data well, as indicated by the large Pearson chi-square (77.55) and the likelihood ratio chi-square (92.19) with 23 degrees of freedom.

A much better fit is obtained with the full additive model (M2) listed in Table F-2 (Pearson chi-square = 27.61 and likelihood ratio chi-square = 29.72, with 18 degrees of freedom). This model states that the general mean effect on the response variable is modified by the main effects of the explanatory variables and that the interaction effects are nil. This is equivalent to saying that the expected odds of a planned release are dependent, in a certain sense, on a foster child's age, race, or ethnicity, prior foster placements, and record of problem behaviors and that these effects are not interactive; that is, the relationship between the response and explanatory variables does not differ across various levels of age, race, prior placements, and problems.[20]

---

[20] One can assess the magnitude of the improvement in fit obtained with the full additive model (M2) by comparing

To test whether or not a given effect in the full additive model is statistically significant, Goodman (1970, 1971) suggests comparing (a) the G^2 for a model that excludes the effect with (b) the G^2 for a model that includes the effect, in order to see how much of an improvement in the fit is obtained. Thus, the difference G^2 (M2) − G^2 (M6) can be used to test the null hypothesis that the main effect of race or ethnicity on planned release is nil. The conditional test for model (M6) given the full additive model (M2), G^2 = 5.16 with 1 df has a descriptive level of significance above 0.05, and the null hypothesis of no race or ethnicity effect therefore is rejected. The remaining main effects, similarly tested, are also significant at the 0.05 level (problem behaviors) and 0.01 level (age and prior placements). The fit of the full additive model (M2), shown in Table F-2, to the data can be improved by taking into account significant interaction effects among the explanatory factors. To obtain a better fit, stepwise procedures outlined by Goodman (1972) were followed to find the most parsimonious model that yielded the best fit. Following these steps, model (M12) was selected as providing the best fit to the observed data. Table F-3 provides estimates of the main and interaction effects for model (M12), as well as the estimates of the corresponding zero-order effects of age, race, rebellious behavior, and prior placement on the expected odds of a planned release from institutional care.

The set of parameter estimates listed in Table F-3 for model (M12) can be used to gain additional insight into the effects of age, race, and problem behaviors on the

---

the difference between the likelihood ratio chi-square (G^2) values of the independence and full additive models, G^2 (M1) − G^2 (M2), to the G^2 value of the independence model. The ratio of these terms is a statistic, introduced by Goodman (1970, 1971), which is somewhat analogous to the usual coefficient of multiple determination, R. The statistic $[G^2$ (M1) G^2 (M2)]/G^2 (M1) can be interpreted as the relative decrease in the weighted unexplained variation obtained when the main effects of the explanatory variables are used to predict the odds of a planned release from institutional care. We see in Table F-4 that the full additive model accounts for a 67.8 percent reduction in the weighted unexplained variation. A remaining 32.2 percent of the variation is due to residual three-, four-, and five-factor interaction effects.

TABLE F-2 Pearson and Likelihood Ratio Chi-Square Values for Some Logit Models Pertaining to Planned Release

Models		df	χ^2	G^2
M1	[C] [APBR]	23	77.55	92.19
M2	[CP] [CA] [CB] [CR] [APBR]	18	27.61	29.72
M3	[CP] [APBR]	22	66.07	77.65
M4	[CA] [APBR]	21	48.48	52.93
M5	[CP] [CA] [APBR]	20	38.98	41.91
M6	[CP] [CA] [CB] [APBR]	19	32.77	35.45
M7	[CPA] [CPB] [CPR] [CAB] [CAR] [CBR] [APBR]	9	4.92	5.74
M8	[CPA] [CPB] [CPR] [CAB] [CAR] [APBR]	10	5.15	6.30
M9	[CPA] [CPR] [CAB] [CAR] [APBR]	11	6.70	7.67
M10	[CPR] [CAB] [CAR] [APBR]	13	8.67	9.73
M11	[CP] [CAB] [CAR] [APBR]	14	10.59	11.80
M12	[CP] [CR] [CAB] [APBR]	16	13.55	15.14
M13	[CP] [CAB] [APBR]	17	18.63	20.21

probability of a planned release from institutional care. The beta (B) estimates in Table F-3 are analogous to regression coefficients, and the sign indicates the direction of an explanatory factor effect on planned release. The beta estimates are the natural logarithms of the corresponding gamma estimates listed in Table F-3. As shown in that table, no prior foster placements, age under 13 years, no record of problem behaviors, and white race are all positively related to planned release.

To examine the manner in which the probability of a planned release is affected by various combinations of the explanatory factors, one sums the partial data effects corresponding to a particular case. The sum can be converted to expected odds by taking its antilog, which then can be transformed into a statement of probability. By performing these steps we calculate that a child who entered institutional care in 1974 with the above characteristics ran a 95 percent probability of experiencing a planned release. The probability declined to 62 percent if the child was between 13 and 15 years old and to 47 percent if the child of this same age group was either black or Hispanic.

To examine the effects of prior placement on a child's subsequent adjustment with natural or foster parents, a series of logit models were fit to a 2^4 contingency table in which the four dimensions pertain to (B) break-down in postinstitutional placement, (C) planned release, (P) prior placement, and (H) foster/parents' home. In this case, variables H and B are considered response variables, and variables C and P are factors that may affect H and B and the relationship between H and B.

The first model (M1) listed in Table F-4 is that of independence within and between the joint response variable of failure in foster/parents home placements (BH) and the joint predictor of planned release and prior placement (CP). Neither the independence model (M1) nor the full additive model (M2) fits the observed data well, as indicated by the large Pearson and likelihood ratio

TABLE F-3 Estimates of the Effects of Background Variables on the Odds of a Planned Release From Institutional Foster Care (for M12)

Factors	Zero-Order	Effects	Partial	Effects
General mean	n.a.*	n.a.*	1.214	0.194
Age				
Under 13 years	1.778	0.576	2.858	1.050
13 to 15 years	0.557	−0.586	0.563	−0.574
16 to 19 years	1.010	0.010	0.621	−0.476
Preinstitutional placements				
None	1.502	0.407	1.445	0.368
One or more	0.666	−0.407	0.692	−0.368
Problem behaviors				
No	1.464	0.381	1.302	0.264
Yes	0.683	−0.381	0.768	−0.264
Race				
White	1.246	0.220	1.331	0.286
Nonwhite	0.830	−0.220	0.751	−0.286
Age x problem				
Under 13 years	n.a.*	n.a.*	0.491	−0.712
13 to 15 years	n.a.*	n.a.*	1.070	0.068
16 to 19 years	n.a.*	n.a.*	1.904	0.644

*Not applicable.

TABLE F-4   Pearson and Likelihood Ratio Chi-Square Values
for a Series of Logit Models Applied to Data on Placement
Stability

Model						df	χ^2	$\underline{G}^2$
M1	[B] [H] [CP]					10	19.42	19.04
M2	[BC] [BH] [BP] [CH] [PH]				[CP]	5	15.29	15.35
M3	[BC] [BH] [BP] [CH] [CP]					6	15.80	15.35
M4	[BC] [BH] [BP] [PH] [CP]					6	15.51	15.41
M5	[BC] [BH] [CH] [PH] [CP]					6	15.93	16.07
M6	[BC] [BP] [CH] [PH] [CP]					6	15.59	15.59
M7	[BH] [BP] [CH] [PH] [CP]					6	17.49	17.04
M8	[BC] [CH] [BPH] [CP]					--	--	--
M9	[BCH] [BPH] [BCP]					3	4.80	4.96
M10	[BCH] [BPH] [BCP]					2	2.94	2.88
M11	[BCH] [BPH] [CPH] [BCP]					1	1.81	1.73

chi-square statistics. The three-factor interaction
model (M11) does provide an acceptable fit. Deletion of
the planned x prior x home interaction term (CPH) from
model (M11) does not significantly affect the goodness-of-
fit. Therefore model (M10) is selected as the most parsimonious model that yields the best fit. Table F-5 on the
following page gives the estimates of the main and interaction affects of model (M10).

TABLE F-5 Estimates of the Effects of Predictor Variables
on the Logit Vector of Return to Parents and Placement
Stability (M10)

Effects	γ	β
Mean		
Stability	1.286	0.252
Parents	1.374	0.318
Main Effects		
Stability x Release		
Planned	1.250	0.223
Unplanned	0.800	−0.223
Stability x Prior		
No prior placement	1.117	0.111
One or more	0.895	−0.111
Stability x Home		
Natural parents	0.812	−0.209
Foster parents	1.232	0.209
Parents x Release		
Planned	0.974	−0.026
Unplanned	1.026	0.026
Parents x Prior		
No prior placement	1.115	0.109
One or more	0.896	−0.109
Planned x Prior		
No prior placement	1.943	0.664
One or more	0.515	−0.664
Interaction Effects		
Stability x Planned x Prior		
No prior placement	1.318	0.276
One or more	0.759	−0.276
Stability x Parents x Prior		
No prior placement	0.612	−0.491
One or more	1.633	0.491
Stability x Parents x Release		
Planned	1.472	0.387
Unplanned	0.679	−0.387

REFERENCES

Bakal, Yitzhak, and Polsky, Howard (1979) Reforming
Corrections for Juvenile Offenders. Lexington, Mass.:
Lexington Books.
Bettelheim, Bruno (1974) A Home for the Heart. New
York: Alfred A. Knopf.
Bowlby, John (1977) The Making and Breaking of
Affectional Bonds, Part I. British Journal of
Psychiatry 130:201-210.
Fanshel, David, and Shinn, Eugene (1978) Children in
Foster Care: A Longitudinal Investigation. New
York: Columbia University Press.
Goldstein, Joseph, Freud, Anna, and Solnit, Albert J.
(1973) Beyond the Best Interests of the Child. New
York: The Free Press.
Goodman, Leo (1970) The Multivariate Analysis of
Qualitative Data: Interactions Among Multiple
Classifications. Journal of the American Statistical
Association 65:225-56.
_____ (1971) The Analysis of Multidimensional
Contingency Tables: Stepwise Procedures and Direct
Estimation Methods for Building Models for Multiple
Classifications. Technometrics 13:33-61.
_____ (1972) A Modified Multiple-Regression Approach
to the Analysis of Dichotomous Variables. American
Sociological Review 37:28-46.
_____ (1975) The Relationship Between Modified and
Usual Multiple-Regression Approaches to the Analysis
of Dichotomous Variables. Pp. 83-110 in David Heise,
ed., Sociological Methodology 1976. San Francisco,
Calif.: Josse Bass.
Handler, Joel (1979) Protecting the Social Service
Client. New York: Academic Press.
Hopkirk, H. W. (1944) Institutions Serving Children. New
York: Russell Sage Foundation.
Illinois Commission on Children (1970) Report. Committee
on Young Children in State Correctional Institutions.
Springfield, Ill.: Commission on Children.
_____ (1973) Illinois Accountability in Providing
Children's Services: Children's Rights.
Springfield, Ill.: Commission on Children.
Illinois Department of Mental Health and Developmental
Disabilities (1971) Mental Health Statistics.
Springfield, Ill.: Department of Mental Health.
_____ (1973) Mental Health Statistics. Springfield,
Ill.:Department of Mental Health.

Janowitz, Morris (1978) The Last Half-Century: Societal
    Change and Politics in America. Chicago: University
    of Chicago Press.
Joint Commission on the Mental Health of Children (1970)
    Crisis in Child Mental Health: Challenge for the
    1970's. New York: Harper and Row.
Lubove, Roy (1975) The Professional Altruist. New York:
    Atheneum.
Matza, David (1966) Delinquency and Drift. New York:
    John Wiley and Sons.
Mayer, Morris Fritz, Richman, Leon H., and Balcerzak,
    Edwin A. (1977) Group Care of Children: Crossroads
    and Transitions. New York: Child Welfare League of
    America.
Miller, Jerome (1973) The Politics of Change:
    Correctional Reform. Pp. 3-7 in Yitzhak Bakal, ed.,
    Closing Correctional Institutions: New Strategies for
    Youth Services. Lexington, Mass.: Lexington Books.
Mnookin, Robert (1973) Foster Care--In Whose Best
    Interest? Harvard Educational Review 43:158-197.
    _____ (1976) Child Custody Adjudication:
    Judicial Function in the Face of Indeterminacy. Law
    and Contemporary Problems 39:226-293.
    _____ (1978) Child, Parent, and the State.
    Stanford, Calif.: Stanford University Press.
Mouzelis, Nicos (1971) Organization and Bureaucracy.
    London: Routledge and Keagan Paul.
Murphy, Patrick T. (1974) Our Kindly Parent--The State:
    The Juvenile Justice System and How it Works. New
    York: Viking.
National Association of Social Workers (1973) Statistics
    on Demographic and Social Welfare Trends. Washington,
    D.C.: National Association of Social Workers.
National Council on Crime and Delinquency (1962)
    Procedure and Evidence in the Juvenile Court.
    Advisory Council of Judges. New York: National Council
    on Crime and Delinquency.
Nonet, Philippe, and Selznick, Philip (1978) Law and
    Society in Transition: Toward Responsive Law. New
    York: Harper and Row.
Ohlin, Lloyd, Miller, Alden, and Coates, Robert (1977)
    Juvenile Correctional Reform in Massachusetts.
    Washington, D.C.: U.S. Government Printing Office.
Rosenheim, Margaret, ed. (1962) Justice for the Child:
    The Juvenile Courtin Transition. New York: The Free
    Press of Glencoe.
Scheff, Thomas J. (1966) Being Mentally Ill: A
    Sociological Theory. Chicago: Aldine.

Schur, Edwin M. (1973) Radical Non-Intervention:
    Rethinking the Delinquency Problem. Englewood Cliffs,
    N.J.: Prentice-Hall.
State of Illinois (1969) A Statement of Program and
    Policy. Springfield, Ill.: Department of Mental
    Health.
Trumball, William M. (1965) Proposed New Juvenile Court
    Act for Illinois. Illinois Bar Journal 53:608-619.
U.S. Department of Justice (1977) Children in Custody:
    Advance Report on the Juvenile Detention and
    Correctional Facility Census of 1974. Law Enforcement
    Assistance Administration. Washington, D.C.: U.S.
    Government Printing Office.
Wald, Michael (1975) State Intervention on Behalf of
    Neglected Children: A Search for Realistic
    Standards. Stanford Law Review 27:985-1040.
Walsh, Thomas, Teitelbaum, Fred, and Testa, Mark (1979)
    Improving the Productivity of Purchased Care.
    Springfield, Ill.: Office of Health Finance.
Young, Tom (1976) Winning and Losing at
    Deinstitutionalization: A Two Case Study of Social
    Service System Reform in Massachusetts and Illinois.
    Unpublished paper, School of Social Service
    Administration, University of Chicago.

Mandated Change in Texas: The Federal District Court and the Legislature

MICHAEL J. CHURGIN

INTRODUCTION

The Texas juvenile justice system has been the subject of constant federal litigation, under the case name Morales v. Turman,[1] in one United States district court during much of the 1970s. In addition, there have been numerous legislative enactments that affect both commitment to juvenile facilities and the operation of these institutions. The interrelationship of the judicial decrees and the legislative (and other state) acts is the subject of this paper.

In order to better understand this relationship of the Texas state government and the federal court, a brief background description is necessary. The Texas legislature only meets biannually unless it is called into special session. These special sessions, however, are limited to specific items designated by the governor. Basic

---

[1] 326 F. Supp 677 (E.D. Tex. 1971) (right of counsel to see confined juveniles); 59 F.R.D. 157 (E.D. Tex. 1972) (discover); 364 F. Supp 166 (E.D. Tex. 1973) (interim order); 383 F. Supp 53 (E.D. Tex. 1974) (final order), vacated 535 F. 2d 864 (5th Cir. 1976) (three-judge court issue), reinstated 430 U. S. 322 (1977) (three-judge court issue), vacated 562 F. 2d 993 (5th Cir. 1977) (remand for evidence as to changed conditions).

legislative sessions last for 140 days. Texas government is based on a weak governor model, a reaction to the sweeping powers exercised by Reconstruction governors during the period following the Civil War. Until 1974 governors were elected for a term of two years rather than the current four years. Few executive departments are under the chief executive's control. Rather, there is an elaborate system of boards and commissions, whose members serve for six-year staggered terms, thus making it difficult for one governor's appointees to dominate a board until a second term. In addition, the governor does not have the power to remove members of the various boards and commissions. Finally, numerous offices are elective in Texas, thus further limiting the governor's authority. The one significant power held by the governor is the term veto in the appropriation process, although legislative lumping of programs into one category limits this as well.

United States District Judge William Wayne Justice has been referred to by some pundits as the "real governor of Texas" (Burka 1978:113). Like Frank Johnson in Alabama, Judge Justice has presided over numerous cases with important statewide ramifications. It has been argued by some that he actually encourages litigation in his court that concerns basic constitutional issues and statewide practices. The seat of his court is Tyler, which is in the eastern district of Texas. Through astute forum shopping, a litigant could place a lawsuit before the judge by picking the appropriate division of the court. It is no accident that the major Texas desegregation case, a suit involving conditions of confinement in state prisons, reapportionment disputes, and other major litigation have found their way into Judge Justice's court. He is willing to address constitutional issues with broad ramifications and to consider the full range of equitable powers possessed by a federal judge. In these respects, he is in sharp contrast to most federal district judges in the state. Texas state government, including the executive, legislative, and judicial branches, has not been sympathetic to innovative actions of this federal court.[2]

---

[2] A former chair of the Texas House Judiciary Committee stated: "We all know that just being a lawyer doesn't make a man a magician or give him supernatural powers. Only an appointment to the federal judiciary can do that" Cited in United States v. De La Torre, 605 F. 2d 154, 156 n. 1 (5th Cir. 1979).

As the Morales litigation unfolded in 1971, the Texas
Youth Council (TYC) consisted of three members who in turn
selected the executive director who ran the daily operations. As a matter of tradition the executive director
and the chair of the council were the significant individuals in terms of administering the system of children's
home and delinquent facilities. The executive director
had been in office since 1957, while the chair of the
council had held that position for 11 years. There was
little accountability of the council to anyone. During
the fiscal year ending August 31, 1971, there were 4,129
admissions to TYC training schools and related facilities
for delinquent youth, with an average daily attendance of
2,442 in five major institutions. A sixth would open in
1972 (Texas Youth Council 1972). (TYC also administers
facilities for neglected and dependent children; the Morales suit did not concern this group and thus legislation
involving these children is not included within the scope
of this paper.) The institutions are large facilities in
basically rural settings.

THE FIRST SKIRMISH

Morales opened in modest fashion. TYC officials denied
attorneys private access to clients. The council operated
closed institutions and did not want outsiders meddling,
even though the basic issue initially at stake concerned
the legality of the commitment and not the running of the
institution. The attorneys requested a federal court order directing unimpeded access to clients. The subsequent
hearing exhibited two basic problems. First, there appeared to be a substantial number of juveniles who had
been denied basic rights at their commitment hearings.
Second, TYC appeared to have no written policies or regulations to guide staff in their treatment of the inmates;
the operation of the system seemed lawless. Judge Justice
issued a modest preliminary order: Lawyers were to be
able to see clients in private, without the presence of a
TYC official in the room, and were to be able to communicate by mail without censorship.[3] However, the case
soon mushroomed into a frontal assault on Texas commitment
procedures in operation and the administration of the institutions. The case continues today.

---

[3]326 F. Supp 677 (E.D. Tex. 1971).

The procedural elements were easily handled and the resulting judicial findings, while not embraced with enthusiasm, did not cause continuous friction between the federal court and the state government. In fact, in retrospect the judicial and legislative initiatives dovetailed well. A decision of the United States Supreme Court in 1967 extended the protection of the due process clause of the fourteenth amendment to juvenile commitments. In re Gault (387 U.S. 1 (1967)) established the right to counsel in these proceedings and the accompanying right to free counsel if indigent. In addition, the Court directed a new level of formality akin to criminal cases in the adjudication of delinquency. Along with her sister states, Texas legislatively mandated compliance with the decision. Similarly, the juvenile judges in Texas, like fellow members of the judiciary nationally, failed to put the decision into effect (Horowitz 1977). Judges either failed to appoint counsel or obtained waivers that were highly suspect.

With the newly acquired right to interview clients, and the discovery of widespread violations of both Gault and the Texas statute, the Morales attorneys requested federal court intervention. In addition to the rampant denial of counsel, certain other practices of the Texas juvenile courts were attacked, including the conduct of the proceedings. Many of these deficiencies of the juvenile justice system had already received the attention of the drafters of the new proposed family code. Title III provided for fairly elaborate due process safeguards for the juvenile commitment process and corrected many perceived problems of the former procedures. The 1971 legislature never enacted the code for reasons unrelated to Title III (Texas Tech Law Review 1974).

During the summer of 1971 the judge sent questionnaires to all delinquent minors who were confined within the Texas Youth Council facilities. The returns showed substantial violations of the right to counsel in Texas juvenile commitments, despite Gault and the subsequent legislation providing for counsel.[4] The Texas attorney general's office checked the accuracy of the results by making inquiries of all of the juvenile courts involved and submitted further evidence that many juveniles who had been denied counsel had not waived counsel.[5] The court

---

[4]383 F. Supp 53, 68-9, n. 11 (6).
[5]Lockamy v. State, 488 S. W. 2d 954 (Tex. Civ. App., Austin, 1972) (appellants' brief at 16-17).

specifically found that over 500 persons who were then
confined in TYC facilities had been committed without
having attorneys. This constituted over 20 percent of the
TYC delinquent population--a staggering statistic showing
widespread violation of state and federal law by the Texas
juvenile courts. The state even agreed to the entry of
an order noting this widespread violation of constitutional rights.[6]

Judge Justice, however, chose not to order the release
of these juveniles without first giving the state courts
an opportunity to do so. (It is also arguable that he
could not release the inmates at once, because state
postconvicton remedies had not first been exhausted.[7]
In a class action petition for habeas corpus that was
filed in Austin, the state capital and official seat of
the Texas Youth Council, the attorneys for the plaintiffs
in Morales sought this relief. The state district judge
was only willing to grant the writ to individuals who had
been denied counsel in the capital's county; the other 500
youth would have to seek relief in their home counties.
The intermediate appellate court disagreed, and in a
somewhat remarkable opinion for a Texas court ordered the
systemwide relief.[8] Step one of deinstitutionalization
had taken place with the release of so many juveniles at
one time. The actual orders had been issued by state
judges, although the federal judge carefully had set the
stage.

With the discharge of the juveniles who had been denied
the right to counsel, Judge Justice turned his attention
to future practices of the Texas juvenile courts in ad-
judicating delinquents. He issued a declaratory judgment
that set forth basic rights of juveniles in the commitment
process.[9] The federal judge had the benefit of the
draft of the family code, which had failed in the previous
Texas legislative session[10] and appears to have judicially implemented some of its provisions. Relying on a
tool that had been used in other cases involving statewide

---

[6]383 F. Supp 53, 68-9, n. 11 (8) (order of October 31,
1972).

[7]See Preiser v. Rodriguez, 411 U. S. 475 (1973).

[8]Lockamy, supra n. 5. The state did not petition the
Texas Supreme Court for review.

[9]383 F. Supp 53, 69, n. 12.

[10]Anonymous source.

practices,[11] Judge Justice required that reports on the activities of the juvenile courts throughout the state be sent to him to ensure that the declaratory judgment was being followed. If compliance was not shown within 180 days, the court reserved the right to enter injunctive relief and to provide for appropriate sanctions.[12]

The judicial timing was masterful. Judge Justice had not released a single juvenile but had put into operation a procedure that released hundreds. Judge Justice did not force a confrontation with state officials and judges (at this time), but he set into motion a method of operating that would yield proper adjudication or would result in subsequent sanctions. The declaratory judgment and reports, while toothless initially, had the potential of force six months later. Finally, as the judgment was entered on the eve of a legislative session and the deadline for compliance was following the legislature's adjournment, the judge gave the lawmakers the opportunity to correct the system. He would hold his hand to see what he was dealt.

The New Juvenile Code

The sixty-third session of the Texas legislature was unique. In 1971 and early 1972 a scandal broke in the state concerning bribery and influence peddling involving the charter of a certain bank. The ensuing imbroglio, popularly known as the "Sharpstown Scandal," resulted in the defeat in the Texas Democratic Primary of numerous long-time conservative political figures. The 1973 legislature was younger than normal and contained more moderate individuals than any previous legislature in recent history. During the legislative session, numerous bills that would have been pigeonholed in committees in previous years now came to the floor and passed. Suddenly, Texas had several examples of pro-consumer acts. In addition, the state now was to operate under new family and penal codes. Title III of the new family code specified the method of operation of the juvenile justice adjudicatory system. It provided a marked improvement over the previous procedural framework and led to further deinstitu-

---

[11]United States v. State of Texas, 321 F. Supp 1043, 1061 (E) (E.D. Tex. 1970).
[12]383 F. Supp 53, 69-70, n. 12 (Directive).

tionalization of juveniles. It now became more difficult
to commit a child to facilities of the Texas Youth Council, and those already confined were to be released.

It is difficult to determine to what extent Judge Justice's declaratory judgment served as a catalyst for the
action of the legislature in reforming the juvenile commitment provisions. Work to revise the juvenile adjudicatory and disposition process had begun as early as 1968
with a committee of the Family Law Council of the State
Bar of Texas (Dawson 1974). As noted earlier, the federal
judge was aware of the new draft code. As enacted by the
legislature, Title III agreed fairly closely with Judge
Justice's declaratory judgment. However, subsequent legislative sessions weakened some provisions of the code,
such as permitting waiver of some rights, including right
to counsel during an interrogation.[13] Following the
entry of the declaratory judgment, Judge Justice issued
no further orders concerning the adjudicatory procedures
of the Texas Family Code. It seems reasonable to infer
that the federal court served as a catalyst for the legislature's action, although it was by no means the only
force for revision of the juvenile code.

Several provisions are noteworthy because of the effect
they had on population levels of the Texas Youth Council.
Under the old statute, persons who had once been committed
to the Texas Youth Council remained under its jurisdiction
until the age of 21; under the new code, TYC control ended
at age 18.[14] Furthermore, the statute, when read in
conjunction with the new age of majority law, appeared to
apply the new age cutoff to persons who had been committed
to TYC under the old provisions.[15] The attorney general
issued a ruling to this effect,[16] and 79 persons were
released from institutions, while numerous others were
discharged from parole status.[17] An effort in a later
session of the legislature to reinstate the old commitment
period for delinquent persons was unsuccessful.[18]

---

[13]Family Code, Sec. 51.09(b), added 1975.
[14]Compare Art. 5143d Sec. 31 with Family Code Sec.
54.05(b).
[15]S. B. 123, 63rd Leg. (1973).
[16]Tex. Att. Gen. Opinion H-83 (August 13, 1973).
[17]Austin American-Statesman (August 31, 1973).
[18]H. B. 943, S.B. 1004, 64th Leg. (1975).

The old statutory scheme, as interpreted by the Texas Court of Criminal Appeals,[19] focused on the age of the juvenile at the time of trial rather than at the age of offense. As a result, several counties simply kept juveniles in custody, awaiting the seventeenth birthday and an adult prosecution.[20] One method was to commit the individual to the Texas Youth Council as a juvenile delinquent for a certain offense and then, when the individual reached 17, try that person as an adult for the very same offense. A federal court declared this procedure to be unconstitutional.[21]

A second and more sophisticated practice was to adjudicate the individual delinquent for an offense but not for the serious felony. The person would be transferred to the Texas Youth Council until age 17, and would then be tried as an adult for the serious felony. Both of these procedures avoided the more cumbersome transfer method provided for in the statute to try a juvenile as an adult, and the Texas Court of Criminal Appeals sanctioned the second avoidance procedure.[22] As a result, in many situations there were long periods of what was, in effect, pretrial detention in TYC facilities until individuals reached the magic age of 17 for an adult trial. Previous efforts by the legislature to make the crucial factor in juvenile jurisdiction the age at the time of the offense were thwarted by the Texas courts through judicial construction of admittedly sloppy legislation.[23] The new family code, however, made the jurisdictional question moot, as it clearly stated that the age at the time of offense was to be the crucial factor.[24]

The only method that could now be used was the specialized transfer procedure. Juveniles who committed serious felonies would never spend any time in TYC facilities. Rather, if convicted, the individual would be placed in

---

[19]Salazar v. State, 494 S. W. 2d 548 (Tex. Civ. App. 1973).

[20]Letter dated April 1, 1980, to author from Bexar (San Antonio) County Office of the Criminal District Attorney.

[21]Sawyer v. Hauck, 245 F. Supp. 55 (W.D. Tex. 1965).

[22]Garza v. State, 369 S. W. 2d 36 (Tex. Cr. App. 1963), but see Hultin v. Beto, 396 F. 2d 216 (5th Cir. 1968).

[23]Foster v. State, 400 S. W. 2d 552 (Tex. Cr. App. 1966), Dillard v. State, 439 S. W. 2d 460 (Tex. Civ. App., Houston [14th Dist.] 1969, writ ref'd n.r.e.).

[24]Family Code, Sec. 51.02(1) (B).

the Texas Department of Corrections.[25] The state has
not maintained statistics concerning the number of juveniles transferred for trial as adults, but from preliminary inquiry it appears that the number increased significantly with the passage of the family code.[26] (Some
counties had never used the transfer procedure under the
old code.) Thus, a small but important group of individ-
uals--the more serious offenders--was removed from TYC
jurisdiction.

The old code contained two vague and overly broad definitions of delinquent conduct: "One who habitually so
deports himself as to injure or endanger the morals or
health of himself or others," and "one who habitually associates with vicious or immoral persons."[27] Both definitions were abandoned by the legislature; no counterpart
exists under the new code. Finally, the legislature imposed new qualifications for the judges, namely the requirement that the judge be an attorney in order to conduct any adjudication of delinquency hearings.[28] In
sum, the new legislative provisions made it more difficult
to commit a child to Texas Youth Council facilities.

Status Offenders

The legislature also redefined delinquent conduct in a
manner to restrict commitment to Texas Youth Council institutions. Following a national trend (Horowitz 1977),
a new category of individuals subject to juvenile court
jurisdiction came into being--children in need of supervision (CINS).[29] Under the former code, persons now to
be classified as CINS were subject to a finding of delinquency and commitment to the training schools.[30] Under

---

[25]Family Code, Sec. 54.02.
[26]Statistics from Bexar (San Antonio), Tarrant (Fort
Worth), and Travis (Austin) Counties.
[27]Art. 2338-1 Sec. 33(f)(g). The former provision had
been upheld by the Texas courts, E.S.G. v. State, 447 S.
W. 2d 225 (Tex. Civ. App., San Antonio 1969, writ ref'd
n.r.e.), cert. denied 398 U.S. 956 (1970).
[28]Family Code, Sec. 51.04(d). This section was weakened
by subsequent legislatures, but the law now (1980) requires an attorney for adjudication hearings.
[29]Family Code, Sec. 51.03(b).
[30]Art. 2338-1 Sec. 33 (c)-(g).

the new code, however, probation was the only alternative, unless there were repeated violations of penal laws or ordinances.[31] Under no circumstances could children in need of supervision be committed to Texas Youth Council facilities, unless there were specific findings of violation of criminal laws. As elsewhere, probation was the favored alternative for these individuals.

Subsequent legislatures reduced the special protections for status offenders. Finding that an absolute ban on placing status offenders within TYC institutions limited placement alternatives, juvenile authorities recommended that commitment to a TYC facility be allowed under certain circumstances, and the 1975 legislature concurred. Persons found to be CINS now were to be placed on probation initially. However, subsequent noncriminal conduct (e.g., truancy or being a runaway) while on probation could be termed delinquent conduct as a violation of "a reasonable and lawful order of a juvenile court" that had been entered as part of the initial disposition hearing.[32] Under these circumstances, CINS could be committed to a TYC facility. To protect these individuals, however, the legislature provided that CINS committed to TYC may not be placed with non-CINS.[33] Instead, the facilities for dependent and neglected children were to be used.

This special restriction was short-lived, and during a subsequent legislative session the limitation was dropped.[34] CINS committed to TYC can now be placed in any facility. There is no available legislative history concerning this decision, but one can surmise that TYC officials reported that CINS often were major management problems and could not be adequately controlled in the facilities for neglected and dependent children. As of 1978, CINS constituted 8 percent of the admissions to training schools, with close to 75 percent of that number having violated a probation order as runaways (Texas Youth Council 1977).

---

[31]Family Code, Sec. 54.04(d).
[32]Family Code, Sec. 51.03(a)(2). See also In the Matter of E.A.R., 548 S. W. 2d 454 (Tex. Civ. App., Texarkana, 1977).
[33]Art. 5143d, Sec. 12(b).
[34]Human Resources Code, Sec. 61.062.

ROUND TWO OF THE LITIGATION

While the 1973 legislature was in session, the trial phase
of Morales was taking place in Tyler. It has been suggested by at least one commentator that Judge Justice expanded the lawsuit from one that was procedural (i.e.,
concerning entry to Texas Youth Council facilities) to one
concerning the very nature of the TYC training schools
themselves (Burka 1978). The federal judge did invite the
United States to participate as a party, an invitation
that was accepted by the Justice Department and its Civil
Rights Division.[35]   With the resources of the federal
government the plaintiffs were able to amass significant
materials showing the nature of TYC facilities.[36]   In
August Judge Justice issued an interim order that provided
emergency relief for the plaintiff class.[37]   The order
established standards concerning the use of physical
force, segregation, conditions of solitary confinement,
use of the maximum security facility, visitation rights,
provision of medical care, hiring of perspective personnel, and communications within and without TYC facilities.
In addition, the court appointed an ombudsman who had the
power to make recommendations and to report to the court
and parties, but had no authority to take action.

The federal court order was followed shortly by an up-
rising at Mountain View, the maximum security facility and
the subject of much of the testimony. This "riot" involved over 100 inmates and received prominent attention
throughout the state. Some blamed the rebellion on the
federal court in that there were now restrictions on the
use of physical force. There were also reports that staff
at the facility had actually encouraged the property damage and riot to embarrass the court.[38]   The failure of
TYC administrators to explain the court order to staff,
the disturbances at Mountain View, the development of

---

[35] Request to the Attorney General of May 17, 1972.
[36] See e.g., Testimony of Peter Sandman, "Abuse and Neglect of Children," Hearings before the Subcommittee on
Child and Human Development, 96th Congress, 1st Session
at 95 (1979), and Factual Appendix prepared for Morales
appeal by the United States.
[37] 364 F. Supp 166 (E.D. Tex. 1973).
[38] Houston Post (September 15, 1973), p. 1; Dallas Morning News (September 16, 1973), p. 45A; Gatesville Messen-
ger (September 13, 1973), p. 1.

dissension within the council, and the trial disclosures all contributed to the resignation of the long-time executive director, James Turman, and the chair of the Texas Youth Council, Robert Kneebone.[39] One observer has indicated that the removal of the executive director from his post was the most significant and important change to take place at TYC as a result of the Morales case. It is clear that the central office in Austin had condoned the brutality, which was described in graphic detail in the trial and in the court's final decision.[40]

As noted earlier, the Texas Youth Council had acted for years with little legislative or executive supervision. With an uninterested governor and a part-time legislature, there was virtually no oversight. In addition, through years of service the executive director and chair of the council had close links with power bases throughout the state. A senate committee report issued in 1969 sharply criticized TYC and recommended reform; it was ignored. One state senator suggested that Turman "got with the house leadership and torpedoed it" and "flopped the whole thing with political maneuvers." A consultant to TYC was the brother of the (then) chair of the House Appropriations Committee. Recommendations that new facilities be built close to population centers rather than in rural areas were ignored by TYC. It constructed two new training schools in the districts of the lieutenant governor and speaker of the house.[41] No one, however, could now ignore the federal court interim order.

It was obvious to most observers that the federal judge's final order under preparation would necessitate sweeping changes in TYC administration. In an attempt to show that the state was ready to act, the governor issued an executive order in October 1973 that noted "a critical need in the state of Texas to upgrade the quality of correctional care, and rehabilitative services for Texas youth, and to coordinate their delivery to the persons in need."[42] He created an interagency task force, and in turn it commissioned a nationally recognized consulting firm to establish a master plan for youth services in the state. (The federal Law Enforcement Assistance Adminis-

---

[39]Austin American-Statesman (October 3, 1973); National Observer (September 29, 1973).
[40]Anonymous source.
[41]Austin American-Statesman (December 6, 1973).
[42]Executive Order, D.B. 9 (October 10, 1973).

tration funded the study (<u>Texas Master Plan</u> 1975)).
Meanwhile, the new administration of the Texas Youth
Council was attempting to implement the court's interim
order. The new chair of the board, W. Forrest Smith, appeared to support efforts for change. With his appointment as the new executive director and with support from
the majority of the council, Ron Jackson implemented new
programs and lessened the emphasis on security.[43] However, there were serious staff problems because most of
the employees who had operated under the old regime were
still in place. The federal ombudsman issued a steady
stream of reports to the parties.[44]

The state attempted to reopen the case in 1974 to show
both the significant changes in the operation of TYC facilities and the council's plan to further upgrade the
system of youth care. The federal judge refused, noting
that evidence had to end at some point, and in August 1974
Judge Justice issued an extremely detailed decision that
set forth numerous constitutional violations in almost all
phases of TYC facility administration.[45] However, as
with his handling of the procedural aspects of the case,
he did not issue any injunctive relief at this time.
Rather, the judge asked for the submission of plans and
encouraged negotiations and agreement on the method of
carrying out the changes within TYC. The emergency interim order was maintained in effect.[46] Every aspect
of institutional life was covered in the court's final
decision, from education to medical treatment to basic
levels of care.[47] Finally, the court indicated that
constitutional treatment could not take place within two
TYC facilities, Mountain View and Gatesville. Appeals
from the order spanned numerous years because of delays
in the appellate court and because of judicial wrangling
over minutia of three-judge court jurisdiction. No implementation plan ever was put into effect by the court.

---

[43]<u>Austin American-Statesman</u> (December 3, 1973, p. 1;
December 4, 1973, p. 22; December 5, 1973, p. 1).
[44]The author has reviewed mounds of files containing
reports from the ombudsman to the court and parties. In
one random month there were 13 reports, some of which
contained multiple incidents.
[45]383 F. Supp 53 (E.D. Tex. 1974).
[46]393 F. Supp at 126.
[47]The Fifth Circuit ultimately complained that the order
was too detailed, 562 F.2d 993 (1977).

No new hearing has been held; the parties are now engaged
in settlement discussions.

TYC Reacts

The new chair of TYC had been converted to the need for
reform and recommended significant new funding in preparing his budget for the 1975 legislature.   "The attorney
general's staff tried desperately to extricate the lawsuit from the depths of defeat, but he just couldn't
change the facts, and the facts were that there were
practices going on none of us wanted to admit, and the
plaintiffs proved they were true." He had become personally convinced that these practices were routinely taking
place.[48]   The federal court order had noted the need
for a "less restricted alternative," and chairman Smith
proposed a subsidy program to establish community-based
corrections, almost a new concept in Texas.[49]

There was considerable reluctance on the part of TYC
to place its institutions under Judge Justice's jurisdiction. One focus of the efforts of TYC and the legislature
in the subsequent years was to show that Texas could put
its own house in order without federal court direction.
Of course, it was the federal court that served as the
catalyst for this newfound interest in juvenile care.
Smith acknowledged the court's value in exposing brutali-
ties, "but it's one thing to tell us we can't beat the
hell out of kids anymore—we've stopped that by now—and
its a wholly different thing for him to tell us how to run
the agency." He indicated that TYC might itself choose

---

[48]Austin American-Statesman (September 9, 1974), p. 17.
[49]Smith represented a two-person majority on the TYC;
the dissenting member favored a go-slow policy on compliance. See, e.g., Austin American-Statesman (March 20,
1974), p. 15. Some found Mr. Smith to be too much of a
convert, and the governor declined to reappoint him in
1975. In leaving office Smith charged that his loss of
reappointment was either because the governor disapproved
of the "new directions I and others have attempted to
chart for the TYC or he is simply unwilling to face pressures by those who would attempt to bring back the old
TYC." His replacement was quite conservative. Austin
American-Statesman (October 25, 1975); Gatesville Messen-
ger (November 6, 1975, p. 1.).

to close the two facilities, but that the agency preferred to wait until it was ready, rather than follow the court's "as quickly as possible" mandate. "If I were the court, I would have entered an order saying, 'TYC, you've been bad as hell in the past, but I've got confidence in you; get to work.'" While in basic agreement with the order, Smith indicated he did not think it could succeed if it were court-enforced. He indicated in a newspaper interview that TYC support is needed to sell the program to the legislature and the people, but that TYC cannot support the specific court order since the judge did not indicate "where the state is today" and that there were serious difficulties--both political and financial--in making such a rapid conversion.[50]

The consultant's report, which was ordered by the governor's task force, was delivered in preliminary form to TYC in late 1974. It was received with little enthusiasm but did serve as a mechanism for TYC to criticize the court order, since the consultant had not recommended the immediate closing of the large institutions. The chair of the House Human Resources Committee criticized the plan as "little more than a 'gimmick' for maintaining TYC's large institutions." "The plan's recommendations had obviously been made on the basis of political pragmatics. The consultants (who developed the plan) found that the institutions and the towns in which they are located--joined by a strange assortment of public officials from these areas, ossified bureaucrats in the TYC hierarchy, and those totally unfamiliar with the trends in modern juvenile corrections--are a vocal pressure group for the maintenance of the status quo."[51]

Once the Supreme Court declined to issue a stay of the final order of Judge Justice, TYC finally began the negotiation process with the attorneys for the plaintiff. It soon became clear that there would be no voluntary submission to federal court jurisdiction or other outside forces in terms of oversight of TYC facilities. However, moving on its own, the majority of the Texas Youth Council recommended a massive budget to show its commitment to

---

[50]Austin American-Statesman (September 9, 1974; September 11, 1974).
[51]Austin American-Statesman (September 30, 1974; November 18, 1974).

community-based programs; in addition, Mountain View was to be closed.[52]

The Legislature Responds

The 1975 legislature was sympathetic to the need for change in the Texas Youth Council and its facilities. While some members wished to wait until the litigation was over, the majority were willing to take steps to show the state's good faith and to show that the state could put its own house in order. The resistance to the court order was still there, but there was a recognition of a need for alteration of the status quo. The federal court had pointed the way, and the legislature seemed willing to pay the price to extricate the TYC from federal court oversight.

The closing of the Mountain View facility served as an important symbol of a commitment to change. With its double rows of barbed wire, the training school looked more like a prison than a youth facility, and from the trial testimony it had been operated as a "bad" prison. The House Social Services Committee noted that "the institutional population of the TYC had dropped drastically in the aftermath of the Morales order" and there was no need for the facility (Texas House of Representatives 1975:29). A letter from the executive director of TYC to the director of the Department of Corrections graphically described the existing situation:[53]

> There are several factors which have caused TYC to contemplate [the abandonment of Mountain View]. First, the number of children we have in our various institutions is only one-half the number we had one year ago. The lowering of the adult age to eighteen, the passage of Title III of the Family Code, which took away from TYC the "children in need of supervision," and the various court decisions concerning due process rights for children have caused our situation.

---

[52]Austin American-Statesman (November 8, 1974; December 5, 1974, p. A13).
[53]Ron Jackson, Executive Director, TYC, to Jim Estelle, Director, Texas Department of Corrections, August 26, 1974. Contained in ombudsman report to Judge Justice of July 14, 1976, enclosing TYC minutes of June 14, 1976.

> Secondly, the TYC is initiating community-based programs which will be extensively utilized in the future methods by which TYC seeks to accomplish its mandate from the Legislature. It is anticipated that a significant number of the children committed to the TYC can be placed in living situations alternative to institutions.

The Department of Corrections was willing to have the new facility to house its burgeoning population, and the legislature approved the transfer. Mountain View no longer was a TYC facility; however, it would continue to serve its function as a prison--now for women instead of juveniles.[54]

Another major legislative effort was the reform of the Texas Youth Council structure. The membership was increased from three to six, and the daily expense allowance was raised and authorized for 90 rather than the previous 60 days. The house committee noted that "the TYC has recently undergone one of the most drastic upheavals experienced by any state agency. . . . The impact of the Morales v. Turman lawsuit has required a reorientation of juvenile corrections in Texas." The increase in size "should make the task of dealing with the court order somewhat easier." The governor immediately appointed the first black to the council and gave the board a much broader geographical base.[55]

------

[54]A subsequent legislature approved the closing of the other Texas Youth Council facility mentioned in Judge Justice's 1974 order (Gatesville) effective in phases during 1979. Enrollment had declined from 1,000 to 300 since the interim order. The Gatesville institution was contrary to TYC's current image as an organization devoted to community-based facilities and institutions that stressed freedom of movement rather than punitive confinement. Once again the facility was converted to a prison for the Texas Department of Corrections. Art. 5119a-1; Austin American-Statesman (February 9, 1978).

[55]Texas House of Representatives (1975:24, 28, 31); Texas Youth Council (1975). Even with the replacement of moderate Smith by a conservative in the fall of 1975 (see n. 49), the council seems to have maintained its somewhat moderate course. The new chair was a Smith adherent, and Ron Jackson remained executive director. Austin American-Statesman (November 20, 1975).

One of the problems that Judge Justice noted in his decision was the seeming lack of rules and regulations governing conduct of staff and the juveniles within their care:

> In fact, almost _any_ action, however arbitrary, by an employee short of physical abuse of a child is probably _consistent_ with TYC 'policy', because that 'policy', as embodied in the minutes [of the Texas Youth Council meetings], is close to undiscoverable and does not constitute a coherent body of regulations that are applied throughout the system; such rules and regulations as exist are local to single institutions or even subdivisions thereof [emphasis in original].[56]

The legislature enacted the state's first administrative procedures act. It required notice and comment and encouraged public participation in rule making. Furthermore, regulations were to be made available to the public and to those affected by the rules.[57] TYC today has an elaborate set of rules governing almost every phase of staff conduct in their treatment of juveniles, and there is a set of regulations governing inmate life that includes a bill of rights and a grievance procedure.[58] At least on paper, there is a rule of law.

The primary achievement of the legislative session was the passage of authorization for community-based juvenile corrections. Two models were proposed and considered in the house. One was modeled on the Federal Juvenile Justice Act of 1974, and the Committee on Social Services recommended this prototype to the house. However, it was rejected on a 63-62 vote, and a substitute was passed. The Texas Youth Council was authorized to contract with local or other state agencies or to provide direct care within the community, including halfway houses, diversion programs, and other services. Unlike the defeated bill, there was no provision for a state advisory committee, and the monitoring function of local boards was unclear. The house committee noted with approval that while "the full force of the Morales decision has not yet been felt, the Youth Council is already on its way toward implementing

---

[56]383 F. Supp at 63-64.
[57]Art. 6252-13(a).
[58]Title 37, Texas Administrative Code, Part III.

many of the reforms suggested by the Federal District
Court, one of the most important of these being the move
toward community-based corrections, rather than institutionalization, for the juvenile offender."[59]   Although
some hostility to the federal judge existed in the legislature, including one unsuccessful attempt to place a
halfway house adjacent to Justice's Tyler home,[60] the
relevant authorization committees seemed mildly supportive
of the goals embodied in the court order and were willing
to give TYC the tools to comply with it.

However, the appropriations committees were less sympathetic, and they added a rider to the money bill that
delegated legislative authority to the governor concerning
the spending of $4 million during the first year of the
community services program and $5 million during the sub-
sequent year.   Any appropriation for community services
was made contingent upon a specific finding by the governor "that the Texas Youth Council has developed and
adopted a plan for allocation of the appropriation for
community assistance which takes into consideration full
utilization of the existing facilities in a given area
prior to the allocation of funds for new facilities in
that same area."[61]   Governor Dolph Briscoe concluded
that there was only partial compliance, and in two actions
authorized the spending of only $2 million.[62] This re-
sulted in the significant diminution of TYC's effort, and
it was done in opposition to the Youth Council (the governor had previously only recommended an appropriation
budget).   The executive director of TYC indicated that he
had received no objections to the community-based programs
from the governor's office.[63]   Several months later the
attorney general, acting on a request from the chair of
the Social Services Committee, ruled that the governor
could not make a partial finding and had to release all
funds.[64]   The ruling came too late in the budgetary
process.   Contracts had already been signed for reduced
services and for a duration of six months or less.   There

---

[59]Texas House of Representatives (1975:24, 28-29); House
Journal, 64th Leg. at 4482-86, 4489-91 (1975).
[60]House Journal, 64th Leg. at 4485 (1975).
[61]Acts 1975, 64th Leg., ch. 743 at 2417, 2503 et seq.
[62]Austin American-Statesman (January 15, 1976).
[63]Austin American-Statesman (January 16, 1976; February
19, 1976, p. 6; May 14, 1976).
[64]Tex. Atty. Gen., Opinion H-822 (May 12, 1976).

was no way that the agency felt it could now spend $2 million in the less than three months remaining in the fiscal year. As a result of the severe initial cutback by the governor, TYC claimed to have diverted only 90 persons from the institutions to the community programs rather than the 400 that they had projected.[65] However, faced with the attorney general's ruling, the governor released the full $5 million effective for the fiscal year beginning September 1, 1976. Under the agency's proposal, rehabilitation services were to be provided in the community for 1,515 individuals, and special testing and medical services for 870 others.[66]

Another legislative effort during the 1975 session was a small appropriation for an ombudsman within TYC to hear grievances of the institutionalized youth. TYC considered this program to be of some importance, in part to show the federal court that it could monitor its own institutions without a federally appointed ombudsman. Shortly after the interim order in 1973, TYC appointed its own ombudsman and placed him in the central office in Austin. According to an intern in that office one summer, one reason the individual was hired was "to prove to the public, if not to the court, that TYC could do a better job on its own of protecting children's rights than the court could force upon it" (Bush 1974:26-29). TYC did not enjoy the federally appointed ombudsman at Mountain View, even though he had been a former caseworker within TYC. Under the court's order there was a constant flow of paper from the ombudsman and from all institutions to the federal court. Anytime an individual was placed in isolation for a certain period, a notice had to be sent to the federal court. In addition, the federal ombudsman reported on all of his investigations and kept the court and plaintiff attorneys informed of TYC meetings, staff conferences, newspaper articles, and other matters that might be of interest.[67]

The operation of the ombudsman was particularly annoying to the staff at Mountain View, where he was housed. In response to one particular report of the ombudsman, the superintendent of Mountain View wrote to Judge Justice:

---

[65]Austin American-Statesman (May 14, 1979; June 9, 1979).

[66]Austin American-Statesman (September 17, 1979).

[67]Testimony, supra n. 36 at 573-4.

> There was no violation of the Order in this case
> (and in many of the unsupported allegations for-
> warded by Mr. Derrick [the ombudsman] without com-
> ment), nor does this represent a matter which
> should be brought to your attention. Yet this re-
> port will be further elaboration of Plaintiff's
> case against Mountain View School for Boys, as
> evidenced by heavy references to Mr. Derrick's re-
> ports in post-trial briefs (which we are then not
> given fair chance to refute). Mr. Derrick has not
> chosen to interpret his function as necessitating
> verification on his part of any reports forwarded.
> He sends to you that which is given to him as is.
> Yet, the weight of his office, as outlined in your
> Order, lends face validity to his reports. . . .
> If this were not the case, then such references to
> his reports (many of which represent unsubstanti-
> ated allegations) would not be referred to so
> heavily by Plaintiffs in support of their claims
> that we are no different than our infamous prede-
> cessors. His covert accusations, by and large, are
> not investigated to any extent by himself or
> Plaintiffs' attorneys who have been conspicuously
> absent and content to rely on the face validity
> of reports forwarded indiscriminately by Mr.
> Derrick.[68]

In short, TYC wanted control over its own institutions.
   The governor did not share TYC's view and vetoed the
appropriation for the internal ombudsman project. Noting
the changes within TYC, the chief executive stated that
"the new direction in which the Council is moving will
obviate the necessity for the ombudsman project." However, if the agency still wanted such an office, it could
find money for it within its own general administration
budget.[69] TYC diverted $100,000 from its community
services budget. The executive director stated that there
was "a need to provide legal services for our kids and
merit in the idea of having someone looking over a state
agency's shoulder." He admitted that with such a large
agency and so many employees, "now and then kids can get
hurt. We found that out in our court suit." The current

---

[68]Ace E. Myrick to Hon. Wiliam Wayne Justice, June 7,
1974.
[69]Senate Journal, 64th Leg. at 2891 (1975).

TYC ombudsman noted that because he was all alone he wouldn't be surprised if "nine out of ten kids in our facilities said they never heard of me or this position."[70] The federal court-ordered ombudsman operated at sufferance. Soon after the U.S. Court of Appeals for the Fifth Circuit vacated Judge Justice's order in 1976, the ombudsman was fired.[71] (As soon as he heard of the TYC action, Judge Justice sent a federal marshall to the federal ombudsman's office to take possession of all of his records.) When the Supreme Court reversed the court of appeals on the jurisdictional issue, the federal ombudsman was not rehired. TYC contended that the agency now had an effective grievance procedure, including its own ombudsman staff.[72]

The 1975 legislature also authorized the construction of two small institutional facilities in areas of the state where none existed. The governor vetoed this budgetary item, finding it inconsistent with the new emphasis of community programs. "With this new program element available to the council, it would be imprudent to expand the institutional capacity at this time."[73] There have been no further legislative efforts to expand the institutional capacity of the Texas Youth Council for delinquent youth. In fact, the 1979 session saw the transfer of the multibuilding Gatesville facility to the Texas Department of Corrections. However, with the increasing population of the state and the rise in juvenile crime reports, there might soon be a need for some more institutional beds despite the functioning community programs.

THE EFFECT OF THE LITIGATION

The actions of the 1975 legislature can be traced to Judge Justice's order detailing widespread relief in almost all areas for the inmates of the Texas Youth Council. The exact impact of these legislative actions is hard to determine. The long, contorted route of the litigation has only recently begun to reveal the condition of the facilities of the Texas Youth Council. No implementation de-

---

[70] Austin American-Statesman (July 17, 1975, p. 9).
[71] Austin American-Statesman (November 28, 1976, p. B2).
[72] Austin American-Statesman (March 22, 1979).
[73] Senate Journal, 64th Leg. at 2891 (1975); Texas House of Representatives (1975:25).

cree was ever negotiated by the parties, and none was entered by the court. However, TYC has acted in the court's
shadow for the whole decade of the 1970s. Even though
there was no longer any need to send daily reports to the
federal district court after 1976, there was always the
possibility that another order would someday be issued.
When the Fifth Circuit initially vacated Judge Justice's
order in 1976, the TYC executive director issued an interesting statement that was self-serving but also showed
that he was aware of the federal district court: "Today's
ruling will in no way lessen the youth council's commitment to providing the best possible care for the children
of Texas. The TYC has gone through significant changes
during the past three years and we're anxious to tell the
court about what our agency is like today."[74]

Unlike other institutional litigation, Morales involved
no constant action by the federal judge once the orders
had been issued. No extensive compliance hearings were
held, in large part due to the unsettled state of the appellate process in reviewing the court's order. The only
continuing contact of the court with the litigation was
the reporting requirement contained in the interim order
of 1973, and this ceased to be in effect in 1976. One
federal judge could not possibly evaluate the constant
stream of reports that came to the court from every TYC
institution housing delinquent youth (concerning placement
in isolation and other serious punishments) and from the
federal ombudsman (containing incident reports and occurrences within the maximum security institution and the
rest of TYC). Occasionally, in a particular case, the
judge would request clarification from the attorney general's office. In addition, the judge backed the federal
ombudsman to make sure that he was given access to the
confined youth and also given notice of all TYC meetings.[75] Beyond this there was no action.

Texas was not proud of the Morales case. Following the
issuance of the court order, the serious deficiencies in
the institutions were admitted by most council members,
the governor, and most members of the legislature. The
new refrain became "we can put our own house in order."
(This is very unlike the current situation concerning the
suit against the state adult prison system, where almost

---

[74] Austin American-Statesman (July 22, 1976).
[75] See, e.g., W.W. Justice to Special Assistant Attorney
General Choate, May 20, 1976.

all state officials take considerable pride in the efficiency, economy, and discipline of the Texas corrections
system.) The state line of argument for the past five
years of the Morales litigation has been that TYC is now
different and has changed so that no federal court interference is necessary. A strong, economy-minded state
legislature and an economy-minded governor provided the
necessary funds requested by TYC to change the focus of
their treatment of confined youth. Of course, the potential for community-based youth corrections to be less expensive than institutionalization no doubt contributed,
to some extent, to the willingness to appropriate the
initial funds. At least in 1975 there appears to have
been a strong commitment to act and to show that the state
recognized its responsibility to its confined youth and
would follow through. The matter still has not been resolved.

Texas rarely concedes anything in litigation. Unlike
other states, it is reluctant to enter into consent judgments, especially in institutional or programmatic litigation. Even while TYC was making changes in its operations, the state waged an aggressive appellate attack on
the federal court order, ultimately winning a new hearing
on current conditions. The initial procedural aspect of
the Morales litigation was the exception; there was no
question as to the illegal confinement of numerous juveniles who had been denied counsel at trial, and long-term
federal court monitoring was unlikely. The substantive
aspect was different, although the state did not appeal
from the orders concerning the most egregious conduct
(e.g., physical abuse, use of tear gas, use of solitary
confinement).[76] Conditions in TYC were deplorable, but
the state insisted on its right to change them. Here the
constitutional mandate as well as specific legal remedies
were less clear, and the state chose to resist. Texas
would not agree voluntarily to any federal court-imposed
changes and accompanying monitoring. It might follow the
final order on its own, but it would never surrender its
prerogatives voluntarily. Another factor was the presence
of the United States as an invited party. The intervention of the federal judge was intrusive enough; the involvement of the Justice Department was beyond the pale.
State officials resented the Civil Rights Division's

---

[76]Morales v. Turman, Memorandum Opinion and Order, June
12, 1980, at 4.

presence in <u>Morales</u> and fought against government involvement in a similar invited role in <u>Ruiz</u> v. <u>Estelle</u>,[77]
the class-action case on conditions in Texas prisons that
was heard by Judge Justice in 1979. Texas would not yield
its authority to the federal judge and the U.S. Justice
Department until it had exhausted every weapon in its
arsenal.

Despite denials by some TYC officials and legislators,
there can be no question that without Judge Justice there
would have been no real push for change within the Texas
Youth Council facilities. His 1974 decision graphically
shows the high level of brutality that characterized the
prior administration of TYC. A somewhat sympathetic TYC
chair and a new executive director seemed to have a commitment to change TYC facilities and the method of treatment. The 1973 and 1975 Texas legislatures were more
progressive (moderate) than usual and implemented most of
the requested legislation. Judge Justice recently described the effect of the litigation: "Given the character
of defendants' defense during the initial trial of this
action and the timing of the purported changes, it is un-
questionable that these changes, if they have occurred,
were a direct result of this action. . . ."[78]

Judge Justice did not end up serving as the classic
powerbroker (Diver 1979), as was characteristic of judges
in some other class litigation in sister states, although
he did even the sides with his invitation to the Justice
Department to join the litigation. The federal judge's
basic approach was to give direction to the council and
to the legislature on needed reforms once the constitutional violations were found. Reports would show compliance or the lack thereof. Had an implementation hearing
been held and had there been evidence of noncompliance
with his order and no movement toward compliance with his
final decision, Judge Justice would not have hesitated to
issue a final decree and to use the full range of his
powers as federal judge. This, however, never came to
pass because of the laborious appellate process. TYC was
left alone during much of the late 1970s and was able, to
its own satisfaction, to show its good faith and its
ability to run its own institutions without direct federal

---

[77]<u>In</u> <u>re</u> <u>Estelle</u>, 516 F.2d 480 (5th Cir. 1975), cert.
denied 426 U.S. 925 (1976), three justices dissenting with
opinion.
[78]<u>Morales</u>, n. 90 at 4-5.

interference. In the final analysis Judge Justice served as a catalyst for state action.

The final order, however, was not designed merely to serve as a catalyst for change. Judge Justice provided a blueprint for a well-run and hopefully rehabilitative juvenile justice system. It was instrumentalism in a close-to-perfect form. TYC operated an unconstitutional system of juvenile corrections. Merely eliminating the barbarity would not be sufficient; the whole structure had to be changed. The final order describes what the new system would look like. The Fifth Circuit's approach in vacating the order in 1977 was different; it is what Owen Fiss calls "formalism represented by the tailoring principle"(1979:56). On remand, Judge Justice must evaluate the TYC operations as they are today and can only enjoin those practices that continue to fail constitutional standards. The federal court cannot remake TYC. By prolonging the appellate process, Texas has succeeded in preventing implementation of Judge Justice's final order. The new case is much more limited in scope.

REFERENCES

Burka, Paul (1978) The Real Governor of Texas. Texas Monthly 6(June):113.
Bush, Steven (1974) Unpublished paper on file with the Criminal Justice Project, University of Texas School of Law, Austin, Texas.
Dawson, Robert O. (1974) Draftsman's Comments. Texas Tech Law Review 5:509.
Diver, Colin (1979) The Judge as Political Power Broker. Virgina Law Review 65:43-106.
Fiss, Owen (1979) Foreword: The Forms of Justice. Harvard Law Review 93(1):1-58.
History of the Family Code (1974) Texas Tech Law Review 5:267-268.
Horowitz, Donald (1977) The Courts and Social Policy. Washington, D.C.: The Brookings Institution.
Texas House of Representatives (1975) Report to the Speaker. Committee on Social Services. 64th Legislature. Austin, Texas.
Texas Master Plan for Youth Development Services, A Summary Report (1975).
Austin, Texas.
Texas Youth Council (1972) Annual Report of the Texas Youth Council to the Governor for the Fiscal Year

Ending August 31, 1971. Austin, Texas: Texas Youth
Council.
_____ (1975) Annual Report. Austin, Texas:
Texas Youth Council.
_____ (1977) Annual Report. Austin, Texas:
Texas Youth Council.

Services for Status Offenders: Issues Raised by Private Provision of Publicly Financed Services

APPENDIX
H

WILLIAM POLLAK

INTRODUCTION

In many states, publicly financed services for status offenders are provided by private agencies. Thus the runaway house, the preadjudication "advocate" service, and the group home are likely to be paid for with public dollars and to be provided by private agencies. The private production of public services for status offenders raises questions concerning the responsiveness and quality of private providers, the management and financing methods used by the public sector, and the tenor of the public/private relationship in which the public sector pays and manages and the private sector produces. These questions form the focus of this paper.

This paper touches on issues relating to the private provision of services, but the well-being of youth, their families, and the communities with which they interact are the ultimate concerns here. This poses a dilemma, for there is considerable controversy about which services to status offenders will best meet those concerns. In light of this controversy, by what standard should the performance of the private sector be judged? The position adopted in this paper is that private sector performance is "good" if service is efficiently produced and meets the needs of youth as seen by the public agencies responsible for them. Other standards might reasonably be advanced. However, this standard seems appropriate in a paper that

examines private production as an alternative to public
production in discharging responsibilities deemed to be
public.

The paper consists of three sections. The first describes the environment of juvenile justice and child welfare systems through which status offenders flow and in
which services for them are financed and provided. This
description, which is based on current arrangements in
Cook County, Illinois, provides background for the issues
addressed in the following sections of the paper. It aids
both in framing the general character of the relationship
between the public sector and private providers that is
examined in the second part of the paper, and in identifying dimensions of public sector financing and management. These dimensions and their influence on availability, appropriateness, quality, and cost of privately
produced services are examined in the third section of
the paper.

The paper is largely based on interviews with direct-
service workers and administrators from both the public
and private sectors in Illinois, primarily in Cook County.
It is obvious that firm conclusions about the influence
of aspects of public management on provider performance
cannot be based on observations gathered in interviews
with participants in the system, and the paper consequently does not attempt to reach conclusions. Rather it
uncovers significant dimensions of public financial and
management arrangements and speculates about how choices
along those dimensions may affect provider performance.
Although the paper does not provide empirical results, it
does frame issues and advance hypotheses. To broaden the
base of the investigation, interviews also were conducted
in a second state, Massachusetts. Although these interviews produced insights consistent with those developed
in Illinois, this appeared to be due to an unusual similarity in the history and character of public/private
relationships in the two states. For this reason, efforts
are made below to speculate on possibilities outside the
range encountered in Illinois and Massachusetts.

In light of the growing importance of privately produced public human services, one would expect that an
expanding literature on service delivery issues could
provide substantial support for the fruits of independent
investigation. Unfortunately, although numerous articles
and books were reviewed, relatively few provided significant help. Two problems limit the utility of the literature that focuses on the trend toward private production

of publicly financed services (i.e., the trend toward "privatization"). First, that literature is dominated by works that document this trend and then turn either to expressions of regret at the autonomy that private agencies tend to lose when public funding increases in importance, or to demands for private agency accountability when the public sector is paying for the services they provide. Relatively few articles go beyond description, explanations of increasing privatization, and simple exhortation to provide either positive analyses of public and private sector interaction and performance or normative analyses of how the public sector should carry out its responsibilities in managing a private provider system. Second, the literature on human services privatization contains few works particularly focused on the juvenile justice system and the services provided within it. Finally, it is worth stressing that in the fairly extensive literature on status offenders, relatively little attention is given to the topic of this paper--the particular issues raised by the private locus of services provided to status offenders. An anthology of papers concerning status offenders, which was compiled by the National Council on Crime and Delinquency (1978), illustrates this point. The volume contains 22 papers covering a variety of topics, including the appropriateness of juvenile court jurisdiction over status offenders, the service needs of families and youth, the character of status offenders and the treatment they receive in juvenile courts, the costs and service impacts of deinstitutionalization, and the merit of voluntary service. In spite of this breadth and the attention given to services and related issues in several papers, the topic of the present paper is nowhere singled out for consideration.

Despite the sparsity of directly relevant works and the resulting need to depend primarily on information and insights developed in interviews, several works were helpful, particularly in framing general service delivery issues relevant to status offenders (see, for example, Edwards et al. 1977, Fisk et al. 1978, Massachusetts Taxpayers Foundation 1980, Nelson 1978, Young and Finch 1977).

STATUS OFFENDER SERVICE ARRANGEMENTS:
CLIENTS, PROVIDERS, AND FUNDING SOURCES

Clients

This paper is concerned with youth who are adjudicated as
minors in need of supervision (MINS) and other youth who
exhibit comparable behaviors, whether or not they touch
some element of the described system or use services under
current arrangments. Although data on this large population are not available, a recent publication of the Illinois Department of Children and Family Services (1980a)
notes that only 2.5 percent of the youth processed by the
police for status offenses were petitioned to the court
as MINS. The department uses this figure and statewide
figures on police contacts to estimate that "as many as
145,000 youth may be at risk of entering the juvenile
justice system for status offenses." According to a report by the Illinois Commission for Delinquency Prevention
(1980), 3,625 MINS petitions were filed statewide in juvenile courts and 1,203 youth were adjudicated MINS in
1979. Of those youth served with MINS petitions who were
referred to the state's alternative-to-detention program
(Illinois Status Offender Service), the majority (63.5
percent) were classified as runaways and most of the remainder (29.5 percent) were classified as ungovernable.
   Numerous services are provided to status offenders.
Residential services include both short-term or emergency
shelter care (including runaway houses) and foster family
care, and longer-term arrangements (e.g., foster family
care, group homes, institutional care, and supervised independent living). Nonresidential services include advocacy service (as an alternative to detention), counseling,
drop-in youth centers, and alternative schools. It would
be useful here to indicate for each the volume of services
provided to status offenders, measured either in service
units or in dollars. However, it is impossible to do this
because data generally do not separate out status offenders from other youth. This is partly because, with one
exception--the Illinois Status Offender Service (ISOS)--
the public programs that finance and the private agency
programs that produce status offender services also serve
other youth.

Providers

Although data on revenues and programs are available by individual human service agencies, nowhere are these compiled in a form that permits analysis within the modest scope of this paper. Nonetheless, it is possible to make a number of qualitative observations about the providers of status offender services. These observations are drawn from interviews and from the literature on nonprofit provider agencies.

All of the private agencies that produce status offender services in Illinois have a nonprofit financial structure. Such agencies contrast with for-profit organizations, whose responses to market and public policy shifts are normally interpreted as the behavioral changes dictated by profit maximization in the altered market or policy environment. No single uniform objective is commonly associated with the nonprofit structure. Our interviews, though not specifically focused on this topic, revealed considerable diversity of objectives among providers, whether objectives are thought of in broad terms, such as growth or innovation, or in more narrow service objectives (i.e., servicing the whole youth community, providing the highest quality treatment services, or maintaining stable foster family settings for particularly troublesome youth). The diversity of objectives fostered by the nonprofit structure makes it likely that a uniform policy will elicit varied responses from different providers and suggests that pursuit of some public aims will be most effective if sought through policies that recognize differences among providers and that take advantage of the potential inherent in this diversity of objectives.[1]

Our interviews revealed other, sometimes related differences among agencies in terms of the following factors: the strength of their ties to other neighborhood or community institutions (e.g., schools and police), agency age, political ties, and degree of formal professionalization. We also discovered considerable variation among agencies in the sources of their financing. Some derive virtually all funding from the sale of services to public human-service programs; others that provide at least some very similar services derive as much as 40 percent of

---

[1]Young and Finch (1977) develop this point in their analysis of foster family arrangements in New York City.

their revenue from endowment, direct contributions, and
indirect contributions through such agencies as the United
Way. It seems probable that the availability of nonpublic
sources of revenue partially insulate agencies from economic pressures and will affect their responsiveness to
economic incentives embodied in public policies.

Finally, the difficulties that nonprofit agencies have
in raising capital to finance physical settings and operating needs were noted in several interviews. These difficulties seem to stem from the unavailability of equity
funding, the unreliability and/or unavailability of donated funds, the difficulty of retaining earnings under
human service reimbursement arrangements, and the very
limited availability of debt financing to nonprofit organizations. In the absence of policies specifically
targeted toward capital funding, these problems can also
inhibit the responsiveness of providers.

Decision Points and Sources of Funding

Youth may follow a variety of routes in getting to one or
another publicly financed service. Ways in which youth
are referred (or refer themselves) to alternative services
and service providers are of interest for several reasons.
It is at those points that (a) key decisions about services for youth are made and (b) one should find individuals who are particularly familiar, at the street level,
with private providers and the issues raised by a private
provider system. Important referral sources are listed
below. Juvenile court judges are not listed here; although they make important decisions that affect status
offenders, they appear less important in Cook County than
the listed decision points in determining which service a
youth will receive and which agency will provide the service (see Table H-1).

The information on funding in the second column is
provided because of its potential for affecting the
availability of services for referred youth. If a referral source does not pay for the services to which it directs or refers clients, then providers must weigh the
cost of accepting the referral, either in terms of other
service that it then will not provide or in financial
terms. If funding is associated with referrals, however,
then the net cost to the provider of serving the referral
is reduced. This will not eliminate problems of service
availability for referrals, but it might reduce them.

TABLE H-1   Funding of Referrals by Referral Source

Referral Source	Service Funding Accompanying Referral
Youth and family	No
Police	No
Illinois Status Offender Service (ISOS)	Yes
Court intake	No
Probation office	No
Department of Children and Family Services (DCFS)	Yes

The funding of referrals also has potential long-term significance beyond its possible influence on availability. If choices about which agency will provide which service to individual youth are made by workers at the decision points, and if funding in fact follows those choices, then the provider system will be forced to respond. Agencies that provide service judged unsatisfactory in type and/or character will not be selected and therefore will find it necessary either to scale down or alter the services they provide; those that provide more satisfactory service will have the option to expand. For this marketlike mechanism to influence the constellation of services and providers over the long run, financing must follow the service and provider choices made on behalf of individual youth at the decision points. For this to be a salutary influence, those choices must reflect understanding of the youth and their needs as well as information about the quality and characteristics of providers. Although this reasoning may be valid when applied to Cook County, which has several private providers of each of the services used by status offender youth, it could not be applied in a small rural county capable of supporting only a single agency. In that case, some other mechanism would be required to ensure responsiveness.

Of the decision points identified here, ISOS and DCFS are the only ones that are also programs that finance services. The police, court intake, and the probation office in Cook County all refer youth to, and in that sense use, services produced by private agencies, but they

do not pay for them. The services they use are financed
by a variety of sources, including the Illinois Commission
on Delinquency Prevention (ICDP), the Illinois Law Enforcement Commission, local government general funds,
CETA, and private contributions made directly and through
the United Way and other conduits.[2] These sources tend
to fund whole programs or parts of programs on a block
grant as opposed to unit-of-service basis. Their funding
choices shape the private provider system but in a different fashion than the unit-of-service funds, which follow service decisions made on behalf of individual youth.
The merits and problems of these two modes of financing
are considered later.

The ISOS Program The Illinois Status Offender Program
(ISOS) is a program of the Illinois Commission on Delinquency Prevention. It is the state's alternative-to-
detention program and has responsibility for detainable
status offenders between police contact and court intake
and between court intake and adjudication. Although the
program uses shelter care and foster family services, its
core service--advocacy--is provided primarily by private
agencies. Virtually all youth served by the program receive this service. Approximately 50 percent receive
short-term foster care and 6 percent stay in shelter care.
Advocacy contracts generally are with multiservice agencies that employ one to three advocates for the ISOS program. Advocates are assigned to individual detainable
youth in Cook County on a geographic basis. They then are
responsible for keeping track of the youth, selecting a
foster or shelter care placement, representing the youths'
interest, keeping in touch with the probation office, ensuring that the youth shows up in court, and reporting on
the youth to the court. In the course of their work,
private agency advocates interact regularly with the police, judges, and workers employed directly by ISOS,
including the court liaison and the workers who assign
advocates. The Cook County ISOS program is responsible
for developing and monitoring its own contracts with private agencies and for referring individual preadjudicatory
youth to its various contractors.

---

[2]ICDP has two major programs--ISOS and a Title XX
donated-funds initiative that finances comprehensive
youth service programs. It is the latter component of
ICDP that is referred to in this sentence. ISOS is considered below.

<u>Illinois Department of Children and Family Services</u> The
Department of Children and Family Services (DCFS) was
created in 1964 as the state's child welfare agency responsible for adoptions and foster family and other child
placement services. Although it always has had responsibility for some adolescents, the age distribution of its
case load and the problems with which it copes were
changed significantly when, in 1972, responsibility for
MINS was transferred from the Department of Corrections
to DCFS. The department now <u>must</u> accept court referrals
of MINS who have violated a court order and <u>may</u> accept
first-time MINS offenders. Although the court may suggest
an out-of-home placement or some other particular service,
the department makes the final selection. In addition to
handling referrals the department also may serve troubled
youth who come directly to it.

Approximately 47 percent of the DCFS case load are
children over 13. However, 17 percent of these are neglected, dependent, and abused children whose cases were
opened at a younger age. Among children between 13 and
17, those in the data category closest to status offender
(i.e., "behavior problem") represent 15 percent. This
figure may understate the prevalence of status offenders
in the case load if some first-offense status offenders
have had petitions changed to "dependent" or "neglected"
so that DCFS can be forced to accept the referral. Of
the adjudicated MINS that it serves, DCFS has placed 51
percent in substitute care; of these, 65 percent are in
group homes or institutions (Illinois Department of Children and Family Services 1980b).

Although DCFS produces some services itself, most are
produced by private agencies under contract. Workers, at
least in Cook County, are not specialized with a particular category of child. If assigned to a MINS, they select
a service and a provider under contract to the agency and
refer the youth to the provider for services. Respondents
indicated that the court favored out-of-home placements
more frequently than DCFS, but that DCFS workers make
fewer foster family, group home, and institutional placements than they would like, because of the scarcity of
placement slots.

Individual caseworkers work in area offices. The administrators of area offices are not assigned a total
budget to be allocated among various services in accordance with their perception of area needs; rather, they
work with budget allocations for individual services that
are made at the state level. Contracts also are generally

not the responsibility of the area office; they are now
centralized in a regional office that develops new resources, develops and negotiates contracts, and is responsible for monitoring and evaluation.

Youth and Families Youth who enter the juvenile justice
system are generally referred, with varying degrees of
compulsion, to private service producers at one or another
decision point identified above. However, troubled and/or
troublesome youth and their families also may voluntarily
seek publicly financed service from a provider, often from
the same providers that serve youth on referral from
either DCFS or the probation office. Comparing the
apparent volume of voluntary self-referred use of status
offender services and the volume use that is formally referred and/or compelled by an element of the juvenile
justice system depends primarily on two matters. The
first concerns how services are measured and defined.
Services both to adjudicated MINS and to youth awaiting
adjudication who have been served with MINS petitions are
certain to be counted as status offender services. The
description of other services as status offender services,
however, is less clear-cut; that is, a drop-in center designed to attract predelinquent youth, a runaway house
available for any youth who finds it, and a counseling
service for adolescents all might be included or excluded
in the definition. The more broadly status offender services are defined, the more significant voluntary self-
referral service choices will appear.
    Second, the volume of self-referrals relative to formal
referrals will depend on service and service impact. Most
obviously, the relative importance of self-referral depends on how the jurisdiction of MINS is handled. If, as
some propose, jurisdiction is removed from the court,
fewer services would be used under court compulsion.
Depending on the alternatives put in place of court jurisdiction, the importance of self-referral and client
choice could increase or decrease. Given the current
structure of juvenile justice arrangements for MINS, however, the relative importance of self-referral services
is determined by the amounts budgeted for various services. If the budgets of those programs that fund youth
service bureaus and other community-based youth services
(largely on a grant basis) were expanded, self-referral
services would be more widely available and probably more
frequently used. If the claims of proponents about the
preventive value of these services are accurate, such ex-

panded funding would increase the relative importance of
self-referral service use not only directly but also indirectly, because the number of cases flowing through the
formal juvenile justice system would then be decreased.
Increased funding of these programs also would expand options and service referrals for the police and probation
offices because, as noted, these decision points depend
on services that they do not finance.

In addition to DCFS and ISOS, the sources that finance
private agency services for status offenders and other
youth exhibiting similar behaviors include (1) the community services component of the Illinois Commission for
Delinquency Prevention (i.e., not ISOS), (2) the Illinois
Law Enforcement Commission, (3) the Cook County Department
of Human Services, and (4) CETA (and some of the organizations and agency associations through which these programs' funds sometimes flow). These four sources finance
on a grant basis programs that take referrals from the
probation office and police as well as voluntary self-
referrals. Although precise figures restricted to MINS
services are not available, it would seem that the total
dollar amounts flowing to status offender services from
these four sources are less than the amounts spent on such
services by DCFS and ISOS (with the former dominating).

Individual private agencies may supply only a single
service but most provide several. They may receive funding from one or several of the sources just mentioned and
often will simultaneously operate programs financed on a
grant basis and programs financed on a unit-of-service
basis. The privately produced status offender services
that tend to be funded on a grant basis by the four above-
mentioned sources, and that tend to be used both by youth
on referral from the police and courts and by youth who
drop in, include counseling, alternative schools, work
training, and drop-in activities. The agencies that provide these services overlap somewhat with those that provide services to DCFS, but respondents indicated that as
a group the former were younger, less professionally oriented, less funded by contributions, more dependent on
public grants and purchases, and more likely to stress the
fact that they were commmunity based (i.e., they had
strong linkages with local schools and police, neighborhood and client participation on board and staff, and,
possibly, local financial participation). In contrast,
agencies that received relatively more of their public
funding from DCFS were more likely to be characterized as
traditional or "establishment," as emphasizing highly

trained professionals who provide clinical treatment (possibly of extended duration), and as having substantial funding from contributions.

PUBLIC/PRIVATE RELATIONS: GENERAL ISSUES

In recent years a number of authors have examined the phenomenon of private production of publicly financed services in general and in the human services. Frequently they list advantages and disadvantages of private production. The advantages of private over public production commonly include the following: The greater ability of private organizations to hire highly qualified staff; the greater ease they have in disciplining unproductive and uncooperative employees; their greater propensity to innovate because of their nature and because they are less burdened by entrenched workers with vested interests in the status quo; the weaker hold in private agencies of routines that serve bureaucratic interests rather than client needs; the greater ease of introducing multiple producers and capturing the cost, quality, and (possibly) client-choice benefits that competition may foster; and the promotion of objectivity that may follow when contracting separates the planning and evaluation functions from day-to-day operations. Disadvantages tend to be given less attention but when listed may include the difficulty of controlling quality, the possibility that public workers who use and monitor private agencies will be "captured" by providers and will act in their own interests rather than those of the public, the opportunity for private corruption of public workers, and the increased possibility of suspension of operations when services are produced by units that are not directly under public control.

Other considerations that are less significant when weighing the long-run merits of private and public production may be more important to explaining why private agencies are increasingly used to produce publicly financed human services. First, it often is easier to get legislatures to increase funding for purchased services than it is to get them to expand public employment to produce service. Second, services to be purchased from private agencies may garner political support in the community that public services cannot obtain. Finally, the public sector can sometimes tap private resources by paying less than full costs for the services that it purchases.

Private (and public) production could be studied in an effort to empirically identify merits and problems and to determine whether or not private production was desirable. Aside from the extreme measurement and analytic difficulties that would plague such an endeavor, it is not clear that the effort would be useful. The merits and problems of private production probably depend on too rich and idiosyncratic a set of historical and institutional factors to yield to any valid summary judgment. And even if a summary asessment were not sought, the utility of such an investigation may still be questioned. Future private production of publicly financed human services seems assured whatever the outcome of such a study. It therefore may be wise to shift from efforts to assess the overall merit of private production to analyses of those public practices that can influence the quality and cost of private status offender services and the responsiveness of private agencies (these issues are addressed later in this paper).

The concern for improving public sector practices is reasonable only to the degree that those practices are malleable--and they sometimes are not. Consider a system in which several private agencies provide a single service. That system is likely to generate more satisfactory service if public sector workers are free to cut referrals to unsatisfactory agencies and to expand the number of youth sent to good agencies. However, instances were encountered in Cook County and in Massachusetts where a private agency successfully used political channels to maintain its flow of clients after public workers and/or administrators had tried to reduce or end public referrals because the agency's program was considered to be unsatisfactory. The public sector workers followed appropriate practices; they were thwarted not because of ignorance or incompetent management on their part but because of political pressures. Even in the context of these examples, however, it is possible that these public practices could be improved. Accurate and conveniently compiled information on the performance of private agencies also is a tool of public sector management. Respondents generally argued that, when available, information is a powerful tool that can win battles even when the other side has political muscle. Thus, with better documentation of the deficiencies of an unsatisfactory provider, state agencies might be able to dominate political efforts to overrule its referral and contracting decisions.

The view that there are significant problems in the
management of most privately provided human service systems was frequently expressed in interviews and was also
mentioned in several articles. Sam Edwards, Bill Benton,
Tracey Feild, and Rhona Millar (1977) closely examined
purchase-of-human-service arrangements under Title XX in
eight states and gathered data from the remaining states
and the District of Columbia. They concluded that although purchased services constitute a major industry
(Edwards et al. 1977:32),

> the organizational concepts which drive the na-
> tional social services program remain geared to
> concepts which recognize only the direct (public)
> service delivery system. . . . The professional
> discipline of staff to run this 'industry' is fo-
> cused on service and service delivery, but not on
> the management of service delivery systems imple-
> mented by providers. . . . The complex issues of
> control and accountability, the use of donated
> funds and unanswered questions on what to purchase
> and why, are recognized by senior state adminis-
> trators; but because of institutional frameworks,
> existing patterns of service delivery and the lack
> of an organizational system designed to deal with
> purchase, they are resolved on an ad hoc basis.

The generally observed difficulties that states have
in structuring and managing private provider arrangements
can be explained in different ways. A historical explanation, implicit in the above-mentioned conclusions of
Edwards et al., would stress that states traditionally
have provided services directly and have not yet adapted
to the different demands of a system in which they finance
and manage, and private agencies produce. This perspective received some support in Illinois, particularly with
respect to MINS. In 1972, when responsibility for them
was transferred from the Department of Corrections to
DCFS, it evidently was assumed that private agencies would
supply services. According to one respondent, in contracting with private agencies for services to younger
children DCFS traditionally responded to privately initiated proposals to serve privately identified needs. However, different procedures were required when DCFS first
sought to serve MINS. Private agencies were accustomed
neither to serving these youth nor to initiating programs
to serve them; therefore, DCFS had to take more initia-

tive. Generally, respondents indicated that it did so with minimal information about the number of youth involved and their characteristics and minimal planning about how to stimulate and manage a flow of services from an array of providers.

The historical explanation seems to identify adaptation in which the state would gradually improve the capacity to manage a system of private providers, but our research did not suggest continuous improvement in management practices. Furthermore, bits and pieces of information gleaned from various interviews suggest an alternative, less sanguine explanation. In this view several considerations combine to put the public agencies in a dependent position relative to the network of private providers. Perhaps the most important consideration here is funding. Public agencies regularly seek to increase their budget allocations from the legislature. Because they lack political strength, they tend to seek allies. Providers are natural allies because they too stand to benefit from larger human service expenditures. In addition, providers may be better placed politically than public agencies. Many traditional establishment agencies have stronger "helping" images than the public programs and have politically well connected boards. Less traditional agencies may have strong community connections that can produce considerable grass roots political support. That the public programs depend on private agencies to generate political support for their budget requests is apparent. So natural is this that one agency director expressed surprise that the state would not reimburse the agency for staff time spent lobbying for the public program on which it depended.

It can also be argued that the state depends on private agencies to partially finance the services for which it is responsible. In Illinois, state agencies are required to reimburse 100 percent of costs. However, this policy is implemented in a fashion that squeezes private agencies very tightly. The state programs often want and get more service than they can or do pay for. But in doing so, they are accumulating a kind of debt to the private sector.

Finally, state programs depend on private agencies for service. State agencies may be unable or unwilling to close an unsatisfactory privately run program—not out of fear of political repercussions but because they need its services. The state programs usually do not produce service directly, and they depend on a private system that operates close to capacity. Indeed, for the same reason, they may find it difficult to negotiate service improvements with a recalcitrant provider if that provider threatens closing rather than changing its practices. These considerations obviously can weaken the public sector's hand in the short run, particularly in dealing with providers of residential care, but it might seem a minor consideration in the longer run when the state should be able to stimulate compensating supply increases. Even this point loses strength to the degree that the preceding point is accurate, for stimulating a compensating service increase is complicated considerably if the state reimburses on a very marginal basis.

In a less sanguine view these elements of public dependence on private providers explain lax public management. A public sector that is indebted to and dependent on its providers is obviously in a weakened position. It is unlikely to manage providers tightly for fear of losing their political support, services, and/or indirect financial aid. If tempted to tighten public control in spite of these realities, efforts may be opposed or directly prevented by private sector political intervention.

This cynical view of public/private relationships stands in direct opposition to a naive view that posits an array of controls that the public sector can freely manipulate to get providers to do its bidding. In the cynical view, failure to use these controls is not really a management problem; rather, it is one symptom of a power relationship in which the public sector cannot control the private sector because it is, in a sense, controlled by the same sector it seeks to manage.

Those who are sympathetic to the cynical view can find evidence to support it. This view was more or less advanced by a former administrator in the Massachusetts human services system as well as by several people in Illinois, including two who have worked in state human service agencies. For evidence, they pointed to an evaluation unit designed and operated to provide information on provider performance that was shut down after a short life--according to one respondent, because providers did not like it. A simple guide for the Chicago area, which described agencies and their services and included somewhat veiled comments about their quality, was produced and found useful by direct service workers. It, too, was dropped and has not been reissued or updated. In both cases, of course, these events can be explained by considerations other than private sector opposition. To disconfirm the cynical view or to accumulate enough evidence to prove its accuracy would require investigations well beyond the scope of this paper. Although the concerns raised by the cynical view are real, they are probably overdrawn in that they rule out the possibility of independent control for the state agencies that finance and use private status offender services.

Diversity of objectives, ideology, and practices among private agencies would seem to strengthen the potential for public influence. Similarly, the balance of public and private power might be tipped more toward the public by changing the jurisdictional level at which services are financed and contracted for. The current relatively strong private agency position is attained under arrangements that lodge those functions at the state level. Shifting responsibilities to lower levels of government might strengthen the public sector institutions; agencies that are powerful at the state level may be weaker at the local level. Of course, if decentralizing public control or taking advantage of agency diversity would strengthen public control over established agencies, the cynical view would argue that these changes will not (cannot) occur.

Finally, it should be noted that these comments are based on conversations held only in Illinois and Massachusetts--two states that, according to respondents, have unusually politicized and powerful private agency sectors. In other states, public management of private service providers may be less inhibited by political intervention. If it is, the cynical view would be less applicable and the possibilities for public control would be greater. For this reason, insights developed in the following consideration of management issues might be more easily applied in the rest of the country than they are in the two states that form the basis for discussion.

ASPECTS OF PUBLIC MANAGEMENT AND PRIVATE PERFORMANCE

Introduction

This section considers options available to the public sector in its management of a system in which private agencies produce services to status offenders. Consideration of these options is useful even though political constraints and the general character of public/private relations may prevent the use or limit the effectiveness of some (or all) in some areas.

Management here refers to those alterable aspects of public programs that affect the provision of service by private agencies. Management, therefore, not only includes the day-to-day internal matters to which the term conventionally refers but also to major structural dimensions of public programs--the financial, referral, and regulatory linkages that tie public programs to the private agency sector.

Analysis of private sector performance and its relation to aspects of public management would be greatly facilitated if we had access to objective measures of private performance under today's arrangements. Unfortunately, but not surprisingly, such information does not exist in any coherent form. Instead, we had to develop insights on the basis of the respondents' subjective impressions concerning the problems and virtues they saw. Interestingly, their comments focused more on the failings of public management (which might induce or permit poor private performance) than they did on performance problems themselves.[3]

The section is organized around three types of problems--quantity, quality, and cost of services. These problems are discussed separately and are preceded by a brief presentation of some structural matters relating to funding that should be clarified at the outset. Although we have already distinguished between grant funding and unit-of-service funding of private agency programs, it is useful here to define pure types of each, and to speculate on the circumstances under which they would be appropriate.

Under pure grant funding, a provider agency is granted a fixed amount of money to support either partially or fully a program whose services and target group are specified in the grant agreement. The grantee maintains responsibility for day-to-day program management and for central program decisions (e.g., who will be served if requests for service exceed capacity, the mix of services that will be provided to individual users, and the overall

---

[3]In an interesting and useful monograph, the Massachusetts Taxpayers Foundation (1980) identifies many problems in Massachusetts' management of its private providers of human services. But although numerous public management failings are cited, virtually nothing is stated about provider performance in terms of availability, service quality, or service costs.

mix of services provided by the program). The initial grant agreement, of course, can restrict the provider's freedom in determining these, but within the grant's specifications the provider has control.

Under unit-of-service funding, a per-unit price is established for each service that the agency provides. Total payments are determined by the volume and mix of services that the agency provides in response to demand decisions made on behalf of (or by) clients. Under what is here termed pure unit-of-service funding, demand decisions are made by public workers employed by the program that pays for service. The public workers (called case managers here) determine who is eligible for service and, either independently or with client consultation, decide which provider will be used (if more than one is available) and what mix of services the individual client will get.

A priori, neither form would seem superior. Rather, their relative merits depend on the characteristics of the service at issue and the situation of its provision. For example, where the state has legal responsibility for a youth, the grant form is inappropriate because it would cede to providers responsibilities that belong to the state. Conversely, if the service is one that must be available in the community for youth to use at their own discretion, pure unit-of-service funding makes little or no sense. The total cost of service that is likely to be used by each individual also is relevant. If this cost is low, and other considerations are constant, it would seem inappropriate to use the pure unit-of-service form which, by adding case management cost to (low) service costs, would add significantly to total costs. Conversely, if the cost of service per individual is high, the case for public case management is strengthened by the lower cost (relative to service costs) of that function and by the desire to have public control over use of a service that imposes significant public costs.

The benefits of quality competition can be obtained under both forms. Under unit-of-service funding, competition would occur through the expansion or contraction of those providers whose service is thought to be desirable or undesirable, respectively, by case managers. Such possible situations as a small number of providers or disinterest of nonprofit providers in expansion might inhibit the effectiveness of this mechanism. But competition obviously can also enhance quality under grants, although the competition in this instance would not be

competition for unit sales but rather episodic competition
for grants when grant programs are initiated and renewed.
Other noncompetitive or "voice" mechanisms can also communicate public preferences to providers under both
forms.[4] This situation can occur under grant funding
in the push and shove of negotiations over the specifics
of the grant document, and can occur under pure unit-of-
service funding in discussions on specific cases between
public case managers and providers and in discussions at
a higher level that communicate public reactions to private agency performance.

The pure forms presented here are, of course, not necessarily followed in practice. Indeed, actual arrangements can be shaped so that one form almost blends into
the other. Thus, a grant for a single-service program can
be very tightly written, with quantities specified precisely so that, de facto, the arrangement differs little
from an impure unit-of-service contract that specifies a
quantity of service and ensures payment whether or not
services are provided. Such possibilities make it clear
that the details of any real arrangement, rather than a
simple rubric, should be examined before conclusions are
reached.

The definitions of pure forms presented above nonetheless are helpful in discussion. Moreover, they facilitate
a couple of comments on departures from the pure forms.
First, consider a program funded on a unit-of-service
basis that is impure in that there is no public case manager. Such a program clearly is inappropriate if it cedes
to the provider responsibility for an individual whose
care is properly a public responsibility. However, even
in one of the many youth service instances in which public
responsibility is not an issue, this impure form is problematic. Its unit-of-service funding gives the provider
a financial incentive to expand service use while providing no countervailing mechanism to control use of a service that absorbs valued public funds. Second, consider
a youth service program arranged for on a grant basis that
is impure in that youth are directed to it primarily by
public case managers. If the case managers are required
to assess client needs and to select and monitor services

---

[4]"Voice" is the term Hirschman (1970) coined to describe
nonmarket mechanisms that can convey the concerns of users
to the providers of service. They are contrasted with
market or "exit" mechanisms in Hirschman's terms.

and providers, then grant funding is inappropriate. It
is not required to control excess service provision since
services are selected by public case managers who have no
financial incentive to over-refer. And if grant funding
is used in concert with public case managers, it can only
weaken their influence. Since agencies are independently
funded by a grant, they have little incentive to meet the
preferences of the case managers. The provider, of
course, may be responsive in all of these ways (i.e., may
supply service to the case manager's preferences and may
negotiate with the case manager over the characteristics
of service that is provided), but the structure of the
arrangement itself does not foster such responsiveness.

Problems Relating to Quantity

Several concerns of respondents related to the quantities
rather than the quality of service. Two concerns over
quantity are distinguished here: (1) the relative quantities of residential and nonresidential services, and
(2) the inadequate quantity of service available for the
most troublesome adolescents.

<u>Residential vs. Nonresidential Services</u> It is frequently
argued that too many status offenders are in residential
care (i.e., foster family, group home, and institutional
care) at least partly because too little provision is made
for nonresidential services that would divert youth or
support a disrupted family, such as drop-in activity and
counseling centers, alternative schools, job-training
programs, short-term crisis intervention, long-term intensive therapy, and homemaker and other family support
services. The first thing to note about this argument is
that the dispassionate newcomer to the area is given
little information with which to assess its validity.
Thus, although increased provision of nonresidential services may be desirable, it is not clear that providing
such services would necessarily lessen reliance on residential care.

Several respondents indicated that what now limits the
quantity of residential care used for youth is not the
sparsity of substitute or preventive nonresidential services but rather the sparsity of appropriate residential
slots. Respondents repeatedly indicated that workers
would like to place more status offenders in residential
care and would do so if they could find vacancies with

foster families or in group homes. If these observations
are accurate, increased nonresidential services are not
likely to offset declines in residential placements for
which there is an existing excess demand. They will do
so only if expanded provision of noninstitutional services
very significantly reduces the flow of status offenders
coming through the courts to DCFS; and while that might
occur, our research encountered no concrete evidence that
it would. In light of these observations, it seems that
the number of youth in residential care is regulated by
the decision mechanism that determines the number of residential slots for youth rather than by the decisions of
judges or DCFS caseworkers who make dispositional decisions about individual youth.

Since decisions concerning individual youth do not appear to determine the aggregate mix of private services
flowing to youth, it is worth considering what may determine this mix. Residential youth services for nondelinquents in Illinois are funded almost entirely by the state
through DCFS. Nonresidential services are financed by the
state through DCFS, the Illinois Commission on Delinquency
Prevention, the Illinois Law Enforcement Commission, and
by public and private programs at the local level. The
DCFS budget contains line items for institutional care in
group homes and for care in foster homes. The line item
appears to be the major determinant of the volume of residential institutional and group home care because, as
noted above, workers' demands for placements exceed
available supplies. Foster family care is funded more on
an open-ended basis. Unavailability of foster care
therefore probably is not due to the constraint of a fixed
budget; rather, it is due to the limited volume of foster
slots that is elicited by the state's foster care reimbursement rates given state efforts to recruit foster
parents for youth.

Budget and reimbursement decisions made at the state
level probably play a central role in determining the
volume and mix of residential services provided to youth.
The same point could be made with respect to nonresidential services, although more of their funding originates
at a lower level. It also appears that these decisions,
overall or in the incremental form in which they annually
arise, are not based on any substantive analysis of the
needs of youth or on a plan that takes into account the
relationship between the needs for some services and the
quantities of other services provided to status offenders.
This observation is meant to be descriptive rather than

critical. It makes little sense to criticize agency and budget officials for making ad hoc decisions on issues about which little of substance is known by anyone.

Emphasis here has been on state-level decisions, but decisions concerning individual youth are made by workers in local offices. A shift toward nonresidential services and care conceivably could originate at the local level. However, area offices of DCFS in Cook County have little incentive to initiate such a shift under current arrangements even if it were desirable. First, it seems likely that nonresidential care places a greater burden on local caseworkers than does a residential placement. Second, area offices do not have control over the allocation of the funds that they use. Consequently, they cannot capture for the support of local nonresidential services and burdensome case management, funds that might be saved if fewer residential placements were made. Savings might be produced, but they would flow to the state rather than to the office that made the effort.

It also should be noted that although DCFS funds both residential and nonresidential services, many of the services that might reduce the need for residential care are funded through other programs. This dispersal of financial responsibility for possible substitute services also would interfere with reasoned allocations even if local units of DCFS were given more budget responsibility.

Finally, there are political matters. Some respondents argued that the older, traditional agencies exert pressure to have the residential care expenditures on which they depend either maintained or increased. It also was felt that the relative power of these agencies, particularly religious ones with provider agencies spread over much of the state, was greater at the state than at the local level. Other agencies that focus more on nonresidential services claim to have greater strength at the community than at the state level.

Although private agencies provide the bulk of status offender services, the decisions governing the mix of residential and nonresidential services seem to be public ones made largely at the state level, both directly through budget allocations and indirectly through decisions on reimbursement rate and other matters. If the private sector influences the mix, it does so through political linkages, with the political strength of different provider groups determining the direction of the private sector's influence.

Certain conclusions can be drawn from the analysis. First, little is known either about the relationships between the availability of and need for various status offender services, or about planning. This "ignorance" complicates the process of making rational allocations of services that substitute for one another and suggests the possible merit of shifting the allocation function from the state to local communities where allocations could be shaped more by the institutions (courts, schools, police, and families) that are affected by and are more familiar with the impact of services on youth behavior. Shifting more financial responsibility to local DCFS offices would move in this direction and would correct some of the incentive problems identified above. However, some respondents argued that formal and informal DCFS ties generally are strong with providers and relatively weak with other community institutions. Even if that is not so, more than decentralization of DCFS budget responsibilities is warranted, because more services than those now funded by DCFS are at issue. It could be argued that control over the mix of all status offender and other youth services should be lodged in a single local organization that has responsibility for all youth and that is sensitive to the consequences to the community of providing an array of services to status offenders as well as to other, more troublesome youth who would, of course, be the responsibility of the local organization.

Services for Particularly Troublesome Adolescents   States experience problems locating private agency residential slots for difficult status offenders. In Illinois, for example, these problems have resulted in out-of-state placements, in the handling of the care of several youth by a special program in the office of the governor (the Governor's Cook County Court Project), and in the creation of a joint public/private program (the Joint Service Program for Adolescents) directed at difficult youth that subcontracts to several facilities and provides auxiliary funding for special services to individual youth.

To a significant degree, the problem of finding slots inheres in the difficulty of dealing with very troublesome youth and is not the unique consequence of private provision. Even if services were publicly produced, there would be problems in locating residential programs in city neighborhoods and finding staff who are experienced and effective in working with difficult youth. In addition, the costs incurred would be high. But the problem of availability is probably exacerbated when private non-profit suppliers, which are not under direct state control, are relied upon for service.

The nonprofit form has merits that make it particularly appropriate for agencies that provide human services. In particular, the form reduces incentives to skimp on quality in order to reduce costs and increase profits. It is also likely to attract administrators and staff who are particularly service-oriented. As noted earlier, however, the nonprofit form fosters independence and diversity of objectives and, relative to for-profit organizations, nonresponsiveness to financial incentives. Those latter characteristics, added to the inherent difficulty of handling very troublesome youth, contribute to the availability problem.

The characteristics of a nonprofit organization prove particularly problematic if its objectives are tied to the provision of services that attract little if any response from troubled youth. This tendency to not respond to a state need for services to difficult youth may be worsened if, as seems the case, many of the traditional providers of residential care (a) are accustomed to children with different problems, (b) have political strength to ward off public pressure, and (c) have sufficient financial resources not to be seriously tempted even by generous reimbursement for a task they don't want to perform. In this context a state's difficulties in locating slots and negotiating tight "no-decline" contracts are easily understood. One person who is involved in arranging contracts noted that providers respond in force to RFPs for counseling; and, in explaining nonresponse to RFPs for shelter care, made the telling comment, "What's in it for a provider?"

Although the state has and will have problems in locating slots for difficult youth, interviews suggested that in seeking such slots a state might not take enough advantage of the existing diversity of objectives among potential providers. For example, one respondent indicated that DCFS repeatedly went back to its traditional providers of residential care and did not seek residential services for difficult youth from new, less traditional agencies. The provision of services to tough kids may be closer to the mission of such an agency. Furthermore, new agencies tend to depend primarily on public funds and therefore might be more influenced by the financial benefits of supplying services to difficult clientele than would an older agency with a more secure financial base.

However, developing new suppliers might require that DCFS
do more than issue RFPs; that is, it might have to provide
initial support and technical assistance to an agency that
in the long run might be useful and self-sustaining. But
that is not, most people argued, something that the department has done. In fact, several respondents stressed
aspects of DCFS operations, such as administrative procedures, that tend significantly to dampen provider participation. Although intrusive regulation and red tape
are endemic and explainable with public agencies, an effort to control them might be particularly productive in
generating a supply of services that are difficult to
obtain.

Problems Relating to Quality

This section is concerned with the quality of various
services supplied to status offenders by private providers. Quality refers to dimensions of services other than
quantity; that is, the matters referred to when service
is assessed as "good" or "bad." Issues and problems in
the assessment of quality are discussed later.
    It is interesting that none of the respondents charac-
terized the general quality of youth services as bad, and
relatively few even singled out particular agencies as
providers of inferior service. However, all with whom the
issue was discussed seemed able to rank providers from
worse to better according to some subjective quality criterion. In addition, many cited public sector management
practices and political realities that they thought inhibited the evolution of the private provider system into
one that provided improved service matched to the needs
of youth.
    Issues of quality under the unit-of-service funded
programs and in the grant-funded programs are treated
separately and in that order, partly because they present
different though overlapping issues and partly because the
grant-funded programs were less thoroughly investigated.
Quality under both arrangements probably depends first on
the motivation and caliber of the private provider agencies. Although service quality is often only one of several agency objectives, and although various agencies have
quite different notions about what constitutes good service, one gets the impression that agencies generally are
committed to providing good and appropriate service to
their clients. In any case the commitment and concern of

providers are taken as givens in this discussion, which focuses largely on public sector management issues as they relate to service quality.

The public sector can affect the quality of privately produced services in several ways, perhaps most importantly through the unit outlays it incurs for service. Indeed, in the absence of adequate resources no management legerdemain can secure the provision of high-quality services. The structural matters discussed below can complement but not substitute for a sufficiency of resources. However, given the level of resources it provides per unit of service, other public sector actions can affect the quality of service: through decisions about which service and which provider will serve individual youth; through public/private discussions on the care of particular individuals; through the negotiating of contracts and the enforcing of contractual obligations and licensure standards; and through the termination of old contracts (at or before term) and the opening of new ones. Comments on quality issues as they arise in the DCFS and ISOS programs are woven through a discussion that is organized around the various means through which the public sector can affect quality, given unit outlays and the quality and commitment of active and latent provider agencies.

Public and Public/Private Decisions Concerning Individual Youth   Public decisions about which service and which agency will serve individual youth can influence quality in two ways: (1) at the individual level, by linking youth to the services and agencies best fitted to their individual needs, and (2) at the system level, by disproportionately channeling youth away from lower quality and toward higher quality agencies. Over time such referral patterns have the potential to increase the ratio of high to low quality service (and providers) and to cause some less satisfactory providers to evolve toward more satisfactory performance.

For these mechanisms to operate effectively, several conditions must hold. First, there must be more than one provider to choose from, preferably several more, and there must be the potential for new providers to emerge. For many services for status offenders, this condition holds in Cook County (although sometimes service is at some distance from the youth's home), but it obviously does not hold in many smaller communities throughout the state. In addition to the ideal of having access to more than one supplier, the system also must have some vacan-

cies. If a system is dominated by one buyer, and if reimbursement policy or other policies foster a situation
in which most providers operate close to capacity, the
caseworker seeking a service slot will not have the luxury
of selecting a good agency from among two or more but will
be content just to locate an agency that will provide the
required service. Competition on the basis of quality
would be muted or nonexistent. Respondents in Massachusetts repeatedly stated that this impediment to quality
competition existed with respect to residential care in
small facilities; in Cook County, though not mentioned in
these terms, it would seem to exist with respect to group
home care and agency-provided foster family care. This
is not surprising. Residential care involves significant
capital and personnel costs that are fixed over the program period. Unless programs are operated at or close to
capacity, these fixed costs will elevate unit costs. In
addition, the tendency of workers to fill any residential
slots that exist would tend to keep vacancy rates low,
particularly if budget or other higher officials see limiting the number of slots as the only means of controlling
utilization.

     For these reasons, there seems to be little competition
for worker referrals on the basis of quality with respect
to group homes and other small-facility forms of residential care. Furthermore, an increase in such competition
has limited potential unless policymakers are willing to
absorb the costs of unused capacity to foster competition.
Although this is a reasonable arrangement in theory, it
is an unlikely eventuality in today's fiscal environment.
Respondents suggested, however, that more choice existed
in selecting among providers of larger facility residential care and nonresidential services for youth. Slack
in the former system is an unplanned by-product of recent
efforts to restrict the use of large institutions. In
Massachusetts one respondent acknowledged this as a factor
that gave the state enhanced market leverage.

     Capacity constraints that limit the effectiveness of
competition in enhancing the quality of residential services may be less problematic with nonresidential services. In part this is simply because physical plant and
other fixed inputs pose less of a barrier to service
expansion with nonresidential than with residential services. Additionally, in Illinois the ability of nonresidential service providers to respond to increased demand
from any particular public agency is enhanced by the fact
that providers generally serve demands from several public

and private sources. Consequently, increased demands from one source can be met not only by increasing total service quantity but also by reducing the degree to which other demands are met.

Marketlike competition to foster high-quality service is made more effective by the existence of slack. Effective quality competition also requires providers that seek to respond to high demands with expansion and/or to low demands with contraction or changes in the quality or character of their service. The issue of responsiveness is discussed elsewhere, but a few comments are appropriate here. Strongly conflicting observations and examples were offered that suggest the existence of real variations in responsiveness among providers. This may reflect the existence both of providers whose notions of desirable service diverge from those of the public sector, and of nonprofit providers that prefer not to grow larger. Thus, even an agency that faces strong economic (i.e., financed) demands for service and that can expand easily may not choose to do so. In some instances unresponsiveness seemed to be facilitated by a financial cushion that made it easier for the provider to bear the financial consequences of nonresponse. However, the expansion of good agencies may sometimes be inhibited by factors other than their own reluctance to grow. Agencies that stand to lose clientele if other agencies grow may intervene politically to protect their flow of clients. One example cited here can illustrate the problem but not evaluate its extent. The response of one Cook County supervisor to the question, "Will good providers get more service?" was, "No, it's very political. One agency that did meet our needs . . . picked up on working with late-age teenagers with special needs . . . but the state has gone after (this agency) for auditing and licensing; it's always under the gun. It's under very particular scrutiny for nonprogrammatic things." The supervisor felt that this nontraditional agency provided good service to youth and was valued by workers. But she thought it was subject to harassment from a higher level in order to control its growth and prevent the contraction of better-connected traditional agencies.

The elements of multiple providers, enough slack, providers whose objective functions and financial condition foster responsiveness, and a political context that permits market responses all are necessary if a marketlike mechanism is to propel the provider system toward higher quality performance. Also required are referrers who are informed about the services and capacities of providers. Indeed, because information about suppliers is so important at the time of referral and at other points in the operation of a private provider system, it is discussed in detail below. Here, however, we note that referrers/case managers are not only potential users of information, but that they are also potential providers of it. They interact with agencies on a day-to-day basis and pick up considerable insight about their process and performance.

Potentials and pitfalls of a market mechanism that is driven by referral decisions on individual youth have just been considered. However, referrer/case managers can also influence the entire private provider system through their consultations and negotiations with agencies concerning services for particular individuals. This point was made several times by people talking about the CHINS program in Massachusetts. An Arthur Young and Company report on service issues in that program included among its summary points the conulsions that "provider staff's perceptions of the quality of their working relationships with Department CHINS workers appear to be one of the primary determinants of the overall quality of service available to a CHINS youth," and "frequent contact between provider agency and Department CHINS workers appears to be important to the development and successful implementation of a long-term plan for CHINS" (1980:IV). A high-level administrator in the Massachusetts Department of Public Welfare was generally skeptical about the state's control over private providers and was not unaware of problems with the CHINS program. She argued, however, that with respect to purchase of service the CHINS program was one of the service accounts they managed best. Among the reasons given was that it was a "closed-referral" program—one in which providers can only serve youth who are referred by a public sector worker. This, she noted, permits public involvement and some control on each case; it also facilitates the acquisition of information about providers by the public agency. In Cook County the potential contribution of worker involvement on individual cases also was noted. But its effectiveness, one area supervisor argued, was limited by the absence both of contracts and specific agency program plans. "If I don't have a contract with a place, I can work only at the case level and initiate a case review. That is helpful, but a program plan gives you a second lever for controlling what goes on so that you don't have to argue on a case-by-case level where there can be disputes about professional skill."

The control and quality stimulus that public referrers/ case managers can provide for a private provider system obviously depends on the quality of the public staff and on the time they can and do give to individual cases at initial referral and as the case is carried. Though important, these matters were not examined. The comments of a high-level state administrator with DCFS experience, however, are germane. He indicated that he did not regard DCFS as a case management system, even though workers make referrals and carry cases as they would under a case manager system. In explaining why, he said that most important was the feeling that DCFS is a provider-oriented rather than a community- or child- and youth-oriented program. He suggested that DCFS is not set up to exercise strong responsibility for youth and to supervise privately produced care, but rather that it operates to pass responsibility for youth (and children) on to the private agencies that it supports. In this connection, the phenomenon of "reverse referrals" is significant. Reverse referrals are instances in which an agency initiates contact with a client, obtains DCFS permission for DCFS funding of the case, and essentially carries the case with minimal or no DCFS supervision. Although this phenomenon (a de facto "open referral" program in Massachusetts' terms) was cited, its prevalence in serving status offenders could not be determined. Knowing the prevalence of this practice, however, would provide some measure of the limitations on the case management control that the public agency exerts.

Information   Information about the quality and types of services provided by various agencies is necessary in a multiagency context if referrals are to channel youth to the best agencies, and if youth are to receive the services that best fit their needs. Independent of the number of providers, information about agencies is necessary if the provider system is to be effectively controlled through the negotiating of new and revised contracts, the enforcement of contractual obligations, and the reasoned shifting of contracted service among providers.

Information, particularly about provider performance, is not easily obtained. Inputs can be measured. Although this makes them common targets of regulatory activity, input information is of limited utility in judging the quality of provider performance. The intangible character of many aspects of the quality of services to youth undoubtedly complicates the collection and compilation of other potentially useful information. Nonetheless, some important aspects of provider performance can be observed and recorded, often in the regular course of referring to and using agencies. These aspects include the agencies' rates of acceptance and rejection of referred youth, both overall and within behavioral and socioeconomic categories; the care taken in preparing service plans; performance, as measured by the completion of service plans as opposed to their premature termination; responsiveness in dealing with public sector staff; public workers' subjective but informed assessments of selected aspects of provider performance; and youths' reactions to agency service.

Although the collection and compilation of such information by service and by agency is not as ambitious as what many have in mind when speaking of "evaluation" and "monitoring," the information would be useful in negotiating with agencies and in shifting service among them. Furthermore, the collection, compilation, and analysis of data would provide information about important aspects of quality and in some cases would be relatively easy and inexpensive to carry out. This is not done, however, either for their own use or for use in dealing and negotiating with providers. DCFS supervisors in Cook County were recently invited to provide their insights at a contract review session held prior to contract negotiations. We were told that only five people attended. The information about providers that workers and supervisors inevitably and continuously acquire does not seem to be used systematically in managing the system. In making referrals, workers undoubtedly draw on their own experience with agencies and on information that they informally acquire from other workers and supervisors.

As for other efforts related to information, the termination of the DCFS' evaluation unit was noted above. Although that unit's performance may have been problematic, continued neglect of the evaluation function should be noted. When asked about DCFS monitoring efforts and capacities, people invariably responded in rather negative terms.

These points suggest that DCFS has insufficient information about providers on which to base crucial departmental decisions. Moreover, there is some evidence that in at least one instance, information that it has was not used. For example, a book was once available describing agencies in the Cook County area and the services they provide. Respondents indicated that workers found it useful and thought it fostered informed choice. Though not terribly complex to prepare initially, and easier still to update, the book is no longer generally available.

The ISOS program faces easier problems in collecting and using information. It deals with each youth for a shorter period of time and uses fewer agencies than DCFS does. Respondents indicated that the program obtained information on the performance of its private agency-based advocates from several sources, namely the court liaison, probation officers, police, and ISOS workers who assign youth to advocates. It also seemed that this information was used in working with providers to shape their performance and to develop new contracts.

Other Public Sector Influences on Provider Performance
The preceding discussion of quality has focused primarily on worker and supervisor influences on quality that occur through placement and negotiation relative to individual youth. We now look briefly at influences that work at a higher level.

Suppose that an absence of slack or the presence of other factors prevents competition for the placement of individual youth from enhancing quality. It still might be possible for public sector to get some benefits of competition through selectively awarding contracts when they are opened or renewed. Clearly, that is not possible in the cases in which the state has trouble generating even a single supplier (e.g., residential care for hard-to-place youth). But even where suppliers are more abundant, terminating contracts or shifting contracted volume among suppliers to raise quality is done infrequently if at all, except where gross malfeasance has occurred. People in both states argued to varying degrees that politics played a part in this, but they also acknowledged the influence of public sector sympathy for the providers with whom they worked.

If conscious shifting of contracted volume has a role to play in fostering quality, it is a latent role. Consequently, other functions that can foster high quality assume greater importance--namely the negotiating, writing, and enforcing of contracts. These matters were not specifically pursued in depth in the interviews, but relevant comments nonetheless revealed a variety of problems. Most important were the weak information that DCFS compiles on providers and the kind of staff that DCFS has. A former administrator in the department stated that "if

you are going to go to a model where the state does contracting and only contracting, you need a totally different staff with totally different training." This individual, who worked in the department in the 1970s, noted
that "no one had a contract--that is, no one had anything
that was legally binding in terms of what they had to do."
The inheritance of this past includes similar current
practices for some services and providers, as well as
providers who strongly and successfully resist contractual
control and even the idea of control.

Issues in the Grant-Funded Programs   Grant-funded programs
are used by youth who find them on their own and by youth
who are referred by other agencies such as the police,
court intake, and the probation office. Alternative
schools, youth centers, and other grant-funded programs
are important resources for probation and the police.
However, because they do not fund the programs that they
use and know, these agencies do not directly influence the
general level at which the programs are funded or the allocation of given funds among types of services and provider agencies.

Interviews with those who fund and monitor the grant-
funded programs suggest there is much cooperation and
considerable ideological sympathy and general agreement
on youth and community needs between the predominantly
nontraditional "community-based" private providers of
grant-funded youth services and the public programs that
do finance them (i.e., ICDP, ILEC, and local government
sources). This relationship has its positive side and
will benefit communities and youth if the shared beliefs
are appropriate. However, so close a marriage can inhibit
attainment of some benefits that might otherwise flow when
purchase of service separates the production of service
from its financing and evaluation. Too close a marriage
can prevent testing of the prevailing ideology and can
discourage both the dispassionate assessment of providers
and hard-headed efforts to keep providers responsive to
changing knowledge and changing youth and community needs.

Cost Issues

The costs that public programs incur in using private
agencies to provide services to status offenders depend
on agencies' costs of production and on the arrangements
that state programs make for paying providers. Although

they are significant and important to public program operations and state administrators, cost issues are complex
and can be analyzed adequately only with knowledge of details. They are dealt with here briefly and only to the
degree permitted by information collected in interviews.

Status offender services in Illinois are paid for on a
grant basis or on a unit-of-service basis, with rates determined either on a negotiated agency-cost-related basis
or on a fixed-rate (per unit) basis. Fixed rates, which
are unrelated to the costs of the providing agency, are
only used to pay for foster family care. The majority of
service provided to status offenders is paid for on a
cost-related basis. The latter method is discussed below.

Basically, as implemented in Illinois, accounts showing
the costs of the object program are used to identify program costs in a prior year. Division by the number of
units of service actually provided (or by a minimum utilization figure equal to a fixed percentage of capacity)
yields a unit-cost figure. The state reviews costs, dis-
allows items not reasonably related to program services,
adjusts for inflation since the prior year, and arrives
at the unit price it will pay. If the provider objects
to some element in the state's procedures (for example,
disallowance of a cost item thought to be justified), the
agency can negotiate for an adjustment.

Several years ago Illinois paid less than full costs,
but it now has a policy of 100 percent reimbursement.
Ideally, this arrangement permits the state to pay no more
than the cost of service, permits agencies to cover all
of the cost of providing care, and provides no incentives
for agencies to skimp on inputs because they have nothing
to gain by doing so. However, even in its ideal form the
procedure has one major flaw; agencies have no incentive
to be economical in producing service because any reimbursable cost will be paid for. The state can try to
provide incentives through the review of accounts and the
disallowance of selected items, but this is difficult to
accomplish and is no substitute for the continuous on-site
efforts to economize that would occur if agencies benefited from being efficient.

As practiced, however, there are additional problems
in the operation of arrangements that attempt to allow
reimbursement for the unit costs incurred in providing
service. The effective use of these arrangements requires
both that agencies be able to isolate the costs imposed
by particular programs and that they actually do so. This
situation presents conceptual and practical problems for

the majority of agencies that produce services financed on unit-of-service and on grant bases by multiple public and private sources. Many private agencies, particularly smaller new ones, may lack the technical accounting skill and/or personnel to handle these tasks. Other agencies may find it in their interest not to allocate the costs of various programs in an accurate manner. Such problems were alluded to in our interviews in Illinois, and the technical problems receive documentation in the Arthur Young and Massachusetts Taxpayers Foundation reports cited above. In such cases the state must have the ability to support agencies that need assistance and the capacity to monitor for error and abuse. Neither the interviews nor the written reports suggest that these two states currently are capable of handling these tasks well. In part this stems from the difficulty of adequately staffing these functions in the public sector. But it would also seem to derive from the inherent difficulties of external policing of the cost accounts of a single program operated in a multiprogram, often multisite, human service agency that employs many inputs that contribute to several programs.

Another practical problem in the administration of cost-based reimbursements derives from tightness in funding. This takes such forms as inflation adjustments that do not match experienced cost increases, the disallowing of costs that may be reasonable (e.g., disallowing recreation expenses in the operation of a group home), and practices that may result in less than full-cost reimbursement under a policy that claims to pay full costs. This raises issues other than fairness, and may create supply constraints such as those discussed above.

It may be argued that such fiscal tightness is an inevitable by-product of the general scarcity of public money and therefore cannot be attributed to a particular manner of payment. Conversely, it may be argued that because specific constraints on payments are the only means by which to control cost under a reimbursement method that provides no incentives for efficiency, these practices can be attributed to the cost-related payment form.

Problems that arise when providers are reimbursed for their unit costs are apparent: Providers have no incentive to be efficient and state agencies find it difficult or impossible to ensure that costs are accurately accounted and paid for. It is difficult, however, to devise better alternatives. Reimbursements for an agency's service that are not directly tied to the agency's unit costs would have the advantage of incorporating an incentive for efficiency but would pose two practical problems. First, such rates must be set at a high enough level to induce the supply of the desired volume of service without being so high as to provide an excessive surplus for providers. Second, rates should be different for services that are provided to youth who impose different costs. If rates are not differentiated to parallel the costs that different youth impose, providers will be reluctant to serve high-cost and/or problematic youth, and workers will have even greater difficulty in placing such youth than they do now.

The need to vary rates for different youth would pose difficult technical and administrative problems. At a minimum, these problems would complicate implementation of reimbursements that are divorced from individual agency costs. However, some states already use similar client-related reimbursements to pay for nursing home care. This indicates that they can be implemented, at least for one human service. Given their potential merit, as well as the incentive and administrative problems of current arrangements, client-related reimbursements probably deserve more study and consideration in the youth service area than they have been given.

CONCLUSIONS

The most controversial issues related to status offender services concern the mix of services that should be provided (institutional vs. nonresidential) and discretion in service use: Should youth be compelled (by courts) to accept service or should all service use be voluntary at the discretion of youth and their families? These issues are beyond the scope of this paper, which focuses only on the questions raised by the production of publicly financed services by private agencies. Numerous advantages are frequently associated with private service production. However, some of these (e.g., quality benefits derived from agency competition) can develop fully only with a greater independence of public and private agencies than is suggested by this study. Effective public management of the private provider system also seems constrained by limitations in public sector information concerning providers' performance, by natural and policy factors that inhibit competition, and by reimbursement arrangements that impose major administrative burdens. Strengthened public management and/or structured change (e.g., changing the level of government responsible for the provision of services) might make the provider system more responsive. But these too could be implemented only if they could survive in a political environment in which the private agencies have considerable power.

REFERENCES

Arthur Young and Company (1980) The Children in Need of Services Program: A Summary of Service Issues. Report for the Massachusetts Department of Public Welfare, Office of Social Services. Boston, Mass.: Department of Public Welfare.

Edwards, Sam, Benton, Bill, Feild, Tracey, and Millar, Rhona (1977) The Purchase of Service and Title XX. Washington, D.C.: The Urban Institute.

Fisk, Donald, Keisling, Herbert, and Muller, Thomas (1978) Private Provision of Public Services: An Overview. Washington, D.C.: The Urban Institute.

Hirschman, Albert O. (1970) Exit, Voice and Loyalty. Cambridge, Mass.: Harvard University Press.

Illinois Commission on Delinquency Prevention (1980) Human Services Policy Papers: Part II, ICDP's Services to MINS Youth. Chicago: Commission on Delinquency Prevention.

Illinois Department of Children and Family Services (1980a) Concepts for Consideration Regarding Services for Troubled Youth. Springfield, Ill.: Department of Children and Family Services.

_____ (1980b) Illinois Human Service Plan, Volume I, Services for Youth: Issues and Options. Springfield, Ill.: Department of Children and Family Services.

Massachusetts Taxpayers Foundation, Inc. (1980) Purchase of Service: Can State Government Gain Control? Boston: Massachusetts Taxpayers Foundation, Inc.

National Council on Crime and Delinquency (1978) Status Offenders and the Juvenile Justice System: An Anthology. Hackensack, N.J.: National Council on Crime and Delinquency.

Nelson, Barbara (1978) Purchase of Service from the Private Sector: Technique and Theory. In George

Washnes ed., <u>Productivity Improvement Handbook for
State and Local Government</u>. New York: John Wiley and
Sons, Inc.
Young, Dennis, and Finch, Stephen V. (1977) <u>Foster Care
and Nonprofit Agencies</u>. Lexington, Mass.: Lexington
Books.

Index

Adoption Assistance and Child Welfare
  Act of 1980, 622, 637, 641-642, 653,
  658-659
Aid to Families with Dependent Children–Foster Care program, 641-659
  eligibility for, 644-645
  federal administration of, 643-644
  federal reimbursement formula for,
    651-652
  federal requirements for court process-
    ing, 652
  number served by, 650
  objectives of, 643
  placements under, 645, 656-657
  and services to status offenders, 655-
    656
  and state programs, 645, 647, 655
  and status offenders, 641, 644-645, 647-
    658
  summary of, 658-659
  support levels under, 651-652
  (see also foster care)
Aid to Families with Dependent Children
  program, 182-183, 646-647
  eligibility for, 182, 642, 645-646
  and foster care, 642-643
  funding levels under, 644
  origins of, 642
  and state programs, 187

AFDC (see Aid to Families with Dependent Children program)
alternatives to institutions, 55-58
  and deinstitutionalization, 272, 322-323,
    346-347, 414-415, 517, 813
  characteristics of, 56
  costs of, 404, 406, 413, 420
  definitional and operational problems
    with, 56
  development of, 104, 106, 110-111, 124,
    429-430, 458, 482, 518, 523
  funding of, 96, 104, 274-275, 279, 289,
    380-381, 430, 448, 483-484, 523-524,
    815-818
  funding problems of, 98, 232-233
  lack of, 88, 104, 118-120, 296, 421, 454-
    455, 481, 502-503, 553
  as a policy goal of deinstitutionaliza-
    tion, 60-61
  use of, 191
  (see also community-based programs;
    foster care; group homes; runaway
    centers)
Angelo v. the People, 19
Arizona
  conclusions concerning deinstitutionali-
    zation in, 286-291
  summary of findings in, 101-102

939

child in need of supervision (*see* status offenders)

child placement
  and deinstitutionalization in Illinois, 825-867
  legal and medical models of, 843-866

child protective services, 383-402

Children's Bureau, 562

child welfare services
  data on, 625-628
  eligibility for, 633-636
  and foster care, 625, 636-637
  funding of, 527
  programs for, 628
  summary of, 636-637

CHINS (*see* status offenders)

commingling, 106, 264, 303, 304-305
  legislation prohibiting, 376
  of status offenders and delinquents, 31, 91, 346
  and Title I, 693-694

Commonwealth of Pennsylvania v. *Fisher*, 22

community-based programs
  in California, 789-790, 815-818
  changes in, 140-142
  definition of, 386-387
  development of, 864-866
  formation of, 135-139
  intake and referral policies of, 149, 150
  and JJDPA, 135-136, 139-140
  purposes of, 128
  services in, 151-153
  treatment philosophy of, 153-154
  types of, 129
  (*see also* alternatives to institutions)

court intake
  diversion role of, 278-280, 356, 488-489
  organization of, 278, 355-357
  role of, 122, 471-475

Crime Control Act (*see* Omnibus Crime Control and Safe Streets Act of 1968)

Dandoy v. *Fisher*, 269

data analysis, 732-739
  on alternative placements, 737-738
  on diversion, 736-737
  on preadjudicated detention, 735-736
  problems with, 10, 272-273, 282-283, 297, 319-320, 391-393

on secure placement, 734-735

decarceration, 105-107
  in Illinois, 839-843
  as JJDPA mandate, 105-106
  opposition to, 105
  as a policy goal of deinstitutionalization, 202-203
  and Title I, 693
  (*see also* incarceration, prohibition of)

deinstitutionalization
  community resistance to, 37-39, 339, 351-352
  concepts of, 43-58
  and concern over juvenile crime, 308-309, 419-420
  conditions favorable to, 116-118, 308
  conditions unfavorable to, 118, 402, 404-406
  costs of, 33-35, 259, 314
  court-centered approach to, 115, 121-124
  criticism of, 328-329, 364-366, 777
  current status of, 30-39, 297, 347-348
  definition of, 5
  and diversion, 50-52, 115, 117-118, 120-121, 419-420
  evaluation of, 47-48, 62-65
  federal role in, 176-177, 214-215, 582
  framework for analysis of, 80-86
  humanitarian concerns about, 30-33
  and local actors, 288, 291, 367, 412-413, 457-458, 554-555
  local implementation of, 115, 361-363
  in Louisiana, 317-318
  in Massachusetts, 336-337
  in Pennsylvania, 414
  policy goals of, 58-62, 205
  potential racist and sexist biases of, 31-33
  professionals' criticism of, 35-37, 259, 324, 339, 364-365, 404, 516
  relationship of federal goals and standards for, 230-231
  research issues for the future, 236-238
  as a social movement, 80-81

delinquency prevention programs, 483

delinquents, legal definition of, 257, 301-304, 306, 375, 378, 381, 545-546

dependency, federal definition of, 182

dependent and neglected youth
  jurisdiction over, 388-391

legal definition of, 257, 301-304, 306,
    375, 378, 381
placement decisions regarding, 525-527
detention, 52-55, 107-110
    arguments in favor of, 365
    in Arizona, 280-285
    in California, 108-109, 785-788
    federal criteria for, 52-53
    federal focus on, 232
    and JJDPA amendments of 1977, 109
    and JJDPA amendments of 1980, 52-
        53, 109, 357
    nonsecure facilities for, 481-482
    prohibition of, 107, 109, 203
    of status offenders, 53-54, 217-219
    in Utah, 453-456
    in Virginia, 473-474, 476, 481-482
    in Wisconsin, 546-553
    (*see also* detention prohibition, con-
        cerns regarding)
detention prohibition, concerns regarding,
    54-55, 88-89, 94, 107-108, 109
    in Arizona, 261
    in Louisiana, 311-312, 323-324
    in Massachusetts, 347, 357
    in Pennsylvania, 385-386, 390-391
detention rates for status offenders
    in Arizona, 258, 280-284, 291-292
    in California, 811-812
    in Louisiana, 319-320
    in Pennsylvania, 400-401, 409-410
    in Utah, 437, 453-454
    in Virginia, 478-481
    in Wisconsin, 551, 552-553
detention, state legislation on, 95
    in California, 792-811
    in Louisiana, 303-304
    in Pennsylvania, 376, 378, 382
    in Virginia, 470
    in Wisconsin, 522-525
diversion, 89, 110-112
    as decarceration, 50
    as divestment, 50-52
    and JJDPA, 51
    in Massachusetts, 358-359
    in Pennsylvania, 393-395, 410-412, 414
    as a policy goal of deinstitutionaliza-
        tion, 59-60
    as referral to community-based serv-
        ices, 51

and juvenile court, 124, 361, 473, 500-
    501
role of police in, 118, 125
state legislation on, 95, 110, 420, 426-
    428
of status offenders, 224-225
types of strategies for, 50-52, 379
studies of, 426-427
in Utah, 435, 437, 449-451
in Virginia, 476
(*see also* diversion programs; police)
diversion programs
    funding of, 275-276, 423, 425
    role of police in, 424-425
    state use of federal funds for, 110
    in Utah, 425, 448-451, 458-459
    (*see also* police)

Education for All Handicapped Children
    Act of 1975, 185-187, 699-719
    child identification policy under, 710-
        712
    costs of compliance with, 714-715
    and deinstitutionalization, 708-709, 712-
        713
    eligibility for, 186
    funding of, 185, 701-702
    and least restrictive setting, 185
    misclassification under, 709-710
    overlap of populations served, 716
    purposes of, 185, 700
    requirements of, 700-702
    and state programs, 187, 701
    and status offenders, 706, 707-708, 717-
        718
    summary of, 717-719
    (*see also* special education programs)
Elementary and Secondary Education Act
    of 1965 (*see* Title I of the Elementary
    and Secondary Education Act of
    1965)
Elmore, Richard, 85-86, 210
Ex parte Ah Peen, 19
Ex parte Crouse, 18

facility analysis
    assessment instruments for, 134-135,
        740-754
    facility-based research, 729-731
    facsimile questionnaire for, 755-780
    methodology for, 128-135

purposes of, 127-128
sampling procedures for, 129-133
selection criteria for, 728-729
site visits for, 133-134
federal court decisions
  and deinstitutionalization, 28, 315, 872-
    897
  and reform efforts, 113, 307-308
  (*see also* individual court cases indexed
    by name)
federal funds
  fungibility of, 189-190
  local awareness of, 362
  response of service levels to, 193-194
  and state deinstitutionalization efforts,
    101, 190-192, 211-214, 285, 431
  state use of, 113-115, 352-353, 423, 519
  (*see also* individual federal programs in-
    dexed by name)
federal influence
  on advocacy and reform groups, 112-
    113, 310-311
  and deinstitutionalization, 211-217, 230-
    234
  in Louisiana, 298-299, 313-315
  in Massachusetts, 337, 366-367
  in Pennsylvania, 415
  on standard setting, 28-29, 230
  types of, 176
  in Utah, 431, 448, 457
  (*see also* federal funds; federal court
    decisions; federal legislation; federal
    programs)
federal legislation
  and deinstitutionalization, 29, 101
  legitimizing function of, 113
  (*see also* individual laws indexed by
    name)
federal program analysis
  data issues in, 780-783
  federal program research, 727-728
  selection criteria for, 727
federal programs
  and alternative services, 191
  and deinstitutionalization, 6
  eligibility for, 195, 196-197
  and funds for status offenders, 194,
    196-197
  incentives to states, 197
  integration into state programs, 186,
    188
  populations served by, 178

and provision of social services, 187,
    190, 192
state implementation of requirements
    for, 188-189
states' interpretation and use of, 177
voluntary provisions of requirements
    for, 189
foster care
  for adolescents, 649
  in Arizona, 264-266
  cost of, 264, 526
  funding of, 264, 265, 276, 280
  in Massachusetts, 345-346
  placements, 194-195, 655-658
  population in, 647-651
  problems with use of, 346
  programs for, 649-655
  relation of state-run and federal pro-
    grams, 658
  and status offenders, 219-220, 503-504,
    543, 659
  in Utah, 456-457
  in Wisconsin, 525-527, 534-535
  (*see also* Aid to Families with Depend-
    ent Children–Foster Care program;
    alternatives to institutions)

Gary W. v. *State of Louisiana*, 93, 315
group homes
  funding of, 520, 521
  in Massachusetts, 345, 351
  in Pennsylvania, 402-406, 414
  placement of status offenders in, 345,
    440-441, 543
  in Utah, 440-441
  in Virginia, 482
  in Wisconsin, 543
  (*see also* alternatives to institutions)

implementation analysis
  backward mapping, 85-86, 202, 210-211
  forward mapping, 85-86
implementation system
  characteristics of, 67-74, 84, 201
  and diffusion of innovation, 81, 206
  factors external to, 83
  federal role in, 70-74, 206-207, 211-217,
    231-235
  and grant-in-aid programs, 67-68
  and influence of law, 78-79
  and lack of statutory coherence, 82-83
  local variations of, 209

and outcome assessment methods, 82-86, 205-207
political support for, 83, 208-209
problems of, 83, 209
and public attitudes, 79
as a social system, 79-80, 84-85
state and local roles in, 72-73, 207, 235-236
and tractability of the problem to be solved, 82, 207-208
variables affecting, 209-211
implementing agencies
autonomy of, 68-69, 204
bureaucratic nature of, 68
characteristics of, 68-70, 82, 201-202
and interest groups and professional associations, 70
and purchase-of-service arrangements, 69-70
response of, 222
incarceration, prohibition of, 88, 524
incorrigible youth, 257
In re Gault, 28, 94, 96, 98, 176, 836, 875
In re Gault and deinstitutionalization
in Arizona, 258
in Louisiana, 307-308
in Massachusetts, 337
in Pennsylvania, 377
in Virginia, 467
in Wisconsin, 516
In re Winship, 307-308
institutional settings, characteristics of, 55-56
institutions for juveniles
closing of, 521
in nineteenth century, 17-19
placement of juveniles in, 438
In the Matter of Ferrier, 19

JJDPA (*see* Juvenile Justice and Delinquency Prevention Act of 1974)
Justice System Improvement Act of 1979, 75, 575-576
juvenile court
attitudes toward families, 124, 494
autonomy of, 76-77, 122-124, 126, 203-204, 344
constraints on, 77-78
disposition options of, 343-344, 471
enforcement powers of, 357, 360-361, 389, 471, 497

establishment of, 15, 20
as lobby group, 261, 262, 362
organization of, 257-258, 373, 422, 467-468, 472-474
placement policies of, 264, 266, 356, 495, 498-502
purposes and practices of, 21-22
reasons for referral to, 396-400
referral of dependent youth to, 392-395
referral of runaways and ungovernables to, 449-451
referral sources to, 343, 355-356, 397-399, 474
referral of status offenders to, 274-278, 343-344, 392-400, 435-437, 442-452, 474-476, 481, 497-499, 539-541
referral of truants to, 452
reform of, 258, 489
as service broker, 121, 123-124, 496, 501-502
as service provider, 121-123, 385, 408-409, 494-495, 500-501
staff of, 500, 505
(*See also* juvenile court, jurisdiction of; juvenile court, referral of status offenders; juvenile court judges.
juvenile court judges
attitudes toward deinstitutionalization, 103, 384, 485-490, 491-492, 518
attitudes toward families, 359
attitudes toward status offenders, 490-491, 496, 507-508
and court policy, 278-279, 361, 421, 434-435, 474, 540
and court staff, 290-291, 488-489, 501
discretion of, 301-304, 317, 362-363, 421, 472, 486-490, 547, 549-550
as interest group, 431-432
as key local actor, 90, 117, 125, 126, 288-292, 448-449, 555
as lobbyists, 304, 358, 360, 421
juvenile court, jurisdiction of, 22, 99, 100
in Arizona, 257-260
in Louisiana, 300-301
in Massachusetts, 355, 360
in Pennsylvania, 375, 388-391
in Utah, 424
in Virginia 466-472, 486-488, 494, 496
in Wisconsin, 520
juvenile court, referral of status offenders to
in Arizona, 274-278

in Massachusetts, 343-344
in Pennsylvania, 392-400
in Utah, 435-437, 442-452
in Virginia, 474-476, 481, 497-499
in Wisconsin, 539, 541
Juvenile Delinquency Prevention and
    Control Act of 1968, 29, 75, 423,
    425, 563
Juvenile Delinquency and Youth Offenses
    Act of 1961, 26, 562
juvenile justice
    differential enforcement of, 226-227
    history of federal concern with, 25-26,
        75, 562-568
    and Law Enforcement Assistance
        Administration, 75
    nineteenth-century concerns with, 15-20
Juvenile Justice Act (see Juvenile Justice
    and Delinquency Prevention Act of
    1974)
Juvenile Justice and Delinquency Preven-
    tion Act of 1974, 5, 29, 30, 75, 177,
    179, 561
    California's response to, 790-792
    compliance with, 99, 262-263, 313-314,
        343, 379-380, 420-421
    and deinstitutionalization, 263, 270-271,
        286, 288, 431, 522
    deinstitutionalization mandate of, 567,
        581-582
    and detention rates, 280-285
    emphases of, 42-43
    and Office of Juvenile Justice and De-
        linquency Prevention, 566
    programs under, 561, 576-583
    reauthorization of, 11, 33
    requirements of, 76, 84
    state participation in, 68, 101, 103-104,
        258-263, 305-306, 426, 428-429
    and status offenders, 567
Juvenile Justice and Delinquency Preven-
    tion Act funds
    and deinstitutionalization, 179, 190-191,
        380, 523-524, 818-823
    as incentive for compliance, 383-384,
        468, 806-810
    as incentive for participation, 114, 259,
        284-285, 311, 428, 522-524
    and state programs, 186
    state use of, 190-191, 312, 420-421, 430,
        814-818

juvenile justice reform
    in California, 27, 794-802
    federal support of, 28-29
    and juvenile court, 20-27
    in Pennsylvania, 379-380
    in Virginia, 466-472
juvenile justice system, 257-263, 266-267,
    296, 299-307
    organizational characteristics of, 76-77
    state concerns with, 26-27, 262-263, 469
    studies of, 423, 427
    youth not served by, 225-226, 305, 395,
        532

Kent v. United States, 28, 307-308
Kobrin, Solomon, and Klein, Malcolm,
    47-48

Labeling (see relabeling)
Law Enforcement Assistance Administra-
    tion, 179
    and federal monitoring procedures, 76
    focus on status offenders, 567-568
    programs of, 568-576, 581-583
Law Enforcement Assistance Administra-
    tion funds
    administrative control over, 570
    and deinstitutionalization, 190-191
    and development of alternative serv-
        ices, 110, 274-275
    maintenance-of-effort provision, 180,
        567, 570-575
    state use of, 113-114, 262, 263, 274-275,
        280, 338, 377, 423-425, 447-448
    threat of loss of, 342
    types of, 180, 568-569
LEAA (see Law Enforcement Assistance
    Administration)
least restrictive alternative, 56, 307, 382-
    383, 524, 544
    (see also alternatives to institutions)
Lessard v. Schmidt, 527
Louisiana
    conclusions concerning deinstitutionali-
        zation in, 329-331
    summary of findings in, 92-94

maintenance-of-effort provision (see Law
    Enforcement Assistance Administra-
    tion funds)

Massachusetts
conclusions regarding deinstitutionalization in, 361-367
summary of findings in, 90-92
Medicaid program, 183-184, 663-679
eligibility for, 183, 195-196, 665, 669
eligibility of status offenders for, 668-
672
federal administration of, 665
funding of, 183, 665-666
and institutional services, 674-678
purposes of, 183, 664
and services to status offenders, 197-
198, 672-674
services under, 183-184, 664-665
state operation of, 667-668
and state programs, 188
summary of, 678-679
(*see also* medical assistance programs,
state)
medical assistance programs, state
coverage of financially needy children,
669-671
coverage of optional eligibility groups
of, 668
and institutional placements for status
offenders, 674
institutional services under, 667, 672,
673, 675-677
limits in use of facilities and services
under, 673-674
and status offenders, 668
mental health facilities
in Arizona, 267-269
development of alternatives to, 527
funding of, 267
inappropriate commitments to, 267,
269, 834-835
partial closing of, 528
placement of status offenders in, 104,
107, 307, 439-440
procedures for committing juveniles to,
267-269, 527-528
as substitute for secure detention, 269
in Wisconsin, 527-528
Miller, Jerome
and deinstitutionalization in Illinois,
829-862 *passim*
and deinstitutionalization in Massachusetts, 338-340

minors otherwise in need of supervision
(*see* status offenders)
MINS (*see* status offenders)
Morales v. *Turman*, 873-897 *passim*

normalization, 11-12
assessment of, 135, 161-163
degree of, 172-174
and family involvement, 163-165
as a policy goal of deinstitutionalization, 61-62
and privacy, 167
and program rules, 165-166
and recreation activities, 169-170
and resident responsibility, 168
of status offenders, 220-221

Office of Justice Assistance, Research,
and Statistics, 575-576
Office of Juvenile Justice and Delinquency Prevention, 5, 75
development of, 576-577
establishment of, 179
focus on serious offenders, 11
purposes of, 561
OJARS (*see* Office of Justice Assistance,
Research, and Statistics)
OJJDP (*see* Office of Juvenile Justice and
Delinquency Prevention)
Omnibus Crime Control and Safe Streets
Act of 1968, 29, 563, 568
out-of-home placements
and eligibility for other programs, 197
normalization in, 221-222
for status offenders, 219

parens patriae, 19-21, 296, 301, 337, 466,
836, 842
Pennsylvania
conclusions regarding deinstitutionalization in, 413-415
summary of findings in, 98-101
People ex. rel. O'Connell v. *Turner*, 19
People v. *Presley*, 835-837, 839, 840
P.L. 89-313 (*see* Title I of the Elementary
and Secondary Education Act of
1965)
P.L. 94-142 (*see* Education for All Handicapped Children Act of 1975)

placements, monitoring and review of, 93, 97, 100, 316-317, 521
police
    attitudes toward deinstitutionalization, 277-278, 449
    discretion of, 125, 303
    diversion efforts of, 118, 275, 424-425, 447-448, 459
    as referral source, 276, 446-447, 539
    (*see also* diversion; diversion programs)
Pollak, William, 223
President's Commission on Law Enforcement and Administration of Justice, 26, 96, 102, 337, 423, 426-427, 516
private providers
    characteristics of, 903-904
    development of, 95, 123, 339-340, 350, 353-354, 440, 483
    funding of, 505, 904-906
    as lobby group, 386
    problems with, 350-354
    public management of, 915-935
    referral of status offenders to, 407-408
    services provided by, 401-406
    and services to status offenders, 104, 349-350, 902
    sources of referral to, 904-910
    state management and monitoring of, 352-353
    state officials' support of, 350
    (*see also* purchase-of-services system)
purchase-of-services system
    characteristics of, 78, 223-224
    evaluation of, 910-915
    in Illinois, 899-936
    in Massachusetts, 348-354
    in Pennsylvania, 374, 386-387, 401-408
    (*see also* private providers)

reform coalitions
    in Arizona, 261-262
    breakdown of, 106, 112, 339-342
    changes effected by, 310, 517, 529, 554, 555-556
    characteristics of, 111-112
    conservative opposition to, 339-340
    fiscal conservatives as part of, 95, 97, 112, 518, 520-521
    legislative efforts of, 377, 379, 383, 516-518
    loss of influence of, 312-313

    in Louisiana, 309-310, 312-313
    in Massachusetts, 90, 337-340
    members of, 90, 309, 468-469, 515-516, 793
    opposition to, 90
    in Pennsylvania, 377, 379, 383
    in Virginia, 468-469
    in Wisconsin, 515-518, 520-521, 529, 554-556
relabeling, 88, 95
    in Arizona, 266-267, 269
    in California, 812
    as commitment to mental health facilities, 269, 326-327, 528
    by contempt charges, 325-326
    of delinquents as status offenders, 327-328
    as a function of age, 343
    in Louisiana, 325-328
    in Massachusetts, 343, 359-360
    for placement purposes, 91
    potential for, 521, 529
    reasons for, 107, 325, 359-360, 365-366
    of runaways as ungovernables, 424, 435
    and Title I, 694
    as upgrading the offense, 325, 365, 385, 393-395, 484-486, 492-493, 551
    in Utah, 424, 435, 443
    in Virginia, 476
    in Wisconsin, 521, 536-539
research design, 6-9, 723-731
residential facilities
    capacity of, 154-161
    and the community, 159-161
    demographic characteristics of youth in, 142-145
    development of, 170-171
    location of, 156, 159-161
    physical autonomy of, 155-156
    physical structure of, 157-159
    policy changes and youth in, 146-147
    problems facing, 174-175
    program characteristics of, 149-151, 171-172
    security and personal freedom in, 156-157
    separation of status offenders from delinquents in, 147-149
    youth in, 142-149
Rosenheim, Margaret, 220
runaway centers, 191, 193, 588-593

Runaway and Homeless Youth Act of 1974 (*see* Runaway Youth Act program)
runaways, 4
  federal responsibility for, 585-586
  jurisdiction over, 423-424
  police referral of, 276-277
  programs for, 179-180
  (*see also* status offenders)
Runaway Youth Act program, 177, 582-595
  in California, 815
  clients of, 195
  effects of, 188
  funding levels under, 587-588
  grants under, 586-587
  growth of centers under, 192
  origins of, 584-585
  use of funds under, 179-180

Sabatier, Paul, and Mazmanian, Daniel, 82, 83-84, 207
shelter care
  as alternative to detention, 109-110
  in Arizona, 279, 284-286
  in Massachusetts, 342-343, 351
  in Pennsylvania, 382, 410
  placement of status offenders in, 551
  referral of status offenders to, 284-285, 286
  in Wisconsin, 523-525, 549-551
Social Security Act of 1935 (*see* Aid to Families with Dependent Children program; Medicaid program; Title IV-B; Title XX)
social services, 190, 192-193, 197
special education programs
  and deinstitutionalization, 715-716
  funding sources of, 717
  response to local pressures of, 717
  in the states, 701-705, 715-716
  (*see also* Education for All Handicapped Children Act of 1975)
state case studies
  selection criteria for, 723-724
  state-based research, 724-726
state corrections department
  in Arizona, 270-273
  commitment to, 536-540, 541-543, 546, 788

commitment of status offenders to, 270-273, 285-286, 438-439, 475-481, 517-518, 529-532, 534-535, 543
  in Louisiana, 305
  prohibition of commitments to, 260, 471, 483, 484
  in Virginia, 483-485
state planning agency
  Arizona State Justice Planning Agency, 263, 275-276
  California Council on Criminal Justice, 796-797, 804-805, 808, 818-821
  Louisiana Commission on Law Enforcement, 310, 313, 314
  Massachusetts Committee on Criminal Justice, 342-343
  role of, 569-570
  Utah Council on Criminal Justice Administration, 423, 426, 428, 429, 450-451
  Virginia Division of Justice and Crime Prevention, 468
  Wisconsin Council on Criminal Justice, 516, 518, 522, 555-556
state social service department
  in Arizona, 260, 264-267
  attitudes toward status offenders, 504
  discretion of, 363
  jurisdiction of, 355, 373, 388-391, 424, 427, 526-527
  jurisdiction over status offenders, 260, 305, 316, 342-345, 348
  in Louisiana, 305, 316
  in Massachusetts, 342-345, 348, 355, 359, 363
  in Pennsylvania, 373, 383-384, 388-391
  role of, 359
  in Utah, 424, 427
  in Virginia, 504
  in Wisconsin, 526-527
status offenders
  attitudes toward, 506-508
  brokering of services to, 503
  definitions of, 4, 43-50
  and delinquents, 48-50
  jurisdiction over, 45-47, 260, 280, 305, 381-382, 386, 388-391, 497-498, 880-881
  and juvenile court, 4
  and the juvenile justice system, 111, 306-307

and labeling decisions, 47-50
legislation concerning jurisdiction over,
    101-102, 426-428
number served, 351-352
numbers of, 4, 298
placement of, 532-546, 553
services to, 91, 219, 402, 404-406, 412-
    413, 502-506
state legislation concerning, 340-342
    (*see also* status offenders, legal defini-
    tion of; status offenders, placement
    decisions regarding)
status offenders, legal definition of
in Illinois, 839
in Louisiana, 305, 306
in Massachusetts, 343
in Pennsylvania, 374-383
in Utah, 427
in Virginia, 470, 500
in Wisconsin, 516
status offenders, placement decisions re-
    garding
in Illinois, 925-929
in Louisiana, 316-317
in Massachusetts, 345-346
in Pennsylvania, 376, 409
in Utah, 456-457
in Virginia, 471-472, 501-502
status offense, definition of, 43-50, 484-
    485

Title I of the Elementary and Secondary
    Education Act of 1965
eligibility for, 184-185, 196
federal funding under, 682-683
and placement decisions, 696-697
placement incentives under, 198
program for handicapped children
    (P.L. 89-313), 690, 695-696
program settings authorized by, 185
programs of, 187-188, 684-696
purposes of, 184-185, 681, 682
state use of funds from, 338
and status offenders, 681
summary of, 696-697
Title IV-A of the Social Security Act of
    1935 (*see* Aid to Families with De-
    pendent Children program)
Title IV-B of the Social Security Act of
    1935

child welfare services under, 181, 621-
    637
eligibility for, 181, 624
funding levels of, 181-182, 622-623,
    629-632
purposes of, 181-182, 622
and services to delinquents, 623
and services to status offenders, 623,
    632
state administration of, 624
and state programs, 187, 628-629
    (*see also* child welfare services)
Title XIX of the Social Security Act of
    1935 (*see* Medicaid program)
Title XX of the Social Security Act of
    1935 programs, 180-181, 598-618
definition of, 599
and deinstitutionalization, 608-609
eligibility for, 180-181, 196, 600-601,
    613-616
federal requirements on, 605-606
funding of, 180, 601, 603, 604, 606-607
goals of, 180-181, 600
and purchase of services, 604-605
and services to status offenders, 194,
    601-602, 608-612
social services provided under, 181,
    607-612
state administration of, 602-605
state implementation of, 187
and state social service programs, 605
summary of, 616-618
truants, 4, 324-325, 424, 451-452 (*see also*
    status offenders)

ungovernables, 4, 300 (*see also* status of-
    fenders)
upgrading (*see* relabeling)
Utah
conclusions concerning deinstitutionali-
    zation in, 457-460
summary of findings in, 102-105

Virginia
conclusions concerning deinstitutionali-
    zation in, 506-509
summary of findings in, 94-96

widening of the net, 92, 224-225, 351-352, 452, 459
Wisconsin
   conclusions regarding deinstitutionalization in, 553-556
   summary of findings in, 96-98
Wyatt v. *Stickney*, 28

Youth Development Bureau, 179

Zald, Mayer, 80, 81, 84-85, 205-206